SOCIOLOGY: MAN IN SOCIETY

SOCIOLOGY: MAN IN SOCIETY

Melvin L. DeFleur
Chairman, Department of Sociology, Washington State University

William V. D'Antonio
Chairman, Department of Sociology, University of Connecticut

Lois B. DeFleur
Associate Professor of Sociology, Washington State University

SCOTT, FORESMAN AND COMPANY   GLENVIEW, ILLINOIS   LONDON

Acknowledgments

American Jewish Year Book: table adapted from *American Jewish Year Book, 1969;* reprinted by permission of American Jewish Committee and the Jewish Publication Society of America.

American Political Science Association: table from "Some Social Requisites of Democracy: Economic Development and Political Legitimacy" by Seymour Lipset, March 1959; reprinted by permission.

American Sociological Association: table and selection from "Urban Structure and Social Participation" by Morris Axelrod; and selections from "Crime and Punishment in the Factory" by Joseph Bensman and Israel Gerver, "Death by Dieselization" by W. F. Cottrell, "Some Social Requisites of Democracy" by James C. Davies, "Some Principles of Stratification" by Kingsley Davis and Wilbert Moore, "Cultural Factors in the Selection of Marriage Mates" by August B. Hollingshead, "The Precipitants and Underlying Conditions of Race Riots" by Stanley Lieberson and Arnold R. Silverman, and "Why I Wanted to Become a Sociologist" by Stuart Rice. For all of these selections, permission to reprint has been granted by the copyright holder, the American Sociological Association.

Annals of the American Academy of Political and Social Science: figures of "Multiple Nuclei Theory" and "Sector Theory" adapted from "The Nature of Cities" by Chauncey D. Harris and Edward L. Ullman, November 1945; reprinted by permission.

Antioch Press: table from *Social Distance* by Emory S. Bogardus; reprinted by special permission of the author from *Social Distance,* Antioch Press, 1959, p. 33.

Appleton-Century-Crofts: selection from *The Study of Man* by Ralph Linton, copyright, 1936; reprinted by permission of Appleton-Century-Crofts, Educational Division, Meredith Corporation. Selection from *In Their Own Behalf: Voices from the Margin* by Charles H. McCaghy *et al.,* eds., 1968; reprinted by permission of the publisher.

The Atlantic Monthly: selection from "What Are You Supposed to Do If You Like Children?" by Anne Bernays, copyright © 1970 by The Atlantic Monthly Company, Boston, Mass.; and "Marriage as a Wretched Institution" by Mervyn Cadwallader, copyright © 1966 by The Atlantic Monthly Company, Boston, Mass.—both reprinted by permission of the publisher and the authors.

Barnes & Noble, Inc.: selection from *New Outline of the Principles of Sociology,* ed. Alfred McClung Lee, 1951; reprinted by permission.

Black Panther Party: Rules of the Black Panther Party; reprinted by permission of the Black Panther Party, Berkeley, California.

The Bobbs-Merrill Company, Inc.: selection from *The Big Con,* copyright © 1940, by David W. Maurer; reprinted by permission of the publishers and the author.

Campaign to Check the Population Explosion: table from *The Population Bomb Keeps Ticking;* reprinted by permission.

The Center for the Study of Democratic Institutions: selection from "The Economy Under Law" by W. H. Ferry; reprinted, by permission, from the Center Pamphlet, *The Economy Under Law,* 1960, a publication of The Center for the Study of Democratic Institutions in Santa Barbara, California.

Chicago Tribune: selection from an editorial, February 19, 1970; reprinted, courtesy of the *Chicago Tribune.*

Committee for Economic Development: selection from "Minimizing Government Control to Strengthen Competitive Private Enterprise" by Milton Friedman in *Problems of United States Economic Development,* January 1958; reprinted by permission of the publisher.

Commonweal: selection from "Priesthood and Revolution" by Herbert McCabe, in *Commonweal,* September 20, 1968, pp. 621–625; reprinted by permission of Commonweal Publishing Co., Inc.

Curtis Publishing Company: selection from *Advice to a Nervous Visitor* by William Golding; reprinted by permission of Curtis Brown, Ltd., copyright © 1963 by Curtis Publishing Company. Selection from "Don't Blame the Ghetto" by David B. Lee, copyright 1965 by The Curtis Publishing Company; as condensed in the April 1965 *Reader's Digest;* reprinted by permission of the publisher and the author.

Joan Daves: excerpts from *I Have a Dream;* reprinted by permission of Joan Daves. Copyright © 1963 by Martin Luther King, Jr.

The John Day Company, Inc.: selection reprinted from *To My Daughters with Love* by Pearl S. Buck, by permission of The John Day Company, Inc., publisher and A. P. Watt & Son, London; copyright © 1967 by the Pearl S. Buck Foundation, Inc.

The Dial Press: selection reprinted from *Nobody Knows My Name* by James Baldwin by permission of the publisher, The Dial Press and Michael Joseph Ltd.; copyright © 1960 by James Baldwin.

The Dorsey Press: selections reprinted with permission of Charles N. Glaab, *The American City: A Documentary History,* pp. 6, 233; with permission of E. Hagen and Massachusetts Institute of Technology, *On the Theory of Social Change,* p. 15; with permission of W. Seward Salisbury, *Religion in American Culture,* p. 325.

Doubleday & Company, Inc.: selection from *Taming Megalopolis,* ed. H. W. Eldridge, © 1967 by H. Wentworth Eldridge; reprinted by permission of Doubleday & Company, Inc. and *Daedalus.* This selection originally appeared in *Daedalus,* Vol. 92, No. 4 (Fall 1963). Table from "The Population of Latin America" copyright © 1964 by Doubleday & Company, Inc., from the book *Population: The Vital Revolution* by R. Freedman; reprinted by permission of Doubleday & Company, Inc. Selection from *World Aflame* by Billy Graham, copyright © 1965 by Billy Graham; reprinted by permission of Doubleday & Company, Inc. and World's Work Ltd. Selection from *The Religious Factor* by Gerhard Lenski, 1963; reprinted by permission.

E. P. Dutton & Co., Inc.: selection from the book *Child of the Dark: The Diary of Carolina Maria de Jesus,* translated by David St. Clair, copyright © 1962 by E. P. Dutton & Co., Inc., and Souvenir Press Ltd; used by permission of the publishers.

Federal Probation: figure from "Capital Punishment" by Thorsten Sellin, September 1961; reprinted by permission of the author.

The Free Press: selections from *The Adolescent Society* by James S. Coleman, 1964; "The Fabulous Races" by Herbert Collins in *Race:*

Individual and Collective Behavior, ed. Thompson and Hughes, 1958; *The Functions of Social Conflict* by Lewis A. Coser, 1956; "Notes on the Sociology of Deviance" by Kai T. Erickson and "Two Studies of Legal Stigma" by Richard D. Schwartz and Jerome H. Skolnick in *The Other Side: Perspectives on Deviance*, ed. Howard S. Becker, 1964; *Structure and Process in Modern Societies* by Talcott Parsons, 1960; *Structure and Function in Primitive Society* by A. R. Radcliffe-Brown, 1952; and *Theory of Social and Economic Organization* by Max Weber, tr. by Henderson and Parson, 1964—all reprinted by permission. Table reprinted with permission of The Macmillan Company from *Social Theory and Social Structure* by Robert K. Merton; copyright 1957 by The Free Press, a Corporation; copyright 1949 by The Free Press.

Harcourt Brace Jovanovich, Inc.: selections from *Social Stratification* by Bernard Barber, 1957; and *They Went to College* by Ernest Havemann and Patricia S. West, 1952—both reprinted by permission. Selection abridged from *Middletown* by Robert S. and Helen M. Lynd; Harcourt Brace Jovanovich, Inc., 1929; reprinted by permission of Harcourt Brace Jovanovich, Inc. and Constable Publishers Ltd. Selection abridged from *City Development*, copyright, 1945, by Lewis Mumford; reprinted by permission of Harcourt Brace Jovanovich, Inc. and Martin Secker & Warburg Ltd.

Harper & Row, Inc.: table adapted from Merrill Kelley Bennett, *The World's Food*, 1954; projected 1980 figures from the United Nations, *Provisional Report on World Population Prospects*, 1964; reprinted by permission. Selections from "What Missing the Newspaper Means" by Bernard Berelson in *Communications Research*, ed. Paul Lazarfeld and Frank Stanton, 1949; *A History of Colonial America* by Oliver P. Chitwood, 1931; *The Negro Revolt* by Louis Lomax, 1962; *The Wasted Americans* by Edgar May, 1964; *Industrial Society* by Delbert C. Miller and William H. Form, 1964; *Community Organizations* by Murray G. Ross, 1967; "Juvenile Delinquency: A Group Tradition" by Clifford Shaw in *Gang Delinquency and Delinquent Subcultures*, ed. James F. Short, Jr., 1968; and *Family and Civilization* by Carle C. Zimmerman, 1947—all reprinted by permission.

Holt, Rinehart and Winston, Inc.: selections from *The Psychology of Rumor* by Gordon Allport and Leo Postman, 1947; and *Premarital Dating Behavior* by Winston Ehrmann, 1959; Henry Holt and Company—both reprinted by permission of Holt, Rinehart and Winston, Inc. Selection from "Some Recent Findings in Human Relations Research in Industry" by Daniel Katz and Robert L. Kahn in *Readings in Social Psychology*, revised edition, ed. G. E. Swanson, *et al.*; copyright 1947, 1952 by Holt, Rinehart and Winston, Inc., adapted and reprinted by permission of Holt, Rinehart and Winston, Inc.

Horizon Press: selection from *The Living City* by Frank Lloyd Wright, copyright 1959; reprinted by permission of the publisher.

Houghton Mifflin Company: figure from *Race and Ethnic Relations*, 3rd ed., by Brewton Berry, 1965, p. 40; copyright © 1965, 1958 by Brewton Berry; used by permission. Selections from "Urbanism and Suburbanism as Ways of Life: A Re-evaluation of Definition" by Herbert J. Gans in *Human Behavior and Social Processes*, ed. Arnold Rose, 1962; *Sociology* by William Ogburn and Meyer Nimkoff, 1964; and *Patterns of Culture* by Ruth Benedict, 1934—all reprinted by permission.

Indiana University Press: selections by Eugene R. Black, Robert C. North, and Edgar Snow, from *The Population Crisis and the Use of World Resources*, ed. Stuart Mudd with Hugo Boyko, Robert C. Cook, Larry Ng, W. Taylor Thom, Jr.; copyright © 1964 by Uitgevery Dr. W. Junk; reprinted by permission of Stuart Mudd and Indiana University Press.

Land Economics: two tables in "The Changing Color Composition of Metropolitan Areas" by Harry Sharp and Leo F. Schnore, May 1962; reprinted by permission.

J. B. Lippincott Company: selections from "Norm-Violating Behavior and Lower Class Culture" by William C. Kvaraceus and Walter B. Miller in *Juvenile Delinquency*, ed. Ruth Shonle Cavan; and *The Family in Various Cultures*, rev. ed. by Queen, Habenstein and Adams—both reprinted by permission of the publisher.

Macmillan and Company Ltd.: selection from "First Essay on Population" by Thomas R. Malthus, reprinted from the Royal Economic Society, 1926, by permission.

The Macmillan Company: selections from *The Elementary Forms of Religious Life* by Emile Durkheim, 1926; *Deviance: The Interactionist Perspective* by Earl Rubington and Martin Weinbert, 1968; *The Social Teaching of the Christian Churches* by Ernst Troeltsch, 1931; "Small Town in Mass Society" by Arthur Vidich and Joseph Bensman in *Readings in Introductory Sociology*, ed. Wrong and Gracey, 1967; and *Religion, Society and the Individual* by J. Milton Yinger, 1957—all reprinted by permission.

McGraw-Hill Book Company: selection from *Slums and Suburbs* by James B. Conant, 1961, McGraw-Hill, pp. 2–3; reprinted by permission. Selection from *The World Cities* by Peter Hall; copyright © Peter Hall, 1966; used with permission of McGraw-Hill Book Company and World University Library, London. Selection from *Power and Privilege* by Gerhard Lenski; copyright © 1966 by McGraw-Hill, Inc., used with permission of McGraw-Hill Book Company. Table from *Sociology of Religion* by Glenn M. Vernon; copyright 1962 by McGraw-Hill Book Company, used with permission of McGraw-Hill Book Company.

David McKay Company, Inc.: three figures from *Theories of Mass Communication* by Melvin DeFleur, 2nd ed., 1970; copyright © 1966 and 1970 by David McKay Company, Inc., reprinted by permission of David McKay Co., Inc.

Michigan Quarterly Review: selection from "The Family in a Cybernetic Era" by Alice Mary Hilton in *Michigan Quarterly Review*, 3 (1964), 29–30; reprinted by permission.

The National Catholic Reporter: selection from "A Newsman's Nightmare of Boston, 1773" by Fred W. Friendly, April 10, 1970, p. 19; reprinted by permission of the author.

The New Republic: selection from "The Nonsense Explosion" by Ben Wattenberg; reprinted by permission of *The New Republic*, © 1970, Harrison-Blaine of New Jersey, Inc.

Newsweek: table from June 20, 1966, p. 90, estimates based on study by Arch Patton of McKinsey & Company, Inc., management consultants; and selection from "Is America a Shay or a Scow?" by Stewart Alsop, copyright Newsweek, Inc., 1970—both reprinted by permission.

The New York Times Company: selections from a *New York Times* editorial, "A Jury's Service," © 1970 by The New York Times Company; "Is It Ever Right to Break the Law?" by Charles Frankel, © 1964 by The New York Times Company; and "It's Not a Bad Crisis to Live In" by Irving Kristol, © 1967 by The New York Times Company—all reprinted by permission.

W. W. Norton & Company, Inc.: selection reprinted from *Civilization and Its Discontents* by Sigmund Freud. Translated from the German and edited by James Strachey. By permission of W. W. Norton & Company, Inc., Sigmund Freud Copyrights Ltd., The Institute of Psycho-Analysis, and The Hogarth Press Ltd. Copyright © 1961 by James Strachey.

Playboy magazine: excerpts from "Pot: A Rational Approach" by Joel Fort, M. D.; originally appeared in *Playboy* magazine, copyright © 1969 by HMH Publishing Co., Inc., reprinted by permission of the author and the publisher.

Prentice-Hall, Inc.: selections from "The Anatomy of Paris" by Honoré de Balzac, "What Makes a Peer?" by Daniel Defoe, "The Powers and Rhythms of London" by Thomas de Quincey, and "Waiting at the Station" by William M. Thackeray—all in *Sociology Through Literature*, ed. Lewis Coser, © 1963. Selections from "World Population Growth" by Harold F. Dorn, and "Population and Economic Development" by Ansley Coale—both in *The Population Dilemma*, ed. Philip M. Hauser, © 1963. Table from "Population Growth in the United States" by Donald J. Bogue in *The Population Dilemma*. Selections from *The Press and America* by Edwin Emery, © 1962; *The Family* by William J. Goode, © 1964; "The Meaning of Work and Adjustment to Retirement" by Herman J. Loether in *Blue-Collar World: Studies of the American Worker*, ed. Arthur B. Shostak and William Gomberg, © 1964; and *Societies: Evolutionary and Comparative Perspectives* by Talcott Parsons © 1966. All of these selections reprinted by permission of Prentice-Hall, Inc.

Princeton University Press: selection from *The Invasion from Mars* by

Preface

Sociology: Man in Society provides students with a readable and intellectually provocative account of modern sociology. It weaves together theoretical concepts, historical perspectives, modern research, and important social issues to offer the student a new way of viewing the social processes of which he is a part. It is intended to aid him in penetrating beneath the superficialities of social life and in understanding the underlying principles that shape it.

Several objectives have guided us in the preparation of this text. First of all, we have attempted to integrate the important theoretical concepts of classic and contemporary sociology with the discipline's accumulation of empirical studies. Instead of trying to catalogue every aspect of modern sociology, *Sociology: Man in Society* thoroughly discusses the concepts, theories, and research that are basic to the discipline. While clearly selective, this coverage includes a broad spectrum of specialized interests and methodological approaches. Throughout the text, examples are integrated with the textual discussion of concepts. These illustrations are drawn from many sources, ranging from quantitative research reports to eyewitness accounts of riots, mass hallucinations, and deviant behavior. We have also evaluated the validity of sociological formulations, distinguishing those that have solid research support from more tentative theories and from sociological speculation.

Second, we have attempted to develop our sociological framework within a context of significant social issues. The text emphasizes that both social stability and social conflict are basic social processes which are important for an understanding of modern society. It maintains that sociology is as much concerned with rock festivals, urban riots, and revolutions in developing countries as it is with the small-group laboratory or the large-scale bureaucratic organization. Social structure and social equilibrium, therefore, provide one important focus, while social change and social conflict provide another.

Finally, we have tried to present an objective picture of sociology as a discipline, treating its controversies and shortcomings along with its contributions and accomplishments. Not trying to idealize sociology, we have presented the debates over ethical neutrality, sociological activism, and radical protest, as well as the basic conceptualizations about which sociologists have long agreed. In addition, rather than emphasizing a particular theoretical perspective to the exclusion of rival points of view, the text discusses the competing orientations of modern sociology while offering balanced critical comment.

The Prologue and Epilogue to *Sociology: Man in Society* reflect the objectives just mentioned. The Prologue, for example, traces in some detail the origins of modern sociology and discusses the various contributions that many individuals have made to the discipline. At the same time, it sets forth the most widely accepted epistemology of contemporary sociology. The Epilogue, on the other hand, brings out a number of the more salient controversies concerning the conduct and funding of sociological research. It also discusses the ways in which sociology is having an increasing impact on public policies.

Sociology: Man in Society has two special features that should be particularly significant for the introductory student. Twenty-six Methodological Essays have been prepared with the help of research specialists to introduce the student to the techniques and procedures commonly used by sociologists in their day-to-day activities. Each essay is set off in a special format and positioned near related textual discussion. While no claim is made that these essays will equip the student to do research on his own, they should give him a feeling for the working tools of the sociologist. They will also help him understand the difficulty of studying sociological phenomena objectively and some of the practical problems that sociologists encounter in attempting to assemble valid and reliable data.

The Viewpoints are the second special feature. Each of the eighteen Viewpoints presents two brief interpretations of a social issue. The Viewpoints in Chapter 2, for example, consist of statements by Barry Goldwater and the SDS concerning the problems of the individual in mass society. The fascinating thing is that they both say almost the same thing! In other cases, however, spokesmen for various groups give diametrically opposing views on a given issue. The Viewpoints are intended to promote sociological discussion of specific issues and to illustrate the need for objective sociological inquiry in unraveling complex problems.

Sociology: Man in Society has been organized for maximum flexibility. The instructor may easily bypass the Methodological Essays and Viewpoints if this appears desirable. Furthermore, the book adjusts easily to courses of differing lengths. For the short course, the first half (the Prologue plus Chapters 1–9) presents sociology's most basic concepts and theories. For a longer course, the next Part (Chapters 10–13) can be added. The "institutional" chapters are grouped conveniently at the end and can be used selectively or omitted entirely. The Epilogue, however, is recommended for all students who are interested in some of sociology's problems as a discipline.

Individual contributions to a book of this type are all but impossible to unravel. The critical readers, who are listed opposite the title page, made innumerable suggestions for improving the manuscript. Each chapter was carefully reviewed in terms of its subject matter, and the book as a whole was closely studied for overall organization and teachability. We would like to thank the critical readers for their valuable assistance and emphasize that they are in no way responsible for any shortcomings in the book.

Many students, both undergraduates and graduates, helped us sharpen our ideas, and many colleagues and friends provided helpful information and references. Special thanks are expressed to Robert Antonio and Gilbert Cardenas for selecting some of the Viewpoints, and to several of our colleagues who worked on the Methodological Essays: David Dodge (Interpreting Statistical Tables), Gary Hesser (Measuring Religiosity), Ira Hutchison (Measuring Conjugal Interaction Patterns), John Maiolo (Ideal Types), and Victor Matthews (Computer Simulation).

We also wish to acknowledge the valuable suggestions obtained from Professors Stan Albrecht, Felix Berardo, Jack Bynum, Fabio Dasilva, James Davidson, John Dryden, John Drysdale, Frank Fahey, Robert Hassenger, Jeff Hubbard, Zahi Kamal, Richard Kurtz, Richard Lamanna, Otto Larsen, Luis Leñero, John Maiolo, Ivan Nye, Walter Slocum, Robert Vasoli, Harwin Voss, Frank Westie, and Andrew Weigert. Dr. Joan Huber Rytina made helpful editorial and substantive suggestions on several sections of the manuscript. Dr. Armand Mauss prepared a thorough index and gave valuable advice on several chapters.

Gary Gereffi, Saskia Haremaker, Mario Renzi, and Jo Ann Richmond aided in tracking down census data, footnote references, tables, and other basic information. Mrs. Loretta Budzinski, Mrs. Harriet Graf, and Mrs. Florence Lawrence deserve a warm note of appreciation for long hours of typing seemingly endless versions of the manuscript, and Janet Mauer richly deserves our thanks for editorial help. To all of our other friends who gave us a helping hand along the way, we express our collective gratitude.

The staff of Scott Foresman's College Division kept us going through many rounds of writing, rewriting, revising, and plain hard work. David Halfen made major contributions along these lines, and David R. Ebbitt was directly responsible for numerous substantive improvements. Judy Green provided irreplaceable editorial work on the manuscript and outstanding captions for the photographs.

Finally, no one is more responsible for the fact that this book finally became a reality than Mrs. Cynthia Adamic, a thorough and demanding editor, a wonderful person to work with, and an outstanding human being.

Melvin L. DeFleur
William V. D'Antonio
Lois B. DeFleur

Contents

Methodological Essays

The Science of Society

A state police car patrols a lonely stretch of highway; in the back seat an observer sits quietly, trying to understand the problem of law and order as seen through the eyes of the police officer. In Chicago, a middle-class man moves into a slum area on the near west side in order to see the world of the inner city as its residents do. In a midwestern town, two interviewers talk to a cross section of people about their attitudes toward the distribution of power and wealth in American society.

A graduate student working for a Ph.D. sends out a questionnaire to members of a professional society to determine the climate of opinion within the profession. A group of undergraduate and graduate students spends the summer in a small Texas town carrying out a basic census and probing the problems of education, employment, and politics in an unincorporated community in which 80 percent of the residents are Mexican Americans.

Several college professors ask their students to fill out questionnaires about their dating patterns and their attitudes toward sexual behavior. Another scholar puts in hours of concentrated effort on the problem of separating reliability and validity in test-retest correlations. A public lecturer tells a large audience that family size must be limited to 2.5 children—and no nonsense!

All of these individuals are sociologists or students of sociology, and their varied activities suggest what sociology is all about—an attempt to examine human social behavior systematically, to understand it, to predict it, and perhaps to do something about it.[1] As this book will make clear, sociology is not a completely unified discipline, never has been, and probably never will be. This may well be one of its most attractive features for the inquiring student. Sociologists differ not only in their areas of interest and choice of research methods but even in their expectations for the discipline as a whole.

Most students turn to sociology hoping that it will help them understand their own social world. They are less concerned with finding an abstract theoretical scheme that will explain the social order and the workings of human groups than they are with discovering what's wrong with society and what, specifically, can be done to improve it. Social problems press in on all sides, urgently demanding solution. It seems fair, then, to criticize "the science of society," if it seems to divorce itself from society's needs:

The real object of science is to benefit man. A science which fails to do this, however agreeable its study, is lifeless. Sociology, which of all sciences should benefit man most, is in danger of falling into the class of polite amusements, or dead sciences.

This statement might well have been made by a disenchanted student or an "anti-sociologist" in 1970. In fact, it was made in 1911 by one of the founding fathers of American sociology, Lester Frank Ward, who went on to suggest a method for breathing "the breath of life" into his discipline.[2]

Most contemporary sociologists agree with Ward that their science should be relevant to the world in which they live—that it should benefit man—but they disagree on specific goals. Does the sociologist have a special obligation to *do* something with his knowledge, to take an active role in trying to bring about changes in social behavior? Or is he obliged, as a scientist, to

---

1. For examples of the kinds of work described in the opening paragraphs, see Jack J. Preiss and Howard J. Ehrlich, *An Examination of Role Theory: The Case of the State Police* (Lincoln, Neb.: University of Nebraska Press, 1966); Gerald Suttles, *The Social Order of the Slum* (Chicago: University of Chicago Press, 1968); W. H. Form and Joan Rytina, "Ideological Beliefs on the Distribution of Power in the United States," *American Sociological Review*, 34 (February 1969), 19–30; John T. Sprehe, *The Climate of Opinion in Sociology: A Study of the Professional Value and Belief Systems of Sociologists* (unpublished Ph.D. dissertation, Washington University, 1967); Texas community study sponsored by University of Notre Dame and Fabens, Texas (in progress); Winston W. Ehrmann, *Premarital Dating Behavior* (New York: Holt, Rinehart and Winston, Inc., 1959); Ira L. Reiss, *The Social Context of Premarital Sexual Permissiveness* (New York: Holt, Rinehart and Winston, Inc., 1967); David R. Heise, "Separating Reliability and Stability in Test-Retest Correlation," *American Sociological Review*, 34 (February 1969), 93–101. The phrase "2.5 children and no nonsense" was used in a talk given by Professor Kenneth Boulding of the University of Michigan in 1962; the same view has been espoused by other leading demographers such as Philip M. Hauser of the University of Chicago and Lincoln Day of Yale University.

2. Lester Frank Ward, *Dynamic Sociology*, 2nd ed., Vol. 1 (New York: D. Appleton & Co., 1911), xxvii.

remain ethically neutral and to concentrate his energies on the pursuit of knowledge about how society works? Indeed, it has often been argued that knowledge per se is the only relevant goal in any of the sciences:

I propose to define science as knowledge of reality because "truth" is used in such a variety of senses. I do not know whether it is possible for us ever to arrive at a knowledge of "the truth" in regard to any important matters. I doubt if it is possible. It is not important. It is the pursuit of truth which gives us life, and it is to that pursuit that our loyalty is due.

The author of this statement, William Graham Sumner, stands with Ward as one of the important early contributors to the development of sociology in the United States. The title of the essay from which the quotation is taken—"The Absurd Effort to Make the World Over"— clearly removes Sumner from the ranks of the activists.[3] Is his position still relevant today?

As a discipline and as a profession, sociology finds itself somewhat divided as the decade of the 1970's opens—and thus very much a part of the world scene. One central issue concerns the obligations of the sociologist as scientist and citizen. As we shall see, efforts to make sociology relevant to the solution of social problems are as old as the discipline itself, but the societal crises of the last decade have given the question of relevancy a new urgency. Some contemporary sociologists argue that "pure science" is a luxury we can no longer afford, that sociologists must actively apply whatever knowledge they have to the solution of society's ills—now. But is it possible to become a social activist and still remain effective as a social scientist? Many doubt that it is and maintain that the sociologist can make his greatest contribution by remaining objective and building up man's store of verified knowledge about how society really works. But again the rejoinder comes back: Is objectivity really possible when the subject matter is one's own society? And must a sociologist abandon a critical area of research if it doesn't wholly lend itself to the scientific method? These are some of the questions being hotly debated by sociologists today.

Another area of debate in contemporary sociology concerns the relationship between social order and social conflict. Do "healthy" human groups tend naturally toward states of stability, equilibrium, and harmony, as some sociologists have theorized? Or are tendencies toward disequilibrium, conflict, and change intrinsic to every social system? If so, how does a human group provide for dissent and change while still maintaining a necessary degree of order, so that members can coordinate their activities and work toward their individual and collective goals? Is conflict necessarily bad? Under what conditions do disorder and conflict become dominating tendencies? These questions are as old as recorded history, yet as contemporary as today's news broadcast. The answers a sociologist gives to them almost inevitably have ideological overtones, for it is difficult to think about stability or change in the abstract. Is a particular pattern of change for "better" or "worse"? Does stability imply "social harmony" or simply the maintenance of the "status quo"?

The crises of the last decade have highlighted the need for an improved understanding of social behavior. The challenges both to sociology and to man as a social being were symbolized at the end of the decade by the achievement of Apollo 11 in putting two men on the moon. It was not only an amazing technological feat, but a feat of teamwork, of social action, of people working together. The careful observer could not help being struck by the contrast between the perfect order of the mission itself and the tensions and conflict of the world the astronauts left behind for a time. If sociology is to be relevant to an analysis of contemporary society, it must help us understand both sides of social life. What are the foundations of order and predictability in smooth-functioning human groups? And what are the sources of conflict and tension both within groups and between groups? These theoretical questions will provide a framework for interpreting many of the concepts discussed in the present text.

Sociology offers no blueprint for utopia or even for the solution of particular social problems. Indeed, for the intelligent student this introduction to the discipline may raise as many questions as it answers. What sociology *can* do is give us new insights into social behavior and the processes through which social patterns can change.

---

3. Quotation reprinted from Maurice Davie, *William Graham Sumner: An Essay of Commentary and Selections* (New York: Thomas Y. Crowell Company, 1963), p. 10.

THE PRESCIENTIFIC ORIGINS OF SOCIOLOGY

Although sociology as an organized inquiry into the fundamental nature of social life dates only to the middle of the last century, efforts to understand and improve society are old indeed. As soon as written languages developed, philosophers, poets, and kings began to record their thoughts about how their society worked and what impact it had on its members.

THE QUEST FOR AN IDEAL SOCIAL ORDER

Ancient systems of law such as the code of Hammurabi, the Laws of Manu, and the Mosaic code were some of the earliest systematic attempts to stabilize the social order and to make it work more justly. Written almost four thousand years ago, Hammurabi's code, for example, dealt with many of the same problems that concern social theorists and lawmakers today. Its 282 laws included provisions for regulating commerce, military and political affairs, the practice of medicine, the treatment of children, and many other kinds of social relationships, including the age-old problems of troublesome neighbors and incompatible husbands and wives:

If any one be too lazy to keep his dam in proper condition, and does not so keep it; if then the dam break and all the fields be flooded, then shall he in whose dam the break occurred be sold for money, and the money shall replace the corn which he has caused to be ruined. . . .

If a man's wife, who lives in his house, wishes to leave it, plunges into debt, tries to ruin her house, neglects her husband, and is judicially convicted: if her husband offers her release, she may go on her way, and he gives her nothing as a gift on release. If her husband does not wish to release her, and if he take another wife, she shall remain as servant in her husband's house.[4]

Like modern legal codes, Hammurabi's laws were based to a large extent upon the customs of his society, deeply established by tradition long before they were written down. But—again like modern laws—they also represented a determined effort to achieve social reform. As Hammurabi stated in the prologue to his code, he was exercising his divine authority as king of Babylonia "to cause justice to prevail in the land, to destroy the wicked and the evil, to prevent the strong from oppressing the weak . . . to enlighten the land and to further the welfare of the people." If these phrases sound like the preelection promises of a twentieth-century politician, it is because the goal of an ideal social order continues to intrigue and elude mankind.

Every philosopher who has tried his hand at designing a perfect society has been sure his proposals were valid. Plato, for example, was much concerned with the nature of justice and spent much of his life elaborating a utopian society in which it could be maximized. His *Republic*, written in the fourth century B.C., is the first really extensive and systematic social analysis produced in the Western world.[5] The utopian society described by Plato was modeled upon the relatively small *polis*, the Greek city-state with which he was familiar. He believed that his ideal society could serve as a guide for those who wanted to insure just treatment for all citizens, relative to their contribution to the society and the level of responsibility they assumed. Plato described in detail his plans for government, family life, economic organization, class structure, and education, all designed to promote harmonious social relationships. No known society has ever tried to put his social system into practice, however, and despite Plato's continued influence on Western thought, his ideas for improving society have remained unproven speculations of unknown practical utility.

THE BEGINNINGS OF SOCIAL THEORY

Every society and every period of history has produced men like Plato who were dedicated to finding a means for constructing a more perfect society, and the brilliance of individual philosophers would lead us to suspect that some

---

4. In Lewis Browne, ed., *The World's Great Scriptures* (New York: The Macmillan Company, 1946).

5. *The Republic of Plato*, trans. Francis P. Cornford (New York: Oxford University Press, 1961).

of them might have produced right answers. But how is it possible to determine when an analysis of society is true and workable and when it is not? Throughout most of history, the great stumbling block for social theorists has been that they lacked a reliable method for verifying their conclusions—for testing them against empirical evidence. Such a method finally became available with the scientific revolution of the seventeenth and eighteenth centuries, but even then it was only gradually applied to studies of society.

A "social scientist" ahead of his time. One of the most remarkable early attempts to develop a "science" of society was that of the Moslem historian-philosopher Ibn Khaldoun (1332–1406). Although he predated the development of the scientific method by several centuries, Ibn Khaldoun contributed to the eventual development of the social sciences with his insistence that human conduct was governed by *natural laws* that could eventually be discovered by observing societal data. He conceived of history as an evolutionary process and maintained that the events and actions of men in the past were the surest guide to what they would do in the future. The true purpose of history, he said, "is to make us acquainted with human society, *i.e.*, with the civilization of the world, and with its natural phenomena."[6]

Ibn Khaldoun used historical data as a means for understanding the ways in which society had changed and progressed from one stage to another. He wrote of religion, government, economics, human nature, the urban versus the rural society, and the bases of social solidarity—the ties that bind men together in a common social order. He was perhaps the first to suggest that the understanding of society could most effectively proceed by systematically observing the uniformities in social phenomena and thus discovering their underlying natural laws.

Social philosophy during the Age of Reason. The foundations of the scientific method were established early in the seventeenth cen-

tury by men like Francis Bacon and René Descartes, who argued that scientists must rid themselves of preconceived notions about the natural order and seek a new understanding through observation, experiment, and reason. In outlining the method of *induction* as a systematic process for accumulating reliable knowledge, Bacon established the basis of the experimental method upon which so much scientific progress has depended. Descartes complemented Bacon's approach by demonstrating the uses of mathematical analysis and logical *deduction* as other avenues toward scientific understanding.

Although the scientific method was not immediately applied to the systematic study of society, the basis of a new science of society was clearly established during the seventeenth and eighteenth centuries, when political and social philosophers began to address themselves directly to the problem of order and conflict in society. Typical of the period was the English political philosopher Thomas Hobbes, who sought a rational justification of political authority that would be consistent with the facts of history and with his own dark view of human nature. Hobbes believed that man in a state of nature was "as a wolf to his fellow man," so that absolute government was essential to prevent social conflict and to maintain an ordered society. In the *Leviathan* (1651), he pictured the state as a great artificial man, "in which the *sovereignty* is the artificial *soul*, as giving life and motion to the whole body."[7]

Hobbes believed that in the distant past people had willingly surrendered their rights to an absolute government in order to protect themselves from each other and so create a workable society. He thus provided one of the earliest statements of a *social contract* theory of government. Later writers, such as John Locke (1632–1704) and Jean Jacques Rousseau (1712–1778), developed important variations of the contract theory, which tries to explain the origins of the state as an agreement among society's members to submit voluntarily to rule in order to stabilize social relationships. Unlike Hobbes, however, both Locke and Rousseau used the concept to challenge authoritarian rule and to demonstrate the people's right to overthrow an unjust government and establish a more equitable "contract."[8] Thus here again we see the social theorist's perennial concern with the relationship of social stability to social conflict and change.

---

6. Charles Issawi, *An Arab Philosophy of History* (London: John Murray, 1950).

7. Thomas Hobbes, *Leviathan* (Oxford: James Thornton, 1881).

8. See John Locke, *Two Treatises of Government* (1690), and Jean Jacques Rousseau, *A Treatise on the Social Compact* (1762).

THE EMERGENCE OF MODERN SOCIOLOGY

Between the beginning of the eighteenth century and the first quarter of the nineteenth, social philosophy in the traditional sense gave way to social science. Dividing into more specialized fields (such as economics, ethics, political science, psychology, sociology, and jurisprudence), the study of social phenomena began to draw on the scientific logic of the physical sciences. The idea of a "social physics," which would provide for students of society what natural science was providing for students of the physical world, was an enticing vision indeed.

AUGUSTE COMTE AND THE "SOCIAL PHYSICS"

Philosophers first became interested in the development and expansion of science as a new epistemology—as a new way of "knowing." They attempted to classify the new sciences and to understand their natural order of development. Many sought clues as to when and how it would be possible to develop a science of society. The French philosopher Henri de Saint-Simon (1760–1825) wrote of *la science politique* (political science) and anticipated many of the ideas later elaborated by Auguste Comte (1798–1857).[9]

It was Comte who gave the name *sociology* to the science of society and who is generally credited with establishing it as a definite discipline. In several important works written between 1830 and 1854, he outlined an elaborate "social physics" to be built upon the foundations of earlier scientific achievements. Comte saw man's intellectual development as an evolutionary process related to the progressive development of science, which he analyzed in terms of his Law of Three Stages: theological, metaphysical, and positive. He saw *positivism*—the use of observation and experimentation to understand natural phenomena—as the key to man's continued progress.[10]

Comte reviewed the existing sciences and classified them into a hierarchy on the basis of their increasing complexity. At the top of the hierarchy he placed sociology, "the queen of sciences," which was to build upon all the others. The major divisions of the new science were to be *social statics*, concerned primarily with the structure of society, and *social dynamics*, concerned with social evolution and change.

The organic nature of society. Although Comte did little research himself and did not try to analyze in detail the nature of the social order, he did outline what sociologists call an organic view of society. Society, he noted, shares many of the observable characteristics of living organisms: it has a *structure*, its parts *function interdependently*, and it has *evolved* from simpler to more complex forms. The particular organizational characteristics of society led Comte to classify it as a *collective* organism, as distinct from an individual animal or plant.

The priesthood of positivism. Comte was a product not only of the scientific revolution but also of the social unrest of his time. The old order had just given way before the French Revolution, and the Industrial Revolution was beginning to have far-reaching social effects. It was Comte's deep dissatisfaction with society as he saw it that led him to stress the need for applying science to the task of "social reconstruction." Comte firmly believed that positivism would eventually yield the knowledge necessary for rebuilding society on a rational basis. This belief led him to suggest that the direction of society should be turned over to a "priesthood of positivism"—a new class of leaders selected for their ability to apply the scientific method and sociological principles to the task of developing effective social policies.

Comte's emphasis on social reform forecast the direction that much sociological research would take in years to come. His scheme for establishing sociologists as the scientific directors of society did not win wide acceptance, but it opened the question of the sociologist's proper role in societal leadership—a question still being debated today. In terms of sociological analysis, Comte's ideas about the organizational nature of society directed the attention of sociologists who followed him to order, consensus, and so-

---

9. Henri de Saint-Simon, *Social Organization: The Science of Man,* trans. and ed. Felix Markham (New York: Harper & Row, Inc., 1964).

10. Auguste Comte, *The Positive Philosophy,* trans. and ed. Harriet Martineau (London: George Bell and Sons, 1915).

cial integration. For Comte as for many other early theorists, social conflict and change were only the means to a desired utopia, not an inevitable part of the social process itself.

CONFLICTING THEORIES OF SOCIAL CHANGE

After receiving its initial outlines in the writings of Comte, sociology became heavily influenced by the social impact of the Industrial Revolution. The social theorists of the nineteenth century became increasingly aware of the social problems that were accompanying the move toward an urban-industrial society and began to question them. Why did they occur? Were they inevitable? The continuing social upheaval and the misery of the masses led many intellectuals to consider the need for social reform. The same conditions gave impetus to the establishment of a wide variety of "utopian" communities in both Europe and the United States.

Of the many nineteenth-century writers who sought answers to the problems generated by the Industrial Revolution, no two offer a sharper contrast than Herbert Spencer, who believed that social progress would come inevitably through *evolution*, and Karl Marx, who advocated reform through *revolution*. Both men have had a continuing influence on sociological thought, especially on theories of social change.

Herbert Spencer. Spencer had an unbounded faith in the natural development of society through evolutionary processes, which would lead, he believed, to "the survival of the fittest" (a phrase later borrowed by Darwin) and thus ultimately to social progress. Spencer was strongly opposed to what he considered the indiscriminate application of legislation as a means of solving social problems. The government, he argued, should adopt a policy of *laissez faire*, so as not to interfere with the "natural selection" of those most fit to survive. He argued against free public education, for example, on the

grounds that a man who really wanted to learn would somehow find the means.

Spencer's approach to societal development did not recognize planned change as potentially resulting in more adequate societal integration. Anything that disturbed the orderly evolution of increasingly improved social forms was considered pathological. Spencer didn't oppose change; indeed, he saw it as part of the life process, in the very nature of things. Nor was he necessarily opposed to conflict, as the phrase "survival of the fittest" makes clear. But he viewed conflict itself as part of an orderly process: what *was* at any time *ought* to be. Those with wealth, power, and property proved by that very fact that they were the fittest and thus deserved what they had. Most contemporary social theorists have recognized this pronounced conservative bias in Spencer's work.

Spencer's interpretation of society in terms of evolution and natural selection—sometimes called Social Darwinism—was related to the elaborate analogy he developed between society and a biological organism. Although this analogy had also been made by Comte and ultimately had roots in the writings of ancient philosophers, Spencer was the first to work out a systematic theory of the structure and functioning of society and of the processes through which it changed.[11] While his organic theory is now mainly of historical interest, modern social theorists who adopt the *functional* approach to the analysis of social systems (page 48) make use of somewhat analogous concepts.

Karl Marx. An analysis totally different from Spencer's was that of Karl Marx, who observed the early form of industrial capitalism in England and concluded that total political revolution was the only realistic means by which social betterment could be achieved. The major points of the Marxian interpretation of society are outlined in the *Communist Manifesto*, which he prepared with Friedrich Engels in 1848, and are further elaborated in his *Das Kapital*.[12] Basically, Marx's theory of society was one of economic determinism; it attempted to account for social structure and social change in terms of the relationships between people and the means of production. Marx saw the social classes as corporate bodies pitted against one another and developing within themselves a strong feeling of solidarity. He believed that the social injustices of this struggle, in which the owners

11. Herbert Spencer, *The Principles of Sociology* (New York: D. Appleton and Co., 1898).

12. Karl Marx and Friedrich Engels, *The Communist Manifesto*, ed. Samuel H. Beer (New York: Appleton-Century-Crofts, 1955) and Karl Marx, *Capital*, ed. Friedrich Engels (New York: International Publishers, 1967).

exploited the workers, could end only when the worker class overthrew the capitalist class and established a dictatorship of the proletariat. This, he maintained, would eventually lead to a classless and collectivistic society, where each would labor according to his ability and each would receive according to his need.

Marx has had an important influence on social theory no less than on political thought.[13] He was the first to develop a systematic theory about one segment of the societal structure—the economic—and to show what its consequences might be for the society as a whole. He was also one of the first spokesmen for a conflict theory of social change. Whereas Herbert Spencer viewed social progress in terms of an orderly unfolding of the evolutionary process, Marx saw progress coming from a consciously fostered clash of major interests and social classes.

Not even Marx, however, saw conflict as an intrinsic part of the human condition; rather, it was only the consequence of certain kinds of social structures. In a sense, Marx was an evolutionist no less than Spencer was, for he saw society inevitably moving toward a utopia in which conflict would finally cease. But unlike Spencer he believed that man could hasten the evolutionary process by active intervention.

THE BEGINNINGS OF SOCIAL RESEARCH

It was only toward the end of the nineteenth century that an international corps of scholars came to think of themselves specifically as sociologists and to write works labeled "sociology." Such pioneers as William Graham Sumner, Lester Ward, Georg Simmel, Ferdinand Tönnies, Émile Durkheim, and Max Weber began to address themselves to the task of understanding society as it actually *was*, not simply as it "ought to be," and to work out methods for studying it objectively. These men began their development of a science of society with little or nothing in the way of special research techniques and with little consensus about what aspects of society were most deserving of study. They had only the social philosophies of the past—and the problems of the present—to suggest where they should focus their attention.

Social thought ever since Plato had approached the study of society on a broad scale, seeking generalizations about such matters as the origins of the state, the moral bases of society, its overall structure, its political functioning, and the direction of its change or development. Working from these same broad concerns, the early sociologists sought to give their new discipline a sharper focus. Durkheim and Weber, in particular, contributed to the development of contemporary sociology by identifying many significant areas of study and by working out early research techniques for accumulating and analyzing sociological data. Durkheim's now famous monograph on suicide, published in 1897, has a special historical significance because it showed that sociology could make a unique contribution to understanding a social problem even as it pursued its primary objective of explaining patterns of human behavior.[14] It greatly furthered our understanding of the act of self-destruction, and it established a crude model for much subsequent sociological research.

By collecting and analyzing the raw data of suicide statistics in various European countries over a period of years, Durkheim was able to place an old form of human tragedy in an entirely new perspective. Specifically, he tried to demonstrate a relationship between (1) the degree to which individuals are integrated into cohesive groups and (2) their proneness to various *types* of suicide. Durkheim found, for example, that the suicide rate for unmarried individuals was higher than for married ones, and he explained these statistics in terms of his belief that the unmarried are likely to have a lower level of social integration and group involvement. Since the emotional attachment of single persons to a meaningful family group is less than that of married persons, he said, they experience a less strong barrier to suicide in times of personal stress.

Durkheim referred to this type of suicide as *egoistic* suicide. He accounted for differences in suicide rates of Protestant and Catholic countries with the same concept, suggesting that suicide rates were higher among Protestants

13. See, for example, Maurice Zeitlin, *Ideology and the Development of Sociological Theory* (Englewood Cliffs, N.J.: Prentice-Hall, Inc., 1968).

14. Émile Durkheim, *Suicide: A Study in Sociology*, trans. John A. Spaulding and George Simpson, ed. George Simpson (New York: The Free Press, 1951).

than among Catholics (though both religions condemned suicide) because the Catholic Church integrated the individual more strongly into group life. For Protestants, a central concept was that each individual stood alone before his Maker; for Catholics, a hierarchical order of the priesthood intervened. Thus, according to Durkheim, the Protestant was more susceptible to egoistic suicide than the Catholic because he was less intimately associated with an organized church and placed largely on his own resources.

Durkheim identified a second type of suicide as *anomic* suicide, and again he saw the structure and characteristics of the individual's group life as providing an important key. If a society or other group was characterized by a high degree of confusion and contradiction in its basic social rules—a condition that Durkheim termed *anomie*—a higher than usual rate of suicide could be predicted, he said. Under conditions of anomie, it is difficult for the individual to know what is expected of him or to feel a sense of close identity with the group. Durkheim demonstrated that rates of suicide rose sharply in a society when established standards and expectations no longer seemed to apply, as during periods of economic depression or inflation, political disturbances, after defeat in war, or under frontier conditions.

The third type of suicide which Durkheim identified, *altruistic* suicide, was also seen as related to the individual's social integration, but in quite a different way. In this case, it was not lack of integration with a group that reduced the barriers to suicide, but rather a close sense of identity with a group. A person may feel such strong ties to a group, Durkheim maintained, that he will place its welfare above his own and willingly accept self-destruction in its behalf. Durkheim illustrated altruistic suicide by noting the different suicide rates among civilians, ordinary enlisted soldiers, and noncommissioned officers. Enlisted soldiers had higher rates than civilians, and noncommissioned officers—who presumably felt the greatest sense of commitment to military norms and goals—had the highest rates of all.

A more contemporary example of altruistic suicide has been provided by the *Kamikaze,* the Japanese pilots of World War II who went to certain death by deliberately diving their planes into American warships. Even more recently, altruistic suicide has been demonstrated by the self-immolation of Buddhist monks in Vietnam and young freedom fighters in Czechoslovakia, both firmly committed to their causes. In general, Durkheim believed that altruistic suicide was more characteristic of folk and traditional societies, where group life is highly integrated, than of urban-industrial societies, which tend to be more individualistic and characterized by some degree of anomie.

Although the more sophisticated research techniques of today make it possible to criticize Durkheim's study on many grounds, it was nevertheless a classic demonstration that the sociologist could shed new light on human behavior by making a systematic analysis of social phenomena. In relating the different suicide rates of different categories of people to the variable of social integration, Durkheim cast doubt upon the "common-sense" assumption that all suicides could be adequately explained in terms of mental or emotional disturbances. Subsequent studies of suicide have refined both Durkheim's methods (see Methodological Essay, page 22) and his conclusions, but all owe an ultimate debt to his early model of sociological research.

THE "AMERICANIZATION" OF SOCIOLOGY

For the first sociologists in Europe, humanitarian motives were far more urgent than the goal of developing a science of societal phenomena. A scientific approach to the study of society was widely sought, but at this stage of sociology's development it was for the purpose of correcting social ills rather than that of acquiring knowledge per se. Thus the term *sociology* came to be understood as practically synonymous with social reform.

Sociology and social problems in the United States. Sociology retained its reformist image as it became established in the United States during the final decades of the nineteenth century. In fact, it appears to have been this very aspect of the new discipline which made it especially attractive to Americans and thus ultimately caused it to flourish in this country as nowhere else.

American society during the late nineteenth and early twentieth centuries was characterized by a number of social displacements and severe

An 1898 view of Orchard Street on New York City's lower east side (below) shows that urban congestion is by no means a recent phenomenon. Under the stimulus of industrialization, American cities grew rapidly after the Civil War, attracting floods of new residents from Europe, as well as from rural areas in the United States. Although the cities represented opportunity, many newcomers found in them a host of new problems. European immigrants received something less than a friendly welcome at the receiving center on Ellis Island, where they were tagged like cattle and inspected for signs of disease (bottom right). In the cotton mills of the South (top right) and in the steel mills of the North, children worked long hours for pitifully small wages. And in New York City and elsewhere, the urban slum was born (far right). These and other problems spawned by industrialization and urbanization led early sociologists to focus their attention on the task of improving man's social condition.

Lewis W. Hine, George Eastman House Collection

Lewis W. Hine, George Eastman House Collection

social problems. The South had yet to recover from the collapse of its economy following the Civil War. Industrialization in the North was proceeding very rapidly, and large numbers of people from rural areas were leaving their farms for urban centers in the search for a better life. The growing cities were also being flooded by foreign immigrants, whose diverse values, cultures, and beliefs sometimes conflicted with established ways. The westward movement was in full swing, adding to the disruption of an earlier way of life.

Large segments of the American population were unable to cope effectively with the many impersonal, seemingly intractable, social and economic difficulties which these changes were generating. Racial, religious, and ethnic prejudices, periodic unemployment, boom-or-bust business cycles, political corruption, the rising incidence of crime, spreading slums, increasing rates of family disorganization, juvenile delinquency, problems of congestion, exploitation, pollution, and a variety of other unsettling features of the new urban-industrial society were blighting the lives of millions of its citizens.

The scientific study of society seemed to many American intellectuals, as it had earlier to many Europeans, to be potentially capable of coming to grips with these problems. If achievable, an accumulation of scientifically verified principles of the functioning of society would perhaps be able to provide a rational basis for bringing about needed social change. Thus, early sociologists in the United States "directed their interest to the conditions or issues associated with the urban poor: pauperism, charity, scientific philanthropy, private and public relief, unemployment, migratory labor, child labor, women wage earners, the labor movement, dependent children, insanity, illness, crime, juvenile delinquency, family instability, temperance, immigration, and race relations."[15] Indeed, sociology began in the United States almost as a social movement, with many of its leaders bent on improving man's lot and doing away with the evils inherent in the new urban-industrial society.

The growth of sociology in the United States. Although the transformation from social philosophy to social science was initially the work of European sociologists such as Émile Durkheim and Max Weber, it was the rapid growth of sociology in the United States that greatly accelerated that change. Publications

dealing with the subject matter of sociology began to appear in this country late in the 1880's, and during the following decade courses in sociology were established in a few institutions of higher learning. The American Sociological Society (forerunner of the present American Sociological Association) was established in 1905 as a professional organization for sociologists. The new discipline found most ready acceptance on the campuses of the Middle West. The newly established land-grant colleges, with their technical and problem-solving orientations, and new privately endowed schools such as the University of Chicago were relatively unhampered by the strong traditions of the older colleges and universities of the eastern seaboard. These new institutions apparently found sociology an exciting young discipline.

Between World War I and World War II the young science of sociology became an established part of the curriculum of almost every college and university in the United States, and since then the discipline has grown at an astonishing rate. Membership in the American Sociological Association, for example, was only 1300 in 1945; by 1970, the number of professional sociologists in the United States had increased tenfold. More significant than mere numbers, however, is the fact that as sociology became firmly established on American campuses it began to shift its focus from social problems and to develop a new identity as a basic science of society, aimed at developing explanatory theories concerning social phenomena of every conceivable type.[16]

THE FOCUS OF CONTEMPORARY SOCIOLOGY

Sociology shares its scientific interest in the social life of man with such disciplines as anthropology, economics, history, political science, and social psychology. Each of these related fields,

15. Roscoe C. Hinkle, Sr., and Gisela J. Hinkle, *The Development of Modern Sociology* (New York: Random House, Inc., 1963), p. 4.

16. For a good review of the circumstances responsible for the development of scientific sociology in the United States, see Talcott Parsons, "The Development of Sociology as a Discipline," *American Sociological Review,* 24 (1959), 547–559.

commonly termed the social sciences, began with some central or specialized focus, such as preliterate society and culture; systems of production, distribution and exchange; the structure and functioning of government; and so on. Sociology, as we have seen, took as its area of study the broad organizational properties of societies and the manner in which they *change*. Historically, it has also had a special concern with the *problem* aspects of society.

Each of the social sciences, including sociology, has gradually extended its area of concern until today it has become increasingly difficult to draw exact lines between them. For example, the interests of the sociologist parallel those of the anthropologist at many points in the study of culture and its relationship to human personality. Political behavior and the forces that shape it concern both the sociologist and the political scientist. Sociologists share with economists the study of work patterns and a concern with the consequences of differential distribution of income within a society. Sociologists and psychologists have developed the interstitial area of social psychology to probe the relationships between the individual and the group.

All of the social sciences, in short, are in some way concerned with discovering the nature of social relationships and their varied influence on human behavior. In its central focus, however, sociology remains distinct from related disciplines. Whereas most of the social sciences are concerned only with particular facets of social life, such as political or economic behavior, sociology is concerned more broadly with "those social elements and relationships found among human beings, whether they are acting as familial groups, say, or as political groups, or in economic pursuits. . . . Sociologists, then, study human interaction *as such*. They try to learn the likenesses and differences among people in groups, no matter what the particular orientation of the group may be."[17]

Although sociologists are ultimately concerned with understanding the structure and functioning of society as a whole, much of their research focuses upon more limited areas of study represented by such established subfields as criminology, urban sociology, marriage and the family, population, intergroup relations, religion, mass communications, and so on. Specialization in sociology, as in the other sciences, helps to define a particular scientist's field of observation and enables him to discern regular patterns of behavior that might otherwise go unnoticed. The new knowledge thus gained often has applications in understanding other areas of behavior, and often it can be synthesized into general principles about human societies. By studying in detail a wide range of both deviant and conforming behavior, sociologists work toward their ultimate task of explaining the nature of society.

SOME COMMON MISCONCEPTIONS

Perhaps because it is a relatively new discipline and not yet completely sure of its own goals, sociology is still poorly understood by the public as a whole. In discussing a contemporary social issue with a small-town lawyer and a local businessman, one of the authors of this text discovered, for example, that the lawyer was convinced that sociology was the same as social work, and the businessman that it was identical with socialism! Such views are by no means rare.[18] With the growing popularity of sociology, journalists and others have contributed to notions that sociologists are primarily social reformers, social critics, or simply dreamy-eyed do-gooders.

Sociology can be sharply distinguished from *social work*, which is a distinct professional field with its own courses of training, technical literature, and professional associations. Persons trained in accredited schools of social work help individuals and families through ameliorative programs sponsored by private agencies and by various levels of government. Undergraduate training in sociology is often helpful for a person going into this field, but the social worker receives his principal training in a specialized course of study, usually at the graduate-school level.

As a social science, sociology should also be distinguished from *social engineering*, which is directed toward planned social change, and other efforts to put the discipline's findings to practical uses, as in government and industry. Persons who have received training in one or

17. Pitirim A. Sorokin, as cited in *A Career in Sociology* (Washington, D.C.: The American Sociological Association, n.d.), p. 5.

18. Ørjar Øyen, "Encounter with the Image of Sociology," *Sociologiske Meddelelser*, 10. Serie, 1 og 3. Laefe, 1965, pp. 47-60.

more of the social sciences may apply their special knowledge in developing programs for communities or societies to aid them economically or in some other way. Thus, farmers in underdeveloped countries can be persuaded to adopt more effective agricultural practices, and families in high birthrate areas can be introduced to techniques for family planning. Both social workers and social engineers rely upon basic information and principles of social behavior developed by sociologists, for without this background of knowledge it would be difficult to design effective programs of social amelioration or planned social change. But their chief task is that of applying sociological knowledge, whereas the social scientist's is that of discovering the underlying principles of social behavior.

Probably most sociologists today think of themselves as *basic* scientists; that is, they are seeking fundamental knowledge about a selected aspect of nature, man's social life, through systematic study. Like other scientists, they attempt to describe and explain what they discover by formulating generalizations, hypotheses, and theories. They also seek to evaluate the validity of their explanations against the hard criteria of factual evidence. The last two sections of this chapter will discuss the basic "rules" of sociological inquiry, which follows the methods and logic of science in general.[19]

In sociology as in physics or chemistry, the line which distinguishes basic and applied science is seldom clear-cut. It is difficult to anticipate either the practical consequences of basic research or the theoretical implications of applied studies. The distinction between basic and applied sociology is further complicated, as we have suggested before, by the question of how this science can best benefit man.

THE DEBATE OVER ETHICAL NEUTRALITY

During the present century, the chief emphasis of sociology has largely shifted from social amelioration to social science. Irving Horowitz, an outspoken critic of this trend, concedes that American sociology has for the most part "accepted the appealing formula of neutrality with regard to political and ideological values."[20] Today, however, there are signs of a renewed emphasis on social reform and social action, as some contemporary American sociologists, including Horowitz, argue vigorously for more direct involvement in society's problems and practical affairs.

The sociologist, such critics maintain, has a moral obligation to take active leadership in the struggle for social justice for the poor, for minorities, and for others who do not enjoy full participation in American society. Echoing Comte, they suggest that the sociologist's technical knowledge gives him a unique advantage in helping the society develop more effective social policies. Most of those who take this position feel that it is impossible to be "value free" in any case. Sociologists would be more realistic, they argue, if they abandoned the model of the ethically neutral physical sciences and tried to use their skills to achieve social betterment.

The popularity of these views has increased somewhat in recent years. The limited success of the civil rights movement, the growing schism between black and white, the failure of poverty programs to achieve very much, and growing distaste for the war in Vietnam all contributed to unfavorable evaluations of American society in the 1960's. As citizens and as social scientists, many sociologists have become increasingly frustrated by the failure of society to achieve needed reforms.[21] They lack confidence in the nation's ability, or even its intention, to bring massive efforts to bear in alleviating the problems of the poor, the city, minorities, or the international situation. Sociologists with an activist orientation feel that they have a special obligation, as students of society, to help lead the way toward societal reform. And they have been particularly insistent about the right of group members to participate more actively in the decision-making processes that affect their lives.

19. George C. Homans, *The Nature of Social Science* (New York: Harcourt Brace Jovanovich, Inc., 1967), p. 4.

20. Irving Horowitz, *Professing Sociology: Studies in the Life Cycle of Social Science* (Chicago: Aldine Publishing Co., 1968), p. 30.

21. The presidential addresses to the American Sociological Association in 1967 and 1968 clearly reflect this frustration, although neither president could be said to be in the vanguard of contemporary activism; see Charles P. Loomis, "In Praise of Conflict and Its Resolution," *American Sociological Review*, 32 (December 1967), 875–890, and Philip M. Hauser, "The Chaotic Society: Product of the Social Morphological Revolution," *American Sociological Review*, 34 (February 1969), 1–18.

Sociologists who continue to advocate a "value-free" position insist that the social scientist must not place moral issues or ideology ahead of the search for valid knowledge about how society works. If sociologists abandon their ethical neutrality, advocates of this position argue, who will develop the field as an objective science? Furthermore, they ask, how can the public or anyone else place confidence in the objectivity of a scientist who uses his discipline as a tool for social change? Isn't there reason to suspect that he may emphasize data consistent with his personal views and discount contradictory data? The technical knowledge of the sociologist is trustworthy and therefore valuable, in short, only insofar as it is free from personal bias.

Advocates of ethical neutrality define the role of the sociologist as that of a technically trained specialist whose task it is to seek *explanations* for social order and social problems. Although his research findings may give direction to the efforts of those who have a mandate from society to initiate programs of social reform, the sociologist himself has no such mandate. As a private citizen he may indeed be obliged to press for social reforms, but his role as citizen must be kept clearly distinct from his role as scientist, which requires that he remain objective. The challenge of separating the two roles has been clearly stated by Stuart A. Rice, who has combined a distinguished career in social research with a longtime interest in social reform:

In my opinion sociologists are obligated, to the best of their abilities as scientists, to analyze and interpret problems affecting society; and to reach and make known the conclusions from their studies, with the data behind them. As citizens they should participate in public affairs. They may express opinions on issues regarding which evidence is partial or nonexistent. But they should not allow such opinions to be understood by others as professional—as expressions of scientific judgment. . . .

When Charles Francis Murphy, sachem of Tammany Hall, was interviewed by New York reporters during John Purroy Mitchel's reform campaign for the mayoralty in 1913, they reported him as saying, "Sure, boys, I'm for the Uplift too, if that's the word." Now, like Murphy, I'm for reform—of many aspects of life and society. My views regarding some social issues derive from evidence and analysis; but respecting a larger number of others they are doubtless emotional and uninhibited by rational examination. Therein is a potential disservice. I may injure both the profession with which you are identifying me and the wider society if my romantic or unreflective support of debatable "causes" is assumed to be an expression of sociology. . . .

There is much to be done. The social stresses are severe. If we, as sociologists, can divorce ourselves from prejudices, wishful thinking and partisanship, creating a true science of society, I believe we can help to relieve stress and further peaceful human relationships. The "heroic task," to quote Manning Nash's review of Gunnar Myrdal's recent *Asian Drama*, is "an understanding of human affairs that will help men intervene in their own destinies with knowledge and deliberation."[22]

A recent survey of the membership of the American Sociological Association by John T. Sprehe suggests the dimensions of the debate over ethical neutrality and shows that, in fact, few sociologists take a completely consistent position on one side of the question or the other.[23] Sprehe used a series of fifteen items to measure the degree to which a respondent felt that his major role as a sociologist was to help change society. Half of the respondents (52 percent) said that the most important aspect of sociological research is its contribution to theory, and an even greater majority (80 percent) supported the importance of rigorous methodology. There was also widespread agreement that the next generation of sociologists will need much more training in mathematics.

Regarding the issue of ethical neutrality, however, a full 73 percent acknowledged that they were not really value free in their own work, even though they might pay lip service to ethical neutrality as an ideal. Further, two out of three respondents maintained that in their teaching sociologists should be free to express their personal values to students. And finally, although a majority considered themselves to be basic scientists, 77 percent felt that active involvement in efforts to remedy social problems

---

22. Stuart A. Rice, "Why I Wanted to Become a Sociologist," *The American Sociologist* (November 1968), p. 285.

23. John T. Sprehe, *The Climate of Opinion in Sociology: A Study of the Value and Belief Systems of Sociologists* (unpublished Ph.D. dissertation, Washington University, 1967). Sprehe reported that 51 percent of the members of the American Sociological Association filled out his questionnaire. Although certain areas of the country and certain age groups were overrepresented, the author believed that the sample of membership was sufficiently representative so as not to bias his findings.

Poverty, racism, overpopulation, impersonalization, alienation—these are some of the dilemmas that Americans face in the 1970's. Since the solution of such problems will require reliable data on many facets of social life, sociological knowledge may increasingly be applied to the amelioration of society's ills.

need not seriously bias the sociologist. In short, the results of this survey were mixed. As the author states it, "it would seem that these respondents favored the application of social science knowledge in society, but they see their own functions as providing knowledge and understanding. In other words, they do not themselves wish to be involved in the much-needed applications of sociology."[24]

The debate over professional goals in sociology is likely to continue, shaping the course that the discipline will take in years to come. We will reconsider this important issue in the Epilogue, after the student has had the opportunity to assess what this relatively new science has been able to accomplish thus far.

THE FORMULATION OF SOCIOLOGICAL KNOWLEDGE

Like other sciences, sociology tries to organize its accumulated knowledge in the form of concepts, generalizations, and theories. *Concepts* identify a specific class of objects, situations, or events that are of special interest to the scientist. *Generalizations* are statements or propositions describing a relationship between two or more concepts. The relationship stated in a generalization may be one that has actually been observed (an empirical generalization) or one that is thought to be potentially observable (a hypothesis). When generalizations have been reasonably well verified by empirical evidence, they can then be brought together into logically related sets of propositions to form *theories*, which provide tentative explanations of how particular classes of events are related to antecedent circumstances and conditions. We will discuss each of these forms of knowledge in turn, with special reference to their uses in sociological research.

CONCEPTS

Ideally, scientific analysis always begins with concepts. A concept in sociology, as in other sciences, is a miniature *system of meaning*—that is, a symbol, such as a word or letter, which stands in an agreed-upon relationship to a particular phenomenon that the scientist is studying. By giving a name or label to a class of events on the basis of those properties which distinguish all members of the class, a concept becomes a kind of "map" of a particular segment of reality. In sociological analysis, the segments of reality identified by concepts are typically qualities, attributes, or properties of social behavior. Examples of concepts are the behavioral territories that sociologists identify by such terms as *role, status, norm, and bureaucracy.*

Variables. Concepts whose properties can vary—that is, come in different amounts, either simply or subtly—are called *variable concepts* or, more commonly, *variables*. To illustrate, sociologists use the term *social cohesion* to describe the degree to which group members share common beliefs, practices, and values and thus act "like one." A group can be more or less cohesive; thus, *cohesion* is a variable concept. Some sociologists feel that at this early stage in the development of the discipline, many sociological concepts must be treated *qualitatively* without attempting to measure them precisely. Other sociologists are convinced of the scientific need for assessing and describing all variables in quantitative terms through the use of such measuring techniques as indices and scales.

The need for precise concepts and terms. Regardless of whether a sociologist approaches a concept quantitatively or not, it serves as a kind of window through which he views whatever phenomenon he has chosen to study. For example, Durkheim viewed the phenomenon of suicide through the concepts of *egoistic, anomic,* and *altruistic suicide* in order to focus on its relationships with other social factors. Because the particular concepts a scientist uses will inevitably affect what he "sees," he must construct his concepts in such a way that they will distort reality as little as possible. This is an especially difficult task for the sociologist, who is concerned with the elusive reality of social acts rather than the more stable properties of things. He must be careful not only to identify the specific attributes a concept will represent, but also to choose a name for the concept that will introduce as few unwanted connotations into his

24. *Ibid.,* p. 220. For a different view, see Stephen E. Deutsch and John Howard, eds., *Where It's At: Radical Perspectives in Sociology* (New York: Harper & Row, Inc., 1970).

meaning as possible. For example, an attempt to study interracial attitudes today must take into account the different connotations of the labels *Negro, black, Afro-American,* and *colored.*

Developing an adequate terminology for sociological concepts is an exacting—and sometimes exasperating—task. It is complicated not only by the fact that almost all of the concepts in the field are undergoing continuous revision and refinement, but also by the fact that many of them deal with aspects of social behavior already understood in part by the layman. Often a new name must be invented to symbolize some newly discovered property of a familiar societal phenomenon, or a term already in popular use must be assigned a new meaning by sociologists, who want to use it in a special way to signify properties of social events which have not previously been studied. Thus, in their search for adequate tools of conceptualization, social scientists often find it necessary to manipulate language in ways that are puzzling or even irritating to the layman, who may object that sociological terminology is a hopeless jargon that obscures communication instead of clarifying it. Sociologists are aware of this difficulty, but they rightly insist on the need for using the symbols of language in whatever way is necessary to define the concepts they must use as tools for systematically exploring the nature of social reality.

GENERALIZATIONS

A generalization is formed by combining concepts into a statement that sets forth some meaningful relationship between them. Usually a generalization states a *quantitative* relationship, predicting that if one variable changes in some regular fashion, predictable changes will take place in another. To illustrate, it can be stated as a generalization that *the birth rate of a society regularly declines as the level of industrialization in that society increases.* Here we have two variable concepts (birth rate and level of industrialization) and a statement of inverse quantitative relationship between them.

This particular generalization was formulated on the basis of numerous studies of the birth rates and levels of industrialization in modern countries, which have actually demonstrated the relationship stated. A generalization

which summarizes factual evidence, as this one does, can be called an *empirical generalization.* It is assumed to be valid insofar as it corresponds with observed realities.

Now let us suppose, for the moment, that extensive data on birth rates and levels of industrialization had not yet been gathered. In such case, the generalization would simply be posing a possible or potential relationship between the two concepts. Only a careful scientific investigation aimed at gathering the relevant evidence would then enable us to evaluate the validity of the stated relationship. Generalizations that have not yet been adequately confirmed by empirical evidence are called *hypotheses.* This type of generalization is important because it helps to define the further research problems that must be studied to clarify the relationship between the concepts.

THEORIES

Generalizations take on increasing importance if they can be combined into *theories.* A theory is a set of interrelated generalizations, combined in such a way that they form a logical system of explanation in which one generalization does not contradict another. Like generalizations, theories not only provide explanations of observed realities but also serve as important sources of new hypotheses.

To illustrate, let us refer to our earlier generalization concerning declining birth rates in societies undergoing industrialization. If we now add the generalization that in such societies *a decline in the death rate regularly precedes a decline in the birth rate,* we can take the two propositions as a related set and logically derive a hypothesis: *The population of a society undergoing industrialization will grow rapidly at first and then level off as a result of successive reductions in death rates and birth rates.* These relationships are illustrated schematically in Figure 1, page 20.

The proposition we have stated here is not a sophisticated sociological theory of population growth, but it serves to illustrate how a logically related set of generalizations is capable of yielding a more comprehensive generalization in the form of a hypothesis. To substantiate this miniature theory, it would be necessary to check the factual evidence through appropriate research on populations undergoing industrialization. (In

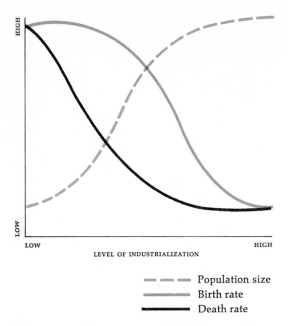

FIGURE 1. **SCHEMATIC DIAGRAM OF GENERAL-IZATIONS CONCERNING BIRTH RATES, DEATH RATES, AND POPULATION SIZE IN AN INDUS-TRIALIZING SOCIETY**

fact, many such studies have already been made. The complex relationships between industrialization and population growth are discussed in detail in Chapter 8, "Demographic Change.")

Explanation. The great importance of theories is that they provide comprehensive explanations of social phenomena. A single generalization may accurately describe how classes of events are related; a theory adds to our understanding by accounting for the antecedent conditions which *lead to* particular events. (Thus, rapid population growth can be explained by changes in birth and death rates resulting from increasing industrialization.) There are many kinds of sociological theories, but all attempt to show that some repetitive social event occurs as an effect of some prior set of circumstances. In other words, they outline the causes of whatever phenomena the theory attempts to explain. This, in the last analysis, is what science is all about.

Theories, like generalizations, have more than an explanatory or predictive value however. Equally important to the scientist, they suggest lines of further inquiry. The old notion of sci-ence as an activity in which discoveries are made accidentally or through flashes of genius does not fit very well with reality. For the most part, scientific progress is built upon painstaking research directed toward testing hypotheses that have been derived in some way from systematic theory.

Validation. The formulation and verification of an explanatory theory is a task of tremendous difficulty in any science. Most theories remain in a state of partial validation for substantial periods of time, as scientists continue to test them against empirical data. Strictly speaking, no theory or hypothesis is ever finally proved; it is valid only in the sense that it has been supported by a substantial amount of empirical evidence. The continued testing and refining of theoretical formulations is basic to the scientific method, and it is made especially necessary in sociology because patterns of social relationship change. A contemporary sociologist must ask, for example, if the relationship Durkheim found between social cohesion and suicide rates still holds in a highly secularized and diversified society.

Most generalizations in sociology state a *probabilistic* relationship between variables, indicating that there is a tendency for them to be related in a statistically meaningful way. Seldom is the relationship an invariant one that permits no exceptions. After examining relevant data in many different communities, for example, sociologists have concluded that juvenile delinquency tends to be concentrated at the bottom levels of the socioeconomic hierarchy, being found with decreasing frequency at higher levels. These probabilistic relationships can be expressed by the following generalization: *The lower the socioeconomic level of a group or social category, the higher the probable incidence of juvenile delinquency within that group or category.* It should be clear that this generalization is not invalidated by the fact that the offspring of wealthy parents occasionally get into conspicuous trouble with the law.

Only in the most highly developed sciences does one find generalizations in the form of invariant laws. Most sciences, including sociology, develop their knowledge in the form of probabilistic statements concerning the relationship between variables. The continuing task, then, is to refine such generalizations so that they permit fewer and fewer exceptions.

Theoretical models. Like the concepts from which they are formed, generalizations and theories serve as "maps" of the behavioral "territories" which they describe. These symbolic representations of sociological realities are sometimes called *models*, because they show the structure of particular relationships. In the present text, most generalizations and theories will be expressed in words and thus may be thought of as *verbal* models. Sometimes social relationships can also be expressed *schematically* by plotting regular patterns of interaction between individuals or groups (page 36). In advanced sociological works, theories and generalizations are sometimes expressed by means of *mathematical* models, which avoid the ambiguities and connotations of ordinary language. Although words are still the most commonly used symbols in contemporary sociology, nonverbal models are likely to be used increasingly as sociologists seek new symbol systems capable of expressing social relationships more precisely.[25]

THE LOGIC OF SCIENTIFIC INQUIRY

Although each science has its own particular subject matter and research techniques, all adhere to the same general logic of inquiry. This system of inquiry, commonly termed the *scientific method*, is a set of rules for ensuring that research will lead to valid generalizations and theories. Every science shares a concern that the data it gathers will accurately reflect the properties of the phenomena it studies. The scientific method has evolved, then, as a basic safeguard against the possibility of arriving at false conclusions or of accepting generalizations that have not adequately been supported by evidence.

To those accustomed to thinking about man and society within the established frameworks of the humanities and religious tradition, the idea of using scientific procedures to study man's social behavior has sometimes seemed outrageous and perhaps a little dangerous.[26] To those accustomed to thinking of science as belonging in the laboratory and dealing only with physical phenomena, it has sometimes seemed presumptuous or a little absurd. Even sociologists have periodically joined in the debate over whether the field can legitimately be called a science. The issue has been slowly resolving itself, however, as sociologists have continued to refine their research techniques and to demonstrate their concern with meeting the broad criteria distinguishing science from other systems of thought.

In outlining the scientific method and showing its applicability to the social sciences, we do not mean to suggest that contemporary sociologists always abide by its rigorous rules. On the contrary, most social research continues to fall far short of the ideal that any description of the method implies.[27] But the practical difficulties that a researcher may encounter in following the scientific method do not detract from its usefulness as a model. In sociology as in other sciences, it provides not only the guidelines to be followed in building a research design but also a means for evaluating research results.

25. For students with appropriate backgrounds, interesting examples of advanced models are readily available. See, for example, Joseph Berger, Morris Zelditch, Jr., and R. Anderson, *Sociological Theories in Progress* (Boston: Houghton Mifflin Co., 1966).

26. For a sociologist's rejoinder to criticisms commonly leveled at the discipline, see Robert K. Merton, "The Case for Sociology," reprinted in *Life in Society,* ed. Thomas E. Lasswell, John H. Burma, and Sidney Aronson (Glenview, Ill.: Scott, Foresman and Company, 1965), pp. 26–29.

27. For a recent discussion of the special problems of methodology in the social sciences, see Gideon Sjoberg and Roger Nett, *A Methodology for Social Research* (New York: Harper & Row, Inc., 1968); also Philip E. Hammond, ed., *Sociologists at Work: Essays on the Craft of Social Research* (New York: Basic Books, Inc., 1964).

FORMULATING RESEARCH QUESTIONS

The scientific method requires that a researcher begin his inquiry with a clearly formulated research question about some specific phenomenon. Although this sounds like a relatively simple task, formulating testable hypotheses is actually one of the most difficult chores that scientists face. It is not enough to identify a problem that needs study, although even this may be difficult, especially during the early

METHODOLOGY   AN EARLY EXAMPLE OF RESEARCH AND THEORY-BUILDING

The methods employed by Durkheim in his classic study of suicide were primitive indeed by today's standards. The statistical records available at the time were scattered and incomplete, and he lacked even the most rudimentary of modern methods for data analysis. Social scientists now command an array of sophisticated techniques for determining how variables are related and for assessing the probability that their findings might be due to chance factors. Moreover, today's computers can perform in an instant work that would have overwhelmed thousands of clerks in the 1890's. Why is it, then, that Durkheim's *Suicide* continues to hold the interest of sociologists?

Aside from its historical importance, the significance of the work is twofold. First, it is still a convincing demonstration that social variables can be of great importance in the causation of an act that on the surface seems explainable only in terms of personal or psychological variables. Second, Durkheim's systematic effort to assemble and interpret relevant data represents an impressive start toward theory-building.

Durkheim's guiding hypothesis was that there are several types of suicide, each with a distinctive explanation based on the individual's involvement in systems of social constraint. As a first step in his study, Durkheim examined the various hypotheses attributing suicide to such extra-social factors as mental illness, racial characteristics, hereditary factors, and "imitation." Eliminating each of these explanations in turn, on the grounds that they failed to account for variations in suicide rates, he then went on to assemble data showing a probable relationship between suicide and certain social variables.

In demonstrating the pattern of suicide that he termed *egoistic,* Durkheim prepared tables and density maps which showed the rates of suicide per million inhabitants for areas of Europe in which there were heavy concentrations of people belonging to particular religious groups. The data showed that suicide rates were related in a regular way to the proportion of individuals affiliated with a given religion in a given population: rates among Protestants were proportionately higher than those among Catholics, and rates among the nonreligious were highest of all. In another comparison, Durkheim found that married persons had relatively low suicide rates, single persons had higher rates, and the widowed had very high rates. On the basis of these statistics, he concluded that the social constraints of religious and family groups served as a deterrent to suicide.

Durkheim demonstrated the *anomic* pattern of suicide by much the same method, using comparisons of suicide rates and indices of social change to show that conditions such as economic crisis and war were accompanied by a significant increase in suicides. Crises in smaller groups—for example, divorce in a family—seemed to have much the same effect, increasing the likelihood that a member would take his own life. Thus, Durkheim concluded that a disruption of group stability and the consequent loss of social constraints increased the probability of self-destruction.

As evidence of an *altruistic* pattern of suicide, Durkheim cited accounts and descriptions of primitive tribes and other groups to show that in certain settings individuals have committed socially approved suicide because of old age, serious illness, the death of a spouse, or the loss of a leader. In such instances, they saw it as their *duty* to take their own lives; failure to do so would have been considered an act of dishonor. Durkheim supplemented these illustrations with data showing differences in suicide rates among military personnel and civilians in various European countries during times of war (page 9). On the basis of both historical and statistical evidence, then, he concluded that intense loyalty to a group, with the reduced individuality this implied, might predispose an individual to take his own life if the welfare of the group seemed to require it.

Durkheim's methodology was considerably more elaborate than this brief summary can suggest, and his *Suicide* still stands as an impressive example of painstaking social research. In terms of theory-building, however, Durkheim's effort was far from complete—he only induced a theory; he did not test it. Subsequent scholars have picked up the task where Durkheim left off, following his leads and testing and refining his hypotheses.

period of a science's development. As we have noted, such pioneer sociologists as Max Weber and Émile Durkheim began their studies with little more than a broad concern about how society worked. But how does one start to investigate anything so complicated as human society? To isolate a problem capable of being studied systematically, the social researcher must first have the insight to see that a possible relationship exists between two or more aspects of some complex societal phenomenon. Durkheim, for example, noted that suicide rates rose or dropped sharply in particular countries during certain periods, and he believed such fluctuations in rates could not be wholly explained by family troubles, mental illness, remorse, or any

of the other reasons that were listed in the official records on suicide. Rejecting the usual explanations of suicide, he then went on to formulate a research problem for investigating suicide in terms of the individual's involvement in social relationships. (See box, page 22.)

The inductive development of new concepts, insights, and inferences is one vital aspect of scientific inquiry. As a science matures, however, investigators find it increasingly possible to derive research problems from theories developed by earlier researchers. Indeed, as we have already suggested, one of the basic values of a scientific theory is that it suggests new lines of inquiry. Often, for example, it is possible to *deduce* from a theory various logical propositions

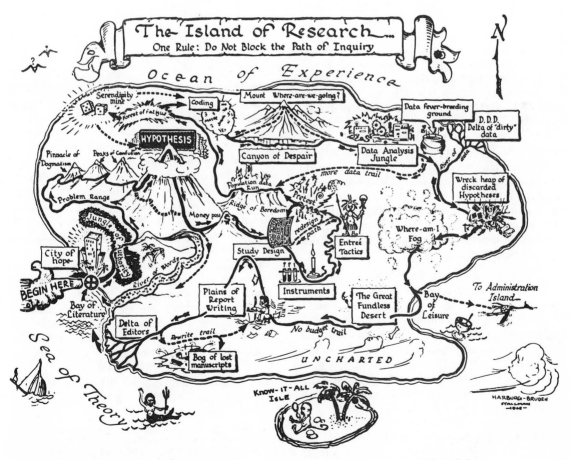

The course of pure science, like that of true love, seldom runs smooth. Here is one sociologist's humorous yet realistic view of the obstacles scientists may encounter in their research.

that can be stated as hypotheses and tested.[28] If such derived hypotheses are supported by subsequent research, they lend weight to the theory. Negative results can be equally important, showing that the theory probably needs revision.

Framing a testable hypothesis. A careful distinction must be made between a research *problem,* which merely identifies an area of concern, and a research *hypothesis* that lends itself to systematic investigation. For example, if the problem is to determine whether all citizens in the United States receive equal treatment under the law regardless of their socioeconomic position, the researcher must frame a tentative statement about the expected relationship between particular variables, predicting that changes in one variable (e.g., income level, as a measurable indicator of socioeconomic position) will regularly correlate with changes in another (e.g., percentage of convictions in criminal courts, as an indicator of treatment under the law). Thus, the hypothesis might be: *Among individuals who have been indicted for criminal offenses, a greater proportion of those from low-income levels are likely to be convicted than of those from middle- and upper-income levels.* Although this proposition deals with only an isolated facet of the larger question regarding equal treatment under the law, it may still be too broad for adequate testing, and the researcher might decide to narrow his study by limiting it to convictions for one class of offense, such as burglary or rape, in the cities of New York and Chicago. Typically, many related studies are necessary before sociologists can make an empirical generalization about any complex social phenomenon.

Establishing a research design. In formulating a hypothesis, the investigator must always think in terms of a *research design.* What are the significant variables being studied, and how can they be measured? What other variables might intervene to cause misleading results, and how can the influence of such variables be controlled or discounted? And since the researcher can study only a selection of the relevant data, how can he make sure that those cases he selects for study are adequately representative of the whole? All of these questions and many others must be answered in the course of defining a research hypothesis that will yield trustworthy results.

GATHERING THE DATA

Once his hypothesis has been clearly formulated, the researcher is ready to subject it to empirical test. Although all of the sciences follow the same general rules for gathering evidence, each has developed devices and techniques appropriate to its own subject matter. The radio telescope of the astronomer is of no use to the paleontologist as he tries to develop generalizations about the fossilized remains of plants and animals, nor is the paleontologist's system of carbon dating useful in studying the motion of the heavenly bodies. No matter how different their research tools, however, all scientists take careful steps to ensure that the evidence they gather will be trustworthy. By one method or another, they try to rule out the possibility that extraneous factors will influence their results and lead to a misinterpretation of the accumulated data.

Controlled observation is most readily accomplished under experimental conditions, where *ideally* all variables are rigidly accounted for. Having hypothesized a relationship between the particular variables he is going to study, the experimenter allows one of them (called the *independent* variable) to change in some regular manner so that he can observe the effect of such change on a second variable (the *dependent* variable). All extraneous variables are carefully controlled so that the experimenter can rule out their effect on the phenomenon he is observing.

Although the classic laboratory experiment is still held up as a scientific ideal, today there are many alternative methods for making controlled observations. Sophisticated statistical and mathematical techniques are now widely used in all the sciences either to hold constant extraneous factors or to measure them so that they can be taken into account in interpreting results. Statistical controls are especially valuable in sociology, which can make only very limited use of the classic laboratory experiment in studying social phenomena. (The varied research methods used by sociologists will be introduced at relevant points in the text. See the listing of Methodological Essays following the Table of Contents.)

---

28. Such deductive procedures are often complex and require familiarity with formal systems of logic. For an example, see Melvin L. DeFleur and Richard E. Quinney, "A Reformulation of Sutherland's Differential Association Theory and a Strategy for Empirical Verification," *Journal of Research in Crime and Delinquency,* 3 (January 1966), 1–22.

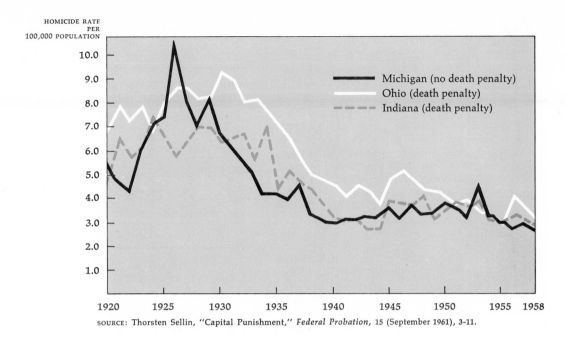

HOMICIDE RATE
PER
100,000 POPULATION

Michigan (no death penalty)
Ohio (death penalty)
Indiana (death penalty)

SOURCE: Thorsten Sellin, "Capital Punishment," *Federal Probation*, 15 (September 1961), 3-11.

FIGURE 2. **DOES THE DEATH PENALTY DETER MURDER?**

ANALYZING THE RESULTS

After the relevant observations have been made under appropriate conditions, research data must be summarized and interpreted. In sociology as in other sciences, this is frequently done today through the use of statistics. Based on probability theory, statistical tests tell the researcher how far he can trust his evidence and how great the likelihood is that chance or extraneous factors might have yielded similar results.

Sociologists seldom try to predict what specific individuals will do, any more than agronomists try to predict which specific stalks of grain in a field will contribute to a high or a low yield. However, different levels of probability can be assigned to different *categories* of persons, in given circumstances, concerning the likelihood that they will engage in particular forms of behavior. Statistical inference need not be the final court of appeal in all cases, especially

for generalizations which do not lend themselves readily to quantitative form, such as generalizations about the effects of urbanization on family life. Nevertheless, at some point a discipline must submit its explanations to a process of verification capable of demonstrating that they are valid within logically sound standards of proof.

Even those sociological explanations that must be regarded as tentative are based upon some degree of empirical analysis and are thus more trustworthy than speculations dictated simply by "common sense." For example, common sense suggests that capital punishment should serve as an effective deterrent to serious crimes such as murder. But what is the evidence? Figure 2 compares the homicide rates of Michigan, Indiana, and Ohio—three adjacent states that are more or less homogeneous culturally—over a period of almost forty years. The homicide rate in Michigan, which had no death penalty, closely paralleled and was often lower than the homicide rate in the neighboring states which *did* have capital punishment. Sociologists have made similar comparisons in other areas of the United States, always with similar results.[29] Empirical analysis, then, raises serious doubts

29. See, for example, Walter C. Reckless, "The Use of the Death Penalty—a Factual Statement," in *Crime and Delinquency*, 15, No. 1 (January 1969), 43–56.

METHODOLOGY   INTERPRETING STATISTICAL TABLES

Modern sociological research makes considerable use of statistical tables, both as sources of data and as a means of summarizing research results. Thus the ability to read tables is an essential skill for the student of sociology.

Before trying to interpret the figures in a table, examine its *title* carefully; it should indicate specifically what data the table presents. The titles of the two tables opposite, for example, indicate that both give suicide rates in the United States for the year 1960, but for different sub-populations. After determining what data a table includes, examine the *source* (or sources) from which the data were obtained. The source information at the bottom of the table will help you judge the reliability of the data being presented; it also gives you the option, if you have a question, of checking the original data for yourself.

Look at the *labels* not only at the top of the various columns but also along the left-hand side of the table. Make sure that you understand them. The data in a table must usually be interpreted with both sets of labels in mind. In Tables 1.A and 1.B the column headings show, in each case, that suicide rates are given for two race groupings and, within each of these categories, for sub-groupings based on sex. But note that the row labels in 1.A indicate regional groupings, whereas those in 1.B indicate age groupings. Thus the two tables show quite different information, even though both are derived from the same basic data—data on the size, composition, and distribution of the U.S. population in 1960 (as reported by the Bureau of the Census) and data on suicides during that year (as reported by the Office of Vital Statistics).

Finally, in order to interpret a table you must understand what *units* are being used—whether the figures represent thousands or millions, for instance, or whether they express percentages or rates. In each of the tables shown here, the title makes clear that the figures are suicide *rates,* and a headnote explains that the rates indicate the number of suicides *for each 100,000* of population. Standardized rates of this sort make possible direct comparisons of the rates for groups (populations or sub-populations) of different sizes.

TABLE 1.A.   SUICIDE RATES FOR REGIONS OF THE U.S., BY COLOR AND SEX, 1960

Rates per 100,000 of population

| | WHITE | | | NONWHITE | | |
REGION	MALE	FEMALE	TOTAL	MALE	FEMALE	TOTAL
North	16.0	5.0	10.4	7.4	2.2	4.7
South	18.5	4.5	11.4	6.0	1.4	3.6
West	22.0	8.4	15.2	12.7	4.9	8.9
U.S.	17.6	5.4	11.4	7.1	1.9	4.4

TABLE 1.B.   SUICIDE RATES FOR AGE GROUPS IN THE U.S., BY COLOR AND SEX, 1960

Rates per 100,000 of population

| | WHITE | | | NONWHITE | | |
AGE	MALE	FEMALE	TOTAL	MALE	FEMALE	TOTAL
20–24	12.0	3.2	7.5	7.4	1.6	4.3
25–29	13.8	4.8	9.2	12.7	3.2	7.6
30–34	15.9	6.8	11.2	13.3	3.9	8.2
35–39	19.6	8.3	13.8	14.6	3.3	8.7
40–44	24.2	8.2	16.1	12.3	4.1	8.0
45–49	30.2	11.0	20.4	12.8	2.7	7.5
50–54	37.6	11.2	24.2	12.2	4.0	8.0
55–59	39.9	10.9	25.1	16.5	3.3	9.8
60–64	40.6	11.2	25.2	17.5	3.0	10.0

SOURCE: *Vital Statistics of the United States, 1960*, Vol. II, *Mortality* (Washington, D.C.: Office of Vital Statistics), pp. 125–379; *United States Census of Population, 1960: United States Summary, General Population Characteristics* (Washington, D.C.: Bureau of the Census), pp. 159, 160, and 167–172.

The comparisons shown in Tables 1.A and 1.B raise many sociological questions. For example, why does the West have higher suicide rates than either the North or the South? Why is there a strong tendency for suicide rates to increase with age, especially for whites? Why do whites have much higher rates than nonwhites? And why are male rates higher than female rates, regardless of color? Note also the striking influence of *combinations* of characteristics (e.g., the rate for white males in the West versus that for nonwhite females in the South). Such variations need to be explained. Would Durkheim's theory help here?

For some recent attempts to explain variations in suicide rates in terms of social variables, see Louis I. Dublin, *Suicide: A Sociological and Statistical Study* (New York: The Ronald Press, 1963); Jack P. Gibbs and Walter T. Martin, *Status Integration and Suicide: A Sociological Study* (Eugene, Ore.: University of Oregon Press, 1964); Andrew F. Henry and James F. Short, *Suicide and Homicide* (New York: The Free Press, 1954); and R. W. Maris, *Social Forces in Urban Suicide* (Homewood, Ill.: The Dorsey Press, 1969).

about the validity of the widespread assumption that the death penalty is an effective deterrent to murder.

In everyday conversation the term *theory* is frequently used as a synonym for *hunch* or *guess*. Friends say, "I don't care about your theories, only about the facts," or "That may be all right in theory, but it won't work in practice." In science, however, theories that have been adequately verified by research *are* "the facts," in the sense that they are the most accurate explanations of reality that scientists have been able to formulate. Furthermore, valid theories *do* "work in practice," providing objective and reliable guides for predicting relationships between several phenomena.

Sociology has not yet developed the ability to make precise predictions in all areas of its concern, but it has been able to demonstrate that social behavior follows remarkably stable patterns, despite the fact that much human conduct may seem unpredictable or a matter of individual choice. For example, it can be safely predicted within small margins of error that during a given year a certain proportion of people in our society will take their own lives, change jobs, commit armed robbery, get divorced, become addicted to drugs, go to college, move from one city to another, have a child, vote Republican, violate their paroles, or engage in numerous other specific forms of behavior. Taken as a whole, man's social behavior seems to follow predictable regularities, and sociology has assumed the task of identifying them more exactly.

SUMMARY

In many respects, the basic goal of contemporary sociology is identical with the goal that social philosophers have pursued throughout the ages —it seeks to understand social organization and social processes, the bases of stability and change. It differs from older forms of knowledge-seeking about society principally in that it uses the methods of science to arrive at increasingly valid and comprehensive explanations of social reality.

To be classified as a science, sociology must first of all have as its main purpose the discovery of the natural properties of the phenomena it investigates. It must attempt to describe these phenomena within systems of concepts and generalizations which portray them as accurately as the development of the field will permit. Furthermore, it must attempt to explain discovered relationships with systematic and logically consistent theories. If it attempts these things, it is a science *in its aims*, regardless of how sophisticated its findings may be at any given time.

A second criterion of a candidate science is that it must base its descriptions and explanations of nature upon controlled observations, using the best techniques available to minimize the possibility of accumulating spurious or erroneous data. If it does this, it is scientific *in its methods*. Sociology is limited in the kinds of experiments that can be meaningfully performed in the laboratory (although many small-scale experiments on social processes *have* been carried out under controlled conditions), but this is not an insurmountable handicap, any more than it has been for astronomy. Scientists have a way of developing research tools appropriate to their particular area of study, and in its short history sociology has already gone far toward refining its methodology. A rapidly advancing computer technology, for example, has made it possible for sociologists to analyze masses of data and to control numbers of variables undreamed of even a decade ago. Thus the charge that the subject matter of sociology is "too complex" for scientific study has become somewhat obsolete.

Finally, to be counted among the sciences, a field must rely upon rigorous rules of evidence for testing the reliability of its hypotheses and generalizations. If it does this, it is a science *in its epistemological procedures*. Sociologists evaluate their evidence according to a specific set of rules based upon statistical probability. Contemporary sociology, then, clearly meets all the basic criteria for a science: in its aims, methods, and rules of evidence it follows the accepted practices of science in general.

THE SOCIAL ORDER

Social Organization

INTERACTION: THE BASIC SOCIAL PROCESS

The Patterning of Social Relationships.   Approaches to the Study of Interaction.   The Focus of Coordinated Interaction: Group Goals.

THE PRINCIPAL COMPONENTS OF SOCIAL ORGANIZATION

Norms as Rules for Interaction.   Social Roles: The Division of Labor.   Integrating the Group Through Social Control. Social Ranking.

THE GROUP AS A SOCIAL SYSTEM

The Equilibrium Assumption.   Functional Analysis.

GROUP TENSION AND CONFLICT

The Breakdown of Social Organization.   Sources of Intragroup and Intergroup Conflict.   Some Positive Functions of Social Conflict.

The human group is to the sociologist what the living organism is to the biologist—the fundamental object of scientific analysis. Thus, a logical way to approach the study of substantive sociology is to examine the concept of *group* from the sociological perspective. What are the essential components of group structure? How do groups maintain themselves? How do they respond to changing needs and demands, to internal and external conflict? Are there limits to the amount of stress a group can tolerate without breaking down?

It is no less difficult to generalize about human groups than about biological organisms; their diversity all but obscures their underlying similarities. Any inclusive definition of *group* must be equally applicable, for example, to a Bantu family, a New York street gang, the board of directors for IBM, the International Red Cross, the U.S. Army, the House of Commons, and even whole communities and societies. Even when we consider only one type of group, such as the small decision-making group, the range of variation is almost infinite. Each group has its own special goals, and each is composed of particular individuals, none of whom are exactly alike or will interact with others in exactly the same way.

Despite great differences in size, complexity, and orientation, however, all human groups fit the general definition of a group as a *number of individuals who interact recurrently according to some pattern of social organization.* Although the pattern may vary dramatically from group to group, the basic components of social organization are always the same. Sociologists identify these as a system of *norms,* or rules for governing the behavior of group members; a system of *roles* for coordinating their activities; a system of sanctions for maintaining *social control;* and a *ranking system* for assigning different degrees of importance to particular roles. As we will illustrate in this chapter and Chapter 2, "Types of Groups," these elements of social organization are common to all groups—ranging from the dyad, as the two-person group is sometimes called, to heterogeneous societies made up of hundreds of millions of members. Even in groups that are not formally organized, social interaction is patterned around "rules" and expectations that are mutually understood by the members. Thus a first step in analyzing the behavior of groups is to analyze their underlying structure.

INTERACTION: THE BASIC SOCIAL PROCESS

The study of social behavior begins with the observation of the transactions that take place between two or more individuals, particularly as these develop into repetitive, somewhat predictable patterns. Given sufficient opportunity to observe the behavior of a group, the sociologist is able to identify the rules and regularities that people are observing as they carry on socially coordinated activities. He can assess the members' mutual expectations of each other, the manner in which they coordinate their activities, the techniques they use for minimizing violations of their shared rules of conduct, the goals they share, their methods of dealing with conflict, and the criteria they use for ranking group members. The sociologist infers the social organization of a group, in short, by observing the interpersonal behavior, or *interaction,* of group members.

THE PATTERNING OF SOCIAL RELATIONSHIPS

Sociologists seldom have an opportunity to observe groups in the process of being formed, but in approaching the subject of social organization, it is nevertheless helpful to think of groups in a developmental way. Stated in the simplest terms, the conditions necessary for the formation of a group are (1) the existence of potential *members* (2) who are either deliberately or unwittingly seeking similar *goals* or satisfactions of some kind and (3) who begin to engage in *coordinated interaction* to attain them.

Transitory versus recurrent interaction. Every human act that somehow influences another individual of whom the actor is aware is a form of social interaction. At the same time, there are many interpersonal events which the sociologist would hesitate to call group behavior. Human groups are based upon interaction involving *meaningful communication.* They are structured around some pattern of social organization and oriented toward the achievement of common goals. In differentiating between group behavior and other forms of interaction, sociologists often make a distinction between transitory and recurrent interaction. Transitory interaction typifies the behavior of such human aggregates as crowds, publics, and audiences, whose members interact only momentarily—though often with great intensity—and then go their separate ways. As we will note in Chapter 11, "Collective Behavior," transitory interaction is relatively unstructured, in the sense that it is not shaped by a system of social organization with specifically relevant norms, roles, and sanctions.

The distinction between transitory and recurrent interaction is not always clear-cut. In some forms of collective behavior, such as casual crowds, interaction is almost wholly unstructured—and it often takes dramatic, unpredictable turns. Such collective phenomena as panics and riots occur in nonrecurring situations for which there are no clearly established behavioral guides. Many kinds of nongroup behavior, however, have a loose pattern of their own, for as people move in and out of similar situations they develop standard ways of responding to them. The kind of transitory interaction that takes place among members of a theater audience, for example, or among strangers at a cocktail party is nonrecurrent only in the sense that the same individuals do not interact on a repeated basis.[1] The situation is repetitive; the participants change.

Interpersonal behavior based on transitory interaction is of considerable interest to sociologists, but their central concern is with the coordinated, recurrent interaction patterns that are characteristic of organized groups. The distinction between group and nongroup interaction can be illustrated with a simple example. Imagine that a number of individuals, most of them strangers to each other but all from the same town, are waiting for a commuter train in a small railway station when suddenly a fire breaks out. Most of the waiting commuters rush to escape the burning building, pushing and shoving one another in their effort to get out unharmed. This clearly is an example of unstructured interaction.

Now let us assume that one individual suddenly takes charge. He directs some of the people to work as a bucket brigade, others to remove valuables from the building, and still others to administer first aid. Interaction would thus become coordinated. However, if everyone

dispersed after the fire and never again worked together, their interaction still could not be classified as group behavior.

But suppose that the experience of the fire made the community more aware of the need for some kind of organized fire-fighting force and that the individuals who had cooperated earlier decided to organize themselves as volunteer firemen to achieve that goal. Their subsequent meetings, drills, planning sessions, and actual fire fighting would constitute a pattern of recurrent, goal-oriented interaction. They would have formed a *group* with a stable and recognizable pattern of social organization.

Informal and formal interaction patterns. Group organization may be based on either formal or informal interaction patterns. *Informal* interaction is typical among family members, friends, and members of other groups whose activities are not governed by a body of official rules. This does not mean that informal interaction follows no rules, only that the rules are implicit, unwritten, loosely formulated, and relatively flexible. The members share a general understanding about the kinds of behavior that are appropriate and acceptable, and they tend to tolerate any behavior that falls within this rather broad range. This informal type of social organization—or *informal structure,* as it is sometimes called—is characteristic of most spontaneously formed groups.[2]

At the other end of the scale, *formal* interaction proceeds on the basis of rules that are clearly specified, usually in a written document. They may be spelled out in a handbook, in the bylaws of an association, or, even more inflexibly, in legal or quasi-legal contracts that specify in detail the behavior each party will tolerate and expect of the other. Social organization based upon formal interactional patterns is characteristic of most large organizations with clearly specified goals. However, informal interaction continues to have an important place even in the most rigid bureaucracy, for every large group tends to spawn a variety of spon

---

1. For a provocative analysis of transitory and related forms of interaction, see Erving Goffman, *Encounters: Two Studies in the Sociology of Interaction* (Indianapolis: The Bobbs-Merrill Co., Inc., 1961).

2. The terms *social organization* and *social structure* will be used synonymously in this text, although sociologists sometimes define them in slightly different ways.

METHODOLOGY   PARTICIPANT OBSERVATION

Participant observation is a method which can be used to obtain an intimate view of the social organization and orientations of a specific group of people. It is also valuable for the exploratory phases of research. Participant observation is exactly what the name implies: the sociologist becomes a group member. He records observations (privately), assesses their implications, makes further observations, modifies his interpretations where needed, and eventually formulates generalizations which appear to describe correctly the group processes under study.

Although the exact steps used in this method are not rigorously codified, William F. Whyte's classic work, *Street-Corner Society,* illustrates the necessary procedures. Whyte used participant observation to study young men in an Italian slum neighborhood. (For some of his findings, see pages 66 and 294.) Essentially, he followed the steps indicated below.

1. *Initial Formulation of Research Objectives.* Whyte questioned the widely held belief that slum neighborhoods are socially disorganized; he suspected that informal and subtle social organization characterized such areas. His research objective was to study slum society for the purpose of determining its organization and its relationship to the larger community.

2. *Initial Contact.* Whyte lived with an Italian family in a particular neighborhood for eighteen months, but later rented a nearby apartment. He made his first contacts with the Nortons—a corner gang he studied intensively—through the local settlement house.

3. *Learning to "Fit In".* He learned to speak Italian and began to participate in neighborhood activities. He identified himself as a writer studying Italian customs and the history of that area of the city. Later, Whyte revealed his purposes to some of the informal leaders of the group. (In some cases, the researcher may not wish to do this.)

4. *Gaining Full Acceptance.* Gradually, Whyte became accepted as a good fellow and was able to participate fully in the activities of the group.

He bowled, dated, played cards, shot pool, and ate and drank with the young men. They trusted and accepted him as a friend.

5. *Systematic Observation.* As their acceptance of him increased, Whyte began to make systematic notes on the group's patterns of interaction, social structure, and way of life. He trained himself to remember details of their social relations in order to make accurate notes later. He accumulated a mass of detailed data.

6. *Avoiding Influence on the Group.* A major problem with any method is to avoid altering the process under investigation by the act of observing. Whyte attempted, not always successfully, to avoid influencing the activities of the group. Above all, he avoided making moral evaluations of their activities. He was there to learn about life in the neighborhood and not to pass judgment on it.

7. *Forming Generalizations.* Whyte used his mass of recorded observations in preparing sociological generalizations about the neighborhood. He organized his material around the components of a social system, describing social control techniques, shared values, and sets of interlocking roles among corner gangs, rackets, the police, political clubs, and numerous other groups. He set forth details on normative systems prevailing in the area. For example, the young men had various codes designating which females could be exploited sexually and which should not. Clear codes prevailed concerning the obligations of friendship and relationships with other gangs, social workers, school, and the larger community. Whyte mapped patterns of leadership and determined the position of each member of the corner gang in its social structure.

In general, Whyte found that it was possible to portray the organizational characteristics of the slum as a complex social system having a latent and informal structure. In this study, participant observation yielded much data on the nature and basis of social organization. While not suitable for some kinds of sociological research, the method is ideal for the type of investigation Whyte conducted.

William Foote Whyte, *Street-Corner Society: The Social Structure of an Italian Slum* (Chicago: The University of Chicago Press, 1948; rev. ed., 1955).

taneous *subgroups* in which interaction proceeds according to informal rules. As we shall have occasion to note, these rules often conflict with those of the formal organization.

Institutionalization. As the members of a group interact over a period of time, their interpersonal exchanges follow increasingly predictable patterns. Members come to know more clearly what is expected of them and what to expect of others as they interact in group situations. Even such two-person relationships as those between physician and patient or teacher and student are based on interactional patterns that have the important characteristic of predictability.

The process of developing orderly, stable, and increasingly predictable forms of recurrent interaction is called *institutionalization.* Patterns of interaction which have become institutionalized are considered binding by group members. Schools, businesses, military units, communities, and societies all have institutionalized pattterns of interaction which members feel they ought to follow. The institutionalization of behavioral norms serves to maintain the structure and stability of the group by providing standard ways for coping with needs and achieving group goals.

APPROACHES TO THE STUDY OF INTERACTION

Although social interaction is a matter of central concern in sociology, sociologists themselves do not completely agree on how it should be defined or how it can best be studied. A brief examination of two contrasting orientations to the study of interaction will demonstrate that such differences can be of more than theoretical concern: the working definition a sociologist chooses will influence what he includes in his observational data and how he interprets his findings.

The *Verstehen* approach. One major approach to the study of interaction was first suggested by the pioneer sociologist Max Weber. Weber defined *social action* (the term he used for *interaction*) as all human behavior oriented toward other people in which *the actor attaches a subjective meaning to what he does.*[3] According to

this view, which has many adherents among contemporary sociologists, the concept of interaction refers not only to what the interacting parties do, but to what they think, feel, and otherwise experience while they are doing it. The observer of social action, therefore, must note and record the subjective experiences of interacting persons as well as their overt behavior. This, of course, is no easy task.

The method Weber suggested for analyzing the subjective elements of interaction was called *Verstehen,* a German word meaning *understanding* or *insight.* The observer is to put himself into the place of the interacting parties, to see the interaction from their point of view. By searching through his own experiences, thoughts, and emotions, he should be able to gain an interpretive understanding (*Verstehen*) of what such interaction would mean to him, the observer, if he were in fact one or both of the interacting parties. His interpretation is then to be recorded as part of his observational data.

The *Verstehen* approach is particularly relevant to social scientists who use the method of participant observation as a major tool for gathering data. This technique often requires that the researcher spend considerable time establishing rapport with the group he wishes to study and immersing himself in their total pattern of living, so that he can see interaction patterns from their point of view. In the late 1930's, for example, William Foote Whyte spent three and a half years living among the members of an Italian slum community in Boston, gathering data for his classic study of *Street-Corner Society.* (See box, page 33.) Elliot Liebow used a similar approach in his recent study of Negro streetcorner men in Washington, D.C., adopting the men's manner of dress and something of their speech patterns in order to interact with them more freely and thus gain insight into their patterns of social behavior.[4]

Some sociologists object that the *Verstehen* approach provides evidence primarily on the

3. Max Weber, *The Theory of Social and Economic Organization,* trans. A. M. Henderson and Talcott Parsons (New York: The Free Press, 1957), pp. 88, 112–123; originally published in 1925.

4. Elliot Liebow, *Tally's Corner: A Study of Negro Streetcorner Men* (Boston: Little, Brown and Company, 1967). For a recent study which in some ways parallels Whyte's, see Gerald Suttles, *The Social Order of the Slum: Ethnicity and Territory in the Inner City* (Chicago: The University of Chicago Press, 1968).

subjective experiences of the observer rather than on those of the actors: there is no way to know whether the actors themselves had the same thoughts and emotions as they carried out their activities. Such critics point out that no other science depends on private data which cannot be verified by other researchers. In reply to this objection, those sociologists who favor the approach argue that the data are not really private. Through his own interaction with others in the various groups of a society, the social scientist comes to share with others the beliefs, thoughts, and emotions that give meaning to social interaction. One of his jobs as a scientist, then, is to be able to distinguish more accurately than the ordinary citizen the significance of the act to the actors involved.

The neopositivistic approach. The neopositivists have a different approach to the study of interaction. Building on the ideas of Auguste Comte and more particularly Émile Durkheim, they maintain that interaction should be defined as behavior that can be seen and recorded by objective techniques. The sociologist should limit himself to the observable facts and avoid subjective interpretations of what the actors might be thinking or feeling. The neopositivists do not rule out such subjective meanings as a legitimate focus of concern, but they insist that they be studied through controlled experiments, tests, scales, and other techniques that remove the need for introspection and insight on the part of the observer. (Sociometry, described in the Methodological Essay on page 36, is but one of many objective techniques for studying interpersonal behavior.)

Those who object to the neopositivistic approach argue that insistence on a strict empiricism ignores many nuances of meaning important to the interacting parties. They maintain that if sociologists restrict their study to behavior that can be measured precisely, their data will be incomplete. Since complicated psychological processes undoubtedly guide the behavior of individuals as they interact with others, why not take these processes fully into account, even though they must be reconstructed through introspection?

Both the *Verstehen* approach and the neopositivistic approach obviously have strong arguments in their favor. The one provides for a more sensitive and complete interpretation of the causes and meaning of interaction; the other is more objective and thus leads to more trustworthy data. Progress in sociology actually depends on the careful application of both. The *Verstehen* approach, for example, is often used to explore research areas that cannot realistically be studied by means of questionnaires, surveys, sociometric devices, attitude scales, and the like. It can also provide the insight that leads to the development of new theories and hypotheses, which can then be studied more systematically by objective and quantitative means.

The sociological and psychological perspectives. Whatever their particular orientation, sociologists differ from psychologists in their overall perspective on human behavior. Psychology is primarily interested in individual behavior; it observes the actions of people as they respond to stimuli in their environment and infers the abstract intrapersonal processes and structures that characterize personality. Sociology, on the other hand, focuses on social behavior; it observes the actions that take place between individuals and infers the abstract interpersonal processes and structures that characterize groups.

Although sociologists and psychologists make their observations from different perspectives, they are interested in many of the same phenomena. Psychologists, for example, study patterns of social organization because groups constitute important sources of stimuli to which individuals must respond as well as sources of rewards and punishments which influence the learning process. Sociologists, for their part, try to understand the personal motives that people have for engaging in group behavior and the kinds of satisfactions they experience as group members. Both disciplines have a special interest in the process of socialization (Chapter 5), by which the individual incorporates into his own personality the values, beliefs, and behavior patterns of the society around him.

For the purposes of the present chapter, which emphasizes group structure and group processes, we will simply assume that individuals participate in group behavior in order to satisfy their own personal needs—some of them biological, some of them learned as the result of social experience. Our point of departure, then, will be to determine what happens when two or more individuals coordinate their activities to achieve shared or interrelated goals.

METHODOLOGY   SOCIOMETRY

Sociometry is an objective technique for assessing patterns of attraction, indifference, or even rejection among the members of a specific group, such as a class in school, a college dormitory, a factory subgroup, or even a small village. These patterns provide indices of friendship, influence, and power among the people being studied, thus demonstrating how the feelings of group members may influence the group's pattern of social organization.

One approach to gathering sociometric data is to observe a group's behavior directly over a period of time and infer the regular patterns of interaction among members. This is difficult to do, however, and can lead to misinterpretation unless all interaction can be adequately sampled. A more common technique involves the use of a questionnaire, in which each member of the group is asked to name the individual with whom he would most like to engage in some specific form of activity. In some cases, he is asked to make several choices, ranking members according to his first preference, second preference, and so on.

A variety of social relationships can be studied—eat with, sit next to, go camping with,

live next to, have as a close friend, etc. Each person making selections is assured that his choices will never be revealed to the other members of the group—an important ethical consideration.

The data obtained are often represented in the form of a *sociogram,* which indicates symbolically the patterns of choice existing between the members at the time the data were gathered. The figure below shows several of the choice patterns that are commonly found. For example, the lines between persons 01 and 05 show a pair who are *mutually attracted,* at least with respect to the kind of interaction being studied. Individual 12 was heavily chosen by other members of the group and can be characterized as a *star.* Person 10 was chosen only once, but since that choice was by the star, he can be characterized as a potential *power behind the throne.* Person 02 chose others, but no one chose him; he can be termed an *isolate.* Individuals 03, 14, 07, and 16 form an interesting *nonreciprocated chain.* Finally, the trio 13, 15, and 09 have mutually chosen each other but are relatively isolated from the remainder of the group; these three form a *clique.*

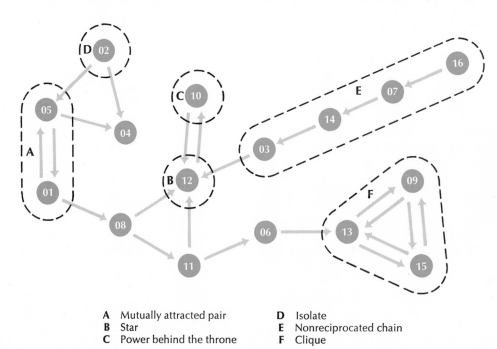

A   Mutually attracted pair   D   Isolate
B   Star   E   Nonreciprocated chain
C   Power behind the throne   F   Clique

THE FOCUS OF COORDINATED INTERACTION: GROUP GOALS

We have postulated that groups are formed so that their members, through coordinated effort, can together achieve satisfactions they could not achieve singly. In other words, one of the necessary conditions for the formation of a group is the existence of *goals* that are valued individually and collectively by the members-to-be. Such goals may be related to money, religion, emotional satisfaction, the control of social deviants, the acquisition of political power, the preservation of historical sites, the defeat of military enemies, the disruption of campus life, the restructuring of a social system, or any one of thousands of other purposes. In general, the satisfaction of individual members is dependent on the degree to which group goals are effectively attained.

Manifest and formal goals. Sometimes when groups are formed, the members have in mind certain clearly specified goals that they can state in explicit terms. A group of political leaders meeting to draft a constitution for a new government may formally state in an official document that their purpose is "to form a more perfect union." A new fraternity may note in its charter that its purpose is "to foster a spirit of brotherhood among its members." Those gathered to participate in a wedding might be told ritualistically that they are "gathered here today for the purpose of joining this man and this woman." In all such cases, the goals to be obtained by coordinated activity are both manifest (that is, clearly understood by the members) and formal. The members willingly submit to the "rules of the game" so that a mutually desired outcome can be effectively achieved.

Latent and informal goals. Sometimes groups form for reasons that the members understand only vaguely, if at all. For example, several boys may begin to engage in acts of delinquency together, motivated by forces of which they are unaware and which they might not acknowledge or understand even if somebody pointed them out. Yet these boys apparently find it more rewarding to steal or commit acts of vandalism together than to do these same things alone.[5] Similarly, several college students may begin playing bridge, studying, going out, and having bull sessions together, always including the same people in their plans. Individually, the students may think of their friends as a group only vaguely, and they would probably be at a loss to explain their common goals.

The goals of such spontaneously formed groups are *informal,* in that they are not officially specified by the group or its spokesmen, and *latent,* in that they are not consciously recognized by the members. Typically, they are closely related to the members' desire for approval, acceptance, and companionship. Without the relatively stable pattern of relationships found even in informal groups, individual members could not achieve these basic satisfactions. The meshing of individual goals, then, is an important factor in establishing and maintaining even the most informal groups.

Mixed goals. Sometimes the manifest goals of a formally organized group are only loosely related to the motivating goals of individual members. An illustration of a group with mixed goals is provided by Hans Toch's analysis of a popular chain of learn-to-dance studios.[6] For the owners and operators, the principal goal of the group is profit. For the clients, a manifest goal is learning to waltz, to tango, or to do the latest popular dance. For many participants, however, learning to dance is not the only goal or even the most important one. Most of the clients are relatively lonely, socially isolated people who participate in the dance lessons and in the studio parties that are arranged (for a price) because these activities offer them an opportunity for companionship. As a commercially available group, the dance studio provides satisfying social relationships for people who are unable, for various reasons, to establish such relationships in other ways.

The housewife who participates in volunteer groups devoted to charity work may also be pursuing mixed goals. Her manifest purpose may be to help others less fortunate than herself, but she probably also has such latent goals as escaping her household routine, making new friends, and winning the approval of those whose opinion she values.

As groups become larger and more structured, their goals become correspondingly more

5. See, for example, Albert K. Cohen, *Delinquent Boys* (New York: The Free Press, 1955).

6. Hans Toch, *The Social Psychology of Social Movements* (Indianapolis: The Bobbs-Merrill Co., Inc., 1965), pp. 91–93.

complex and varied. The social organization of a community, for example, is made up of countless components, ranging from small, intimate groups (e.g., individual families and informal groups of friends, neighbors, and coworkers) to formal associations (e.g., schools, businesses, and civil groups) and other large organizations. The community as a whole has the general goal of providing a stable human environment where its citizens can live and work together in reasonable harmony and efficiency. But within this broad framework, each of the many formal and informal subgroups also has its own set of goals, which may be closely related to, independent of, or directly opposed to those of other subgroups as well as to those of the community. To a greater or lesser extent, such diversity of goals is characteristic of most human groups.

THE PRINCIPAL COMPONENTS OF SOCIAL ORGANIZATION

Sociologists make a clear distinction between groups and social categories. A *social category* may be defined as a number of individuals who share a common characteristic or, in some cases, a cluster of characteristics.[7] There is an almost unlimited number of ways in which people can thus be categorized: men under 35, people with incomes above $10 thousand, people with a common national origin, blue-eyed blonds, salesmen, and women might all be classified as social categories. They are alike in some specified way, but they don't share norms, roles, goals, and the other elements of social organization which characterize groups.

Although social categories, by definition, are unstructured, they are often a factor in the structuring of organized groups. A group may recruit or exclude certain categories of people (e.g., a business may hire only college graduates), or it may use membership in a particular social category as a basis for allocating roles, regardless of the qualifications of the particular individuals involved (e.g., in most companies, women are excluded from top executive positions). In addition, social categories sometimes provide the basis for the development of new groups. College students, for example, can be

classified as a social category simply by reason of their all going to school. Because of their common problems, interests, and goals, students have developed patterns of social interaction among themselves and formed groups of many kinds. Occupational, ethnic, and age categories have similarly provided a basis for the development of many organized groups.

Basically, it is the emergence of some pattern of social organization that distinguishes a group from a social category or some other conglomerate of human beings. Groups establish general rules, or *norms,* which apply more or less uniformly to all members of the group. To achieve a necessary division of labor, they also develop institutionalized expectations, which sociologists call *roles.* Roles assign distinctive rights, duties, and obligations to particular members of the group. Groups institute techniques of *social control* to ensure that members will behave according to both the general rules and the specialized expectations. And finally, groups develop a *ranking system,* by means of which members are accorded different levels of prestige, power, and privilege. Norms, roles, social control, and ranking are the principal components of social organization, and they can be found in the organizational pattern of every human group. We will examine each of these important concepts in turn.

NORMS AS RULES FOR INTERACTION

Norms are shared convictions about the patterns of behavior that are appropriate or inappropriate for the members of a group. They are the rules of the game defining what group members may, ought, should, must, cannot, and should not do in varying situations. Some norms are universal in their application; that is, they apply to every member of the group, no matter how important or unimportant he may be. The rule specifying monogamy in marriage, for example, is a universal norm in our society; the requirement of loyalty to other members is a universal norm in most close-knit groups; aca-

---

7. Sociologists use a number of other terms to refer to the same idea. Such labels as *statistical aggregate, collectivity, conglomerate,* and even *plurel* are more or less synonymous with social category.

demic honesty is a universal norm in every school. At the societal level, universal norms are sometimes classified as *folkways* or *mores* (pages 88, 90), depending on how critical they are to the society's survival. Both types of norms are sometimes formulated into law.

Many norms have only a specialized application, in that they are relevant to certain categories of members but not to others. Girls in our society are expected to play with dolls, but the same behavior is considered inappropriate for boys and for adults. Sometimes a norm provides for *alternative* forms of behavior, any one of which is acceptable. A hostess can serve her dinner guests meat, fish, or poultry prepared in any one of a thousand ways and still conform to the norms governing what is appropriate when company comes to dinner. She may not, however, serve them cornflakes or dog food.

Formal and informal norms. The process by which norms develop within a particular group is not always understood. Formal norms, which are rationally designed to govern behavior within a deliberately organized group, are simply imposed on group members by their leaders or by some higher authority. The rules found on many college campuses requiring women students to keep certain hours are a ready example of imposed, formal norms. Legal statutes such as criminal codes, civil codes, and traffic regulations are other examples, as are the official rules of clubs, businesses, and other associations organized for specific purposes.

Some norms, however, seem to emerge spontaneously. Even the most casual kind of group, such as a play group on the schoolyard, works out informal norms with which members are expected to comply. The boy who tattles, who fails to fight fairly, or who becomes identified as a sissy is violating important norms of his group, and his deviation will somehow be punished. Sometimes informal norms that emerge spontaneously become widespread social habits over time. No one knows, for example, why most men in the United States began to feel they must shave every day, when at an earlier time most men wore beards, and no one knows why beards have recently made a limited comeback. If an emergent norm becomes institutionalized, the individual who does not conform to it becomes subject to either mild

To be effective, both formal and informal norms must be supported by group consensus.

or strong disapproval, depending on how important the norm is considered.

To be effective, both formal and informal norms must be supported by group *consensus:* the majority of members must regard the norm as appropriate and as sufficiently important to demand conformity. In the absence of such consensus, a norm loses its compelling quality. In the United States, for example, widespread support for the norm forbidding any kind of work on the Sabbath has long since been lost, and though some states still have "blue laws" prohibiting most kinds of business activity on Sunday, they are seldom strictly enforced.

The differential importance of norms. The extent to which a group demands conformity to a norm depends on how much the norm contributes to the group's purposes and how deeply it is rooted in sentiment and tradition. Some norms are only vaguely formulated and loosely adhered to; others are precisely spelled out and rigidly enforced. The host inviting friends to an open house may specify the hours as from 5:00 to 7:00, but he knows that most guests will not arrive before six and can only hope that all of them will leave before midnight. But the next day in his role as a college professor, the same person may insist that his students be on hand promptly at 9:00 for the beginning of a class and that they stay until he dismisses them.

Many norms, such as the custom of saying "hello" or "I'm glad to meet you," are simply established rituals for making social relationships more pleasant and predictable. People may be offended by the violation of such norms, but they are likely to shrug off their annoyance or disappointment without reprimanding the offender. He may be rude, but his rudeness does not constitute a serious threat. Other norms, however, such as the army's prohibition against desertion, are deemed critical to the achievement of group goals, and their violation is severely punished.

The number of norms to which an individual is expected to conform is immense. Most people belong to a great many groups, and each group imposes on them a number of formal and informal norms which control his behavior in a wide variety of ways. But if norms reduce the freedom of the individual, they also make his life less complicated and confusing by making social relationships more predictable. In most of his interpersonal dealings, he knows what he can expect of others as well as what others will expect of him.

SOCIAL ROLES: THE DIVISION OF LABOR

Collective action is often far more effective than individual action in achieving desired goals because groups make possible a division of labor. *Specialization* is a key concept here. If a group can somehow get each member to carry out certain specific activities consistently and can somehow restrain him from engaging in other activities, the behavior of all members can be coordinated to attain the group's goals. The development of a division of labor based upon specialized expectations for different members is called *role allocation.*

A social role defines the rights, duties, and obligations of any group member who performs a specialized function within the group. In formal groups, most key roles are explicitly defined, perhaps in a series of job descriptions or a manual of procedure. In informal groups, they are more likely to be "understood."

Whether formal or informal, however, the roles of a given group are interpreted in much the same way by all the members. For example, each member of a given family understands the rights, duties, and expectations of the father, mother, and offspring. Insofar as they share more-or-less common definitions of these roles, their definitions constitute a particular subclass of *norms.*

These shared definitions of various roles organize the behavior and expectations of the group as a whole. Each person, including the one actively playing a given role, can predict what the behavior associated with that role will be. For example, the child who has misbehaved dreads the father's return from work because his reactions as the family disciplinarian can be predicted. The father for his part knows that he must punish the child, even though he dreads the prospect. The mother expects the father to carry out his responsibilities but she will comfort the child after he has been spanked. Thus, the behaviors and anticipations of the entire family are organized by their mutual understanding of the place each has in the family's system of roles. It is in this sense that *roles are configurations of norms.* They not only differentiate the behavior of individual members into specialized activities but also unify the behavior of the group into an organized system of mutual expectation.

The allocation of specialized roles. Every group, either deliberately or unwittingly, allocates roles in terms of distinctive expectations for different members. By this means, the activities of one are effectively related to the activities of others as all pursue their individual and collective goals. Although role specialization is most easily recognized in formal organizations, it is also characteristic of informal groups. On the surface, most girls in a teen-age clique might seem to be behaving in essentially similar ways; however, extended observation of any such group would probably reveal that one girl was the unofficial leader, that one or two others took over the direction of particular activities, and that even the followers fit into the group in different ways.

When spontaneously formed groups persist over time, informal role specialization tends to become increasingly pronounced. For example, if one member repeatedly smooths over quarrels, the other members may learn to turn to him whenever strife occurs. Another role often found in informal groups is that of the joker.[8] Many groups also have an opinion leader, a person who is more closely in contact with outside sources of information than the other members of the group. The opinion leader relays the information, ideas, and rumors he picks up from various sources and helps interpret this material for the group.[9] Though individual members may be unaware of their own specialized roles in an informal group, this aspect of group structure is very real in its consequences.

The coordination of roles. The allocation of specialized roles provides one major element of a group's social organization; the coordination of these roles into an overall system of reciprocal relationships provides another. Consider the role system of a typical family. The role of husband has no meaning unless it is linked with the *complementary role* of wife. The same is true of father

and child, brother and sister, uncle and nephew, and so on. All social roles can be viewed as complementary to other roles. There can be no physician without a patient, no teacher without a student, and no friend without another. Thus, the activities or expectations relevant to a given role are reciprocally linked with other roles in an interdependent system.

In small, spontaneous groups the pattern of role coordination and interdependency is usually quite simple and only vaguely defined. The members seldom need formal direction in working together. A more clear-cut division of labor is usually found in formally organized groups, even if they are small. A committee charged with the task of reaching a specific goal normally has a chairman and may also have a secretary. Sometimes several subcommittees are designated. In such cases, roles are clearly specified, and interrole linkages are carefully coordinated. A baseball team is another example of a small group with a clearly defined division of labor. The role system is formally specified in the rules (norms) laid down by baseball officials, and the pattern of coordination between roles is well understood by the players, manager, coaches, and most people in the grandstand.

In large businesses and other associations, the division of labor becomes highly elaborate. Those responsible for designing the organizational pattern of a corporation must give detailed attention to both the allocation and the coordination of interdependent roles. Often they rely on detailed job descriptions to give formal definitions of the various occupational roles within the organization, from clerk-typist to section manager. They may use time-and-motion studies to determine the most efficient pattern of movement for workers on an assembly line. And always they create an organizational chart, showing lines of communication and responsibility as they stem from the head of the organization on down through lower levels of management.

Essentially, it is the need for coordinating roles that is responsible for the development of *leadership.* As we have already noted, spontaneous leaders develop in informal groups when members repeatedly turn to the same person for advice, for suggestions, or for direction in achieving group goals. In formally organized groups that require more definite leadership, authority is specifically delegated: certain individuals have a clearly defined right to coordinate the activities of others. Very different criteria and

8. Jacqueline D. Goodchilds, "The Effects of Being Witty on Position in the Social Structure of a Small Group," *Sociometry,* 22 (1959), 261–272.

9. Bernard R. Berelson, Paul F. Lazarsfeld, and Hazel Gaudet, *The People's Choice,* 2nd ed. (New York: Columbia University Press, 1948).

procedures are used to select leaders in different types of groups, but always the basic reason for a leader is the need for coordinating the members' specialized activities.

Role expectation and role behavior. As the preceding discussion has suggested, a social role can be thought of either as a set of organized expectations concerning the activities appropriate to a given position or as the actual behavior of the role incumbent—of the group member who carries out the role. Although the concepts of role *expectations* and role *behavior* are closely related, the distinction between them is important. If the way a group member acts out his role is fairly consistent with the group's expectations of the role, group interaction will proceed harmoniously; but if an incumbent's role performance does *not* match the group's expectations, conflict is likely. This is especially true when the gap between role expectations and role performance widens to a point where achievement of the group's goals seems threatened. Thus, most groups develop a system of rewards and punishments to ensure that members will carry out their roles according to expected patterns.

INTEGRATING THE GROUP THROUGH SOCIAL CONTROL

Groups of all types attempt to maintain the stability of their social organization by developing techniques of social control. *Social control* can be defined as the application of sanctions to ensure that members will (1) abide by the group's norms, (2) perform required roles in a prescribed manner, and (3) coordinate their activities in such a way that group goals can be achieved. *Negative sanctions* are meted out as punishment or the threat of punishment to members who violate norms or fail to perform their roles adequately; their purpose is to check deviation. *Positive sanctions*, on the other hand, are used to reward members who meet or exceed the group's expectations; thus, they serve to reinforce approved patterns of behavior. Both kinds of sanctions are considered necessary to maintain the organization of a group and to increase the probability that its goals will be attained.

Tolerance limits. Although some groups are much stricter than others in demanding conformity from their members, most of the rules in any group provide for a *range* of tolerable behavior. Except for norms that are deemed critical, such as the societal norm prohibiting murder, some degree of deviation is permitted before negative sanctions are invoked.

Tolerance limits are seldom precisely defined, but the members of a group soon learn from experience how much leeway they have in interpreting particular norms and roles. For example, some motorists regularly drive at speeds slightly over the posted limit on the assumption that they probably will not be stopped for this minor infraction of the law. Many drivers, in fact, follow a rough-and-ready formula for speeding: speeds up to five miles an hour beyond the limit will usually be tolerated by the police. They have conceived a tolerance limit that realistically defines the point beyond which negative sanctions will be invoked.

Sometimes a literal enforcement of a group's rules arouses considerable hostility among the members, especially if the rules seem relatively unimportant. In military establishments located in combat zones or other hardship areas, for example, traditional discipline and rituals are often greatly relaxed. If a new officer arrives and insists on strict adherence to the norms associated with formal military protocol, he will be cordially hated by his men, who may even try to subvert his authority in serious ways.

The administration of sanctions. The negative sanctions used by various groups range from subtle gestures like raising an eyebrow to show a member he has committed a social error to such drastic acts as executing an individual who has violated the norm forbidding murder or treason. In small, intimate groups sanctions are usually verbal, but occasionally they involve the administration of physical punishment under the guise of a game. In a classic study of a group of factory workers, Roethlisberger and Dickson noted that the men had developed an informal norm specifying the number of units that each member of the group should produce as a fair day's work. If a given member greatly exceeded this norm, producing so many units that the other men might appear to be slackers, sanctions were employed to bring him back into line. His friends would call him a rate-buster and other less flattering names, all in a semihumorous vein but not entirely in fun. A really serious violation was punished through the game of "binging," a form of horseplay in which the men exchanged blows to the upper arm, with the rate-buster always getting the worst of it.[10]

Similar sanctions are sometimes used by students who resent an individual whose grades are "too high." Although the superior student may receive positive sanctions from his professor, in the form of praise and a good grade, he may be subjected to negative sanctions from his fellow students. Joking references to him as a "curve breaker," "brown nose," or "grind" are actually techniques of control aimed at lowering his performance to a level where he will no longer pose "unfair" competition.

In most small groups, sanctions are devised spontaneously and can generally be administered by any member. In large groups, social control is likely to be much more formal and sanctions are usually meted out according to official policies. Most formal organizations have a wide variety of positive and negative sanctions. An obvious example from the business world is the practice of awarding or withholding promotions and pay increases on the basis of merit, that is, for adequate or inadequate role performance. Many groups also use symbolic sanctions. College students are given grades; military cadets are given decorations or demerits; successful managerial personnel in corporations are given a more prestigious title, a rug on the floor, a private secretary, a reserved parking space, or a key to the executive washroom.

The authority to apply formal sanctions is an important basis of control for those charged with the task of coordinating the organizational machinery of an association or other large group. The head of a formal organization is respected—and sometimes feared—largely because he has been vested with the final authority to give or withhold official rewards.

The interplay of formal and informal sanctions. Since most large groups incorporate a variety of spontaneous subgroups, individual members are subject to both formal and in-formal social controls. If an official norm conflicts with one supported by a subgroup, the individual must make a choice. Often he will decide to violate a norm of the larger group, rather than one upheld by people with whom he more closely identifies. In some circles of young people it became popular during the late 1960's to shout "Hell, no, we won't go!" in response to a military conscription notice. Many young men were willing to face the negative sanctions of the federal government, knowing that their actions were receiving positive sanctions from their peers.

An effective dovetailing of formal and informal controls can produce a tenacious adherence to norms and a conspicuous overperformance of roles, as often demonstrated by the performance of small military units in combat. In a study seeking to explain the extraordinary effectiveness of the German army on several fronts during most of World War II, Shils and Janowitz tested the hypothesis that the key factor in motivating the determined resistance of the average German soldier was "the steady satisfaction of certain primary personality demands afforded by the social organization of the army" rather than the technical quality of the German high command or the ideological strength of National Socialism. The data obtained supported the hypothesis by showing that as long as the soldier felt a special loyalty to his squad or platoon and identified himself emotionally with other squad members, his morale remained high and he was extremely effective as a soldier. The researchers found further that the effectiveness of the army as a whole seemed to be enhanced, not endangered, by the fact that the focus of attention of the smaller units was very narrowly restricted and oriented toward their own group of comrades.[11]

SOCIAL RANKING

As a group's pattern of social organization becomes institutionalized, the various roles that have been delineated tend to be ranked hierarchically. Various criteria may be used as a basis of such ranking. For example, a specific role may be accorded high rank because of the higher degree of authority it carries relative to other roles in the group. Or, a given role may be ranked high because it presupposes a talent

---

10. Fritz J. Roethlisberger and William J. Dickson, *Management and the Worker* (Cambridge, Mass.: Harvard University Press, 1939), Part 4.

11. Edward A. Shils and Morris Janowitz, "Cohesion and Disintegration in the Wehrmacht in World War II," *The Public Opinion Quarterly*, 12 (1948), 280–315.

Groups use a wide range of techniques to encourage approved patterns of behavior and to check deviation. The enthusiasm of crowd members in honoring American astronauts for a successful moon landing serves as a positive sanction, as does the formal presentation of an Academy Award. Techniques used to discourage disapproved behavior can range all the way from a dirty look to the exercise of legal force.

that few men possess. Other roles may be associated with unusual wealth or require a long and demanding period of training. Some roles may be ranked low in the system because they carry little power, few privileges, or limited responsibility. Whatever the criteria, the shared judgments of the group members form some system of social ranking.

Ascribed and achieved criteria. Sociologists make a distinction between ascribed and achieved criteria of social ranking. *Ascribed* criteria are those about which the individual can do little or nothing. Almost every society, for example, ranks its members on the basis of age and sex, with the role of female generally being ranked below the role of male and the role of child being ranked below that of adult. Lord Chesterfield reflected the traditional thinking about a woman's proper role in a letter of advice to his son (1748):

Women, then, are only children of a larger growth; they have an entertaining tattle, and sometimes wit; but for solid reasoning, good sense, I never knew in my life one that had it, or who reasoned or acted consequentially for four and twenty hours together. . . . A man of sense only trifles with them, plays with them, humors and flatters them, as he does with a sprightly forward child; but he neither consults them about, nor trusts them with, serious matters . . . .

Unlike age, sex, and family background, *achieved* criteria are those about which the individual can do something. He may undertake costly and difficult training in order to enter a professional occupation that is accorded high rank in his society. He may campaign vigorously in order to get elected to an important political office. He may assume great responsibility in order to be promoted to the executive ranks in some business group.

Ascribed and achieved criteria are used not only for judging the relative rank of different roles in a group but also for selecting individuals to fill them. A child cannot expect people to respond to him in terms of adult roles, and a female may be channeled out of certain occupations which have been traditionally allocated to males. Race and ethnicity are sometimes similarly used as ascribed criteria for barring whole categories of people from certain types of roles.

Groups vary in the extent to which they depend upon ascribed or achieved criteria for allocating people to roles and for according high or low rank to the roles they play. Ascribed criteria, mainly age and sex, are almost universally used as bases for the ranking system of the family. In groups with a more elaborate division of labor, such as those typically found in modern business, education, and government, roles are generally ranked according to the degree of skill or training they require, and individuals are assigned to them on the basis of ability to perform adequately. However, the fact that we apparently need laws to guarantee equal employment opportunities for minority-group members, women, and older workers suggests that relatively few roles in such groups are filled on the basis of ability alone.

Status. The confusion of meanings associated with the term *status* clearly demonstrates the need for an increasingly precise terminology in the social sciences. Some sociologists, for example, use the term *status* to refer to a role's position within an orderly structure of roles, with no implication of rank. Thus, it is possible to think of the status system of a baseball team simply as the nine positions that comprise the group's role structure. Other sociologists have used *status* to identify the concept we have termed *social rank.* Compounding the confusion, nonsociologists often use *status* to indicate the possession of unusually great wealth or prestige.

In the present text we will try to clarify these related aspects of social organization by making a consistent distinction between the concepts of status and social ranking. The term *social ranking* will be used, as in the section above, to refer broadly to the differential ranking of roles in a group. The term *status* will be used more specifically to designate the level of *prestige* that is accorded a group member by virtue of the particular role he plays. Status (prestige) is thus seen as a *consequence* of social ranking: an individual enjoys a high level of status or suffers a low one because the role allocated to him is ranked high or low in the group's hierarchy of roles.

It should be noted that a person's status in one group may be quite different from his status in another. A department head has high status in his own work group but may have relatively low status in the overall corporate structure. His secretary has even less status in the corporation, but she may enjoy high status as the president of her church group or women's club.

At the community level status is a consequence of social ranking in a cluster of interrelated systems. This complex aspect of social organization will be analyzed in detail in Chapter 7.

Esteem. The level of status accorded to an individual as the result of his role in a social system is independent of the level of *esteem* accorded to him as a person. The distinction between status and esteem can be simply illustrated by analyzing the criteria we might use in rating the personnel in a dentist's office—typically, the dentist, a dental technician, and a receptionist. A patient seeking the professional services of this group could easily distinguish the three roles in terms of the status they carried, and his ranking would be the same regardless of the individuals involved. The hierarchy might be quite different, however, if the patient were to rate the role incumbents in terms of their personal qualities. The dentist himself might be a disagreeable grouch, and his technician might be cold and officious. The receptionist, on the other hand, might be a pleasant woman who made trips to the dentist less an ordeal.

In this example the patient's rating of the three individuals in terms of their personal qualities might be just the reverse of the way he would rate their relative status. Status, in other words, derives from a role, whereas esteem derives from the personal qualities of an individual. The two concepts are related only to the extent that outstanding role performance generally commands admiration.

THE GROUP AS A
SOCIAL SYSTEM

In the preceding sections we have examined norms, roles, sanctions, and ranking systems in terms of their importance to group *structure*. To complete our analysis of social organization, we must bring the time variable into the picture and consider the group as an ongoing *process*. For a human group is not static; like its members, it responds to the environment and changes over time, even as it maintains its basic identity.

Although contemporary sociology no longer uses elaborate organic analogies, such as those proposed in the nineteenth century by Auguste Comte (page 6) and Herbert Spencer (page 7), an organic perspective remains relevant to those modern sociologists who view every group, large or small, as a *social system*.[12] The concept of *system* is used in sociology much as it is in the physical and biological sciences: it defines a configuration of parts that are in a relationship of interdependency. Thus we can speak of the sun and the heavenly bodies that revolve around it as the *solar system*; of man's body with its interrelated parts and functions as a *biological system*; of a group with its integrated pattern of social organization and behavior as a *social system*. Each system, whether living or nonliving, has a characteristic structure and a characteristic pattern of functioning. Finally, each is composed of subsystems and is itself part of a larger system, or *field*.

The analysis of a group as a social system requires two stages. First, it is necessary to observe the interaction of group members over a period of time in order to infer the group's structure—the specific norms, roles, systems of ranking, and social control that make up its pattern of social organization. Second, it is necessary to define the ways in which these structural elements are *interrelated* and *interdependent*—how they function together as an ongoing whole.

An analysis of this type is made more difficult due to the fact that no group exists in a social vacuum. Each has transactions with, or is part of, other groups. Thus, the Smith children are a subgroup of the Smith family and perhaps of a playground group. The family as a whole is a subgroup of the neighborhood, which is a subgroup of the community. The community itself is one of countless subgroups of the society. Individually or as a family, the Smiths also belong to a variety of educational, occupational, recreational, religious, and political groups—all of which are also community and societal subgroups. The *internal system* of any particular group, then, must be analyzed in the context of the *external system*, or total environmental field, in which it operates.

The task of actually unraveling all the patterns of interdependency within a group, and between a group and its social environment, is

---

12. See, for example, Talcott Parsons, *The Social System* (New York: The Free Press, 1951).

nearly an impossible one. The patterns are almost infinitely complex, and they are continuously changing. Nevertheless, a social systems perspective can be extremely useful to the sociologist as he searches for relationships of cause and effect. The concept of interdependency implies, for example, that a disturbance or change in one component of a social system will have repercussions throughout the system. Thus, a sociologist who is trying to account for some distinctive pattern of behavior within a particular subgroup—whether the pattern be drug taking, political apathy, early marriage, or emphasis on material possessions—may analyze the relationship of the subgroup to the rest of the system in his search for possible causes. In this way, a social systems perspective often leads to the discovery of sociological relationships that might otherwise go unnoticed.[13]

THE EQUILIBRIUM ASSUMPTION

In sociology as in other disciplines, a systems perspective assumes that systems have a tendency to resist disintegration and to maintain their equilibrium. In the human biological system, certain drives propel the organism to seek the food, water, sleep, and oxygen it needs in order to survive. If the organism is invaded by disease-causing microorganisms, it forms antibodies to fight the invaders. If danger threatens, automatic changes in body chemistry help the individual cope with the emergency.

Sociologists who utilize the social systems perspective note that groups have a similar tendency to maintain themselves and to resist disturbances from outside. When a group's equilibrium is upset, whether by internal or external forces, the patterns of relationship that existed prior to the disturbance tend gradually to be restored.[14] A group's system of sanctions, for example, serves not only to prevent deviation but also to bring deviators back into line.

Most systems theorists recognize that the concepts of stability and equilibrium are relative. Stable groups change over time, just as stable individuals do. Indeed, unyielding resistance to change can sometimes boomerang and lead ultimately to a group's disintegration, for groups must adapt to changing circumstances if they are to survive and be effective. To say that a group

has a tendency toward equilibrium and stability, then, means only that changes usually come gradually, without disrupting the basic structure of the system.

FUNCTIONAL ANALYSIS

An important corollary to the equilibrium assumption is that *every component of a social system makes some contribution to the system's equilibrium.*[15] Thus, any repetitive form of behavior, any role or norm or other element of a group's social organization, can be analyzed in terms of the *function* it has in maintaining the group and enabling it to operate effectively. Research aimed at discovering such relationships is known as *functional analysis.*

Latent and manifest functions. Functionally oriented sociologists usually distinguish between the latent and manifest functions of an established pattern of social relationships.[16] *Manifest* functions are those which are built into a social system by design; like manifest goals, they are well understood by a group's members. *Latent* functions, by contrast, are unintentional and often unrecognized. They are the unanticipated consequences of a system that has been set up to achieve other ends. The system of free public education in the United States, for example, has the manifest function of opening educational opportunity to all citizens and thereby increasing their ability to participate equally in a democratic society. In practice, however, the system has had the unintended effect of educating new members of society selectively, opening opportunity for some and closing it for others. (Both the manifest and latent functions of the American educational system will be examined in detail in Chapter 18.)

13. George C. Homans, *The Human Group* (New York: Harcourt Brace Jovanovich, Inc., 1950).

14. Charles P. Loomis, *Social Systems: Essays on Their Persistence and Change* (Princeton, N.J.: D. Van Nostrand Co., Inc., 1960). See also Walter Buckley, *Sociology and Modern Systems Theory* (Englewood Cliffs, N.J.: Prentice-Hall, Inc., 1967).

15. This view was once very popular in anthropology. See A. R. Radcliffe-Brown, *The Andaman Islanders* (New York: The Free Press, 1948), p. 397.

16. Robert K. Merton, *Social Theory and Social Structure* (New York: The Free Press, 1957), pp. 19–84.

Almost every pattern of social organization has similarly unexpected effects. In a corporation, the management may establish a tight system of control in order to make employees more productive, only to make them dissatisfied and perhaps *less* productive. In a family, the parents may try to let a child develop as much independence as possible, only to have him think they don't care what he does. In making a functional analysis of any group, the sociologist tries to determine both the latent and manifest functions of each aspect of social organization and to show how they interrelate. The Methodological Essay on page 76 describes the application of functional analysis to the study of bureaucratic organizations.

Function and dysfunction. The equilibrium assumption, more than any other aspect of the social systems perspective, can have an important influence on the direction of social research, for it orients the sociologist who accepts it to search for the effects of particular organizational patterns *on the stability of the system as a whole.* Some functionally oriented sociologists maintain, for example, that the unequal distribution of wealth, status, and power in a society is necessary for motivating individuals to fill difficult societal roles and to perform them adequately. Seen in this light, social stratification is integrative rather than divisive: it may penalize some individuals and groups, but it has a positive function for society as a whole. In Chapter 7, "Social Stratification," we will weigh this theory against the arguments of Karl Marx and others who have related social stratification to theories of social conflict.

In making a functional analysis of any social arrangement, it is important to distinguish the consequences for different parts of the system. Functionally oriented sociologists say that a given practice is dysfunctional if it somehow hampers the achievement of group goals or disrupts the group's equilibrium. Thus, the practice of retaining a fireman on diesel trains, which have no practical use for a fireman, can be viewed as dysfunctional from the point of view of a company that is trying to operate a railroad for profit. The practice may be functional, however, from the point of view of the railroad workers, in that it retains jobs for those who might otherwise be displaced. The terms *functional* and *dysfunctional,* in short, are relative to the particular group that is being analyzed.

Whether an activity is seen as functional or dysfunctional is often a matter of perspective. Thus, a student strike is likely to be regarded as dysfunctional by university administrators, since it disrupts the normal operation of the school. From the perspective of the students, however, the disruption may be viewed as a necessary step toward changing the structure of the university and making it function more effectively.

GROUP TENSION AND CONFLICT

Thus far we have emphasized the relatively stable and predictable patterns that develop in groups as their members engage in coordinated interaction over a period of time. This emphasis was deliberate in order to provide a theoretical framework for analyzing social behavior. In a sense, we have constructed an idealized model of a smooth-functioning, stable group.

In the world of social reality, of course, few groups remain completely harmonious and stable over long periods of time. Even in the absence of conflict, a group changes as its members change and as new goals command their attention. Much more dramatic, however, are the disruptions that occur when conflict develops within a group—or between constituent groups in a larger setting, such as a community or society. The episode described below, drawn from the recent history of our own society, serves to illustrate the sociological implications of both *intra*group and *inter*group conflict.

THE BREAKDOWN OF SOCIAL ORGANIZATION

In August 1968, the Democratic party held its national convention for the purposes of nominating presidential and vice-presidential candidates and writing a campaign platform. The attention of the nation, and indeed of the world, was concentrated on this group as it sought to achieve its goals. The news media had made elaborate preparations. Television cameras, reporters, and newspaper photographers covered every important area near the convention hall, the party's headquarters, and other strategic points.

Prior to the convention, a number of dissenting groups had made it known that they would come to Chicago in strength to demonstrate their dissatisfaction with the incumbent administration's handling of the war in Vietnam and other issues.[17] Some of the dissenters were enthusiastic young supporters of Eugene McCarthy, who had challenged President Johnson and the Democratic party organization in seeking the presidential nomination. Others included

socialists, anarchists, New Leftists, Yippies, communists, and a variety of moderate liberals. These groups were by no means united in philosophy or goals. In fact, they represented almost every possible position on the political spectrum from the middle through the far left. However, they all shared one goal: they wanted to make their dissatisfaction known.

Spokesmen for some of the more extreme elements among these groups maintained that one of their purposes in coming to the city was to provoke the Chicago police into a massive overretaliation so that, as they put it, "the worst aspects of establishment fascism would be revealed." A few protest leaders threatened to disrupt the city as well as the convention itself. As *Time* magazine later noted:

Chicago's newspapers repeatedly listed diabolical threats aimed at the city, ranging from burning Chicago down by flooding the sewers with gasoline, to dumping LSD in the water supply, to having 10,000 nude bodies float on Lake Michigan. Also widely accepted was the boast that from 100,000 to 200,000 demonstrators would descend on the city.[18]

In the face of these threats, city authorities mobilized twelve thousand policemen and six thousand Illinois National Guardsmen to maintain order during convention week. Additional military units were brought into the Chicago area from out of state to be ready if reinforcements were needed.

Protesters, members of the news media, and the police department readied themselves for the week of the convention against an emotionally charged background of tension, mutual distrust, and suspicion. From the start, the more radical demonstrators were openly antagonistic to the police, whom they referred to individually and collectively as pigs. Moderates and radicals alike protested the city's refusal to grant them permits for parades and rallies. The police, mobilized for

---

17. This description of the convention week disturbances in Chicago is drawn from the Walker Report to the National Commission on the Causes and Prevention of Violence, *Rights in Conflict* (New York: Bantam Books, Inc., 1968). The study team directed by Daniel Walker was composed of 212 investigators, who interviewed over 3000 witnesses and reviewed countless films and photographs taken by the news media, police photographers, and private citizens.

18. *Time*, December 6, 1968, p. 34. Actually, according to reliable estimates, only about 5000 protesters arrived from out of town. Other thousands came from the city itself.

the possibility of a serious disturbance, regarded the protesters as the potential enemy. Police officials were also critical of the news media, charging that they had sometimes staged incidents to create news. In any case, the presence of newsmen would, for some demonstrators, be an invitation to start trouble. The police also maintained that the cumbersome television equipment and the popping of the news photographers' flashbulbs interfered with the policemen's ability to pursue their duties. Members of the media, for their part, insisted on their right to be present wherever news might be expected to break. They spoke of their obligation to keep the public informed and complained of harassment by the police and convention officials.

The public, looking on, was apprehensive. People had mixed feelings about the demonstrators. Some were concerned that the elaborate police preparations would unnecessarily provoke strong countermeasures. Others warned that police overreaction could seriously endanger the right of Americans to dissent publicly. Most Chicagoans, however, were not particularly sympathetic toward the protesters, whom they lumped together as an oddball group, best typified by the Yippies. At best, they were "weirdos" or "irresponsible kids who needed to grow up"; at worst, they were actors in "a communist plot." Mayor Daley was not alone in insisting that the demonstrators should be kept in line by whatever means became necessary. The police were very much aware of these sentiments.

As the week of the convention approached, thousands of demonstrators concentrated in the city's Lincoln and Grant parks. On Sunday night, the eve of the convention's opening, the police acted on the city's decision to enforce an ordinance specifying that Lincoln Park be cleared of people by 11:00 p.m. As the police swept through the park, where the Yippies and others had established their headquarters, they met unexpectedly strong resistance. Soon rocks, bottles, and other debris were being hurled at them. They were taunted and jeered in vile terms.

For a time, the police took these provocations in stride. They arrested numerous demon-strators and continued their sweep of the area. However, resistance grew increasingly intense. Some demonstrators hurled plastic bags filled with human excrement. Unverified reports indicated that other demonstrators sprayed officers with cans of oven cleaner, threw potatoes with razor blades imbedded in them, and used sharpened sticks as spears. The level of verbal obscenity used by the demonstrators was said to have exceeded anything previously encountered by an American police force.

The melee on Sunday night turned out to be only a prelude to the violence that marked convention week. As the resistance of the demonstrators grew, the countermeasures used by the police became increasingly rough. Soon, policemen were making few distinctions between the different types of people they encountered in the areas where trouble occurred. Bystanders, peaceful demonstrators, newsmen, and rioters alike were subjected to police attack, without regard for age or sex. As the demonstrators and some onlookers struck back, police discipline sometimes collapsed completely. Ignoring the orders of their superior officers, policemen flung themselves into the crowds, beating their tormenters with clubs, shouting obscenities, kicking and striking anyone who came in their way. Some demonstrators were repeatedly beaten even after they had fallen and ceased to resist.[19]

The confrontation between the police and the protesters reached its climax on the night of Wednesday, August 28. Americans who had turned on their television sets to watch the convention proceedings were startled and disturbed at the scene they witnessed in front of convention headquarters at the Conrad Hilton Hotel. They saw American policemen clubbing and kicking people while shoving them into waiting vans. They saw newsmen with bloodied heads and smashed equipment. (Fully sixty newsmen out of three hundred covering the events had their equipment damaged, suffered physical injury, or were arrested.) The Walker Report to the National Commission on the Causes and Prevention of Violence later termed the breakdown of police discipline a police riot. An official observer from the Los Angeles Police Department said about the events of Wednesday night:

There is no question but that many officers acted without restraint and exerted force beyond that necessary under the circumstances. The leadership at the

---

19. The Walker Report documents numerous incidents of violence on the part of both police and demonstrators; see esp. pp. 235-285.

Goal conflicts, normative confusion, and breakdowns in communication all helped set the stage for the violence that erupted in Chicago during the Democratic Convention in August 1968.

point of conflict did little to prevent such conduct and the direct control of officers by first line supervisors was virtually non-existent.[20]

The violence of convention week touched off an intense debate over the moral, legal, and political implications of what had happened. No one was without an opinion, and emotions ran high. There were loud denunciations of the Chicago police, Mayor Daley, and the Democratic party—and equally loud ones of the demonstrators. Moderate views on either side were in the minority.

Whatever the final interpretation of this episode, it provides a dramatic example not only of the kinds of social conflict that can be generated between groups but also of the kinds of disruptions that can occur within a group, even one so firmly committed to the principles of order and discipline as a major metropolitan police force. In the following section we will examine the sources of such conflict in terms of what we have already learned about social organization.

SOURCES OF INTRAGROUP AND INTERGROUP CONFLICT

Social instability and disorder can stem from a variety of causes, many of them related to group structure. A conflict in goals, a breakdown in the usual channels of interaction and communication, normative inconsistency, role conflict and strain, the ineffectiveness of available sanctions, and disturbances in status relations are but a few of the possible sources of tension and disharmony within groups and between groups. Such breakdowns in social organization can help explain the violent events that occurred in Chicago as well as the less dramatic forms of conflict that occur in all human groups.[21]

---

20. *Rights in Conflict,* p. 2.

21. Sociologists recognize that breakdowns in group patterns sometimes occur because members are mentally disturbed or temporarily overwhelmed by strong emotion. However, social conflict more often involves clinically normal people and can be traced to problems in social organization. The present section, therefore, focuses upon *structural* sources of instability and conflict.

Conflicts in group goals. In the Chicago incident there was an obvious conflict between the manifest and formal goals of the police force and the informal goals of some of its members. The official purpose in bringing large numbers of policemen to confront the demonstrators was to maintain order. However, as the Walker Report indicates, an individual goal of some policemen during the incident was to punish rather than to control. Even more significant was the polarity and potential for conflict between the goals of the two groups—the demonstrators and the police. Although such goal conflicts did not in themselves lead directly to the confrontation and the breakdown of police discipline, they were clearly contributing factors.

The effects of a conflict in goals can be illustrated in the context of many kinds of groups. The administrative policy of a university, for example, may require that faculty members "publish or perish" at the same time that it stresses the importance of undergraduate teaching. Although these goals are not necessarily incompatible, many faculty members feel that they only have time to pursue one at the expense of the other. The result can be dissatisfaction on the part of everyone. Students are likely to feel that they are being shortchanged by the emphasis on publication and research. Professors are aware that if they divert too much time from research they may be passed by when it comes to promotions or raises. The eruption of student protests in the late 1960's reflected this conflict and many others between the goals of students, faculty, administrators, and society as a whole. In a university or any other complex group, some conflict in goals is inevitable. The integration of goals, in such cases, may mean simply that the formal and informal goals of one subgroup don't negate the goals of another.

Breakdowns in communication. During the Chicago convention disturbances, communication broke down at every level—between the demonstrators and the authorities, among the demonstrators themselves, and within the police force. The Walker Report describes the confused reactions of the demonstrators on Sunday night after the police announced that Lincoln Park must be cleared:

Confusion followed. Some [demonstrators] urged avoidance of conflict, others urged active resistance to the curfew. Two other recommendations were dispersal in small groups and street demonstrations. . . .

In the middle of a large group, one youth suddenly got up and yelled, referring to the marshalls [from one of the more organized protesting groups, the National Mobilization Committee to End the War in Vietnam], "Fuck the marshalls! Down with the leaders!" Someone else was giving instructions to a crowd of demonstrators who did not wish to receive them. "Daley gives orders," someone yelled, "don't you give us orders, you fascist." There were other objections in the same vein, and one witness says he was afraid that violence would break out within the demonstrating group itself. . . .

. . . Mobilization marshalls were yelling: "This is suicide! Suicide!" They urged people to flee the park and told them they could sleep on the grounds of the McCormick Theological Seminary, apparently unaware that seminary officials had already denied such use.

As the marshalls bellowed their announcements through a microphone, Yippies shouted them down as authoritarian. Some Yippies even attempted to take the microphone away.[22]

During the height of the violence between police and demonstrators, communication between police officials and their men similarly collapsed. Those in charge repeatedly ordered their subordinates to avoid unnecessary force, only to have their commands ignored.

As we will note in Chapter 11, "Collective Behavior," communication difficulties are usually a key element in riots, panics, and similarly unstructured situations. Less obvious, perhaps, is the importance of communication patterns to the stability of both formal and informal groups. For example, the fate of the average high-school clique after graduation day can be partly explained by the fact that regular and open channels of communication cannot be maintained. Even when members of the group remain in the same community or neighborhood, marriage, job responsibilities, and changing interests divert time and attention. Members communicate less frequently and less openly, until finally the group loses its identity. From time to time there may be abortive attempts to reestablish old ties through reunions, but somehow it is never quite the same. Certainly, more than a simple reduction in communication has taken place; the original goals of the group are no longer partic-

ularly important to the members. Yet, the disruption of the original patterns of interaction and open communication cannot be discounted as having contributed to the group's dissolution.

Normative confusion. Émile Durkheim developed the concept of *anomie* (page 9) to describe a social situation in which rules of conduct are so weakened or confused that they no longer provide effective behavioral guides. Certainly normative confusion was a contributing factor in the police-protester confrontations that occurred in Chicago during the Democratic convention. The title of the Walker Report, *Rights in Conflict*, suggests a fundamental difference between the norms of the conflicting groups. The demonstrators were exercising their right to dissent; the police were acting on the city's acknowledged right to protect its citizens and its property. Thus normative behavior for one group was, in the eyes of the other, deviant and potentially disruptive.

As previously suggested, there was also a great deal of normative confusion among the demonstrators themselves. Many of the protesting groups had no unified program, and the differences between one group and another were often greater, initially at least, than differences with the police. Many demonstrators were determined to act within the law; others were equally determined to flout it.

Finally, there was a confusion of norms even within the police force itself. A few months before the convention, Mayor Daley had publicly rebuked the Chicago police for showing too much restraint in dealing with arsonists and looters during the riots that had followed the assassination of Martin Luther King.[23] By some policemen, this was interpreted as an official "green light" to handle rioters roughly—despite police regulations that clearly forbid the use of force except as a last resort. Furthermore, there was a discrepancy between official police norms, which define the officer's task as that of maintaining order, and the informal norms of particular policemen who felt that people looking for trouble deserved rough treatment. Adding to the confusion were the normative attitudes of the public, many of whom demanded that the police

---

22. *Rights in Conflict*, p. 148.
23. The mayor's widely publicized remark, which he later modified, was that the police should "shoot to kill arsonists and shoot to maim looters."

be given more power in order to maintain "law and order."

Such normative confusion undoubtedly contributed to the eventual breakdown of order within the police department, just as normative differences between police and protesters established the basis for a confrontation between the two groups. During the violence of convention week, relatively few people knew clearly what to expect of others, or what was expected of them.

Normative confusion can similarly disrupt a family, a peer group, a business office, or any other group. Parents who are inconsistent in enforcing the rules they set down for their children often find that the children become a problem; not knowing what is expected of them, they don't know how to behave in order to avoid friction with their parents. Employees who make their own rules can disrupt the smooth operation of a business and cause dissension among their own informal group of co-workers. A dating couple with conflicting norms of sexual behavior soon fights or breaks up.

Role conflict. Role conflict, like a conflict in norms, is a cause of disruption in all kinds of groups, both large and small.[24] Sometimes conflict is actually built into a role definition. For example, the role of college professor, as we have already noted, often involves conflicting expectations for scholar and teacher. Similarly, the role of supervisor in a business group typically involves one set of role expectations from management and quite different expectations from those being supervised. Even the general sex roles in our society involve some built-in contradictions.[25] Parents may remind a daughter in college that she is expected to study hard, make good grades, and prepare herself for a career; at the same time, they may anxiously inquire whether she has met "any nice young men," clearly implying that they envision her only career as that of wife and mother, and that

they think of college as a place for girls to find husbands.

Role conflicts of this type are sometimes referred to as *internal* role conflicts, since conflicting expectations are inherent in the roles themselves. *External* role conflicts, by contrast, are generated by the incompatible demands of two or more different roles. A man's role as husband and father requires that he devote himself to his family, whereas his role as employee may require that he spend most of his time and energy on his job. A college student whose friend asks for help in cheating on an examination also faces an external role conflict: his role as a member of an academic community requires that he refuse the request; his role as friend includes the expectation that he will provide the requested aid.[26] Such conflicts are of more than theoretical concern. In 1965 a number of cadets were expelled from the United States Air Force Academy for their failure to report other cadets who had cheated on an examination. In the minds of some parents (in their role as defender-of-offspring), the scandal at the Academy was not so much the exam episode as it was the Academy's interpretation of loyalty-to-friends as grounds for expulsion. In this instance, as often happens, role conflict was closely interrelated with a conflict in norms.

In the breakdown of police discipline during the Chicago convention, the role of law enforcement officer was clearly incompatible with the role of outraged private citizen. The one role called upon the individual policeman to maintain a professional calm and to use only the force necessary in controlling the demonstrators. The more general role of red-blooded American male defined the appropriate response to extreme provocation in a different way: insult for insult and blow for blow were the "natural" reactions, at least by the definition of those policemen whose discipline collapsed. Many of the demonstrators faced a similar conflict between their role as law-abiding citizens respecting the city's need to maintain order and their role as political activists expressing their dissatisfaction with the status quo.

Ineffectiveness of social control. A group's system of social control can be effective only to the extent that sanctions are considered meaningful and that most members support the authority of those empowered to administer them. For reasons we have already cited, mem-

24. See, for example, Jack J. Preiss and Howard J. Ehrlich, *An Examination of Role Theory: The Case of the State Police* (Lincoln, Neb.: University of Nebraska Press, 1966), esp. pp. 94–121.

25. See Mirra Komarovsky, "Cultural Contradictions and Sex Roles," *American Journal of Sociology*, 52 (November 1946), 184–189.

26. Rose K. Goldsen, Morris Rosenberg, and Robin M. Williams, *What College Students Think* (Princeton, N.J.: D. Van Nostrand, Co., Inc., 1960).

For a system of social control to be effective, group members must accept as legitimate the authority of those empowered to administer formal sanctions.

bers of the Chicago police force had reason to doubt that they would be punished for violating the department's official rules of conduct when called upon to handle a riot. The fact that there were relatively few suspensions or dismissals after the convention disturbances tended to support their conviction and raised the question of whether the department's internal system of controls could be effective under similar circumstances in the future.

The confrontation itself, of course, provides an even more dramatic instance of the breakdown of social controls. Many of the more radical demonstrators denied the authority of the police altogether; the officers were pigs doing the dirty work of a corrupt society. Even those demonstrators who were initially intent on an orderly protest soon came to feel that the police had seriously overstepped their authority—and had thereby lost the right to be obeyed. Social controls were further weakened, as they were

in the police department itself, by the fact that sanctions could not be applied effectively when deviation became widespread.

In his classic study of a maximum security prison as a social system, Sykes has shown that similar factors work to undermine the effectiveness of a prison's system of internal controls.[27] At first glance, a maximum security prison would seem to be a social system in which control is absolute: guards and prison officials are given complete authority by the state and can effectively enforce whatever rules are needed to govern a population of captives. In fact, however, rule violations are frequent and the guards are relatively powerless to prevent them.

One reason that prisoners misbehave despite the near certainty of punishment is that

---

27. Gresham M. Sykes, *The Society of Captives: A Study of a Maximum Security Prison* (Princeton, N.J.: Princeton University Press, 1958).

the sanctions used as punishment are often relatively meaningless to inmates. For minor violations of rules, the prisoner may lose certain privileges. He may be barred from his prison job and be forced to remain idle. But since most prison jobs are boring and unpleasant, this does not provide much of a deterrent. The prisoner may be restricted in his movements—not allowed to leave the cell block except for meals. However, since he really can't go anywhere except within the prison walls, and usually in a group under guard, this doesn't seem very important either. Punishments such as the cancellation of visiting privileges and the restriction of mail are similarly meaningless because even well-behaved inmates are allowed little mail and few visitors. Even more severe punishments, such as being placed in solitary confinement on a diet of bread and water, are not especially dreaded by an inmate accustomed to the harsh environment and unappetizing food that are a regular part of prison life.

A really effective system of social control is one where those controlled subscribe to the legitimacy of the authority of those who exercise the sanctions and to the necessity of the norms that govern the group. Although prison officials, supervisors, and guards are committed to the necessity and rationality of the regulations they impose, prisoners are not. The inmates readily admit that prison officials have the legal right to control them, but they are not committed to the rules in such a way that they willingly enforce them on themselves. In most groups, as we noted earlier in this chapter, members readily control their own behavior because they don't want to violate the rules which are important to their group. In "the society of captives," self-enforcement of the norms is weak at best, and compliance to the authority of the guards is grudging. It is nearly impossible to exercise effective social control within such a setting, and those in power are faced with a continuous repetition of violations.

Disturbances in social ranking. If anything is clear about the conflict between police and protesters in Chicago, it is that the role of policeman was ranked quite differently by most demonstrators than by the officers themselves or the public as a whole. Even before their initial efforts to clear Lincoln Park, the police were

taunted with cries of "fascist pig," "oink," "shithead," "mother fucker." Not all of the demonstrators joined in the name-calling, but most were at least skeptical of police motives and concerned about the issue of police brutality. Whatever prestige the police had in the eyes of the protesters was almost completely eroded during the course of the confrontation.

The same was true in reverse. The police, by and large, regarded the demonstrators not as citizens exercising their right to dissent but as hooligans and un-American radicals intent on disrupting the convention, the city, and the country. In the eyes of many officers (and of many private citizens), the undisciplined Yippies were typical of all. After the first violence of Sunday night, distaste for the protesters grew. A tape of the police department's radio log gives this sampling of police attitudes:

Police Operator: "1814, get a wagon over at 1436 North Wells. We've got an injured hippie."
Voice: "1436 North Wells?"
Operator: "North Wells."
In quick sequence, there are the following remarks from five other police cars:
"That's no emergency."
"Let him take a bus."
"Kick the fucker."
"Knock his teeth out."
"Throw him in a wastepaper basket."[28]

The negative evaluation of the police by the demonstrators and of the demonstrators by the police made their behavior toward the other unpredictable. The police could not expect that their orders would be obeyed; the demonstrators could not expect that their rights would be respected. The established relationship between the law and the citizen broke down.

The disruption of an established ranking system is a frequent source of conflict within groups as well as between groups. Sometimes the source of instability is excessive competition, as in a business group where managerial personnel vie with each other for positions of greater power and prestige. In most kinds of groups, competition can serve either as an incentive to excel or as a source of conflict. If competition becomes cutthroat or divisive, members may withdraw from the group or lose interest in working for its goals.

Other kinds of disruptions occur when status relationships are unclear or when they

---

28. *Rights in Conflict* p. 183.

seem unfair to individual members. In formally organized groups, the clouding of role distinctions often becomes a source of friction. The manager who is a "good guy" and develops personal ties with the people under him is in some ways an ideal boss; but the reduction of social distance between a supervisor and those underneath him can create jealousies among co-workers and also make it difficult for the manager to maintain the "company perspective" required by his role. In informal groups, by contrast, the deemphasis of status distinctions is expected; members of a peer group are supposed to be equal, though in fact they have different roles, and the member who gets "uppity" soon finds himself on the outside.

Ranking systems, perhaps more than any other aspect of social organization, touch closely upon the emotional and psychological needs of individual members. Not every member can be or wants to be at the top of every system, but every person needs the feeling that he is respected. As one police officer asked after an encounter with some of the demonstrators, "Why do you call us pigs?"[29] His question is not wholly unlike the one that black children have often asked their parents: "Why do they call us niggers?"

SOME POSITIVE FUNCTIONS OF SOCIAL CONFLICT

Sociologists have long recognized that social conflict and social tension are normal parts of group life. But what of their consequences? In the short term, conflict is disturbing to the individuals involved and disruptive of the group in which it occurs. Sometimes, indeed, it can result in a group's dissolution. The effects of conflict are not always wholly negative, however, even for a group in danger of being destroyed.

Conflict can clarify issues. Few Americans would regard the convention week violence in Chicago as anything but deplorable, whether they sided with the demonstrators or with the police. Yet it is possible that the widespread public discussion precipitated by the incident and by the subsequent trial of demonstration leaders will eventually lead to a clarification of basic issues. (See Viewpoints on the facing page.) What are the citizen's rights when he is

in the act of dissent and what are the limitations on those rights? Where should the line be drawn between the legitimate and the excessive use of force in controlling civil disorder?

The upheavals that have erupted in the black ghettos of many American cities have similarly served to focus attention on a critical societal issue, that of racial justice. The new black militancy has had mixed effects on the attitudes of white Americans, but at least massive indifference to the problem of racial discrimination has given way to massive awareness. Problems affecting the members of a group cannot be solved until they are seen and examined—whether the group is a society, a business, or a family.

Conflict can integrate a group. The nineteenth-century German sociologist Georg Simmel was among the first to write about how intergroup conflict could reduce tensions within a group by providing an external target for resentments and hostilities.[30] The way in which conflict with outsiders tends to draw the members of a group more closely together can be observed in many contexts. The confrontation between police and protesters in Chicago had a divisive effect on the community and the society, but it solidified group feeling within the police department and also served to unify the protesting factions. A religious sect that breaks away from an established Church to initiate some type of reform is likely to become increasingly close-knit as conflict develops with the larger group. A society fighting for its very existence against a common enemy, as Great Britain did during World War II, often exhibits a powerful sense of determination and will to resist as individuals subordinate their personal interests to the welfare of their country. The motivation to work together for common goals typically weakens after the external threat has been met or the conflict resolved.

Conflict can stimulate change. The development of the United Nations as a means for systematically reducing the risk of war resulted directly from the global conflict, the Second World War. Management-labor conflict in the

---

29. *Ibid.*
30. Georg Simmel, *Conflict and the Web of Group Affiliations,* trans. Reinhardt Bendix (New York: The Free Press, 1955), pp. 92–93.

VIEWPOINTS   **THE CHICAGO VERDICT**

The verdict in Chicago's flamboyant conspiracy trial stands as quiet justification of the jury system. Despite chaotic and partisan proceedings in the courtroom, the jurors evidently managed to remember the basic issues. They were given precious little help from a judge who often acted as though in alliance with the prosecution and from defendants who, more interested in discrediting the courts than in looking to the legal process for vindication, richly deserved contempt sentences—though not of the severity they received.

Yet the jury ignored both the contemptuous behavior of the defendants and the vindictiveness of Judge Hoffman. By acquitting all the accused of conspiracy but finding five of the seven guilty of crossing state lines with intent to incite riot, the jury has opened the way for a clear test of the constitutionality of the 1968 riot act, in which conspiracy is not involved.

Far more important than the question whether the defendants were guilty of inciting to riot—as much of the evidence indicated they indeed were—is the question of the right of the Federal Government to prosecute anyone joining a protest demonstration across a state boundary. Such an interpretation of the Government's power—and in the present temper of the Justice Department, this is not a theoretical question—would make it all too easy to label as law-breakers that perennially unpopular species, the "outside agitator." If this law is sustained, it will be a first step to denying the aggrieved in any state the right to receive support from "alien" sympathizers in any other.

These are the principles at stake, and they should not be overshadowed by outrages committed in Chicago in 1968, whether by police or demonstrators, nor by the more recent outrages in the court, whether by demonstrators or judge. The real issue is the constitutionality of the law under which the defendants have now been convicted by the Chicago jury; and this is the issue of basic importance that will surely be taken on appeal to the higher courts.

New York Times editorial
February 20, 1970

The jury's verdict in the Chicago riot-conspiracy trial was a triumph of justice against unparalleled and almost insuperable efforts to obstruct it. The verdict should restore public faith in the judicial process and particularly in the jury system, which revolutionaries in this country have done their utmost to destroy.

Altho all seven of the defendants were acquitted on the general charge of conspiracy, five of them were convicted of doing individually what all seven had been accused of conspiring to do. The conspiracy count alleged that all seven defendants conspired to travel in interstate commerce and use its facilities with intent to incite riots during the Democratic convention in 1968 and committed specific acts of violence in furtherance of that intent. All were acquitted on this charge, but David Dellinger, Rennard C. Davis, Thomas E. Hayden, Abbot H. Hoffman, and Jerry C. Rubin were convicted on specific counts of coming to Chicago with "intent to incite, organize, promote, and encourage a riot" and of committing specific acts to accomplish that purpose. . . . Lee Weiner and John Froines were acquitted on all counts. . . .

The conspiracy count has been widely publicized as the nub of the government's case, and defamers of Chicago no doubt will find satisfaction in the verdict of acquittal on this charge. They had ridiculed the government's contention that the Chicago riots were planned long in advance by revolutionaries who came here for the specific purpose of disrupting the convention. The jury, however, did find that five of the defendants did precisely what all seven had been accused of conspiring to do. . . .

The anti-riot statute, adopted in 1968, had been widely misrepresented by liberal newspapers, ignoramus columnists, and irresponsible lawyers as an attempt to suppress freedom of thought, by punishment for a "state of mind." The language of the statute, however, is explicit. Both under the conspiracy and the substantive sections it is necessary to prove not only "intent" but specific actions to promote or incite a riot.

Judge Hoffman has been abused by the same revolutionary and irresponsible elements that have defamed Chicago and derided the riot-conspiracy trial. . . . These pettifoggers should wait and see what the Supreme Court says. Meanwhile, the whole country should be grateful to Judge Hoffman, the jury, and United States Atty. Thomas Foran, and his staff for doing their duty.

Chicago Tribune editorial
February 19, 1970

United States has helped to improve working conditions, to raise the standard of living for most Americans, and to create the machinery for settling disputes that might disrupt the economy. Racial conflicts in recent years have led to new laws and the reinforcement of old laws aimed at eliminating racial discrimination, particularly in such areas as voting, housing, education, and employment. Technological change has been stimulated throughout the country's history not only by the urgencies of war but also by that institutionalized form of conflict known as business competition.

Conflict, in short, can provide a powerful stimulus to social and cultural change—or, as Lewis Coser terms it, to creativity:

Conflict within and between groups in a society can prevent accommodations and habitual relations from progressively impoverishing creativity. The clash of values and interests, the tension between what is, and what some groups feel ought to be . . . have been productive of vitality.[31]

The effects of intragroup and intergroup conflict, then, are generally a mixture of good and bad. The question for the student of social behavior is not whether conflict can be avoided but rather how much and what kind of conflict a particular group can accommodate while still maintaining enough order and stability to resist disintegration. He must also be ready to evaluate the significance of disintegration itself. There is no basis for assuming that the dissolution of a group always has negative consequences.

---

31. Lewis A. Coser, *The Functions of Social Conflict* (New York: The Free Press, 1956), p. 153.

SUMMARY

The sociological perspective on human behavior focuses on interaction—the events that take place *between* individuals—rather than individual behavior and personality. Group behavior is distinguished from other kinds of social behavior by the fact that it is shaped around some pattern of social organization. The prerequisites to the development of a group are the existence of potential members who are seeking interrelated goals and who undertake some form of coordinated interaction to achieve them.

A group's pattern of social organization serves to coordinate the members' activities as they work toward their individual and collective goals. Group norms are rules of conduct, emerging from recurrent interaction, that define the specific forms of behavior that members expect of each other. Some types of norms lead to similarities of behavior among members; others define the specialized role activities expected from persons occupying distinct positions within the group. When such roles are coordinated into an integrated system, the group achieves a division of labor. Coordination of the roles in a group and enforcement of general behavioral norms are achieved through a system of social control, which depends upon the selective application of both positive and negative sanctions. Every group also has some type of ranking system, by which greater rewards are associated with some roles than with others.

The social systems perspective on groups emphasizes the integrated functioning of groups as they persist over time. It assumes that groups tend toward equilibrium, resisting both internal and external disruptions, and that each component of the group's structure makes some contribution toward maintaining the equilibrium of the group as a whole. If this perspective is understood to imply that the disruption of a group's established patterns necessarily harms the group, then a conservative value bias almost inevitably enters into the analysis of conflict and dissent.

Social conflict typically occurs, both within groups and between groups, when goal conflicts develop, when normal communication and interaction patterns break down, when norms become confused or don't seem to apply, when there are conflicts in roles, when social controls are meaningless or otherwise ineffective, and when status relationships become confused or unacceptable. In most instances of social conflict, a variety of these factors work together to disrupt established patterns of social behavior.

Although social conflict is generally seen as something to be avoided, it often has positive consequences. It can focus attention upon issues that need to be solved if the group is to function effectively; it can integrate the members of a group around a common purpose; and it can stimulate social and cultural change. In most groups, and certainly at the level of modern society, some form of dissent and conflict seems as probable as any tendency toward equilibrium. The task of sociological analysis is to understand the interplay of these two tendencies in order to better explain social behavior.

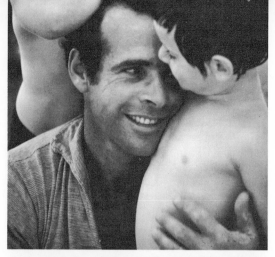

2
Types of Groups

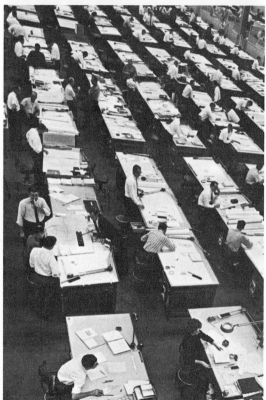

Every science must develop some systematic basis for classifying the phenomena being studied. Thus biologists classify living forms according to class, genus, and species, and chemists use the periodic table to classify chemical elements into related groups. In all sciences, the reasons for classification are essentially the same: it provides a framework for the orderly accumulation of knowledge about similarities and differences among the various phenomena with which the discipline is concerned.

In their efforts to develop a system for classifying human groups, sociologists have considered such varied criteria as size of membership, the significance of group goals for the members, the basis of membership, and the formality or informality of interaction patterns. Some of the most commonly used systems simply identify the ends of a particular continuum. For example, groups can be classified as either *primary* or *secondary*. A primary group, as defined by Charles Horton Cooley, is any small, intimate group that is especially important to the individual as a source of emotional satisfaction.[1] A secondary group is distinguished by the fact that it is relatively impersonal; it is not necessarily "secondary," however, in terms of its effects on the individual's life.

Another traditional classification is that of *in-group* and *out-group*. The term *in-group* refers broadly to any social unit of which the individual considers himself a member and with which he feels "a consciousness of kind." An *out-group*, by contrast, is any social unit with which he feels no sense of identity. This classification, which was developed around the turn of the century by William Graham Sumner, is based almost entirely on the subjective feeling of individuals —feelings of "we" versus "they."[2]

A third classification system distinguishes between *membership* and *reference* groups. A membership group is what the name implies—a group to which a given individual actually belongs. A reference group, by contrast, is one whose opinions are important to him whether he is a member or not. Thus an undergraduate student who hopes to gain admission to medical school may adopt the opinions of the American Medical Association on social issues relating to the practice of medicine, such as how best to provide medical care for the poor. Although he is not himself a member of the AMA, the student is nevertheless using it as a reference group in forming his opinions. A practicing doctor who actually belongs to the AMA, on the other hand, may wholly disagree with its official stand on social and political issues. For this individual, the AMA would be a membership group but not a reference group.[3]

Groups, like other objects of scientific study, can also be classified on the basis of their structural characteristics. The components of social organization discussed in Chapter 1—goals, norms, roles, and so forth—are common to all groups, but within this general framework there are significant patterns of variation that help differentiate one type of group from another. This chapter will examine some of the distinctive structural patterns that typify groups at various levels of size and complexity, ranging from small, intimate groups to whole societies.

1. Charles H. Cooley, *Social Organization* (New York: Charles Scribner's Sons, 1929).

2. William Graham Sumner, *Folkways* (New York: The New American Library, Inc., 1960), p. 27; originally published in 1906.

3. At the opposite extreme from the simple dichotomies discussed here are various elaborate systems for classifying groups on the basis of highly abstract qualities that can be identified only through the use of sophisticated statistical techniques or the consideration of mathematical models. See, for example, James S. Coleman, "Mathematical Models and Computer Simulation," in *Handbook of Modern Sociology*, ed. Robert E. L. Faris (Chicago: Rand McNally & Company, 1964), pp. 1027–1059.

SMALL GROUPS

At least two quite different kinds of small groups play key roles in modern social life. The first of these is the *primary group*, which has always had a central place in sociological analysis because of its importance in shaping the individual's attitudes and values. The other is the formally organized *decision-making group* —such as the committee, the advisory panel, or the board of directors—which has become increasingly important in directing the affairs of government, business, and other segments of our urban-industrial society.

PRIMARY GROUPS

Of special significance to individuals are the many small, spontaneous groups they form for no other reason than the personal satisfaction they afford. Charles Horton Cooley, who first formulated the concept of primary groups, defined them thus:

By primary groups I mean those characterized by intimate face-to-face association and cooperation. They are primary in several senses, but chiefly in that they are fundamental in forming the social nature and ideals of the individual. The result of intimate association, psychologically, is a certain fusion of individualities in a common whole, so that one's very self, for many purposes at least, is the common life and purpose of the group. Perhaps the simplest way of describing this wholeness is by saying that it is a "we"; it involves the sort of sympathy and mutual identification for which "we" is the natural expression.[4]

The formation of primary groups begins early in life when children find playmates whose company they particularly enjoy. As the years go by, they continue to seek close association with others who are like them in age and interests. Primary groups of this type are usually termed *peer groups* by sociologists. Common examples are cliques in school, boys' gangs, dating couples, and close friends at work. Our need to associate with others in intimate, face-to-face interaction is so strong that we continue our interest in peer-group activity until we die. The old man's cronies are just as important to him as were his special friends at any other age.

The family (Chapter 16) is a special kind of primary group, so essential both to individuals and to society that its formation is usually legitimized by the community through religious and legal rituals. The rights, duties, obligations, and privileges that make up family roles are deeply embedded in societal traditions and are surrounded by formal norms and legal sanctions. While other primary groups can disband voluntarily if the members wish it, the dissolution of a family can only be accomplished through institutionalized means. In most societies, these are prescribed by law.

The concept of *primary group* obviously encompasses a wide range of social behavior. How is it possible, then, to distinguish primary groups, as a type, from other small groups

whose members associate on a friendly basis? The answer lies in their distinctive pattern of social organization. A group can be classified as primary to the extent that its goals, interaction patterns, norms, role structure, methods of social control, and ranking system fall into the characteristic pattern described below.

Primary group goals. People engage in primary interaction because they enjoy the interaction itself—the group is maintained more for its own sake than for the purpose of accomplishing specified goals. Being with others and interacting on a close, personal basis is fulfilling regardless of the particular activities the group may engage in—whether playing cards, washing the dishes, going to church, or smoking "pot."

To the extent that interaction is *not* an end in itself, the group is less a primary one. Some

4. Cooley, *op. cit.*, pp. 23–24.

From childhood to old age, primary groups are especially important as sources of emotional satisfaction.

families develop dislikes and hostilities toward each other and act out their roles ritualistically without enjoyment. Although such families may remain intact until their members die, they have ceased to be primary groups in the fullest sense once their members fail to derive personal satisfaction from the interaction.

Patterns of interaction. Interaction in the primary group is based upon open communication and generally involves a face-to-face relationship. Although primary group interaction can be carried on through long periods of time without face-to-face communication, as when a family is divided by war, normally the members are not spatially separated.

Physical nearness, or *propinquity,* is an important condition for developing and maintaining the open channels of communication that are characteristic of primary groups. In a true primary group the level of self-disclosure is high: members let down their guards and talk openly

about their feelings and ideas. Thus they come to know each other well and to be genuinely concerned about each other as individuals. The members of a primary group respond to each other in terms of their complete personalities rather than merely in terms of their role performance. For example, a woman may be a terrible cook, an inept driver, a very poor golfer, and an unskilled hostess. Her husband, however, can ignore these faults or even find them endearing: he responds to his wife as a *whole* person rather than as a set of specific skills.

Primary group norms. Primary groups develop especially strong informal norms. As with all groups, norms emerge from the interaction of members and serve to make their behavior in the group stable and predictable. Many of the norms of a given primary group are *unique* in that they pertain only to the members of that particular group and are not shared by outsiders. Indeed, they may not even make sense to nonmembers. The normative use of certain words in ways that nonmembers do not understand is a common practice, and some primary groups even develop these into elaborate argots that permit private communication. Special uses of language are found in almost every family—each has its own inside jokes, its special nicknames or terms of endearment, its use of phrases carried over from the children's early years. Other informal norms may regulate the use of space, clothing, or other possessions.

Although every primary group has many norms that are unique, primary groups are also principal agencies for transmitting and interpreting the norms of the larger society. This is particularly true of the family, where the child acquires the normative orientations of his parents toward politics, minority groups, cultural tastes, religious beliefs, status striving, and many other broad issues. An almost equally strong influence is exerted by other primary groups as the individual makes his way through life. The teen-age peer group, for example, transmits norms concerning hairstyles, dance forms, modes of dress, sexual conduct, smoking, drinking, and other aspects of behavior. Comparable influences could be cited among adult peer groups. Indeed, one of the reasons for applying the term *primary* to family and peer groups is the important part they play in shaping the individual's overall attitudes and behavior.

Although primary groups are by no means unique in their development of strong informal norms, their norms are especially significant because of the importance the individual attaches to them. The normative orientations, beliefs, and definitions of conduct that we acquire from our primary groups are not easily displaced or altered. This is an important aspect of socialization (Chapter 5).

Role expectations and social solidarity. Role expectations in a primary group are based upon the strong "we" feeling noted by Cooley. Members are bound together by their feeling of sameness and common identity rather than by the fact that their roles are mutually interdependent and create a division of labor. This does not mean that the members of primary groups do not develop specialized roles; as we have already noted (page 41), they obviously do, though the roles are usually informal. But the interlinking of roles is less important in binding

the members of a primary group together—in creating social solidarity—than are the reciprocal bonds of affection, friendship, and loyalty which lead, in Cooley's words, to a "certain fusion of individualities in a common whole."

This essential characteristic of primary groups is well illustrated in *Street-Corner Society* (page 33), in which William F. Whyte contrasts the organizational patterns of Doc's streetcorner gang with those of Chick's club. Chick and his friends are college students learning to orient themselves to the structural patterns of the larger American society. Doc and his gang are oriented inward toward the Cornerville slum in which they live. Both groups live within Cornerville and know each other well. As Doc told Whyte:

Bill, I owe money now, but if I was paid all the money owed me, I would have a gang of money. I never saved. I never had a bank account. . . . If the boys are going to a show and this man can't go because he is batted out, I say to myself, "Why should he be deprived of that luxury?" And I give him the money. . . . And I never talk about it.

Again, in discussing the difference between Chick's club and his own gang, Doc said:

Chick says that self-preservation is the first law of nature. Now that's right to a certain extent. You have to look out for yourself first. But Chick would step on the neck of his best friend if he could get a better job by doing it. . . . We were talking one night on the corner about that, and I was sucking him in. I got him to admit it—that he would turn against his best friend if he could profit by it. . . . I would never do that, Bill. I would never step on Danny even if I could get myself a $50.00-a-week job by doing it. None of my boys would do that.

Nor would Doc advance himself socially if he had the chance to live life over:

I suppose my boys have kept me from getting ahead. . . . But if I were to start over again—if God said to me, "Look, here, Doc, you're going to start over again, and you can pick out your friends in advance," still, I would make sure that my boys were among them—even if I could pick Rockefeller and Carnegie. . . . Many times people in the settlement [a social welfare agency in the area] and some of the Sunsets [a socially mobile girls' club] have said to me, "Why do you hang around those fellows?" I would tell them, "Why not? They're my friends."[5]

Informal social control. Members of a primary group enforce the norms and roles of the group informally, using a great variety of techniques as both positive and negative sanctions. The wife who proudly presents her husband with a freshly baked pie may not realize that she is exerting social control by the exercise of a positive sanction, but from a sociological perspective she is. The husband who shows his appreciation with a hug and a kiss is reinforcing his wife's exemplary role performance by the application of another type of informal sanction. Such simple gestures as laughing at the jokes of a fellow member or smiling in approval can be used as positive sanctions. Negative sanctions can be exercised by yawning, grinning, or even "looking blank" when some other form of response is hoped for.

Much of the control that maintains the social organization of a primary group is self-generated and self-administered: the anticipation of disapproval or rejection is usually sufficient to deter a member who contemplates some act that would upset the other members. If he has in fact already offended the other members, his feelings of guilt or anxiety may serve as more severe negative sanctions than open criticism from the others.

Reduction of social distance. Ranking systems develop within primary groups as the members work out an informal system of roles with accompanying distinctions in rank. However, primary interaction tends to minimize distinctions among members, especially those originating in other contexts, such as wealth, education, or occupational role.

In the Air Force, for example, bomber crews are made up of commissioned officers and several grades of enlisted men who represent different levels of status in the military hierarchy. Flying together day after day, often on dangerous missions, these teams frequently develop into close-knit primary groups despite military norms proscribing personal friendships between commissioned officers and enlisted

men. Similarly, college students from quite different social backgrounds often join together in primary groups that minimize differences in wealth or social standing. One of the important consequences of primary interaction, then, is the *reduction of social distance* between people from dissimilar backgrounds.

FORMAL DECISION-MAKING GROUPS

Increasingly important in modern society are small groups, such as committees, commissions, councils, juries, boards of supervisors, and other appointed or elected groups, which are formed for the specific purpose of making decisions and formulating policies within larger organizational structures. Much of the available information about the dynamics of such groups has been obtained from experimental studies of "artificial" groups in laboratory settings, since it is generally impossible to observe "natural" decision-making groups in actual operation. Legal proscriptions forbid the presence of outsiders in jury rooms, and the demands of security prohibit the presence of observers in many kinds of industrial and governmental policy-making groups. In spite of these obstacles, however, social scientists have accumulated an impressive amount of information about the social organization and patterns of interaction that are characteristic of small task-oriented groups.

The interplay of formal and unstated goals. The goals of a decision-making group are typically related to policy making, allocation of resources, distribution of rewards, approval of proposals, or other similar issues. The group's decisions can be of considerable importance to the members of the larger group it serves or to others with whom they are associated. This often makes the small decision-making group an arena for power struggles and competitive maneuvering.

Interaction in such a setting can be extremely subtle, as members attempt to influence each other and to promote decisions that will favor their special interests. Often there is a "hidden agenda"—members have goals they hope to attain but do not reveal as the group goes about completing its formal assignments.

---

5. William Foote Whyte, *Street-Corner Society: The Social Structure of an Italian Slum,* rev. ed. (Chicago: The University of Chicago Press, 1955); quotations from pp. 106–108.

Seating arrangements and protocol are sometimes matters of major importance in formal decision-making groups. Here members of the UN Command to the Korean Armistice Commission sit directly opposite their counterparts from North Korea as they negotiate for the release of the U.S.S. Pueblo and its crew. The conference table is positioned precisely on the 38th parallel between North and South Korea.

Typical patterns of interaction. As noted by Bales and Strodtbeck,[6] interaction in decision-making groups seems to develop in stages. At the start, the members are essentially concerned with *collecting information*: they ask for orientation, give information, and make factual analyses concerning the problem at hand. The second phase is primarily devoted to *evaluating the information* at hand. Members offer their own opinions on the issue and react positively or negatively to the views of other members. In the third phase, the group concentrates on *reaching a decision*. Emotional strains are most likely to develop at this stage, as members become more open in their criticisms, form or resist coalitions, and support some individuals and reject others.

Once the group has arrived at a decision or agreed on the formulation of a policy, the pattern of interaction typically shifts to an attempt at *restoring equilibrium*. Rates of negative reaction fall off and positive reactions increase. The members joke and laugh, releasing tension and emphasizing group solidarity. These successive patterns of interaction can be observed in almost every small decision-making group, whatever the nature of its task.

Formal and informal roles. Titles such as "foreman of the jury," "chairman of the board,"

6. Robert F. Bales and Fred L. Strodtbeck, "Phases in Group Problem-Solving," *Journal of Abnormal and Social Psychology,* 46 (1951), 485–495.

or "executive secretary of the commission" refer to rather well-defined roles in particular kinds of decision-making groups. These formally designated roles, however, allow for considerable variation in performance. Some leaders are authoritarian while others are democratic. The harmony or strain within the group as it proceeds toward its task can be closely related to the role performance of the designated leader.

In groups that meet repeatedly, particular members are likely to assume informal leadership roles. Someone other than the formal leader often emerges as the "best idea man"—the one who gives guidance to the group, contributes suggestions for solving its problems, and generally offers the most effective ideas for reaching its goals. However, the person playing the "best ideas" role is not necessarily the one whom the group likes the best. A social-emotional leader often emerges and serves to minimize friction in the group. Studies have shown that the person who assumes the role of "best idea man" frequently becomes the least liked member of the group, while the social-emotional leader becomes the best liked.[7]

Social control. When a decision-making group operates within the context of some larger group, as is usually the case, the formal controls of the larger group carry over into the smaller one. Thus, role performance in a management group may be closely related to the general occupational role a person plays. The system of sanctions that characterizes the control system of the business, educational institution, or other association also applies to role performance within the smaller group.

In addition to formal controls, decision-making groups rely heavily on informal controls that are similar to those of primary groups. Much of the interaction that takes place in such groups is congenial and polite. Words or gestures signaling approval serve as positive sanctions, while disapproving comments, signs of rejection, and other culturally understood gestures serve as negative sanctions. Eventually, of course, a decision-making group reaches the stage where members must vote on the issue or otherwise formally declare their positions. As already noted, criticism of individual members is likely to become much more open at this point than during the earlier stages of collecting and evaluating information.

Ranking systems. Investigators have found that the status individuals have outside a decision-making group helps determine the position they enjoy within the group. For example, businessmen and professional people appear to have greater influence on jury decisions than individuals from occupational roles of lesser prestige. Similarly, men seem to emerge as task leaders more often than do women, who tend to specialize in the social-emotional roles. Thus, both role-playing and relative rank within a small decision-making group are influenced by the status and roles that members have outside the group.[8]

Sometimes the informal hierarchy that emerges in a decision-making group is the product of a struggle for position in the early meetings. Until the informal ranking system has been worked out, the members are generally less effective in moving forward in their task than they are after the hierarchy has settled into a stable pattern. Actually, the pattern that evolves may represent a complex of several different ranking systems, each based on different criteria. For example, groups typically develop a *hierarchy of relative popularity*, in which members are ranked on the basis of personal attractiveness. As we have already noted, a member's popularity within the group is often related to the type of informal role he assumes. He may have quite a different ranking in the *hierarchy of relative power*, which emerges as some individuals prove more able than others to influence the decisions of the group.

Neither of these informal hierarchies is necessarily related to the system of formal ranking, where designated leaders are supposed to have the greatest prestige. The formal leader may be one of the least popular members of the group, and he may actually have less influence on group decisions than the "idea man" or some other informal leader. As in all formally organized groups, the informal structure that emerges is an essential and important aspect of social organization.

7. Robert F. Bales, "The Equilibrium Problem in Small Groups," in *Working Papers in the Theory of Action*, eds. Talcott Parsons, Robert Bales, and Edward Shils (New York: The Free Press, 1954), pp. 111–161.

8. Fred L. Strodtbeck and R. D. Mann, "Sex Role Differentiation in Jury Deliberations," *Sociometry*, 19 (1956), 3–11.

ASSOCIATIONS: FORMAL ORGANIZATIONS

Much of the activity of modern urban-industrial society is carried out through large, formally organized groups called *associations*, in which the prevailing pattern of social organization is *bureaucracy*. Blau and Scott state the matter thus:

If the most dramatic fact that sets our age apart from earlier ones is that we live today under the shadow of nuclear destruction, the most pervasive feature that distinguishes contemporary life is that it is dominated by large, complex, and formal organizations. Our ability to organize thousands and even millions of men in order to accomplish large-scale tasks—be they economic, political, or military—is one of our greatest strengths. The possibility that free men become mere cogs in the bureaucratic machineries we set up for this purpose is one of the greatest threats to our liberty.[9]

The bureaucratization of social organization in associations is the keynote of Western industrial society. In nineteenth-century America, only the government was perceived as bureaucratic; the emerging industrial empire was locally owned and run by entrepreneurs and their families. The largest of all the industrial trusts, Rockefeller's Standard Oil, was smaller than are any of the present-day companies that originated when the trust was split. Occupational roles were still very much oriented to small enterprises and even to semifeudal relationships. But all that has changed, and government now is only one of many bureaucratic organizations.

To understand the basis for classifying a group as an *association*, we will examine the formal characteristics of bureaucracy as seen from the perspective of the sociologist. Although government, military, and industrial organizations come closest to being "pure" bureaucracies, elements of bureaucratic organization can be found in associations formed for widely varied purposes. Max Weber, who systematically analyzed bureaucracy as an "ideal type,"[10] commented on its wide utility:

This type of organization is in principle applicable with equal facility to a wide variety of different fields. It may be applied in profit-making business or in charitable organizations, or in any number of other types of private enterprises serving ideal or material ends. It is equally applicable to political and to religious organizations. With varying degrees of approximation to a pure type, its historical existence can be demonstrated in all these fields.[11]

Weber found elements of bureaucratic organization as far back as ancient Egypt and Rome, but these were only partial forms, still dependent on personal relations, feudal loyalties, and the arbitrary use of power by those in control. Bureaucracies as rationally conceived instruments for efficiently accomplishing complex tasks began to achieve their present form only with the Industrial Revolution, which led to an increasing division of labor.

FORMAL BUREAUCRATIC STRUCTURE

Although the term *bureaucracy* is associated in the popular mind with a cumbersome, bungling, inefficient machinery that defies the dictates of common sense, actually the principles underlying bureaucratic organization are *rationality* and *efficiency*. A bureaucracy is deliberately structured so that specific goals can be accomplished with maximum speed and efficiency and with a minimum of interpersonal friction. The duties and responsibilities of individuals are supposed to be clearly defined and highly specialized, and all roles presumably are intermeshed in a complex organizational structure that is stable, predictable, and self-perpetuating. Individuals can come and go, live out their careers and retire, with no appreciable effect on the efficiency of the total operation. Interpersonal relations tend to be formal and impersonal. Weber insisted, indeed, that bureaucratic efficiency is achieved in direct proportion as social relationships are kept free of emotional involvement.

---

9. Peter M. Blau and W. Richard Scott, *Formal Organizations* (San Francisco: Chandler Publishing Co., 1961), p. ix.

10. The term *ideal type* in sociology refers to an abstract model that isolates and accentuates the distinguishing characteristics of some social phenomenon. It is a theoretical tool, not intended as an accurate description of reality. The construction and use of ideal types is described in the Methodological Essay on page 86.

11. Max Weber, *Theory of Social and Economic Organization*, trans. A. M. Henderson and Talcott Parsons (New York: The Free Press, 1957), p. 334; originally published in 1925.

The importance of formal goals. If an organization is to function efficiently and rationally, its goals must be specifically defined. Ideally, the definition of goals determines the structure of a bureaucracy and the resources it needs:

The nature of the goal provides the criteria to be used in the recruitment of personnel and determines what resources are required and the priorities for their acquisition. It also furnishes a basis (relative contribution to the attainment of the objectives) for determining the amount of compensation participants receive and, in part, for allocating authority among them. It should be apparent, then, that to the extent that organizational goals are diffuse or lacking in clarity and to the extent that multiple, possibly conflicting goals are being pursued, the organization will lack the rational basis for making these critical decisions.[12]

Multiple goals do not necessarily create a problem unless the pursuit of one goal interferes with the pursuit of another. In organizations as large and complex as those found in government, such conflicts are not uncommon. One section of the Department of the Interior, for example, may be working to create more dams to reduce flood damage and to better utilize the available water supply, while another section may be working to preserve areas of natural beauty that the dams would destroy. On a much broader scale, requirements for military and defense spending have seriously interfered with our government's ability to pursue programs aimed at correcting some of our problems at home.

Whether an association is organized for political, economic, educational, or charitable purposes, the pursuit of conflicting goals is clearly inconsistent with the principle of rationality upon which the efficiency of a bureaucracy depends. The principle of rationality also breaks down when the individual members of an association are unaware of its goals or are misinformed about them. Although it seems obvious that participants must know what is expected of them if they are to do their jobs well, studies in various countries have shown that

members of large-scale organizations are often poorly informed about group goals.[13]

Generally, the effectiveness of a bureaucracy also suffers if it fails to consider the personal goals of its members. A truly rational system is one in which individuals can achieve their own goals effectively by fulfilling their formal roles and working for organizational objectives. In business associations, for example, formal incentives such as salary, title, and job security satisfy the personal goals of individual participants and at the same time encourage them to carry out the purposes of the company for which they work. A little later in this chapter, we will use an actual case study to show how the goals and interests of individuals work to modify the formal structure of a bureaucracy.

Channeled interaction. In marked contrast to the open communication of primary groups, communication in a bureaucratically organized association proceeds through clearly defined channels. Reports, requests, orders, and policy decisions are all passed from one level in the hierarchy to another, and almost everything must be put in writing. Probably no feature of bureaucratic organization is more subject to criticism from insiders and outsiders alike than the requirements for red tape and paper work, yet formal patterns of communication are necessary to maintain the effective operation of a bureaucracy. When subordinates bypass their immediate supervisors and communicate directly with superiors several steps removed, lines of authority and responsibility break down, and the whole carefully designed organizational structure is weakened.

Official norms. Like channeled communication, the application of general rules to particular cases is one of the most characteristic features of bureaucracy. Rules of procedure are formally standardized so that particular tasks can be performed uniformly, regardless of who is performing them. In addition to defining standard operating procedure (in bureaucratic jargon, SOP), the formal norms of a bureaucracy typically prescribe the type of clothing that is appropriate (in some cases the wearing of uniforms and insignia), the hours of work, and the use of tools and materials. Sometimes there are even norms defining the kind of behavior that is expected of members in their life outside the organization. A school board may specify that

12. W. Richard Scott, "Theory of Organizations," in *Handbook of Modern Sociology,* ed. Robert E. L. Faris (Chicago: Rand McNally & Company, 1964), p. 492.

13. *Ibid.,* pp. 492–493.

the teachers it hires should not smoke or drink alcohol in public; a corporation may insist that its executives take an active role in community affairs.

The formal norms of a bureaucratic organization range from simple rules for writing memoranda to procedures governing a wide range of behaviors. (See "Rules of the Black Panther Party," opposite.) The purpose of bureaucratic norms, however, is in every case the same—to bring order and efficiency to the processing of a multiplicity of cases, so that every individual's problem becomes a simple matter of bureaucratic routine, and to ensure that the whole structure operates predictably.

Fixed roles. The allocation of roles in a bureaucratic structure creates a clear-cut and relatively fixed division of labor. The sphere of responsibility associated with each role is clearly defined, often in an official job description. Individuals are expected to perform their duties in a specified way, to avoid ad-libbing, and to refrain from assuming the obligations of others.

The division of labor in a bureaucratic organization is based on the assumption that job specialization will lead to increased competence in a limited sphere of activity. It also has the effect of freeing the organization from unnecessary dependence on individuals. The maxim that "no one is irreplaceable" is true to the extent that his role is clearly defined and calls only for a specific set of skills. Ideally, the way a particular role is performed does not change with the role incumbent.

The formalization of roles also minimizes the possibility that friction between individuals will interfere with overall operating efficiency. With responsibility in the division of labor clearly fixed, two members in interlocking roles can, in theory at least, carry out their assigned tasks even if they thoroughly dislike each other. This assumes, of course, that they do not informally subvert their roles in subtle ways.

The fixing of duties and responsibilities in an organization obviously increases its stability and thus the likelihood that its goals will be attained. The work of the organization can proceed in an orderly and predictable fashion, unaffected by changes in personnel or by the personal characteristics of the people who occupy particular roles. The dehumanization of roles, which Max Weber saw as an essential of bureaucratic efficiency, has been seen by many as

a threat to human dignity and freedom. As we shall see shortly, however, the impersonality of bureaucratic organizations is often more apparent than real.

Control by consent and contract. Roles in a bureaucracy are organized into a strict hierarchy, with every role coming under the supervision of a role higher in the structure. Authority—the right to give commands and expect them to be obeyed—is clearly channeled and delimited, and it is vested in the role itself, not in the individual. Every self-respecting association has an organizational chart that designates lines of authority, channels of communication, and areas of responsibility.

In most associations, social control is based on voluntary submission to authority. The individual consents to follow the orders of his superior because he considers them legitimate and necessary. In joining the organization he has, in effect, accepted a *contract* that obligates him to follow the rules. In return for his services he can expect a secure place in the organization and other appropriate compensation, such as a guaranteed salary and a chance of promotion. Whether or not a legal contract is involved, the arrangement is essentially legalistic in that it formally specifies what each party can legitimately expect of the other. The contractual basis of bureaucratic organization is the basis not only for control by consent but also for the group's solidarity. Individuals are bound to the organization by the obligation they have assumed and not necessarily by loyalty, sentiment, or any of the other ties that hold members together in many other types of groups.

Most associations use both positive and negative sanctions to reinforce control by consent. The gold star awarded to schoolchildren for not being late and the gold watch presented to the faithful employee for twenty-five years of service are positive sanctions that reinforce well-understood norms in their respective associations. Low grades, unfavorable work assignments, and failure to promote are typical negative sanctions in groups relying mainly on control by consent. Much stronger negative sanctions may be used in associations where membership is involuntary and consent is minimal. Prison inmates, for example, may be physically punished or placed in solitary confinement for failing to conform to formal prison norms. As recently as World War II, an American soldier

RULES OF THE BLACK PANTHER PARTY

Central Headquarters
Oakland, California

Every member of the *Black Panther Party* throughout this country of racist America must abide by these rules as functional members of this party. *Central Committee* members, *Central Staffs,* and *Local Staffs,* including all captains subordinate to either national, state, and local leadership of the *Black Panther Party* will enforce these rules. Length of suspension or other disciplinary action necessary for violation of these rules will depend on national decisions by national, state or state area, and local committees and staffs where said rule or rules of the *Black Panther Party were violated.*

Every member of the party must know these verbatim by heart. And apply them daily. Each member must report any violation of these rules to their leadership or they are counter-revolutionary and are also subjected to suspension by the *Black Panther Party.*

The Rules Are:

1. No party member can have narcotics or weed in his possession while doing party work.
2. Any party member found shooting narcotics will be expelled from this party.
3. No party member can be *drunk* while doing daily party work.
4. No party member will violate rules relating to office work, general meetings of the *Black Panther Party*, and meetings of the *Black Panther Party anywhere.*
5. No party member will *use, point,* or *fire* a weapon of any kind unnecessarily or accidentally at anyone.
6. No party member can join any other army force other than the *Black Liberation Army.*
7. No party member can have a weapon in his possession while *drunk* or loaded off narcotics or weed.
8. No party member will commit any crimes against other party members or *black* people at all, and cannot steal or take from the people, not even a needle or a piece of thread.
9. When arrested *Black Panther* members will give only name, address, and will sign nothing. Legal first aid must be understood by all Party members.
10. The Ten Point Program and platform of the *Black Panther Party* must be known and understood by each Party member.
11. Party Communications must be National and Local.
12. The 10-10-10-program should be known by all members and also understood by all members.
13. All Finance officers will operate under the jurisdiction of the Ministry of Finance.
14. Each person will submit a report of daily work.
15. Each Sub-Section Leader, Section Leader, Lieutenant, and Captain must submit Daily reports of work.
16. All Panthers must learn to operate and service weapons correctly.
17. All Leadership personnel who expel a member must submit this information to the Editor of the Newspaper, so that it will be published in the paper and will be known by all chapters and branches.
18. Political Education Classes are mandatory for general membership.
19. Only office personnel assigned to respective offices each day should be there. All others are to sell papers and do Political work out in the community, including Captains, Section Leaders, etc.
20. *Communications*—all chapters must submit weekly reports in writing to the National Headquarters.
21. All Branches must implement First Aid and/or Medical Cadres.
22. All Chapters, Branches, and components of the *Black Panther Party* must submit a monthly Financial Report to the Ministry of Finance, and also the Central Committee.
23. Everyone in a leadership position must read no less than two hours per day to keep abreast of the changing political situation.
24. No chapter or branch shall accept grants, poverty funds, money or any other aid from any government agency without contacting the National Headquarters.
25. All chapters must adhere to the policy and the ideology laid down by the *Central Committee* of the *Black Panther Party.*
26. All Branches must submit weekly reports in writing to their respective Chapters.

Source: *The Black Panther*, Monday, Feb. 17, 1969. Reprinted by permission.

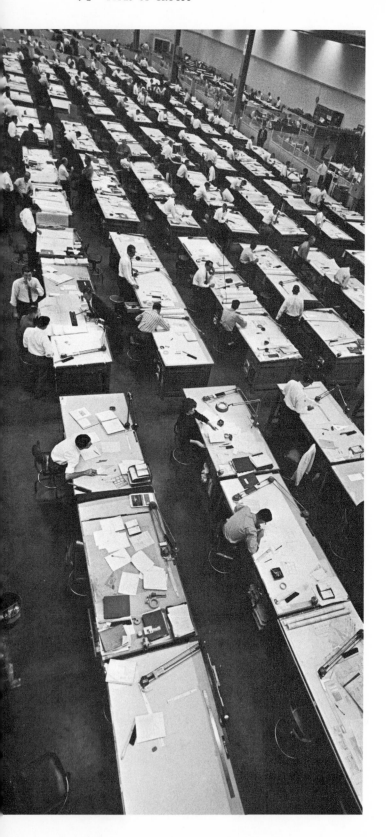

was executed for deserting in the face of the enemy. In most formal organizations, however, the need for strong negative sanctions is minimal.

Ranking based on competence. Theoretically at least, all roles in a bureaucratic organization call for specialized skills; this is the basis of the division of labor. Not all roles are equally easy to fill, however, nor equally crucial to the attainment of basic group goals. Differences in the kinds of specialized skills required by particular roles and differences in the amount of responsibility and authority they carry thus become the criteria for developing a ranking system.

In many associations the ranking system consists of three general levels that are based on the kinds of competence required to fill the roles within each stratum. At the bottom of the pyramid are the *workers* or *followers*, the rank-and-file members who do the routine work of the association according to established procedural norms. The roles at this level call for specialized competence, but the skills are not difficult to acquire; members can be easily replaced.

The *functionaries*—supervisors and middle managers—are essentially administrators: their task is to implement the policies and directives they receive from above. Thus, their skills usually relate to the handling of people rather than things, and the ability to interact smoothly with others—superiors, inferiors, and equals—becomes crucial. The most capable administrator is the one who can best coordinate the activities of those below him with his section's activities and with those of related sections. This requires that he maintain harmony and minimize interpersonal conflict. The functionaries, in short, specialize in getting others to do their assigned jobs without having to apply negative sanctions.

At the top level of the pyramid are the *policy makers*, whose roles require them to generate ideas which, when implemented, will move the association toward its goals. Generally, the skills necessary at this level depend upon accumulated

The allocation of roles in a bureaucratic structure creates a clear-cut and relatively fixed division of labor. Individuals are expected to perform their duties in a specified way, to avoid ad-libbing, and to refrain from assuming the obligations of others.

years of experience and a substantial degree of creative talent. The policy makers are much less easily replaced than those occupying roles in the strata below because their specialized skills are in much shorter supply.

The prestige associated with different levels within a bureaucracy is made evident not only through the differential distribution of rewards but also through the use of visible status symbols. The blue collar and the white collar in an industrial association signify widely understood status differentials. In a nightclub or restaurant the different ranks of the busboys, ordinary waiters, wine steward, and maître d'hôtel are easily recognized by their distinctive uniforms. In the Ku Klux Klan an ordinary member wears a relatively simple sheetlike robe, whereas a Grand Dragon or an Imperial Wizard is resplendent in brightly colored robes of silk and satin. In a business corporation upper-status levels are seldom distinguishable in terms of clothing, but they are made apparent by special titles, mode of office decor, the privilege of having a private secretary, and other visible symbols of prestige.

THE INFORMAL STRUCTURE

On paper, various individuals may appear to be similarly qualified for a particular role in an organization. In fact, however, no two people will carry it out in exactly the same way or with exactly the same effect. Each person brings to the group his own attitudes, prejudices, and other personality characteristics that lead him to play his assigned role in ways not prescribed by its designers. As a result of recurrent interaction, each develops feelings of like or dislike, of loyalty or distrust, for other members of the group organization. And each has primary-group loyalties and personal goals that may seem more important to him than the goals of a large, impersonal group.

Sometimes the formal structure of an association is informally modified simply because it is inadequate for getting a job done. When the rules fail to provide for particular problems that come up, individuals are forced to invent their own solutions or to follow unofficial procedures that other workers have made standard. In other cases, the formal structure, though well-designed in terms of organizational goals, may fail to account for the goals and needs of the people who must carry it into effect. Thus, an association designed to utilize volunteers in rank-and-file positions may have difficulty in recruiting individuals because the work is not personally rewarding. Similarly, a carefully designed wage-incentive plan may not do much to motivate workers whose roles provide little else in the way of job satisfaction.

In general, the development of an informal structure in an association injects new and unofficial goals into the group; it redefines channels of communication and interaction in ways that are not part of the official plan; it redefines formal norms or invents new ones to meet changing problems that are not covered by the existing rules; it results in the reinterpretation of roles that are theoretically fixed; it supplements official techniques of social control with informal sanctions; and it leads to informal ranking systems that alter the formal hierarchy in subtle ways.

Sometimes the informal structure implements the formal structure in achieving organizational goals. Individuals may create new procedures to get a job done more efficiently or may feel so committed to the organization that they go beyond the simple requirements of their roles. In other cases, the informal structure that emerges is clearly at cross-purposes with the large-scale goals of the organization, as when workers develop their own norms concerning the length of coffee breaks and lunch periods, what constitutes a fair day's work, or the legitimacy of pilfering company supplies. Regardless of whether the informal structure subverts or supports the formal structure, however, *it is an integral part of the group's social organization.*

THE DYNAMICS OF BUREAUCRACY: A CASE STUDY

The interplay of formal and informal structure in directing the ongoing activity of an association has been clearly demonstrated by Peter Blau, an American sociologist who has done continuing research on the manner in which bureaucratic organizations actually attempt to achieve their goals. In 1949, for example, Blau studied the division of a state employment

METHODOLOGY THEORY AND RESEARCH

Blau's study *Dynamics of Bureaucracy* provides an excellent example of the interplay of theory and research in sociology. This is an analysis of two bureaucratic organizations, a federal enforcement agency and a state employment agency. The basic concepts that Blau used came from Weber, but the theoretical orientation that guided his research was functional analysis (page 48). Thus, the study focused on the consequences of particular interaction patterns and organizational arrangements for the functioning of the agency as a whole.

Blau relied on three basic research techniques: participant observation (page 33), use of statistical records (page 389), and interviews (page 492). Participant observation went on daily in each departmental office for three months. During the same time office operational records were carefully examined. Following the observation period in each case, all members of the departments that had been studied—a total of eighty-five persons—were interviewed in their homes.

Blau himself has pointed out the limitations of his study. In the first place, the findings for the organizations studied may not be representative of other bureaucratic organizations. The two agencies that granted Blau permission to carry out his research were relatively new ones; a number of private agencies and older public ones refused to participate. Blau acknowledged that this process of self-selection might bias his findings: the agencies that were willing to be studied showed by that fact alone that they were more flexible than the organizations that would not participate. A further limitation was that only single departments of the two agencies were studied, representing but a small segment of their total social structure. Thus, there is some question about the significance of the observed practices for the functioning of either agency as a whole.

But if selectivity had disadvantages, it also had some important advantages, especially in enabling Blau to use a variety of research techniques and to study the functioning of the departments in depth. For example, through participant observation he gained the impression that competitive practices set up in the employment agency interfered with productivity. An analysis of office records confirmed this impression: the more competitive a group was, the lower its productivity. Blau then hypothesized that a group's productivity was affected by its degree of social cohesion. He tested and confirmed this hypothesis by observation and interviews, using a specially created index of social cohesion.

The multiple techniques Blau used also allowed him to test the reliability of his conclusions. For some social-interaction situations, the responses obtained in interviews with departmental personnel proved to be unreliable when compared with the findings obtained through observation and the analysis of office records. By carefully checking one research technique against another, Blau was able to develop more thorough and accurate explanations for his research questions, even if the range of generalization was limited.

Like most field research, Blau's study shows the almost inevitable discrepancy between a research plan worked out in advance and actual research procedures. Blau maintained a flexible approach and periodically revised his research design to fit the circumstances and new research needs. Blau sums up the challenge:

"The researcher who compulsively insists on following his predesigned plan will miss [some] rare opportunities. Conversely, the one who is seduced by every new lead will find he has failed to collect information on the theoretical problems that had prompted his research. A research schedule that is recurrently revised but that is quite closely followed guards against these dangers. . . . At the very least my research schedule prevented me from inadvertently forgetting to obtain some information that was essential in terms of my theoretical framework."

Peter M. Blau, *Dynamics of Bureaucracy: A Study of Interpersonal Relationships in Two Government Agencies,* 2nd ed., rev. (Chicago: The University of Chicago Press, 1963); quotation from p. 274.

agency serving the clothing industry of a large city. Using the research techniques described in the box on page 76, he made a detailed analysis of the agency's organization, with respect both to its internal functioning and its relationship with the public.[14]

Blau observed a clear-cut difference between what the interviewers in the employment office were trained to do and what they actually did on the job. For example, they were taught to fill out all job requests for workers in detail, to find the best client for a given vacancy, and to provide counseling for a client if he needed it. But these procedures just did not fit the reality of their office situation. Employers needed workers at once or not at all, and the level of skills required was usually so low that there was little apparent need to try to find the best-qualified workers. As a result, the interviewers usually selected the first available client who met the minimum qualifications. Thus, while adjusting to the reality of the situation, they were still able to satisfy the needs of the employers and to some extent the needs of the clients.

The interviewers also adjusted to the reality of how they were being evaluated. The employment agency was dependent on appropriations from the state legislature, which judged its performance on the basis of the number of job placements it made. In this situation, the counseling of clients, especially of unskilled workers looking for unskilled jobs, seemed a questionable use of time. Thus the interviewers eliminated counseling for the great majority of clients, in order to make the greatest possible number of placements.

Even the receptionists faced difficulty in role performance. Their task was the seemingly routine one of assigning potential clients their first appointment with an interviewer. Because jobs were scarce at certain times, the regulations called for delays in appointments of from thirty to sixty days. But often the receptionists faced clients who were desperate for work, and if they knew that job openings had just come in, they would arbitrarily schedule appointments to fit the job needs. This had the effect of improving their relations with the clients, but it often led to overcrowding in the office, with too many

applicants for the few jobs available. It also meant that applicants were not treated equally—though equal treatment is a basic premise of bureaucratic organization. Again, however, the major organizational goal of maximizing placements was achieved.

Blau found that the system for rating an interviewer's performance had the effect of improving supervisor-interviewer relationships while increasing tensions between the interviewers themselves. Performance ratings were based to a considerable degree on objective criteria (e.g., number of referrals made). This meant that the supervisor could place the onus for criticism on the record, without having to make a subjective evaluation or to criticize the interviewer as a person.

Blau also had the opportunity to test the importance of impersonality to the agency. He found that interviewers were not satisfied with their work when they had to follow strictly bureaucratic procedures. The pressures to maximize referrals and find clients in a hurry for low-skill jobs led to a work routine that many found boring. The interviewers' most satisfying experiences came when they were "doing something more than was called for." They particularly liked to help clients who were "very personable and very anxious to work." On balance, these clients tended to be middle-class, white-collar workers, who represented only a small percentage of the whole.

Blau found that the agency was continually adjusting internally to try to achieve efficiency of operation and that many of these adjustments were brought about by actions taken by personnel at all levels of the hierarchy. Furthermore, adjustments were often deemed necessary because of pressures brought to bear by elements outside the bureaucratic organization, such as the state legislature, clients, and employers. Because a bureaucracy does not operate in a vacuum, those occupying particular roles must continually revise the rules to meet the exigencies of daily needs. In the case of the state employment agency, some revisions led to increasing friction within the agency while decreasing friction between the agency and its public.

The findings of this study supported Blau's thesis that bureaucracies contain and develop the seeds, not necessarily of their own destruction, but of their continuous transformation. The conditions that Blau found to be crucial to the

---

14. Peter M. Blau, *Dynamics of Bureaucracy: A Study of Interpersonal Relationships in Two Government Agencies,* 2nd ed., rev. (Chicago: The University of Chicago Press, 1963); originally published in 1955.

self-adjustment process and thus to the maintenance of efficient operation were:

(1) at least some security in employment; (2) the absence of basic conflict between work group and top management; (3) a professional orientation toward the performance of duties; (4) established work groups that command the allegiance of their members; (5) organizational needs that are experienced as disturbing.[15]

The first three characteristics listed by Blau are consistent with the principles of formal bureaucratic structure, but the last two clearly fall outside Weber's typology of an ideal bureaucracy. Whereas efficiency theoretically requires that work relationships be kept impersonal, Blau found that such personal interaction patterns as joking and complaining were in fact helpful in creating and maintaining social cohesion. This, in turn, became the basis for the establishment of informal work groups which, by developing their own unofficial norms, were able to adjust to the practical, ongoing needs of the organization. In some ways, Blau's findings parallel those of Shils and Janowitz (page 43), who determined that primary-group relationships were essential in maintaining the effectiveness of the German *Wehrmacht*.

Judging from the research of Blau and others, it seems clear that the effectiveness of a bureaucracy is not necessarily dependent on impersonality. Contemporary man, though increasingly hemmed in by rules and regulations, apparently remains very much an individual, capable of having an impact on the large formal organizations around which so much of his life revolves.

COMMUNITIES

The term *community* is derived from the Latin word for *fellowship* and was used at one time to refer to the warm, affective relationships that could be expected among closely knit groups of people. Gradually, its meaning came to be broadened to refer to an aggregate of people living together in a particular geographical area and bound together politically and economically. We will use the term *community* in this rather broad sense, as roughly synonymous with village, town, or city.

Like the other groups we have examined thus far, the community has a distinctive pattern of social organization. Every village, town, and city has its goals, a role structure and division of labor, typical patterns of interaction, norms for regulating behavior, techniques of social control, and a system of social ranking. Because of these organizational features, communities are groups in every important respect, even though most people are not accustomed to thinking of them in that way.

Unlike most groups, communities have distinct *spatial locations.* Not only is the community itself defined in terms of a fixed geographic area (nomadic communities are a rare exception to this rule), but even the specialized groups within it, such as schools, businesses, families, and churches, are located according to characteristic ecological (spatial) patterns. This is not meant to suggest that a community is simply an aggregation of buildings, streets, and people— or, as one wag put it, a lot of families connected by a common set of sewer pipes. Like a society, it is an *integrative social system* that ties together the activities of the various groups of which it is composed. By interacting together, its families, business enterprises, religious organizations, schools, civic groups, political parties, and other constituent groups create a complex behavioral system that is a group in its own right.

There are, of course, a great many kinds of human communities, ranging from the simple nomadic food-gathering and grazing communities of primitive man to the massive urban centers of modern industrial nations. Important similarities can be found, however, even among communities that are in many ways quite different, especially when they are classified on the basis of size. Small communities have a great many organizational features in common, whether they are herding communities in Lapland, agricultural villages in Thailand, or rural centers in the United States. Similarly, urban centers in all parts of the world—and even in different periods of history—are somewhat alike in basic social organization despite whatever other differences they may have.

15. *Ibid.*, p. 256.

PRIMARY AND SECONDARY GOALS

The primary goals of communities have always been basically economic. In earlier times they were also closely related to defense. Primitive food-gathering communities, for example, were formed as early hunters and gatherers discovered that by banding together they could ensure themselves a more adequate food supply and defend themselves more effectively against their enemies.

Similar goals are basic to the agricultural village, a form of community organization that has been common in most parts of the world from earliest times to the present, although it is rarely found in the United States. In this pattern, family dwellings are clustered together in a village that is surrounded by the fields and pastures of the residents. Agricultural workers leave the village every day to go out and work their fields, returning to the village at night. This pattern of community organization has for centuries provided groups of families with a means of defense as well as with an effective system for producing, storing, and distributing food and for exchanging goods. It makes an interesting contrast to the organizational pattern of the American frontier, where single families lived in relative isolation on the land they worked and where small towns developed primarily as regional trade centers.

Even today, the growth and decline of particular communities is closely related to economic factors. Typically, a number of individuals are first attracted to a specific location because it offers some kind of economic resource. Soon others come along to service those involved in the primary economic activity, and the nucleus of a community is established. Nothing testifies more dramatically to the importance of economic goals in building a community than the ghost towns of the American West, where entire towns were abandoned almost intact once their economic bases collapsed. (See also the case study of "Caliente," a railroad town, in Chapter 6, "Social and Cultural Change," pages 195–196.)

Economic goals related to such activities as industry, trade, and tourism continue to be of primary importance even in an established community. Once its economic development is assured, however, a community diverts an increasing amount of attention and effort to such secondary goals as promoting the arts, improving the educational system, beautifying the area, and providing recreational facilities. Though of secondary importance in maintaining the community, these emergent goals are closely related to the basic need of every individual to interact socially with other human beings.

PATTERNS OF INTERACTION IN TOWN AND METROPOLIS

Patterns of interaction vary considerably with the size of a community. In a rural hamlet, a given individual may interact directly with almost every other resident at some time during a given week or month. Even in a small town of several thousand people, the spatial proximity of residents gives one the impression that he knows almost everyone in town, even though his circle of acquaintances may number only two or three hundred persons. In contrast, the resident of a large city might conceivably roam the streets for a week without ever seeing a familiar face. Although his circle of acquaintances might actually be larger than that of his small-town cousin, the sheer size of the city, in terms of both population and area, lessens the probability of his meeting someone he knows.

Interaction in a small community involves close and frequent contact among friends, relatives, and acquaintances. Because of this and because there may be little else to compete for his attention, the typical small-town resident tends to become greatly involved in the lives of his fellow townsmen. Details concerning their marriages, illnesses, drinking habits, and changes in employment become subjects for gossip and often matters of personal concern.

The resident of a big city has proportionately more contact with people he does *not* know on a personal basis. The clerk who waits on him in a department store, the bus driver who gets him to work, the teller who handles his bank deposit, and the landlord who collects his rent may all be strangers with whom he interacts only in impersonal role-playing situations. Even the friendships he forms at work do not necessarily carry over to his leisure hours, since the individuals involved are likely to live in scattered parts of the city. At home, the relative anonymity of urban life and the rapid turnover of residents in many areas work against the development of strong neighborhood ties.

It should not be assumed, however, that everyone in a large metropolitan area lives a bleak and isolated existence. In middle-class suburbs, for example, close interpersonal ties develop in a relatively short time. A chief complaint of many suburbanites, in fact, is lack of privacy! Even in the inner-city, many residential areas are stable neighborhoods where families interact on a somewhat regular basis.[16] And in both the suburbs and the city, numerous voluntary associations—such as the PTA, lodges, churches, clubs, and charitable groups—provide many opportunities for interaction with other members of the community.

In Chapter 9, "The Urban Transition," we will examine further evidence showing that the image of the urban community as a "lonely crowd" has been vastly exaggerated. Nevertheless, it is a fact that interaction among urban dwellers is, on the whole, *less primary* than that among residents of a small town. In some parts of the city, particularly in the rooming-house areas adjacent to the central business district, anonymity and social isolation are undeniable realities. Here the indigent and the homeless lead lives unrelated to the overall life of the community and largely devoid of close interpersonal ties. Nearby, the well-to-do residents of modern high-rise apartment buildings may lead almost equally anonymous lives, often by choice. Even the largest city, however, is a web of interdependent interaction. Anyone doubting this need only observe the near-chaos that can result when basic services (police, transportation, fuel delivery, garbage disposal) are disrupted for even a few days.

NORMS AT THE COMMUNITY LEVEL

The norms of a small community are more homogeneous than those of a large city, and they are more widely understood and accepted. Shared convictions about what is right or wrong,

16. See *Street-Corner Society,* cited above, and Gerald Suttles, *The Social Order of the Slum* (Chicago: The University of Chicago Press, 1968), a recent study of neighborhood patterns in Chicago's near west side.

Life in an urban community tends to be more impersonal than that in a small town. But even the largest city is a web of interdependent interaction, and near-chaos can result when basic services are interrupted for a few days. Here garbage and trash are piled high on a sidewalk in front of a Greenwich Village coffee house in New York City, where a sanitation workers' strike in February 1968 created a city-wide health emergency.

fair or unfair, proper or improper have been passed on from generation to generation and have thus become deeply institutionalized. The community provides a *locus* where the basic values of the society are interpreted and reinforced through the repeated interaction of community members.

In addition to clear rules governing ethical conduct, the normative system of a small town typically includes widely accepted guidelines governing many routine activities. There is a shared understanding about what is appropriate in respect to such matters as dressing, eating, talking, borrowing, worshiping, and burying the dead. The greater the isolation and the smaller the community, the more homogeneous and unchanging its norms are likely to be. The isolated mountain village in the Appalachians still retains a structure of norms that shapes life much as it was in nineteenth-century rural America. The greater the degree of contact with the outside world, the less likely it is that a traditional pattern survives. If a small town is located on good highways, is within the reach of a television signal from a larger city, is served by a bus line, and receives a newspaper from an urban area, its norms tend to become increasingly heterogeneous, like those of larger communities. To a great extent, urbanism today is "a state of mind," only loosely related to place of residence.

Unlike the average small town, an urban community brings together people from a wide variety of ethnic, religious, racial, regional, educational, and occupational groups, each with its own conceptions concerning proper behavior. The majority of the population are likely to agree on certain fundamental rules of conduct, such as respect for a person's life and property, but there is no consensus on norms governing many aspects of behavior nor is there any real basis for developing one. A large city must therefore rely on formal norms to regulate conduct much more than a small community does. In addition to the usual criminal codes, the statutes of a city may include everything from rules for parking one's car to rules for wrapping one's garbage.

In a diverse population, such as that found in a large urban complex, the concepts of *conformity* and *nonconformity* become extremely relative: what seems odd or improper to one segment of the population may be normative behavior for another. In terms of the informal

norms of his own particular subgroup, the average hippie is no less a conformist than is the "proper Bostonian." Both support ethical standards, modes of dress, and forms of behavior that are not shared, nor necessarily approved, by other groups in the community.

The largeness of a city and the relative anonymity of its residents make it possible for many minor deviations in behavior to go unnoticed. There is also a greater acceptance of varying behavioral norms. People expect their families, friends, and business associates to behave in a particular way, but they tend to accept or at least to tolerate some nonconformity in the behavior of others. A middle-class businessman, for example, may be amused at the city's hippie community or charmed by its foreign sections, feeling that both add "character" to the city. In matters that concern him more closely, however, he expects adherence to his own set of norms: the bearded artist may no longer seem amusing when he becomes a prospective son-in-law, and old-world customs may no longer seem quaint when practiced by the neighbors next door.

THE COMMUNITY AS A SYSTEM OF ROLES

Communities of every size have a role structure that creates a division of labor. In a small community, however, roles tend to be much more closely integrated than they are in a large modern city: typically, the role an individual plays in the family, as appropriate to his age and sex, relates to the role he plays in the occupational system of the community and in its political, recreational, and religious life. Where the principal economic activity is farming, for example, the family is likely to have a distribution of roles whereby each member has not only a family role but a corresponding role in the operation of the farm. Even the young children have economic roles, such as feeding the small animals and gathering the eggs. Religious activities are similarly interwoven with family life, with an older member of the family usually taking the role of religious leader and teacher of the young. The integration of different roles within the family setting is less often found in the United States today than in earlier times or in other parts of the world, but some aspects of the pattern can still be observed in many small American communities.

In a modern urban community, by contrast, there is relatively little integration or continuity among the different roles a person plays. Economic roles are largely a matter of individual rather than family choice, and they vary widely among persons of the same age, sex, and general educational background. It is relatively uncommon to find a modern urban family in which a child is trained systematically to take over the occupational role of his father. On the contrary, most children—and many wives—have only a vague idea of what the father does on his job. His role as breadwinner is something quite apart from his role as father and husband.

Many of the roles in an urban setting are played out within bureaucratic associations that operate quite independently. The group structure of the community includes a school system with various courses of study, many different religious groups, and a wide range of clubs, organized charities, and other voluntary associations—offering the individual community member a variety of roles from which to choose.

MECHANISMS OF SOCIAL CONTROL

In a small town, most members have internalized the values, attitudes, and other shared convictions of the community to the point where they accept the group's standards unquestioningly as their own. Furthermore, the consequences of misconduct are generally clear. The small-town resident knows that he is under constant surveillance and that any misconduct will become a matter of general concern. As in larger communities, the police and the courts are authorized to use formal sanctions when necessary, but the fear of gossip and of social rejection keeps much potential deviation in check.

Even though informal controls are especially effective in the small community, the system does allow for some deviation. Patterned evasions and specific forms of illicit activity are often winked at by the authorities and largely accepted by most residents. Drunkenness, "helling around" on the part of young males, bootlegging, and prostitution can be found in otherwise straight-laced small towns. However, even patterns of deviation are likely to be integrated into the group's normative system: young men are *expected* to sow their wild oats, and no one really minds the town drunk—unless he happens to be the doctor, the banker, or some other "regular" citizen who has a "duty" to behave conventionally.

In the large city, where norms are less uniform and the factor of surveillance is much reduced, social control is somewhat more likely to require the threat and occasional use of force. The vast majority of city residents, of course, submit voluntarily to the rules of the community. Through interaction with family, school, and other agents of socialization, they have developed internalized controls much like those of small-town residents. And although the potential wrongdoer is less subject to community pressure, he nonetheless fears the rejection of his family and friends. To the extent that his reference groups support the official norms of the community, he is likely to behave in a generally approved way.

The problem of social control is usually most difficult in economically deprived areas of the city where community identification is weak. A number of sociological factors may work together in such areas to subvert the development of effective informal controls. The residents may represent a mixture of backgrounds and have conflicting loyalties and norms. They tend to be cut off from the mainstream of community life not only by ethnic differences but also by poverty and a lack of economic opportunity. The population usually includes a large transient element that feels no identity with the neighborhood, its residents, or the community as a whole. Schools may be substandard. The rate of family breakdown is often high. Under these conditions there is little opportunity for people to internalize the community's system of norms, and some degree of social conflict therefore becomes almost inevitable.

No community, regardless of size, can rely exclusively on self-applied sanctions and informal controls to ensure uniform adherence to community norms. In general, however, a community that must rely heavily on the formal sanction of force has experienced some breakdown in other important aspects of its social organization.

COMMUNITY STRATIFICATION

At the community level, the system of social ranking is a *stratified* one; that is, a number of roles ordinarily carry the same general social rank and thus constitute a relatively homogeneous stratum. In a typical community in the United States, for example, men who work at unskilled jobs make up a single stratum of relatively low rank, regardless of their particular occupations. Those who have white-collar jobs constitute a stratum that is ranked somewhat higher, and professional people make up a still higher rank. Usually members are ranked as *families:* a man's wife and children are accorded the same general rank as he is, even if there is some basis for ranking them differently.

In Western societies, most communities rank their families into a stratified *class system.* Even in a very small town, where the variation or distinction between those at the top and those at the bottom is relatively small, social class is important and residents are sensitive to differences that outsiders would not notice. Such communities seem almost classless, however, in comparison to large metropolitan areas, where members of the highest and lowest socioeconomic classes have such totally different life styles that they might well be living in different societies.

The criteria used as bases for social stratification usually are related to the community's economy and its system of values. In primitive hunting or food-gathering communities, a man's social rank is typically based on his skill as a hunter or his courage as a warrior. These are qualities necessary to the community's survival and thus tend to be valued highly. In an agricultural community, the stratification system is more likely to be based upon ownership of land or livestock. As communities grow in size and their economies become more complex, the criteria by which an individual and his family are ranked become increasingly varied. In a large urban-industrial community, education, income, occupational role, life-style, material possessions, and purchasing power are commonly used bases for social differentiation, with the man's occupation being probably the single most important criterion. The way a given occupation is ranked, however, depends not only on its monetary rewards but on the difficulty of its role requirements and on its perceived contribution to the life of the community.

In most modern industrial societies, social stratification systems are based largely on achieved criteria and thus tend to be relatively open. An individual can move up in the system, at least within limits, if he meets the criteria used for assigning a higher rank; if he "falls on bad times," he is likely to move down. In stratification systems based largely on ascriptive criteria, by contrast, there is relatively little social mobility in either direction. As we noted in Chapter 1, probably no ranking system is based entirely on either ascribed or achieved criteria, but one or the other usually predominates.

Few facets of man's organized social life have received more attention from sociologists than the complex phenomenon of social ranking at the community and societal levels. The large body of research and theory that has been accumulated in this area will be examined in detail in Chapter 7, "Social Stratification."

SOCIETIES

Despite the vastness of particular societies, the great complexity of their organizational structures, and the indirectness of the ties between members, societies nevertheless meet our broad definition of a group as "a number of individuals who interact recurrently according to some pattern of social organization" (page 31). The elements of social organization take unique forms at the societal level, to be sure, but the same thing is true with all types of groups. Although the pattern of organization is different in form, it is not basically different in kind.

Like a community, a society is an integrative system that coordinates and binds together the great many smaller groups of which it is composed. It is the largest group with which most people can feel a sense of personal identity, and in some ways it is the most important in its effects on his life. A society is the only group, for example, that can legitimately claim the power of life and death over an individual. It also plays a very significant role in shaping the kinds of interaction that take place in other groups and in shaping their norms, roles, sanctions, and ranking criteria. A society, in short, is an enormously complex pattern of social organization that interrelates its members in patterns of mutual dependency and provides them with guidelines for all areas of social behavior.

When a society places a high value on a goal—such as putting the first man on the moon—its members are willing to expend their energy and resources in pursuing it. In Chicago, as in many other cities, thousands of people turned out to see the Apollo 11 crew and show approval of their accomplishment.

SOCIETAL GOALS

Like many other groups, societies often have formally stated goals. The Preamble to our own Constitution, for example, states the people's intent "to form a more perfect Union, establish Justice, insure domestic Tranquility, provide for the common defence, promote the general Welfare, and secure the Blessings of Liberty to ourselves and our Posterity." Other basic goals of our society—equally important and sometimes conflicting—can be inferred from the choices we make as a nation.

A societal goal—whether military, political, social, or economic—is meaningful and operative only if it expresses the *shared values* of a majority of the society's members, who must individually and collectively work to achieve it. Societies, like individuals, have only limited resources and therefore must decide how they want to use them. Thus, when we say that a society places a high value on something or considers it an important goal, we mean quite simply that its members are willing to expend their energy and resources in pursuing it and that they give it priority over other attractive alternatives.

The shared values of a society, whatever they may be, help shape its basic institutions and the social activities of its members. American society, for example, has traditionally placed a high premium on individual freedom and achievement. This individualistic component in our value system is expressed variously in our political institution (democracy), economic institution (competitive capitalism), and dominant religious institution (Protestantism). It finds further expression in the average American's search for personal satisfaction in his marriage and job, in his desire for material possessions and other symbols of personal success, and in the money and energy he devotes to pursuing his individual interests and having a good time. Our society has been so organized, in other words, that individualistic goals can be pursued through interaction with other members.

Individualism is only one of many important components of the traditional American value system; others will be detailed in the next chapter, which considers societal values in the overall context of culture. Here, the point is simply that the values shared by a society's members determine the society's goals and thus give shape and direction to its basic organizational patterns. Societal goals, of course, are enormously complex, as are the processes involved in shaping and implementing them. A potential source of conflict in all societies is that patterns of social organization, once established, tend to resist change, whether or not they continue to be effective means for achieving societal goals. In the long run, however, the stability of a society requires that its institutions accommodate themselves to the values and expectations shared by most members. (For a more detailed analysis of the relationship between consensus and social conflict, see Chapter 14, "The Political System.")

GENERAL PATTERNS OF INTERACTION

Interaction among a society's members usually takes place within the context of smaller groups, each with its own characteristic pattern of interpersonal relationships. By studying a cross section of specific groups, however, sociologists are able to identify broad interactional patterns that seem characteristic of a whole society. In some societies, for example, relationships between people tend to be informal and relatively intimate, regardless of the group context in which interaction takes place. Interaction in other societies tends to be more formal, ritualistic, and impersonal. Sociologists have long been concerned with analyzing such differences and with studying the changing patterns of interaction that have characterized Western societies.

The trend from status to contract. One of the early students of societal interaction was Sir Henry Maine, the British legal scholar whose work *Ancient Law* was first published in 1861.[17] Maine was principally interested in tracing the development of law as an index of societal development, but one aspect of his work pointed to an important change that was occurring in the interaction patterns of Western societies.

Maine noted that the "tie between man and man" had for centuries been shifting from relationships where rights and duties were defined by family obligation and fealty to a form where the individual was increasingly free to act *independently* in entering into reciprocal and binding interactions with others. He called attention to the increasing use of the *contract* as a means of specifying interactive obligations between persons. This change enabled the individual to enter freely into the terms of formal agreements made between contracting parties. In an earlier time, the duties of the individual were defined for him by his family and by tradition. Maine suggested that this change in the character of interactive relationships could be called a trend from *status to contract*.[18] Although most of Maine's work is primarily of legal-historical interest, the trend he noted became a central focus of sociological concern for more than a century.

***Gemeinschaft* and *Gesellschaft*.** The industrialization of Western societies has been accompanied by a move toward increasingly impersonal forms of interaction. An early analysis of this trend was Ferdinand Tönnies' *Gemeinschaft und Gesellschaft*, first published in Germany in 1887 and still considered a classic.[19] The words *Gemeinschaft* and *Gesellschaft*, defining two quite different kinds of social relationship, do not translate simply into English. The former is sometimes identified as *community* and the latter

17. Sir Henry Maine, *Ancient Law*, 5th ed. (New York: Henry Holt Co., 1885); see esp. pp. 163–165.

18. The reader will note that this use of *status*, referring to social position based on ascriptive qualities of family, is distinct from the general use of *status* in this text to refer to prestige or social honor; see page 46.

19. Ferdinand Tönnies, *Community and Society (Gemeinschaft and Gesellschaft)*, trans. Charles P. Loomis (East Lansing, Mich.: Michigan State University Press, 1957).

METHODOLOGY   IDEAL TYPES

Sociology, during its formative years, was characterized by many attempts to create typologies that would give direction to research and theory-building. Comte developed three basic typologies to explain man's intellectual development, Durkheim attempted to explain social change in terms of mechanical and organic types of social solidarity (see page 92), and Tönnies formulated contrasting types of social relationships that he termed *Gemeinschaft* and *Gesellschaft*. It was Max Weber, however, who systematically developed the concept of the *ideal type*.

As methodological tools, Weber intended ideal types to be mental constructs—precise concepts developed from scientific observations—that could be used in making a comparative analysis of two or more social phenomena. Thus, a sociologist can compare the distribution of authority, say, in organizations A and B by comparing the pattern in *each* organization with that in Weber's model of bureaucracy.

Weber proposed three criteria for the construction of ideal types. First, they are to *accentuate,* even exaggerate, reality rather than to describe it accurately. Thus, when Weber characterized bureaucratic organization (pages 70–75), he was abstracting characteristics that could be observed, in some form or other, in a variety of existing organizations, such as corporations and government bureaus. Ideal types, as such, *do not exist in reality.*

The second criterion for ideal types is related to the first: they are not ready-made constructs but rather must be *contrived* by the social scientist. Their purpose is to help us conceptualize social phenomena, much as our systems of weights and measures help us to conceptualize and observe the physical world. When a physicist conceptualizes one horse power in terms of raising 33,000 pounds one foot per minute or 550 pounds one foot per second, he is using a completely arbitrary abstraction as an aid in relating himself to the phenomena he studies. Ideal types serve a parallel purpose for the sociologist.

The third criterion of ideal types is that they should generate hypotheses and give direction to empirical research. Thus, in studying the dynamics of bureaucracy, Peter Blau (page 76) used Weber's ideal type of bureaucracy as a starting point and derived the hypothesis that adherence to well-defined bureaucratic procedures leads to more efficient and productive behavior. The fact that Blau's research did not confirm this hypothesis does not mean that Weber's ideal type is incorrect or useless. Since ideal types are abstractions, their accuracy is less relevant than their usefulness as a framework for examining reality and for building tested generalizations and theories.

Weber was careful to point out that ideal types are not "ideal" in the sense of representing a desired state of affairs. Nevertheless, many contemporary sociologists have abandoned Weber's original term in favor of *pure type, constructed type,* or *model,* which are free of the value connotations associated with the word *ideal.* Few sociologists, however, question the continuing utility of Weber's basic conceptions. The ideal types he constructed have generated a great deal of fruitful research and led to a refinement of his early theories about such phenomena as bureaucracy, social action, authority, and political power. More important perhaps, his development of the ideal type as a methodological tool has provided modern sociologists with one means for opening new areas of research and theory-building. Studies of urban-rural differences, the culture of poverty, the professionalization of work roles, the anatomy of confrontation and conflict—all these and many other areas of contemporary research have been influenced by Weber's early contribution.

For further reading on ideal types, see H. H. Gerth and C. Wright Mills, *From Max Weber. Essays in Sociology* (New York: Oxford University Press, 1958), pp. 59 ff., and Don Martindale, *The Nature and Types of Sociological Theory* (Boston: Houghton Mifflin Company, 1960), pp. 381–383. Martindale also has compared Weber's views with those of recent works; see "Sociological Theory and the Ideal Type" in *Symposium on Sociological Theory,* ed. Llewellyn Gross (Evanston, Ill.: Harper & Row, Inc., 1959), pp. 57–91.

as *society,* but Tönnies' concepts imply more than the meanings we usually attach to those words.

Essentially, the term *Gemeinschaft* implies a binding interactional relationship based on *sentiment.* Tönnies identified several types of social relationships as being primarily *Gemeinschaft* in character. Those who are united by *kinship* usually form a *Gemeinschaft,* as do those who live in a particular *locality* over a long period of time. People who band together because they are *likeminded* and wish to pursue a common goal, such as a religious brotherhood, may similarly form a *Gemeinschaft.*

The *Gemeinschaft* relationship is an intimate one, not unlike that found in primary groups. The close interpersonal ties that bind lifelong friends and neighbors in a rural village provide one familiar example. The members of the community are concerned with each other's welfare; they stand ready to lend a helping hand; they may do things for each other without thought of repayment or personal gain. The *Gemeinschaft* relationship is one of mutual trust and concern and willing cooperation for common goals. The actors feel a reciprocal and binding sentiment toward each other. The *Gemeinschaft,* in short, welds people into a common unity; it is in this sense that the term means *community.*

The *Gesellschaft,* on the other hand, is an interactional system characterized by *individualism* and *mutual distrust.* As Tönnies put it:

Here everybody is by himself and isolated, and there exists a condition of tension against all others. Their spheres of activity and power are sharply separated, so that everybody refuses to everyone else contacts with and admittance to his sphere, i.e., intrusions are regarded as hostile acts.[20]

In the *Gesellschaft,* interpersonal relationships are basically competitive. People struggle with each other to gain a personal advantage. There is no mutual sentiment that generates trust and reciprocal concern. Under such a condition, the *contract* becomes the principal instrument for defining the obligations of interaction: "For everything pleasant which someone does for someone else, he expects, even demands, at

least an equivalent." [21] Tönnies saw the urbanization of society, even in his time, as leading to an increase in the *Gesellschaft* relationship.

In reality, of course, no society is based exclusively upon the interactional model of either the *Gemeinschaft* or the *Gesellschaft:* all societies are some blend of the two. Tönnies constructed these concepts as "ideal types," that is, as abstractions to aid in understanding basic organizational trends in Western society. (See box, page 86.) He did not imply that there was a simple evolutionary development of society from a predominance of one to a predominance of the other, but he did point out that rural society is based much more on *Gemeinschaft* interaction, while urban society has a higher frequency of the *Gesellschaft* relationship.

Communal and associative relationships. Max Weber elaborated Tönnies' theme about forty years later. In *The Theory of Social and Economic Organization,* published in 1925, Weber suggested the terms *communal* and *associative* to describe two types of social relationship corresponding closely to *Gemeinschaft* and *Gesellschaft.* A social relationship of the communal type is based upon a "subjective feeling of the parties . . . that they belong together." The associative relationship, on the other hand, is "one resting upon a rational motivated adjustment of interests or a similarly motivated agreement [arranged] by mutual consent." [22] As we have noted, this kind of interaction typifies bureaucratically organized groups—hence their classification as *associations.*

The trend toward mass society. The trend toward more formal, superficial, and impersonal relationships as noted by Tönnies, Weber, and others has led some sociologists to characterize modern society as a *mass* society. The interactional ties between people, they say, have become less meaningful in terms of human qualities—less dependent upon friendship, tradition, and kinship. Individuals are reluctant to enter into relationships with each other unless protected by legal contracts or other formalized rules.

There is little doubt that there has been a decline, overall, in interaction based on sentiment and an increase in contractual relationships. The change, however, is by no means complete. Much human activity continues to be focused in primary groups, where social rela-

20. *Ibid.,* p. 65.
21. *Ibid.,* p. 78.
22. Weber, *op. cit.,* pp. 136–137.

tionships are essentially *Gemeinschaft* in character. Even bureaucracies, as we have noted, are not nearly so depersonalized in fact as they would seem to be in theory. Furthermore, the relative impersonality and great size of mass society can have the positive effect of providing people more freedom of choice in selecting their friends and running their own lives.

SOCIETAL NORMS

Societal norms determine the ways in which most groups within a society are organized and operate. They also provide the individual with guides to conduct that are above and beyond the norms of particular groups.

Most persons bring to each of the groups they join a number of prior ideas about how they should play their roles in that group. For example, newlyweds begin their family life with a great many preconceptions about what the relationships should be between husband and wife, between parents and children, and between the family and the community. They share with their society a *common core* of mutual expectations concerning the rules of conduct in the family relationship. While it is true that each individual family will modify these societal norms or perhaps work out private norms that pertain only to their unique group, they will generally follow the institutionalized expectations of their society.

Precisely these same observations can be made of other kinds of groups. The business corporation, the peer group, the religious congregation, and the school all derive their particular systems of norms from a common core of behavioral expectations. The individual normative systems of elementary schools in the United States, for example, resemble each other to a striking degree, despite sometimes considerable variations from community to community and from state to state. Without some core of norms shared by most members of society, social life would be almost wholly unpredictable.

Folkways. Every society has a number of norms that do not specifically apply to any particular group but are simply institutionalized expectations about social conduct. Americans, for example, take a dim view of the person who refuses to bathe regularly; the customary ex-

pectation is that an individual will take enough baths to avoid becoming an olfactory problem. This is not a norm of a specific group, such as the PTA, the Moose lodge, or the local supermarket, but rather a *general* norm endorsed by most members of society.

The classic statement on general societal norms is that of the American sociologist William Graham Sumner. In *Folkways*, published in 1906, Sumner outlined several categories of societal norms and illustrated them profusely with examples drawn from a great many societies in different historical periods.[23] A society's folkways are norms the members have hit upon more or less by chance and established as common practices. They specify modes of dress, etiquette, language usage, and other routine matters not regarded as having much moral significance. Whether one shakes hands when he is introduced to another, raises his palms, or bows and sucks in his breath is determined by his society's folkways.

No one knows precisely how the particular practices of a given society begin or how they become institutionalized. As Sumner put it, "The operation by which the folkways are produced consists in the frequent repetition of petty acts, often by great numbers acting in concert or, at least, acting in the same way when face to face with the same need."[24] Many long-established folkways probably once had an adaptive or functional origin, but it is generally impossible to trace their exact beginnings. The custom of hand-shaking, for example, probably originated as a gesture to show that the individual carried no weapon. The custom of shaving has been attributed to Darius' order for his troops to remove their beards, so that the enemy could not use them as a "handle" to pull the men from their horses.

In societies undergoing rapid change, new folkways are constantly created and old ones abandoned. As technical innovations, such as the telephone, the automobile, and television, have become integral parts of modern life, each society has developed its own norms to govern their use. No one knows why Americans answer the phone with "Hello" and the British identify themselves by stating "Smith here," or why the Mexicans say "Bueno" (good) and the Spaniards

---

23. Sumner, *op. cit.*
24. *Ibid.,* pp. 18–19.

VIEWPOINTS THE INDIVIDUAL IN MASS SOCIETY

A first task of any social movement is to convince people that the search for orienting theories and the creation of human values is complex but worthwhile. . . . Our own social values involve conceptions of human beings, human relationships, and social systems.

We regard *men* as infinitely precious and possessed of unfulfilled capacities for reason, freedom, and love. In affirming these principles we are aware of countering perhaps the dominant conceptions of man in the twentieth century: that he is a thing to be manipulated, and that he is inherently incapable of directing his own affairs. We oppose the depersonalization that reduces human beings to the status of things. . . .

Men have unrealized potential for self-cultivation, self-direction, self-understanding, and creativity. It is this potential that we regard as crucial and to which we appeal, not the human potentiality for violence, unreason, and submission to authority. The goal of man and society should be human independence: a concern not with image of popularity but with finding a meaning in life that is personally authentic. . . .

Human relationships should involve fraternity and honesty. Human interdependence is contemporary fact; human brotherhood must be willed, however, as a condition of future survival and as the most appropriate form of social relations. Personal links between man and man are needed, especially to go beyond the partial and fragmentary bonds of function that bind men only as worker to worker, employer to employee, teacher to student, American to Russian.

Loneliness, estrangement, isolation describe the vast distance between man and man today. These dominant tendencies cannot be overcome by better personnel management, nor by improved gadgets, but only when a love of man overcomes the idolatrous worship of things by man. . . .

We would replace power rooted in possession, privilege, or circumstance by power and uniqueness rooted in love, reflectiveness, reason, and creativity. As a *social system* we seek the establishment of a democracy of individual participation, governed by two central aims: that the individual share in those social decisions determining the quality and direction of his life; that society be organized to encourage independence in man and provide the media for their common participation. . . .

Students for a Democratic Society
Port Huron Statement

The root difference between the Conservatives and the Liberals of today is that Conservatives take account of the *whole* man, while the Liberals tend to look only at the material side of man's nature. The Conservative believes that man is, in part, an economic, an animal creature; but that he is also a spiritual creature with spiritual needs and spiritual desires. What is more, these needs and desires reflect the *superior* side of man's nature, and thus take precedence over his economic wants. Conservatism therefore looks upon the enhancement of man's spiritual nature as the primary concern of political philosophy. Liberals, on the other hand—in the name of a concern for "human beings"—regard the satisfaction of economic wants as the dominant mission of society. They are, moreover, in a hurry. So that their characteristic approach is to harness the society's political and economic forces into a collective effort to *compel* "progress." In this approach, I believe they fight against Nature.

. . . Man's most sacred possession is his individual soul—which has an immortal side, but also a mortal one. The mortal side establishes his absolute differentness from every other human being. *Only a philosophy that takes into account the essential differences between men, and, accordingly, makes provision for developing the different potentialities of each man can claim to be in accord with Nature.* . . . The Conservative knows that to regard man as part of an undifferentiated mass is to consign him to ultimate slavery.

Secondly, the Conservative has learned that the economic and spiritual aspects of man's nature are inextricably intertwined. He cannot be economically free, or even economically efficient, if he is enslaved politically; conversely, man's political freedom is illusory if he is dependent for his economic needs on the State.

The Conservative realizes, thirdly, that man's development, in both its spiritual and material aspects, is not something that can be directed by outside forces. Every man, for his individual good and for the good of his society, is responsible for his *own* development. The choices that govern his life are choices that *he* must make: they cannot be made by any other human being, or by a collectivity of human beings. . . . The conscience of the Conservative is pricked by *anyone* who would debase the dignity of the individual human being. Today, therefore, he is at odds with dictators who rule by terror, and equally with those gentler collectivists who ask our permission to play God with the human race.

Barry Goldwater
The Conscience of a Conservative

"Habla" (talk), but each custom satisfies the need for a ritual of common use. People follow the established folkways of their society because they provide convenient techniques for handling a host of routine situations.

A basic characteristic of a folkway is that the intensity of feeling associated with it is relatively low. If a person chooses to dress in an unconventional manner, to answer the telephone in a unique way, to eat odd combinations of food, or to display strange table manners he may be regarded as an eccentric or someone to be avoided, but he will usually be allowed to go his own way. Violations of the folkways do not generally provoke strong reactions. However, the very existence of alternative or competing folkways may in some cases constitute a beginning point for social conflict. In our own society, immigrants with "foreign ways" and young people who adopt nonconforming dress may be viewed with hostility by the majority simply on the basis of their distinctive folkways, whether they deviate from society's more fundamental norms or not.

Mores. Like folkways, *mores* come down to us from the past, but unlike folkways they are associated with intense feelings of right and wrong. The mores define rules of conduct that are simply not to be violated. If they are, the violator is rejected by society and punished severely. Sometimes the penalty is death.

The mores of a society cover a variety of behaviors, but all of them concern acts that threaten critical values. Cannibalism, incest, and infanticide, for example, arouse almost "universal" feelings of disgust and condemnation among members of Western societies. Even if we had no specific laws governing such acts, they would still be regarded as wrong.

Of particular significance are the mores governing sexual conduct. Since the family is such a significant group for the survival of society, it is not difficult to understand why strong norms have developed to ensure its stability. Societies differ considerably in the specifics of their sex codes, but whatever their rules, they take strong measures against the individual who deviates conspicuously from accepted practices.

Folkways and mores are the two extremes on a continuum of societal norms. The folkways govern routine behavior and do not carry strong sanctions for violators; the mores regulate more critical forms of behavior, and deviants are sub-ject to severe disapproval and punishment for transgressions. Many societal norms fall somewhere between these two extremes. Public drunkenness, for example, is not such a serious transgression that the individual is forever banished from the company of his neighbors, yet in some segments of society such activity causes a considerable amount of gossip and a degree of social rejection. Similarly, divorce, premarital promiscuity, welching on a bet, and open gambling are regarded as serious affronts by some groups. The norms governing such matters are neither folkways nor mores but have some characteristics of both.

Laws. Laws are formalized codes of conduct stating fixed punishments that have been promulgated by an official body of leaders within the society. Like folkways and mores, these norms vary in the intensity of feeling and emotional reaction that are associated with them. Unlike folkways and mores, however, laws have a clear-cut origin.

Some laws concern matters of only limited public concern. Nearly every community has statutes that prohibit littering, jaywalking, and parking in certain areas. However, violators of such norms are seldom sent to jail. These regulative statutes are designed to eliminate confusion and inconvenience in routine situations. Many of them are simply formalized folkways. Other laws concern such serious matters as homicide, robbery, and assault. For the most part, these are adequately regulated by the mores, but experience has shown that self-applied sanctions alone are not adequate to control the behavior of some. As societies have become more complex, it has been increasingly necessary to formalize norms—to give them official recognition and to back them with penal sanctions exercised by the state.

Almost all of the really significant societal norms have been formalized into legal statutes. This implies a very close relationship between mores and the law. Legal statutes with strong support in the mores are those that are most uniformly enforced. Others, for which an adequate basis in the mores has slipped away or for which no basis ever really existed, are difficult to enforce and are likely to be ineffective. The notorious failure of Prohibition is a dramatic illustration that laws not rooted in the informal norms of a people are largely unenforceable.

Young people who adopt nonconforming dress and hairstyles may be viewed with hostility by the majority simply on the basis of their distinctive folkways, whether they deviate from society's more fundamental norms or not.

ROLES AND ROLE COMPLEXES

General roles. Society as a whole defines a number of general roles which cut across particular groups. Such characteristics as age, sex, race, and occupation provide bases for general role patterns to which individuals are expected to conform in all their interactions with other societal members. For example, the rights, duties, and obligations associated with the role of child are much more restricted than those ascribed to the role of adult. Some societies develop fairly elaborate role patterns associated with age. In our own society, the role of child is considered as somewhat distinct from the role of teen-ager; young adulthood entails a different set of expectations than middle age; and still different institutionalized expectations are associated with old age.

Male and female roles provide another example of general roles at the societal level. We begin training boys and girls to perform different roles at a very early age. If little Johnny smashes his thumb with a hammer and runs howling to mother, he is told that "big boys don't cry." If the same thing happens to little Suzy, mother comforts her and tells her to "go ahead and cry."

Societal roles for male and female include not only differential patterns of emotional expression but also distinct clusters of interests, different positions in the division of labor, different modes of dress and adornment, different speech habits, and different bodily gestures.

These expectations vary widely from society to society, and they change with the age of the individual. Nevertheless, such roles are general in that they apply *uniformly* to every male or female in a given society. Each male of a particular age is expected to display a certain restricted range of "appropriate" behaviors.

In the United States, general roles have also been prescribed on the basis of race. In the Deep South, in particular, the Negro traditionally was expected to be subservient, to doff his hat in the presence of a white person, to go to the back door at the homes of white families, and so on. The Negro role was a general one in that *every* black was expected to behave in this manner in his contacts with whites. It mattered little if he were more highly educated, wealthier, or more law-abiding than the white individuals with whom he was interacting.

The division of labor and social solidarity. The division of labor in a society is a tremendously complex system that coordinates not only general societal roles but also the roles developed in various specialized groups. One of the most significant analyses of this aspect of social organization is that of Émile Durkheim, who compared the role structure and division of labor in small traditional societies with that of industrial societies. His *Division of Labor in Society*, published in 1893, remains one of the most important theoretical statements concerning the society as a special type of group.[25] Durkheim's central thesis was that the division of labor in a society determines the type of solidarity that binds its members and welds the society into a cohesive whole.

In primitive societies and in small agricultural societies, the division of labor is relatively simple and restricted. Every adult male plays roughly the same roles as every other adult male in the society, and he plays them in about the same way. The same thing is true of females. In societies of this type, the similarities among people are much greater than the differences. Largely by virtue of their role *similarities*, people tend to identify with each other and to subscribe wholeheartedly to the values and beliefs of the society as a whole—which are generally identical with their own. Durkheim called the type of social solidarity based upon common sentiments *mechanical solidarity*, because he considered the attraction patterns between like individuals to be somewhat analogous to the attraction patterns between similar molecules in a chemical compound.

By contrast, urban-industrial societies have an extended division of labor characterized by a high degree of *specialization*. Occupational roles, for example, become increasingly dissimilar as systems of mass production are developed, as more and more goods of different types are produced, and as more and more specialized services are needed. Individuals find their way into these specialized roles and pursue occupations that may be totally different from those of their neighbors. With the rise in special-purpose associations, other roles open up which further distinguish one member of the society from another. More and more functions are removed from the family and are taken over by outside groups. Medical facilities, school systems, government agencies, labor unions, and many other groups assume responsibility for different tasks in the society and provide additional role specialization for the individuals who participate in them.

Durkheim maintained that an extended division of labor increases the differences among people and thus eliminates the basis for developing mechanical solidarity. The members of a complex industrial society are nevertheless linked to each other in one very important way: the very specialization that separates them makes them *mutually dependent*. Durkheim referred to this type of social cohesiveness as *organic solidarity*, because it is based on an interdependence of specialized functions like that in an organic system. Even in the absence of common attitudes, beliefs, and values, the members of a modern industrial society are effectively bound together by their need for each other's services. Indeed, the members of such societies are in many ways *more* dependent on each other than the members of simpler societies, who are economically self-sufficient to a much greater degree.

Durkheim's analysis of the social significance of the division of labor generally supports the assumption of equilibrium tendencies in society (page 48). In both traditional and industrial societies, according to this view, the lives of individuals are linked together in such a way as to ensure the stability of the group as a whole.

---

25. Émile Durkheim, *The Division of Labor in Society*, trans. George Simpson (New York: The Free Press, 1947).

THE PROBLEM OF SOCIAL ORDER
AND CONTROL

At the societal level as in other types of groups, the most effective type of social control is essentially *voluntary* control—that is, most people willingly submit to the rules and regulations that society imposes on them. There is a minority in every society, however, that does not conform. These two facts demand sociological explanation. What produces willing conformity in some people, and what explains the conspicuous deviation of others?

Voluntary control and conformity are closely related to the kinds of training a society's members receive as children and even as adults. Through the process of *socialization* (Chapter 5), the individual internalizes the attitudes, values, beliefs, and patterns of behavior supported by those with whom he associates, particularly his family, teachers, and friends. Their definitions of right and wrong, of acceptable and unacceptable behavior, become *his* definitions almost automatically. To the extent that their standards reflect societal norms, he is likely to conform willingly to society's rules.

What, then, is the explanation for deviant behavior? Why does a particular individual or group fail to accept society's norms and to follow its rules? In general, sociologists search for the causes of deviant behavior through the analysis of social and cultural systems. They look to the social conditions that shape people's values and define their life possibilities. When individuals have different goals from those supported by societal consensus, or when they find society's goals outside their personal reach, they are unlikely to internalize society's norms or to follow its rules voluntarily. If the goals and institutions of a society are meaningless to substantial segments of the population—if the social system does not provide for their needs—voluntary social control is unlikely to check behavior that deviates from conventional norms. People who cannot obtain satisfaction within the system are likely to seek it through nonconforming activities.

Some degree of deviance seems inevitable in all societies, given the fact that people are first socialized into the ways of the primary group, with its *Gemeinshaft*-like relations, and then become members of secondary groups based largely on *Gesellschaft*-like relations. Both personal discomfort and social conflict may be the inevitable result, even if people try not to be deviant. One of the great challenges to the sociologist is to understand the ways in which primary and secondary group structures overlap, conflict, and thus threaten both individual and societal stability.

SOCIETAL STRATIFICATION

Social stratification has been studied most often at the community level, where patterns of selective interaction between the members of different strata can most readily be observed. A community's system of social ranking, however, reflects the ranking system of the society as a whole.

The implications of stratification for determining the distribution of power, wealth, and prestige have been recognized ever since men first became concerned with the systematic study of society. Both Plato and Aristotle wrote extensively on social stratification, not only as it existed in the societies they knew but as they thought it ought to be. Aristotle, for example, distinguished three basic classes: the rich, the poor, and the middle class. Thus class to Aristotle was clearly an economic concept, but it had significant social and political consequences. Political stability, he said, depended on the existence of a large middle class. Its members were the least likely either to shrink from rule or to be overly ambitious for it. They were economically secure and neither anxious nor envious of the rich.

Aristotle was certain that the best legislators would come from this middle class. He felt that the rich were spoiled by their wealth and would never be able to submit to authority. If allowed to rule, they would become despots. The poor, on the other hand, were too accustomed to exploitation. They were too subservient to rule, knowing only how to obey. That state would be most secure, Aristotle maintained, which had a large middle class, with the rich and the poor on either side not too large. Only in this way could stratification be an integrative force in society.

In the eighteenth and nineteenth centuries, changes brought about by the Industrial Revolution generated new interest in this aspect of social organization, particularly in the role of the

When individuals find society's goals outside their personal reach, or when they have different goals from those supported by societal consensus, they are unlikely to internalize society's norms or to follow its rules voluntarily. Much of the looting that followed the assassination of Martin Luther King, Jr. (right) and much of the rioting that occurred at a Chicago rock festival in July 1970 (above) involved youngsters who apparently felt no qualms about their actions.

economic system in differentiating the population into distinct social classes. In the late 1700's, it was held as axiomatic that, as Thomas Malthus put it, "... in every society that has advanced beyond the savage state, a class of proprietors, and a class of laborours, must necessarily exist. . . ." [26]

The capitalistic economic institution of the industrializing nations began to produce social classes based less upon such criteria as nobility of birth, ownership of land, or inherited caste position and more upon the relationship of the individual to the means of production and his ability to accumulate wealth through his occupational pursuits. For the most part, the older social order had been regarded as natural and just, but increasingly in the nineteenth century new political philosophies challenged the assumption that any group had a natural right to dominate others.

The Marxian theory of class conflict. One of the most significant nineteenth-century theories of societal stratification was that forcibly outlined by Karl Marx (pages 7–8), who maintained that the relationship between social classes had been one of continuous exploitation of the weak by the strong. Marx linked the class struggle closely to both the political process and the economic system, proclaiming the latter to be the determining force for change. He believed that class struggle would eventually culminate in the establishment of a classless society. Marxian theory is a clear example of a social theory that accounts for the emergence of new social forms through conflict.

The current worldwide struggle between Communist and non-Communist societies is partially a product of differing interpretations of societal stratification. The question of whether Marx' theory was valid or not has perhaps been less significant than the fact that people have reacted variously to the challenges it posed (see page 180). Nevertheless, it is clear that the capitalist societies have not collapsed as Marx predicted they would. There have been significant developments that he did not foresee, such as the modifications of the relationships between the classes that have taken place throughout the non-Communist Western societies, the radical

26. Thomas R. Malthus, *First Essay on Population* (1798). Reprinted for the Royal Economic Society (London: The Macmillan Company, 1926), p. 283.

transformation of capitalism, and the gradual emergence of government as a countervailing force to private initiative. Nor have either proprietors or laborers united into a single corporate class with feelings of group solidarity and hostility to the other class. It seems increasingly clear, moreover, that possession of wealth is not the only criterion of societal stratification.

To a considerable extent our awareness of the limits of a single-dimensional approach to stratification stems from sociological research carried out during the past forty years, with the focus on American society (see Chapter 7). Studies have demonstrated that our society is indeed a stratified one and that the system of social ranking greatly influences every individual's life chances. The available evidence supports the hypothesis that the same is true of other societies, including the Communist ones.

SOCIAL INSTITUTIONS

In the foregoing sections, the nature of societies as human groups has been reviewed. Their patterns of social organization were examined in terms of norms, roles, social control, and other organizational components. At the same time, it was noted that societies are not only groups in their own right but also integrative systems that bring together large numbers of other groups—communities, associations, families, etc.—into predictable patterns of relationship.

In their efforts to understand how societies develop, function, and change, sociologists have developed numerous conceptual approaches for studying societal structure. One of these is to view societies as organized around a number of *social institutions*. This term refers to certain specific areas of human social life that have become broadly organized into discernible patterns. For example, a society will normally have some form of political activity. This activity, considered in all its aspects, would include groups, roles and norms within specific groups, social processes, beliefs, practices, attitudes, and so forth. All of these social phenomena would be part of the political institution of that society. Thus, a social institution includes all "institutionalized" forms of behavior pertaining to certain broad, goal-oriented activities within the society.

There are several basic social institutions that can be identified in all societies—the *eco-*

nomic, educational, familial, political, and *religious* institutions. Most modern societies have many more (e.g., scientific, military, recreational, etc.). Any broad, goal-oriented area of behavior that is firmly established in a society can be regarded as a social institution. (The sociological term *social institution* obviously differs from everyday usages, that is, a prison or an orphanage as an "institution.") The idea of social institutions in no way interferes with the analysis of social behavior in terms of groups and their social organization. In fact, institutional analysis presumes an understanding not only of the social organization of human groups but of culture and numerous social processes that will be discussed in later chapters.

SUMMARY

In this chapter we have differentiated several basic types of groups in terms of their distinctive patterns of social organization—their characteristic goals, patterns of interaction, norms, roles, sanctions, and systems of social ranking. Like other systems of classification in sociology, this one is intended as an aid in the orderly accumulation of knowledge about man in society.

Of special significance both to the individual and to the various social systems of which he is a part are *primary groups* such as his family and peer groups. The cohesion of such groups depends less on formal organization than it does on the mutual bonds of affection between members, on their sense of oneness. Primary groups are of central importance in shaping the attitudes, values, and goals of the individual. They are often his most important reference groups.

Decision-making groups, though also small, are much more formally organized than primary groups. Interaction is task-oriented rather than people-oriented. Sociological research has shown that the decision-making process in groups such as committees, councils, and juries typically proceeds through several stages, as the members collect information, evaluate it, reach a decision, and then dissipate the interpersonal tensions that have developed. Although interaction in such groups follows a formal pattern, an informal organizational structure usually emerges that helps give direction to the decision-making process.

Another type of formal group that has assumed increasing prominence in modern society is the large, bureaucratically organized *association.* Associations are organized around structural forms that stress the principles of rationality and efficiency. The norms, roles, sanctions, and other aspects of a bureaucracy's formal organization are designed to achieve particular ends, much as the parts of a machine are designed to perform specific functions. In the course of their actual operation, however, such organizations develop an informal structure that may either support or subvert the official one. Interaction in a bureaucracy is theoretically depersonalized, but studies have shown that primary relationships continue to be important and that individuals are sometimes more significant than formal rules in determining the group's effectiveness.

Social organization at the *community* level is enormously complex, but communities nevertheless have all of the structural characteristics necessary to classify them as groups. Although there are many types of communities, differing in size and complexity and purpose, all are integrative social systems that link together the activities of their various constituent subgroups. One distinctive characteristic of the community, as compared with most other types of groups, is that it has a fixed spatial location and consequent ecological patterning.

The most complex human group, and in some ways the most important, is the *society.* Much classical sociological theory has been devoted to describing and analyzing societal organization and its direction of change over time. Such concepts as *status-to-contract, Gemeinschaft* and *Gesellschaft, communal* and *associative* relationships, and *mass society* illustrate the range of sociological formulations that have been developed as aids in understanding societal organization.

The elements of social organization are the same in societies as in smaller groups, though they take distinctive forms. Societal norms, for example, can be identified as folkways, mores, and laws. Characteristic patterns of expectation define general roles in society, such as those based on the ascriptive criteria of age and sex. The division of labor at this level of social organization is especially significant in holding the group together as a cohesive social system.

Like most systems developed thus far for classifying human groups, the classification used in this chapter is oversimplified and makes no systematic attempt to account for the wide range of differences to be found within each type. It is useful, nonetheless, in analyzing the distinctive characteristics of groups with different patterns of social organization and in illustrating the sociological perspective on man's social behavior.

3
Culture

THE NATURE AND IMPORTANCE OF CULTURE

Culture, Society, and Social Organization.   Human Evolution and the Development of Culture.

COMPARATIVE CHARACTERISTICS OF CULTURE

Cultural Variability.   Cultural Integration.   Cultural Relativity.

THE CONTENT AND STRUCTURE OF CULTURE

The Analysis of Culture Traits.   Trait Configurations. Cultural Themes and Emphases.

The first two chapters have emphasized the significance of social organization as a sociological concept. A second broad concept that is essential for understanding the structure and interrelationships of human groups is *culture.* This is not the culture we associate with sophisticated appreciation of literature and the fine arts. To the sociologist, every person who learns and follows the way of his society is "cultured." A comic book or a tin whistle is as truly a cultural object as a Bible or a bassoon; the barroom limerick and the folk ballad are as much a part of our cultural heritage as the sonnet and the oratorio. While aware of the different valuations people place on these things, the sociologist recognizes all of them as parts of the design for living—that is, the culture—of the society in which they occur.

As used by sociologists, *culture* refers to the total pattern of beliefs, customs, institutions, objects, and techniques that characterize the life of a human community. A culture may include a stone ax or a spaceship, a rain dance or a meteorological report, a chant or an aria, a totem or a trinity—everything a people believes, values, and shares through words and other symbols, along with the artifacts, or material elements, created out of these shared ideas and aspirations.[1]

Clearly, cultures are almost infinitely variable: the way of life of any given people shows numerous institutionalized behavior forms that are unique to that people. Cultures may be well integrated and harmonious, but they may also be characterized by such disharmony and disjunction that conflict rather than equilibrium seems to be the normal state. Cultural variability is particularly evident in standards of behavior: what appears to be a meritorious act in one cultural setting may be judged as a serious transgression of norms in another. Thus, to understand the behavior of any group, the sociologist must be familiar with its culture.

1. This definition is a composite based upon a number of analyses in standard sources. For example, see E. B. Tylor, *Primitive Culture,* 7th ed. (New York: Brentano's 1924), p. 1; A. L. Kroeber, *The Nature of Culture* (Chicago: The University of Chicago Press, 1952), esp. Parts 11 and 14, pp. 104–107 and 118–135; Ralph Linton, *The Tree of Culture* (New York: Alfred A. Knopf, Inc., 1955), p. 29; and Abram Kardiner, *The Individual and His Society* (New York: Columbia University Press, 1939), pp. 5–6.

THE NATURE AND IMPORTANCE OF CULTURE

Culture is often referred to as the social heritage of a society. Because each generation passes on to its offspring the design for living that it acquired from its forebears, man is relieved of the necessity for working out all over again the solutions to innumerable recurring problems. We Americans living today did not have to invent the wheel, learn to control fire or harness steam, create a spoken and written language, discover metallurgy, devise ways for growing, harvesting, and storing food, or develop a system of laws. These things, plus untold others, were already available. Earlier generations left us an elaborate cultural heritage, which we will transmit, along with some modifications and additions, to our children.

Culture represents man's solutions to problems. The members of every society face a number of identical problems simply because they share certain fundamental biological characteristics. Our hair grows; something has to be done about it. We all get uncomfortably hot or cold; techniques for cooling, warming, and sheltering the body must be provided. Food and water are necessary for individual survival; procreation and childbearing are essential for societal survival; death is inescapable.

All men share these problems, but the solutions they arrive at are astonishingly variable. The hair styles, clothing habits, architectural forms, dietary practices, family structures, and funerary rites that have been devised by different peoples at different times in history are almost incredible in their diversity. Nevertheless, each society's solutions "work." While some may seem inefficient, illogical, even absurd by our own cultural standards, the culture of every society includes workable solutions to the problems imposed by nature.

Beyond these physical problems, man also faces more abstract issues. His presence on earth and his relationship to the cosmos are matters for speculation, and he devises legends, myths, folk tales, religions, and philosophies to explain them. These, too, have great variety, yet each must more or less satisfy the members of the society in which it develops.

In order to maintain societal continuity over a long period, a people must create social institutions—complex configurations of cultural elements developed around specific cultural forms. Each society has some set of religious beliefs and practices, a political process, some form of organized family life, an economic system, and some established means for educating new generations to its ways.

Although scientific studies continue to find gaps in the theories that once fenced man neatly off from other creatures, it still seems clear that even the simplest human society has developed cultural forms to a far greater degree than any other living things. For practical purposes, it can still be said that men have cultures and animals do not.

CULTURE, SOCIETY, AND SOCIAL ORGANIZATION

A clear distinction needs to be made between *culture* and *society*. We have already defined society as a relatively large number of individuals who are engaged in repetitive interaction according to a pattern of social organization. Culture is the *specific* system of norms, beliefs, practices, techniques, and objects that the people of a society have inherited from their forebears, have invented, or have adopted from other sources.

In a sense the distinction between society and culture is an artificial one. A culture requires a society to create and maintain it. Yet cultures are certainly independent of particular members of society. In fact, the entire membership of every society regularly undergoes complete replacement through death and birth. For the purposes of studying cultural phenomena, we could conceivably ignore the individuals who make up a given society at any particular moment and examine only the cultural patterns.

The study of culture requires that cultural elements and patterns be inferred from the behavior of societal members. But once this has been done, cultural phenomena become scientific data in their own right. They possess characteristics and attributes that are analytically independent of the society with which they are associated. Thus, we can compare the cultural patterns of one society with those of another in cross-cultural studies, some of which may in-volve different historical periods. We can examine the content and structure of a given culture and its processes of growth and change. We can reach conclusions about the functions of any item in a culture and about the degree to which it is integrated into larger cultural patterns.

The concept of *culture* needs to be distinguished not only from *society* but also from *social organization*. A convenient way to do this is to provide an example of social organization without culture:

Termites, like bees and ants, are social insects living in colonies. Like bees and ants they work together, performing special tasks for the good of the colony, but, unlike them, they live together continuously, instead of interruptedly, in the nests or burrows. This colonial habit has given rise to different kinds of individuals . . . fitted structurally to perform definite functions in the life of the colony: soldiers for defense, a king and queen for reproduction, often replaced or supplemented by the supplemental reproductives; and usually . . . workers for the collection of food, the care of the king, queen, soldiers and young . . . .[2]

By stretching things a bit, we might interpret such insect phenomena within a framework of behavioral regularities (norms), a division of labor (specialized roles), group goals, social ranking, etc. But the termite colony operates on very different behavioral principles than those of human groups. The role specializations are *built into* the individual members of the colony through inheritance, and such concepts as learning have little bearing on the way in which the social insects carry on their collective life. We do not presume that the insects have the ability to modify their own shared solutions to the problems of living in their environment; they cannot mutually adopt new ways.

Thus the termites do not have culture in any accepted sense of the term. Although their life is *organized* in that it follows predictable patterns and *social* in that it is based on interrelated and mutually dependent forms of interaction, the colonies have no accumulated social heritage that each new generation must learn. They have social organization, but they have no culture.

Social organization as it develops in human groups is not based on biological inheritance.

2. Charles A. Kofoid, ed., *Termites and Termite Control* (Berkeley: University of California Press, 1934), p. 8.

Learning plays a fundamental role. As was explained in Chapter 1, social organization refers to the pattern of shared expectations that guides the behavior of a group's members as they interact with one another. Through the development of institutionalized—that is, stabilized—patterns of expectation, groups are able to carry on their interpersonal relationships in such a way that transactions among members become highly predictable. Every group develops a somewhat unique pattern of social organization, but the culture in which it operates helps to define the goals it sets, the norms its members follow, its techniques of social control, its criteria for status, and other aspects of its social organization.

This principle is easily illustrated. Our culture includes the belief that every human being has dignity and worth, even when he is so old and ill that he can no longer contribute to the society. Therefore we think it important that our aged have some economic security and some guarantee of medical attention. With this goal broadly defined, our society has established formal associations whose specific task is to administer provisions of the law so that old people have at least their minimum needs satisfied. We do this by a system of taxation and distribution that is consistent with our economic institutions and our general values.

If our culture defined the worth of the human individual differently, we might have developed other forms of dealing with the aged. At one extreme, we could have adopted a plan like that followed by some traditional Eskimo groups and sent the aged out to die. They could have been identified as no longer capable of contributing to the welfare of the society and as therefore representing a danger to its survival.[3] Or we could have followed the course of those societies that look upon their old people with special reverence and give their comfort and well-being the highest priority. Our culture prescribes a middle way, and the groups we set up to handle the problem reflect our cultural values.

In general, then, the culture of a society gives direction to and sets limits on the pattern of social organization that will be worked out

within the society. A group cannot legitimately be formed in a society for the pursuit of goals that its culture does not tolerate; it cannot easily utilize sanctions that violate basic cultural values; it cannot prescribe roles that are outside cultural limits. Thus culture sets the broad limits for the development of specific patterns of social organization of particular groups within the society.

HUMAN EVOLUTION AND THE DEVELOPMENT OF CULTURE

From the biological standpoint, man is little more than a middle-sized, rather weak, terrestrial biped.[4] He lacks the fangs, claws, and strength of most large carnivores, and his relatively hairless hide offers little protection from the elements or from enemies. How is it that such a poorly equipped creature has been able to gain dominion over all other animal species and achieve extraordinary control over the physical environment? The answer lies in man's enormous learning ability as compared to that of other creatures. This capacity provides a necessary condition for the development of culture. It was his learning potential that permitted man to develop language. With these prerequisites to culture, he underwent the long evolutionary process that eventually separated him distinctly from all other animals.[5]

The biological evolution of man over eons of time need not concern us here, and we will note only two of the basic steps in the development of his material culture. The first was the use of simple tools. Once man taught himself to fashion crude weapons by striking one stone against another to create a sharp edge, he could greatly expand his food supply; he became increasingly the hunter rather than the hunted. There is evidence to suggest that there was a substantial growth and spread of human population as a result, for the new technology gave man an important edge over competing species in the struggle for survival.[6] A second cultural spurt occurred when man mastered techniques for producing his own food. This advance led to another considerable growth of population and a great many cultural changes. In particular, stable community life followed in the wake of the development of agriculture and animal husbandry.

3. George P. Murdock, *Our Primitive Contemporaries* (New York: The Macmillan Company, 1934), p. 214.

4. Linton, *op. cit.*, p. 7.

5. *Ibid.*, p. 8.

6. Edward S. Deevey, Jr., "The Human Population," *Scientific American*, 203 (September 1960), 195–203.

This detail from a Paleolithic cave painting in France is among the oldest known examples of man's pictorial art. It indicates that early man used symbols to communicate with others about the basic necessities of life—the hunt, the community, and so on. But as man's culture developed so also did his means of expression; the two went hand in hand. Today our symbolic development has reached the stage of an elaborate written language, which enables us not only to communicate about such things as food and shelter but also to express complex and abstract systems of reasoning.

The significance of tools and farming in human history are obvious enough, but the role of speech may not be fully recognized. Yet the importance of language in the development and transmission of culture can scarcely be overemphasized. Language is both an integral part of culture and an essential prerequisite to its growth. Little can be said about its origin, however, for spoken languages leave no physical traces, and the systems of writing man has developed are only a few thousand years old.[7]

Although we do not know how languages originated, we are beginning to understand the essential place of language in human life. Without it, the development and elaboration of culture could never have taken place. Man was able to assign agreed-upon meanings to *symbols*— gestures and objects but also utterances and, long afterward, written marks.[8] Through the use of these verbal symbols, one individual was able to convey meaning to another, and communication as we know it began. It was through language that early man was able to grope toward the first forms of coordinated group activity, to cooperate in the hunt, and to develop simple communities with an interlocking division of labor. Through the use of language symbols,

man has been able to deal both with things— spears, horses, shoes, transistors—and with abstractions—evil, loyalty, holiness, democracy. He has been able to record his ideas and transmit them to others.

If man's manipulation of symbols went no further than the everyday use of language for interpersonal communication, his culture would never have developed to its present elaborate state. His progress has depended largely on the application of reason—on his ability to think in consistent, orderly steps from premises to conclusions. Since ancient times man has developed various formal systems of reasoning, from the syllogisms of Aristotle to the most abstract modern mathematics. Today he has embarked on an era in which machines—computers— perform some of the more laborious systematic manipulations of symbols. Thus cultural development depends upon, and is synonymous with, symbolic development.

7. *Ibid.*, p. 53. See also Edward Sapir, "Communication," *Encyclopedia of the Social Sciences*, 4 (1942), 78.

8. Alfred R. Lindesmith and Anselm L. Strauss, *Social Psychology*, 3rd ed. (New York: Holt, Rinehart and Winston, Inc., 1968).

COMPARATIVE CHARACTERISTICS OF CULTURE

Three general characteristics of culture stand out clearly as one examines the styles of life found in different societies around the world. First, cultural solutions to identical problems show great *variation* from one society to the next. Second, unless subject to internally generated strains or to drastic changes imposed from without, cultures tend to become consistent and *integrated*; this tendency is especially apparent in relatively isolated societies. Finally, cultural standards are *relative*: judgments concerning morality, beauty, logic, propriety, and the like are meaningful only within the cultural framework of the society involved. These three ideas merit more detailed consideration.

CULTURAL VARIABILITY

One of the most fascinating aspects of human life is the great variety in the solutions people of different societies develop for the problems of life. Descriptive anthropologists, or ethnographers, have studied the cultural patterns of hundreds of societies living in all parts of the globe, and this literature has made possible a great many cross-cultural comparisons. No two societies have independently approached in identical ways the satisfaction of their needs for food, shelter, and clothing. Endless differences exist not only in the forms of technology societies use to satisfy basic needs but in their systems of courtship, family organization, kinship structures, inheritance rules, value commitments, religious concepts, health practices, political processes, and all other forms of organized social activity. Yet, as we pointed out earlier, in spite of these innumerable variations, all cultures seem to "work." They provide the means by which the members of a society can cope with their environment and coordinate their lives.

The great variation that exists in the cultural patterns of mankind raises a number of sociological questions. How did they come about? Why is it that some people have developed very complex forms of art, social organization, technology, and religion while others have retained simpler forms? Are there variations in inherited ability that have brought some groups to the space age while others continue to use stone implements?

The available evidence suggests that cultural differences are not due to variations in native learning capacity. Although comparative testing is difficult, the members of all human societies appear to have about the same average level of native intelligence. Aldous Huxley argues, indeed, that man's intellectual capacity has changed very little over the last twenty or thirty thousand years:

The native or genetic capacities of today's bright city child are no better than the native capacities of a bright child born into a family of Upper Paleolithic cave-dwellers. But whereas the contemporary bright baby may grow up to become almost anything—a Presbyterian engineer, for example, a piano-playing Marxist, a professor of biochemistry who is a mystical agnostic and likes to paint in watercolours—the paleolithic baby could not possibly have grown into anything except a hunter or food-gatherer, using the crudest of stone tools and thinking about his narrow world of trees and swamps in terms of some hazy system of magic.[9]

As Huxley's statement implies, some of the important variables contributing to cultural differences are the kind of *environment* within which the society exists, the kinds of *materials* available within this environment, the amount of *contact* the society has with other people from whom they can borrow ideas, and, of course, the richness of their *cultural heritage* from the past. Some societies, because of their geographical location, are well endowed with natural resources and have been able to profit from contact with others, enriching their culture through the use of borrowed solutions. Others, located in particularly harsh environments or in isolated parts of the world, have few resources and have been involved in little cultural cross-fertilization.

Western man has been able to build upon the cultural heritage of all the great civilizations of the Mediterranean area—of Egypt and the Near East, Greece, Rome, and Islam—and certainly this heritage helped the West to reach its present sophisticated level of technology. But the bequests of cultural ancestors hardly constitute a full explanation of the differences between cultures. Why has the West, which has progressed so far in science and technology and produced so many material comforts and con-

veniences, failed to achieve comparable advances in ethical and cosmological concepts and in poetic and architectural forms? (It could be argued that in these latter respects the achievements of the ancient Greeks and Hebrews remain unsurpassed.) Why did Western science come to a halt for centuries, while educated men devoted their attention to logic and theology? And why did India and China, with their own rich cultural heritages, take different roads from that followed by Western man?

The failure of Eastern societies and earlier Western societies to create a scientific and technological revolution on the order of the one that began in Europe in the seventeenth century cannot be explained by cultural heritage alone. Nor can it be attributed to a lack of intelligence. Men of intellect in every society direct their energies according to their goals. And when a society applies itself to certain pursuits at the expense of others, it is reasonable to assume that its basic beliefs and values are responsible. The medieval European was influenced by religious convictions that directed attention away from the things of this world. The ancient Greeks had a more secular orientation, but although they were very curious about man and his universe they placed little value on working out practical applications of their intellectual theories. The Chinese, after making remarkable progress in science and technology, became more concerned with the maintenance of tradition.

Once we recognize that the failure of some peoples to invent steam engines or electric dynamos or atomic bombs may be either because they lacked the appropriate background and resources or simply because they felt no urge to work in such directions, we may better appreciate the ways in which other societies have succeeded in meeting their needs. Cultural forms that at first glance seem merely colorful or exotic may upon closer analysis prove to be very practical and extremely clever solutions to particular problems. Take, for example, the problem of shelter. The tepee of the American plains Indian was constructed of poles and hides. It was easily taken down when the tribe had to move to better hunting grounds. It furnished shade during the scorching summers and turned aside the coldest blasts of sub-zero winters. Its

9. Aldous Huxley, "Human Potentialities," in *Science and Human Affairs*, ed. R. E. Farson (Palo Alto, Calif.: Science & Behavior Books, 1965), p. 69.

As early man used available materials and technology to provide shelter for himself and his family, he developed forms of architecture that are in some ways reflected in the architecture of today. The circular hut and the geodesic dome are similar in form even though they were developed from different materials and for different purposes. The gypsy wagon was originally a special adaptation to a no-madic way of life. Its present-day counterpart—the mobile home—is actually intended to provide inexpensive housing rather than mobility.

ventilating flaps and hole at the top let fresh air in and smoke out while its double wall could hold in a fire's warmth in chilly weather.[10] Working with minimal resources, the Eskimo came up with his ingenious igloo. Dwellers in the hot and humid rain forest in the South Pacific used available materials to produce a cool, airy shelter that withstood monsoons but permitted the lightest breezes to circulate at night. Other peoples far removed from the Western cultural heritage did not stop with the building of suitable shelters but went on to construct elaborate temples and palaces, like the great stone buildings of the Mayans in Central America and the sophisticated courts of old China.

Cultural variability arises from other sources as well. Human beings have an interesting tendency to preserve cultural practices that were at one time necessary and logical but that later become unnecessary and even illogical. Thus, items that have long outlived their utility may be retained in a culture. For example, it was at one time both necessary and rational for the American family to have one or more dogs. There was farm work to be performed by these animals; they could herd stock, assist with hunting, guard against hostile Indians, and aid in the protection of the family when help could not be summoned. Today, the average American has no practical need for a dog's services. Yet, because we have retained friendly attitudes toward these beasts as part of our cultural heritage, they remain in our homes. From any logical standpoint their presence is absurd. They are troublesome as well as costly. But moved by thoughts of "man's best friend," "a boy and his dog," and other cherished clichés, Americans willingly spend well over a billion dollars a year to keep these animals in their dwellings.

Many Americans become sorely agitated over the idea of using dogs as laboratory animals in medical experiments. They do not become nearly so upset over the similar plight of other animals, such as white rats, largely because they associate different cultural values with these creatures. Indeed, Americans sometimes seem more concerned about dogs than about their fellow human beings. Not long ago a Chicago newspaper reported that over five hundred readers had called to offer a home to a puppy that had been found with its ears mutilated, while not a single call had been received about

a four-year-old child who had been bitten over 95 percent of his body by a pack of dogs.

In some cases cultural variability may be due to factors that are quite apparent. Arabic has terms for camels of every size, age, shape, color, odor, state of health, and degree of strength.[11] Similarly, Eskimo languages have a very large number of words for snow in various forms, densities, etc. But the causes of many other cultural variations are by no means obvious. For example, it is difficult to explain why one people adopts monogamous marriage while another adopts polygyny. One problem in tracing the origins of cultural forms is that preliterate peoples leave no record of the beliefs and values that give rise to their social organization. While historians can frequently discover the reasons for particular cultural developments in literate societies by examining their literature and other written records, explanations of cultural choices by the preliterate must usually be far more tentative.

CULTURAL INTEGRATION

A listing of the techniques and artifacts that a people use, or a detailed description of their marriage customs, religious rituals, or other practices, does not provide an adequate view of their culture. A particular culture is more than the sum of its individual elements; it becomes understandable only when it is viewed as an organized pattern, as a more or less integrated whole.

Cultures differ significantly in the extent to which they are internally consistent in their patterns of value, belief, and behavior. If the principles to which people commit themselves while acting as family members, say, or in practicing their religion, are inconsistent with what they do and believe while engaging in economic or political behavior, we can say that their culture is poorly integrated, that it incorporates built-in strains. A fully integrated culture is one in which there are no significant contradictions between people's beliefs and their actions, or between one set of actions or beliefs and an-

---

10. Murdock, *op. cit.,* pp. 268–269.

11. Otto Klineberg, *Social Psychology,* rev. ed. (New York: Holt, Rinehart and Winston, Inc., 1954), p. 50.

other. To illustrate differences in cultural consistency, we can compare the culture of the Zuñi, an Indian group that has lived for centuries in the Rio Grande Valley of New Mexico, with the culture of the United States as a whole.

Zuñi culture. The Zuñi, like the Acoma, the Hopi, and several other nearby groups, are contemporary survivors of pre-Columbian Pueblo Indians who formerly existed in substantial numbers in northwestern New Mexico.[12] The Zuñi live in one of the most desert-like environments in the United States. Rainfall is scanty, and the summers are searingly hot. The Indians are farmers. They learned many centuries ago to grow corn, which became their basic food, as well as other minor crops. Spanish explorers found the Zuñi grouped in seven villages (which the Spaniards referred to as the Seven Cities of Cibola), but most of them are now concentrated in a single large pueblo.

The Zuñi have been well aware of their precarious dependence upon the whims of nature. In their desert environment, agriculture is a risky venture at best, but the Zuñi long ago invented ingenious techniques for growing their food under forbidding conditions. In addition to planting, tending, and harvesting the corn, they have always given over much of their lives to learning and performing the intricate ceremonies and rituals that make up their religious system. These observances are intimately associated with the traditional agricultural techniques—that is, they represent attempts to control the environment by pleasing the gods and spirits that the Zuñi feel are responsible for fertility and rain. The central theme that threads through all the elaborate calendric observances, the rain dances, and the other religious rituals is water. The activities of the priests, the succession of dances, and the sacred objects are all in some way a part of efforts to assure a sufficient supply of moisture. Much of this old culture remains intact today.

The Zuñi live an intensely social life. The physical structure of their pueblo is such that families are in close contact with each other.

Although close physical proximity and scarce resources are conditions that might lead to interpersonal and interfamilial conflict, the Zuñi culture mitigates against such disruption. Individualism, emotion, and personal strivings are not approved of, and conflict is kept at a minimum.

The Zuñi family system reflects the fact that the principal social system is the village, or pueblo, itself. Marriages are rather casually arranged and are not occasions for great public ceremony.[13] Divorce is relatively simple and causes neither social upheaval nor public censure. But the Zuñi have a means of preserving familial continuity and order in the face of changes in marital partnership. One of the many organizational structures that help to integrate the society is the matrilineal family. It is the women who own and inherit the house, the sacred objects, the family lands, and the supplies of stored corn. The man comes to his wife's house and lives there with the old mother, her husband, and the other married daughters and their husbands. This group is also the major economic unit in the production of corn. If divorce occurs, the husband returns to the home of his own mother with little more than his spare moccasins and a few of his personal religious objects. The wife arranges for a new marriage, and another male enters the household. In spite of the relative ease of divorce, however, most Zuñi marriages are enduring ones, for the Zuñi character is essentially peaceful.

According to Ruth Benedict, in the traditional culture of the Zuñi there is no struggle for power in political affairs. Indeed, a man who seeks a position of authority or leadership is strongly disapproved of; offices of any kind are avoided and will be undertaken only with great reluctance and at the insistence of the others. Personal competitiveness is considered an unwholesome trait; if an individual gives evidence of it, he will be discouraged by the rest.

The ideal man in Zuñi is a person of dignity and affability who has never tried to lead, and who has never called forth any comment from his neighbours. Any conflict, even though all right is on his side, is held against him. Even in contests of skill like their foot-races, if a man wins habitually he is debarred from running. They are interested in a game that a number can play with even chances, and an outstanding runner spoils the game: they will have none of him.[14]

12. Carl C. Seltzer, "Racial Prehistory in the Southwest and the Hawikuh Zunis," *Papers of the Peabody Museum of American Archaeology and Ethnology,* 23, 1.

13. Ruth Benedict, *Patterns of Culture* (Boston: Houghton Mifflin Company, 1961), pp. 74–75.

14. *Ibid.,* p. 99.

Viewed as a whole, the Zuñi culture is a remarkably integrated one. Religious values and beliefs are closely tied to the agricultural system that constitutes the economic base. Zuñi family structure and customs support and aid in preserving the stability of the society and in maintaining the orderly succession of inheritance and property ownership. Zuñi attitudes toward competitiveness and rivalry limit interpersonal conflict and strain even though the people live in a physically concentrated village. What the Zuñi do, what they believe, and what they hold in high value form an integrated configuration. This does not mean that there is never any conflict or that every single aspect of their culture is closely and perfectly linked with every other one. But compared with most other societies, the Zuñi have developed a very harmonious cultural system. They have maintained their own way of life in the face of the powerful impact of the invading Spaniards, who attempted religious conversion by force and who tried to use them as slave labor. They have also resisted the seductive American culture that came to the area in the mid-nineteenth century. While they have accepted and incorporated many items from both Spanish and American culture, in large part the Zuñi continue to live now much as they have for centuries.

American culture. Americans lack the long history of continuous cultural evolution in a local region that has permitted the Zuñi and many Asian, African, and European peoples to develop a unified set of traditions, customs, and values. American society has been formed relatively recently of people who brought with them a great diversity of orientations and practices from many distinct sources. Furthermore, Americans have not developed their way of life under a single set of environmental conditions. Farming in New England, planting in the Carolinas, ranching in Texas, trapping in the mountains, and following the sea along the coasts were only a few of the contrasting forms of economic activity that characterized the new society.

Our basic values, therefore, do not come from a single cultural heritage but rather reflect many different aspects of our society's experience. Our emphasis on individual success, for example, stems from three basic sources: the *Puritan heritage*, which has survived from the colonial period, the *frontier spirit*, which dominated the westward movement of population over more than two centuries, and the *capitalistic ethic*, which has been the impetus behind our increasingly industrial social order. These orientations have all contributed to our belief that each man should struggle to rise in the status system, to "get ahead," to succeed; and as a result the acquisition of material goods, economic independence, and symbols of prestige are goals that we as a people hold very high.[15] (For a more detailed discussion of American value orientations, see pages 120–122.)

As our society has grown, it has developed a greatly expanded division of labor. Occupational specialties, plus numerous regional variations, have given rise to a host of distinctive ways of life. This diversity has tended to weaken the psychological bonds that unite more homogeneous societies. For example, among the Zuñi all families follow the same economic pursuit. They have a much more restricted division of labor and rather uniformly subscribe to the same way of life. The feeling of "likeness" that results provides a strong basis for societal solidarity. Our expanded division of labor increases the functional dependency of one occupational group upon the next, and thus is a source of unity in itself; but it also tends to produce conflict, strain, and feelings of "we" versus "they" as the various groups competitively seek their specialized goals. Psychological unity is further weakened by the class structure, with some people enjoying an extremely abundant material life while others are in greater or lesser degree deprived. In a society devoted to the ideals of "equality" and "democracy," this disparity has done little to weld the members into a like-minded whole. Economic inequality has always been one of the most significant sources of disharmony among the American people.

Religious disunity in American society has also weakened cultural integration. The various major religions practiced in the United States did not grow out of attempts to cope with nature in any immediate sense, as did the religion of the Zuñi. Most were brought here from the Old World, and they have served more often as focuses of division than of harmony. Further-

---

15. Richard Weiss, *The American Myth of Success* (New York: Basic Books, Inc., 1969). The author points out that the Puritan divines who offered guidance to colonial New Englanders always treated material success "in the context of a larger framework of values." But in the Puritan heritage these other values were not always visible.

more, religion in our culture is not closely integrated with other areas of life as it is in the culture of the Zuñi. Although the fundamental teachings of all our major religions stress basically the same ideals, religious ideals are largely ignored when Americans turn their attention to business enterprises or international affairs; to these activities we apply other sets of values.

Our political system is openly based on conflict. We divide ourselves into political parties with different orientations, competing for the votes of blocs and special interest groups. Our periodic election campaigns provide the basis for perpetuating conflicting orientations and political antipathies. Furthermore, our political deeds seldom match our political words; we publicly subscribe to ideals that we fail to practice. Most notably, we profess to cherish the ideal of equality, while regularly denying opportunity to some members of our society on the basis of such considerations as skin color or religious belief. The great "American Dilemma" is that in practice we often flout the very ideals and values that we proclaim to be the basis of our democracy.[16] We even periodically go to war to "preserve peace." Whatever the historical reasons for these cultural contradictions, they have been sources of division and disharmony among the American people.

There are many other sources of conflict in our society that stem from cultural orientations. We change so rapidly that the members of each new generation despair the "old-fashioned" ways of their parents. Our society is split by ideological groups and interest blocs that often pursue their own goals at the expense of the others. We need mention only a few of the conflicting segments of our society to indicate the many possible sources of strain: labor versus management, haves versus have-nots, segregationists versus integrationists, blacks versus whites, Protestants versus Catholics, Christians versus Jews, manufacturers versus consumers, liberals versus conservatives, federal bureaucracy versus local government—the list is almost endless.

It should be noted, however, that even though American culture embodies many sources of conflict, the result is not chaos. For the most part the struggles that take place in our society follow the established "rules of the game." Labor and management or segregationists and integrationists may be in open and bitter disagreement; but if such conflicts erupt into violence and social disorder, the society invokes both formal and informal mechanisms of control. Internal conflicts usually are tolerated only if they occur within the limits of an established cultural framework.

Even so, our culture (like the cultures of most other rapidly changing industrial societies) is much less closely integrated than that of the Zuñi. This does not mean that one culture is "good" and the other "bad," nor does it mean that one will endure and the other will decline. History makes it clear that societies can function adequately without a high degree of cultural integration. Indeed, there are many social theorists who argue that conflict can be a creative force, that it is necessary to stimulate change. Without making value judgments, then, we can only say that the Zuñi and American cultures are very different. We have our configuration, often characterized by conflict; the Zuñi have theirs, usually characterized by harmony. For many of us, life among the Zuñi might be downright boring. For them, life in the general American society might be an impossible nightmare.

CULTURAL RELATIVITY

A third major characteristic of culture is the relativity of the standards that societies use for making judgments and evaluations concerning truth, beauty, morality, and the "correctness" of particular patterns of behavior. The women of one society starve their way to beauty while the women of another gorge their way to the same goal. Our society finds dogs lovable; some other societies find them delicious. Muslims and Jews think it wrong to eat pork; Hindus have religious scruples against slaughtering cattle; most Western peoples, including Americans, are repelled, esthetically if not morally, at the thought of eating lizards, grasshoppers, locusts, ants, and termites, although millions of other peoples eat them regularly.[17] Condemnation of cannibalism is by no means universal. Societies may revere youth or age, music or money, wisdom or war.

A major question with respect to cultural standards concerns their *validity*. Are the many

---

16. Gunnar Myrdal, *An American Dilemma: The Negro Problem and American Democracy*, rev. ed. (New York: Harper & Row, Inc., 1962).

17. Marston Bates, *Gluttons and Libertines* (New York: Random House, Inc., 1968).

METHODOLOGY COMPARATIVE STUDIES

Sociologists often use cross-cultural and intersocietal comparisons to study particular facets of social organization or culture as they occur in different settings. The comparative approach is not a specific method of research but rather employs a wide range of sociological techniques.

Comparative studies usually have either one of two general objectives. Most often, perhaps, the goal is to reconstruct the origins of a particular sociocultural phenomenon. Thus a study might seek to account for the development of a value orientation (such as that associated with Western capitalism), a specific type of technology (such as weaving), or a given social movement (such as temperance). Typically, comparative studies of this type include societies or subgroups in which the trait configuration does *not* appear as well as those in which it does. Thus Weber found clues to the origins of the "spirit of capitalism" (page 181) by studying not only capitalistic societies in western Europe but also non-Western societies in which capitalism failed to develop.

A somewhat broader goal than tracing the origins of a particular configuration is that of establishing generalizations that will apply uniformly to all groups of a given kind—to all decision-making groups, for example, or to all large communities. A well-known comparative study of this type is the Inkeles and Rossi research which attempted to demonstrate that modern industrial societies such as the United States, Great Britain, the Soviet Union, Japan, New Zealand, and Germany all have very similar occupational ranking systems. (For an analysis of comparative studies on occupational ranking systems, see pages 225–227.)

In *The Rules of the Sociological Method* (1895), Durkheim distinguished three basic designs for comparative studies, all of which are widely used today. One approach is to compare variations among different categories or groups of people within a single society at a given point in history. This design is obviously useful in studying configurations of norms or values in the various American subcultures.

A second approach is to study specific differences in societies or other groups that are basically similar. An example of this design is David Sudnow's comparative study of two large hospitals. Although the two institutions were alike in many respects, one served a well-to-do clientele whereas the other administered mainly to the poor. Sudnow compared the act of dying in these two settings and found drastic differences in the formal systems for dealing with the death of a patient, in cultural rituals, in medical practices, and in meaning to hospital staff.

A third type of comparative study focuses on specific similarities among societies or other groups that are basically different. Thus D'Antonio and Form discovered underlying similarities in the community power structures of El Paso, Texas, and Ciudad Juarez, Mexico. Separated by a river and an international border, these communities differ sharply in cultural, linguistic, political, economic, ecological, and ethnic characteristics. However, the researchers found them to have at least one thing in common: commitment to a very similar democratic ideology with an actual power structure at considerable variance with the one that ideology implies.

One of the most elaborate sources of data for cross-cultural and intersocietal comparisons is the Human Relations Area Files (HRAF) developed by George Murdock and Associates. Essentially, this is a system for accumulating and storing retrievable information on societies around the world. The files now contain nearly eight hundred categories of information on more than four hundred societies. These materials have proved to be a rich source of secondary data for a variety of research purposes.

For more details on the comparative approach see Robert M. Marsh, *Comparative Sociology* (New York: Harcourt, Brace & World, 1967). The studies referred to above are Alex Inkeles and Peter N. Rossi, "National Comparisons of Occupational Prestige," *American Journal of Sociology*, 61 (1956), 329–339; David Sudnow, *Passing On: The Social Organization of Dying* (Englewood Cliffs, N.J.: Prentice-Hall, Inc., 1967); and William V. D'Antonio and William H. Form, *Influentials in Two Border Cities* (South Bend, Ind.: University of Notre Dame Press, 1965). See also George P. Murdock, *Outline of World Cultures*, 4th rev. ed. (New Haven, Conn.: HRAF Press, 1963).

differing norms concerning morality, beauty, and truth equally valid, or is there one universal moral code, one correct logic, one ultimate criterion of truth, one true standard of beauty? This question becomes particularly perplexing when posed in the context of religion. Is there one true form of religious belief, or do all the world's religious faiths have equal validity? Because these issues involve personal commitment and subjective value judgments, scientific sociology can never address them directly. Cross-cultural studies that compare and contrast the standards of different cultures are not concerned with questions of right and wrong. They prove only one thing, namely, that whatever the individual's beliefs—whatever standards he invokes in matters of morality, beauty, or rationality—his convictions are by no means subscribed to by all mankind.

Although many attempts have been made to establish universal standards of "right" and "wrong," they have never been accepted by all men at any point in history. Human societies have been as varied in their standards of morality, esthetics, rationality, and religious conviction as they have been in such matters as hairstyles, food tastes, clothing, and bodily adornment. Perhaps some perspective on this matter of relativity can be gained by a brief look at the sex standards of several cultures.

Contrasting sex standards. Standards for sexual behavior not only differ greatly from one society to the next but also vary over time within a given society as it undergoes cultural change. In swiftly developing industrial societies, such change can take place as rapidly as from one generation to the next. Early in the present century, for example, American women wore dresses that concealed them from neckline to shoe top, and the sight of a woman's calf was considered to be a strong erotic stimulus for males. Only a few decades later the same society accepts the bikini calmly and experiments with see-through garments and see-all theater.

In the late 1920's, Margaret Mead studied the relationships between the sexes prior to marriage among adolescent groups in Samoa.[18] It was commonly expected in this society that young men and women would have a number of romances in which premarital sex relationships were accepted naturally. There was no feeling of shame or guilt attached to such conduct. The standards of the society defined such behavior as permissible and proper. As the young people approached adulthood, however, they were expected to locate and settle upon mutually satisfactory partners. Once marriage had taken place, no sexual license was tolerated, and the punishments for breaking this rule were severe.

At about the same time, another anthropologist, Bronislaw Malinowski, studied the sexual behavior of the Trobriand Islanders, a Melanesian people of the New Guinea area.[19] Here, sexual behavior was also very permissive. Parents engaged in intercourse without taking special precautions to prevent children watching. Trobriand children had complete sexual freedom except for incest taboos. The games in which they imitated adult copulation were considered amusing by their elders. During adolescence, the young men lived in special "bachelor" houses to which they brought their girl friends for casual affairs. After marriage, however, complete fidelity was expected of both partners.

The permissive standards of the Trobriand Islanders regarding premarital sex contrast sharply with the standards that prevailed for centuries in China and with those that recently prevailed in Victorian England and among upper-class families in Latin America. In these societies contacts between the sexes prior to marriage were rigidly controlled. In rural China, for example, a young man was required to marry a bride from a neighboring village. The girls of his own village were defined as unavailable for mating and procreation. He did not, of course, have to make his own marital selection. This was done for him by the elders of his family in consultation with the parents of the bride. Betrothals were arranged through a broker, sometimes during the infancy of both parties. It was not unusual for the bride and groom to see each other for the first time at the marriage ceremony.

Can the sexual behavior of the young people in any of the societies we have described be considered immoral? The sociologist would say that it is possible to make such an evaluation only when individuals violate the standards that prevail *within their own culture*. If adolescents in Victorian England had behaved in the manner

18. Margaret Mead, *Coming of Age in Samoa* (London: J. Cape, 1929).

19. Bronislaw Malinowski, *Sex and Repression in Savage Society* (New York: Harcourt Brace Jovanovich, Inc., 1927).

Ethnocentrism carried to extremes can be ultimately self-destructive, closing the door to innovation and to peaceful interaction with other groups.

of the Trobriand Islanders, for example, they would clearly have been immoral by the standards accepted in Victorian England. But there is no basis for judging such conduct immoral on grounds that it violates our own standards or some assumed universal standard. (It might be mentioned, incidentally, that the Micronesians, among other peoples, find kissing unthinkable.[20])

Sexual behavior, then, like other types of behavior associated with standards of right and wrong, must be interpreted in the context of the society's culture. To impose our own standards arbitrarily on societies that do not subscribe to them requires that we assume that ours is the best of all possible cultures, that ours are the most wisely developed rules for behavior, and that the ways of others are by definition inferior. Such an assumption is an example of *ethnocentrism.*

Ethnocentrism. All known societies are ethnocentric, and almost all groups within a given society are ethnocentric with respect to one another. Stated simply, ethnocentrism is the tendency of a group to regard its own ways as superior and to look down upon the ways of all others. Ethnocentrism fosters a feeling of superiority on the part of the members of a group as they judge nonmembers. This attitude finds expression in the names and labels that the group uses to characterize itself and others. For the ancient Greeks, for example, all non-Greeks were "barbarians." The ancient Hebrews believed themselves to be the "chosen people," their god to be the only god. Christian Europe viewed all non-Christians as "pagans," "infidels," or "heathens," and Islam returned the compliment. Our language is replete with epithets suggesting that some particular group or segment of society is less worthy than another. Racial, ethnic, and religious categories are frequently denigrated by such labels. City people deplore the ways of "country bumpkins" or "hicks," while rural folk regard "city slickers" with dark suspicion. Young people are amused at the ways of "old fogies" or outraged by those of the "Establishment," while adults condemn the antics of these "wild kids." The "hip" cannot abide the "straight," and vice versa. Even the professional criminal expresses his ethnocen-

---

20. Bates, *op. cit.*, p. 23.

trism by labeling the law-abiding citizen as a "sucker."

Ethnocentrism is an obvious source of misunderstanding and conflict *between* groups, but it is a source of unity and stability *within* groups. By maintaining ethnocentric attitudes toward outsiders, a group promotes its own solidarity, maintains loyalty, and builds morale. Such attitudes as patriotism, nationalism, and feelings of ethnic superiority serve to reinforce the cultural norms prevailing among a people and preserve the stability of their culture and social organization. Whether ethnocentrism is seen as functional or dysfunctional, then, is partly a matter of perspective. Even from the standpoint of a particular group, however, ethnocentrism carried to extremes can be ultimately self-destructive, closing the door to innovation and to peaceful interaction with other groups.

THE CONTENT AND STRUCTURE OF CULTURE

The average person looks at culture much as he looks at art: he doesn't understand it, but he knows what he likes. The difficulty of studying culture is well recognized by social scientists, who over the years have developed a number of theoretical tools to aid them in the task. In general, they use either one or two broad strategies. The *analytic* approach focuses on small units of culture; the *synthetic*, on broad cultural patterns.

Much of what we know about culture represents the work of anthropologists, who have directed their efforts primarily to the study of preliterate societies. Thus, their research has paralleled and complemented that of sociologists, whose interests have focused for the most part on the urban, industrial societies. These two fields now share a large number of perspectives that together have proved useful in interpreting, classifying, and comparing cultures.

THE ANALYSIS OF CULTURE TRAITS

The *analytic* approach to the study of culture seeks to identify, describe, and classify individ-ual culture *traits*—the smallest meaningful units of cultural content. For example, the bow and arrow is often cited as an example of a culture trait. One may note immediately that this weapon involves a combination of several parts: the arrow shaft, the arrowhead, the feather fletching, the bow itself, and the bowstring. Physically, the apparatus can readily be reduced to these separate units. Behaviorally, however, it cannot. One might try to throw the arrow shaft or use the unstrung bow as a club, but separately the parts would be little more than a jumble of sticks, feathers, and string. Only when they are assembled as a unit do they provide a workable cultural solution to a problem.

In the case of more complex elements, the task of identifying traits can be very difficult indeed. For example, is the electronic computer a culture trait in our society? What about the refrigerator, the automobile, the atomic bomb? These represent solutions to problems that other societies solve with such units as the abacus, the cold stream, the horse, and the war club; and in the sense that they would be behaviorally meaningless if disassembled into a heap of unconnected parts, each is a trait—an elementary unit of our fantastically complex mechanical culture.

The refrigerator is a fairly "universal" trait in our society—a widespread solution to a problem. The same is true of the automobile. The other devices, however, are highly "specialized" traits; they pertain only to specialized groups. Certainly they are not a part of the culture of the common man, though he would recognize them as being part of the way of life of his society as a whole.

Actually, the problem of deciding what is a trait and what is a combination of traits is a very secondary concern to most social scientists. The main object of the analytic approach is to identify those cultural items that can be classified, traced from one society to another, or observed in terms of the contribution they make to the culture as a whole. The question of ultimate units, then, is not crucial. For a given trait the matter can often be adjudicated somewhat arbitrarily.

Culture traits are by no means limited to weapons and machines. A specific hairstyle can be a trait. So can a type of dance, a particular superstition, or a given attitude toward marrying one's cousin. The entire culture of a society is made up of traits, which fall into different categories. Mechanical objects such as fish spears, guns, and movie cameras might form one class, for example, and nonmaterial traits such as folk tales, puberty rites, beliefs, and values might form another. There is no standard system for classifying culture traits, but most social scientists recognize the usefulness of the general categories described below.

Material traits. The material or technological traits in a culture include all the artifacts—the man-made things—a society uses: weapons of war, articles of clothing, agricultural implements, jewelry, industrial machines, household furnishings, transportation devices, and scientific apparatus. Some social scientists would also include the various techniques required to use the physical objects, on the theory that the technology of a society comprises not only its devices but the skill patterns and lore that their human users must have in order to apply them to the solution of problems.

Normative traits. The normative or regulative traits of a society make up a major category of its nonmaterial culture. They include all the institutionalized expectations that the members of the society follow in their dealings with each other. The society's folkways, mores, and laws would be included here, as would institutionalized role patterns common in the society and any other rules of conduct that serve to make interaction more predictable.

It is at this point that the concepts of culture and social organization most closely parallel each other. Norms, roles, and other institutionalized expectations are given specific direction and definition by culture. They also constitute the basis for the organization of behavior within the society. Thus, this regulative category of culture traits holds special significance for the sociologist. In searching for the causes of some particular form of behavior in a group (whether crime, divorce, combat effectiveness, suicide, or acceptance of innovation), it is to the normative culture—that is, to the basis of social organization—that he often turns first for clues.

Cognitive traits. A third broad category of culture traits is made up of the various beliefs a society shares about the nature of reality—an aspect of the nonmaterial culture made possible through and especially influenced by the use of language. Within this rather heterogeneous

category would be included such matters as scientific theories, basic religious concepts, political beliefs, myths, legends, and other kinds of cognitive elements of culture. While language plays an important part in all aspects of culture, it is clearly paramount here, and for this reason some social scientists prefer to call the category *symbolic* culture.

Values. A fourth major category of culture traits is made up of the values and other deep-seated sentiments the members of a society share—the emotionally held orientations of a people. These are the basic sentiments by which men orient themselves toward the higher goals and ideals by which they interpret what is worthwhile, what is sordid, what is humorous, what is sacred. In some ways this aspect of non-material culture is the most difficult category of all to separate clearly from the others. The deep-seated values people hold are symbolically expressed and are often linked to norms and beliefs. In practice, moreover, people themselves seldom think of their values as separate from other aspects of culture. For purposes of cultural analysis, however, it is often convenient to make this distinction: the identification of the basic values and sentiments held by a group can provide considerable insight into the reasons for their behavior.

TRAIT CONFIGURATIONS

The classification of traits into rough categories sheds light on the structure of culture and also provides a tool for studying specific traits. However, in terms of what people actually do, the categories obviously overlap. The artifacts and other material elements of a society's culture, for example, may reflect a people's beliefs and values and be regulated in many ways by their norms. In the United States, the automobile is as much a way of life as it is a material possession. Similarly, any one of the mores of our society is not only a normative rule prohibiting some act such as murder or incest but also a set of cognitive and value traits defining that act's importance and its moral significance. The study of individual traits, then, must be supplemented by the study of cultural configurations—patterns of interrelated traits that together account for some broad pattern of behavior. Among the types of configuration that have been identified through the synthetic approach are culture complexes, social institutions, and subcultures.

Culture complexes. A culture complex is a cluster of related traits around which people organize some aspect of their lives. A good example from a primitive society is the hunting-fishing complex of the traditional polar Eskimo. This complex includes a number of material traits: the kayak, the harpoon, and various other fishing devices, specialized clothing, and other artifacts. It also includes a considerable body of technical lore. There are norms differentiating the roles men and women play in the activity and other norms governing the types of animals to be hunted at various times. Folktales, legends, and myths about hunting and animals abound in this culture, and they are a part of the complex. Values and sentiments are also included. Some types of animals are sacred; others are highly prized for food or other purposes. Various religious concepts, technical skills, material objects, and sets of beliefs, then, form an identifiable and meaningful configuration within the culture, and this complex constitutes a major component of its overall structure.[21]

In our own society we organize our lives around a number of culture complexes. Each of the spectator sports makes up such a complex. From the standpoint of the culture as a whole, for example, basketball is a configuration including backboards, nets, balls, whistles, uniforms, a large building with a polished wood floor, and a host of other material objects. The norms surrounding it include standards of appropriate dress for players, officials, and members of the audience. Rules of conduct define the roles of each member of the team, appropriate behavior by spectators, recruitment of players, the general conduct of the game, and much more. An elaborate set of shared beliefs surrounds the sport. Legends of earlier great teams, outstanding coaches, and memorable games are retold. The traditions of schools and their records of wins and losses are recounted. Details of the lives and past performances of star players are discussed avidly by the fans. Values are also prominent. The supporters of each team place high importance on victory. Spectators often

travel hundreds of miles at considerable inconvenience and expense to watch their favorites play. There are general values pertaining to the presumed sportsmanship and character-building virtues of the game. A similar summary could be made for every other spectator sport in American society.

Illustrations of such complexes can be drawn from many areas of culture. Concerning relationships between the sexes, Emilio Willems has described an interesting and antithetical set of dual complexes that help structure upper- and middle-class Brazilian culture:

The female role is centered around a cluster of values which may be characterized as *virginity complex.* The belief that the virginity of unmarried females ought to be preserved at any cost has so far tenaciously resisted change. Such institutional arrangements as segregation of the sexes, chaperonage and family-controlled courtship, which are to be regarded as component traits of the virginity complex, have undergone so many changes, at least in the larger cities of Brazil, that the original pattern is hardly recognizable. However, under the somewhat deceiving appearance of changing intersexual relationships and vanishing family controls, the old rule that females should abstain from premarital sexual experiences has been rigidly maintained. Carefully conducted interviews carried out over a period of nearly twelve years showed that even the most liberal-minded men were apt to become suddenly intransigent if asked how they envisaged the prospect of marrying somebody with premarital sexual experience. Most men feel they would make fools of themselves if they married a girl who had been deflowered by somebody else.

The male role is centered around a set of values which may properly be called *virility complex.* A young Brazilian is expected to get actively interested in sex at the age of puberty. Even before puberty the average boy becomes used to the sexual bravado of older companions. He learns that regular sexual intercourse is not only believed to be physically healthy, but above all an essential attribute of manhood. There is a generally accepted opinion that early and frequent sexual intercourse is stimulated by peculiar racial qualities and the physiological effects of a tropical climate. This point of view, which is presumed to be scientific, entitles men to feel irresponsible in sex affairs. Marriage is not expected to channelize or to restrict his sexual activities. Normally a male feels free to have intercourse with as many different women as may be available.[22]

21. Murdock, *op. cit.,* pp. 192–220.

22. Emilio Willems, "The Structure of the Brazilian Family," *Social Forces,* 31, No. 4 (August 1953), 340–341.

The hippie subculture is based on a search for a community-oriented way of life. It is not only a rejection of the impersonality of industrial society, but it is an attempt to develop close interpersonal ties—Gemeinschaft relationships—with other individuals. Some of the hippies who have left the urban centers, such as New York's East Village (above), feel that the self-sufficiency of an agricultural commune is more conducive to a spirit of mutual trust and dependence. At a hippie commune in northern New Mexico, for example, some people build their homes out of mud and logs (top left); others live in teepees (top right). They grow most of their own food and pray for rain, a good harvest, and to be left alone in peace.

In this respect, the Brazilian culture is clearly structured differently from our own. We share some of the elements of this same complex because the Brazilian and American cultures both have their origins in western Europe, but we do not support quite such a glaring double standard for males and females.

An important part of our own culture is the *romantic complex* that has long governed relationships between the sexes. This is a combination of traits from each of the four general categories of culture discussed earlier. For example, we subscribe to the belief that both males and females should have freedom to select suitable mates on their own. We place great value on this practice, maintaining that marriage is really proper only where both parties first "fall in love"—though no one seems able to define this state very adequately. Forming matches through rational selection by parents, for economic reasons, by a marriage broker, or for purposes of mutual convenience seems "un-American."

Young men and women in our society are expected to locate their mates through some mysterious chemistry of spontaneous mutual attraction. (In earlier generations they were supposed to be "properly introduced.") They are expected to attend various social functions together, largely at the financial expense of the male. Only gradually do they become permissive in terms of lovemaking, though this process seems to be speeding up with each generation. Through increasingly exclusive interaction and progressively deeper emotional involvement, a couple that dates regularly is presumed to be heading ultimately toward matrimony.

A host of traits makes up this general complex. These include material artifacts and symbols such as gifts, stereotyped ideas such as romantic music and moonlight, and even exotic practices such as carving hearts and initials on the trunks of trees. Elaborate norms govern types of dates, exchanges of gifts, the use of endearments, and the times, places, and stages of lovemaking. Viewed objectively, this complex is as bizarre and colorful as any that has been developed by any primitive tribe in the world.

Social institutions. Social institutions can be studied not only as patterns of social organization but also as configurations of culture traits. The family, for example, is more than a subunit of the community and society; it is a culturally defined pattern of roles, norms, beliefs, sentiments, and values. Similarly, the economic institution is not simply the system of production and exchange that a society has established but an elaborate configuration of many different kinds of traits. In the United States, for example, it is made up of material or technological elements such as steel mills, automobile factories, computers, research and testing centers, transportation systems, and stock exchanges; normative elements such as trade regulations and commercial folkways; our culturally defined attitudes and beliefs about economic activities; and the underlying values that guide our behavior as producers and consumers. These various kinds of traits all come together in the incredibly complex pattern that we identify as "our economic institution." Each of a society's major institutions can be viewed in much the same way, as an integrated complex of material and nonmaterial traits.

Subcultures. The term *subculture* refers to a pattern of norms, beliefs, attitudes, values, and other cultural elements that are shared within particular groups or segments of a society but that do not normally characterize the society as a whole. Subcultures can include special vocabularies or argots that are not understood by persons who are not members of the specific group.[23] Specialized modes of dress, foods, forms of religion, political beliefs, and attitudes toward the law are some of the many other possible bases for subcultural distinctions within a society.

Modern urban and industrial societies in particular are characterized by numerous subcultures. The source of these patterns lies in the extensive social differentiation found in such societies. In a diverse population, persons with similar attributes tend to be drawn to each other and to develop common ways of coping with the larger social environment. Thus, such characteristics as occupation, religion, or even a mutually practiced form of deviant behavior can draw people together and promote the development of a subculture.

The medical profession provides a good illustration of an occupational subculture: physicians share a common background of extensive

---

23. David Maurer, *The Big Con* (Indianapolis: The Bobbs-Merrill Co., Inc., 1940); see esp. Chapter 9.

training, a common set of goals in the healing of the sick, a professional association that tends to unify their orientations and attitudes, a complex technical jargon, a vast number of specialized material traits, and a set of values pertaining to the practice of their art.

The medical subculture differs greatly from that found among, for example, cab drivers in a large city. The cab drivers' orientation toward their clients is different; they have a totally different argot; their association (if they are unionized) promotes a different orientation; the material traits of their trade have little in common with those of physicians; and ideals pertaining to the practice of their trade have not been highly developed.

Occupation is only one of many bases for social differentiation and the development of subcultures. In societies occupying large land areas, the geographic regions are likely to have had very different histories of development and to have drawn their populations from quite different sources. The result is a blending of traits into regional subcultures. In the United States, for example, a person from the Deep South or from New England can be easily identified from his speech patterns. Regional subcultures are likely to involve special folkways, tastes in food, styles of architecture, and even political orientations.

Religious differences can also lead to the development of subcultures. In our society, Jews, Catholics, and the various Protestant denominations all have their cultural specialties—that is, distinctive traits that are not shared uniformly by the remainder of the society. These often form the basis of a subculture, especially among individuals who also share a common national origin.[24] A few religious groups like the Amish have highly integrated subcultures that include not only distinctive religious practices but modes of dress, vehicles, farming methods, attitudes toward schooling, and many other traits that set them quite apart from the larger society.

Of particular significance in most societies are the subcultures associated with social class and status differences. In a highly stratified society each broad stratum develops particular attitudes, practices, norms, values, and beliefs not uniformly shared by the members of other classes. Most middle-class Americans, for example, place great value on upward mobility, individual responsibility, resourcefulness, and personal initiative. They share norms concerning

dress, etiquette, and "manners" that persons higher or lower in the socioeconomic hierarchy do not always subscribe to. The analysis of "class" subcultures has been very useful in explaining the wide range of behavior patterns found in many modern societies.

In our own complex society there are subcultures associated with almost every area of life. Teen-agers, college students, and military personnel all support appropriate subcultures. So also do the devotees of camping, photography, horse racing, dog breeding, sailing, and hot-rodding. We can even speak of a male subculture and a female subculture insofar as distinctive norms, attitudes, interests, activities, clothing styles, and types of material possessions are identified with each of the two sexes.

Most subcultures exist harmoniously within the cultural complex supported by society as a whole. Deviant subcultures, by contrast, are configurations of behavioral practices, attitudes, values, and other traits that are widely disapproved. Some deviant subcultures are grudgingly tolerated by the society (e.g., the subculture of the hippies), but others so seriously transgress the general societal norms that they are defined as unlawful. The subculture of the drug addict or the professional criminal, for example, effectively removes him from the mainstream of societal life.

Sociologists find the concept of subculture extremely useful as a theoretical tool. It can be applied not only in analyzing the structure and content of a particular society's culture but also in explaining patterns of individual and group conduct that fall outside the range of generally approved behavior. In a large society such as ours, the individual obtains many of his behavioral definitions from the various subcultures in which he participates. Although he shares in the culture supported by society as a whole, his own particular social milieu provides him with the basic attitudes, norms, and values around which he organizes his life. If the forms of conduct approved by his subcultures conflict with those supported by the general culture, he may collide head-on with the norms of "conventional" society. The importance of subcultural influences

---

24. See, for example, Nathan Glazer and Daniel P. Moynihan, *Beyond the Melting Pot* (Cambridge, Mass.: The M.I.T. Press, 1963). The authors argue that "the melting pot" has failed to work in New York City at least, where ethnic and religious subcultural configurations continue to flourish.

VIEWPOINTS   THE INCONSISTENT AMERICAN

We [Americans] expect too much of the world. Our expectations are extravagant in the precise dictionary sense of the word—"going beyond the limits of reason or moderation." They are excessive.

When we pick up our newspaper at breakfast, we expect—we even demand—that it bring us momentous events since the night before. We turn on the car radio as we drive to work and expect "news" to have occurred since the morning newspaper went to press. Returning in the evening, we expect our house not only to shelter us, to keep us warm in winter and cool in summer, but to relax us, to dignify us, to encompass us with soft music and interesting hobbies, to be a playground, a theater, and a bar. We expect our two-week vacation to be romantic, exotic, cheap, and effortless. We expect a faraway atmosphere if we go to a nearby place; and we expect everything to be relaxing, sanitary, and Americanized if we go to a faraway place. We expect new heroes every season, a literary masterpiece every month, a dramatic spectacular every week, a rare sensation every night. We expect everybody to feel free to disagree, yet we expect everybody to be loyal, not to rock the boat or take the Fifth Amendment. We expect everybody to believe deeply in his religion, yet not to think less of others for not believing. We expect our nation to be strong and great and vast and varied and prepared for every challenge; yet we expect our "national purpose" to be clear and simple, something that gives direction to the lives of nearly two hundred million people and yet can be bought in a paperback at the corner drugstore for a dollar.

We expect anything and everything. We expect the contradictory and the impossible. We expect compact cars which are spacious; luxurious cars which are economical. We expect to be rich and charitable, powerful and merciful, active and reflective, kind and competitive. We expect to be inspired by mediocre appeals for "excellence," to be made literate by illiterate appeals for literacy. We expect to eat and stay thin, to be constantly on the move and ever more neighborly, to go to a "church of our choice" and yet feel its guiding power over us, to revere God and to be God.

Never have people been more the masters of their environment. Yet never has a people felt more deceived and disappointed. For never has a people expected so much more than the world could offer.

Daniel J. Boorstin
The Image: A Guide to Pseudo-Events in America

Since you will arrive [in the United States] in September I had better give you a warning. You will see [Americans] first during a curious male festival which is very ancient and deep-seated. At that time the shops exhibit pictures of dead animals and surround them with clusters of guns and saw-edged knives. In the skirts of the woods you will find groups of young men and boys, armed with every sort of weapon from air guns to antique muzzle-loaders. The countryside resounds with a constant popping and banging, and the steady crash of boughs brought down by the fusillade. This is very exciting and male. . . .

But September is a thing apart. Americans are not like that. They enjoy their woods as much as you, after the first fury is over. . . . With a gun out of his hand, the hunter becomes an amiable gas-station attendant, a student, a banker, perhaps, and just as human as you are.

For the Americans are not at all what anyone thinks who has only seen them outside their own country, or on films, or listened to propaganda about them. Sometimes over here [in Europe] their political image seems too like saber-rattling. At home they have none of the truculence nor the world outlook that their politicians are fashioning into an image for them. For one thing that really hurts them bitterly is the fact that they are not—or their image is not—universally loved; for they do not yet understand that power is not loved, but feared and hated. The acid of this is seeping slowly into the American consciousness.

At home they are the mildest and gentlest of people. Approach them as a stranger in their country and they will go to endless trouble to help you. In Texas a group of them from whom I tried to borrow some tool or other for changing a tire simply took the whole job off my hands, did it with a kind of casual efficiency and left us feeling we had conferred a favor on them by allowing them to help. Out of hundreds of ordinary Americans I met from one end of the country to the other, there was not one who did not want to explain and show, to guide, advise, and help. Their principal desire, as I conceive it, is to be left, each one in his own landscape, troubling no one and being troubled by nobody. He is neither a warmonger nor a conscious exploiter. He cares far less about the world outside America than his political spokesmen would have us believe. He is friendly and parochial, not so much a man of his state, as a man of his country.

William Golding
"Advice to a Nervous Visitor"

in shaping an individual's attitudes and standards of conduct will be considered more fully in Chapter 5, "The Socialization Process," especially pages 150–153.

CULTURAL THEMES AND EMPHASES

Our discussion of subcultures should make clear the difficulty of describing a culture in terms of overall traits. The culture of the inner-city slum seems worlds apart from that of the nearby Gold Coast or that of an Iowa farm town. Yet we still speak of "the American culture" and recognize that it is somehow distinct from the cultures of other societies. A core of common experiences and traditions provides a measure of cultural unity even in a society as diverse as ours. As a people, we tend to interpret events in somewhat similar ways and to place value on similar goals. One approach to the study of culture, then, is to abstract the qualities that seem to give a particular culture its distinctive character.

Ethos. In a classic work first published at the turn of the century, William Graham Sumner revived the ancient Greek term *ethos* to mean "the sum of the characteristic usages, ideas, standards and codes by which a group was differentiated and *individualized in character* from other groups." Thus, the ethos of a society is the set of guiding beliefs that give the people of that society a distinguishable makeup.[25] While difficult to measure and define, this attribute of a people is not difficult to note through observation. The general character of Mexican culture or German culture stands in contrast to the culture prevailing in the United States. Because of the difficulties of working with concepts at such a high level of abstraction, however, the use of this term is declining in contemporary sociological literature.

Ethic. Max Weber effectively captured two major cultural themes in *The Protestant Ethic and the Spirit of Capitalism* (page 181).[26] Based on an ambitious comparative study of religious and economic institutions in both Western and non-Western societies, this classic work advanced the thesis that capitalism developed in western Europe as an outgrowth of the devel-

opment of Puritanism. Weber abstracted the value orientations associated with Calvinism—individualism, hard work, frugality, rationality—and showed how they became readily translated into economic activity. Thus, the configuration of attitudes and values associated with a new religious orientation became the guiding spirit behind the growth of entrepreneurial capitalism. The Puritan ethic continues as a basic value orientation in most Western cultures today, though it has long since lost much of its religious meaning.

American value orientations. The continuing influence of the Puritan ethic is apparent in Robin Williams' analysis of dominant cultural themes in the United States.[27] Williams identifies fifteen major value orientations that seem to guide the behavior of the American people. The fact that not all of them are consistent may help to explain some of the conflicts that Americans have regularly experienced both as individuals and as a nation.

1. *"Achievement and Success."* In our highly competitive society we value the success story—the Horatio Alger myth of moving from rags to riches, the Abe Lincoln legend of progress from log cabin to White House. For the common man, this lore translates into the dream of occupational and economic success.

2. *"Activity and Work."* The United States is a land of busy people who stress disciplined, productive activity as a worthy end in itself. Especially valued is work that brings mastery over the environment or an improvement in socioeconomic position.

3. *"Moral Orientation."* Americans tend to be moralists, judging the world in terms of right and wrong. Even those who do not follow some specific moral code tend to evaluate the behavior of others within an ethical framework.

4. *"Humanitarian Mores."* As a people, Americans believe in being kindly and helpful and in coming spontaneously to the aid of oth-

25. William Graham Sumner, *Folkways* (New York: The New American Library, Inc., 1960), p. 48; originally published in 1906.

26. Max Weber, *The Protestant Ethic and the Spirit of Capitalism*, trans. Talcott Parsons (London: George Allen & Unwin Ltd., 1930); originally published in 1920.

27. Robin M. Williams, Jr., *American Society: A Sociological Interpretation*, 2nd ed. (New York: Alfred A. Knopf, Inc., 1960).

ers. Although the history of the United States is not without episodes of national brutality, these are widely condemned. Traditional sympathy for the underdog, generosity toward victims of war or disaster, and the ubiquitous charity drive are behavioral illustrations of American humanitarianism.

5. *"Efficiency and Practicality."* The streamlined efficiency and tremendous productivity of United States industry provide Americans with a standard against which they judge the rest of the world. Coupled with this is the high value Americans place on the practical solution that "gets things done."

6. *"Progress."* Orientations toward the future are more approved than orientations toward the past. Americans share a conviction that things should constantly get better and better, and they work toward that end. Optimism and "boosterism" express the belief that man's social condition can be improved.

7. *"Material Comfort."* Americans value "the good life" and constantly seek to improve their standard of living. They like to enjoy material possessions and physical comforts of all kinds. Consumption appears to be challenging production as a major national goal.

8. *"Equality."* Even though the United States is a stratified society, its members constantly avow a commitment to equality. Beginning as a society that accepted indentured servitude and slavery, Americans have consistently sought ways of improving the lot of those at the bottom of the socioeconomic structure.

9. *"Freedom."* This term has almost a religious connotation for Americans, and the "free-

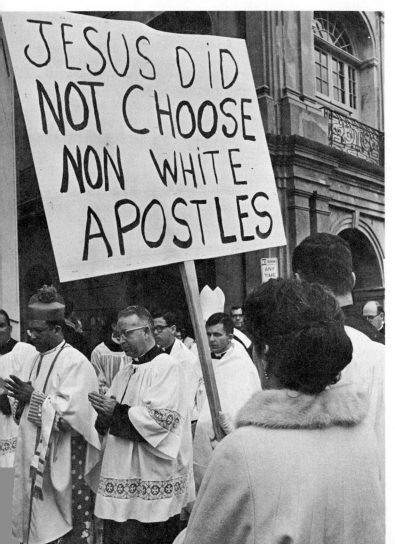

The inconsistent values of American culture help to explain some of the conflicts that Americans have experienced both as individuals and as a nation.

dom" of the individual is seen as one of the great advantages of the American political system. In spite of abundant restraints on their behavior, people in the United States feel that they are, and must remain, "free."

10. *"External Conformity."* Although they regularly appeal to the virtue of "rugged individualism," Americans are conformists to a considerable degree. They show great uniformity in such matters as dress, housing, recreation, manners, and even the expression of political ideas. Thus, the behavior of Americans implies a value orientation that most of them verbally disavow.

11. *"Science and Secular Rationality."* Americans highly esteem the applied sciences as means for asserting mastery over the environment. Their belief in the potential of science amounts almost to a religious faith. In many ways the scientific orientation reflects other values that are highly prized in the American culture, such as diligence, honesty, pragmatism, and efficiency.

12. *"Nationalism-Patriotism."* The sentiments that Americans attach to their nation-state are of overwhelming importance to them. "Americanism" is almost a rigid orthodoxy, and "un-American" things are viewed with suspicion and disapproval. Most Americans feel that their country "has been good to them," and few express any desire to live elsewhere.

13. *"Democracy."* Although the Constitution makes no direct reference to democracy, Americans are convinced that it is the essence of their form of government. They subscribe deeply to the principle that every man should have a voice in his political destiny.

14. *"Individual Personality."* To Americans, every individual should be independent, responsible, and self-respecting. They question seriously any notion that the group should take precedence over the individual. The freedom of the individual is carefully safeguarded by law.

15. *"Racism and Related Group-Superiority Themes."* A strong countercurrent in the American value system is the differential evaluation of racial, religious, and ethnic groups. Despite their commitment to the principles of equality and democracy, Americans as a group continue to downgrade some categories of citizens. This poses one of the chief value conflicts in American culture.

Williams' analysis of American value orientations is only one of many attempts to abstract and synthesize some of the basic attitudinal complexes that help distinguish a particular culture. Formulations of this type are necessarily imprecise, and many of those that have been developed are highly controversial. Despite their limitations, however, such constructs can be very useful in providing the sociologist with new insights into the culture of a society and thus into the characteristic behavior of its members. In general, the study of trait configurations such as value orientations, subcultures, and social institutions permits a more meaningful description of a culture than an analysis of individual traits out of context.

SUMMARY

Culture is a broad concept that serves as a general label for a society's entire design for living. It is the social heritage of a people, representing their accumulated solutions to the problems of coping with nature and with each other. But culture does not remain static as it is passed on from one generation to the next. New traits and trait complexes are continually being added to the existing cultural base, and not infrequently traits are subtracted. The addition of the automobile as a material trait in American culture, for example, led to the loss of the horse-drawn carriage. Nonmaterial traits such as food preferences, scientific theories, and values also change over time.

Human evolution and cultural evolution appear to have been closely related. As man slowly developed into his present biological form, he also slowly accumulated the beginnings of culture. His acquisition of language enabled him to coordinate his behavior with that of others and to pass on his knowledge and beliefs to the next generation. His ability to manipulate symbols systematically—to reason—accelerated the rate of cultural growth and permitted man to solve increasingly elaborate problems.

Despite the striking differences among the cultures that different societies have developed, each cultural system has seemed to provide a workable design for living. Cultural standards are relative, and judgments concerning morality, beauty, logic, and so forth can only be made within the framework of a particular culture. Cultural relativity notwithstanding, however, the tendency toward ethnocentrism seems well-nigh universal.

Cultures differ greatly not only in content but also in the degree to which they form an integrated, consistent pattern. In general, the cultures of modern industrial societies are much less closely integrated than those of small pre-literate societies. Contemporary American culture, for example, contains many built-in sources of conflict and strain. Acceptable patterns of behavior are fairly well defined, however, just as they are in the more harmonious culture of the Zuñi.

Social scientists use various complementary approaches in studying the content and structure of a culture. One approach is to isolate particular traits that can be traced from society to society or that diffuse within a society. Another is to abstract meaningful configurations of traits such as culture complexes, social institutions, sub-cultures, and basic value orientations. Though imprecise, such abstractions aid greatly in understanding the characteristic behavior of people within a given society.

PART II

SOCIETY
AND THE
INDIVIDUAL

4

Personal Organization

In the preceding chapters, we have deliberately deemphasized the individual in order to show that social organization and culture can be studied and understood at their own level, without appealing to psychological explanations. But pedagogical strategy aside, sociologists are interested in the individual as well as in the groups that he devises. They look at the relationship between personal and social behavior in two complementary ways. First, a person's habits, beliefs, motivations, and sentiments significantly influence how he will interpret the norms of his groups; how he will act out his roles; how he will respond to systems of social control, and so on. Second, the social and cultural characteristics of a person's groups—especially his family, his peer groups, and his society—help determine what kind of person he becomes.

To make clear what is meant by *personal organization*, we will discuss what behavioral scientists believe to be the major characteristics of human personality and the ways in which human personality is dependent upon biological and constitutional factors. Finally, we will examine the role of social processes in the development of personal organization.

THE STRUCTURE OF PERSONALITY

By observing how an individual responds to his environment, it is possible to infer concepts defining the orderly, predictable, and patterned elements in his behavior. Basically, these characteristic patterns are what is meant by *personality* or *personal organization*. Among those concepts that have been widely used in analyzing the structure of personality, we will discuss

briefly motivation, the cognitive structure, the habit structure, trait configurations, acquired predispositions, and unconscious processes.

TYPES OF MOTIVATION

Certain very fundamental sources of motivation appear to be products of the organic nature of the individual. He has biological needs for food, water, and air which must be satisfied if he is to survive. If even temporarily deprived, serious disequilibria occur in the functioning of the organic system. Other needs or imbalances may be caused by inadequate diet, sexual deprivation, salt denial, changes in bodily temperature, etc.[1] When an organic imbalance occurs, the individual typically experiences an urge to obtain whatever will redress the imbalance and thereby restore equilibrium. These basic motivational patterns are usually referred to as *biological drives.*[2]

Many needs and motives derive from sources other than organic ones. Through habitual exposure to certain gratifying experiences, the individual may develop an *acquired need* (a learned need) to have similar experiences.[3] For example, the person who continually enjoys music of a given type, specific forms of food, or the company of particular friends may feel uncomfortable when deprived of these pleasures. Although we would not refer to the urge to satisfy such needs as drives, acquired needs—ranging from the need for approval to the need for pizza—provide the motivation for much of human behavior. Clearly, the acquisition of such motives can occur only through participation in social and cultural processes.

THE COGNITIVE STRUCTURE

The individual's cognitive structure consists of the concepts and beliefs that aid him in interpreting the world around him.[4] Although a product of the individual's own experiences, it normally reflects values and beliefs that are widely shared in his cultural environment. If the culture defines the world as flat, then the individual normally believes it to be flat; if it defines the members of a particular social category as inherently superior or inferior, then in the absence of contrary definitions the individual will generally believe them to be so. Much the same

1. David Krech, Richard S. Crutchfield, and Egerton L. Ballachey, *Individual in Society* (New York: McGraw-Hill Book Company, 1962), pp. 71–73.

2. S. Stansfeld Sargent and Robert C. Williamson, *Social Psychology*, 3rd ed. (New York: The Ronald Press Company, 1966), pp. 191–192.

3. *Ibid.*

4. Theodore M. Newcomb, Ralph H. Turner, and Phillip E. Converse, *Social Psychology* (New York: Holt, Rinehart and Winston, Inc., 1965), pp. 27–33.

could be said of thousands of other examples. The patterns of conceptualization and belief that exist in the individual's social environment are the principal sources from which he draws his own *definitions of reality*. Our senses, after all, provide us with only limited information about the world as it really is. For example, we never "see" electromagnetic radio or television waves, but our scientists have established shared beliefs that tell us the waves exist, and we confidently believe them. In earlier societies learned men taught their societies that there were witches, evil spirits, and magic spells. For those societies, these were realities.

Every man's beliefs and other cognitive orientations toward his world are reinforced continually by the existence of similar beliefs and orientations among his trusted associates. *Consensus*, or the sharing of belief, is our chief means of defining reality. The less we are able to experience that reality directly and immediately, the more important is the process of *consensual validation* of our beliefs about it. Because of this principle of the *social definition of reality*, group participation is an important source of the individual's cognitive structure.

THE HABIT STRUCTURE

The term *habit* can refer to almost any regularly patterned way of acting, feeling, or thinking that an individual has acquired through learning. In some ways, the concept of habit is so broad and inclusive that it becomes difficult to identify any form of learned behavior that is not a habit in some sense. The individual develops, for example, literally thousands of responses that are consistent with societal folkways and cultural definitions concerning such everyday matters as eating, cleanliness, modes of dress, the use of technical devices, and so forth. While these are undoubtedly part of his personal organization, they are relatively insignificant aspects of his basic personality structure. Of much more central importance are his habitual ways of perceiving the world around him, his characteristic modes of thinking and remembering, and his characteristic patterns of emotional response. The significance of these habit patterns can be reviewed very briefly.

Perception. The process through which the human individual translates the data from his senses into internal meaning experiences is called *perception*. The meaning that an individual associates with some stimulus event detected through his senses will depend greatly upon what he has learned about interpreting similar events. In interpreting social phenomena, his habits of perception will be greatly influenced by his own pattern of social experience.

For example, in a classic study of the social stratification system of an American community, Davis, Gardner, and Gardner found by sociological analysis that the community had six rather well-defined social classes. However, they also discovered that the members of each of these social classes perceived the social class system in a different way: those at the bottom saw only two classes above them, whereas those at the top saw four levels below them. The sociological analysis indicated patterns of selective perception of the social structure, which were somewhat unique to each class.[5]

Emotional response systems. An individual's emotional responses are greatly influenced by learning, even though emotion itself is a physiological phenomenon not subject to conscious control. People of different societies often give quite different emotional reactions to the same stimuli. Through a long learning process, each person must acquire his society's habitual modes of interpreting emotional responses.

Thought processes. The individual must habitually associate specific word-symbols, either written or spoken, with specific inner meaning experiences. The ways in which he makes these associations are not capricious but, rather, are a matter of established conventions within his society. The individual must learn the particular language conventions that join symbols and their referents in his society. Once he begins to acquire these language habits, he can partially bridge the gap between his own inner processes and the experience systems of others. He can participate in the communication processes, which include not only interpersonal communication but also self-communication in the form of thought and memory. Thus, communication habits underlie the individual's ability to talk, write, read, think, and remember. There is, of course, more to these activities than

5. Allison Davis, Burleigh B. Gardner, and Mary R. Gardner, *Deep South: A Social Anthropological Study of Caste and Class* (Chicago: The University of Chicago Press, 1941).

symbolic habits alone. There are important physiological correlates, for one thing. But in terms of personal organization of behavior, symbolic habits are major components of personality.

TRAIT CONFIGURATIONS

In everyday conversation we often refer to particular individuals as being good-natured or nasty, stingy or generous, sincere or untrustworthy, optimistic or pessimistic, hardworking or lazy. Our language includes literally thousands of such terms to describe some enduring or repetitive characteristic of a person's behavior.[6] To the long list of descriptive words used by laymen, the social and behavioral sciences have added such terms as *introverted, masochistic, inner-directed,* and *peer-oriented*—each used to identify, as precisely as possible, some organized pattern of response to a particular kind of event.

The term *trait* is used in the social and behavioral sciences to refer to any characteristic that can be observed or measured. Usually it is a discrete and small unit of analysis. (See, for example, the discussion of culture traits in Chapter 3, page 113.) As we are using it here in analyzing personality structure, the concept of *trait* actually refers to an organized cluster of characteristics, which together add up to some repetitive way of behaving. This does not mean that a particular trait causes a pattern of behavior; it simply gives the pattern a name.

The concept of personality trait is an elusive one, and behavioral scientists do not wholly agree on how to identify or study traits. It is widely recognized, however, that every individual tends to develop characteristic ways of responding to similar situations and that these patterns of response are to a large extent products of his involvement in social interaction.

---

6. Webster's *New International Dictionary* has been found to include almost eighteen thousand trait names; see Gordon W. Allport and H. S. Odbert, "Trait Names: A Psycho-Lexical Study," *Psychological Monographs,* 47, No. 211 (1936).

7. The nature of dispositional terms has been clarified by Carl G. Hempel, "Fundamentals of Concept Formation in Empirical Science," *International Encyclopedia of Unified Science,* 2, No. 7, 24–25.

8. The most complete contemporary statement on the nature and functions of attitudes as they relate to human personality is Newcomb, Turner, and Converse, *op. cit,* esp. pp. 17–153.

ACQUIRED PREDISPOSITIONS

In addition to various habits, traits, belief systems, and motivations, there are a number of distinctive types of response patterns that behavioral scientists refer to as *predispositions.* In general, these describe some regularity in the manner in which a person appears inclined to accept or reject some thing, situation, or event that occurs periodically in his environment.[7] Most predispositions fall into the class of preferences, attitudes, or values.

Preferences. A person's preferences are his tendencies to accept or reject a wide variety of objects. We all have specific tastes in foods; we are attracted to or reject certain types of automobiles, clothing, furniture styles, architectural forms, color schemes, and so forth. Any one preference, such as liking blue better than green, is insignificant, but all of a person's preferences together determine much of what is patterned and predictable in his behavior.

There are no grounds for assuming that preferences are inherited. They appear to be acquired from others with whom the individual engages in meaningful interaction.

Attitudes. Predispositions toward complex classes of phenomena are called *attitudes*[8] and can be thought of as more comprehensive than preferences. Each person is presumed to have a number of these relatively stable tendencies to accept or reject certain broad classes of stimuli, such as minority groups, economic policies, religions, and so on. Like preferences, these tendencies are products of social learning.

Attitudes provide the individual with ready-made modes of response to rather broad categories of stimuli. The prejudiced person, one with an emotionally charged negative attitude toward some social category, does not have to decide how he will respond to every member of that category. He can reject them "categorically" without bothering to consider them as individuals. Since such attitudes make it simpler for the prejudiced person to respond to a complex environment, they are very resistant to change. (For one method of measuring attitudes, see the Methodological Essay on page 132.)

Values. Each person develops a set of very broad and rather abstract predispositions that identify the general goals he feels are important

Attitudes provide the individual with ready-made modes of response to rather broad classes of stimuli. The prejudiced person, one with an emotionally charged negative attitude toward some social category, can reject all members of that category without bothering to consider them as individuals.

and worth pursuing.[9] We saw earlier that the value culture of a society consists of such convictions shared by its members. Here, we refer to the same phenomena, but at the level of the individual. For example, the materialistically oriented individual who runs after a "fast buck" in some shady enterprise can be contrasted with the more altruistically oriented person who deliberately enters an occupation where the principal reward is serving others. Materialism and altruism would be examples of personal values.

UNCONSCIOUS PROCESSES

Some personality theorists place great emphasis upon motivations, orientations, emotions, and other personality components of which the person is not consciously aware. Some of these are said to be products of man's biological system; others are thought to develop during his early exposure to his family.

The best known formulations of this type are the theories of human psychic structure and process advanced by Sigmund Freud and the modifications of these ideas by his followers.[10] Essentially, Freud divided the human psyche into three major aspects: id, superego, and ego.

9. Gordon W. Allport, Phillip P. Vernon, and Gardner Lindzey, *A Study of Values: A Scale for Measuring the Dominant Interests in Personality*, 3rd ed. (Boston: Houghton Mifflin Company, 1960).

10. Sigmund Freud, *An Outline of Psychoanalysis*, trans. James Strachey (New York: W. W. Norton & Co., Inc., 1949).

The *id* is the aspect of personality that motivates the individual toward seeking physically pleasurable gratification. The *libido* drive—the basic source of human energy—finds expression through the id, with the individual unconsciously seeking to express his instinctive cravings. Sexual gratification or, more accurately, bodily gratification in general plays an important part in this conceptualization.

The *superego* is the aspect of the psyche that has acquired the moral norms of the society. The superego constantly imposes the demands of the orderly society against the bumptious id to prevent it from achieving gratification in ways that, by his society's definition, are morally unacceptable.

The *ego*, the conscious and directive function of the personality, is balanced between the id and the superego and is under constant pressure to retain control. Thus, the ego exercises various adaptive mechanisms to prevent the id from becoming the dominant motivating force over the individual. Through *sublimation,* for example, the ego *redirects* impulses of the id toward activities that are socially acceptable.

The idea of unconscious psychic processes remains a topic of chronic debate. Such concepts as id, superego, and ego are difficult, if not impossible, to test on the basis of observable evidence. Like many other personality concepts, however, they are theories that their authors feel can account for much of human behavior.

THE BIOLOGICAL BACKGROUND OF PERSONALITY

The human personality is a product of the interplay between the biologically inherited potentialities of the individual, plus other constitutional factors, and the social and cultural systems in which he develops. In spite of this complexity, we can reach some conclusions about the nature of the biological contribution to personality.

THE ABSENCE OF HUMAN INSTINCTS

In the nineteenth century it was assumed that the structure of the individual's personality came to him at birth and emerged as the individual matured. Many people still assume that a person's patterns of behavior are inherited. For example, "bad blood" is said to be responsible for an individual's criminal acts. Although there is still some debate about the exact role of genetic factors in shaping personality, the biological and behavioral sciences have long since abandoned instinct theories as general explanations of human behavior.

Instincts can be defined as behavior patterns that are (1) *unlearned*—inherited through genetic transmission in some manner, (2) *universal*—found in every member of the species in much the same form, and (3) *complex*—requiring the coordination of various specific behaviors. Animals seem to have many blind inherited patterns connected with such complex activities as mating, rearing of offspring, migration, etc., but modern science places no credence in the instinct idea as applied to human beings. For every proposed instinct, too many exceptions can be found. Even something as seemingly fundamental as self-preservation can scarcely be universal when thousands of people who are not insane take their own lives every year in most major societies. Similarly, a motherhood instinct is difficult to justify when infanticide is a regular and expected practice in some societies. Also, as will be seen later, individuals raised in relative isolation show no evidence of such patterns.

Although man does inherit many reflexes and other unlearned behavioral patterns of a relatively simple nature, there is no scientific basis for assuming that he inherits predispositions that will lead him automatically to develop some specific kind of personal organization.

LIMITING AND FACILITATING FACTORS

Although there is no evidence that personality is inherited as such, biological factors play both a direct and indirect part in shaping an individual's personal organization. His intelligence, aptitudes, temperament, and energy level, for example, are all determined in part by heredity, and all influence the kinds of experiences he will have and the kind of person he will become. The term *constitutional factor* is used broadly to refer to any organic or physical characteristic—whether a product of inheritance, diet, disease, plastic surgery, or physical fitness exercises—that limits or facilitates the individual's ability to develop in particular directions.

METHODOLOGY MEASURING ATTITUDES

Sociologists use several techniques for assessing attitudes. One of the earliest of these to be developed, and one still widely used, is the *equal-appearing intervals scale.* In constructing such a scale, the researcher first selects a particular *attitude object* (topic or situation) toward which he wishes to measure individual predispositions. He then prepares a large number of statements—usually fifty or more—representing a range of opinions about the attitude object.

The investigator's next step is to make an objective determination of how favorable (or unfavorable) an attitude each item expresses. He accomplishes this by having the items evaluated by a number of judges (not by the subjects whose attitudes are eventually to be measured). Each of the judges independently examines each item and assigns it a position on an *attitude continuum,* indicating his impression of the degree of positive or negative feeling the item expresses. The judgments for each item are then plotted in a curve that shows how they are distributed. The figure below, for example, shows the distribution of judgments on an item being evaluated for a scale designed to measure attitudes toward the legalization of marijuana. The item stated: "The use of marijuana should be rigorously prohibited by federal legislation."

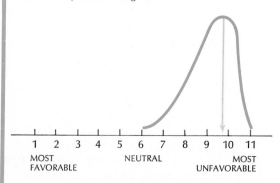

The rating for this item was 9.7—the median (or midpoint) in the distribution of judgments. This median represents the *scale value* of the item, indicating where the statement falls on the attitude continuum. On the continuum illustrated here, a scale value of 9.7 shows that the item is considered to express an attitude highly unfavorable to legalizing marijuana.

Once a scale value has been obtained for every item initially prepared by the researcher, the next step is to make a selection of items for actual use in the final measuring instrument. The researcher automatically discards ambiguous items—those which have low, "fat" distribution curves, indicating that the judges did not closely agree on how the item should be rated. A relatively tall and narrow curve, by contrast, indicates that all the judges classified the item in much the same way:

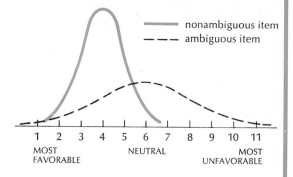

From the nonambiguous items the investigator selects about twenty that fall more or less evenly along the attitude continuum (some items at the two extremes, some in the neutral area, and some along positions in between). Each of the items finally selected is examined for clarity, appropriateness of language, and other criteria.

The final list of items constitutes a scale in which each statement has a known value along the attitude continuum. The items are arranged in random order before being presented to the subject, who is asked to read each statement, to decide whether he agrees or disagrees with the opinion it expresses, and to record his endorsement or rejection of the statement. A subject's *attitude score* can quickly be determined by averaging the scale values of all items he endorsed.

For a detailed treatment of the various methods used in measuring attitudes, see Allan L. Edwards, *Techniques of Attitude Scale Construction* (New York: Appleton-Century-Crofts, 1957).

Intelligence and learning capacity. An individual's learning capacity seems to be limited by his heredity, although exactly how is by no means clear. Certainly the intelligence level eventually developed by a given individual is not a simple product of genetic transmission; it is heavily influenced by the learning environment he is exposed to. There are many people who could never develop into geniuses, regardless of how rich their sociocultural environment might be. By the same token, there is no assurance that inherited high potentials will be developed, especially if the individual is in a limiting sociocultural environment.

Aptitudes. Like intelligence, aptitudes have long been thought to be partly determined by inheritance. The evidence on this issue is not entirely conclusive, but aptitudes seem to set an upper limit on the development of certain complex skills. For example, some people simply do not have the prerequisite quickness and coordination to develop into highly skilled athletes, although such skills can certainly be improved through training. Furthermore, the whole idea of aptitudes may have little application to many kinds of activities, such as learning a language, performing common occupations, or engaging in other social activities.

Temperament and energy level. For one reason or another, some persons are nervous, quick-moving, and responsive. Others appear to be much slower to react and are more calm and deliberate in coping with their environment. We do not know just why this is the case. There is a good possibility that inheritance plays some part, but knowledge is limited on this point.

There is also reason to suspect that genetic factors play a part in a person's general *energy* level. The metabolic processes differ from person to person, and these appear to place limits on his general rate of activity. Here, however, it is difficult to sort out the influence of such factors as nutrition or even the influence of cultural norms concerning the value placed on hard work, self-discipline, and high levels of activity.

Categories based on race and sex. Some constitutional factors influence in an indirect but very clear manner the kind of social experiences and general sociocultural environment

a person will be exposed to. Physical criteria place a person in certain significant social categories with important ascribed statuses that sharply structure his sociocultural experiences. The female child, for example, experiences different expectations and training in most societies than the male child. The various racial categories have the same effect. A black child born into a predominantly white society that ranks this racial category low in ascribed status encounters quite a different sociocultural environment than does a similar child in a society composed entirely of Negroes.

There are many other subtle influences that operate on the individual because of constitutional factors. For example, each society holds to some set of standards concerning physical attractiveness. If the society values the tall, muscular, blond male with a symmetrical profile, a person whose inherited physical structure is that of a short, fat brunet with irregular features will receive quite different responses than the former. Beauty may be only skin-deep, but such factors can have important consequences for personality development.

PERSONALITY AS SYSTEM

The components of personality discussed in the foregoing sections are not isolated or distinct; they are linked to each other in systemic configurations. Individuals of higher intelligence, for example, are likely to acquire different beliefs, attitudes, and values than persons of lesser ability. Similarly, differences in aptitudes can limit the skills that an individual might develop in coping with certain aspects of his environment. Persons with specific traits, attitudes, and beliefs that are attractive to others may receive quite different responses than persons whose personality characteristics are regarded as objectionable. Thus, some elements of personality can influence the shaping of others.

Relationships between certain types of personality variables have been widely studied. For example, perception has long been thought to be dependent upon values. This relationship has been demonstrated many times by psychological studies, of which the following experiment by Bruner and Goodman is typical.

The subjects of the experiment were thirty ten-year-old boys, half from relatively rich families and half from poor families. They were asked to estimate the size of various coins (socially valued objects); the hypothesis was that the poor boys would tend to overestimate their size. To test this hypothesis, a small circle of light was projected onto a screen. The diameter of the circle was easily adjustable by turning a single knob. The idea was for the subject to match the size of the coins with the circle of light. Each subject was tested with coins of various denominations. A separate control group was similarly tested, but with cardboard discs (nonvalued objects) rather than coins. In general, both the poor boys and the rich boys overestimated the size of the coins, whereas the control group did not overestimate the size of the discs. However, as predicted, the poor boys overestimated the coins to a considerably greater degree than did the rich boys.[11]

Although this study was once quite controversial, subsequent research has tended to confirm its conclusions. The evidence seems clear that perception is related to value and need, as well as to other variables.

There is also abundant evidence that attitudes play an important part in shaping what a person "sees" in a complex set of social stimuli. For example, Hastorf and Cantril showed students a motion picture taken of a football game between rival schools. Following the game, each college had publicly accused the other of deliberate and unnecessary roughness. This motion picture was shown to a sample of students at each of the institutions involved. In each case, the students "saw" about twice as many infractions committed by their rival as by their own team.[12]

In other words, the various components of personality influence each other in numerous ways. In this sense, they form a *system* whose attributes are more than simply the sum of its parts. The human personality is a dynamic process that is constantly adjusting to the internal and external environment of the individual.

Some theorists maintain that human personality does not necessarily constitute a harmonious system. On the contrary, theorists such as Freud (page 131) have described the human personality as a system in which the components are in *conflict* with each other for control of the human being. According to such theories, the behavior of the individual at any given moment can be thought of as a product or resolution of this conflict.

Most theories concerning the structure of personal organization see personality as a system that tends toward equilibrium.[13] The behavior of the person at any particular time is directed toward restoring equilibrium that has been disturbed by the impact of external or internal stimuli. The action or mediation of predispositions, such as attitudes and values, directs the person's behavior as he seeks to return to a more comfortable state of balance.

Describing the precise nature of personality, its components, and systematic properties is a research responsibility of the sociologist as well as of the psychologist and psychiatrist. Sociological studies of the *social and cultural sources* of personality and psychological functioning of the human being have made important contributions to our understanding of personality.

THE SIGNIFICANCE OF SYMBOLIC INTERACTION

The essence of the social act is meaningful communication. It is through symbolic interaction with others that the infant gradually develops a personality, an ability to function as a conscious, thinking human being. Communicative interaction with significant other persons on a regular basis is also necessary for the maintenance of personal organization. In the present section, the basis of the communicative act and the contribution that this fundamental form of

11. Jerome S. Bruner and C. C. Goodman, "Value and Need as Organizing Factors in Perception," *Journal of Abnormal and Social Psychology*, 42 (1947), 33–44.

12. Albert H. Hastorf and Hadley Cantril, "They Saw a Game: A Case Study," *Journal of Abnormal and Social Psychology*, 49 (1954), 129–134.

13. For example, the term *balance theory* is often used to designate the tendency for the cognitive structure to shift toward a state of harmony, balance, or equilibrium, in which no beliefs or attitudes are dissonant. There have been several rather distinct formulations of such a theory. For example, see Fritz Heider, *The Psychology of Interpersonal Relations* (New York: John Wiley & Sons, Inc., 1958); Leon Festinger, *A Theory of Cognitive Dissonance* (Evanston, Ill: Row, Peterson, 1957); Dorwin Cartwright and Frank Harary, "Structural Balance: A Generalization of Heider's Theory," *Psychological Review*, 63 (1956), 277–293.

VIEWPOINTS   PERSONALITY AND THE SOCIAL ORDER

The development of the individual seems . . . to be a product of the interaction between two urges, the urge towards happiness, which we usually call "egoistic," and the urge towards union with others in the community, which we call "altruistic." . . . In the process of individual development, . . . the main accent falls mostly on the egoistic urge (or the urge towards happiness); while the other urge, which may be described as a "cultural" one, is usually content with the role of imposing restrictions. But in the process of civilization . . . the most important thing is the aim of creating a unity out of the individual human beings. It is true that the aim of happiness is still there, but it is pushed into the background. It almost seems as if the creation of a great human community would be most successful if no attention had to be paid to the happiness of the individual. . . .

Just as a planet revolves around a central body as well as rotating on its own axis, so the human individual takes part in the course of development of mankind at the same time as he pursues his own path in life. . . . So, also, the two urges, the one towards personal happiness and the other towards union with other human beings must struggle with each other in every individual; and so, also, the two processes of individual and of cultural development must stand in hostile opposition to each other. . . .

[Civilization] does not trouble itself enough about the facts of the mental constitution of human beings. It issues a command and does not ask whether it is possible for people to obey it. On the contrary, it assumes that a man's ego is psychologically capable of anything that is required of it, that his ego has unlimited mastery over his id. This is a mistake; and even in what are known as normal people the id cannot be controlled beyond certain limits. . . .

For a wide variety of reasons, it is very far from my intention to express an opinion upon the value of human civilization. I have endeavored to guard myself against the enthusiastic prejudice which holds that our civilization is the most precious thing that we possess or could acquire and that its path will necessarily lead to heights of unimagined perfection. I can at least listen without indignation to the critic who is of the opinion that when one surveys the aims of cultural endeavor and the means it employs, one is bound to come to the conclusion that . . . the outcome of it can only be a state of affairs which the individual will be unable to tolerate.

Sigmund Freud
Civilization and Its Discontents

[According to] the popular individualistic view of things, the social order is thought of as something apart from, and more or less a hindrance to, a man's natural development. There is an assumption that an ordinary person is self-sufficient in most respects, and will do very well if he is only left alone. But there is, of course, no such thing as the absence of restraint, in the sense of social limitations; man has no existence apart from a social order, and can develop his personality only through the social order, and in the same degree that it is developed. . . .

A child comes into the world with an outfit of vague tendencies, for all definite unfolding of which he is dependent upon social conditions. If cast away alone on a desert island he would, supposing that he succeeded in living at all, never know speech, or social sentiment, or any complex thought. On the other hand, if all his surroundings are from the first such as to favor the enlargement and enrichment of his life, he may attain the fullest development possible to him in the actual state of the world. In so far as the social conditions have this favoring action upon him he may be said to be free. And so every person, at every stage of his growth, is free or unfree in proportion as he does or does not find himself in the midst of conditions conducive to full and harmonious personal development. Thinking in this way we do not regard the individual as separable from the social order as a whole, but we do regard him as capable of occupying any one of an indefinite number of positions within that order, some of them more suitable to him than others.

So far as discipline is concerned, freedom means not its absence but the use of higher and more rational forms as contrasted with those that are lower or less rational. A free discipline controls the individual by appealing to his reason and conscience, and therefore to his self-respect; while an unfree control works upon some lower phase of the mind, and so tends to degrade him. It is freedom to be disciplined in as rational a manner as you are fit for. . . .

The social order is antithetical to freedom only in so far as it is a bad one. Freedom can exist only in and through a social order, and must be increased by all the healthy growth of the latter. It is only in a large and complex social system that any advanced degree of [freedom] is possible. . . .

Charles Cooley
Human Nature and the
Social Order

social interaction makes to psychological organization will be examined briefly.

Man is not unique in being able to communicate with other members of his species. Many kinds of living creatures are able to exchange signals of some sort and to influence each other's behavior. Only man, however, has the ability to base his communication on *arbitrary* and *conventionalized symbols.* By examining the principles underlying the communication processes of more elementary forms of life, we can learn something of the impact of human communication on psychological structure.

INSTINCTUAL COMMUNICATION AMONG INSECTS

Life in an anthill, a beehive, or a termite colony involves a rather complex division of labor with specialized functions being performed by different types of individuals with distinct bodily structures. The ability to communicate is a prerequisite to the successful coordination of this organized system. For example, worker bees that have located sources of nectar engage in one of several characteristic dances upon entering the hive. This stimulates other workers to proceed on their own, in the correct direction and for the proper distance, to the place where food has been located.[14] At first glance this behavior appears to be communication that includes such abstract concepts as food source, direction, and distance. Actually, of course, the bee does not need such concepts or anything remotely resembling them. Intricate biological mechanisms possessed by every single individual of that physical type control and automatically govern the motions of the bee. We need not assume abstract thought or even conscious processes. The bees who observe the dance and then go to the food source are also driven by inherited mechanisms, which require no learning whatever. It is as though each bee were governed by a bank of very elaborate, but microscopic, computers based upon biological principles and carefully programed to provide all of the response systems the organism needs. Our ignorance about such instincts is abysmal, but much of the often amazing behavior of many of the world's "simple" creatures is controlled by them. The insect's biological makeup determines the kinds of communicative acts that he can accomplish; he can perform only those that

his genetic structure permits; and he automatically performs them upon receiving the proper stimuli.

ANIMAL COMMUNICATION THROUGH LEARNED NATURAL SIGNS

At the intermediate levels of animal life, the members of different species use characteristic cries or other signals to communicate such things as danger, food, and sexual excitement. In some cases, these communicative acts seem to be entirely instinctive. In others, *learning* adds to the animal's communicative repertoire.

Dominance hierarchies. An illustration of communication based on learning but limited by biological structure can be provided by animals that travel or live together in flocks, herds, or other kinds of groupings. In such collective situations, the males fight to determine their position in the dominance hierarchy with the stronger and quicker animals emerging victorious and dominant over their competitors.[15]

If such animals spent all their time fighting, there would be little time left for eating, reproducing, or anything else. Thus, most animal groups develop some method of reinforcing the relationship of dominance and submission between a given pair without the necessity of repeated combat. For example, chickens use a system of pecks to maintain their hierarchy. Horses maintain theirs by a biting-kicking order. Baboons and monkeys that travel in groups use a system of mounting, whereby a dominant male will occasionally jump on the back of a former competitor as a reminder of who is superior. Such actions represent a shortened or truncated form of a more elaborate series of acts. The chicken who merely pecks his former rival to reinforce the dominance-submission hierarchy is using the beginnings of the act of combat as a substitute for the entire act. The competitor who displays submission by not countering the peck is also responding to the beginnings of the aggressive series by giving up when the peck occurs rather than by doing so only after a thorough and painful beating. Obviously, the estab-

---

14. Karl von Frisch, "Dialectics in the Language of Bees," *Scientific American,* 207, No. 2 (August 1962), 78-87.

15. A. M. Guhl, "The Social Order of Chickens," *Scientific American,* 194, No. 2 (February 1956), 42-47.

lishment of these habits occurs only after the two animals have engaged in combat several times and it has been clearly demonstrated that one is dominant.

Gestures as natural signs. When an animal learns to respond to the beginning phases of an act in much the same way that he formerly responded to the entire act or series of acts, he is responding to a *gesture*. We may define *gesture* as a truncated act that stands for the entire act. Thus, the type of animal communication we have described is a kind of conversation of gestures in which learned *signs* (substitute stimuli) stand for more complex experiences that the animal has had in the past. A moment's thought will suggest that the signals these animals exchange concerning not only dominance but also food, danger, etc., can be accounted for within this framework. These gestures are *natural* signs: the behaviors used fall completely within the natural repertoires of the animals who use them; they do not select them arbitrarily. In this sense, they are limited by their biological structure and inherited patterns; the chickens cannot arbitrarily decide to let a wiggle of the left wing stand for dominance or establish the convention among themselves that three claw taps on the ground will be a sign for submission. Such agreements would involve *arbitrary* and *conventional* signs, which are the basis of true language and are beyond the ability of any animal species other than man.

Two animals can communicate via gestures as natural signs because they have learned individual habit patterns that mesh and interlock: the signs have quite different meanings for each animal and thus elicit quite different responses. In fact, it is precisely because of these differences that the two animals can influence each other. *The animals do not share common meanings;* they have acquired *distinct but coordinated meanings* that are aroused by the natural sign.

We need not assume that the animals are internally or consciously aware of initiating or responding to the natural signs they use. They may be, but such an assumption is not needed to explain their communicative acts. Learned responses once established can be as automatic as the blind mechanisms of instinct.

---

16. This is the central thesis of the symbolic interactionists. See George Herbert Mead, *Mind, Self and Society: From the Standpoint of a Social Behaviorist*, ed. Charles W. Morris (Chicago: The University of Chicago Press, 1934).

HUMAN COMMUNICATION THROUGH SIGNIFICANT SYMBOLS

But what of human communication? In what ways does it differ from the kinds already discussed? As with lower forms of life, man's communicative behavior is in part limited by his biology. To communicate, an individual must use the muscular, skeletal, and neural structure of his body. If these are impaired, he will not be able to perform well. But apart from such considerations, biological inheritance plays no significant role in man's communicative behavior.

Arbitrary and conventional signs. The basis of human communication is the *symbol*. The symbol is first of all a sign—a substitute stimulus—that stands for something else, usually an object or an idea. While animals are limited to natural signs, human beings use signs that are both *arbitrary* and *conventional*. They are arbitrary because man can use almost any kind of a stimulus as a substitute for almost anything he wishes. He can use bodily gestures or other kinds of gestures, such as the astounding variety of grunts, pops, whistles, hums, and whines capable of being produced by the human voice. Or, he can scratch characters in clay, form tokens of metal, and imprint designs with dark liquid on a light surface. However, once a given stimulus has been selected as a sign for a particular referent, then a *rule* must establish that specific stimulus as a sign for that particular referent. When rules of this type are established, symbols become *conventional*. The essence of language is that its symbols are conventional and therefore a part of shared culture. Thus, all words (symbols) of a language are both arbitrary and conventional.

Significant symbols and the sharing of meaning. Symbols that are both arbitrary and conventional are called *significant symbols*. When a person uses a certain word, it is a significant symbol if it arouses within him approximately the same meaning (internal responses and experiences) that is aroused in the person toward whom it is directed. Two human beings are in communication when these sets of internal responses and experiences *parallel each other rather closely.*[16] Once a given symbol has been conventionalized within a group, each human being in that group can experience the same general meaning when confronted with either

Gestures encompass a wide range of human behavior—from the simple to the very complex. The grasp of a child's hand, the peace sign, and the symbol for black power are gestures that have a general meaning for most people in American society. But some gestures, when used by formal groups, become standardized to ensure that very specific meanings are being communicated. The members of the Board of Trade, for example, use an out-turned palm to signal an offer to sell and a palm turned inward to indicate an offer to buy. Fingers indicate the price.

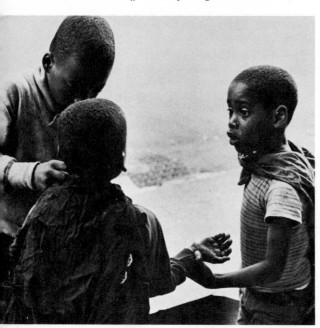

the symbol or its referent. Of course, no symbol will evoke exactly the same internal experiences in any two people. Nevertheless, once this habit has been learned, a person can respond to the symbol in much the same way that he responded when he first experienced the symbol's referent.

But why is communication such an important issue? Why is it so necessary to distinguish clearly between the communication processes of lower animals and those of man? The answer is readily apparent. Whereas communication only acts to facilitate certain activities for lower animals, language is essential for the development of man's human nature. Only through the use of language can man participate in the social process with other men. Through such participation the individual derives his concept of self, his ability to engage in thought, and his set of internal controls—his human nature.

THE EMERGENCE OF MIND AND SELF

Much modern sociological thinking concerning the relationship between individual human nature and the communication-based social order stems from the work of two pioneer sociologists, Charles Horton Cooley and George Herbert Mead. Modern research on the nature and functioning of human mental processes as a product of involvement in social interaction has strongly supported the theoretical insights of these earlier writers.

THE "LOOKING-GLASS SELF"

Shortly after the turn of the century, Charles Horton Cooley formulated a theory concerning the emergence of the self through a process of social interaction. Cooley maintained that the development of a social self and of human personality in general began very early in life. The primary group, which in the earliest years meant the family, was the source of the experiences necessary for the emergence of the infant's self-image. Later, peer groups and other associates provided additional social contexts within which the individual could continue to develop as a social being.

Distinguishing self from others. As Cooley observed the process in his own children, he saw that the human voice, facial expressions, and other activities of surrounding adults are, at the beginning, like any other attractive phenomena in the environment of the young infant. Slowly, however, through an accumulation of interactive experience, the child begins to attach special meaning to other human beings. Gradually, he begins to perceive the limits of his own body and to define himself as an object that is different from the physical environment and distinct from the other human beings around him. This first crude differentiation of self from others is aided by the very words we use to make such distinctions. The social nature of self-realization is implied by the word I, which automatically indicates the existence of non-I's, that is, of others who must be taken into account.

As the child comes to distinguish between self and others, he gradually becomes aware that others are evaluating him; they are judging his appearance and conduct according to rules and standards. These standards and rules must be understood before the individual can begin to evaluate *himself* as a social object. He is certainly not born with such an ability; he can only acquire it through involvement in a complex and subtle interaction within groups where these rules and standards prevail. As the individual learns these evaluative criteria, he can make more and more sophisticated judgments about his own appearance and behavior. A *self-image,* in other words, emerges as a product of group involvement and communication with others.

Seeing ourselves in the evaluations of others. Cooley's phrase *the looking-glass self* makes clear the process by which we arrive at self-evaluation. As Cooley himself stated it in 1902:

> Each to each a looking glass
> Reflects the other that doth pass.

As we see our face, figure and dress in the [mirror], and are interested in them because they are ours, and pleased or otherwise with them according as they do or do not answer to what we should like them to be; so in our imagination we perceive in another's mind some thought of our appearance, manners,

By drawing and cutting out life-size figures of themselves, the children in this experimental kindergarten are in fact learning to distinguish self from others. They can evaluate their own paper "self-images" in relation to the "images" of their peers.

aims, deeds, character, friends, and so on, and are variously affected by it.

A self idea of this sort seems to have three principal elements: the imagination of our appearance to the other person; the imagination of his judgment of that appearance; and some sort of self-feeling, such as pride or mortification.[17]

It is thus that the individual builds a set of beliefs and evaluations about himself as a human being. His self-image is his socially derived understanding of his qualities, attributes, and characteristics, as these are evaluated according to the shared criteria of his society.

The identification of this important aspect of human nature as a product of behavior and the tying of its origins to the social process itself constituted a radical departure from earlier traditions, which proclaimed man's nature to be entirely spiritual or a strict product of biological endowment. For Cooley, it was the "imaginations which people have of one another" that constitute the "solid facts of society" and enable us to understand individual human nature.[18]

Although Cooley emphasized the childhood years as the most crucial for the development of the looking-glass self, it should be obvious that this process continues through the life cycle of the individual. As the person moves successively from infancy to childhood, through adolescence, young adulthood, middle age, and into the older years, the social mirror around him responds to him in ever changing ways. He must learn to read these successive looking glasses and to redefine himself in realistic and appropriate terms as each new stage is reached. At some point he must stop thinking of himself (and behaving) as a young and vigorous person. He has to face the fact that he is middle-aged, or eventually, an old man or woman whose life is nearly over. These successive self-images may not come easily, but they are an important aspect of human nature at each life stage.

MIND, SELF, AND THE SIGNIFICANT SYMBOL

Cooley's ideas suggested to others the importance of the interplay between society and

---

17. Charles Horton Cooley, *Human Nature and the Social Order* (New York: Schocken Books, Inc., 1964), p. 184; first published in 1909.

18. *Ibid.*, p. 121.

the individual in understanding human nature. One of the most important thinkers to follow his lead was George Herbert Mead, the philosopher-sociologist whose main ideas were formulated early in the present century. His theories concerning the relationship between mind, self, and society added a great deal to our understanding of the mental functioning of the human being.

We noted earlier that human communication in its elementary form consists of one person directing significant symbols toward another, with the reasonable assurance that the internal experience (meaning) aroused by the symbols will be parallel in himself and the other party. Mead formulated this interpretation and coined the term *significant symbol.*

The social nature of mind. Mead's theory of communication clarified the act of thinking, which he explained as an internal response to self-directed symbols. The individual responds to these self-directed symbols in the same way that he responds to symbols directed toward him by others. In this view, the individual's mind is very closely tied to his language ability. Cognitive processes of the individual and the language of his society are in many ways the same process. They are mental or social, depending upon whether one views them as individual internalized habits or institutionalized collective processes.

Mead believed that mind and self emerged jointly from the individual's experience in the social order:

Mind arises in the social process [when that process enters into] the experience of . . . the given individuals involved in that process. When this occurs the individual becomes self-conscious and has a mind; he becomes aware of his relations to that process as a whole, and to other individuals participating in it with him. . . ."[19]

Thus, as Mead delineated the process, the individual becomes a social person (acquires a human nature) as he acquires the response abilities called *mind.* It is important to recognize, however, that the acquisition of mind and of self

19. Anselm Strauss, ed., *George Herbert Mead on Social Psychology: Selected Papers* (Chicago: The University of Chicago Press, 1964), p. 195.

take place at the same time. Although we can discuss and analyze these aspects of personality separately, they are interlocking parts of an ongoing system.

Genesis of the self. Self, like mind, has its genesis in communication, the basis for interaction with other people. It is through this social interaction that the individual defines himself. The earliest interactive experiences, which initiate the development of the self, are somewhat like the conversation of gestures in animals. The process actually begins, according to Mead, in the interplay between the newborn infant and his parents, especially the mother. The infant's crying and other behavior are a constant source of stimuli. We do not assume that the child is consciously trying to convey meanings, such as being hungry, cold, or wet. However, the mother responds to these stimuli by providing a bottle, her breast, cuddling, or other forms of relief. From the point of view of the infant, the process of communication has begun. The child's cries become patterned, and the mother begins to distinguish between the pain cry, the hunger cry, and so on.

As the areas of communication expand, the child learns to elicit from the mother appropriate behaviors by particular kinds of cries and noises. The child, in other words, learns to stimulate his mother and to respond to her in a variety of patterned ways. What began as a conversation of gestures from the infant's point of view becomes communication with significant symbols as the child anticipates his mother's response. The child's symbols are calling out the responses he anticipates in the other.

Play and the game. As the child develops skill in communicating through the use of significant symbols, he gradually becomes able to take the role of the other. For example, he can pretend that he is the mother, who is punishing the child (himself) for a naughty act. He begins to understand the point of view of another person and to exercise the attitudes and orientations of that person toward himself. Similarly, he *plays at* being a teacher, policeman, doctor, or father. His imaginary role-taking is at first limited, however, to one role at a time.

Gradually, as the child develops, role-taking expands into what Mead called the *game.* The child who plays a game, even one as simple as hide-and-seek, must simultaneously grasp not only his own role but also the roles of all the other players in an organized system. Baseball provides a clear example of what Mead meant by the game: each participant must not only learn to take mentally the role he is playing but also must understand fully the roles of all the other players on his team and the other team as these operate in a coordinated system. Only by grasping the roles of all the others simultaneously and by seeing both himself and others from an outside point of view can he effectively act out his own part.

All social activity is a game in this sense. The individual must understand and must incorporate into his own makeup the attitudes and expectations of others with whom he interacts. Mead referred to this aspect of personality as *the generalized other*: as the individual mentally assumes the roles of other people, their attitudes "organize into a sort of unit, and it is that organization which controls the response of the individual." [20] From the game, then, the individual develops an internal sense of *other* from which he derives his own definitions for appropriate behavior.

The I and the Me. Although Mead postulated that the self develops in the fullest sense only as it mirrors the expectations of others, he also recognized a creative and spontaneous aspect of self. He labeled these two complementary aspects of personality the *I* and the *Me*.

The *I* is unfettered by the generalized other; it encompasses that which is personal, distinct, and unique about the individual, that which permits him to be creative and nonconforming. The *Me*, on the other hand, is the predictable reflection of the social group; it is the product of socialization (Chapter 5). If our selves had only the *I* aspect, social behavior would be unpredictable and organized group activity would be impossible. If, on the other hand, our selves had only the *Me* aspect, there would be no art, invention, or social change.

20. *Ibid.,* p. 218.

A child's imaginary role-taking is at first limited to one role at a time; he plays at being a father, teacher, or soldier. Gradually, however, the child is able to play a game, for which he must simultaneously grasp not only his own role but also the roles of all the other players in an organized system.

THE DENIAL OF GROUP EXPERIENCE

We have repeatedly suggested that the individual acquires much of what we know as human nature through cultural exposure and interaction with others. We have also noted that this social experience is limited or facilitated by various constitutional factors. If, then, personality is a product of the interplay between biological factors and the sociocultural environment, a simple prediction can be made: human beings who are denied normal participation in group processes should show noticeable deficiencies or impairment in personal organization. The sections that follow summarize the impact of such isolation on both human infants and adults.

---

21. Robert Briffault, *The Mothers: A Study of the Origins of Sentiments and Institutions* (London: George Allen & Unwin Ltd., 1927), pp. 23–24.

ISOLATION IN EARLY LIFE

Experiments to determine how children learn to speak are as ancient as history itself. Herodotus reports that Psammetichus, King of Eygpt, had several children raised by nurses who were forbidden to speak to them in order to find out if the children would first utter the Egyptian tongue or some other. Reportedly, when the children tired of the goat's milk they were being fed, they asked for bread in the Phrygian tongue. When Emperor Frederick II attempted to repeat the experiment, the children died, which confirmed the existing belief that children raised without speech would have no souls and, therefore, lack vitality. King James IV of Scotland arranged for two children to be placed on the island of Inchkieth in the care of a woman who could not speak. He was seeking proof for the widely held belief that children raised under these circumstances would speak Hebrew, the tongue of Adam. According to the reports of the experiment, when the children came to the age of speech, "they spak guid Hebrew." [21]

Whatever the validity of these early reports, contemporary observations do not support the idea that children come into the world naturally predisposed to speak one language or another. In fact, the absence of communicative contact with other human beings in early life appears to have very drastic consequences for the developing infant. While we lack controlled experimental evidence, some reliable information on the effects of isolation from groups in early age is available from case studies of children who, for one reason or another, have been raised under conditions of substantial isolation from group life. Although limited, the data from these "natural experiments" illustrate what happens when human beings are denied normal participation in group processes.[22] Two specific cases can be cited where extended observations were made on the development of such children when they were placed in a socially stimulating environment after their discovery. (The names of these children have been fictionalized.)

The case of Anna. Anna was the second illegitimate child of a sturdy young woman who lived on and operated her grandfather's farm. The grandfather was a man of stern morals and strongly disapproved of this new evidence of his granddaughter's indiscretions. Efforts were made to place the newborn child up for adoption. This did not work out for various reasons, and after only a few months the mother was forced to take the infant home in spite of the grandfather's wrath. To avoid trouble, Anna was confined on the second floor in an attic-like room.

Anna was left almost without attention. Ordinarily, it seems, Anna received only enough care to keep her barely alive. She appears to have been seldom moved from one position to another. Her clothing and bedding were filthy. She apparently had no instruction, no friendly attention.

It is little wonder that, when finally found and removed from the room in the grandfather's house at the age of nearly six years, the child could not talk, walk, or do anything that showed intelligence. She was in an extremely emaciated and undernourished condition, with skeleton-like legs and a bloated abdomen. She had been fed on virtually nothing except cow's milk during the years under her mother's care.[23]

After she was discovered, Anna spent about a year and a half in a county home. She learned to walk, to feed herself, to understand simple commands, to be more or less neat, to remember people, etc. She made little progress toward speech; she could only babble like a normal child of about one year of age. At this time, she was placed in a private home for retarded children where she received more adequate training. Approximately four years after discovery, the school reported on her condition:

Anna had reached 46 inches in height and weighed 60 pounds. She could bounce and catch a ball and was said to conform to group socialization, though as a follower rather than a leader. Toilet habits were firmly established. Food habits were normal, except that she still used a spoon as her sole implement. She could dress herself except for fastening her clothes. Most remarkable of all, she had finally begun to develop speech. She was characterized as being at about the two-year level in this regard. She could call attendants by name and bring in one when she was asked to. She had a few complete sentences to express her wants.[24]

Unfortunately, Anna died at the age of ten, about a year after this report. She had made some additional progress; she could string beads, identify colors, play lovingly with a doll, wash her hands, brush her teeth, and help other children. There is little doubt that Anna was seriously retarded as compared to normal children of her own age, but considering that when found she was an apathetic and animal-like creature, her psychological development at the time of her death provides a striking contrast. She was unmistakeably acquiring a human personality, including the ability to use language.

Anna's retardation appears to have been a product of both the impoverished social environment of her early life and inherited limitations on her capacities for development, although the latter cannot be fully confirmed. The mother was tested for intelligence, and even though she had

22. In an earlier era, much was made of reports of so-called feral children who supposedly were raised by animals. These reports have been largely discredited as failing to meet adequate scientific standards of reporting. For this reason, they will be ignored in the present discussion, even though their conclusions are entirely supportive of the issues as discussed.

23. Kingsley Davis, "Final Note on a Case of Extreme Isolation," *The American Journal of Sociology,* 52 (March 1947), 433.

24. *Ibid.,* p. 434.

completed the eighth grade, her I.Q. of 50 was considerably below normal. In spite of the possibility of genetically linked limitations on her potentialities, Anna's progress after being removed from social isolation provides a dramatic demonstration of the significance of social interaction for personality development.

The case of Isabelle. Only nine months after the plight of Anna first came to light, another child of almost identical age was discovered living under isolated conditions. In this case, the child was not completely alone during her isolation. Isabelle was the illegitimate offspring of a deaf-mute mother, who had been confined with her. This young mother was not feebleminded. She had suffered severe brain damage at the age of two, which limited her sight to one eye, and as a result of the injury she could neither talk, hear, read, nor write. She was able, however, to communicate with her family in a limited way with crude gestures. When this unfortunate young woman became pregnant at the age of twenty-two, her family was both shocked and ashamed. They locked her up in a darkened room during her pregnancy. After Isabelle's birth, both remained involuntarily confined in this room for six and a half years. Finally, the mother escaped. She fled with her child in her arms, and was immediately brought to the attention of authorities, who placed both her and Isabelle in a children's hospital.

Since the mother was unable to communicate except through gestures, Isabelle's environment during her confinement had been one entirely without speech and normal human social interaction. At first, in her new environment, she could make only strange croaking sounds. She was as terrified by strangers as is a wild animal just after capture. She was, from the point of view of human personality development, about as bad off as Anna. Her physical condition was somewhat better, but she was a wan and thin child with legs badly bowed from a rachitic condition caused by improper nourishment and lack of sunshine. The soles of her feet came nearly flat together so that she could not walk.

At first, the authorities were puzzled and thought her to be feebleminded. She was completely unable to respond to human speech. When it was finally established that she was neither deaf nor feebleminded, an expert university teacher of speech undertook to give her language training.

Isabelle's progress under this tutelage was truly remarkable. Within two weeks she was making her first attempts to identify toys by name when they were presented to her (ball, car, etc.). Within two months, the child knew dozens of words and could volunteer simple sentences. After a year of effort Isabelle could write, count up to twenty, add up to ten, and give a simple summary of a story which had been read to her. After a year and a half of training, the following was written as part of a report on her progress:

(1) Vocabulary between 1,500 and 2,000 words.
(2) Questions asked by Isabelle:
    Why do crayons break? Why does the hand move around the clock? Why does the paste come out if one upsets the jar? Do you go to Miss Mason's school at the University? Are you going to Church tomorrow? Does your dog sleep in your bed? What did Miss Mason say when you told her I cleaned my classroom?[25]

In short, at the age of eight years, the child had made almost spectacular progress to a point where she was becoming like a normal child of her age. After six and a half years of silence and isolation, she was an energetic, rapidly progressing, and happy youngster. Appropriate surgery had corrected her leg deformity, and she showed few signs of her period of isolation. Isabelle had passed through all the stages of learning that normal children experience, but in a much shorter time. Eventually, Isabelle entered a regular school and made entirely normal progress.

The conclusions from these two cases parallel those of the limited number of other cases of young children found living under severely isolated conditions. When denied interaction with others, children fail to develop human personality structure in anything like the normal pattern. Their biological processes, inherited capacities, and other constitutional factors do not provide a basis for acquiring a human nature in the psychological sense.

Spitz' foundling-home study. The evidence from a study by Rene Spitz suggests that even

---

25. Marie K. Mason, "Learning to Speak After Six and One-Half Years of Silence," *Journal of Speech Disorders*, 7 (1942), 303.

a limited reduction of human contact can have serious effects on infants.[26] Spitz compared the mortality rates of children under one year of age in a foundling home and in the nursery of a women's penal institution. Although hygienic conditions were good in both institutions, those in the foundling home were somewhat superior. However, 37 percent of the children in the foundling home died during the period of the study, usually from common infant diseases, whereas none of the children in the nursery died. In addition, the children in the nursery were more proficient in learning how to sit, walk, and talk.

The following differences were observed in the two institutions: (1) toys were common in the nursery, but uncommon in the foundling home; (2) the children in the nursery could see what was going on and had a pleasant view of the outdoors, but in the foundling home, sheets were hung from the children's bedrails, effectively cutting off the outside world; (3) while the children in the nursery moved around their cots, the foundling-home children lay in one position for hours; (4) the foundling home had one nurse for each seven or eight children, while the nursery had the children's mothers, as well as four nurses.

The amount of attention appeared to be the most significant factor. In a follow-up study Spitz observed that the foundling home had modified its practices as a result of the original study. The children were now put to play on the floor of a large, sunny room, but they still did not develop to their normal age level. Although not conclusive, Spitz' study strongly suggests that maternal love and affection are essential for the growth of a child's personality.

SOCIAL ISOLATION AND ADULT PERSONALITY

Scientists believe that the human individual is dependent upon social interaction for *maintaining* as well as for developing a personal organization. If this is true, then adults who undergo long periods of isolation from meaningful human contact can be expected to show some signs of personality impairment.

Again, reliable data are meager, since lengthy isolation experiments would be unthinkable. However, from time to time men have either voluntarily or involuntarily been subjected to extreme isolation from their fellows. Explorers, prisoners, men lost in the wilderness, and others cut off from human associations almost uniformly report serious effects on their personal organization.

The experiences under severe isolation of the famous Antarctic explorer, Admiral Richard E. Byrd, have been summarized by the social psychologist Robert E. L. Faris in the following terms:

His first reaction after being left by his men at the lonely outpost on March 28th, was a general feeling of peacefulness. Within about ten days he noted a fear of boredom, then of loneliness. By the end of the first month it took some moments after awakening in the morning to collect his wits, and he found himself wondering where he was and what he was doing there. The silence depressed him, and he became irritable and reported that he had difficulty in concentrating. A month and a half after being alone he reported that his table manners had deteriorated to the point where they were atrocious. He also wrote on May 11th, after about forty-four days of solitude, that he found it hard to think in words.[27]

The effects of prolonged isolation on personal organization have also been observed in prison settings. During the early part of the nineteenth century, for example, the states of Pennsylvania and New York established prisons where inmates were held in complete solitary confinement during their entire sentence. Each prisoner was provided with a Bible, work, and ample time for him to pray and meditate upon his sins. The hope was that he would undergo inner reformation and find the determination to return to the ways of the Lord. Unfortunately, the prolonged isolation had serious effects on personality. The prisoners became eccentric, apathetic, and reclusive. Many developed severe mental disorders, and attempted suicides appear to have been quite common. The system was eventually abandoned.[28]

---

26. Rene Spitz, "Hospitalism," in R. S. Eissler *et al.*, *The Psychoanalytic Study of the Child*, Vol. 1 (New York: International Universities Press, 1945), pp. 53–72.

27. Robert E. L. Faris, *Social Psychology* (New York: The Ronald Press Company, 1952), pp. 342–343. This summary is taken from Richard E. Byrd, *Alone* (New York: G. P. Putnam's Sons, 1938).

28. Donald R. Taft and Ralph W. England, *Criminology* (New York: The Macmillan Company, 1964), pp. 404–407.

More recently there have been various controlled experiments to test the effects of isolation on prisoners. In one such study, a psychologist obtained forty volunteers among long-term inmates in a penitentiary, half of whom were required to stay in solitary confinement for a period of four days. The other half followed their normal prison routine and thus served as a control. Immediately following the period of isolation, a series of psychological tests was administered to both groups. On certain of the tests, the solitary-confinement group performed somewhat less adequately than the control group. Since the period of confinement was only four days, it is unlikely that the experience had any effects that would be noticeable to casual observation.[29]

29. A. J. W. Taylor, "Social Isolation and Imprisonment," *Psychiatry*, 24, No. 4 (1961), 373–376.

Overall, the effects of social isolation from human groups seem to be reasonably clear, even though the evidence is unsystematic. To be reared under conditions of extreme social isolation denies the developing child a crucial source from which human personality is developed. He may be able to function adequately as a biological organism, and he may have the inherited potentiality to develop a truly human nature if removed from isolation, but until he is able to interact with other people through the use of significant symbols he will not develop either self or mind, as we have outlined them.

For the normal adult, conditions of extreme social isolation will impair personal organization. Adherence to social norms and the habits of associating symbols with their referents are complex skills that will deteriorate if not practiced. Prolonged isolation may lead to severe mental disorders.

SUMMARY

The sociologist looks at the relationship between the individual and society in two complementary ways. First, every individual plays some part in shaping the social process. Although group behavior can be analyzed in its own terms, it is nonetheless the product of interaction between particular individuals, each trying to satisfy his own needs and achieve his own goals. Second, group processes have an important influence on the development of individual personality.

The term *personality* refers to the structure or organization of the individual's psychological behavior. This structure includes *aptitudes, perception, attitudes, self-image, traits, motivation, unconscious processes,* and the like. These aspects of personality interlock in an ongoing system, the nature of which is much debated by theorists.

The human individual inherits a number of constitutional potentialities and limitations that influence the development of his personal organization. He does not have the inherited instincts that enable some animals to engage in remarkably complex behavior without prior learning, but his capacities to learn and to acquire certain types of skills nevertheless appear to be directly related to his genetic heritage. Other constitutional factors such as sex, race, and general appearance also have an indirect influence on personality development, for by placing an individual into significant social categories they help determine how other members of society will respond to him. This, in turn, influences his self-image and his characteristic patterns of behavior.

The individual enters into social interaction with others mainly through the use of language, which effectively links him to the experience systems of others through conventionalized gestures and significant symbols. This ability sharply separates him from other animals. It is only through meaningful communication with others that man becomes truly a human being.

5

The
Socialization
Process

Socialization is the complex process of learning whereby man the biological being becomes man the truly human being, capable of functioning adequately as an individual and as a group member. The newborn infant has the capacity for developing in an almost infinite number of ways, but his subsequent development is never random. Through meaningful interaction with his parents, peers, and other members of his society, he acquires a pattern of personal organization that mirrors the social world around him. As Ruth Benedict has stated it, "By the time he can talk, he is the little creature of his culture, and by the time he is grown and able to take part in its activities, its habits are his habits, its beliefs are his beliefs, its impossibilities his impossibilities."[1]

The socialization process explains not only the continuity of societies through successive generations but also the very ability of a society's members to interact in a meaningful way. All human beings who participate in a given culture learn to take many of the same things for granted. A common language, a core of common knowledge, common ways of handling routine situations, a shared technology and material culture, shared social institutions—all provide the basis for purposeful interaction. Unless socialization worked to make all members of a society in some ways alike, group behavior—even group conflict—would be impossible.[2]

Because socialization is basic to societal continuity and stability, there is a tendency to think of it simply as indoctrination. However, the socialization process helps to explain the *differences* among a society's members as well as the similarities. Pressures to conform to any prescribed set of standards are greatly modified by the fact that socialization is accomplished through many different agents—family, school, church, peer groups, occupational groups, the mass media, and various other formal and informal "teachers"—each of which promotes its own values and behavioral patterns. What a person comes to learn in each context depends, then, on the total pattern of his socializing experiences.

Nor is the individual a passive entity, wholly ready to be molded by outside forces. As we noted in reviewing Mead's theory of the "I" and the "Me" (page 142), there is a creative and spontaneous aspect of self that remains unfettered by others. Each human being responds to his environment with behavioral tendencies that are typical for *him*. These tendencies seem to be the product not only of previous experience but also of constitutional factors such as intelligence, aptitude, and temperament. Because each individual learns from each situation in his own way, socialization can result in an almost unlimited variety of personality configurations.

Even from a societal perspective, the goal of training new members to participate in a shared social process leaves room for individuality and change. Indeed, most societies provide some kinds of socialization to *guarantee* social and cultural change. The fact that scientists, philosophers, artists, engineers, and others are deliberately encouraged to be innovators suggests that societal goals include more than mere efforts to maintain stability.

With these perspectives in mind, we will begin our analysis of the socialization process by examining the relationship between the personal organization of the individual and the social organization of the groups in which he participates. Next, we will single out particular agents of socialization and examine the special part they play in shaping personality. And finally, we will consider the socialization process as it affects the individual during various stages in his life cycle. For as our discussion will make clear, socialization does not end with childhood or adolescence. It is a continuing process of adjustment to changing expectations and demands.[3]

1. Ruth Benedict, *Patterns of Culture* (Boston: Houghton Mifflin Company, 1934), pp. 2–3.

2. Social scientists have been no less fascinated than travelers have with the observation that different cultures seem to produce distinct personality types. See, for example, Abraham Kardiner, *The Psychological Frontiers of Society* (New York: Columbia University Press, 1945); Margaret Mead, *Soviet Attitudes Toward Authority* (New York: McGraw-Hill Book Company, 1951); Ruth Benedict, *The Chrysanthemum and the Sword* (Boston: Houghton Mifflin Company, 1946); Ralph Linton, *Cultural Background of Personality* (New York: Appleton-Century-Crofts, 1945). For an excellent synthesis of the literature on the relationship between culture and personality configurations, see S. Stansfeld Sargent and Robert C. Williamson, *Social Psychology*, 3rd ed. (New York: The Ronald Press Company, 1966), pp. 39–90.

3. For an extensive review of the concept of socialization, see John A. Clausen, ed., *Socialization and Society* (Boston: Little, Brown and Company, 1968).

SOCIAL ORGANIZATION AND PERSONALITY

The same elements of social organization that give stability and direction to *groups* serve also to help shape the personal organization of the *individuals* who participate in them. It is by interacting repeatedly with others in group situations that a human being develops his personal standards of conduct and the distinctive pattern of habits, attitudes, beliefs, and values that we refer to as "personality." Groups shape people no less than people shape groups.

THE INTERNALIZATION OF NORMS

Anyone who has observed a child learning to guide his own personal conduct according to accepted standards has seen the socialization process at first hand. As the child matures, he learns how to feed and dress himself, develops habits of cleanliness, learns how to play with other children, and gradually masters thousands of other aspects of "appropriate" behavior. When an individual of any age comes to accept as his own a behavioral norm to which his group is collectively committed, he is said to have internalized that norm. *Internalization,* then, is a consequence or product of socialization. It explains the individual's tendency to behave in relatively predictable ways even in the absence of formal group pressures.

Group norms and individual behavior. The compelling influence of group norms on individual behavior has been clearly demonstrated in controlled laboratory experiments (see page 152). In a classic study by Muzafer Sherif, for example, subjects were asked to judge the apparent movement of a pinpoint of light some distance away from them in a darkened room. The light was actually stationary, but under such conditions a light appears to move (the so-called *autokinetic effect*). When subjects were asked to make judgments in small groups, their responses over a number of trials tended to *converge* on a common average distance of perceived movement. Thus, a "norm" was established. When

these same individuals were later tested in isolation from others, they continued to confine their reports of perceived movement within the limits established earlier by their group. By contrast, individuals who were tested without the prior experience of establishing a group norm were much more variable and erratic in their judgments of how far the light "moved."[4]

Everyday observations of human behavior confirm the experimental findings of Sherif, Asch, and others regarding the compelling influence of group-established norms. A person who is home alone all day does not revert to completely unorganized personal behavior. Although he may not bother to conform to all the standards he uses in public, he is not likely to gobble his food like an animal, cease to bathe, or go naked. Nor does he abandon somewhat less obvious norms, such as the standards of logic, morality, artistic beauty, and humor which through socialization have become part of his personality.

Selective internalization. The norms an individual internalizes reflect the totality of his social experience, which is in some ways unique. Even within a given group, no two members encounter precisely the same norms in precisely the same way. More significant for the socialization process, however, is the fact that every individual belongs not just to one group but to many, each with its own set of "rules." When the norms of one group conflict with those of another, as often happens, the individual can only accept one set of standards at the expense of the other. The "choice," seldom a fully conscious one even among adults, depends largely upon which group provides him with more satisfaction and has become more important to him as a reference group. Typically, an individual internalizes *some* norms from *each* of his membership and reference groups, but the influence of his primary groups—of his family and his peers—is usually greater than that of more impersonal groups.

The effects of differential association have been clearly illustrated in studies of deviant groups in which members are regularly exposed to norms quite different from those of society

---

4. Muzafer Sherif, *The Psychology of Social Norms* (New York: Harper and Brothers, 1936).

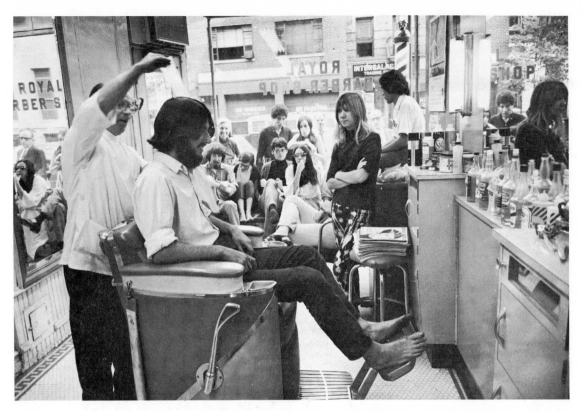

Every person belongs to many groups, each with its own set of "rules." When the norms of one group conflict with those of another, as often happens, the individual can only accept one set of standards at the expense of the other.

as a whole.[5] In an intensive study of lower-class delinquent boys Kvaraceus and Miller found, for example, that the appearance of "toughness" was paramount:[6]

The street-corner boy will say, "Man, I ain't been home or ain't slept for two nights. I've been on the prowl." Or: "They grilled me and beat me with a hose but I didn't admit nothing." Similarly: "My old man and me had one helluva fight. Man, he beat me up good."

Another quality embodied in the norms of the streets and alleys is the ability to outsmart others:

Skill in duping and outsmarting the other guy as well as the ability to avoid being duped by others indicate a lower-class concern with "smartness." . . . The models of estimable achievement in the area of "smartness" are the con man, the fast-man-with-a-buck, the bunco operator, whose victims are seen as suckers and dupes.

The normative culture of lower-class delinquents also stresses the excitement to be found in taking risks and in flouting the norms of the community as a whole:

---

5. The principle of *differential association* is central to a well-known theory of criminality developed some years ago by Edwin Sutherland. See Chapter 12, "Deviance" pp. 394–395; also Edwin H. Sutherland and Donald R. Cressey, *Principles of Criminology*, 5th ed. (New York: J. B. Lippincott Company, 1955), pp. 77–80.

6. William C. Kvaraceus and Walter B. Miller, "Norm-Violating Behavior and Lower Class Culture," reprinted in *Readings in Juvenile Delinquency,* 2nd ed., ed. Ruth Shonle Cavan (New York: J. B. Lippincott Company, 1969), pp. 37–47; quotations from pp. 40–41. See also James F. Short, Jr., and Fred L. Strodtbeck, *Group Process and Gang Delinquency* (Chicago: The University of Chicago Press, 1965).

METHODOLOGY   **THE LABORATORY EXPERIMENT**

In recent decades the *small-group laboratory experiment* has become a convenient sociological research tool. In such a study, the investigator attempts to reproduce certain fundamental social processes in the laboratory setting. Key advantages of the laboratory study are its simplicity, the close observations that it permits, and the high degree of control that can be exercised. The experimenter can select the members of his groups; he can dictate the rules of their interaction; and he can eliminate behaviors that would confound the interpretation of his results.

The basic purpose of a laboratory experiment is to study the cause-effect relationship between two variables: the experimenter systematically changes one of them (called the *independent variable*) in order to calculate its effect on another (called the *dependent variable*). Extraneous factors that might affect the dependent variable are held constant or else measured so that their influence can be taken into account; these are called *control variables*. Usually the researcher begins by preparing an *experimental design,* a formal statement in which he defines the variables, describes the conditions under which observations are to be made, and specifies the procedures for measuring and recording results.

One commonly used type of design for assessing the influence of extraneous variables involves the use of a *control group.* The experimental conditions for the control group are identical to those for the experimental group *except* that the independent variable is not introduced.

A classic example of a small-group laboratory experiment with a control group is that reported by Solomon Asch on the effects of group pressure (the independent variable) on individual judgment (the dependent variable). Several experimental groups were used, each consisting of eight people who were "confederates" of the researcher and one naive subject who knew nothing of the true purpose of the experiment. The groups were shown a series of eighteen panels, each of which contained three horizontal lines of slightly different lengths, ranging from two to ten inches. With each panel, the group was also shown a separate "comparison" line. Members were asked to judge which of the three panel lines most closely matched the length of the comparison line. Things were arranged so that the actual subject always stated his opinion last.

In six of the eighteen trials, all of the confederates gave uniformly *correct* answers by choosing a line from the panel which exactly matched the comparison line in length. In such trials, the subject experienced nothing unusual. However, in twelve of the trials the confederates uniformly chose a line from the panel which *did not match* the comparison line. The "errors" made by the eight confederates were large, ranging from .5 to 1.75 inches. Obviously, in the error trials, the subject had to choose between going along with the majority and making an independent judgment. The subjects reported being under stress when making independent judgments; many simply conformed to the majority.

Numerous trials were run and the results were repeatedly confirmed. However, a control group without confederates showed very different results: there was no evidence of conformity or emotional stress. Overall, the experiment illustrated the powerful influence of group norms on individual behavior.

Critics of small-group laboratory research point out that the situations created by the experimenter are artificial: people in "real life" would behave differently. This is undoubtedly true. However, the same argument could be made concerning experiments in the physical sciences; numerous phenomena are studied under conditions that would never be found in nature. The advantage is that all laboratory experiments—physical, biological, and social—permit variables to be manipulated, controlled, and observed in simple and flexible ways. Such procedures may seldom duplicate nature, but they yield important insights into the characteristics of the phenomena under study.

Solomon E. Asch, "Effects of Group Pressure Upon the Modification and Distortion of Judgments," in *Readings in Social Psychology,* eds. Eleanor E. Maccoby, Theodore M. Newcomb and Eugene L. Hartley (New York: Holt, Rinehart and Winston, Inc., 1958) pp. 174–183.

The desire for excitement is reflected in prevalent patterns involving drinking, gambling and playing the numbers, goading ("testing") official authorities such as teachers and policemen, picking up girls, going out on the town, participating in a "rumble," destroying public property, stealing a car and joy riding.

In some cases the standards of the larger society seem all but irrelevant to the member of a deviant group. As Clifford Shaw noted some years ago, "The cultural standards of his group may be such as not to tolerate socially approved forms of expression; they may represent a complete reversal of the standards and norms of conventional society."[7] For the most part, however, an individual can scarcely avoid internalizing at least some conventional norms. The school, television, the movies, and usually his family expose him to the standards of behavior considered acceptable by society as a whole.

For both the "conformist" and the "deviant," socialization involves the selective internalization of norms from a great many different groups. The conflict faced by those who participate in a deviant subculture is different in degree, but not basically different in kind, from the conflict experienced by a middle-class person when he must choose, consciously or unconsciously, between the norms of his parents, his spouse, his church, his peer groups, and his business associates.

THE ORGANIZING INFLUENCE OF ROLES

The view that human social activity is organized into systems of roles is sometimes called the "dramaturgical" theory of behavior. Social roles are in a very real sense the parts we play in the dramas of everyday life, and like their counterparts in the theater they must be learned.

Role socialization. Groups can function smoothly only if the individuals who fill particular roles "learn their lines" and perform more or less as expected, so that their behavior can be coordinated with that of other "actors" in the cast. Learning to play a real-life role generally requires the acquisition not only of specialized skills but also of supportive attitudes, values, and emotions. Learning the role of "mother," for example, involves much more than acquiring the skills taught in a child-care course; it also means acquiring the attitudes and motivations that make caring for one's children seem an important and gratifying task.

Preparation for many adult roles begins with *anticipatory socialization* in childhood.[8] Girls begin learning the attitudes and skills they will need as mothers by watching and helping their own mothers keep house, by playing with dolls, and by reading books and watching films that portray the joys and responsibilities of motherhood. Parallel experiences prepare individuals for other family roles such as father, brother, sister, grandparent, aunt, or uncle and also for many specialized roles outside the family. The miniature cars and toy tools that we give to young boys are clearly related to our expectations for them as adults. So too, perhaps, are the toy guns and soldiers, the plastic hand grenades, and the various other items of military paraphernalia that have become standard accouterments of childhood.

General and segmental roles. General societal roles such as those based on age, sex, and occupation (page 91) are perhaps the most significant ones in the socialization process, for they organize a great many different facets of personality and behavior.[9] Whatever specialized roles a married woman may have outside her family, she usually identifies herself first of all as a wife and mother, and her overall behavior and attitudes are generally consistent with the expectations for those roles. For men, a particularly significant general role is the occupational one. An individual who has been socialized into the role of lawyer has a different configuration of attitudes, values, skills, motives, and goals

7. Clifford Shaw, "Juvenile Delinquency: A Group Tradition," in *Gang Delinquency and Delinquent Subcultures,* ed. James F. Short, Jr. (New York: Harper & Row, Inc., 1968), p. 83.

8. The term *anticipatory socialization* came originally from studies related to promotion in rank in military groups, but the concept has been broadened to include any type of socialization that rehearses in advance the assumption of future roles, either through overt play or in fantasy. See Robert K. Merton and Alice S. Kitt, "Contributions to the Theory of Reference Group Behavior," in *Continuities in Social Research: Studies in the Scope and Method of "The American Soldier,"* eds. Robert K. Merton and Paul F. Lazarsfeld (New York: The Free Press, 1950).

9. Talcott Parsons, "Age and Sex in the Social Structure of the United States," *American Sociological Review,* 7 (1942), 604–616.

Mark Vlach, Age 9

Through anticipatory socialization, children begin to learn the skills and attitudes that are required for their adult roles. Toy guns, plastic helmets, and various other items of military paraphernalia are related to a role that young boys may assume later in life. They learn not only to "play at" war but also to acquire the attitudes, values, and emotions of the "soldier" role.

than if he had become a plumber, stock broker, jazz musician, physician, or cab driver. The endless variety of occupational roles in a modern urban-industrial society goes far toward explaining the great heterogeneity of its population.

The various segmental roles a person plays from time to time—as a motorist, member of the PTA, golf partner, airline passenger, voter, or customer at the supermarket—have a less pervasive influence on personality organization than general roles, but they too are part of the socialization process. Individually and collectively, they involve patterns of expectation that help shape the "inner man" as well as his outward behavior in specialized situations.

Although roles do not quite "make the man," any more than clothes do, people do indeed change with the roles they play. The college freshman who comes home for Christmas vacation is not quite the same person who left his family a few months earlier, any more than the President of the United States is still a country schoolteacher or a grocer's son. Each new role the individual assumes in the course of his life has the effect of somewhat altering his behavior patterns, including his way of looking at life.

Adjusting to new roles. Sometimes the assumption of a new role requires extensive resocialization. Society provides countless experiences to prepare girls for the roles of wife and mother, but such anticipatory socialization is of little use to a young woman who launches on a career, especially if the career she chooses is not generally considered an "appropriate" one. Childhood socialization may help prepare a girl for the role of nurse or teacher, but it is unlikely to prepare her for a typically male role such as lawyer, engineer, or plumber—much less for a deviant role such as being a prostitute.

The extensive resocialization required to become a successful prostitute has been demonstrated in a study by Bryan, who interviewed thirty-three call girls ranging in age from eighteen to thirty-two. That prostitution is actually a difficult "profession" to enter becomes clear in the following remarks by a girl who had tried to begin on her own:

"I met this guy at a bar and tried to make him pay me, but the thing is, you can't do it that way because they are romantically interested in you, and they don't think that it is on that kind of basis. You can't all of a sudden come up and want money for it, you have to be known beforehand. . . . I think that is what holds a lot of girls back who might work. I think I might have started a year sooner had I had a connection. . . . You can't just, say, get an apartment and get a phone in and everything and say, 'Well, I'm gonna start business,' because you gotta get clients from somewhere. There has to be a contact."[10]

The aspiring prostitute must form a relationship with a professional who will serve as a contact and also provide the necessary amount of training. The trainer may be an established prostitute or a pimp who manages several girls. Frequently a prostitute will develop a deep emotional attachment to her pimp and give him

more of her earnings than their agreement requires.

Once a teacher-learner relationship is established, training begins in earnest:

The classroom is, like the future place of work, an apartment. The apprentice typically serves in the trainer's apartment, either temporarily residing with the trainer or commuting there almost daily. The novice rarely serves her apprenticeship in such places as a house of prostitution, motel, or on the street.[11]

Becoming a prostitute means acquiring new attitudes toward self, new ways of handling emotional feelings toward the sex act, and new role relationships with men. The training provided by a professional contact promotes such resocialization.

Any significant change from one general role to another is likely to involve some degree of resocialization. When couples marry, for example, each partner serves as an agent of socialization for the other. Only if each participant can adjust to new role expectations is the marriage likely to be a satisfying one. The arrival of a child requires further adjustments. Suddenly, roles are not what they were before. The child serves as a focus for the resocialization of both husband and wife, as they adjust their behavior patterns and attitudes to the requirements of their new roles as father and mother.

GROUP CONTROLS AND INTERNALIZED CONTROLS

From a group perspective, positive and negative sanctions are techniques to encourage adherence to established norms and to check potential or actual deviation. They are directed primarily toward *acts*, not toward individuals. But from the perspective of the group member whose behavior is rewarded or punished, sanctions are experienced very personally: they cause either pleasure or distress.

According to one well-developed theory of learning, an individual experiences *positive gratification* when he is rewarded or sustained by the treatment he receives from others, *negative gratification* when he is punished or made to feel uncomfortable. Positive gratification has the effect of *reinforcing* the behavior that elicited the reward, increasing the probability that the indi-

10. James H. Bryan, "Apprenticeships in Prostitution," *Social Problems*, 12 (Winter 1965), 289.

11. *Ibid.*, p. 291.

vidual will behave in a similar way when next he finds himself in similar circumstances. Negative gratification has the opposite effect, reducing the likelihood that the punished act will be repeated. Behavior patterns that are repeatedly rewarded tend to become firmly established over time, whereas those that have resulted in negative gratification tend to be eliminated.[12] Although this is by no means a complete explanation of social learning (it omits, for example, the crucial factor of imitation), the concepts of gratification and reinforcement go far toward explaining the complex process by which an individual comes to internalize the norms of his groups.

Ordinarily, of course, the members of a group do not monitor each other's behavior so thoroughly that *every* approved act is rewarded and *every* nonconforming act is punished. As Doby has noted, reinforcement is likely to occur only intermittently:

A child does not always get rewarded or punished for a given type of response. The rewards and punishments sometimes follow a given response and sometimes they do not. This is true all through life. An investor does not make a profit on every investment. Nor does a fisherman catch a fish every time he goes fishing, but he keeps on going fishing.[13]

Experimental studies of learning in animals have demonstrated that behavioral responses reinforced on an intermittent basis are particularly resistant to extinction. This raises the possibility that socialization may actually be facilitated by the fact that positive and negative sanctions are administered somewhat irregularly.[14] In any case, reinforcement in socializing situations apparently occurs often enough, and in patterns sufficiently related to group-supported norms and roles, so that the individual comes to organize his behavior around group expectations. Gradually he begins to apply to *himself* the same standards that other people have used in judging him.

The effects of sanctioning on personality formation are most readily observed in early childhood, when parents use rewards and punishment as deliberate techniques for teaching the child approved forms of behavior. As the individual matures and begins to participate more fully in social life, sanctioning becomes increasingly complex. For example, many of the sanctions commonly used by groups depend for their effectiveness on prior experience. Unlike the food pellets and electric shocks used in animal experiments, the rewards and punishments used to encourage adherence to group expectations often have no inherent ability to gratify the human organism or to cause it distress: people must *learn* to be rewarded by such symbolic gestures as diplomas, titles, praise, and applause. Among the most significant symbolic sanctions are those that are applied informally, often without conscious intent. The intense loyalty that most people reserve for their primary groups attests to the potential effectiveness of informal rewards—a smile, a word, a spontaneous gesture of friendship—in encouraging adherence to group norms.

Social control in most human groups seldom requires physical punishment or other strong sanctions. Through the socialization process, an individual internalizes the standards of the groups that are important to him and thus monitors his own behavior. The feelings of "pride" that come with self-approval have much the same effect as rewards given by others; the feelings of distress and anxiety that we commonly term "bad conscience" can be every bit as painful as punishment administered by a group. Often social norms are internalized so completely that the mere contemplation of some act of deviation will result in self-recrimination and private embarrassment. In extreme cases self-sanctioning may be so severe that an individual will commit suicide rather than suffer his own self-imposed feelings of guilt.

GROUP RANKING SYSTEMS AS INFLUENCES ON PERSONALITY

Group ranking systems have the effect of narrowing the range of contact among members. In a large university, for example, undergraduate students interact most often and most intimately with other undergraduates; graduate students,

---

12. For a fuller explanation of this theory of learning see, for example, Ernest R. Hilgard and Gordon H. Bower, *Theories of Learning*, 3rd ed. (New York: Appleton-Century-Crofts, 1966).

13. John T. Doby, *Introduction to Social Psychology* (New York: Appleton-Century-Crofts, 1966), pp. 172–173.

14. See Albert Bandura and Richard H. Walters, *Social Learning and Personality Development* (New York: Holt, Rinehart and Winston, Inc., 1963), p. 5.

with other graduate students; faculty members, with other faculty members. The same principle holds true in all stratified groups: interaction between individuals in one stratum and those in another is largely limited to formal contacts. Much informal social learning, therefore, is a product of reciprocal influences between people who have the same general rank and perspective.

The impact of ranking systems on the socialization process becomes dramatically clear at the community level, where a person's position in the class structure narrowly channels his exposure to cultural norms. Because interaction between the members of different social classes is severely limited, each of the classes tends to develop and maintain a distinctive subculture and thus to transmit distinctive values and patterns of conduct to new members.

Summarizing research on social class differences in the United States, Barber has noted a number of behavioral patterns that seem to distinguish lower-class people in general from people in the middle class:

Lower class people . . . participate in fewer voluntary associations and other organized activities. They have less facility in reading and writing. They read fewer magazines and listen to the "less serious" radio and television programs. They know less about political issues and have less expressed interest in them. They are less critical of the sources of the daily news. They are more timid about expressing their opinions to poll interviewers and more often give "don't know" answers. They know less about such matters that concern their economic and social interests as income taxes, price controls, birth control, and consumer's cooperation. They have lower occupational aspirations and tend to go into blind-alley jobs. They have lower expectations for future income and they are much less likely than people in the middle class to say that the future holds good opportunities for them to improve their educational, occupational, or economic position.[15]

These characteristic patterns of belief, interest, motivation, and attitude are perpetuated by the socialization process. As Cohen and others have noted, children in middle-class families are exposed to a set of values representing a kind of tempered version of the Protestant Ethic (page 120), an orientation to which lower-class families are much less deeply committed.[16] The central value in this orientation is *achievement.* Middle-class norms define "getting ahead" as a kind of moral obligation. An individual without ambition to improve his position in society is seen as somehow lacking in character. Members of the middle class have great faith in "rationality"—in what can be accomplished by planning ahead and by allocating time, money, and energy efficiently. Children are taught the value of foregoing immediate gratification and rewards in the interest of attaining long-range goals.

The value orientations of most lower-class people place much less emphasis on future achievement. Although ambition is by no means deplored, economic security is generally stressed more than upward mobility or long-range goals. Members of the lower class are much less likely than middle-class people to put much faith in careful, long-range planning. Life over the short term seems unpredictable enough; enjoyment should be taken when it can. If a lower-class family receives an unexpected financial windfall, it is likely to spend the money right away for something that can be enjoyed "here and now." A middle-class family, by contrast, is inclined to save for "a rainy day."

Middle-class families stress the value of self-reliance and self-improvement. When a boy becomes old enough to start thinking about work, he is taught that the most desirable job is one in which he can exercise his ability and initiative to get ahead. A lower-class boy, by contrast, is more oriented toward valuing a job that offers security and immediate rewards.

Different orientations to achievement are reflected even in attitudes toward recreation. Middle-class parents believe firmly that children should spend their leisure time doing something that is "worthwhile," such as learning to play a musical instrument, participating in sports, or pursuing a hobby. Members of the lower class are much more tolerant of youngsters who spend their free time doing "nothing" or "just hanging around" with their friends.

Middle-class children are taught that good manners, courtesy, and proper clothes are important in building and maintaining pleasant social relationships. Lower-class families are less concerned with "propriety," at least as it is

15. Bernard Barber, "Social Class Differences in Educational Life Chances," *Teachers College Record,* 63 (1961), 108.

16. The following summary of middle- and lower-class characteristics has been adapted from Albert K. Cohen, *Delinquent Boys* (New York: The Free Press, 1955), pp. 84–87.

commonly defined, and they care less what "other people" think. The two classes also have different attitudes about the appropriateness of physical violence as a means for settling disputes. If a middle-class boy comes home with a bloody nose or a black eye, his parents are likely to lecture him about fighting and to encourage him to make friends with his opponent. A lower-class boy, on the other hand, may be told that he should learn how to use his fists so that people won't push him around.

The significance of differences between middle- and lower-class orientations is not that one is necessarily "better" than the other, but that American society is run, for the most part, by the middle class. Middle-class standards have become a kind of measuring rod for assessing the behavior and values of all in a number of important areas of life. Thus, an individual who has internalized a different set of standards may find it difficult to fit in (much less to excel) in school, in business, and in many other activities. For such an individual, the net result of socialization may be to severely limit his opportunities for upward mobility in a society that stresses success.

AGENTS OF SOCIALIZATION

The personal organization of the individual is shaped by the total pattern of his social experience, but certain types of groups and institutions can be singled out for the special part they play in the socialization process. Some of the principal agents of socialization, such as the family and the school, have a clear mandate from society to "train" new generations of members—to transmit the society's cultural heritage and to teach its accepted ways of acting, thinking, and feeling. Agents such as peer groups and the mass media, by contrast, do most of their "teaching" incidentally, influencing how the individual perceives and responds to his social world. Other more specialized agents of socialization are the various formal groups an individual joins in the course of his life; to a greater or lesser extent, each one of them remolds the individual's attitudes, beliefs, and motivations to make him an effective group member.

THE FAMILY

The family has been central to every theory of personality formation, socialization, and child-rearing that has been formulated within the behavioral sciences.[17] It is the family that has always borne the major responsibility for teaching the child the essentials of social order and culture in his society and for guiding his personal development.

Psychoanalytic interpretations. Freud's theories of personality (page 131) have greatly influenced psychological interpretations of the family's role in the socialization process. In Freudian theory it is specifically the task of the family to develop the child's superego, that is, to instill in him the moral values and norms of his society so that he obtains effective guides for controlling his behavior according to culturally approved patterns.

Freud also made much of the various stages of psychological development within the context of the family. He wrote extensively about the *Oedipus complex* and the *Electra complex*. According to these theories, the young child develops a sexual attachment for the parent of the opposite sex. Consequently, he feels jealous and hostile toward the parent of the same sex, even though society insists that he love this parent, too. The child must resolve this dilemma (through adequate socialization) in order to become a mature and socially adjusted adult.

Freud's theory of the *Oedipus complex* has been much modified and seriously questioned by anthropological and sociological research. The distinguished anthropologist Bronislaw Malinowski studied the society of the Trobriand Islanders, in which the maternal uncle had the major responsibility for socializing the young male.[18] At the same time, the child lived in a monogamous family situation much as we do. In this situation, there was hostility toward the uncle (who was often a hard task-master), but seldom was there hostility or resentment toward the father. The child in this society was much aware of the sexual relationship between the

---

17. See Gardner Murphy, *Personality: A Biosocial Approach to Origins and Structure* (New York: Harper and Brothers, 1947), esp. Ch. 37, "The Family as Mediator of Culture," pp. 842–865.
18. Bronislaw Malinowski, *Sex and Repression in Savage Society* (New York: Humanities Press, 1927).

father and mother, who went to no special pains to conceal this activity from the child. Malinowski's research raised serious doubts concerning the *source* of the presumed hostility toward the father in the Western family. It may not be sexual in nature but simply due to the role of the father as a primary agent of socialization, disciplining the child and making him learn acceptable modes of conduct.

Sociological interpretations. In primitive and traditional societies, the family is the principal agent of socialization throughout a long period of childhood and even adolescence. This has become much less true in urban-industrial societies such as the United States. There are several reasons why this is the case. For one thing, more and more outside groups are taking

over child-rearing and socialization tasks that were formerly carried out by the family. Nursery schools and kindergartens take over part of the socialization of the very young. When a child enters school, he encounters not only a formal system of socialization but also informal systems among his peers. Others, such as boy scout leaders, also act as agents of socialization when the child is away from home during substantial parts of the day. For the working mother, the problem is compounded by having to leave the child in the care of others for long periods of time. The implications of this for the emotional security and overt behavior of the children involved is still a matter of much debate.[19]

In the lowest socioeconomic levels of society, the impact of the working mother may be more obvious. Among Negro families in urban slums, for example, about a third are fatherless through desertion or divorce. The relative instability of the Negro family and the role of the

19. Alex Inkeles, "Society, Social Structure and Child Socialization," in Clausen, *op. cit.*, pp. 121–122.

Today, in both affluent and poor urban homes, there may be no steadily present male role of any kind for a boy to model himself after.

mother as the principal economic provider has been widely documented.[20] In such families, children of pre-school age may simply be left home in the care of slightly older siblings while the mother tries to earn a livelihood. Consequently, their socialization process is unenriched by the experiences that adults in other social classes normally provide for children. One result can be "cultural deprivation," which can permanently handicap the child for school work.

In urban society, the father is often away from the home during the greater part of the child's waking hours. By contrast, in the rural home the father was more often occupationally visible to the children as he carried out his farming duties. Indeed, boys were normally required to help in the tasks.

Today, in the usual urban home, the presence of the mother provides the girl with an appropriate role model, but the boy has little or no direct experience with the occupational aspects of the male role. In fact, with the father absent during the day and often preoccupied with his own pursuits on weekends, there may be no steadily present male role of any kind for the child to model himself after. The result of such a situation for the male child may be what Parsons has called "sex-role blurring."[21] With the mother as the main socialization agent, the boy may take on many of the mannerisms, attitudes, and orientations of the female. He may enter the teen years with a somewhat feminine self-image which will require drastic revision.

Girls or boys raised in families where an opposite sex sibling is present seem to take on different traits than do those in families where the children are all of the same sex. In exploring this problem, Brim found that girls with brothers have more masculine traits than girls without brothers.[22] At the same time, they did not evidence fewer feminine traits; rather, they seemed to have a broader behavioral repertoire. The pattern with boys was similar, except that the boys seemed to displace some masculine patterns with feminine ones.

Overall, then, the socialization experiences of the child and the role of the family as an agent in this process depend upon a host of factors, such as the rural or urban characteristics of the family, the occupational activities of the parents, the family's position in the social class structure, its organization in terms of the presence or absence of either parent, and the sex composition of the offspring themselves.

THE PEER GROUP

Next to the family, the peer group is probably the most influential agent of socialization in the life of the individual. In the earliest years, the child in a peer group plays at society. He develops ideas about norms, roles, systems of social control, and conceptions of differential ranking. The child also learns fundamental skills in dealing with others. He learns what their tolerance limits are, how to cooperate, to share, and to develop friendships; he acquires the ability to predict what others will do under a wide variety of circumstances. These social skills and orientations permit the child to interact successfully within his miniature model of society. If he does not, he will be unceremoniously excluded from the group.

The peer group is not an agent of deliberate socialization. Its major purpose for its members is *recreational*. It exists because the members enjoy peer group interaction for its own sake. Nevertheless, "cliques" and "gangs" unintentionally exert a great amount of pressure on their members to acquire the values, orientations, and outlooks of the group. Thus, the individual member usually internalizes strongly the codes and expectations of his peer group so that his position in this highly valued group will not be jeopardized.

Peer groups and other-directedness. David Riesman has suggested that the peer group is becoming *the* most important agent of socialization in modern society. He has described three very different types of general personality structure that result from distinctive patterns of socialization.[23] In the primitive and traditional societies, the coherent culture and stable patterns of social organization provide an adequate basis for behavioral definition. Socialization in such societies usually results in a "tradition-

---

20. Jessie Bernard, *Marriage and Family Among Negroes* (Englewood Cliffs, N.J.: Prentice-Hall, Inc., 1965), pp. 13–21.

21. Parsons, *op. cit.*

22. Orville G. Brim, Jr., "Family Structure and Sex Role Learning by Children: A Further Analysis of Helen Koch's Data," in *Selected Studies in Marriage and the Family*, rev. ed., eds. Robert F. Winch, Robert McGinnis, and Herbert R. Barringer (New York: Holt, Rinehart and Winston, Inc., 1962), pp. 275–290. This article was adapted from *Sociometry*, 21 (1958), 1:1–16.

23. David Riesman, in collaboration with Reuel Denney and Nathan Glazer, *The Lonely Crowd* (New Haven, Conn.: Yale University Press, 1950).

directed" man, one who looks to the accepted ways of his society for guidance in personal conduct.

The "inner-directed" man, on the other hand, is most often found in a society undergoing rapid normative change. Since the external codes around him do not provide stable guides for personal conduct, such guidance must come from within. The socialization processes of such a society (as, for example, in nineteenth-century America) emphasize strong personal ideals and inner moral convictions to give adequate direction to personal behavior.

In modern society, Riesman says, people tend to be "other directed." They look to their peers for ideas as to how they should behave. There is a considerable need for social approval and a great fear of social rejection. The "other-directed" man has neither a strong social order with stable and deeply institutionalized behavioral norms to serve as his guide, nor a strong and independent set of internal convictions about what constitutes proper conduct regardless of his situation. Instead, he has a particular sensitivity to the probable approvals and disapprovals of his peers, which he uses to define his responses to a wide variety of life situations.

The "generation gap." In many contemporary societies, the importance of the peer group can be seen in the growing disparity between the norms of young people and their parents. By the time the individual is a young teen-ager, the peer group is making demands on him to think, act, and feel in ways that are often in sharp contrast to the norms of older generations. Modern youth cultures have emerged that emphasize new art forms, less rigid sex mores, innovative modes of dress, protest, colorful hairstyles, experimentation with drugs, and many other deviations from the accepted practices of most parents. Quite often, parental values and expectations are either subverted or openly rejected.[24]

While this gap between generations appears to be increasing in the United States, adoles-

cence is not a period of conflict in every society. Among the Hopi Indians, for example, it is a period for gradually assuming adult roles.

As the Hopi boy approaches adolescence his economic responsibilities increase. He now accompanies his father or grandfather to the fields or grazing areas. By the age of fourteen he is expected to have mastered most agricultural skills and to be able to take charge of his own herd and his mother's fields. In winter he accompanies his elders into the kiva [men's ceremonial chamber] where the men's handcrafts, including weaving and moccasin making, are taught him. Here also he is expected to learn tribal lore and master the rituals of . . . the wider Hopi society.[25]

As we see from this passage, adolescence for the Hopi is a period in which youths greatly increase their interaction with *adults* as their "significant others." As they move toward becoming what their parents and grandparents have been before them, their ideas of self gradually become mature.

By contrast, in contemporary Western urban society the generations tend to become compartmentalized, with young people during adolescence *decreasing* their involvement with adults. This is partly a consequence of shifting the responsibility for socialization from the family to other agencies.

The school has become the locus of activities for children and adolescents whose labor is no longer needed by society. One sociologist has suggested that this has had the effect of cutting adolescents off from the rest of society and making them carry out their whole social life with others of their own age. Of the high-school-age individual, Coleman says:

With his fellows, he comes to constitute a small society, one that has most of its important interactions *within* itself, and maintains only a few threads of connection with the outside adult society. In our modern world of mass communication and rapid diffusion of ideas and knowledge, it is hard to realize that separate subcultures can exist right under the very noses of adults—subcultures with languages all their own, with special symbols, and most importantly, with value systems that may differ from adults'. . . . To put it simply, these young people speak a different language. What is more relevant to the present point, the language they speak is becoming more and more different.[26]

24. Kingsley Davis, "The Sociology of Parent-Youth Conflict," *American Sociological Review*, 5 (August 1940), 523–535.

25. Stuart A. Queen, Robert W. Habenstein, and John B. Adams, *The Family in Various Cultures,* rev. ed. (New York: J. B. Lippincott Company, 1961), p. 60.

26. James S. Coleman, *The Adolescent Society* (New York: The Free Press, 1961), p. 3.

Today's young people are demanding not only more personal autonomy but also a restructuring of society itself. To many adults, their behavior appears to be irresponsible rebellion against legitimate authority and responsible socialization. To the youths involved, rebellion is in part a rejection of dependency on their parents and other adults and in part a protest against the whole impersonal system that has gradually been replacing the family in the socialization process. These emerging conflicts may further compartmentalize the generations in our society and make socialization in adolescence even more heavily influenced by peers rather than parents.

THE SCHOOL

Much of the deliberate socialization that occurs in our society falls on the shoulders of various bureaucratically organized associations. Socialization responsibilities that are allocated to the family in primitive and traditional societies are in our society usually the province of such groups as the school, the work organization, the church, and the military. Of these groups, the school has the most universally recognized responsibility for transmitting the ways of the general society to younger members, while other types of associations concentrate on more specialized socialization tasks.

In its formal structure, the school is a rationally organized bureaucracy—a social machine designed to "process" batches of human beings who are fed into the system at the bottom and who are expected to emerge some years later with useful and socially approved modifications in their knowledge, skills, values, attitudes, and general orientations to society. As the statistics on dropouts and delinquency make clear, however, the school does not always succeed in its task. To understand some of the reasons for its failures, we need to look beyond the formal structure of the school and examine the ways in which it is linked to other groups and to social processes over which it has little control. Of special significance are the values and loyalties that individual teachers and learners bring to the school situation.

Most of the teachers in our schools are recruited from the middle class. This back-ground, plus their own "processing" in teacher training institutions, results in special viewpoints and outlooks. Normally, teachers are very strongly committed to the set of norms and orientations that we previously described as "the middle-class value system." They see themselves as the protectors of the "American way of life," which means life as middle-class people define and live it.

At the same time, many schools draw large proportions of their students from working- and lower-class homes. As we have indicated, such children are seldom very strongly committed to the middle-class ideals and values which teachers will use to evaluate their merits and performance. As a consequence, lower-class children have a good chance of being perceived as poor performers, uncommitted to traditional values, and unwilling to make the sacrifices needed for

The generation gap is evident as these two students look at material for a contemporary course at the University Center for Adult Education in Detroit.

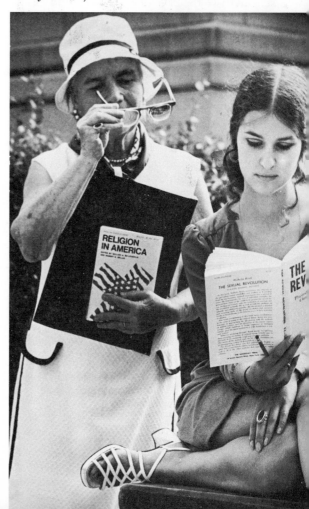

attaining the all-important "success." The following excerpt from a book by Herbert R. Kohl shows a clash between working- and middle-class culture in a school situation. Compare these two poems by sixth-grade children:

SHOP WITH MOM
I love to shop with mom
And talk to the friendly grocer
And help her make the list
Seems to make us closer.
　　　　　　—Nellie, age 11

THE JUNKIES
When they are
in the street
they pass it
along to each
other but when
they see the
police they would
run some would
just stand still
and be beat
so pity ful
that they want
to cry

　　　　　　—Mary, age 11

Nellie's poem received high praise. Her teacher liked the rhyme "closer" and "grocer," and thought she said a great deal in four lines. Most of all the teacher was pleased that Nellie expressed such a pleasant and healthy thought. . . . I was moved and excited by Mary's poem and made the mistake of showing it to the teacher who edited the school newspaper. She was horrified. First of all, she informed me, Mary couldn't possibly know what junkies were, and, moreover, the other children wouldn't be interested in such a poem. There weren't any rhymes or clearly discernible meter. The word "pityful" was split up incorrectly, "be beat" wasn't proper English and, finally, it wasn't really poetry but just the ramblings of a disturbed girl.[27]

As this example points out, the school is potentially an arena for a serious conflict of values. In the eyes of children who have not internalized the middle-class ethic of ambition, self-discipline, manners, individual responsibility, and the like, school can be perceived as a punishing activity where they are doomed to experience few successes and many failures. School may even appear as an *enemy*, designed to hurt and embarrass them. This conflict between the middle-class expectations of teachers and the lower-class orientations of many students can seriously subvert the best intentioned efforts of the educational system to train all citizens equally for adult roles and responsibilities.

Also important in the informal structure of the school are the subcultures that are fostered and maintained by students themselves. Much "lore" is perpetuated about particular teachers, other students, courses of study, sex, and ways to "beat the system." Modes of dress, dance forms, and speech mannerisms peculiar to the age group are innovated, diffused, and adopted as part of these ever-changing subcultures. While such subcultural content may or may not be directly subversive to the larger intellectual goals of the school, it is generally not particularly supportive. At best, it is merely distractive.

In addition to school-wide subcultural patterns, the informal structure of the school includes the many cliques and subgroupings into which students divide themselves. These also support particular subcultural values and orientations that play a part in the socialization process. Much sociological research has explored the nature of these clique structures and their meaning to the child, particularly in the high school.[28] Generally, there are elite groups at the top of the status system, outcasts at the bottom, and various kinds of groups in between.

In many ways, the relationship between the child and these informal structures defines the socialization experience he will receive from the school. They modify the efforts of the formal system to transmit and instill community-approved values, motivations, and skills. In some cases cliques are totally destructive of socially approved goals and values. Under certain circumstances, they can provide alternative ways for obtaining social approval, a positive self-image, and personal esteem through outright delinquency and vandalism.[29] In other

---

27. Herbert R. Kohl, *Teaching the "Unteachable"* (New York: The New York Review, 1967), p. 15.

28. Robert S. and Helen M. Lynd, *Middletown: A Study in American Culture* (New York: Harcourt, Brace & World, Inc., 1929); August B. Hollingshead, *Elmtown's Youth* (New York: John Wiley & Sons, Inc., 1949); Patricia C. Sexton, *The American School: A Sociological Analysis* (Englewood Cliffs, N.J.: Prentice-Hall, Inc., 1967).

29. Cohen, *op. cit.*, pp. 121–179.

cases they may link the individual quite directly with the values of "Main Street" in ways which the school cannot accomplish.[30]

AGENTS OF SPECIALIZED SOCIALIZATION

Specialized groups such as churches, corporations, the military services, labor unions, and other associations of all kinds provide specialized socialization for particular segments of the society. Of these, we will look at the corporation and the military services, both of which attempt to "reshape" their recruits so that they will behave more effectively as group members.

The corporation. William H. Whyte, Jr., has analyzed the process by which "executive material" is recruited, evaluated, and utilized in various levels of management. He places particular emphasis upon the way the corporation shapes and influences the values and activities of those whom it retains and moves up the ladder.[31] Whyte contends that the organization serves as a powerful agency for suppressing the creative innovator, the driving self-motivated individualist identified in popular thought as a potential captain of industry. While such two-fisted types were destined in the "rough-and-tumble" days of American industry to drive quickly to the top, he states, today's corporations will quickly channel them out of their management systems as unorthodox and even dangerous.

Today the "organization man" is more likely to move upward through the administrative hierarchy. He fits in smoothly with the modern committee approach to management; he "does not think up ideas himself, but mediates other people's ideas, and so democratically that he never lets his own judgment override the decisions of the group."[32]

In his dealings with subordinates, the organization man is concerned primarily with "human relations" and with the techniques of welding employees into a loyal and smoothly running team. He is a generalist rather than a specialist, a practitioner of persuading other people to work.

Whyte sees the corporation as demanding this type of personality configuration and the system of higher education as operating so as to provide it. One may or may not agree with

all points of this interesting analysis, but undoubtedly the corporation is becoming increasingly important as an agent of socialization and as an influence on the prior socialization of its recruits.

The military services. Military socialization has been the topic of humor and fiction, of controversy, and of systematic sociological analysis.[33] While the several branches of the military vary considerably in the details of their approach to deliberate socialization, they share certain goals and procedures. A brief sociological description of the socialization process in the Marine Corps, often ranked as one of the best fighting groups in the world, will give some insight into the reasons for its effectiveness.

The Marine-to-be arrives at the training base psychologically structured as a civilian. His past socialization, self-image, and general orientations tend to support his identity with his former life. The Corps systematically suppresses this identity in order to transform the recruit into a Marine.

First, his physical body is transformed. His head is shaved. His civilian clothes are removed and he is issued shapeless dungarees that make him look like something out of a Li'l Abner cartoon strip.

The Marine "boot" is crowded into a barracks with others like himself. He is not even permitted the individual touch of pasting his own selection of pictures inside his locker box. Like each man around him, he has a given number and kind of undershirts, socks, shoelaces, belts, etc. The last external vestiges of individuality have been removed; he is as much like the others as it is possible to be. Lest he retreat vicariously into his former identity, his communication with his past is temporarily restricted. He is permitted to write to his immediate family but, for the moment, to no one else. He is restricted to his immediate barracks or camp area.

To hasten the systematic suppression of his civilian self-image, his new drill instructor and his assistants demand a degree of physical per-

30. Sexton, *op. cit.,* p. 93.

31. William H. Whyte, Jr., *The Organization Man* (New York: Simon & Schuster, Inc., 1956).

32. *Ibid.,* p. 150.

33. Sanford M. Dornbusch, "The Military Academy as an Assimilating Institution," *Social Forces,* 33, No. 4 (May 1955), 316–321.

formance that the recruit cannot meet. Running five miles around a parade ground before breakfast is calculated to exhaust all but the most extraordinary physical specimens. Complex commands confuse him. Official policies to the contrary, he is degraded by kicks in the posterior, by raps on his helmet with a stick, and by some of the vilest name-calling and general verbal abuse that human beings have ever invented. Those in charge have traditionally taken great delight in inventing degrading punishments of an absurd nature for picayune infractions. Marines for years have found themselves engaged in such unusual activities as scrubbing extensive latrine areas with a toothbrush or chanting self-accusations while running up and down the platoon area.

After many days of this, the individual comes to the conclusion that he is, in fact, an unworthy and low individual who is a disgrace to himself, his family, his country, and most of all to the Marine Corps, just as he has been told over and over. By careful manipulation of the mechanisms underlying the looking-glass self, those in charge have seriously challenged his former concept of self.

While this has been going on, however, other things have also been happening. First, no one can be more miserable than the Marine "boot." The shared punishment and the shared pride in each individual's ability to "take all that can be dished out" welds the trainees together into a brotherhood that becomes an effective substitute for former "significant others" and reference groups. This is the germ of the *esprit de corps* that the whole process is designed to foster.

Secondly, the recruit gradually becomes able to perform the arduous physical tasks that are demanded of him. Constant exercise, good diet, and regular hours provide the basis for a physical transformation that gives him a great boost in morale. He becomes able to do with ease what formerly appeared to be superhuman tasks.

Finally, the sergeant in charge one day tells the group, somewhat begrudgingly, that maybe they aren't such a bad bunch after all. As the group increases in proficiency, additional praise is given. This is almost always praise for the group rather than for specific persons, so as to reinforce the group identity of the individual. Gradually, the new Marine is given more freedom, snappier uniforms, and increased praise. The rewards for conformity are sweet. Systematically, his self-concept has been rebuilt as a member of the Corps, and he has intense pride in his new status. At the end of the training period, when there is a "graduation ceremony" for his platoon, he feels that he has made the grade and thinks of himself as a Marine. His new value system follows a profile carefully designed to make him a reliable and effective combat soldier.

THE MASS MEDIA

The average child in American society today spends an astonishing amount of time with television and the other mass media. On the basis of nation-wide studies, Professor Wilbur Schramm has concluded that "From ages three through sixteen, he spends more time on television than on school."[34] Television viewing takes up about one sixth of the waking hours of the statistically average child. There is evidence that viewing is heavier in the lower class than in the middle class, but the total time spent with *all* communication media by American children as a whole probably accounts for more of their time than any other activity except sleep.

What does this all mean in terms of socialization? Heavy exposure to media is easy to document, but unraveling the influence of media on children is not a simple task. Sociological research has revealed two major types of socialization influences on children: the *cultural norms theory* of media influence and the *incidental learning function* of mass communications.[35]

The media and cultural norms. The basic idea of the cultural norms theory is that the media can provide for audience members a "definition of the situation" on a variety of issues. By emphasizing certain topics, stressing particular interpretations, or overusing specific themes (it is hypothesized), the media may create the distorted impression that their "defi-

34. Wilbur Schramm, *Television in the Lives of Our Children* (Stanford, Calif.: Stanford University Press, 1961), p. 30.

35. Although television and the other media have been charged with everything from causing juvenile delinquency to ruining the cultural tastes of the nation, research has thus far failed to turn up any convincing evidence of immediate and direct causal links between the media and particular patterns of social behavior. For a detailed discussion of this issue, see Chapter 13, "Mass Communication."

nition"—or set of norms—is a reflection of the real society. For example, if sexual promiscuity is regularly portrayed as widely practiced, the young viewer may accept such definitions as normative in the society. When he must define his own overt behavior in such a situation, norms internalized from media sources may guide his conduct. This same type of relationship may prevail with respect to such matters as the use of alcohol, tobacco, drugs, and even violence. If violence is depicted repeatedly (by movies, television, comics, etc.) as a socially acceptable means of settling differences, this may provide the individual with norms for so defining his own behavior when confronted with a situation where violence is one option open to him.

The cultural norms theory takes into account the factor of differential association. That is, most persons are exposed to many sources of norms, which accept *and* reject such things as sexual promiscuity, drug abuse, and violence. Therefore, the media are only one source among many for defining norms. However, for individuals who lack counter associations, the media may play a rather decisive role in providing behavioral definitions. Unfortunately, there is insufficient research on the cultural norms theory to provide a basis for accepting or rejecting it. Nevertheless, it does suggest ways in which indirect forms of socialization can result from long-term exposure to certain types of media content.

The media and incidental learning. The media constitute an important source for learning about society. However, this is incidental learning, an unplanned by-product of entertainment. Through television, the movies, and other media, the child catches glimpses of an adult world of which he is not yet a part, but which holds great fascination for him. In this way, he acquires conceptions of people's values, numerous social roles, and other kinds of social knowledge without really seeking it.

Incidental socialization is not entirely understood, but there is a growing suspicion on the part of social scientists that it may be important in giving the child incorrect interpretations about his society. To explore the potential role of the media in this regard, a team of sociologists monitored six months of television broadcasts as they appeared on the screens of a small midwestern community. The goal of the research was to study the world of work as it was portrayed in ordinary television fare.[36] Over 450 fairly detailed occupational portrayals were noted and analyzed. The labor force as it was depicted on television was then compared with the actual labor force in the state where the study was conducted. Data were obtained from the Bureau of the Census concerning the proportions of the state's labor force that were in different categories of work.

The televised occupational distribution departed from reality in a number of significant ways. For example, no factory worker appeared among the 450 occupations portrayed on T.V., though such workers constituted more than one fifth of the actual labor force in the state where the study was made. About a third of the workers portrayed on television were professionals, though in fact professionals made up only about one tenth of the labor force. A full third of the televised workers were engaged in occupations associated with the law.

If a child had only television upon which to form beliefs about the adult world of work, he might acquire some strange ideas. Not only were there the over- and under-representations mentioned, but numerous other distortions were evident. But the real issue raised by such research is, of course, its impact on the young audience: Do children actually develop badly distorted ideas about the world of work as a consequence of socialization from television?

To study this question, a second research project was designed to follow up the analysis of occupational portrayals on T.V. This follow-up study was done with school children in the same community. Special questionnaires were devised for interviewing a sample of 237 children. The idea was to measure how much they knew about the roles and requirements of the jobs under study and how well they could rank the jobs into a socioeconomic hierarchy that would correspond to adult rankings of the same occupations. Three types of jobs were studied: those with which the child had extensive personal contact; those which he encountered mainly on television; and those which were present in the community but not particularly visible to the child either directly or through the medium.

---

36. Melvin L. DeFleur, "Occupational Roles as Portrayed on Television," *Public Opinion Quarterly*, 28 (Spring 1964), 57–74.

The research team discovered that the children were most familiar with occupations with which they had had some form of personal contact. However, occupational roles that had been frequently portrayed on T.V. were understood almost as well. The children had a poor understanding of jobs that were present in the community but not visible to them.

Overall, this study showed that television can be a rich source for incidental learning about occupations. Children of all social levels were able to describe the duties, modes of dress, and relative social rank of such roles as butler and head waiter, even though they had never encountered them in person. At the same time, the findings indicated that there were numerous distortions and stereotypes in the ideas the children entertained about the occupational roles studied.[37]

The findings of such research are significant for understanding not only the role of the media in the socialization process but how they operate in conjunction with other sources of learning. Modern society requires that a child make a complex series of decisions concerning his relationship to the labor force—decisions that may have the most profound effect upon his future way of life. Yet, systematic agents of planned socialization (schools, churches, and the like) provide scant help in informing him objectively of the characteristics and consequences of most occupational roles. In this area and in many others, the media become important agents of socialization by default. In providing the child with incidental information about the social world, some of which is inaccurate, they help shape his ideas about what life as an adult should be like.

SOCIALIZATION
AND THE LIFE CYCLE

Experiences in infancy and childhood are especially crucial in shaping personality, but the socialization process never ends. As the individual moves through his life cycle, he assumes a progression of general roles such as worker, spouse, parent, widower, and retired person. Finally, as the end of his life span nears, he must face the unpleasant reality of being a dying person. Each of these broad roles involves special demands and expectations. So too do the hundreds of limited or specialized roles that an individual occupies in the course of his life. As we noted in introducing this chapter, socialization is a continuing process of adjustment to changing expectations and demands.

SOCIALIZATION
IN ADOLESCENCE

In American society today, adolescence is no longer simply "that period in the life of a child when he is no longer regarded as a child but not yet accorded the roles and status of a full-fledged adult."[38] Not only are young people increasingly isolated from adult society, but in addition, the period of adolescence itself is being extended in time. It once ended with graduation from high school or even earlier. With entry into the labor force and early marriage, prior generations were adults for the most part in their late teen years. Today, adolescence for many individuals stretches from age ten or eleven to the time they leave college at age twenty-two or so and take their first adult jobs. The increasing emphasis on advanced degrees means that a sizeable proportion of young people may remain adolescents, in the sense of being functionally dependent on support from others, into their late twenties or early thirties.

These trends, however, are not uniform at all levels of the society. Several rather distinct patterns of adolescence are discernible, each with its special problems of socialization. At the bottom of the socioeconomic scale, the school dropout rate is high. Clearly, youths who leave school before graduating from high school are not being socialized for the adult roles that are commonly associated with the "American way of life." Hence they do not so much reject the larger society as *become rejected by it.* They are barred from being a part of the "adolescent society" that continues on in the schools, and they cannot effectively enter the conventional adult world. For this group, adolescence ends early, but adulthood offers limited opportunities and rewards.

37. Melvin L. DeFleur and Lois B. DeFleur, "The Relative Contribution of Television as a Learning Source for Children's Occupational Knowledge," *American Sociological Review,* 32, No. 5 (October 1967), 777-789.

38. For a fuller discussion on the meaning of the term *adolescence,* see Hollingshead, *op. cit.,* pp. 5-7.

VIEWPOINTS   **ON BEING A WOMAN**

Somewhere along the line my brother and I managed to receive an utterly different education regarding ourselves and our own expectations from life. He was taught many things but what he learned was the need to develop a kind of inner necessity. I was taught many things but what I learned, ultimately, was that it was the prime vocation of my life to prepare myself for the love of a good man and the responsibilities of home-making and motherhood. All the rest, the education, the books, the jobs, that was all very nice and of course, why not? I was an intelligent girl, shouldn't I learn? *make* something of myself! but oh dolly, you'll see, in the end no woman could possibly be happy without a man to love and children to raise. What's more, came the heavy implication, if I *didn't* marry I would be considered an irredeemable failure.

How did I learn this? . . . The lessons were implicit and they took place in 100 different ways, in a continuous day-to-day exposure to an *attitude,* shared by all, about women, about what kind of creatures they were and what kind of lives they were meant to live; the lessons were administered not only by my parents but by the men and women, the boys and girls, all around me who, of course, had been made in the image of this attitude. . . .

Women . . . have never been prepared to assume responsibility; we have never been prepared to make demands upon ourselves; we have never been taught to expect the development of what is best in ourselves because no one has ever expected *anything* of us—or for us. Because no one has ever had any intention of turning over any serious work to us. Both we and the blacks lost the ballgame before we ever got up to play. . . .

In a time when all the real problems are solved, man makes up new ones in order to go on solving. He must have work, work that he considers real and serious, or he will die, he will simply shrivel up and die. That is the one certain characteristic of human beings. And it is the one characteristic, above all others, that the accidentally dominant white male asserts is not necessary to more than half the members of the race, i.e., the female of the species. This assertion is, quite simply, a lie. Nothing more, nothing less. A lie. That energy is alive in every woman in the world. It lies trapped and dormant like a growing tumor, and at its center there is despair, hot, deep, wordless.

Vivian Gornick
"Next Moment in History"

If it weren't for the disturbing quality that lurks behind every word of Women's Liberation literature, you might be tempted to write off the substantive stuff (men are sexual vampires, marriage is stunting and exploitative—that kind of complaint) as merely whacky. But it is difficult to ignore a movement whose pervasive theme is so resentful, envious, and despairing, and which draws to its liberated bosom thousands of females who would rather break down than build up. Sadder still, while Liberation is irresistible to women who want to be men, it is poison to women who want to be women. . . .

At the root of Liberation's determination to disintegrate the sexes is the disabling anxiety that *different* means the same thing as *inferior.* Anybody can see that women are as valuable as men, but they are no more the same than ears and eyes are. Women are biologically, constitutionally, and emotionally different from men. Why is this palpable fact so hard for so many women to swallow? Are we as confused as all that? . . .

No one with any brains would deny that women represent the largest wasted labor force in America, nor that, except for several crucial years, we need and should be given the opportunity to put our gifts—intellectual, artistic, political, whatever—to work on a regular, equal-pay basis. But when Liberation insists that women can be absolute "equals" with men in these spheres, they're ignoring what it's all about. For if women are willing to acknowledge the remotest emotional obligation to husband and children, especially to children during their fragile first five or six years of life, then they can't summon the time, physical energy, and psychic equipment to do two jobs simultaneously. You can't split a woman's life down the middle and expect each half, like a severed worm, to go happily crawling off, to survive and function in perfect health. . . .

Some women . . . may *enjoy* having their kids around, giving them lunch, talking with them, trying to discover the shape of *their* personalities, presiding over domestic war and peace, taking them to buy shoes, even kissing them. Here in sentimental form is what is missing in the Liberation's manifesto, which, like scores of radical solutions for injustices, bases its corrective assumptions on selective, fragmentary reasoning. Marlene Dixon says, "All women suffer from economic exploitation, from psychological deprivation, and from exploitive sexuality."

She didn't ask me.

Anne Bernays
"What Are You Supposed to Do
If You Like Children?"

For those who go to college, expectations can become a major problem during late adolescence. As the individual approaches graduation, he must begin to think seriously about a job and usually also about marriage and a family of his own. Often he is unprepared for this change in roles. Graduate school may be an attractive alternative to joining the larger society, which he has been either overtly or covertly rejecting for a period of years. Such alternatives as the Peace Corps also seem to have acted as important vehicles for helping adolescents achieve some sort of adult self-identity without committing themselves completely to the ways of adult society.

While these patterns of adolescence are discernible in American society, they are by no means the entire story. Some perspective is needed here. Probably the majority of college students are still concerned primarily with finding their own place in an affluent society. They may not be prepared for adult roles in a specific sense, but their socialization has made them flexible. They have been subjected to a variety of socializing environments and they have learned to "play it cool." Perhaps the specific cultural content of socialization during this period is not as important as the learning of a process. The very discontinuity between adolescence and its prior and subsequent periods teaches youth that change is continuous, that it is often unpredictable, and that one might as well be prepared to endure the difficult adjustments it involves.

SOCIALIZATION IN ADULT LIFE

The meaning of adulthood is changing as people can expect to live longer and are required to fill changing roles. The roles of husbands and wives, fathers, mothers, and breadwinners are more complex than ever before in history. Discontinuity in the socialization process may be inevitable in modern society.

The adult female role. During early childhood girls undoubtedly internalize various domestic and child-rearing aspects of their adult roles through anticipatory socialization. However, during the period of adolescence the process is interrupted. The emphasis for the young female is deflected to romantic and "glamour" roles during the dating and courtship stage. During this period very little emphasis is placed on the acquisition of domestic skills or on learning what it takes to be a good wife.

Within a relatively few years after marriage the female may experience an identity crisis that centers around the very acquisition of adequate role definitions for her adult years. For example, a woman in our contemporary middle-class society will normally have borne all her children within six or eight years after marriage. Within five years she will no longer be the dominant influence on their socialization. Modern industry, with its prepackaged frozen meals, ready-made clothing, and electrical household appliances, has reduced her homemaking activities to a minimum. Her counterpart in the early part of the century had more than a full-time job just getting the meals and doing the housework. Today, these activities occupy only part of the adult female's time.

The scope of both her motherly role and her domestic responsibilities are sharply reduced by the time she reaches her late thirties. With average life expectancy well into the seventies, she has more than half of her adult years ahead of her. Yet, she has no demanding and complex role responsibilities comparable to those of the male toward which to direct her energies.

There are alternatives among her choices for avoiding "social death" at mid-life. Many women (close to 40 percent) return to the labor force. While some do so because of perceived economic necessity or advantage, many do so to give their lives greater meaning. Others enter the world of civic affairs or club work. Still others attempt (often with limited success) to return to the glamour and romantic roles of their adolescence. Research is badly needed on the relationship between the female's adolescent roles and her subsequent role choices. We know little about the way in which earlier socialization affects her patterns of choice in adult life.

The adult male role. The male in an industrial society also faces strains and stresses that were unknown in earlier generations. His self-image and indeed his entire personal organization must be altered as he enters the impersonal roles of the labor force, the responsibilities of marriage, and the demands of parenthood. A

Where and how do the elderly citizens of our society live? Who cares for those who are not able, physically or economically, to care for themselves? A small portion of retired couples and individuals can afford to take it easy in a warm climate. Others make new friends, pursue new hobbies such as music, or involve themselves in volunteer work. But the vast majority of our aged—who are not so fortunate—spend the remaining years of their lives in other ways. Some must depend on their children for economic support, even though they feel cut off from family activities. And many of our elderly citizens have no alternative other than the lonely existence of an expensive rest home.

man must somehow learn to integrate his many roles and acquire the ability to move easily among them. His world of work may have little to do with his home and family.

Perhaps even more than the wife, the husband must handle transition through self-socialization. As he works up through the ladder of promotion, he widens his sphere of responsibilities and occupational contacts. He will probably change jobs at several points in his lifetime. He may move from one city to another, from small town to the city, from the city to the suburbs. All of these changes require resocialization, including adjustment to new life styles. The upwardly mobile middle-class male and his wife may experience pressures to alter their habits of dress, their manner of speech, their tastes in food, and even their religion and politics. We still know very little about how the socialization process facilitates such transitions or how it enables an individual to maintain his basic personality structure while adjusting to new roles and expectations.

THE END OF THE SOCIALIZATION PROCESS

It is doubtful that becoming old was ever very easy for man, but it is made more and more difficult in modern society for two reasons. First, our society venerates youth, not old age. Secondly, old age is marked by the loss of significant roles that in younger years serve as important sources of personality maintenance.

The decline of group involvement. In older years, group ties that formerly linked the individual with significant others gradually collapse. As health fails and the individual is less and less active, group supports to the more meaningful aspects of life become harder to maintain.

We saw earlier that isolation from social interaction had a very serious impact on the maintenance of personality in adult years. Consequently, the aged will suffer personality impairment as isolation from others increases. What often seems to be physical decline in ability among the aged may in part be a result of progressive disengagement from social interaction. As long as the individual is under the pressure of complex role expectations from others, he has every prospect of maintaining

alertness into advanced years. In fact, numerous statesmen, scientists, musicians, jurists, and educators have produced some of their finest work in their later years. However, if the individual begins to lose his skills in the area of language and symbolic interaction, he will be less able to communicate with others and increasingly unable to use language internally in the process of thinking.

The role of elder. In our society, the question "Who am I?" is generally answered in terms of occupational role. Consequently, retirement from the labor force, which comes as a sudden and sharp break, creates an identity problem for the older male. In earlier times the individual withdrew from economic pursuits in a much more gradual way. In fact, traditional societies usually increased the responsibility and general status of an elder. Because he had lived longer than anyone else, he knew more and thus had a very important role to play. There was no rapid explosion of new scientific knowledge to displace his patiently accumulated lore. A good illustration is provided by the role of elder in the Chinese family under the traditional clan system:

Retirement did not mean loss of authority in decision-making. The elders were always consulted, and theirs was the final "yes" or "no," if they chose to take part in family councils. Withdrawal from such activities did not mean complete loss of other functions, such as scholarly pursuits and religious duties, art and hobbies, or the care and education of grandchildren. Certainly it meant no loss of position or status in the household, for the place of the elder was at the top of the hierarchy.[39]

Throughout most of human history, the elderly have had a scarcity value; only a handful of people survived to old age. The intergenerational continuity of the society guaranteed them a role in the socialization of younger generations. They retained a sense of being useful and important all during the time they were being slowly phased out of communal life.

The aged in contemporary society. In our society, there is little dignity in being among the elderly. The scientific accomplishments of in-

39. Dorothy R. Blitsten, *The World of the Family* (New York: Random House, Inc., 1963), p. 121.

dustrialized society have prolonged the lives of our aged until most people over sixty-five now have a life expectancy of between ten and fifteen years. But the technical revolution has also brought marked changes in the structure of the family and in the role of the aged in community life. Like adolescents, the elderly are not needed in the contemporary labor market. The information explosion in all fields has made their knowledge obsolete, and rapid changes in cul-

tural definitions have even made their morals and manners out of date. At best, the "golden years" of senior citizenship mean taking it easy in a warm climate and staying out of the hair of the rest of society. More often, they mean poverty, boredom, and loneliness. There is a crucial need to locate meaningful roles for the elderly members of our society and to provide adequate socialization to prepare them to play these roles.

SUMMARY

Socialization is the complex process of social learning whereby an individual internalizes the norms, values, beliefs, and expectations of other society members. From a societal perspective, socialization is necessary to ensure social order and the continuity of culture from one generation to the next. The socialization process accounts not only for the likenesses among a society's members, however, but also for some of the differences. Because each individual participates in a different combination of groups and subcultures, and because each responds to his social environment in his own way, socialization produces a wide range of personality configurations and behavior patterns.

Every group in which the individual participates serves as an agent of his socialization, but some have a greater influence than others. The family and the school, for example, have a special mandate from society to train new generations of members—to teach the knowledge, skills, attitudes, values, and general orientations that are needed to function effectively as an individual and group member. Not all of the learning that takes place in these settings is intended, however, and some of it may run counter to the norms and values that the society formally supports.

Peer groups have a special importance as agents of socialization during all stages of life, simply because the individual values them so highly as sources of emotional support. Desire for the esteem of one's close friends exerts a strong pressure for conformity to their standards. Groups with specialized goals, such as business organizations and the armed services,

are often important agents of socialization in adulthood, remolding the attitudes and behavior patterns of the individual so that he will function effectively in a specified role. What an individual learns in any of these contexts depends on the total pattern of his socializing experiences.

Socialization proceeds throughout the entire life span as the individual assumes changing roles and encounters changing needs and demands. Although anticipatory socialization helps people prepare for some of their future roles, often there is very little continuity between one stage of life and the next. Adolescents, for example, are effectively isolated from adult society by various conditions of modern life and thus develop subcultures of many kinds. These subcultures play an important part in shaping the values and expectations of young people, but they may be dysfunctional in terms of preparing adolescents for their later roles as adults.

Adult socialization tends almost inevitably toward discontinuity and conflict, for the individual must move quickly into changing role relationships of fundamental importance. Job requirements, the marital relationship, parenthood, and so on necessitate major adjustments in orientation. The processes of socialization by which adults make these transitions are not well understood. In old age, the loss of many former roles creates an identity crisis and again requires the formation of new habits and attitudes. Psychiatrists and sociologists are anxious to improve their knowledge of the socialization process in older people in order to learn how personality organization can be maintained through the last years of life.

PART III

STABILITY AND CHANGE

6
Social and Cultural Change

From the perspective of the individual, nothing in life seems more certain than change. This is no less true for the person living in a primitive village in India or Africa than it is for the sophisticated urbanite in a highly industrialized society. We all face the regular seasonal and yearly cycles as well as the cycle of birth, childhood, adolescence, marriage, procreation and child-rearing, old age, and death. In American society, as we noted in the previous chapter, the life cycle itself is getting more complicated: adolescence has been prolonged into several stages, there are increasingly varied job opportunities from which to choose, and many individuals are changing jobs several times during their adult years.

To the extent that such changes follow established patterns, they are really part of the socialization process, not illustrations of social and cultural change. For example, starting nursery school or kindergarten is a new situation for a child and marks a definite change in his life. But if the experience is expected of most children in his community, then it is part of the socialization process. We become interested in nurseries and kindergartens in relation to social and cultural change only when they are introduced into communities or societies that have not previously had them. We might then look to the conditions of life that have made it possible and desirable to create these organizations, the values and beliefs that seem to sustain them, and the possible consequences stemming from their introduction, such as changes in daily family routine, changes in authority patterns, and changes in educational policies.

Socialization and change are in many ways opposing processes: the former makes our behavior somewhat predictable and conforming; the latter disrupts stable patterns and urges us into new ways of thinking and acting. In this chapter we will examine some of the factors that seem to stimulate change; the patterns by which changes typically originate and spread; the social institutions most responsible for initiating change; and some of the reasons for resistance to change.

In analyzing the complex phenomenon of change, sociologists often use the terms *social change* and *cultural change* synonymously. Such usage is less than precise, however, for the two terms reflect the conceptual distinctions we have already noted (page 100) between social organization and culture. Thus *cultural* change refers to the emergence of new traits and trait complexes, to changes in a culture's content and structure; *social* change, on the other hand, refers to alterations in the patterns of social organization of specific groups within a society or even of the society itself. For example, expansion of a society's division of labor may create new roles for women, and this change in turn may alter the organizational structure of the family and kinship network. An expanded division of labor may also bring about a more open class system. Primary group ties may be replaced gradually (or not so gradually) by more bureaucratic and contractual relationships. All such changes are examples of change in social organization.

In reality, of course, it is usually very difficult to isolate a particular change and to classify it as clearly cultural or social. We may ask, for example, whether the widespread adoption of the automobile as an item of material culture was a contributing *cause* or only one kind of *effect* of the changing structure of American society early in the present century. It clearly made possible the further expansion of the suburbs; it contributed to changes in the norms concerning contacts between the sexes; it helped reduce distinctions in the way of life between city and country. However, trends toward industrialization and urbanization were already well under way at the time the automobile was introduced, and perhaps it was widely adopted simply because it "fit in" with those ongoing patterns of social change. Because of this mutual dependency between social and cultural change, we will often refer simply to the basic phenomenon of change; when possible, however, we will make the appropriate distinctions.

FACTORS STIMULATING CHANGE

People often speculate on why there should be more creative activity in some societies than in others, and among only a few rather than a majority of individuals. We may agree with Ralph Linton that change is a result of "the restless energy of the human mind."[1] But why, then, are men in some societies seemingly more "restless" than those in other societies? And why

1. Ralph Linton, *The Study of Man: An Introduction* (New York: Appleton-Century Co., 1936), pp. 87 ff.

is social and cultural ferment so much more characteristic of some periods of history, such as our own, than of others?

In trying to answer these questions, social scientists have identified a number of factors that have helped stimulate social and cultural change in the past. Here we will consider the potential importance of the physical environment, population growth, ideology, and individual leadership. It should be recognized from the start, however, that changes in a group's living patterns can never be explained in terms of simple cause and effect. As Parsons warns,

no claim that social change is "determined" by economic interests, ideas, personalities of particular individuals, geographical conditions, and so on, is acceptable. All such single-factor theories belong to the kindergarten stage of social science's development. Any single factor is always interdependent with several others.[2]

The analysis that follows can only suggest the complexity of factors influencing the direction and pattern of change. An interplay of forces is always at work, and change in one part of a system invariably affects other parts as well—often, as we shall see, with wholly unforeseen results.

THE PHYSICAL ENVIRONMENT

Obviously the physical environment cannot in itself cause social or cultural change to occur; it merely provides conditions that may be more or less *conducive* to change. It is man as a social being who decides how those conditions will be met. This principle can be clearly illustrated by recounting the socioeconomic history of a single small area in the United States, the Muskingum Valley of Ohio.

The Muskingum is the great watershed of eastern Ohio which feeds eventually into the Ohio River. The nineteenth-century settlers who cleared the hilly area in order to farm the land lacked knowledge about the use of trees and terrace farming in protecting the land from flooding and soil erosion. By the beginning of the twentieth century, floods were occurring regularly, and finally, after the great flood of 1913 struck a tremendous blow to the area, the people decided to act. They organized a special committee into a public corporation, the Musk-

ingum Watershed Conservancy District, and this agency in turn was able to obtain the aid of several departments of the federal government that were then becoming increasingly concerned about soil erosion and flooding. As a result of steady collaboration between the Conservancy District and government at the federal, state, and local levels, the land of the Muskingum Valley has now been reclaimed, floods are a matter of history, and the area has become a vacationland for many Ohioans and residents of surrounding states.

History provides countless examples of how the physical environment can stimulate social and cultural change. Natural disasters such as floods, droughts, and earthquakes have periodically disrupted life for large numbers of people, forcing them to abandon not only their homes but their traditional patterns of life. Throughout history, geography has played a part in shaping boundary lines and political alliances. Climate has often turned the balance in war. And the distribution of natural resources has given direction to patterns of settlement and conquest.

It was the lure of gold and silver, for example, that brought Cortes to Mexico and Pizarro to Peru during the early part of the sixteenth century, thus altering the course of history for both the New World and the Old. And three centuries later it was the discovery of gold in California that led to the rapid settlement of the American West. Indeed, much of the social and cultural history of the United States can be clearly related to the presence and location of natural resources—its navigable rivers and lakes, its forests and mineral deposits, its areas of rich farm land, its open plains.

The story of the white man's coming to the New World makes clear the complexity of processes by which societies and cultures change. The Europeans who were attracted to North and South America by the promise of opportunity helped to shape their new environment and were in turn shaped by it. They brought with them the social and cultural traditions of the countries from which they had come; but in response to new conditions, and in response to each other, they developed distinctive culture traits and distinctive patterns of social organization. And finally, in building their own new societies they largely destroyed the culture

---

2. Talcott Parsons, *Societies: Evolutionary and Comparative Perspectives* (Englewood Cliffs, N.J.: Prentice-Hall, Inc., 1966), p. 113.

TABLE 6.1. **POPULATION OF THE WORLD, IN MILLIONS, 1000–1980**

YEAR	EUROPE AND RUSSIA	INDIA AND SOUTHWEST ASIA	CHINA, JAPAN AND SOUTHEAST ASIA	AFRICA	THE AMERICAS	WORLD
1000	47	80	85	50	13	275
1100	54	83	97	55	17	306
1200	68	85	111	61	23	348
1300	81	83	125	67	28	384
1400	54	73	142	74	30	373
1500	80	83	160	82	41	446
1600	102	98	181	90	15	486
1700	130	131	256	90	10	617
1800	205	190	405	90	29	919
1900	421	325	545	120	144	1,555
1980	456	1,001	1,427	449	635	4,268

SOURCE: Adapted from Merrill Kelley Bennett, *The World's Food* (New York: Harper & Brothers, 1954), p. 9. Projected 1980 figures from the United Nations, *Provisional Report on World Population Prospects* (New York, 1964).

In addition to pointing up the dramatic growth of world population in the last two centuries, this chart reflects some interesting historical developments in various regions. Between 1300 and 1400 the population in Europe and Russia declined drastically, mainly as the result of the Black Plague; in 1500 the population was still slightly below that of 1300. By 1600, while European population had again risen significantly, that of the New World had been all but destroyed by European conquest. In 1800 the population of North and South America was still less than those continents had possessed four hundred years previously. Africa experienced a slow, even growth from 1000 to 1600, but during the following two centuries the population remained stationary because of the deprivations of the slave trade and an almost static balance between high birth rates and high death rates.

and social organization of the Indian peoples who had been settled in the Americas for many centuries.

POPULATION GROWTH

It has probably been true throughout history that any significant increase or decrease in the size of a population has tended to disrupt patterns of social life. Rapid population growth has posed the threat of an inadequate food supply; serious declines in population, on the other hand, have meant the possibility of not enough people to keep a society going or to defend it from enemies.

History shows that famines, plagues, and warfare have periodically checked population growth and even depleted human populations. Thus the Black Death that swept through west-

ern Europe during the fourteenth century sharply reduced the size of a population that had been increasing steadily for several centuries (see Table 6.1). We may speculate that such changes in population size would lead to changes in family structure as well as other aspects of social organization. In a society whose numbers had been depleted by the plague, we might expect an increased emphasis on early marriage and a high birth rate. During periods of sustained population growth, on the other hand, delayed marriage or enforced bachelorhood might be the preferred patterns. Records of feudal Europe do in fact indicate that many men did not marry. We need not assume that people at that time were concerned about keeping population growth within bounds. Rather, limited resources and patterns of social organization simply made marriage impractical for a great many individuals. Laws of primogeniture, specifying that a family's entire property should pass to the eldest son, had the indirect effect of encouraging celibacy, for younger sons had few options open to them other than military service or a life in the Church.[3]

3. For historical detail on these points, see John T. Noonan, Jr., *Contraception: A History of Its Treatment in the Catholic Theologians and Canonists* (Cambridge, Mass.: Harvard University Press, 1965), pp. 228–230.

In our own time, the population explosion that has taken on such critical overtones since World War II is clearly altering patterns of social behavior. Cities are mushrooming. Housing is often in short supply. Environmental pollution has become a widespread reality. In the developing nations, where population growth has generally outstripped economic growth, increasing numbers of people go jobless and hungry. These problems have spurred the development and distribution of more effective contraceptive devices such as the Pill and IUD (intrauterine device), while also increasing the frequency with which sterilization and abortion are practiced. Governments, religious groups, population experts, and individual married couples all have their own perspectives on the issue of population growth, but all seem to be moving in the direction of an increased emphasis on effective family planning. And in the process, traditional values and beliefs are being subjected to question. What is the real meaning of sexual morality? What are the primary obligations of parents? What role should a woman have in the family and in society?

The relationship between population trends and social change defies any simple analysis. In the Western world, the Industrial Revolution combined with accompanying improvements in agriculture, sanitation, and medicine to lower death rates and thus to increase population growth during the eighteenth and nineteenth centuries. But population growth then combined with other variables to promote new patterns of social organization and to complete the transformation to urban-industrial society. And this transformation, in turn, led to changes in family structure and a gradual reduction in birth rates. The question of whether this cycle will repeat itself in the developing countries has been the subject of considerable debate, but present circumstances suggest that it may not. (See Chapter 8, "Demographic Change.")

IDEOLOGY

In all human groups, beliefs and values—manifested in norms and goals—are important guides to behavior. A complex of beliefs and values providing an overall rationale for a society is termed an *ideology*. Ideologies obviously help to sustain societies. But how, and to what extent, do they also act to stimulate change?

Marxism. According to Karl Marx (page 7), every social order of the past contained the seeds of its own destruction in the economic structure imposed by the ruling class. The exploitation of the weak by the strong made class conflict inevitable, and it was such conflict that had led to the establishment of successive new systems of order. In the history-making *Communist Manifesto*, written in collaboration with Friedrich Engels and published in 1848, Marx declared:

The history of hitherto existing societies is the history of class struggles.

Freeman and slave, patrician and plebian, lord and serf, guild-master and journeyman, in a word oppressor and oppressed, stood in constant opposition to one another, carried on an uninterrupted, now hidden, now open fight, a fight that each time ended, either in a revolutionary re-constitution of society at large, or in a common ruin of the contending classes.[4]

Marx expected the revolutions of the twentieth century to occur in countries with an advanced industrial base, for he theorized that class consciousness, so vital to the development of the next stage of disorder and conflict, only developed in modern capitalistic societies, where people were drawn together in city and in factory. The final outcome of the class struggle, he believed, would be the emergence of a classless society.

Marx was convinced that it was the economic structure of a society that provided the impetus for social conflict and change, not the beliefs and values of its members: "It is not the consciousness of men that determines their existence, but rather it is their social existence which determines their consciousness."[5] Yet it is one of the interesting facts of history that Marxism itself has become an ideology. Millions of people have come to believe and to act on at least some parts of Marxian theory, and in so doing they have shown that beliefs can indeed influence human behavior. It seems likely, in fact, that *belief* in Marxian ideology has been a greater force for social change than have the

4. Karl Marx and Friedrich Engels, *The Communist Manifesto*, ed. Samuel H. Beer (New York: Appleton-Century-Crofts, 1955).

5. Karl Marx, *A Contribution to the Critique of Political Economy* (New York: International Publishers, 1969); see also Karl Marx and Friedrich Engels, *The German Ideology* (New York: International Publishers, 1947), esp. pp. 7–25.

economic forces that Marx saw at work. Most "Marxian" revolutions have taken place not in advanced industrial societies, as he predicted they would, but in preindustrial or at best incipient-industrial societies. Equally contrary to Marxian theory, the more industrialized nations of the world have been able gradually to modify their social structures without experiencing extreme class conflict.

To a remarkable degree, the history of Marxism illustrates one of the basic principles of sociology: If men define situations as real, they are real in their consequences.[6] Thus people have defined social reality in terms of Marx's interpretation of it (or often in terms of their own interpretation of Marx's interpretation) and have worked at making it real for themselves. They have carried out revolutions in its name, even if the circumstances existing before the revolutions differed markedly from the conditions that were presumed to be essential to Marx's predictions.

The Protestant Ethic. One of the most determined efforts yet made in the social sciences to establish a relationship between ideology and sociocultural change was that made by the German sociologist Max Weber, whose writings were to an important degree an effort to confront the Marxian theory of economic determinism. Weber was careful to insist that he did not intend to offer a one-sided theory of his own as an alternative to Marx; rather, he wanted to establish the principle that *ideas* as well as technological developments and the economic structure could be determining factors in bringing about change. To do this, Weber set out to identify the major factors responsible for the rise of rational capitalism—the type of capitalism

characterized by double-entry bookkeeping, uniform pricing, systematic planning, and the insistence upon competence rather than familial considerations as the basis for business relations.[7]

Weber acknowledged that many factors were responsible for the rise of rational capitalism and of the metropolitan city that was its locus. Improvements in sanitation and preventive medicine, the increase in agricultural productivity, inventions leading to the Industrial Revolution, and better methods of transportation were all necessary conditions for the rise of modern capitalism. But Weber believed that no one of these factors, nor all of them together, provided a sufficient explanation for the larger sociocultural changes that had taken place. He also rejected the idea that the modern world was nothing more than a simple continuation of an inexorable evolutionary process.

Through a wide-ranging historical analysis, Weber attempted to show that the religions of China, India, and ancient Israel developed everyday ethics or ideologies that were in varying ways inimical to the development of modern capitalism. Adherence to tradition, stereotyping, otherworldly orientations, and closed-class or caste systems of stratification all acted to impede the development of the capitalistic spirit upon which the modern Western economy was to be built. Weber also carefully contrasted the beliefs and values of Roman Catholicism and Lutheranism with those of Calvinism. It was Calvinism, he maintained, which paved the way for the emergence of modern capitalism, for in providing man with a "this-worldly asceticism" it altered the focus of his attention and gave him a different perspective on life. Over time this perspective has become embodied in what is popularly called the Protestant Ethic (page 120). It might more accurately be labeled the "Puritan Ethic," since it was an outgrowth of Calvinism rather than of Protestantism generally.

In the years since Weber wrote, his theory has been both defended and denounced by other scholars.[8] The thesis he advanced in *The Protestant Ethic and the Spirit of Capitalism* (1920) was substantially strengthened by his careful comparative studies, and though his theory cannot be proved, it is nonetheless plausible. Most social scientists today would agree, in any case, that values and beliefs must be recognized as potential forces of change and also of resistance to change.

6. The principle of "the self-fulfilling prophecy" was first developed by W. I. Thomas in *The Child in America: Behavior Problems and Programs* (New York: Alfred A. Knopf, Inc., 1928), p. 81; for a further elaboration of the idea, see Robert K. Merton, *Social Theory and Social Structure*, rev. ed. (New York: The Free Press, 1957), pp. 421–434.

7. Weber's best-known work, published in 1920, is *The Protestant Ethic and the Spirit of Capitalism* (New York: Charles Scribner's Sons, 1958), but the full scope of Weber's thesis cannot be appreciated without reference to several other works, notably *Ancient Judaism* (New York: The Free Press, 1952); *The Religion of China* (New York: The Free Press, 1951); *The Religion of India* (New York: The Free Press, 1958); and *General Economic History* (New York: Collier Books, 1961).

8. For a recent critique, see Kurt Samuelsson, *Religion and Economic Action* (New York: Harper & Row, Inc., 1961).

In modern times the term charisma has been applied to leaders as different as Robert Kennedy and Mao Tse-tung; both of them articulated a new vision for their people and tried to lead men to significant social and cultural change. At left is Robert Kennedy as he campaigned for the 1968 presidential nomination. The photograph above, which was taken in 1967, shows some of the fifty thousand soldiers who swam the Yangtze in honor of Mao.

LEADERSHIP

Leaders succeed in bringing about change to the extent that they are able to establish social movements—to get followers who believe in their cause and act accordingly. Often such movements succeed only after near disasters or apparent failures.

The charismatic leader is especially important in giving direction to sociocultural change. In the biblical tradition, the term *charisma* means a "gift of grace," divinely given. Weber used the term to describe "a certain quality of an individual personality by virtue of which he is set apart from ordinary men and treated as endowed with supernatural, superhuman or at least specifically exceptional powers or qualities."[9] The prophets of the Old Testament are historical examples of leaders with charismatic qualities. They spoke out against the rulers of the day, warned of doom, and in the name of their God Yahweh urged a return to the old ways. In a strictly historical sense, Christ may be seen as the great charismatic leader whose teachings changed the history of the Western world, much as Muhammad changed the history of parts of Asia and Africa. But charisma is not a phenomenon of the past, nor is it limited to religious leaders. In modern times the term has been applied to leaders as different as Gandhi, Pope John XXIII, Martin Luther King, Jr., Adolf Hitler, Franklin D. Roosevelt, John F. Kennedy, and Fidel Castro. All have spoken for a cause and helped lead men to significant social and cultural changes.

Charismatic leadership does not function in a vacuum. On the contrary, the effectiveness of a charismatic leader in bringing about change seems largely dependent on the existence of certain conditions—such as severe stresses and strains in the social system—to which he can offer a meaningful alternative. The mere existence of such conditions, however, does not by itself guarantee that change will take place. For example, living conditions in 1958 were much worse in some other countries of the Western Hemisphere, such as Haiti and Paraguay, than they were in Cuba; but a revolution began in Cuba because new values, beliefs, and norms were emerging there and because a charismatic leader was available to provide direction.

The significance of the Cuban revolution was not simply the overthrow of the dictator Fulgencio Batista but more profoundly the emerging leadership of Fidel Castro and his attempt at the total transformation of Cuban society. Castro spoke out in the name of a cause, and the cause was not merely doctrinaire communism or anti-yankee nationalism: it was the cause of total social revolution. The goal was to change the cultural and social life of a country by direction and tight control. Whatever the ultimate success of the Cuban revolution, it had become clear by the late 1960's that similar revolutions could not easily be exported to other countries like Venezuela and Bolivia, where the conditions were different and indigenous leadership was lacking.

Charismatic leadership, while clearly a source of change, does not continue indefinitely. Sometimes a social movement dies with the death of its leader, but often the passing of the leader ushers in a period of consolidation, during which an attempt is made to institutionalize his ideas and to translate them into organized social structures. This was the case in the Soviet Union following the death of Lenin.

A movement for change must itself undergo change if it is to have a lasting effect. Ideas must be put to work, and sometimes they have to be modified. Often this creates a conflict within the movement between bureaucrats and ideologists. The former become increasingly concerned with developing, and then with strengthening and maintaining, social organizations and related cultural complexes that reflect the movement's basic tenets. The latter try to keep their leader's "message" intact and protect his principles from compromise. Such differences in viewpoint sometimes erupt into severe conflict, as happened in Red China during the middle of the 1960's. The Cultural Revolution led by Mao's "Red Guards" was an attempt to restore ideological purity to the process of constructing a new China. The technical experts who had been directing China's program of economic development were charged with corrupting the revolutionary movement. The real answer to China's future, the ideologists argued, lay in absorbing the "thought" of Chairman Mao Tse-tung, which would bring inevitable improvement in all areas of personal and social endeavor. The Cultural Revolution was more than a political

---

9. Max Weber, *Theory of Social and Economic Organization,* trans. A. M. Henderson and Talcott Parsons (New York: The Free Press, 1957), p. 358.

power struggle; it was an effort to reshape the thought patterns of an entire people.

Probably the most significant social movement in the United States during the last ten years has been the civil rights movement. A number of leaders, both black and white, have been identified with it and no single man has controlled it, but during its formative years Martin Luther King, Jr., was clearly its most influential leader. His assassination in the spring of 1968 by no means brought an end to the civil rights movement, but it deprived the movement of whatever unity it had previously had. Both before and after King's death, many individuals have spoken up and tried to provide leadership, some urging violence, some urging restraint, many urging that white Americans support massive and far-reaching programs for change. The civil rights movement has even drawn strong counterleadership, as typified by former Alabama governor George Wallace, with his espousal of a return to "the old days" through a special form of "state's rights."

Relatively few men have the special gift of leadership that we term *charisma*. More often than not, a leader is less an innovator than one who provides direction for the felt needs of the members of a particular group. He does this by being able to approximate the values and beliefs of those people more closely than anyone else. He identifies himself with their aspirations and adheres more closely to the norms they generally accept. He is able to lead, in short, because he can anticipate that his orders will be obeyed, that people will follow. In contrast, the charismatic leader has the capacity to articulate a new vision for his people. In times of conflict and stress, leadership can become the crucial factor in determining the direction of change.

SOME PATTERNS OF CHANGE

Evolution, diffusion, and *invention* are among the terms traditionally used in describing basic patterns of change. In recent times we have also become increasingly concerned with possibilities for *guided* change. This section will examine each of these concepts in turn, concluding with a brief discussion of the kinds of problems that develop when some facets of a social system change more slowly than others.

EVOLUTION

In the nineteenth century the concept of evolution assumed a central place in explanations of human development and change. Most influential were Charles Darwin, whose theory of natural selection provided a solid base for biological evolution, and Herbert Spencer (page 7), who systematized a theory of social evolution. Spencer saw evolution as a unilinear development—a continuing process by which matter was synthesized at ever higher levels of complexity. He maintained that man in society has been like other living forms in following an inevitable course from amorphous and homogeneous structures to increasingly differentiated and specialized ones. In an effort to support this theory, Spencer traced the development of marriage and the family from an original state of promiscuity, through stages of polyandry and polygyny, to the final and, in his view, most highly developed stage of monogamy.[10] Spencer maintained that social evolution was in the natural order of things and that man could not hope to alter the process by legislation.

In the United States, William Graham Sumner became the most outspoken theorist of social evolution. In a famous dictum that has influenced political thinking for the past half century, he argued that "stateways" could not change "folkways"—that social change would come only in its own good time.[11] His argument is echoed today by those who oppose civil rights laws on grounds that morality cannot be legislated.

Some other sociologists contemporary with Sumner, while accepting much of evolutionary theory, rejected the notion that man could not control change. Lester Frank Ward, for example, saw society as the final state of a "long, unbroken series of cosmic aggregations leading from the ultimate material atom up to the social aggregate."[12] Evolution brought on ever new syntheses from the continuing conflict and collision of creative energy. Out of these syntheses the human intellect gradually emerged, and it was precisely in the intellect that Ward found evidence that evolution for man was *not* like all

10. Herbert Spencer, *The Principles of Sociology* (New York: D. Appleton & Co., 1898).

11. William Graham Sumner, *Folkways* (Boston: Ginn and Company, 1906), pp. 87–88.

12. Lester Frank Ward, *Dynamic Sociology*, 2nd ed., Vol. 1 (New York: D. Appleton & Co., 1911), 451.

previous biological evolution. Ward believed that through scientific intelligence man could bring about social laws to effect desired changes.

For Karl Marx, as we have seen, the basic mechanism of social evolution was conflict, the continuing struggle between the exploiters and the exploited. Presumably the struggle would continue through successive stages of social order until the final stage of a classless society had been reached, at which point the evolutionary process would cease. Marx believed in the inevitability of the changes he foresaw, but he also believed that man could hasten the evolutionary process by his active involvement in class conflict.

Despite their differing orientations, evolutionary theorists seem to have agreed that man is in the process of increasing his level of social and cultural differentiation. A pattern of differentiation can indeed be observed, whether viewed as the inevitable outcome of forces beyond man's control or as the product of his own intelligence.[13] The evolutionists, especially Marx, also did much to help social scientists focus on the interdependence of the parts of society. It is now generally recognized that a change in any one part of the social system, such as the economic or political institution, may have repercussions throughout the whole system. Several specific illustrations of this phenomenon are included elsewhere in this chapter.

CHANGE THROUGH BORROWING AND DIFFUSION

Most societies are very ethnocentric: they judge their own ways to be superior to those of other people and assume them to be the products of their own invention. This tendency to ignore the role of *diffusion*—the transfer of cultural and social elements from one society to another—is nowhere more apparent than among the people of the United States. Because we live in a period of great technological advancement, we are prone to think that our own culture is largely self-created. Anthropologists are continually reminding us, however, that we also are great culture borrowers. The following passage by Ralph Linton is often quoted to make the point:

13. For a recent discussion of the process of differentiation, see Parsons, *op. cit.*, esp. pp. 20–25 and 113–115.

Our solid American citizen awakens in a bed built on a pattern which originated in the Near East but which was modified in northern Europe before it was transmitted to America. He throws back covers made from cotton, domesticated in India, or linen, domesticated in the Near East, or wool from sheep, also domesticated in the Near East, or silk, the use of which was discovered in China. All of these materials have been spun and woven by processes invented in the Near East. He slips into his moccasins, invented by the Indians of the Eastern woodlands, and goes to the bathroom, whose fixtures are a mixture of European and American inventions, both of recent date. He takes off his pajamas, a garment invented in India, and washes with soap invented by the ancient Gauls. He then shaves, a masochistic rite which seems to have been derived from either Sumer or ancient Egypt.

Returning to the bedroom, he removes his clothes from a chair of southern European type and proceeds to dress. He puts on garments whose form originally derived from the skin clothing of the nomads of the Asiatic steppes, puts on shoes made from skins tanned by a process invented in ancient Egypt and cut to a pattern derived from the classical civilizations of the Mediterranean, and ties around his neck a strip of bright-colored cloth which is a vestigial survival of the shoulder shawls worn by the seventeenth-century Croatians. Before going out for breakfast he glances through the window, made of glass invented in Egypt, and if it is raining puts on overshoes made of rubber discovered by the Central American Indians and takes an umbrella, invented in southeastern Asia. Upon his head he puts a hat made of felt, a material invented in the Asiatic steppes.

On his way to breakfast he stops to buy a paper, paying for it with coins, an ancient Lydian invention. At the restaurant a whole new series of borrowed elements confronts him. His plate is made of a form of pottery invented in China. His knife is of steel, an alloy first made in southern India, his fork a medieval Italian invention, and his spoon a derivative of a Roman original. He begins breakfast with an orange, from the eastern Mediterranean, a canteloupe from Persia, or perhaps a piece of African watermelon. With this he has coffee, an Abyssinian plant, with cream and sugar. Both the domestication of cows and the idea of milking them originated in the Near East, while sugar was first made in India. After his fruit and first coffee he goes on to waffles, cakes made by a Scandinavian technique from wheat domesticated in Asia Minor. Over these he pours maple syrup, invented by the Indians of the Eastern woodlands. As a side dish he may have the egg of a species of bird domesticated in Indo-China, or thin strips of the flesh of an animal domesticated in Eastern Asia which have been salted and smoked by a process developed in northern Europe.

When our friend has finished eating he settles back to smoke, an American Indian habit, consuming a plant domesticated in Brazil in either a pipe, derived from the Indians of Virginia, or a cigarette, derived from Mexico. If he is hardy enough he may even attempt a cigar, transmitted to us from the Antilles by way of Spain. While smoking he reads the news of the day, imprinted in characters invented by the ancient Semites upon a material invented in China by a process invented in Germany. As he absorbs the accounts of foreign troubles he will, if he is a good conservative citizen, thank a Hebrew deity in an Indo-European language that he is 100 percent American.[14]

American culture, of course, is not the only one with widespread origins. Murdock estimates that about 90 percent of every culture known to history has acquired its elements from other peoples.[15] There are very clear reasons for this. One important function of culture traits is that they help people solve problems. A society facing a problem for which it has developed no adequate solutions is generally willing to borrow an approach that has proved effective elsewhere.

The process of cultural and social diffusion. A considerable amount of culture borrowing is very indirect; that is, the culture in which a given trait originated may be far removed in space or time (or both) from a people who have more recently acquired that trait. The spread of smoking tobacco provides one interesting illustration of indirect intersocietal diffusion. The habit of smoking originated in tropical America, where the tobacco plant is indigenous. Over centuries it was acquired and cultivated by one neighboring Indian group after another until it traveled up Central America and spread out north, east, and west across the North American continent. Sometimes the tobacco was rolled into a crude cigar, and sometimes it was crushed and stuffed into a reed. Every conceivable variation on the pipe has been found in ancient Indian sites, with the stem and bowl put together in different ways and with carvings and art forms characteristic of the people who used it.

Among the Eskimos, on the other hand, no ancient remains of the pipe have been found. These people did not smoke, for their climate prohibited the growing of tobacco and they were too far removed from its sources to have acquired it by trade. In recent centuries, however, the Alaskan Eskimo acquired both the pipe and tobacco along with the word *tawak,* a corruption of the Spanish word *tabaco* with which this plant seems to be identified nearly the world over. The Eskimos borrowed this culture trait from traders coming across the Bering Strait from Siberia. The traders, in turn, had tobacco because it had earlier spread across Europe and Asia from Spain, whose explorers got it from the Indians of tropical America. Thus, tobacco reached the Eskimos of Alaska by a journey of diffusion around the entire world.[16] Although not every cultural form that moves from one society to another travels this far, the concept of intersocietal diffusion provides an important perspective on the process of culture borrowing and on the accumulation of traits in a given culture.

The concept of diffusion also applies to exchanges of culture traits between subgroups *within* a complex society. Many new cultural forms that originate within specialized groups of a society, as part of a specific subculture, are later taken on by other groups. For example, jazz and the blues were developed by American Negro musicians in New Orleans; but as blacks moved north to Chicago and other urban centers, they took their music along, with the result that jazz and the blues have become part of the social heritage of the nation as a whole. Many traits of our popular culture—hair styles, clothing styles, dance forms, and slang—similarly spread from a distinct subculture to society as a whole.

Patterns of diffusion. When a new culture trait or complex is introduced to a group and eventually becomes widely adopted, it follows a characteristic pattern as it spreads through the population. A few individuals may see what they believe to be the advantages of the new trait— perhaps a material item, perhaps a belief or idea—as soon as it is introduced, and they adopt it almost immediately. After these *innovators* have accepted the trait and its merits have been demonstrated, it begins to spread gradually to

---

14. Linton, *op. cit.,* pp. 326–327.

15. George P. Murdock, *Our Primitive Contemporaries* (New York: The Macmillan Company, 1934).

16. This account is summarized from Alfred L. Kroeber, *Anthropology: Culture Patterns and Processes* (New York: Harcourt, Brace & Co., 1923), pp. 211–214.

Fads and crazes generally involve limited segments of society and seldom become popular again once they have been abandoned. Dance marathons were one of a variety of ludicrous—and in this case, inhuman—fads popular during the 1930's. Two decades later, college students took to stuffing telephone booths and automobiles. The hula hoop, probably the greatest flash-selling item in the history of toys, was one fad that became popular with almost every segment of the American public. From their introduction in 1957 to their decline in the latter part of 1958, almost thirty million of these plastic rings were sold.

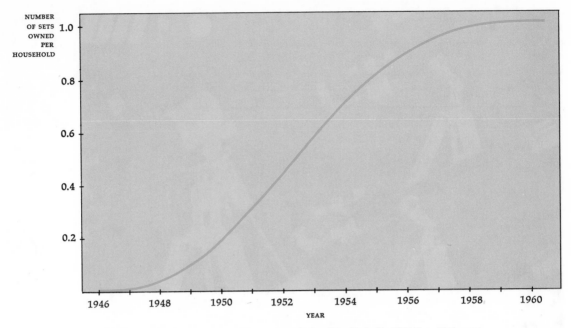

SOURCE: Melvin L. DeFleur, *Theories of Mass Communication* (New York: David McKay, 1966), p. 73.

FIGURE 6.1.   **THE DIFFUSION CURVE FOR TELEVISION, 1946-1960**

growing numbers of people. Usually it is only after a substantial number of *early adopters* have made it a standard form among themselves that the *majority* of the group or society begin to adopt it. Some *late adopters* may not accept the trait until long after the majority have made it part of their culture, and a few very conservative individuals may never take it up at all.[17]

A *diffusion curve* can often be plotted for a given innovation by noting its spread through a specific population over time. Figure 6.1, for example, shows the spread of television in the United States between 1946 and 1966 in terms of the number of sets owned per family. It should be noted that in studying the diffusion of a material trait, such as television or tobacco, it is the population's *behavior* in relation to the new item, and not the item itself, that most interests the student of social change.

If a particular culture trait becomes widely diffused through a society, it is a potential folk- way. However, to qualify as a folkway, it must become firmly established. As was suggested in Chapter 2 (page 88), two important dimensions of folkways are the degree to which they are widely practiced (have diffused through the entire society) and the degree to which they have become an accepted element of the culture (have become *institutionalized*). Diffusion and institu- tionalization are key aspects of a society's mores as well as its folkways. The additional element identifying the mores, of course, is that the intensity of feelings associated with them is high. A diffusion curve showing the adoption and subsequent retention of one of a society's folkways or mores would resemble the top pat- tern shown in Figure 6.2.

Even when a particular cultural element is widely adopted by the members of a society, there is no guarantee that it will remain forever a part of their culture. Our vocabulary makes note of this by labeling as *fashions* those cultural forms that become generally accepted but are periodically subject to change. Clothing styles obviously fall in this category. So too do our changing preferences for certain styles of furni- ture, certain sports, and certain breeds of dog. As shown in Figure 6.2, a curve tracing the diffusion of a fashion differs significantly from the curve for a folkway. Since substantial seg- ments of the society never adopt the fashion, the

---

17. Everett Rodgers, *Diffusion of Innovations* (New York: The Free Press, 1962).

FOLKWAYS AND MORES

FASHIONS

FADS AND CRAZES

FIGURE 6.2. **CHARACTERISTIC DIFFUSION AND OBSOLESCENCE PATTERNS**

curve does not rise as high as that of a folkway. In addition, it shows only a very short institutionalized phase or none at all. After reaching its peak of adoption, a fashion typically follows a pattern of declining usage and gradually becomes *passé*.

The behavior patterns we label as *fads* and *crazes* appear and disappear even more quickly than fashions. They generally involve limited segments of society and typically are regarded by the majority as examples of pure foolishness, or worse. They are also distinguished by the fact that they never achieve a permanent place even in the subculture of a given group. Whereas fashions are likely to be cyclical (witness the ups and downs of hemlines and the recurrent appearance and disappearance of shoulder pads), particular fads and crazes seldom become popular again once they have been abandoned. And usually they are abandoned just as quickly as they are adopted.

Obsolescence and displacement. A pattern of declining usage identifies *obsolescence*, which we may define as the abandoning of previously established modes of conduct toward some cultural item. Thus, diffusion and obsolescence are

natural counterparts. One indicates the phase of increasing acceptance of a new cultural element, and the other indicates its declining usage.

The diffusion of a new culture trait sometimes causes another trait to become obsolescent. The neighborhood movie, for example, has been to a considerable degree displaced by the increasing diffusion of television in American society. *Displacement*, then, refers to the decline of one cultural form brought about by the increasing adoption of a more effective *functional alternative*—that is, a cultural item that performs essentially the same function as the displaced item but that comes to be preferred.

Sometimes a cultural item diffuses through a society, achieves institutionalization, and becomes obsolescent only to rise again and achieve increasing adoption through revival. Victorian furniture followed such a pattern. It began to disappear from American homes after the turn of the century, but in the past two decades it enjoyed renewed popularity. Now its fashionability appears once again to be declining.

Some implications of diffusion. Although people ordinarily adopt new traits because there seems to be some advantage in doing so, the diffusion of a social or cultural trait is not necessarily beneficial, either in the short run or in the long run. A classic example of the mixed results of diffusion involves the American Indians and their contacts with the white man. The Plains Indians, for instance, incorporated the horse and the rifle into their own way of life and suddenly found their social patterns radically altered. The horse increased their mobility, and together with the rifle it vastly improved their hunting ability. The buffalo became their staple of life, and their meager agricultural economy was generally abandoned. As a result, the Plains Indians became more numerous and more prosperous; cultural diffusion was initially an advantage. When the buffalo was effectively eliminated by the white man, however, the culture of the Plains Indians was seriously disrupted. In this case, diffusion was not a continuous process, leading to *acculturation* and gradual *assimilation* of the Indian into the dominant American society. Rather, it did away with most of the traits and complexes of their original culture and left them either unable or unwilling—perhaps both—to accept a different way.

In considering the implications of diffusion we must remember, finally, that it is not limited to material items like furniture and guns and music; in the long run the most important kind of diffusion may be the spread of beliefs and ideas between societies. Thus during the nineteenth century, the political ideals generated by the American and French revolutions diffused slowly throughout Latin America, where some societies even adopted constitutions based on the French or American model. The diffusion of democratic values was very uneven, however, and met with great resistance by entrenched leaders who wished to maintain the status quo. Most Latin American societies now find themselves in a state of political and social turmoil, faced with the increasing probability of revolutionary convulsions in the decades ahead. Not only in Latin America but in the world as a whole, the diffusion of opposing ideologies has become a major source of conflict both within societies and between them.

INVENTION

Much cultural and social change is a product of man's ability to invent, to create some-thing that has not previously been part of his culture or society. We tend to think of inventions as mechanical devices and technical artifacts, but they may just as well be new songs, art forms, religious beliefs, games, or other nonmaterial products of the creative mind. Or they may be new forms of social organization such as bureaucracy or the voluntary association.

Although it is debatable whether anyone ever had an entirely original idea, invention becomes possible because individuals are capable of taking existent ideas and structural patterns and casting them in a new light. For example, until a young man named Hank Luisetti began to play basketball, the only way to try for a basket was to use both hands in shooting the ball. Luisetti introduced the one-handed shot in 1938 and revolutionized the game. The new shot not only challenged traditional beliefs and norms about how the game should be played, but it also radically altered the structural patterns of offensive and defensive play. Still, these changes did not destroy the original game. Typically there is continuity in a pattern of social behavior even as it undergoes change.

The exponential principle. Many inventions involve much more than a simple new grouping of a few traits, and often it is clear that they are not the product of a single inventor. In every case, however, they represent new forms that individuals or groups of individuals have devised from the existing culture base. Many significant inventions involve grasping some new principle about the relationship between known concepts. Classic examples of this are Newton's gravitational laws, the periodic table of chemistry, and Harvey's discovery of the circulation of the blood.

The possibilities for invention in a society are closely related to its existing cultural content. A society that lacks a technology for working with glass and a knowledge of optical principles can scarcely be expected to invent a microscope. By contrast, a society that has the technology for working in various metals to reasonably close tolerances, that has available the wheel, the piston, and the connecting rod, and that understands something of the expansive power of confined steam is one in which some reasonably bright tinkerer is likely to come up with the idea of a steam engine. This would be especially true if there were a number of ready applications for a source of cheap and dependable power.

The relationship between the number of traits making up the culture base of a particular society and the number of inventions that can potentially be made from them forms an exponential curve (Figure 6.3). The exponential principle is based on the elementary mathematics of combinations. If, for example, a hypothetical culture contained only 100 traits, there would be 4950 possible ways in which these could be paired together as potential inventions. (The formula for the number of pairs in n objects is $n(n-1)/2$. Where $n = 100$, the number of possible pairs is 4950.) If the number of traits in the culture base were merely to double to 200, the number of pairs that could be made would increase fourfold to a startling 19,900. The possibilities for invention increase even more dramatically when we consider the additional combinations that could be made by using three, four, or more traits.

The exponential principle thus helps explain why the flow of inventions in our society has reached such astounding proportions. It is not so much that we are an especially clever or inventive people as it is that we have accumulated an enormous culture base. Because each new invention stimulates others, we may expect the technologically advanced societies of the world to experience cultural accumulation at an ever increasing pace.

Invention and social change. The history of man has been written in large part around invention and technological advancement—the increasingly sophisticated control of heat energy; the invention of the wheel, the steel plow, and gunpowder; progress in medicine and sanitation; the development of the printing press, radio, and television; the invention of the automobile and the airplane. But how did it all begin, and why has technological advance brought more significant social change to some societies than to others?

We can only speculate with Hagen, Linton, and other students of social change that early inventions were due in part to the random discoveries of intelligent men and in part to man's ability to become dissatisfied with present solutions to his problems.[18] Probably few inventions were the result of conscious efforts to bring on change, for it is only in modern times that we find societies actively encouraging change. The fact is that throughout most of history, the preferred course has been maintenance of the status quo. Individuals were permitted to be creative so long as their inventions did not threaten the power structure or basic values of the society, and only in times of great stress, when traditional solutions proved inadequate to need, were innovators regarded with hope and expectation. As Hagen notes, "if there are no serious internal stresses and no disturbing forces from the outside, cultural change in any society proceeds at a snail's pace."[19]

The history of man reveals periods of little change interspersed with periods of great innovation, all in very uneven patterns. Throughout the Middle Ages, for example, trade routes between societies were opened, closed, and then

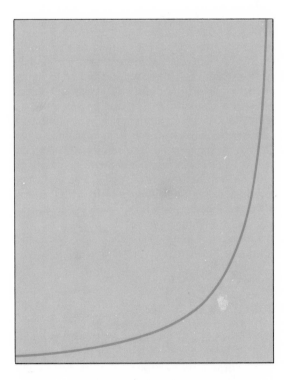

FIGURE 6.3.   **THE EXPONENTIAL PRINCIPLE**

The potential for technological advance follows an exponential curve. As the culture base grows larger, the number of conceivable inventions increases at an ever more rapid rate.

18. See Everett E. Hagen, *On the Theory of Social Change: How Economic Growth Begins* (Homewood, Ill.: The Dorsey Press, 1962), pp. 13 ff.; and Linton, *op. cit.,* pp. 306 ff.

19. Hagen, *op. cit.,* p. 15.

reopened. Hagen asserts that reopening them seemed to stimulate change but not necessarily initiate it. The pattern of developments leading to the Industrial Revolution is similarly lacking in simple cause-and-effect relationships. The number of scientific inventions doubled from the fourteenth to the fifteenth century and then tripled in the sixteenth century. But not all societies participated on an equal basis in the growth of science, not even those that had contributed significant scientific inventions. Scholars are still seeking a full explanation of why the Industrial Revolution should have reached its culmination in the last half of the eighteenth century in England rather than somewhere else. It was certainly not because all the great inventions had occurred there. A partial explanation may lie in the fact that technological change in England was coupled with changing ideas about the individual and his society.

Changes in various parts of the social system tend to stimulate and feed on each other. When inventions are accepted as part of the culture, they may bring on the appearance of new groups (the factory and the corporation), require the development of new role relationships (bureaucratic authority and specialists such as engineers, accountants, and advertising men), and even alter family life styles and structures (the husband and even the wife may be removed from the home during a significant portion of the day, and this in turn may alter the power structure of the family). In the last analysis inventions are fundamentally series of new ideas in the minds of men, ideas that may eventually alter the structures of the social groups within which men live. It is impossible to anticipate all the long-range consequences of any invention, but man proceeds ahead with the optimistic belief that invention means progress.

GUIDED CHANGE

Diffusion and invention and perhaps some kind of evolution have been major patterns of change throughout history. These patterns continue to be important in the modern world, but today we see an increasing tendency for men to initiate change and attempt to control its direction. The reclamation of the Muskingum Valley in Ohio (page 178) illustrates one effective program of guided change. A similar example on a much larger scale was the creation of the Tennessee Valley Authority (TVA), a complex program of flood control, rural electrification, and agricultural development that radically altered the way of life for people in the several states of the TVA region. Programs of urban renewal, programs to combat poverty, programs to implement the civil rights movement, programs to reduce environmental pollution—all represent ambitious efforts to guide the direction of change in American society today.

Ideally, a program of guided change involves (1) a clear and unambiguous definition of a problem that demands solution; (2) careful study "of the nature, meaning, and implications of the problem; (3) a decision regarding ultimate solutions; and (4) action on the solution agreed upon."[20] But although social planning can only proceed on the assumption that workable solutions are available, the actual course of planned change seldom if ever runs smoothly. The funds necessary for implementing a program of guided change may not be forthcoming. The people whose cooperation is needed may fail to cooperate. Changes in one area of social life may increase strains and stresses in other areas. And the more encompassing the goals of a program, of course, the more difficult it is for the planners to see all the variables involved, much less control them.

Demographic change. Efforts to introduce preventative medicine and improved sanitation to the underdeveloped areas of the world illustrate some of the complexities of social planning. Such programs have had pronounced success since World War II, but the increase in life expectancy and the reduction of infant mortality have enormously accelerated population growth, creating severe social and economic problems. (See Chapter 8, "Demographic Change.")

One by-product of the population explosion has been an increased emphasis on family planning. Indeed, programs to control population growth can be seen as a worldwide effort at guided change, an effort that now officially involves even the United Nations. A review of the literature on the subject reveals a pattern of continuing evaluation of existing programs, attempts to coordinate programs at the national

---

20. Murray G. Ross and B. W. Lappin, *Community Organization: Theory and Principles,* 2nd ed. (New York: Harper & Row, Inc., 1967), p. 139.

and international levels, an effort to define the problem more clearly and to anticipate the ramifications of various possible solutions, and an increasing awareness of the necessity to motivate those most important to any program's success, the people involved—in this case, individual husbands and wives. There is also an increasing tendency to tie family planning in with agricultural and industrial development and to attempt to allocate available funds according to some overall planning scheme.[21]

Urban planning. Population growth and population movement have put tremendous pressures on cities in all parts of the world and led to an increasing awareness of the need for urban planning. Urban planning is still in its infancy in the United States, but it already has a history of some success in many of the societies of western Europe. One of the most remarkable examples of this kind of change is the attempt to halt the physical growth of London. Great Britain's planners actually stopped this growth at the point it had reached in the summer of 1939, and a Green Belt five miles wide has been maintained around London ever since. Strategically placed around the outer rim of the Green Belt are eight New Towns, each planned for low-density population and traditional British housing patterns, with few multistory buildings. To minimize commuting problems, the British have attempted to relocate industry and to place shopping centers for maximum accessibility.

Critics acknowledge that these planned communities have been unusually successful; in fact, community planners have come from all over the world to study them for the lessons they offer. But their very success, together with factors not foreseen when they were created, have tended to create new problems even as old ones were being solved. Chief among the factors that have worked to lessen the success of this experiment has been the unexpected population growth in England since World War II. Added to this, an economic boom further attracted people to the London area, raising the population density and threatening the housing patterns that were so highly valued.[22] The planners simply did not foresee any of these possibilities.

Perhaps the chief lessons to be learned from the London example are that social systems are dynamic and that change, whether guided or not, may introduce new problems that in turn will create new pressures for change. This principle seems to be valid whether the unit of analysis is a school system, a city, or a whole society.

CULTURAL AND SOCIAL LAG

We have seen that cultural and social patterns diffuse through a society at different rates and reach different proportions of the population. Some patterns become institutionalized, while others become obsolescent and are abandoned. There is also a general tendency toward increasing differentiation, heterogeneity, and complexity. In the short run, at least, neither cultures nor societies change in a steady and coordinated way.

Some years ago, William Ogburn noted that material or technological aspects of culture tend to soar ahead in their rate of change, while norms, beliefs, values, and patterns of social organization change much more slowly. The result of such differing rates of change is a phenomenon he termed *cultural lag.* Several sociologists have expanded Ogburn's idea and provided insights into the problem of cultural lag in American society. Hauser gives the following illustration:

The right to bear arms, important in 1790, is today a fine example of cultural lag. With almost three fourths of the American people urban and about 65 percent metropolitan, a gun is certainly not needed to obtain food or for protection from wild animals or hostile Indians. The widespread prevalence of guns throughout urban and metropolitan America gives the United States the highest gunshot death rate of any nation in the world. We kill or maim tens of thousands of people a year compared with dozens in other comparable populations in which the gun is prohibited to the private citizen. In the United Kingdom, a society not too dissimilar from our own in many respects, not even the police force, except under special conditions, is permitted to bear arms. The right to bear arms in contemporary America is

21. See, for example, Bernard Berelson *et al., Family Planning and Population Programs: A Review of World Developments* (Chicago: The University of Chicago Press, 1966).

22. Peter Hall, *The World Cities* (New York: McGraw-Hill Book Company, 1966), pp. 48–52.

A largely unforeseen consequence of urbanization, air pollution has become a serious social problem. And it has created, in turn, new pressures for change—both in our attitudes toward and in our use of the environment. Here the city of Denver, once acclaimed for its clean mountain air, is covered by a blanket of smog.

a cultural atavism—a survival from the past which works much mischief in contemporary society.[23]

As Hauser points out, some cultural "lags" may pose a threat to society, while others are insignificant. "In the trivial category is the persistence of the string designed to keep collars closed against inclement weather before the advent of the pin and the button. The string has become the necktie, a relatively harmless if not always esthetic vestige which has acquired a new function, decoration."[24] In a later section (page 203) we will discuss some of the factors that may cause man to resist change—a tendency that often cannot be overcome by the mere accumulation of facts or logical arguments.

AGENTS OF CHANGE

To some extent, all institutional sectors of a society are instruments through which social and cultural change are effected as well as instruments for maintaining stability. But certain social institutions seem more central than others in initiating and directing change. In modern society these are the economy, government, and the educational system.

23. Philip M. Hauser, "Population and Social Problems," in *Contemporary Civilization: Issue 5,* ed. James Findlay (Chicago: Scott, Foresman and Company, 1971).
24. *Ibid.*

THE ECONOMY

Economic organizations must seem to most Americans to be the great fount of change and progress in this society. In fact, patriotic literature continues to wax strong on how an economic system based on free enterprise made this a great society. We are encouraged to believe that any product of the American economy is automatically better than foreign products and that economic growth and progress are synonymous.

In some respects, change has been built into daily life as a part of the economic cycle. Automobiles, the great backbone of the American economy, are a case in point. New models are made to appear out of date within three to five years, with advertising very heavily used to strengthen the felt need for change. On the surface, most of the change initiated by the automotive industry is technical rather than social. In fact, however, the automobile manufacturers have encouraged subtle changes in our values and our beliefs about the use of money and have helped make the car a part of our status-ranking system. A further by-product of rapid obsolescence is that millions of used cars, often in good condition, are available to provide transportation for the poorer members of the society.

The Industrial Revolution of the eighteenth and nineteenth centuries created the giant corporation, the assembly line, and mass production, in themselves vital social and cultural changes which in turn triggered other changes throughout the whole social system. In general, Americans place great value on economic and technological progress, but this analysis tends to obscure the fact that economic change is seldom entirely free of disruptive consequences. Technological development in the United States, for example, has resulted in the decline or quiet "death" of many cities that once flourished as centers of commerce or industry.

Industrial growth during the nineteenth and twentieth centuries was marked by a change from small, locally owned enterprises to giant corporations with plants in many different areas. The entrepreneurs of the nineteenth century had their roots in the towns where they developed their factories; they identified with the towns and had a commitment to them. But the growth of the corporation brought many changes, not the least of which was the corporate executive. Seldom did he remain in one town with one factory during the whole course of his career. He moved at the direction of his corporation, which often found it more profitable to close a plant in a small town and start a new one in a more desirable location. New England is full of towns that time has passed by, their abandoned old factories testifying to the fact that "progress" for the textile industry meant relocation in the South, where labor was cheaper and raw materials were closer at hand.

The problems caused by such relocations led W. F. Cottrell to study the sociological implications of economic change. And so he became involved in his now classic study, "Death by Dieselization."[25] Cottrell's purpose was to examine a community faced with radical change in its economic structure in order to observe the effect of economic change throughout the social structure. He selected a one-industry town, which was "ideal" in that other economic factors did not enter in to complicate the case.

Caliente, as Cottrell called the town of his study, was located in the American Southwest. It had come into existence in order to service the steam locomotive, which in the beginning required frequent stops. Long before Caliente finally came to grief at the hands of the diesel engine, many other railroad towns felt the negative effects of engineering progress, for with improvements in locomotive construction during the early part of the twentieth century, trains were able to travel longer and longer distances without needing to be serviced. Because Caliente was midway between terminals six hundred miles apart, however, these technical improvements actually represented a gain for the town. Trains still stopped at Caliente, and they now needed more servicing.

Thus Caliente grew and prospered with the railroad, and the people did not anticipate that technological advancement would reverse the trend. They built homes; put in a water system in cast iron pipes; established businesses; built a twenty-seven-bed hospital, school buildings, a theater, and even a park. These activities reflect the customary expectations of any "solid" and "sound" American community. But the people of Caliente went further than establishing the bare essentials; like their counterparts in other American communities, they established

25. W. F. Cottrell, "Death by Dieselization," *American Sociological Review*, 16 (June 1951), 358–365.

a Chamber of Commerce, a Masonic Lodge, a Rotary Club, and other civic organizations. Caliente was a community with a solid social structure, growing and optimistic.

Caliente was suddenly threatened with extinction in the mid-1940's when the railroad announced that it would no longer maintain its facilities in the town. In Cottrell's words, "The location of Caliente was a function of boiler temperature and pressure and the resultant service requirements of the locomotive." World War II, which had originally brought increased prosperity to Caliente, had also hurried the demise of the steam locomotive. The war effort used up the old steam engines, and the government helped to underwrite the costs of their replacement with diesels. The new diesel engines were more efficient than previous engines and required fewer stops for servicing. Thus Caliente, a division point essential to the steam engine, rapidly became obsolete. A change that benefitted most of American society sealed the fate of a one-industry town.

Nearly everyone in Caliente experienced some loss. The railroad had owned thirty-nine homes, a clubhouse, and a hotel in town. These became virtually worthless, but at least the company could write them off. The workers, who had seniority only in the local union, lost a great deal more. For many, technical advance meant that their old skills and talents were obsolete. A boilermaker might be reduced to an unskilled laborer. Moreover, three out of every four men had to look for new jobs, since the diesel engine reduced overall labor needs. The local merchants also lost badly. The younger ones could move out, but even they lost, for their property became worthless. The bondholders and the homeowners both lost; it was hard to foreclose on a dead town, and the 135 homeowners had no one to sell to.

Cottrell observed that those people who had been the most "moral" in the American sense—that is, had lived by the values, goals, and norms of American culture—had suffered the most. Friendships rapidly cooled and the community structure, built on a seemingly solid foundation, began to disintegrate. The local owners who had assumed family and community responsibility lost the most; the nomads who ran national chain stores lost the least.

The early reaction of the people was to band together to save the town; they saw the community as a real, meaningful entity, and they tried to attract new industry. But no one wanted to come to Caliente. As hope for new industry faded, the people began to develop a feeling of bitterness against the railroad. They acknowledged that nobody wanted to stand in the way of progress, but they could not believe that true progress would ignore loyal employees, their families, and the community which had developed in the American way through decades of service and good citizenship. They found it difficult to justify cold-blooded profit-motive decisions. The workers tried to get union backing to set up new rules that might aid them in retaining their jobs. They argued for "make-work" rules. They fought for "justice," for the things they had a "right to expect." But Caliente was dead, the victim of collective forces beyond the control of community leaders, forces that have their source in the vast systematic networks of social interdependence.

In the course of the past century, American society has seen the birth and death of many Calientes. Technological change has had repercussions throughout all sectors of the social system, and while change has been functional for many sectors, it has brought tension and hardship to others. Often the negative consequences of technological change have not been foreseen; and in any case, the culture provides no easy answers about what should be done in such situations. In fact, the culture has included values and beliefs extolling technology even at the expense of individuals or small towns.

In the decades since the 1940's the federal government has become increasingly concerned about the possibility of dislocations caused by technological change, and new laws and programs have been introduced in an effort to counteract at least the worst of its negative effects. The fact remains, however, that changes in a society's economic structure, like changes instituted in other sectors of society, often have unforeseen and far-reaching effects.

THE GOVERNMENT

The organizational structure of American government exists on three loosely related levels, the local, state, and federal; and within each level there are loosely related organizational structures with executive, legislative, or judicial responsibilities. At any given time each

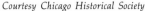

As long ago as the 1850's some of America's cities were experiencing the positive and negative consequences of technological change. Prior to the Civil War, Galena and Chicago were two of the most prosperous cities in Illinois. Galena, in fact, was the state's wealthiest city, the lead mining capital of the world, and the major commercial port on the upper Mississippi. Today, however, Galena is often described as the "town that time forgot." In 1853 the leaders of Galena rejected an opportunity for the city to become a railroad center, and from that time on, Galena's commerce and industry became smaller and smaller. No longer the bustling community of a past century (bottom left), the town now has a population of only 4500. Having changed very little since the days of its decline, Galena today (bottom right) attracts visitors because of its historical significance. Chicago, on the other hand, made the more progressive move of adopting the railroad, and the economic consequences have been obvious. Above are two views of Chicago's Water Tower on Michigan Avenue. A comparison between the drawing at the left, which was done more than a century ago, and the recent photograph at the right indicates the development of what is now America's second largest city.

of these structures may be seeking to maintain stability or to foster change in particular areas of American life. Government at the federal level is especially likely to act as a stimulant to change, not only because it has the power to initiate and implement far-reaching programs but also because it serves as a focal point for the diffusion of ideas between the different segments of society. It is at the federal level, too, that competition between the two major political parties becomes most intense, stimulating the emergence of leadership and the development of programs designed to attract voter support.

The federal government has greatly extended its areas of activity in the last several decades, but it probably always has been an agent of change as well as of the status quo. Thomas Jefferson, one of the chief architects of the Republic, was well aware that government had a role in fostering change no less than in maintaining stability. In a memorable statement now emblazoned on a wall of the Jefferson Memorial in Washington, D.C., he declared:

I am not an advocate for frequent changes in laws and institutions. But laws and institutions must go hand in hand with the progress of the human mind as that becomes more developed, more enlightened, as new discoveries are made, new truths discovered and manners and opinions change with the change of circumstances. Institutions must advance also to keep pace with the times. We might as well require a man to wear still the coat which fitted him when a boy as civilized society to remain ever under the regimen of their barbarous ancestors.

The federal government has ranked with the economic sector as the pacesetter for change in the United States. In earlier days it fostered change through the support it gave to building roads, canals, and railroads, through land acquisition and suppression of the Indians, through the development of the land-grant colleges. In the contemporary period it has fostered change in ever expanding areas, including many that closely affect the individual citizen. Since 1935, for example, it has developed programs involving social security, health, welfare, and civil rights. Its recent decision to help sponsor family-planning clinics for the poor (page 269) may eventually change the cultural and structural patterns of some five million American families.

The government often fosters change even in its own structure. It has created various agencies, bureaus, and commissions that in turn work changes in societal life patterns over a period of time. We have witnessed fundamental changes in the pattern of relationships between federal and local government; in cultural beliefs about the role of federal government; and in the definition of societal goals and the proper means to achieve them.

The role of the federal government in actively fostering social and cultural change is clearly seen in its recent effort to alter the racial status-ranking system of American society, an effort that began with experiments in integrating military troops during World War II.[26] The critical public event that gave impetus to this move toward change was a 1954 decision by the United States Supreme Court in the case of Brown vs. the Board of Education of Topeka. In this decision the Supreme Court declared that racially segregated schools were not and could not be equal and that the separation of whites and blacks in the public schools was therefore unconstitutional. The repercussions from this event are still being felt throughout the nation, illustrating the manner in which one segment of government may sometimes encourage or even impel other segments to become agents of change. Thus, the school desegregation decision led to a crisis in Little Rock in the fall of 1956, when the governor tried to block the desegregation of the high school. President Eisenhower sent federal troops to Little Rock to see that the law of the land was upheld. Two years later, Congress passed its first civil rights legislation in over sixty years.

Government activity in the area of civil rights has stimulated a gradual change in American folkways and mores, which now seem to be moving into closer correspondence with the society's formally stated ideals. But among some segments of the white population, the government's firm stand on civil rights has had the counter effect of stiffening resistance both to racial integration and to the "intrusion" of the federal government in matters traditionally left to the individual and to the states. A further effect that could not be foreseen has been the increasing frustration and bitterness of black Americans as they perceive that their rising expectations are not quickly being met.

---

26. For an account of these experiments, see Samuel A. Stouffer *et al.*, *The American Soldier* (Princeton, N. J.: Princeton University Press, 1949).

VIEWPOINTS   TECHNOLOGY AND THE FUTURE

We do well to remember that today's young people, those who protest against the inroads of technology, were born directly into this amazing age. They have never lived without central heating, the telephone, the automobile, the twin confusers radio and television, indoor plumbing. They have never lived with the sixty hour week, or one Sunday suit, or a smallpox epidemic. They have little vision of what things were like before. In effect, they are the Rip Van Winkles of our time, opening their eyes onto discoveries already in being. No wonder they take some of those discoveries for granted, and view others with suspicion or hostility. . . .

The truth is that technology grows out of a basic human instinct, the instinct to do things better, faster and easier. It began with the roller and the wheel and the lever, and it is reflected in the fascination that people everywhere find in using tools and gadgets. I can't believe that anything terrible has happened to the immortal soul when a woman in Burma sits down to her sewing machine, or when a doctor in Africa saves a child's life with a tank of oxygen. . . .

Our young people are concerned about the quality of life today. So am I. But I believe that the wise use of technology offers hope for a more rewarding way of life, both on and off the job.

Our young people are upset about what is happening to our water, land and air resources. So am I. But I know that in order to provide the food, energy and simple necessities that they want for the better, more liberated life, without further spoiling our environment, we are going to have to turn more and more to technology to solve some of the problems that it has created.

I am not foolish enough to believe that technology can solve all our problems, but I believe we can't solve most of them *without* technology. Technology wisely used can give us the time to overcome the flaws in our personal relationships. Technology wisely used can help provide the abundant and secure life we need to ensure justice and equal opportunity for all. Technology used with imagination can help eliminate the abrasive, underlying inequities that lead to conflict between men and nations. I wish that all these matters might be resolved by simple changes in human attitudes—soul power, if you wish—but nothing in history leads me to that expectation.

Fred C. Foy
"Some Kind Words for a New Villain"

As a biologist, . . . I believe that continued pollution of the earth, if unchecked, will eventually destroy the fitness of this planet as a place for human life. . . .

If we are to survive, we need to become aware of the damaging effects of technological innovations, determine their economic and social costs, balance these against the expected benefits, make the facts broadly available to the public, and take the action needed to achieve an acceptable balance of benefits and hazards. Obviously, all this should be done *before* we become massively committed to a new technology. One of our most urgent needs is to establish within the scientific community some means of estimating and reporting on the expected benefits and hazards of proposed environmental interventions *in advance*. Such advance consideration could have averted many of our present difficulties with detergents, insecticides, and radioactive contaminants. It could have warned us of the tragic futility of attempting to defend the nation's security by a means that can only lead to the nation's destruction. . . .

The obligation which our technological society forces upon all of us, scientist and citizen alike, is to discover how humanity can survive the new power which science has given it. It is already clear that even our present difficulties demand far-reaching social and political actions. Solution of our pollution problems will drastically affect the economic structure of the automobile industry, the power industry, and agriculture and will require basic changes in urban organization. To remove the threat of nuclear catastrophe we will be forced at last to resolve the pervasive international conflicts that have bloodied nearly every generation with war.

Every major advance in the technological competence of man has enforced revolutionary changes in the economic and political structure of society. The present age of technology is no exception to this rule of history. We already know the enormous benefits it can bestow; we have begun to perceive its frightful threats. The political crisis generated by this knowledge is upon us.

Science can reveal the depth of this crisis, but only social action can resolve it. Science can now serve society by exposing the crisis of modern technology to the judgment of all mankind. Only this judgment can determine whether the knowledge that science has given us shall destroy humanity or advance the welfare of man.

Barry Commoner
Science and Survival

Other government efforts to guide change have had similarly mixed consequences on American society. Simply by expanding its areas of activity, the federal government has become by all odds the nation's largest single employer. Thus when it alters its programs or reallocates funds, the jobs of countless individuals are affected. A further effect of government "bigness" has been the impact of federal spending not only on particular industries but on the economy of the country as a whole. In recent years this has become a matter of increasing public concern, as has the question of national priorities.

The changes that have begun to sweep over the underdeveloped countries promise to be even more fundamental than those now being debated in American society. Indeed, the twentieth century is likely to become known as the century of revolutions that gradually transformed the traditional societies of the world, drastically altering not only their political structures but also their cultural patterns. And in these societies no less than in our own, the central government is becoming the dominant agent for change. Although individual men, charismatic and otherwise, are providing the lead, in the long run it appears that revolutionary changes only become institutionalized when a formal machinery of government develops and becomes sufficiently strong and stable to plan, guide, and perhaps force change in the larger society. The central governments of the developing nations—with their control of financing, their access to the myriad agencies of the United Nations, and their increasing awareness of the relationship between population growth and societal development—will almost certainly be primary instruments of social and cultural change through the remaining years of this century.

EDUCATION

Although education has often been championed in the United States as the best hope for changing the world, in fact our formal system of education is primarily an agent of socialization. This is especially true at the elementary and secondary levels, but even today's "multiversity" serves the socializing functions of putting a polish on the adolescent, preparing him for the world of work, helping him find a marriage partner, and passing on the accepted knowledge of the past that will enable him to get along in the roles society has to offer him.

But the school is also dedicated to the principle that it should help teach young people to be inquiring and creative. This goal of formal education is often preached as a primary purpose of the college-university system in our complex society. In addition, the university has traditionally been the center for basic research, involving not only the quest for new knowledge but the questioning of established beliefs about man and the universe. In fostering such research and in stimulating individuals to think along new lines, higher education becomes an important agent for social and cultural change.

Despite the widely held assumption that people develop new attitudes and values as a result of their college experience, empirical evidence suggests that this may not be the case. Jacobs pioneered research in this field with a provocative study called *Changing Values in College*.[27] On the basis of data gathered from some thirty colleges and universities, he concluded that in general students' values do *not* change in college, that higher education tends to put a polish on values already instilled, and that only a few small colleges, known for the high quality of their liberal education, seem to have any major impact on values. Despite the many criticisms of the Jacobs study, other research has generally supported his main conclusions, suggesting that college serves mainly to bring out tendencies already within the individual, to sharpen his attitudes and norms, to make him more conscious of the general cultural milieu. The fact that college campuses have recently become a locus for social protest suggests the need for further research on this question.

Whether or not students' values are significantly altered by higher education, American universities have clearly stimulated many kinds of cultural and social change. As centers of basic research in both the physical and the social sciences, they have led the way toward technological advance and toward a changed understanding of man and his universe. They have also become increasingly involved in applied research, working in close cooperation with both industry and government. Many members of the

---

27. Philip E. Jacobs, *Changing Values in College* (New York: Harper & Row, Inc., 1957).

academic community have expressed concern over the implications of such involvement, fearing that it will subvert the basic goals of the university and make it the handmaiden of government or special interest groups. Some critics argue for a return to the ivory tower; others, for a new kind of commitment to the needs of society as a whole. In the years ahead we can expect a continuing reexamination of the relationships between the university, government, and society.[28]

RELIGION

It may be hypothesized that whether or not religious organizations stimulate change will depend largely on cultural variables. At first glance it would seem that if the orientation of values and beliefs is other-worldly, directing man's attention to God and personal salvation, the effect may well be to support tradition. If, on the other hand, values and beliefs direct man toward his neighbor and toward horizontal relationships generally, then change would seem more probable. But is this necessarily the case?

Latin America provides some striking examples of how religious organizations can be agents of change as well as of the status quo. Both functions are illustrated in Willems' study of the growth of Protestantism in Brazil and Chile.[29] Population pressures combined with the "revolution of rising expectations" have led millions of peasants to flee the hacienda. And they have also fled the ritualistically rigid Catholicism that was identified with it. It is estimated that between 5 and 10 percent of the Brazilian and Chilean populations have converted to Protestantism since the turn of the

century, with most of the conversions coming since 1930, about the time when general sociocultural ferment began to manifest itself in Latin America. But the conversion to Protestantism has been selective: the Pentecostal sects have won the most converts among peasants moving to urban areas, whereas the more traditional denominations have made little impact. According to Willems, as the peasants moved into urban areas they sought out religious groups that were the most opposed to the traditional Catholicism of rural Latin America. The Pentecostal Churches they joined emphasized egalitarianism and local autonomy. In fact, says Willems:

The more pronouncedly the internal structure and inherent value system of a Protestant body deviates from those of traditional Latin American society, the more attractive it has proved to be to the masses. This tendency has found its most radical expression in the Pentecostal sects that have substituted a classless society for the traditional class system. In order to preserve this classless society, they consistently deny the validity of all those conventional values that ordinarily lead to social differentiation. This is what we call subverting the traditional social order in the language of religious symbolism.[30]

Several further points are worth noting with regard to the growth of Pentecostalism in Latin America. The sects have an absolute prohibition on drinking, smoking, and gambling, with the result that the members are likely to be steady workers who are attractive to employers and thus are becoming increasingly integrated into modern economic life. An unintended consequence of their practices and beliefs may well be a new form of the so-called Protestant Ethic, which will differentiate them from the masses whether they intend it or not. Furthermore, their distrust of authority represents an important break with the traditional dependency patterns of the past, whereby the peasants looked for guidance to either the patrón or the bishop or the political leader. The Pentecostal sects may be considered as types of voluntary associations that can be positively functional in a rapidly changing society.

For its part, the Roman Catholic Church, increasingly cognizant of its precarious position in a revolutionary setting, has shown signs of overcoming the encrustations of centuries of tradition. Whether it will become an agent for

28. The issue of the relationship between social science and practical politics came to a head in 1964 with the "Rise and Fall of Project Camelot," a U.S. government-sponsored research project designed to "determine the feasibility of developing a general social systems model which would make it possible to predict and influence politically significant aspects of social change in the developing nations of the world." For a detailed account of the project and its implications, see Irving L. Horowitz, ed., *The Rise and Fall of Project Camelot* (Cambridge, Mass.: The M.I.T. Press, 1967).

29. See Emilio Willems, "Protestantism and Culture Change in Brazil and Chile," in *Religion, Revolution and Reform: New Forces for Change in Latin America*, ed. W. V. D'Antonio and F. B. Pike (New York: Frederick A. Praeger, Inc., 1964).

30. *Ibid.*, p. 108.

change in Latin America or will be increasingly irrelevant to the social revolutions that have begun there remains problematic at this writing.[31] It is clear, in any case, that the impact of religion on social change depends upon the culture and organization of the society as well as the nature of the religious institution itself.

LEISURE ACTIVITIES
AND THE MASS MEDIA

The increasing numbers of organizations devoted to leisure activities—sports, television, movies, and the like—have become new agents of change in American society and elsewhere. Although they might properly be considered part of the economy, their specialized nature and the increasing numbers of people they involve justify their classification as a new type of social institution.

Leisure activities. The growing popularity of mass entertainment and organized sports has made social mobility increasingly possible and rapid for individual members of America's minority groups; and in the process, it has had some effect in altering the status-ranking system of our society. Top athletes and entertainers have become popular heroes, and increasing prestige and wealth are now attached to the roles they play. Blacks and other minority-group members have been able to share in the rewards of this system by virtue of the fact that proven ability is almost the only criterion of rank. Not every door has always been open, of course; it was not until 1948, for example, that organized baseball admitted Jackie Robinson as the first black player on a major league team. But despite vestiges of prejudice, the sports and entertainment worlds have come closest to providing a model for a truly open-class American society.

The growing emphasis on leisure activities has brought many other changes in American society. One effect of the camping boom, for example, has been a change in the attitudes of American citizens toward their national and state parks. Growing numbers of people have come to appreciate the parks and other areas of natural beauty—and to fear that they will be spoiled by overuse. Camping has also been associated with a new kind of informality in social relationships. Families who find themselves neighbors on a campground become acquainted immediately, are eager to help each other, become close friends within a day or two, and then just as suddenly are gone off to new "instant friendships." Perhaps we have here a further manifestation of the changes in American social and cultural patterns which William H. Whyte noted in his studies of Park Forest, Illinois, during the 1950's.[32] Americans seem to be developing shallow roots that they can sink quickly in strange grounds, knowing that they will take hold. While the faces of the people differ, the values and norms remain the same. Apparently, one of the changes brought about by a mass-market economy has been the belief that all middle-class people are pretty much like oneself.

The mass media. Although the mass media may be thought of generally as agents of socialization, in that they distribute information about the society, they have also been responsible for social and cultural change. The development of television, for example, created a large new industry and many new occupations, and it brought changes in other industries as well—witness the decline of the neighborhood theater and subsequent changes in the film industry, the marked growth of advertising budgets, and the increasing professionalization of sports. There has been little empirical research dealing with the impact of television on social patterns, but few doubt that it has had some effect. In many American homes, television scheduling helps determine mealtimes and bedtimes. New Year's Day has become a day for watching three football games. Morning programs for preschool children are translated into a chance for mothers to do their housework.

The potential effect of the media in shaping attitudes and behavior has been the subject of considerable debate (see Chapter 13, "Mass Communication"). Because media influence is modified by many factors, it is probably less powerful than many people think. It is clear, however, that the media do have at least an indirect influence on attitudes, if only because they make people aware of events outside their immediate experience. Through television, we

31. For some sharply differing viewpoints on this question, see D'Antonio and Pike, *op. cit.,* esp. Chapters 1, 2, 4, 6, 9, and 12.

32. William H. Whyte, *The Organization Man* (New York: Simon & Schuster, Inc., 1956).

know our political leaders as personalities, and whether we like them or not can be as important to us as the views they represent. We witness crime, racial strife, and the horrors of war in the quiet of our own living rooms and make our judgments. We see that new fashions are catching on and take a jaundiced look at our own tired wardrobes. Whatever other effects television may have had in the United States, it has clearly contributed to the rapid diffusion of knowledge, ideas, and cultural patterns.

Television is considered as a great potential agent for change in developing areas of the world, where it may serve as a fundamental teaching device. To date, however, most of the changes brought about by television in all parts of the world have been peripheral or unplanned.

RESISTANCE TO CHANGE

Even within a society that is undergoing steady and often rapid change, there may be significant pockets of resistance to new ideas and behavior patterns. Even such a practical innovation as the auto seat belt has proved a difficult item to get accepted completely in the United States. We are a society that prides itself on rationality, efficiency, and good common sense. Yet millions of drivers take to the road without buckling up even after seat belts have been installed in their automobiles by law.

Resistance to change becomes most pronounced when traditional values and beliefs are involved. In India millions of people are ill fed and even starving, yet over 200 million edible cows, sacred to the Hindus, roam freely through the villages and farmlands. It is extremely unlikely that the eating of beef will diffuse as an innovation in India in the near future. It is more likely that Indians will accept as an innovation the government's massive program of birth control, since it does not run counter to religious proscriptions.

AN INNOVATION THAT FAILED

The field experiment described on page 204 suggests that resistance to cultural change is not easily overcome by logical argument alone. An appeal to "the facts" may have little or no effect if the facts run counter to well-established beliefs. In Peru, a major public-health effort has been to introduce such hygienic measures as boiling contaminated water. But after two years of work in Los Molinos, a rural town of two hundred families, a local hygiene worker persuaded only eleven housewives to boil their

Resistance to change becomes most pronounced when traditional values and beliefs are involved. In India millions of people are ill fed and even starving, yet over 200 million edible cows, sacred to the Hindus, roam freely through the villages and farmlands.

METHODOLOGY   THE FIELD EXPERIMENT

The small-group laboratory experiment (page 152) makes use of "artificial" groups that have been created especially for the purpose of the experiment: members are selected by the researcher, and social organization is determined by the research design. The *field experiment*, by contrast, utilizes existent groups, in which members have already worked out a pattern of social relationships. The researcher then systematically varies the experiences of the groups in order to determine what effects particular variables may have in shaping the members' behavior. The field experiment is thus quite different from field studies using the method of participant observation (page 33), in which every effort is made to *avoid* disturbing the ordinary functioning of the group being studied.

A classic study carried out by Kurt Lewin and his students during World War II illustrates the type of strategy a researcher may use in designing a field experiment. This particular study had a practical goal: to discover ways of persuading housewives to serve their families "intestinal" meats (beef hearts, sweetbreads, and kidneys) and thus help compensate for the wartime shortage of regular meats, which were strictly rationed and sometimes not available at all. Intestinal meats are high in nutritional value and relatively inexpensive, but most housewives had a deep-seated aversion to such meats (criticizing their odor, texture, appearance, etc.) and avoided serving them even when they could not get other meats. Lewin and his associates explored the hypothesis that if housewives discussed the merits of intestinal meats among themselves and publicly committed themselves to a *group decision* to try them, they would be likely to adopt the use of these foods on more than a one-trial basis. This ex-periment was one of a series of studies on the effects of group decision in changing individual conduct.

To test their hypothesis, the researchers selected for study six groups of Red Cross volunteers organized for home nursing. The groups ranged in size from thirteen to seventeen members. Three of the groups heard extensive lectures by a home economist, who emphasized the nutritional and economic advantages of intestinal meats and suggested ways of preparing them so that they would be odor-free, attractive, and "delicious." The lecturer told of her success in serving the meats to her own family, and she stressed that using them was a way of contributing to the war effort.

The other three groups heard very brief talks that simply summarized the above points. But these women were then led into a discussion of how "housewives like themselves" might be persuaded to use intestinal meats. The discussions brought out the usual aversions, but they also brought out ways of overcoming them, plus numerous points in favor of the meats. At the end of these discussions, the members were asked for a show of hands to indicate their willingness to serve one of the meats within the next week. Most of the women agreed.

A follow-up study showed that only 3 percent of those in the control groups who received the lecture treatment had gone ahead and used one of the meats. For those who participated in the groups that had made a joint decision to try the meats, the figure was 32 percent. Clearly, public commitment to a group decision was an important factor in overcoming individual resistance to change. Further study indicated that the effects of this group decision lasted over relatively long periods of time.

Kurt Lewin, "Group Decision and Social Change," in *Readings in Social Psychology*, 3rd ed., ed. Eleanor Maccoby, Theodore Newcomb, and Eugene Hartley (New York: Holt, Rinehart and Winston, Inc., 1958), pp. 197–211.

water. Every effort was made to convince the others, including lectures by a physician and visits to every home, but most people refused to take up this innovation.[33]

The water used in the town comes from irrigation ditches, a spring, and a public well. All of this water is subject to pollution. Typhoid and other water-borne diseases are a constant problem. The people of Los Molinos have little knowledge of germ theory and take no precautions to insure that their water is free of bacteria. They send their children to fetch it home in open containers from the nearest of the three sources.

When the germ theory was explained to the residents, they did not really believe it. How could such creatures fail to drown in the water? Furthermore, if germs are so small that they cannot be seen or felt, how can such delicate things survive? There are enough *real* threats in the world to worry about—poverty and hunger—without bothering oneself about animals that one cannot see, hear, touch, or smell.

In addition to this failure to comprehend the threat of bacteria, the people of the village also support a system of belief that identifies boiled water with sick people. This set of beliefs is complex and identifies certain foods, liquids, medicines, and other substances as inherently "hot" or "cold." Once an individual is sick, it would be unthinkable for him to eat and drink certain substances. Above all, he should avoid extremes in hot and cold. Since raw water is thought of as a "cold" substance, he should avoid it just as he should brandy, which is a "hot" substance. However, the cold quality of water can be eliminated by boiling it. Thus, boiled water is used by the sick as a result of a system of cultural beliefs. It has nothing to do with contamination by bacteria. Thus identified, boiled water has an unacceptable connotation for the healthy. Because of these cultural factors, the innovation of boiling water as a health measure was rejected in Los Molinos.

OVERALL RESISTANCE TO CHANGE

Resistance to change is not always limited to specific items or practices; sometimes whole societies are relatively impervious to change.[34] Among Western societies, Spain stands out as the prime example of overall resistance to change. During the medieval period, Spain was an open society "where close contact between the peoples of the peninsula had led to a mutual tolerance among the three main communities of Christians, Jews, and Moors."[35] But in 1492 Ferdinand and Isabella completed the Christian reconquest of Spain from the Moors. This marked the beginning of a new era for Spain, in which it gradually became a closed society, successfully resisted the Protestant Reformation, became the most rigidly orthodox and stratified of Catholic societies, colonized Latin America, and achieved first place as a world power. But with the close of its *Siglo de Oro* (literally "Century of Gold," the sixteenth century) Spain became a second-rate power, maintaining a state of stability that effectively cut it off from the mainstream of Western life with its increasing tempo of economic, political, and religious change.

The history of Spain demonstrates that a society can effectively resist change for long periods if it can develop a social structure and undergird it with values, beliefs, and norms that are felt to be meaningful to the people involved. In fact, so successful was Spain in integrating its social and cultural systems that the revolution of the Latin American colonies was not a revolution against the system as such, but only against control from Spain. The New World leaders maintained the culture and structure almost intact. And even though they superimposed constitutional forms of government that in many ways resembled that of the United States, they were able to give such values as freedom and democracy a very limited meaning. Freedom meant the right of the patrón to organize social life on his hacienda as he saw fit; democracy meant government by the aristocratic elite. Equality and achievement were not valued as the rights of all men. As one Latin American phrased it: "God created the rich and the poor; the poor are supposed to work as best they can with their limited capacities, and respect the orders of the rich. The rich are supposed to take

33. Edward Wellin, "Water Boiling in a Peruvian Town," in *Health, Culture, and Community,* ed. Benjamin D. Paul (New York: Russell Sages Foundation, 1955).

34. Social scientists have studied a number of communities and small societies that have maintained a more or less stable equilibrium and persistence of pattern over time. See, for example, Horace Miner, *St. Denis: A French-Canadian Parish* (Chicago: The University of Chicago Press, 1939).

35. Henry Kamen, *The Spanish Inquisition* (New York: The New American Library, 1968), p. 2.

care of the poor."[36] This social system, with its integration of economy, religion, education, and government, maintained itself for well over three centuries and proved extremely resistant to the increasingly open tendencies of the rest of the modern world.

CHANGE IN PERSPECTIVE

Writing on the eve of World War II, Ogburn and Nimkoff pondered the future:

What will be the probable rapidity of change in the future? Many people refer to our times as an age of change, with the possible implication that prior to the present there was a stationary culture, and that in the future there will probably be a stabilization of the forces of change. In other words, some observers seem to think that the present is an age of transition between two periods of peace and quiet. Of this theory it may be said there is little evidence to support the idea that culture actually was stationary in the epoch immediately preceding the present. The past would seem to be characterized by slower changes; in modern times the changes have been faster. Moreover, a truly stationary society has seldom existed in the past few thousand years. In the period of pre-history, when there were no written records, changes would have to occur within the lifetime of a man or at least within his memory, if they were to be noted. If changes did not occur within such a span of time, for all historical purposes the society would be stationary. But today many profound changes may occur within the lifetime of an individual.[37]

In the quarter-century that has passed since these words were written, the world has witnessed rapid and at times violent change. And there appears to be little reason to believe that there will soon be a stabilization of the forces of change. Indeed, the pace of change has quickened, both within our own society and in the world at large, and some of the interactive effects seem less and less subject to control. In most societies today, change has become the dominant theme of human life.

Several years ago a number of social scientists and philosophers tried to analyze the problem of coping with political, social, and economic change in the developing world. One group urged caution and warned of the dangers of unguided change. A second group argued that the secret of how to get rich quick—industrialization—was already "out of the bag," creating the demand for immediate progress. Population pressures plus the pressures resulting from the revolution of rising expectations have created an explosive situation, they maintained; a world half rich and half poor in this situation cannot maintain a stable equilibrium. Professor Leonard Reissman reminded both groups that social scientists simply do not know enough to guide the practitioners of change. He suggested that if leaders of the developing countries want industrialization, they will have to go after it and hope for the best, recognizing that they can neither predict nor prevent the myriad of other consequences that are sure to come with it.[38]

Hagen warns that the secret of economic development is not entirely technological and that both lag and resistance to change may continue because of a society's social organization and culture:

The transition to economic growth occurs rather gradually and over a considerable period of time. Although contact with the technologically advanced societies is a necessary condition for rapid technological progress (barring a long, slow process paralleling the technological history of the West), such progress does not occur merely because of this contact. In some countries, it has not occurred after a prolonged period of considerable contact; in others with less contact it has proceeded. Low-income countries cannot simply imitate techniques in use in the West; technological progress in these countries requires a high degree of creativity, as it did in the West. The innovations required are not only technoeconomic changes but also social ones. The latter may be the more complex. The transition to economic growth is accompanied by major political and social change. The causes must be forces which affect many aspects of human behavior.[39]

---

36. Statement made by a Mexican landowner at a public meeting held in Ciudad Juarez, Mexico, during July 1962. The landowner was protesting against recent statements by the Catholic Church on the need for land reform and decent wages. He argued that the teachings were Communistic and opposed to the social order established by God. The meeting was attended by one of the authors of this text.

37. William F. Ogburn and Meyer F. Nimkoff, *Sociology* (Boston: Houghton Mifflin Company, 1940), p. 803.

38. K. H. Silvert, *Discussion at Bellagio* (New York: American University Field Staff, 1964).

39. Hagen, *op. cit.*, pp. 34–35.

SUMMARY

Just as there are a variety of factors that may be necessary conditions for change in society, so are there a variety of patterns and possible agents of change. Social or cultural change may be initiated in any of the several institutional sectors of society, and the consequences may reverberate throughout the other sectors. Often one change stimulates others; the amount, direction, and velocity of change seem to vary with the complexity of the cultural base and the degree of structural differentiation in a society.

For the most part, social and cultural change have been less the result of planning and initiative than of social and cultural forces accumulating over time. But the scope of guided change, as opposed to unplanned or spontaneous change, increases with the modernization of society and also with the development of its political institutions. Social life has come to revolve around larger and larger sociocultural units. One effect of this trend is that individuals and small groups are increasingly challenged by external forces as they pursue their own goals.

The challenge for the social scientist today is to try to comprehend more fully the mechanisms of change and to identify the conditions under which a society alters its culture and social institutions while still maintaining some degree of order and stability. Sociologists are recognizing the need for reinterpreting concepts like integration and equilibrium, which used to seem so central in explaining order in society. Apparently man can live in modern society, with its increasing differentiation of structure and cultural pattern, and remain adaptive even in a situation of rapid change. In ensuing chapters we will explore the implications and limitations of this generalization as we examine modern urban society and some of the institutional sectors that cross-cut it.

7

Social
Stratification

As we noted in Chapters 1 and 2, social ranking is a basic component of social organization found in all human groups. In this chapter we will take a closer look at the phenomenon of ranking as it operates in the community and society—the ranking of individuals and families into strata that share unequally in the distribution of societal rewards. Ranking of this type is referred to as *social stratification.*[1]

The technological basis of the society is an important factor in determining which strata are most highly rewarded and what the rewards will be. Although stratification systems show great variety, all known societies have been found to be stratified on one basis or another. Among the Siriono Indians of the Brazilian jungle, the hereditary chiefs were admired as big men, able hunters, and good leaders and were accorded such privileges as having more than one wife and occupying the center of the large house in which the band lived.[2] In modern industrial societies the crucial strata are occupational, and the order in which they are ranked goes far to predict how wealth, prestige, and power will be distributed. Thus physicians and lawyers receive higher rewards in American society than ditch-diggers and clerks regardless of how well they perform their roles. *Within* occupational categories, those individuals who are judged most competent are likely to be most highly rewarded; but this evaluation is only a secondary factor in the stratification system.

As we shall see, social stratification tends to be transmitted from one generation to the next. The family is ranked as a whole, and its position in the hierarchy is crucial in determining the range of opportunities available to its members. This is not to say the ditch-digger's son cannot become a doctor—only that, given his family's rank, his chances of becoming one are much inferior to those of a doctor's son. So too are his chances of marrying a doctor's daughter.

In the following sections we shall examine the major theories developed to explain the phenomenon of social stratification, the basic conceptual tools needed for its analysis, and the major research findings about stratification in American society. Finally, we shall discuss social mobility and its implications, both in the United States and cross-culturally.

OPPOSING THEORIES OF STRATIFICATION

It is one thing to point out that all human societies are stratified; it is another to try to explain why this is true. Most of the explanations cluster around two general theories we have already encountered. One focuses on integration, order, and equilibrium; the other on conflict, cleavage, and change. The equilibrium or *functional* theory (pages 48–49) implies that stratification is simply one of the mechanisms that help maintain social stability. It is an integral part of every society and is undergirded by a broadly accepted system of values, beliefs, and sentiments. Conflict theory, on the other hand, implies that stratification is basically a mechanism of coercion: those in a position to benefit from the system impose it on the rest of society's members. In this view, social dissension and change are at least as much a part of the "natural" condition of society as are stability and equilibrium. As we have suggested in earlier chapters, conflict and functional theories are not necessarily mutually exclusive. Social reality provides evidence to support both.

CONFLICT THEORY

Without doubt the best-known of the conflict theorists has been Karl Marx (pages 7–8). According to Marx's theory of stratification, rewards have been distributed unequally in all known societies because of the continuing struggle between classes. It has always been the rulers (the owners of property) versus the ruled (the nonpropertied). Whatever class is in control tends naturally to exploit the propertyless and to build a system of stratification that seems to serve its own ends. The family perpetuates the system, passing on either wealth, property, and education to the next generation, or else poverty and ignorance.

As we have seen, Marx believed that class conflict was the mechanism through which a

1. For an introduction to the concept of stratification, see pages 82–83 and 94.
2. Allan R. Holmberg, *Nomads of the Low Bow: The Siriono of Eastern Bolivia* (Garden City, N.Y.: Doubleday Anchor Books, 1969).

classless society would eventually evolve. He declared that the modern capitalistic system was doomed because, like all earlier socioeconomic systems, it contained the seeds of its own destruction. By bringing the oppressed people together in city and factory, it provided the conditions necessary for the development of class consciousness; gradually the proletariat would come to perceive their self-interests and would revolt against the bourgeoisie. After a brief dictatorship the workers would establish a classless society in which the state would maintain control of banking, industry, and agriculture. In the long run, political power, along with class distinctions, would disappear because "political power, properly so called, is merely the organized power of one class for oppressing another."[3] Marx concluded that "In place of the old bourgeois society, with its classes and class antagonisms, we shall have an association in which the free development of each is the condition for the free development of all."[4]

For Marx, then, stratification was both an instrument by which one class oppressed another and ultimately the means (through the development of class consciousness) by which a classless society might be brought into being. His writings represent both a grand-scale theory and an ideology for action, both keen insight into the social forces that make history and polemic against these forces. The study of social stratification has been in large measure a reaction to and confrontation with Karl Marx.

Conflict theory continues to have strong proponents. For example, Dahrendorf carries on the argument that social structures are naturally coercive, though he focuses his attention not on class antagonisms as such but on the differential distribution of authority within social organizations. He hypothesizes that the patterns of domination and subjection that inhere in organizational arrangements lead to "systematic social conflicts of a type that is germane to class conflicts in the traditional (Marxian) sense of this term."[5]

FUNCTIONAL THEORY

Out of the writings of Comte, Durkheim, and others has come the theory that people build complexes of rules, roles, and social structures to live by in accordance with their fundamental value patterns. Society is an orderly system of human relationships because people are goal-oriented and because they accept certain values and beliefs as fundamental to the achievement of their goals. According to this theory, stratification has positive consequences for a social system because it reflects and reinforces the value-belief system.

Kingsley Davis and Wilbert Moore have stated this general view of stratification most clearly.[6] According to them, stratification is universal because every society must distribute its members in the different positions that make up its division of labor. And it also must insure that the individuals who fill particular roles will be motivated to meet the expectations associated with them. Not all roles are of equal difficulty: it takes less skill to be a bat boy than a pitcher in baseball, less skill to be a hospital orderly than a surgeon. And some difficult roles involve unattractive labor. A medical doctor must spend many years in specialized training, much of it far more exhausting than inspiring. In some ways, the work is "dirty," dealing as it does with diseases, infections, foul odors, and the like. But human life is highly valued and so are persons who can help save life. To outweigh the difficulties involved in playing such a role, significant rewards must be offered, and these are built into the system. According to Davis and Moore: "If the rights and perquisites of different positions in a society must be unequal, then the society must be stratified, for that is what stratification means."[7]

In general, the greatest rewards are associated with those roles which (1) have the greatest importance for the society and (2) require the

3. Karl Marx and Friedrich Engels, *The Communist Manifesto*, ed. Samuel H. Beer (New York: Appleton-Century Crofts, Inc., 1955), p. 32.

4. *Ibid.*

5. Ralf Dahrendorf, *Class and Class Conflict in Industrial Society* (Stanford, Calif.: Stanford University Press, 1959), p. 165. See also Celia Heller, "Unresolved Issues in Stratification Theory," in Heller, ed., *Structured Social Inequality: A Reader in Social Stratification* (New York: The Macmillan Company, 1969), pp. 479–531. Heller notes that recent events in Europe (e.g., the general strike in France in 1968) and in the United States (e.g., the Poor People's Campaign and the grape pickers' strike) support the theory of continuing class conflict in modern industrial societies.

6. Kingsley Davis and Wilbert Moore, "Some Principles of Stratification," *American Sociological Review,* 10 (April 1945), 242–249.

7. *Ibid.*, p. 243.

greatest training or talent. As Davis and Moore note, however, societies do not over-reward positions that are easy to fill, even if they are important. Thus, until the rapid growth of population resulted in a shortage of teachers to man the crowded classrooms, the rewards received by teachers were particularly small as judged against the importance of their role for society.

The central argument of the Davis-Moore position is that unless roles are rewarded unequally, some jobs won't get done. Since in fact the jobs *do* get done in all societies, stratification must be built into the system, whether consciously or not. In this view, stratification has the consent of the people, even those who do not get a major share of the rewards. There is passive acceptance of the large bonuses given to top executives of corporations, just as there is acceptance of the bonuses professional teams give to rookie players. Even those workers at the lowest end of the pay scale raise no serious protest about the generous rewards received by business executives. Nor do they hesitate to approve similarly generous rewards for their own leaders.

Seen in this light, social stratification appears to be basically integrative. It ensures that the important jobs will get done, and it may even provide a certain amount of psychological security to the individual: he knows his place; he has the respect of his fellows; he does his job and is rewarded accordingly. The city councilman doesn't believe that he should have as much power as the mayor, nor does the bat boy expect to receive as much money or applause as the star pitcher. Satisfaction is a highly relative matter; in the perspective of this theory of stratification, it means that people accept differential rewards because they accept the value system and the rules that go with it. They believe they are getting essentially what they deserve to get.

The functional theory seems most applicable to an open-class society, one in which the most talented can come to the fore and be recognized. It is possible to glance quickly at American society and say, "Yes, this is how the system works." We value entertainment, for instance, and we reward those who provide it. Barbra Streisand, Joe Namath, and Bill Cosby might serve as examples of the open-class system that permits the talented to find their way to the top and to be rewarded accordingly. But if we analyze the system more carefully, we find it necessary to question at least parts of the theory. Do the professions—including politics—really attract the most talented? Are top business positions filled by giving everyone equal access to valued roles, or are there biases along the way favoring certain people over others? Can the theory account for the fact that, outside sports and show business, blacks are grossly underrepresented in the middle and upper levels of the occupational ladder? Furthermore, how does the theory explain the more than chance pattern of succession in occupations? It has been found that almost 20 percent of American medical doctors are children of medical doctors. This tendency toward succession is evident throughout business and the professions.[8]

The functional theory of stratification seems to ignore the fact that people are literally born into different social strata. And since socialization varies by class and status, some people are relatively advantaged and others disadvantaged, regardless of their potential ability to play a particular role. Although it is true that the broad range of the middle class of American society includes some 50 to 65 percent of the people and that through societal consensus and the school system they compete more or less equally, the fact remains that those at the top enjoy special privileges and those at the bottom suffer special deprivations. In the long run, continued succession at the top and bottom may produce dysfunctional consequences.

Acknowledging that many more people have the capacity to become medical doctors than actually do, Davis and Moore assert that most potential doctors are discouraged by the prospect of the long training process. Hence, it is necessary to offer high prestige and wealth to attract enough people to meet the need. But do the medical schools in fact lack applicants, or is it true instead that there are not enough medical schools to train all those who apply for admission? And is it possible that some medical organizations would, if necessary, try to restrict enrollments in order to preserve the scarcity value of the profession?

8. See Charles F. Schumacher, "The 1960 Medical School Graduate: His Biographical History," *Journal of Medical Education*, 36 (May 1961), 398–406. In a study of the academic profession, Clifford Kirkpatrick and Melvin DeFleur found that more than a third of the sons of Indiana University faculty members had achieved Ph.D.'s; see "Influence of Professors on the Flow of Talent to the Academic Profession," in *Social Forces*, 38, No. 4 (May 1960), 296–302.

If functional theory does not wholly fit the facts of life in American society, it seems even less applicable to those traditional societies stressing the belief that "God created the rich and the poor"—unless one assumes that God also made the rich uniformly more talented than the poor. History, of course, suggests otherwise. We must conclude, then, that functional theory best fits those patterns found in the middle strata of a relatively open society. It assumes that roles are filled largely on the basis of achieved rather than ascribed criteria, and it also assumes that education is readily accessible to help people prepare for the roles to which they aspire.

DIMENSIONS OF STRATIFICATION

Max Weber challenged the simplicity of Marx's system of stratification, which focused so strongly on economic factors. Weber analyzed stratification into three main orders, which he called *class, social honor,* and *party*.[9] A class is made up of people who share the same life chances based on their occupational roles and/or their inherited wealth. Social honor is the status or prestige individuals enjoy. Party means political power, which Weber defined as ability to command the behavior of others, even over opposition.

All three orders of stratification are interrelated. Parties may represent status groups and economic interests. Social honor may result from class—either occupation or wealth or both—and in time the prestige may come to outweigh the facts of profession or possessions. Similarly, the power of wealth may be translated, to a degree, into political power. But here Weber made a sharp distinction: class and political power do *not* have a one-to-one relationship, as Marx contended. Control of the means of production does not automatically confer political dominance. Weber also believed that, in the short run, class consciousness is not a necessary element of class stratification.

In American sociology Weber's *party* is usually called *power,* and we shall follow this usage. Political parties are obviously concerned with power, and use of the term emphasizes its close relationship with class and status. Broadly conceived, power is the ability to control the decision-making process—to initiate policies and to see that they are implemented.

STATUS

Status refers to the amount of prestige that accrues to an individual in his social roles. It provides him with self-respect, with a sense of worth. Desire for these feelings is built into the individual early in the socialization process. As we pointed out in earlier chapters on personality development, an individual's self-respect is relative to the groups that are most significant to him—in our society usually his family, his peer groups, and his occupational group.

Acquisition of prestige. In the past, valor in battle and the accumulation of wealth were common ways by which people who were not born with high status could acquire it. Daniel Defoe in a poem called "What Makes a Peer?" noted how well the English had managed to develop their nobility, despite the fact that the ancestors of these gentlemen were mainly foreign and of questionable background:[10]

> Wealth, howsoever got, in England makes
> Lords of mechanics, Gentlemen of rakes.
> Antiquity and birth are needless here;
> 'Tis impudence and money makes a peer.

Defoe's poem, written in the seventeenth century, touches on the shift from wealth to prestige that Weber noted. Wealth may have made the difference in the first place, but, over time, antiquity and family would become telling characteristics of status. And with the latter went the prestigious traditions—of speech, manner, taste, and education. Thackeray noted what these status differences meant in nineteenth-century England:[11]

9. Max Weber, "Class, Status, and Party," in *From Max Weber: Essays in Sociology,* ed. Hans Gerth and C. Wright Mills (New York: Oxford University Press, 1946), pp. 180–195.

10. Reprinted in Lewis A. Coser, ed., *Sociology Through Literature* (Englewood Cliffs, N.J.: Prentice-Hall, Inc., 1963), p. 131.

11. William Makepeace Thackeray, *Sketches and Travels in London;* reprinted in Coser, *op. cit.,* pp. 138–139.

Throughout most of history, status symbols have been used to indicate the prestige associated with various social roles. In early twentieth-century England, for example, one could determine the different degrees of "social honor" by scanning the hats worn at the Ascot races. Those of wealth and lineage wore top hats and took the top position. Straw hat and bowler indicated the success of the nouveaux riches, while members of the lower strata, who had the poorest view of the race, wore cloth caps.

They [the lower strata] are not like you, indeed. They have not your tastes and feeling: your education and refinements. They would not understand a hundred things which seem perfectly simple to you. They would shock you a hundred times a day by as many deficiencies of politeness, or by outrages upon the Queen's English—by practices entirely harmless, and yet in your eyes actually worse than crimes—they have large hard hands and clumsy feet. The woman you love must have pretty soft fingers that you may hold in yours: must speak her language properly and at least when you offer her your heart, must return hers with its *h* in the right place, as she whispers that it is yours, or you will have none of it. If she says, "Hedward, I Ham so unappy to think I shall never behold you again",—though her emotion on leaving

you might be perfectly tender and genuine, you would be obliged to laugh.

The "correct" use of language—particularly pronunciation, usage, and grammar—continues to be much more a matter of social etiquette than of communication. "Bad" English, while usually perfectly understandable, is still the mark of the lower strata.

In American society, the path from wealth to social distinction has been shortened. The men who made enormous fortunes in the nineteenth century were often crudely spoken, bad mannered, and uneducated; but their grandchildren—if not their children—were able to qualify as old families of established position

In the United States the structure of relationships between whites and blacks has had many characteristics of a caste system.

and snub the new rich as vulgar social climbers. Meanwhile, the old, old families—those that had reached America earliest and had either brought with them or soon achieved a respected gentility—looked down on both generations of wealth in the smug conviction that lineage, not money, was the only sound basis of prestige.

For all of us, prestige is a reward to be ardently sought and ferociously defended. Lenski points out that the quest "influences almost every kind of decision from the choice of a car to the choice of a spouse. Fear of the loss of status, or honor, is one of the few motives that can make men lay down their lives on the field of battle."[12]

Closed status systems. There have been numerous occasions throughout history when differences in prestige became so pronounced as to create more-or-less closed status groups. The most extreme form of the closed status group is the *caste.* In a caste system, a person is born into a particular caste and must remain in that caste until he dies, regardless of his achievements. His occupation and marriage opportunities are both prescribed by the fact of caste. Patterns of stratification are deeply institutionalized and are supported by religious beliefs, custom, and law. In essence, all forms of social interaction are narrowly prescribed by the particular style of life of the caste to which individuals belong by fact of birth. India provides a classic example of a stratification system built around closed status groups. Although the Hindu caste system there has been formally abolished by law, the traditional castes continue to limit the life chances of millions of citizens.

In the United States, the structure of relationships between whites and blacks has had many characteristics of a caste system.[13] Being black has automatically put an individual into a low status group and limited his access to wealth and political power. The persistence of these patterns of discrimination for more than a hundred years after the signing of the Emancipation Proclamation illustrates the strength of

---

12. Gerhard Lenski, *Power and Privilege: A Theory of Stratification* (New York: McGraw-Hill Book Company, 1966), p. 37.

13. For two of the early community studies treating this phenomenon, see John Dollard, *Caste and Class in a Southern Town* (New Haven: Yale University Press, 1937) and St. Clair Drake and Horace Cayton, *Black Metropolis* (New York: Harcourt Brace Jovanovich, Inc., 1945).

status systems supported by traditional folkways and mores.

Elements of a closed status system also permeate many other sectors of American life. Religion, ethnicity, sex, lineage, and education have all tended to preserve closed status groups.[14] Although these variables have lost some of their significance over the last century, they continue to influence not only life styles but also life chances. Jews may still have difficulty getting a job or receiving promotion in New York banks, and Catholics and Jews as well as blacks may still be excluded from certain private clubs. Women are still not accepted in most occupations on an equal basis with men, and life chances are probably still better for graduates of Yale, Harvard, and Princeton than for graduates of state universities or less prestigious private institutions.

Open status systems. The Protestant Reformation, the Industrial Revolution, and the gradual development of political democracy have combined in most of the Western world to disrupt the traditional system of assigning prestige on the basis of ascribed characteristics. Thus, with the reservations already noted, American society, like other industrialized societies, has a relatively open status system—that is, people move up or down on the status scale depending on their level of achievement, especially their achievement in occupational roles. Socialization in an open society tends to blur differences of birth and to emphasize the right of all to acquire a fair share of society's rewards, including the reward of prestige. Social honor is not the exclusive possession of one group, as it has tended to be in traditional societies.

A majority of Americans today have sufficient income to purchase most of the basic symbols of status, including education. Almost anyone can achieve some increase in prestige, and maintaining closed status groups is increas-

ingly difficult. Yet status differences continue to be a source of conflict in American society, even excluding the black-white dilemma. Although our values and norms minimize the importance of status, most Americans are very conscious of it. At the least, they want to keep up with the Joneses. Perhaps status is most significant today at the level of primary-group activity, where it continues to influence patterns of friendship, dating, and marriage.

CLASS

The concept of social class refers to a stratum or aggregate of persons who share more or less the same economic privileges in a society. These privileges derive largely but not exclusively from the occupational role or roles of the household breadwinner(s). Inherited wealth is the other major source.

Class fluidity. Even in an open society, social prestige can be increased only gradually over a relatively long period of time. Economic position, by contrast, can change very rapidly. Compared to status groupings, then, social classes are relatively fluid.

The concept of class fluidity becomes meaningful only in a dynamic industrial society where occupational roles are sharply differentiated and where new, specialized roles develop that are open to some degree of competition. In traditional societies, occupational roles as well as status tend to be determined at birth. This was the case in feudal Europe, and it is still the case in most of the developing world.

An increasingly significant phenomenon of industrial society is the working wife. In 1950 about 24 percent of married women in the United States were part of the labor force; by 1970, the figure had risen to almost 40 percent.[15] The overall effect of this trend may be to ensure an even greater fluidity of social classes, for the additional income a wife brings in may alter radically the privileges a family can enjoy. A striking example of how the pattern works is found in the border area between the United States and Mexico. As of 1963, some fifteen thousand Mexicans crossed the border daily from Ciudad Juárez in the state of Chihuahua to work in El Paso, Texas. Among them were thousands of women who worked in the textile

---

14. The most elaborate attempts to measure the impact of status groups on the American community have been made by W. Lloyd Warner and his associates (page 216). See, for example, W. Lloyd Warner and Paul S. Lunt, *The Status System of a Modern Community* (New Haven: Yale University Press, 1942) and W. Lloyd Warner and Leo Srole, *The Social Systems of American Ethnic Groups* (New Haven: Yale University Press, 1945).

15. U.S. Bureau of the Census, *Statistical Abstract of the United States, 1969* (Washington, D.C.: Government Printing Office, 1969), p. 220.

plants and earned between $40 and $50 a week. While the status level of the job was low, the income level was higher than that of a Ciudad Juárez bank teller. Many of these factory workers paid a special tuition to send their children to school in El Paso on the presumption that such education would improve their children's life chances.[16]

Measuring class and class consciousness. Contemporary sociological interest in class differences can be traced to the community research carried out in the thirties and forties by W. Lloyd Warner and his associates, which demonstrated empirically the existence of social classes in American society.[17] The fact that people with no knowledge of sociology readily classify families as being "lower-middle" class or "upper-middle" class, "upper-lower" class or "lower-upper" class, is direct testimony to the impact of the Warner studies on American thinking about stratification.

Warner's approach to measuring class has been widely criticized for its failure to distinguish between class and status and its tendency to assume that power is largely a function of wealth. But these criticisms should not be allowed to obscure the importance of Warner's contribution. He and his colleagues provided both a set of concepts for dealing with class differences and a means for measuring such differences systematically (see Methodological Essay, page 218).

Subsequent studies of the stratification patterns in American communities have followed Warner's lead and used both objective and subjective measures of class. With the objective approach, variables such as income, occupation, education, and place and type of residence are used as indices of class. With the subjective approach, individuals may simply be asked to assess their own class position. Studies of both types have consistently shown the existence of some three to six classes in American communities. An additional distinction is sometimes made between "blue collar" and "white collar" workers. These terms imply differences not only in wealth but also in status between those in the working and lower classes and those in the middle and upper classes. Thus they do not identify social classes as such but simply provide a general orientation to the stratification system in American society, which

is tied closely to the system of occupational ranking.

Research has shown that most Americans are aware of a class structure but that many people misperceive their own position in it.[18] One recent study, using both open-ended and pre-coded questions, confirmed the tendency noted over the last quarter-century toward self-identification with the middle class.[19] In response to an open-ended question asking the subject to identify his own class in his own words, nearly three-quarters of the adults in a national sample identified themselves as being "average" or as falling somewhere within the broad range of the middle class. Only 11 percent acknowledged being in the working class or lower class. In the same study, the five-option class question brought forth somewhat different responses but showed the same basic pattern. The class options offered were: upper, upper-middle, middle, working, and lower class. In this situation 61 percent of the sample identified themselves as middle or upper-middle class and 34 percent as working class.

The authors of this study found that a broad range of interclass contacts among the people in their sample was no less important than economic factors in determining class consciousness. Overall, the study revealed not only that wealth and prestige mingle in the minds of

16. See William V. D'Antonio and William H. Form, *Influentials in Two Border Cities* (South Bend, Ind.: University of Notre Dame Press, 1965), Ch. 2.

17. Among the best-known studies are those of "Yankee City" (Newburyport, Massachusetts): W. L. Warner and P. S. Lunt, *The Social Life of a Modern Community* (1941) and *The Status System of a Modern Community* (1942); W. L. Warner and L. Srole, *The Social Systems of American Ethnic Groups* (1945); and W. L. Warner and J. O. Low, *The Social System of a Modern Factory* (1947), all published by Yale University Press. Another influential group of studies was the series on "Jonesville" (Morris, Illinois, also called "Elmtown," "Hometown," and "Prairie City"): W. L. Warner, R. J. Havighurst, and M. B. Loeb, *Who Shall Be Educated* (New York: Harper & Brothers, 1944); W. L. Warner and Associates, *Democracy in Jonesville* (New York: Harper & Brothers, 1949); W. L. Warner, M. Meeker, and K. Eels, *Social Class in America* (Chicago: Science Research Associates, Inc., 1949); and A. B. Hollingshead, *Elmtown's Youth* (New York: John Wiley & Sons, 1949).

18. A pioneer study of class consciousness was that of Richard Centers, *The Psychology of Social Classes* (Princeton, N.J.: Princeton University Press, 1949).

19. Robert W. Hodge and Donald J. Treiman, "Class Identification in the United States," *American Journal of Sociology*, 73, No. 5 (March 1968), 535–547.

adult Americans, but that most of them feel they belong to an open, more or less middle-class society, one with which they can readily identify.

POWER

Max Weber defined power as "the probability that one actor within a social relationship will be in a position to carry out his own will despite resistence."[20] Power, in other words, is the ability to make and implement decisions, with or without the consent of those who will be affected. Control of decision-making is an important measure of rank in all human groups, but it is especially significant at the level of community and society, where those with power can determine the general life chances of those without it. Power, thus conceived, is not only a reward of the stratification system but a means for determining the distribution of other rewards.

In traditional societies, the rewards of power, wealth, and status have generally gone hand in hand. It has been accepted as "natural" that the rich should rule, that rulers should be rich, and that all others should serve and obey. These principles are only now being challenged in the developing societies, where an unequal power distribution has been strongly supported by tradition and religious belief. When power struggles have occurred, they have been primarily struggles among those already in the top strata; whatever the outcome, power has remained concentrated in the hands of a few. The typical Latin American "revolution," for example, has meant little more than a changing of the palace guard. Only in Mexico and Cuba have the rights of the old elites been challenged in any fundamental way.

In Western societies, the trend over the last several centuries has been toward the diffusion of power. Traditional systems of authority have gradually given way to legal-rational systems, in which power is vested not in a class of individuals but in a system of offices with clearly defined prerogatives and responsibilities. Political power is distributed to the citizenry through the vote and through access to public office. As

20. Max Weber, *The Theory of Social and Economic Organization* (New York: The Free Press, 1957), p. 152.

The variety of homes that fall into the category of "middle class housing" reflects, to some extent, the variety of individuals who consider themselves "middle class."

METHODOLOGY MEASURING CLASS AND STATUS

No one way to measure social class or status is universally accepted, and all methods have been subject to serious criticism. Many sociologists continue to use variations of the two techniques developed by W. Lloyd Warner in his pioneering studies of the class structure in American communities.

Warner's first technique was called *Evaluated Participation* (E.P.). Assuming that people in the same community evaluate each other and are aware of the ranking system that emerges, the researchers asked informants to identify and rank local social classes and to place community members in these ranks. The investigators noted the use of symbols indicating class structure ("Main Line," "high hat") and remarks about personal traits that carried connotations of class and status ("leader," "immoral"). Each informant placed the person to be ranked above, equal to, or below himself or else specifically assigned him to a social class. This information became the basis for determining how many classes existed in a community and which persons belonged to each. Warner and his associates identified six classes: upper-upper, lower-upper, upper-middle, lower-middle, upper-lower, and lower-lower.

Warner developed a second measurement technique because the first, requiring extensive interviewing, was expensive. The *Index of Status Characteristics* (I.S.C.) was based on the observation that four factors had high correlation with the class placement obtained by E.P. These were occupation, source of income (inherited wealth, salary, wages, welfare payments), house type, and dwelling area. Occupation was given a weight of 4; source of income, 3; house type, 3; and dwelling area, 2. An individual could receive a score of 1 (high) to 7 (low) on each item. Thus, a score of 12 to 22 placed him in the upper class, while 52 to 66 placed him in the upper-lower class. The I.S.C. is thought to give at least an approximate measure of the class and status of persons in small cities.

Ruth Rosner Kornhauser has criticized the Warner approach to stratification on several grounds. First, his techniques lump together the three orders of stratification that Weber singled out. Warner had originally thought that economic factors would contribute most heavily to a definition of class position, but he discovered that some families who had lost their wealth retained a measure of prestige, while some high-income families had relatively low prestige. Finding that wealth alone was not a sufficient indicator of stratification position, Warner added the factors of prestige and power to his index. But since all three dimensions of stratification are combined, we have no way of knowing how they interrelate—for example, how long prestige remains when wealth is gone, or under what circumstances wealth is converted to power.

Second, although wealth, power, and prestige are combined, prestige is stressed. Prestige is a legitimate focus of study, but it may be more relevant in explaining the habits of the rich than in explaining the protests of the poor.

Third, Warner's measure of prestige is suited primarily to small communities where people are aware of one another's ancestry and reputation. Furthermore, Warner may not have correctly described the status structure even of a small town, for he relied primarily on upper-middle-class and upper-class informants. Those who have money tend to see the class structure in terms of manners and are capable of making finely honed distinctions. The poor tend to see a simpler division into "haves" and "have-nots."

In summary, the Warner approach to stratification gives us a good picture of the styles of life of various strata, especially in small communities, but does not tell us very much about what the lower strata want or what will happen if they try to get it. The study of power hierarchies based on economic interests might be a more fruitful focus of investigation if one wants to explain what is going on in American cities today.

For Warner's discussion of his methods, see W. Lloyd Warner, Marchia Meeker, and Kenneth Eels, *Social Class in America* (Chicago: Science Research Associates, 1949). For criticism of the Warner approach, see the work cited above: Ruth Rosner Kornhauser, "The Warner Approach to Social Stratification," in *Class, Status, and Power: A Reader in Social Stratification* (New York: The Free Press, 1953), pp. 224–255. Another comprehensive criticism is found in Milton Gordon, *Social Class in American Sociology* (New York: McGraw-Hill Book Company, 1963), pp. 85–123 and 210–233.

political parties have come into being to compete for control of the government, they have become brokers for a wide variety of social aggregates, all seeking the rewards that political power can give.

The complexities of social stratification become clear when we try to analyze the extent to which competition for power in a democratic society reflects competition between classes. In Great Britain and some of the Continental countries, political parties have seemed to reflect class interests more strongly than they have in the United States. The value-orientations of American society support an open class system as being morally right, and most political leaders have avoided making a direct appeal to class differences. Both parties have nominated men of inherited wealth as presidential candidates, and both have nominated men of humble origin—from Andrew Jackson and Abraham Lincoln to Lyndon B. Johnson and Richard M. Nixon. Still, the generalization is often made that the Democrats represent the working class and the intellectuals, whereas the Republicans rep-

___

21. *Newsweek*, March 17, 1969, p. 136.

resent the interests of business and property. The legislative actions of the two parties lend some support to this contention, though not to the point of establishing class cleavages (see Table 7.1, page 220).

Whatever the allegiances of our major parties, competition for power *within* them seems to be weighted in favor of those who have inherited or achieved a favored position in society. In theory, any American boy has an equal chance of growing up to become President, but those actually selected as presidential candidates have hardly represented a complete cross-section of American society. (See inset, below.) All have been middle or upper class, and all have enjoyed high status prior to nomination. Furthermore, though possession of wealth is not in itself a guarantee of political power, access to wealth has increasingly become a necessary condition for winning political office. In 1968, Richard Nixon spent $8.5 million and Hubert Humphrey spent $4 million just in campaigning for nomination. Campaign costs for other would-be nominees were $6 million for Nelson Rockefeller, $7 million for Eugene McCarthy, and $6 million for Robert Kennedy.[21]

___

WHAT PRESIDENTIAL CANDIDATES ARE LIKE

1. Between the ages of fifty and fifty-four when first nominated, with Democrats closer to fifty than the Republicans.

2. Born in New York and Ohio more often than any other state, the former tending to be the principal natal state of Democrats.

3. Most often sons of professional persons, farmers, or public officials; the Democratic nominees close to the norm for the entire group.

4. Almost invariably professional persons, particularly lawyers . . . .

5. Most have read or otherwise studied law in preparation for the bar, but they were not always holders of B.A. or LL.B. degrees; Democrats nominated the only Ph.D. (Wilson).

6. Most nominees were Presbyterians or Episcopalians, with a preponderance of Democrats in the former. Democrats are also distinguished for having placed the first member of the Catholic faith (Smith) at the head of its ticket and for

having elected the first Catholic (Kennedy) . . . .

7. The average presidential nominee in either major party had governmental experience in at least two or three offices, usually at the state or federal levels of government. Democrats have drawn more frequently [than Republicans] from United States senators and state governors and less frequently than Republicans from the military.

8. The nominees, without major differentiation between parties, have held executive positions at one or another level of the party organization.

The presidential nominee, whether he wins or loses, is only a titular leader of his party, under contract to run with the general support of the party. In the literal sense of a contract, the national convention offers him the nomination, which he may or may not accept. He holds no formal office in the party, although he has all kinds and degrees of informal influence.

Reprinted from Ralph M. Goldman, *The Democratic Party in the United States* (New York: The Macmillan Co., 1966), p. 129; based on statistical analyses of all presidential nominees from 1831 to 1956 (up to and including Eisenhower).

TABLE 7.1 **PARTY VOTING RECORDS ON MAJOR DOMESTIC BILLS, 1933–1968**

Bill	Party	House YEA	House NAY	Senate YEA	Senate NAY	Year
TVA (created public corporation to develop and sell electric power, control flooding, etc.)	Dem.	284	2	48	3	1933
	Rep.	17	89	14	17	
Security and Exchange Act (provided for regulation of stock exchanges and trading practices)	Dem.	254	11	47	1	1934
	Rep.	22	73	15	12	
Wagner Act (created National Labor Relations Board and strengthened labor's bargaining position)	Dem.	voice		49	4	1935
	Rep.	vote		12	8	
Social Security Act (provided for old-age benefits based on earnings before age 65)	Dem.	287	13	60	1	1935
	Rep.	77	18	14	5	
Soil Conservation and Domestic Allotment Act (provided payments to farmers for soil conservation)	Dem.	246	25	49	9	1936
	Rep.	20	64	5	11	
National Housing Act (created U.S. Housing Authority to administer construction loans to cities and states)	Dem.	239	38	55	8	1937
	Rep.	24	48	6	8	
Wages and Hours Act (provided for minimum hourly wage and limited work week)	Dem.	247	41	voice		1938
	Rep.	31	48	vote		
School lunch program	Dem.	164	45	38	4	1946
	Rep.	110	56	11	17	
Taft-Hartley Act (placed restrictions on organized labor, enabled states to enact "right-to-work" laws)	Dem.	106	71	20	22	1947
	Rep.	225	11	48	3	
National Housing Act (authorized funds for public housing construction and for urban redevelopment)	Dem.	192	55	33	2	1949
	Rep.	34	131	24	11	
Civil Rights Act (created Civil Rights Commission, barred interference with voting rights)	Dem.	128	82	23	15	1957
	Rep.	151	15	37	0	
Labor Reform Bill (Landrum-Griffin bill, aimed at eliminating corruption within unions)	Dem.	156	122	approved		1959
	Rep.	147	3			
Area Redevelopment Bill (authorized grants and loans to economically depressed areas)	Dem.	208	42	48	11	1961
	Rep.	43	125	15	16	
Minimum Wage Bill (raised minimum hourly wage and expanded coverage)	Dem.	208	43	51	11	1961
	Rep.	133	35	14	17	
Education Bill (extended National Defense Education Act and federal aid for impacted school areas)	Dem.	221	23	52	7	1961
	Rep.	157	9	28	0	
Tax Revision Bill (revised taxes and closed tax loopholes)	Dem.	218	34	40	14	1962
	Rep.	1	162	19	10	
Civil Rights Act (banned discrimination in public places, in employment, and in labor unions)	Dem.	152	96	46	21	1964
	Rep.	138	34	27	6	
Bill Establishing Antipoverty Program	Dem.	204	40	51	12	1964
	Rep.	22	145	10	22	
Medicare (provided medical care payments for those 65 and older)	Dem.	248	42	55	7	1965
	Rep.	65	73	13	14	
Aid to Education (provided federal assistance for elementary and secondary schools)	Dem.	228	57	55	4	1965
	Rep.	35	96	18	14	
Voting Rights Bill (provided for federal officers to register black voters in noncomplying counties)	Dem.	221	61	47	17	1965
	Rep.	112	24	30	2	
Demonstration Cities and Metropolitan Development Act (provided for an extensive attack on urban blight)	Dem.	162	60	39	9	1966
	Rep.	16	81	14	13	
Truth-in-Lending Bill (required lenders to disclose annual percentage cost of credit)	Dem.	218	3	56	0	1968
	Rep.	165	1	36	0	
Housing and Urban Development Act (included provisions for helping low-income families buy homes)	Dem.	156	43	40	3	1968
	Rep.	72	92	27	1	
Open Housing Bill (banned racial discrimination in housing)	Dem.	150	88	42	17	1968
	Rep.	100	84	29	3	

Obviously, a serious contender for the presidency must be either rich in his own right (like Rockefeller and Kennedy), close to the party apparatus (like Nixon and Humphrey), or a symbol for a cause that people will contribute to (like McCarthy). Nor are large campaign expenditures limited to the contest for the presidency. Nelson Rockefeller was reported to have spent at least $5 million on his reelection as governor of New York in 1966. At the senatorial level, costs run from a quarter of a million to a million dollars. In 1968 total campaign spending for all offices—federal, state, and local—was $250 million dollars, an increase of 25 percent over 1964.[22]

Given the increasing importance of political office in American society, we need to examine carefully the variables like wealth, education, and occupation that are replacing lineage, religion, and race as limiting factors in the struggle for political power. In particular, we need to study the manner in which these variables act to affect party organization and thus to determine our candidates for public office. These are some of the issues that we will consider in Chapter 14, "The Political System."

AGENTS OF STRATIFICATION

The social institutions having the greatest impact on the stratification system in American society are the family, the school, the occupational system, and the government. All of these institutions help maintain the system, even as they provide some means for changing it. The family, for example, is the primary agent for perpetuating class differences, despite the fact that most families strive to improve their own class position. The school is designed as the great social equalizer, but in fact the schools tend to sort out society's members and to give some better life chances than others. The occupational system is the main vehicle for upward mobility, but job opportunities are not open to everyone on an equal basis. The government has taken

an increasingly active part in altering some aspects of the stratification system, but the question of a middle- or upper-class bias remains. In the sections that follow we will examine the role played by each of these social institutions in determining the distribution of status, wealth, and power. The focus of our discussion will be primarily, but not exclusively, on American society.

THE FAMILY

Many sociologists agree with William J. Goode that the family is "the keystone of the stratification system, the social mechanism by which it is maintained."[23] The class and status of an individual's family help determine not only his educational and job opportunities but also his opportunities for social interaction. For the most part, people go to school with, become friends with, work with, and spend their leisure with other people at the same general social level. Thus when it comes to choosing a marriage partner, the choice is pretty well limited to someone of the same class and status.

From the standpoint of maintaining the stability of the family, intraclass marriage tends to be functional. Similar backgrounds enhance the probability that husbands and wives will share a wide range of interests, attitudes, and values and be better able to rear their children with a minimum of conflict. In turn, the children learn the values and attitudes of their own family, come to see them as right, and seek out other young people of similar viewpoint. As the saying goes, they feel comfortable with "their own kind." But this very pattern of "like seeking out like" tends to perpetuate the inequalities between the classes, at least in the short run. In effect, it makes it much easier for the "uppers" to keep the "lowers" in their places.

Whatever criteria a society uses for determining social rank—whether lineage and landed wealth or education and occupational achievement—the upper classes have the most resources at their disposal, and the futures of their children are most assured. As Goode notes, "in all family systems, upper class children obtain unearned advantages, entirely irrelevant to their skills or intelligence."[24] Those with little talent are generally able to bypass open competition in the job market, thus limiting the opportunities for those who have more ability but less in-

22. *U.S. News and World Report*, November 11, 1968, p. 52.
23. William J. Goode, *The Family* (Englewood Cliffs, N.J.: Prentice-Hall, Inc., 1964), p. 80.
24. *Ibid.*, p. 84.

fluence. A major weakness of the functional theory of stratification, as we noted earlier, is that it fails to account for the importance of family in determining occupational role. Regardless of how much talent they have, the poor seldom get to the top of the occupational ladder, and the rich seldom fall to the bottom.

Still, Goode offers a comforting thought to families waiting their turn on the ladder. His historical analysis shows that the uppers as a general class aggregate have never had long-term insurance against loss of position. In most societies ineptness, plain stupidity, low fertility, and unexpected disasters have resulted in some measure of downward mobility from the upper class. The scholar Hsu reports that there was considerable movement downward among the Chinese nobility, partly as a consequence of their children being overprotected. "Often, the family head permitted his sons to become wastrels, enjoying their irresponsibility and loose or luxurious way of living as a sign of his own worldly success. Since they were not held to performance standards as youngsters, how-

ever, they were unable as adults to hold the family or its property intact." [25] Barber found substantially the same pattern in a number of European countries.[26]

But though the families at the top may be unable to stay there forever, there is little probability that most families will ever get there at all. Life chances are greatly limited by the fact of birth, and few families move very fast or very far. Despite ever more eloquent declarations about human equality, it continues to be true that the goods of society are unequally divided and that more go to some families than to others. This in turn helps determine whom people will interact with, go to school with, dine with, and eventually marry. Most important for American society, it still greatly influences the job market opportunities of men and women, black and white.

---

25. *Ibid.*, pp. 85–86.
26. Bernard Barber, *Social Stratification: A Comparative Analysis of Structure and Process* (New York: Harcourt Brace Jovanovich, Inc., 1957).

Access to wealth has increasingly become a necessary prerequisite for winning political office. And with skyrocketing campaign costs has come a proliferation of fund-raising dinners, which may require those who attend to pay anywhere from $50 to $1000 a plate.

THE SCHOOL

Until the last century, formal education beyond the rudimentary level was pretty much limited in all societies to the children of the wealthy. They were to be educated in the fine arts to be gentlemen, and a small number of elite schools served their needs. Barber, after reviewing the evidence from the United States and western Europe, states: "On the whole, schools formerly served primarily to help the upper classes maintain their established position, only secondarily to permit some mobility within the bourgeois middle classes and from the bourgeoisie into the nobility." [27]

Today, while they have certainly not been eliminated, the elite schools have had to modify their functions to fit in with modern industrial society. The public universities themselves have become the agents for access to valued occupational roles of industrial society. Lenski puts the point more broadly when he says that "Educational status has become increasingly important as a resource in the struggle for power and privilege." [28] It is a truism that "you can't get anywhere today without an education."

But the different social classes do not have either the same awareness of this fact or the same access to different types and amounts of education. We are rapidly coming to realize that by the time a child is ready for kindergarten, his chances of being able to benefit from the school system that is available to him are closely linked to the class orientation of his family (see Chapter 5, pages 162–163). Furthermore, educational facilities themselves are unequal, as Conant points out in his trenchant analysis, *Slums and Suburbs:*[29]

The contrast in money available to the schools in a wealthy suburb and to the schools in a large city jolts one's notions of the meaning of equality of opportunity. The pedagogic tasks which confront the teachers in the slum schools are far more difficult than those which their colleagues in the wealthy suburbs face. Yet the expenditure per pupil in the wealthy suburban school is as high as $1,000 per year. The expenditure in a big city school is less than half that amount. An even more significant contrast is provided by looking at the school facilities and noting the size of the professional staff. In the suburb there is likely to be a spacious modern school staffed by as many as 70 professionals per 1,000 pupils; in the slum one finds a crowded, often dilapidated and unattractive school staffed by 40 or fewer professionals per 1,000 pupils.

Chances for education vary by whether a person is born in the slums or the suburbs, into a lower, a middle, or an upper-class family, and into a white or a nonwhite family. But stratification and its consequences may not stop there. It still makes a difference what college a person graduates from. Some years ago, Havemann and West found that "at all types of colleges, the graduates from wealthy family backgrounds wind up making more money than those from poorer family backgrounds. . . . But among both the self-help students and the family-supported students, considered separately, the type of college plays a great part in later financial success." [30] Their study showed that the graduates of the Big Three (Harvard, Yale, Princeton) earned more than any other group of college graduates, $2000 per year more on the average than Big Ten graduates, and $3000 more than the graduates of all other midwestern colleges.

The Ivy Leaguers did better financially even if their college grade records were poorer than those of graduates of lesser known schools. It may be argued, of course, that Yale, Harvard, and Princeton provide a better education than any other group of schools in the country and thus attract the most talented young men. But this would only be another example of how stratification perpetuates inequality.

The structure of inequality becomes most clearly apparent in comparisons between whites and blacks. In 1960 the median number of school years completed by blacks twenty-five years old and over was 8.2, compared to 10.9 years for whites; by 1968 the figures had risen to 9.3 years for blacks and 12.1 years for whites.[31] Thus despite the civil rights movement, blacks remained relatively as disadvantaged in terms of education as before. At each level of educational attainment, furthermore, they continued to make significantly less money on the average than whites at the same level (Figure 7.1, page 224). Education clearly

---

27. *Ibid.*, p. 391.
28. Lenski, *op. cit.*, p. 392.
29. James B. Conant, *Slums and Suburbs* (New York: McGraw-Hill Book Co., 1961), pp. 2–3.
30. Ernest Havemann and Patricia S. West, *They Went to College* (New York: Harcourt Brace Jovanovich, Inc., 1952), p. 181.
31. *Statistical Abstract of the United States, 1969*, p. 106.

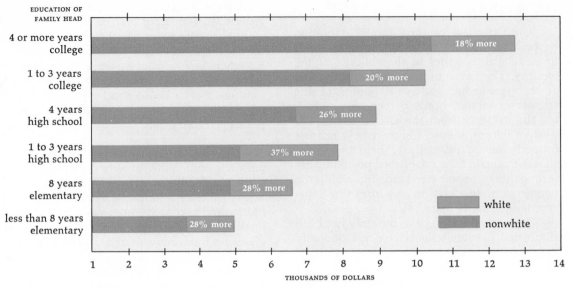

SOURCE: *Statistical Abstract of the United States, 1969*, Table 478, p. 325

FIGURE 7.1.   **MEDIAN FAMILY INCOME FOR WHITES AND NONWHITES BY LEVEL OF EDUCATION, 1967**

opens opportunities for blacks as it does for other Americans, but it does not enable them to compete on an equal basis.

In the Soviet Union, too, education appears to make a difference. With rapid industrialization, it has become the stepping stone to occupational success, in political as in economic and scientific roles. Schooling is said to be universal and free in the USSR, but Barber reports that "since the thirties children of the new middle and upper classes have had various differential advantages."[32]

As Lenski observes, the school serves to pass on the political ideology of the nation-state and thus to sanction the power arrangements that are in existence at any given time.[33] In the Soviet Union young people learn the virtues of Marxism Russian-style and grow to become firm supporters of the internal power arrangements. In the United States, the educational system has supported the general democratic ideology and sanctioned the prevailing power and other stratification arrangements.

THE OCCUPATIONAL SYSTEM

The family sets you up, the school applies the polish, and then there you are—with a job.

What kind of job? One that will pretty much determine your share of the power, prestige, and wealth available in the society. There has probably been no point in history when the job itself counted for so much as it does in industrial society today. Industrialization brings an ever growing range of occupations, requiring ever more complex skills. For individuals who can work their way through the school system, there are occupations offering considerable wealth, prestige, or power, and sometimes all three. Let us examine each of these variables and their distribution within the occupational structure of society.

Income. It is easy to say that, because of greater energy, industry, talent, or luck, some people earn more than others. We are all aware that professional men and women, business executives, administrators, and the like earn more than filing clerks, garage mechanics, and garbage collectors. Income seems to be a function of the evaluation of the importance of the occupation to the society—until one looks carefully at a list of occupations and observes the

32. Barber, *op. cit.*, p. 403.
33. Lenski, *op. cit.*, pp. 393 ff.

variation in income even within the professional category (Table 7.2).

Data show that in 1967 the median income for *all* employed male citizens was $6610. Self-employed professionals had the highest median income, $14,135, while armed forces personnel and farm laborers had median incomes below $1700 per year. The median income for employed females was generally less than half that of males in each occupational category.[34] The corporate rich, who comprise only 1 percent of the labor force, receive about 8 percent of the total income. As you examine "What the Top Brass Earn" (Table 7.3, page 226), you might ponder the question of whether or not such earnings are functional for the society. Among questions that might be asked are: What would be the incremental gain for all wage earners if this 8 percent of the total income was divided more or less equally among all? What would be the psychological gains or losses to the system as a whole? Does it really matter that these great differences occur in a relatively free society in which the basic needs of most people are rather adequately met?

Industrial psychologist Edward Lawler reported that "work motivation studies invariably show that executives rate the chance to realize their potential, to function professionally and do a good job—in short, psychic rewards—far ahead of financial reward."[35] Perhaps the income itself is a kind of psychic reward, an indication that others appreciate the quality of the job performance. Thus, income may become an important measure of self-respect beyond the status symbols and other privileges it purchases.

Prestige. Occupational prestige has become one of the most widely studied aspects of stratification and is one of the few areas in which comparative analysis of several countries has been attempted. In a classic study published in 1956, Inkeles and Rossi compared the ranking of occupations in six industrialized countries (the United States, Great Britain, the Soviet Union, Japan, New Zealand, and Germany) and found remarkable similarities. They concluded on the basis of their data that "there is a relatively invariable hierarchy of prestige associated with the industrial system, even when it is placed in the context of larger social systems

---

34. *Statistical Abstract of the United States, 1969*, p. 327.
35. Quoted in *Newsweek*, June 20, 1966, p. 90.

TABLE 7.2. PROFESSIONAL OCCUPATIONS RANKED BY MEDIAN INCOME, 1959 AND 1949

	1959			1949
RANK	MEDIAN INCOME		RANK	MEDIAN INCOME
1	$15,013	Physicians & surgeons	1	$8,302
2	12,392	Dentists	3	6,448
3	11,261	Lawyers & judges	4	6,248
4	10,514	Airplane pilots & navigators	6	5,263
5	10,279	Osteopaths	2	6,458
6	9,178	Veterinarians	20	4,220
7	9,127	Aeronautical engineers	9	4,828
8	8,948	Chemical engineers	7	5,005
9	8,868	Architects	5	5,509
10	8,772	Optometrists	18	4,343
11	8,710	Electrical engineers	11	4,657
12	8,639	Metallurgical engineers	12	4,657
13	8,522	Miscellaneous engineers (except mining)	8	4,965
14	8,497	Mechanical engineers	13	4,594
15	7,965	Natural scientists (not elsewhere classified)	19	4,245
16	7,868	Social scientists	16	4,446
17	7,790	Industrial engineers	15	4,519
18	7,773	Civil engineers	14	4,590
19	7,669	Personnel & labor relations workers	10	4,754
20	7,510	College faculty, deans, & presidents	17	4,366
21	7,385	Pharmacists	21	4,170
22	7,245	Chemists	22	4,091
23	6,758	Accountants & auditors	26	3,977
24	6,745	Authors	24	4,033
25	6,463	Chiropractors	28	3,471
26	6,333	Artists & art teachers	27	3,552
27	6,159	Farm & home management advisors	23	4,059
28	5,975	Radio operators	25	4,016
29	5,967	Funeral directors & embalmers	34	3,179
30	5,794	Draftsmen	29	3,470
31	5,709	Teachers (elem. & secondary)	30	3,465
32	5,692	Photographers	38	2,941
33	5,640	Actors	32	3,260
34	5,591	Therapists & healers (not elsewhere classified)	36	3,011
35	5,519	Sports instructors & officials	31	3,330
36	5,481	Social & welfare workers (except group)	33	3,196
37	5,394	Athletes	45	2,336
38	4,873	Foresters & conservationists	37	2,997
39	4,757	Musicians and music teachers	41	2,700
40	4,614	Technicians: medical & dental	39	2,908
41	4,592	Librarians	47	2,294
42	4,486	Surveyors	40	2,773
43	4,400	Nurses, professional	42	2,645
44	4,395	Recreation & group workers	35	3,155
45	4,151	Clergymen	43	2,410
46	3,674	Entertainers	48	2,217
47	3,483	Dancers & dancing teachers	44	2,385
48	3,241	Religious workers	46	2,316

SOURCE: *United States Census of Population, 1960: Occupational Characteristics* [PC(2)-7A], Table 25; *United States Census of Population, 1950: Occupational Characteristics* [P-E No. 1B], Table 19.

which are otherwise differentiated in important respects."[36]

Follow-up research by R. W. Hodge and his associates at the National Opinion Research Center of the University of Chicago (NORC) has shown a similarity in occupational prestige rankings even between developed and under-developed countries.[37] Using data from a series of studies done over a period of time, the NORC researchers compared each of twenty-three foreign countries with the United States and found a high overall correlation among occupational prestige hierarchies. They then divided the twenty-three countries into Western and non-Western, noting that the per capita average of the GNP (Gross National Product) was never less than $450 in the Western countries, never more than $300 in the non-Western. The authors found that "despite their divergence in level of GNP, the two groups of countries do not differ significantly in their similarity to the United States in prestige evaluations."[38] This evidence suggests that there may be "social structural features that all societies, whether industrialized or not, have in common."

After considering several structural explanations for their findings (which they describe

as exploratory rather than definitive), the authors offer the following speculation about the meaning of their data:

Development hinges in part upon the recruitment and training of persons for the skilled, clerical, managerial, and professional positions necessary to support an industrial economy. Thus, acquisition of a "modern" system of occupational evaluation would seem to be a necessary precondition to rapid industrialization, insofar as such an evaluation of occupations insures that resources and personnel in sufficient numbers and of sufficient quality are allocated to those occupational positions most crucial to the industrial development of a nation. In one important regard, then, adoption of an occupational-prestige

36. Alex Inkeles and Peter N. Rossi, "National Comparisons of Occupational Prestige," *American Journal of Sociology,* 61 (1956), 329–339; quotation from p. 339.

37. Robert W. Hodge, Donald J. Treiman, and Peter H. Rossi, "A Comparative Study of Occupational Prestige," in *Class, Status, and Power: Social Stratification in Comparative Perspective,* ed. Reinhard Bendix and Seymour M. Lipset, 2nd ed. (New York: The Free Press, 1966), pp. 309–321.

38. *Ibid.,* p. 320. The Gross National Product is the total value of the goods and services produced in a given year by a particular country. For the purposes of this study, the GNP of several nations was computed in American dollars.

TABLE 7.3. **WHAT THE TOP BRASS EARN**

The money earned by chief executives varies both by size of company and by industry. Based on the cash paid to top officers in 1965, the table below shows what a top executive would earn—exclusive of stock options and other fringe benefits—while working for companies of the following sizes and industries:

| | COMPANY SALES OF: | | | |
	$40 MILLION	$100 MILLION	$400 MILLION	$1 BILLION
Drugs and cosmetics	$75,000	$108,000	$189,000	$274,000
Consumer products	90,000	123,000	176,000	266,000
Office equipment	84,000	115,000	187,000	259,000
Steel and iron	72,000	102,000	175,000	249,000
Chemicals	63,000	92,000	158,000	228,000
Nonferrous metals	63,000	94,000	155,000	215,000
Building materials	67,000	92,000	149,000	205,000
Machinery	74,000	98,000	150,000	199,000
Electronics	74,000	98,000	149,000	196,000
Tobacco	79,000	102,000	151,000	196,000
Petroleum	87,000	108,000	152,000	189,000
Aircraft and missiles	87,000	106,000	145,000	177,000
Public utilities	60,000	79,000	123,000	162,000
Air transport	87,000	97,000	113,000	126,000

SOURCE: *Newsweek,* June 20, 1966, p. 90; estimates based on McKinsey & Co. study.

hierarchy similar to that of industrial nations may be a prerequisite for development, notwithstanding the fact that increased development may in turn induce further similarities in occupational prestige evaluations.[39]

The authors have suggested an intriguing possibility, though they leave unanswered the question of how knowledge about such occupations comes to these underdeveloped countries in the first place. Their explanation certainly supports in some way, and is derivative from, the functional theory of stratification.

The NORC data on occupational ranking in the United States have led Hodge, Siegel, and Rossi to conclude that occupational prestige hierarchies are not only "similar from country to country but also from subgroup to subgroup within a country."[40] Such consensus can best be explained, the authors believe, by analysis of the occupations themselves: "The prestige position of an occupation is apparently a characteristic of that occupation, generated by the way in which it is articulated into the division of labor, by the amount of power and influence implied in the activities of the occupation, by the characteristics of incumbents, and by the amount of resources society places at the disposal of incumbents."[41]

Comparing the prestige of various occupations in 1947 and 1963, the NORC studies found that ratings were remarkably stable (Table 7.4, page 228). Why was there so little shift? Apparently neither the nature of the occupation, its perceived importance, nor the rewards attached to it changed very much. The authors assert, in fact, that when ratings from the NORC surveys are compared with findings from earlier research, the prestige of occupations has changed very little since 1925.

Occupation and power. Occupation is the chief source of income and prestige for the individual male and indirectly for his wife and children. And income and prestige continue to be unequally distributed between occupations. Is this true also for power? Ignoring the "one man-one vote" aspect of power, and acknowl-

edging a significant change from the early days in the United States when property ownership was a prerequisite for voting, let us briefly examine several aspects of power related to occupations.

The first deals with the amount of power in an occupational role itself. Power is most clearly delineated in bureaucratic organizations. The closer a role is to the top of the bureaucratic structure, generally the more authority is attached to it. The power enjoyed by the role incumbent depends not on his authority alone, however, but also on the amount of influence he wields. Whereas authority is rather specifically delimited, influence may vary according to the incumbent's interest in enlarging his power resources, his ability to persuade, and his ability to manipulate people. At the lower end of the bureaucratic structure, where the great majority of workers are located, there is little authority and even less ability to influence decision-making as an individual. We may hypothesize that many persons who become active in labor union affairs have personalities that orient them toward power; since they find little opportunity to fulfill their aspirations in the normal routine of the job, they may turn to union offices to find an outlet.

The informal work norms that all work groups seem to develop are a manifestation of the influence that workers can exercise in their occupational roles. Such informal work norms are found not only among manual workers in the factory but also in the white-collar bureaucratic roles. In his study of two bureaucratic government agencies (page 76), Blau found that employees actually developed work patterns significantly at variance with established rules and authority. Although Blau's concern was more with the dynamics of bureaucracy than with power per se, we should not overlook this interesting evidence of power even at the lower levels of the bureaucratic organization.

The power an individual derives from his occupational role is not readily transferable to the members of his family, nor does it necessarily carry over to the roles he has outside his job. Power, in short, is much less generalized than status and class. Nor is power all of one kind. A corporation president may exert ultimate control over decision-making in his company, but his power as a business executive does not approach in range or consequences the power of a Supreme Court Justice, who helps define the law of the land.

---

39. *Ibid.*
40. Robert W. Hodge, Paul M. Siegel, and Peter H. Rossi, "Occupational Prestige in the United States: 1925–1963," *American Journal of Sociology,* 70 (November 1964), 286–302.
41. *Ibid.*

TABLE 7.4. OCCUPATIONAL PRESTIGE RATINGS, 1963 AND 1947

OCCUPATION	1963 SCORE	1947 SCORE	OCCUPATION	1963 SCORE	1947 SCORE
U.S. Supreme Court Justice	94	96	Newspaper columnist	73	74
Physician	93	93	Policeman	72	67
Nuclear physicist	92	86	Reporter on a daily newspaper	71	71
Scientist	92	89	Radio announcer	70	75
Government scientist	91	88	Bookkeeper	70	68
State governor	91	93	Tenant farmer—one who owns livestock and machinery and manages the farm	69	68
Cabinet member in the Federal Gov't.	90	92	Insurance agent	69	68
College professor	90	89	Carpenter	68	65
U.S. Representative in Congress	90	89	Manager of a small store in a city	67	69
Chemist	89	86	A local official of a labor union	67	62
Lawyer	89	86	Mail carrier	66	66
Diplomat in U.S. Foreign Service	89	92	Railroad conductor	66	67
Dentist	88	86	Traveling salesman for a wholesale concern	66	68
Architect	88	86	Plumber	65	63
County judge	88	87	Automobile repairman	64	63
Psychologist	87	85	Playground director	63	67
Minister	87	87	Barber	63	59
Member of the board of directors of a large corporation	87	86	Machine operator in a factory	63	60
Mayor of a large city	87	90	Owner-operator of a lunch stand	63	62
Priest	86	86	Corporal in the regular army	62	60
Head of a dept. in state government	86	87	Garage mechanic	62	62
Civil engineer	86	84	Truck driver	59	54
Airline pilot	86	83	Fisherman who owns his own boat	58	58
Banker	85	88	Clerk in a store	56	58
Biologist	85	81	Milk route man	56	54
Sociologist	83	82	Streetcar motorman	56	58
Instructor in public schools	82	79	Lumberjack	55	53
Captain in the regular army	82	80	Restaurant cook	55	54
Accountant for a large business	81	81	Singer in a nightclub	54	52
Public school teacher	81	78	Filling station attendant	51	52
Owner of a factory that employs about 100 people	80	82	Dockworker	50	47
Building contractor	80	79	Railroad section hand	50	48
Artist who paints pictures that are exhibited in galleries	78	83	Night watchman	50	47
			Coal miner	50	49
Musician in a symphony orchestra	78	81	Restaurant waiter	49	48
Author of novels	78	80	Taxi driver	49	49
Economist	78	79	Farm hand	48	50
Official of an international labor union	77	75	Janitor	48	44
Railroad engineer	76	76	Bartender	48	44
Electrician	76	73	Clothes presser in a laundry	45	46
County agricultural agent	76	77	Soda fountain clerk	44	45
Owner-operator of a printing shop	75	74	Share-cropper—one who owns no livestock or equipment and does not manage farm	42	40
Trained machinist	75	73			
Farm owner and operator	74	76	Garbage collector	39	35
Undertaker	74	72	Street sweeper	36	34
Welfare worker for a city government	74	73	Shoe shiner	34	33
			Average	71	70

SOURCE: Robert W. Hodge, Paul M. Siegel, and Peter H. Rossi, "Occupational Prestige in the United States: 1925–1963," *American Journal of Sociology*, 70 (November 1964), 286–302.

In both business and government, the power that derives from authority is quite clearly delimited. But what of power based on influence? In Chapter 14, "The Political System," we will examine the theory of the *power elite,* which maintains that men who have reached the top in certain occupations (primarily top military officers, corporate executives, and leaders in the executive branch of government) form an interlocking elite that now largely controls decision-making in American society. Thus far no one has been able to confirm the major proposition of this theory through empirical testing, and many social scientists feel that it represents a greatly oversimplified picture of the power structure of American society.

Political decision-making in the United States does not seem to be the exclusive prerogative of any one group at either the community or national level. Business influence is clearly a factor to be reckoned with, but this is not to say that business leaders are always unified in their interests or that they always get their way. Labor legislation of the late 1920's and early 1930's, culminating in the Wagner Labor Act of 1935, provided labor unions with the means of countering to some extent the power of business leaders within the political as well as the economic system. Most major occupational groups now have their own political lobbies, which try to control decision-making at local, state, and national levels according to their perceived interests. At all levels of government, most decisions are reached through contest and compromise.

An interesting new development in the struggle for power has been the upsurge of protest movements. These have involved not only minority group members and students but also such occupational groupings as policemen, firemen, school teachers, and clergy. What is common to the efforts of these aggregates of people is their desire for more autonomy, for more control over the decision-making that directly affects their lives. It is a strongly held belief among their leaders that only as they increase their power will they be able to influence the distribution of prestige and wealth.

---

42. For a detailed discussion of the long struggle between labor unions and government, see Joseph Shister, *Economics of the Labor Market* (New York: J. B. Lippincott, Co., 1949), esp. pp. 277–310.

THE GOVERNMENT

Marx perceived governments primarily as the agents of the bourgeoisie aligned inevitably against the proletariat. Whether one agrees with his analysis or not, governments have indeed often served as agents of the status quo. It has been remarked that the law is written by people of middle-class and middle-status background to be applied against people of lower class and status. The strong anti-labor posture of the United States government during the nineteenth and early twentieth century lends support to this argument,[42] as do the inequalities of our present tax structure (Figure 7.2, page 230). It remains true, furthermore, that those occupying the important positions in government are drawn almost exclusively from the middle and upper classes.

But it is difficult to maintain that government in the United States has acted solely as an agent of the status quo. Like governments in most other societies, it has taken an ever more active role in initiating and directing social change; and in doing so, it has come increasingly to act in behalf of all the people. Today business, as well as labor, is regulated. And if government has continued to protect the privileges of the middle class, it has at the same time tried to extend those privileges to more and more members of society. Land-grant colleges, child-labor laws, Federal Housing Administration mortgages, the GI Bill, minimum-wage laws, federal aid to college students, and school desegregation are examples of government action that has been an impetus to social mobility if not a direct causal factor. Recent civil rights legislation is designed to affect the power of the black *vis à vis* the white through better voting guarantees, at the same time that it attempts to make possible a more equitable distribution of other societal privileges.

The government at both local and national levels has acted as an employer and thus as a vehicle for mobility of large numbers of persons from the minority groups in American society. The rights of citizens to vote and to run for elective office have also contributed to the mobility of minorities—both immigrant ethnic groups in earlier times and black Americans more recently. The election of black mayors in Gary, Indiana, and Cleveland, Ohio, in 1967 and 1969 may have marked a major step in the

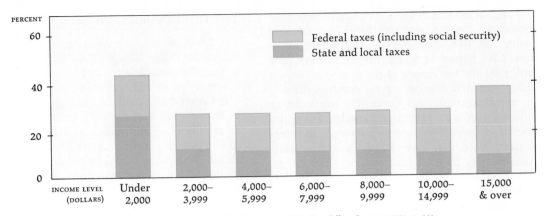

SOURCE: *Economic Report of the President*, U.S. Government Printing Office, January 1969, p. 161.

FIGURE 7.2   **TAXES AS PERCENT OF INCOME, BY INCOME LEVEL, 1965**

process by which blacks could expect to achieve status, power, and some degree of economic well-being through the agency of government.

SOCIAL MOBILITY

The history of the United States shows a broad and steady trend toward increasing equality in the distribution of societal rewards. While a small percentage of families at the top still receive a disproportionate share of the wealth in American society, there is so much more of it to go around today than there was even twenty-five years ago that most citizens can now be classified, on the basis of both objective and subjective criteria, as part of a broad middle class. (See Figure 7.3.) If differences in prestige are still considerable, mobility has made them less significant for individual self-images and for the life chances of people generally. Most Americans apparently see themselves as pretty much like everyone else, and most apparently are fairly well satisfied with their lot.

In a classic case study of stratification patterns in New Haven, Connecticut, Robert Dahl has shown that a major factor in the reduction of inequalities over the past 150 years has been the dispersal of wealth, prestige, and power.[43] The fact that these societal rewards are to some extent separable in American society

has made upward mobility possible for successive aggregates of people. The businessmen-entrepreneurs of the nineteenth century gained wealth and then power. Sons and grandsons of European immigrants gained political power and then wealth and prestige. Meanwhile, the old established families retained prestige but often lost power and sometimes wealth as well.

One of the thorniest questions in social research today is whether the process of reducing and dispersing inequalities in American society still continues or whether new forms of cumulative inequality have developed.[44] Of special concern is the plight of those who now seem trapped at the bottom level of society, the urban and rural poor. The percentage of American families living below the poverty line has dropped by more than half since 1947 (Figure 7.3), but those families who have not crossed the line actually have a smaller share of total family income today, proportionate to their numbers, than they did a generation ago.[45] Thus relative

43. Robert A. Dahl, *Who Governs? Democracy and Power in an American City* (New Haven: Yale University Press, 1961).

44. For viewpoints contrasting with Dahl's thesis, see C. Wright Mills, *The Power Elite* (New York: Oxford University Press, 1956) and G. William Domhoff, *Who Rules America?* (Englewood Cliffs, N.J.: Prentice-Hall, Inc., 1967).

45. See, for example, Leon H. Keyserling, *Progress or Poverty* (Washington, D.C.: Conference on Economic Progress, 1964), p. 27; also Pamela Roby, "Inequality: A Trend Analysis," in *Annals of the American Academy of Political and Social Sciences* (September 1969), pp. 110–117.

to the rest of the population, and perhaps even in absolute terms, the very poor in American society have been downwardly mobile. The very fact that the society has preached upward mobility so loudly and so long increases the bitterness and frustration of those who find themselves cut off from the good things upward mobility can bring (though not from the mass media that advertise these good things) and thus contributes to the tendency toward alienation and conflict.

The overall success of the American system makes critical analysis of it difficult. Because the great majority of Americans now live comfortably, enjoy adequate prestige, and participate at least minimally in the political process, it is easy to conclude that the system does indeed guarantee all men the opportunity to get ahead. But the fact that most Americans have come to enjoy a good life also highlights the inequalities that still persist. If some aggregates of people remain almost wholly cut off from access to wealth, prestige, and power, and if some others enjoy a disproportionately large share of these societal rewards, then there is a basis for arguing that the system guarantees the prerogatives of the "haves" at the expense of the "have-nots." Even if a social scientist takes a middle position (the system is basically functional but it also has built-in conflicts and inequalities) his analysis is almost inevitably biased by ideological commitments. No matter how hard he strives for objectivity, it makes a difference, in the end, that he is part of the system and makes his analysis from that perspective. It is important to keep these limitations in mind as we examine the evidence regarding mobility patterns in the United States and compare them with those in other societies.

CAUSAL FACTORS IN MOBILITY

Patterns of social mobility in the United States have been closely tied to the changes that have accompanied industrial progress—an expanded and altered labor market, increased horizontal and geographical mobility, changing fertility patterns, and a growing emphasis on education. All of these factors have interacted in complex ways not only to facilitate upward mobility but also to change the rules of the game.

Changes in the labor market. An important measure of mobility in a society is the degree to which sons succeed their fathers in their occupations. Perfect succession would imply not only a closed stratification system but also a stable occupational structure, in which the available jobs changed little from one generation to the next. In industrial societies, the trend has been in the other direction: stratification systems have become relatively more open, and both the number and variety of jobs have steadily increased.

Between 1870 and 1970, the labor force in the United States grew from thirteen million

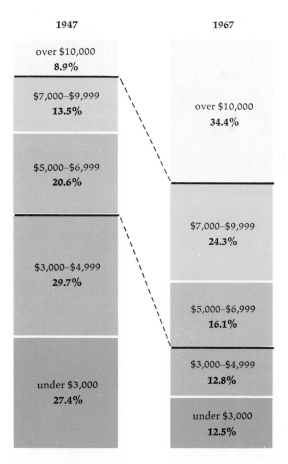

SOURCE: *Statistical Abstract of the United States, 1969,* Table 474, p. 323.

FIGURE 7.3. **PERCENT OF AMERICAN FAMILIES AT DIFFERENT INCOME LEVELS, 1947 AND 1967, IN CONSTANT (1967) DOLLARS**

persons to about seventy-five million. In the process, there has been a dramatic shift away from farming and unskilled jobs toward clerical, service, business, and professional jobs (Table 7.5). In 1900 almost 40 percent of all those in the labor force were in agriculture, whereas today farm workers constitute less than 5 percent of the work force. An economy dominated by modern technology, with thousands of occupations requiring varying levels of skill, is bound to offer far more opportunities for mobility than an economy dominated by farming. Thus the industrial-agricultural revolution has been a stimulus to upward mobility in at least two ways: first, in the increase in the absolute number of jobs; second, in the change in the job structure—the increase in white-collar jobs relative to farming and blue-collar jobs.

But while economic expansion and a changing job structure have clearly stimulated mobility, they have also played a part in slowing its pace, especially over the last fifty years. Mechanization, specialization, and the trend toward "bigness" have made it much more difficult and costly for a man to get ahead by setting up his own business. They have also raised the educational requirements for most jobs and

created many more steps to climb in the move from bottom to top. Empirical research since the 1920's has consistently produced evidence challenging the reality of the American Dream that a man could raise himself from rags to riches if only he had ability and ambition. An early study by Sorokin, for example, showed that most men entered the occupational world at about the same level as their fathers and that only a very small proportion moved up more than a step or two.[46] Robert and Helen Lynd's studies of "Middletown" (Muncie, Indiana) showed a similar pattern: although "anyone" might theoretically work his way up to the job of foreman in the factory, the probabilities were extremely low.[47] Subsequent research by Warner and others points to the conclusion that

46. Pitirim Sorokin, *Social Mobility* (New York: Harper and Brothers, 1927).

47. Robert and Helen Lynd, *Middletown* (New York: Harcourt Brace Jovanovich, Inc., 1929) and *Middletown in Transition* (New York: Harcourt Brace Jovanovich, Inc., 1937). See also Warner and Low, *The Social System of a Modern Factory, op. cit.,* and Eli Chinoy, *The Automobile Worker and the American Dream* (Garden City, N.Y.: Doubleday & Company, Inc., 1955).

TABLE 7.5. **PERCENT OF AMERICAN WORKERS IN MAJOR OCCUPATIONAL GROUPS, 1900 TO 1969**

	1900	1910	1920	1930	1940	1950	1960	1969
TOTAL LABOR FORCE (IN 1000's)	29,030	37,291	42,206	48,686	51,742	59,648	66,681	76,520
White-collar workers	17.6	21.3	24.9	29.4	31.1	37.5	43.1	47.6
Professional & technical workers	4.2	4.7	5.4	6.8	7.4	7.5	11.2	14.3
Managers, officials, & proprietors	5.8	6.6	6.6	7.4	7.3	10.8	10.5	10.3
Clerical workers	3.0	5.3	8.0	9.1	9.6	12.8	14.7	17.1
Sales workers	4.5	4.7	4.9	6.3	6.7	6.4	6.6	6.0
Blue-collar workers	35.8	38.2	40.2	39.6	39.8	39.1	36.3	35.7
Craftsmen & foremen	10.5	11.6	13.0	12.8	12.0	12.8	12.8	12.9
Operatives	12.8	14.6	15.6	15.8	18.4	20.4	18.0	18.5
Non-farm laborers	12.5	12.0	11.6	11.0	9.4	5.9	5.5	4.3
Service workers	9.0	9.5	7.8	9.8	11.7	10.9	12.5	12.6
Private household workers	5.4	5.0	3.3	4.1	4.7	3.1	3.3	2.2
Other service workers	3.6	4.6	4.5	5.7	7.1	7.8	9.2	10.4
Farmworkers	37.5	30.9	27.0	21.2	17.4	12.4	8.1	4.0

SOURCE: Bureau of the Census, *Historical Statistics of the United States, Colonial Times to 1957,* p. 74 (for data before 1950); *Statistical Abstract of the United States, 1969,* p. 222. Data beginning 1950 not strictly comparable with earlier years.

VIEWPOINTS   **BLACK VIEWS OF THE AMERICAN DREAM**

People are continually pointing out to me the wretchedness of white people in order to console me for the wretchedness of blacks. But an itemized account of the American failure does not console me and it should not console anyone else. That hundreds of thousands of white people are living, in effect, no better than the "niggers" is not a fact to be regarded with complacency. The social and moral bankruptcy suggested by this fact is of the bitterest, most terrifying kind.

The people, however, who believe that this democratic anguish has some consoling value are always pointing out that So-and-So, white, and So-and-So, black, rose from the slums into the big time. The existence—the public existence—of say, Frank Sinatra and Sammy Davis, Jr. proves to them that America is still the land of opportunity and that inequalities vanish before the determined will. It proves nothing of the sort. The determined will is rare—at the moment, in this country, it is unspeakably rare—and the inequalities suffered by the many are in no way justified by the rise of a few. A few have always risen—in every country, every era, and in the teeth of regimes which can by no stretch of the imagination be thought of as free. Not all of these people, it is worth remembering, left the world better than they found it. The determined will is rare, but it is not invariably benevolent. Furthermore, the American equation of success with the big times reveals an awful disrespect for human life and human achievement. This equation has placed our cities among the most dangerous in the world and has placed our youth among the most empty and most bewildered. This situation of our youth is not mysterious. Children have never been very good at listening to their elders, but they have never failed to imitate them. They must, they have no other models. That is exactly what our children are doing. They are imitating our immorality, our disrespect for the pain of others.

All other slum dwellers, when the bank account permits it, can move out of the slum and vanish altogether from the eye of persecution. No Negro in this country has ever made that much money and it will be a long time before any Negro does.

James Baldwin
Nobody Knows My Name

I attended a New York City junior high school where a man teacher was chased around the classroom by pupils armed with window poles. All the teacher could do was pull down the shades so that no one outside would witness his humiliation. The only way many teachers could have any calm in their classes was to let students read comic books. If you left the building during lunch hour, you would be robbed by older boys from neighboring schools. Narcotics and obscenity mingled on the scene with chalk and blackboards.

The school was in the Harlem ghetto, about which so much has been written recently—a lot of it nonsense from white men who care only about the spectacular; a lot of it from Negroes who are performing scapegoat artistry. Many of these want to place the blame for the Negro's inability to gain full citizenship and social acceptability completely on White America. But the Negro must accept his share of responsibility. Too many are too anxious to blame the ghetto for everything.

Often this may be justified; some Negroes are not strong enough to escape. But for many others, the slavery of the ghetto is self-imposed. The real problem they ignore is that they don't try hard enough to improve their lives—they are defeated unnecessarily. . . .

Many of my friends have accomplished whatever in life they've wanted to do—from the mastery of half a dozen languages to traveling around the world, from directing in the theater to successful writing, from civic leadership to political affairs and public service. Raised in the Harlem ghetto, they have never used it as an excuse for not having high hopes and acting upon them.

Other friends will never get away, even though they have the ability. Their defeatist attitude hinders them. I've listened to many excuses: "You can't beat the white man, so why try?" . . . "Accept life; don't batter your head against a strong wall." . . . "We're in a prison from which there is no escape."

Yes, the ghetto is a prison. But there are no walls, no bars, no fences. *It is a prison of the mind.*

I believe that the most important task before today's Negro is to realize that nothing is impossible if he's willing to work and fight for it. The organizations—NAACP, CORE, and the others—cannot do it alone. The major portion of the job is going to have to be done by the individual.

David B. Lee
"Don't Blame the Ghetto"

upward mobility has become for most people a gradual and slow process at best.

As the structure of the job market has changed and education has become increasingly important, intragenerational mobility has largely given way to mobility from one generation to the next. Kahl has estimated that between 1920 and 1950 total intergenerational mobility was about 67 percent; that is, 67 percent of the sons were mobile relative to their fathers. Industrial and economic expansion—the creation of new jobs—accounted for almost one third of this mobility, most of which was moderately rather than dramatically upward (e.g., from clerks and salesmen to semi-professionals).[48] Individual success stories are not wholly a thing of the past, however. Kahl's study showed that in 1952 some 69 percent of American business leaders had managed to rise to their positions, rather than simply succeeding their fathers; and 18 percent of this business elite had come from blue-collar families.[49] More recent research points to education as the key factor in determining a man's chances for occupational advancement, but suggests that his education, in turn, "depends to a considerable degree on the socioeconomic status of his father."[50] Upward mobility, obviously, is not equally available to all.

Horizontal and geographical mobility. The term *horizontal mobility* refers to movement from one position to another where there is little or no change in rank. Typically it involves a lateral move from one social system to another—from business to business, from rural area to city, from region to region, or even from country to country. Thus horizontal mobility and geographical mobility often go hand in hand.

Although horizontal and geographical mobility tend to be overlooked in discussions of stratification, they may be vital preconditions for vertical mobility—for movement up or down in the stratification system. A man cut off from hope of advancement in a small, family-owned company may take a similar job in a larger company where he has a better chance of moving up. One who has become lost in the shuffle in a large company may move to a different company where he can make a fresh impression on the management and/or find a better use for his skills. Lateral movement of this sort has become increasingly typical of white-collar and professional workers, many of whom

see job changes as requisite to occupational advancement, especially early in their careers.

The major population movements in the United States over the past hundred years have been similarly impelled by strivings for upward mobility. In Chapter 9, we will examine in detail the migrational patterns that have been associated with the period of rapid urbanization in American society—the movements from farm to city, from East to West, from South to North, from North to South, and from city to suburb (see pages 283 ff.). Here we may simply note that all have involved the search for greater opportunity and a better way of life. The nineteenth-century adage "Go West, young man" was more than a call to adventure; it was the recognition that *there* lay opportunity, not only in the open lands but even more in the booming new cities. In the present century, economic and technological change have increasingly moved the locus of opportunity to the cities, making urbanization—the movement of peoples from rural areas to cities—a necessary condition for whatever upward mobility has occurred.

Differential fertility. Demographic evidence shows that beginning in the nineteenth century members of the middle and upper classes began to restrict their family size and to produce fewer children on the average than did members of the lower class. Kahl has estimated that at least 7 percent of the intergenerational mobility that took place in the labor force between 1920 and 1950 could be attributed to differential fertility rates between those with blue-collar occupations (including farmers) and those with white-collar occupations.[51] He found that professional men, for example, were producing less than one son each on the average—not enough even to replace themselves—whereas farmers were producing between one and two sons each on the average. Thus a particular population was available to take advantage of the jobs being created by an expanding economy.

The evidence today suggests, however, that high fertility is more likely to impede than to

48. Joseph Kahl, *The American Class Structure* (New York: Holt, Rinehart & Winston, Inc., 1961), pp. 257–262.

49. *Ibid.*, pp. 267–268.

50. Peter M. Blau and Otis D. Duncan, "Occupational Mobility in the United States," in Heller, *Structured Social Inequality, op. cit.*, pp. 340–352.

51. Kahl, *op. cit.*, pp. 257–262.

facilitate upward mobility for members of the lower class, especially for the very poor. The pattern of early marriage and lack of family planning makes it difficult if not impossible for many lower-class parents to finish their educations and thus to compete for good jobs. The children of such families, in turn, are cut off by their parents' poverty from the educational and other opportunities necessary for their own advancement. Thus low socioeconomic position perpetuates itself or becomes worse. With the growing national consensus in favor of family planning, class differences in fertility can be expected to become less significant in determining patterns of mobility either up or down. (For a more detailed discussion of these issues, see Chapter 8, "Demographic Change," especially pages 264–270.)

Differential socialization. Whereas the schools and other agents of socialization tend to open opportunities for the children of the middle and upper classes, they often have the effect

---

52. See Conant, *op. cit.*

of curtailing chances for the children of the poor. All the research since the 1920's has shown that children from lower-class families are much more likely than those from middle- and upper-class families to drop out of school. According to the hypotheses being tested currently, dropping out is caused by a lack of relevant motivation in the home, a clash between the norms and general behavior patterns learned in the homes of the poor and the middle-class norms and behavior demanded in the school, and a bias against the children of the poor in the schools themselves. The schools in lower-class neighborhoods are often poorly equipped and poorly staffed, and too often the children are shunted into dead-end programs.[52] Thus, it would appear that differential socialization may well be a major causal factor in either promoting or impeding upward mobility.

The importance of socialization in determining mobility patterns can also be illustrated by the changing role of women in contemporary society. There has been little research on female mobility, primarily because the status and class positions of family members continue to be so heavily dependent on the husband. Many wives

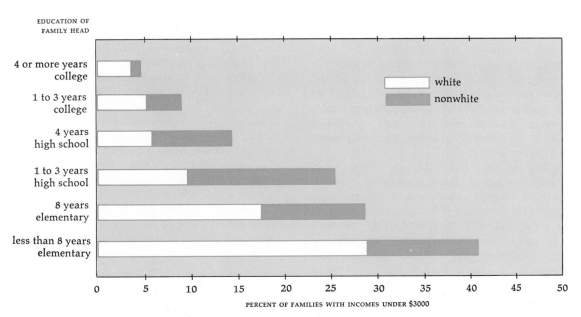

EDUCATION OF
FAMILY HEAD

4 or more years college
1 to 3 years college
4 years high school
1 to 3 years high school
8 years elementary
less than 8 years elementary

white
nonwhite

0   5   10   15   20   25   30   35   40   45   50

PERCENT OF FAMILIES WITH INCOMES UNDER $3000

SOURCE: *Statistical Abstract of the United States, 1969*, Table 478, p. 325

FIGURE 7.4. **EDUCATION FACTOR IN POVERTY OF FAMILIES, WHITE AND NONWHITE, 1967**

enter the labor force only after the family's position is fairly well established; and despite the continuing movement of wives into the labor market, a majority of wives still do not work for wages outside of the home. Nevertheless, for an increasing percentage of females, high school and college education has become a key mechanism for mobility. Education functions directly to improve their preparation for a career in the labor market and indirectly to provide them with an opportunity to seek out a marriage partner in a setting favorable to upward mobility. Education has also helped improve the overall status of women and given them at least a foothold in the contest for political power at both local and national levels.[53] At the same time, however, socialization continues to limit women's opportunities to move upward on their own. Women are socialized not to be overly ambitious for a career, and men are socialized to think of the worlds of business and politics as their own. The middle- or upper-class daughter who rises to the top job is no less exceptional in most fields (including those in which women predominate, such as professional education) than is the working-class son who becomes a captain of industry. The difference is that women have access to societal rewards through their husbands, whereas men must make it on their own or not at all.

Mobility and national values. In the United States, government legislation since the nineteenth century has been an impetus to mobility, as was noted earlier. We might also ponder the importance to mobility in American society of the statements in our Declaration of Independence that "All men are created equal" and that they are equally entitled to the "pursuit of happiness."

On the other hand, the rate of individual mobility has not increased much in recent years. There is considerable movement within the blue-collar and white-collar ranks, but those at the top and at the bottom tend to stay there. It is too early to tell whether society will alter the pattern for those now at the bottom, and there is little in the value system to urge a change at the top. Perhaps a major reason why there has been little organized grumbling against the stratification system in American society is that so few have fallen relative to the number who have risen.

The growing strength of the civil rights

movement during the 1960's gives grounds for hope that some of the most serious inequalities in contemporary American society, those between blacks and whites, are now gradually being reduced. Black employment, for example, rose by 20 percent between 1960 and 1968, and significant numbers of nonwhite workers shifted to better jobs (Figure 7.5). White employment during the same period increased by only 15 percent. Despite the gains made by blacks, however, the percentage of black workers employed as unskilled laborers or in service and farm jobs in 1968 was still more than double the percentage of white workers (44 percent compared to 19 percent).[54] The decade of the seventies should tell whether we have witnessed only token changes in the stratification system or whether black Americans are on their way toward achieving genuine equality.

MOBILITY IN INTERNATIONAL PERSPECTIVE

One way to define the "revolution of rising expectations" now taking place in the developing societies around the world is to say that it is a drive for vertical upward mobility—in fact, for a transformation in the structure of stratification. To the extent that governments are now acting as agents to stimulate social change, they are also acting as agents of mobility. For example, land reform programs in Latin America and elsewhere are designed not only to change farming practices and patterns of land ownership but also to make new sources of wealth available and to create new patterns of distribution. The evidence from Mexico shows that such objectives can be achieved; but even there, after more than thirty-five years of sustained government activity, the results, while encouraging, are still spotty.[55]

We have already observed that studies of occupational prestige over time show a rather consistent pattern of similarity among societies,

---

53. For a discussion of female mobility, see Lenski, *Power and Privilege, op. cit.,* pp. 416–417.

54. U.S. Department of Labor, *Manpower Report of the President* (Washington, D.C.: U.S. Government Printing Office, 1969), pp. 39–41.

55. Patterns of social and economic change in modern Mexico are analyzed at length in Chapter 8, pp. 253–257.

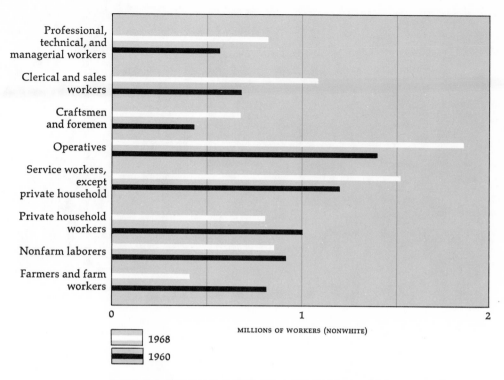

SOURCE: *Manpower Report of the President,* U.S. Department of Labor (1969), p. 40.

FIGURE 7.5. **SHIFTS IN OCCUPATION FOR NONWHITE WORKERS, 1960–1968**

including some of the less developed ones. The findings of cross-cultural studies of mobility, while still far from conclusive, seem to point in the same direction; that is, there seems to be no great difference in the amount of mobility in the United States as compared with that in the other highly industrialized societies of the Western world.

Lenski has recently attempted to systematize and analyze a variety of research findings on mobility in different societies.[56] In the more industrialized societies of the world, intergenerational mobility averaged about 30 percent in jobs not involving movement in or out of agricultural occupations, with the United States at the top with 34 percent and Italy at the lower end of the ladder with 22 percent. There was

a range also in total mobility, with the United States showing a distinct but not a great lead over the other societies studied. And the net general drift was upward in all societies, after deducting for rates of downward mobility. This is not surprising since all these societies are undergoing similar changes in their economies, toward occupations demanding increasingly complex skills.

As Lipset and Zetterberg point out, Europe and the United States share important structural features.[57] Both have experienced differential fertility by social class; both have experienced the industrial-agricultural revolution, with its great change in occupations; and both have experienced the great social and economic changes made possible by the increase in access to formal education and by the decline of privately owned businesses in favor of corporate structures. Lipset and Zetterberg have hypothesized that while Americans are exposed to stronger norms and more vivid models encour-

56. Lenski, *op. cit.,* pp. 410 ff.

57. Seymour M. Lipset and Hans Zetterberg, "A Theory of Social Mobility," in Bendix and Lipset, *Class, Status, and Power, op. cit.,* pp. 561–573.

Although apartheid in theory endorses the parallel development of South Africa's ethnic groups, what in fact has resulted is an extreme segregationist policy that severely curtails personal contacts between its peoples. Racially mixed groups are not allowed in public, and nonwhites may neither attend the cinema, theater, or opera in a white district without a special permit. Predictably, color makes the job in South Africa, and only whites are eligible for highly skilled or executive positions. The two workers at left center, standing rigidly at attention, are undergoing an interview in the personnel bureau of a diamond mine. Educational facilities, once open to all, are now strictly segregated. This photograph (below), showing university students protesting racial discrimination, was taken thirteen years ago; today they would be jailed for six months.

aging mobility than Europeans are, the aristocratic traditions of Europe may make for stronger ego needs which pressure for upward mobility. Thus the general congruence of mobility patterns in Europe and America.

At the present time, the most accurate statement on mobility in international perspective would seem to be that the rate for the United States appears to be somewhat higher but that there is a tendency toward convergence based on the level of industrialization of any particular society. Future trends in mobility and perhaps in stratification itself will depend on such factors as growth of the economy, fertility trends, educational opportunities, and socialization.

SUMMARY

Stratification refers to interaction patterns that result in the unequal distribution of wealth, prestige, and power. Their unequal distribution over time leads to the development in community and society of social strata; within each stratum people share more or less the same chances relative to the three basic rewards.

There is much evidence that in earlier historical periods there was a more or less complete convergence of rewards among strata, so that those with the most wealth also had the highest prestige and the most power. In its most extreme form, such convergence led to the formation of closed systems or castes. In more recent times, there is evidence of a shift in the reward patterns; for example, those with the greatest wealth may not have high prestige or the most power.

Just as the family, the school, the economy, and the government act variously as agents of socialization or social change, so also do they act as agents to maintain or alter stratification patterns. Socialization and change provide crucial elements of functional and conflict theories, especially as they relate to stratification. Functional theory helps best to explain stratification in a society dominated by a value-belief system that emphasizes achievement, equality of opportunity, and mobility and where organizational structure supports the realization of these values. The family and school become agents that foster stability and equilibrium for the large majority of citizens and subtly cultivate the continuity of stratification, with only gradual modifications in the distribution of rewards. Values and beliefs, from whatever source, become the firm foundation for the system. The goals and norms to achieve them are defined so that society's members learn to accept them as legitimate and proper. Over time, a strong moral tone tends to become built into the system of stratification.

At the same time, functional theory provides a less than adequate explanation for the built-in inequalities in the family and the school systems and is even less able to account for the rising levels of protest against the more extreme forms of inequality in societies. Conflict theory seems to help greatly to account for the processes of change that are increasingly important phenomena of the contemporary world. In its more extreme form, conflict theory holds that conflict is an inevitable part of stratification itself—that as long as there is inequality in the distribution of the rewards and the distribution is determined by who controls decision-making and the productive forces of the economy, there is bound to be conflict. The "have-nots" will not passively accept their lot.

The main theme of agrarian life was stability. The main theme of contemporary industrial and urban life is change. With regard to stratification, change means new value orientations about mobility—movement up or down the stratification ladder, leading to a redistribution of the rewards both on an individual and a societal level. Occupation has become the direct source of the rewards to be distributed. Industrial urban society provides an ever-growing variety of occupations of varying levels of prestige, income, and power, and so far no society has devised a means by which all its members can have equal access to these occupations. But if the reality of mobility in these societies has not matched the rhetoric, it can nevertheless be said that mobility has been sufficient to blunt criticism of the system in most Western societies.

The question remains whether sufficient rewards can be distributed to those at the bottom level of society so that the differences between levels, while they may continue to be large in absolute terms, will not be perceived as important enough to challenge. Certainly one of the features of life in our time is the challenge being raised against all elements of stratification in both the developing and the developed societies. In this challenge the struggle for the redistribution of power seems at least as important as the struggle for the redistribution of wealth. And not least among the factors influencing this struggle is population growth, to which we next turn our attention.

8
Demographic Change

In the last three decades the world has been rocked by two great explosions—the literal explosion of the atomic bomb and the figurative explosion of the world's population. Indeed, during the last decade the mass media have focused attention increasingly on the population explosion as the more serious of the two threats to mankind. Why? Simply because the world's societies have responded even less successfully to the challenge of controlling their own runaway growth than to the challenge of controlling nuclear weapons. If the current rate of growth continues, the population of the world will double by the time most readers of this text are fifty years old. What kind of society, what kinds of group life will this mean—for you readers and your children, and for the billions of other human beings who may never have a chance to learn to read?

No social problem is more closely tied to questions of human values than the problem of checking population growth. If there is a universal human value, then surely it is the value of "being alive." To be born is good and to die is bad—it is as simple as that. Most people feel that they wouldn't have missed this world for anything; until recently most have not even considered the question of whether a conscious effort should be made to limit births.

Paradoxically, those who seem to get the least from their stay on this earth, as measured by ordinary material and social criteria, are today the most prolific. How can we explain the fact that people who are apparently doomed to live in poverty, who fail to achieve either material or psychic well-being even by the standards set by their own society, bring more children into the world than those with great advantages? Do societies or groups that consciously try to restrict population growth place less value on human life than those that do not?

It is not our purpose as sociologists to try to pass judgment on different value patterns and their behavioral consequences. It is our task, however, to examine the tensions and problems brought on by rapid population growth and to consider the sociological implications of varying behavior and attitudes toward "the problem of people." In this chapter we will begin with a historical overview of the growth of human populations, to show the background and dimensions of the so-called "population explosion." Then, through case studies of Mexico,

Communist China, and the United States, we will point up some of the implications of the current population trends for societies in different stages of economic development and population growth. Finally, we will consider differences in attitudes and behavior regarding family planning in various parts of the world, together with prospects for change.

Throughout the chapter we will try to make clear the differences between the industrially advanced, urban societies that have already undergone a demographic transition from high to relatively low rates of population growth (for example, the United States, the countries of western Europe, Canada, Australia, and Japan) and the underdeveloped or developing nations that have yet to experience this transition and are currently growing very rapidly (the countries of Latin America and Africa and some Asian countries, especially India, Ceylon, Pakistan, and Communist China). As we will see, the patterns and problems of population growth vary markedly in these different parts of the world.

POPULATION GROWTH— THE LESSONS OF HISTORY

World population is currently growing at the rate of about 2 percent a year, faster than ever before in history. With total population now close to 3.5 billion, this means an increase of almost 70 million people each year—more than the current population of Great Britain.

The limited evidence available suggests that the total population of the world at the beginning of the Christian era was about 250 million people. It took roughly 1650 years for the figure to double to half a billion, but in the next three hundred years it doubled and redoubled, reaching two billion by 1930 (Figure 8.1, page 244). World population is expected to reach four billion by 1975, doubling in less than fifty years; and if current birth and death rates remain unchanged, it will continue to double about every thirty-five years. Thus, although a world population growth rate of 2 percent per year may not sound particularly dramatic, its effects will be readily apparent in our lifetimes.

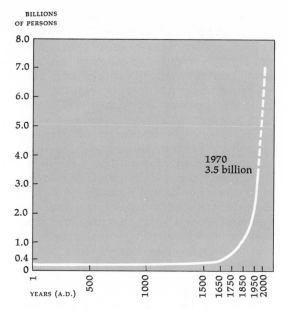

BILLIONS
OF PERSONS

1970
3.5 billion

YEARS (A.D.)

SOURCE: Harold F. Dorn, "World Population Growth," in *The Population Dilemma*, ed. Philip M. Hauser (Englewood Cliffs, N.J.: Prentice-Hall, Inc., 1963), p. 10.

FIGURE 8.1   **GROWTH OF WORLD POPULATION SINCE 1 A.D.**

MALTHUS' GLOOMY PROPHECY

Thomas Robert Malthus (1766–1834), an English clergyman, mathematician, and economist, was the first to write systematically about the possible consequences of unchecked population growth. In his *Essay on the Principle of Population*, first published in 1798, he set forth the theory that human populations could—and under the right circumstances *would*—grow by geometrical progression (2, 4, 8, 16, 32, 64, 128), whereas food production could increase only arithmetically (1, 2, 3, 4, 5, 6, 7) and would reach some ultimate limit. He predicted that whenever a population grew to the point where it could no longer be supported by the available food supply, the death rate would inevitably rise to bring the two forces again into balance.[1]

Malthus based his theory on the belief that man's biological drive for sexual gratification was essentially incompatible with his material needs, especially his need for food. It is a law of nature, he said, that "the power of population is indefinitely greater than the power in the earth to produce subsistence for man." Malthus predicted that all of man's efforts to improve his standard of living were in the long run destined to fail. Any increase in the food supply would only further stimulate population growth, so that the benefits would be quickly wiped out.

Historically, famine, plagues, and wars had functioned as *positive checks* to keep populations in balance with the available food supply, and Malthus believed that these disasters were divinely ordained. In his later writing he urged that man try to avert future disaster by applying the *preventive check* of "moral restraint" to limit reproduction. But he feared that the sexual drive was too strong for most people to accept what he considered to be the only morally defensible means of reducing fertility—postponement of marriage and continence in marriage.

The Malthusian principle became synonymous with a gloomy prophecy that living standards for the great masses of men were doomed to remain low, and as such it stirred both controversy and concern.[2] Prime Minister William Pitt of England, for example, withdrew proposed legislation that would have provided relief payments in direct relation to family size, for Malthus' theory had led him to fear that such a law would only encourage more rapid population growth and thus lead to increased poverty. Fifty years later Karl Marx denounced the Malthusian doctrine as just another defense of the status quo. Poverty, he claimed, resulted not from a shortage of resources but rather from the capitalist system of production and distribution.

In retrospect, we can see that Malthus' theory had several weaknesses. In the first place, it assumed that postponement of marriage and continence would continue to be the only morally acceptable means for limiting reproduction. Malthus did not anticipate the development of effective mechanical and chemical means of contraception, nor could he have known that within 150 years after his death most of the world's major religious bodies would have accepted the need for some form of family planning and birth control.

1. Thomas R. Malthus, *An Essay on the Principle of Population* (Homewood, Ill.: Richard D. Irwin, Inc., 1963).

2. For critical commentary, see Judy K. Morris, "Malthus in Retrospect," *Population Bulletin* of the Population Reference Bureau, 22, No. 1 (February 1966), 28 ff., and William Petersen, *Population*, 2nd ed. (New York: The Macmillan Company, 1969), pp. 141 ff.

Perhaps even more important in upsetting Malthus' formula have been the revolutionary changes in agricultural methods and technology. In Malthus' time, it was the practice in farming to leave one third of the land fallow each year so that the soil could recover its fertility. If this system had continued and there had been no other changes in agricultural techniques, Malthus' dire forecast might indeed have come true already. But the introduction of crop rotation in the mid-nineteenth century increased land utilization by 50 percent. Shortly after Malthus' death, too, came the important discovery of chemical fertilizer. This development and subsequent improvements in farming techniques—irrigation, hybridization of seed, pest and weed control, better drainage systems, more efficient tools—have helped increase agricultural yields in the developed world ten times over those of Malthus' day. World population in the same period has increased less than four times. Thus the Malthusian day of reckoning has at least been postponed.

THE DEMOGRAPHIC TRANSITION IN THE INDUSTRIALIZED WORLD

Concern over today's population explosion tends to obscure the fact that throughout most of human history rates of population growth were little more than enough for man to replace himself. Probably never before 1800 did the world's population growth rate reach 0.5 percent, or a fourth of its present level. (See the definitions of demographic terms, below.) Birth rates were generally much higher than now, but high fertility was necessary to compensate for high rates of mortality, especially among infants and children. As noted in the chapter on social change, the ravages of war and disease periodically brought actual *declines* in population on both a regional and a world scale.

The Industrial Revolution. In western Europe, a major turning point in population trends came with the Industrial Revolution, which saw the beginning of a gradual reduction in death

BASIC DEMOGRAPHIC TERMS

Demography is the statistical study of populations, their size, distribution, and composition. It is concerned with such matters as the changes over time in fertility, mortality, and migration and with the factors related to these changes. In the present chapter we will focus primarily on four basic demographic concepts: population growth rate, death rate, birth rate, and fertility rate.

The term *population growth rate* refers to the rate, usually given as an annual percentage, by which a population is changing in size, either growing or declining. For the world as a whole, the growth rate depends on the relationship between births and deaths in a given year: it is obtained by subtracting the total number of deaths from the total number of births and then calculating what percentage the remainder is of the world population for that year. Thus, if there are as many infants born to the world in a year as there are people dying, the population remains stable; any excess of births or of deaths leads respectively to growth or to decline. For a given nation or community, the population growth rate for any year must include not only the net difference

between births and deaths (*natural growth*) but also the net difference, if any, between in-migration and out-migration. During the late nineteenth and early twentieth centuries, for example, migration was a significant factor in boosting annual growth rates in the United States.

Birth rates and *death rates* are generally figured on the basis of every 1000 persons in a given population for a given year. Thus a birth rate (or death rate) of 20 means that there were twenty births (or deaths), on the average, for every 1000 persons in the total population. Often specific death (mortality) rates are calculated on the basis of some variable such as age, occupation, race, or sex. The *infant mortality rate,* for example, indicates the number of infants per 1000 live births who die during the first year of life.

Finally, the term *fertility rate* refers to the number of births in a particular population relative to every 1000 women of childbearing age (usually defined as women from fifteen to forty-five). Fertility relates only to actual births and should thus be distinguished from *fecundity,* which refers to the biological capacity for producing offspring.

Traditional agricultural methods in much of the underdeveloped world don't keep pace with the reproductive power of the people. Thus the gloomy predictions of Robert Malthus may eventually become a reality.

rates. Since 1800, when Malthus wrote, successive advances in medicine and sanitation have lowered death rates in most of the industrialized nations from levels of 25 to 30 per 1000 population to current levels ranging from 7 to 11 per 1000. In the United States, mortality rates in the last two decades have stabilized, at least temporarily, in the area of 9 or 10 per 1000.

As death rates began to drop in the Western world, rates of population growth accelerated accordingly, causing many people to fear that Malthus' prophecy would soon be fulfilled. By the middle of the nineteenth century, however, it was apparent that more rapid population growth was being accompanied by a steady *improvement* in standards of living. The revolution

in agriculture was promising to ensure an increasingly adequate food supply, and industrial expansion was bringing greater prosperity to growing numbers of people. Population growth, in fact, came to be seen as a necessary stimulant for economic development: if the economy was to grow, more people were needed to produce— and, in turn, consume—more goods. As we shall see, the same argument is sometimes used today to defend unchecked population growth in the developing countries, but circumstances are so different that the argument has little bearing. In fact, rapid population growth may well have the *opposite* effect, negating the potential gains from agricultural and industrial development.

Declining growth rates. In western Europe and the United States, per capita income was already much higher by the middle of the nineteenth century than it is today in the developing areas of the world, and the population base was much smaller. Furthermore, changes in the rate of population growth occurred more slowly and were closely tied to an overall pattern of technical, economic, and social change.[3] Death rates, for example, declined only gradually during the nineteenth and early twentieth centuries, as medical science slowly improved; and by the time they had dropped significantly, birth rates had also begun to decline. Birth rates in the industrialized countries have continued to fall during the present century, reaching a current low in the United States, for example, of about 17 per 1000—compared with about 30 in 1910 and about 55 in 1800. Meanwhile, death rates have tended to level out at about 10 per 1000.

The lowering of birth rates in the industrialized countries has been related to a number of factors. In the first place, the marked reduction in infant and child mortality meant that parents no longer needed to have eight or ten children to be sure that some would survive to adulthood. Equally important, industrialization and urbanization were gradually changing the character of family life: the family was becoming less and less a self-sufficient and self-contained productive unit. As rapid progress in industrialization brought greater job specialization and thus an increased need for formal education, children moved out of the labor force and into school to train for specialized roles. Thus they ceased to be economically productive members of the family unit and became instead a family expense. The changing structure of the labor force and the extension of the educational system, especially in the United States, led in turn to new opportunities and a gradually improved status for women. It became less and less true that a woman's only place was in the home. All of these changes have worked together in the industrialized nations to create favorable attitudes toward the conscious limitation of family size. These attitudes, even more than the devel-

opment of effective contraceptives, have been responsible for gradually decreasing birth and fertility rates and thus for holding population growth rates, over the long term, to fairly moderate levels.

Over a period of two hundred years, then, the now developed world has experienced what demographers call a "demographic transition," moving from high mortality rates and high fertility rates to low mortality and low fertility. Death rates started to drop before birth rates did, causing population growth rates to rise rapidly for a time. Gradually, however, birth rates also began to fall, and rates of growth in most of the industrialized nations now seem to be stabilizing at relatively low levels. During the 1960's the United States and the Soviet Union, for example, had annual growth rates ranging from a high of 1.65 percent to a low of less than 1 percent. Japan and most countries of western Europe had even lower growth rates, ranging from 0.5 to 0.75 percent. Because of the large population base in most of the industrialized nations, even moderate growth can be expected to bring its share of problems—crowded housing, jammed highways, air and water pollution—but it seems unlikely to reverse the trend toward steadily increasing prosperity.

DEMOGRAPHIC CHANGES IN THE DEVELOPING WORLD

Birth and death rates in the industrialized countries gradually arrived at their present levels as a result of modifications that took place over two centuries. By contrast, the developing nations in Asia, Africa, and Latin America have experienced a precipitous drop in their death rates over a period of only twenty to thirty years, without an accompanying drop in birth rates (Figure 8.2, page 248). As Dorn states the matter, "It is the combination of a medieval birth rate with a twentieth-century death rate that is responsible for the current high rate of population increase."[4]

The revolution in mortality control. Since World War II, public health programs involving the widespread use of antibiotics, vaccines, and insecticides—all imported from the industrialized nations—have caused death rates in the developing world to plummet from 35 or 40 per

---

3. See George J. Stolnitz, "The Demographic Transition," and J. J. Spengler, "Population and Economic Growth," in *Population: The Vital Revolution*, ed. R. Freedman (New York: Doubleday & Company, Inc., 1964).

4. Harold F. Dorn, "World Population Growth," in *The Population Dilemma*, ed. Philip M. Hauser (Englewood Cliffs, N.J.: Prentice-Hall, Inc., 1963), p. 16.

BIRTH AND DEATH RATES IN THE DEVELOPED
AND UNDERDEVELOPED COUNTRIES, 1850–1950

PROJECTED POPULATION GROWTH IN DEVEL-
OPED AND UNDERDEVELOPED AREAS, 1950–2000

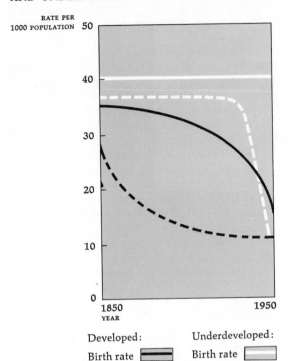

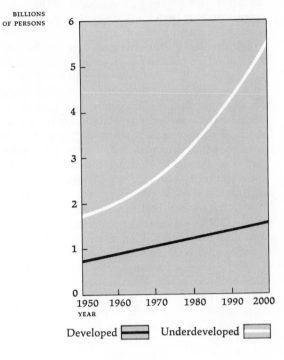

FIGURE 8.2 **POPULATION TRENDS IN THE DEVELOPED AND UNDERDEVELOPED COUNTRIES**

1000 population to averages between 10 and 20 per 1000. In a few countries, death rates are now comparable to those in the industrialized world. Birth rates, however, have remained at their previous high levels or gone higher, averaging about 40 per 1000 population and in some countries reaching as high as 50 per 1000. One long-range consequence of the drop in mortality is that more husbands and wives will live throughout their entire period of fertility and therefore be able to produce even more children. These are the facts that give substance to the phrase "population explosion."

In the developing world as a whole, population growth rates now average about 2.2 percent a year; in many countries, especially in Latin America, annual growth rates exceed 3 percent. If present trends continue, then, the developing countries can be expected to double their populations within the next twenty-five to

thirty-five years—about twice as fast as the industrialized nations. Already they account for almost 70 percent of the world's total population, and by the end of the twentieth century the figure will probably have risen to nearly 80 percent. The changing distribution of the world's population becomes dramatically clear in the case of Latin America: in 1900 only one out of every thirty-seven persons in the world was a Latin American, but by 1980 the figure is expected to be one in twelve.

Traditionalism versus change. In the industrialized nations, as we have seen, a broad pattern of social change accompanied economic growth and helped shape population trends. The decline in death rates was only gradual, and it was followed sooner or later by a compensating decline in birth rates. But this historical process is not repeating itself in the developing nations, where Western technology is being imported by societies which, for the most part, are still traditional in orientation. It has been relatively simple and inexpensive to lower death rates dramatically over a very short period of time; in Ceylon, for example, the death rate dropped 40 percent in a single year following the widespread use of residual insecticides to combat malaria. It is proving very difficult, on the other hand, to implement programs of birth control, which depend for their ultimate success not on technical knowledge and government support but on the attitudes of individual couples.

The complexity of social and cultural change is nowhere more apparent than in the area of population dynamics, for here the values, beliefs, and behavior patterns of traditional or folk societies stand in marked contrast to those that have evolved in urban, industrialized societies. In most of the developing countries, for example, almost everyone marries, and almost everyone marries young, which means that the wives have a long reproductive period. In addition, the desire for male heirs continues to be strong. Sons carry on the family name, provide the hard labor still so necessary for economic survival, perform key roles at religious ceremonials, and often are considered proof of the father's masculinity. Not least important, sons are a form of social security: if parents should survive to old age, they must, under present circumstances, rely on their sons to take care of them.

Studies in many countries of the developing world consistently show that between 60 and 80 percent of both men and women say they want to limit their family size. Yet the fact is that most do not.[5] One explanation is that many people in these societies seem unaware that the death rate has been dramatically reduced: they continue to assume that some of their children will probably die. Thus when they say that they want only three or four children, they seem to mean three or four who will survive to adulthood and old age.

Another factor that helps account for the continued high birth rates in these societies is that there is little social mobility and that little value is placed on such mobility. Children aspire to be what their parents were, a value orientation that tends to discourage individual motivation and patterns for change. To the extent that people think at all about the relationship between family planning and economic well-being, they tend to have a false picture of the situation. For example, Stycos found that women living in rural Peru and lower-class women in general have the mistaken notion that urban and upper-class women have larger families than they themselves have.[6]

Even among the upper classes, there is no clear-cut pattern that would provide a model for successful, large-scale family planning. As long as traditional patterns are maintained, those who try to plan their families may feel like, and be perceived as, outsiders. Yet the hard fact is that unchecked population growth threatens to preclude the achievement of social and economic goals in the developing nations. Indeed, where food supplies are already inadequate, the challenge of checking this rapid growth may soon be a matter of survival.[7]

POPULATION GROWTH AND ECONOMIC DEVELOPMENT

Most societies and their leaders proclaim themselves in favor of higher living standards, more adequate food supplies, technical innovation, and economic growth. But how can such aspirations be achieved and what relationship, if any, exists between socioeconomic development and population growth?

Some leaders of the developing countries, pointing to the history of the industrialized nations, assert that rapid population growth is a necessary stimulant to economic expansion. Eugene Black sums up their thinking as follows:

5. For a critical summary of the research on attitudes toward family size, see Bernard Berelson, "KAP Studies on Fertility," in *Family Planning and Population Programs*, ed. B. Berelson *et al.* (Chicago: The University of Chicago Press, 1966).

6. J. M. Stycos, "Social Class and Preferred Family Size in Peru," *American Journal of Sociology*, 70, No. 6 (May 1965), 651–658; see also Frederick Seitz, in Preface to *The Growth of World Population*, National Academy of Sciences, No. 1091 (1963), 22–26.

7. For discussions of the relation between agricultural and population growth, see William and Paul Paddock, *Famine 1975!* (Boston: Little, Brown and Company, 1968), and Paul R. Ehrlich, *The Population Bomb* (New York: Ballantine Books, 1968). See also *The Population Crisis: Implications and Plans for Action*, eds. Larry K. Y. Ng and Stuart Mudd (Bloomington, Ind.: Indiana University Press, 1965).

Some people argue that a big population implies a good market for the businessman's product: he can use mass production techniques and charge low prices. They insist, too, that with a growing population, the businessman constantly finds demand exceeding his estimates. Optimism and production run high; new products win ready acceptance, while obsolete industries die painlessly; the incentive to invest is strong and social mobility and change are encouraged. The burden of social costs is spread widely. By contrast, they suggest, a declining or even stationary population brings pessimism and economic stagnation; there is insufficient reward for private enterprise, and the state is thereby forced to intervene increasingly in fields better left to the private citizen.[8]

In Latin America, where the populations of most countries are increasing at the rate of about 3 percent a year, many people point to the vast expanses of empty space to demonstrate the need for more people. Bolivia, for example, has as much land area as prewar Germany but only about four million people, less than one tenth the population of West Germany alone; hence the conclusion that Bolivia is not threatened by its current rate of population growth but actually needs more people to stimulate economic development. It is argued that population control will follow naturally, as it did in western Europe and the United States, once economic development has taken place. But are these in fact the lessons from history?

Parallels and contrasts. It is true that the current rate of population growth in Latin America is no greater than that of the United States between 1790 and 1860, but different patterns of settlement and of social and economic change are leading to quite different consequences. Like the United States during its frontier days, Latin America has considerable land-use potential that remains untapped, even allowing for its extensive mountainous areas and impenetrable jungles; but rather than spreading out to develop virgin lands, its peoples are swarming to the already crowded cities. In Brazil, for example, the urban population increased 70 percent between 1950 and 1960, while the rural population increased only 18 percent. A 1960 census showed that six hundred new urban places had grown up in the same ten-year period.[9]

The phenomenon of urban growth in Latin America—which has parallels in the developing countries of Asia and Africa—cannot be compared to the urbanization of the Western world, for it has not been stimulated by industrial and economic growth. Some of the most spectacular population growth, in fact, has occurred in cities where job opportunities are conspicuously lacking. (See Chapter 9, "The Urban Transition.") In most cases the central administration is finding it increasingly difficult to provide the new arrivals with even the basic necessities— water, sewage disposal, lighting, and roads—to say nothing of schools and hospitals. And the economic and social problems created by mass migration to the cities are aggravated by high rates of population increase within the cities themselves.

As Black points out, the theory that rapid population growth will automatically stimulate economic development simply does not apply in most of the developing world, where there are already too many unskilled hands without prospects for productive employment. In India, with twice the population of the United States in half the land area, the masses go barefoot not because they do not want shoes, but because the system cannot produce shoes at prices they can afford. The fact is that in India two thirds of every dollar earned must be spent on food in order to maintain even a substandard diet. In most of the developing countries, bare survival is the primary concern of the masses, and populations are growing so rapidly that economic expansion is scarcely enough to keep standards of living from falling even lower.

The burden of child dependency. Economic growth is dependent on the ability of a society to direct a portion of its resources into investment—into the addition of new factories and other productive facilities, including the means for training and retraining workers.[10] But in countries with rapid population growth, the

---

8. Eugene R. Black, "Address to the Economic and Social Council of the United Nations," in Ng and Mudd, *op. cit.*, p. 41. From a different but related perspective, David Heer argues that "large governmental expenditures on health and education will enhance the reduction in fertility obtainable from an increase in national economic level alone." See David M. Heer, "Economic Development and Fertility," *Demography*, 3, No. 2 (1966), 423–444.

9. T. Lynn Smith, "The Population of Latin America," in Freedman, *Population: The Vital Revolution*, p. 186.

10. The following discussion is based largely on Ansley Coale, "Population and Economic Development," in Hauser, *The Population Dilemma*, pp. 49 ff.

In recent years the application of modern medicine has vastly improved the health of the underdeveloped world. India, for example, launched a massive campaign against smallpox in 1962, and within two years 64 percent of the population—or 279 million people—had been vaccinated. Thus in India, as in many countries, high birth rates are no longer offset by high death rates.

need for capital investment confronts tremendous pressures for immediate consumption. One effect of the precipitous drop in death rates in the developing countries has been to radically alter their age structures. Whereas only 20 to 30 percent of the populations of the industrialized countries are under fifteen years of age, in the developing nations the proportion reaches nearly 50 percent. These children are essentially consumers rather than producers, and the task of providing them with education, housing, clothing, and other basic necessities puts an unusually heavy drain on the economy. Unless birth rates decline, the burden of child dependency will become greater with each generation.

Density of the labor force. Over the long term, rapid population growth also threatens to glut the labor market, creating a high density of workers relative to the amount of capital available for investing in new productive facilities and thus for making new jobs. Brazil's labor force, for example, is expected to grow from its present level of 38 million to 161 million within sixty years if population continues to grow at the rate of 3 percent a year. It is doubtful that any economy can expand fast enough to create jobs for so many new workers.

Economists estimate that to keep per capita income from declining, the amount of national income allocated to investment must increase annually at a percentage three times greater than the annual percentage increase of the labor force. Thus, if the number of workers increases by 3 percent a year, as in Brazil at the present time, the rate of investment increase must be about 9 percent just to keep productivity *at the same level*. A further increase in investment is necessary to effect a net gain in per capita income. Yet most of the developing countries have been unable to expand their economies at a sustained rate of even 5 percent a year—less than enough to keep pace with a 2 percent annual increase in the number of available workers. If present trends continue, therefore, economic "growth" may mean little more than growth in the number of people available for employment. Standards of living will improve very little, and they may deteriorate. As Coale has noted, the problems created by the lack of adequate productive facilities are "compounded by the lack of education and training on the part of the labor force itself."[11] The provision of such training, of

11. *Ibid.*, p. 66.

This family, like 100,000 other Calcuttans, has no home but the open sidewalk. Living conditions are equally grim in the bustees, or slums, where families live in houses that are ten-feet square, windowless, and infested with rats. With a population that has doubled over the last twenty-five years to 7.5 million, the outlook for Calcutta is almost hopeless.

course, creates a further drain on available capital.

A developing country with a low rate of population growth would seem to have it easier all around. In the short run, its burden of child dependency is relatively much less than that experienced by a population with a high fertility rate. A smaller percentage of the national wealth is drained off by nonproductive consumers, so that more capital is available for investment. Over a period of several generations, the differences between a slowly growing population and a rapidly growing one increase as differences in the comparative density of the two labor forces become more marked. Here density refers not to geographic density but rather to the density of workers *relative to available capital.* One of the most densely populated areas of the world is the narrow strip of land running from Boston, Massachusetts, to Washington, D.C., which has an aggregate population of some 28 million, or more than two thousand people per square mile. Yet the median family income here in the early 1960's was $6600, well within the range of the American middle class. In this area, as in less populous parts of the industrialized world, the density of the labor force is low relative to the level of capital available for investment. The opposite is true throughout the developing world.

The prospects for change. In the industrialized nations, as we have noted, the decline in birth rates was a *consequence* of the sociocultural changes that accompanied economic growth. In the developing nations, by contrast, a reduction of birth rates seems to be a necessary *prerequisite* for economic and social progress. A country that can reduce its rate of population growth to about 1 percent a year will have much better prospects for raising the living standards of its people than one whose growth rate remains at 2 or 3 percent a year. While the differences in life chances for the two populations will be relatively small for the first generation, they will become progressively greater as differences in the comparative density of the two labor forces become a decisive factor. Coale estimates, for example, that a 50 percent reduction in fertility, accomplished over a period of twenty-five years, might lead to a 40 percent gain in per capita income at the end of thirty years; a 100 percent gain in sixty years; and a 500 percent gain in 150 years.[12] These economic changes would lead to changes in other patterns of social behavior, including probably an upgrading of education and new roles and higher status for women and children. Such sociocultural developments would be likely to further depress fertility rates, as they have in nations that have already experienced modernization.

Although there is clearly a need to better understand the complex relationship between population growth and economic development, there seems little doubt that the current population explosion is impeding, not helping, the process of modernization in the developing countries. That this explosion has created a crisis of worldwide proportions is amply demonstrated by recent efforts of the United Nations to deal effectively with population growth by means of programs aimed both at decreasing fertility and at increasing economic productivity.[13] Fortunately, medical and industrial technology has given man the means for achieving these goals, but whether he will use this technology effectively hinges largely on questions of attitude and belief. As we shall see, the "problem of people"—that is, rapid population growth and its consequences—takes on different dimensions in different societies, but in every society it is increasingly complex.

MEXICO—THE PROBLEMS OF A NEIGHBOR

Among the nations of the world that we label underdeveloped or developing, Mexico stands out as one that has made remarkable progress toward achieving its social and economic goals.[14] In the aftermath of a political revolution dating back to 1910, Mexico has implemented an ideology of social progress that is only now beginning to emerge in most other countries of the developing world. The ideals of the Mexican Revolution—now broadly accepted by all major political factions—included agrarian and labor reform, the extension of educational opportunity, the assimilation of isolated Indian villages into national life, the improvement of living standards, and the development of a political democracy.

During the past thirty years Mexico's political structure has been the most stable in Latin America. The *Partido Revolucionario Institucional* (PRI) has firmly dominated most aspects of national life, steering Mexico between the economic orientations of socialism on the one hand and twentieth-century capitalism on the other. Under the land reform program initiated in 1915, millions of acres of agricultural lands, formerly concentrated in large private holdings and operated under a system of peonage, have been confiscated by the government and redistributed to the peasants under the *ejido* system.[15] The *ejidos* (literally, *common lands*) are owned collectively by the agricultural workers (*ejidatorios*) who farm them. Many of the *ejidos* are

12. *Ibid.*, pp. 68–69.

13. "United Nations General Assembly Resolution on Population Growth and Economic Development," in Ng and Mudd, *op. cit., The Population Crisis.* On Dec. 10, 1966, twelve members of the United Nations signed the historic "World Leaders' Declaration on Population," which declared family planning to be a basic human right and warned that "too rapid population growth seriously hampers efforts to raise living standards . . . ." By January 1968, eighteen more nations had signed the document. See *Population Crisis Newsletter* (February 1968), p. 3.

14. The following discussion is based largely on "Mexico: The Problem of People," *Population Bulletin* of the Population Reference Bureau, Inc., 20, No. 7 (November 1964). See also Luis Leñero Otero, "The Mexican Urbanization Process and Its Implications," in *Demography*, 5, No. 2 (1968), 866–873.

15. For a discussion of the *ejido* system, see Eyler N. Simpson, *The Ejido: Mexico's Way Out* (Chapel Hill, N.C.: University of North Carolina Press, 1937).

held by either a single family or a small village. Though geared primarily to the production of subsistence foods, the Mexican land reform program has done much to increase agricultural output as well as to improve the lot of the peasant.

Government in Mexico has been similarly responsible for accelerating industrial growth, for modernizing communication and transportation facilities, and for improving public education and public health. In the thirty-year period between 1930 and 1960, real wages per capita about tripled in Mexico. Compared with most of its Latin American neighbors, then, Mexico has made an enviable record of social and economic progress over the last several decades. It is against this setting that we will examine the difficulties this nation is experiencing as a result of rapid population growth.

BACKGROUND OF THE PROBLEM

Disease, warfare, internal strife, and conditions of near-servitude for the masses all helped to keep Mexico's population at fewer than 10 million until late in the nineteenth century. By 1900 its population had grown only to 13.6 million—several million less than the current population of New York State. Since then, however, it has quadrupled (Figure 8.3).

Net in-migration has been inconsequential in accounting for Mexico's rapid growth during the last several decades. As elsewhere in the developing world, the primary factor has been a sharp decline in the death rate, which began earlier in Mexico than in most of the developing countries because of public health measures instituted by the government. In 1930 the mortality rate in Mexico was 26.6 per 1000 population; by 1963 it had been cut to 10.4. The birth rate, in the meanwhile, increased slightly, from 43 per 1000 in 1930 to about 46 per 1000 in 1960.

The combination of a high birth rate and low death rate has boosted Mexico's rate of population growth to more than 3 percent a year. There is little chance that this will be reduced in the near future, for the mothers of the next generation are already born. In 1960, 48 percent of all brides in Mexico were under twenty years of age; these women were born after Mexico's "population explosion" had already begun.[16] How many children will these young women

want? Will they even ponder such a question? Since there appears to be little likelihood that fertility patterns will change significantly within the next ten years, projections of population growth during this period are based mostly on what is expected to happen to mortality rates, which are still relatively high in Mexico's isolated rural areas. Depending largely on the success of the public health measures in these areas, it is projected that Mexico's population will probably grow to somewhere between 65 and 70 million by 1980. How will this affect the family, the community, and the nation?

GROWTH VERSUS PROGRESS

Despite tremendous economic gains over the last several decades, rapid population growth has meant that Mexico still cannot produce enough food for its own people, much less provide them with sufficient schools and adequate housing, though these are nationally stated goals. Mexico's gross national product (the total amount of goods and services produced within a country in a given year) tripled between 1940 and 1960, but in the same period the population doubled. Thus, the number of Mexicans living at a bare subsistence level remained as great as before.[17]

Food production. At present Mexico is one of the few developing nations in which the average diet meets the minimum daily nutritional requirement of 2500 calories. This figure is only an *average*, however; some nine million Mexicans still suffer from malnutrition. Almost a fourth of Mexico's people never have fish, meat, eggs, or milk.

Whatever its problems, Mexico is more fortunate than many countries in that its land and coastal waters are capable of producing all the food it will need for the foreseeable future. Some 74 million of its 487 million acres are cultivable by today's technology, and less than half this land is now being farmed. Thus Mexico

---

16. This figure compares with 2.1 percent for the United States in 1960 and 14.4 percent for France. In 1940, by contrast, the respective percentages were Mexico, 76 percent; United States, 11.6 percent; and France, 19.5 percent.

17. "Mexico: The Problem of People," p. 181.

clearly has the potential for greatly increasing its agricultural productivity—*if* ways can be found to provide adequate irrigation and to make farming techniques more efficient.

To date, rural isolation in Mexico has served to work against the widespread introduction of modern agricultural technology. The *ejido* system of farming, so strongly built into the revolutionary ideology, is not adequate for current needs. One reason is that most of the *ejido* parcels are small—usually ten acres or less for each *ejidatario*—and many are unsuited to mechanized farming. Lack of machinery and mechanical knowledge, illiteracy, and traditional cultural patterns also stand in the way of modernization. Unfortunately, special government agencies set up to provide financial and technical assistance have provided only sporadic help.

Despite agricultural progress, Mexico is still not self-sufficient in corn, its basic food. In 1960 the corn yield per acre was only fifteen bushels, compared to an average yield of fifty-three bushels in the United States. (On individual farms in our Midwestern corn belt, per acre yields run as high as 150 bushels.) That there is a potential for marked improvement has been clearly demonstrated by those Mexican farmers who have broken with tradition to apply modern agricultural methods. One of these is Jesus Reyes, who was a boy during the early years of the Mexican Revolution; in his own words, he was "an eye witness to the most crucial times, the violent days of Carranza, Zapata, Villa, de la Huerta."[18] With a will to get ahead, Reyes bought his present farm in 1945—sixty-six acres of poor, thin soil which barely covered the rocks in some spots. He drilled over 120 feet to get water and then, with the aid of the National Corn Commission, got special seed and fertilizer. Now, with certified seed, irrigation, and fertilizer, he is able to get up to a hundred bushels of corn per acre. He is alert to agricultural experimentation and uses pesticides. This modern farmer in ancient Mexico has a home with indoor plumbing, television, and even a telephone. In his own words, "Now, thanks to the Lord, we live like people."

Reyes is an innovator who hopes that others will follow his example; and many have. Many more, however, continue to farm as did their fathers before them, using the same native corn, unfed and unirrigated.

Why do they cling to the old ways? They can see. They can reach out and touch Reyes's towering corn. But they do not change. Even men who work on Reyes's farm follow the old ways on small plots of their own. Why? "*Así es!*—that's the way it is." It is said with a shrug that answers everything and nothing.[19]

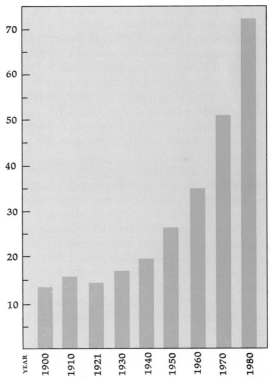

SOURCE: *Population Bulletin*, 20, No. 7 (November 1964).

FIGURE 8.3. **GROWTH OF MEXICO'S POPULATION, 1900–1980**

The decrease in Mexico's population from 1910 to 1921 was an effect of the Revolution and outmigration. In the following decades, political stability and the introduction of public health measures brought the beginning of rapid population growth, and by 1960, Mexico had the third largest population in the Americas. The projection for 1980 is based on a current annual growth rate exceeding 3 percent.

18. *The Quiet Revolution* (Skokie, Ill.: International Minerals and Chemical Corporation, 1965) pp. 8-11.

19. *Ibid.*, pp. 10-11.

Although men like Reyes helped to increase Mexico's per capita food production by 40 percent in the decade of the 1960's, about half of Mexico's cultivated land is still worked by traditional methods on small farms. To make these farms more efficient, the Department of Agrarian Affairs and Land Settlement is trying to organize the *ejidos* into cooperative units large enough for mechanized farming and modern farm technology, but this effort is opposed by many of the *ejidatarios*. For them, the *ejido* remains a symbol of freedom and dignity, won after generations of servitude, and they fear the loss of their independence. When and under what circumstances can the proper motivations be developed so that these farmers will become more like Jesus Reyes? During the 1960's, Mexican agriculture produced about 20 percent of the total gross national product, while it employed more than half the entire labor force. By contrast, in the United States only 5 percent of the labor force was in agriculture in 1967, and agriculture produced 3 percent of the GNP. These figures sharply reveal the difference between a developing and an industrialized economy.

Industrialization. Among the developing nations, Mexico is one of the world leaders in industrialization, but here, too, it faces great pressures. Its task is not merely to match the developed nations in industrial efficiency and productive capacity but also to create enough new jobs for its expanding labor force. The rapid population growth of recent years means that about 400,000 persons will be entering the Mexican labor market *each year* between now and 1980. New jobs are being created at less than half that rate.

Economists remind us that making jobs has become an expensive process. In the United States, where the costs of productive facilities and job training run unusually high, a new job is now capitalized at somewhere between $50,000 and $100,000.[20] The cost per job is usually less in developing economies, but it is still high relative to the amount of capital available for investment, especially considering the number of new jobs needed to achieve and maintain full employment. Even if it cost only $10,000 to capitalize a new job, Mexico—which had a GNP of only $21.75 billion in 1966—would have to spend $4 billion *annually* to create jobs for the 400,000 people joining the labor force each year. In fact, the problem is much

more serious than that, for Mexico is actually capitalizing new jobs at a cost near $40,000. Why is the figure so high? Because new plants are being automated, and relative to cost and productive capacity, they provide fewer jobs than older plants. In the cotton textile industry, employment actually dropped about 29 percent during the 1950's, while the value of production increased 177 percent.[21]

Automation is probably necessary if Mexico is ever to compete on equal terms with the already advanced industrial nations, but it greatly complicates the economic problems of a developing nation with a surfeit of labor. Many millions of Mexicans are either unemployed or employed at such low levels of skill and income as to preclude their being able to "live like people," in the words of Jesus Reyes. Certainly they are unable to stimulate demand for the goods being produced in Mexico's factories. After modernizing their productive facilities, many industries are operating at only 25 to 50 percent of capacity simply because too few people can afford their products. If Mexico's population continues to grow at the present rate, the economic and social problems created by a glutted labor market will probably become increasingly severe.

Education. In Mexico as in other developing countries, rapid population growth has created a heavy burden of child dependency. In 1960 some 44 percent of Mexico's population was under fifteen years of age, compared with 31 percent in the United States and 25 percent in western Europe. This large proportion of young people puts a heavy strain on Mexico's resources.

Although the Mexican government has been committed since the Revolution to wiping out illiteracy and providing at least a primary education for every child, rapid population growth and limited capital have thus far kept the goal out of reach. By 1960 almost two thirds of Mexico's people could read and write, yet the population had grown so rapidly in the preceding decade that in 1960 there were 1.5 million more illiterate Mexicans than there had been ten years earlier. During this same decade Mexico

---

20. To capitalize a new job is to invest money so as to provide a job that was not previously available in the marketplace.

21. "Mexico: The Problem of People," p. 195.

built an average of 850 elementary schools a year, and elementary-school enrollment increased from 2.8 to 5.4 million children. But despite these gains, 4.3 million children between the ages of five and fourteen were not in school in 1960—a slightly greater number than in 1950.

Looking ahead to 1980, the problem is staggering, for if the current rate of population growth continues, the number of children between five and fourteen will by then reach 19 million—a number almost equal to Mexico's total population in 1940. Even though the federal government (which largely finances the public schools) is allocating some 25 percent of its total budget to education, there is no guarantee that it will be able to provide even the rudiments of education for this many youngsters. And the real challenge is to do much more, for educational requirements become increasingly great as industry is automated and the economy grows more complex. A lowering of the birth rate between 1970 and 1980 would begin to reduce the need for additional elementary facilities and thus make more capital available for developing new secondary and technical schools; but so far Mexico's leaders have not acknowledged that family planning and a lowering of the birth rate may be necessary if the country is to achieve its social and economic goals.

BIRTH CONTROL: THE CURRENT SITUATION

Although few Mexicans may perceive the long-range effects of unchecked population growth on national goals, many are acutely aware of the personal hardships that sometimes come with "too many children." Abortion rates in Mexico appear to be typical of those in Latin America, with at least one induced abortion for every four or five live births. But even though abortion has become a major health problem, by 1970 the Mexican government had shown no signs of making family planning a part of its

national health program. Pope Paul's 1968 encyclical "On Human Life," reinforcing the traditional stand of the Roman Catholic Church against the use of contraceptives, can be expected to have an inhibiting effect on any direct action the government may have been contemplating. It will almost certainly have some effect on the attitudes of Mexico's nominally Catholic population. At its annual meeting held in August 1968, the Roman Catholic hierarchy of Mexico gave its full support to the papal encyclical, urging the faithful to obey the ban against artificial contraception.[22]

Judging from reaction in other parts of the world, however, it is not expected that the papal pronouncement will have much effect on couples already using contraceptives. A survey in August 1968 showed that there was no disposition to halt or even modify the family planning programs that have recently been developed in Mexico under private auspices and with the aid of the International Planned Parenthood Federation. It was estimated that these programs were serving about eighty thousand Mexican women, primarily with the Pill and the IUD.

Obviously, family planning will have to be instituted on a much broader scale before it significantly affects the future of the nation as a whole. Although the fertility rate will probably drop very little in the next ten years, forces for change are already at work. In the final section of this chapter we will examine some of the factors that may gradually alter attitudes toward family size not only in Mexico but elsewhere in the developing world.

THE PEOPLE'S REPUBLIC OF CHINA

In the twenty-odd years since the Communists under Mao Tse-tung established the People's Republic of China, mainland China has probably added some 200 million to its population —the equivalent of the entire population of the United States. Although accurate census figures are lacking, the population of Communist China is now estimated at approximately 800 million, making it by far the most populous country in the world. How does this developing giant—a

22. As reported in *The New York Times*, Aug. 12, 1968. See also comments by Dr. Julian Samora, Coordinator of Ford Foundation Population Programs in Mexico and Central America, in *National Catholic Reporter*, August 1968, p. 4. In private correspondence, Dr. Luis Leñero of the Instituto Mexicano de Estudios Sociales states that their research findings show that Catholics in Mexico may not be more influenced by the recent encyclical than Catholics elsewhere.

"young" nation built on one of the great civilizations of the ancient world—react to the "problem of people"?[23]

THE RESTRUCTURING OF A SOCIAL ORDER

When the Chinese Communists formally assumed power in October 1949, they inherited a country impoverished and disorganized, the victim of years of warfare, colonial exploitation, government corruption, and internal strife. It took some 85 percent of the population to produce the food supply (at that time the percentage for Mexico was a little more than 50 percent and for the United States about 12 percent). The Communists came to power confident of their ability to bring about a radical social revolution—to remodel an agrarian, family-oriented society into a prosperous industrial society built on the theories of Marx and Lenin as interpreted by Mao Tse-tung.

The Communists acknowledged their lack of administrative experience, appeared eager to learn, and sought to compensate for lack of expertise with tight central controls and ideological zeal. They were able to achieve some things rapidly, such as ridding the streets of thievery, beggary, and filth, putting an end to government corruption, and halting inflation. They pushed land reform ruthlessly, destroying the class of large landowners and giving small plots to the peasants. Even more basic, perhaps, was the Communists' attack on China's traditional family system, which diverted loyalty from the state to the clan.

Clan structure, long considered the heart of the Chinese family system, dates back to the eleventh century.[24] The clan is literally an association of families sharing a common ancestry. It is patrilineal and to a degree patriarchal. Over the centuries, the clan assumed a variety of socioreligious functions—maintenance of clan genealogies and ancestral shrines, promotion of ancestry worship, provision of clan schools which stressed filial duty and disseminated Confucian ethics. Great emphasis was placed on father-son loyalty, and marriages were arranged by the clan in order to ensure its continued stability. Thus the individual was encouraged to put the welfare of the clan before other considerations and to focus his efforts on building

its wealth and prestige. Traditional clan structure was obviously inimical to Communist ideology and to the goals of the Revolution.

The beginnings of industrialism during the nineteenth and early twentieth centuries had put considerable strains on the clan system long before the Communists came to power, but Communist pressures greatly accelerated the disruption of family patterns. Under a new marriage law enacted in 1950, children were declared free to choose their own marriage partners, and women were given equal rights with men in all things, including occupational choice and divorce. In order to increase production and to free more hands for work, the Communists also established communal work forces, communal dining halls, and communal nursing schools, which effectively separated the members of the family during much of the day. Some of these programs have met with resistance, but family patterns in China are undoubtedly changing. For the urban Chinese, at least, the family's main functions are now seen as the procreation of children and the sharing of leisure time. Thus the Communist effort to shift the focus of family life from the clan to the community is having the ultimate effect—clearly unintended—of making Chinese family patterns more congruent with those in the industrialized West.

MARX AGAINST MALTHUS

Its vast areas, the relative isolation of many villages and regions, and the lack of effective administrative organization have prevented China from ever accurately recording its population. Three censuses were taken between 1909 and 1928, but all were incomplete and inconclusive. In 1933 the League of Nations estimated the population of China at 450 million people.[25]

---

23. Much of the following discussion is taken from John S. Aird, "China: A Demographic Crisis," *Population Bulletin* of the Population Reference Bureau, Inc., 19, No. 5 (August 1963).

24. Ping-ti Ho, "An Historian's View of the Chinese Family System," in *Man and Civilization: The Family's Search for Survival*, eds. Seymour M. Farber *et al.* (New York: McGraw-Hill Book Company, 1965), pp. 15–30.

25. For elaboration see Leo A. Orleans, "The Population of Communist China," in Freedman, *Population: The Vital Revolution*, pp. 228 ff.

Soon after taking power in 1949, the Communists established the State Statistical Bureau to coordinate all government statistical work. A national census was planned to provide basic information for the first Five-Year Economic Development Plan, to be launched in 1953, and also for the registration of voters for the first national elections, to be held in that same year. For ideological reasons, the Census Bureau was not allowed to seek help from the West; it received limited help from the Soviet Union. Western scholars have critically examined the information the Chinese have given out concerning this census and have accepted the results with great reservations.[26]

The Chinese reported a population of 583 million people. The urban population was said to be only 13 percent of the total, or 77 million people, though no clear-cut criteria were set forth to define what was meant by "urban." (Since then the government has tried to control the flow of the population to urban places but has not been entirely successful. Current urban population is estimated at between 100 and 110 million—approximately the same as the United States urban total.) The Chinese also acknowledged a birth rate of 37 per 1000 population and a death rate of 17. Thus the growth rate was stated at 2 percent, or an increase between twelve and seventeen million a year. Western demographers wondered if either figure could be accepted: a birth rate closer to 45 and a death rate closer to 25 or 30 seemed more probable, though this would not appreciably change the overall growth rate.[27] In any case, the Chinese appeared to be satisfied with their census and bravely declared that the size of their population meant more hands for production.

China's new leadership firmly rejected the Malthusian argument that rapid population growth would prevent the people from ever satisfying their needs. In the Communist view, the problem was not one of numbers per se but of how the economic system was organized—specifically, of the relation between labor as a productive force and those in control of pro-duction. China's large population and rapid rate of growth had been a danger, the Communists maintained, only under the old clan-capitalist-landlord system, which wasted human labor. Under a restructured political and economic system, China's huge population would no longer be a liability. Through the rational use of human labor as a valuable resource, productivity could quickly be raised "and the living conditions of the people—even the living conditions of a population that was rapidly expanding—could be steadily improved. It was possible, now, to abolish unemployment, poverty, vagrancy, hunger, pestilence, war and untimely death."[28]

The first Five-Year Plan. In the words of one Chinese economist, the first Five-Year Plan, 1953–1958, was "trial and error" on a national scale. Top priority was given to heavy industry, particularly to steel production. The evidence suggests that some quotas were met and that industrial production in general rose, but progress was uneven. The attempts to meet quotas for certain selected industries showed little concern about the consequences for the rest. Relative demand was barely considered.

As far as agriculture was concerned, the Plan clearly failed. The early land reform program by which small farms had been given to peasants was gradually replaced by agricultural collectivization. By 1956, 96 percent of all peasant holdings had been forced into cooperatives where property and tools were held in common and labor was centrally managed. Lack of good statistics makes it virtually impossible to say whether the new system worked well or not, but peasant resentment was reported to be widespread. Poor food crops were apparently one tangible result. Another was the attempt by millions of peasants throughout the 1950's to enter the cities, with counter attempts by the government to force them back to collectivized farms in order to improve agricultural production.

Poor food crops in 1954 and again in 1956 may have played some part in encouraging the government to modify its stand on population control. At the Eighth Congress of the Chinese Communist Party in 1956, Premier Chou En-lai declared: "To protect women and children and bring up and educate our younger generation in a way conducive to the health and prosperity of the nation, we agree that a due measure of

---

26. See, for example, Aird, *op. cit.*, and Orleans, *op. cit.*

27. In 1959 the Chinese announced that the death rate had been reduced to 11 per 1000, quite comparable to the rates in the most advanced nations of the world. As far as can be ascertained, some 40 percent of China's population is now under fifteen years of age.

28. Robert C. North, "Communist China and the Population Problem," in Ng and Mudd, *op. cit.*, p. 91.

In China, as in most parts of the world, ideological beliefs and values largely determine the way population growth is viewed and what, if anything, is done about it. Prior to the 1960's the Chinese Communist leaders advocated the Marxist position that a large population is conducive to economic growth. Ideological zeal, central controls, and an emphasis on community, they believed, would help to compensate for a lack of technology. It soon became evident, however, that China's economy was not keeping pace with its population. Communal work forces (left), though consistent with Maoist doctrine, were not increasing agricultural production. Many individuals, such as the stocking-maker at right, whose output is only one stocking an hour, were unable to produce more and better goods. Today China's problems remain basically the same, but the ideology has changed somewhat to fit the demands of the times. The government has instituted family planning projects, and it is believed that China has also undertaken a massive fertility control program.

birth control is desirable."[29] However, the Chinese leaders continued to reject the Malthusian argument that unchecked population growth will outstrip economic growth regardless of economic policies, insisting that their program was designed simply to protect the health of mother and child and to provide women with adequate time for work and study.

The Great Leap Forward. In 1958, ideological fervor reached new heights, and the government launched its "Great Leap Forward." The immediate goal was to double overall production in a single year. Great Britain's production was to be matched within fifteen years. At the same time, the party reverted to its original position on birth control and announced that population growth was a creative force. Several reasons have been suggested for this change in attitude toward birth control: conflict between population control and Marxist ideology; a possible labor shortage; a lack of cheap, effective contraceptives; and the continued strength of the folk heritage among the overwhelmingly rural and uneducated population.

But the "Great Leap" turned out to be only a stumble. Despite the high priority given to agriculture by Mao Tse-tung and other leaders, and despite attempts to inflate the statistics, nothing could hide the fact that between 1958 and 1961 agricultural growth failed to keep up with, much less surpass, population growth.

One of the casualties of the "Great Leap" was the Chinese Census Bureau. The ideological fervor of 1958–1959 included denunciation of bourgeois statistics on birth and death. At the same time, the statisticians were forced to produce figures to support Mao's propaganda claims, and the result was total disruption of the Census Bureau. By the early 1960's the government still lacked trained and reliable personnel to handle vital statistics, which are generally deemed essential for effective planning in a complex society. Nevertheless, some Western scholars believe that the regime probably knows enough about its urban population, its labor force, and its educated people and skilled laborers to get by. In fact, Orleans doubts that a difference of 25 or even 50 million people above or below the figures the Chinese leaders are currently using would alter their goals and policies.[30]

Birth control: the current situation. With the passing of the "Great Leap," the government has moved slowly but steadily toward programs of family planning. Edgar Snow, reporting on his most recent visits to China, stated that there were adequate supplies of contraceptives available, even in remote clinics, although the demand was light. He found also that party members frowned upon "undisciplined procreation" and that young party leaders seemed to be opting for more study and delayed marriage. Men were not marrying until twenty-five or twenty-seven and women until twenty-one or twenty-three. In an interview with Snow in 1964, Premier Chou En-lai declared:

We do believe in planned parenthood, but it is not easy to introduce all at once in China and it is more difficult to achieve in the rural areas, where most of our people live, than in the cities. The first thing is to encourage late marriages. The years 20 to 30 are very important to mental and physical development—years when scientific and artistic growth often occur most rapidly. Among various means of deferred parenthood, sterilization is only the last, and only applies to those already burdened by too many children.[31]

In reply to a question as to whether it would be possible to reduce the population growth rate to 1 percent by 1970, Premier Chou said that experts had been sent to study the pattern followed in Japan but it was doubtful that the growth rate could be noticeably reduced by 1970. He continued with his explanation:

For example, as a result of the improved living conditions over the past two years, our rate rose again to 2.5 per cent! Therefore, China's purpose in carrying out planned parenthood is entirely positive. Planned parenthood, on the basis of increased production for consumption, is conducive to raising the living standard of the people. This is a matter of fundamental importance. That is why we have been studying it very carefully during the past two years.

THE LESSONS OF CHINA AND MEXICO

This discussion of China cannot be comparable to that of Mexico for several fairly obvious reasons. In the first place, China not only

29. As quoted by Aird, *op. cit.*, p. 125.
30. Orleans, *op. cit.*, p. 238.
31. Edgar Snow, "Population Control in China: An Interview with Chou En-lai," in Ng and Mudd, *op. cit.*, pp. 101–102.

METHODOLOGY A NOTE ON THE CENSUS

Although governments have always been interested in knowing facts about their citizens, for military, tax, and other purposes, information has been sporadically gathered and often has provided only rough estimates. The United States has the world's oldest regular census of population, the first one dating back to 1790. A major reason for this is the nature of the composition of the House of Representatives, as established by the Constitution. The number of representatives from each state is based on the population of that state relative to the population of the other states.

As our society has grown more complex, our census taking has gone far beyond mere head counts. We have censuses of manufacturing, farming, and business every five years. In addition, we have added a great array of questions to our decennial census, dealing with such matters as housing, education, occupation, income, migration, and commuting. In the 1960 census effort, some 180,000 persons were hired to handle the various phases of work. Because of the amount and variety of data that must be obtained, the Bureau of the Census uses *samples* as a basis for much of its information (see Methodological Essay, "Sampling," page 300).

By law citizens are required to answer all the questions asked of them by the census taker. This requirement holds for all societies that take regular censuses. Government officials argue that a reliable census could not be obtained otherwise, and the individual citizen as well as the society would suffer from the lack of accurate information.

Actually, in the 1970 census about 80 percent of all United States families had to answer only some twenty-two to twenty-four questions. Only a minority of families had to fill in longer forms. Thus sampling procedures have reduced the amount of work and number of families involved while still making it possible to accumulate important information. And to those who worry about the confidentiality of the census procedures, the Bureau of the Census proudly claims that there is no known case

in which a census employee violated his oath of confidentiality.

The census-taking process, like so many activities in and out of government, has been a stimulant to technological change. For example, by 1890 it had become literally impossible to handle the desired data by existing methods. Herman Hollerith of the Bureau of the Census invented a procedure by which he was able to record the data about each person on special cards by a key-punch process. Thus came into being the cards that are so much a part of our lives today, and with these cards came the counter-sorter machines, forerunners of the computers.

The decennial census provides data on some 18,000 incorporated places in the United States, some 35,000 townships, and 31,000 counties. For the big cities, data are also available on areas known as *census tracts* and even city blocks. Census tracts are geographical areas of a city, usually set off by streets or other natural boundaries, which are more or less homogeneous with regard to physiographic land use, demographic characteristics, socio-economic status, and indices of social disorganization. The population size of a census tract is relatively small, varying between one thousand and fourteen thousand persons, with the average around three thousand.

Almost every governmental agency at federal, state, and local levels uses census data to project such needs as schools and water supplies. Business and industry are also major users, for they must project their production and sales according to the expected size and needs of varying age groups. Finally, the census data provide social scientists with crucial facts about society—facts that raise many questions about education, income, marriage patterns, and earning power. For example, why should income be distributed as it is? What is happening to social mobility in the society? Why are people having only two, three, or four children? These and other questions raised by census data form the basis for much sociological research and theory-building.

This discussion of the census is based on Conrad Taeuber, "Taking an Inventory of 180 Million People," in *Population: The Vital Revolution*, ed. Ronald Freedman (Chicago: Aldine Publishing Co., 1965), pp. 84–99; and Estie Stoll, "Census or Nonsense," *The Sciences*, 9, No. 11 (November 1969), 24–29. Summaries of the statistics obtained by the Bureau of the Census include *Current Population Reports*, *Historical Statistics of the United States* (*Colonial Times to 1957*), and the *Statistical Abstract of the United States*.

lacks good statistics but closely guards whatever data it does have. Western observers can only surmise the current facts about China's population and its economic growth on the basis of information the government provides. Mexico, by contrast, has developed a good census bureau and makes its statistics readily available to outside economists and population specialists.[32]

A more fundamental difference, of course, exists between the two countries themselves. The Mexican Revolution is now more than fifty years old, and party control—though tight in some ways—is orderly and not without some semblance of democratic process. Opposition to the ruling party is open and legal, and there is a free interchange of ideas. Government programs have evolved into a mixture of state control and free enterprise, of socialist ideology and pragmatism. Mexico, moreover, is open to the influence of cultural patterns from the industrialized countries of the West, which support norms generally favorable to family planning and population control.

Despite differences, however, the case studies of Mexico and China both indicate some of the ways in which population growth relates to other facets of societal life. Political, religious, and familial beliefs and values largely determine the way population growth is viewed and greatly influence what, if anything, will be done about regulating it. Meanwhile, the growth itself, through its effect on the economy, threatens to frustrate the people's aspirations for higher living standards. Whatever else the studies of China and Mexico may show, they suggest that there is little reason to expect a significant lessening of the population crisis in the decade of the 1970's.

THE UNITED STATES

The United States may be taken as representative of the developed Western societies. It provides us with the most up-to-date statistics on population trends and their implications for industry, education, government welfare, recreation, and the like. These statistics reveal that its more than 200 million citizens live in a highly industrialized society geared to steadily increasing affluence. Birth control is practiced effectively by the majority of married couples and is supported by family, religious, and governmental norms.

IS THERE A POPULATION PROBLEM?

During the 1950's and 1960's the United States experienced a moderate overall growth rate of about 1.65 percent per year, very similar to that of the Soviet Union. As the decade of the 1970's began, the birth rate had reached a low of about 17 per 1000 population and the growth rate appeared to be stabilizing at around 1 percent a year. Thus the pattern in the United States is now close to that in Western Europe.

This leveling off of the growth rate does not tell the whole story, however, for we are now moving into an era when the number of women of childbearing age will be increasing rapidly. Table 8.1 shows that the number of women in the most fertile years, ages 20–29, will double between 1960 and 1990, after holding steady for the preceding thirty years. This projection is not based on mere speculation; the figure for 1990

TABLE 8.1. **NUMBER OF WOMEN OF CHILD-BEARING AGE IN THE UNITED STATES, 1930–1990**

YEAR	NUMBER OF WOMEN AGE 20–29 (millions)	NUMBER OF WOMEN AGE 15–44 (millions)
1930	11	29
1940	12	32
1950	12	34
1960	11	36
1970	15	43
1980	20	54
1990	22	70

SOURCE: Donald J. Bogue, "Population Growth in the United States," in *The Population Dilemma*, ed. Philip M. Hauser (Englewood Cliffs, N.J.: Prentice-Hall, Inc., 1963), p. 76.

32. As a matter of fact, a main characteristic distinguishing between modern and archaic census enumerations is accessibility. The modern census dates from the second half of the eighteenth century. Prior to that time, information on the number and characteristics of population was kept secret since it indicated strengths or weaknesses of interest to possible military foes.

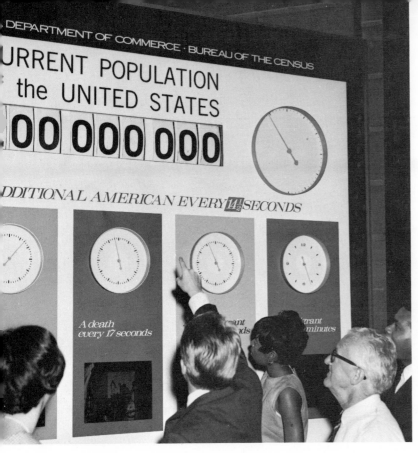

The Census Clock in the lobby of the Department of Commerce building in Washington registered the 200 millionth American at about 11 a.m. on November 20, 1967. Since that time we have increased the total by more than 5 million, and our population will probably reach 300 million before the year 2000.

represents women who have already been born. Thus, without a further drop in the fertility rate, the number of births per year in the United States will increase significantly over the next few decades.

Between 1960 and 1970, the United States population increased from 180 million to more than 205 million. It will probably reach 300 million before the year 2000. Does such growth constitute a problem? Many think that it does.[33] At the very least it seems to threaten the quality of American life, especially in the large urban areas where most of the growth is taking place. Let us consider the question in the light of just three crucial areas of social life: education, jobs, and black-white relations.

Education. The "baby boom" that followed World War II has by now placed great strains on all levels of our educational system, and its full consequences are yet to be felt. High-school enrollment, for example, increased by 50 percent between 1960 and 1970, from ten to fifteen

million students, and it will continue to rise throughout the seventies. This rapid expansion of the educational system has necessitated constant increases in taxes and school bond issues—occasioning, in a few communities, taxpayer revolts that have actually forced the closing of schools for a time. But shutting down schools does not seem like a viable alternative to footing the bill, given the values, beliefs, and norms of American society and the fact that people without at least a high-school education have little occupational future.

The challenge, of course, is not only to provide enough schools but also to reach the students and to make their education meaningful. About 70 percent of young people of high-school age were completing twelfth grade by the end of the 1960's, compared to less than 50 percent in 1930 and only 10 percent in 1900. Nevertheless, it is estimated that some seven million boys and girls did not finish high school during the 1960's. Thus, even though the percentage of dropouts is decreasing, their numbers are large, creating serious problems for society. These young people may be effectively blocked off from the better jobs, not necessarily because

33. See, for example, Lincoln and Alice Day, *Too Many Americans?* (Boston: Houghton Mifflin Company, 1964).

BIRTHS PER
1000 WOMEN

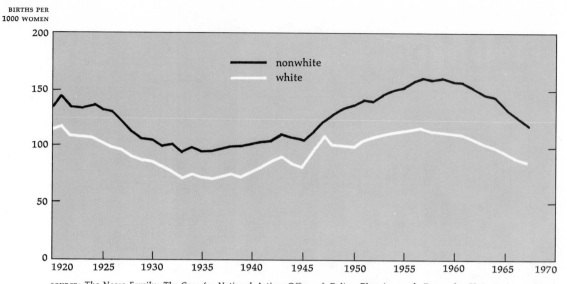

SOURCE: *The Negro Family: The Case for National Action*, Office of Policy Planning and Research, U.S. Department of Labor, March 1965, p. 26; *Statistical Abstract of the United States, 1969*, Table 57, p. 48.

FIGURE 8.4.   **FERTILITY RATES FOR WHITE AND NONWHITE WOMEN IN THE U.S., 1920–1967**

they are unable to handle the work but because, as dropouts, they are unlikely to be hired. What will be the long-range effects on their role behavior in family and community?

Population growth and rising educational aspirations have also put great pressure on the college-university system, which must expand its facilities, create new teaching ranks, and experiment with new teaching methods in order to meet the changing needs of a student population larger than any in human history. College enrollment should reach eight million during the 1970's.

Jobs. The expansion of the teaching profession and the disappearance of unskilled jobs are only two of many changes in the labor picture. During the 1960's the labor force was increasing by about 1.3 million persons per year. In contrast to the developing countries, however, the United States had sufficient capital available for new investment to absorb most of the new workers, and their earning power has been a further spur to the economy.

The composition of the labor force is changing no less rapidly than its size. Some 45 percent of women between the ages of twenty and twenty-four are now in the labor force, as

are 30 percent of those in their teens. Yet women are still largely an untapped labor market resource in American society. As the number of highly educated women grows and as the activities related to motherhood are increasingly restricted to the years between twenty and thirty-five, more and more women are likely to be seeking jobs demanding superior skills.

Blacks and whites. Demographic questions related to education and jobs in the United States are complicated by the distinctive patterns that prevail among different segments of the population, especially among blacks and whites. In 1960 there were 20.7 million nonwhites (mostly blacks) in the United States, making up 11.4 percent of the total population. The Bureau of the Census estimates that the black population will double to 41.5 million by 1990 and make up some 14.5 percent of the total.[34] This

---

34. This percentage will still be smaller than at some earlier points in the country's history. In 1790, the year of the first recorded census, blacks made up nearly 20 percent of the total population; in 1850, they made up 15.7 percent of the total. See Philip M. Hauser, "Chaotic Society: Product of the Social Morphological Revolution," *American Sociological Review*, 34, No. 1 (February 1969), 1–19.

growth is made more significant by the fact that blacks are now heavily concentrated in the large cities. During the past fifty years the black population has changed from 73 percent rural to 73 percent urban. Thus the black American is now even more urban than the white American, though he does not enjoy the fruits of urbanization to nearly the same degree. (See Chapter 9, "The Urban Transition.")

Nonwhite fertility has run steadily ahead of white for the past fifty years in the United States, and there is no indication that the gap is closing (Figure 8.4). Apparently one key variable is education. Among both whites and nonwhites, women who marry young to husbands who have not completed high school have significantly larger families than women who marry later and whose husbands have had one or more years of college (Table 8.2). Since years of schooling is closely correlated to earning potential, it is scarcely surprising to find an inverse relationship between family income and family size (Table 8.3). Again, the relationship generally holds among whites as well as among nonwhites, but in the United States the problem of too little education and too little income is overwhelmingly a black one.[35] Racial discrimination tells much of the story, but its effects seem to have been compounded by patterns of early marriage and high fertility. In his widely discussed report on the Negro family, the urban affairs expert Daniel P. Moynihan has summed up the situation thus:

A cycle is at work; too many children too early make it most difficult for the parents to finish school. . . . Low education levels in turn produce low income levels, which deprive children of many opportunities, and so the cycle repeats itself.[36]

In terms of education, labor force trends, and the special problems of black Americans, then, there is indeed a "people problem" in the United States. Population growth has not threatened our food supply or glutted our labor market, as it has in the developing countries, but it is closely intertwined with our problems of race relations, air and water pollution, traffic congestion, rising taxes, and urban decay. Because it is as much a problem of values as it is a demographic-economic problem, government programs to encourage family planning can be only a partial solution at best.

TABLE 8.2. **NUMBER OF CHILDREN EVER BORN TO WOMEN AGE 35–44, RELATED TO AGE AT MARRIAGE AND EDUCATIONAL-OCCUPATIONAL LEVEL OF HUSBAND, WHITE AND NONWHITE, 1960**

	CHILDREN PER WOMAN	
	WHITE	NONWHITE
Wives married at 14–21 to husbands who are laborers and did not go to high school	3.8	4.7
Wives married at 22 or over to husbands who are professional or technical workers and have completed 1 year of college or more	2.4	1.9

SOURCE: 1960 Census, *Women by Number of Children Ever Born,* PC (2) 3A, Table 39 and 40, pp. 199–238. Data are for wives married only once, still living with their husbands.

TABLE 8.3. **FAMILY INCOME AND FAMILY SIZE, NONWHITE, 1960**

FAMILY INCOME (1959)	NUMBER OF CHILDREN PER MOTHER AGE 35–39 (1960)
Under $2,000	5.3
$2,000 to $3,999	4.3
$4,000 to $4,999	4.0
$5,000 to $5,999	3.8
$6,000 to $6,999	3.5
$7,000 to $9,999	3.2
$10,000 to $14,999	2.9
$15,000 and over	2.9

SOURCE: 1960 Census, *Women by Number of Children Ever Born,* PC (2) 3A, Table 38, p. 188.

---

35. The Bureau of the Census has reported that "in 1966, after six consecutive years of economic expansion, 41 percent of the nonwhite population was poor, as compared with 12 percent of the whites"; *Current Population Reports,* "The Extent of Poverty in the United States: 1959–1966," Series P. 20, No. 54 (Washington, D.C.: U.S. Government Printing Office, 1968). The Bureau's statistics for 1968 show that the average level of schooling achieved by blacks twenty-five years old and over was 9.3 years, compared to 12.1 years for whites in the same age category; *Statistical Abstract of the United States* (Washington, D.C.: U.S. Government Printing Office, 1969), p. 106.

36. U.S. Department of Labor, *The Negro Family: The Case for National Action* (Washington, D.C.: U.S. Government Printing Office, 1965), p. 27.

VIEWPOINTS POPULATION GROWTH IN THE UNITED STATES

We are living today in a country of more than 200 million people; 70 percent of the population is urban; population density along our east and west coasts is increasing even faster than the population of India, and in spite of our affluence and ingenuity, we are beginning to have trouble in buying clean air, pure water, or simply a piece of unoccupied space.

The real threat facing us is not creeping socialism or creeping capitalism, but rather creeping populationism. The growth of our population, generation by generation, year by year, is putting pressure on many of the resources we value; not only our lands and waters, our forests and plains, but also our schools and hospitals, our roads and cities, our recreation and, ultimately, of course, our whole standard of living. . . .

During a normal lifetime the average American will devour 28,000 pounds of milk and cream, 10,000 pounds of meat, and 26 million gallons of water; he will require 21 million gallons of gasoline and $8,000 worth of school construction. He will purchase $6,000 worth of clothes and $7,000 worth of furniture. And to supply these demands, America will produce nearly 50 percent of the world's industrial pollution. In this vast consumptive process, Americans pay the garbage collectors nearly $3 billion every year just to collect the debris.

These numbers translate into the gradually deteriorating pictures of everyday life—dirty air, dying waters, slum-ridden cities, crowded parks, bumper-to-bumper traffic, a greater and greater struggle for less and less space—and with every half century, the appalling expectation that our population will double and redouble and double again. Until we see that an end is in sight, until we recognize that population and pollution are one and the same, . . . we will not find a lasting solution. We are in effect chasing our own tails in an endless and seemingly insane cycle of production, reproduction, construction and destruction. . . .

The time has come to look—without blinking or averting our eyes—at where we stand today in the population crisis. What was appropriate for Adam and Eve in biblical times or for our own forebears who crossed and populated a continent is no longer appropriate in a world of more than three billion people where two-thirds of all children are poor, hungry, or dirty, and without much hope of improvement.

Senator Bob Packwood
Speech in the Senate of the United States

Crowded, crowded, crowded, we are told. Slums are crowded, suburbs are crowded, megalopolis is crowded and more and more people are eating up, burning up and using up the beauty and wealth of America—turning the land into a polluted, depleted sprawl of scummy water and flickering neon, an ecological catastrophe stretching from the Everglades to the Pacific Northwest. Crisis. Crisis. Crisis. . . .

To be sure, much of the concern about population growth is sane, valid, and important. . . . While America could support twice its current population and probably four times its current population—growth can obviously not go on forever and it is wise to understand this fact now rather than a hundred years from now. It is also wise to begin to act upon this knowledge . . . . Our problems in the future probably will be easier to handle with somewhat fewer people than with somewhat greater numbers.

But what is wrong, and dangerous, and foolhardy is to make population a crisis. Doing so will simply allow too many politicians to take their eyes off the ball. When Explosionists say, as they do, that crime, riots, and urban problems are caused by "the population explosion," it is just too easy for politicians to agree and say sure, let's stop having so many babies, instead of saying let's get to work on the real urban problems of this nation. . . .

When the Explosionists say, as they do, that it's because we have so many people that Lake Erie is polluted then once again we are invited to take our eye off the tens-of-*billions*-of-dollars ball of environmental safety and we are simultaneously invited to piddle around with 25-*million* dollar programs for birth control, which are nice, but don't solve anything to do with Lake Erie. . . .

Lake Erie, the Hudson River, the Potomac are ecological slums today. If the US population did not grow by one person over the current 205 million Americans, these bodies of waters would *still* be ecological slums. These waters, and any others now threatened, will be decent places only if men are willing to devote resources to the job. That is not a function of population growth, but of national will. It can be done if we, as a nation, decide that we want it done and are willing to pay for it. It is as simple as that and it has relatively little to do with whether the national decision involves 250 or 300 or 350 million Americans.

Ben Wattenberg
"The Nonsense Explosion"

CHANGING POLICIES AND ATTITUDES TOWARD BIRTH CONTROL

Until the 1960's the United States government avoided taking a direct stand on the issue of population growth. Its major activities in this area were in developing a sophisticated census and in supporting research into reproductive physiology. However, beginning with the Kennedy administration, the government has taken an increasingly strong stand in favor of family planning, based on its growing awareness of the seriousness of the population problem, both at home and abroad.

A great amount of evidence has been amassed in support of government-financed programs, much of it dealing with attitudes toward family planning. One important finding has been that the poor would like to have many fewer children than they do. Reporting on a study of low-income families in Chicago, Donald Bogue said in 1965:

The most important finding was that despite their actual high fertility, these groups said they wanted smaller families than do more well-to-do people. . . . The incidence of unwanted and accidental pregnancy is very high among these low-income and low-education groups; nevertheless, they endorse the idea of family planning more strongly than does the general population.[37]

Other studies in the early 1960's showed that some five million American women in the fertile age group—from fifteen to forty-four—were too poor to afford medical services and that many of them were generally ignorant of birth control. Through the activity of the Planned Parenthood Association and state-supported welfare departments, perhaps 500,000 of these women—about 10 percent—were receiving some family-planning assistance.

National opinion polls taken several times during the 1960's revealed that an increasing majority of Americans (57 percent of Catholics, 64 percent of Protestants, and 89 percent of Jews in 1967) approved of federal aid for family-planning clinics.[38] With the support of this growing public consensus, the federal government has begun to move ahead rapidly with birth-control programs not only at home but abroad, where technical training has been provided to medical personnel. Spending for foreign and domestic programs increased from a mere $2.3 million in the fiscal year 1965 to $14.7 million in 1966 and $25.3 million in 1967. During the presidential election campaign of 1968, the platforms of both the Democratic and Republican parties for the first time contained statements supporting population control programs. In the same year Congress again increased appropriations for population control, projecting the allocation of $143 million for domestic and international programs by 1970.

It seems likely that the federal government is going to be more and more involved in the issue of population control. Figured at an average cost of $25.00 per year per woman, family-planning services for the poor in the United States will cost somewhat in excess of $100 million annually when the program reaches full operation; and future involvement at the international level can be expected to be much more costly. By the end of the sixties, however, total expenditures for population control still formed an insignificant part of the federal budget (Table 8.4).

---

37. Testimony by Donald Bogue taken at subcommittee hearings on Senate Bill S1676 and found in Hearings Report Part 2A, p. 1005, 1965. See also Harold L. Sheppard, "Effects of Family Planning on Poverty in the United States," a staff paper by the W. E. Upjohn Institute, Kalamazoo, Mich. (Oct. 1967).

38. "The Emerging Consensus," *Population Bulletin* of the Population Reference Bureau, Inc., 21, No. 3 (August 1965); "Planned Parenthood-World Population: Memorandum #4.21," OEO (August 15, 1968); and "Roman Catholic Fertility and Family Planning: A Comparative Review of the Research Literature," *The Population Council*, No. 34 (October 1968), 20–21.

TABLE 8.4. **COST OF SELECTED GOVERNMENT PROGRAMS**

(1969 Estimates for 1970 Budget)

Space Program	$3.2 billion
Grants to States for Welfare	$3 billion
Health and Death Control Programs	$2.5 billion
Food for Peace Exports	$1 billion
Crime Control	$868 million
Oceanography	$472 million
Supersonic Plane (pilot model)	$126 million
Air Pollution Control	$80 million
Population Control (domestic)	$65 million
Population Control (foreign)	$51 million

SOURCE: Based on figures in Emerson Foote, *Must We Have Population Control by Starvation, Disease and Death?*, pamphlet published by Campaign to Check the Population Explosion, 60 E. 42nd Street, New York.

Many demographers have pointed out that the government's efforts to limit population growth in the United States are somewhat offset by the fact that it continues to reward people for having children. Kingsley Davis has proposed that in order to effectively limit population growth governments might

cease taxing single persons more than married ones; stop giving parents special tax exemptions; abandon income-tax policy that discriminates against couples when the wife works; reduce paid maternity leaves; reduce family allowances; stop awarding public housing on the basis of family; stop granting fellowships and other educational aids (including special allowances for wives and children) to married students; cease outlawing abortions and sterilizations; and relax rules that allow use of harmless contraceptives only with medical permission.[39]

Even assuming that such policies could win public acceptance, it is difficult to predict what their effects might be in the United States or elsewhere. National fertility patterns, as we have seen, are shaped by a host of different variables, and in the final analysis it is the behavior of millions of individual couples that determines how rapidly a population will grow. As Dr. Davis notes:

Logically, it does not make sense to use *family* planning to provide *national* population control or planning. The "planning" in family planning is that of each separate couple. The only control they exercise is control over the size of *their* family. Obviously, couples do not plan the size of the nation's population, any more than they plan the growth of the national income or the form of the highway network.[40]

Among American couples, there has clearly been a growing sentiment in favor of family limitation and family planning. A series of surveys carried out in 1955, 1960, and 1965 showed a steady increase in the use of contraceptives by married women in the United States, especially among nonwhites, Catholics, and younger women.[41] These studies also revealed that the Pill, introduced in 1960, changed patterns of fertility regulation significantly. By 1965 it was being used by 33 percent of white women and by 29 percent of nonwhite women. Catholics had adopted it almost as frequently as Protestants.

Even more significant than the develop-

ment of new contraceptives, however, has been the development of attitudes strongly favorable to family planning among the American people as a whole. According to a Gallup Poll taken in 1968, shortly after the appearance of Pope Paul's encyclical reaffirming the Church's opposition to the use of contraceptives, 65 percent of American Catholics believed it was possible to practice contraception and still remain "a good Catholic."[42] Apparently the widespread acceptance of the Pill in the United States during the 1960's was closely related to the fact that a growing percentage of American couples, regardless of religious affiliation, had become motivated to plan the number and spacing of their children.

ATTITUDES TOWARD FERTILITY— THE CRUCIAL VARIABLES

We may expect that a significant lowering of birth rates in the developing countries will ultimately depend, as it has in the United States and other industrialized societies, on changes in patterns of value and belief. In this final section we will examine attitudes toward fertility and family planning in Latin America and in the Muslim countries of Asia.

LATIN AMERICA

Nowhere is the question of population control more complicated than in Latin America, for here is a portion of the world which until fairly recently was considered to be underpopulated. Many Latin American leaders complained that the slow economic growth of their countries was due to a lack of people, and several countries (notably Brazil, Chile, and Argen-

---

39. Kingsley Davis, "Population Policy: Will Current Programs Succeed?", *Science* (November 10, 1967), p. 738.
40. *Ibid.*, p. 732.
41. Charles F. Westoff and Norman B. Ryder, "Methods of Fertility Control in the United States: 1955, 1960 and 1965," in *Family and Fertility*, ed. William T. Liu (Notre Dame, Ind.: University of Notre Dame Press, 1967).
42. As reported in an Associated Press article by George Cornell, *The New York Times* (September 27, 1968).

tina) tried to encourage immigration. But, as we have seen, it becomes daily more difficult to maintain the thesis that social and economic development in Latin America is being hampered by lack of people. In fact, the opposite thesis seems more plausible.

The beginnings of Latin America's population explosion can be traced back to 1920 (Table 8.5). Its growth rate was not affected by either World War, nor was it greatly affected by the depression of the 1930's. At the present time the population of Latin America is increasing by about nine million people per year.

The forces of traditionalism. Although established patterns of value and belief are now being challenged from many sides, the impact of tradition remains strong in Latin America. Thus it is unlikely that fertility rates will drop very significantly in the near future.

Well over 90 percent of Latin Americans are at least nominally Catholic—that is, have been baptized in the Catholic Church. Whatever else their Catholicism means depends on the criteria used. Formal liturgical worship is most likely to be found in the cities and to be practiced by the middle and upper classes, which make up only a small segment of the total population. Probably no more than a fourth of Latin American Catholics attend church more than once a month. Among the poorer classes, particularly among the Indians, there is a folk Catholicism that is only loosely related to the formal structure of the Catholic Church. The great majority of the poor see a priest or other functionary once a year at most. Nevertheless, these people identify themselves as Catholics and adhere to many of the traditional teachings of the Catholic Church, including the belief that children are a gift of God and therefore to be welcomed without question.

Church teachings about the blessings of a large family have found reflection and support in familism—the configuration of values and behavior patterns associated with family life in Latin America. Traditionally in Latin America, the good family has been the large family. The ideal for the male has been that he should be *macho*—brave, virile, and able to produce children. Premarital sexual activity has been expected of males, and in some parts of Latin America extramarital sex has also been normative. The Latin American woman, for her part, has found her identity in motherhood. If she has not always been well loved as a wife, as

TABLE 8.5. **POPULATION GROWTH IN LATIN AMERICA SINCE 1900**

YEAR	MILLIONS OF PEOPLE (*estimates*)
1900	43
1920	89
1940	125
1960	202
1970	250

SOURCE: T. Lynn Smith, "The Population of Latin America," in *Population: The Vital Revolution*, ed. R. Freedman (New York: Doubleday & Company, Inc., 1964).

a mother she has been worshiped. Large families, then, have traditionally been a means of fulfillment for both men and women.

In most Latin American countries, government itself has been a force of traditionalism, at least until recently. Political regimes have typically allied themselves with the Church hierarchy in efforts to maintain the status quo; in several countries such alliances still exist, making government action in the area of fertility control extremely unlikely. In any case, most Latin American leaders either have not been interested in population questions or else have believed that their countries were underpopulated.

Social ferment. Today the traditional patterns of Church, family, and government in Latin America are all in a state of ferment. The situation is not everywhere the same, however, and it is by no means clear what new patterns will eventually emerge. Certainly there is no basis for the easy generalization that change will be in the direction of the dominant Western pattern as exemplified by Europe or the United States. Nor is it clear that this pattern is necessarily the desirable one for Latin America.

Traditional family patterns in Latin America have been greatly disrupted by the phenomenon of rural-urban migration, the flood of humanity pouring into the older cities and making new cities out of small towns. Extended kinship ties are subject to increasing strain in this new kind of urban life. Lack of housing and lack of jobs force people to keep on the move. Beyond this is the fact that industrialization requires new work patterns and challenges many of the values and attitudes that have long undergirded fami-

Traditionally in Latin America, the good family has been the large family. The woman, for her part, has found her identity in motherhood. If she has not always been well loved as a wife, as a mother she has been worshiped.

lism. The traditional role of women is being questioned increasingly by both sexes.

In many parts of Latin America, the ferment for change within the Catholic Church acts as a further stimulus in altering traditional family patterns. In the 1965 Schema on the Church in the Modern World, Church leaders formally recognized the right of husband and wife to decide how many children they would have and when they would have them. Furthermore, the statements on conjugal love as a fundamental good of married life placed Catholic teaching very much in line with that of other Western religious groups. Now that women are formally recognized as equal partners in the marriage enterprise, it can be expected that their status will rise.

Government leaders, too, have started to take a fresh look at the status quo. Most Latin American governments have now instituted formal demographic studies that will give them more precise information about the nature of their own populations, and some have even

given support to the establishment of family-planning programs. The outstanding example is that of Chile.

Under the leadership of President Eduardo Frei, himself a practicing Catholic, the Christian Democratic party has allowed the use of national health facilities in Chile for experimental family-planning programs. This move reflects a grave concern over rising rates of illegal abortion. A series of studies on induced abortion carried out by Chilean physicians during the 1950's and 1960's showed that 25 to 30 percent of the women questioned had had at least one induced abortion; that some middle-class women were resorting to sterilization to prevent further conceptions; and that in some cases churchgoing Catholic women had higher rates of induced abortion than did Protestant Evangelicals.[43] These findings, together with the re-

---

43. Herman Romero, "Chile," in Berelson *et al.*, *Family Planning and Population Programs*, pp. 235–247.

sults of attitude studies showing that a majority of women (around 75 percent) and their partners felt that birth control should be made universal and that the Church had no right to interfere in such matters, led the government to institute an aggressive anti-abortion campaign. By 1965 it was estimated that some 100,000 women were using some form of contraceptive device, with an interuterine device (IUD) preferred about ten to one over other methods. "Doctors assert almost unanimously that objections, principally religious or moral, are exceptional."[44]

Elsewhere in Latin America, studies show that increasing percentages of adults want small families but that they are generally ignorant about fertility control or hesitant to use birth-control methods other than rhythm until Catholic Church leaders give their permission.[45] In Brazil, a family-planning agency is now struggling to convince both the people and the government of the need for family planning. As in Chile, the major focus is against induced abortion. But as of this printing, Brazilian law forbids the sale or use of contraceptives except for medical reasons. It seems likely that the law is being stretched, for in 1968 there was a reported sale of some sixty million birth-control pills in Brazil. Still, political opposition to family planning remains strong, with political leaders making statements like these: "Birth control may be useful to the United States but not to Brazil, which is not sufficiently populated"; "It is absurd to think of birth control by the government in a country as big as ours. What we need is better living conditions." In Colombia, on the other hand, the government has embarked on a national birth-control and family-planning program despite strong opposition from the Church. National polls show strong popular support.

Commenting on the current situation in Latin America as a whole, Stycos notes that many of Latin America's intellectuals still see programs of fertility control as directly linked to such dangers as socialism, depopulation, and

decatholization and as a threat to the fertility mystique that has given meaning to Latin American family life. He concludes that outside efforts to encourage birth-control programs may in fact have had the effect of stiffening resistance to change:

Beneath what appears to be an illogical argument about population density and an irrational fear of international genocide lie the deeper and perhaps more justified sentiments of national pride and resentment over a melancholy history of relations with powerful nations. It will not be easy to treat the symptoms of this malaise while leaving its roots untouched.[46]

THE MUSLIM COUNTRIES

Generally the birth rate among Muslims has been higher than that of any other major religious group—in excess of 40 per 1000 and ranging as high as 62 per 1000 in Pakistan.[47] There appear to be several factors in the religion of Islam and its related family life that are conducive to high fertility.[48] For the most part, Muslims still live in folk-peasant conditions, with high mortality. Sons are considered necessary to continue the family line, to guarantee land ownership and an adequate labor supply, to give support in old age, and to offer prayers after death.

For the Muslims as for no other major religious group, religion and family life are completely intertwined. The Koran (the holy book of the Muslims) allows men to have more than one wife, supports patrilineal, patrilocal, and male dominance patterns, and gives sexual pleasure a positive emphasis unknown in Christian teachings. Custom encourages early marriage: in ten Muslim countries for which data are available, 70 to 86 percent of all females aged fifteen to forty-four are married, and less than 3 percent of Muslim women remain unmarried at forty-five. Almost all widows and divorcees remarry. In most Muslim countries in the mid-1960's less than 10 percent of the women had any formal education.

There has continued to be strong anti-Western, anti-Christian, and anti-Jewish feeling among the Muslims. This has made them hostile to Western ways, Western medicine, Western urban patterns, and to birth control as a Western means to diminish their numbers. To date,

44. *Ibid.*, p. 243.
45. See *Demography*, 5, No. 2 (1968), esp. 785–893.
46. J. M. Stycos, "Opposition to Family Planning in Latin America: Conservative Nationalism," in *ibid.*, p. 854.
47. Peterson, *Population*, pp. 591–602.
48. The following discussion of the Muslim countries is based on Dudley Kirk, "Factors Affecting Moslem Natality," in Berelson *et al.*, *Family Planning and Population Programs*, pp. 561–579.

Faced with a population explosion which threatens to wipe out economic gains, many governments have given high priority to massive family planning programs. Throughout India this familiar sign (*above*) urges family planning with the slogan "two's enough." The poster at left advertises IUD's; it appears in front of a store selling contraceptives in East Pakistan.

malnutrition, disease, and high infant mortality have all tended to keep the population growth rate in Muslim countries below that in most other parts of the developing world. Thus the effect of modern health measures, as they are accepted, may be to increase an already high rate of growth.

In none of the Muslim countries from which data were gathered in the mid-1960's did a majority of the people know any modern method of birth control. Such knowledge was limited to educated urbanites. Most couples said they wanted only three children, especially if one or two of the children already born were male. But actual family size was considerably larger. In Turkey, for example, women past childbearing age (over forty-five) reported an average of 6.3 pregnancies during their child-bearing years, 5.8 live births, and 4.1 living children. Very little evidence of fertility control

was found except in the cities. In Beirut, however, 60 percent of the uneducated and 83 percent of the educated women reported some attempt to limit the size of their families.

The governments of Turkey, Tunisia, the United Arab Republic, and Pakistan have recently decided to initiate family-planning programs, but national levels of fertility will not begin to be affected until the mid-1970's. While the programs will have to contend with the traditional patterns, values, and beliefs outlined above, there is nothing in Muslim religion specifically opposed to birth control, and the evidence from Turkey indicates that a majority of couples favor the government policy. It may well be that during the 1970's not religion as such but rather education (especially education related to knowledge of changing conditions) will differentiate the high fertility countries from the low.

SUMMARY

The population of the world is increasing at a rate unprecedented in history, with the overwhelming preponderance of growth occurring in the underdeveloped and developing nations. This growth is largely the result of the precipitous drop in death rates in these areas. And herein lies one of the important differences between the "two worlds." It took more than a century and a half for the death rates to drop to their current low levels in the industrialized areas of the world. In the developing areas the drop has occurred in less than thirty years. One of the most significant immediate consequences of these demographic changes has been a radical alteration in the age structure of many societies, leading to a fantastic increase in the percentage of population under twenty years of age.

The population explosion is occurring both in rural and in urban areas and is partly a cause and partly a consequence of urbanization. The overall pattern of change has directly challenged age-old beliefs and values about family life and family size. At the same time, the recent development of effective and easily applied methods of contraception has brought the countries of the developing world within reach of fertility control, which, if accomplished, can restore the balance between birth and death rates and perhaps make it possible for the first time for the great majority of mankind to share a life of material well-being.

The evidence shows that governments, which have been largely responsible for the rapid reduction of mortality rates in the developing countries, have now begun to take an active role in reducing birth rates. As Professor Ryder notes, "It seems that the future fertility of modern nations will depend primarily on the relative success with which their respective governments can bring individual decisions about childbearing into correspondence with demographic requirements of the society."[49] Thus there is a new awareness of the mutual dependence of society s most basic social unit, the family, and its largest and in some ways most pervasive unit, the government.

49. Norman B. Ryder, "The Character of Modern Fertility," *Annals of the American Academy of Political and Social Science*, 369 (January 1967), 36.

9

The Urban Transition

The establishment of permanent settlements began with the domestication of plants and animals at least six thousand years ago, but the urbanization of man is essentially a phenomenon of the past two centuries. It is reputed that Rome in its heyday may have had more than 300,000 inhabitants, but by the fourth century its population had declined to some 15,000 people. At no time before the nineteenth century did the proportion of city dwellers ever reach more than 5 percent of the total population of the earth. Technical know-how in such areas as agriculture, commerce, sanitation, transportation, and industry was so limited that cities as we know them today simply could not develop.

Although the growth of cities has been closely associated with the idea of "progress," even the most casual observer is aware that city growth and urbanization have caused numerous problems. Indeed, feelings of anti-urbanism have been one concomitant of urbanization.[1] Balzac painted Paris in the first half of the nineteenth century as a city of feverish activity whose inhabitants, driven by the desire for money and pleasure, ignored the fact that the city was destroying the beauty and wisdom of man, making him a mere cog in a huge machine. And for those readers who may think that air pollution is a modern phenomenon of the city, Balzac complained that "half of Paris sleeps amidst the putrid exhalations of courts and streets and sewers."[2] However, Thomas de Quincey described his first visit to London in 1800 as a heavenly occurrence and likened it to the wonders of nature—a "mighty wilderness," "some vast magnetic range of Alps," "A Norwegian maelstrom," "the roar of Niagara."[3]

Benjamin Franklin was very much an urbanite, and he saw the culture of the city with its library, university, and other amenities as the key to the Enlightenment. Thomas Jefferson, by contrast, saw agrarianism as the continuing hope for the future. In 1787 he wrote to James Madison: "I think our governments will remain virtuous for many centuries as long as they are chiefly agricultural; and this will be as long as there shall be vacant lands in any part of America."[4]

One of the most outspoken recent critics of urbanism was the brilliant and controversial architect Frank Lloyd Wright. Of "sidewalk happy" urban man Wright said: "if he is properly citified, the citizen has long lost sight of the true aim of normal human existence. He has accepted not only substitute means but substitute aims and ends...."[5] In *The Living City*, Wright set down his vision for building the urban center of the future:

Infinite possibilities exist to make of the city a place suitable for the free man in which freedom can thrive and the soul of man can grow, a city of cities that democracy could approve and so desperately needs.... [The individual] at home ... will be organically related to landscape, to transport and distribution of goods, to educational entertainment and all cultural opportunity.[6]

Yet this city of the future would be far different from the city as we know it today, for Wright wanted to spread the families out over the countryside and to provide an acre of land for each, in effect making the city coterminous with the nation. The trend over the past two hundred years has been very much in the opposite direction: populations have become increasingly concentrated in cities and the areas immediately surrounding them. This trend has been most pronounced in the industrialized societies of the Western world, where urbanization is already virtually complete. The developing societies of Asia, Africa, and Latin America seem now to have begun moving in the same direction.

In this chapter we will examine some of the factors that have propelled the growth of urban areas as well as the social and cultural changes that have accompanied such growth. We will attempt to understand how urban life differs from rural life and to assess the kinds of social organization that are both cause and consequence of urban life as we know it today.

1. For a critical review of anti-urban attitudes, see Morton and Lucia White, *The Intellectual Versus the City* (Cambridge, Mass.: Harvard University Press and M.I.T. Press, 1962).

2. Honoré de Balzac, "The Anatomy of Paris," in *Sociology Through Literature*, ed. Lewis Coser (Englewood Cliffs, N.J.: Prentice-Hall, Inc., 1963), p. 247.

3. Thomas de Quincey, "The Powers and Rhythms of London," in *ibid.*, pp. 233–236.

4. Quoted in Charles N. Glaab, *The American City: A Documentary History* (Homewood, Ill.: The Dorsey Press, 1963), p. 6.

5. Frank Lloyd Wright, *The Living City* (New York: Horizon Press, 1959), p. 21.

6. *Ibid.*, pp. 29, 82.

THE CITY IN HISTORICAL PERSPECTIVE

The city as a distinct pattern of group living has been in existence for at least six thousand years. As soon as people began joining together in permanent agricultural settlements, they developed new forms of social organization that made them a community rather than a mere aggregate of family units. For whatever reasons, they evolved new patterns of life that increasingly differentiated them from people living in rural areas.[7]

THE PREINDUSTRIAL CITY

Urban life is ultimately dependent on the existence of food surpluses. Thus it is not surprising that the earliest cities emerged in environments where the soil was especially fertile and where there was sufficient water available to sustain both farm and city. The emergence of the preindustrial city also depended on the existence of relatively large rural populations on which the city could draw. Historically, disease and famine have kept death rates higher in urban areas than elsewhere, so that cities have been barely able to maintain their size without a constant influx of people from outside.

The first known cities emerged in the fertile valleys of the Tigris and Euphrates rivers, regions where agriculture was well developed and where there was much contact between peoples of diverse cultures. It may be surmised that these contacts themselves helped stimulate permanent settlement. Evidence of other very early cities has been found in the Nile River Valley, the Indus Valley of present-day Pakistan, the Yellow River Valley of China, and in several parts of Mesoamerica. In all of these areas, the ability to produce larger and larger surpluses of food gave people increasing freedom to pursue non-agricultural activities and led to a gradual specialization of arts and crafts. Archeological finds in the valleys of the Tigris and Euphrates show that even the earliest cities supported skilled artisans. They also supported a literate elite.

As preindustrial cities evolved, they developed characteristic organizational forms. (1) Political control was usually theocratic—the king and the high priest were one. (2) The center of the city was the area of highest prestige, and the elite lived there. The poorest people lived on the fringes of the city and had the least protection from attack by enemies. (3) Artisans established themselves in special quarters or streets, further sharpening differences in social ranking.

In many ways the organizational structure of the preindustrial city worked to maintain a rigid system of social stratification. Wealthy families controlled the government and religious activities and set the norms for work. The fact that they lived close together in the center of the city made it easy for them to communicate among themselves and helped maintain their distinctive patterns of life. Religious orthodoxy stressed the moral rightness of the established social order. Formal education was exclusively limited to the elites, and it was geared to traditional religious-philosophical knowledge. In addition, the elites' disdain for manual labor and concern for abstract learning discouraged contact between them and the artisans, who focused their energies on practical efforts.

Even while supporting the status quo, however, the preindustrial city clearly acted as an agent of social and cultural change. As a major transportation center, the city was a natural receptacle for new ideas and inventions, and these in turn flowed from the city to outlying areas. The concentration of artisans in one area served to stimulate technological innovation. And not least important, new forms of social organization had to be developed to accommodate the increasing numbers of people in one location and to coordinate their specialized activities. The organizational problems concerned especially the collection and distribution of goods between city and farm country and the protection of the city from outside enemies. Thus, the preindustrial city brought the gradual development of new forms of political, military, and economic organization.

The first cities to be planted in the American colonies followed the general model of the

7. The following discussion draws heavily on Gideon Sjoberg, "The Origin and Evolution of Cities," Philip M. Hauser, "Urbanization: An Overview," and R. M. Adams, "The Origin of the City," all in *Metropolis in Crisis,* ed. Jeffrey K. Hadden, Louis H. Masotti, and Calvin J. Larson (Itasca, Ill.: F. E. Peacock Publishers, Inc., 1967); also Max Weber, *The City,* trans. and ed. Don Martindale and Gertrude Neuwirth (New York: Collier Books, 1962).

preindustrial city as it had evolved in Europe. They were built to provide protection for their residents and to facilitate trade and commerce. They also served as bases for the movement of populations into undeveloped territories. To a great extent, their growth was a function of location, especially regarding water transportation facilities and the accessibility of agricultural support.

Although the New World offered social mobility for many, the colonial city was not without class distinctions. The old aristocracy was gone, but a new one—composed of landowning patricians—emerged. Below the patricians was a small class of merchants, clerks, and the like. At the bottom of the hierarchy was the largest class, composed of the artisans and unskilled manual laborers.[8]

Although the colonial city was free of some of the problems that beset modern cities, it had problems enough of its own. Chitwood describes it as follows:

As the colonial city owed its importance to commerce rather than to manufacturing, it was free from many of the nuisances that are commonplaces of this industrial age.... On the other hand, the townsmen of that age had to forego certain comforts which we could not be deprived of today without great inconvenience. In none of the cities was there running water in the houses, and there was probably not a bathtub in any American home before the Revolution. Water was obtained from surface wells and was always liable to pollution by disease germs....

None of the colonial cities had any arrangement for disposing of garbage, and New York was the only one that attempted to clean the streets. Ashes and garbage were thrown into unsanitary heaps in the alleys and on vacant lots. In some cities and towns hogs were allowed to roam through the streets and act as scavengers by eating up the scraps of meat and vegetables that had been thrown out by the housewives.... These unsanitary conditions persisted long after colonial times and are matters of comment by travelers in the middle of the nineteenth century.[9]

---

8. For an account of the history of the American city see Glaab, *op. cit.* For an analysis of stratification in the preindustrial American city, see Robert A. Dahl, *Who Governs?* (New Haven, Conn.: Yale University Press, 1961), Book 1.

9. Oliver P. Chitwood, *A History of Colonial America* (New York: Harper and Brothers, 1931), p. 580.

10. See Hauser, *op. cit.,* pp. 59–61.

11. Sjoberg, *op. cit.,* p. 53.

THE EMERGENCE OF THE INDUSTRIAL CITY

Although cities have been in existence for six thousand years or more, only recently have they housed a significant proportion of the world's population. In 1800 the number of people living in cities of 20,000 or more made up only 2.4 percent of the world total; by 1950 the percentage had increased ninefold.[10] The rapid course of urbanization in the nineteenth and twentieth centuries becomes even more dramatic if we look only at those societies that have experienced the full impact of industrialization. In the United States, the first official census in 1790 showed a total of only twenty-four urban places, just two of which had populations in excess of 25,000. Altogether, city dwellers made up less than 3.5 percent of the population. A hundred years later, there were five metropolitan areas having a population of a million or more each, and the urban population had increased to almost 30 percent of the total. Today, an estimated 70–75 percent of Americans live in places officially defined as *urban* (see inset, page 280).

In the United States as in other Western societies, urbanization in the late eighteenth and early nineteenth centuries was directly tied to the changes being wrought by the Industrial and Agricultural Revolutions. But the emergence of the industrial city, like the emergence of industrialism itself, reflected more than an improved technology. Essential to both was a practical orientation that had been growing in the West for more than a century, stimulated first by the Protestant Reformation (page 181) and then by the new philosophy of science. As Sjoberg notes:

With the development of the experimental method ... the learning of the elite became linked with the practical knowledge of the artisan, the barber-surgeon and the like; the result was a dramatic upsurge of knowledge and a fundamental revision of method that has been termed the scientific revolution. Such was the basis of the industrial revolution and the industrial city.[11]

The emergence of the industrial city has brought marked changes in man's basic patterns of social organization. The economic and political institutions have become increasingly dominant, while the sphere of religion has narrowed.

DEFINING URBAN POPULATIONS

In 1960 the United States Bureau of the Census defined as *urban* any locality with a population of 2500 or more persons, whether that locality is incorporated or not. Thus the urban population, as officially defined, includes the residents of many places that we would normally think of as small towns. Other countries tend to restrict the term *urban* to localities in which the population is 20,000 or more persons. Whatever cutoff point is used, however, the objective is essentially the same: to locate areas in which economic activities are predominantly nonagricultural.

In earlier eras, persons who earned their livelihood within the city usually lived within its political boundaries. Today, however, the formal boundaries of a city are much less likely to delimit activity. Millions of people who work in the city live in "dormitory suburbs" or nearby small towns; other millions live in the city but shop and engage in other forms of interaction outside it. Increasingly, daily life focuses in and on the *metropolis*—a central city and the area immediately surrounding it, including many communities that were once largely self-sufficient.

In order to deal with this complex phenomenon, the United States Bureau of the Census has developed three special concepts to identify and analyze units of population that are functionally integrated even though they may be broken up by various political boundaries. The most general concept, *urbanized area,* was developed to provide a meaningful separation of rural and urban populations in areas surrounding large cities. An urbanized area includes at least one city of 50,000 or more inhabitants, plus all closely settled territory surrounding it. Everyone who lives within an urbanized area is counted as part of the urban population, even though some may live in unincorporated places of less than 2500 people.

A *Standard Metropolitan Statistical Area* (SMSA) is defined somewhat more specifically as an integrated unit. According to the Bureau of the Census, an SMSA is "a county or group of contiguous counties which contains at least one city of 50,000 inhabitants or more or 'twin cities' with a combined population of at least 50,000. In addition to the county or counties containing such a city or cities, contiguous counties are included in an SMSA if, according to certain criteria, they are essentially metropolitan in character and are socially and economically integrated with the central city." The Bureau of the Census delineated 212 SMSA's on the basis of the 1960 census. In addition, it delineated two unique complexes of SMSA's as *Standard Consolidated Areas:* New York–Northeastern New Jersey and Chicago–Northwestern Indiana. These large metropolitan complexes are functionally unified in many ways, but they do not meet all the criteria of social and economic integration that would be necessary to classify them as single SMSA's.

Recently the term *megalopolis* has come into popular use to designate a chain-like linkage of metropolitan areas that creates an almost unbroken urbanized area over a broad geographical region. Although this concept is less precise than those used by the Bureau of the Census, it nevertheless has a good deal of descriptive value. The most fully developed megalopolis in the United States runs southward along the northeastern Atlantic seaboard from Boston, Massachusetts, to Washington, D.C., and into northern Virginia. In 1960 this area encompassed a population of almost 37 million people in its maze of interlinked urban and suburban areas. Similar chains of metropolitan areas are developing between Detroit and Chicago, along the California coast, and in Texas, where Dallas and Forth Worth are gradually becoming linked up with Houston and San Antonio. The development of megalopoli clearly implies an ever growing level of interdependency among urban populations in a given region, despite the fact that local government is still geared to traditional city patterns.

The United Nations has been working, so far unsuccessfully, to develop a standard set of concepts for identifying urban populations and delimiting urban boundaries. For a fuller discussion of this point and an elaboration of the concepts used by the U.S. Bureau of the Census, see Jack P. Gibbs, ed., *Urban Research Methods* (New York: D. Van Nostrand Co., Inc., 1961).

A more fluid system of social stratification has evolved. More and more areas of activity have come to revolve around large, bureaucratic organizations. Individuals and groups have become increasingly interdependent, while at the same time losing some of their sense of common identity. The extent and significance of these changes has been a major focus of sociological concern from the early nineteenth century to the present.[12]

The spatial patterns of the city have changed no less than its patterns of life. No longer is the central core the area of highest prestige: people of wealth have moved to the outskirts, and the center of the city has largely been relegated to the poor and the powerless. This pattern has become particularly evident in the United States, where the line setting off the inner city is today drawn almost literally in black and white. In the developing societies, as we shall see, the preindustrial pattern still persists: the central city is occupied by the middle and upper classes and is surrounded by rapidly growing rings of slums. Inherent in both patterns is the potential for social conflict.

URBANIZATION: THE AMERICAN EXPERIENCE

The major cause of urban growth in the United States and elsewhere has been the movement of rural people to cities. Only recently have urban death rates been lowered to the point where city populations can grow rapidly without an influx of people from outside. Historically, rural areas have produced people and cities have consumed them.

The United States was well set for urbanization by 1800. It had a gradually developing industrial and agricultural technology, rich farm lands capable of yielding an abundance of food, and a system of waterways that could be used for transporting goods. If anything was lacking

it was experience in the practical arts of building and governing cities, which were bringing together ever increasing numbers of people from a wide variety of cultural backgrounds. But whether the cities were ready for them or not, the people flocked in, presumably in the hope of improving their life chances. During the nineteenth century the urban population of the United States increased about seven times faster than that of the nation as a whole.

FROM TOWN TO METROPOLIS

Despite the steady progress of urbanization after 1800, the agrarian tradition remained strong in the United States, and many of the newly emerging cities continued to reflect rural and preindustrial patterns. This may help explain America's tendency to evaluate urban life even today in terms of preindustrial patterns—and by comparison to find it wanting. In *Middletown,* Robert and Helen Lynd report the recollections of a physician who had grown up during the middle of the nineteenth century in the open country near Muncie, Indiana, when the population of that city had reached about six thousand people:

The log farmhouse of his father was ceiled inside without plaster, the walls bare save for three prized pictures of Washington, Jackson, and Clay. All meals were cooked before the great kitchen fireplace, corn pones and "cracklings" and bread being baked in the glare of a large curved reflector set before the open fire. At night the rooms were lighted by the open fire and by tallow dips; there was great excitement later when the first candle mold appeared in the neighborhood. Standard time was unknown; few owned watches, and sun time was good enough during the day.... When the fire went out on the family hearth the boy ran to a neighbor's to bring home fire between two boards; it was not until later that the first box of little sticks tipped with sulphur startled the neighborhood....

Social calls were unknown, but all-day visits were the rule, a family going to visit by horseback.... Social intercourse provided a highly important service; there were no daily papers in the region, and much news traveled by word of mouth. Men and women went miles and spent days in order to hear champions argue disputed political or religious points.[13]

12. For a review of the early theories of Tönnies, Weber, Durkheim, and others, see Chapter 2, pp. 85–87 and 92. Later urban theorists have pursued much the same themes; see "Theories of Urban Life," beginning on p. 286.

13. Robert S. and Helen M. Lynd, *Middletown* (New York: Harcourt Brace Jovanovich, Inc., 1929), pp. 11–17.

These photographs, which were taken from the same spot forty-four years apart, point up the fact that the west coast has experienced a more dramatic growth than any other section of the country. In 1922 (left) Los Angeles was a relatively small city with about half a million inhabitants, but by 1966 (right) it had become a huge metropolis. Today Los Angeles has a population of almost three million and ranks as the third largest city in the United States.

The consequences of industrialization and the accompanying rural-urban migration did not become widely evident until the end of the nineteenth century, when as the historian A. M. Schlesinger has observed, "urbanization for the first time became a controlling factor in national life."[14] Its effects were felt first in the older commercial and industrial centers along the east coast. In a critical portrait of New York City, Lewis Mumford suggests the extent to which life there had been transformed by the 1870's:

Within the span of a generation, the open spaces and the natural vistas began to disappear. . . . Vanishing from the consciousness of most Manhattanites were the open markets that had once brought the touch of the sea and the country to its streets, connecting farmstead and city home by means of little boats that plied the Hudson and Long Island Sound.

. . . The water and the soil, as the prime environment of life, were becoming "immaterial," that is to say, they were of no use to the canny minds that were promoting the metropolis, unless they could be described in a legal document, appraised quantitatively, and converted ultimately into cash.

Meanwhile, the city as a whole became progressively more foul. In the late seventies the new model tenement design, that for the so-called dumbbell apartment, standardized the habitations of the workers on the lowest possible level, encouraging for twenty years the erection of tenements in which only two rooms in six or seven got direct sunlight or a modicum of air. Even the best residences were grim, dreary, genteelly fusty. If something better was at last achieved for the rich in the 1890's, on Riverside Drive and West End Avenue, it remained in existence scarcely twenty years and was replaced by mass congestion.[15]

Today New York City is the focal point of the United States' first megalopolis, and it has come to characterize both the worst and the best about American urban life in the final third of the twentieth century. In terms of noise, congestion, air pollution, and housing conditions,

it has continued in the direction that Mumford deplored, becoming "progressively more foul." For many people, these disadvantages are balanced by the fact that the city offers them a wide choice of employment opportunities, cultural stimulation, and increased freedom to live their own lives. But for others the modern city has provided little of value; for blacks especially, it has meant entrapment in a ghetto that offers little hope of escape. We will take a closer look at these and other realities of contemporary urban life later in the present chapter.

POPULATION TRENDS

Kingsley Davis has delineated five major population shifts during the period of urbanization in the United States: (1) the movement from East to West, which continues even into the 1970's; (2) the movement from South to North, and more recently from North to South; (3) the movement from rural to urban, now pretty much completed; (4) the particular and increasing participation of blacks in the three movements listed above; and (5) the new movement, the deconcentration of the white population out from the central city to the suburbs.[16]

East to West. The movements noted by Davis, particularly that from East to West, are partly reflected in Table 9.1 (page 284), which shows the largest cities in 1820, 1900, and 1970. Three trends are noted: the continued growth and dominance of some cities; the fading of others; and the inclusion of midwestern and western cities in the top ten as the westward trend intensified. Much of the process can be explained in terms of transportation technology, from ocean to rivers and lakes (often by way of canals), then the coming of the railroads, and finally the highways. Location, accessibility, and technology have helped cities like New York, Cleveland, and Chicago outstrip those such as Boston, Cincinnati, and New Orleans.

Today, the two most highly settled areas of the country are the east and west coasts, but the west coast has achieved this position in half the time it took the east coast to do it. Los Angeles is one of the few major American cities to become developed *after* the introduction of automobiles and paved roads, and its ecology differs in many ways from that of cities in the East and Midwest: it is less a city than a sprawling series

---

14. Quoted in Glaab, *op. cit.*, p. 173.

15. Lewis Mumford, *City Development* (New York: Harcourt Brace Jovanovich, Inc., 1945), pp. 34–35.

16. See Kingsley Davis, "The Urbanization of the Human Population," *Scientific American* (September 1965), 41–53; also Davis, "Urbanization—Changing Patterns of Living," in *The Changing American Population; A Report of the Arden House Conference,* ed. Hoke S. Simpson (New York: Columbia University Press, 1962), pp. 59–68.

TABLE 9.1. **TEN LARGEST CITIES IN THE UNITED STATES, 1820, 1900, AND 1970**

1820		1900		1970	
New York, N.Y.	123,706	New York, N.Y.	3,437,202	New York, N.Y.	7,771,730
Philadelphia, Pa.	63,802	Chicago, Ill.	1,698,575	Chicago, Ill.	3,325,263
Baltimore, Md.	62,738	Philadelphia, Pa.	1,293,697	Los Angeles, Cal.	2,782,400
Boston, Mass.	42,541	St. Louis, Mo.	575,238	Philadelphia, Pa.	1,926,529
New Orleans, La.	27,176	Boston, Mass.	560,892	Detroit, Mich.	1,492,914
Charleston, S.C.	24,780	Baltimore, Md.	508,957	Houston, Texas	1,213,064
Washington, D.C.	13,247	Cleveland, Ohio	381,768	Baltimore, Md.	895,222
Albany City, N.Y.	12,630	Buffalo, N.Y.	352,387	Dallas, Texas	836,121
Providence, R.I.	11,767	San Francisco, Cal.	342,782	Washington, D.C. (est.)	764,000
Salem, Mass.	11,346	Cincinnati, Ohio	325,902	Indianapolis, Ind.	742,613

SOURCE: Bureau of the Census.

of suburbs. Like older cities, however, Los Angeles has grown more by happenstance than by design. With a complicated maze of highways making up for the lack of adequate public transportation, it suffers the same traffic congestion that has long plagued the east coast.

The steady movement of population from East to West has been stimulated both by the opening of new economic opportunities in the West and by the fact that immigration to the United States has been primarily from Europe rather than from Asia. More than 20 million people arrived from Europe during the four decades when immigration was heaviest, between 1880 and 1920. Many of the new arrivals settled permanently in New York City and other parts of the East, but many others joined the growing stream of Americans who were moving toward the West.

South to North and North to South. The migration from South to North began as a trickle in the nineteenth century but was greatly accelerated by the need for industrial workers during World Wars I and II. Although this pattern of migration has involved whites as well as blacks, the exodus of the black population from the South has been particularly marked (see Chapter 10, pages 321–322). Whereas the vast majority of blacks once lived in the southern states, the percentage has now dropped to about half (Table 9.2). Most of the migration has been to the large cities of the North, in some of which black minorities are rapidly becoming majori-

ties. This is true despite the fact that the movement northward has slowed somewhat: the black population in the cities is now experiencing a high rate of natural growth, while the white population dwindles as a result of the steady exodus to the suburbs.

The years since World War II have also seen a considerable movement of whites from North to South. The most significant difference between this pattern of migration and the countermovement from South to North is less a matter of race, however, than of educational level and occupational skills. For the most part, those who have moved South are white-collar and professional people, some of them moving to take new jobs and others to enjoy a comfortable retirement. If only by virtue of their spending power, they have helped enhance the economy of the southern states. By contrast, the majority of those migrating to the North, whether black or white, have been poorly educated, unskilled workers from impoverished rural backgrounds. Few have been prepared to find good jobs or otherwise to cope with the hard realities of life in a large northern city.

Rural to urban. Despite the great claims that have been made for the values and virtues of rural life, urban growth has been primarily a function of the flight from the farm. In the United States, this pattern was already clearly apparent toward the end of the nineteenth century: the 1890 census showed that nearly 40 percent of the nation's 25,746 townships had lost population over the previous decade.[17] Rural to urban migration has greatly accelerated in the present century, as changes in agricultural technology have made the large farm increasingly productive and the small one decreasingly profitable. In 1790, 95 percent of Americans lived on farms. Today, the figure has dropped to 5 percent. Thus, little farm population is left to continue the pattern of rural-urban migration. It has become increasingly difficult, furthermore, to make significant distinctions, other than occupational ones, between urban and rural life. Thus the urbanization of the United States is now virtually complete.

City to suburbs. Perhaps the significant distinction that can now be made is not between rural and urban but rather between the inner city and the suburbs. We will give special attention to slums and suburbs in a later section, but it should be reiterated here that a dramatic change is taking place in the nature of the population in the central city, as the poor become concentrated there and the middle and upper classes move out. The 1970 Census showed, for the first time, that more Americans lived in the suburbs of big cities (74.2 million) than in the cities themselves (62.2 million).

The movement toward suburbia is not new, but it has been proceeding at a vastly accelerated rate over the last few decades and has been increasingly tied to patterns of racial segregation. (See, for example, Table 9.3, opposite, and Table 9.4, page 286.) Farley and Taeuber summarized their recent study of urban population trends as follows:

We examined special census data for 13 cities to assess trends in population, migration, and residential segregation from 1960 to mid-decade. In these cities, the demographic trends of the 1950's are continuing. There is a net out-migration of white population, and in several cities a decline in total population. Negro population is growing rapidly, but natural increase rather than net in-migration increasingly is the principal source. The concentration of whites in the suburbs and Negroes in the central cities is continuing. Within the cities, indices of racial residential segregation generally increased. The combination of small increases in residential segregation

and large increases in the Negro percentage has greatly intensified the magnitude of the problems of segregation and desegregation of neighborhoods, local institutions, and schools.[18]

These population patterns have created not only a personal crisis for those who are trapped in the slums but a crisis for the city as a whole. Though suburbanites continue to depend on the city for their livelihood, they contribute disproportionately little to its maintenance and to the provision of crucial public services. The poor who are left behind cannot pay for such services themselves. Thus a downward spiral sets in,

---

TABLE 9.2. **PERCENT DISTRIBUTION OF BLACKS IN THE UNITED STATES, BY REGION, 1940–1968**

	1940	1950	1960	1968
South	77	68	60	53
Northeast	11	13	16	18
North Central	11	15	18	22
West	1	4	6	8

SOURCE: Bureau of the Census, *Current Population Reports*, Series P-23, No. 26, July 1968, p. 3. By the standard Census definition, the South includes Delaware, the District of Columbia, Kentucky, Maryland, Oklahoma, and West Virginia as well as the states of the Confederacy.

TABLE 9.3. **PERCENTAGE OF WHITES IN CENTRAL CITIES OF TWELVE LARGEST SMSA'S, 1930–1960**

SMSA	1930	1940	1950	1960
New York	95.1	93.6	90.2	85.3
Los Angeles–Long Beach	95.0	94.0	90.2	84.7
Chicago	92.9	91.7	85.9	76.4
Philadelphia	88.6	86.9	81.7	73.3
Detroit	92.2	90.7	83.6	70.8
San Francisco–Oakland	95.1	95.1	88.2	78.9
Boston	97.1	96.7	94.7	90.2
Pittsburgh	91.7	90.7	87.7	83.2
St. Louis	88.5	86.6	82.0	71.2
Washington, D.C.	72.7	71.5	64.6	45.2
Cleveland	91.9	90.3	83.7	71.1
Baltimore	82.3	80.6	76.2	65.0
TOTAL 12 SMSA's	92.4	91.0	86.3	78.6

SOURCE: Harry Sharp and Leo F. Schnore, "The Changing Color Composition of Metropolitan Areas," *Land Economics*, 38 (May 1962), 169–185.

---

17. Glaab, *op. cit.*, p. 176.
18. Reynolds Farley and Karl E. Taeuber, "Population Trends and Residential Segregation Since 1960," *Science*, 159 (March 1, 1968), 953–956.

with a further deterioration of already deteriorated housing, inadequate educational opportunities, high rates of unemployment, family breakdown, and welfare dependency. These are the conditions that give meaning to the phrase, "the crisis of the cities." We will examine them more closely a little later in this chapter.

THEORIES OF URBAN LIFE

With the dramatic move toward urbanization in the nineteenth and twentieth centuries has come the growth of sociology as a scientific discipline. In fact, the development of sociology in the United States has so closely paralleled the development of the industrial city that sociologists have often been linked primarily with urban problems. The work of pioneering sociologists at such places as the University of Chicago, with their studies of the city's ghettos, gold coasts, and gangs, and the establishment of such specialized subfields as delinquency, ecology, and collective behavior all reflect the sociological orientation toward urban life.[19]

The sociologist is interested in the city, because it is the locus of and stimulant for new forms of social organization and culture. As we have emphasized, these new forms are likely to produce tensions and strains that become manifested as social problems. In trying to explain these problems, the urban sociologist has sometimes begun with empirical research and worked toward general theory, and sometimes he has begun with a theory and let it provide direction for his research. In both cases, he has tried to understand how new forms of social organization affect man's ways of thinking and behaving.

THE MAKING OF URBAN MAN

One crucial aspect of the changing nature of interpersonal relations has been the changing locus of social action. According to theorists of urban life, the focus of interaction has moved away from the family and has centered increasingly around economic and governmental organizations. In the process, authority and status distinctions, once clearly defined by birth and based on family ties and tradition, have come to be defined more by contracts or other formal agreements and based on rational considerations and calculations of individual advantage. At the same time, a more complex division of labor and the new organizations of urban life have inevitably led to a breakdown in the uniformity of beliefs and sentiments, sanctified by time and tradition, that have been considered characteristic of the small town and the rural community. New beliefs and sentiments have developed that require men to be more impersonal, formal, and autonomous in their behavior.

Despite the disappearance of many traditional restrictions on behavior, urban man is far from being either normless or free. Rather, he is bound by a complex body of rules and contractual obligations that constrain his social actions quite as much as did the traditional patterns. The change in human relationships accompanying the rise of industrial cities did not do away with rules, beliefs, and sentiments. It only altered them.

TABLE 9.4. **PERCENTAGE OF NONWHITES IN SUBURBS OF TWELVE LARGEST SMSA'S, 1930–1960**

SMSA	1930	1940	1950	1960
New York	3.8	4.6	4.5	4.8
Los Angeles–Long Beach	2.7	2.3	2.7	4.1
Chicago	2.0	2.2	2.9	3.1
Philadelphia	6.7	6.6	6.6	6.3
Detroit	2.9	2.9	5.0	3.8
San Francisco–Oakland	4.1	3.6	6.8	6.8
Boston	1.0	0.9	0.8	1.0
Pittsburgh	3.8	3.6	3.5	3.4
St. Louis	6.1	6.7	7.3	6.3
Washington, D.C.	19.0	13.7	8.7	6.4
Cleveland	1.1	0.9	0.8	0.8
Baltimore	13.8	11.9	10.2	6.9
TOTAL 12 SMSA's	4.0	3.9	4.4	4.4

SOURCE: Harry Sharp and Leo F. Schnore, "The Changing Color Composition of Metropolitan Areas," *Land Economics*, 38 (May 1962), 169–185.

19. During the first half of the twentieth century the sociology department at the University of Chicago became preeminent and literally showed the way in using the city as a sociological laboratory. The term "Chicago School" thus came to denote not only a specific group of scholars but also empirical research oriented to the problems of city life.

THE FOLK-URBAN CONTINUUM

In the present century Robert Redfield and Louis Wirth of the University of Chicago, working respectively in the fields of anthropology and sociology, further refined the theories of societal organization developed by early sociologists such as Tönnies and Durkheim. While the efforts of Redfield and Wirth were not directly collaborative, they tended to complement each other in important ways. Subsequent studies have shown that their theories had very serious limitations, as we will note below, but their work further illuminated some aspects of urban life and paved the way for continued research.

Redfield's "folk society." Redfield readily acknowledged that his folk society was an "ideal type"[20] (perhaps approximated in reality by preliterate societies studied chiefly by anthropologists) and that his typology was influenced by the writings of Maine, Tönnies, Durkheim, and others.[21] According to Redfield, the folk society is small, containing no more people than can come to know each other well. It is isolated, preliterate, and homogeneous—both culturally and physically. In theory at least, these attributes create a high degree of group solidarity. Isolation also makes for economic independence in the form of a subsistence economy. The technology is very simple, and the division of labor exists primarily along sex and age lines.

In the "ideal" folk society, communication is face-to-face, and problems are met in conventionalized ways. Over a period of time traditional patterns of belief and behavior become systematized into a coherent and self-consistent *culture*. Oral tradition is sacred. There is no check on the past and no tendency to criticize the present, because alternative ways are unknown. Behavior is spontaneous and uncritical, following long-established folkways: "That is the way

to do it because that is the way it has always been done."

Kinship is central to all experience in the folk society: the family is the central unit of action. All activities are ends in themselves, including those of an economic nature. People help each other not because they expect favors in return but because family and community ties make such expectations obligatory. Life is one large web of activity from which nothing can be separated without affecting the rest. As Redfield stated it in his preface to Horace Miner's *St. Denis: A French-Canadian Parish*, "Life is like a wheel turning."

In the folk society, status is largely fixed at birth. On those rare occasions when an individual does rise to a higher level of status, there is a norm that declares the change to have been foreordained. There is no objectivity or systematized knowledge as such; one simply accepts what *is* as what *ought* to be. The folk society, as Redfield developed it, posits the idea of a functionally integrated system, a system in equilibrium.

Redfield never delineated the urban community as an "ideal type," but he indicated that it could be identified by its differences from the folk society. For example, the solidarity built on uninterrupted face-to-face relationships so characteristic of the folk society is lacking in the urban community. Because it is too large to permit affective interpersonal interaction among any large number of citizens, impersonal relations become the norm. More than that, the urban system is so complex and differentiated that it is literally impossible for any group of citizens to be socialized into all the norms, beliefs, and sentiments that it incorporates. Diversity of beliefs and norms leads to tolerance and critical scrutiny; life becomes more secular; and the family is now only one among several important groups within which the individual acts. Change rather than stability becomes an important part of the daily round. Social action becomes a means to an end and is no longer valued in itself. The same is true of work: individuals become instruments by which large-scale organizations achieve their goals, and the workers come to perceive their work not as satisfying in itself but as a means to other ends, such as salary and status.

Redfield suggested that much could be learned about the identifying characteristics of the modern urban community by contrasting it

20. See the Methodological Essay on the "ideal type" as a theoretical and research tool, p. 86.

21. See Robert Redfield, "The Folk Society," *American Journal of Sociology,* 52 (January 1947), 293–308, for the most complete statement of his ideal type. There are many earlier references in Redfield's research writings on Tepatzlan and other Mexican communities and in his introduction to Horace Miner's *St. Denis: A French-Canadian Parish* (Chicago: The University of Chicago Press, 1939). In later writings Redfield also delineated another type, the peasant community, which represented a mixture of characteristics from both the folk and the urban communities.

with the folk society. For example, the contrasting typologies should provide the basis for developing and testing hypotheses about urban life. Thus, it might be predicted that when primitive and peasant communities come into contact with an urbanized community, the members tend to adopt the characteristics of the latter. It could also be hypothesized that the elements of social organization are closely interdependent, so that change in one element tends to bring about change in others. Contact between different types of communities might thus be expected to have far-reaching consequences.

Wirth's theory of urbanism. In 1938, even before Redfield had spelled out his theory of the folk society in all its detail, Louis Wirth published his famous essay on "Urbanism as a Way of Life." Wirth's essay was in a sense the culmination of many years of research and writing by the men of the "Chicago School," and it became the point of departure for urban sociology during the ensuing generation.[22] Wirth defined the city as "a relatively large, permanent, dense settlement of socially heterogeneous individuals." He then examined the characteristics of *large size, dense population,* and *heterogeneity* to ascertain what consequences they had for urban living.

According to Wirth, density and size affected social relationships in a number of ways. In the first place they led to heterogeneity, since an increase in the number of people in a community naturally led to an increase in the possible range of ideas, cultural patterns, occupations, and personal traits. Furthermore, the rapid growth of the cities through immigration would continually reinforce heterogeneity as a basic characteristic of urban life.

Another consequence of size and density was that one person could not know as many others so intensively as in the folk society. As the number of potential interactors *increased,* the intensity of the interaction *decreased.* People would come to see only part of the personality of others—to see them in segmentalized roles. *Social relationships then would become more formal, often impersonal, superficial, transitory, and segmental.* As a further consequence, individuals would become more reserved and indifferent in their attitude toward others, thus protecting themselves from the personal claims and expectations of people they didn't know.

Wirth maintained that another important consequence of urbanism was a greater tolerance for individual differences. In part, this would be an inevitable result of increased heterogeneity in the population. Furthermore, some role demands would require tolerance whatever one's personal attitudes. For example, a clerk selling stamps at the post office window cannot discriminate against customers whatever their religion or color or ethnic background.

According to Wirth, primary relationships learned in the family would not serve in the larger milieu of the city. As a result, kinship bonds would weaken, the family would decline in importance relative to other social groups, and the neighborhood would lose much of its significance. The consequence of these changes would be an undermining of the traditional bases of social solidarity. Faced with these losses, the individual would have to turn to new forms of social organization in order to fulfill his needs.

THE "SMALL-TOWN FOLK" AS THEORISTS

The tendency to see the folk way of life as promoting an integrated order and hence "good," and to see urbanism by contrast as promoting personal and social disorganization and therefore "bad," is a popular way to read folk-urban theory. This tendency is found not only among "alienated intellectuals" but also among those Americans who have continued to live in small towns. In their study of a small country town called Springdale, for example, Vidich and Bensman found that most of the three thousand residents were still stongly tied to Jeffersonian agrarianism. They seemed to pity the poor city people who lived in a bustling, jostling, nerve-racking, impersonal environment. Here is how the authors summarized the average Springdaler's belief—whether well founded or not—that his was the better of two worlds:

1. The basic traditions of American society—"grassroots democracy, free and open expression, individualism—are more firmly located in rural society. The American heritage is better preserved in the small town because it can resist bad city influences and thereby preserve the best of the past."

---

22. See Louis Wirth, "Urbanism as a Way of Life," *American Journal of Sociology,* 44 (July 1938), 1–24.

2. The future hope of American society lies in rural life because it has resisted all "isms" and constitutes the only major bulwark against them.

3. Much of the progress of society is the result of rural talent which has migrated to the cities. In this way rural society has a positive influence on urban life; rural migrants account for the virtues of city life. "Everyone knows that most of the outstanding men in the country were raised in small towns," and Springdalers proudly point to several local names that have made good on the outside.

4. "When you live in a small town you can take or leave the big cities—go there when you want to and always come back without having to live as they do." There is the belief that "if more people lived in small towns, you wouldn't have all those problems."[23]

While the Springdalers spoke eloquently about the virtues of rural life, the researchers found that clear-cut status distinctions prevailed there no less than in the city and that most people could and did rank each other on the basis of their economic worth. Perhaps ironically, those town folk who were most strongly linked to the city were in the best position to improve themselves socially, economically, and politically in Springdale. And whether he realized it or not, the Springdaler's image was strongly influenced by the mass media, particularly by television. The question of whether he could "take or leave" the big city was perhaps not so simple as he wanted to believe.

As a further sidelight on this study, we may note that the "Springdales" of this country must share responsibility for the urban problems they deplore. Political scientists have pointed out that the residents of small towns have long had a disproportionate influence on urban places through their control of state legislatures. State legislatures were constituted so as to give control to the rural area and small towns in the era before the rise of the industrial city. Thus, many of the faults that small-town people see in the city are directly or indirectly caused by the power structure at state government levels, which has allowed the small town to stifle the

attempt by city people to confront their problems. Furthermore, many residents of small towns earn their living in the city and take their money back to the small town. In doing so, they fail to support the tax structure of the city while providing more than enough revenue for their small-town needs.

THE ECOLOGICAL APPROACH

Much of the material on which Wirth based his ideas was drawn from the work of other sociologists at the University of Chicago during the 1920's and 1930's, some of whom emphasized the importance of ecological processes —especially of competition for land—in determining the spatial patterning of the city. These sociologists argued that natural forces operate in human communities, as they do in plant and animal communities, to create areas that are clearly differentiated in terms of how the land is used.[24] Thus some segments of the city are allocated to business or industrial use and others to different patterns of housing. The various areas tend to be *segregated* (in the sense of being more or less isolated and self-sufficient) and to resist the intrusion of other types of land use. When *invasion* can no longer be resisted successfully, *succession* occurs: a different pattern of land use becomes predominant, and the displaced pattern re-creates itself in a different (usually adjoining) locality. Thus as a city grows, its spatial organization is continually being modified.

One member of the Chicago group, Ernest W. Burgess, hypothesized that the impersonal process of land-use competition led to the development of a series of concentric zones spreading out from the city's center, each reserved for particular activities and for occupancy by particular segments of the population (Figure 9.1, A). At the heart of the city is the central business district, an area of intensive land use that plays host to throngs of workers and shoppers by day but whose nighttime population is largely limited to transient hotel residents. Immediately surrounding the business district is a zone in transition, which is continually threatened by the invasion of commercial activities from the expanding city center. Generally a blighted area, it is associated with cheap housing, residential instability, and high rates of crime, delinquency, and vice. Its population

23. Arthur Vidich and Joseph Bensman, *Small Town in Mass Society* (Princeton, N.J.: Princeton University Press, 1958); as summarized in Dennis Wrong and Harry Gracey, eds., *Readings in Introductory Sociology* (New York: The Macmillan Company, 1967), p. 365.

24. See Robert E. Park, Ernest W. Burgess, R. D. McKenzie, and Louis Wirth, *The City* (Chicago: The University of Chicago Press, 1925).

consists for the most part of racial and ethnic minorities, migrants from rural areas, social outcasts, and others who for one reason or another cannot move to more desirable residential areas. Ringing this transitional area is a zone of working-class homes, surrounded in turn by middle- and upper-class residential areas in the zones farther out.

While Burgess apparently intended his scheme of concentric zones as a hypothesis to be tested, it became popularized almost as a general theory. Subsequent research has shown that the zonal pattern exists, at least to a degree, in a number of American cities, especially those that developed rapidly (as Chicago did) during the period of heavy European immigration in the nineteenth century. However, the zonal theory does not seem very applicable to cities built before the Industrial Revolution (e.g., Boston and New Haven) or to cities built in the twentieth century after the coming of the automobile. Peculiarities of topography, such as the presence of hills, rivers, and lakes, can also have important effects on the course of a city's development. Even Chicago, which Burgess used as his model, developed not as a series of concentric circles but rather as a series of half-circles, cut off on one side by Lake Michigan. Land use along the lake shore, furthermore, follows quite a different pattern than it does elsewhere in the various zones.

A modification of Burgess' scheme was developed in the 1930's by Homer Hoyt, who envisioned the structure of the city in terms of *sectors* or quadrants (Figure 9.1, B). Hoyt stressed the importance of transportation arteries (main streets, rail lines, and waterways) in determining the spatial organization of the city and the direction of its growth. Concentrating his study primarily on rental values and residential patterns, he found that high-rent areas tend to move out toward the periphery of the city but to stay within their original sectors. The expansion of low-rent residential areas generally follows a similar pattern, as does that of industrial sections. Thus according to Hoyt's theory, a land-use map of a city would look more like a series of arms radiating from the center than a series of concentric circles.

Still another theory of ecological patterning is the *multiple nuclei* theory developed by Chauncey D. Harris and Edward L. Ullman (Figure 9.1, C). These ecologists argued that land use within a city is organized around a number of distinct nuclei, each distinguished by its own special functions and requirements. The differentiation of these areas, they believed, resulted from the interplay of four main factors. (1) Certain activities require specialized facilities (manufacturing, for example, requires large blocks of land and good shipping facilities). (2) Certain related activities, such as retail stores, tend to group together because they benefit from each other's presence. (3) Certain dissimilar activities, such as residential development and industrial development, are detrimental to each other and thus tend to locate in separate areas. (4) Certain activities cannot afford to locate where property values are high (bulk wholesaling, for example, and low-income housing). Harris and Ullman argued that as a city grew in size, its nuclei would increase in number and become more specialized in their activities.

Gradually, ecologists have come to recognize that the organization of people in urban space reflects the interplay of many factors and cannot be accounted for simply by competitive economic processes. Nor can their behavior be explained solely in terms of such variables as size, density, and heterogeneity. Cultural factors continue as independent variables, and folk-like features of organization may be influential in the larger urban milieu as well as in the small town.

REALITIES OF URBAN LIFE

Gideon Sjoberg, Leo Schnore, Herbert Gans, and others have argued that Wirth overstated his case that the city is rapidly becoming a *Gesellschaft*.[25] They point out that there is insufficient data to prove that size, density, and heterogeneity are the only independent variables operating, or that they necessarily have meant the end of primary or *Gemeinschaft* relationships. Anonymity, impersonal interaction, segmentation of roles may all be present as the result of

25. For a detailed critique of the Chicago school and Wirth in particular, see Gideon Sjoberg, "Comparative Urban Sociology," in *Sociology Today*, ed. Robert K. Merton *et al.* (New York: Basic Books, Inc., 1959), pp. 334–359; Leo Schnore, "Community," in *Sociology: An Introduction*, ed. Neil Smelser (New York: John Wiley & Sons, Inc., 1967), esp. pp. 105 ff.; and Herbert J. Gans, "Urbanism and Suburbanism as Ways of Life: A Re-evaluation of Definitions," in *Human Behavior and Social Processes*, ed. Arnold Rose (New York: Houghton Mifflin Company, 1962), pp. 306–323.

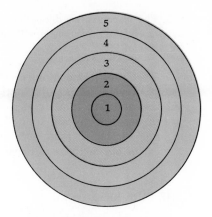

A. CONCENTRIC ZONE THEORY

1. Central business district
2. Zone in transition
3. Zone of workingmen's homes
4. Residential zone
5. Commuter zone

SOURCE: Adapted from Ernest W. Burgess, "The Growth of the City," in *The City*, ed. R. E. Park, E. W. Burgess, R. D. McKenzie, and L. Wirth (Chicago: University of Chicago Press, 1925).

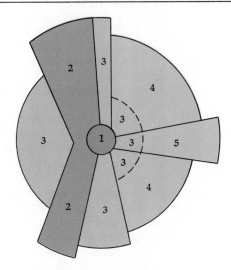

B. SECTOR THEORY

1. Central business district
2. Wholesale, light manufacturing
3. Low-class residential
4. Medium-class residential
5. High-class residential

SOURCE: Homer Hoyt, *The Structure and Growth of Residential Neighborhoods in American Cities* (Washington, D.C.: Federal Housing Administration, 1939); drawing adapted from Chauncey D. Harris and Edward L. Ullman, "The Nature of Cities," *Annals of the American Academy of Political and Social Science*, 242 (November 1945).

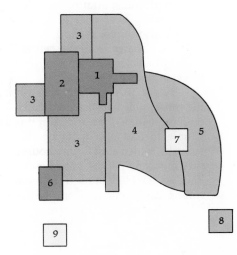

C. MULTIPLE NUCLEI THEORY

1. Central business district
2. Wholesale, light manufacturing
3. Low-class residential
4. Medium-class residential
5. High-class residential
6. Heavy manufacturing
7. Outlying business district
8. Residential suburb
9. Industrial suburb

SOURCE: Adapted from Chauncey D. Harris and Edward L. Ullman, "The Nature of Cities," *Annals of the American Academy of Political and Social Science*, 242 (November 1945).

FIGURE 9.1. **THEORIES OF URBAN ECOLOGY**

urbanism—but do these patterns constitute *all* the interaction, *all* the significant forms of social organization to be found in urban life? Have they totally replaced the patterns implied by Tönnies' term *Gemeinschaft?*

Herbert Gans has pointed out that Wirth's formulation was largely derived from and supported by research in the city's transient district—that is, the gold coast and the slums that generally surround the central business district. Of all the residents of the city, Gans argues, Wirth's thesis best fits the transients. Here the heterogeneity of the population does indeed lead to anonymity, impersonality, and superficiality. But on careful analysis, Gans concludes, the social features resulting from urbanism are not so much a direct consequence of size, density, and heterogeneity as they are of *residential instability.* In fact, he says,

heterogeneity is itself an effect of residential instability, resulting when the influx of transients causes landlords and realtors to stop acting as gatekeepers— that is, wardens of neighborhood homogeneity. Residential instability is found in all types of settlements, and, presumably, its social consequences are everywhere similar.[26]

Gans next questions whether the outer city, the area of working-class and middle-class residences, accurately mirrors Wirth's theory. Gans hypothesizes from the little hard evidence available that these neighborhoods might best be described as "quasi-primary." That is, "the interaction is more intimate than a secondary contact, but more guarded than a primary one." Sociability rather than formality is the keynote of social contact, even in voluntary associations such as PTA's and civic associations. On the basis of empirical research conducted since Wirth formulated his thesis, Gans develops three propositions:

1. As concerns ways of life, the inner city must be distinguished from the outer city and the suburbs; and the latter two exhibit a way of life bearing little resemblance to Wirth's urbanism.

2. Even in the inner city, ways of life resemble Wirth's description only to a limited extent. Moreover, economic conditions, cultural characteristics, life-cycle stage, and residential instability explain ways of life more satisfactorily than number, density, or heterogeneity.

3. Physical and other differences between city and suburb are often spurious or without much meaning for ways of life.[27]

The latter proposition is particularly interesting in view of popular notions about the suburbs and how they differ from the city. Let us turn now to an examination of life in suburbia in order to place it more accurately within the context of our analysis of urbanism.

THE SUBURBS

The suburbs seem to have two characteristics that presumably set them apart from the city: they are generally outside the political boundaries of the city, and they are residential areas of comparatively low density. The second characteristic is not peculiar to the suburbs, for the density of sectors housing the middle and upper classes in the city is often as low as that of the suburbs. Indeed, many of these outer-city sectors were once suburbs themselves. Contrary to much popular belief, the suburbs are not entirely a twentieth-century phenomenon.

Development in the nineteenth century. Glaab reports that as early as 1823 New York City realtors were advertising "country" lots that were within fifteen to twenty-five minutes of the central business district by foot.[28] And so it was with other American cities during the nineteenth century. The suburbs grew and flourished as improved transportation made it possible to move easily over ever greater distances. The growth of suburbs, in short, was determined not only by distance from the central business district, but also by the amount of time it took to traverse that distance.

By the 1870's Chicago had become one of the most suburban-oriented cities in the world, with more than one hundred trains daily moving people in and out of its nearly one hundred suburbs, which at that time housed an estimated fifty thousand people. Lake Forest and Highland Park were widely praised for the beauty of their rolling landscape, and one writer in particular

26. Gans, *op. cit.,* p. 311.
27. *Ibid.,* p. 315.
28. Glaab, *op. cit.,* p. 229.

felt that the development of the suburbs demonstrated man's ability to be both practical and esthetic:

The controversy which is sometimes brought, as to which offers the greater advantage, the country or the city, finds a happy answer in the suburban idea which says, both—the combination of the two—the city brought to the country. . . . The city has its advantages and conveniences, the country has its charm and health; the union of the two (a modern result of the railway) gives to man all he could ask in this respect.[29]

Twentieth-century suburbia. What is new about the suburbs today is the rapid rate at which they are attracting new residents, almost all of them white, and the fact that they may be extracting more wealth from the central city than they return to it. The suburbanite may indeed have the best of both worlds. But where does this leave the central city?

Another characteristic of our modern suburbs is that they are decreasing in density. The suburbs geared to subway transportation and built for New Yorkers between the two World Wars had densities of ten to fifty dwellings on each acre. The post–World War II suburbs like Levittown on Long Island averaged seven houses per acre. The suburbs built between 1945 and 1960 are from fifteen to twenty-five miles from Times Square, and the most recent are zoned in lots of from one half to two thirds of an acre each.[30]

There is no evidence that the movement to suburbia will abate in the near future. The automobile has provided people with a flexibility never before possible. Also significant has been the gradual reduction in the official work week from forty-eight to forty hours or less. An employee can now spend eight or ten hours a week commuting without increasing his total time away from home.

Life style. How, if at all, do suburbanites differ in *behavior* from the city residents of mid-

dle- and upper-class neighborhoods? Again, there is not enough sound empirical evidence to support any theory, but it seems increasingly certain that the writings of popular critics like William H. Whyte do not offer an accurate picture of suburban reality. Whyte's essays on suburbia at most support the hypothesis that these people live lives of quasi-primary patterns. How is this different from city life? Gans remarks: "It is true that the upper-middle-class housewife must become a chauffeur in order to expose her children to the proper educational facilities, but such differences as walking to the corner drug store and driving to its suburban equivalent seem to me of little emotional, social, or cultural import."[31]

Are the quasi-primary patterns of suburban life basically different from the neighborhood patterns known to the parental generation? We may hypothesize that they are no more homogeneous—that the homogeneity of ethnic and religious neighborhoods of a generation ago is being replaced by the homogeneity of occupational and educational neighborhoods of this generation. Summarizing research on occupational and residential distribution, Schnore concludes that "Generally, 'social distance' is a good predictor of spatial distance, since men who are like each other in occupational terms tend to reside in the same areas."[32] Larger and older cities exhibit the pattern more clearly than newer and smaller cities do, but in either case the differences are not so much between urban and suburban as between neighborhoods. It is not yet clear how much racial homogeneity is a function of the above. The test will come soon.

As to whether the suburbs produce any notable changes in family life styles, that too is uncertain. It is popularly maintained that the suburbs are good for the family, but in comparison to what? The city as a whole? The inner-city slums? Or the outer-city residential areas? How, if at all, do husband-wife patterns in the residential sectors of the city differ from those in the suburbs? And if peer groups dominate the lives of teen-agers in the suburbs, do they not also dominate the lives of city teen-agers? How, if at all, is the suburban do-it-yourselfer different from his city counterpart? Data from a study of New England communities showed that the populations in both urban and suburban residential areas exhibited varying degrees of heterogeneity regarding income, ed-

---

29. *Ibid.*, p. 233.

30. See Peter Hall, *The World Cities* (New York: McGraw-Hill Book Company, 1966), esp. pp. 196–199.

31. Gans, *op. cit.*, p. 313; see also William H. Whyte, Jr., *The Organization Man* (New York: Simon & Schuster, Inc., 1956).

32. Schnore, *op. cit.*, p. 125.

ucation, occupation, and ethnic status with no significant differences discernible between urban and suburban.[33]

In a recent study, Ross attempted to compare the life styles of upper-middle-class whites in two New York City neighborhoods, one in the central city and one on the periphery. In both cases those surveyed were apartment-house dwellers. Ross could find no important differences between the two groupings. He suggested that "city-suburban differences in life style are primarily the product of underlying differences in class, ethnicity and family status."[34]

THE INNER-CITY SLUMS

We have already indicated that it is *perhaps* in the slums that Wirth's theory of urbanism comes closest to portraying reality. It is here that density and heterogeneity may combine with size to bring on social disruption, anomie, a sense of not belonging to the larger society, of not fitting in, a breakdown of family life, and growing impersonality and anonymity. But are these *necessary* conditions of urban life, even in the inner city?

Street-Corner Society. At the time Wirth was writing his famous essay and his colleagues at the University of Chicago were examining the behavior of dwellers in the inner city, William Foote Whyte was making his community study of Cornerville, the Italian subcommunity of Boston that he described in his book as a *Street-Corner Society* (1943). Whyte's introductory comments to this classic book are instructive:

In the heart of "Eastern City," there is a slum district known as Cornerville, which is inhabited almost exclusively by Italian immigrants and their children. To the rest of the city it is a mysterious, dangerous, and depressing area. . . .

Respectable people have access to a limited body of information upon Cornerville. They may learn that it is one of the most congested areas in the United States . . . that children overrun the narrow and neglected streets, that the juvenile delinquency rate is high, that crime is prevalent among adults, and that a large proportion of the population was on home relief or W.P.A. during the depression.

In this view, Cornerville people appear as social work clients, as defendants in criminal cases, or as undifferentiated members of "the masses." . . .

. . . The middle-class person looks upon the slum district as a formidable mass of confusion, a social chaos. The insider finds in Cornerville a highly organized and integrated social system.[35]

Not only was life within Cornerville highly organized, but Whyte also found that there existed between Cornerville and the larger community definite patterns of social organization involving politics, the rackets, and methods of social control. This does not mean, however, that Whyte found no evidence for the patterns implied by Wirth's theory. On the contrary, the comparison between Doc's gang and Chick's club (page 66) reveals that the latter—in attempting to move beyond Cornerville, to go to college and to learn the ways of the larger community—did behave in more formal, segmental ways which led to social disorganization when the two groups attempted to collaborate. Not size, density, and heterogeneity but differing values, norms, and goals brought on the distinctive behavior manifested by these two groups.

The "deprived" and the "trapped." As we have noted, Gans maintains that economic condition, cultural characteristics, life-cycle stage, and degree of residential instability explain ways of life in the inner city more satisfactorily than do size, density, and heterogeneity. In support of this contention, he identifies five different types of inner-city residents: (1) the "cosmopolites," chiefly intellectuals and professionals who want to live near the city's cultural facilities; (2) the "unmarried or childless" who also live in the inner city by choice and are generally middle class in their orientations; (3) the "ethnic villagers," including some second- and third-generation Europeans as well as more newly arrived Puerto Ricans, who maintain close kin-

33. See Mary G. Powers, "Socio-Economic Heterogeneity of Urban Residential Areas," *Canadian Review of Sociology and Anthropology*, 1, No. 2 (August 1964), 129–137.

34. H. Laurence Ross, "Uptown and Downtown: A Study of Middle Class Residential Areas," *American Sociological Review* (April 1965), pp. 255–259; quotation from p. 256.

35. William F. Whyte, *Street-Corner Society: The Social Structure of an Italian Slum*, rev. ed. (Chicago: The University of Chicago Press, 1955), pp. xv–xvi. A more recent study shows how these patterns maintain their continuity as well as undergo change in Chicago's near west side; see Gerald D. Suttles, *The Social Order of the Slum: Ethnicity and Territoriality in the Inner City* (Chicago: The University of Chicago Press, 1968).

ship and in-group ties and have little contact with other people except in their occupational pursuits; (4) the "deprived"; and (5) the "trapped."[36] The latter two have become increasingly predominant in the inner city and are of special concern to us here.

As Gans notes, the "deprived" and the "trapped" are distinguished from the other groups in that they lack residential choice. They live in the inner city by necessity, whether they want to or not. The "deprived" population includes

the very poor; the emotionally disturbed or otherwise handicapped; broken families; and, most important, the non-white population. These urban dwellers must take the dilapidated housing and blighted neighborhoods to which the housing market relegates them, although among them are some for whom the slum is a hiding place, or a temporary stop-over to save money for a house in the outer city or the suburbs.

The "trapped" are the people who stay behind when a neighborhood is invaded by non-residential land uses or low-status immigrants, because they cannot afford to move, or are otherwise bound to their present location.[37]

The "deprived" and "trapped" who make up so much of the inner city's population today are different in many ways from the "ethnic villagers" who predominated two or three generations ago and who can still be found in lesser numbers today. Undoubtedly the most significant difference is that they find it so much harder to move out. For those who are black, problems of poverty are vastly compounded by problems of racial discrimination. Even the stable working-class blacks are caught in the inner-city trap. The very fact that they have achieved some success in education and jobs may make them more rebellious: studies of the urban riots that occurred during the late sixties have suggested that it was not the newcomers

to the ghettos but second- and third-generation slum dwellers who showed the most despair and participated most actively in the destruction.[38]

Hall's picture of the black areas in New York City conveys some of the reality of what it means to be "trapped"—almost literally—in the deteriorated sections of a modern metropolitan center:

The Negro population of New York records a lower average income, a smaller percentage of owner-occupancy, a higher degree of overcrowding, and a higher tendency to occupy old buildings than the population at large. In Harlem the red brick houses, built mostly to accommodate white middle-class citizens who left after 1890, have become one of the most concentrated areas of Negro population on the North American continent. Between 110th Street on the south and 155th Street on the north, between 8th avenue on the west and the East and Harlem rivers to the east, live some quarter-million Negroes. Here are found all the signs of extreme poverty and physical degradation: the pawnbroker's shops, the horrifying advertisements for rodent and pest exterminators in every druggist's window, the aimless unemployed teen-agers on the street corners. And, since 1940, the position of the Negroes has relatively deteriorated. New waves of Negroes and Puerto Ricans have arrived much more quickly than the city could renew the housing stock. Urban renewal, initiated under the 1949 Housing Act, has been carried out through private redevelopers on a commercial basis. In many cases this has exacerbated the problem: between 1950 and 1957, fully half the residents of demolished dwelling units in the city were Negro, while only 5 per cent of new construction was taken up by non-whites. . . .

The Negroes thus find themselves under almost impossible pressure. The white areas are closed to them, and give way slowly and reluctantly if at all. Any dispersion is apt to be into the immediately neighbouring blocks, which rapidly lose their white populations.[39]

Urban renewal programs, representing a massive outpouring of planning and capital, provide an excellent illustration of the way in which the urban planner, despite his technical neutrality, has been primarily an agent of the middle and upper classes. Most renewal programs to date have almost literally traded poor people for wealthy ones in the central city. A distinguished professor of urban planning describes the "economics" of slum clearance:

---

36. Gans, *op. cit.*, p. 309. The second type could also include hippies and others who reject middle-class orientations and live in the slums by choice.

37. *Ibid.*, pp. 309–310.

38. *Report of the National Advisory Commission on Civil Disorders*, (New York: Bantam Books, 1968), pp. 110–111. See also Nathan S. Caplan and Jeffrey M. Paige, "A Study of Ghetto Rioters," *Scientific American*, 219 (August 1968), 15–21.

39. Hall, *op. cit.*, pp. 193–194.

A major goal of most urban renewal projects has been that of providing decent housing for low-income families. More often than not, however, the residential units that replace the urban slum are either too expensive for a poor family to afford or not much more livable than the housing they were forced to abandon. The families who live in the public housing project shown above, for instance, have simply been transplanted from a horizontal slum to its high-rise equivalent of concrete and wire gratings. The attractive town houses pictured at left were also built as part of an urban renewal program, but their rents are prohibitively high for the people who once lived in this location. Overall, slum-clearance programs in our major cities have been of much greater benefit to members of the middle and upper classes than to the urban poor.

[A city] may acquire a slum area under eminent domain, clear it of its buildings and sell it to a developer. No one today can afford to build for the poor without subsidy. On expensive central land, it is nearly impossible to build at all except for the rich, and even that must be done at high density by means of apartment towers. On central land, the city can be quite certain that it is exchanging the poor slum dwellers for wealthy apartment dwellers. The cost of this operation to the city is one third of the difference between what it paid for the area to its previous owners and what the developer pays the city for it. The federal government pays the other two thirds. The profits to the city will be increased tax revenue resulting from newer and more expensive property plus the savings in city services. This is likely to prove profitable to the municipal corporation. For instance, one large recent project cleared an area where the average income of families was $234 per month and built there apartments with an average rent of $200 per month. Only families with a monthly income of $1000 or more would normally pay such rents.[40]

The poor receive little or no benefit from this kind of planning. In fact, the housing supply for their income level is usually decreased rather than increased by such planning, thus further exacerbating the problem in other slum areas. It is not surprising that such programs have come under attack by increasingly vocal voluntary associations. It remains to be seen whether the new approach represented by the federal government's Model Cities Program can produce the planning that is needed and apparently desired.

The growing crisis of the cities. The black ghettos of the modern metropolis are the areas in which a heavy density of population seems to contribute most directly to personal and social disorganization. Heterogeneity is also a contributing factor, insofar as blacks with differing backgrounds and values have all been forced together in the central city. But as Gans points out, these conditions are a consequence of such handicaps as racial discrimination and low income, not an inevitable result of urbanism itself. Lack of residential choice forces the deprived "to live amid neighbors not of their own choosing, with ways of life different and even contradictory to their own. If familial defenses against the neighborhood climate are weak, as is the case among broken families and downward

mobile people, parents may lose their children to the culture of 'the street.'"[41]

Urbanism, as we have seen, does not necessarily breed alienation and discontent. The crisis of today's central city has deep-seated roots in the past. It seems to be less a product of "size, density, and heterogeneity" than it is of the passive or overt opposition of a predominantly white, middle-class society to the integration of its black population. The lack of structural relationships between the slums and the rest of the city now makes it unlikely that the slum dweller will learn the norms and roles that could make such integration possible.

Thus far, at least, education and occupation have worked more to perpetuate differences than to overcome them. In fact, despite the thrust of the civil rights movement and government efforts to combat poverty, the gap between the residents of the inner and outer city seems to be growing, not shrinking. A 1966 report of the Bureau of the Census showed, for example, that while 28 percent of all blacks twenty-five years old and older had completed at least four years of high school, some 52 percent of whites in the same age group had done so—an increase of 10 percent for whites since 1960, compared to an increase of 8 percent for blacks. A similar trend prevails with regard to family incomes.[42] These patterns, with their consequences for socialization and stratification, led the Kerner Commis-

---

40. William Alonso, "Cities and City Planners," in *Taming Megalopolis*, ed. H. W. Eldridge (New York: Doubleday & Company, Inc., 1967), pp. 580–596; quotation from pp. 589–590. For a detailed account of the housing problem see Lawrence M. Friedman, *Government and Slum Housing* (Chicago: Rand McNally & Company, 1968).

41. Gans, *op. cit.*, p. 311. For a challenging analysis of the effects of this life on Negro family structure see Lee Rainwater and William K. Yancey, eds., *The Moynihan Report and the Politics of Controversy* (Cambridge, Mass.: The M.I.T. Press, 1967). See also Michael Harrington, *The Other America* (New York: The Macmillan Company, 1962). Harrington's critical essay actually became the impetus for public concern about the deprived and the trapped in the early 1960's. This reveals how effectively sociological data can be used by a social critic to "create" a social problem, for one way to define a social problem is to say that it exists only when it is consciously recognized as such by the group or society within which it exists.

42. For a detailed discussion on the differential effect of education in metropolitan areas, see James B. Conant, *Slums and Suburbs* (New York: McGraw-Hill Book Company, 1961). For further evidence on the extent of housing segregation throughout the United States, see Karl E. and Alma F. Taeuber, *Negroes in Cities: Residential Segregation and Neighborhood Change* (Chicago: Aldine Publishing Company, 1965).

In a few more years, lacking effective public action, this is how [our] cities will likely look:

Central business districts in the heart of the city, surrounded by mixed areas of accelerating deterioration, will be partially protected by large numbers of people shopping or working in commercial buildings during daytime hours, plus a substantial police presence, and will be largely deserted except for police patrols during nighttime hours.

High-rise apartment buildings and residential compounds protected by private guards and security devices will be fortified cells for upper-middle and high-income populations living at prime locations in the city.

Suburban neighborhoods, geographically far removed from the central city, will be protected mainly by economic homogeneity and by distance from population groups with the highest propensities to commit crimes.

Lacking a sharp change in federal and state policies, ownership of guns will be almost universal in the suburbs, homes will be fortified by an array of devices from window grills to electronic surveillance equipment. . . .

High-speed, patrolled expressways will be sanitized corridors connecting safe areas, and private automobiles, taxicabs, and commercial vehicles will be routinely equipped with unbreakable glass, light armor, and other security features. . . .

Streets and residential neighborhoods in the central city will be unsafe in differing degrees, and the ghetto slum neighborhoods will be places of terror with widespread crime, perhaps entirely out of police control during night-time hours. Armed guards will protect all public facilities such as schools, libraries, and playgrounds in these areas.

Between the unsafe, deteriorating central city on the one hand and the network of safe, prosperous areas and sanitized corridors on the other, there will be, not unnaturally, intensifying hatred and deepening division. Violence will increase further, and the defensive response of the affluent will become still more elaborate.

Individually and to a considerable extent unintentionally, we are closing ourselves into fortresses when collectively we should be building the great, open, humane city-societies of which we are capable.

Final Report of the National Commission on the Causes and Prevention of Violence

All facts and figures about particular cities and suburbs have only a passing relevance to the people who happen to be temporarily living there. Americans are a moving people. (Within New York City itself more than half the population has not lived at its present place of residence for longer than five years.) The "urban population" and the "suburban population" are not fixed and exclusive entities. When we resoundingly declare that "we must do something for the people of our cities," we tend to forget that, by the time any program is put into operation, a lot of *these* people are not going to be living in *this* city—or any other, probably.

If anything is certain about the direction in which American society is moving, it is this: more and more people are going to be living in suburbs. . . . This trend has existed for over a century—disguised, to be sure, by successive annexations of suburbs by the city government—and it is as powerful as ever today. . . .

I find it as difficult as the next man to cope with New York City today. But intolerable? No. One simply has to keep reminding oneself that the fruits of social change—even of social progress—are always bitter-sweet. . . .

I think that things will get worse before they get better—more and more poor people are migrating to our big cities, and there is no way by which an increase in urban discomfort and urban turbulence can be avoided. But I do think that, eventually, things will get better. For our new urban poor are 100 per cent American, and the desire for suburban home and late-model automobile is bred into their bones. They will abandon the city for the suburbs as soon as it is financially possible for them to do so. If our city governments could provide jobs for these people, it would be sooner rather than later. But our urban poor will doubtless survive the economic mismanagement of our cities. They will make it on their own—to the suburbs: what is now a trickle of Negroes and Puerto Ricans will become a stream and then a flood. By the time some of the fancier new programs for "rehabilitating" the "local community" of Bedford-Stuyvesant begin to have an appreciable effect, many of the people who constitute this "community" will have been largely dispersed and the area itself will be—who can say what it will then be? At that point, we shall be living in a very different world, and coping with some very different "urban crisis."

Irving Kristol
"It's Not a Bad Crisis To Live In"

METHODOLOGY **SAMPLING**

Preliminary steps in most social research are defining the particular population to be studied and then selecting a sample of its members for actual observation. A *population* may include all members of a society (or even all mankind), but in most research it is considerably more specific, e.g., the residents of "Springdale" or Chicago, the nonwhite population of New York City, middle-class and working-class families in Cleveland, married couples in New Haven. The population to be studied is seldom so small, however, that the researcher can observe every member. Rather, he must select a representative *sample* of the population and use it in making inferences about the whole.

A sample is said to be *representative* (or *unbiased*) if it accurately reflects the characteristics of the entire population, or at least those characteristics that may be relevant to the research problem. For example, if the population being studied is 55 percent male and 45 percent female, the sample should include males and females in these proportions. The same is true for any population characteristic that may have some influence on research results (e.g., age, income level, level of educational attainment, racial or ethnic background). Although the distribution of relevant characteristics is not always known, the composition of a properly designed sample will be likely to resemble closely that of the whole population.

In sociology as in other kinds of scientific research, samples are drawn from populations according to carefully specified procedures based on probability theory. In selecting particular cases for study, the researcher uses a *sampling design* that exactly specifies the method for choosing cases that will yield an unbiased estimate of how a given variable is distributed in the population as a whole. An estimate is judged to be *unbiased* if repeated samples produce almost identical results; this indicates that similar results would probably be obtained by studying the entire population. Even if a researcher uses only one sample in a given study, the use of a standard sampling design creates a high probability that his estimates will closely approximate population values. His sample is likely to contain some error, but the error probably will not be large.

At the very least, results obtained by studying carefully selected samples will be consistently more accurate than those obtained from haphazard observations.

Of the various sampling designs used in social research, the one most readily understood is the *simple random design*. The use of this design depends upon the availability of a *sampling frame* which correctly lists all members of the population. Cases are then selected from this list by any procedure that gives each member an equal probability of being included in the final sample. For instance, a name card for every person may be placed in a large drum. The drum is rotated thoroughly before the first name is drawn and also between subsequent drawings. After a name card has been selected, it is usually returned to the drum to equalize probabilities; however, no name can be included in the sample more than once. The drawing of names continues until a sample of the desired size has been selected.

Because a simple random sample of an entire population is seldom practical, various logical substitutes are frequently used. One of these is the *area sample,* in which the units selected are city blocks, census tracts, counties, or other spacial configurations. Those living (or working) in the selected area units then become the subjects for study. If it is impossible to interview or otherwise study all relevant members of these units, further sampling becomes necessary. In a typical *multistage sample*, a random selection of area units is followed by a random selection of households within each unit. Sometimes the precise person to be interviewed in a given household is also determined by random means. Complex designs provide for substituting alternate subjects in place of those "not at home."

Sampling theory and procedures have become highly sophisticated. There are sampling designs to take care of almost any conceivable problem, and elaborate computations may be required to compute estimates of population values from sample data. Essentially, however, all sampling designs are systematic procedures for selecting representative cases for study and for making unbiased estimates about the way in which given variables are distributed in a particular population.

For a discussion of sampling theory as applied to social research, see Bernard Lazerwitz, "Sampling Theory and Procedures," in *Methodology in Social Research,* ed. Hubert M. Blalock, Jr., and Ann B. Blalock (New York: McGraw-Hill Book Company, 1968), pp. 279–328.

sion in 1968 to sound the warning that urban America "is moving toward two societies":

The future of [the] cities, and of their burgeoning Negro populations, is grim. Most new employment opportunities are being created in suburbs and out-lying areas. This trend will continue unless important changes in public policy are made. . . .

To continue present policies is to make permanent the division of our country into two societies; one, largely Negro and poor, located in the central cities; the other, predominantly white and affluent, located in the suburbs and in outlying areas.[43]

PRIMARY AND SECONDARY RELATIONSHIPS

Until recently, most theorists of urban life have tried to explain the growth of cities and their consequences for man largely in terms of dichotomies. All of the typologies we have dis-cussed suggest that in moving from the folk-rural community to the urban community, man has evolved new forms of social interaction. Such theories maintain that these new forms of interaction not only manifest themselves in the world of work but alter other forms of social relations as well. Thus the family, which had stood for so many millennia as the basic unit of social organization, is seen as gradually giving way to other institutions. More important, urban theories have implied that the love, affection, warmth, and loyalty that were presumably part of folk-family life are largely lost in the city. A growing body of empirical evidence has made it necessary to modify these broad assertions.

The urban family. In a study of marriage patterns in New Haven, Connecticut—a large industrial community with all the marks of ethnic and religious diversity that characterize the urban way—Hollingshead found that the

norms restricting marriage by race, religion, ethnicity, and social class were almost as strong for young people in the late 1940's as they had been in their parents' generation. Of those studied, 97 percent of the Jews and 93 percent of the Catholics were married to coreligionists. Hollingshead also noted that "class position and education stratified the three religious pools into areas where an individual was most likely to find a mate."[44] More recent studies show that inter-ethnic and interreligious marriages are becom-ing increasingly common, but they do not sup-port the hypothesis that urbanism eliminates the family as a mechanism of social control, or that the family is without warmth and affection. Rather, they raise important questions about the *meaning* of the changes that have taken place in family structure and function. This issue will be examined in detail in a later chapter on the family.

Sussman's research on family-help patterns raises further questions about the meaning of size, density, and heterogeneity and the pre-sumed loss of familistic values and sentiments. Sussman's research was prompted specifically by the challenge posed by urban theory.[45] Building on earlier research findings that chal-lenged the theory of the isolated nuclear family, Sussman decided to examine kin and family relationships among a sample of middle-class and working-class families in Cleveland, Ohio. He found that practically all the families in the sample were actively engaged in interfamily help patterns. About 70 percent of the working class and 45 percent of the middle class had relatives living in their neighborhood; furthermore, the automobile and other modern means of trans-portation made it possible for relatives not living in the same neighborhood to help each other. Among the most common forms of help given within a month of the research interview were the following: help during illness (reported by 76 percent); financial aid (53 percent); care of children (47 percent); personal or business ad-vice (31 percent); and valuable gifts (22 percent). The middle-class families more than the work-ing-class ones were able to provide advice, valu-able gifts, and baby-sitting care. In view of these findings and similar ones by other re-searchers, as cited in his article, Sussman ques-tioned why sociological theory has given so much emphasis to the decline of primary rela-tionships in the urban milieu. His conclusion is worth noting:

43. *Report of the National Advisory Commission on Civil Disorders, op. cit.,* pp. 21–22.

44. August B. Hollingshead, "Cultural Factors in the Selection of Marriage Mates," *American Sociological Review,* 15 (1950), 619–627; as reprinted in R. Winch, R. McGinnis, and H. Barringer, eds., *Selected Studies in Marriage and the Family* (New York: Holt, Rinehart and Winston, Inc., 1962), p. 489.

45. Marvin B. Sussman, "The Isolated Nuclear Family: Fact or Fiction," *Social Problems,* 6, No. 4 (1959), 333–340.

The urbanite is said to be dependent upon secondary rather than primary group relationships. This view may exist because of a time lag between urban and family theory and research. It may also reflect a cultural lag between what was believed to be a generation ago (or may actually have been) and what exists today. The writings of such men as Durkheim, Simmel, Tönnies, and Mannheim contain early twentieth-century views of family and social life in a growing urban industrial society. Durkheim's research on suicide indicated weaknesses in family structure and the effects of isolation upon the individual. In no way did he indicate the basic features of family structure which did, do today, and will tomorrow sustain its continuity on through time. In other words, a theoretical view tinted towards the ills of social and family life was implanted and subsequent research sought to ferret out the disorganizing features of social life.[46]

Urban man in bureaucracy. With urbanization, American society has become increasingly a complex of bureaucratic organizations; and just as there has been a strong tone of anti-urbanism accompanying urban growth, so also has the word *bureaucrat* come to be a derogatory epithet. This is not surprising when one considers the strong strain of individualism that has for so long pervaded the American value system, but the fact remains that bureaucratic organization is essential to accomplish the tasks of our highly industrialized, urban society.

The statistics on the changing occupational structure of American society during the last sixty years clearly illustrate what is meant by saying that urban man has become bureaucratic man: perhaps as many as 85 percent of all Americans employed today work for some type of bureaucratic organization. Whether urban man's occupation be that of machine toolist or college professor, priest or physician, department store clerk or accountant, corporation president or assistant personnel director, a major facet of his role is that it is defined to some extent by bureaucratic rules and regulations. In addition, urban man must spend a good portion of his nonworking hours interacting with others in bureaucratic roles as he attempts to take care of his personal and family affairs. These are the patterns giving rise to the fear that urban man may become a mere cog in the elaborate machinery he has set up to achieve his complex goals.

Impersonality and formality have traditionally been considered the hallmarks of bureaucracy. Indeed, in analyzing bureaucracy as a distinct form of social organization, Max Weber theorized that bureaucratic efficiency was directly dependent on the depersonalization of interaction within the organization. However, as we noted in our earlier discussion of bureaucratic organization (pages 70–78), there are dynamic forces at work within bureaucracies that Weber did not take into account. Just as research on the city and on residential patterns has failed to support the urbanism thesis of Louis Wirth, so studies of actual bureaucracies have failed to show that primary-group relationships disappear in bureaucratic organizations or that such relationships are inimical to bureaucratic efficiency.[47] Indeed, Blau's analysis of the operation of a state employment agency (page 76) showed that one condition *necessary* to the efficient operation of the agency was the establishment of informal work groups that commanded the allegiance of their members.

Although the problems associated with bureaucracies are real, bureaucratic organization is nonetheless one of our most important social inventions, enabling man to achieve complex goals that would otherwise be out of reach. The available evidence suggests, furthermore, that the danger of man's sacrificing his individuality to bureaucratic efficiency has been exaggerated. Patterns of primary relations learned through socialization in the family and peer groups are carried by urbanites into their job situations. These tend to modify in some degree the formal structure of the job environment, but without necessarily endangering its goal achievement. However rigid and impersonal a bureaucracy may be in theory, individuals can find ways to modify the structure so that it provides for the satisfaction of their basic psychological needs.

The voluntary association in urban life. The role of the voluntary association in community life has been the subject of scholarly discussion for many years. As early as 1835 the French observer Alexis de Tocqueville noted that one of the most striking features of Ameri-

---

46. *Ibid.*, p. 339.
47. For an extensive discussion of this and related problems of bureaucracy, see Robert K. Merton *et al.*, eds., *Reader in Bureaucracy*, rev. ed. (New York: The Free Press, 1965), and Peter M. Blau and W. Richard Scott, *Formal Organizations* (San Francisco: Chandler Publishing Co., 1962).

Most urban sociologists agree that the story of "life in the big city" is not completely one of alienation and impersonalization. People can—and do—have fun in a large metropolitan area, and there is often a significant amount of primary and secondary interaction. Children usually make use of whatever is available to them—such as an open fire hydrant on a hot summer day—while older urban dwellers take advantage of the city's many facilities for culture and amusement. Some may take their families on an outing to the zoo; others join their cronies for a chess game in the park.

can society was the manner in which people at the local level banded together to form voluntary associations to meet specific needs or solve community problems. Although American life has altered greatly since de Tocqueville wrote, we are still very much a nation of joiners. Arnold Rose has estimated that in the United States today there are at least 100,000 voluntary associations to meet specific needs.[48] A 1963 survey of Prince George's County, Maryland (an area of middle-class commuters bordering the nation's capital) found some 1800 voluntary associations serving a population of less than 400,000 people.[49]

Voluntary associations may be primarily community-service oriented, like the Rotary and the Lions Club; civic-political, like the NAACP and the League of Women Voters; occupational, like the Chamber of Commerce; or socioreligious, like many of the Protestant churches, especially the more fundamentalist ones. That voluntary associations are no longer the exclusive preserve of the white middle class, if indeed they ever were, is evidenced by the rise of a wide range of black associations in recent years. These range in style and purpose from local groups protecting their own interests, such as Chicago's Woodlawn Association and Poor Peoples' Coalition, to national associations like the Southern Christian Leadership Conference founded by the late Martin Luther King, Jr., the Student Non-Violent Coordinating Committee, the Black Muslims, and the Black Panthers. More and more voluntary associations are forming on college campuses, ranging in philosophy from the Students for a Democratic Society to its right-wing counterpart, the Young Americans for Freedom.

The struggle for autonomy and for the right to participate in decisions affecting their own lives has also led to the rise of associations for policemen, public school teachers (The American Federation of Teachers) and even clergymen (The National Priests Association). Perhaps one of the main reasons for the turmoil of urban life is the discovery by masses of previously unorganized people that they can help control the course of their own lives through free organizations. As Daniel Bell has suggested in a recent essay:

It is the extended network of voluntary associations which has been the source of so much independent initiative, in politics and social life, in the United States. One might argue that with our increasing urbanization such civic consciousness would diminish and that in this decline one could find the source of the dis-orientation that individuals feel in the large, urban environment. And yet I would argue to the contrary. In American life today there is probably more voluntary association, more local community and suburban newspapers and more participation in a variety of organizations, professional, hobby and civic, than at any previous period in American history.[50]

Recent surveys show that a majority of people in American society are members of at least one voluntary association. Data gathered in 1953 by Wright and Hyman, for example, showed that the more urban the area studied, the more likely were American adults to belong to a voluntary association. In fact, in metropolitan areas 25 percent of the adults belonged to at least two such organizations, as compared with only 9 percent of the adults in rural areas.[51] A partial explanation for this pattern may be that voluntary associations provide the means by which an urbanite can exert initiative in shaping community life while also satisfying his personal need for social attachments.

Blanket comparisons can be somewhat misleading, however. In a more detailed study, Axelrod found that although a majority of the population of the Detroit metropolitan area were members of at least one formal group, less than half of this majority considered themselves active members. Furthermore, formal group membership within this community varied according to family income, education, and occupation (Table 9.5). In contrast, *informal* group association was found to be almost universal, with a majority of those surveyed—regardless of income or education—reporting relatives as the people they associated with most frequently. Axelrod concluded his study with the following comment:

---

48. Arnold M. Rose, *The Power Structure* (New York: Oxford University Press, 1967), p. 218.

49. H. J. Ehrlich and W. V. D'Antonio, "Voluntary Association Leaders in a Suburban County," unpublished study.

50. Daniel Bell, "Toward a Communal Society," *Life*, May 12, 1967.

51. Charles R. Wright and Herbert H. Hyman, "Voluntary Association Memberships of American Adults: Evidence from National Sample Surveys," *American Sociological Review*, 23 (June 1958), 290, Table 4.

Formally organized associations have unquestionably an important role in the urban community. The ultimate logic of urban life might conceivably still be towards a universal and intensive membership in such groups. However, in the present scene their direct influence does not touch a large part of the population.[52]

Research on voluntary associations has led to the hypothesis that those in the lower classes and those belonging to minority groups are less likely to be "joiners" than are those who enjoy a more privileged position in American society. A recent study of voluntary-association membership in a southwestern metropolis showed the possible significance of such factors. Mexican-Americans reported lower rates of membership in both church-related and nonchurch-related associations than did white non-Mexican-Americans. And membership for both Anglo- and Mexican-Americans tended to be positively correlated with economic position; that is, the higher the economic position, the greater the probability of membership in at least one voluntary association, with the correlation consistently stronger for Anglos.[53]

The question of black participation in voluntary associations has been summarized in a recent research article which suggests that lower-class blacks may be *more*, rather than less, active than middle-class whites in voluntary associations, perhaps as an attempt to compensate for their rejection by white society.[54] Data from the study, made in a city of 140,000 persons, showed that 72 percent of the blacks interviewed belonged to at least one nonchurch or labor-union related voluntary association. For whatever reasons, the black has indeed become a joiner. Thus, social class does not necessarily correlate negatively with membership in voluntary associations.

It seems clear that the voluntary association has had a considerable impact on urban life, but we are far from understanding just what this impact has been. Evidence accumulated by Axelrod and others casts doubt on the assertion

TABLE 9.5. **EXTENT OF PARTICIPATION IN FORMAL GROUPS RELATED TO FAMILY INCOME, EDUCATION, AND OCCUPATION (BASED ON A DETROIT SAMPLE, 1952)**

	PERCENT WHO WERE MEMBERS	PERCENT WHO WERE ACTIVE MEMBERS
Family Income		
Under $3000	42	8
$3000–3999	66	9
$4000–4999	67	14
$5000–5999	62	12
$6000–6999	65	12
Over $7000	81	21
Education		
0–6 years	52	2
7–8 years	60	9
9–12 years	63	14
Some college	78	19
Occupation of Family Head		
Service worker or laborer	50	19
Operative	40	8
Craftsman, foreman, etc.	40	11
Clerical, sales, etc.	62	21
Professional, manager, proprietor, etc.	61	11

SOURCE: Morris Axelrod, "Urban Structure and Social Participation," *American Sociological Review*, 21, No. 1 (February 1956), 15.

that the voluntary association has taken the place of primary groups in urban society. Rather, it seems to supplement them and to provide yet another setting in which both formal and informal interaction can take place.

URBAN MAN IN THE DEVELOPING COUNTRIES

Urbanization in the developing countries of Asia, Africa, and Latin America is proceeding much more rapidly than it did in the industrialized nations, and it is impelled less by economic development than by rapid population growth. In general, it represents a very uneven and unstable kind of social and cultural change. The lack of commerce and industry to support the

---

52. Morris Axelrod, "Urban Structure and Social Participation," *American Sociological Review*, 21, No. 1 (February 1956), 13–18.

53. J. F. Barbosa-Dasilva, "Participation of Mexican-Americans in Voluntary Associations," *Research Reports in the Social Sciences*, 2 (Spring 1968), 33–43.

54. Mario Renzi, "Negroes and Voluntary Associations: An Open Question," in *ibid.*, 63–71.

population and the retention of traditional systems of stratification mean that most people in the cities are condemned to poverty, with little hope of improving their lot. The problems associated with inner-city slums in the United States extend throughout most of the urban areas in these countries, often in exaggerated form.[55]

In most cities of the developing world physical facilities such as housing, sanitation, and transportation are wholly inadequate to serve the needs of a large population. In one Indian city of over two million people, for example, there are only twenty thousand motor vehicles—less than one for every two hundred inhabitants. The new immigrants who crowd to the cities have little control over their environment, either politically or otherwise. They live in squalor, with grossly inferior housing, inadequate diets, and none of the basic facilities we take for granted.

AN INSIDER'S VIEW OF POVERTY

Squalor, of course, is not new to history, nor is it confined to the cities of the developing nations. What *is* new in this pattern of urbanization is that such vast numbers of human beings

---

55. For detailed discussions of urbanism in the developing world, see Gerald Breese, *Urbanization in Newly Developing Countries* (Englewood Cliffs, N.J.: Prentice-Hall, Inc., 1966) and Sylvia Fava, ed., *Urbanism in World Perspective* (New York: Thomas Y. Crowell Company, 1968). Both sources have been helpful in preparing this brief analysis.

In the favelas of Rio, one of Brazil's worst slums, vast numbers of human beings live under conditions barely capable of sustaining life. As one resident has put it, "I was in the favela breathing the smell of excrement mixed with the rotten earth.... I have the impression that I'm a useless object, destined to be forever in a garbage dump."

live under conditions barely capable of sustaining life. The following excerpts from the diary of Carolina Maria de Jesus, a resident of one of Brazil's worst slums, tell more than statistics do. The entries were written in May 1958, but they are no less relevant today:

May 20: . . . At 8:30 that night I was in the favela [slum area] breathing the smell of excrement mixed with the rotten earth. When I am in the city I have the impression that I am in a living room with crystal chandeliers, rugs of velvet, and satin cushions. And when I'm in the favela I have the impression that I'm a useless object, destined to be forever in a garbage dump.

Sometimes families move into the favela with children. In the beginning they are educated, friendly. Days later they use foul language, are mean and quarrelsome. They are diamonds turned to lead. They are transformed from objects that were in the living room to objects banished to the garbage dump.

For me the world instead of evolving is turning primitive. Those who don't know hunger will say: "Whoever wrote this is crazy." But who has gone hungry can say:

"Well, Dona Carolina. The basic necessities must be within reach of everyone."

How horrible it is to see a child eat and ask: "Is there more?" This word "more" keeps ringing in the mother's head as she looks in the pot and doesn't have any more.

May 21: I spent a horrible night. I dreamt I lived in a decent house that had a bathroom, kitchen, pantry, and even a maid's room. I was going to celebrate the birthday of my daughter Vera Eunice. I went and bought some small pots that I had wanted for a long time. Because I was able to buy. I sat at the table to eat. The tablecloth was white as a lily. I ate a steak, bread and butter, fried potatoes, and a salad. When I reached for another steak I woke up. What bitter reality! I don't live in the city. I live in the favela. In the mud on the banks of the Tiete River. . . .

Yesterday I ate that macaroni from the garbage with fear of death, because in 1953 I sold scrap over there in Zinho. There was a pretty black boy. He also went to sell scrap in Zinho. He was young and said that those who should look for paper were the old.

One day I was collecting scrap when I stopped at Bom Jardim Avenue. Someone had thrown meat into the garbage, and he was picking out the pieces. He told me:

"Take some, Carolina. It's still fit to eat."

He gave me some, and so as not to hurt his feelings, I accepted. I tried to convince him not to eat the meat, or the hard bread gnawed by the rats. He told me no, because it was two days since he had eaten. He made a fire and roasted the meat. His hunger was so great that he couldn't wait for the meat to cook. He heated it and ate. So as not to remember that scene, I left thinking: I'm going to pretend I wasn't there. This can't be real in a rich country like mine. I was disgusted with that Social Service that had been created to readjust the maladjusted, but took no notice of we marginal people. I sold the scrap at Zinho and returned to Sao Paulo's back yard, the favela.

The next day I found that little black boy dead. His toes were spread apart. The space must have been eight inches between them. He had blown up as if made out of rubber. His toes looked like a fan. He had no documents. He was buried like any other "Joe." Nobody tried to find out his name. The marginal people don't have names.[56]

PATTERNS OF CHANGE

Although industrialization is proceeding slowly in the developing nations, the cities are growing rapidly, and the ensuing misery is building despair, frustration, and perhaps the seeds of revolution. In Latin America alone, seven countries report urban areas of over one million people, and in Argentina some 52 percent of the total population lives in cities of 100,000 or more. For Latin America as a whole, the figure reaches 27 percent. What are the consequences of such a disorganized, conflict-ridden situation?

Certain key cities of the developing world, usually the capitals, have somewhat unique characteristics. The capital is typically the main point of contact with the outside world, and thus it continually increases its importance as the center of power. It further acts as a special agent for implementing and diffusing change in the society, becoming in the process the point of concentration for the nation's talent and manpower.[57] This tendency of the prime city to build upon and expand the functions it had during

---

56. *Child of the Dark: The Diary of Carolina Maria de Jesus,* trans. David St. Clair (New York: Signet Books, 1962), pp. 38–41.

57. See Breese, *op. cit.,* Chapter 2.

colonial days has led to severe centralization and bureaucratization, and in many ways it has worked against the development of the country as a whole. This is especially evident in the way national funds for investment are allocated. Unfortunately, the concentration of wealth and power in one city also tends to make it even more attractive to the migrant seeking escape from rural poverty. From a distance, the prime city seems full of special promise, but in fact it is unprepared to offer even marginal support to most of its flood of new residents.

FAMILY TIES AND VOLUNTARY ASSOCIATIONS

Studies of urban life in the developing nations suggest that family and kinship ties continue to be vitally important to the new urbanites, just as they are to the residents of American cities. On the basis of her study of the West African cities of Brazzaville, Dakar, Lagos, Leopoldville, and Stanleyville, for example, Joan Aldous has concluded that "the extended family is indeed functional. Besides filling recreational, religious, legal or economic needs of urbanites it substitutes for a nonexistent public social welfare program. Kinsmen provide for the elderly and support the sick, the jobless and the destitute. . . ."[58]

There is also evidence that urbanization has led to the growth of voluntary associations in the developing countries. Kenneth Little, for example, reports the existence of a wide variety of voluntary associations in the urbanized areas of West Africa.[59] Some are traditional, serving mainly tribal or kin needs and catering largely to the poor and unskilled, the unlettered. Some are mixtures of traditional and modern organization and aims, designed for mutual aid and benefit and for status and class-oriented activity related to occupations; they are not unlike the guilds of medieval Europe. The modern associations, particularly those that are primarily social, are modeled closely on European lines.

Little found not only special associations for men and for women but also some that were mixed. These, he pointed out, provided a means whereby males and females could meet socially under the new conditions of urban life. Many of the associations also helped new members adjust to the ethos of the city, thus serving as substitutes for traditional agencies of socialization and social control.

58. Joan Aldous, "Urbanization, the Extended Family, and Kinship Ties in West Africa," in Fava, *op. cit.*, pp. 297–305.
59. Kenneth Little, "The Role of Voluntary Associations in West African Urbanization," in *The Substance of Sociology*, ed. Ephraim H. Mizruchi (New York: Appleton-Century-Crofts, 1967), pp. 362–378.

SUMMARY

In this chapter we have traced briefly the historical development of urban life and some of the efforts to explain the impact of urbanization on society and the individual. In the cities of antiquity, primary relations remained predominant, although there were the beginnings of bureaucratic organization. The preindustrial city in Europe was a model of ordered relations built on status groups and caste-like structures. This type of city was gradually replaced in the West by the industrial city; in Latin America and other developing areas of the world, the preindustrial pattern is still the predominant one.

In the development of the industrial cities of the United States, masses of migrants first established more-or-less exclusive residential areas where they managed to maintain their traditional ways of life as best they could. But gradually work patterns, transportation, and such other ecological factors as size, density, and heterogeneity threw these people into extensive contact with "strangers." As a result, impersonal and formal relations (summed up in such terms as *Gesellschaft* and *organic solidarity*) became increasingly the order of the day. People who for one reason or another inhabited transient areas of the city were most directly challenged by anonymity.

The research data available suggest, however, that the anonymity and impersonality of city life have been exaggerated. Apparently the city offers a continuum of social relations to urban man: isolation and anonymity (the dweller in furnished rooms or the transient in the favela); a mixture of formal and informal relationships (the corporation, the assembly line); the continued warmth of the homogeneous neighborhood (Little Italy, Chinatown, the upper-middle-class suburb). Despite the increasing bureaucratization of urban life, primary-group relationships are still of central importance to most individuals.

Historically, the major distinctions in pre-industrial cities were between the town dwellers and those who lived outside the walls. With industrialization, the distinction changed to that between the traditional folk society and the new life patterns of urban man, wherever his actual residence. In the coming era of the megalopolis, the distinction may be between those who live within a megalopolis and those decreasing few who are untouched by its predominant pattern,

either physically or psychically. The anomaly is that such isolates will as likely be found within the inner-city slums as in isolated rural areas.

Although the process of urbanization, now nearing completion in the developed societies, has often been loudly decried, most people have accepted the urban way as the most satisfactory means of achieving their goals. Whatever the threat to traditional values, norms, customs, and systems of social control, the patterns of social organization offered by urban life have won the day over those of rural folk-society. And despite tremendous obstacles posed by population growth and the struggle for change, they seem to be winning the day also in the developing areas of the world.

Urban life with its diversity of groups—often with competing goals, values, norms, and means of social control—makes highly probable the existence of tension and conflict, both at the personal and group level. Thus, one of the major concomitants of urbanization becomes the necessity of learning to live with loose structural arrangements, and of knowing when and how to rely on formal and informal patterns of behavior.

PART IV

SIGNIFICANT SOCIETAL CONCERNS

10
Intergroup Relations

Due to a variety of social and historical circumstances such as wars, migrations, and changes in political boundaries, the populations of most larger societies are composed of many kinds of people. In these societies, distinct racial and subcultural divisions develop complex patterns of intergroup relations, which change or stabilize over time. Intergroup relations can range all the way from total rejection or complete dominance of one group by another to complete mutual acceptance.

The present chapter will analyze the origins and nature of the more significant of these relations. An attempt will be made to understand their patterns of development and the social mechanics of their maintenance, particularly in American society. We will examine the bases for distinguishing various categories commonly called "minority groups," and we will review the historical experience of several major minorities in American society. Against this background, the full range of patterns of intergroup relations that can characterize minorities and dominant segments of society will be summarized. Finally, the nature of prejudice, both as a psychological and as a cultural phenomenon, will be examined. This concept is particularly important for understanding the perpetuation of patterns of inequality in intergroup relations.

MINORITY GROUPS

The analysis of intergroup relations begins with the concept *minority group*. It should be noted at the outset that the term *group* as used in this context departs from our earlier definition of a group as a number of individuals who interact on a regular basis according to some pattern of social organization. Actually, most minority segments of our population, such as blacks, Puerto Ricans, Orientals, and Mexican Americans, could be more accurately classified as social categories (page 38). But the term *minority group* has long been used by sociologists and others to designate certain subdivisions of a population that occupy lower levels in a system of social ranking, and though it contradicts our technical definition of *group*, we will follow this traditional usage in the present chapter.

THE ATTRIBUTES OF MINORITY GROUPS

There is no simple way to describe the basis Americans use in designating—and treating—a segment of the population as a minority group. Each part of the population now thought of as a minority group has shared a unique set of historical experiences, giving it a somewhat distinctive place in the American social structure. Each has its own general position in our system of social ranking; each faces a somewhat distinct situation with respect to prejudice and discrimination; and each has a peculiar place in the political and economic system of the country.

There are many kinds of minority groups—almost any conceivable trait or characteristic can be used as a basis for distinguishing one category of persons from the remainder of the population and ascribing a low rank to it. In the United States such criteria as race, religion, language, national origin, political affiliation, and even modes of dress are all regularly used as bases for identifying one minority group or another. There is little in the way of systematic theory to explain how any given attribute becomes a criterion, but at least three major attributes seem to characterize minority groups.

Relative size. Usually a minority group is considerably smaller than the dominant segment of the society. This simple numerical fact has significant implications for the people in question because it tends to place them at a disadvantage in both political and economic activities. In American society the largest minority group (blacks) constitutes only 12 percent of the population at the present time. Other minority groups make up smaller fractions of our total population. (See Figure 10.1, page 314.)

On the other hand, numerical inferiority is not always a clear indicator of minority status. For example, in the Union of South Africa only about 20 percent of the people are white. The remaining 80 percent of the population is made up of several categories of nonwhites. But the numerically inferior whites are dominant both politically and economically. By no stretch of the imagination could they be considered a minority group as sociologists use the term. (See photo essay pages 238–239.)

Dominance. A major attribute of minority position is that of being dominated in some way

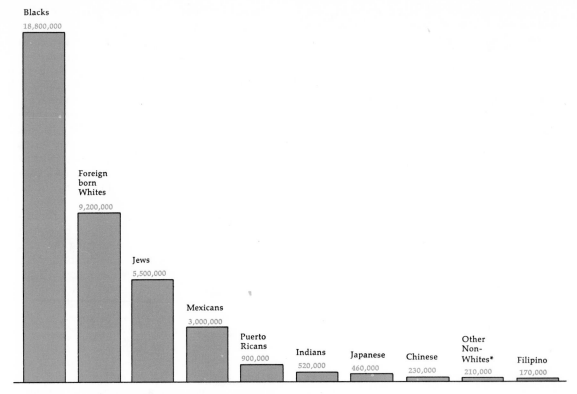

*Includes Asiatic Indians, Koreans, Polynesians, Indonesians
SOURCE: Brewton Berry, *Race and Ethnic Relations*, 3rd ed. (Boston: Houghton Mifflin Company, 1965), p. 40.

FIGURE 10.1. **PRINCIPAL RACIAL AND ETHNIC MINORITIES IN THE UNITED STATES, 1960**

by other segments of the population.[1] The composition of the dominating segment of society varies as one considers each specific minority group. Collectively, for example, blacks have been dominated by whites (including members of other minority groups), and the same is generally true for Indians. Jews and Catholics, on the other hand, are not necessarily dominated by all who are not Jewish or Catholic. Racial factors complicate the pattern; it would be difficult to specify the exact composition of the dominating segments of society for each minority group. In general, however, it can be said that native-born, white, Anglo-Saxon Protestants—the so-called WASPS—have managed to remain dominant over other categories in American society.

The most exaggerated form of dominance is slavery, but there are many other kinds. Peonage and debt-servitude fall just short of slavery in the control that is exercised over the individual. At the other extreme are forms of dominance that seem to permit total political and economic freedom but subtly deny access to education, employment, or advancement. All possible forms of dominance, including slavery, military subjugation, peonage, economic suppression, and various forms of discrimination, have existed at one time or another in American society.

Visibility. Minority groups vary greatly in the degree to which they are "visible" within a society. Religious and cultural practices other than language use are less easily "seen" by the casual observer than skin color or other obvious hereditary physical traits, but use of a "foreign" language creates high visibility. Some sign of

1. James W. Vander Zanden, *American Minority Relations,* 2nd ed. (New York: The Ronald Press Company, 1966), pp. 10–12.

minority identity is essential for the enforcement of unequal treatment. Insofar as a group succeeds in minimizing the differences between itself and the dominant group, it can merge into the larger society and escape treatment as a minority group. This is precisely what has happened with a number of minority groups that were formerly identified in terms of national origins. In earlier years in American society, persons of Italian, Polish, Scandinavian, and other European origins were accorded minority positions because of language and other cultural differences. As these disappeared, such groups merged with the dominant population—though some scholars reject the theory that the merger has been by any means complete.[2]

THE TREATMENT OF MINORITY GROUPS

Minority groups are usually accorded fewer privileges, lower status, less power, and fewer opportunities than other segments of the population. In American society these conditions have been more severe for some minorities than for others. But whatever the situation of a particular minority, at least two consequences of minority position have been felt in greater or lesser degree by all such groups.

Exclusion. Even the most favorably treated minority groups are usually excluded from *some* significant forms of interaction with the majority. These exclusions may range from ostracism that forces a minority to live on an isolated reservation or in a segregated ghetto to more subtle forms such as avoidance by the dominant group of close personal interaction with members of the minority. Such exclusions, whether severe or seemingly inconsequential, identify the member of the minority group, both in his own eyes and in the eyes of others, as a "second-class citizen." Acts of exclusion are an important basis for intergroup hostility.

Categorical treatment. Associated with exclusion is *categorical treatment*.[3] The individual

2. The traditional concept of the United States as a melting pot is challenged in Nathan Glazer and Daniel P. Moynihan, *Beyond the Melting Pot* (Cambridge, Mass: M.I.T. Press, 1963).

3. George E. Simpson and J. Milton Yinger, *Racial and Cultural Minorities*, 3rd ed. (New York: Harper & Row, Inc., 1965), p. 16.

member of a minority group is more or less automatically assigned the qualities presumed to be shared by all the members. Regardless of his personal attributes, he is thought of and treated as "one of them"—a category—and not as an individual. Thus, if he is identified as a member of a low-ranking minority group, even a highly educated professional man may be thought of as having all the traits commonly attributed to that group—including, perhaps, ignorance. Such categorical treatment is obviously inconsistent not only with simple logic but with the accepted American value that every person should be treated on his own merits. Systematic exclusion and categorical treatment of minority-group members obviously complicates the problem of easing intergroup tensions.

RACE AND ETHNICITY

To the ordinary American, whose beliefs and orientations tend to be internalized counterparts of the prevailing culture around him, the question, "What are the races of mankind?" seems to have a patently obvious answer. Within his perspective there are blacks and, of course, whites. There are also Indians and Orientals. Beyond this, his conceptual apparatus gets a little vague.

Equally problematic in this respect is the term *ethnic group*. The layman tends to think along the lines of familiar nationalities—Italians, Russians, Germans, and so forth. But the citizens of a given nation-state may or may not constitute an ethnic group in the sociological sense. For sociologists, an ethnic group is one whose members are bound together by a common culture regardless of their national identity. The boundaries of states shift with the fortunes of war and politics, and people move from country to country; but the bonds of ethnicity prevail over long periods of time.

THE CONCEPT OF RACE

If the layman's approach to classifying the races is vague and inadequate, the scientific approach must be characterized as inconsistent or even self-contradictory. Responsible scientists, mainly physical anthropologists and geneticists, have proposed systems of racial classification that provide from three categories to more than thirty.[4] These systems are generally based upon characteristics such as skin color, nose shape, hair texture, eye color, blood type, gene frequency, head measurement, facial structure, lip form, and other morphological or biological criteria.

No matter what scheme scientists may utilize, laymen will probably continue to classify the races and respond to them in ways provided by their own cultures. In the United States we employ what Simpson and Yinger have labeled the "administrative" concept of race as our official system for classification.[5] In large part this system follows our historical usages of racial classifications from the era of slavery and the frontier. Certain "racial" categories have been established by official acts or by popular practice, and if a person is classified in one of these categories, it will have numerous effects on his life activities. For example, prior to 1960 the Bureau of the Census usually recorded any person who had traceable black ancestry as a "Negro," though he might be more Caucasian in his physical appearance than many of his "white" neighbors. Similarly, a person who was regarded in his community as an "Indian" was so classified in the official records.[6]

The administrative concept of race has had exceedingly severe consequences for some groups. In our own society at one time, such a classification literally meant the difference between life as a slave and life as a free citizen. In Hitler's Germany, to be classified as a "non-Aryan" effectively denied the individual access to the normal life of his society. In particular, to be classified in the Nazi era as a member of the "Jewish race" made the individual a candidate for the gas chamber.

---

4. Stanley M. Garn and Carleton S. Coon, "On the Number of Races of Mankind," *American Anthropologist*, 57 (1955), 996–1001.

5. Simpson and Yinger, *op. cit.*, pp. 29–30.

6. For the first time, in the 1960 Census, respondents had an opportunity to classify *themselves* with respect to race. It was thought that this would affect the results, but there was no indication that it did.

In the United States all minority groups have been excluded from some significant forms of interaction with the majority. Jews, for example, have been excluded from numerous occupations, kept out of certain residential areas, and denied access to some hotels and restaurants. Such exclusions identify the member of the minority group as a "second-class citizen" and thus are an important basis for intergroup hostility.

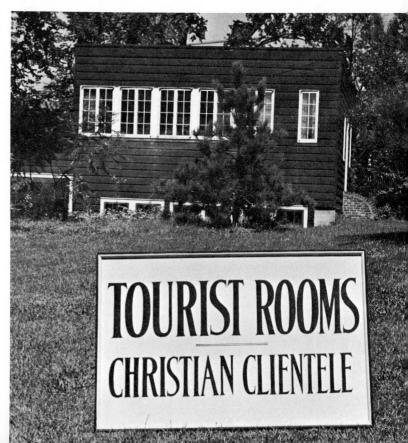

The racial categories employed by laymen have little relationship to the various scientific systems for distinguishing between subgroups of mankind. They are *sociocultural* classifications that have developed historically or that have been invented to enforce domination over oppressed groups. From another point of view, they are part of the technique by which the *status quo* can be maintained. The essential point is that sociocultural definitions of race do not correspond to either scientific systems of classification or other objective criteria. Such definitions are products of those experiences of a society that underlie the development of its entire culture and its intergroup traditions.

THE CONCEPT OF ETHNICITY

As we have already indicated, an ethnic group is one whose members are bound together by common cultural ties. This implies that even though they may be spatially separated, such people have a sense of common identity; they feel a "consciousness of kind," an in-group loyalty and "we-ness." Generally, ethnic groups follow folkways, mores, and customs that distinguish them from others around them. Religion and language often serve as especially integrative focuses of allegiance.

Most modern societies are ethnically heterogeneous. The United States has numerous ethnic groups in its population (Figure 10.1), and many retain identifiable subcultures. The Soviet Union is composed of more than a hundred ethnic groups, many with their own languages, customs, and religions.

In the United States, the position of a given ethnic group in the hierarchy of dominance appears to be governed largely by such factors as its ability to avoid being "visible," the amount of time its members have been present in the population in substantial numbers, and the extent to which they have become "Americanized." In the mid-nineteenth century, such groups as the Irish and the Germans occupied very low positions in the social hierarchy. To-

ward the end of the century, when large numbers of Poles and other eastern Europeans and Italians arrived, these new minorities tended to replace the Irish and Germans in the ranking scale. The immigrant ethnic groups of the nineteenth and early twentieth centuries are now substantially assimilated into American culture, and new groups, such as the Puerto Ricans, are occupying the lower levels of the ethnic stratification system. In the case of the Puerto Ricans, the problem of assimilation is complicated by the factor of mixed racial composition.

THE HISTORY OF AMERICAN MINORITIES

To the majority of its own people, the United States stands for equality of opportunity, treatment, and legal status for all citizens. In its practices, however, the nation falls far short of these stated ideals. While Americans of almost every persuasion endorse the general principles of democracy, they vary sharply in the degree to which they are willing to practice those principles in their relationships with members of minority groups.[7] This is the great "American Dilemma"—the continuing struggle between our ideals of equality for all and the hard realities of prejudice and discrimination toward minority groups.[8] Much change has occurred in some areas of our minority relations, but the hierarchy of dominance still exists, and present trends toward social equality are far from complete.

The system of intergroup relationships prevailing in the United States today was forged over a period of three hundred years. The orientations and values defining these relationships have in large part been handed down to us from earlier generations, like our language and our basic social institutions. This does not justify existing practices, but it helps explain the difficulties we encounter in trying to change them. Therefore, even though majority-minority relations in the American society undergo change from generation to generation, our current structure of intergroup relations needs to be understood in terms of our heritage. In the sections that follow, data will be assembled on the nature of minority groups in the United States at differ-

7. Frank R. Westie, "The American Dilemma: An Empirical Test," *American Sociological Review*, 30, No. 4 (August 1965), 527–538.

8. Gunnar Myrdal, *An American Dilemma: The Negro Problem and American Democracy*, rev. ed. (New York: Harper & Row, Inc., 1962).

ent points in our history, on their relations with the societal majority, and on the social and cultural processes by which these relations have been altered or maintained over time.[9]

BLACKS

In the year 1619, settlers in the new Virginia Colony purchased twenty blacks from a "Dutch man of warre." Thus began the influx of African Negroes into the southern region of colonial America. In the North, the first blacks were brought to the Massachusetts Bay Colony in 1638, just eleven years after the settlement was established.[10] Since these early times, the destiny of the black minority has been inextricably interwoven with that of the society as a whole. American history is black as well as white, although most history books have failed to make this clear.

Many of the blacks who arrived during this early period were technically classified as servants rather than slaves. However, slavery by custom preceded slavery by statute. When the several colonies began to clarify their laws and make clear distinctions between indentured servitude and slavery, the latter became the category reserved for blacks, and the fate of black people in America was sealed for hundreds of years.

The institutionalization of slavery. Meanwhile, the New England slave trade had begun on a regular basis. In 1644 the first slaves were imported directly from Africa (earlier arrivals had come by way of the West Indies).[11] By the end of the seventeenth century, slavery had been given legal status in all of the American colonies. A newly imported black man could be bought in Boston at a price ranging from £30 to £50.

Although there was scattered opposition, slavery became an established institution in colonial America, as it was in most of the world.[12] Even after the African slave trade was outlawed by the United States and the major European powers in the early nineteenth century, the slave population in America continued to grow. In 1800 there were a million slaves in the United States; by 1860 the number had increased to nearly four and a half million.

For economic reasons, the slave population was concentrated primarily in the southern states. It was the vast agricultural land of the South and the major southern crops—cotton, sugar cane, tobacco—that required quantities of cheap, unskilled labor. In the northern states, a relatively small number of slaves served primarily as domestic servants. There were also numerous free blacks who practiced trades and crafts, and a movement for complete emancipation was under way throughout the region by the beginning of the nineteenth century.

In the late eighteenth century, however, a series of technological advances in the British textile industry gave the southern plantation economy a strong boost. By making possible the cheap and efficient production of cloth, the new spinning jenny and the power loom greatly increased the demand for raw cotton. Then, in 1793, the invention of the cotton gin by the American Eli Whitney drastically reduced the cost of separating cotton fiber from the seeds, making cotton the cheapest and most popular fiber in the world. Huge tracts of virgin land were put under cultivation, and the demand for black field hands increased.

From time to time the slaves struck back at their masters in scattered revolts and uprisings, and these outbursts were greatly feared by the white population. The net result was the accumulation of increasingly severe laws that placed total control over slaves in the hands of their owners. An owner could punish his slave as he chose or even put him to death without interference by the law. The slightest indication of a possible revolt brought harsh and brutal suppression.

Although the history of the South records incidents of good and kindly treatment of slaves, the majority were poorly fed, dressed, and housed, even by the rude standards of the day. Whipping and other forms of corporal punishment were common; torture and mutilation were not unknown. Considering that this system of social relationships existed for more than two hundred years, it is little wonder that last-

---

9. Although coverage of racial and ethnic relations in other countries would be desirable if space permitted, we will restrict our coverage to the United States and make only brief reference to situations in other parts of the world.

10. Benjamin Brawley, *A Social History of the American Negro* (New York: The Macmillan Company, 1921), p. 9.

11. Lorenzo J. Greene, *The Negro in Colonial New England* (Port Washington, N.Y.: Kennikat Press, Inc., 1942), pp. 20–21.

12. Brawley, *op. cit.*, p. 12.

The members of an ethnic group are bound together by common cultural ties and have a sense of common identity. They feel an in-group loyalty and are proud of the folkways, mores, and customs that distinguish them from other groups.

ing hostilities toward whites have been passed on as a strong element of contemporary black culture.

The culture of slavery. The institution of slavery developed an elaborate system of rituals to govern relationships between blacks and whites. This system of racial "etiquette" called for the black to exhibit overt and symbolic indications of humility and inferiority in the presence of a white. It required the white to treat the black in the most condescending and patronizing manner possible. Some of these practices continue to exist, especially in the South, as part of the cultural heritage from the days of slavery. Surviving elements of this system are deeply resented by most blacks today.

More than anything else, the system of slavery demanded that the black be defined as biologically, morally, and intellectually inferior.

Elaborate arguments were invented to "prove" that he was subhuman, childlike, animalistic, and generally deserving of enslavement. Religious arguments based upon isolated biblical references were particularly persuasive in justifying his bondage. In many states it was forbidden to teach blacks to read and write.

These cultural definitions of the black made it far easier to deal with him as "property" and to justify this treatment within a moralistic-legalistic framework. It was so effective that even today our culture is replete with epithets, stereotypes, racial jokes, and muddled arguments concerning the alleged "natural inferiority" of blacks that were vital ideological underpinnings of the system of slavery.

Racial mixing. Racial mixing began almost as soon as blacks arrived in the colonies. Most common were biological unions between white masters and slave women, but in the early period there were a number of instances of white indentured women marrying blacks in similar servitude and of free white women marrying slaves. The white community disapproved of all such marriages in the strongest possible terms. Eventually, an elaborate legal apparatus was developed (particularly in the South) in an attempt to prevent interracial marriage.

There was also much illicit intercourse between Negroes and whites. Such relationships were not confined to any particular class; both upper- and lower-class white males enjoyed the favors of slave women. Free mulattoes and whites frequently mixed, and there was sexual promiscuity between white women and male slaves. Several notorious divorce cases in early New England involved such contacts.[13]

The end result of this interbreeding is that today there are but few racially "pure" blacks in the United States. This situation poses some curious problems concerning the definition of the terms black and Negro. It would appear on rational grounds that in a two-category system an individual who is more than 50 percent white in ancestry should be technically classified as "white." Cultural patterns, however, do not follow genetic principles. Such was the impact of the powerful historical feelings against racial intermixing that any offspring of a black-white union was automatically classified as a "black." This sociocultural definition has prevailed; a great many whites retain the view that a person is a black if he has any black ancestry at all. As a result, the increase in "mixed" couples, which is particularly evident on college campuses, is looked on by some whites with fear and horror.

Thus, the period of slavery laid a deep foundation for the system of relationships between the races that was to prevail in the years that followed. This foundation was strengthened by the events of the Civil War and the Reconstruction period.

Emancipation. After studying the Civil War intensively for more than a century, historians are still not in agreement concerning its causes. One major factor, however, was the debate over the acceptance or prohibition of slavery in the new states and territories of the West and the implication this had for the Senate's balance of power between slave and nonslave states. Bitter sectional arguments rose over the fugitive slave laws, states' rights, the Underground Railroad,

and a host of other problems, and the moralistic outcries of abolitionists added fuel to the fires of dissent. An accumulation of such difficulties drove the two regions further and further apart. In February 1861, the Confederate States of America was formally established, and on April 12, 1861, the Confederacy opened fire on Fort Sumter, launching four years of bloody war.

During the conflict, the issue of emancipation was a thorny one. Slave-holding border states had remained loyal to the Union, and President Lincoln was anxious not to lose their support. Eventually, he drafted a document that freed *some* slaves but not others. The document declared to be free "those slaves residing in territory in rebellion against the Federal government" (over which the Union actually had no control). Announced just after the Union victory at Antietam in September 1862, the Emancipation Proclamation had great popular appeal. Slavery was finally abolished by the Thirteenth Amendment in December 1865.

Reconstruction. When the war was over, the South lay in physical, economic, and social ruin. The destruction of communities, farms, and transportation facilities was severe. More significant, the entire social and economic system founded on slavery had been all but destroyed. Nevertheless, most southern states quickly enacted the so-called Black Codes to repress the former slaves and keep them in a servile position.

The political fate of the rebellious states remained to be decided. A great struggle ensued between harsh retributionists and those who favored more gentle treatment of the South, including Lincoln and his successor, Andrew Johnson. The retributionists finally prevailed: in 1867 a Congress controlled by Radical Republicans passed a series of Reconstruction Acts that demanded new state constitutions and new state governments in ten southern states. According to southern tradition, the period that followed was one of utter degradation, in which northern "carpetbaggers" and southern "scalawags" ran corrupt political machines with the support of army troops and shamelessly manipulated the votes of illiterate ex-slaves. Some modern historians present a considerably different picture

13. Greene, *op. cit.*, p. 206.

of the Reconstruction period, but there can be little disagreement about its aftermath.[14]

The ideology of "white supremacy." After about six years the Reconstruction administrations in the southern states collapsed. Technically, the nation was united again. But any intelligent analysis of race relations in the South since that time must take into account the events—and particularly the folklore—of Reconstruction.

In spite of the surge of northern idealism and humanitarianism associated with the freeing of the slaves, there was no *cultural* basis upon which to establish equality for blacks. The sociologist W. E. B. DuBois, who devoted his life to the study of his people, concluded: "To the northern masses, the Negro was a curiosity, a subhuman minstrel, willingly and naturally a slave, and treated as well as he deserved to be."[15] Although northern workers had hated the idea of slavery, partly because it posed a serious potential threat to their own economic situation, they were not ready to treat the black as an equal. Northern relief over the demise of slavery as an institution was accompanied by little social acceptance of the people who had been freed. In the South there was a clear determination to suppress the black's attempt to escape his "place" at the bottom of the social structure. The ideology of black inferiority, which had been refined over two centuries to justify slavery, continued in full force even in the face of changes in the black's legal status.

Few blacks left the South after the war. Most simply returned to the fields that they had always known, now as free men but in fact little better off than they had been in slavery. The old paternalistic relationships between planter and field hand had scarcely been disturbed. A system of peonage based upon debt-servitude and sharecropping began to spread. The net of economic bondage replaced the chains of slavery.

Now, however, blacks were competing in the labor force directly with landless whites. The postwar period was not a prosperous one for the South, and jobs were scarce. Poor whites deeply resented their Negro competitors. Gradually, legislative changes in the southern states disenfranchised the black, and by the beginning of the twentieth century the policy of "white supremacy" had been firmly established. Poll taxes, literacy tests, property ownership requirements, and other restrictions effectively denied the black his vote. "Jim Crow" laws sanctioned a rigid pattern of segregation in public and private facilities of all kinds. Negro education was all but blocked. In general, the black was denied equality and assigned a place in the social structure as, in effect, a subordinate caste.

Every effort was made during the ensuing years to ensure that the black "remained in his place." One of the most terrifying of the techniques employed was the lynching. Blacks were brutally beaten, hanged, and even burned at the stake. These acts were often justified by the claim that the victim had raped a white woman. Most were, in fact, results of homicides, often with little regard as to whether the black who was chosen to be punished had actually done the deed. The number of such lynchings increased sharply in the South in the 1890's, during the period when most of the laws legalizing white supremacy were passed, and there was another flare-up in the 1920's, associated with Ku Klux Klan activity.

The great migrations to the "Black Metropolis." Prior to the First World War, the impersonality and unknowns of the large northern city held no special attraction for black field hands, but the war found northern industries caught in a severe manpower shortage, and recruiting agents descended upon the South and urged blacks northward in the tens of thousands. Often, free transportation was provided along with the guarantee of a job in industry. Blacks moved to Chicago and other industrial centers of the North; those who came early sent for their families and relatives. Even though conditions in these cities were far from ideal, they offered a significant improvement over the grinding toil, social humiliation, and abject poverty that blacks had experienced in the South.

Whites in these urban centers viewed the new arrivals with mixed feelings. Their labor was indispensable, but they were not welcomed as neighbors. A struggle for living space was the inevitable result. Black ghettos were established and became desperately crowded. Rents skyrocketed; families doubled up. Pressures to en-

14. Louis B. Wright *et al., The Democratic Experience,* 2nd ed. (Glenview, Ill.: Scott, Foresman and Company, 1968), pp. 221–223.

15. William E. B. DuBois, *Black Reconstruction in America* (New York: Harcourt Brace Jovanovich, Inc., 1935), p. 60.

The civil rights movement of the late 1950's and early 1960's was based on a philosophy of passive resistance and was aimed primarily at eliminating legal injustices in the South. During the last several years, however, blacks have increased their organizational efficiency and turned their attention to economic oppression in the North. The early civil rights picture shows a lone demonstrator attempting to be served at a lunch counter in Nashville, Tennessee. Packages were placed on the other stools to prevent blacks from sitting down. In the more recent photograph, Jesse Jackson directs a meeting of Chicago businessmen and presents some future plans of Operation Breadbasket.

large the "black belts" were resisted, and a new kind of conflict between black and white was generated. Numerous frictions and frustrations resulted from these confrontations. Lines of segregation hardened, along with feelings of antagonism on both sides. Minor incidents of violence became increasingly common. Then, as war industries closed and the returning soldiers arrived home, the manpower shortage became a manpower surplus. Blacks found themselves "last hired and first fired." By 1919 a wave of interracial conflicts erupted in northern cities. Unlike more recent riots, in which burning and looting have figured heavily, these upheavals were open fights between blacks and whites.

But the blacks were in the northern cities to stay. An educated business and professional class emerged, while the flow of unskilled and poorly educated rural people from the South continued. The "Black Metropolis" had become a social reality of American urban life. Organizations were founded to obtain justice for blacks through civic programs and the courts. The Urban League and the National Association for the Advancement of Colored People became national in scope and developed their integrationist strategies.

During World War II a second great migration was launched by the same general conditions that had led to the first. Manpower shortages in northern industries swelled the stream of black migrants from the South and intensified the race problems in metropolitan areas. Overcrowding, segregation, job ceilings (only lower-status jobs for Negroes), discrimination by the armed services, white resentment, and a host of other factors stretched tempers to the breaking point; and once again race riots flared in northern industrial communities.

The postwar period saw a great increase in mechanization on southern farms. Mechanical tools replaced black hands in the planting, cultivating, and harvesting of crops. Government agricultural programs and the economic squeeze on farmers created a national trend toward larger and larger farm units. Thus, many rural southern blacks were forced out, losing even the marginal subsistence roles as sharecroppers and field laborers that had been theirs since the Civil War. They owned no land, and they were no longer wanted for work on the lands of others. As a result, additional thousands of black families migrated to the industrial cities of the North, hoping for good jobs but seldom finding them. As the numbers of urban blacks have increased, so too have their frustration and their demands

for more jobs, better housing, and a place in the society that economists and advertisers call affluent.

Civil rights and passive resistance. The most recent major effort to alter the racial structure in the United States came not from the Black Metropolis in the North but from the South itself. In 1955 a massive boycott by blacks effectively eliminated segregation on city buses in Montgomery, Alabama. From such confrontations emerged the Reverend Martin Luther King, Jr., and other black leaders who sought to achieve rapid social change by nonviolent means. The passive resistance doctrines of Mohandas Gandhi, the renowned spiritual-political leader of India, were applied to the problem of eliminating segregation in the South. Blacks and sympathetic whites undertook to challenge the system by which public facilities of all kinds were operated on a two-caste basis. "Freedom riders" on interstate trains and buses tested new federal laws and their enforcement in southern states. A wave of "sit-ins" by Negro college students broke the ban on serving blacks at lunch counters outside black neighborhoods. There were "wade-ins" at swimming pools and even "kneel-ins" at all-white churches.

Although public schools had been desegregated legally in 1954 in a historic Supreme Court decision, most southern communities either refused to comply or complied only with token integration. In 1957, when the Governor of Arkansas used the National Guard to prevent nine black students from entering a high school in Little Rock, President Eisenhower sent federal troops to enforce the desegregation order. Finally, as increasing pressures were applied, the old patterns began slowly to give way. By 1963 the drive for full civil rights for blacks reached national proportions. Jim Crow in a formal legal sense was all but dead so far as the voting booth, public facilities, and educational institutions were concerned. Even the old laws against interracial marriage were eventually abandoned. Based upon high ideals and democratic principles, the civil rights movement was widely supported by liberal whites, many of whom joined the demonstrations and marches as active participants. Indeed, some gave their lives, along with blacks working for the same cause.

The cost of progress was high. Some blacks were murdered; many more were beaten and abused. At Little Rock, the University of Mississippi, and Birmingham, white southern resentment flared into open aggression. But the civil rights movement itself stuck to its passive philosophy, its peaceful forms of protest, and the concept of social change within the structure of law.

The urban riots and black militancy. The civil rights movement in the South achieved significant legal and social changes. But it did little or nothing to ease the plight of the black masses in the pressure cookers of the North. It was fine that the southern black was now able to vote, and it was a real gain when southern lunch counters opened their doors to black customers; but this progress did little to alter the daily struggle for existence of blacks in the blighted northern ghettos. It was economic as well as social oppression that triggered the explosion in the Black Metropolis.

Faced with continued poverty, closed opportunity, *de facto* school segregation, substandard housing, and numerous other indignities, the frustrated and bitter urban masses in northern ghettos provided ready audiences for those advocating forceful action. Many black leaders began to reject such ideas as "working within the system," "nonviolent means," "gradualism," and even the concept of "integration." They pointed out that these were the white man's ideas (as "Negro" was a white man's label) and that their acceptance meant that racial reform could proceed only as fast as the white establishment would permit. In order to win "freedom now," they argued, black men must separate themselves from the white community and build an independent position of power.

The new "black power" movement was essentially a separatist movement, directed toward such goals as economic and political independence and the reestablishment of racial pride, but for some it was a call to violence. Leaders such as Stokely Carmichael and H. Rap Brown called for militant strategies, even armed resistance against the "honkeys." The Black Panther organization advocated extracting an eye for an eye when dealing with the white police. After all, such militants maintained, ghetto blacks had nothing to lose even if they brought the city down about their ears.

In the mid-1960's, the Black Metropolis blew up in the face of incredulous whites. During the 1965 Watts riot (analyzed in Chapter 11, "Collective Behavior"), "Burn, baby, burn" became the slogan of destruction. By the end of the decade firebombing, looting, sniping, and near-anarchy had broken out for short periods in most major cities in the United States, including the nation's capital.

These chaotic events are so recent that it is not yet possible for most citizens, white or black, to view them objectively, but it is clear that the urban disorders of the sixties were significantly different from the "race riots" of earlier years. For one thing, the recent urban eruptions have not been primarily physical clashes between particular groups of blacks and whites but rather widespread disorders aimed at the most visible symbols of white society—property, the police, local merchants, and public officials. Black leaders advocating nonviolent approaches to the solution of black problems have been castigated no less than whites. Even Martin Luther King, Jr., was not immune from criticism by black militants, who declared that he was no longer in step with the times. The rioting that followed King's assassination in April 1968 was a kind of grim tribute by that segment of black America that had ceased to have faith in his dream.

The conditions underlying contemporary racial strains have been created by three centuries of suppression and by economic, political, and demographic change. They are imbedded in a complex of deeply institutionalized and emotional norms among both whites and blacks. These aspects of the society are so complex and so difficult to manipulate that the prospects for immediate and complete solution are drastically limited, even assuming improved good will on the part of both whites and blacks. There is some evidence, however, that closer association of the races can result in better understanding. Deutsch and Collins, in their study of interracial housing,[16] found that blacks and whites required to live in integrated apartment buildings in New York City because of public housing codes got to know each other and even became good friends, whereas blacks and whites in segregated public housing in Newark kept their distance and tended to be mutually antagonistic.

One major trend that can be anticipated for the future is the gradual control of some major cities by blacks. The demographic trends for urban populations are sufficiently clear: as many as twenty of our principal urban centers may have black majorities by the end of the

---

16. Morton Deutsch and Mary F. Collins, *Interracial Housing* (Minneapolis: University of Minnesota Press, 1951).

VIEWPOINTS THE STRUGGLE FOR RACIAL EQUALITY

It would be fatal for the nation to overlook the urgency of the moment and to underestimate the determination of the Negro. . . . There will be neither rest nor tranquility in America until the Negro is granted his citizenship rights. The whirlwinds of revolt will continue to shake the foundations of our nation until the bright day of justice emerges.

But there is something that I must say to my people who stand on the warm threshold which leads into the palace of justice. In the process of gaining our rightful place we must not be guilty of wrongful deeds. Let us not seek to satisfy our thirst for freedom by drinking from the cup of bitterness and hatred. We must forever conduct our struggle on the high plane of dignity and discipline. We must not allow our creative protest to degenerate into physical violence. Again and again we must rise to the majestic heights of meeting physical force with soul force. The marvelous new militancy which has engulfed the Negro community must not lead us to a distrust of all white people, for many of our white brothers, as evidenced by their presence here today, have come to realize that their destiny is tied up with our destiny and their freedom is inextricably bound to our freedom. We cannot walk alone. . . .

I say to you today, my friends, that in spite of the difficulties and frustrations of the moment I still have a dream. It is a dream deeply rooted in the American dream.

I have a dream that one day this nation will rise up and live out the true meaning of its creed: "We hold these truths to be self-evident; that all men are created equal."

I have a dream that one day on the red hills of Georgia the sons of former slaves and the sons of former slaveowners will be able to sit down together at the table of brotherhood. . . .

I have a dream that my four little children will one day live in a nation where they will not be judged by the color of their skin but by the content of their character. . . .

This is our hope. This is the faith with which I return to the South. With this faith we will be able to hew out of the mountain of despair a stone of hope. With this faith we will be able to transform the jangling discords of our nation into a beautiful symphony of brotherhood. With this faith we will be able to work together, to pray together, to struggle together, to go to jail together, to stand up for freedom together, knowing that we will be free one day.

Martin Luther King, Jr.
"I Have a Dream" Speech

It is clear that when this country started to move in terms of slavery, the reason for a man being picked as a slave was one reason: because of the color of his skin. If one was black, one was automatically inferior, inhuman, and therefore fit for slavery. So that the question of whether or not we are individually suppressed is nonsensical and is a downright lie. We are oppressed as a group because we are black, not because we are lazy, not because we're apathetic, not because we're stupid, not because we smell, not because we eat watermelon and have good rhythm. We are oppressed because we are black, and in order to get out of that oppression, one must feel the group power that one has. . . .

It is impossible for white and black people to talk about building a relationship based on humanity when the country is the way it is, when the institutions are clearly against us. We have taken all the myths of this country and we've found them to be downright lies. This country told us that if we worked hard we would succeed, and if that were true we would own this country lock, stock, and barrel. It is we who have picked the cotton for nothing; it is we who are the maids in the kitchens of liberal white people; it is we who are the janitors, the porters, the elevator men; it is we who sweep up your college floors; yes, it is we who are the hardest working and the lowest paid. And that is why it is nonsensical for people to start talking about human relationships until they're willing to build new institutions. Black people are economically insecure. White liberals are economically secure. Can you begin an economic coalition? Are the liberals willing to share their salaries with the economically insecure black people who they so much love? Then if you're not, are you willing to start building new institutions that will provide economic security for black people? That's the question we want to deal with.

. . . We are on the move for our liberation. We have been tired of trying to prove things to white people. We are tired of trying to explain to white people that we're not going to hurt them. We are concerned with getting the things we want, the things that we have to have to be able to function. The question is, can white people allow for that in this country? If that does not happen, brothers and sisters, we have no choice, but to say very clearly, move on over, or we're going to move on over you.

Stokely Carmichael
Speech on "Black Power"

seventies. As the proportion of black citizens increases in these cities, black public officials will undoubtedly replace white administrators. Whether these population and political changes will result in realistic solutions to the problems of urban blacks remains to be seen.

Another significant trend among black Americans is occurring in our nation's high schools and colleges, where there are mounting efforts to establish Black Studies programs. As these programs gain increasing academic respectability, they will help the country gain a new sense of the black man's identity and contributions to American society. As the culture of the black man in America becomes identified and appreciated, perhaps relations between black and white in our society will gradually be restructured on a more rational basis.

JEWS

There are more Jews in the United States than in any other country in the world (see Table 10.1), yet Jews account for only about 3 percent of our total population. Historically, the Jews are people of Mediterranean Caucasian origin who have mixed with various ethnic stocks. Unlike

TABLE 10.1. **ESTIMATED JEWISH POPULATION BY COUNTRIES, 1968**

COUNTRY	JEWISH POPULATION
United States	5,870,000
Soviet Union	2,594,000
Israel	2,436,000
France	535,000
Argentina	500,000
England	410,000
Canada	280,000
Brazil	140,800
Republic of South Africa	114,000
Rumania	100,000
Hungary	80,000
Iran	80,000
Morocco	50,000
All other countries	596,200
Total	13,786,000

SOURCE: The American Jewish Year Book, Vol. 70, 1969.

blacks, they are not defined in American culture as a distinct "race." Rather, they have been distinguished from other groups in our society primarily on the basis of religious beliefs and a strong sense of community with other Jews, both here and abroad.

Jews have been a part of American society since colonial times. The story of their experiences as a minority group in the United States is in many ways unique.

The immigrant Jew. The history of Jews on the North American continent began in 1654 with the arrival in New Amsterdam (New York) of twenty-three Jewish refugees from Brazil. These first immigrants were Sephardic Jews, whose ancestors had lived in Spain and Portugal and who followed the Spanish Jewish rites. There was a trickle of Jewish immigration from Europe throughout the colonial period, and by the time the United States was created, there were approximately 2500 Jews in the new nation, most of them living in towns and cities along the Atlantic seaboard. Fifty years later their number had swelled to perhaps fifteen thousand.

Even in this early period there were substantial differences among American Jews in language, degree of religious orthodoxy, education, and general cultural orientation. Those who had established themselves—often as artisans or merchants—felt socially superior to new arrivals and were concerned lest an influx of "foreign" Jews cause an increase in anti-Semitism.[17] The first large influx began in the 1840's, as a part of the wave of immigration caused by political and economic difficulties in Europe and the freedoms and opportunities offered by the United States. The vast majority of Jewish immigrants were from Germany, especially from southern German towns and villages. By 1880 American Jews numbered a quarter of a million.

The new immigrants took part in America's westward movement, often as traders and peddlers. A considerable number established themselves as pioneer merchants and bankers in the new towns and cities. Many of those who settled in the older urban centers opened stores and factories. Jews played a major role in developing America's ready-made clothing industry. By the

17. Nathan Glazer, "Social Characteristics of American Jews, 1654–1954," *American Jewish Year Book* (1955); and *American Judaism* (Chicago: The University of Chicago Press, 1957).

late nineteenth century there was hardly a form of business or professional activity in which Jews were not represented.

Then, around 1880, there began the torrent of immigration that was to bring more than two million Jews to the United States within forty years. Again the cause was both positive—America's promise—and negative—Europe's pain. In eastern Europe, particularly in Russia, Poland, and Rumania, persecution of the Jews had reached new heights: entire Jewish communities had to flee for their lives. As the new arrivals streamed into New York, the old pattern repeated itself. American Jews looked on the "foreigners" with despair. And these Jews from eastern Europe were truly foreign in many respects, for they had been isolated from western European culture.

Yiddish-speaking and mostly poor, the new arrivals settled in ghetto-like concentrations in New York and other big eastern cities, often taking menial jobs in firms and factories established by Jews who had come before them.[18] The ecology of immigration tended to perpetuate the cultural patterns they had brought from the Old World; but like their predecessors they were determined that their children would rise in the New World, and they were convinced that education was the ladder. No American minority has placed greater stress on schooling or benefited more from it.

The most recent wave of Jewish immigration (from 1936 to 1946) resulted from the Nazi program of Jewish extermination. The social characteristics of the Jews who immigrated at this time tended to be very different from those in the third wave. Most were middle class and well educated, they had fewer problems in adjusting to the new society, and they had less tendency to form neighborhood concentrations within the urban community.

American Jews today. Although about two fifths of all the Jews in the United States live in New York City,[19] Jews live in communities both large and small in all parts of the country, and about 100,000 live on farms.[20] Today Jews are distinguishable from other American citizens of the same social rank mainly by their ancient religious and cultural heritage and by very little else.[21]

In the process of assimilation, there has been a de-emphasis on traditional and orthodox religious forms which once were an important basis of Jewish unity and which preserved a sense of apartness from the general society. Increasingly, the daily lives of most Jews have become secularized. But most still retain an active psychological identification with their religion, just as do those Christians who have similarly abandoned most traditional rituals.[22]

Because of the long history of persecutions of Jews, American Jews tend to feel a strong bond of sympathy, identification, and kinship with their coreligionists abroad. The horrors of the Nazi exterminations greatly reinforced these feelings and created among Jews a special emotional frame of reference concerning the emerging state of Israel. As the first national homeland for Jews since they were dispersed from the ancient land of Canaan (roughly the site of modern Israel) by the Romans in the first century A.D., it is regarded as a haven that must be preserved.

In spite of our formal policies concerning religious freedom, there have been periods of virulent anti-Semitism in the United States. The 1920's saw a wave of prejudice toward Jews develop, in part as a reflection of the anti-Jewish feeling being generated in Europe during a period of political and economic crisis. In some parts of the United States, restrictive covenants in real estate contracts were used to keep Jews out of certain residential areas. Jews were also denied access to hotels and restaurants in some areas, and a number of colleges and universities had quotas for Jews. They were systematically excluded from numerous occupations.

For the most part, the more open forms of discrimination have disappeared. Aiding in the fight against such discrimination have been such organizations as the American Council for Judaism, the American Jewish Committee, the American Jewish Congress, and the Anti-Defamation League of B'nai B'rith, all of which have been aggressive in forcing an end to restrictive covenants, quotas, and other formal systems of exclusion. In recent years, both prejudice and

18. Milton M. Gordon, *Assimilation in American Life* (New York: Oxford University Press, 1964), p. 185.

19. Glazer and Moynihan, *op. cit.*, p. 138.

20. David Goldberg and Harry Sharp, "Some Characteristics of Detroit Area Jewish and Non-Jewish Adults," in *The Jews: Social Patterns of an American Group* ed. Marshall Sklare (New York: The Free Press, 1958), p. 112.

21. Gordon, *op. cit.*, p. 190.

22. Herbert J. Gans, "American Jewry: Present and Future," *Commentary*, 21, No. 5 (May 1956), 422–430.

The largest group of Spanish-speaking Americans is composed of citizens of Mexican birth or descent. Those pictured here are from the Brownsville area of Texas but have moved into Indiana to find agricultural work during the summer months. Many of them continue to migrate from place to place and must work long hours for low pay just to maintain themselves. The individuals who remain in the North have a very difficult time finding good jobs; they usually have no alternative but to take on the heavy, dirty, or dangerous work that no one else wants.

OTHER MINORITIES

While blacks and Jews constitute the largest minorities in the United States, several other sizable groups share this status. Within our borders there are a number of Spanish-speaking groups, a sizable Oriental population, and our American Indians. In addition, there are people from many lands who retain elements of their national cultures, and there are religious groups whose ways of life set them distinctly apart from the larger society. It is not possible to comment on the origins and characteristics of each of these segments of our society. The present section will consider briefly only the Spanish-speaking, Oriental, and Indian minorities.

Spanish-speaking minorities. The United States has over six million Spanish-speaking people living within its borders. These Americans are not a single cultural group but rather several distinct minorities who came to this country at different times from different places under widely varying conditions.

The oldest segment is made up of the so-called Hispanos of the Southwest—descendants of the people of Spanish origin who occupied that region before New England was first settled.[23] In 1848, following the Mexican War, Mexico ceded a vast area to the United States, including what are now the states of California, Nevada, and Utah, most of Arizona and New Mexico, and parts of Colorado and Wyoming. Under the terms of the Treaty of Guadalupe Hidalgo, American citizenship was granted to those in the area who wished to remain on their land. Most elected to stay, and their descendants now constitute about half a million people. The largest proportion resides in New Mexico and until recently has tended to remain in somewhat isolated rural villages.

The largest group of Spanish-speaking Americans is composed of citizens of Mexican birth or descent. There are almost five million of these Mexican Americans, or Chicanos (as they sometimes call themselves), now living in this country, most of them in the states along the border and in Colorado.[24] The great majority are unskilled or semiskilled workers, and the group as a whole suffers serious discrimination. According to one writer, Mexican Americans in the Southwest are "worse off in every respect than the nonwhites (Negroes, Indians, and

discrimination against Jews appear to be slowly declining. Legal reforms (restrictive covenants are unenforceable) have hastened this. The dropping of quotas and the lessening of job discrimination have been accompanied by an increasing assimilation of Jews into the main cultural, social, and economic streams of American society, even though undeniable forms of discrimination remain in some areas and latent hostilities still characterize some segments of the population.

23. Carey McWilliams, *North from Mexico* (Philadelphia: J. B. Lippincott Company, 1949); for a more recent exposition of the problem of the Mexican Americans in the Southwest, see Julian Samora, ed., *La Raza: The Forgotten Americans* (South Bend, Ind.: University of Notre Dame Press, 1966).

24. John H. Burma, *Spanish-Speaking Groups in the United States* (Durham, N.C.: Duke University Press, 1954).

Orientals), not to mention the dominant Anglos (everybody else)."[25]

A third Spanish-speaking minority has come from the island of Puerto Rico, which the United States acquired at the close of the Spanish American War in 1898. Puerto Ricans have been American citizens since 1917 and may come to the mainland as they wish. Following World War II, migration to the United States from Puerto Rico rose sharply. According to the 1960 United States Census, there were nearly 900,000 persons of Puerto Rican birth or parentage in this country.[26] The great majority of these people remain concentrated in New York City, though some have now begun to settle in other areas. For those Puerto Ricans who are darkskinned (some, in fact, are blue-eyed blondes), acceptance in the United States has been complicated by traditionally strong patterns of prejudice and discrimination against nonwhites.[27]

Finally, political events in Cuba since Castro's takeover in 1959 have produced an exodus of Cubans to the mainland. As early as 1966 there were approximately 300,000 Cuban refugees in this country,[28] and the influx has continued. Many of these people were middle class in their own land, but as has been the case with other immigrant groups, most have had to enter the new society at the bottom. Some of these exiles have dispersed throughout America, but over half are still living in the Miami region, and the majority retain hope that they can return to their own country.

It is difficult to form generalizations that apply to all Spanish-speaking people. Since the Hispanos of the Southwest have tended to remain quite rural and isolated until recently, they have not undergone the assimilation that might be expected considering they were the earliest of the Spanish-speaking groups to become citizens. For the same reason, they have encountered very little formal discrimination. The much larger Mexican-American group, however, has been discriminated against in every way, and there is growing impatience and militance in the *barrio*, or ghetto. On the one hand, there is the desire to merge with the dominant group. Some studies indicate that second and third generation Mexican Americans are undergoing rapid assimilation. In Los Angeles, for example, Mexican Americans are marrying out of their ethnic community to a much greater extent than ever before.[29] At the same time, there are movements

to unite the Chicanos, to teach them pride in their own culture, and to win a better position in American society for what has been described as "the nation's second biggest deprived minority."[30]

The Cuban refugees have encountered some difficulties, particularly in areas where there are large numbers of them. Some of the Cubans are slowly rebuilding a somewhat normal life in this country, but others are more or less marking time pending a return to their homeland. In southern Florida, for example, they tend to be concentrated in ghettos, occupying low-status positions and making little effort to learn American customs or language. This minority probably will be integrated into the dominant society very slowly.

With their mixed racial characteristics and their continuing close ties to their homeland added to the barrier of language, the Puerto Ricans have had a particularly difficult time finding a place in the dominant society. Their large concentration in the ghettos of a single urban center has created many problems in education, employment, and cultural assimilation for them, as well as for the community as a whole. In recent years, the city of New York has tried, through public and private organizations, to meet these problems, but although a few Puerto Ricans have moved out of the ghetto and are making better adjustments, progress is very slow. There are substantial individual differences in status within our various Spanish-

25. Helen Rowan, "A Minority Nobody Knows," *The Atlantic* (June 1967), p. 47.

26. U. S. Census of Population, 1960, *Puerto Ricans in the United States*, viii.

27. C. Wright Mills, Clarence Senior, and Rose Goldsen, *The Puerto Rican Journey* (New York: Harper & Row, Inc., 1950).

28. *Cuban Refugee Problem*, Hearings before the Subcommittee to Investigate Problems Connected with Refugees and Escapees of the Committee on the Judiciary, U.S. Senate, 89th Congress, 2nd Session (March 1966), pp. 129–131.

29. Frank G. Mittelbach, Joan W. Moore, and Ronald McDaniel, "Intermarriage of Mexican-Americans," Advance Report 6, Division of Research, Graduate School of Business Administration, University of California at Los Angeles (November 1966).

30. *Time*, July 4, 1969, p. 17; see also W. V. D'Antonio and Julian Samora, "Occupational Stratification in Four Southwestern Communities: A Study of Ethnic Differential Employment in Hospitals," *Social Forces*, 41, No. 1 (October 1962), 18–25; and W. V. D'Antonio and W. H. Form, *Influentials in Two Border Cities* (South Bend, Ind.: University of Notre Dame Press, 1965).

speaking minorities, but by and large few of their members are yet able to enjoy equal participation within the larger society.

Orientals. Two quite different Oriental minorities, the Chinese and the Japanese, live in the United States, with their largest concentrations along the Pacific Coast and in Hawaii. Their histories are dissimilar except in one respect: both have suffered particularly severe persecutions at the hands of white Americans.

The Chinese began to arrive in large numbers in the middle of the last century, during the gold rush boom on the West Coast. Later, Chinese "coolie" labor was imported to help build the first transcontinental railroads.[31] Because there were few women in the West, the Chinese also took over such tasks as washing and cooking; the Chinese laundry and the Chinese restaurant, which are so familiar in urban America, resulted from this adaptation.

The gold rush and the years of growth that followed brought far more people to California than could be absorbed into the economy, and within a few decades many whites found themselves competing directly with cheap Chinese labor. The result was a wave of bitter anti-Chinese feeling. During the late 1800's the Chinese were beaten, burned out, stoned, kicked in the streets, and otherwise harassed until many returned to China. Eighteen were lynched in a single race riot in Los Angeles in 1871. Because of their treatment, most of the Chinese who remained in this country withdrew to enclaves in urban centers where they could insulate themselves from American society and retain their own cultural patterns.[32]

Legislation with respect to the Chinese has been extremely suppressive. The Chinese Exclusion Act of 1882 virtually ended Chinese immigration. California enacted numerous laws that denied the Chinese access to schools, jobs, and homes. Only in the last few years have these discriminatory laws been declared unconstitutional. Today, however, the Chinese are one of the favored minorities, admired for their industry and intelligence and respected for their achievements in business, the sciences, and the arts. Until the recent revival of Chinese immigration gave them new life, the older "Chinatown" ghettos were tending to disappear.[33]

Japanese immigration into the United States did not begin in substantial numbers until about the beginning of the present century. Just prior to World War II about 90 percent of the Japanese in the United States were concentrated along the Pacific Coast, with the majority in California.[34] Soon after their arrival, the Japanese began to feel the impact of the same prejudices that were directed toward the Chinese. Legislation and many informal practices were quickly established to exclude the new group from schools, the labor force, and other areas of social life. Japanese immigration was stopped by federal law in 1924. With other Orientals, the Japanese were regarded by the white majority as a "yellow peril" that somehow threatened the American way of life. In fact, the Japanese in America were a frugal, hard-working people who established family farms and businesses and who were upwardly mobile in the manner strongly approved by the American value system.

When Pearl Harbor was bombed in 1941, a wave of anti-Japanese hysteria overwhelmed the United States. All Americans of Japanese ancestry were suddenly considered security risks and potential traitors. Early in 1942 it was decided to evacuate all Japanese Americans from the Pacific Coast and place them in internment camps in the interior. Over 100,000 people of Japanese extraction, about two thirds of whom were American citizens, were forced to sell—or abandon—their homes, farms, and businesses and live in government-controlled camps for the duration of the war or else leave the country.[35] After the war's end, Japanese Americans could not easily pick up their former pursuits, and many never returned to the West Coast. Their dispersion to various other parts of the country has perhaps hastened their assimilation into the mainstream of American society. In any case, Japanese Americans have enjoyed an increasing measure of acceptance in recent years. Like the Chinese (and the Jews among Caucasians), they have insisted that their children receive as much education as possible, and their economic adjustment has been very successful. Despite the

31. B. Schrieke, *Alien Americans* (New York: The Viking Press, Inc., 1936), pp. 8–10.

32. David Te-chao Cheng, *Acculturation of the Chinese in the United States* (Philadelphia: University of Philadelphia Press, 1948).

33. Rose Hum Lee, "The Decline of Chinatowns in the United States," *American Journal of Sociology*, 54 (1949), 422–432.

34. Vander Zanden, *op. cit.*, p. 259.

35. Leonard Broom and Ruth Reimer, *Removal and Return* (Berkeley: University of California Press, 1949), pp. 202–204.

improved standing of both our Chinese and Japanese minorities, however, many of the patterns of prejudice and discrimination against Orientals remain as part of our culture.

American Indians. Historically, no minority in the United States has suffered greater injustice than the American Indian. The Indians encountered by the invading white man had been established on this continent since the dawn of recorded time. The various tribes had their own cultural patterns, well adapted to their particular needs and to the particular areas where they lived. They were little attracted by European culture with its monotheistic religion, strange economic systems, and unfathomable technology.

Today some 600,000 American Indians survive in the United States. They are living under conditions of poverty which, because of geographical isolation, are hidden from most Americans. The majority are still faced with the dilemma of what to do about adapting to the society of their conquerors.[36]

Indians have never shared a single culture. There are more than two hundred reservations in the United States, established for the various tribes through special treaties with the federal government. Each tribe has different problems and a different culture, and each has accommodated itself differently to the mainstream of American society. Some individuals who have left their reservations and moved to cities have given up their traditional cultural patterns; others have sought to maintain tribal customs and organization in their new surroundings. Still others live on the reservations part of the time and work outside at other times.

Various segments of the dominant society have held widely divergent views concerning what the relationship of the white man to the Indian should be. From early times, humanitarian and religious groups worked to educate and assimilate Indians. Others wanted to leave them alone. Still others demanded that they be exterminated. For more than two centuries the federal government has shifted from one policy to another, to the vast confusion and disgust of the Indians.

Our first policy was to move Indians off lands wanted by white settlers. By the middle of the nineteenth century, the official policy was to segregate Indians on reservations. The Indians became wards of the government and until recently were denied citizenship. Later, attempts were made to break up the tribal organizations and bring about "Americanization" through schooling of the young and suppression of the old ways.

In the present century, attempts at assimilation were replaced by efforts to achieve cultural pluralism. At one time the tribal lands were to be broken up into individual holdings. Then efforts were made to restore them as communal holdings. More recently, the federal government has placed more power over Indians in the hands of the individual states. Thus we have collectively vacillated between policies of extermination, wardship, assimilation, cultural pluralism, acceptance, rejection, and individual freedom.[37]

Through all this the Indians have somehow managed to survive. The impact of cultural conflict, social rejection, and economic denial has caused problems of every conceivable kind for these people, but Indian groups still retain many elements of their ancient cultural heritage. The future remains in doubt. Those whites concerned with the plight of the Indian cannot agree—nor do today's Indians agree among themselves—on the extent to which the Indian should be assimilated into our urban, industrial society or on the means by which such assimilation, if desirable, can best be accomplished.

THE STRUCTURE OF INTERGROUP RELATIONS

It should be clear from the history of American minorities that there are many possible patterns of relationship between dominant and minority groups, and that relationships are likely to change over time. At one point tensions may flare into open conflict; at another, some new mode of accommodation may evolve.

Initially at least, the structure of intergroup relations is shaped mainly by the dominant group—that is, what happens to the minority is

36. Daisnke Kitagawa, "The American Indian," in *Minority Problems: A Textbook of Readings in Intergroup Relations*, eds. Arnold M. Rose and Caroline B. Rose (New York: Harper & Row, Inc., 1965), p. 26.

37. Brewton Berry, *Race and Ethnic Relations*, 3rd ed. (Boston: Houghton Mifflin Company, 1965), pp. 233–241.

in many respects a result of policies adopted, either formally or informally, by those with the greatest power. The relationship initiated by a dominant group can range from an attempt to exterminate the minority to efforts to absorb it completely through intermarriage or a merging of cultures.

Whatever the policy of the dominant group, the structure of intergroup relations is fully established, of course, only with the minority's response. The members of a minority group may resign themselves to discriminatory treatment (sometimes even to the extent of becoming prejudiced against themselves) or they may employ various kinds of active strategies for improving their relative position in the society. Similarly, they may either welcome or reject efforts of a dominant group to assimilate them.[38]

When particular members of a minority group band together in an organization, their behavior becomes truly *group* behavior and, in this context, their response to minority position may become more clearly defined. Some of the organizations formed by minority-group members are primarily defensive: the NAACP, the Urban League, and the Anti-Defamation League, for example, are collective efforts to protect minorities from injustice. Other organizations are basically political, seeking the election of candidates who will work for the interests of the minority. Still others may develop as separatist movements or as efforts to subvert the power of the dominant group. All such organizations may play some part in shaping the complex structure of intergroup relations. At the very least, they give focus to feelings of "we" and "they."

In the following sections we will examine four characteristic patterns of relationship between dominant and minority groups: aggression, segregation (or avoidance), pluralism, and merger through assimilation or amalgamation. As we shall see, much the same strategies are used by both dominant groups and minorities, though they are usually directed toward different goals.

---

38. James Vander Zanden, a sociologist who has specialized in the study of minority relations, has developed a systematic classification of minority reactions. He identifies four major types: acceptance, aggression, avoidance, and assimilation. A given minority group may use any or all of these reactions. See Vander Zanden, *op. cit.*, pp. 337–421.

39. George P. Murdock, *Our Primitive Contemporaries* (New York: The Macmillan Company, 1934), pp. 16–18.

AGGRESSION

In its most extreme form, aggression by a dominant group may be directed toward wiping out a "troublesome" minority. In the history of European expansion, for example, aboriginal peoples often were simply annihilated. The Spanish slaughtered the Indians of southern Argentina in systematic military campaigns; the English in Tasmania hunted the aborigines for sport and for dog food;[39] the white man in North America wiped out a number of important Indian tribes, particularly along the Atlantic seaboard. Probably the most shocking systematic attempt to destroy an entire people, however, was not an assault on aborigines by colonizers but the genocide policy of the Nazis toward European Jews.

Except during the Indian wars, American minority groups have seldom employed the strategy of open aggression. Although rebellious slaves were numerous in the antebellum South, only a few slave revolts involved significant numbers. As we have seen, however, some American blacks are now convinced that they must fight for their rights. Indeed, some believe that blacks face annihilation unless they fight back—that they must fight to survive.

More typically, however, aggression by either a dominant or minority group is not fully open or direct. For example, intergroup antagonisms are often expressed through *symbolic* aggression: the dominant group maintains a culture of jokes, epithets, and other symbolic devices that perpetuate its prejudices against the minority; the minority develops its own jokes, epithets, and other verbal means of ridiculing or denigrating the dominant group. An old example is the black's use of "ofay" to refer to a white.

Another way of acting out one's hostilities is through *covert* aggression. Members of the dominant group may use it to circumvent civil rights legislation. For example, they may obey the letter of the law by serving a customer belonging to the minority but provide such slow, reluctant, rude, or inferior service that he is made perfectly aware that he is unwelcome. On the other side, the member of the minority may use covert aggression to avoid overt retaliation. If he is employed by a member of the dominant group, he may deliberately do poor work. During the period of slavery, blacks sometimes mutilated themselves so that they could neither

American Indians have long been the victims of extreme forms of discrimination, and the indications of their suffering are still appalling. The life expectancy of an Indian, for example, is twenty-seven years less than that of a white American, and an Indian family living on a reservation—as most of them do—has an annual income of about $1500. But many American Indians are no longer willing to accept such injustices; they will not wait patiently while government agencies decide what is to become of them, their land, and their culture. The occupation of Alcatraz by some one hundred Indians in 1970 (bottom left) was largely a symbolic protest, but it was indicative of an increasing trend toward activism.

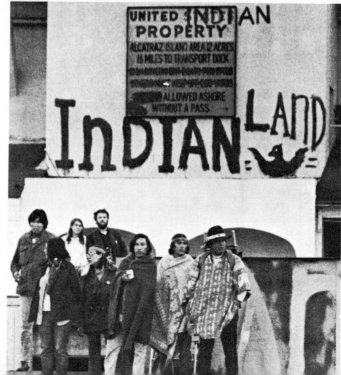

work for their white masters nor be sold. Some apparently committed suicide with similar motivation.

SEGREGATION OR AVOIDANCE

As practiced by the dominant group, a segregation policy can range from imposition of rigid spatial limits on the movements of a minority in ghettos, pales, reservations, concentration camps, or other special areas to the use of discriminating practices that exclude the minority group from more or less important areas of social and economic life. The United States has had a long history of segregation. All the principal minorities have been systematically excluded from full access to employment, education, housing, and political life. Some have been refused admission to trains and buses, restaurants, swimming pools, theaters, parks, and even churches. While many overt forms of discrimination have been declared illegal in recent years, many other types of segregation continue to be practiced, particularly those that result from informal policies and are not subject to regulation by the law. A comparison of the white and nonwhite populations in the United States with respect to housing, income, and other indices of stratification makes it clear that, despite progress, we are still a long way from realizing the American ideal of equal opportunity for all citizens (Table 10.2, page 338).

As the history of the United States makes clear, social segregation does not necessarily depend on physical segregation. Under our system of social stratification, blacks and various other minority-group members are automatically assigned low positions on the social scale. They are thus effectively "kept apart" even when they are not segregated geographically. If blacks living in a predominantly white community are shunned by most of their neighbors, they are victims of segregation no less than if they were forced to live in an all-black ghetto. In almost all societies, members of minority groups generally find it much more difficult than others to achieve upward social mobility. Even when they are able to reach a relatively high economic level, they seldom make comparable gains in social prestige or power.

Segregation of the minority by the dominant group has its equivalent in minority efforts to avoid contact with those who treat them as inferiors. While intergroup contacts are extremely difficult to avoid completely in a society like ours, many individual members of minority groups attempt to minimize them. This may mean choosing not to enter a restaurant where there is any possibility of being refused service. Or it may mean general avoidance, such as choosing to live and work in a neighborhood inhabited chiefly by one's own group.

Efforts toward insulation may also take the form of collective avoidance, through migration or through separatist social movements. From the end of the nineteenth century, for example, many Jews were attracted by the Zionist movement to establish a nation of Israel where all Jews could escape the ill treatment that had been theirs through centuries of persecution. A little-known example of collective attempts at separatism was that of the former planters and plantation owners who emigrated to the Belem region of Brazil after the Civil War in an attempt to reestablish the kind of society they had had in the antebellum South. Among American blacks, "back-to-Africa" movements have had little support, but a significant number of writers, artists, and musicians avoid American forms of discrimination by living in Europe. As other examples of separatism among American minorities, the Black Muslims preach separation, some Indian tribes try to keep contacts with whites to a minimum, and a number of religious sects avoid worldly society.

PLURALISM

Of the many separatist efforts in the course of American history, few have succeeded for long. A more promising pattern of intergroup relations is cultural pluralism, which permits a minority group with a distinct cultural background to retain differences in customs and traditions while its members cooperate in political, economic, and other aspects of societal life. There has clearly been an element of pluralism in the development of intergroup relations in the United States. Immigrant groups often settled in enclaves of the city or in rural areas where they retained their language, their religion, their dietary practices, and other continuing ties to the culture of their origin.

In the earlier decades of this century, the dominant group scoffed at "foreign ways" and exerted strong pressure on immigrants to aban-

During World War II the Japanese experienced an extreme form of segregation in the United States; more than 100,000 persons were evacuated from their homes and forced to live in war relocation camps. This 1942 photograph shows Japanese-Americans, immigrants, and American-born alike arriving at an Alien Reception Center in Manazar, California.

don them. It was felt to be vitally important to absorb the newcomer as soon as possible, to "Americanize" him and erase visible signs of his foreign origin. More recently, some of the cultural differences retained by *some* of our ethnic groups have come to be valued—for example, types of food, music, and other art forms. For the groups themselves, they have become less a liability and more a source of in-group pride and distinction. It is doubtful, however, that ours will ever be a truly pluralistic society. Our standardized school system, communication media, mass-produced consumer goods, and great mobility all tend to create a society with increasingly uniform folkways.

ASSIMILATION OR AMALGAMATION

In the United States, assimilation has been the common pattern by which minority groups have merged into the mainstream of social life. Successive waves of immigrants have adopted the language, values, beliefs, and other cultural elements of American society, while that society has taken over some of their foods, words, decorative motifs, or other cultural elements. Merger can also occur through amalgamation, the biological mixing of groups. In Hawaii, for example, mixing of the races is proceeding steadily as Caucasians, Orientals, and Polynesians intermarry. The American black, as we have indicated, has mixed biologically with whites for centuries. If present trends continue, we shall ultimately have a nation of considerable racial homogeneity, despite strong opposition to amalgamation by many members of both the dominant group and minority groups.

Minority groups have mixed feelings about cultural assimilation. For some minority-group members, assimilation represents a means by which prejudice and discrimination can be escaped. An individual may decide that he wants to become completely assimilated so that he can "pass" for a member of the dominant group. A great many Americans have changed their

TABLE 10.2.   COMPARISON OF SOCIAL AND ECONOMIC CONDITIONS OF WHITES AND NONWHITES IN THE UNITED STATES, 1960 AND 1966

INDEX OF STRATIFICATION	1960 WHITE	1960 NONWHITE	1966 WHITE	1966 NONWHITE
Place of residence				
Percent living in central cities	30	51	27	56
Percent with housing not meeting specified criteria	13	44	8	29
Education				
Percent of males 25–29 years old having completed 4 or more years of high school	63	36	73	53
Employment				
Unemployment rate	4.9	10.2	3.3	7.3
Percent of workers with white-collar jobs or jobs as craftsmen or operatives	79	43	81	50
Income				
Percent of families below the poverty level	15	49	10	35
Percent of families with incomes of $7000 or more	41	17	55	28
Median family income of nonwhites as percent of median family income of whites	—	55	—	60

SOURCE: *Social and Economic Conditions of Negroes in the U.S.*, Current Population Reports, Series P. 23, No. 24, October 1967.

"difficult" foreign names through legal action, and members of religious minorities cease to profess the "foreign" faith of their forebears. Some "Negroes" with sufficiently light skins choose to pass for whites. But while complete integration is the goal of many American blacks, others are fiercely opposed to the idea of being absorbed into the mainstream of "white" society. Similarly, some American Jews are deeply concerned that the old traditions of the Jewish people will die out in the United States through secularization. For many individual members of minority groups, cultural pluralism—not assimilation—remains the ideal.

THE NATURE OF PREJUDICE

Although civil rights legislation has opened many new doors to minority groups in the United States, these changes in the formal norms of our society have done relatively little to alter the structure of intergroup relations. Whatever the law of the land, the treatment of blacks and other minority groups continues to be based on the institutionalized patterns of prejudice and discrimination that have become deeply engrained in our culture. To understand why a society formally dedicated to the concept of equality continues to rank differentially and to reject certain of its members, we must examine the nature of prejudice as both an individual and a group phenomenon.

THE PSYCHOLOGY OF INDIVIDUAL PREJUDICE

Viewed from the standpoint of the individual, prejudice is an attitude based upon *antipathy*. Most writers on the subject note that prejudice is a particularly rigid type of attitude—an emotional bias that is not easily changed through persuasion or through exposure to factual evidence that contradicts the beliefs on which it is based.[40]

Some theorists have termed prejudice a "prejudgment," in the sense that it is a judgment

40. For a very comprehensive survey covering many approaches to the understanding of prejudice, see Gordon W. Allport, *The Nature of Prejudice* (Reading, Mass.: Addison-Wesley Publishing Company, 1954).

made without reference to knowledge or experience.[41] This implies that prejudice includes a generalization that all members of a given minority uniformly possess certain characteristics. Prejudice is in this sense a *categorical* aversion to each and all members of the relevant group. In short, racial or ethnic prejudice can be defined for present purposes as *an emotional, relatively inflexible and categorical antipathy toward the members of a minority group, individually and collectively.*

Before turning to a sociological perspective on prejudice, it will be useful to review some of the theories that psychologists have developed to explain the origins of prejudice in the individual.

The scapegoat theory. Psychologists have noted that an individual who is frustrated in his effort to achieve highly desired goals tends to respond with a pattern of aggression. If it is possible to direct his aggression at the actual cause of his frustration, he may do so; if not, he tends to displace it on a scapegoat—a person, object, or group that is close at hand and incapable of offering effective resistance. Thus the frustrated office worker may criticize his wife rather than his employer for his failure to be promoted; or the unskilled worker who cannot find employment may blame "Wall Street" for his plight.

The projection theory. Projection refers to the tendency of an individual to assign to others modes of behavior, motives, or other characteristics that are in fact part of his own personality but that he cannot acknowledge, perhaps even to himself, because they are considered socially unacceptable. For example, a white American of puritanical heritage may view sexual matters as "dirty" or sinful, while at the same time sharing a normal human desire for sexual activity. According to the projection theory, such an individual may resolve his internal conflict by projecting his guilt-arousing desires onto other individuals and then condemning those individuals as immoral. Thus many white people, it is theorized, project their own inhibited sexual impulses onto blacks and use this as the basis for disliking or distrusting them. The familiar theme of "Negro man rapes white woman," which has touched off so many tragic lynchings in the South, is said to be better understood in the light of the projection of gross sexuality onto the black. The theory offers one possible explanation of why white reactions to such charges tend to be out of proportion to the number of such events that have actually occurred.

The authoritarian personality theory. An explanation of individual prejudice that was especially popular following World War II is the idea that prejudice is a fundamental aspect of the personality structure of certain types of people raised under particular circumstances. In a widely read work called *The Authoritarian Personality*, T. W. Adorno and his colleagues presented a number of measuring scales and clinical data identifying broad personality patterns that could be labeled "authoritarian."[42] The authoritarian personality was said to be one in which such traits as ethnocentrism, intolerance of ambiguity, conventionalism, political conservatism, and preoccupations with power were predominant. In general, it was found that prejudice against minority groups is typical of the authoritarian personality. The research underlying this theory has been strongly criticized on technical grounds.[43]

Research on the psychological origins of prejudice continues. The theories reviewed above indicate something of the range of ideas that have been brought forth to explain the phenomenon of prejudice in terms of individual psychological structure and functioning.

PREJUDICE AS A CULTURAL PHENOMENON

Prejudice must be viewed not only as an attitudinal-emotional phenomenon of the individual but also as a *group* phenomenon. That is, it is part of the established or institutionalized culture of the society as a whole, and it is a particularly significant part of certain regional and social-class subcultures within the society.

From this standpoint, prejudice is part of the general folkways and other norms that are transmitted to new generations through socialization. Learning to be prejudiced and acquiring

41. E. Franklin Frazier, *The Negro in the United States* (New York: The Macmillan Company, 1949), p. 665.

42. T. W. Adorno *et al.*, *The Authoritarian Personality* (New York: Harper & Row, Inc., 1950).

43. Theodore M. Newcomb *et al.*, *Social Psychology* (New York: Holt, Rinehart and Winston, Inc., 1965), p. 441.

habits of discrimination against minorities can come about in much the same way as acquiring preferences for certain forms of recreation or habits of eating. In this sense, prejudice as a personal trait is no more an indicator of underlying personality difficulties than one's tastes in reading or personal attire. It is a product of socialization—an outcome of the particular experiences one has had in associating with people who share and transmit a particular cultural theme. By this means, a person can easily learn to be prejudiced against the members of a minority group even though he has little or no actual contact with them and despite the fact that his economic status or other situation may not be affected in the slightest by their presence or absence in his society.

Through the process of *differential association* (page 150), the individual can be more thoroughly exposed to cultural norms of either prejudice or nonprejudice. Our society contains both cultural themes. Typically, parents and peers indoctrinate the child in the prevailing prejudices and patterns of discrimination that exist in his community.

As a result of this pattern, college students often encounter a kind of "prejudice crisis" as part of their educational experience. At an earlier age they probably acquired the shared antipathies toward minority groups that are a part of the culture of many communities in this country. Later, because of the greater emphasis on norms of equality encountered in the college or university setting, they find themselves challenging their own prejudices. To some degree they may undergo resocialization, depending upon the peer culture or other influences they encounter. This can be an unsettling experience. It can leave the individual intellectually committed to newly acquired liberal norms but with an underlying emotional commitment to the prejudices learned at an earlier age.

This dualism can create a difficult conflict for the individual when he is faced with a situation in which he must publicly reveal his position. If he acts overtly in a nondiscriminatory manner, he may suffer negative sanctions at the hands of reference groups from his home community. If he acts in accord with his old emotional prejudices, he will have to face the psychological task of reconciling his discriminatory behavior with his newly acquired liberalism.[44] Many people manage to avoid this dilemma by *compartmentalizing* the two cultural themes, i.e.,

by putting them in separate categories. Thus they continue to act on their prejudices yet subscribe firmly to the notion of equality.

Viewing prejudice as a cultural phenomenon also enables us to understand why some members of minority groups are prejudiced against members of other minorities and even against themselves! For example, research has indicated that black children of preschool age have learned that their color and racial charac-

---

44. Lawrence S. Linn, "Verbal Attitudes and Overt Behavior: A Study of Racial Discrimination," *Social Forces*, 43, No. 3 (March 1965), 353–364.

Typically, parents and peers indoctrinate children in the prevailing prejudices and patterns of discrimination that exist in their community. Thus individuals can easily learn to be prejudiced against the members of a minority group even though they have little or no actual contact with them.

teristics are negatively evaluated by their society.[45] This can pose emotional disturbances and crises concerning the worth of the self. Although the young blacks later begin to acquire group identifications and new in-group norms that aid in countering self-devaluation, these problems continue to trouble many of them throughout their lives.

In addition, the Negro-as-an-American is exposed to norms of prejudice and discrimination toward other minority groups. In fact, some writers indicate that minority groups may be more prejudiced toward one another than is the case of the dominant group toward any particular minority. In some cities Polish Americans have been particularly hostile toward blacks, and in the black ghetto there is often virulent anti-Semitism. Louis Lomax, a black writer, wrote of walking one night through the streets of Harlem and coming upon a street-corner speaker. The scene that he describes illustrates the castigation of Jews, who for many urban blacks represent white businessmen in general:

"Now gather round," the speaker said, "I want to tell you about the white man."

"Say on, brother," some sister yelled from the crowd.

"Did you ever—hear me now—did you ever know a white man to do anything right?"

The crowd roared with scornful laughter.

"Hell no," a man screamed out. "Right ain't in them!"

"Tell them about it," a woman joined in.

"Now listen," the speaker said. "I want you to understand how the white man, particularly the Jew, keeps you in the economic locks. Am I right or wrong?"

"You right," the crowd shot back.

"Now, now, now," the speaker stammered for emphasis, "this is the way it is. You get up early every morning with roaches and rats running round your bed. Is that right?"

"That's right."

"You stumble over to your child's bed to make sure the rats ain't done bit his ears off. Is that right?"

"That's right."

"Then you make it through falling plaster to a leaky water closet to wash your face."

"Yes, sir . . . that's it, that's it."

"Your finally get the sleep out of your eyes and put on some clothes that are just about worn out but you ain't finished paying for them yet."

"Say on brother. The white man ought to be killed!"

"Then, then, then—hear me now—then you go down in the subway and make it down to the garment district to meet the man. Am I right or wrong?"

"You right."

"And this is where the economic locks come in; you go downtown to work for Mr. Eisenberg."

"Yeah!"

"You work all day, eight hours a day, five days a week for forty-four dollars."

"That's right."

"And while you making forty-four dollars, Mr. Eisenberg is watching you sweat and grunt and he makes forty-four hundred dollars. Am I right or wrong?"

"You right; great God, you right!"

"Say on."

"Tell it like it is."

"Oh don't worry, brother, I'm going to tell it just like it is; I'm going to bring it right down front so everybody can smell it!"

"Now—and watch this—you all work all day for Mr. Eisenberg, you come back up here to Harlem and buy your clothes from Mr. Gosenberg."

"Yeah."

"You buy your jewelry from Mr. Goldberg."

"Yes."

"You pay rent to Mr. Fineberg."

"Yes."

"You get borrowed money from a finance company headed by Mr. Wienberg."

"Yes, tell it."

"Now what you don't know is that Mr. Eisenberg and Mr. Gosenberg and Mr. Fineberg and Mr. Goldberg and Mr. Wienberg is all cousins. They got you working for nothing, and they take back the little nothing you make before you can get home with it. That's how they got you in the economic locks.[46]

As this dialogue points out, the culture of prejudice affects *all* groups in our society. It defines the personal antipathies of minority groups toward one another in much the same way that it defines the antipathies of the majority toward various minorities.

45. Kenneth B. Clark and Mamie P. Clark, "Racial Identification and Preference in Negro Children," in *Readings in Social Psychology*, 3rd ed., ed. Eleanor Maccoby *et al.* (New York: Holt, Rinehart and Winston, Inc., 1958), pp. 602–611.

46. Louis E. Lomax, *The Negro Revolt* (New York: Harper & Row, Inc., 1962), pp. 179–180.

The origins of prejudicial norms. Cultural norms related to racial and ethnic minorities develop in the way that other kinds of norms develop. In some cases it is possible to trace their specific point of invention; in other cases they seem to have been borrowed from other societies; in still other cases their origins are simply obscured in the mists of the past.

It is clear that a society in which various groups of unlike people are pitted in competition with each other for scarce values offers a fertile site for the unwitting "invention" of prejudices. In fact, some social scientists maintain that prejudices have originated in societies explicitly for the purpose of assuring the economic or political dominance of the majority. For example, in American society we have always competed for wealth, power, or other rewards. Thus, prejudices toward various minorities could easily be attributed to the problems posed by strong intergroup competition. Such prejudices also could have been perpetuated as a means of consolidating and holding gains when one group emerged as clearly dominant. Over time, such norms tend to become institutionalized as a part of the general culture and begin to play a part in the socialization of the next generation.

In our discussion of America's Chinese minority, we reviewed a specific instance of prejudice rising out of competition. During a time of economic crisis, substantial segments of the white population of the Pacific Coast found themselves in direct competition for jobs with newly arrived immigrants from the Orient. In the struggle the Chinese became the objects of intense prejudice and discrimination, where earlier they had been valued for the essential services they were performing.

The hypothesis that the culture of prejudice arises out of intergroup competition for scarce values and that it is perpetuated as a means of maintaining the position of the dominant group receives indirect support from evidence that unlike groups have often lived together without developing mutual prejudices. Ralph Linton has described the historical situation of the Puyallup Indians of the Puget Sound region of the present state of Washington. When white men first began to settle the region in small numbers, the settlers and the Indians developed a harmonious and symbiotic—or mutually advantageous—relationship. Indians worked for the whites and were treated fairly. There was mutual respect on

both sides. In the absence of white women, many settlers legally married Indian women. These unions provoked no social stigma. The two groups worked together, traded together, and adopted numerous customs from each other. Then, following the Civil War and the more general opening of the West, large numbers of whites came into the area. The white man's culture was more vigorously established. The partially assimilated and cooperative society of an earlier time was overwhelmed.[47] The point of the example is that in this somewhat unique situation of symbiosis, the usual intergroup prejudices did not develop. The factors of competition and discrimination were absent, making mutual antipathies unnecessary and even dysfunctional.

Norms of prejudice may also be part of a traveler's baggage. When millions of European immigrants came to this country, they brought with them the cultures of prejudice that they shared in their countries of origin. Anti-Semitism crossed the Atlantic, along with anti-Catholicism and the innumerable cross-border animosities spawned by ethnocentrism overseas.

Social distance hierarchies. One of the most stable aspects of the culture of prejudice has been revealed by the accumulated behavioral research on *social distance*. These investigations probe the degree to which people are willing to admit members of racial and ethnic categories to intimacy in social relationships.[48] The basic technique for obtaining measures of social distance is described in the Methodological Essay opposite.

One interesting finding of research in social distance is that members of minority groups appear to share the views of the dominant group. Blacks, for example, will place their own group at the top of the scale of preference, but in all other respects their rankings are almost identical to those of whites.[49] This phenomenon has been studied among such diverse classes of respon-

47. Ralph Linton, *Acculturation in Seven American Indian Tribes* (New York: D. Appleton-Century Company, 1940), p. 37.

48. For a very different approach to the study of social distance between black and white, see Frank R. Westie and Margaret Westie, "The Social Distance Pyramid: The Relationship Between Caste and Class," *American Journal of Sociology*, 63, No. 2 (September 1957), 190–196.

49. Eugene Hartley, *Problems in Prejudice* (New York: King's Crown Press, 1946).

METHODOLOGY   MEASURING SOCIAL DISTANCE

Beginning in 1924, Professor Emory S. Bogardus developed a scale for the quantitative measurement of the *social distance*—"degree of sympathetic understanding"—subjects feel exists between themselves and members of other groups. This scale is still a valuable means of obtaining information on the social distance between the subject and some specified category of others (usually members of minority groups). It has revealed rather stable hierarchies of social distance, which are part of the culture of prejudice.

The scale was originally constructed by using the procedure discussed in connection with the equal-appearing-intervals attitude scale (page 132). Some sixty statements, expressing varying degrees of social distance, were prepared. These were submitted to one hundred judges, who rated them on a seven-point scale according to the amount of social distance they were thought to express. The greater the social distance, the higher the rating. A score representing the average of the judges' ratings was obtained for each statement, and items that had received decidedly mixed ratings were deleted. A final scale was formed, with one item at each of the seven points along the continuum.

With this scale, the subject checks those statements that describe relationships he feels he would tolerate between himself and members of the group in question. For example, check those statements below that indicate relationships you would be willing to enter into with, say, *Australians:*

—— to close kinship by marriage   (1)
—— to my club as personal chums   (2)
—— to my street as neighbors   (3)
—— to employment in my occupation   (4)
—— to citizenship in my country   (5)
—— as visitors only to my country   (6)
—— would exclude from my country   (7)

The numbers at the right indicate the number of points associated with each statement. The larger the number, the greater the implied social distance. These numbers are not shown to actual subjects.

With this scale, the sociologist can assess the feelings of a set of subjects toward a number of different groups or categories (e.g., religious, racial, or nationality groups). Sometimes, fictional groups are included to see if subjects are realistic in their responses.

Response categories are arranged in such a way that the subject can easily check those statements that express his feelings of social distance for each group. In responding, he is instructed to use his *first reaction* toward the group in question. This procedure appears to yield more reliable results than if the subject were to carefully weigh his responses.

Once the subjects have responded to a set of groups in this manner, a score is obtained for a particular group by averaging the *point values* of the subjects' *lowest* responses with respect to that group. (Subjects sometimes check more than one category for each group.) This pooled score is the *distance quotient*, or DQ, for that group. A DQ of 1.00 would indicate that all subjects had checked statement 1 for the group in question, showing that they felt little or no social distance between that group and themselves. A DQ of 7.00, on the other hand, would indicate a maximum of social distance, or strong rejection.

When the DQ's of a number of groups are ranked from highest to lowest, they constitute a *social distance hierarchy* (See Table 10.3) for the subjects who responded to the scale. The study of such hierarchies reveals some of the prejudices subscribed to by the persons under investigation. Comparable research conducted at various points in time over the last forty years indicates that such hierarchies tend to be relatively stable.

See Emory S. Bogardus, *Social Distance* (Yellow Springs, Ohio: The Antioch Press, 1959).

dents as college students, business men, children, Jews and other religious groups, and American Orientals. Minor shifts appear in the relative position of one group or another, but overall our social distance hierarchy is very consistent. (See Table 10.3.)

Stereotypes, epithets, and clichés. Another significant aspect of the culture of prejudice is the lack of objectivity and the fictional quality of the beliefs that one group entertains about another. The development of unrealistic ideas about men who are different from oneself is as old as the history of intergroup contact.

Stereotypes are clusters of beliefs that are uniformly applied to certain groups of people.

They are prejudicial to the group involved when they connote a negative image and when they are categorical in nature. Thus, when an individual maintains that blacks are superstitious, lazy, happy-go-lucky, ignorant, and naturally musical—a stereotype long reinforced by Hollywood movies—he is entertaining an unrealistic set of conceptions. The simplest reflection would indicate that this or any other set of traits does not uniformly apply to all blacks any more than some analogous set of traits applies to all whites. Yet categorical thinking about minority groups is a very real part of the culture of prejudice.

Epithets pose a related problem. As part of the culture of prejudice we perpetuate the use

TABLE 10.3. **RACIAL AND ETHNIC DISTANCE IN THE UNITED STATES IN 1926, 1946, AND 1956**

GROUP	RANK 1926	GROUP	RANK 1946	GROUP	RANK 1956
English	1	Amer. (nat. white)	1	Amer. (nat. white)	1
Amer. (nat. white)	2	Canadians	2	Canadians	2
Canadians	3	English	3	English	3
Scotch	4	Irish	4	French	4
Irish	5	Scotch	5	Irish	5
French	6	French	6	Swedes	6
Germans	7	Norwegians	7	Scotch	7
Swedes	8	Hollanders	8	Germans	8
Hollanders	9	Swedes	9	Hollanders	9
Norwegians	10	Germans	10	Norwegians	10
Spanish	11	Finns	11	Finns	11
Finns	12	Czechs	12	Italians	12
Russians	13	Russians	13	Poles	13
Italians	14	Poles	14	Spanish	14
Poles	15	Spanish	15	Greeks	15
Armenians	16	Italians	16	Jews	16
Czechs	17	Armenians	17	Czechs	17
Indians (Amer.)	18	Greeks	18	Armenians	18
Jews	19	Jews	19	Japanese Amer.	19
Greeks	20	Indians (Amer.)	20	Indians (Amer.)	20
Mexican Amer.	21	Chinese	21	Filipinos	21
Mexicans	22	Mexican Amer.	22	Mexican Amer.	22
Japanese Amer.	23	Filipinos	23	Turks	23
Japanese	24	Mexicans	24	Russians	24
Filipinos	25	Turks	25	Chinese	25
Negroes	26	Japanese Amer.	26	Japanese	26
Turks	27	Koreans	27	Negroes	27
Chinese	28	Indians (East)	28	Mexicans	28
Koreans	29	Negroes	29	Indians (East)	29
Indians (East)	30	Japanese	30	Koreans	30

SOURCE: Emory S. Bogardus, *Social Distance* (Yellow Springs, Ohio: Antioch Press, 1959), p. 33.

of unflattering names for various groups. These connote negative images and are deeply resented by those to whom they refer. Although one might protest that names are not important, such terms as "nigger," "wop," "spic," "mick," "kraut," "gook," and "kike" are emotional terms that suggest undesirability and social rejection.

The same general situation is embodied in other verbal practices. In our common language and slang we maintain numerous *clichés* that tend to perpetuate prejudicial norms. For example, such phrases as "jew him down," "mighty white of you," and "working like a nigger" help to support negative stereotypes and maintain shared antipathies.

Stereotypes, epithets, and clichés of the type illustrated here are part of the culture of prejudice in two ways. They are themselves widely shared habits of belief and verbalization and are in this sense part of the folkways of society. At the same time, they are techniques for maintaining prejudice at the personal level. The individual who entertains such beliefs and habitually uses such epithets and clichés would have a difficult time in adopting more realistic views of the minority groups involved. Although members of the dominant group use them casually, they are stinging insults to the minority groups that are victims of the antipathies they express.

SUMMARY

The concept *minority group* implies a relationship of differential status and power between one group and another, a relationship that does not necessarily depend on the relative size of the two groups. There are many types of minority groups: almost any distinguishable characteristic can serve to set one category of people apart as somehow "inferior" to the dominant segment of society. The most commonly used criteria of minority-group identity are race and ethnicity, though both concepts are extremely vague. The definitions of race used popularly and even officially in the United States, for example, have no scientific foundation. Nevertheless, they are very real in their consequences. To be labeled a nonwhite is to be automatically assigned a low position in our system of social ranking.

In reviewing the history of intergroup relations within the perspective of American society, we have outlined the experiences of blacks, Jews, Indians, Orientals, and Spanish-speaking peoples in our country in order to show how the present structure of our dominant-minority relationships has emerged over the years. As the history of American minorities makes clear, intergroup relations do not follow a single pattern and seldom are completely stable. The structure of relationship that prevails at any given time between a dominant group and a particular minority is a product of historical circumstance as well as of the posture each group assumes toward the other. Common patterns of dominant-minority relationship are aggression, segregation, pluralism, and fusion through assimilation or amalgamation. Although the dominant group is primarily responsible for defining the broad structure of intergroup relations, the pattern that emerges also depends on the response of the minority group.

Discrimination against minority groups is perpetuated largely through prejudice, a negative emotional bias that is highly resistant to change and is applied categorically to all members of the group in question. Prejudice is usually viewed as an individual phenomenon with its origins in various psychological processes. However, it must also be viewed collectively as part of the culture that is passed on from generation to generation through the socialization process. The culture of prejudice contains not only a relatively stable set of social-distance relationships between various groups but also beliefs and verbal habits that support prejudice, such as negative stereotypes, epithets, and clichés. The view of prejudice as a cultural phenomenon does much to explain the persistence of discriminatory practices in a society that formally avows the equality of all its members.

II
Collective Behavior

From time to time throughout history men have been swept up in spontaneous forms of behavior that follow neither logic nor past experience nor the established conventions of society. They have participated in riots, lynchings, ecstatic religious revivals, wild outbursts of financial speculation, migrations, manias, crazes, and a great variety of unusual social movements. Some of these phenomena occur within relatively small aggregates, where people are in close spatial proximity. Others are more diffuse, sometimes involving large numbers of people or taking place over long periods of time.

Sociologists use the term *collective behavior* as a rather loose label for such events. The term is somewhat misleading since all kinds of social interaction are in a sense "collective," but its use has become traditional in referring to social behavior that does not follow an organized pattern of conventions and expectations. Essentially, collective behavior differs from group behavior in that it is relatively unstructured and therefore relatively unpredictable. Those involved do not know what they can expect of others or what is expected of them. As a result, their behavior often takes unexpected turns.

The most dramatic forms of collective behavior usually take place when people are confronted with a situation to which they feel compelled to respond but for which they have no previously acquired guides to action. They have to do *something*, but they lack established social or cultural routines for handling the situation. Thus the teen-age girls who went to theaters to hear Frank Sinatra sing in the 1940's felt they had to respond to their idol with something more than applause. They swooned. A generation later their daughters reacted to the Beatles by shrieking and throwing jelly beans. In both cases, the response quickly became routine.

The thousands of Americans who were convinced by a radio play in 1938 that the country was indeed being invaded by Martians also had to do *something*:

Long before the broadcast had ended, people all over the United States were praying, crying, fleeing frantically to escape death from the Martians. Some ran to rescue loved ones. Others telephoned farewells or warnings, hurried to inform neighbors, sought information from newspapers or radio stations, summoned ambulances and police cars. At least six million people heard the broadcast. At least a million of them were frightened or disturbed.[1]

Even though collectivities lack a pattern of social organization, collective behavior is seldom if ever completely unstructured. Probably only the most extreme danger could lead to an instance where each individual in an aggregate might act wholly on his own, completely oblivious to the influence of others. Most types of collective action are quite clearly combinations of structured and unstructured behavior. A typical audience, for example, has many elements of social organization even though it is not a group. There are general norms of audience behavior, and sanctions are available for controlling anyone who fails to follow them. Because the structure of an audience is very loose, however, behavior can quickly become disorganized and unpredictable: a wildly enthusiastic audience at a rock concert may unexpectedly become a mob that tears the theater apart; at the cry of "fire," previously sedate theater-goers may begin to stampede. By contrast, some forms of collective behavior, such as social movements (page 183), become *more* rather than less structured as time goes on, evolving roles and a system for ranking them as well as special norms and techniques of social control. What began as a collectivity thus becomes an organized group.

Sociologists are interested in collective behavior not only because it is a fascinating phenomenon in its own right but also because it frequently is a stimulant to sociocultural change. The Paris mob was instrumental in destroying monarchy in France during the French Revolution. Crowd reaction to the rhetoric of Adolf Hitler opened the way to Nazi control of Germany in the 1930's. In the United States, urban riots have stimulated new social programs and at the same time brought increased demands for stronger law enforcement. Indeed, "law and order" has become a significant issue largely because of the many recent instances of collective behavior.

The "tulip mania" that occurred in Holland in the seventeenth century shows how collective behavior can take strange turns with unpredictable results.[2] The tulip, said to have been introduced from Turkey in 1559, was at first a rarity

1. Hadley Cantril, "The Invasion from Mars," in Eleanor Maccoby *et al.*, *Readings in Social Psychology* (New York: Holt, Rinehart and Winston, Inc., 1958), pp. 291–292.

2. Charles Mackay, *Extraordinary Popular Delusions and the Madness of Crowds* (New York: L. C. Page, 1932), pp. 89–97. (Reprint of the original 1841 edition.)

in Holland, prized only by a few horticultural enthusiasts; but before long every man of wealth had a collection of the plants, and soon the enthusiasm spread to the middle class. Bulbs were scarce, and their prices rose rapidly as demand increased. People became less and less interested in the flowers as such and more and more interested in the profit to be made from buying and selling them. In the 1630's a rage for tulip bulbs swept Holland. Some bulbs sold for the equivalent of thousands of dollars— many times the value of their weight in gold. Then, mysteriously, prices began to level off. The shrewder speculators quietly disposed of their holdings. As prices slipped, public confidence melted away. Thousands were ruined when they were unable to sell bulbs for which they had paid enormous sums. The price of tulips fell to almost nothing.

This widely documented case of a mania surrounding a specific cultural element provides an interesting example not only of spontaneous collective behavior but also of the lasting impact such an incident can have. To this day, Holland remains the world center of tulip growing. Thus the society as a whole was altered by an instance of collective behavior.

Unfortunately, collective behavior is one of the most difficult of all areas of human social conduct to study within the scientific perspective. One cannot tap a rioter on the shoulder and begin an interview by saying, "Pardon me, sir, but I notice you're looting this store. Would you mind answering a few questions for scientific purposes?" As a rule, the researcher is confined to studying reconstructed accounts of such events, obtained after the fact from people who either participated or observed. In the case of some of the more persistent forms of behavior such as social movements—the current civil rights movement, for example—the behaviors of participants and the organizational aspects of the activity can be studied more leisurely. Even here, however, it is difficult to locate, trace, and understand all the relevant phenomena. And the task becomes almost impossible in the case of historic outbursts like the dance mania that struck medieval Italy and the obsession with witches that swept Europe in the sixteenth and seventeenth centuries and spread to the New England colonies.

For these reasons, the study of collective behavior tends to be more discursive than empirical, to be based more on theoretical specula-tion than upon rigorously accumulated data. In the present chapter, attention will be focused first on theories of crowd behavior and then on some of the processes by which crowds or other collectivities become transformed from peaceful assemblies to active, emotional aggregates such as mobs. These theoretical formulations will then be applied to the analysis of an actual instance of collective behavior, an urban riot.

THEORETICAL APPROACHES TO THE STUDY OF CROWDS

Crowds are common in ordinary life, well within the range of experience of every individual. They range from small clusters of street-corner gawkers to huge gatherings of spectators at scheduled events. Casual crowds that form spontaneously and crowds of the audience type that come together purposefully share many characteristics. Under certain circumstances, they can become transformed into highly expressive aggregations within which dramatic forms of collective behavior occur.

Traditionally, crowds have been studied in terms of their impact on the individual. Both classic and contemporary writings in sociology have made this "social psychology" of crowds a major focus of theoretical attention. But crowds must also be understood within a theoretical framework derived from concepts of social organization. In the sections that follow, several types of crowds will be analyzed from these two distinct perspectives.

ORGANIZATIONAL CHARACTERISTICS OF CROWDS

There have been many attempts to classify crowds, and no completely standard taxonomic system has yet been adopted by sociologists. For present purposes, a relatively simple scheme will serve to focus attention on the salient concepts. For example, no elaborate distinction need be made between crowds and audiences; they share enough characteristics so that the actions of both may be regarded as variants of crowd behavior. More important are the general features and patterns of the acts the members engage in and

VIEWPOINTS LAW AND ORDER

"Civil disobedience," a seditious slogan of gross irresponsibility, has captured the imagination of citizens who are morally, mentally, and emotionally immature. It has been spread at street corner rallies by those who would use it as an avenue to personal power and prestige. And it has been spread in the false guise of academic freedom in the halls of public and private institutions that have permitted emotional and often obscene harangues against morality and reason. What they really seek is license, not freedom.

I am greatly concerned that certain racial leaders are doing the civil rights movement a great disservice by suggesting that citizens need only obey the laws with which they agree. Such an attitude breeds disrespect for the law and even civil disorder and rioting. The citizen has no latitude as to what laws he must obey. If he feels a law is wrong or unjust, he has recourse to established constitutional procedures to have it changed through his legally elected representatives.

It is reprehensible for any person to select those laws he will obey and those he will ignore. Such defiance is a form of anarchy. It is shameful and disgraceful for persons in high authority to condone or urge the breaking of established laws.

I have also become increasingly concerned about the influence wielded upon the impressionable minds of our youth by some so-called educators, such as the college professor who reportedly urged a group of students at the University of California to burn their draft cards, refuse to pay income taxes, and, if necessary, go to jail for their actions.

Civil disobedience is not, and must not become, an accepted norm of behavior in a society of free men. It leads to anarchy, and preempts all possibility of rational discussion or appeal.

No longer can respectable citizens complacently stand by while celebrity status is accorded those with sick minds and corrupt souls who tamper with and ridicule our orderly processes of government under law.

We must choose between law and anarchy, freedom and chaos.

Is America as a nation being swept by an epidemic of spiritual malnutrition? I fervently hope not; but the danger signs are all too clear. I fear that the public may be coming to accept widespread lawlessness as an unavoidable adjunct to our way of life.

J. Edgar Hoover
"The Faith of Freedom"

Civil disobedience is a grave enterprise. It may sometimes be justified, but the provocation for it has to be equally grave. Basic principles have to be at issue. The evils being combated have to be serious evils that are likely to endure unless they are fought. There should be reasonable grounds to believe that legal methods of fighting them are likely to be insufficient by themselves.

Nor is this the only limitation on the individual's moral right to disobey the law. The most important limitation is that his cause must be a just one. . . .

But who is to make these difficult decisions? Who is to say that one man's moral principles are right and another man's wrong? We come here to the special function that civil disobedience serves in a society. The man who breaks the law on the ground that the law is immoral asks the rest of us, in effect, to trust him, or to trust those he trusts, in preference to the established conventions and authorities of our society.

He has taken a large and visible chance, and implicitly asked us to join him in taking that chance, on the probity of his personal moral judgment. In doing so, he has put it to us whether we are willing to take a similar chance on the probity of our own judgment. . . .

This, indeed, may be the most important function of those who practice civil disobedience. They remind us that the man who obeys the law has as much of an obligation to look into the morality of his acts and the rationality of his society as does the man who breaks the law. The occurrence of civil disobedience can never be a happy phenomenon; when it is justified, something is seriously wrong with the society in which it takes place.

But the man who puts his conscience above the law, though he may be right or he may be wrong, does take personal moral responsibility for the social arrangements under which he lives. And so he dramatizes the fascinating and fearful possibility that those who obey the law might do the same. They might obey the law and support what exists, not out of habit or fear, but because they have freely chosen to do so, and are prepared to live with their consciences after having made that choice.

Charles Frankel
"Is It Ever Right to Break the Law?"

the meaning these acts have for them. We may classify crowds, for example, on the basis of whether the members have gathered spontaneously or for a scheduled event, whether they are behaving peacefully or violently, and whether they are preoccupied mainly with personal, subjective experiences or with events and objects external to themselves.

In addition, we may analyze crowd behavior on the basis of its *organizational* characteristics. Students of collective behavior usually emphasize its lack of social organization; in fact, they point to the unstructured nature of the settings in which such behavior occurs as one important feature that permits the action to take the form it does. As we suggested earlier, however, the unstructured nature of the setting for collective behavior is neither absolute nor constant. In some instances, certain components of social organization may be present in elementary form; in others, the situation may approach a more truly unstructured character. The following discussion, then, will include not only the major crowd forms but also the varying organizational characteristics of such crowds.

The casual crowd. Some years ago, Blumer proposed a relatively simple way of classifying crowds.[3] For example, one important and obvious category of crowd behavior is provided by the *casual* crowd. Onlookers come together spontaneously for brief periods when their attention is drawn to some commonly perceived event. They do very little but view that event and are thus mainly a passive and fleeting aggregate of persons.

As sociologists have pointed out, the members of a casual crowd share no collective goal and do not interact in any recognized pattern to achieve norms, a division of labor, techniques of social control, or a hierarchy of social ranking. Although they define their behavior in terms of norms, roles, social control, etc., these derive from other groups or from the more general folkways rather than from conventions established within the crowd itself. In this sense, the casual crowd is one of the least structured of all human collectivities. It lacks completely any form of social organization generated within itself.

The conventionalized crowd. The conventionalized crowd is one which assembles for a specific purpose. Its behavior is essentially like that of the casual crowd, except that it is usually expressed in established ways. The church congregation is quiet and respectful; the audience in the concert hall applauds politely; the fans at a ball game roar their approval and disapproval.

Clearly, some of the prerequisites and components of group structure discussed in Chapter 1 are present in the typical conventionalized crowd. The members of an audience, for example, are usually pursuing some kind of mutual goal, namely the purpose for which they are assembled. On the other hand, this goal is normally pursued as an individual matter, not by means of coordinated interaction among all members. If the members do interact, their interaction is generally brief and impersonal.

The conventionalized crowd normally imposes certain simple norms and roles on its members. For example, the person who laughs when hushed silence is more appropriate or who makes an unnecessary commotion may be deviating from expected and approved patterns. The roles of participants vary in different types of conventionalized crowds: the behavior permitted and even expected of an enthusiastic fan at a boxing match would certainly be regarded as conspicuously deviant at a religious gathering. When individuals deviate from expected norm and role expectations, attempts at informal social control are likely to be forthcoming. In the case of conspicuous nonconformity, fellow members of an audience may first ask the offender to desist and then, if he continues, demand that he leave.

While these elements of social organization are generally observable in conventionalized crowds, other important elements are usually absent. There is no allocation of specialized roles forming a coordinated division of labor. Consequently, there is no system of differentially rewarded and differentially ranked positions. The conventionalized crowd, in other words, is a *quasi group*. It lacks important elements of social organization, and whatever structure it does have is extremely unstable and relatively useless in the face of crisis.

The active crowd. Neither casual nor conventionalized crowds take collective action with

---

3. Herbert Blumer, "Elementary Collective Groupings," in *New Outline of the Principles of Sociology,* ed. Alfred McClung Lee (New York: Barnes & Noble, Inc., 1951), pp. 178–179.

respect to objects or individuals external to themselves. In contrast, the active crowd is one that openly engages in more volatile forms of behavior directed toward persons, things, or events. For example, damage to property or injuries to persons may result from the externally focused behavior of an active crowd, such as a mob participating in a riot. On occasion, a conventionalized crowd of sports fans becomes an active crowd.

The active crowd is normally very lacking in structure. As Blumer describes it:

It has no heritage or accumulation of tradition to guide its activity; it has no conventions, established expectations, or rules. It lacks other important marks

4. *Ibid.*, p. 180.

of a society, such as an established social organization, an established division of labor, a structure of established roles, a recognized leadership, a set of norms, a set of moral regulations, an awareness of its own identity, or a recognized "we-consciousness."[4]

The expressive crowd. Still different is the expressive crowd, in which the subjective experiences of the members themselves are the principal feature of attention. A highly emotional religious revival meeting is an example. In the context of such a crowd, exaltation, grief, joy, fear, and other emotions can be generated in ways unlikely to be experienced by individual members in isolation. Another example is the rock music festival, where members of the au-

Occasionally a conventionalized crowd of sports fans becomes an active crowd. In 1966, for example, this soccer game in Lima, Peru, turned into the worst riot in sport history; scores of people were trampled to death and nearly five hundred were injured. The riot was set off by one man, who walked onto the field to protest a referee's decision.

A teen-age audience at a Beatle concert may begin as a conventional gathering but will generally become an expressive crowd. This photograph points up the fact that members of expressive crowds seldom monitor their own behavior, let alone the behavior of their fellow members.

dience react in a wide variety of ways to the emotional impact of the music.

Although the expressive crowd may develop initially as a conventionalized collectivity, it soon becomes a *nongroup*. As emotional processes become more intense, the concept of "expectation," which is basic to the ideas of norms and roles, no longer applies. Members of expressive crowds seldom monitor their own behavior, let alone the behavior of their fellow members. Thus, norms and roles in the usual sense of institutionalized expectations cease to be relevant in such settings. The concepts of social control and social ranking are similarly irrelevant.

On the other hand, as we will point out later, certain forms of behavior can be uniformly, if temporarily, adopted by members of active and expressive crowds. Such behavioral forms serve as *apparent norms* to give definition and guidance to overt action. But they do not become institutionalized and are therefore not true norms.

THE SOCIAL PSYCHOLOGY OF CROWD BEHAVIOR

One important focus of attention in the study of crowds is on the social psychology of crowd behavior. In a crowd, an individual may behave quite differently than he would when acting alone or as a member of a more conventional group. Both sociologists and social psychologists have tried to understand why this is so.

LeBon's analysis. The classic analysis of the crowd is that of Gustave LeBon, whose *Psychologie de foules*, a work first published in Paris in 1895, gave direction to the study of the social psychology of crowd behavior.[5] LeBon was interested in the role of crowds in the new type of society that had emerged in Europe in the nineteenth century. Increasing secularization and industrialization were the dominant social

5. Gustave LeBon, *The Crowd: A Study of the Popular Mind* (New York: The Viking Press, Inc., 1960).

trends of his time, and he felt that, as older societal forms were giving way to a newer urban and industrial social order, crowd behavior was assuming increasing importance. "The age we are about to enter," he said, "will in truth be the *era of crowds.*" In many respects, history has validated LeBon's prediction. During the twentieth century we have experienced many dramatic instances of crowd behavior—in the totalitarian states of the 1930's and 1940's, for example, and more recently on our campuses and in our urban centers.

A major focus in LeBon's work is the psychological impact of the crowd on its individual members. He concluded that the persons forming a crowd underwent marked changes that led them to behave in new ways:

Whoever be the individuals that compose it, however like or unlike be their modes of life, the fact that they have been transformed into a crowd puts them in possession of a sort of collective mind which makes them feel, think and act in a manner quite different than that in which each individual of them would feel, think and act were he in a state of isolation.[6]

While the term "collective mind" has been abandoned by most behavioral scientists as misleading, the idea that a crowd can produce profound changes in the psychological functioning of its individual members is still a viable hypothesis. Ordinary observation of individuals cheering, jumping, and screaming at an exciting basketball game reveals that they are swept up in enthusiasms and emotional displays that could scarcely be generated in solitude. In the more ominous situation of the lynch mob, persons who would not individually think of themselves as killers can collectively commit acts of extreme violence.

LeBon's attempts to account for the behavior of individuals in crowd situations were much influenced by the new emphasis on psychiatry, which had come into vogue in his time. LeBon felt that the *anonymity* the crowd provides somehow strips away the checks on behavior that are generally operative under ordinary circumstances. This, he felt, permits the individual to be responsive to *unconscious motivations.* LeBon believed that several factors lead to this change

in psychological functioning when the ordinary person becomes a member of a crowd. First, he said, the individual in a crowd acquires a "sentiment of invincible power." This allows him to yield to impulses which he would have resisted had he been alone. Second, *contagion* aids in spreading sentiments and orientations throughout the crowd, and at the same time the member of the crowd becomes highly *suggestible* to influences from his fellow members. LeBon saw in this situation a close analogy between the man in the crowd and the person in the grip of a hypnotic trance:

Such is approximately the state of the individual forming part of a psychological crowd. He is no longer conscious of his acts. In his case, as in the case of the hypnotized subject, at the same time certain faculties are destroyed, others may be brought to a high degree of exaltation. Under the influence of a suggestion, he will undertake the accomplishment of certain acts with irresistible impetuosity. This impetuosity is the more irresistible in the case of crowds than that of the hypnotized subject, from the fact that the suggestion being the same for all individuals of the crowd, it gains strength by reciprocity.[7]

Thus, the key concepts in LeBon's analysis of the social-psychological impact of the crowd on its members are: *anonymity, unconscious motivations, contagion, suggestibility,* and *reciprocal influence.* While many aspects of LeBon's work can be severely criticized within contemporary perspectives, these concepts recur in analyses of crowd behavior right up to the present time.

Blumer's analysis. In the 1940's, Herbert Blumer analyzed the active crowd in more contemporary terms. His conceptualization is clearly influenced by that of LeBon:

The character of the [active] crowd can be appreciated better by understanding the condition of the typical member. Such an individual loses ordinary critical understanding and self-control as he enters in rapport with other crowd members and becomes infused by the collective excitement which dominates them. He responds immediately and directly to the remarks and actions of others instead of interpreting these gestures, as he would do in ordinary conduct. His inability to survey the actions of others before responding to them carries over to his own tendencies to act. Consequently, the impulses aroused in

---

6. *Ibid.,* p. 27.
7. *Ibid.,* pp. 31–32.

him by his sympathetic sharing of the collective excitement are likely to gain immediate expression instead of being submitted to his own judgment. It is just this condition which is the mark of suggestibility; it explains why the role of suggestion is so pronounced in the crowd.[8]

Blumer has also suggested the salient social-psychological characteristics of the *expressive* crowd. In many respects it is like the active crowd, except that unlike the former it lacks a focused objective or goal. As a result, it develops no plan of action. The members of the crowd are in a state of excitement, but with no objective to focus on, they lack the means to achieve release of tension. Instead, they engage in mutual and reciprocal stimulation, which produces still higher levels of excitement. In such a situation, the expression of feelings and the release of tension can become ends in themselves. Thus, the actions of the expressive crowd often include such behaviors as shouting, leaping, screaming, weeping, and laughing. In more extreme cases, especially when coupled with religious stimulation, behavior may take the form of glossolalia ("speaking in tongues") or uncontrollable physical spasms.

The religious type of experience in the expressive crowd provides Blumer with a useful illustration:

The stimulation that the individual receives from those with whom he is in rapport lessens his ordinary self-control and evokes and incites impulsive feelings which take possession of him. He feels carried away by a spirit whose source is unknown, but whose effect is acutely appreciated. There are two conditions which are likely to make this experience one of ecstasy and exaltation, and to seal it with a sacred or divine stamp. The first is that the experience is cathartic in nature. The individual who has been in a state of tension, discomfort and perhaps anxiety, suddenly gains full release and experiences the joy and fullness that come with such relief. This organic satisfaction unquestionably yields a pleasure and exhilaration that makes the experience momentous. The fact that this mood has such complete and unobstructed control over the individual easily leads him to feel that he is possessed or pervaded by a kind of transcendental spirit. The other condition which gives the experience a religious character is the approval and sanction implied in the support coming from those with whom he is in rapport. The

fact that others are sharing the same experience rids it of suspicion and enables its unqualified acceptance.[9]

Thus, according to Blumer, both the active crowd and the expressive crowd provide similar social-psychological environments for their members. In each, the anonymity of the setting permits the individual to engage in forms of behavior that he would control in other kinds of situations; the excitement of the event makes him less critical of his own acts as well as of the behaviors of others. Feelings and emotions spread contagiously; the fact that many people are acting in unison legitimizes what is occurring; and the individual becomes open to suggestion from those around him. In the active crowd, suggestion focuses attention on some goal or objective, and emotional excitement is released in accomplishing this objective. In the expressive crowd, no such objective is formulated, and tensions must be individually released in forms of emotional behavior.

THE SOCIAL DYNAMICS OF COLLECTIVE BEHAVIOR

It is difficult to develop generalizations that apply equally to such varied forms of collective behavior as panics, riots, crazes, manias, and social movements, but in most cases four distinct processes seem to be involved. First, for the participants, conventional systems of norms and other features of organized social behavior become ineffective or inadequate. Second, emotional forms of behavior replace more rational response systems. Third, rumor (or some other form of informational input) aids in creating new interpretations or definitions of the situation and sets the stage for suggestibility and overt response. Finally, behavioral forms—such as running, praying, buying, looting, burning—diffuse through the crowd to bring collective behavior to an overt level. These interactional processes are defined as the "social dynamics" of collective behavior.

8. Blumer, *op. cit.*, pp. 180–181.
9. *Ibid.*, pp. 183–184.

INADEQUACIES OF EXISTING STRUCTURES

Dramatic forms of collective behavior do not ordinarily develop unless existing patterns of social organization become inadequate to guide and stabilize the behavior of individuals as they interact with each other. Structural inadequacies of this sort can originate in a number of ways.

Crisis-related inadequacies. Perhaps the easiest to understand of the various forms of structural inadequacy underlying collective behavior are those that result from crisis. In the typical audience situation, for example, the usual roles, norms, and procedures for social control provide no clues as to how one should behave if a fire or explosion occurs. On a sinking ship, panic is more likely if the passengers and crew are untrained in the use of lifeboats and life jackets and in the procedures for abandoning ship than if they have had drills in such matters.

Clearly, the patterns of social organization that stabilize behavior in normal times are not designed to meet the needs of the public when crisis strikes. On the other hand, populations can withstand extremely trying circumstances if

they are provided with suitably institutionalized forms of social organization. The populations of London, Berlin, and Tokyo, for example, were well trained in procedures for taking shelter, fighting fires, caring for the injured, and so on during the bombing raids of World War II. In each case, they survived harrowing situations without collapsing into chaos.

Intercultural conflict. In addition to temporary or crisis-related inadequacies of social organization, there are other ways in which institutionalized social arrangements can become inadequate as guides to stable behavior. Populations undergoing rapid cultural transition provide fertile ground for the development of certain kinds of collective behavior. Groups that have recently migrated from a rural to an urban environment would be included here, as well as populations whose traditional native culture is breaking down under the impact of more advanced societies. Persons caught up in such intercultural conflicts are especially likely to become involved in collective behavior.

In 1890, while first suffering the rigors of adjusting to life on reservations, American Indian tribes took up the "ghost dance," a ceremony that was supposed to cause the white man to disappear and the buffalo—and the Indians' ancestors—to return. Thus, through this religious movement, the unhappy present would be wiped out and the past restored.[10]

10. James Mooney, *The Ghost Dance Religion and the Sioux Outbreak of 1890* (Chicago: The University of Chicago Press, 1965).

In an expressive crowd, such as a religious revival meeting, tensions are released individually through emotional behavior. Since the release of tension often becomes an end in itself, the members of an expressive crowd usually engage in such behaviors as shouting, leaping, screaming, weeping, and laughing.

Intracultural discontinuities. Students of societal organization have long pointed out that social breakdown and disorder are far more likely in societies characterized by a complex division of labor, great social differentiation, and social heterogeneity than in traditional societies that are characterized by simpler role structure, homogeneous beliefs and values, and reciprocal binding ties of sentiment among members. (It will be recalled that Durkheim discussed such conditions as the basis for the distinction between mechanical and organic solidarity.[11])

As we have noted in earlier chapters, American society is characterized by many social and cultural discontinuities. It has not only an astronomical number of occupational specialties but many other sources of social heterogeneity, stemming from religious, ethnic, economic, regional, political, and racial differences. This heterogeneity provides a ready source of conflict. Goals, norms, roles, social ranking, and other aspects of organization differ substantially among our various groups, regions, classes, races, and occupations. The result is a social order that cannot encompass the needs and goals of all. Almost no one is *entirely* satisfied, and the majority are clearly dissatisfied in one way or another. As is evident on many college campuses today, these dissatisfactions can lead the individual to participate in various forms of collective behavior as he seeks solutions.

EMOTIONAL CONTAGION

Perhaps no interactional process is so important in generating certain types of collective behavior as that by which emotional orientations are spread from person to person in crowd situations. It is through this process of "emotional contagion" that the members of a crowd can become increasingly unified in their psychological outlook and increasingly committed to dramatic forms of action. The usual rational, self-imposed restraints on behavior deteriorate to allow the individual to be guided by impulse and emotion. Emotional contagion is especially important in those situations bordering on panic or riot. It is through this contagion that excited crowds can become destructive mobs, frightened audiences can bolt in screaming stampedes, highly stimulated congregations can be carried into religious ecstasy.

Homogeneity of members. Emotional contagion is more likely to occur among members of crowds that have common characteristics than it is among more heterogeneous aggregations. For example, an audience composed of young girls is more likely to experience waves of "swooning" in response to a popular singer than an audience made up of persons of different ages and both sexes. Similarly, a new craze or fad is more likely to spread among some specific segment of the population than among people from all walks of life. Homogeneity among members permits them to see each other as persons "like themselves." They are more available to each other as role models than are dissimilar persons.

Similarity of emotional mood. The initial mood that people share is an important factor in the development of emotional contagion. People who are assembled for a religious service, for example, usually share feelings of awe, reverence, or humility. This provides an important basis for psychological unity. People so unified can be led to states of religious exhilaration by an enthusiastic evangelist more easily than can an audience of people with initially mixed emotional states.

Focused attention. Emotional contagion is easier to stimulate in situations where people are focusing their attention on some dramatic and commonly perceived object than in situations where they are distracted by many different stimuli. For example, focused attention can be provided by a dramatic speaker, an incident involving police officers and a suspect, a fire in a theater, or any other event that commands the undivided attention of participants. Such focused attention distracts the individual from his thoughts or from contemplation of rational alternatives to present behavior.

Distraction from self. In large aggregates such as crowds, the individual is relatively anonymous. This alone reduces the necessity for constant self-monitoring. Constraints that are usually effective when the individual is in the presence of others who know him well, and whose reactions to his behavior are important to him, do not operate in the situation of anonymity. Furthermore, with his attention focused

---

11. See Chapter 2, page 92.

upon some dramatic event, the individual becomes less attentive to his own emotions and other reactions. He is, in other words, distracted from evaluating his own behavior and thus less subject to self-imposed restraints.

Suggestibility. The individual who loses awareness of self is open to suggestions from external sources. If he is surrounded by people who are exhibiting signs of growing excitement and tension, these emotional states become powerful suggestions for similar feelings in him. Suggestibility leads, therefore, to the adoption of the emotional states of others under conditions where the individual is giving little thought to his own responses and feelings but is concentrating on some strong external stimulus.

Reciprocal stimulation. Under conditions of focused attention, anonymity, narrowed field of consciousness, limited self-evaluation, and high suggestibility, the process of reciprocal stimulation can raise emotional levels quickly and sharply. For example, if a large number of people are verging on some strong emotional state such as fear, ecstasy, or anger, an observable manifestation of feeling on the part of one actor can call out a *similar* response on the part of another. This, in turn, can *reinforce* the emotions of the original actor and lead to an even stronger manifestation, which serves to stimulate the other person to a still greater response. Thus, an aggregate of persons can mutually reinforce each other's emotional responses and lead each other to emotional states of quickly mounting intensity.

Selective perception. Persons tend to see situations within selective frameworks even under the most ordinary circumstances. Their attitudes, needs, values, and other psychological predispositions all influence the meaning they assign to the events around them. When people are under the grip of strong emotions, this general principle operates very effectively. The person under the influence of strong religious emotion, for example, is far more likely to read divine implications into events coming to his attention than he would in calmer circumstances.

Selective perception often works through the process of emotional contagion to provide the participants in collective behavior with shared interpretation of a situation. Thus, by many of those radio listeners in 1938 who were convinced that our planet had been invaded by Martians, normal traffic outside on the street was "seen" as people fleeing the city.[12]

Under certain unsettling background conditions, new frames of reference can spread among the members of a population in such a way that a set of events will be perceived in a manner unrelated to reality. Situations of this type are sometimes referred to as *collective delusions.* They are most likely to develop when a population, already in a state of generalized tension, is confronted with a stimulus situation that appears to pose some kind of threat. The people involved share a pressing need to understand and cope with the threat, but little objective information is available to aid in the development of interpretive frameworks that are closely tied to reality. Under such conditions, people normally seek orienting frames of reference through interaction with others. Thus, socially derived interpretations of reality are substituted for objective definitions.[13]

Collective delusion is well illustrated by the Seattle "windshield pitting epidemic," which was studied in detail by Medalia and Larsen.[14] This phenomenon occurred in the spring of 1954, when the people of this western city became concerned that a strange agent was causing pits in the windshields of their cars. At first, the damage was attributed to vandals with air guns, and people took simple precautionary measures such as placing cardboard or plywood over their windshields when leaving their cars on the street. Soon, however, it became apparent that there were other forces responsible. Stories were circulated about the mysterious development of pitted windshields on cars that had been in locked garages or in protected underground storage areas. The mass media focused increasing attention on the issue in news broadcasts and in the press. Within a few days the entire community was in a state of excitement over the strange phenomenon.

Various explanations were advanced and circulated. Most popular was the idea that the pits had something to do with fallout from the

---

12. See Cantril, *op. cit.,* p. 295.

13. For further discussion of this process, see Chapter 13, p. 418.

14. Nahum Z. Medalia and Otto N. Larsen, "Diffusion and Belief in a Collective Delusion; The Seattle Windshield Pitting Epidemic," *American Sociological Review,* 23, 2 (April 1958), 180–186.

H-bomb tests that had been conducted in the Pacific only three weeks earlier. The Cold War focused attention on the Russians, who were held responsible by some. Other residents felt that the pits were a manifestation of God's displeasure with man's wickedness. A few advanced alternative explanations related to meteoric dust, malicious boys, and even mad scientists. Through emotional contagion, the level of excitement in the community grew to near-panic proportions. Finally, civic leaders appealed to state and federal authorities for help.

Meanwhile, careful research by physical scientists revealed no cause for the windshield pits, other than normal road damage. Studies by Medalia and Larsen established that the "windshield blight" was an instance of collective behavior resulting from new shared interpretations that had diffused through the community against a background of generalized tension concerning the bomb tests. People were looking *at* their windshields rather than merely *through* them. Pits caused by normal road damage were being interpreted in a new way.

The case of the "phantom anesthetist" of Mattoon, Illinois, provides yet another example of how perceptual distortion can become "contagious."[15] In September 1944 many of the people in this small community became deeply alarmed over a "mad gasser" who, they thought, was prowling their streets at night, spraying a "sweet sickly-smelling gas" into bedrooms. This gas was said to paralyze its victims for a period of two hours or more but not to harm them permanently. The gas seemed to disappear without a trace once the victims recovered.

This incident got its start when a middle-aged lady called the police to report that she and her daughter had been so victimized. The local newspaper ran a front-page story on the event the next day, complete with pictures. That night, several other persons phoned the police to report that they had been similarly attacked. By the second night, dozens of gassings were reported. During several succeeding evenings the mad gasser terrorized the entire community. The state police were called in along with other authorities. Elaborate measures were taken to apprehend the phantom anesthetist, but even though people kept reporting that he had struck, he was never seen. After a few days, no more gassings were reported, and the people of Mattoon stopped talking about the incident.

Here, again, the background of tension produced by the war years, with the ever present fear of such dangers as sabotage, secret weapons, and germ warfare, provided an important element. The role of the press in spreading

15. Donald M. Johnson, "The Phantom Anesthetist of Mattoon: A Field Study of Mass Hysteria," *Journal of Abnormal and Social Psychology* (April 1945), pp. 145–186.

During the "windshield pitting epidemic" of 1954, pits caused by normal road damage were being interpreted in a new way. As these photographs from a Seattle newspaper illustrate, people were looking at their windshields rather than merely through them.

an interpretive framework within which events in the environment could be interpreted was clear. Suggestion and rumor also played their parts. Finally, thanks to selective perception, any hissing sound heard after dark became the anesthetist's sprayer; any odd smell was the dreaded gas; any dim figure seen down the street was the mad gasser making his rounds.

In general, then, the process of emotional contagion involves a complex set of changes among those participating in some form of collective behavior. It is a process whereby excitement and various other emotional states spread through an aggregate of persons and provide the members with a psychological unity.

RUMOR

The exchange and spread of information by rumor is one of the most significant processes underlying the development of collective behavior in general. As we have seen, it plays a major role in collective delusion. In a very real sense, rumoring is itself a form of collective

behavior and can be studied as such in its own right.[16]

A rumor can be defined as an unverified report that is passed along from person to person, usually by word of mouth. It has no clearly identified source to establish its authenticity, but it answers a felt need for information and is therefore likely to be accepted at face value. Rumors usually develop within a context of ambiguity and stress, as when basic norms or beliefs are challenged, when physical danger looms, when our welfare seems to be at stake. Such situations arouse anxieties and concern. It is these feelings which provide the motivation for both listening to and passing on what we hear. As in the case of collective delusions, socially derived interpretations of reality may compensate for the lack of objective definitions.

The study of the rumor process has had a long tradition in the social sciences. One investigative approach has been to study artificially created "rumors" in a controlled laboratory setting, where rumor-like experimental messages are told and retold from person to person. A second major strategy has been to investigate actual rumors that have been generated spontaneously in situations of tension, in settings ranging from army camps to small towns and from prisons to college campuses. In each type of study, distortion in message content seems to have followed a typical pattern.

---

16. See Tomatsu Shibutani, *Improvised News: A Sociological Study of Rumor* (Indianapolis: The Bobbs-Merrill Company, Inc., 1966), especially pp. 95–128.

DAILY JOURNAL-GAZETTE

WEATHER
ILLINOIS: Fair tonight and Sunday. Warmer tonight. Little change in temperature Sunday.

Seventieth Year. No. 197   MATTOON, ILLINOIS, SATURDAY EVENING, SEPTEMBER 9, 194   All Phones 250   Price 5 Cents

"Mad Gasser" Adds Six Victims!

Stage Set for Siegfried Battle

5 WOMEN AND BOY LATEST OVERCOME

STRENGTH OF LINE SOON TO BE TESTED

Tight Censorship Believed to Be Favorable Indication

BY J. C. OESTREICHER
(I. N. S. Foreign Editor)

The stage was set today for a week-end test of the war's greatest enigma—strength or weakness of the Siegfried line.

Four powerful Allied armies swept from the west and south against the fortification's outposts, moving to within 18 miles of the German frontier at one point and promising an early arrival at the Belfort gap...

Doubts U. S. Land of Equal Chance

Chicago — (INS) — W. Lloyner, University of Chicago anthropologist, contended it "mythical" to believe every American school boy has an equal chance to reach the White House.

It's mythical, he said, because the American school system operates as a conservative force to keep most people in the class from which they spring.

Professor Warner asserted that the schools fail to provide equal opportunity because America has a complex and varied class system, more subtle than the distinctions of wealth. The schools fail to break class barriers, he said, being designed to fit into the distinctions. Using 100 as the average intelligence quotient, Warner declared:

"America cannot boast of equality of educational opportunity un...

VIET FORCES SWEEP INTO BULGARIA

Near Junction With Yugoslav Troops of Marshal Tito

BY NATALIA RENE
(I. N. S. Staff Correspondent)

Moscow—The rapidly expanding Soviet drive which has enveloped practically the whole of Romania swept into Bulgaria today on a 135-mile front, hammered westward at the gates of Yugoslavia and pushed northward beyond the liberated city of Sibiu in the direction of tottering Hungary.

Official confirmation of persistent...

Allied Leaders to Study Future of Italy

BY KINGSBURY SMITH
(I. N. S. Staff Correspondent)

Washington — It was learned authoritatively today that the future of Italy will be discussed at the forthcoming meeting between President Roosevelt and British Prime Minister Winston Churchill.

This conference between the two Allied leaders, which is expected to be held shortly in Canada, will deal with European political problems in addition to drafting plans for the final defeat of Japan next year.

Churchill, who recently visited Rome, is understood to favor a more lenient policy toward the Italians now. The British have been pursuing a cautious policy in Italy pending some indication as to which way that country would swing after the war. There was some fear in British circles that it might go...

ISOLATIONISM IS DEAD, SAYS GOV. DEWEY

G. O. P. Presidential Nominee Travels to Michigan

BY LEO W. O'BRIEN
(I. N. S. Staff Correspondent)

Aboard Dewey Campaign Train, Enroute to Michigan—Gov. Thomas E. Dewey traveled toward his native state of Michigan today for conferences and a week-end with his mother, after telling the people that American isolationism is dead and that peace plans must be lifted entirely out of politics.

The Republican presidential nominee, in a speech at the Louisville armory, where an audience of 12,500...

125 RETAILERS HEAR SPEECH ON AVIATION

Douglas Representative Speaks at Fall Meeting

Geoffrey F. Morgan of Chicago, a member of the speakers' bureau of the Douglas Aircraft Company, thrilled 125 persons at the fall dinner meeting of the Retail Division of the Mattoon Association of Commerce in the Masonic Temple Friday night with an address on future aviation.

Mr. Morgan, introduced by H. B. Ewing, chairman of the retail group, who presided at the dinner, spoke on the subject, "The Shape of Wings to Come."

4 in One House; Another Home Visited 4 Times in 2 Nights

Springfield, Ill.—(INS)—Failure to identify the gas sprayed into Mattoon homes by a phantom-like "mad anesthetist" was announced today by Richard T. Piper, chief of the Bureau of Criminal Identification and Investigation of the Illinois Department of Public Safety.

Piper said that State Chemist John Sutter reported to him that evaporation of the chemical stains on a cloth used by the mad anesthetist in attacking his victims had made the drug impossible of identification. But Piper, chief of the Bureau, had tested the stains for all known liquid cases without success.

The "mad gasser" incident began with a single telephone call and spread throughout the community by rumor, suggestion, and extensive news coverage. This front-page headline and story appeared in Mattoon's daily newspaper on September 9, 1944.

Experimental studies—the embedding pattern. Typical of the laboratory studies of rumor-like messages are those of Allport and Postman.[17] One subject, selected as the starter, is presented with a complex story or set of ideas. These stimulus materials are often reinforced with a drawing, photograph, or motion picture. It is the task of the first subject to relate what he has seen and heard to the next subject, who has not previously been exposed to the materials. This subject passes the information on to the next, and so on down the line. The version of the story reproduced at each stage is recorded and studied for content changes.

A number of investigations have shown that the general patterns of change that a message follows as it moves from person to person through these artificially constructed networks are fairly uniform.[18] The kinds of content distortion that occur in serial retelling have been termed the *embedding pattern*. The key elements in this pattern are leveling, sharpening, and assimilation:

Leveling has been defined as follows: "As rumor travels it tends to grow shorter, more concise, more easily grasped and told. In successive versions, fewer words are used and fewer details are mentioned."[19]

Sharpening has been defined as "the selective perception, retention, and reporting of a limited number of details from a larger context."[20] By this process certain central details remain in the story, becoming the dominant theme, while others drop out.

Assimilation refers to the way in which items in the rumor are sharpened, leveled, or otherwise altered in accordance with attitudes, cultural themes, stereotypes, and the like. Assimilation distorts rumor content in the direction of established habits and conventions.[21]

Researchers are in substantial agreement that experimental messages studied under the conditions described tend to become reduced in length, edited in content to a more concise form, and, finally, fused with a combination of common cultural themes plus the attitudinal and interest biases of the subjects who actually do the retelling.

17. Gordon W. Allport and Leo Postman, *The Psychology of Rumor* (New York: Henry Holt and Company, 1947).
18. T. M. Higham, "The Experimental Study of the Transmission of Rumour," *British Journal of Psychology* (March-May 1951), pp. 42–55.
19. Allport and Postman, *op. cit.*, p. 75.
20. *Ibid.*, p. 86.
21. *Ibid.*, pp. 99–155.

The embedding pattern has been found not only in the laboratory setting but also in experimental studies in which messages were deliberately started in communities so that their pathways and distortions could be traced as they were passed from person to person. For example, one group of sociologists deliberately started a six-word message in a small community and allowed it to diffuse through the population for a period of three days.[22] A randomly selected sample, constituting 17 percent of the housewives, was selected to "start" the message, a simple commercial slogan which was devised for the research. The slogan extolled the merits of a particular local brand of coffee ("Gold Shield Coffee—Good as Gold!"). Each starter was given a pound of this coffee and told that interviewers would call at every house in town within three days to see who knew the slogan. The starters were also told that everyone who knew the slogan when the interviewers called would receive a free pound of coffee as a reward. To provide additional interest and motivation in the project, thirty thousand leaflets were scattered over the community from a plane. These leaflets informed the population about the slogan-spreading venture and pointed out that the free coffee would be given to those who could find out what the slogan was.

At the end of three days, 84 percent of the housewives in the community knew some version of the slogan, although even the simple six-word message had in many cases become badly garbled. The pathways of these messages were traced out step-by-step by having each participant recall whom she had heard it from and whom she had told. A total of ninety networks, some of great complexity, were reconstructed. By this means it was possible to assess the state of the message at each successive step or "remove" from the original starters. Clear patterns of leveling, sharpening, and assimilation were discovered: the message was distorted along exactly the same lines as those passed on under the more controlled conditions of the laboratory.

---

22. Melvin L. DeFleur, "Mass Communication and the Study of Rumor," *Sociological Inquiry*, 32, 1 (Winter 1962), 51–70.

23. Warren A. Peterson and Noel P. Gist, "Rumor and Public Opinion," *The American Journal of Sociology*, 57 (September 1951), 159–161.

24. Warren A. Peterson, "A Field Investigation of Sociology Examination Rumors," unpublished document.

Field studies—the compounding pattern. In both laboratory experiments and field experiments, the element of anxiety or stress usually associated with "real" rumors is absent. To understand the effects of stress in altering rumor content, we shall examine some typical findings from studies of spontaneous rumors. Typical of the field studies of rumor is that of Peterson and Gist, who investigated the diffusion of rumors in a small community during a period of public concern about the rape and murder of a fifteen-year-old girl.[23] A central theme emerged to the effect that Mr. X. (who had employed the girl as a baby-sitter) left the party that he and his wife were attending, returned to his home, entered the house, raped and murdered the girl, and returned to the party after changing his clothes. Developing around this central theme was a series of infinitely elaborated and distorted interpretive accounts concerning the activities, characteristics, motivations, background, and reactions of Mr. X. Stories were circulated concerning his relationship with his wife, details of the crime, the activities and suspicions of the police, and a multitude of related topics. Actually, Mr. X was completely exonerated after thorough police investigation. He had nothing to do with the crime.

A markedly similar pattern has been observed in an educational setting that generated rumors of a very different sort.[24] On the campus of a Midwestern university, a completely false rumor developed that a copy of the final examination given to all students in introductory sociology had been stolen. Widely diffused a short time before the examination was scheduled, this rumor created a great deal of concern. The central theme became compounded with further propositions concerning the identity of the persons who had stolen the exam, the students who were in possession of it, what the sociology department intended doing about it, what students could expect concerning the threat to their grades, and so forth.

Both these situations illustrate the *compounding pattern* of rumor distortion. People wanted and needed information to define the situation, but little was forthcoming from official sources. In such cases, one rumor simply *demands* another. If one hears that a girl has been murdered, the questions of who did it and under what circumstances become natural ones. Similarly, if an exam has been stolen, certain obvious questions impose themselves. Under conditions creating anxiety or distress, any scraps of explanatory information are eagerly sought after and enthusiastically transmitted. The fact that their source may have been someone's fertile imagination can easily be overlooked.

Although the embedding pattern is generally associated with non-threatening situations and the compounding pattern with threatening ones, the two patterns may not be mutually exclusive. As yet, social scientists have not been able to follow and record with great accuracy the exact distortions that occur in rumors spread through communities or organizations under stress. It is entirely possible that embedding and compounding *both* take place, at least in part. The central theme of a rumor may become shorter and more concise and may be distorted to fit with shared attitudes and cultural expectations; but this embedding process may be obscured by the growth and spread of additional rumors concerning other details of the original stimulus event. The confirmation of this hypothesis must await further research.

These various issues concerning the nature and functions of rumor have been discussed at some length because of the important role of rumor in many forms of collective behavior. In earlier chapters we have stressed that interpersonal activity of every type is dependent upon communication based upon significant symbols. Collective behavior is no exception. Rumors play a part in mobilizing participants, in orienting them individually to the events they will respond to in a collective manner, and in spreading shared definitions of appropriate action. These functions of rumor in the development of collective behavior will be illustrated in detail in a later section.

BEHAVIORAL CONTAGION

Behavioral contagion is that process by which excited bystanders may be transformed into people who *act*. Just as emotions sometimes diffuse through the members of a crowd or other collectivity, so also do patterns of overt behavior. Thus normally "sensible" people may suddenly find themselves stampeding for the exit of a theater or sports arena, selling their assets at a large loss in a financial panic, or setting buildings afire in a riot.

The social sciences have by no means developed a complete understanding of the nature of behavioral contagion. In many respects, it

seems to resemble what some of the sociologists of the late nineteenth century referred to as "imitation." Kurt and Gladys Lang have pointed out that sociological pioneers such as Walter Bagehot and Gabriel Tarde developed elaborate explanations of a wide range of societal phenomena on the basis of presumed instincts for imitation that all men were said to possess.[25] While we no longer attempt to explain imitative behavior in terms of instincts, it remains true that behavioral forms of many kinds spread rapidly from one person to others in a variety of circumstances. Lang and Lang maintain that the basis of such imitation is learning:

Children do ape their elders, and many of the behavioral forms in crowds, in fashion, as well as in highly conventionalized activity have the outward appearance of imitation. More recent psychological theory has located the sources of imitative behavior in learning.[26]

A more sociological explanation of the basis of behavioral contagion would recognize that people in stressful situations of collective behavior are faced with powerful urges to act but often lack socially validated guides to action. If some *innovator* suddenly commits an overt act, such as throwing a rock at a police car, bolting for the exit in the face of a fire, or scrambling to withdraw funds from the bank, this can serve as an *apparent norm*. That is, it can provide a social definition, which may seem to be shared by others, as to what the appropriate or expected patterns of behavior in the situation are. If several others suddenly take up the actions of the innovator, it is likely that most of those present will follow suit. Thus the spread of action forms in collective behavior can be regarded as a special case of diffusion processes. The rapidity with which the new behavior spreads through the relevant population does not alter this interpretation. The quick transformation of excited bystanders into overtly acting participants may be interpreted as an instance of the rapid emergence and sudden sharing of an apparent norm. (Since the new norm may be quickly abandoned, it may not represent "learning" in the sense of the establishment of a stable habit.)

In general, therefore, the social dynamics of collective behavior are the necessary and suffi-

25. Kurt Lang and Gladys Engel Lang, *Collective Dynamics* (New York: Thomas Y. Crowell Company, 1961), pp. 210–211.

26. *Ibid.*, p. 212.

cient conditions that (1) define existing forms of social organization as inadequate for some substantial number of persons, (2) excite these persons through the reciprocal generation of emotional orientations, (3) spread common interpretive rumors through the population, and (4) set off epidemic-like diffusions of overt behavioral forms in their midst. These concepts can now be used as a framework within which to describe and analyze a concrete instance of collective behavior—an urban riot.

THE ANATOMY OF A RIOT

Within the last few years, American society has witnessed a disturbing incidence of riots within the black ghettos of its cities. But riots are certainly not new, nor are they confined to urban ghettos. Americans can read of a riot in the newspapers or see a report of one on television almost any day of the year. Large-scale political riots in Africa, Asia, Europe, the Near East, and Latin America have all been fully reported in our news media. In our own country, institutional riots take place regularly in prisons and schools. Our nation's history includes such incidents as the draft riots in New York during the Civil War and the Boston police-strike anarchy of 1919.[27] It also records prior large-scale clashes between blacks and whites in Chicago, Detroit, and other cities, especially following World Wars I and II. Yet for many Americans these earlier upheavals always seemed somehow remote, involving "other" people in "other" places or times. The recent riots in our urban centers cannot be so easily dismissed. For the growing number of citizens who are concentrated in or near major cities, the events have taken place only a few minutes

away by car. Many people have been killed, and many more have been seriously injured. And perhaps most alarming of all for the ordinary citizen, the agents of law enforcement have seemed helpless to control the situation.

The scope of the recent urban riots and their nearness to the majority of the nation's population have stimulated a number of official inquiries into their causes. They have also resulted in many attempts to assign blame. The riots have been variously attributed to Communist conspirators, Black Power militants, recent migrants, local agitators, the criminal element, and youthful school dropouts. Careful analysis, however, has failed to indicate that they were precipitated by any of these categories in an organized manner. While members of all the categories (and others) were involved, there is no sound basis for assuming that any of them either caused or controlled the upheavals.[28]

But how do such events take place? What triggers a riot and how does it spread? In attempting to understand how such crises occur and through what stages they progress, we may examine the Watts riot, which occurred in Los Angeles in 1965. This riot attracted international attention, and its details have been painstakingly reported.[29] The reports provide a useful illustration of the anatomy of a riot.

INADEQUACIES IN THE AMERICAN SOCIAL STRUCTURE

From a sociological point of view, urban ghetto upheavals such as the Watts riot can best be understood as incidents of collective behavior that develop stage by stage until they erupt into widespread and destructive civil disorder. Such events have occurred not only among blacks in our own time but among every kind of population experiencing the appropriate social conditions. They are, in other words, the end product of forces generated within the society as a whole.

The sociologist Neil Smelser has suggested a useful explanation of the development of incidents of collective behavior in general. He has indicated the necessary and sufficient conditions that accumulate one by one until the behavior is touched off.[30] This general scheme in much modified form, plus theoretical concepts described earlier in this chapter, will be used as a framework for analyzing the course of events that led to the Watts riot and the conditions that sustained it for nearly a week.

---

27. Randolph Bartlett, "Anarchy in Boston," *The American Mercury*, 36 (1935), 456–464; also William H. Lofton, "Northern Labor and the Negro During the Civil War," *The Journal of Negro History*, 34 (1949), 251–273.

28. See, for example, Anthony Oberschall, "The Los Angeles Riot of August 1965," *Social Problems*, 15, 3 (1968), 322–341.

29. See Jerry Cohen and William S. Murphy, *Burn, Baby, Burn* (New York: E. P. Dutton & Co., Inc., 1966); *Violence in the City—An End or a Beginning,* Governor's Commission on the Los Angeles Riots (December 2, 1965); and Oberschall, *op. cit.*

30. Neil Smelser, *Theory of Collective Behavior* (New York: The Free Press, 1962).

Along with a widespread belief in police brutality there existed in Watts a deep hostility toward the police as the representatives of those who refused to accept black Americans. If a breakdown of social order was to occur, it was likely to be precipitated by an incident involving the police.

Chronic societal discontinuities. Black Americans experience a world of discriminatory societal norms; they have traditionally been allocated the more menial occupational roles and been assigned the most degrading of statuses within the society. Elements in our system of informal social control have long been aimed at "keeping them in their place." These aspects of our societal organization and cultural practices have left a heritage of bitterness that is highly conducive to resentment and even retaliation on the part of our black minority. Perhaps the remarkable thing is not that we have finally had a number of urban riots but that they did not come sooner and on a larger scale.

Flaws in the existing social structure are in themselves not causal. Rather, they provide situations that can become aggravated, providing other factors are present, to a point where violence can flare. They are *necessary* preconditions without which the riots would not have happened, but they are not *sufficient* conditions in themselves to trigger violent upheavals.

Acute local discontinuities. The chronic societal conditions that have been conducive to urban violence have existed for decades in our nation and in some ways were even worse in earlier times than they are now. Why, then, have ghetto riots flared up only within the last few years? A partial explanation is that particular kinds of problems have become acute in these areas, and these problems have created tensions and strains that led the people involved one step closer to upheaval. Smelser has referred to such conditions as "structural strain." Within an immediate social environment, inconsistencies, conflicts, and deprivations are generated that are more acutely frustrating and irritating than those that are more general to the nation. These constitute a second set of structural strains that operate as necessary conditions leading toward crisis.

The people of Watts, for example, are mostly relative newcomers to the Los Angeles area; by far the majority of them came from the South. Some came during World War II, drawn by the economic opportunity provided by an aircraft industry that was experiencing a shortage of labor. Others came more recently from rural regions of the South, where the average unskilled black has had no better prospect than a lifetime of grinding toil as a poorly paid field hand. Many chose Los Angeles because relatives or friends were already there. Others were attracted by the climate, the old idea of moving west to a better life, and a thousand other personal reasons. But whatever their motivation in coming to Watts, the majority anticipated a better way of life where the traditional problems of a minority would be minimized.

On the surface, Watts does indeed seem to offer a better environment, at least compared to the sharecropper's shack or the urban tenement of the eastern city. The houses are small but neat; there are grass and trees; the streets are wide and free of trash. Population density is high, to be sure, but not nearly so high as in some areas of other cities. Less visible, however, were a number of other factors. The area was characterized by official apathy and neglect.[31] There was little in the way of economic opportunity for the residents. Stores, operated for the most part by white owners, charged more for goods than did stores in other areas of the city. Unemployment rates were excessively high, especially for younger males. The lack of adequate public transportation facilities aggravated the unemployment problem by making it difficult for those without cars (about half the people in Watts) to take jobs in many parts of the city. Educational levels were excessively low. The surrounding white population was indifferent. Watts was an area of heavy relief burdens, broken homes, high rates of crime and delinquency—in general, a problem area with respect to almost every index of personal and social disorganization. The response of the larger community was mainly to make certain that the area was heavily policed.

Personal responses of bitterness and frustration may become cultural norms of alienation and dissatisfaction when shared with others who have had similar experiences. These provide collective orientations that help make chronic problems acute. Both the migrant from the South and the older resident of the Watts area found that the great struggle for civil rights had brought very little concrete improvement. New patterns of discrimination had been substituted for more familiar ones; total indifference had replaced more obvious prejudice; and unem-

ployment had taken the place of poorly paid agricultural work.[32]

THE SPREAD OF A GENERALIZED BELIEF

In areas where people with similar grievances are concentrated, chronic problems tend to be perceived as acute. Before a violent collective response can erupt, however, the situation of strain must be clearly *focused* and made more meaningful in concrete terms to the potential actors. One of the ways in which this takes place, according to Smelser, is through the growth and spread of a "generalized belief." Specific targets for hostility must be identified. These must be interpreted as major *sources* of the dissatisfactions and strains impinging upon the potential actors. For the people of Watts, this specific target became the police.

It is difficult to say whether or not the police in this urban area were any more abusive in their contacts with black residents than police are in similar areas elsewhere. The limited evidence available suggests that they probably were. The important point is that a belief had built up among this population that white officers were unnecessarily harsh and discriminatory in their enforcement of the law where black citizens were concerned.

At best, the job of the police in a situation of this type is difficult. More than occasionally, it is also dangerous. Daily in ghetto areas, numerous incidents of police-citizen contacts occur that would be handled very differently in a white middle-class suburb. On the other hand, many blacks interpreted every act of the police within a selective framework that was a product of their collective past. Even if the Los Angeles policemen had all been courtly gentlemen in every contact with a black (which they certainly were not), they would still have been perceived through minds conditioned by deep resentments, and they would still have been damned for the actions of other policemen who had done unspeakable things to blacks in the name of white supremacy.[33]

Another factor that made the police a specific target for feelings of hostility was that they were the ever present and highly visible agents of the dominating white establishment. It was abundantly clear that the white community was more interested in keeping the lid clamped down in the ghetto than in helping to solve its problems. Thus, whether right or wrong, justi-

31. Raymond J. Murphy, "Postscript on the Los Angeles Riots," in *Problems and Prospects of the Negro Movement,* ed. Raymond J. Murphy and Howard Elinson (Belmont, Calif.: Wadsworth Publishing Co., 1966), pp. 231–234.

32. Oberschall, *op. cit.,* pp. 331–332.

33. "Unlawful Police Violence," United States Commission on Civil Rights, *Justice,* No. 5 (Washington D.C.: U.S. Government Printing Office, 1961).

fied or exaggerated, along with a widespread belief in police brutality there existed in Watts a deep hostility toward the police as the representatives of those who refused to accept black Americans. If a breakdown of social order was to occur, it was likely to be precipitated by an incident involving the police.

THE PRECIPITATING INCIDENT

The kinds of incidents that touch off riots are often said to be casual and insignificant in themselves. Perhaps any one of a hundred events occurring against the background of conditions in Watts could have ignited the spark. But careful examination of the kinds of incidents that have in fact incited people to such violence indicates that they may have particular characteristics. For example, Lieberson and Silverman recently studied available accounts and records of seventy-six race riots that occurred in the United States between 1913 and 1963. They noted that: ". . . race riots almost always involve some confrontation between the groups in which members of one race are deeply 'wronged' in fact or in rumor by members of the other."[34]

However, even if such an incident does occur, this does not mean that a major upheaval of violence will inevitably follow. People are not especially prone to rioting under any circumstances. Incidents occur every day, but riots do not. It takes a great deal of provocation for people to engage in burning, looting, and killing, even when all the background elements are present. Incidents must have special characteristics before they can touch off widespread violence. Those characteristics were present in an incident that took place on the evening of August 11, 1965, at the corner of 116th Street and Avalon Boulevard in Watts. The events that occurred at that place and time illustrate well the pattern by which a casual crowd is transformed into a destructive mob.

Mobilization of potential actors. One obvious factor that is required before large numbers of people can develop the behavior forms of the active crowd is that they must first assemble. Usually they do so because something captures their attention and draws them to the scene. But what are the conditions under which casual crowds gather quickly to watch an event that they can interpret against a background of acute strains? Among the most significant is the state of the weather! Few riots occur in the winter or in a heavy rain; people stay inside, and it is difficult to attract a casual crowd. In the summer, however, especially on hot humid evenings, residents of places like Watts are likely to escape their small, stuffy living quarters by sitting on steps and the lawn or strolling in the streets. Such was the case on the evening in question. It had been the hottest day of the summer, and the early evening offered little relief. The yards and streets of the neighborhood were filled with people.

Into this setting drove two young men in an old sedan. A highway patrol motorcycle, with siren screaming and red light blazing, was in close pursuit. The two young blacks had been drinking and had been clocked driving at fifty miles an hour in a thirty-five-mile-per-hour zone. As the vehicles stopped, the event drew the attention of the curious for several blocks around. The officer approached the car and began to investigate the situation. A crowd gathered almost immediately. Within a few moments it was apparent to everyone that the offenders were under the influence of alcohol. The members of the crowd joked good-naturedly. Meanwhile, more and more people gathered just to "see what was going on."

The officer was a model of politeness, but at the same time he was firm. He made the suspect try to walk a straight line—a task he was patently unable to perform. The crowd was amused. Relationships between the suspect, the officer, and the crowd were cordial; they kidded with each other.

The effects of emotional contagion. The incident was coming to a close. A police transport car arrived to take away the driver, who had been placed under arrest, and a wrecker had been summoned to remove the automobile. The policeman's back-up motorcycle officer had also arrived on the scene. However, as the police wrecker was preparing to remove the car, the suspect's mother arrived in a state of agitation. She began to try to persuade the wrecker operator to release the car to her so that she could drive it home. When it was discovered that the automobile was actually registered in her name, the officer in charge granted her request, and the car was released. It was still only a routine situ-

---

34. Stanley Lieberson and Arnold R. Silverman, "The Precipitants and Underlying Conditions of Race Riots," *American Sociological Review*, 30, 6 (December 1965), 888.

ation. By this time a substantial number of on-lookers had gathered, but they showed no signs of hostility.

Suddenly, the mother turned on her son and began to berate him for being drunk and for misbehaving with her automobile. The son tried to plead with her for forgiveness. When she rejected his pleas, the son's mood changed quickly and dramatically. He became angry and shouted that the police would never take him to jail. He declared that they would have to kill him first. He was screaming obscenities in a fit of rage, and the officer was unable to calm him. A minor struggle ensued, and the suspect attempted to strike the officer. The crowd grew silent.

The officers converged on their subject with handcuffs, determined to get him under control. By this time the officers were surrounded by a huge crowd that was becoming sullen. The transport-car officer radioed quickly for additional help; he also removed his (unloaded) shotgun from his car and held it where the crowd could see it. A wave of tension swept through the crowd. The situation had quickly grown potentially dangerous.

At that moment, the first of the reinforcements arrived. The policemen had armed themselves with clubs. The suspect meanwhile was still resisting violently and shouting abuse. One officer had had enough. He struck the suspect sharply on the head with his club. This succeeded in quieting him down, but it also caused him to begin bleeding as the handcuffs were clamped on.

At this point, the crowd began to stir. A few individuals shouted insults at the patrolmen. Suddenly the other suspect started fighting the police. The mother grabbed her son and tried to pull him away from the officers, setting off a general pushing and shoving melee as members of the crowd tried to assist her. The situation was deteriorating; the police were losing control. But additional squad cars arrived at that very moment, and the officers succeeded in pushing the crowd back.

These elements of the incident had served to heighten emotions considerably. The process of emotional contagion and reciprocal influence were transforming the blacks from a passive collection of bystanders into a hostile and aggressive crowd that needed only a little more stimulation to respond with overt action. The usual norms and guides to behavior which restrain even the angry individual and keep his aggressive tendencies in check were crumbling. Hecklers in the crowd began shouting proposals for retaliatory measures to a highly suggestible and emotional mob that was almost ready for action. Yet even at this point a riot had not been touched off. The situation could have gone either way. Unfortunately, certain key elements now entered that led to disaster. *Selective perception* was one such element.

An important detail in the developing situation had been the clubbing of the suspect. Perhaps in calmer circumstances the majority of the onlookers would have agreed that he richly deserved to be forcibly controlled for his behavior; but under the charged emotional pressures of the moment this event was selectively perceived, raising the issue of police brutality.

Given this perceptual framework, two additional events supplied further evidence, as far as the crowd was concerned, of intolerable acts of brutality on the part of the police. One of these took place when the main suspect was being placed in the police transport car. As an officer was pushing the still resisting subject into the vehicle, he had to shove the man's legs in forcefully with his knee and quickly slam the door. Police are taught to do this rapidly so as not to remain long with their backs to a hostile crowd. To onlookers, however, it appeared that the officer had kicked the handcuffed and bleeding suspect and then slammed the door on the man's feet. Those who "saw" this shouted in angry protest, and this interpretation diffused quickly through the remainder of the crowd in the form of *rumor*.

The crowd became extremely agitated at this evidence of brutality. Rocks and bottles began to appear in many hands. By this time everyone was milling and shouting. As new police reinforcements arrived, they were greeted with angry insults and corrosive verbal abuse by the entire crowd. Yet even in this last moment of boiling anger, no rock or bottle had been thrown. Behavioral contagion had not yet occurred.

Meanwhile, a young black woman who worked as a barber in a nearby shop had been attracted to the scene. Swept up in the emotion of the crowd, she found herself face to face with a white officer just as the police were preparing to leave. In a state of emotional compulsion, she stepped forth, with her blue barber's smock flapping loosely, and spat on the officer.

Two nearby policemen saw the act and rushed over to grab her. They reached into the

The Watts riot of 1965 provides a clear example of what can happen to a crowd when emotional and behavioral contagion sets in. The weather on August 11 was unseasonably warm, and thus an unusually large number of people happened to witness a routine arrest for drunken driving. Into this scene stepped the driver's irate mother, who became belligerent as the police began to take her son away. Gradually, the tenor of the arrest became more emotion-charged, the size of the crowd increased, and its attention became fully focused on the struggle between the police and the driver. All that was needed to make the situation erupt was one person to commit an overt act of violence. He did, and the crowd followed his example. Although many Watts residents took part in the looting and rioting that followed, others, as the picture below shows, watched in stunned silence.

crowd and dragged her out. Members of the crowd tried to pull her back. The woman screamed abuse and fought to get away. Finally, the police succeeded in handcuffing her and half-carried, half-dragged her, still protesting, to a car. This episode spawned a second rumor. The story shot rapidly through the crowd that the police were manhandling a pregnant woman. The blue barber's smock was seen as a maternity dress! This was the straw that broke the camel's back.

The diffusion of overt action. Shouts arose of "Let's get them cops!" "Kill the bastards." "Selma!" "Bogulusa!" "Smash those white sons-of-bitches!" The officers sensed that the end was at hand and ran to their vehicles to get clear of the area. Just as they attempted to leave, the riot broke. Bolder innovators threw the first stones, and the idea diffused rapidly through the rest of the crowd. The last station wagon in the police convoy was deluged with bricks, bottles, and stones. The mob surged forth in a frenzy of destruction.

THE RIOT

The precipitating incident set in motion new frames of reference, definitions of the situation, motivations to action that served as focal points for the mobilization of thousands of additional people. The original active crowd surged out from the site of the precipitating incident and provided stimuli and interpretations that drew increasing numbers into immediate participation in the excitement.

Recruitment of additional participants. Perhaps the most significant element in the recruitment of additional participants was the rumors growing out of the original incident. The story of the police mistreating the handcuffed and bleeding suspect was distorted to a point where the man was said to have been viciously beaten and repeatedly kicked while helplessly manacled. The story of the "pregnant woman" and her brutal manhandling by the police was regarded as an especially ugly affair for which the police deserved punishment. The original spectators, moreover, reported that they "had seen it with their own eyes."

This tapestry of half-truths based upon selective perception and distorted rumor was a clear call to action for thousands of young men and teen-agers. The accounts of how the police cars were stoned by the crowd provided heady suggestions for further action. Soon, all cars containing white passengers going through the area were being stoned. From that point it was an easy step to stopping the cars, dragging out their terrified occupants, and beating them senseless. This pattern of generalized retaliation against all whites spread swiftly. A bus was stopped, its windows smashed, and its passengers attacked with bricks and two-by-fours. White children were beaten along with their parents, who had innocently driven into the riot area.

During this period many blacks in the area were horrified by what they saw their fellow residents doing to innocent people. Some tried to intervene to aid the victims of the mob. In a few cases they were successful, but often they were unable to help. Teeth were knocked out, eyes were gouged, bones were broken, and people were severely bruised by kicks and by blows with bottles and boards.

More and more automobiles containing whites were stoned and their occupants mistreated while the police tried desperately to seal off and contain the violence. An area of some twenty square blocks was loosely surrounded, but rioters spilled out across back alleys and through yards between the intersections.

The police had largely withdrawn from the main area of the riot. A few probing teams entered it from time to time in an attempt to disperse concentrations of people, but they lacked sufficient manpower for any really effective sweeps. By this time, television cameras had arrived to record and broadcast what was happening.

The seeming inability of the police to control the situation or to force the rioters off the streets served to make the actions of the mob more bold. The police served as a continuing focus for aggression. They were under a constant barrage of rocks and bottles. The rioters taunted them repeatedly with verbal abuse.

During the remainder of the first night of the riot, the police continued to avoid a total confrontation. It was apparently their strategy to let the rioters blow off steam, and then, when things had calmed down, to quietly restore order. As reasonable as this strategy seemed, it was not altogether effective. When sunrise came, nineteen policemen had been injured, sixteen other persons were seriously hurt, thirty-four had been arrested, and fifty vehicles, including two fire trucks, had been damaged or burned.

Burning and looting. The phrase "Burn, baby, burn" was a catchy saying of "Magnificent Montague," a black disc jockey with a large audience in Los Angeles. Its intent was to get all his listeners into a receptive mood for the records he played on his program. Unintentionally, the phrase became both a rallying cry for teen-agers and a suggestive stimulus to action as the riot progressed.

No one knows who set the first building on fire, but the pattern became widespread as the riot entered its second night. At first the rioters continued doing what they had done the night before—stoning and overturning cars and beating motorists. Initially, only automobiles were set on fire, but soon stores and other buildings were being put to the torch. As firemen responded and attempted to control the flames, they were pelted with rocks and harassed with sniper fire. The police had the additional duty of trying to protect the firemen who were being shot at.

The area of the riot was expanding block by block. Buildings in a wide area were burning, and authorities began to fear a fire storm of the type that had wrought such terrible damage on wartime cities under bombing attack. These patterns continued for five more days until parts of the city looked like the devastated and gutted communities in postwar Europe.

The norm of looting arose at the same time. Windows and storefront barricades were smashed, and blacks entered to carry off whatever they could remove. The most frequent targets were liquor stores and places where appliances such as television sets were sold. Supermarkets were another favorite; entire families joined the fun of wheeling away carts overflowing with foodstuffs. There was some selectivity in these attacks: stores and businesses known to be owned by blacks were sometimes (but not always) left unscathed.

As has already been suggested, not all the black residents of the area responded to the riot in the same way. Some provided the active hard core. These were mainly younger men, who set the fires, systematically stripped stores, and sniped at the police and firemen. Others—men, women, and children—were drawn in when free

food, clothing, liquor, and appliances were right there for the taking. Somehow the fact that these goods belonged to "Whitey" made it seem legitimate to take them. One witness reported that a youngster loaded down with booty said, "That don't look like stealing to me. That's just picking up what you need and going."[35] The majority of residents of the area simply stood on the sidelines and either threw an occasional rock or joined in the general shouting and screaming at the police. Still others refrained from taking any part at all and remained in their homes.

Oberschall has summarized and analyzed the statistics on arrests during the riot. He has concluded that the 3371 adults and 556 juveniles who were arrested did not represent any unusual concentration of the criminal element, brand-new arrivals, school dropouts, or juvenile delinquents. The rioters were apparently drawn from almost all segments of the population of the area, although most were from the lowest socioeconomic stratum.[36]

THE RESPONSE OF THE LARGER COMMUNITY

After much delay, the National Guard was called in to restore order. This was not an easy task. Some ten thousand black rioters had been roaming the streets in a wild rampage for several days. During the peak of the disorders, 13,500 National Guardsmen were required to bring the area under control.

In addition to this use of military force, many ordinary citizens in the white community were prepared to take individual action. There was a rush to buy firearms, and those who already had them in their homes brought them out and oiled them up "just in case." On the other hand, this riot was quite unlike those in the past in which pitched battles took place between groups of whites and blacks. In Watts (as in the riots that erupted after the murder of Martin Luther King, Jr.) the main thrust of the violence was against the police and against property in the area, especially that owned by whites. Little or no effort was made to attack white people in other areas of the city.

Overall, the conflagration raged for six days. A total of thirty-four people lost their lives. Most were black. Thousands were injured. Some

35. *Time,* August 20, 1965, p. 17.
36. Oberschall, *op. cit.,* pp. 326–329.

METHODOLOGY THE CASE STUDY

The sociological case study is a detailed description of an event of theoretical significance, based upon systematic observation carried out within a framework of sociological concepts. Typically, the researcher uses local records, intensive and extensive interviews with informants and others, participant observation, and many other techniques.

To illustrate the case study, we may examine briefly the "Leeville Lynching," as summarized by Hadley Cantril in his well-known work *The Psychology of Social Movements.* This event took place during the 1920's in a small Texas community after a black farm laborer was reported to have raped the wife of his white employer. Some people said the woman had invited the sexual attentions of the black man; she claimed, however, that he had forced his way into her home with a shotgun when her husband was absent and had assaulted her repeatedly. Whatever the true story, medical evidence indicated that sexual activity had indeed occurred.

After attempted flight, the farm hand was apprehended by a deputy sheriff, charged with the crime, lodged in the county jail, and swiftly brought to trial. Local whites talked among themselves that he would "get what was coming to him." On the morning of the trial, many white people came to Leeville to see what would happen. As the trial proceeded, the crowd grew larger and increasingly hostile. Texas Rangers were on hand to keep order, but the crowd was convinced that the Rangers would never shoot to protect the black defendant. Shouting and heckling increased as the day wore on. Many rumors were passed around. The precipitating event, "which changed the huge curious crowd into a vicious mob, was the bringing of the woman from the hospital in an ambulance and carrying her on a stretcher into the courtroom. . . . After that the crowd went wild." Members of the mob stoned the courthouse, tried repeatedly to break in, and eventually set it on fire. "The fire department used its ladders to carry the people from the second floor courtroom. There was some objection to the rescuing of the judge, county attorney, sheriff, and Rangers. 'Let the bastards burn up with the nigger,' was the cry."

The governor of Texas sent a small detachment of the National Guard to reinforce the Rangers, but by this time the mob had grown so belligerent that the troops were no match for them. A violent confrontation ensued, and the defenders were forced to retreat. The would-be lynchers used stolen dynamite to blast into the building and get the accused, who was killed by the explosion. When his corpse was brought out, the crowd shouted, "Take him to niggertown." As the case study reports, "the body was fastened behind a Ford roadster. . . . About five thousand howling, yelling people fell into a midnight parade behind the corpse. Someone struck up the strains of 'Happy days are here again,' and soon hundreds joined in. . . ."

The dead man was drawn up on a tree limb and a nearby drugstore was ransacked for burnable material to place under it. Some claimed that the corpse was desexed before the fire was set. A great cheer went up as the flames engulfed the man's body. Children danced as they watched it blister and burn.

After burning the corpse, the mob fell to looting the homes and businesses of blacks. Numerous buildings were set on fire with gasoline; the fire department was not permitted to put water on any fire if the property were not owned by whites. Meanwhile, the two thousand black citizens of Leeville were forced to hide.

The next day, the National Guard arrived in strength and restored order. Civil authorities eventually indicted fourteen persons, but only one man was ever sentenced (for arson). Even he was out of prison in a short time by order of the governor.

Clearly, this instance of collective violence has parallels with the upheaval in Watts, though the precipitating events were quite different and the racial characteristics of the participants were reversed. Comparisons of such case studies indicate that the sociological variables shaping crowd action have a similar impact regardless of the exact situation and regardless of who is involved. Case studies of this type are an essential part of sociological knowledge, and they contribute significantly to the development of adequate theories.

Hadley Cantril, *The Psychology of Social Movements* (New York: John Wiley and Sons, 1963); quotations from pp. 99, 100, and 102. Cantril's summary of the "Leeville Lynching" is based on a case study by Durward Pruden (unpublished M.A. thesis, Southern Methodist University, 1930).

$40 million worth of property was destroyed, including six hundred buildings that were burned down or severely damaged. At the time, it was the worst civil disorder ever to take place in the United States.

The Watts riot illustrates almost every mechanism and concept that sociologists have ever used in attempting to understand collective behavior. Against a configuration of general background conditions, acute local strains developed. These were coupled with a generalized belief in police brutality. As the precipitating incident progressed, the social-psychological environment of the active crowd transformed normally law-abiding people into a mob ready to do violence. When emotional contagion—involving selective perception—and rumor concerning police brutality finally touched off the riot, ordinary norms became largely ineffective; new apparent norms spread, and the riot sustained itself for six full days as a relatively unstructured situation, without institutionalized organization or leadership, in the face of repeated attempts at control.

Whatever one's evaluation of this incident of collective behavior, it had significant implications for the larger society. In fact, it can be said with substantial justification that American society has never been quite the same since the Watts riot. The upheaval focused the anguished attention of a nation upon one of its urban black ghettos. It also appears to have served as a stimulus to black populations living in similar circumstances in other parts of the nation. In the several years since the Watts riot took place, upheavals of an almost identical nature have taken place in almost every major city in our nation. Some of these have been even more devastating in terms of loss of life and property than the disorders in Watts. As a direct result of these incidents of collective behavior, many new laws have been passed by federal, state, and local authorities. Some of this legislation is aimed at suppressing potential riot leaders; other laws are aimed at some of the underlying conditions that led to the riot itself. Thus, the disturbance at Watts has led to numerous and specific forms of social change.

SUMMARY

Collective behavior differs from group behavior in that the former takes place in relatively unstructured settings and is therefore relatively unpredictable. Collective behavior takes many different forms, but the study of crowds has been a focus of special interest. Several types of crowds have been identified, including the casual crowd, the conventionalized crowd, the active crowd, and the expressive crowd. Each of these types has different organizational characteristics, ranging from the almost complete lack of organization in the casual crowd to the substantial degree of organization that characterizes the conventionalized crowd.

Gustave LeBon's early analysis of the social psychology of the crowd continues to be the definitive statement. It has been brought up to date by Herbert Blumer and other more modern writers, but LeBon's focus on anonymity, unconscious motivations, contagion, suggestibility, and reciprocal influence still provides the basic framework for understanding crowd behavior.

The social dynamics of collective behavior can be analyzed in terms of the social and psychological factors necessary to precipitate collective action. These include background factors, such as inadequacies in existing social arrangements that occur because of crises, intercultural conflict, and intracultural discontinuities. In incidents of collective behavior, emotional orientations spread through emotional contagion. This process is a complex one which in itself involves a number of necessary conditions. Rumor also plays a part in the development of collective behavior, although it can be studied as collective behavior in its own right. Two important patterns of rumor have been identified: the embedding pattern and the compounding pattern. Most rumors probably involve both. An analysis of the riot that erupted in the Watts section of Los Angeles in the summer of 1965 provides a clear illustration of the theoretical formulations developed by LeBon and other students of collective behavior.

12
Deviance

In the summer of 1968, the following incident was reported by a nineteen-year-old inmate in a Philadelphia prison:

On Tuesday morning, the first week of June at about 9:30 A.M., I was in my cell 412 on D block and I had started to clean up. A tall, heavy-set fella came into the cell and asked for a mirror and shaving brush and a comb, and that my cell partner said he could borrow.

He then said that he heard something about me concerning homosexual acts. I told him what he had heard was not true. He then started to threaten me and if I didn't submit to him. Then I hit him with my fist in his face before he could hit me. Then about three more men came into my cell, and they started to beat me up, too. I fought back the best I could and then I fell on the floor and I got kicked in the ribs. Three guys were holding me while the other one tore my pants off; I continued to fight until one of the guys knocked me out.[1]

Sodomous rape and other types of homosexual activity are by no means rare in jails and prisons. How can we explain such acts? Perhaps our first reaction is to attribute them to psychological maladjustment. A fraction of American males is homosexual, and presumably this fraction is represented in prison populations. Thus it is possible to assume that sexual assaults in the prison setting are a product of the same types of individual maladjustment found in the community as a whole.

The problem with such an interpretation is that it does not account for all the relevant data. For one thing, prisoners who commit such acts do not think of themselves as "queer." They think of themselves as sexually dominant "he-men" and consider their *victims* the "homosexuals." Furthermore, while some homosexual activity is to be expected in an all-male society like a prison population, studies have shown that sexual assaults are more common in certain *types* of penal institutions than in others. To account for this we would have to hypothesize either that different types of prisons systematically draw from populations with differing rates of homosexual behavior or that *features in the social system of the prison itself are related to variations in rates.* The latter hypothesis provides a more comprehensive explanation of the data.

Whether or not the rate of sexual deviance is abnormally high in a given institution seems to depend in large part upon the role characteristics, norms, stratification patterns, system of social control, and other organizational characteristics of that institution. If the inmate subculture equates physical-sexual prowess with prestige and self-esteem *and* if officials ignore inmate complaints concerning assaults, then conditions are highly conducive to such incidents. Aggressive men will establish dominance by using younger and weaker men sexually. For the more aggressive male, the prisoner role provides few nonsexual channels through which dominance can be exerted. Only sexual and physical prowess stand between him and feelings of masculine inadequacy.

Deviant behavior in such instances is, therefore, a product of a complex interplay between the nature of the social system *and* the personal characteristics of the human beings within it. This interplay, in fact, is an appropriate starting point for studying deviant behavior more broadly. The sociologist is concerned with a great variety of persistent forms of deviance, most of which are engaged in by clinically normal people.[2] To understand such phenomena as crime, delinquency, sexual deviance, alcoholism, and drug addiction (to mention only a few of the more common forms of deviant behavior), it is necessary to examine the features of the sociocultural environments in which such acts occur as well as the characteristics of the persons who commit them.

The present chapter seeks to view deviant behavior broadly. After defining deviance and considering its social significance, we will discuss it in a sociological perspective. Crime and delinquency, as major forms of deviance, will be covered in some detail. We will then examine sociological theories concerning particular types of deviance. Finally, the problem of controlling deviance will be discussed, particularly in terms of contemporary systems for curbing crime and delinquency.

---

1. Allan J. Davis, "Sexual Assaults in the Philadelphia Prison Systems, and Sheriff's Vans," *Trans-action*, 6, No. 2 (December 1968), 10. Investigations of various local and county institutions in other sections of the country—e.g., Chicago and Cook County—have revealed the widespread occurrence of similar incidents.

2. See Albert K. Cohen, "The Study of Social Disorganization and Deviant Behavior," in *Sociology Today,* ed. Robert K. Merton, Leonard Broom, and Leonard S. Cottrell (New York: Basic Books, Inc., 1959), pp. 461–484.

Deviant behavior may have positive social consequences, even when it disrupts the stability of a society. During the early 1900's the Suffragettes were often considered "disruptive" and "deviant" as they staged demonstrations, picketed the White House, and even went to jail in their attempt to extend the voting right to women. But the end result of this early feminist movement was the passage of the Nineteenth Amendment. Similarly, the Women's Liberation Movement—considered "deviant" by the majority today—may ultimately be viewed as a positive force for social change.

WHEN IS BEHAVIOR DEVIANT?

In a general sense, *deviant behavior* can be defined as any kind of conduct that in some way fails to meet shared behavioral expectations. From the standpoint of the group within which it occurs, deviant behavior is usually considered undesirable, since it threatens shared values and interferes with the smooth functioning of the group. It is wrong, however, to assume that all deviant behavior is socially "bad." Some deviant acts have positive consequences for the group or society in which they occur. As Kai Erikson has noted, deviance can help a group define its own identity and thus increase its sense of solidarity:

People who gather together into communities need to be able to describe and anticipate those areas of experience which lie outside the immediate compass of the group—the unseen dangers which in any culture and in any age seem to threaten its security. Traditional folklore depicting demons, devils, witches and evil spirits may be one way to give form

to these otherwise formless dangers, but the visible deviant is another kind of reminder. As a trespasser against the group norms, he represents those forces which lie outside the group's boundaries: he informs us, as it were, what evil looks like, what shape the devil can assume. And in doing so, he shows us the difference between the inside of the group and the outside. It may well be that without this ongoing drama at the outer edges of group space, the community would have no inner sense of identity and cohesion, no sense of the contrasts which set it off as a special place in the larger world.

Thus deviance cannot be dismissed simply as behavior which *disrupts* stability in society, but may itself be, in controlled quantities, an important condition for preserving stability.[3]

Even when deviance disrupts the stability of a group, the consequences are not uniformly bad. The innovator who takes up some new item of culture, some new belief or behavioral practice, is usually departing from the norms of his

---

3. Kai T. Erikson, "Notes on the Sociology of Deviance," in *The Other Side: Perspectives on Deviance,* ed. Howard S. Becker (New York: The Free Press, 1964), p. 15. See also Robert A. Dentler and Kai T. Erikson, "The Functions of Deviance in Groups," *Social Problems,* 7 (Fall 1959), 98–107.

group and his society, but without this type of deviance there could be no social change. The politician who succeeds in cutting red tape to better serve his constituents is also engaging in deviant behavior, but his deviance is positively valued, at least by those he serves. Furthermore, if everyone was a thoroughgoing conformist in all things, life would be impossibly dull.

In recent years our nation's campuses have seen numerous forms of militancy, confrontation, and violent upheaval, many of which included deviant behavior in the fullest sense. A college student who takes over a dean's office and rifles his files is no less deviant than a ghetto resident who loots a liquor store. Each is violating norms, roles, and other behavioral expectations of the larger community that provide the social context of his activities.

Although both ghetto and campus violence have immediate negative consequences in the form of property damage, social disruption, and outraged feelings, they appear to be leading to at least *some* positive consequences. Our new national awareness of the problems of urban blacks has produced some new social programs aimed at amelioration and is sure to produce more. Colleges and universities are moving to-

ward greater internal democracy. Students are now participating in educational decision-making in many schools. Institutions of higher education have begun to redefine their responsibilities toward minority groups and toward the surrounding communities. As a result of student protests, they are reassessing their policies toward war-related research, involvement with agencies such as the CIA, and military training (ROTC) on the campus. In general, they are exchanging isolation from social and political issues for moral commitment. At the same time, most schools have shown a strong tendency to set clear limits to the dissent and disruption they will tolerate within their jurisdictions. Thus, their goals, external boundaries, internal operating norms, and systems of social control have been clarified, and in many instances altered, partly as a result of the deviant behavior of some students.

DEFINING DEVIANT BEHAVIOR

In sociological terms, deviant behavior involves an *actor*, a *norm*, an *act*, and an *audience* that defines that act as nonconforming to a degree exceeding the tolerance limits of the majority. The concept of limits of permissiveness is important for understanding deviant behavior.

Tolerance limits. It is virtually impossible for anyone to conform absolutely and at all times to every norm or other expectation he encounters. Conformity and deviation are matters of degree, and most norms are surrounded by some range of toleration for violators. Hypothetically, the tolerance limits associated with a norm can be exceeded either positively or negatively. Roles and rules can be so meticulously fulfilled and observed that the perfection of the performance will arouse the ire of the very group that supports the expectation. But even though such positive deviance may on occasion be annoying, it is seldom regarded as serious. Violations of institutionalized expectations in a negative direction, on the other hand, are the source of great societal concern. This is the type of behavior that the present chapter will focus on.

Several factors are important in determining the limits of tolerance associated with various behavioral expectations in a given group. They include the significance of the norms to the group, the situation within which the violation occurs, and the characteristics of the nonconforming individual. Each will be briefly examined.

Differential importance of norms. In all groups, distinctions are made concerning the relative importance of norms. As we noted in Chapter 2, at the societal level the folkways are norms of minor significance, and deviations from them are seldom regarded as a serious threat. Of greater significance by far are the mores. These are usually considered of the utmost importance in preserving societal values. Legal penalties reflect the seriousness with which a society regards violations of its norms. Contrast the fine for a parking violation with the punishment for committing a felony. The less the importance of a norm to a group, the greater the degree of nonconformity that will be tolerated. The reverse is also the case. For norms of major significance, tolerance limits are narrow.

Situation of the act. Another factor that affects the degree to which departures from expectations are tolerated is the situation in which the deviating behavior occurs. We know that in most communities excessive drinking is viewed with greater tolerance on New Year's Eve than it is ordinarily. On Halloween, acts that would be classified as vandalism on other occasions are considered mere mischief. In wartime, taking of the life of another is considered excusable; we may even give the killer a medal. Thus, a great variety of situational factors affect the tolerance limits surrounding a given expectation.

Characteristics of the violator. A more subtle factor that operates in defining limits of tolerance involves the characteristics of violators of norms. For example, a small child may grab a candy bar in a supermarket or destroy someone's flower bed. An adult who did the same thing would be reported for shoplifting or vandalism, but a slapped hand is usually the maximum punishment for the youngster.

Similarly, other category and role memberships affect reactions to nonconforming behavior. We find that various forms of mischief are tolerated when committed by college students as compared to nonstudents of the same age. The college professor who dresses oddly or forgets appointments may be looked on with amused affection; similar behavior by men in other occupational roles evokes quite different reactions. Distinctions are also made between the sexes: the woman driver, for example, may be excused for a violation that a man would be fined for.

The social rank of the violator can be an important factor in tolerance. In traditional societies, those of noble or royal blood have been free to violate many societal rules; and even in a democratic society such as ours, all rules do not apply equally to all in practice. The sons of physicians or bankers are often able to break the rules with impunity, while the same violations may get the sons of janitors or laborers into serious difficulties. Studies conducted by the NAACP in the eleven southern states indicate that during the past twenty years a black man convicted of raping a white woman had close to a 50 percent chance of receiving the death sentence; a man convicted of raping a woman of his own race stood a 14 percent chance.[4] These statistics demonstrate how widely tolerance limits may vary.

---

4. Louisville *Courier-Journal*, December 4, 1966, p. A-22.

THE RELATIVITY OF CONFORMITY AND DEVIATION

An act that violates the norms of one particular group within a society may represent conformity from the point of view of another group. Furthermore, the norms of particular segments of a society may require quite different behavior than the norms of the society as a whole. In some respects, then, conformity and deviation are *relative* to the particular groups making the analysis.

Subculture. In Chapter 3, we pointed out the need for interpreting a given act, belief, or norm within the framework of the particular cultural system of which it is a part. This same principle of *cultural relativity* applies to conduct within a society made up of a number of subgroups with distinctive sets of norms.

American society, like most large modern societies, is composed of a number of distinct groups that support their own subculture. Within such subcultures, there may be substantial variation from the larger culture, not only in norms but in beliefs, values, material traits, and perhaps even language. Thus, the society as a whole may have one set of "official" norms, but the norms that some members of the society are actually expected to follow on a day-to-day basis when interacting with their fellows may be quite different from those of the majority.

This may pose no particular problem as long as these subcultural norms do not contradict or come into conflict with norms that are of major significance to the society as a whole. However, when the content of a subculture clashes head-on with significant norms to which the majority of the society has given official endorsement, the problem of interpreting deviant behavior is made more difficult.

Research has shown that groups such as teen-age gangs, homosexuals, drug addicts, certain types of criminals, and some urban slum-dwellers support subcultures whose basic values, beliefs, normative practices, and shared attitudes run counter to those to which the majority of the society subscribe. Individuals participating in such "deviant subcultures" and sharing the orientations of their groups are both deviants and conformists. They are deviants

from the perspective of the larger society, but they are conformists by the definitions of their own subculture. This point becomes clear in Leznoff and Westley's study of the homosexual community:

Since the homosexual group provides the only social context in which homosexuality is normal, deviant practices moral, and homosexual responses rewarded, the homosexual develops a deep emotional involvement with his group, tending toward a ready acceptance of its norms and dictates, and subjection to its behavior patterns. . . .

A prohibition against sexual relationships within the group, in a manner suggestive of the incest taboo, indicates the extent to which the group culture is oriented to this function. The quotation which follows is indicative of this taboo:

"As far as I know, people who hang around with each other don't have affairs. The people who are friends don't sleep with each other. I can't tell you why that is, but they just don't. Unless you are married [a stable social and sexual relationship between two homosexuals is frequently referred to as 'marriage'] you have sex with strangers mostly. I think if you have sex with a friend it will destroy the friendship. I think that in the inner mind we all respect high moral standards, and none of us want to feel low in the eyes of anybody else." . . .

Within these groups the narration of sexual experiences and gossip about the sexual exploits of others is a major form of recreation. The narration of sexual experiences . . . allocates prestige among the members because of the high evaluation placed upon physical attraction and sexual prowess. Yet it creates hostility and sexual rivalry. The intense involvement of homosexuals in the results of this sexual competition is illustrated in the following statement which was overheard in a restaurant:

"Who wouldn't blow up. That bitch is trying to get her [the substitution of the female for the male pronoun is a common practice within homosexual groups] clutches into Richard. She can't leave anybody alone. I wouldn't be surprised if she ended up with a knife in her back. I don't mean to say I'm threatening her. But she's not going to get away with that stuff forever . . . playing kneesies under the table all night long. I had to get her away from Richard. That lousy bitch. From now on she better keep away from me."

. . . Gossip about sex, the adoption and exaggeration of feminine behavior, and the affectation of speech, represent a way of affirming that homosexuality is frankly accepted and has the collective support of the group.[5]

The individual in such a subculture is in a situation of potential conflict. If he conforms to the demands of society, he risks social ostracism or other punishment by his immediate group, which is of considerable importance to him. If he conforms to the norms and expectations of his group, he becomes a deviant by the definitions of the official norms of his society, which is also a matter of some significance.

Time periods. Deviant behavior is not only relative to specific subgroups within the society but relative over time within the larger culture. That is, types of behavior that are strongly disapproved at one time in a society may become widely accepted at a later time. Earlier in this century, smoking by women was regarded as a sign of immorality. The wearing of wrist watches by men was once thought to be foppish and sure evidence of femininity. Thus, in attempting to determine and interpret what is regarded as deviant behavior within a given group, the time factor as well as an awareness of the multiplicity of normative systems must be kept in mind.

On the other hand, even the most complex society retains a *central core* of norms to which its citizens are expected to conform. And while these "official" norms may not be equally valued or equally observed by all individuals or segments of society, they constitute the most obvious focus for sociological studies of deviant behavior.

---

5. Maurice Leznoff and William A. Westley, "The Homosexual Community," *Social Problems*, 3 (April 1956), 257–263.

Many individuals support subcultures whose basic values and norms run counter to those of the majority of society. The members of the Boston Huns motorcycle club, for instance, bid farewell to their leaders by showering the casket with beer and throwing the empty containers into the grave. They are deviants from the perspective of the larger society, but they are conformists by the definitions of their own subculture.

SOCIOLOGICAL PERSPECTIVES ON DEVIANCE

In our culture there is a clear "psychologizing" tendency; that is, when asked to account for the actions of a given individual, the ordinary person usually begins with presumptions about the relationship between inner psychological predispositions and overt acts. This tendency is very clear in the case of deviant behavior. In everyday discourse, acts of deviance are usually discussed within a framework of "poor adjustment" or even "mental illness." The implication is that there has to be something mentally wrong with a person who seriously flouts the mores, violates the law, or commits some other conspicuous act of nonconformity.

There is abundant evidence from which to conclude that serious mental disorders are *not* concentrated more highly among deviants than they are among conforming populations of the same socioeconomic characteristics.[6] As we have already indicated, the bulk of deviant behavior in our society is committed by clinically normal people. This does not mean that psychological variables may not be extremely significant in explaining particular cases of deviance. Obviously, individual needs, attitudes, motivations, habits, tensions, and stress are important in understanding deviant as well as conforming behavior. But the sociological approach is also needed if we are to understand the characteristic patterns of deviance found in particular groups and societies. For the sociologist, the focus is less on individual personality than on such factors as primary-group involvement, subcultural content, role definitions, socialization practices, normative conflict, and other social and cultural phenomena. The sociological approach, in brief, stresses that human behavior is in large part a product of the *social systems, structures,* and *processes* that men use to relate themselves to one another.

In the present section, the sociological approach to the study of deviance will be illustrated by two somewhat distinct theoretical formulations. The first, which can be called the *anomie theory,* was developed some years ago by Robert K. Merton in an attempt to provide a broad explanation for various distinctive patterns of deviance. The second, which will be termed *labeling theory,* is a newer and more tentative theoretical formulation that is primarily concerned with deviance as a form of role playing. As will be clear, these two theories do not offer competing explanations of the same phenomena; they are actually aimed at somewhat different aspects of deviance. They are useful as illustrations because they indicate the kinds of concepts and variables that enter into the sociological study of deviant conduct.

ANOMIE THEORY

In a well-known attempt to formulate a rather general theory of deviant behavior, Robert Merton observed that there were significant variations in rates of deviance in different groups in our society.[7] The starting point for understanding Merton's analysis is to make note of the relationship between the *cultural* goals that our society stresses and the *institutionalized means* that are culturally defined as legitimate in our society for working toward those goals. One major goal in our culture, for example, is the acquisition of wealth. Yet many Americans lack access to culturally approved means by which to achieve that goal. Since they remain under pressure to "succeed," they may lose interest in the legitimacy of the means: what counts for them is the end result. Such lack of integration between culturally approved ends and means, Merton maintained, leads to the strains associated with *anomie* or normlessness.

Given the conditions of anomie, what are the principal ways by which individuals at different points in the social structure can deal with the conflict between cultural goals and institutionalized means? In an attempt to answer this question, Merton devised a typology of *modes of adaptation* (Table 12.1, page 382) that has contributed to a better understanding of certain kinds of conforming and deviant behavior.

Conformity. First, individuals can accept both the cultural goals and the culturally approved means for reaching them. This is the response selected by most members of American society. Obviously the conformist must have

---

6. Karl F. Schuessler and Donald R. Cressey, "Personality Characteristics of Criminals," *American Journal of Sociology,* 55 (March 1950), 476.

7. Robert K. Merton, *Social Theory and Social Structure* (New York: The Free Press, 1956), p. 140.

TABLE 12.1. **MERTON'S TYPOLOGY OF MODES OF INDIVIDUAL ADAPTATION**

MODES OF ADAPTATION	CULTURE GOALS	INSTITUTIONALIZED MEANS
I. Conformity	+	+
II. Innovation	+	−
III. Ritualism	−	+
IV. Retreatism	−	−
V. Rebellion	±	±

SOURCE: Robert K. Merton, *Social Theory and Social Structure* (New York: The Free Press, 1956), p. 140.

access to legitimate means for achieving cultural goals or else be willing to accept the fact that they are out of his reach.

Innovation. Second, individuals can subscribe to a cultural goal (e.g., accumulation of wealth) without accepting the institutionalized means for attaining it. This type of adaptation Merton calls *innovation.* The individual uses methods other than those that are culturally approved, and he engages in some form of norm-violation. This type of adaptation is particularly evident in the lower strata of our society, where there is the conventional emphasis on monetary success but little access to the conventional and legitimate channels for achieving such success. Thus, we find that innovative but illegitimate means are frequently used by the poor in order to get money and be "successful." This familiar pattern of behavior has led Merton to hypothesize the following:

It is only when a system of cultural values extols, virtually above all else, certain common success-goals for the population at large while the social structure rigorously restricts or completely closes access to approved modes of reaching these goals for a considerable part of the same population, that deviant behavior ensues on a large scale.[8]

The innovation mode of adaptation to the squeeze between goals and means has received substantial attention in the sociological literature on crime and delinquency.[9]

Ritualism. The third type of adaptation that Merton discusses is *ritualism,* which involves a

rigid adherence to rules prescribing the "proper" way of doing things. In this case, however, the cultural goals have been abandoned or rejected. This mode of adaptation is illustrated by those bureaucrats whose main mission in life is to enforce petty rules and by others who persist in ritualistic conformity almost as an end in itself. The terms *over-conformity* and *over-compliance* are used in describing such behavior. Merton points out that ritualism is not usually regarded as seriously deviant behavior; though it can be annoying, ordinarily it does not exceed the tolerance limits of the community or society.

Retreatism. The fourth type of adjustment to conflict between cultural goals and accepted means is *retreatism,* which entails abandoning both cultural goals and the institutionalized means for attaining them. Merton describes retreatist individuals as "in the society but not of it" and as constituting the "true aliens." The retreatist adaptation is characteristic of tramps, alcoholics, drug addicts, and some psychotics. Another contemporary example is the hippie, who turns his back on the struggle for material success and many other socially approved values. Bahr, in his study of homelessness and disaffiliation in New York, related anomie and the type of retreatism manifested by skid-row residents.[10] Research is beginning to make available additional data concerning this adaptation.

Rebellion. The fifth form of adaptation is *rebellion.* This consists not only of rejecting the cultural goals and norms but also of attempting to develop new or modified goals and new means of reaching them. This is often the response of groups who form new social movements, as typified by the student (and post-student) radicals who came into prominence in the United States and western Europe late in the 1960's.

The Merton scheme is relatively simple and quite general. Probably because of this, it has provoked much interest and debate and is regarded as the most influential recent formulation

8. *Ibid.,* p. 146.

9. See, for example, James F. Short, "Gang Delinquency and Anomie," in *Anomie and Deviant Behavior,* ed. Marshall B. Clinard (New York: The Free Press, 1964).

10. Howard M. Bahr, *Homelessness and Disaffiliation,* Columbia University Bureau of Applied Social Research Report (August 1968), pp. 104–117.

in the sociology of deviance. Large numbers of empirical studies have focused on various aspects of the scheme, and there have been several important additions and reformulations.[11] The work of Cloward and Ohlin on juvenile gangs, discussed on page 401, is a good example of contemporary research using Merton's theory as its starting point.

LABELING THEORY

As was pointed out in the Prologue, sociologists trying to explain some repetitive type of behavior often formulate sets of generalizations—theories—that provide a possible explanation of certain phenomena but may not yet have been confirmed by extensive research. An excellent example of a theory under development is the *labeling* approach to the study of deviance. Gibbs has referred to the theoretical formulation associated with this approach as the "new conceptions" of deviant behavior; they concentrate less on the acts themselves and instead focus on the actors and their perceptions of each other.[12]

From this perspective, the primary questions are not who is deviant or what the qualities of the deviant act are but how the group *comes to define* a given individual as deviant; how the group members *change their responses* to him once he has been so defined; and what the *consequences for his future behavior* are. A basic premise of this theory is that *labeling* a person as a deviant is tantamount to assigning him a new role that will determine the nature of his future social transactions with the conforming community. Howard S. Becker comments on the effects of being labeled as a criminal:

To be labeled as a criminal one need only to commit a single criminal offense, and this is all the term formally refers to. Yet the word carries a number of connotations specifying auxiliary traits characteristic

of anyone bearing this label. A man who has been convicted of housebreaking and thereby labeled criminal is presumed to be a person likely to break into other houses; the police, in rounding up known offenders for investigation after a crime has been committed, operate on this premise. Furthermore, he is considered likely to commit other crimes as well, because he has shown himself to be a person without "respect for the law."[13]

Various studies are attempting to unravel the impact of the stigma that comes from being officially labeled a criminal or suspected criminal. The results of a field experiment by Schwartz and Skolnick point to the consequences of various types of criminal records for unskilled workers seeking jobs.

Various types of legal records are systematically related to job opportunities. It seems fair to infer also that the trend of job losses corresponds with the apparent punitive intent of the authorities. Where the man is *convicted,* that intent is presumably greatest. It is less where he is *accused but acquitted* and still less where the court makes an effort to emphasize the *absence* of a finding of guilt. Nevertheless, where the difference in punitive intent is ideally greatest, between conviction and acquittal, the difference in occupational harm is very slight.[14]

Numerous examples could be cited with respect to other forms of deviance. If a person becomes known as a homosexual, an alcoholic, a user of narcotics, a cheat at cards, or simply a liar, people will change their expectations of him. With the label goes a new role, and the imputation of "auxiliary traits" may follow. Thus, the alcoholic may be thought to be sexually promiscuous and the user of narcotics untrustworthy in money matters, whether or not there is factual evidence to support the suspicions.

There seems little doubt that labeling leads to redefinitions of the system of relationships and expectations between the person labeled and the conforming community. In some ways, the process resembles the categorical treatment accorded to members of minority groups in our society and the imputation of cultural stereotypes concerning their presumed traits. (These issues are reviewed in Chapter 10, "Intergroup Relations.")

One additional issue concerning labeling theory merits comment. Up to now, little has

---

11. Marshall B. Clinard, ed., *Anomie and Deviant Behavior* (New York: The Free Press, 1964).

12. Jack P. Gibbs, "Conceptions of Deviant Behavior: The Old and the New," *Pacific Sociological Review,* 9 (Spring 1966), 9–14.

13. Howard S. Becker, *Outsiders: Studies in the Sociology of Deviance* (New York: The Free Press, 1963), p. 33.

14. Richard D. Schwartz and Jerome H. Skolnick, "Two Studies of Legal Stigma," in *The Other Side: Perspectives on Deviance, op. cit.,* pp. 103–118.

Persons who cannot achieve society's goals through legitimate means may retreat from society altogether—abandoning the goals as well as the institutionalized means for attaining them. Retreatism is characteristic of the skid-row alcoholic and the drug addict. As Merton has put it, these individuals are "in the society but not of it"; they constitute the "true aliens."

been said concerning the *consequences* of an individual's being labeled in terms of his future behavior. In Chapter 4 we examined the theory that an individual's evaluation of self is basically a reflection of other people's reactions to his conduct (see pages 139–140). If this "looking-glass" theory of self is sound, we might expect that the person whose social relationships have been restructured by a deviant role-assignment would come to think of himself as a deviant person and develop stable patterns of deviant behavior along the lines of his new social and self definitions. Some theorists believe that this does indeed happen:

Take the case, for example, of a woman who is rather casual about sexual contacts. Over a period of years, she engages in sex relations more or less promiscuously. If one day she should suggest or hint at receiving a gift for her sexual favors or if one of her friends presents her a gift or some money shortly after the sex act, her status has been redefined. Hereafter, other people may come to think of her as a prostitute and she may, reciprocally, come to think of herself in these same terms. When this happens, casual sex promiscuity has become transmuted into a deviant occupational role.[15]

In other words, labeling theory has the potential of going beyond the question of how the group comes to define and label a deviant, or how group members alter their social expectations and behaviors in relation to him. The theory poses the question of the possible *emergence of stable patterns of deviance* out of the changed system of interaction between the labeled person and the conforming community. This aspect of labeling theory remains somewhat controversial, and further research is needed to explore its validity.

From the foregoing reviews of anomie and labeling theory, the discerning student will probably have already noted that the psychological and sociological approaches to deviance are not mutually exclusive. Since individuals incorporate what they learn from their social order and culture into their personality structures, their motives and personal orientations, or their states of "adjustment" and "maladjustment," are not independent of the social milieu

in which they live. But a person's environment does not wholly shape his behavior patterns; each individual responds in a unique way. Both the social environment and relevant psychological factors must be taken into account in understanding deviant behavior.

CRIME AND DELINQUENCY AS MAJOR FORMS OF DEVIANCE

Such formulations as anomie theory and labeling theory are sociological attempts to explain, respectively, how and why certain characteristic patterns of deviance emerge in a society and how certain individuals become increasingly committed to playing deviant roles. However, the sociological study of deviant behavior extends considerably beyond these broad concerns. Sociologists also attempt to develop more specific theories to explain alcoholism, drug addiction, suicide, sexual crime, and every other form of deviance with which society is particularly concerned.

The Merton theory indicates that under certain conditions of anomie individuals will turn to an innovative mode of adaptation and engage in deviant behavior in order to attain particular goals. But the theory says nothing concerning what norms will be violated, with what frequency, or by what specific categories of persons. It is to such empirical questions that the present section turns in examining data on two specific types of deviance, crime and delinquency.

PROBLEMS OF DEFINITION

A completely rigorous system for distinguishing between crime and other kinds of serious violations of norms is unnecessary for the layman. For the specialist, however, it is essential. The police and the courts, for example, must determine with great care whether a given act constitutes a crime; otherwise the innocent may suffer and the guilty go unpunished. The sociologist views crime from a different perspective, but he needs an equally rigorous system of classification. Scientific research must begin with

---

15. Earl Rubington and Martin Weinberg, *Deviance: The Interactionist Perspective* (New York: The Macmillan Company, 1968), p. 7.

an accurate conception of exactly *what* is being studied if the results are to be meaningful.

Unfortunately, the task of constructing a really precise set of categories within which human acts can be defined as criminal or noncriminal poses very great difficulties. Beyond such rather clear-cut violations as robberies and burglaries, there is a great "gray" area in which it is difficult to draw a sharp line between criminal and noncriminal behavior. Even when the law is used as the criterion, the problem of identifying a crime is complicated by many factors, some of them related to the issues discussed in the first section of this chapter. Tolerance limits vary for different types of laws: some are more important than others. The situations surrounding the violation can be significant, and even the personal and social characteristics of the person committing the act can play a part in determining whether or not it is actually classified as a crime.

Situations of definitional confusion. A simple illustration will serve to indicate some of the factors that make it difficult to differentiate between criminal and noncriminal behavior. From 1908 until 1966, when the state legislature legalized the sale of alcoholic beverages, Mississippi was a "dry" state. Yet few in Mississippi went without liquor if they wanted it. The concept of the differential importance of norms is relevant to understanding the Mississippi situation. It was estimated that $40 million worth of illegal spirits, mostly brought in from neighboring states, was sold yearly in Mississippi. Bootleggers were so prosperous and so well protected by local law enforcement personnel that they were able to offer curb service and home delivery with impunity. In spite of constant pressure by groups of ministers to establish narrower tolerance limits, the laws prohibiting the sale of liquor were seldom if ever enforced. For many years, Mississippi legislators, it was said, drank wet and voted dry. They defended their stand with the wry remark that "the wets have their liquor and the drys have their laws."

Under these circumstances, was the purchase of liquor in Mississippi a crime? If so, then a great proportion of residents of the state might have to be classified as criminals.

Another confusing situation exists in connection with the use of drugs. Both in the United States and abroad, more and more young people have been experimenting with drugs. The extent

to which drug use has been increasing is suggested by statistics from California, where "in 1967 juvenile arrests for marijuana went up 181 percent over 1966 and dangerous-drug arrests (most amphetamines and amphetamine-barbiturate combinations) went up 89 percent. There were only a few 'hard' narcotic arrests in the state among juveniles, but the increase for these was over 300 percent."[16] This same study showed that youthful drug experimentation sometimes takes exotic directions, as in the case of this "mod" group:

Starting out with alcohol, with glue, gasoline, or lighter-fluid sniffing, they progressed to marijuana and, in high school, to barbiturates, amphetamines, and more marijuana. Experimenters of an extraordinary order, they might also try nutmeg, sniff burning plastic, crush aspirin in cokes, soak inserts from inhalers in beverages, inject wine intraveneously, and smoke genuine tea.[17]

It is difficult to estimate the percentage of young people who are using drugs. Talk of "grass" and "acid" is commonplace, but this cannot be interpreted to mean that most students actually use marijuana or LSD. Heaviest use seems to be in urban institutions in the West, while lightest use seems to be in the South. In the late sixties DeFleur and Garrett studied one western university in depth and also summarized the results of eighteen other surveys of student drug use.[18] Estimates of the percentage of students involved ranged from a low of 6 percent for one large eastern university to a high of 33 percent at a western urban university. The median was approximately 20 percent. Most of the studies seemed to indicate that the majority of "users" were one-time experimenters, while a smaller segment were weekend or occasional users. Thus, the drug problem on the campus may not be as large in scope as many people suppose it to be. Nevertheless, among the young in general there has undoubtedly been a great increase in the use of drugs in the last decade.

The use of marijuana represents one of the grayest of all gray areas so far as distinguishing

---

16. Richard H. Blum *et al.*, *Students and Drugs* (San Francisco: Jossey-Bass, Inc., 1969), p. 13.

17. *Ibid.*, p. 20.

18. Lois B. DeFleur and Gerald R. Garrett, "Dimensions of Marijuana Usage in a Land Grant University," *Journal of Counselling Psychotherapy*, Fall 1970.

VIEWPOINTS **MARIJUANA**

What should we do about drug abuse—that appalling menace hanging over so many of our young people today?. . .

When a young person smokes marijuana in a cigarette or pipe, the inhaled smoke produces intoxication somewhat similar to the state produced in adults by several strong alcoholic drinks. The effect is felt within a few minutes and seldom lasts longer than twelve hours.

Besides causing dilation of the pupils and red margins of the eyelids, it can engender feelings of extreme well-being, confusion, irritability, distortion of time and space, or loss of memory. Continued use is likely to be accompanied by lethargy, neglect of personal appearance, and a recurrent cough, like that of chronic cigarette smokers.

Other telltale signs and symptoms in chronic users are poorer grades in school, a sudden change in pals, a sharp decrease or increase in pocket money—depending on whether the person buys or sells pot—a radical change in dress such as unkept hair, avoidance of parents when coming home later and later at night, and (most revealing) irrational remarks while under the influence of "grass."

Authorities say that marijuana smokers become so wrapped up in the use of the drug they have no time or interest for anything else. Ultimately they will fail to reach their goals or accomplish any of the things of which they are capable. They can, in fact, drop out of society. . . .

The AMA, the National Research Council, the National Education Association, the U.S. Department of Health, Education, and Welfare, and most other researchers and physicians all preach the same message: *Pot is a dangerous drug. Don't take a chance.*

Physicians and educators try to make young pot smokers see that the fleeting pleasures they enjoy are not worth the risk of a criminal record. Use of marijuana is illegal in every state, and the penalties are rough. Most states have set a minimum sentence of two years in prison for conviction for use or possession of marijuana.

One of the major dangers, the AMA warns, is that marijuana smokers may move on to other harmful drugs as they seek a greater "kick" and marijuana fails to provide it—a tragic step toward a life of waste and misery. . . .

Effective resentment against prohibited drugs is gradually being aroused. Parents, teachers, and youth should be on the alert to detect drug use and drug traffic—that is, users or "pushers"—and report them to the school principal or the local police.

Louis W. Sauer, M.D.
"Drug Abuse Among Teenagers"

It is my considered opinion, after studying drug use and drug laws in 30 nations and dealing with drug-abuse problems professionally for 15 years, that the present marijuana statutes in America not only are bad for the offending minority but are bad for the vast majority of us who never have lit a marijuana cigarette and never will. . . .

Banning marijuana not only perpetuates the rebelliousness of the young but it also establishes a frightening precedent, under which puritanical bias is more important to our legislators than experimentally determined fact—something every scientist must dread. Dr. Philip Handler, board chairman of the National Science Foundation, bluntly told a House subcommittee investigating drug laws, "It is our puritan ethics . . . rather than science" that say we should not smoke marijuana. . . .

Marijuana causes a moderate increase in heartbeat rate, some redness of the eyes and virtually no other physical effects. Contrary to the belief of both users and policemen, pot does not dilate the pupils—this myth apparently derives from the tradition of smoking [marijuana] in a darkened room; it is the darkness that dilates the pupils.

Pot does not affect the blood-sugar level, as alcohol does, nor cause abnormal reactions of the involuntary muscles, as LSD often does, nor produce any effects likely to be somatically damaging. . . . Nor does it dull the mental faculties, as [can be seen by] reviewing the scientific evidence. (I might add, here, that the highest honor students at certain Ivy League colleges are frequently pot users, and one study at Yale found more marijuana smokers at the top of the class than at the bottom. . . .

Thus, treating marijuana in a sane and rational way presents no threat to our society, whereas continuing the present hysteria will alienate increasing numbers of the young while accelerating the drift toward a police state. I take no pleasure in the spread of even so mild a drug as marijuana. . . . While I agree with the psychedelic generation about the absurdity and injustice of our criminal laws relating to drugs, I am not an apostle of the "turn on, tune in, drop out" mystique. I recognize that drugs can be an evasion of responsibility. . . .

But, meanwhile, I must protest—I will continue to protest—against the bureaucrat who stands with cocktail in one hand and cigarette in the other and cries out that the innocent recreation of pot smoking is the major problem facing our society. . . .

Joel Fort, M.D.
"Pot: A Rational Approach"

criminal behavior is concerned. DeFleur and Garrett report that 95 percent of those who had had some experience with marijuana wanted laws related to the drug to be made more lenient or to be abandoned altogether. Less predictably, 41 percent of students who were nonusers recommended the same changes. By the definitions of the larger society, those who use the drug—even once—are criminally deviant. In most states they are guilty of a felony. By their own definition, however, most young people who use marijuana are simply doing what lots of others in their reference groups are doing—ignoring a law that they regard as senseless and unjust.

Dry states that drink wet and adolescents who smoke pot illustrate some of the more obvious difficulties in trying to define crime. Often the problem is more subtle. For example, in our criminal court procedures, persons suspected of having committed a serious crime may be prosecuted on a lesser charge simply because there is more adequate evidence for obtaining a conviction. Or a suspect may agree to confess to a lesser crime in order to obtain a lighter sentence. In such situations, what is the *true* crime?

In spite of all these subtleties, *some* working definition of crime is needed for the purpose of research. Although sociologists who specialize in criminology continue to seek a more precise conceptualization, many settle on a relatively simple definition: *crime is behavior that violates formally promulgated criminal statutes*. This definition may not adequately come to grips with all the difficult issues in the "gray" areas, but at least it provides a necessary starting point for analysis.

Criminal codes as norms. Many European nations have uniform criminal codes that apply to all parts of the country, but in the United States communities, states, and the federal government have all developed their own sets of codes and statutes. As a result, an act defined as a crime in one jurisdiction may not be so defined in another.

Criminal codes in the United States have their origins in three major sources. First, our basic laws were taken over from the English common law. Second, additions and periodic modifications have been made by legislatures and other official bodies. Third, the manner of interpreting the law undergoes change through the actions of the courts. Ultimately, the law is what the courts say it is. Precedents set by courts in one state, for example, can influence the interpretation and application of similar laws in other states. Thus, the criminal codes are not a fixed and unchanging set of rules but undergo constant evolution and development.

In spite of these variations and changes, several underlying principles characterize legal codes in American society and sharply distinguish them from other kinds of norms.[19] The criminal laws are, first of all, *promulgated by political authority.* Norms of other kinds, no matter how important they may be, are not law, and only violations of rules made by the state can be crimes. Second, while most norms are informal "understandings," a law is a *specific rule.* It strictly defines the precise activity that constitutes a violation. Third, in terms of social control, the laws are presumed to be *uniformly applied.* That is, according to legal theory, they are supposed to be enforced in the same way regardless of the characteristics of persons who violate them. Furthermore, social control is specific in that each law carries *penal sanction.* Persons found guilty of violating the law are to be punished within the range of sanctions the law specifies.

Finally, sanctions for violating a criminal law are administered through *agencies of the state.* The apprehension of violators, the determination of guilt or innocence, and the application of punishments are the responsibility of the police, the courts, and the penal institutions. However, an important trend in the American system is the emergence of administrative bodies for handling some forms of criminal behavior. For example, the juvenile offender, the chronic alcoholic, and the narcotics addict are increasingly being handled by personnel operating special rehabilitation centers and programs rather than through courts and jails. This slow shift away from total reliance on enforcement agencies for handling law violators will probably continue.[20]

The law and the juvenile. Generally, individuals must be of a specified legal age (usually

---

19. See Edwin H. Sutherland and Donald R. Cressey, *Principles of Criminology,* 7th ed. (Philadelphia: J. B. Lippincott Company, 1966).

20. William J. Chambliss, *Crime and the Legal Process* (New York: McGraw-Hill Book Company, 1969), pp. 5–7.

METHODOLOGY   RESEARCH USE OF OFFICIAL RECORDS

An important aspect of the culture of contemporary urban societies is their preoccupation with record-keeping for official purposes. Every significant event in the life of a citizen is usually noted in some fashion in public documents. Records are made of his birth, education, employment, marriages, divorces, arrests, court convictions, organizational memberships, political participation, and finally his death. If present trends continue, the Age of the Computer will probably make record-keeping even more elaborate, accurate, and detailed.

Although official records are rich sources of data for sociologists, they are by no means ideal for research purposes. They consist largely of observations made and recorded for specific purposes by non-sociologists, who usually work within the framework of complex legal and administrative regulations. For example, a number of states prohibit by law the recording of the racial characteristics of individuals involved in many public transactions, ranging from obtaining a marriage license to applying for employment. While these proscriptions protect individual rights to privacy and may reduce certain forms of discrimination, they can limit the relevance of official files for the sociologist who is studying racial issues.

Even such seemingly accurate data as records of births and deaths are not without error. Some births are never registered and some deaths remain unreported. Furthermore, the social and cultural circumstances surrounding such events can lead to distorted official records. For example, because of sympathy for family members in a case of suicide, some physicians list a more "acceptable" cause of death in the public records. Similarly, some states prohibit recording a birth as illegitimate on the assumption (probably correct) that the child might be stigmatized later. For the sociologist attempting to assess suicide rates or the incidence of illegitimate births in a given area, such practices can introduce errors of unknown proportions.

In spite of such problems, *certain types* of official records can provide useful data for *certain types* of sociological investigations. For example, one rich source of secondary data for the criminologist is police records on specific types of crimes. Police files on a serious crime, in particular, contain detailed reports of investigating officers, statements of witnesses, comprehensive descriptions of the crime, and a wealth of detail about the situation in which it occurred. Such files often contain photographs, diagrams, ballistic reports, medical data, various documents, personal histories, and other facts about both offenders and their victims. Since this information is normally assembled by the police to be used as a basis for possible prosecution, the sociologist who uses such data must examine it very critically for possible bias.

The potential usefulness of official records in social research is illustrated by one of the landmark studies in criminology, Marvin Wolfgang's investigation of criminal homicide. This study was based upon the complete records of the Homicide Squad of the Philadelphia Police Department over a five-year period, during which time files were developed on 588 criminal homicides. Wolfgang found that homicide in Philadelphia tended to be largely an unplanned act involving a stabbing or shooting. It was committed disproportionately by black offenders against black victims. It was mainly an act of a male aggressor against a male victim. The vast majority of participants knew each other. The age group 20–24 years showed the highest rate of incidence. Homicide was found to vary seasonally in the city under study and to be significantly related to both days of the week and hours of the day. The weekends had the highest rates, and especially high concentrations appeared during the late hours of Saturday night. Alcohol was prominently present in a large number of the crimes studied. Nearly two thirds of the offenders and half of the victims had prior criminal records.

Although basically descriptive research, this study provided many new insights into the patterns of circumstance that may lead to criminal homicide. It has stimulated much further research and also attempts to develop more adequate theory.

Marvin E. Wolfgang, *Patterns in Criminal Homicide* (New York: John Wiley & Sons, Inc., 1966); first published in 1958.

eighteen) before they can be held fully responsible for their actions. Under certain conditions, particularly in the case of such serious crimes as murder and rape, the young offender may be dealt with as an adult by the criminal courts; but for most offenses the juvenile is treated as a "delinquent" rather than a "criminal" and is handled through special procedures and agencies.

The concept of delinquency implies more than the violation of a criminal law by a young person. Political bodies have enacted delinquency laws that indicate, sometimes vaguely, the reasons for which a youngster may be brought before special juvenile authorities. These include many kinds of behavior not covered in the adult criminal statutes. For example, children are often referred to juvenile courts for such things as "habitual truancy," "incorrigibility," "being ungovernable," "knowingly associating with vicious or immoral persons," "running away from home," or "habitually using vile, vulgar language in public places."

Thus even in a legal sense, *delinquency* is very loosely defined. In large part it depends on what local juvenile authorities regard as undesirable for young people, and this will vary from jurisdiction to jurisdiction and from one time period to another. Furthermore, many youngsters commit acts that *could* be brought to the attention of some court but are not. Also, because of protective attitudes toward the young, many juvenile cases are handled on an unofficial basis. This increases the difficulty of formulating a precise definition of delinquency, of assessing the real extent of delinquent behavior, and of identifying the types of norms usually violated by "delinquents" in our communities.

THE SCOPE AND DISTRIBUTION OF CRIME AND DELINQUENCY

The absence of uniform definitions of crime and delinquency adds to the overall problem of determining how many violations of a given type occur in a given area over a specific period of time. Most of the available statistics are simply *estimates* of greater or lesser accuracy, and they must be interpreted with a great deal of care.

The Uniform Crime Reports. Our major source of information concerning crime is the Federal Bureau of Investigation. Data on crimes are collected by the FBI from reports prepared by police departments throughout the United States. Approximately 95 percent of the population is covered in these reports. Each year, the FBI summarizes the various data it has collected in its *Uniform Crime Reports for the United States.* These reports contain a number of indices on various types of crime for different types of cities and sections of the country. For the most part, the measure of crime is expressed as a *rate,* in terms of the number of crimes of a given type for each 100,000 persons in the population.

The amount of crime is very difficult to measure with accuracy. Several different indices of crime are used, each of which provides a somewhat different picture. For example, one important index is "crimes known to the police." This consists of all crimes reported to the police and recorded by them, whether or not anyone is ever caught and convicted. Many crimes are never reported to the police, and there are ample grounds for concluding that some police reports of crime are incomplete or inaccurate. Other measures of crime include "crimes cleared by arrest" and "convictions." Data on prison populations are also available.

It is obvious that none of these several indices is an accurate measure of crime itself. And with each succeeding step from crimes known to the police, to arrests, to convictions, to prison populations, the possibility that the true crime rate is being underestimated is greatly increased. Therefore, it is difficult to know in any absolute sense what the dimensions of our crime problem really are. The index that appears to approach the true crime rate most closely is "crimes known to the police," and this is the index most frequently used to study trends and comparisons of crime rates.

In studying trends related to serious crime, seven major offenses are used in the United States as *index crimes:* murder, forcible rape, robbery, aggravated assault, burglary, larceny, and auto theft. Recent *Uniform Crime Reports* indicate that crime in the United States has been increasing at a much faster rate than the population (see Table 12.2). The FBI has estimated that the overall crime rate (total number of offenses per 10,000 population) rose 99 percent between 1960 and 1968. Serious crimes, though constituting a small part of the total, increased at a comparable pace: the combined rate for crimes of violence (murder, rape, robbery, and aggravated assault) rose 85 percent; that for

TABLE 12.2. **TOTAL ARREST TRENDS, 1960–1968**

	Total Number of Persons Arrested, All Ages		Percent Change, 1960–1968		
Offense Charged	1960	1968	TOTAL, ALL AGES	UNDER 18 YEARS OF AGE	18 YEARS OF AGE AND OVER
Total	**3,501,905**	**4,146,684**	+18.4	+100.4	+4.3
Criminal homicide:					
(a) Murder and nonnegligent manslaughter	4,970	8,310	+67.2	+127.0	+62.3
(b) Manslaughter by negligence	1,971	2,086	+5.8	+6.8	+5.8
Forcible rape	7,309	9,747	+33.4	+55.4	+28.6
Robbery	33,587	59,523	+77.2	+144.0	+55.5
Aggravated assault	55,564	82,242	+48.0	+115.2	+39.1
Burglary—breaking or entering	125,376	189,213	+50.9	+69.9	+33.7
Larceny—theft	205,686	339,165	+64.9	+79.7	+50.8
Auto theft	57,805	98,962	+71.2	+68.1	+76.0
SUBTOTAL FOR ABOVE OFFENSES	492,268	789,248	+60.3	+78.5	+46.6
Other assaults	131,133	182,795	+39.4	+139.6	+27.9
Forgery and counterfeiting	21,618	25,946	+20.0	+102.0	+13.7
Embezzlement and fraud	35,358	46,418	+31.3	+149.2	+28.3
Stolen property; buying, receiving, possessing	10,139	28,773	+183.8	+253.6	+158.2
Weapons; carrying, possessing, etc.	33,289	65,463	+96.7	+63.9	+105.0
Prostitution and commercialized vice	28,033	39,469	+40.8	+86.3	+40.1
Sex offenses (except forcible rape and prostitution)	47,046	36,370	−22.7	−19.0	−23.7
Narcotic drug laws	31,752	134,006	+322.0	+1860.4	+235.7
Gambling	121,117	68,247	−43.7	+14.3	−44.4
Offenses against family and children	41,048	37,459	−8.7	−33.7	−8.4
Driving under the influence	145,184	218,783	+50.7	+90.9	+50.4
Liquor laws	90,324	145,969	+61.6	+135.8	+42.3
Drunkenness	1,249,612	1,070,668	−14.3	+109.9	−15.6
Disorderly conduct	422,249	461,957	+9.4	+102.9	−2.7
Vagrancy	135,164	75,447	−44.2	+3.9	−47.1
All other offenses (except traffic)	466,571	719,666	+54.2	+112.7	+19.0
Suspicion (not included in totals)	113,948	73,067	−35.9	−22.3	−38.9

SOURCE: FBI, *Uniform Crime Reports, 1968,* p. 112; based on comparable reports from 1,944 cities representing 82,384,000 population and 690 counties representing 17,645,000 population. For narcotic drug law violation, the trend is largely influenced by the large cities.

serious crimes against property (burglary, larceny, and auto theft), 101 percent. Although such statistics must be interpreted with caution, there seems little doubt that rising crime rates are indeed a legitimate cause for national concern.

Statistics on delinquency. Statistical data on juvenile delinquency suffer from the same kinds of inadequacies found in the data on crime, and additional problems are generated by the vague and flexible definitions of delinquency itself. There are two main sources of statistical data: juvenile court data collected by the Chil-

dren's Bureau and published in its annual report, *Juvenile Court Statistics,* and the FBI *Uniform Crime Reports.*

The information collected by the Children's Bureau is provided by local authorities on a voluntary basis, as is the data included in the FBI reports. *Juvenile Court Statistics* reports various kinds of information, including the reasons for referral to the court, the disposition of cases, characteristics of the children referred, and other types of data. Some reports on trends in the number of court cases handled are also given.

In the FBI reports, information on delinquency is largely limited to data on police arrests. It should be kept in mind that "arrest" data is quite different from information on "crimes known to the police." For a sizable proportion of the crimes reported, particularly theft cases, arrests are never made. Classifications of arrest data are made according to age and type of offense. Thus, it is possible to compare the percent arrested for various offenses in the age group under eighteen—the juveniles—with the percent arrested at other age levels. Trends over time can be studied by means of these data for arrests of different age groups.

Although the validity of the data on delinquency has been challenged by a number of specialists,[21] there seems little doubt that delinquency has been increasing rapidly in the United States, perhaps even more rapidly than adult crime. As indicated in Table 12.2, the number of juvenile arrests involving serious offenses rose almost 80 percent between 1960 and 1968, while the size of the juvenile population increased by a much smaller percentage. Arrests for aggravated assault more than doubled. It should be noted, however, that violent crimes against persons still make up a very small portion of the total for both juveniles and adults.

CHARACTERISTICS OF OFFENDERS

Official statistics on deviant behavior give indications of how crime and delinquency are distributed among different kinds of persons in our society. Apparently not all types of people are equally likely to become involved in law-violating behaviors. While there may be biases in our law enforcement and judicial procedures that differentially affect distinctive groups, the variations found in the crime and delinquency rates are rather striking.[22]

Age and sex. Males are more frequently involved than females in both adult crime and juvenile delinquency (see Table 12.3). Taking all offenses together, males are arrested by police approximately seven times as frequently as females; among juveniles, the ratio of boys to girls appearing in juvenile courts is about five to one. Some writers have attempted to link these differences to biological or psychological factors, but most criminologists stress the importance of social and cultural factors that influence the two sexes differently.

The criminal statistics show a disproportionately high incidence of serious crime among young persons. By far the greatest proportion of those arrested for serious crimes are under twenty-five years of age (see Table 12.4, page 395). There are variations in age, however, according to the type of crime. A minority of those arrested for murder, manslaughter, and aggravated assault in 1968 were under twenty-five, whereas the young dominated the arrest records for rape, robbery, burglary, and theft. The juvenile courts dealt most often with fifteen- and sixteen-year-olds; FBI arrest data show concentrations at sixteen and seventeen. Apparently many youngsters gradually reduce their participation in delinquent and criminal activity as they mature.

Race. Indications of differential involvement in criminal activities according to race are found in many statistics (see Table 12.5, page 397). Arrest data show that the rate for blacks is approximately three times that for whites. Also, most prisons have substantially greater proportions of black inmates than would be indicated by the proportion of blacks in the general population.

Interpretations of these variations by race are complicated by several factors. First, there is the influence of socioeconomic variables. A high proportion of blacks are in the lower levels of our class structure, and these people in general, black and white, have higher involvements in crime than the average. Thus, high crime rates among blacks can be explained in part by anomie theory: the poor lack legitimate means to achieve many of the goals set by our culture. There is also much evidence that blacks are discriminated against in the legal process.

Data from official sources show that in some areas the incidence of delinquency among black youths is as much as five times that of young whites. However, there are the same problems in interpreting this racial difference as exist in the case of adults. For example, one study of cases processed through the juvenile courts found that black youngsters were committed to institutions at younger ages, for less serious crimes, and with fewer prior court appearances

---

21. See Sophia M. Robison, *Juvenile Delinquency,* 2nd ed. (New York: Holt, Rinehart and Winston, Inc., 1960).

22. See, for example, Ruth Shonle Cavan, *Juvenile Delinquency,* 2nd ed. (New York: J. B. Lippincott Company, 1969); and Walter C. Reckless, *The Crime Problem* (New York: Appleton-Century-Crofts, 1967).

TABLE 12.3. **TOTAL ARRESTS, DISTRIBUTION BY SEX, 1968**

OFFENSE CHARGED	NUMBER OF PERSONS ARRESTED			PERCENT MALE	PERCENT FEMALE
	TOTAL	MALE	FEMALE		
Total	5,616,839	4,891,343	725,496	87.1	12.9
Criminal homicide:					
(a) Murder and nonnegligent manslaughter	10,394	8,722	1,672	83.9	16.1
(b) Manslaughter by negligence	3,144	2,824	320	89.8	10.2
Forcible rape	12,685	12,685		100.0	
Robbery	69,115	65,241	3,874	94.4	5.6
Aggravated assault	106,475	93,256	13,219	87.6	12.4
Burglary—breaking or entering	256,216	245,526	10,690	95.8	4.2
Larceny—theft	463,928	350,818	113,110	75.6	24.4
Auto theft	125,263	119,088	6,175	95.1	4.9
SUBTOTAL FOR ABOVE OFFENSES	1,047,220	898,160	149,060	85.8	14.2
Other assaults	239,918	212,484	27,434	88.6	11.4
Arson	9,121	8,386	735	91.9	8.1
Forgery and counterfeiting	34,497	26,971	7,526	78.2	21.8
Fraud	56,710	43,113	13,597	76.0	24.0
Embezzlement	5,894	4,736	1,158	80.4	19.6
Stolen property; buying, receiving, possessing	37,769	34,847	2,922	92.3	7.7
Vandalism	110,182	102,949	7,233	93.4	6.6
Weapons; carrying, possessing, etc.	83,721	78,428	5,293	93.7	6.3
Prostitution and commercialized vice	42,338	9,197	33,141	21.7	78.3
Sex offenses (except forcible rape and prostitution)	47,573	41,897	5,676	88.1	11.9
Narcotic drug laws	162,177	137,960	24,217	85.1	14.9
Gambling	76,909	70,539	6,370	91.7	8.3
Offenses against family and children	51,319	46,802	4,517	91.2	8.8
Driving under the influence	307,231	287,601	19,630	93.6	6.4
Liquor laws	215,376	189,700	25,676	88.1	11.9
Drunkenness	1,415,961	1,316,905	99,056	93.0	7.0
Disorderly conduct	593,104	513,788	79,316	86.6	13.4
Vagrancy	99,147	89,063	10,084	89.8	10.2
All other offenses (except traffic)	643,404	547,397	96,007	85.1	14.9
Suspicion	89,986	75,792	14,194	84.2	15.8
Curfew and loitering law violations	98,230	79,193	19,037	80.6	19.4
Runaways	149,052	75,435	73,617	50.6	49.4

SOURCE: FBI, *Uniform Crime Reports, 1968*, p. 118; based on reports from 4,812 agencies representing an estimated 1968 population of 145,306,000.

or institutional commitments than were white youngsters.[23]

Social class. Official statistics indicate strikingly that the largest proportion of criminals in this country come from the lower socioeconomic levels. Prison data show that from two thirds to three quarters of the inmates are members of the lower strata. The crimes they commit most frequently are crimes against property—usually some form of theft.

As we have already noted, anomie theory helps to explain the high incidence of crime among the poor, especially the high incidence of theft. The statistics may be somewhat distorted, however, by biases in law enforcement and judicial processes. Widespread concern has recently been voiced over the legal treatment that poor people receive, whatever their race.[24] Substantial numbers have faced courts with no legal counsel. A particularly vivid contrast is provided by examining the treatment those of

23. Sidney Axelrad, "Negro and White Male Institutionalized Delinquents," *American Journal of Sociology*, 57 (May 1952), 569–574.

24. Jerome E. Carlin, Jan Howard, and Sheldon L. Messinger, "Civil Justice and the Poor: Issues for Sociological Research," *Law and Society Review*, 1 (November 1966), 9–90.

higher socioeconomic levels receive in the hands of the law. It is well known that law-breakers of white-collar or professional rank often escape detection and, if caught, have a better chance of escaping punishment. Nevertheless, the percentage of lower-class individuals represented in the crime statistics is so disproportionately large that most criminologists believe it cannot be entirely explained away in terms of police or court bias.

In juvenile delinquency, also, the official statistics indicate that a very high proportion of children who are officially labeled delinquent and who are sent to juvenile institutions are from the lower class. However, studies of delinquency that have relied not on official court records but on responses to questionnaires have shown some very interesting results.[25] Under anonymous conditions, many young people of higher socioeconomic levels will admit engaging in a range of behaviors that could have justified referral to juvenile courts. Given the very ambiguous nature of delinquency laws, probably almost all juveniles at one time or another commit acts that *could* be reported to authorities. Even so, there is reason to suspect that, particularly in large cities, a higher proportion of lower-class youngsters than middle- and upper-class ones are consistently involved in delinquent behavior.

Differentials in crime and delinquency rates are also associated with locality. Urban areas tend to have higher crime rates than rural areas, and in general larger communities have higher rates than smaller ones, particularly for more serious crimes. Within the larger communities, crime rates tend to be greater near the city center, lower in the outlying districts. All such variations must be taken into account in developing explanations of crime and delinquency.

SPECIFIC THEORIES OF CRIMINALITY AND DELINQUENCY

Prior to the twentieth century, most theories of crime and delinquency depended on a unitary definition of crime (which more or less equated all types of crime) and stressed some *single factor* as "the cause." Theologians, reformers, physiologists, economists, physicians, and psychologists all tried one formulation or another. Such concepts as sin, poverty, constitutional factors, broken homes, malfunctions of the glands, and mental defects were all advanced as *the* explanation for crime.

Later, when sociological work on the nature and causes of crime began, it became increasingly obvious that crime was not a unitary category. Studies of particular kinds of crimes indicated that, in a behavioral sense, some types had very little in common with others. Furthermore, as knowledge increased concerning the scope and distribution of various kinds of crime in different segments of the population, it became increasingly clear that no single factor could possibly account for the many forms of crime or their uneven social distribution. For a while, a *multiple-factor* theory was widely advocated: crime was said to be caused in different ways by the operation of various combinations of the variables previously used in single-factor theories. But this shed little real light on the problem, and it became widely recognized that completely new kinds of theories were needed. In the 1930's, sociologists began to develop alternative approaches to understanding both adult crime and juvenile delinquency as products of group experience.

"DIFFERENTIAL ASSOCIATION" THEORIES

The issue of inherited versus acquired tendencies toward criminality constituted one of the great debates within criminology for many years. Only in recent decades has the view become widespread that men are not born criminals. Sociological research on the causal process was largely responsible for this change.

Sutherland's theory. An important example of the sociological approach to criminality is the *differential association* theory, first developed by Edwin H. Sutherland in the late 1930's.[26] Suth-

25. See, for example, James F. Short, Jr., and F. Ivan Nye, "Reported Behavior as Criterion for Deviant Behavior," *Social Problems*, 5 (1957–1958), 207–213; Austin L. Porterfield, *Youth in Trouble* (Fort Worth, Texas: The Leo Potishman Foundation, 1946), pp. 37–51.

26. See Albert K. Cohen, Alfred Lindesmith, and Karl Schuessler, eds., *The Sutherland Papers* (Bloomington, Ind.: Indiana University Press, 1956), pp. 13–29. Sutherland's differential association theory has recently been restated and reformulated as a mathematical model; see Melvin L. De-Fleur and Richard Quinney, "A Reformulation of Sutherland's Differential Association Theory and a Strategy for Empirical Verification," *Journal of Research in Crime and Delinquency*, 3, No. 1 (January 1966), 1–26.

TABLE 12.4. **TOTAL ARRESTS OF PERSONS UNDER 15, UNDER 18, UNDER 21, AND UNDER 25 YEARS OF AGE, 1968**

OFFENSE CHARGED	NUMBER OF PERSONS ARRESTED		PERCENTAGE			
	GRAND TOTAL ALL AGES	UNDER 25	UNDER 15	UNDER 18	UNDER 21	UNDER 25
Total	**5,616,839**	**2,828,822**	10.0	25.9	38.8	50.4
Criminal homicide:						
(a) Murder and nonnegligent manslaughter	10,394	4,157	1.6	9.9	23.6	40.0
(b) Manslaughter by negligence	3,144	1,411	1.0	7.8	25.3	44.9
Forcible rape	12,685	8,171	3.9	20.2	43.1	64.4
Robbery	69,115	51,943	11.9	33.1	56.2	75.2
Aggravated assault	106,475	48,436	5.6	16.5	29.8	45.5
Burglary—breaking or entering	256,216	213,651	26.3	54.7	72.0	83.4
Larceny—theft	463,928	358,414	28.9	54.0	68.1	77.3
Auto theft	125,263	111,109	16.4	60.7	79.0	88.7
SUBTOTAL FOR ABOVE OFFENSES	1,047,220	797,292	22.6	48.8	64.8	76.1
Other assaults	239,918	109,400	6.9	17.6	30.0	45.6
Arson	9,121	7,327	43.1	62.8	72.9	80.3
Forgery and counterfeiting	34,497	17,691	2.4	12.0	29.9	51.3
Fraud	56,710	18,583	1.4	4.5	14.2	32.8
Embezzlement	5,894	1,892	1.0	4.2	14.2	32.1
Stolen property; buying, receiving, possessing	37,769	26,356	12.0	34.6	54.4	69.8
Vandalism	110,182	98,430	48.5	75.2	84.1	89.3
Weapons; carrying, possessing, etc.	83,721	42,350	5.0	17.8	33.3	50.6
Prostitution and commercialized vice	42,338	24,135	.2	2.1	16.7	57.0
Sex offenses (except forcible rape and prostitution)	47,573	24,305	9.4	23.9	36.2	51.1
Narcotic drug laws	162,177	124,296	3.8	26.6	56.5	76.6
Gambling	76,909	11,851	.4	2.6	6.8	15.4
Offenses against family and children	51,319	15,132	.2	1.2	11.8	29.5
Driving under the influence	307,231	57,304		1.0	6.5	18.7
Liquor laws	215,376	177,931	2.5	31.8	75.3	82.6
Drunkenness	1,415,961	226,381	.3	2.6	7.8	16.0
Disorderly conduct	593,104	308,407	8.4	21.7	37.3	52.0
Vagrancy	99,147	42,005	2.0	11.1	29.0	42.4
All other offenses (except traffic)	643,404	391,497	12.5	31.8	47.2	60.8
Suspicion	89,986	58,975	7.1	24.5	47.7	65.5
Curfew and loitering law violations	98,230	98,230	25.1	100.0	100.0	100.0
Runaways	149,052	149,052	39.5	100.0	100.0	100.0

SOURCE: FBI, *Uniform Crime Reports, 1968*, p. 117; based on reports from 4,812 agencies representing an estimated 1968 population of 145,306,000.

erland's theory of criminality stressed the importance of the socialization process in predisposing some people to criminal conduct. By interacting in primary groups where he is exposed more to norms favoring crime than to norms opposing it, an individual comes to internalize a pro-criminal orientation and to learn the attitudes and skills associated with that orientation. In other words, his socializing experiences "prepare" him to participate in an established criminal subculture, much as the socializing experiences of other people prepare them to participate in conventional society. (See the discussion of selective internalization in Chapter 5, pages 150–151.)

Sutherland's theory of subcultural socialization is thus an extension into criminology of the ideas of earlier sociologists such as Cooley and Mead, who stressed the importance of the primary group in shaping individual personality and conduct. While in recent years many other promising sociological formulations have been advanced to help explain the causes of crime, the theory of differential association remains one of the principal frameworks for current research on criminality. Today Sutherland's theory is not considered to have uniform application to *all* forms of crime, but it does identify a set of background conditions that may contribute to the development of deviant orientations.

The group context of delinquency. Early attempts to identify the causes of criminal behavior made no special distinction between juvenile and adult crime. It has become increasingly recognized, however, that the conditions associated with juvenile misconduct may be quite different from those associated with adult criminality.

The systematic study of juvenile delinquency by sociologists in the United States began in the 1920's with the work of Thrasher, Reckless, Shaw, McKay, and others, who emphasized the social disorganization and culture conflicts present in the interstitial areas of large cities, where delinquency rates were particularly high. These pioneers drew attention to the group nature of delinquency, noting that over 90 percent of the delinquent offenses brought to the attention of the courts involved two or more boys.[27] More recent studies have further established the importance of group processes in juvenile misbehavior.

The theory of the reaction subculture. During the 1950's and 1960's the most significant advances in understanding delinquency have been related to the study of *gang* delinquency in urban areas. Several recent theories stress the role of social and cultural factors that impinge upon lower-class youth and may lead them to engage in various forms of misconduct. An excellent example of such a theory is that of Albert K. Cohen. His ideas, which build upon differential association concepts, have stimulated a great deal of contemporary interest in gang delinquency among American sociologists.

In brief, the Cohen theory states that many urban, lower-class boys are raised under conditions where they learn different motivations and value orientations than those required for achieving the goals our society heavily stresses.[28] As they begin to reach adolescence, such boys find themselves unable to compete successfully with boys from middle-class backgrounds, whether at school or on the job. In a society where middle-class values are used as the measuring rod, these boys always come out a poor second. Thus, they are continually frustrated in their desire for social approval, status rewards, and self-esteem.

When a number of such boys are thrown together in the neighborhood and the school, they may form groups and begin to develop subcultures that more adequately meet their needs for success and self-approval. Such groups gradually develop codes of conduct, beliefs, attitudes, and values that are in many ways the *opposite* of middle-class standards. While it may not be a deliberate or conscious process, a "reaction" subculture emerges, characterized by behavior and attitudes that are negations of middle-class ways.

Often such groups begin to engage in vandalism, violence, and nonutilitarian theft "just for the hell of it." Such activities provide opportunities for the development of status within the group and for enhancing self-esteem. Thus, participation in a deviant subculture represents a solution to problems of adjustment that are generated by the social structure. It provides the boys with a social and cultural environment that meets their needs for self-esteem, and it alleviates their status frustrations. As their delinquent activities and other interactions continue, the members of such groups become more and more isolated from conventional society and increasingly dependent upon one another.

Further research is needed to test the validity of Cohen's theory. Although it is far from being a full explanation of gang delinquency, it has done much to focus attention on this type of group deviance and the study of its underlying causes.[29]

---

27. See, for example, Clifford R. Shaw and Henry D. McKay, *Social Factors in Juvenile Delinquency,* National Commission on Law Observance and Enforcement, 2, No. 13 (Washington, D.C.: Government Printing Office, 1931), 194–195.

28. Albert K. Cohen, *Delinquent Boys: The Culture of the Gang* (New York: The Free Press, 1955). The differences Cohen has noted in the value orientations taught by the lower and middle classes are discussed in Chapter 5 of the present text, pages 157–158.

29. For other theoretical approaches to gang delinquency and some of the relevant research findings, see Richard A. Cloward and Lloyd E. Ohlin, *Delinquency and Opportunity: A Theory of Delinquent Gangs* (New York: The Free Press, 1963); Walter B. Miller, "Lower Class Culture as a Generating Milieu of Gang Delinquency," *Journal of Social Issues,* 14 (April 1958), 5–19; and James F. Short, Jr., and Fred L. Strodtbeck, *Group Process and Gang Delinquency* (Chicago: The University of Chicago Press, 1965).

TABLE 12.5. **TOTAL ARRESTS BY RACE, 1968**

	TOTAL ARRESTS						
OFFENSE CHARGED	TOTAL	WHITE	NEGRO	INDIAN	CHINESE	JAPANESE	OTHERS*
Total	**5,349,450**	**3,700,012**	**1,471,730**	**119,265**	**1,666**	**4,186**	**52,591**
Criminal homicide:							
(a) Murder and nonnegligent manslaughter	**9,458**	3,536	5,699	93	2	2	126
(b) Manslaughter by negligence	**2,965**	2,184	733	18		7	23
Forcible rape	**11,607**	5,967	5,406	84		9	141
Robbery	**59,424**	21,550	36,862	485	3	16	508
Aggravated assault	**93,972**	46,039	46,198	814	24	23	874
Burglary—breaking or entering	**241,455**	156,196	80,627	1,582	81	194	2,775
Larceny—theft	**448,392**	299,304	140,406	2,976	339	605	4,762
Auto theft	**116,745**	72,875	40,969	943	40	141	1,777
SUBTOTAL FOR ABOVE OFFENSES	**984,018**	607,651	356,900	6,995	489	997	10,986
Other assaults	**226,488**	136,055	86,148	1,559	64	100	2,562
Arson	**8,498**	5,653	2,709	64		7	65
Forgery and counterfeiting	**31,176**	22,576	8,140	237	10	19	194
Fraud	**54,931**	42,479	11,921	234	10	22	265
Embezzlement	**5,241**	4,252	952	16	1	1	19
Stolen property; buying, receiving, possessing	**31,398**	19,231	11,739	131	8	9	280
Vandalism	**101,915**	79,667	20,865	489	28	59	807
Weapons; carrying, possessing, etc.	**77,844**	37,912	38,575	366	17	30	944
Prostitution and commercialized vice	**34,418**	12,267	21,737	96	14	41	263
Sex offenses (except forcible rape and prostitution)	**44,853**	33,796	10,130	238	17	47	625
Narcotic drug laws	**137,598**	105,886	29,608	270	70	218	1,546
Gambling	**63,506**	18,692	40,111	18	119	662	3,904
Offenses against family and children	**49,956**	33,704	15,529	446	9	5	263
Driving under the influence	**298,664**	241,899	50,586	4,250	86	249	1,594
Liquor laws	**204,214**	176,045	23,573	3,632	62	39	863
Drunkenness	**1,393,886**	1,011,138	292,596	81,465	198	442	8,047
Disorderly conduct	**560,537**	348,179	195,577	8,595	120	74	7,992
Vagrancy	**89,472**	66,827	20,516	1,168	41	90	830
All other offenses (except traffic)	**617,347**	450,071	153,604	6,178	190	668	6,636
Suspicion	**89,006**	48,188	40,318	399	5	3	93
Curfew and loitering law violations	**97,540**	76,282	18,656	850	47	288	1,417
Runaways	**146,944**	121,562	21,240	1,569	61	116	2,396

* Includes race unknown.

SOURCE: FBI, *Uniform Crime Reports, 1968,* p. 120; based on reports from 4,758 agencies representing an estimated 1968 population of 135,545,000.

THE IDENTIFICATION OF "BEHAVIOR SYSTEMS"

Sociologists recognize that it will be possible to develop valid theories of crime in general only after they learn much more about the various crimes in particular. Thus much contemporary research is directed at the intensive study of distinctive patterns of criminal behavior.

The task of developing theories about specific crimes is complicated by the fact that the *legal* definition of a criminal act for which a person can be prosecuted in court may not always coincide with the *behavioral* definition of the offense he actually committed. For example, a crime such as "disorderly conduct" can mean almost anything in behavioral terms. A person arrested on such a charge may have participated in a riot, exchanged verbal insults with another person, or have become involved in a tavern brawl. Vagrancy is another loosely defined offense. Persons have been jailed on this charge for everything from hitch-hiking to petty larceny to prostitution. Even when the charge is much more specific, the act may have been committed in a variety of circumstances and for a variety of reasons. Neighborhood youngsters who "borrow" a car for a joyride and professional thieves who steal a car for an organized ring that will alter and resell it may both be charged with auto theft.

Considerations of this type have led sociologists to place less emphasis on classifying crime in terms of the specific statutes violated and more on grouping together *offenses* and *offenders* with a high degree of behavioral similarity. They can thus search for common components in the development of a particular class of behaviorally similar offenses. This *behavior systems* approach is one of the more promising new directions of contemporary criminology.

Bloch and Geis have outlined some of the major components of such a typological approach.[30] Essentially, they see a given crime that occurs with some regularity as a product of two somewhat separate sets of factors. The first is the *sociocultural matrix*—the general conditions that make a particular type of crime both feasible and profitable in a particular society. The other element in the equation is the *criminal pattern* itself, which develops as a response to the opportunities the sociocultural matrix provides.

Bloch and Geis illustrate these two concepts with the example of confidence games used to cheat older well-to-do women. They note that in our society considerable wealth falls into the hands of widows, many of whom migrate to subtropical regions of the United States, along with other older people, in search of a pleasant retirement. Thus our affluent society and the greater longevity of women have supplied confidence men with an aggregate of individuals particularly vulnerable to victimization.

In response to these "rich pickings," there has developed a class of confidence men who pose as investment counselors with various schemes for easy profit. They practice their "con games" over and over, cheating first one older widow and then another. The techniques they use, their attitudes, the values they support, the special language they employ, and their loyalty to each other have produced a clear-cut behavior system. Differing from other confidence men, who use other strategies for cheating other types of victims, they form a behaviorally homogeneous set of offenders and offenses. The juncture of a particular sociocultural matrix and the particular criminal behavior system that has risen in response to it, then, constitutes a "type" of crime that has little in common with other legally similar offenses.

Many such criminal behavior systems have been identified by sociologists. In this section we will look at three broad classes of crime that have been quite widely studied: *professional* crime, *organized* crime, and *white-collar* crime.

Professional crime. For the layman, it is often difficult to conceive of criminals and their acts as "professional," but certain kinds of criminals have many of the characteristics of legitimate professionals in our society, such as doctors and lawyers. These criminals commit their illegal acts with great skill, which results from considerable training, internship, and practice. Professionals are found in various forms of crime, such as pickpocketing, shoplifting, confidence games, check forgery, counterfeiting, and so forth.[31]

Professional criminals regard themselves as the elite of the criminal world and view with disdain the bumbling, often violent amateur who frequently gets caught. Other distinctive attitudes, values, perceptions, and even speech ways are shared by different types of professional criminals. Their way of life is strongly reinforced by high involvement with other professionals and by very little involvement with other segments of society. Needless to say, given such thorough integration into a career and supportive subculture, the prospects for rehabilitating professional criminals are not promising. Maurer describes the lure of the "big-con" profession in the following way:

Because of the advantages which accrue to his profession, a confidence man, once he has established himself, seldom changes it for another in the underworld. He may "pack the racket in" and go into legitimate business (where some have notable suc-

30. Herbert A. Bloch and Gilbert Geis, *Man, Crime and Society* (New York: Random House, Inc., 1962), pp. 577–584. See also Marshall B. Clinard and Richard Quinney, *Criminal Behavior Systems* (New York: Holt, Rinehart and Winston, Inc., 1967); and Don C. Gibbons, *Society, Crime and Criminal Careers; An Introduction to Criminology* (Englewood Cliffs, N.J.: Prentice-Hall, Inc., 1968).

31. See, for example, Mary Owen Cameron, *The Booster and the Snitch* (New York: The Free Press, 1964); Edwin M. Lemert, "The Behavior of the Systematic Check Forger," *Social Problems*, 6 (Fall 1958), 141–149; and Edwin H. Sutherland, ed., *The Professional Thief* (Chicago: The University of Chicago Press, 1937).

cess), but as long as he remains "on the grift" he prefers to play the confidence games. To step back down the scale permanently, returning to thievery or professional gambling, would be to lose professional status; more than that, there is a thrill about big-con work which no other branch of the grift [theft] can duplicate. The confidence man extends himself fully while he works; all his faculties and abilities are called into play; each mark [victim] is a new challenge to his ingenuity; and, perhaps most important, the stakes for which he plays are very high. "Once a heavy gee [safeblower], always a heavy," said the Postal Kid [a famous con-man]. "And it's the same with the con. When the mark is being played for a big chunk, there is a kick in it just like there is to the heavy when a big peter [safe] is being knocked off."[32]

Organized crime. Organized crime has been defined as "any crime committed by a person occupying a position in an established division of labor designed for the commission of crime."[33] Through various sources such as government investigations a picture of this type of crime can be put together. First of all, organized crime depends on a structured group with distinctive qualities. This group, which carries out illegal activities, is frequently described as *feudal* in its organization. That is, there exists a very clear-cut hierarchy of participants, with those at the top having concentrated personal power and expecting intense loyalty from lesser members of the organization (Figure 12.1, page 400). Usually these organizations operate over rather large, well-defined, protected geographical areas, which they think of as their "territory."

Basically, these groups are in business, and their goal is extensive profits. Cressey describes a nationwide alliance of such groups and has this to say about its activities:

The members of this organization control all but a tiny part of the illegal gambling in the United States. They are the principal loan sharks. They are the principal importers and wholesalers of narcotics. They have infiltrated certain labor unions, where they extort money from employers and, at the same time, cheat the members of the union. The members have a virtual monopoly on some legitimate enterprises, such as cigarette vending machines and juke boxes, and they own a wide variety of retail firms, restaurants and bars, hotels, trucking companies, food companies, linen-supply houses, garbage collection routes, and factories. Until recently, they owned a large proportion of Las Vegas. They own several state legislators and federal congressmen and other officials in the legislative, executive, and judicial branches of government at the local, state, and federal levels. Some government officials (including judges) are considered, and consider themselves, members.[34]

Like professional criminals, members of organized criminal groups share distinctive attitudes and values and often a special vocabulary. However, they are much more involved with conventional society and its values. It is a fact that many of the activities of organized crime could not continue if these "services" were not demanded by the law-abiding part of our society. It is also a fact that the costs to the nation, both tangible and intangible, are enormous.

White-collar crime. Certain types of illegal activities are labeled "white-collar" crimes because the offenders are of relatively high socio-economic status and the crimes are committed in connection with their occupational pursuits.[35] Probably the distinguishing feature of this type of crime is that the violator does not think of himself as a criminal—nor is he usually regarded as one by the public. Persons who commit white-collar crimes normally live respectable and law-abiding lives, but under certain circumstances—frequently through associates on the job—they become exposed to norms favoring such illegal acts as tax evasion, the manipulation of accounts, and employee theft.

32. David W. Maurer, *The Big Con* (New York: Signet Books, 1962), p. 145.

33. Donald R. Cressey, *Theft of the Nation* (New York: Harper & Row, Inc., 1969), p. 313. See also Gus Tyler, *Organized Crime in America: A Book of Readings* (Ann Arbor, Mich.: University of Michigan Press, 1962); Thorsten Sellin, "Organized Crime: A Business Enterprise," *The Annals of the American Academy of Political and Social Science,* 347 (May 1963), 12–19; and President's Commission on Law Enforcement and Administration of Justice, *The Challenge of Crime in a Free Society* (Washington, D.C.: Government Printing Office, 1967).

34. Cressey, *op. cit.,* p. xi.

35. See Edwin H. Sutherland, *White Collar Crime* (New York: Holt, Rinehart and Winston, Inc., 1961); Gilbert Geis, "Toward a Delineation of White Collar Offenses," *Sociological Inquiry,* 32 (Spring 1962), 160–171; and Richard Quinney, "The Study of White Collar Crime: Toward a Reorientation in Theory and Research," *Journal of Criminal Law, Criminology, and Police Science,* 55 (June 1964), 208–214.

White-collar criminals typically develop elaborate rationalizations to justify their behavior, and usually they receive differential treatment in the hands of the police, the courts, and other agencies. Indeed, because of status considerations and the differential importance of norms, most of the acts of white-collar criminals never become part of the official crime statistics. This makes it exceedingly difficult to calculate the extent of white-collar crime. The President's Commission on Crime and Law Enforcement has estimated that the direct cost to business is significant:

Employee theft, embezzlement, and other forms of crime involving business, which appear in relatively small numbers in the police statistics, loom very large in dollar volume. Direct stealing of cash and merchandise, manipulation of accounts and stock records, and other forms of these crimes, along with shoplifting, appear to constitute a tax of one to two percent on the total sales of retail enterprises, and significant amounts in other parts of business and industry.[36]

---

36. *The Challenge of Crime in a Free Society, op. cit.*, p. 32.

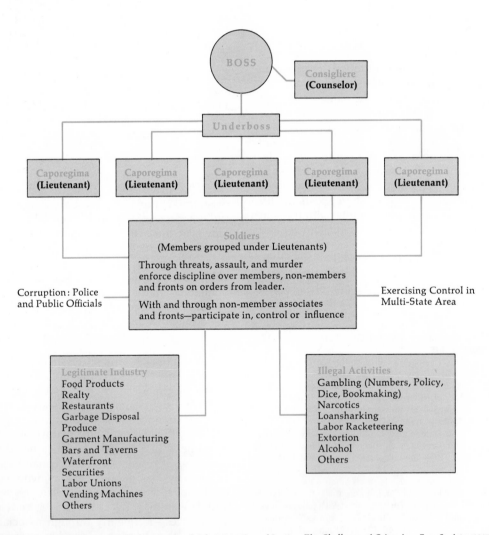

SOURCE: President's Commission on Law Enforcement and Administration of Justice, *The Challenge of Crime in a Free Society*, 1967, p. 452.

FIGURE 12.1. **AN ORGANIZED CRIME FAMILY**

Not all white-collar criminals are guilty of wrongdoing *against* their companies; some break the law *for* their companies. In one well-publicized case, twenty-nine of the leading electrical companies and forty-five of their high executives were convicted of price-fixing violations. Heavy fines were levied against the companies, and seven of the executives actually served short jail terms. The other executives, however, received no jail terms or suspended sentences. In spite of the extent of the violations, the companies were not hurt in any substantial way, and of the executives who did not remain in their jobs many found other employment without difficulty. Overall, it appears that the behavior system of white-collar crime is quite different from that of organized or professional crime, and that one of its most distinctive characteristics is the relative lack of stigma attached to it.

Delinquency behavior systems. The behavior systems approach has been less extensively applied in studies of delinquency than in studies of adult crime, partly because delinquency itself remains a rather vague conception. However, the literature does include descriptions of such distinctive patterns of delinquency as juvenile vandalism, youthful auto theft, and use of narcotics by minors.[37] Even more directly related to the behavior systems approach is the work of sociologists who have attempted to identify the characteristics of various types of gangs and their behaviors.

Cloward and Ohlin have described three types of juvenile gangs, each having a distinctive subculture.[38] They also specify the cultural and structural conditions out of which each of these types of gangs is likely to develop. Drawing on Merton's anomie theory, Cloward and Ohlin hypothesize that delinquent subcultures arise because of the "disparity between what lower-class youth are led to want and what is actually available to them."

Adolescents who form delinquent subcultures ... have internalized an emphasis upon conventional goals. Faced with limitations on legitimate avenues of access to these goals, and unable to revise their aspirations downward, they experience intense frustrations; the exploration of nonconformist alternatives may be the result.[39]

The patterns of behavior of a gang with a *criminal subculture* are primarily oriented toward material gain through illegal pursuits such as theft and extortion. In order to achieve these ends, the gang must establish connections with various adult criminal groups in the area. The adult groups provide certain facilities, such as outlets for stolen goods, and they serve as training grounds where the juveniles can acquire the skills, values, and attitudes they will need if they are eventually to move into the adult groups. Thus, before the juvenile gang with a distinctly criminal subculture can develop, adult criminal groups must be present in the neighborhood or area in which these juveniles live, and there must be opportunities for the integration of the youths into criminal behavior patterns.

The second type of gang is one that develops a *conflict subculture*, in which the main emphasis is on assaultive behavior and violence. These gangs, with their rumbles, assaults, and aggressive actions, attract widespread attention, but probably they are not as numerous as the public believes. The members turn to violence as a means to obtain status; few other opportunities exist for them. Gangs with a conflict subculture are most likely to develop in disorganized areas or neighborhoods, where there is much instability and transiency. Adult criminal groups are generally not highly developed in such areas, so the delinquent gangs have little or no opportunity to integrate their activities with those of experienced criminals.

The third gang pattern is identified with a *retreatist subculture.* Retreatist groups emphasize sensuous pleasures, "kicks," and withdrawal from the conventional world; many of them are drug consumers. Cloward and Ohlin label the youths who participate in these groups as "double failures": they have failed to attain success in the conventional world and they have also been unable to make it through illegitimate avenues in the criminal or conflict gangs. In the face of such a double failure, the adolescent may turn to drugs and in this way retreat or escape from his problems.

---

37. See Marshall B. Clinard and Andrew L. Wade, "Toward a Delineation of Vandalism as a Sub-Type in Juvenile Delinquency," *Journal of Criminal Law, Criminology, and Police Science,* 48 (January-February 1958), 493–497; Erwin Schepses, "Boys Who Steal Cars," *Federal Probation,* 25 (March 1961), 56–62; and Isidor Chein and Eva Rosenfeld, "Juvenile Narcotics Use," *Law and Contemporary Problems,* 22 (Winter 1957), 52–69.

38. Cloward and Ohlin, *op. cit.*

39. *Ibid.,* p. 86.

This overview of criminal and delinquent behavior systems has suggested that behaviorally similar offenses may recur when conditions in the broad social structure and the culture produce similar opportunities for certain forms of crimes. The major advantage of this relatively new theoretical approach lies in its major premise—that the attitudes, specific techniques, values, and other behavioral characteristics of criminals who repeatedly commit particular kinds of offenses may form a behavioral configuration that can be used as a more meaningful basis than legal definitions for typing or classifying crime. However, it should be noted again that the identification of a behavior system is not the same as the development of a causal theory. It is only a tentative first step in the task of explaining why certain kinds of people are drawn into particular patterns of criminal conduct.

CONTROLLING DEVIANCE

Although some types of deviant behavior can make a positive contribution to society, the major forms of deviance—crime, delinquency, drug usage, suicide, etc.—are regarded as serious threats both to the persons involved and to the social order itself. Control of such conduct is one of the great problems of contemporary society. In spite of our technical sophistication, we have yet to devise the social machinery we need for effectively reducing crime, delinquency, and other forms of deviant behavior.

SOCIAL CONTROL IN THE HETEROGENEOUS SOCIETY

In the small homogeneous society, extensive behavioral conformity is insured by the fact that socializing experiences are very much the same for all members. Societal norms tend to be consistent with each other and to be strongly supported by tradition. There is an element of sacredness about them. Social control, then, is primarily dependent on self-sanctioning. Even on those occasions when external sanctions are required, they seldom involve formal punishment. Deviants can usually be brought back to conformity through the use of gossip, ridicule, or humiliation.

The need for formal agencies of control. Even in a complex, urban society such as ours, social control rests largely on the internalization of shared norms. Most Americans behave in socially acceptable ways because they seldom conceive of behaving otherwise. And as in simpler societies, fear of disapproval from family, friends, and neighbors is usually adequate to keep potential deviators in check. Nevertheless, the great diversity of the population, the limitations on effective communication between various segments, and the competitive struggles between groups with different interests have all led to an increasing need for formal mechanisms of control. Deviance of all sorts has become a problem of societal concern in the United States. More and more laws, larger and more mobile police forces, increasingly complex legal processing, and new types of penal institutions are being used in the attempt to stem the apparent increase in criminal behavior, and more and more formal associations are trying to cope with mental illness, alcoholism, drug addiction, and other problems.

The difficulties of controlling deviance are immense. Crime and delinquency, as well as other deviations, have been an integral part of our society since the beginning, and no quick effective means of eradicating them has been or is likely to be developed. An additional consideration in a democratic society is how to control deviance without infringing upon individual rights and freedoms. The issue is one of maintaining order and at the same time protecting basic values.

The discretionary treatment of deviants. In our earlier discussion of labeling theory (page 383), we pointed out that the labeling of an individual as a deviant has particular significance if it is done by formal social-control agencies. Given the evidence that such labeling may not only affect an individual's relationships with conforming society but also contribute to the development of habitual patterns of deviance, it becomes important to ask what criteria are used in applying the "official stamp" of deviance. On the basis of their research on police contacts with juveniles, Piliavin and Briar conclude that police officers apply many consid-

Gangs with a conflict subculture are most likely to develop in disorganized neighborhoods—such as Chicago's Woodlawn area—where there is much instability and transiency. The members of these gangs turn to assaultive behavior and violence in order to obtain status; few other opportunities exist for them.

erations unrelated to actual offenses to decide whether a given youngster should or should not be turned over to juvenile authorities:

[Those] police officers studied . . . were permitted and even encouraged to exercise immense latitude in disposing of the juveniles they encountered. That is, it was within the officers' discretionary authority, except in extremely limiting cases, to decide which juveniles were to come to the attention of the courts and correctional agencies and thereby be identified officially as delinquents. . . . In exercising this discretion, policemen were strongly guided by the demeanor of those who were apprehended, a practice which ultimately led . . . to certain youths (particu-

larly Negroes and boys dressed in the style of "toughs") being treated more severely than other juveniles for comparable offenses.[40]

Studies of this type underscore the fact that deviance—particularly *who* is deviant—is in part a product of a social judgment. An individual who breaks the law may or may not be labeled a criminal or juvenile delinquent because of the discretionary power of officials and agencies to apply such labels. His fate may be more related to how he dresses, the words he uses, and his general demeanor in interactions with authorities than to the kind of offense he committed. Thus far we have little systematic information about such issues. The labeling and discretionary processes constitute an area of much-needed research.

40. Irving Piliavin and Scott Briar, "Police Encounters with Juveniles," *American Journal of Sociology*, 70 (September 1964), 214.

SOCIETAL RESPONSES TO CRIME AND OTHER DEVIANCE

It will be recalled that a basic component of the criminal law pertaining to most forms of deviance is the provision for *penal sanctions.* That is, the group conceives of imprisonment and related forms of punishment administered by the state as devices to induce conformity. It remains an open question, however, whether punishment is actually an effective method for maintaining social control.

The justification of punishment. Although punishment as a response to wrongdoing is very old and widespread, the justifications for its use have differed from group to group. What are the justifications in our society?

Probably the most frequent reason given for the use of punishment is *deterrence.* It is widely assumed that if we punish people for their misdeeds, it will not only deter them from repeating such actions but also discourage others from engaging in criminal acts. Many researchers in the social sciences seriously question this assumption. Most studies to date, however, have dealt only with the efficacy of the death penalty as a deterrent to murder (see page 25). As Gibbs has pointed out, deterrence research must be extended to other types of penalties before sociologists can generalize about the effectiveness of punishment in preventing serious crimes. In his own research, Gibbs found that both certainty and severity of imprisonment were related to the criminal homicide rates in forty-eight states.[41] On the basis of these findings, he concludes that we must consider the relationship between punishment and deterrence as still an open question.

Another justification for punishment in our society is *reformation.* In a restrictive setting such as a prison, attempts are made to help the offender develop attitudes and skills that will facilitate his reentry into society. The emphasis on reform and rehabilitation has greatly increased among penologists, but the general public still holds very strongly to the more traditional concept of punishment.

In addition to deterrence and reformation, many people believe that punishment is necessary to *protect society* from criminals and their acts. If criminals are removed from the environ-ment through imprisonment, exile, or even execution, then life is relatively safer for the group. Another justification—very ancient but probably not too widespread today—is *retribution.* The wrongdoer must pay for his actions; in this way society can "get even" with him. Crimes such as murder, rape, and child molestation are especially likely to call forth angry demands for vengeance on the offender.

Forms of punishment. The most widely used penal sanction in Western society is imprisonment, a form of punishment that is basically consistent with our cultural values and beliefs. Liberty and freedom are so cherished that the denial of them represents a severe punishment for most people. Reduction in the use of most kinds of corporal punishment reflects not only an increased emphasis on rehabilitation but also the steady growth of humanitarian attitudes. The trend away from capital punishment has been particularly noteworthy. Even though some states are reluctant to abolish it altogether, each year fewer and fewer executions take place.

As Cressey has suggested, societal attitudes toward punishment for wrongdoing can be classified on a continuum from "purely punitive" to "purely nonpunitive."[42] In the United States the trend has clearly been toward increasingly nonpunitive attitudes, although widespread concern over rising rates of crime and delinquency have recently led some of the public to argue for a harsher approach. Whatever the public attitude, contemporary penologists and criminologists are generally agreed that punitive punishment and rehabilitation are basically incompatible.

The modern emphasis on rehabilitation is reflected in the increased use of probation and parole. Probation basically involves the suspension of sentence with provisions for supervision and guidance in the community. Parole, on the other hand, is a procedure through which the offender is released from prison after having served part of his sentence. He is supervised in

41. Jack P. Gibbs, "Crime, Punishment, and Deterrence," *Southwestern Social Science Quarterly,* 48 (March 1968), 515–530.

42. Donald R. Cressey, "Hypotheses in the Sociology of Punishment," *Sociology and Social Research,* 39 (July–August 1955), 394–400.

the community by a parole officer for a specified period of time. Other efforts to help the offender make his way back into community life include "halfway houses," community centers, and training programs. Within prisons themselves there have been significant advances in the development of special programs aimed at helping the individual rather than punishing him. However, most prisons still have a basically punitive atmosphere, and there is probably some justice to the charge that they serve more as training grounds for a criminal career than as effective rehabilitation centers. In any case, an estimated two thirds of all inmates return to prison at least once. Seemingly, many of our current practices and penal programs will have to change if the goal of reform is actually to be achieved.

RESPONSES TO THE JUVENILE OFFENDER

Prior to the establishment of juvenile courts around the turn of the century, youthful law-breakers were regarded more or less as small adult criminals. Today, however, the societal response to the juvenile offender is quite different from that to the adult criminal. The goals of the juvenile court are (in theory, at least) to understand, protect, and redirect the youngster who has gotten into trouble. He is regarded more as someone who has not yet been completely socialized and less as a rational individual who can weigh the consequences of his actions.

Most prisons still have a basically punitive atmosphere, and there is probably some justice to the charge that they serve more as training grounds for a criminal career than as effective rehabilitation centers. An estimated two thirds of all inmates return to prison at least once.

The procedures of the juvenile court stress flexibility. Treatment of the youngsters' problems (whether they be educational, psychological, or social) is more frequently the goal than punishment, retribution, or the protection of society. Indeed, redirecting the juvenile has been considered so important that programs of treatment have sometimes disregarded his legal rights. These have recently been reaffirmed in a series of court decisions, with the result that juvenile procedures are now undergoing some modification.

In providing treatment for the juvenile offender, a considerable effort is made to keep the youngster in the community rather than in an institution. He may be required to go to a special school, live in a foster home, or remain under probationary supervision. He may also receive some type of psychotherapy. Although these treatment procedures have met with only limited success, they tend to be more effective than simply locking the offender up.

Juvenile institutions tend to be used as a last resort for those who cannot be treated by alternative means. Even so, such institutions are thought of as "schools" for "reform" and "training" rather than as jails. Most are designed around very different principles than are adult correctional establishments, although in the case of very serious crimes, a juvenile may be sent to an adult penal institution.

New programs are constantly being devised and studied in an effort to provide more adequate means for the prevention of delinquency. The three main areas of concern have been employment opportunities, educational services, and community organization. All of these stress the provision of opportunities to youth who are not adequately participating in the society. Settlement houses, detached workers, recreation programs, job centers, part-time work programs, and many other organized efforts are aimed at directing the activities and attentions of delinquency-prone individuals into legitimate channels.[43]

Unfortunately, in spite of the many efforts to prevent delinquency and to treat the youthful offender, there is considerable doubt concerning the effectiveness of current procedures. Many of the programs aimed at preventing and controlling delinquency have not been adequately evaluated, but most of the assessments that have been made are not encouraging. The following example is not atypical:

The Midcity Project conducted a delinquency control program in a low-class district of Boston between the years 1954 and 1957. A major objective of the Project was to inhibit or reduce the amount of illegal activity engaged in by resident adolescents. Project methods derived from a "total community" philosophy which has become increasingly popular in recent years and currently forms the basis of several large-scale delinquency control programs. On the assumption that delinquent behavior by urban lower-class adolescents, whatever their personality characteristics, is in some significant degree facilitated by or actualized through certain structural features of the community, the Project executed "action" programs directed at three of the societal units seen to figure importantly in the genesis and perpetuation of delinquent behavior—the community, the family, and the gang. . . . It is now possible to provide a definite answer to the principal evaluative research question—"Was there a significant measurable inhibition of law-violating or morally disapproved behavior as a consequence of Project efforts?" The answer, with little necessary qualification, is "No." All major measures of violative behavior—disapproved actions, illegal actions, during-contact court appearances, before-during-after appearances, and Project-Control group appearances—provide consistent support for a finding of "negligible impact."[44]

If delinquency has its roots in conditions of the social structure, such as those that have been discussed in this chapter, there is probably little hope that present techniques can reverse the current trend toward higher rates of youthful crime. Clearly, new approaches and massive efforts will be required. In particular, until the causes of delinquency are better understood, there remains considerable doubt that truly effective procedures for its prevention and treatment can be devised.

---

43. See Stanton Wheeler and Leonard S. Cottrell, Jr., *Juvenile Delinquency: Its Prevention and Control* (New York: Russell Sage Foundation, 1966); also Virginia Burns and Leonard Stern, "The Prevention of Juvenile Delinquency," in *Task Force Report: Juvenile Delinquency and Youth Crime,* President's Commission on Law Enforcement and Administration of Justice (Washington, D.C.: Government Printing Office, 1967).
44. Walter B. Miller, "The Impact of a 'Total-Community' Delinquency Control Project," *Social Problems,* 10 (Fall 1962), 168 and 184.

SUMMARY

In this chapter we have examined deviant behavior as a product of the complex interplay between the social system and the personal characteristics of the individuals who act out roles within it. An act of deviance can be defined broadly as any behavior that exceeds the tolerance limits associated with some shared behavioral expectation. Tolerance limits are influenced by the importance of the norm or other expectation violated, by the situation in which the act occurs, and by the characteristics of the violator. Conformity and deviation are both relative: behavior that is considered deviant in one group may be normative behavior in another.

Whereas psychological explanations of deviance stress personality disturbances and maladjustments that lead to deviant acts, sociological explanations focus on the social structure and on patterns of interaction between the individual and other members of his society. Anomie theory and labeling theory represent different but complementary approaches to the study of deviance as a social phenomenon. Both have provided starting points for useful research.

In studying crime and delinquency as major forms of deviance, sociologists have been plagued by the difficulty of establishing precise definitions. There are also serious problems in determining the extent and distribution of crime and delinquency. The best available evidence suggests that there are significant variations among different age, sex, race, and social-class groupings in the United States. These variations extend not only to the prevalence of crime but also to types of offense. The task of identifying all these patterns and unraveling their causes is immense. Sutherland's differential association theory has been especially useful in guiding research aimed at explaining the development of criminal orientations among certain segments of the population. A relatively new approach to understanding crime centers on the identification of distinctive behavior systems.

The control of deviance is a major concern in all societies, as it is in smaller groups. The most effective control is the voluntary control which most individuals impose on themselves, by virtue of having internalized the shared norms of their society. However, heterogeneous societies have found an increasing need for formal sanctions administered through official agencies of the state. Society's usual response to adult crime is to punish the offender, usually by imprisonment. The response to the juvenile offender has centered much more on reform and rehabilitation. None of the many approaches devised thus far has been particularly effective either in deterring crime and delinquency or in rehabilitating those who have become involved. This gives increased urgency to the task of identifying, and if possible correcting, those aspects of the social system that contribute to the development of deviance.

ТАК
СГОРАЕТ ЗДОРОВЬЕ...

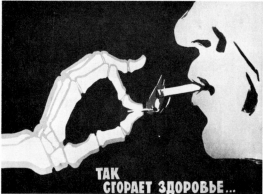

13

Mass Communication

Earlier chapters have noted the fundamental importance of communication processes in the acquisition of human personality, in the maintenance of a group's social organization, and in the generation of social conflict. To understand the organization and functioning of a group so complex as a whole society, we need to examine the communication system at all its various levels.[1] One of these levels, *mass communication,* presumes the use of mechanical and electronic devices. As modern societies have grown larger and more complex, they have come to rely upon such media to achieve certain group goals, such as spreading the news, presenting mass entertainment, selling goods, engineering political consent, and so on. Sociologists are vitally interested in the ways in which different types of societies have developed distinctive systems of mass communication for pursuing these goals. They are also interested in the organizational characteristics of contemporary American systems of mass communication and the social effects these systems deliberately or inadvertently achieve.

The process of *persuasion*—often carried out by means of the mass media—has become increasingly important in modern society. Political leaders give speeches in order to gain widespread consent concerning courses of action or public policy. Businesses advertise in order to sell their products. And a multitude of special-interest groups try to persuade people to reduce littering, make donations, quit smoking, prevent forest fires, register guns, despise Communists, attend church, buckle seat belts, and so forth.

Finally, *public-opinion* formation is closely related to mass communication and persuasion. Alterations of public opinion often give new directions to a society, while stable public opinion can be an important factor in resistance to social change. Public opinion can be heavily influenced by the way events are treated by the mass media, and changes in public opinion are often attempted through the use of mass persuasion. For these reasons, the present chapter discusses all three topics.

SOCIETAL SYSTEMS OF MASS COMMUNICATION

While human beings have been using speech to communicate with each other for millions of years, they have been communicating through written symbols for a mere 250 generations (about six thousand years). And while many societies have had written languages, before the present century only a tiny minority of the world's people were able to read. In fact, it is only within the last hundred years or so that sufficient numbers of people in *any* society have been literate enough to make a newspaper aimed at a mass audience feasible.[2]

In primitive and traditional societies, people could coordinate social activities and keep abreast of local affairs simply by talking to each other. Geographical isolation, low levels of technology, and unawareness of the outside world made mass communication irrelevant. However, as societies became more complex, techniques were needed to coordinate the activities of spatially dispersed groups and to mobilize the sentiments and loyalties of large numbers of people.

These techniques were slow in coming. In fact, only during the twentieth century has technology advanced sufficiently to permit the development of communication devices that can span great distances and bring the same message to huge numbers of people simultaneously. Today, motion pictures, radio, television, and printed matter—newspapers, books, and magazines—are reaching hundreds of millions of ordinary people. Few societies remain untouched by mass communication.[3]

The mass communication system of a country is made up of the totality of the media through which relatively large audiences are quickly reached with a given message. Each specific medium constitutes a somewhat separate subsystem; but all of the media influence each other.

Each subsystem is made up of a complicated set of interlocking *components.*[4] For example, the medium will operate very differently depending upon whether *ownership* is vested in a private corporation, a government bureau, a political party, or some other social organization or individual. Much will also depend on who is responsible for the actual *production* of content.

1. Charles R. Wright, *Mass Communication* (New York: Random House, Inc., 1959), p. 11.

2. Melvin L. DeFleur, *Theories of Mass Communication,* 2nd ed. (New York: David McKay Co., Inc., 1970), pp. 10–13.

3. Daniel Lerner, *The Passing of Traditional Society* (New York: The Free Press, 1958).

4. DeFleur, *op cit.,* pp. 155–172.

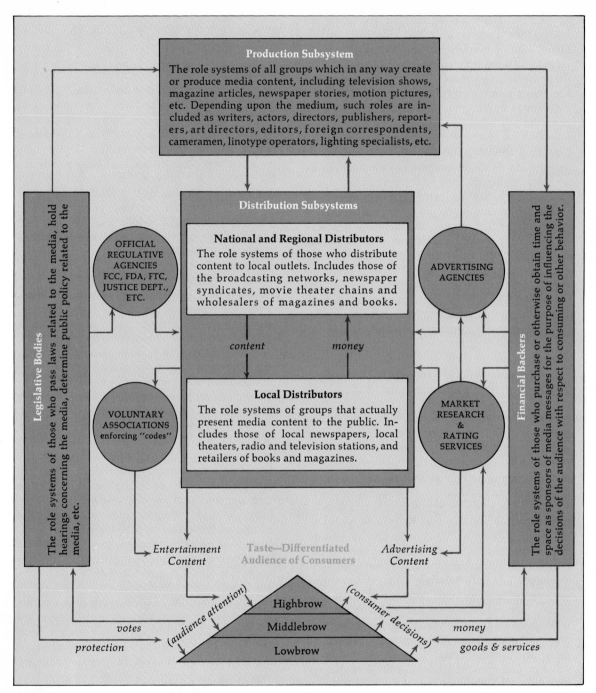

EXTERNAL SOCIAL AND CULTURAL CONDITIONS OF AMERICAN SOCIETY

SOURCE: Melvin L. DeFleur, *Theories of Mass Communication*, 2nd ed. (New York: David McKay Company, Inc., 1970), p. 166.

FIGURE 13.1. **MASS COMMUNICATION IN AMERICAN SOCIETY**

Depending upon the society, this may be a government propaganda ministry or some combination of advertising agencies, commercial sponsors, and broadcasting networks. *Control* over content may be in the hands of an independent newspaper editor and his staff, a state regulatory agency, a ministry of education, or a privately owned motion picture corporation. Content may also be subject to codes and regulations exercised by censorship boards. The components that *distribute* content to consumers are another important aspect of the system. They may have freedom to select or edit material from their sources, or they may be required to transmit content directly from producers without alteration.

Finally, *audiences* are important components of the system. A given audience may be highly educated or largely illiterate, stratified or relatively undifferentiated, affluent or poor. It may be concentrated in urban centers or dispersed thinly over a vast territory. An audience may or may not be able to feed information back to the content producers in such a way that its tastes and interests are taken into account. (See Figure 13.1.)

The historical experiences of a society shape its general culture, its principal values, its interests and tastes, and the nature of its political and economic institutions. A society's culture and social structure, in turn, shape its system of mass communication. Much can be learned about the process and effects of mass communication in different societal contexts by comparing briefly the systems that prevail in two of the principal societies of the world, the United States and the Soviet Union.

THE MEDIA IN THE UNITED STATES

Although printing is several hundred years old, the media that make up the complex mass communication system of the United States are for the most part products of the twentieth century. Even the daily newspaper did not reach its peak of circulation to American families until about the time of the First World War, when more daily newspapers were sold per household than at any time since. (See Figure 13.2.)

5. Edwin Emery, *The Press and America* (New York: Prentice-Hall, Inc., 1962).

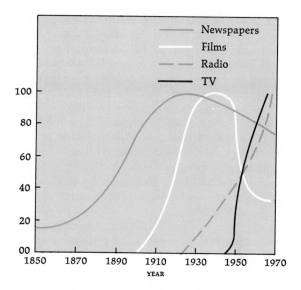

SOURCE: Melvin L. DeFleur, *Theories of Mass Communication*, 2nd edition (New York: David McKay, 1970), p. 74. The units on the vertical axis have been "standardized" so that each curve reaches its peak at the same point. This procedure facilitates comparison of one curve with another.

FIGURE 13.2. **DIFFUSION CURVES FOR NEWSPAPERS, FILMS, RADIO AND TELEVISION**

Household radio was not a reality until the 1920's, and it did not reach its "golden age" until the 1940's. Television, the newest of our major media, was adopted by the American public as recently as the 1950's.

The early press. The societal context within which the media were established played a major role in shaping their present form. For example, the newspaper began its major diffusion during the second half of the nineteenth century, a period of upheaval and rapid change in American society.[5] There was an expanding frontier, a great Civil War, mass immigration from Europe, increasing urbanization, and rapid industrialization.

Against the background of this transition from traditional to modern society, with its inevitable cultural conflict and anomie, the first mass medium had to define its responsibilities to the public—its code of ethics—and establish its financial base. Our modern newspapers developed out of the Colonial Press, as the papers of the thirteen colonies are collectively called.

Small in size and circulation, these papers were written for and read by an educated elite and were devoted more to political commentaries and literary essays than to news as we think of it today. They were also expensive, with subscriptions paid in advance by the year.

One of the most significant heritages of the period of the Colonial Press was the conviction that the government should not have the power to restrict the communication of ideas. For generations, political essayists and pamphleteers in England had been hampered by prior government censorship and fear of government reprisal. Englishmen on both sides of the Atlantic resented this control. In the American colonies a system of licensing and prior censorship was intended to prevent "seditious libel," as unwelcome political criticism in print was officially known. In 1735 an immigrant printer, John Peter Zenger, was put on trial in New York for publishing seditious libel in his weekly journal. Leading citizens rallied to his support, and his lawyer, Andrew Hamilton, argued with consummate skill that speaking and writing the truth was so basic a freedom that the jury should take matters into its own hands, regardless of the existing laws against criticism of the government. The jury did so, and Zenger was acquitted. Although laws against seditious libel remained in force for many years and editors continued to be harassed by colonial governors, the Zenger case is often cited as a turning point in the struggle for freedom of the press.[6]

In 1791 the First Amendment to the Constitution was ratified, prohibiting Congress from abridging the freedom of the press along with other fundamental freedoms of American citizens. Thus, from the advent of the nation, the press in the United States has developed under the protection of the Bill of Rights.

The mass press. In the 1830's a new kind of newspaper appeared on the streets of New York. It sold for a penny, which was less than it cost to produce. The publishers made their profit by selling advertising space. The concept of "news" was redefined. Less attention was given to complex political and economic issues, and more and more space was devoted to the kinds of things ordinary people liked to read about. High on the list were crimes, accidents, human interest stories, reports of bizarre happenings, and exposés of sin in high places.

By the end of the nineteenth century, newspaper publishing empires had been built up by such men as William Randolph Hearst and Joseph Pulitzer. Huge metropolitan dailies and newspaper chains engaged in bitter circulation wars. Under the impact of this competitive struggle, concern over ethics and responsibility in publishing declined sharply. Yellow journalism came into its own as the century ended.

Theirs was a shrieking, gaudy, sensation-loving, devil-may-care kind of journalism which lured the reader by any possible means. It seized upon the techniques of writing, illustrating, and printing, which were the prides of the new journalism, and turned them to perverted uses. It made the high drama of life a cheap melodrama, and it twisted the facts of each day into whatever form seemed best suited to produce sales for the howling newsboy.[7]

Another splurge of sensationalism marked the 1920's, but the Depression years had a sobering effect on the press. With the passing decades, business failures and mergers reduced the number of newspapers in America. Competition also decreased: many cities soon had only a single paper or two papers with a single owner. And frequently, thanks to the growth of newspaper chains and wire services, the "local" paper was owned by a corporation based a thousand miles away, and it filled its news columns with material supplied by a syndicate.

The salient aspects of newspaper publishing in the United States are clearly a product of the societal context within which the system developed—a context based upon American cultural values, which support private enterprise and the profit motive. These values, plus the heritage of the Colonial Press and the protection of the Constitution, give individual and corporate owners a maximum of freedom from governmental restraint. The medium obtained its profit not from its readers but from those who wished to attract the attention of potential customers to their advertising messages. To capture this attention, it gave its readers what it believed they wanted. In short, newspaper content was aimed at selling newspapers and attracting attention to advertisements in order to make money.

---

6. Edwin Emery et al., *Introduction to Mass Communications*, 2nd ed. (New York: Dodd, Mead & Company, 1965).

7. Emery, *op cit.*, pp. 415–416.

In the United States the broadcast media's stress on entertainment has usually been accompanied by a lack of interest in educational programming. As evidenced by the popularity of "Sesame Street," however, entertainment and education can go hand in hand. This daily television series teaches preschool children through a wide variety of techniques, including cartoons, films, and the attention-getting gimmicks used in much of commercial advertising.

The broadcast media. The broadcast media in the United States have had a very different history from the press.[8] The federal government controls the frequencies, transmitting power, and transmitting times of radio and television stations through the Federal Communications Commission (FCC). During the 1920's, when the uncontrolled growth of broadcasting produced chaotic conditions, Congress established the principle that the *air waves belong to the people.* Thus a federal agency could issue licenses and control transmitters in the interests of the people. There are also numerous state and local statutes pertaining to broadcasting.

In spite of these controls, however, the parallels between the broadcast media and newspaper publishing are numerous. The FCC is supposed to award a license to broadcast when such action is "in the public interest, convenience, or necessity," and when frequencies and channels are available, requests for licenses are seldom refused. The FCC is supposed to encourage competition, and it is prohibited from censoring program content. Under certain con-

ditions, broadcasters are required to provide equal time to political parties, and they must agree to offer a certain amount of "public service" broadcasting, to refrain from using obscene material, and to regulate the amount of time devoted to commercials.

Like newspapers, radio and television stations are privately owned and make their profits from advertising. Indeed, advertisers play an even more central role in broadcasting than in newspaper publishing. The newspaper publisher sells empty space to the advertiser and fills the rest of the paper with news, columns, and features. The broadcaster sells the advertiser empty time, but the advertiser chooses the material—the program—that will expose audiences to his commercials. Thus the advertiser on radio and television exerts a much greater influence on content than the newspaper advertiser.

Overall, the mass communication system prevailing in the United States is characterized by private ownership of the media and is dedicated to corporate profits. The organizations that produce content differ greatly from medium to medium. Newspapers and broadcasting, in particular, serve commercial sponsors who compete for audience attention to advertising appeals.

8. Gleason L. Archer, *History of Radio to 1926* (New York: The American Historical Society, Inc., 1938).

Within this system, control over content is exercised to a considerable extent *by the audience* itself. Material that fails to attract and sustain interest tends to be quickly eliminated from the system. Thus the interests and tastes of readers, viewers, and listeners serve as indirect but powerful controls. That is, the audience can choose among alternatives or refuse to "attend" at all. Some control is also exercised more directly through the application of various industry codes, which keep material generally within the bounds of public standards. Governmental regulation and control play only a minimal role.

The central emphasis of mass communication in the United States is on *entertainment.* Generally, the major media aim their content at the broadest stratum of their audiences in order to win the attention of the largest number of consumers for mass-use products. One major result is that the system continually produces a "mass culture" keyed to popular tastes. As will be indicated in greater detail, there has been much controversy and debate among students of the system concerning the direct and indirect effects of this mass culture.

MASS COMMUNICATION IN THE SOVIET UNION

The social, political, and economic conditions prevailing in the Soviet Union during the time when its present system of mass communication developed differed greatly from those in the United States during the comparable period, and the Soviet system thus differs radically from its American counterpart.[9]

Historical background. While American culture includes a belief in the *right* to free communication, such a belief is not a part of the Russian tradition. The autocratic regimes of the czars had always controlled the press. Thus the controls on communication under the Soviet system do not represent a dramatic change. For all practical purposes, however, Russia's mass communication system does not extend much further back in time than the beginning of the USSR. During the period immediately following World War I, the entire Russian social structure underwent violent upheaval. In 1917 the czarist government was overthrown, and the Bolsheviks, led by Nikolai Lenin, seized control. The

leaders of the new Communist government set about to consolidate their power and to achieve the drastic social changes that their ideological system dictated.

The unification of the Soviet peoples would have been a formidable task under any circumstances. The territory that now makes up the Union of Soviet Socialist Republics constitutes about one sixth of the earth's surface. Here live more than 225 million people, representing about 140 distinct ethnic groups and a great variety of religions, languages, life styles, and degrees of technological advancement. All of this implies an audience for mass communication that is in some ways unique. The population of the USSR is obviously one of great heterogeneity; it ranges from nomadic illiterates to educated urbanites. Social differentiation was even more pronounced in the 1920's, the first decade of the new regime, and it was this population that Lenin was determined to weld into a nation that would be one of the world's great powers.

The goals of the Soviet media. Lenin understood that the Russian people had to be instructed and persuaded into accepting the party's goals and decisions, and he saw clearly that the mass media of communication were an important element in achieving these ends. This meant that the media had to be in the hands of those who were guiding the revolution. "Class consciousness" had to be developed among the people. They also needed education, and they needed to be made selectively aware of the rich cultural traditions of their past. Moreover, communication links had to be established between the leaders and the masses so that political policies and decisions could be communicated and explained to every eye and ear.

From the beginning, then, the party was seen as a kind of "teacher" whose task was to educate and indoctrinate the masses concerning

9. The present section is based on Alex Inkeles, *Public Opinion in Soviet Russia: A Study in Mass Persuasion*, 2nd ed. (Cambridge, Mass.: Harvard University Press, 1950); Gayle O. Hollander, "Recent Developments in Soviet Radio and Television News Reporting," *Public Opinion Quarterly* 31, No. 3 (Fall 1967), 359–365; Mark W. Hopkins, "Lenin, Stalin, Khrushchev: Three Concepts of the Press," *Journalism Quarterly*, 42, No. 4 (Autumn 1965), 523–531; and Richard R. Fagen, "Mass Media Growth: A Comparison of Communist and Other Countries," *Journalism Quarterly*, 61, No. 4 (Autumn 1964), 563–572.

their political thought, their national directions, and their social destiny. All decisions were to be worked out by party leaders and communicated to the people via mass media in order to obtain compliance and support. In order to achieve these goals, a governmental agency was established, under the firm control of the top party leaders, to oversee all the mass communication media. Alex Inkeles has described this organization as it operated during the late 1940's:

The Department of Propaganda and Agitation of the Central Committee is charged with general responsibility for molding and mobilizing public opinion in the Soviet Union so that it will effectively support and facilitate the achievement of those long and short-range ends which the party leadership has defined as the goals of the nation as a whole. It unifies and gives central direction to the vast and multiform activities designed to influence public opinion which are carried on by the party, and the government and public agencies under the party's supervision.[10]

There has been little significant change in this structure or its goals up to the present time.[11]

Private ownership of the media does not exist in the Soviet Union. All of the various facilities for the production and distribution of mass communication content—books, films, radio and television broadcasts, magazines, and newspapers—are operated by a complex of governmental bureaus whose task is defined by a mandate from the party.

The Soviet press. Control of the press has been maintained by three principal means. First, editorial personnel are selected on the basis of their loyalty to the regime. This eliminates the need for an elaborate and cumbersome system of censorship. Second, party directives provide guidelines within which the press must operate. Third, formal supervisory machinery monitors the press and sees that it is carrying out the policies of the party within the system of rules and regulations it is supposed to follow. Such surveillance exists not only at the national level but at regional and even local community levels. This system ensures that the press functions in the manner intended—as an instrument of social control, as a transmitter of political propaganda,

and as a means for the selective dissemination of information.[12]

Broadcasting in Russia. Of all the media, none contrasts more sharply with its American counterpart in its pattern of historical development than the Soviet system of broadcasting. This system was developed during the period prior to World War II, when Russian energies were being devoted mainly to the establishment of heavy industry, to the building of a vast military machine, and to the reorganization of agriculture. Little was left in the way of resources for producing consumer goods such as individual radios. Yet it was important for the government to reach the masses with broadcasts as a means of ensuring ideological commitment and compliance. Millions of people had to be reached, and vast distances had to be spanned. The financial, demographic, and geographical difficulties, plus the urgency of the party's political goals, gave rise to a unique system.

Soviet broadcasting was not conceived of as a means of providing entertainment but rather as a channel of communication between the party and the masses. By the 1940's the system consisted of a number of powerful radio transmitting stations in all the principal urban centers and local communities. These formed a tightly controlled network. While some broadcasts originated from regional centers, most originated from Moscow itself, to be rebroadcast within a given region. Local stations originated some material, but they were under careful supervision.

The Soviet citizen did not receive these broadcasts in his home on his own radio set, at least not during the decade following the Second World War. Broadcasts were received by a powerful receiver that served as a local "radio diffusion exchange." They were then sent *by wire* into individual homes, apartments, factories, barracks, etc., which were equipped with simple speakers. The radio diffusion exchange served from a few dozen to several hundred subscribers in this manner. The subscriber could listen or not as he wished, but his program choices were limited to what was on the exchange.

This system had several advantages from the Soviet point of view. First, and most important, it was far cheaper to establish than a system in which each family would be provided with its own receiver. (The average Russian family at that time could barely afford the small sub-

10. Inkeles, *op. cit.*, p. 30.
11. Hopkins, *op. cit.*, pp. 527–531.
12. *Ibid.*

These photographs point up the fact that the Soviet press functions primarily as an arm of the Communist party. The picture at the top was released in April 1969, by a Czech news agency. It shows the former leader of the Czech republic, Alexander Dubček, standing beside President Ludvik Svoboda, who is holding his hat in his hand. The second photograph was later released in the Soviet Union. Note that buildings have moved and Dubček has disappeared, except for one well-polished toe.

scription fee; to purchase a radio set would have been out of the question.) Second, the system permitted a maximum of control over what the Soviet people would hear. This was felt to be essential during the authoritarian regime of Joseph Stalin. Broadcasts from foreign lands could be received only on clandestine sets, and the government could partially block such reception by "jamming" the signals.

The system was well adapted to bringing educational and cultural content, as well as political propaganda, to a wide audience. The technical properties of the broadcasts were excellent: the central receiver was of high quality, and transmission through wires did not lower fidelity appreciably.

In the years since Stalin's death in 1955, the radio system has been greatly expanded, and television broadcasts have become popular. Moscow now has three television channels, and there are at least two channels in most other large cities.[13] Television broadcasting hours are generally limited to about seven per day—a limitation that is common in many countries. In equivalent purchasing power, a Soviet television set costs as much as we pay for a new standard-model car. Despite the high price, by 1963 there were approximately eleven million television receivers in operation in the Soviet Union. (In the same year Americans owned 66.6 million sets.)

The old system of wired receivers for radio broadcasts has been expanded greatly: the number of wired loudspeakers increased from 13.8 million in 1953 to 33.7 million in 1963. But independent receiving sets are also common. Formerly trusted only to loyal party members, by the mid-sixties these radios were in the hands of more than 35 million citizens.[14] Foreign broadcasts are now regularly received in the Soviet Union by those who own short-wave receivers. Their number is unknown but is thought to be substantial. The jamming of outside broadcasts ceased in 1963, except in time of crisis as during the Soviet invasion of Czechoslovakia in 1968.

Politics versus profits. The changes in the Russian broadcasting system in the post-Stalin

era have had a substantial impact on the handling of news by all Soviet media. As people became able to receive reports from foreign broadcasts, the Soviet approach to reporting had to be "liberalized." News was released faster, and less reliance was placed upon centralized party-line interpretations. But much of the old mass communication system persists. The media are still defined by party officials as agencies for furthering the Marxist-Leninist theories upon which the system was founded. The only group whose members are seen as legitimate interpreters of these theories is the Communist party. The main purpose of the media remains that of strengthening the role of party leaders as teachers and guides of the Soviet people.

One significant change in the Soviet mass media is the increased use of advertising. In the days of chronic shortages of consumer goods, there was little need to create demands, but in recent times many shortages have ended. The supply of watches, dresses, canned goods, film, and other products now exceeds demand. Advertising has been recognized as a necessary marketing tool. At present, not only do more advertisements appear in Soviet newspapers (except *Pravda* and *Izvestia*), but posters, billboards, and handbills also present commercial messages. Even radio and television carry commercials.[15]

But while advertising is used to reduce surpluses, it does not represent private enterprise. Overall, the Soviet system of mass communication is not concerned with profit. The sharp contrast between the Soviet and American systems can be understood only in terms of distinctive historical developments within societies with very different social and political institutions.

MASS COMMUNICATION AS A SOCIAL PROCESS

The process of mass communication, like many other forms of human behavior, has been viewed by behavioral scientists primarily in *stimulus-response* terms. That is, message content presented to an individual via a mass medium has been regarded as constituting particular kinds of *stimulus* events, and the activities of attending

---

13. Hollander, *op. cit.*, pp. 359–361.
14. *Ibid.*
15. Carter R. Bryan, "Communist Advertising: Its Status and Function," *Journalism Quarterly*, 39, No. 4 (Autumn 1962), 500–506.

to, understanding, and responding to this content have been regarded as particular forms of *responses.*

Social scientists have tried to explain the ways in which these stimuli and responses are linked. Much effort has been devoted to the development of generalizations concerning *how* and *why* particular kinds of individuals *select* and come to *respond to* particular types of message content in given ways.[16] These generalizations constitute statements about variables, processes, or factors that *intervene* between the stimuli and audience responses. These intervening variables are thought to modify or mediate the impact that message content can have on the behavior of the receiving audience member. Some of these generalizations deal with the *psychological nature* of the responding individual. Others are concerned with the location of the audience member in the principal *social categories* of his society. Still others relate to *interpersonal networks* and other groups in which the message receiver is involved.

THE INFLUENCE OF INDIVIDUAL DIFFERENCES

General psychological theory makes it clear that every person does not respond in the same way to stimulus events in his environment. The unique pattern of a person's needs, attitudes, habits, and values will determine what he will selectively attend to in his environment, what he will selectively interpret, and what he will act upon. This *principle of selectivity* is well established and has been adequately documented by research.[17]

In terms of mass communication, this means that selective attention, perception, and action enter into the communicative behavior of the audience member. From the great variety of available content in print, on film, and through broadcasts, the member of the audience picks out, concentrates upon, and interprets messages. He attends most closely to those that are (1) related to his interests, (2) consistent with his attitudes, (3) congruent with his beliefs, and (4) supportive of his values.[18]

For example, research has established that new car owners are much more likely to read advertisements for the car they have just purchased than are owners of the same make but an earlier model.[19] In a study of smokers and nonsmokers, the former were significantly less likely to read articles on the relationship between smoking and health. (Only 32 percent of male smokers read such articles as compared to 60 percent of nonsmoking males).[20] A study of popular material such as movie magazines and daytime serials revealed that the highest exposure was to be found among women who were in lower socioeconomic strata, who were not "gregarious," and who confessed to feeling "blue and depressed" on occasion.[21]

The *interpretation* that people place on communications is similarly influenced by their personal attributes. Kendall and Wolfe, for example, report a study in which a campaign intended to reduce prejudice through the use of cartoons backfired among more prejudiced respondents.[22] Such persons misinterpreted the intent of the cartoons and saw them as supporting their own attitudes (rather than ridiculing bigotry, which the cartoons were intended to do).

Even if a group of people are similarly exposed to a given communication and interpret it in similar ways, there is no guarantee that they will *act* uniformly in response to the communication. Numerous experiments have firmly established the principle that personal attitudes, values, and other prior orientations greatly influence the way individuals respond or fail to respond to mass-communicated messages.[23]

16. Wilbur Schramm, ed., *Mass Communications* (Urbana, Ill.: University of Illinois Press, 1949), pp. 387–429.

17. See, for example, Douglas Waples *et al.*, *Why They Read* (Chicago: The University of Chicago Press, 1940).

18. For a basic discussion of the psychological principles underlying perceptual selectivity, see David Krech and Richard S. Crutchfield, "Perceiving the World," in *The Process and Effects of Mass Communication*, ed. Wilbur Schramm (Urbana, Ill.: University of Illinois Press, 1954), pp. 116–137.

19. Danuta Ehrlich, Isaiah Guttman, Peter Schonbach, and Judson Mills, "Postdecision Exposure to Relevant Information," *Journal of Abnormal and Social Psychology*, 54 (1957), 98–102.

20. Charles F. Cannell and James C. MacDonald, "The Impact of Health News on Attitudes and Behavior," *Journalism Quarterly*, 33 (1956), 315–323.

21. Elihu Katz and Paul Lazarsfeld, *Personal Influence* (New York: The Free Press, 1955), pp. 309–320.

22. Patricia L. Kendall and Katherine M. Wolfe, "The Analysis of Deviant Cases in Communications Research," in *Communications Research 1948–49*, ed. Paul Lazarsfeld and Frank Stanton (New York: Harper and Brothers, 1949), pp. 152–179.

23. See Carl I. Hovland, "Effects of the Mass Media of Communication," in *Handbook of Social Psychology*, ed. Gardner Lindzey (Cambridge, Mass.: Addison-Wesley Publishing Co., Inc., 1954); and Joseph T. Klapper, "What We Know About the Effects of Mass Communication: The Brink of Hope," *Public Opinion Quarterly*, 21 (1957), 453–474.

SOCIAL CATEGORIES AND AUDIENCE UNIFORMITIES

Patterns of attention to and consumption of mass communication content are roughly similar for people who have a number of common *social characteristics*. Age, sex, level of income, religious affiliation, rural-urban residence, occupation, and educational attainment are indicators of shared patterns of communications behavior. For example, it has been found that the heaviest readers of the "true confessions" type of magazine are younger married women with lower levels of income and educational attainment who

24. George Gerbner, "The Social Role of the Confession Magazine," *Social Problems*, 6, No. 1 (1958), 29–40.

reside in small towns in the Midwest and South.[24]

One of the earliest trends in the empirical study of mass communication behavior in American society involved heavy reliance on such indices. The goal was to describe the ways in which such behaviors as newspaper reading, radio listening, book selection, and motion picture attendance were influenced by the position of the individual within simple social categories. The underlying assumption was that, in spite of the great diversity of modern society, audience members who have similar social characteristics will share common orientations and patterns of usage concerning the mass media. Such a formulation is more descriptive than explanatory, but it is undoubtedly true that people who have

Many countries have stepped up their anti-smoking campaigns through the use of posters and television commercials, but it is still too early to tell whether or not these campaigns will have a significant affect on people who already smoke. Perhaps the principle of selectivity will function here as it has in the past, and smokers will effectively screen out the anti-smoking messages because they are inconsistent with a smoker's actions. The photograph on the left is from an American commercial which emphasizes the fact that a father may unwittingly socialize his son in both good and bad habits—such as smoking. Posters like the one on the right may be seen throughout the Soviet Union; the caption reads, "How you burn up your health."

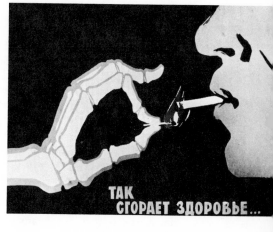

similar attributes relate themselves to the media in roughly similar ways. For this reason, the influence of social categories on the mass communication process remains an important consideration.

THE ROLE OF SOCIAL RELATIONSHIPS

Systematic investigation of the process of mass communication was for many years founded upon the assumption that audiences in modern urban societies where the media were flourishing had mainly *Gesellschaft* characteristics. That is, students of the media assumed that "mass" audiences for "mass" communications acted in relatively individualistic ways in terms of their responses to media content. One well-known student of the media stated the issue in this way:

Until very recently, the image of society in the minds of most students of communication was of atomized individuals, connected with the mass media, but not with one another. Society—the "audience"—was conceived as aggregates of age, sex, social class, and the like, but little thought was given to [informal interpersonal relations].[25]

Almost by accident a major sociological investigation uncovered the significant role played by informal social relationships in the mass communication process. Early social theorists such as Gabriel Tarde had suspected this but had lacked evidence.[26] Then, in a study of hundreds of people who were responding to a mass communicated presidential election campaign, it was noted over and over again that for many of those being studied, one of the most significant sources of information about the campaign was *other people*. In other words, not everyone was attending to the mass media first-hand to get information concerning the candidates, the issues, etc. Many were getting the information from other people who were in contact with the media directly and who were passing on information about the campaign.[27]

This seemingly simple discovery stimulated systematic efforts to understand the role played by *informal interpersonal relations* in the mass communications process. These research efforts led to the conclusion that informal social relationships play a significant role in modifying the manner in which a given individual will attend to, interpret, and act upon a message directed toward him by the mass media. In fact, it was discovered that there are many persons involved in the mass communication process whose first-hand exposure to a given medium is quite limited. If such people obtain information from the medium, in large part they do so indirectly by getting it from others who do attend in a direct sense. Information, in other words, moves through two basic stages. First, it goes from a given medium to a core of relatively well-informed individuals who attend directly. Second, it moves from those persons through interpersonal channels to people who depend upon others for their information. Sometimes, it may pass through many steps in this process of "message diffusion."

This kind of communication process has been labeled the "two-step flow of communication."[28] The key individuals, who are in contact with the media and who transmit information to others, are generally called "opinion leaders." Such key communicators not only pass on information to others but also inevitably play some part in influencing the interpretations and lines of behavior of those to whom they pass on ideas. For this reason, they are said to engage in "personal influence," even though their activities as influencers may be unintended and even unwitting.

Wherever media are used to suggest new courses of action or new ideas, social relationships become important in determining how people will respond. Physicians adopting new drugs may do so because of the personal influence of other physicians who have read about the drugs in medical journals.[29] Similarly, interpersonal influence plays a part when farmers take up new agricultural practices, when house-

---

25. Elihu Katz, "Communications Research and the Image of Society: Convergence of Two Research Traditions," *American Journal of Sociology*, 65, No. 5 (1959), 436.

26. Terry N. Clark, ed., *Gabriel Tarde on Communication and Social Influence* (Chicago: The University of Chicago Press, 1969), pp. 57–58.

27. Paul Lazarsfeld, Bernard Berelson, and Helen Gaudet, *The People's Choice* (New York: Columbia University Press, 1948).

28. Elihu Katz, "The Two Step Flow of Communication: An Up-to-Date Report on an Hypothesis," *Public Opinion Quarterly*, 21, No. 1 (Spring 1957), 61–78.

29. James S. Coleman, Elihu Katz, and Herbert Menzel, *Medical Innovation: A Diffusion Study* (Indianapolis: The Bobbs-Merrill Co., Inc., 1966).

wives begin using new household products, when women accept new fashions, when teachers adopt new educational techniques, and so forth.[30] The mechanisms of the two-step flow of communication are widely found wherever there is a flow of ideas from media to audience.

EFFECTS OF THE MEDIA

The ever increasing availability of mass communications has stimulated a considerable amount of research and endless public speculation concerning their possible *effects*.[31] Do comic books cause delinquency? Are movies lowering moral standards? How much do newspapers and television mold public opinion, either deliberately or inadvertently?

The high level of popular interest in media effects is understandable in light of the astonishing amount of time that Americans spend with the media. For example, the statistically average child spends about twenty hours a week watching television.[32] He also spends time with movies, books, comics, magazines, and radio. The average family in our society buys a ticket to a motion picture about once a week, reads more than one daily newspaper, subscribes to several magazines, owns three or more radios, and has at least one television set.[33] The American public is also buying and presumably reading an ever increasing number of books. Paperback books alone roll off our nation's presses at the rate of more than a million a day. The volume of book publishing has increased by 600 percent during the last decade. Americans now spend about $2.5 billion a year on books.[34]

What effects the media have on their audiences is a question to which an impressive amount of social science research has attempted to provide answers. Although it seems clear that the media are not the all-powerful influence that they once were thought to be, they may have a variety of effects that are not yet fully understood. The difficulty in setting forth a simple list of the social and individual effects of mass communication was indicated some years ago by Bernard Berelson, who summed up the problem by noting that "Some kinds of *communications* on some kinds of *issues*, brought to the attention of some kinds of *people* under some kinds of *conditions*, have some kinds of *effects*."[35]

SOCIAL EFFECTS

In our own society the media have changed a number of patterns of social organization. New communications groups have arisen to play important parts in business, entertainment, the arts, government, and even religion. The creation of a host of work roles centering around the media and related activities has altered the structure of the labor force.

Mass communications also change our culture. New products, advertised to millions via television, magazines, and newspapers, can achieve widespread adoption almost overnight. The rapid spread of other cultural forms, such as speech mannerisms, fads of all kinds, and other innovative patterns, can be triggered by the media. The continuous creation of mass culture, in the form of popular music, sports, television programs, the movies, the comics, etc., provides another source for social change. While much of it disappears as rapidly as it is transmitted, some elements are selected by the viewing, reading, and listening public and retained as a part of the permanent social heritage.

Simply by their *presence* the media have altered the nature of societal communication norms. Large audiences have been created that *expect* the media to provide a continuous flow of news, entertainment, political commentary, and other types of messages. People depend upon the media for various forms of gratification based upon this content. If denied such com-

30. C. Paul Marsh and A. Lee Coleman, "Group Influences and Agricultural Innovations: Some Tentative Findings and Hypotheses," *American Journal of Sociology*, 61, No. 6 (May 1956), 588–594; also Katz and Lazarsfeld, *op. cit.*

31. For example, see Hovland, *op. cit.*; Joseph T. Klapper, *The Effects of Mass Communication* (New York: The Free Press, 1960); and Otto N. Larsen, "Social Effects of Mass Communication" in *Handbook of Modern Sociology*, ed. Robert E. L. Faris (Chicago: Rand McNally & Company, 1964), pp. 348–381.

32. Wilbur Schramm *et al.*, *Television in the Lives of Our Children* (Stanford, Calif.: Stanford University Press, 1961), p. 27.

33. DeFleur, *op. cit.*

34. *Time*, December 16, 1966, pp. 100–101.

35. Bernard Berelson, "Communications and Public Opinion," in *Communications in Modern Society*, ed. Wilbur Schramm (Urbana, Ill.: University of Illinois Press, 1948), p. 178.

METHODOLOGY   CONTENT ANALYSIS

To understand the effects of communications, investigators need accurate measures of the way in which given topics or ideas are portrayed. For example, how many acts of violence appear in a televised Western drama? What political values are emphasized in a comic strip such as Little Orphan Annie? How do magazine stories portray minority groups during a given period? While not all such questions could be answered by sociological investigations, studies of content can offer valuable hypotheses.

Content analysis is a widely used procedure for the quantitative study of messages. In all types of content analysis, defining the purpose of the research is a necessary first step. The study may be designed to gain an accurate description of what has been said via a given medium, or its goal may be to analyze trends in media content. Often it will test some hypothesis from a sociological theory.

Before undertaking his analysis, the investigator must carefully delineate the *universe,* or group of cases, from which samples of content are to be drawn. This may be all issues of a given newspaper published during a specified year; all issues of a given magazine for a defined period; all rumors recorded by an observer in a given community during a period of stress; or any other defineable set of communications. Once the content universe has been defined, it is usually necessary for practical reasons to select a representative *sample* of messages in that universe for actual analysis. If the sample is properly selected, it will provide the basis for making valid generalizations about the larger group of communications with which the research is concerned. (See the Methodological Essay on sampling procedures, page 300).

The sampling design for a study using content analysis must designate a *sampling unit* as well as the procedures to be followed in selecting cases for study. A sampling unit is a specific form of communication content. For instance, in an analysis of rumors in a given community, the sampling unit might be sentences in the rumor messages as recorded by an observer. In a study of newspaper stories on a presidential campaign, the sampling unit might be paragraphs, key words, column inches, or even entire articles. In a laboratory study of content change in messages passed from person to person, attention might be focused on a theme or key phrase.

In content analysis as in other kinds of research, the *size* of the sample is an important consideration. If the sample is too small, it will provide an unreliable basis for making inferences about the larger universe from which it was drawn. If too large, it will be wasteful of time and money; equivalent information might be obtained more efficiently by studying a smaller number of cases. Sample size is usually determined by specialists from appropriate mathematical formulas that indicate what size sample is needed to obtain a given level of precision in the results.

Once these preliminary steps have been completed, the procedures for making the actual analysis of content can be designed. The method for measuring content may be as simple as merely counting the number of phrases, sentences, key words, or paragraphs dealing with a particular topic. In measuring newspaper and magazine content, some researchers employ a basic space unit (BSU) which is an area one printed column wide and one twentieth of a column deep. If it is necessary to refer to the context within which a given sample unit appears in order to determine and classify its meaning, the *context unit* to be employed for such purposes should be clearly specified as well as the sampling unit.

After counting the number of units containing the issues, themes, words, or other categories of content under study, the investigator must subject his results to a *statistical analysis* (page 577) in order to determine, for instance, the percentages of sampling units that contain a given meaning or implication. The kinds of statistical analysis employed in a particular study will depend, of course, upon the purpose for which the study was designed. Typically they involve the computation of coefficients of correlation and other complicated statistical indices. As in most other types of sociological research, procedures for analyzing results are generally specified before the gathering of data begins.

For a detailed discussion of the procedures used in content analysis, see Richard W. Budd et al., *Content Analysis of Communication* (New York: The Macmillan Company, 1967).

munications, they feel deprived.[36] Even in relatively underdeveloped societies, populations quickly develop media-related habits, once mass communications become available to them in a form they understand.

Mass communications have had a substantial impact upon the American political process. A political leader can be helped by good press relations and hurt by bad ones. "Guest" appearances on popular television shows enable him to get his message, or at least his "image," across to millions. Unless a candidate shows up well on television, he may have a limited chance of getting elected. Correctly or incorrectly, many politicians and political experts believed that a major factor in the defeat of Richard Nixon by John F. Kennedy in the presidential election of 1960 was that Kennedy showed up better in their television debates.[37] The staging of the nominating conventions of the national political parties has been much influenced by the presence of television.

The media have had other influences on our political institution. Constant surveillance by the media quickly reveals "credibility gaps" when public officials attempt to withhold information or manipulate the news. Such constant monitoring makes it increasingly necessary for political leaders to be deeply concerned about their relations with the press and the networks. In this sense, the media have increased the degree of social control that can be exercised by voters over those whom they have placed in office.

The mass media perform what Lazarsfeld and Merton have called a "status conferral" function.[38] That is, the media lend a certain amount of prestige to those people on whom they focus their attention. In the minds of ordi-

nary members of society, if people "count" they will be reported on by the media. By the same logic, if they are given attention by the media they must surely be important. Many of the "celebrities" whose names appear in the newspapers and whose faces appear on television are celebrated chiefly, or solely, because of these appearances. Similarly, the media have been accused of creating "pseudo-events"—that is, puffing an incident of no special significance into an event simply by giving it extensive coverage and thus defining it as of great importance.[39]

Other social effects can be briefly mentioned. It has been hypothesized that the media "create" social problems by focusing public attention on certain dramatic forms of deviance which, objectively speaking, have very low incidence (e.g., narcotics addiction).[40] Television has been accused of contributing to violence in the cities by giving extended coverage to rioting blacks. On the other hand, the television appearances of blacks not only as individual performers and in all-black shows but in company with whites on a basis of equality may contribute to an easier relationship between the races. Also, there have been conclusions that the media, by continually portraying romantic themes, have influenced the basis of mate selection in the United States; and it has been suggested that the media have been an important factor in diffusing the urban culture to rural areas.

Even more speculatively, Marshall McLuhan has suggested that the very course of human history is shaped by the form of information available in a given age. According to McLuhan, the electronic media of today, especially television, have a deep impact on the kinds of relationships that are developing among the entire population of our planet. "The medium is the message," he believes, in that it adds unique dimensions to the transmission of ideas.[41]

36. See Bernard Berelson, "What Missing the Newspaper Means," in Lazarsfeld and Stanton, eds., *op. cit.*, pp. 111–129; and Penn Kimball, "People Without Papers," *Public Opinion Quarterly*, 23, No. 3 (Fall 1959), 389–398.

37. See Sidney Kraus, ed., *The Great Debates* (Bloomington, Ind.: Indiana University Press, 1962), pp. 195–200.

38. Paul F. Lazarsfeld and Robert K. Merton, "Mass Communication, Popular Taste and Organized Social Action," in *The Communication of Ideas*, ed. Lyman Bryson (New York: Harper and Brothers, 1948), pp. 95–118.

39. Daniel Boorstin, *The Image: A Guide to Pseudo-Events in America* (New York: Harper & Row, 1964).

40. Jeffrey Hubbard, *Mass Communication and Social Problems*, unpublished doctoral dissertation, 1970, Washington State University.

41. Marshall McLuhan, *Understanding Media: The Extension of Man* (New York: McGraw-Hill Book Company, 1964).

42. Klapper, *The Effects of Mass Communication, op. cit.*

ATTITUDE AND OPINION EFFECTS

The most comprehensive survey of the effects of the mass media on individuals to date is that of the sociologist Joseph Klapper, who examined hundreds of research articles, books, and other sources of objective data concerning the influence of the media.[42] From these sources,

he developed five major generalizations that seemed to emerge from the accumulation of studies up to that time (1960). At the risk of some oversimplification, these can be summarized as follows:

1. Mass communication is usually *not* in itself a necessary and sufficient cause of audience effects; it achieves influence among and through a set of *mediating factors.*

2. Because of these mediating factors, mass communication is usually a contributory agent which *reinforces* (rather than changes) some existing condition (vote intentions, tendencies regarding delinquency, opinions, attitudes, etc.).

3. On some occasions, mass communication may achieve change. If this is the case, one of two conditions is likely to exist. Either:

a. mediating factors will be found to be inoperative, leading to direct media effects; *or*

b. mediating factors that normally favor reinforcement will be found to favor change.

4. There are some situations in which mass communication does seem to produce direct effects, but these occasions are rare.

5. The way in which mass communication achieves effects, either directly or as a contributory agent, can depend upon many indirect factors, such as the source of the message, the type of medium used, the nature of the situation in which the communication is received, public opinion trends of the time, and so forth.

These generalizations do not represent a systematic theory about mass-communication effects. They are simply the conclusions that appeared to Klapper to be most supported by research evidence. To illustrate in more concrete terms ways in which the media have been shown to be influential, we may for the moment focus on opinions and attitudes, leaving aside such matters as "cultural" tastes, buying, voting, or other forms of behavior. In terms of opinions and attitudes, the accumulated mass media research seems to indicate that under various conditions, mass communication can lead to *creative effects, reinforcement, minor change, conversion,* or have *no effect* at all.

Creative effects tend to occur when people have few if any prior attitudes and knowledge about an issue. Where the issue is undefined in terms of existing cultural norms or personal

*A politician's television "image" has become a signifi-
cant factor in the winning—and maintaining—of
political office. Many people believe, for instance, that
the Kennedy-Nixon television debates contributed to
Nixon's defeat in 1960. But once in office, a political
leader is still under the constant surveillance of the
television camera. As indicated by these photographs
of Lyndon Johnson, the many moods of a public figure
may be readily apparent to television viewers.*

psychological considerations, the treatment
given to it by the mass media can weigh heavily
in the creation of attitudes and opinions.

A good example of a creative effect can be
seen in a study by Lang and Lang entitled "The
Unique Perspective of Television and Its
Effect."[43] The research involved a comparison
of the manner in which a public event appeared
to persons who actually viewed the event and
to another audience that saw it only on television. The first group made careful notes on a
parade honoring a national hero (Douglas
MacArthur), which they watched first-hand as
it passed through the streets of Chicago. Another
panel of researchers saw only "on-the-spot"
reports of the parade on television. Comparisons
revealed that the latter group, which saw it only
on television, thought the parade was exciting
and thrilling, while the group that was actually
there found it dull and disappointing. By developing excitement and interest with close-ups,
dramatic camera angles, and a constant flow of
suggestions from announcers, the medium had
literally created opinions and impressions in the
minds of its viewers that did not occur to eye-
witnesses.

The *reinforcement* of attitudes and opinions
is frequently achieved by mass communication
and has been widely documented. The idea is
simply that a person selects material from the
mass media that is consistent with his existing
beliefs. His consumption of what he selects
reinforces the very attitudes that led him to
select it in the first place. Many political
speeches at election time appear to be designed
around this effect. They are intended more to
supply the party faithful with reinforcements for
their existing beliefs than to convert opponents.

The classic study of the reinforcement effect
is that of Lazarsfeld, Berelson, and Gaudet, *The
People's Choice.*[44] This was an exhaustive study
of the presidential election of 1940, in which it
was found that the majority of voters knew
whom they would vote for even before the candidates were officially selected at the national
conventions. Those studied paid attention to
mass media material consistent with their attitudes and finally voted according to their original predispositions. Some who had not formu-

---

43. Kurt Lang and Gladys E. Lang, "The Unique Perspective of Television and Its Effect," *American Sociological
Review*, 18, No. 1 (1953), 3–12.

44. *Op. cit.*

lated a vote intention by May of the election year were "activated" by mass communications before the election in November, but few were converted from one side to the other.

Minor changes in opinions and attitudes are relatively frequent. This type of influence is often observed in experimental studies in which subjects are exposed to persuasive communications incorporating various types of appeals. For example, in communities where persuasive leaflets were dropped to try to alter attitudes toward donating blood to a visiting "bloodmobile," few sweeping changes in opinions or attitudes were noted; but minor shifts in attitude were common, and the leaflets appear to have kept donation rates from dropping as much between visits of the bloodmobile as they had in prior years.[45]

As we have already noted, *conversion* through mass communication is rare. Only under very unusual conditions is it possible for mass-communicated messages to change people's attitudinal convictions. However, there is evidence from cases *not* involving mass communication that when a communicator has a total monopoly, and especially when he is able to control all other mediating factors, conversion is possible. During the Korean War, for example, the Chinese systematically attempted to convert American soldiers away from their loyalties to their own country and toward an acceptance of communism. Through enormous effort, it was possible to achieve this difficult form of conversion in several cases.[46]

As we have seen, a great variety of effects theoretically can occur as a result of mass communications. But though we live in a sea of persuasive messages, we tend to build up "mental callouses" that effectively screen out much of their influence. Campaigns aimed at persuading us to stop smoking, drive more safely, quit littering, or otherwise change our patterns of belief and conduct have only a limited chance of success. The people who attend most intensely to such communications are generally those who are already convinced. Thus a television program devoted to the evils of racial prejudice will draw a large audience mainly from the victims of such prejudice and from liberals who are already sympathetic. While it may reinforce the beliefs of such persons, it will be ignored by the bigots toward whom it is actually directed.

MASS MEDIA AND SOCIAL RESPONSIBILITY

Public controversy concerning the social impact of mass communications has centered around three major categories of people: the highly vocal *intellectual critics*, those who *own or manage* the mass media, and those who do *research* on the media within the empirical perspectives of the social sciences. Each of these categories represents distinct views with respect to evaluating the social role of the media.

The intellectual critics feel that the mass media have a clear responsibility to help build a better society by educating the public and improving its literary and artistic tastes. They tend to be bitter because, in their view, the media are operated as commercial enterprises that have never accepted this responsibility. Some believe that esthetic standards and cultural tastes are deteriorating largely because of the influence of the media. They are convinced that mass culture, deliberately manufactured by the communications industry, is false and shallow. Some believe, too, that there is also a causal relationship between the rise of the mass media in the twentieth century and the rise in the rates of deviance during the same period. The media are seen as playing an insidious role in generating crimes of violence, sexual irresponsibility, juvenile delinquency, and other threatening trends.

On the opposite side of this controversy are the owners and managers of the media, whose first concern is to operate a business that will yield a profit. They reject the idea that they must assume a special responsibility for cultural uplift, mass education, or moral reform. Media content is determined in general by relatively simple economics: to maintain the support of advertisers, the content must capture the attention of potential consumers. This means "giving the public what it wants."

Between these groups is the social researcher, whose role is to gather objective information concerning all aspects of mass com-

45. William R. Catton, Jr., unpublished study from "Project Revere," 1960, University of Washington.

46. Edgar H. Schien, "Reaction Patterns to Severe, Chronic Stress in American Army Prisoners of War of the Chinese," *Journal of Social Issues,* 13 (1957), 21–30.

munication and the ways they relate to other social processes. To date he has found little solid evidence to indicate that the mass media have contributed to our major social ills, but neither is he prepared to support the contention of television network executives, for example, that the medium's continuing emphasis on violence, crime, and other forms of deviance is having no effect on viewers. The social scientist prefers to remain isolated from the debates between critics and media managers until more solid evidence has been accumulated. Often, because he refuses to support one side, he is accused of being an agent of the other.

MASS PERSUASION

Persuasion can be defined as an attempt to achieve some form of behavioral change on the part of an audience through communication. The term is a broad one and includes face-to-face communication as well as communication through the mass media. The term *propaganda* is used in various ways, but in the present context its meaning is limited to *message content* that is designed to have persuasive effects. As such, it carries no connotation of either "good" or "bad."

Persuasion through the use of mass-communicated propaganda has become a very important social process, but there is little scientific understanding of how the process works. Mass advertising, political campaigning via the media, charity appeals, and other attempts to influence public action through mass communication are in large part carried out without any systematic theoretical basis. Sometimes a clever advertisement or an engaging political appeal will be highly successful, but little is known about *why* particular efforts succeed. With present knowledge it is impossible to develop a completely successful persuasion campaign at will, but two general strategies are widely followed. One emphasizes the psychology of the *individual;* the other emphasizes the sociocultural variables that affect the individual as part of a group.

PSYCHODYNAMIC PERSUASION

Rightly or wrongly, it has been assumed that an effective—that is, persuasive—media message is one that is capable of altering one or more psychological variables within the individual in such a way that he will respond overtly (by voting or spending money, for example) in ways desired and suggested by the communicator. It is assumed, in other words, that internal psychological processes have predictable dynamic relationships with overt behavior and that altering the former will lead to correlated changes in the latter in a manner desired by the persuader (Figure 13.3).

We may elaborate this theoretical scheme by conceiving of the human personality as a "system" that seeks to maintain its equilibrium; when its equilibrium is disturbed, the individual experiences discomfort. Thus (according to the theory), if a persuasive message can attract the attention of the individual and temporarily create disequilibrium in the personality system, the individual will tend to seek a course of action that will restore equilibrium and thus relieve his discomfort. If the persuasive message also includes suggestions as to *how* the individual can act to restore equilibrium, presumably he will follow the desired course of action. If in fact he does, then effective persuasion has been accomplished.

These ideas are illustrated by the common use of fear-threat as a means to persuade with mass communications. For example, if the object of a short-run persuasion campaign is to get people to remove dangerous medicines from the reach of children, the communication might portray a child gasping for life beneath an open medicine cabinet after having obviously swallowed a poison. This is presumed to pose a considerable fear-threat for the audience mem-

propaganda (persuasive message)

↓

alters internal psychological process

↓

achieves change in overt behavior

FIGURE 13.3. **THE PSYCHODYNAMIC STRATEGY FOR ACHIEVING PERSUASION**

ber and to create a state of punishing disequilibrium in his personality system. The communication can then suggest the means by which the threat can be avoided and equilibrium can be restored—namely, by locking dangerous medicines away in a safe place. The fallacy of a fear-arousing approach is that the audience member may take a quite different route to avoid the threat that has been created. For example, he may avoid, deliberately misunderstand, or repress the message.[47] In addition to fear, many psychological variables have been used in media propaganda as a basis for the psychodynamic strategy of persuasion—sex urges, status drives, health preoccupations, vanity, greed, and others.

Propaganda based on the psychodynamic strategy assumes that *attitudes* are psychological variables directly correlated with particular patterns of *overt behavior.* Thus a media campaign may be undertaken to reduce racial or ethnic prejudice (attitudinal variable) on the grounds that if this can be accomplished, then discriminatory behavior (overt action) will be reduced. One reason why the psychodynamic strategy often fails is that, as suggested, human beings do not always show such neat relationships between their psychological structure and their patterns of overt behavior. For example, the individual with prejudicial attitudes may not engage in overt acts of discrimination,[48] while the person who gives verbal approval to the idea of punishing litterbugs may himself throw trash on the highway. Despite such complications, the psychodynamic strategy for mass persuasion remains a major one.

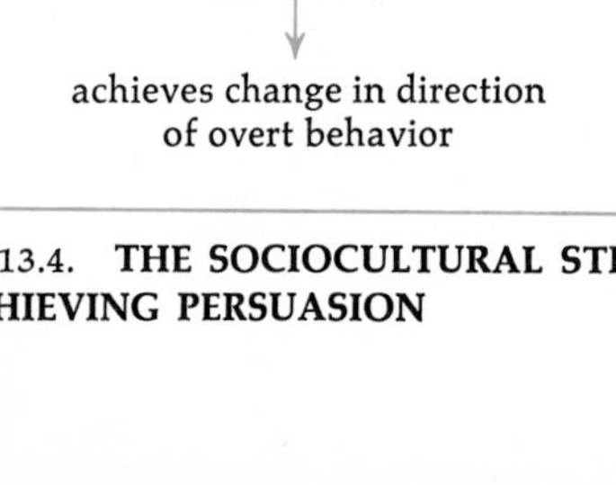

propaganda (persuasive message)

↓

defines (or redefines)
sociocultural processes of group(s)

↓

forming or altering definitions
for socially approved behavior
for group members

↓

achieves change in direction
of overt behavior

FIGURE 13.4. **THE SOCIOCULTURAL STRATEGY FOR ACHIEVING PERSUASION**

SOCIOCULTURAL PERSUASION

The sociocultural strategy of mass persuasion concentrates on defining or redefining, through the use of the media, certain *patterns of expectation* that serve as behavioral guides for members of groups. The task is simplest when the members have no clearly defined expectations with respect to the object of the persuasive appeal. Persuasion is much more difficult to achieve when established patterns of expectations and behavior have to be supplanted with new ones.

Although sociocultural strategy must still take account of the perceptual, cognitive, and attitudinal characteristics of group members as individuals, it assumes that external, group-validated guides to action have a strong impact on shaping behavior, and these become the chief target for manipulation (Figure 13.4).

Many variables are used to provide the individual, through media messages, with what appear to be group-supported modes of conduct toward an object, event, or issue. Social-organizational concepts such as norms, roles, and systems of social control play an important part, for they aid the individual in interpreting ambiguous situations and defining appropriate modes of action. If he can be convinced through mass-media messages that there is *consensus* in the group with respect to a particular pattern of response, then he feels pressure to act in that manner, under the conviction that he is *conforming to expectations.* Actions taken in the belief that they represent conformity to group expectation are not likely to arouse anxieties or otherwise disturb psychological equilibrium. On the contrary, they are likely to be rewarding to the individual.

To illustrate the achievement of persuasion through the use of the sociocultural strategy, we may examine the tactics commonly used by charity drives. Although the "community fund" type of charity campaign uses elements of both

47. Irving L. Janis and Seymour Feshbach, "Effects of Fear-arousing Communication," *Journal of Abnormal and Social Psychology,* 48 (1953), 78–92.

48. The literature on this issue is summarized in Melvin L. DeFleur and Frank R. Westie, "Attitude as a Scientific Concept," *Social Forces,* 42, No. 1 (1963), 17–31; and Lyle Warner and Melvin L. DeFleur, "Attitude as an Interactional Concept: Social Constraint and Social Distance as Intervening Variables Between Attitudes and Action," *American Sociological Review,* 34, No. 2 (1969), 153–169.

psychodynamic and sociocultural strategy, we will stress the latter for illustrative purposes.

An important step in the campaign is to announce (via the mass media) the community *quota* that the drive expects to reach. This is a formulation of an apparent *collective goal,* and it has a certain compelling quality because it is portrayed as the goal of the whole community. The appearance of widespread approval is often achieved by getting socially eminent persons in the community to participate in the announcement. The mass media generally give prominent coverage to these events ("status conferral").

Another step is to announce to the members of the community that their *fair share* is some specified portion of their monthly or weekly income. Again, media campaigns assure that this message is understood by all. The concept of a fair share is especially compelling because it has the appearance of a widely approved *norm.* No one wants to be "unfair." If the members of the community can be convinced that others are giving according to this norm, then they feel pressure to perform according to the shared expectations.

Along with mass-communicated propaganda, an equally important part of the campaign is to create as many *roles* and *counter-roles* as possible within the economic groups of the community. Thus every place of business or division within a bureaucracy is asked to have its own "chairman" for the drive. Each member of the group must play a counter-role to this chairman's role. For example, IBM cards are often distributed so that each member can "pledge" a donation to be collected later. The person who does not choose to play this counter-role must make his *deviance* known by signing the card to indicate refusal or by telling the chairman of his group. Thus, role and counter-role provide a structure that places considerable social pressure on the individual to make a donation.

Even more compelling is the use of neighborhood collectors. These persons call on the residents of their area and request a donation. The role of "good citizen" and "neighbor" thus includes donating to the cause. It is socially embarrassing to refuse a neighbor a reasonable and socially approved request, and refusal risks informal sanctions. No matter how many other charities he has already given to, the individual is unlikely to refuse another contribution in this context.

With skillful use of the media, then, plus manipulation of the sociocultural milieu, this strategy of persuasion can be very successful. The variables utilized in the persuasive campaign to give the potential donor a "definition of the situation" include norms, roles, and informal sanctions as well as the deep-seated values that underlie all charitable activities.

PUBLIC OPINION IN MODERN SOCIETY

Perhaps no other idea concerning the media is so firmly implanted in the popular mind as the notion that they have great power in manipulating public opinion. In the present section the nature of public opinion, some of its consequences, and the relationship it has to mass communication in a democratic society will be briefly examined.

THE SIGNIFICANCE OF THE MEDIA FOR PUBLIC OPINION

The significance of the mass media in the formation of public opinion has been a subject of considerable controversy for decades. Those who are generally critical of the media and those disenchanted with contemporary society seem especially prone to attribute to mass communication an overwhelming power to mold and manipulate public opinion at will. They note that governmental power, even in democratic societies such as the United States, has been increasingly removed from local authority and concentrated in the hands of remote figures at the national level. This tends, they say, to separate the average citizen from events and controversies that may affect his destiny. Lacking first-hand information upon which to make up his mind or to take action, he is seen as increasingly at the mercy of those who control the media in that they can feed him selected information, predigested opinion, and restricted courses of action. Under such conditions, the ordinary citizen (so such critics maintain) is reduced to little more than an automaton who regurgitates the manufactured opinions he has been fed and carries out only those programs of action that have been laid out for him.

There seems little basis for attributing such power to the media, especially in societies where they are not under monopolistic control. In a totalitarian regime, there is little doubt that the media can play a prominent role in the mobilization of public opinion through the use of propaganda.[49] But even in the totalitarian system, public opinion is not a simple product of mass communication. Public opinion in the authoritarian regime is also manipulated by controlling the educational system, suppressing groups (such as churches) that compete for individual loyalties, using a single tightly organized political party, punishing dissidents, staging mass meetings, parades, and demonstrations, and so on.

The more complete the monopoly over all opinion-producing information, the more likely it is that public opinion can be controlled from the top. Even in a dictatorship, however, absolute control over every citizen's opinions on all topics is still highly unlikely. No known system can force media audiences to pay attention, and even if attention is gained, there is no assurance that opinion formation or change will follow in exactly the manner desired by the communicator.

In a democratic society, information monopolies seldom exist. The media, under distributed ownership and control, serve as voices for *competing* points of view rather than for a solitary one. A great variety of pressure groups, political factions, and special-interest associations vie with each other for public attention. Still, it cannot be denied that mass communication plays an important part in the formation and crystallization of public opinion even in democracies. In the section that follows, we will examine a theory that attempts to explain the opinion-formation process, including the part played by the media.

A THEORY OF PUBLIC-OPINION FORMATION

Before attempting to analyze the complex process by which public opinion is formed, it is necessary to clarify the meaning of the terms *mass, public,* and *opinion* as they are used in sociology.

The mass. There has not yet emerged any single definition of *mass* that would be endorsed by every sociologist. Perhaps the most helpful way to view the idea of the mass is to regard it as a convenient abstraction that may have no actual point-by-point correspondence with any specific aspect of social reality. Thus, we will define *mass* as a large number of individuals who exist within a society but who have no social connections with one another. The mass, in theory at least, exemplifies the *complete absence of social organization.*

While there is probably no aggregate that actually corresponds to the mass, there are certain characteristics that could theoretically be assigned to such a collectivity if it did exist. For example, the members would be drawn from every conceivable social category and stratum; they would be unknown to each other and would be physically separated from each other. In other words, they would not engage in interaction, have a sense of belonging to the mass, or even be aware of their fellow members.

The classic statement on the nature of the mass has been made by Herbert Blumer:

[The] mass is devoid of the features of a society or community. It has no social organization, no body of custom or tradition, no established set of rules or rituals, no organized group of sentiments, no structure of status roles, and no established leadership. It merely consists of an aggregation of individuals who are separate, detached, anonymous, and thus, homogeneous as far as mass behavior is concerned. It can be seen, further, that the behavior of the mass, just because it is not made by preestablished rule or expectation, is spontaneous, indigenous, and elementary.[50]

It is difficult to think of the human individual in a state where his behavior is *not* guided and influenced by norms, roles, social-control mechanisms, etc. The term *mass* provides a needed abstraction to identify behavior in which large numbers of individuals can potentially act simply on their own, each responding to his

---

49. Daniel Lerner, *Propaganda in War and Crisis* (New York: George W. Stewart, 1952); Leonard Doob, "Goebbel's Principles of Propaganda," *Public Opinion Quarterly,* 14 (1950), 419–442; Martin F. Herz, "Some Psychological Lessons from Leaflet Propaganda in World War II," *Public Opinion Quarterly,* 13, No. 3 (1949), 471–486.

50. Herbert Blumer, "Elementary Collective Behavior," in *New Outline of the Principles of Sociology,* ed. Alfred McClung Lee (New York: Barnes & Noble, Inc., 1951), pp. 185–189.

VIEWPOINTS   **TELEVISION COVERAGE OF THE NEWS**

As with other American institutions, perhaps it is time that the networks were made more responsive to the views of the nation and more responsible to the people they serve.

Now I want to make myself perfectly clear. I'm not asking for Government censorship or any other kind of censorship. I'm asking whether a form of censorship already exists when the news that 40 million Americans receive each night is determined by a handful of men responsible only to their corporate employers and is filtered through a handful of commentators who admit to their own set of biases. . . .

Our knowledge of the impact of network news on the national mind is far from complete, but some early returns are available. Again, we have enough information to raise serious questions about its effect on a democratic society. Several years ago Fred Friendly, one of the pioneers of network news, wrote that its missing ingredients were conviction, controversy and a point of view. The networks have compensated with a vengeance.

And in the networks' endless pursuit of controversy, we should ask: What is the end value—to enlighten or to profit? What is the end result—to inform or to confuse? How does the ongoing exploration for more action, more excitement, more drama serve our national search for internal peace and stability?

Gresham's Law seems to be operating in the network news. Bad news drives out good news. The irrational is more controversial than the rational. Concurrence can no longer compete with dissent. One minute of Eldridge Cleaver is worth 10 minutes of Roy Wilkins. The labor crisis settled at the negotiating table is nothing compared to the confrontation that results in a strike—or better yet, violence along the picket lines.

Normality has become the nemesis of the network news. Now the upshot of all this controversy is that a narrow and distorted picture of America often emerges from the televised news. A single, dramatic piece of the mosaic becomes in the minds of millions the entire picture. . . .

We'd never trust such power . . . over public opinion in the hands of an elected Government. It's time we questioned it in the hands of a small and unelected elite.

The great networks have dominated America's airwaves for decades. The people are entitled to a full accounting of their stewardship.

Vice President Spiro T. Agnew
Address to the Mid-West Regional
Republican Committee

What alarms me in the current climate of attack on the news media is the possibility that the Boston Tea Party, the most precipitous demonstration in history, would not be broadcast today.

On the night of Dec. 16, 1773, 153 men boarded three of his majesty's ships at anchor in the Boston harbor. In the most notorious "board-in" in history, they dumped 342 chests of fine tea into the water, chanting what may have been the first protest song: "Rally Mohawks, bring out your axes, and tell King George we'll pay no more taxes." Some historians say it was only 50 protesters, so you can see that crowd reporting was an inexact science even in those days.

That illegal march on Griffin's wharf was certainly newsworthy to the staffs of the Boston *Gazette* and the Newport *Mercury*, whose extensive coverage in turn incited other tea parties. But if the Tea Party were to occur tomorrow, it might not be televised, for the vice president of the United States says that television coverage of such embittered protest creates "a narrow and distorted picture of America."

After all, the Boston Tea Party was one of those inflammatory demonstrations by wild-eyed radicals in beads and long hair, including some effete snobs from Harvard and Princeton. The Tory press at the time described them as "truly immoral men . . . religious hypocrites, treacherous and seditious . . . of morose and sour tempers". . . .

Had I been a news director at the time, and if we could have put in a microwave link to Griffin's wharf and gotten enough light on the ships, I would have broadcast it live and in color. Some of the "Indians" would have cursed us; some of the affiliated stations might have objected to our preempting prime time shows, and some viewers would probably have called to say, "Why don't you ever broadcast some good news?" . . .

We still live in a time when some Americans don't want to be told the facts, a time when what Americans don't know could kill us all. Politicians—Democrat and Republican, American and foreign—are by their very nature inclined "to fool some of the people some of the time." The role of the news media is to prevent that—to report all political pronouncements from all sides, and then to say, in effect, "Yes, but . . . " It is all part of a delicate process of collection, interpretation and diffusion of controversial information, a process that can be stunted at birth, or contaminated in maturity.

Fred W. Friendly
"A Newsman's Nightmare of Boston, 1773"

environment in terms of his own private attitudes and needs. If mass behavior becomes organized, if members begin to influence each other and to develop *shared* orientations or expectations of each other, then mass behavior ceases and the actions of the participants become group behavior.

Individual versus public opinion. Several different behavioral phenomena are often identified as "opinion."[51] First, there are the *private opinions of individuals.* The sociologist's understanding of this concept is not much different from the layman's: private opinion refers to a given person's verbalized or communicable set of interpretive beliefs concerning some issue or situation.

Individuals formulate private opinions in part on the basis of their personal attitudes and values concerning the issue at hand. They may draw upon norms they have internalized. They may also use their interpretations of the views of their reference groups, or other sociocultural sources, to formulate their opinions.[52] *Public opinion*, on the other hand, is a sociological rather than a psychological concept. Its formation, as we shall see, involves elaborate interactional processes.

Publics. The term *public* has been used in a variety of ways by social scientists. As used in connection with public opinion, it refers to much more than simply a large number of people. To begin with, we may think of a number of *potential* publics existing in a given population.

How does a given public, then, emerge and become recognizable? A public becomes defined in a preliminary way when some issue or event captures the attention of a large number of individual members of the mass—say as a response to some significant item presented by the media. This shared attention provides a necessary basis for the formation of a public. But while attention is a necessary condition, it is not a sufficient condition. That is, there must be something about the phenomenon being attended to that is provocative, controversial, or unclear— something that makes the situation "unstructured" for the emerging public. We can say, then, that a public emerges from the mass when the attention of a relatively large number of people is focused upon some issue or event to which they cannot easily respond in terms of inner guides or established cultural norms.

The formation of public opinion. An important principle of human behavior that is relevant to the formation of public opinion is the so-called *reality principle*—the tendency of people to use social sources in order to assign meaning to unstructured events. When human beings are confronted with an ambiguous event and lack adequate information and relevant norms to react to it, *they usually try to establish orienting frames of reference through interaction with others.*

To illustrate, we may assume that a major news event has been noted by the mass media. If the news event is of a familiar category (e.g., an auto crash, an earthquake, a revolution in South America), it may not constitute an unstructured situation that requires the formation of public opinion. Those who attend to the event can follow their personal predispositions or the usual norms. They might comment on the riskiness of automobile travel, feel sorry for the earthquake victims, or deplore the instability of foreign governments. After having done so, however, they would probably forget the whole thing. But, let us suppose that the news event is both ambiguous and more demanding of orientation and response. For example, through what stages might public opinion develop in a community where college students have just rioted for the first time? In such a situation we should be able to trace the emergence of public opinion as people seek socially derived definitions with which to interpret an unfamiliar and disturbing event.

Perhaps the initial response of community members is a generalized castigation of the participants, but as it becomes evident that there are several sides to the issue, they may find it increasingly difficult to react to the situation in clear-cut terms. The greater the degree of the public's attention, the more confusing the situation becomes. This is no social disruption in a distant land; it is a situation in their own city regarding which they personally must formulate appropriate modes of orientation and action. As the attention of many individuals focused on this unstructured event, a public would emerge from the mass and the formation of public opinion would be well under way.

The process of public-opinion formation

51. For an analysis of several approaches to this concept see Daniel Katz, *et. al.*, eds., *Public Opinion and Propaganda* (New York: Holt, Rinehart and Winston, Inc., 1954).

52. *Ibid.*, pp. 86–158.

would continue as various interpretations of the event were circulated among the members of emerging public. In this case, the final shaping of public opinion might depend greatly upon the distribution of attitudes toward higher education. Conservatives might call for unqualified reprisals against the rioters, while strong liberals might urge complete tolerance. Various interest groups and factions might add their collective voices to the debate. Spokesmen for student demonstrators might denounce university officials. The administration would probably attempt to justify existing policies. Right-wing student leaders might denounce the rioters and their supporters as Communists and anarchists. Some politicians would undoubtedly blame everything on anyone but themselves.

The mass media would play a significant role throughout these developments. Not only would they present news information, but they would publicize the comments of spokesmen for various sides of the ensuing debate and perhaps note the development of consensus by one segment of the public or another.

The formation of public opinion would thus proceed as an exceedingly complex process of debate, discussion, and exchange—influenced by mass communication, the psychological makeup of individual members of the public, networks of informal interaction, special-interest groups, public leaders, spokesmen for various associations, and so on.[53] Out of all this, a limited number of shared interpretive frameworks would emerge and eventually become dominant. One large segment of the public might develop consensus, in greater or lesser degree, that the rioters were unjustified and deserved little consideration and possibly even severe sanctions. Another substantial faction might agree that the whole unfortunate incident was a symptom of the failure of bureaucratic institutions to adapt to changing needs and maintain that the rioters deserved to be helped rather than punished.

As these opposing views became established, undecided members of the public would be attracted to one side or the other, and public opinion would become increasingly stabilized. Public opinion would be clearly *divided*, but within the opposing blocs a considerable amount

of consensus and uniformity would have developed. Thus, we could identify as *public opinion* the newly formulated and shared convictions of the members of the public concerning the appropriate way to interpret the event under consideration.

For the members who share a given view, their interpretations constitute a *normative* set of convictions. Since the interpretations are shared, they have *social validation*—they are seen as legitimate guides for orientation and action. In a sociological sense, therefore, public opinion is a newly established norm that has not been fully institutionalized.

FUNCTIONS OF PUBLIC OPINION

Once formed, public opinion serves as an important means of social control, both over members of a community or society and over those who lead them. It also serves to clarify ambiguous situations to which people must respond, and to promote integration and social solidarity within groups or population segments that share common views.

Cultural adaptation. If a population has had experience with an unstructured situation of a given type and has created norms of interpretation within which to adapt to it, such a population is in a position to handle more easily another situation or issue of this same type. What was in the first instance a matter of controversy and debate has now become more understandable and routine. For example, in 1940 when selective service legislation took effect, the draft created considerable controversy. There were debates and demonstrations, sometimes of a very stormy nature. Until the controversy over Vietnam occurred, however, new draft calls created little more than a ripple of protest from those immediately involved. The majority of Americans accepted the draft as inevitable and used established norms of orientation within which to interpret it.

When the norms of public opinion become both widespread and institutionalized, they are part of the *culture* of a people. It is in this sense that public opinion serves as an important means of cultural adaptation. Through the process of public-opinion formation, interpretive norms are invented and institutionalized to give

---

53. This is a modernized theory of the formation of public opinion based on James Bryce, *The American Commonwealth* (London: Macmillan and Company, 1889).

By presenting news information and by publicizing the various sides of an ambiguous issue, the mass media play a significant role in the formation of public opinion. Television coverage of the Vietnam War—and of the differing viewpoints involved—has certainly enabled many viewers to decide where they stand on this controversial subject. Although public opinion on the war is divided, there is a considerable amount of consensus within the opposing blocs. In some cases, it may be that the mere presence of the mass media contributes to clear definitions of situations that would otherwise be ambiguous. For example, there was little doubt in the minds of the American people as to who killed Lee Harvey Oswald because he was shot by Jack Ruby before an audience of millions of television viewers. Similarly, the overwhelmingly favorable response to the Apollo 11 moon landing was undoubtedly influenced by the fact that millions of people saw it happen.

structure and cultural organization to what were previously unstructured situations.

Social control. At least in societies where the ordinary citizen has a voice in the selection of his leaders, public opinion concerning the actions of those leaders provides a measure of social control over public policy. But that control is by no means complete. Even in democracies there is seldom a one-to-one correspondence between public opinion and political decisions. Public opinion in such a situation serves as a means of social control in two ways. First, the actions of leaders may cause strong reactions, controversies, and debate. Public opinion may form against them and their policies, resulting ultimately in their being ousted. Second, and perhaps more important, the *potential* of outraged public opinion may check a leader and prevent him from acting in an unpopular way, precisely because he anticipates that a public upheaval and outcry would follow. This is particularly true in a society characterized by intense media surveillance of public officials.

In much the same way, negative public opinion serves as an important means of maintaining individual conformity. The anticipation that one might become the focus of negative community discussion is an effective informal sanction for most persons. Although this may seem to be a different use of *public opinion* than that discussed in earlier sections, from a theoretical point of view it is the same process on a smaller scale. In such an instance, the unconventional or openly deviant behavior of an individual community member would be the "issue" touching off gossip and debate. Eventually, shared interpretations would develop, and the community would orient itself to the deviant in new ways. Possibly, if errant behavior continued, the individual would cease to be widely discussed, on the grounds that such activities were normal for this eccentric person and could be routinely expected. (See the discussion of labeling theory, pages 383, 385.)

Social solidarity. When public opinion is unified, it helps to integrate a community or a nation behind collective goals. It is difficult under any circumstances to marshal the support of the diverse and heterogeneous populations of urban industrial societies. These differentiated populations are not bound together by that "reciprocal, binding sentiment" which provides the basis for the integrated *Gemeinschaft*.

When such societies face great crises, such as war, the need to achieve social solidarity becomes critical. Stronger links must be forged between each individual and the larger society so as to effectively harness the energies of every citizen to the national purpose. It becomes essential to mobilize his sentiments, enlist his loyalties, instill in him a hatred of the enemy, maintain his morale in the face of privations, and direct his energies to making a maximum contribution to the collective effort. An important means of accomplishing these goals is through propaganda intended to achieve uniform public opinion. If the attention of relevant publics can be elicited via mass-communicated propaganda, and if appropriate norms supportive of the national purpose can by such means be developed and maintained, then collective plans of action for meeting the crisis can be more easily implemented.

Supportive public opinion can make or break such plans of action. Excellent illustrations of this point are provided by comparing the behavior of Americans during World War II with their conduct during the war in Vietnam. Although considerable division of opinion concerning American participation existed in 1939, consensus was gradually developed; and from Pearl Harbor on, public support of the war effort was both widespread and powerful; sacrifices were willingly made in almost all social spheres. Response to the conflict in Vietnam has been very different. Dissident segments of the population, openly critical of the conduct of the war and often very negative concerning the United States participation in it, appeared early and multiplied rapidly. Lack of unified public opinion regarding the essential nature of the war contributed to domestic disunity. Tax increases that were said to be required to meet the costs of the conflict were resisted; the system of selective service was openly criticized. Even the military aspects of the war—how many men should be sent, what weapons should be used, what places should be bombed—became objects of conflicting public opinion. The nation, in short, lacked the consensus of supportive opinion that leads to social solidarity behind a unified national purpose. Indeed, by 1970 the disunity in public opinion had become as great a national concern as the war itself.

SUMMARY

In order to understand the organization and functioning of a society, including the dynamics of social change, one must examine its system of communication. In an urban, industrial society one major type of societal communication is achieved through the various mass media. Mass-communication systems use print, film, and broadcasting to reach large audiences. Such systems include role structures related to ownership, production, control, distribution, and consumption of content.

The mass-communication system of a given society is shaped by its general culture. It operates within the society's political and economic institutions and is a product of their historical development. The mass-communication systems of the United States and the Soviet Union illustrate these principles.

The process of mass communication has been conceptualized by social scientists primarily within a stimulus-response perspective. Media messages provide stimuli to which audience members respond. Intervening between the stimulus and the response are three major classes of variables that have a mediating effect on the process: a person's psychological structure, social category, and informal relationships all influence the way he will attend to and respond to mass-communicated material.

The media achieve a variety of effects. By their very existence they alter the organizational characteristics and operation of a society. For the individual they may alter beliefs, attitudes, or overt forms of behavior. The concept of media responsibility has been much debated, with intellectual critics generally seeing the media as harmful to society and owners and operators of the media rejecting such conclusions. Social scientists attempt to accumulate research findings to settle such debates with objective generalizations.

The media are widely used in attempts to achieve mass persuasion. One common strategy presumes a psychodynamic relationship between personality components and behavior. Another common strategy attempts to redefine the individual's definition of the sociocultural structure around him.

The media play a part in the formation of public opinion. Issues are brought to the attention of potential members of the public by the media, and the media help develop normative interpretations of unstructured situations. Resulting public opinion serves several significant functions for the society. It is a mechanism of cultural adaptation, a means of social control, and, under certain circumstances, the basis of social solidarity.

PART V

SOCIAL INSTITUTIONS

14

The Political System

Political power, as we noted in Chapter 7, is not only one of the rewards of a society's stratification system but a means for determining the distribution of wealth and prestige. Thus *politics* has been defined, not inaccurately, as being concerned with "who gets what, when, and how."[1]

In the United States as in many other countries, existing power arrangements are under attack today by a growing minority of citizens who are demanding—in one way or another—a more audible voice in the political process. To some student radicals here and abroad, the governments of the Western democracies are dishonest, hypocritical, and immoral, fit only to be destroyed. To some black militants, American democracy is a fraud that has promised freedom and equality but kept black citizens in economic and psychological chains. To some activists of a very different sort, aggressive defenders of the status quo, freedoms guaranteed by the Constitution must be revoked in order to save the constitutional system.

A much larger portion of this active minority seeks to make its voice heard not in order to subvert the existing system but in order to reform it. While the black militant rejects "white" politics, many more blacks continue to work for Black Power through voter registration and at the polls. While the campus radical carries out his program of "violent confrontation," many other college students look for leaders within the system whom they can trust and for whom they can work with enthusiasm and dedication, as they worked for Eugene Mc-Carthy and Robert Kennedy in 1968.

Meanwhile, the majority—young and old, black and white—neither attempts to destroy the political system nor seeks to change it. These ordinary voters (and nonvoters) watch the demonstrations and counterdemonstrations—the marches, sit-ins, take-overs, riots—and wonder if such direct methods of influencing government policy will replace the casting of ballots. Uneasiness and confusion are widespread.

The purpose of this chapter is to provide some understanding of the basic forces involved in the political process. First, it examines the

1. Harold D. Laswell, *Politics: Who Gets What, When, How?* (New York, McGraw-Hill Book Company, 1936).

2. Max Weber, *The Theory of Social and Economic Organization* (New York: The Free Press, 1957), p. 152.

3. *Ibid.,* p. 154.

concepts of legitimacy, authority, and influence—the underpinnings of political power. Next, it discusses the relationship between consensus, which holds political systems together, and conflict, which may operate either to improve a system or to tear it apart. Finally, it takes a detailed look at political decision-making in the United States, at both the local and the national levels, and touches on some of the factors that create political—and apolitical—attitudes among a society's members.

THE FOUNDATIONS OF POLITICAL POWER

As noted in Chapter 7, "Social Stratification," Max Weber called attention to the concept of power—the ability to make and implement decisions—as central to the political process. Weber defined power as "the probability that one actor within a social relationship will be in a position to carry out his own will despite resistance."[2] Thus conceived, power is a significant part of all social interaction. Any individual whose behavior, or expected behavior, is taken into account by others in a given situation has some degree of power, whether it be the power of a father over his children, a professor over his students, or a department head over his staff of employees. But power is a matter of degree, with people having greater or lesser amounts, depending on the roles they play in society. The important measure of power is the ability to affect decision-making.

THE CONCEPT OF LEGITIMACY

According to Weber, political power is first and foremost the kind of power exercised by the state, and it is distinguished by the state's authority to use force or violence, if necessary, as an instrument of policy. In fact, the state—the central political authority of any country—only remains a state, Weber maintained, "if and in so far as its administrative staff successfully upholds a claim to the monopoly of the *legitimate* use of physical force in the enforcement of its order."[3] Weber did not mean that the power of the state is "legitimate" in some absolute sense, only that the state *claims* it is legitimate and is able to make good this claim in the eyes of its people. The perceived legitimacy of the government provides the "inner justification" for what that government does.

The importance of shared norms and values.

The concept of legitimacy is very useful in analyzing political systems, for it links the visible machinery of government—administrative offices, law courts, police, and so forth—to the subjective values responsible for creating that machinery and for keeping it in existence. As Seymour Lipset has noted, any kind of political system can be considered legitimate if it is able "to engender and maintain the belief that existing political institutions are the most appropriate or proper ones for the society."[4] Indeed, this belief may be more important to the stability of the system than its success in performing the basic functions of government. A state may be *effective*, Lipset says, but still suffer a "crisis of legitimacy" if its values are rejected by significant segments of its population. Groups within a society

will regard a political system as legitimate or illegitimate according to the way in which its values fit in with their primary values. Important segments of the German army, civil service, and aristocratic classes rejected the Weimar Republic not because it was ineffective, but because its symbolism and basic values negated their own. Legitimacy, in and of itself, may be associated with many forms of political organization, including oppressive ones. Feudal societies, before the advent of industrialism, undoubtedly enjoyed the basic loyalty of most of their members. Crises of legitimacy are primarily a recent historical phenomenon, following the rise of sharp cleavages among groups which have been able, because of mass communication resources, to organize around different values than those previously considered to be the only legitimate ones for the total society.[5]

Legitimation—the establishment of legitimacy—is what stops a person from questioning institutionalized norms. If, for example, you share the values defining property as a legitimate institution, you will accept the right of the police, as an agent of government, to protect it, using force if that becomes necessary. If you do not accept those values, you may take property belonging to someone else—and then reject the right of the police to arrest you for theft. In terms of your system of values, the state's use of force in such cases would be arbitrary and illegitimate.

Legitimate force versus coercion. Although the state has a monopoly on the legitimate use of force, extending to life-and-death control of the citizen under certain circumstances, its power does not rest mainly on force or even on the threat of force. Rather, it rests on a system of *authority*, in which the right to use force is only one factor. Any system of authority is "legitimate" to the extent that it is perceived as valid by those who submit to it, regardless of the goals or actions of the particular government in power.

When individuals, groups, or societies are forced to behave in ways *contrary* to what they believe right, they are said to be "coerced." In political sociology, the term *coercion* denotes a form of power based on the illegitimate use or threat of force. In other words, the coercive decision-maker acts outside the norms established by or with the consent (whether tacit or explicit) of the members of the political community. Thus a criminal group that can force the local government to do its bidding in one or several areas of community life may be said to have coercive power in those areas.

The most extreme form of political coercion is the violent overthrow of a legitimately established government. Those responsible for such revolutions usually make every effort to achieve legitimacy, claiming, for example, that they are acting on behalf of "the people." Apparently, political power based on coercion is most likely to exist in societies with weak, poorly structured political institutions and organizations or in societies where the established institutions have collapsed under stress (for example, Russia in 1917 and China during the 1940's). In general, however, not even the most totalitarian governments are maintained primarily by coercive force, unless their authority is being seriously challenged.

Coercive power should not be confused with the *legitimate* use of force by established governments. Political power is considered coercive only when force is used *arbitrarily*, in

---

4. Seymour M. Lipset, "Some Social Requisites of Democracy: Economic Development and Political Legitimacy," *American Political Science Review*, 53 (March 1959), 86–87.
   5. *Ibid.*

a manner inconsistent with the government's recognized functions. Coercive power is never power by "right" or authority; it always depends on the threat or use of force, against the will or wishes of the people.

TYPES OF AUTHORITY

In a now classic formulation, with implications that reach far beyond political sociology, Weber delineated three types of authority as bases for the legitimate exercise of power: traditional, charismatic, and legal-rational.[6] In all of them, authority is a group-centered phenomenon; it refers to the *right* to make and/or implement decisions that have been made through some accepted structural arrangement. Except in the case of charismatic authority, the right to decide is vested in some organizational role, not in an individual as such. Authority is legitimate by definition; to speak of an organization as "losing authority" means that the legitimacy of the control it exercises is being questioned.

Traditional authority. The oldest form of power known to man is traditional authority, in which legitimation has been handed down from the past. There is a sacred quality to such authority; it is upheld by the belief that "It is being done this way because this is the way it has always been done." Such control is generally based on a set of unwritten rules or laws. The recruitment of persons or groups of persons to positions of traditional authority is not based so much on technical competence (the basic criterion under a system of legal-rational authority) as on family ties. Commands are legitimized partly in terms of tradition and partly by the fact that the rulers enjoy almost unlimited loyalty from their subjects.

What, then, are the limits of traditional authority? What is there to prevent all traditional leaders from acting arbitrarily and coercively? The answer is the tradition itself: its sacredness acts as a curb on the leader's power as much as a means by which he may extend that power. The task of those in authority is not to legislate new rules but to find *precedents* to justify any apparent novelty.

Examples of whole societies ruled entirely by traditional authority are now hard to find

anywhere in the world, but the authority on which many so-called modern political systems operate includes a measure of the traditional. For example, the United States Constitution is in one sense a sacred document, accepted as the unquestioned foundation for American political policy. Thus many conservative American politicians claim that much liberal legislation of the past forty years is illegitimate and coercive because they feel it violates the original intent of the Constitution. An example of an authority system based almost wholly on tradition is provided by the Hopi Indians, whose family organization is examined in Chapter 16.

Charismatic authority. The nature of charismatic authority and the important role it plays in social change have been discussed in Chapter 6 (pages 183–184). The charismatic leader's claim to legitimacy lies primarily in his own inner perception of his power. If he attracts followers, then his perception is verified, for himself and others. Another characteristic of charismatic authority is that it lacks stable social organization. It has no set of rules, traditional or rational, by which to guide conduct, and there are no tests for competency beyond the "gift of grace" itself. Most important, charismatic authority is *in conflict with routine.*

One of the great challenges to charismatic authority is the problem of developing a stable political system. The charismatic leader himself is generally not concerned about routinization, but his movement can persist over the long term only if it develops some kind of social organization. This means that it must evolve into either a traditional or a legal-rational system of authority.

Legal-rational authority. The hallmark of legal-rational systems of authority is bureaucratic organization (pages 70–75). In government as in business or elsewhere, this pattern of social organization places definite limits on the exercise of power by causing power to inhere in a social role or position rather than in an individual and by defining the amount of power to be manifested in a given role. The obligation to obey is based on "the rule of law," not upon a sense of loyalty to any individual. In this, legal-rational authority differs from both traditional and charismatic authority.

In many of the developing nations of the world, systems of legal-rational authority are

6. Weber, *op. cit.,* pp. 329 ff.

superimposed on systems of traditional authority. The potential for conflict between the two
is illustrated in a study by Fallers, who analyzed
the clash of bureaucratic with traditional values
among the Soga people in the Uganda Pro-
tectorate.[7] To transform the traditional political
system of rulers and chieftains into a rationally
organized civil service, the British established a
bureaucratic system of local government there
which, at the administrative level of the district,
was staffed entirely by native-born Sogas. The
new system involved two major departures from
the traditional one: (1) Instead of hereditary
succession, possession of the necessary qualifications became the criterion by which offices
were filled. This was less disruptive than it
might have been, since many chieftains and
chieftains' descendants were in fact qualified and
thus were appointed to help administer the
districts. (2) The tribute formerly paid to all
chieftains by their subjects was abolished; the
new "bureaucratic chieftains" were to be paid
a salary by the central government.

At the district level, the new system worked
reasonably well. But the basic unit of Soga life
was still the village, and there were many villages in each district. Each Soga village was
presided over by a petty chieftain, or "headman," who owed allegiance to the tribal chief
but exercised virtually undisputed authority in
purely village matters. For instance, by Soga
custom the headman possessed "reversionary
rights" to most land farmed by the villagers—that is, the land was considered ultimately to belong to him and might therefore
revert to him any time he chose to claim it. From
the central government's point of view, the
headman had no such rights at all, since none
had been granted to him by law.

The total incompatibility of the headmen's
traditional values and the central government's
legal-rational values became clear when the
government tried to draw the headmen into the
bureaucracy by offering them a salary. This
they refused, although abolition of the tribute
formerly paid them by the villagers had deprived them of their traditional source of income. Instead, they attempted to secure a new
income by regularly asserting their "reversionary rights" and terminating their retainers'
"leases" as often as possible (the headmen received a fee every time a piece of land was
reassigned). The central government regarded
this practice as illegal but found it hard to stop,
since the district officials could not function
without the headmen's cooperation. At the same
time, the practice was definitely an abuse of the
headmen's traditional authority and therefore
tended to diminish the standing of the headmen
in the eyes of their people.

Thus the headmen's alternative to accepting
salaries from the government involved the risk
of their authority altogether. Why did they persist in refusing to go on the government payroll?
The reason, according to the author of the study,
was that they realized that their authority, which
was local and personal in nature, would undoubtedly be destroyed if it were subjected to
impersonal, centralized bureaucratic control. In
any case, they did not regard exercise of their
reversionary rights as illegal. As far as they were
concerned, the government was trying to steal
"their" land, and if they became paid officials,
they would be admitting that the land was not
really theirs. One headman put the issue very
clearly when he said, "If you pay me to wash
my table, it will then become your table."

INFLUENCE

There is still no general agreement among
political sociologists as to whether influence is
a type of authority or something else altogether.
Here it will be treated as a distinct element in
the power equation. Roughly defined, influence
is the sum of all the resources a participant in
a decision-making situation can bring to bear in
order to ensure the outcome he favors. It is more
personal than authority, inhering in the individual more than in the office. Influence may be
derived from a position of formal authority, but
it may also be derived from knowledge, personal
charm, wealth, persuasiveness, and many other
sources.

The interplay of influence and authority is
the very stuff of political decision-making, especially under a democratic form of government.
When power is diffused and lines of formal
authority are unclear, a contest for control usually determines who makes the decisions.
D'Antonio and Form have described the elements of conflict at the local level:

7. Lloyd A. Fallers, *Bantu Bureaucracy: A Study of Integration
and Conflict in the Political Institutions of an East African People*
(Cambridge, England: Heffer, 1956). The following account is taken mainly from material on pp. 152–174.

Although Eugene McCarthy failed to win the Presidential election of 1968, his campaign has had a lasting influence on the conduct of American national politics. Ostensibly, McCarthy's candidacy provided a much needed outlet for the anxieties of many American citizens frustrated by the United States continued involvement in Vietnam. Many believe, furthermore, that McCarthy's impressive showing in the New Hampshire primary helped convince President Johnson not to run for a second term. More than this, however, McCarthy brought into action a new style of campaigning very literally concerned with the People, young and old. It is a style based on the idea that the President and any political leader or candidate must fully respond to his people or be rejected by them.

Conflict over who will control derives from many sources, only a few of which may be identified here. First, the authority of several interrelated positions, agencies or institutions is seldom so clearly defined as to eliminate a struggle over who has the right to decide. Second, and very important in a democracy, people in positions of authority have to justify themselves continually to those who may be affected by their decisions. Thus, the city council's right to levy taxes is restricted by its ability to convince the electorate or specific interest groups that the tax is needed and is reasonable. Failure to do so creates an issue—a question of who will control—for both the council and the people have some authority in this case. Third, the influence of persons or groups may operate either to activate authority or to impede its application. For example, respected citizens or groups may call on the city council to act in a given way. The council has to weigh the consequences of obeying or not obeying. Although such persons of influence do not have legitimate authority over the

council, they may, in fact, constitute an informal government. Fourth, and this is the obverse of the third, there is a tendency for persons in authority to extend their control beyond its legitimate limits by acquiring the "influence of office."[8]

When persons in authority lack influence in their own right, outsiders may be expected to move in to fill the gap. When persons with influence lack access to positions of authority but insist on using their resources anyway, the political system may be seriously jeopardized. (Consider, for instance, a city in which the top police officials are in the pay of the underworld.) Between these extremes lie the efforts of interested groups and individuals to help shape the decision-making process. Whether such efforts

8. W. V. D'Antonio and W. H. Form, *Influentials in Two Border Cities: A Study in Community Decision-Making* (South Bend, Ind.: University of Notre Dame Press, 1965), p. 12.

At the national level, the Republican and Democratic parties are mainly concerned with nominating candidates for President and Vice-President and then trying to get them elected. Particularly since 1968, the entire nominating procedure has come under severe criticism as both cumbersome and undemocratic.

are perceived as legitimate or not is determined ultimately by the society's values, as is the legitimacy of authority itself.

Political parties. Of all the nongovernmental organizations that wield political influence in American society, the Republican and Democratic parties come closest to also having authority. This is because they appear to have no serious rivals at the national level and because the leader of one or the other is regularly President of the United States. The key features of the major American parties are decentralization, minimum active participation by the citizenry (except at election time), and pragmatic rather than revolutionary ideology.

The basic unit of party organization is the precinct, a polling district fixed by the state laws and city ordinances governing elections. There are about 130,000 precincts in the United States, each including from two hundred to one thousand voters. Each party has its own precinct workers, and their activity in "getting out the vote" is the key to party success.[9]

During the heyday of political "bosses" and city "machines" (corresponding roughly to the period of heavy immigration and rapid urbanization between 1870 and 1925), the local party served as a kind of informal welfare agency, giving service and jobs in exchange for votes. During the past thirty or forty years, however, the power of political machines has progressively waned until, in most cities at least, machines—that is, party organizations that tightly control large blocs of votes—have all but disappeared. Their loss of power has been the result of such changes as the establishment of the social security system and formal welfare agencies—which have rendered many of the services of the precinct worker unnecessary —and the introduction of civil-service bureaucracies, federal voting laws, and (not least important) voting machines. Changes in transportation and communication patterns have further disrupted the power of the local party

organization by reducing the significance of the precinct as a social unit.

At the national level, the major activity of both the Republican and Democratic parties has been and continues to be nominating candidates for President and Vice-President and then trying to get them elected. All other activities are clearly subordinate. Since presidential elections occur only every four years, the national party structure has an *ad hoc* quality quite unlike that of a typical bureaucratic organization. For instance, members of both the Republican and the Democratic national committees serve without pay. Since this service on the committees costs both money and time, members tend to be drawn from the upper levels of business and law more than from other occupational sectors; and they may be therefore somewhat less than responsive to new movements and tendencies among the party rank and file. On the other hand, potential presidential candidates do well to spend time cultivating the state committees, since these groups select the delegates to the national conventions. Particularly since 1968, the entire nominating procedure has come under severe criticism as both cumbersome and undemocratic. Some writers have urged that it be replaced by nationwide primary elections.

Interest and pressure groups. A group that attempts to exert political influence without being either a political party or a part of government is generally known as an *interest group*. Interest groups have been functioning since the earliest days of the Republic, and so long as they are independent of government control, they can help to develop and sustain democratic processes. But to be effective they must have access to sources of power; without such access autonomy is politically useless. Thus very small groups must somehow be able to make their needs known to larger, more powerful groups.

The term *pressure group*, journalistic in origin, is often used interchangeably with *interest group*. Here, it will be used to denote an interest group with an ideology sufficiently distinct to keep it more or less permanently organized. Not all interest groups can be active all the time: "All the conceivable adjustments between all citizens cannot be made simultaneously and openly through the processes of government. The political system would not stand the strain."[10] But a great many organizations actively exert pressure year in and year out through *lobbying*, which

---

9. For several related views on party organization, see Henry A. Turner, ed., *Politics in the United States* (New York: McGraw-Hill Book Company, 1955), esp. the articles by Warren Moscow, Sonya Forthal-Spiesman, and Robert L. Morlan.

10. David B. Truman, *The Governmental Process: Political Interests and Public Opinion* (New York: Alfred A. Knopf, Inc., 1959), p. 356.

usually involves personal contact with legislators. The list of organizations that spend $50,000 or more each year on lobbying in Washington usually includes the AMA, the AFL-CIO, the American Farm Bureau Federation, the U.S. Savings and Loan League, the National Association of Electric Companies, the International Brotherhood of Teamsters, the National Association of Letter Carriers, and the National Education Association.[11] Veterans' organizations are a powerful force, and the interests of racial and religious groups are increasingly if not always effectively represented.

Successful lobbyists (whose activities are regulated by law) are paid large sums for their services. For instance, in 1965 Oscar Chapman, a former Secretary of the Interior, was being paid $50,000 a year for representing Mexican sugar producers in Washington.[12] The producers needed this representation because of the sugar quota system, under which the United States agrees to import a specified amount of sugar every year from certain foreign countries at a guaranteed price. Which foreign countries shall be allowed to sell how much sugar at this price is decided, in effect, by the House Agriculture Committee. In 1965 the price the United States was prepared to pay for quota sugar was about $5 per hundred pounds *higher* than the price on the world market. Thus the Mexican quota of 385,000 tons was worth some $30,800,000 to the sugar producers. It is clear that, as the person responsible for seeing that this quota was not reduced, Mr. Chapman was earning his fee.

Lobbying is unlikely to become a burning public issue, since most Americans have never heard of lobbyists like Mr. Chapman or of arrangements such as the sugar quota system (although they themselves ultimately subsidize the artificially high price of quota sugar). But political theorists have begun to question whether the traditional picture of democratic pluralism—that is, of free and open competition among a variety of special interest groups—can be said to fit the facts of American political life.[13] What well-paid lobbyist represents the ordinary individual's interests before the Congress? What is "free and open" about a competition for influence between the consumer and, say, General Motors? Unless some influential section of the government steps in on the side of the individual, it is hard to be optimistic about his chances. (See a later discussion of this point on page 467.)

CONSENSUS AND CONFLICT

Every society accumulates some body of values, beliefs, and sentiments in terms of which its members find meaning and regularity in life. This pattern of shared norms is often called a *consensus*. It may well be that the existence of a consensus is the ultimate basis of social order, for legitimacy rests, in the last analysis, on the support of the ruled. There is much debate, however, over how much support is necessary to keep a political system operating effectively and over how that support can be established and maintained, especially in a large, heterogeneous society. Legitimacy is not something that rulers can give themselves, however much they may try. Ralph Linton has stated the problem as follows:

In spite of some 6,000 years of experimentation, the problems of organizing and governing states have never been perfectly solved. The modern world, with the whole experience of history to draw upon, still attacks these problems in many different ways and with indifferent success. One thing seems certain. The most successful states are those in which the attitudes of the individual toward the state most nearly approximate the attitudes of the uncivilized individual toward his tribe. If the members of a state have common interests and a common culture, with the unity of will which these give, almost any type of formal governmental organization will function efficiently. If the members lack this feeling of unity, no elaboration of formal governmental patterns or multiplication of laws will produce an efficient state or contented citizens. How such unity may be created and maintained in great populations and especially in fluid ones where the individual's close, personal contacts are reduced to a minimum is probably the most important problem which confronts us today.[14]

11. Robert K. Carr *et al.*, *American Democracy*, 5th ed. (New York: Holt, Rinehart and Winston, Inc., 1968), pp. 123–124.

12. As reported in a dispatch from the *Chicago Daily News*, reprinted in the *New York Post*, August 20, 1969, p. 54.

13. The principal statement of this point of view is Henry S. Kariel, *The Decline of American Pluralism* (Stanford, Calif.: Stanford University Press, 1967). See also Lester W. Milbrath, *The Washington Lobbyists* (Chicago: Rand McNally & Company, 1963).

14. Ralph Linton, *Study of Man* (New York: Appleton-Century-Crofts, 1936), p. 252.

CONSENSUS AND THE POLITICAL STRUCTURE

As a result of their different experiences, societies develop not only different types of political systems but also different underlying patterns of consensus. This was one of the topics explored by Gabriel Almond, who classified contemporary political systems into four main types: (1) *Anglo-American* (including some members of the British Commonwealth); (2) *Continental European;* (3) *preindustrial* or *part-industrial;* and (4) *totalitarian.*[15] Almond's purpose in making this classification was to compare political structures, not values. But each of the systems he identifies is more than just a set of formal arrangements. "Every political system," he notes, "is embedded in a particular pattern of orientations to political action."

Viewed in this way, consensus becomes not just the sum of individual opinions on this or that (which is the way we in the United States, habituated to polls of every kind, naturally tend to regard it) but the *political aspect of culture.* Just how much difference the cultural approach can make is clear from Almond's comparison of the Anglo-American type of political system with the Continental European one. Frenchmen, Germans, and Italians (the principal components of the Continental European category) are undoubtedly as much in favor of individual freedom as Americans or Englishmen. But, for largely historical reasons, they do not have the same kind of political culture. And this, it seems, has prevented them from being as successful in maintaining democratic institutions.

The Americans and British, according to Almond, have developed a "secular political culture" that is more or less common to *all* groups and individuals taking part in the political process. Politics is seen as a vast market: people "set themselves up in political business" and then bargain with each other. Continental Europeans, on the other hand, are distributed among three major political subcultures: preindustrial (chiefly Catholic peasants); transitional (the "older middle-class elements"); and industrial (for example, the factory workers on

whose votes the Communist parties of both France and Italy depend so heavily).

The Continental European type of political system has not succeeded in reconciling these three subcultures. As a result, Almond says, people tend to be disillusioned with politics in general. "The political actors come to the market not to exchange, compromise, and adapt, but to preach, exhort, convert, and transform the political system into something other than a bargaining agency." Under certain circumstances —war or the threat of war, severe economic depression, anything that calls the effectiveness of the system into question— democratic institutions tend to be replaced by charismatic leaders. The Anglo-American system, on the other hand, seems better able to keep its leaders in check. No matter how charismatic they may be, they are always conscious that they are accountable to the public and may be replaced.

CONSENSUS IN A DEMOCRACY

Democracy as an ideology is based on the premise that the integrity of the individual is worth protecting at any cost. The individual is considered to have been born with a natural right to develop his own beliefs and opinions, even if they diverge from those of the majority. While the will of the majority is supposed to prevail in all matters affecting the society as a whole, the minority is free to try to influence the majority in any lawful way it chooses. Thus democratic political institutions face a major problem: how much dissent, and what kinds of dissent, can the society accept and still maintain political stability?

The ordering of conflict. In the Anglo-American political structure, consensus makes legitimate the existence of opposition and thus of conflict. It orders the conflict, restricting it by reasonably well-defined sets of rules. Thus virtually every adult citizen not only has the right to vote but is given a choice of candidates and parties. Votes are cast in secret, and precautions are taken to assure that they are counted correctly. It is expected that the winner will be allowed to take office without having to use violence. The loser gives up office knowing that

---

15. Gabriel Almond, "Comparative Political Systems," *Journal of Politics,* 18 (1956), 391–409. See also Heinz Eulau, Samuel Eldersveld, and Morris Janowitz, eds., *Political Behavior* (New York: The Free Press, 1956), pp. 253 ff.

he can return to power if he wins next time. Thus the entire system rests on trust and compromise—a remarkable testimony to the strength of the consensus that supports it.

The limits to dissent. Different societies prescribe different limits to dissent. For instance, Mao Tse-tung, chairman of the Chinese Communist party, denies the right of "reactionaries" (i.e., old warlords, former landlords, bureaucratic capitalists, and the like) to participate at all in the political processes of the "people's democracy":

The democratic system is to be carried out within the ranks of the people, giving them freedom of speech, assembly, and association. The right to vote is given only to the people and not to the reactionaries. These two aspects, namely, democracy among the people and dictatorship over the reactionaries, combine to form the people's democratic dictatorship.[16]

In contrast, American society, at least in the years since women won the right to vote, has been extremely reluctant to limit the right of formal political participation. Those whose right to participate is challenged, for whatever reason, are entitled to seek redress through the courts. For example, in October 1968 a three-judge federal court affirmed the right of the Communist party of Minnesota—defined by the Communist Control Act of 1954 as an "agency of a hostile foreign power"—to place its candidates for president and vice-president on the Minnesota ballot. At the same time the court questioned the constitutionality of two sections of the Communist Control Act which maintained that the Communist party in the United States, as a "clear, present, and continuing danger" to American security, was not entitled to "any of the rights, privileges, and immunities attendant upon legal bodies."[17] It is quite clear that a major factor in this judicial decision was the desire of the court to protect rights that it regarded as fundamental to the American political system.

In recent years dissent has been an increasingly serious issue in American society, largely as a result of the Vietnam War. In the late 1960's, opposition to the war became so intense that some government spokesmen and their supporters accused the most violent dissenters of disloyalty and sedition. On the other hand, some members of black militant and student radical groups denied their opponents any right to be heard. The young radicals had a philosophical ally in Herbert Marcuse, who found liberal protection of the political and civil liberties of conservatives to be immoral. Thus, both those defending the status quo and those violently opposed to it questioned one of the fundamental rights guaranteed by the Constitution.

WHAT MAKES DEMOCRACY POSSIBLE?

In nearly all societies today, "freedom" has become one of the values to which appeal is most often made. While the precise meaning of *freedom* varies, it is probably true to say that most people associate it with the individual's right to choose between alternatives. Freedom of this kind cannot exist unless choices become available in the first place and unless individuals realize they *are* available. An individual or group that lacks knowledge of possible choices lives in the unfreedom of ignorance.

Both the distribution of ignorance and the availability of choice are determined by the existing social structure. The history of post-feudal man is largely the history of attempts to change that structure. From that history one lesson in particular emerges: the road to freedom is a long one. In America, the colonists fought for political independence from the mother country and framed their own Constitution, with its Bill of Rights and its carefully designed system of checks and balances. Nearly two hundred years later, legislators and federal courts continue to adapt the system to changing needs and conditions while attempting to preserve the freedoms it was designed to protect. Meanwhile, democracy is held up as an ideal to peoples, usually from areas lacking the natural advantages of the North American continent, who have only recently achieved the same degree of independence as the American colonists in 1776.

The emergence of dozens of new nations in the period since World War II and the political instability many of them have experienced in the face of competing ideologies have led

---

16. Quoted from "The Role of Ideology," by Mao Tse-tung, in *Chinese Society Under Communism*, ed. William T. Liu (New York: John Wiley & Sons, Inc., 1967), p. 104.

17. As reported in *Civil Liberties*, No. 259 (December 1968).

political sociologists to reopen the classic question of what makes democracy possible.[18] It should be emphasized that this is a quite different question from whether democracy in some form is *desirable*. There is not much debate over the latter, at least among American social scientists.

Class structure. In the fourth century B.C. Aristotle argued that democracy is not possible when there are great disparities in wealth.[19] On the other hand, he said, when the majority of the people are in the middle class, and neither the rich above nor the poor below are too far removed from them, the broad value consensus necessary to democracy can develop, permitting orderly dissent and conflict in the body politic. Aristotle's reasoning seems to be that a democratic consensus can be achieved only when men are freed from hunger and ignorance, because only then will they be free from exploitation. And only those who are free from exploitation can develop the internal restraints that make possible democracy's unique balance between consensus and conflict.

Political traditions. Modern researchers tend to agree with Aristotle but are quick to point out that general economic betterment does not necessarily build democracy. There is no easy formula by which to transform a traditional society into a modern democracy. For instance, it is obvious that a democratic type of consensus cannot develop unless people have experience in democratic institutions. But free, open, and honest elections, which Americans take to be a major sign of a democratic society, may not be possible or relevant in the early stages of political development. Indeed, there is little in the socialization processes of most underdeveloped countries to prepare their citizens to be voters. Such societies are usually composed of various traditional socioeconomic groupings—tribes, estates, or autonomous villages—with few or no ties to the central government. The autonomy of a traditional village or landed estate means

not some form of local democracy but monolithic or oligarchic rule. It is one of the paradoxes of political organization that totally autonomous communities tend to be *less* competitive and *more* monolithic, and to provide *less* individual freedom for their members than do communities that are more dependent on a central government.

Economic development and related factors. A study by Lipset, much influenced by the Almond study described previously (page 449), set out to determine exactly what social and economic conditions were associated with stable democratic government.[20] Lipset classified forty-eight countries as stable and unstable democracies and dictatorships (Table 14.1, page 452) and then compared groups of these countries with respect to wealth, industrialization, educational level, and urbanization. He concluded that all these factors could be regarded as aspects of the same thing—namely, economic development. The higher the level of economic development, the more likely that there would be both democracy and political stability. There were very few exceptions to this pattern, and they could be explained in terms that confirmed the author's general thesis.

But it cannot therefore be concluded that economic development by itself leads to democracy and stability. Many other things are necessary—among them a "secular political culture" that is shared by the population as a whole. Thus in the United States we all tend to recognize the same national heroes. Although some segments of the population have culture heroes that the rest of the country would not recognize as such, admiration for, say, George Washington, Thomas Jefferson, and Abraham Lincoln is very nearly universal. In France, on the other hand, the culture heroes of the political left are entirely different from those of the political right. The French Revolution, unlike the American Revolution, remains politically controversial.

In order to contribute to stable democracy, the secular political culture must be sufficiently homogeneous to keep the conflict between politically organized groups at a relatively low level. The type of political regime that "gets in first" acquires a tremendous head start in legitimacy over all other possible contenders. Lipset is therefore inclined to be pessimistic about the chances of democracy in most developing na-

---

18. See Edward G. McGrath, ed., *Is American Democracy Exportable?* (Beverly Hills, Calif.: Glencoe Press, 1968).

19. Aristotle, *Politics*, Book IV, Chapter 11; see also R. Bendix and S. M. Lipset, eds., *Class, Status and Power: A Reader in Social Stratification* (New York: The Free Press, 1961), pp. 17–18.

20. Lipset, "Some Social Requisites of Democracy," *op. cit.*

tions, especially the Asian ones. Perhaps Western-style democracy, especially the Anglo-American kind, is unrepeatable.

A THEORY OF REVOLUTION

Man as a role-playing animal tends to perceive his gratifications and deprivations in relation to those of his neighbors. Thus, the fact that he "has it pretty good" or that "things aren't as bad as they used to be" is generally scant comfort to someone who sees that other people have things much better. This tendency, which has been documented and analyzed in many different kinds of group situations, is known to social psychologists as *relative deprivation*.[21] A related finding indicates that when someone finds his lot improving, he raises his expectations and is likely to react negatively to any blockage or reversal of his progress.

Davies has adapted these principles to a tentative theory of revolution: "Revolutions are most likely to occur when a prolonged period of objective economic and social development is followed by a short period of sharp reversal."[22] This theory contradicts the romantic view that the totally downtrodden "seethe with revolt." On the contrary, they are overwhelmingly preoccupied with just staying alive. They are not organized politically; nor are they committed to any political ideologies. And revolution—the attempt to change society completely by political means—depends on the development of just such a commitment.

The patterns of change in England and the United States during the last two hundred years suggest that the slow, often grudging, but steady granting of political reforms in a period of more or less continuous industrial expansion may be sufficient to prevent the kind of frustration that leads to revolution. This frustration, as Davies points out, need not be concerned mainly with physical well-being. Rather, it may center on questions of justice and self-respect. But in ei-

21. See Herbert H. Hyman and Eleanor Singer, eds., *Readings in Reference Group Theory and Research* (New York: The Free Press, 1968).
22. See James C. Davies, "Toward a Theory of Revolution," *American Sociological Review*, 27, No. 1 (February 1962), 5–19; quotation from p. 6.

TABLE 14.1.   CLASSIFICATION OF EUROPEAN, ENGLISH-SPEAKING, AND LATIN AMERICAN NATIONS BY DEGREE OF STABLE DEMOCRACY

EUROPEAN AND ENGLISH-SPEAKING NATIONS		LATIN AMERICAN NATIONS	
STABLE DEMOCRACIES	UNSTABLE DEMOCRACIES AND DICTATORSHIPS	DEMOCRACIES AND UNSTABLE DICTATORSHIPS	STABLE DICTATORSHIPS
Australia	Austria	Argentina	Bolivia
Belgium	Bulgaria	Brazil	Cuba
Canada	Czechoslovakia	Chile	Dominican Republic
Denmark	Finland	Colombia	Ecuador
Ireland	France	Costa Rica	El Salvador
Luxemburg	Germany (West)	Mexico	Guatemala
Netherlands	Greece	Uruguay	Haiti
New Zealand	Hungary		Honduras
Norway	Iceland		Nicaragua
Sweden	Italy		Panama
Switzerland	Poland		Paraguay
United Kingdom	Portugal		Peru
United States	Rumania		Venezuela
	Spain		
	Yugoslavia		

SOURCE: Seymour M. Lipset, "Some Social Requisites of Democracy: Economic Development and Political Legitimacy," *American Political Science Review*, 53 (March 1959), 74.

Man tends to perceive his gratifications and deprivations in relation to those of his neighbors. Thus, the fact that he "has it pretty good" or that "things aren't as bad as they used to be" is generally scant comfort to someone who sees that other people have things much better.

ther case, it seems reasonable to hypothesize that industrialization instills rising expectations and thus creates conditions that can lead to revolution.

The failure of orderly change. There is little probability of revolution when there is stability, either of the "no hope, no expectations" type or of the "continuing hope" type—when growing and changing needs and expectations can be and are satisfied. The difficulty for developing countries is that no one has yet discovered how to lead them from "no hope" to "continuing hope" without resorting to violent conflict of some sort. Fidel Castro, for instance, as a young lawyer running for election to the Cuban legislature in 1952, became altogether disillusioned with legal means of instituting social change when Fulgencio Batista made

23. From an interview with Fidel Castro in *Playboy*, 14 (January 1967), 63–64.

himself dictator that year through a coup d'état. As Castro later recalled:

I already had some very definite political ideas about the need for structural change. Before the coup, I had been thinking of utilizing legal means, of using Parliament as a point of departure from which I might establish a revolutionary platform and motivate the masses in its favor—not as a means of bringing about these changes directly. I was now convinced that it could be done only in a revolutionary way. I had acquired enough sense of reality to understand that.

. . . In Cuba, people had been talking so long about revolution and revolutionary programs that the ruling class paid no attention anymore. They believed that ours was simply one more program, that all revolutionaries change and become conservative with the passage of time. . . .[23]

It is clear that the Cuban ruling classes, like those still in power in many developing countries, considered basic reform neither desirable nor possible. The challenge to such countries, then, is not only economic but also political. There is a need for a national consensus that recognizes the rising expectations of the majority, who now live below the poverty line, and that provides the means for these people to improve their lot without resorting to violence. Conflict can remain orderly, as we have noted, only insofar as the out-groups in any situation continue to perceive that they can achieve their goals by following what D. B. Truman has called "the rules of the game."[24] If they perceive their goals to be blocked or the means to achieve them to be unacceptable, they may begin to question the rules and, under certain circumstances, to challenge them through the use of force.

Revolution in the U.S.A.? The role of consensus in a society's political life should now be clear. "Political stability and instability," as Davies notes, "are ultimately dependent on a state of mind, a mood, in a society."[25] Currently, the mood in American society is more uncertain than it has been in over a century. The existence of near-universal consent to the political system

can no longer be taken for granted. Not only the capacity but even the motivation of government is being widely questioned.

But if revolution is in the air, there is considerable vagueness as to who is going to overthrow the present political system and to what end. That millions of Americans are poor is fully established. It is unlikely that most of these poor fail to perceive how much worse off they are than other Americans. And the systematic exclusion of those at the bottom of the socio-economic scale from policy-making positions would seem to discourage them from believing that they can improve their situation by working within the system. Does this mean that the poor will rise up in revolution?

As a group, the poor in America have no unity. Poor whites and poor blacks form no common front. Some attempts have been made to unite the various minorities, but Indians and Puerto Ricans, Alaskan Eskimos and Mexican Americans, even urban blacks and rural blacks

---

24. Truman, *op. cit.*, pp. 393, 513, and elsewhere.
25. Davies, *op. cit.*, p. 6.

The nation-wide postal strike of March 1970 was indicative of the fact that the great American consensus is apparently being eroded. In Manhattan some fourteen thousand mailmen opposed federal law by walking off their jobs on March 3, causing Post Office Department officials to suspend mail service in New York City.

have different problems and different interests. And the American poor, unlike the poor in many other countries, constitute a minority of the population. A revolution of "the poor" seems very unlikely at the present time.

What, then, of a black revolution? The outbursts of burning and looting that have occurred in black ghettos have represented rebellion against the law but, even more, against a socioeconomic condition created by racial discrimination. These riots have been the work of a minority of frustrated urban blacks. A minority within this minority is avowedly revolutionary, calling for black separation and war against Whitey. But the great majority of American blacks are interested primarily not in destroying the present political system but in improving their position in it. While feelings of frustration and bitterness are so intense for some that violence seems to them the only means by which a fair share of wealth, power, and prestige can be achieved, neither logic nor ideology supports seizure of the United States by black Americans.

At the same time, it can be said that the poor in the United States, spearheaded by the blacks, are involved in what Kenneth Keniston has called "a continuation of the old and familiar revolution of the industrial society, the liberal-democratic-egalitarian revolution that began in America and France at the turn of the 18th century and spread to virtually every nation in the world."[26] Aimed at an equitable distribution of societal rewards—wealth, prestige, and power—this "revolution" has fairly well met its promise for most Americans. But, as noted in our discussion of social stratification (Chapter 7), the very successes of the American system have also made its failures more glaring.

Violent revolution in the United States is being preached not only by a radical black minority but also by a minority of young (and not-so-young) white Americans. This minority is divided into a number of factions, which form shifting alliances among themselves and, at times, make common cause with nonviolent, nonrevolutionary civil rights and antiwar organizations. While some of the so-called student radicals may have ties with the Communist party, the American revolutionary wing, like similar student groups in western Europe, is characterized by a strong anarchistic bent, as its violent attacks on campus and civic authorities attest.

The student revolutionists have worked out techniques that make university officials, police forces, and political leaders appear to be either cowardly or brutal and generally shameful; but these revolutionists seem to pose no direct threat to the political system. This is not because of their lack of numbers: revolutions are always launched by minorities and usually by middle-class minorities like this one. But, thus far at least, they have come up with no coherent program of their own that bridges either the generation gap or the gap between them and the majority of their contemporaries, particularly among the lower-middle class, the working class, and the poor. When student revolutionaries launch attacks on authority in the name of ending the Vietnam War or opening university enrollment to blacks and the curriculum to Black Studies, campus support is often widespread—particularly if the administration is pushed into taking repressive action. These are popular causes. But the revolutionists' call for the violent destruction of the American system awakens no such enthusiasm. Nevertheless, the student radicals are contributing to the social and political uneasiness of the times.

And a revolution of a new kind *is* taking place—the cultural revolution of the young.[27] Participants in this cultural revolution far outnumber the campus political revolutionists. Like the political revolutionists, they are predominantly white and middle class. Like them, too, they look with distaste on "the establishment," "the system"—in short, the way things are, and the way things are run, in affluent, industrialized, computerized (to them, dehumanized) America today. According to Keniston, theirs is "a newer revolution concerned with newer issues, a revolution that is less social, economic, or political than psychological, historical, and cultural. It is less concerned with the quantities of things than with their qualities, and it judges the virtually complete liberal revolution and finds it wanting."[28]

It is possible that this alienation of many young people from the "system" (whose moral legitimacy they reject) is a more serious threat to the status quo than the "nonnegotiable de-

26. Kenneth Keniston, "You Have to Grow Up in Scarsdale to Know How Bad Things Really Are," *New York Times Magazine*, April 27, 1969, p. 129.

27. See Theodore Roszak, *The Making of a Counter Culture* (New York: Doubleday & Company, Inc., 1969).

28. Keniston, *op. cit.*

VIEWPOINTS   REVOLUTIONARY TRENDS IN THE UNITED STATES

The most important political conflict in the United States today is the generational conflict.

We are all under the influence of a collective historical unconscious.

Communism to us means not Stalin, but the heroic romantic Fidel/Che/Viet Kong.

Hitler to us represents words on paper.

We are optimistic and idealistic about the future. Our 1984 will be great.

The economy is rich; overproduction is the problem; now everyone can dig life, and we know it. Life can be a trip.

We want a communal world where the imagination runs supreme, and where human institutions respond to human needs. Feeling and emotion will go unsuppressed. Everything will be free. People will go to museums to look at dollar bills. There will be no nations, only rich communities and rich cultures. . . .

The generational revolt in Amerika is not explained by Freud or Marx. It is a war between historical generations, and the future belongs to us because Amerika is defending institutions and ideas like ownership and nation—and these institutions no longer respond to needs.

We did not build CBS, the Democratic Party or the Catholic Church, and we want no place in them.

Vietnam is a case of the past trying to suppress the future.

The Amerikan economy has rendered white middle-class youth and black working-class youth useless, because we are not needed to make the economy run. Uselessness breeds revolution. The only exciting and meaningful thing to do in Amerika today is to disrupt her institutions and build new ones.

Subvert!!

That's the task of every young person. Spread ideas that undercut the consistent world of Amerika, and then top it off by burning her symbols—from draft cards to flags to dollar bills. . . .

Previous revolutions aimed at seizure of the state's highest authority, followed by the takeover of the means of production. The Youth International Revolution will begin with mass breakdown of authority, mass rebellion, total anarchy in every institution in the Western world. Tribes of long-hairs, blacks, armed women, workers, peasants and students will take over.

The yippie dropout myth will infiltrate every structure of Amerika. The revolution will shock itself by discovering that it has friends everywhere, friends just waiting for The Moment.

Jerry Rubin
Do It! Scenarios of the Revolution

Sinking the system is . . . the announced objective of the revolutionary young and the black militants. But there has always been the quality of a play-acting nose-thumb, rather than real revolution, about the uprisings of the young and the blacks. Their revolution has not smelled real, simply because the radical young and the black militants do not have either the numbers or the power to make a revolution. Both together represent a small national minority.

The mailmen [who broke the law to go on strike in March 1970], by contrast, represent something close to a national majority. They are, by and large, good family men, steady wage-earners, perfectly representative of what the sociologists call the Lower Middle. If the Lower Middle is to begin thumbing its nose at the government, then the comfortable American bourgeoisie has real reason to worry, and worry hard.

The Declaration of Independence proclaims that "governments are instituted among men, deriving their just powers from the consent of the governed. . . ." But what happens when the governed do not consent?

The mailmen were, of course, perfectly aware that their strike was against the law, and that the government had power—on paper—to put them in jail for striking. But they did not believe that power was just, and more important, they did not believe that it would be exercised. So they struck. . . .

. . . It has been entertaining to read the agonized tut-tuttings of the same editorialists who have been so wonderfully sympathetic when the student radicals or the black militants break the law. When the Lower Middle gets angry enough to defy the law, those famous limousine liberals have reasons to fear for their limousines and, just conceivably, for their lives.

For at least symbolically, the defiance of the mailmen was not play-acting—it was genuinely revolutionary. When large numbers of ordinary citizens decide that they can profitably defy the government, then a political system really can go to pieces—"all at once and nothing first, just as bubbles do when they burst."

There is not much doubt, either, about the kind of vengeful and profoundly illiberal regime that could replace the burst bubble. "You don't need a weatherman to know which way the wind blows," wrote Bob Dylan. Indeed you don't. It blows, hard and strong, toward the right. It could be blowing toward some peculiarly American version of Fascism.

Stewart Alsop
Column in *Newsweek*

mands" and "confrontations" of the avowed revolutionists, black or white, poor or middle class. It is also possible that, in time, the attempt of the "counter culture" to find a better way of living will be translated into political terms and that the "newer revolution" will not only complete the old but transform politics and society.

POLITICAL DECISION-MAKING IN THE UNITED STATES

Political sociologists, while recognizing the importance of formal political structures, are primarily interested in the *total* process by which political decisions are made. An important aspect of this process, as was pointed out earlier in this chapter, is the interplay of authority and influence. No simple distinction can be made between public and private spheres of control, nor between formal and informal power arrangements. Indeed, the view of political life as a total decision-making process tends even to obliterate the distinctions between federal, state, and local governments, since all interact with each other and since very similar processes go on at each level. With these considerations in mind, let us examine the decision-making process as it can be observed in the American political system.

COMMUNITY POWER STRUCTURES

Most of the research on political decision-making in the United States has focused on the interplay of authority and influence at the local level. More than a hundred cities have been studied in order to provide empirical answers to the question: Who governs, how, and with what consequences?[29] There has been an attempt to find regularized patterns within the community whereby decisions are made and implemented through the exercise of authority, influence, and possibly even coercion. These studies have been concerned not only with political parties and governmental bodies but with *all* groups whose activities affect the community and therefore can be taken as evidence of participation by the groups in its power structure.

The diffusion of community power. As we have noted throughout this book, the urbanization of the American population has meant increased contact between diverse peoples, lessened independence for each community, and a broadened range of extracommunity and nonpolitical involvements. With respect to community decision-making, one important consequence of these changes seems to be that power at the community level is becoming more diffused.[30] The increased heterogeneity of American cities means that social differences based on such ascribed characteristics as lineage and religion have become relatively less important in determining who will be influential. Furthermore, the growing number of issues to be resolved at the community level, and the growing complexity of those issues, have rendered simple power arrangements obsolete. In short, neither monolithic, one-man control by a political boss nor oligarchic control by a small, cohesive group of community leaders seems to be consistent with the complex fabric of contemporary urban life.

Studies to examine the power structure in American cities with populations of 25,000 or more have produced evidence that the prevailing pattern is amorphousness—that there is no stable pattern at all. And to the extent that there is a recognizable trend in community decision-making arrangements, it is toward increased decentralization and pluralism.

Walton points to three trends that have contributed to the decentralization of community power:[31] (1) The continual movement toward absentee-owned industry. More and more corporations that originally were locally owned are becoming parts of national and international organizations. The one-industry town run by a single family has all but disappeared from the American scene. (2) The tendency of local gov-

---

29. Two recent summaries of findings are to be found in Claire Gilbert, "Some Trends in Community Politics," *Southwestern Social Science Quarterly,* 48, No. 3 (December 1967), 373–382; and John Walton, "The Vertical Axis of Community Organization and the Structure of Power," in the same edition of the same journal, pp. 353–368. The following discussion draws heavily on these findings and on D'Antonio and Form, *op. cit.*

30. The best documentation in support of this hypothesis can be found in Robert A. Dahl, *Who Governs? Democracy and Power in an American City* (New Haven, Conn.: Yale University Press, 1961).

31. Walton, *op. cit.,* p. 354.

ernments to become more and more involved with state and federal government. (3) The tendency for other groups within the community to have outside ties. Local professional and voluntary associations typically are affiliates of national associations; the organized life of the city is closely intertwined with that of its surrounding suburbs.

Organizations with extracommunity ties add new dimensions of power. For example, nationally owned industries can threaten to pull out of a community if their demands are not met; local government officials can go to Washington for help; a local interest group can call on the resources of a national movement. All of these patterns of influence are part of the growth process of the modern metropolis, and all of them point to the deconcentration of community power.

The deemphasis of political conflict. More and more local governments have turned to nonpartisan elections and a council-manager system of government in the belief that party politics engenders conflict, is inadequate for coping with important issues on a reasonable basis, and thus is "bad" for the community.[32] The council-manager system, by contrast, is set up on the model of business efficiency and prides itself on being free of both corruption and conflict. This twentieth-century structural form currently seems to be the middle-class ideal in the United States. It is predicated on the belief that citizens can resolve all issues on the basis of merit after reasonable discussion. Theoretically, power rests in the hands of a team of technical experts who can resolve all issues without conflict.

Partial support for this theory has been provided by comparative studies of communities with council-manager systems of government and those in which there are regular two-party contests for all positions of power. In one study of sixty-eight cities, for example, Gilbert found that 71 percent of the council-manager governments had low conflict levels, whereas the same proportion of the more political governments had medium to high conflict levels. (It should be noted that Gilbert had to create a special instrument to measure conflict levels, and that this represented an ex post facto analysis of the cities being studied.)[33]

Possibly the most important single finding

to emerge from this type of research has been that business and professional groups prefer a low level of conflict—"Are we going to have a government run in a businesslike manner or return to politics as usual?" They therefore incline toward government of the council-manager type. This has serious implications for the future of the democratic process at the community level. For instance, research in El Paso revealed that one consequence of a low conflict level in government was to exclude the large minority of Mexican-Americans (identified in the study by their Spanish surnames) from competitive participation.[34] Local governments based on the council-manager model seem more likely than others to have business and professional leaders as informal influentials on almost all issues, business and professional leaders as elected public officials, a minimum of representation for working classes and minority groups, and an increasingly heavy reliance on professional experts such as urban planners.

The available evidence suggests that political conflict becomes minimized in communities with a high proportion of middle-class citizens. In some communities pluralism, as measured according to competition for power by ethnic groups and perhaps by organized labor, can and does lead to factionalism and introduces a higher level of conflict into the decision-making process. But this raises the question of whether conflict is necessarily dysfunctional for the system—and, if dysfunctional, from whose viewpoint. In general, those who deplore all conflict as disruptive are those who already enjoy the advantages of wealth, status, and power. The real question, then, is how *much* conflict and what *types* of conflict are consistent with the democratic system.

---

32. The major types of municipal government in the United States are mayor-council and council-manager. Mayor-council governments may have either a strong mayor and a weak council (as in most of the largest cities) or a strong council and a mayor who is essentially a ceremonial figure. Under the council-manager plan, voters choose a small number of councilmen to set policy, usually in a nonpartisan election, and the councilmen hire a professional administrator—the city manager—who is responsible to them.

33. Gilbert, *op. cit.*, pp. 377–378.

34. El Paso had a weak mayor-council type of government but a competitive one-party primary. Conflict there had been minimized by the fact that labor unions were weak or nonexistent. See D'Antonio and Form, *op. cit.*

This roadside view in New Haven, Connecticut illustrates the bewildering hodgepodge of overlapping governments that is typical of most metropolitan areas in the United States. The lack of coordination among local governments is not only inefficient and expensive but also disconcerting to citizens, who often don't know who is responsible for what.

Politics as an avenue to influence. Traditionally in American society, the most important function of pressure groups at the local level has been to provide the lower classes with access to political power. For example, through ward political activity in the late nineteenth century, ethnic clubs were developed. In exchange for their votes, members of these clubs were given access to party office and, through the parties, to public office. Thus political parties become brokers of group interests. There is no reason why they should not also mediate the demands of the very latest interest groups, such as the Black Power movement.

Elsewhere in this text we have noted that one trend of the future may be the gradual con-

trol of major American cities by blacks. But the election of blacks as mayors of a few important cities should not be mistaken for significant black participation in political decision-making throughout the community. Effective control still seems to be a long way off. For example, a recent study of Chicago—a city whose population is almost one third black—found that blacks were systematically excluded from important policy-making positions, both public and private (Tables 14.2 and 14.3, pages 460–461).[35] In Cook County, which comprises most of metropolitan Chicago, only 2.6 percent of such positions were filled by blacks—despite the fact that more businesses are controlled by blacks in Chicago than in any other major northern city. The point is that they are not *major* businesses.

The authors of this study concluded that the power of the few black policy-makers in Chicago

35. Harold M. Baron, "Black Powerlessness in Chicago," *Trans-action*, 6, No. 1 (November 1968), 27–33.

TABLE 14.2. **THE EXCLUSION OF BLACKS FROM POLICY-MAKING POSITIONS IN GOVERNMENT, COOK COUNTY, ILLINOIS, 1965**

	POLICY-MAKING POSITIONS	POSITIONS HELD BY BLACKS	PERCENT
Elected Officials			
U.S. House of Reps.	13	1	8
State Legislature	120	10	8
Cook County—nonjudicial	34	3	9
Chicago—nonjudicial	59	7	12
Cook County—judicial	138	8	6
TOTAL	**364**	**29**	**8**
Appointive Supervisory Boards			
TOTAL	**77**	**10**	**13**
Local Administrative Positions			
City of Chicago	156	2	1
Chicago Board of Education	72	7	9
Metropolitan Sanitary Dist.	7	0	0
Cook County Government	13	1	8
TOTAL	**248**	**10**	**4**
Federal Government			
Civil Service	368	8	2
Presidential Appointments	31	1	3
TOTAL	**399**	**9**	**2**
GRAND TOTAL	**1088**	**58**	**5**

SOURCE: Harold M. Baron, "Black Powerlessness in Chicago," *Transaction*, 6, No. 1 (November 1968), Table 1.

was even less than it appeared, because they were nearly always excluded from the very top positions. No black had ever been elected to a legislative position in Chicago unless he had run in a district with a black majority; it was not enough (regardless of the candidate's merits) for blacks to be the largest single minority group in the district. Nevertheless, the authors concluded that increasing numbers of blacks *will* succeed in reaching policy-making positions. But having won admittance to the system, will this enable them to represent the best interests of their black constituents? Social scientists cannot yet venture an answer to this important question.

The question of business influence. Early studies of community power structures produced some evidence that men known as community leaders, whether inside or outside of political parties, are more likely to have come from the business sector of the community than from any other single sector. Perhaps more time and energy have been devoted to testing this hypothesis than any other concerned with the study of community decision-making.[36] In a sense, the hypothesis is a modified statement of the Marxian proposition that the economic institution is the controlling one in society.

The proposition of predominant business influence has two aspects: first, the assertion that business is the sector of the community that produces most of the decision-makers; second, the assertion that the businessmen comprising the leadership group do in fact act as an oligarchy, a small cohesive group that generally manages to control things. There is considerable evidence to support the first assertion, but the significance of this evidence remains subject to debate. For example, one simple reason why community leaders are likely to come from the business sector may be that there are so few career politicians at the local level. The assertion that businessmen have emerged as a new oligarchy, however, is challenged by evidence that businessmen often appear in opposing factions and that they do not necessarily gain their objectives.

One way to measure the influence of business or any other institution upon community decision-making is to try to spell out in detail the kinds of issues that come before a community. The most common issues of community-wide concern include attracting new sources of jobs, building new hospitals and schools, urban renewal, the war on poverty, local elections, and public welfare programs. The numerous studies that have been done on these issues reveal a number of things: (1) issues are less and less often the concern of only one institutional sector; (2) only a small number of persons are involved in the dynamics of resolving issues; (3) there is some overlap of personnel from issue to issue, but it is not great; (4) specialists, technical experts, and other noninfluentials can and do initiate and help resolve

36. For example, see Delbert C. Miller, "Industry and Community Power Structure: A Comparative Study of an American and an English City," *American Sociological Review*, 23 (February 1958), 9–15; Floyd Hunter, *Community Power Structure* (Chapel Hill, N.C.: University of North Carolina Press, 1953); and W. V. D'Antonio and H. J. Ehrlich, eds., *Power and Democracy in America* (South Bend, Ind.: University of Notre Dame Press, 1961).

important issues; (5) the business, political, and legal sectors of the community are the most involved; (6) the working class (through ethnic clubs, labor unions, and political parties) does exert some influence on certain decisions; (7) there is no preset pattern determining that issues will be settled within either the public or the private domain.

The controversy over the question of the extent of business influence in community decision-making has stemmed in part from different methodological approaches to the problem of community power. (See the Methodological Essays, pages 462 and 463.) Some sociologists have analyzed community power in terms of formal *positions* of authority; others have tried to determine which individuals in a community have the greatest *reputation* for power. In addition, political scientists have analyzed power structures by attempting to discover which individuals are carrying through or blocking community *issues*. Not surprisingly, these three approaches present different data and lead to contrasting hypotheses and theories. In recent years, however, most students of community power have combined at least two and usually all three approaches.

The most important finding that can be generalized from all studies to date is that no single pyramid of power has been uncovered in any American community. There is increasing evidence of patterns of power wherein fluid coalitions develop over specific issues and leadership is drawn from a large pool of citizens. At the same time, the decision-making game is clearly not yet open to everyone on an equal basis.

PATTERNS OF INFLUENCE AT THE NATIONAL LEVEL

The basic structure of the federal government in the United States as set forth in the Constitution is based on the separation of powers, a principle derived mainly from the writings of the eighteenth-century French historian and jurist, Baron de Montesquieu. Briefly, his idea was that kings and emperors were able to rule tyrannically because they exercised many

37. Montesquieu, *The Spirit of Laws* (first published 1748), Book 11, Chapter 6.

TABLE 14.3. **THE EXCLUSION OF BLACKS FROM POLICY-MAKING POSITIONS OUTSIDE OF GOVERNMENT, COOK COUNTY, ILLINOIS, 1965**

	TOTAL ESTABLISH-MENTS	% OF BLACK POLICY-MAKERS				
		NONE	1-5%	6-15%	16-50%	51%+
Business Corporations						
Banks	102	98	0	4	0	0
Insurance	30	28	0	0	0	2
Nonfinancial Corporations	240	240	0	0	0	0
Legal Professions	54	54	0	0	0	0
Universities	7	5	0	2	0	0
Voluntary Organizations						
Business & Professional	5	3	2	0	0	0
Welfare & Religious	14	2	4	7	1	0
Labor Unions						
Internationals	4	0	1	1	2	0
District Councils	23	13	0	5	5	0
Locals	33	14	2	8	7	2
TOTAL	512	457	9	27	15	4

SOURCE: Baron, *op. cit.*, Table 3.

different *kinds* of power. At the very least, Montesquieu argued, the same man should not be allowed to make the laws, carry them out, and judge people accused of breaking them.[37] The first, second, and third articles of the Constitution deal respectively with legislative, executive, and judicial powers and grant these powers to separate bodies and individuals. The same principle is basic to the distribution of power among federal, state, and local governments.

In practice, the literal separation of powers has been impossible to sustain. Through its ever increasing size and the vast resources at its command, the executive has become by far the most powerful branch of government. At the same time, the giant bureaucracies, civil and military, that have been created as administrative agencies within the executive branch have become policy-making bodies in their own right. Similarly, the judicial branch of American government, as represented by the Supreme Court, has periodically been accused of usurping

METHODOLOGY   **THE POSITIONAL AND REPUTATIONAL APPROACHES TO THE STUDY OF COMMUNITY POWER**

One of the most hotly contested issues in political sociology today is how best to study community power structures. Over the years three distinct approaches have emerged: the identification of those in positions of authority; the identification of those having a reputation for being influential in the community; and the analysis of how decisions are actually made on important community issues. As might be expected, the *positional, reputational,* and *issues* approaches yield different kinds of data and have been partly responsible for conflicting hypotheses and theories about the structure of community power.

The simplest and probably the most objective approach to the study of community power is the positional approach. Here, community decision-makers are defined as those persons who occupy the formal positions of authority in the community's institutionalized political, economic, and civic structures. Because they have authority, they are assumed also to have power. This approach makes no provision for the fact that persons not in formal positions of authority may exert influence or coercion on those who are, and thus be the effective decision-makers. Furthermore, even if a more perfect correlation existed between authority and control, identifying the persons in the top positions of authority would be only a first step in analyzing community power.

A more sophisticated approach, though a highly controversial one, is the reputational approach first developed by Floyd Hunter in the early 1950's. Here the investigator seeks out some fifteen to twenty-five persons who are presumed to be closely familiar with various aspects of community life. These persons, called "knowledgeables," usually occupy minor positions of authority in the major institutional sectors. They are interviewed about major local issues and problems and about the persons in the community whom they consider to be most influential. The investigator may ask them to compare influential persons within and between institutional sectors or simply to list an overall category of influential persons. Another question often asked in some form is: If you had to select a committee whose objective would be to get community approval on some issue, e.g., a school bond issue, which persons would you select for that committee in order to ensure its success, regardless of whether or not you know them personally? The hypothesis is that the names listed for this committee and those selected as generally influential will be highly correlated.

After interviewing the "knowledgeables," the researcher generally proceeds to the reputed "influentials" themselves, asking them similar questions. The influentials may or may not be asked to rank the persons selected by the knowledgeable judges. On the basis of the answers given by both knowledgeables and influentials, the researcher attempts to construct a picture of the power structure.

Critics of the reputational approach point out that the reputation for power is not a *demonstration* of power; at most, it represents power *potential.* Although this assertion is true, it is equally true that there has to be some reason why certain people are considered influential, and that generally the reason is their perceived ability to influence decision-making. Either they have done so in the past, are doing so at the present time, or are believed to be able to do so whenever they choose.

Another criticism leveled at the reputational approach is that the information gathered from informants is ambiguous because the investigator cannot always be sure that they are thinking in terms of recent or important issues. However, defenders of the approach insist that they can determine the scope of power that a reputed influential actually has through the use of probing questions.

Contemporary researchers using the reputational approach have modified Hunter's original techniques and have become increasingly careful in interpreting the data they obtain. But while recognizing the limitations of the approach, they insist on its continuing usefulness. It is important to know how community leaders *perceive* the power structure, they argue, because people *act* according to their perceptions of reality. Furthermore, the approach has yielded data showing that community power structures are much more complex than any analysis of formal authority would suggest.

For a detailed critique of the various research approaches to the study of community power, see Arnold M. Rose, *The Power Structure* (New York: Oxford University Press, 1967), pp. 255–280. For an elaboration of the reputational approach, see Floyd Hunter, *Community Power Structure* (Chapel Hill, N.C.: University of North Carolina Press, 1953).

METHODOLOGY   **THE ANALYSIS OF COMMUNITY DECISION-MAKING (THE ISSUES APPROACH)**

The *positional* approach implies that the power structure of a community is fully reflected in its formal systems of authority. It makes no provision for the fact that a person who has a position of high authority does not always enjoy a like degree of power, nor does it provide a means for measuring the influence of persons who lack formal authority but act as powers behind the throne. Used alone, this approach leads to the depiction of community power structures arranged in terms of simple hierarchies. The *reputational* approach, on the other hand, has been criticized for assuming that a reputation for influence necessarily implies some degree of actual power. For these and other reasons, the positional and reputational approaches have increasingly been combined with the newer *issues* approach.

The issues (or decision-making) approach was first systematically developed by Robert Dahl, a political scientist, and his associates. It assumes that power inheres in those persons who successfully carry through—or successfully block—action on community issues. Thus the key in determining the power structure is a detailed analysis of actual issues and the manner in which they are resolved. Dahl used the following operations to estimate the relative influence of different actors:

1. Restrict attention to "comparable" respondents who participate in a "single" scope.

2. Examine decisions where the number of direct participants is more or less the same during the period under investigation.

3. Assume that the following collective actions are responses of roughly the same strength or extent: (a) when a proposal initiated by one or more of the participants is adopted despite the opposition of other participants; (b) when a proposal initiated by one or more of the participants is rejected; (c) when a proposal initiated by one or more of the participants is adopted without opposition.

4. Determine the number of successful initiations or vetoes by each participant and the number of failures.

5. Consider one participant as more influential than another if the relative frequency of his successes is higher, or if the ratio of his successes to his total attempts is higher.

In his study of the power structure in New Haven, Connecticut (see page 230), Dahl chose for study three issue areas that cut across a wide variety of interests and participants: community redevelopment, public education, and nominations in the two major parties. In the area of redevelopment, eight major decisions were carefully examined for the period between 1950 and 1959. In the same time period there were also eight major decisions involving public education. In the political area, the period used for study was 1941 through 1957, during which time there were nine elections and eighteen important nominations by the two major parties.

The results of Dahl's New Haven study and of other studies using the same basic approach suggest that in most American communities there is little overlap among leaders or influentials from issue to issue. Some sociologists have argued that this demonstrates the pluralism of community power structures, whereas others have argued that the apparent diffusion of power may well be an artifact of the number and/or the nature of the issues chosen for study. Critics of the issues approach note that it fails to take account of those participants who lose out in issue contests, and also of important issues that may be settled behind the scenes. Another criticism sometimes leveled at this approach is that the issues chosen for analysis have usually been essentially political in nature. However, this does not reflect any inherent weakness of the method itself: issues-analysis can be applied effectively to issues that fall outside the political sphere (e.g., establishment of a charity fund or of a private hospital) no less than to those within it. The reputational approach, when used in conjunction with the issues approach, provides one means for identifying key issues of general community concern.

In recent years, studies of community power in the United States have tended to use a combination of the positional, reputational, and issues approaches. Overall, their findings have confirmed some degree of pluralism; a strong middle-class background for the overwhelming majority of influentials; and rather loose coalitions of influentials in the economic, political, and legal spheres of community life.

For Dahl's description of the issues approach as applied to his New Haven study, see Robert A. Dahl, *Who Governs? Democracy and Power in an American City* (New Haven, Conn.: Yale University Press, 1961), esp. pp. 332–333.

the authority of both the executive and the legislature.[38]

Contest and compromise. The forces of urbanization and technological change, together with the problem of providing for the national defense, have had an even greater impact on the national government than on the individual citizen. For as the society has grown more complex, so also has the machinery of authority. Inevitably, this has meant an increasing contest for power between the public and private sectors and within government itself.

One of the best examples of how far the traditions of American government can be stretched to maintain governmental effectiveness is the legislation dealing with the control of atomic energy.[39] At the end of World War II, Congress was faced with the problem of what to do with a multimillion-dollar program developed during the war under conditions of the greatest secrecy. This was the Manhattan Engineer District (MED), the unique organization that had produced the first atomic bombs. Now it had to be replaced by a permanent organization that would not only continue to produce atomic weapons but would pioneer the use of atomic energy for nonmilitary purposes.

For reasons of national security, such an organization would have to keep at least some of its operations secret. At the same time, since large sums of public money would have to be appropriated for it, some way had to be found of ensuring its accountability. Debate in Congress over what kind of organization was needed soon began to center on the issue of military versus civilian control. Because so much would

---

38. One of the best studies of the Supreme Court is still C. Herman Pritchett, *The Roosevelt Court: A Study in Judicial Politics and Values, 1937–1947* (Chicago: Quadrangle Books, Inc., 1969). See also Glendon Schubert, *Judicial Policy-Making* (Glenview, Ill.: Scott, Foresman and Company, 1965).

39. Among recent works, the most comprehensive is: Harold P. Green and Alan Rosenthal, *Government of the Atom: The Integration of Powers* (New York: Atherton Press, Inc., 1963).

Although increasing numbers of blacks are casting ballots at election time, there has not been a significant change in the influence of the black minority in political decision-making.

have to be done in secret, the individuals in charge of this organization would be extremely powerful. And there was the issue of whether any government agency should be allowed complete control over such an important area of scientific research as nonmilitary uses of atomic energy.

Finally, the all-civilian Atomic Energy Commission (AEC) was created—five men with equal powers, appointed by the President but functioning independently of him as a kind of high-level policy-making board. Day-to-day operations were placed under a general manager, the Commission's chief executive officer, who could be either a military officer or a civilian. The chief of the Military Applications Division *had* to be a member of the military. In addition, Congress retained some supervisory control through the unique device of the Joint Committee on Atomic Energy (JCAE), composed of members from both the House and Senate. The AEC was explicitly required to keep the JCAE "fully and currently informed" so that the JCAE could at any time recommend legislation on atomic energy to the Congress. As one study noted at the time, in effect this made Congress a party to all decisions of the AEC with regard to the industrial and commercial applications of atomic energy.[40] The AEC's proposed budgets were to come before the House and Senate Appropriations Committees in the usual manner.

More than twenty years later, most of the essential features of the original Atomic Energy Act of 1946 survive virtually unchanged. From being a "watchdog," the JCAE has developed into a major initiator of policy. At the same time, in the opinion of most researchers and others experienced in this field, American policy in the field of atomic energy is initiated not just by the JCAE or the AEC but by *all* the major branches and agencies of government, including the presidency. Despite the continuing need for secrecy, which makes it hard for public opinion

to function effectively in this area, there is no question of military domination. The arrangement has been so successful that some members of Congress have urged that a joint committee be similarly established to oversee the Central Intelligence Agency.

Is there a power elite? During the 1950's, Floyd Hunter and C. Wright Mills both developed the thesis that America's top leadership formed something approaching a power elite—a kind of conspiracy on the part of a few to dominate the majority.[41] Hunter's depiction of the national power structure has been criticized as biased and inaccurate. Mills' theory, carefully documented with examples, is much harder to refute. It depicts a self-conscious elite whose members belong to the upper class and occupy upper-status positions in business, the military, and the executive branch of government. Mills' analysis of the social intermingling among business, military, and political leaders, of the movement from the military to business and from business to top political posts, of the domination of the political elite by the military and business elites, and of the importance of large campaign contributions by business leaders to political parties and politicians raises challenging questions about the relationship between influence and authority at the national level. The data presented, however, offer no proof of the existence of a power elite—that is, of a group that can and does get its way on most important national issues. As Mills' critics have pointed out, for every instance he presents of an elite controlling a decision, another instance could be cited in which the presumed elite failed.

Perhaps the chief merit of Mills' work was that it compelled others to produce alternative theories about the national power structure. One of the most carefully reasoned of these is the "multi-influence hypothesis" of Arnold Rose. Rose's main thesis, which is not unlike the one that has emerged from studies of community decision-making, is stated as follows:

Segments of the economic elite have violated democratic political and legal processes, with differing degrees of effort and success in the various periods of American history, but in no recent period could they correctly be said to have controlled the elected and appointed political authorities in large measure. The relationship between the economic elite and the political authorities has been a constantly varying one

40. James R. Newman and Byron S. Miller, *The Control of Atomic Energy* (New York: McGraw-Hill Book Company, 1948), p. 122.

41. See Floyd Hunter, *Top Leadership, U.S.A.* (Chapel Hill, N.C.: University of North Carolina Press, 1959); and C. Wright Mills, *The Power Elite* (New York: Oxford University Press, 1956). For criticism of this thesis, see Robert A. Dahl, "A Critique of the Ruling Elite Model," *American Political Science Review*, 52 (June 1958), 463–469; and Daniel Bell, "The Power Elite Reconsidered," *American Journal of Sociology*, 64 (November 1959), 238–250.

A reawakening of political interest and activity at the grassroots level indicates that today's average American is ready to assert his territory, power elite or not. The photograph at the right, taken by Dorothea Lange in the 1930's, shows an early example of the little man's protest against the power structure in American society.

Dorothea Lange, The Oakland Museum Collection

of strong influence, cooperation, division of labor, and conflict, with each influencing the other in changing proportion to some extent and each operating independently of the other to a large extent.[42]

Rose concluded that there are a *number* of power structures in American society and that no unified elite is in control of all or any of them. Within each such structure, however, a small number of persons hold the largest share of power. If businessmen have a disproportionate influence on government, it is because they enjoy advantages of education, knowledge, and money. But Rose felt businessmen had been less successful in influencing government since the 1930's than they were prior to that era. He was encouraged, moreover, by the resurgence of political activity on the part of voluntary associations, especially those concerned with such issues as civil rights and help for the elderly. Finally, he argued that the political elite controls the economic elite at least as much as the latter controls the former.

Rose asserted that politicians usually follow their own convictions in voting on legisla-

tion. It would therefore seem important to know whether their convictions are affected by their class and status—and if so, in what ways. For instance, according to a survey made by the Associated Press, "at least one of every five U.S. senators is considered to be a millionaire."[43] Does this make them more conservative or more liberal? And if some millionaire senators are liberal and others conservative, on what factors do these differences depend? Is personal wealth relevant at all here? These are the kinds of questions that need to be answered before we can make any firm generalizations about the national power structure in the United States. It seems safe to say that, as with community decision-making, power is more accessible to middle- and upper-income citizens than to those from the lower class. That national policy is thereby biased in their favor has yet to be conclusively proved.

42. Arnold M. Rose, *The Power Structure: Political Process in American Society* (New York: Oxford University Press, 1967), p. 2.
43. As reported in "One in Five Senators Is a Millionaire," by Harry Kelley, *South Bend Tribune*, March 6, 1968, p. 28.

The limits of influence. Early in 1958, President Dwight Eisenhower, worried about the increasingly negative public attitude toward foreign aid, decided to do something to alter public opinion. He asked Eric Johnston to bring together leaders of business and public affairs to discuss ways of keeping the people better informed about foreign policy and the national interest. The conference, held in Washington on February 25, 1958, was attended by some 1067 national leaders, who heard a bipartisan array of distinguished political leaders plead for support of foreign aid. Mr. Johnston himself admonished them that the day was only a beginning, a day for planting seeds which were to be nourished and cultivated in the months and years ahead.

In his book *National Leadership and Foreign Policy*, James Rosenau analyzes the results of a questionnaire survey of these leaders and then explains why the seeds that were planted in 1958 still have not taken root among the masses and why, given the complexities of our political structure, they may never do so.[44] How is it that these leaders, representing the highest income levels and most prestigious occupations in American society, and overwhelmingly favoring foreign aid, were unable to muster their power to make such aid more attractive to the American people? Certainly the group had many characteristics of a power elite, but its members—America's national nongovernmental leaders of business and public affairs—failed to mobilize public opinion.

Rosenau asserts that "leaders tend to specialize in 'issue areas,' and few local opinion-makers occupy positions which enable them to circulate opinions on international affairs." Conversely, it appears that national leaders may not be able to exert influence at the local level. Top General Motors executives may have more in common with top labor union leaders than either group has in common with GM branch managers or local union officials. Their lines of communication carry them to the executive branch of the federal government and not to the Congress. But congressmen listen to local leaders, and if those leaders lack an international perspective, issues such as foreign aid may continue to be roughly handled by congressmen,

who are more concerned with issues like unemployment and crime in their home districts. Members of the House of Representatives were ignored in the 1958 conference, with disastrous results.

If the study reveals a good deal about the limited power of occupational leaders at the national level, it also reveals a good deal about the power of Congress vis-à-vis the President and national leaders. It suggests further that local leaders may not be without some influence on national and international issues.

The power of the citizenry. Pessimism has often been expressed over the chances of an individual to influence the power structure at any level unless he is already part of it. In particular, the competition of well-financed pressure groups and giant corporations, all served by professional lobbyists, would appear to be too great. Nevertheless, the unaffiliated crusader does occasionally succeed in playing the role of giant killer. A recent example is Ralph Nader, who almost single-handedly, through his writing and public appearances, compelled the Congress to pass automobile safety legislation. He then went on to expose additional causes for consumer concern and to lead a corps of volunteers—Nader's Raiders—in investigations of the federal bureaucracy. Earlier, Rachel Carson's *Silent Spring* sounded the first clear warning against DDT and aroused sufficient public dismay to keep the danger from being ignored or forgotten. A century ago, persistent lobbying of state governors and legislatures by Dorothea Dix raised standards of care for the mentally ill all across the nation.

What chance has the ordinary individual of getting the government to act? In fact, the chances are much better than one might suppose, provided that: (1) there is a growing public awareness of a need for action; (2) the individual forms his own pressure group; and (3) the issue is one in which the government possesses some policy-making authority and on which it may be looking for an opportunity to act. Congressional hearings are set up for the very purpose of producing legislation, and, as Nader's experience indicates, the individual who speaks out authoritatively at a hearing may attract powerful support.

The legislator as broker. Since members of the House of Representatives must face the

44. James Rosenau, *National Leadership and Foreign Policy: A Case Study in the Mobilization of Public Support* (Princeton, N.J.: Princeton University Press, 1963).

electorate every two years, they are campaigning almost constantly. Because they are maintained in office only so long as they demonstrate their awareness of what their constituents think and want, they are especially capable of helping to formulate consensus on the national level. But to do this in a society as diversified as ours takes time and debate.

Federal aid to education is a case in point. This issue involved racial and religious controversy as well as concern for local autonomy and fear of federal control. From the first unsuccessful attempts to get aid bills passed to the voting of billions of dollars for education during the last two years of the Johnson administration, almost twenty years went by. Congress acts when it finds a sufficient consensus among the people, not before.

Another vital function of the congressman is to explain federal programs to the people. The federal government is now involved in one way or another in almost every community in the land, but often it has difficulty winning acceptance for its programs at the local level. This is where members of Congress come in. As one of them has put it: "These activities of explaining, justifying, interpreting, interceding, all help . . . build acceptance for government policy, an essential process in democratic government, and an especially important one, . . . given the circumstances of American social diversity and a decentralized party system." [45]

In many ways, then, the American legislator acts as a broker between the local citizens, to whom he is responsible, and the executive. If he plays the role well, he not only improves his chances of survival with the voters but also increases his influence with the executive—which in turn helps him to further increase his influence at home.

POLITICAL SOCIALIZATION

Political attitudes, like other aspects of culture, are transmitted from one generation to the next by the process of socialization (Chapter 5). In democratic and totalitarian countries alike, young people are indoctrinated with the belief that their country is "best of all" and that its institutions are fully legitimate. A society approaches Linton's political ideal of the primitive tribe (page 448) to the extent that its members accept the political culture as right, moral, and the best possible solution to the problem of maintaining social order.

THE INFLUENCE OF FAMILY AND CLASS

In American society, there is some controversy over whether the home, the school, or some other agency of socialization such as television is most influential in forming children's political attitudes. But it seems that, regardless of what the school or the mass media could do in this area, the family is still dominant. Unconscious, casual learning is more vital to political socialization than formal learning. Very little about political parties, the reasons for their existence, or the differences between them is taught in American schools; indeed, the whole subject of political conflict is played down. Thus the child learns about Republicans and Democrats by taking over the attitudes of his parents. Some children rebel completely against their parents' political values, of course, and many—especially the better educated and the upwardly mobile—change their views somewhat as they grow older. But the great majority do not, at least not in any important respect.

There appears to be very little we learn in childhood that may not affect our political behavior as adults, for political behavior is not something apart. In effect, we *are* politically as we live and think socially. Thus, the middle-class child is developing political attitudes when he learns who "the poor" are and what makes up "a slum," and when he comes to recognize the various ethnic and other minority groups in his society. The whole spectrum of class-related values—degree of ability to trust other people, degree of personal autonomy permitted or obedience demanded, degree of willingness to plan ahead, and so on—all arise through socialization, and all shape political thinking and perception.

45. John Brademas (Congressman, 3rd District, Indiana), "The Emerging Role of the American Congress," *Proceedings of the Indiana Academy of Social Sciences* (1968).

DIFFERENTIAL SOCIALIZATION

Increasingly, political socialization in the United States is becoming problematic. Rising levels of educational sophistication make it less and less likely that society's members will accept without question the belief that existing institutions are necessarily "best." Furthermore, given the size and complexity of modern American society, *uniform* political socialization is virtually impossible. Family and school, ethnicity, and

46. Gabriel Almond and Sidney Verba, *The Civic Culture: Political Attitudes and Democracy in Five Nations* (Princeton, N.J.: Princeton University Press, 1963).

social class all act as differential factors in socialization, whether political or otherwise.

Political socialization in support of democratic pluralism seems to work most effectively in American society for the middle and upper classes, whose position it tends to support. But even among these dominant segments of the population the level of political apathy appears to be relatively high. For example, turnout in American presidential elections among those qualified to vote has averaged only about 60 percent in recent years, as compared with figures of between 70 and 90 percent for most other industrial democracies.[46] If other types of political activity are taken into account, the percent-

Next to the family, the school is probably the most influential agent in the formation of children's political attitudes. In totalitarian and democratic countries alike, the educational system indoctrinates young children with the belief that their country is "best of all" and that its institutions are fully legitimate.

age of the politically active is much lower. In one study, for instance, a representative sample of the American electorate was classified in terms of five different criteria of political participation.[47] Only 10.3 percent were rated "very active," and 16.8 percent as "active"; the remainder—72.9 percent—were either "inactive" or "very inactive."

Significantly, the level of political apathy becomes disproportionately high among those people in American society who are poor and subject to discrimination—although these individuals are precisely the ones who would seem to have the most to gain from making use of the democratic political institutions. In the study just cited, only 12 percent of those at the lowest income level fell into one of the "active" categories, compared with 69 percent of those at the highest income level. Differences in education appeared to reinforce this effect. An individual with a college education was over five times as likely to be "very active" as one with only a grade-school education. The same general picture is reflected in many other studies, before and since.[48] In general, it can be said of American society that the more a group is deprived and discriminated against, the lower is its level of political participation. Voter turnout among American blacks, in particular, has always been low, even in areas where there has been no attempt to prevent blacks from registering or voting.[49]

From what we know of the socialization process, it is not surprising to find data indicating that political apathy is readily transmitted from parents to children. One study of schoolchildren, for example, revealed that more than twice as many of those with college-educated mothers had taken at least some interest in a presidential election campaign, as compared with those whose mothers had only completed grade school. At the ninth-grade level, three times as many children with low-income parents admitted to showing hardly any interest, as compared with children of high-income parents.[50]

The authors of another study, the most comprehensive ever made, found that lower-class children of all ages had less confidence in their own and other people's ability to influence the government than did children from the classes above them. Consider, for example, the attitude of this boy from a working-class home:

"Richard, if the President did something that people didn't like what could they do?"

"The people can't do anything. They can't go to the White House and tell him what to do because he makes all the decisions. If the people don't like it, too bad for them."[51]

Studies such as these raise the question of whether the socialization being accomplished through the school and other agents is effectively maintaining the political consensus upon which our system of government depends.

47. R. E. Agger and V. A. Ostrom, "Political Participation in a Small Community," in Eulau, Eldersveld, and Janowitz, eds., *op. cit.*, pp. 138 ff.

48. See especially Lester W. Milbrath, *Political Participation* (Chicago: Rand McNally & Company, 1965).

49. *President's Commission on Registration and Voting Participation* (Washington, D.C.: Government Printing Office, 1963). Compare Donald R. Matthews and James W. Prothro, *Negroes and the New Southern Politics* (New York: Harcourt Brace Jovanovich, Inc., 1966).

50. From a study by H. H. Remmers, summarized by Herbert H. Hyman in *Political Socialization: A Study in the Psychology of Political Behavior* (New York: The Free Press, 1969), Chapter 3.

51. Robert D. Hess, "Political Attitudes in Children—Do Our Schoolteachers Subvert Solid Social Growth?" *Psychology Today*, 2, No. 8 (January 1969), 28. The data are from Robert D. Hess and Judith V. Torney, *The Development of Political Attitudes in Children* (Chicago: Aldine Publishing Company, 1967).

SUMMARY

Modern political sociology can trace its beginnings to Max Weber, who shifted the focus of analysis from political ends to political means. This involved paying more attention to the phenomenon of *power*. All political power can be classified as legitimate or illegitimate. *Coercion*, based on the illegitimate threat or use of force, is a sign of political weakness. The power of stable political systems, by contrast, is based on some pattern of legitimate *authority*: traditional, charismatic, or legal-rational. The third kind of power, *influence,* can be considered a mixture of legitimate and illegitimate power. Under the American system, political influence is often channeled through the political parties and through interest and pressure groups.

No political system can operate for long without at least some degree of *consensus,* a pattern of shared norms and values that provides the basis for legitimate authority. Democracy is especially dependent on consensus because it makes many demands on the cooperation and self-restraint of its citizens. Even nations that are formally democratic may lack stable democracy because they have failed to develop that particular pattern of consensus which Almond has called a "secular political culture."

Political stability is threatened when substantial numbers of people perceive their goals as blocked under the existing system. Usually the effect of total deprivation is political apathy, but when the deprived begin to see their lot as capable of improvement, they are likely to lose their apathy and start making demands that may lead to revolution, especially if there is no basis for hoping that improvements can be effected *within* the system. These conditions presently exist in many of the developing countries. In the United States, a number of political, ideological, and economic factors work against the likelihood of a violent revolution; but with a significant minority feeling economically deprived and politically ineffective, and with a growing number of middle-class youth feeling alienated from the political system along with the rest of the established culture, political stability in America nevertheless remains problematical.

The structure of political decision-making in the United States demonstrates the society's traditional concern for democratic freedom and the diffusion of power. In general, local governments seem to be becoming more rather than less pluralistic, a trend that is largely the result of growing economic and political interdependence. Studies show that community leadership tends to come from the business sector, especially under the council-manager system, but such studies have failed to disclose evidence of unified power structures or to determine the effects of business influence on community government.

The formal structure of the federal government, as of American government generally, is based on the diffusion of power, but total separation of executive, legislative, and judicial powers has been impossible to maintain. Studies of the national power structure, like those of community power structures, disclose a pattern of multiple influences, despite some plausible attempts to show the existence of a power elite. The ability of national leaders to exert their influence is more limited than is often supposed, especially at the local level. The ordinary citizen, though relatively powerless as an individual, can sometimes still make his influence felt. Congress is the organ of government most responsive to the wishes of the people, and it usually acts when it finds a consensus.

How effectively adults relate themselves to the political system can be shown to stem from their early political socialization, in which the influence of the family is predominant. Studies of political socialization in the United States show that it is most effective, in terms of maintaining a political consensus, for members of the middle and upper classes. Its effectiveness is progressively diminished by low income and low status, which have been shown to correlate with a lack of interest in politics and feelings of political ineffectiveness.

15

The Economic Order

THE DEVELOPMENT OF MODERN INDUSTRIALISM

The Preindustrial Organization of Work. The Factory System. The Rise of the Corporation.

INDUSTRIAL ORGANIZATION: MANAGEMENT

The Formal Bureaucratic Structure. Informal Patterns of Interaction.

INDUSTRIAL ORGANIZATION: LABOR

Labor Unions. Human Relations and the Worker.

THE WORKER IN INDUSTRIAL SOCIETY

Work and Alienation. Occupational Choice and Occupational Mobility. Unemployment. Technological Displacement. Retirement. Changing Attitudes Toward Work.

Industrialization, as we have seen, is not simply a matter of economics. On the contrary, it is accompanied by social processes, such as urbanization, that involve fundamental changes in people's lives. As a result of industrialization, society itself comes to be organized along different lines. Neither its institutions nor its values can ever be the same again.

A society's economic institution consists of the arrangements it makes for the production, distribution, and consumption of goods and services. To date, sociological research has been devoted primarily to the empirical study of contemporary work organizations and work groups and to the analysis of labor force statistics. Despite Max Weber's brilliant use of history, the historical approach is not nearly so common. In this chapter, however, all three approaches will be combined as we seek to construct a general picture of economic man.

THE DEVELOPMENT OF MODERN INDUSTRIALISM

Although the Industrial Revolution is usually said to date from approximately 1780, the origins of the American economic institution go back to much earlier times. Trade is as old as civilization, and tools are at least as old as man. Before the modern union there was the medieval guild, and before the medieval guild there was the guild, or *collegium,* of the Roman Empire. Our direct line of development, however, is from western Europe in the Middle Ages.

THE PREINDUSTRIAL ORGANIZATION OF WORK

Between the tenth and the thirteenth centuries western Europe experienced a period of remarkable commercial growth. In the south, Italian cities expanded rapidly, while in the north thriving towns developed. Peddlers banded together in merchant guilds to control

trade, and in the towns workers formed craft guilds to shut out competition. Indeed, the towns themselves formed leagues for commercial purposes.

The guild system. The guild and the town were interdependent. It will be remembered from Chapter 9 that political autonomy (to at least some degree) and the presence of a market were among the defining characteristics of an urban community. The medieval craft guilds, each representing a specific craft, depended on the urban market for their existence. At the same time, the prosperity of the town depended on the economic well-being of the guilds, and it was the prosperous town that could purchase and maintain autonomy by providing income for the great lord or king.

Fundamental to the development of the guilds was the freedom of the townsmen. Neither slaves nor serfs could legally enter into the contractual relationships upon which these organizations were based. But towns opened the way to personal liberty for medieval man: "In general, a man who lived in a town for a year and a day was a free man, whatever his previous status . . . .[1]

The guild member was free in the sense that he was neither a slave nor a serf, but once admitted to the guild, he was by no means free to do whatever he wished. In addition to controlling recruitment, guild leadership determined the rank of its members. Indeed, the guild's system of social stratification was a rigid one. After three to twelve years of training, the apprentice would usually become a paid journeyman, working under the supervision of a master craftsman. More years would have to elapse before he could hope to become a master himself. All this was done in the name of upholding standards of craftsmanship. Work methods changed very little over centuries, because using methods with which the guild's elderly leaders were not familiar would have been subverting their authority. On the positive side, standards of craftsmanship, fostered by guild examinations and supervision, were very high, as medieval artifacts show, and so too, presumably, was the level of satisfaction that a skilled craftsman could derive from his work.

The domestic or "putting out" system. Under the classic form of the guild system—the form that prevailed, for instance, in late fourteenth-century Florence—the individual producer took care of the entire production process. He designed the product, obtained the raw materials and, with the help of his apprentice, if he had one, worked on every stage of the item until it was completed. He also sold it, usually directly to a purchaser though sometimes to a middleman.

It was this middleman, often himself a member of a merchants' guild, who finally undermined the craft guilds' economic and political independence. As markets expanded, craftsmen came to depend increasingly on merchants to sell their goods. Those who simply waited for prospective customers to visit their workshops and look over the finished goods could not sell nearly as much as those who regularly filled orders for shop owners and traders. And the merchants, being continually in touch with consumers, had a clear idea of what was in demand.

Soon the merchants were telling the craftsmen what to produce. When they also began to supply raw materials and take complete charge of marketing the products of the craftsmen, the formerly independent artisans were well on their way to becoming mere employees. The emphasis in production shifted from all-round quality to unit cost, from finely wrought individual items (a masterpiece was originally the sample of his skill that a journeyman produced to gain the rank of master craftsman) to large batches of goods of lower but more uniform quality.

To take advantage of expanding markets and to meet the demands of their customers, merchants also created the domestic or "putting-out" system. Briefly, this meant that several families, working in their own homes, regularly produced work for one merchant, who provided the raw materials or unfinished goods and paid by the piece. The system appeared in medieval Italy and by the fifteenth century was providing serious competition for the guilds, which tried —on the whole unsuccessfully—to regulate and even to suppress it. By the seventeenth century the putting-out system was the mainstay of the English woolen industry. Rural families supplemented the husbands' meager seasonal earnings as farm laborers by spinning the yarn brought to them in their cottages by clothiers' agents. Hence the term "cottage industries."

Increased production, spurred by population growth and expanding overseas trade, required increased specialization. Spinners spun wool into yarn that was passed along to weavers,

and so on until the finished, dyed cloth was produced. Within his home shop, the craftsman broke his work down into steps so that his wife and children, as well as any apprentices he might have, could help in the production process. Often these steps were simple enough to be performed by workers with very little skill. Thus division of labor and specialization within the work force grew.

The production process moved completely out of the control of the worker, who depended on the entrepreneur for the materials he worked with and for the distribution and sale of what he produced. No longer did the producer deal directly with the consumer; indeed, the two never met. Production had become impersonal.

THE FACTORY SYSTEM

By the middle of the eighteenth century, the idea of craftsmen producing goods for entrepreneurs had become well established throughout most of western Europe. In Great Britain a combination of factors—demographic, economic, political, technological, and social —opened the way for the development of the factory system and the emergence of an entirely new kind of relationship between capital, technology, and labor.[2]

Investment capital. Manufacturing consumer goods was an unusual way of making money in a society still dominated by landed aristocracy. Those not of noble birth who had succeeded in making money had usually done so in foreign or domestic trade, not by investing in land, buildings, machines, raw materials, and labor. All these things, once acquired, constituted *fixed capital*—capital that retains the same form over a long period. As Max Weber points out, investment by private entrepreneurs in fixed capital really marked the beginning of modern capitalism.[3]

In eighteenth-century Britain, entrepreneurs were able to obtain credit from country banks, but they received no help from the government. Their chief source of investment capital was

2. Much of the material in this section is based upon Wilbert E. Moore, *Industrial Relations and the Social Order* (New York: The Macmillan Company, 1951), pp. 17–39.

3. Max Weber, *General Economic History*, trans. Frank H. Knight (New York: Collier Books, 1961), p. 100.

their own profits, which they patiently plowed back into their infant businesses.

Machines and power. Machines and mechanical tools of various kinds had been used in agriculture and manufacturing since antiquity. So had water power. But the mechanical devices of the late eighteenth century were vastly superior, and the rediscovery of steam power—which, thanks to an advanced metallurgy, could now be adequately controlled—allowed them to run with a speed and uniformity impossible for the unaided human hand.

By 1780 a succession of mechanical innovations had revolutionized the British cotton industry. And in 1785 the steam-powered loom was introduced. While decades passed before it was widely adopted, this device freed manufacturers from the necessity of building their mills near running streams in the countryside and opened the way for the development of the factory town. With the application of steam power, the process of rationalizing production could be greatly improved—manufacturers could plan ahead. Later advances, such as harnessing electrical power and refining assembly-line techniques, were basically extensions of this rationalizing process.

The labor market. The factory system could not have come into existence without a large labor pool. In England, for instance, thousands of people were evicted from the land under the Enclosure Acts, and many were forced to seek work in the new factories and mills. Their only alternatives were to beg, starve, or endure the shame and discomfort of the local workhouse for the indigent. This situation, plus the fact that great numbers of Britain's rural poor were resigned to a hand-to-mouth existence in any case, helps to explain why a typical factory worker was prepared to put in a dawn-to-dusk day for wages that would buy little more than bread. Only by having the entire family working was it possible to eke out a living.

There is a temptation to think of the early factory employers as wicked men, exploiting women and children as well as male workers. Though some of them undoubtedly were cruel and callous, it must be remembered that this *type* of employment had never existed before. Society had not caught up with the task of defining the rights and obligations of employers in this new relationship. All previous types of employment,

except for the use of slaves in agriculture and mining, had been on a far smaller scale and had involved a far more personal association between employer and employee. The seventeenth-century baker's apprentice was not paid, but he was looked after; his master's obligation to him was a moral as well as a legal one. Relations between the factory owner and his "hands" were legal only. It was hard for an independent entrepreneur with a large investment to protect to feel any kind of moral obligation toward the ragged strangers he would have to lay off any time the market took an unfavorable turn.

From the point of view of early industrial capitalism, free labor was much superior to slave labor because in slack periods workers could be dismissed to shift for themselves. On the other hand, with workers coming and going, it was necessary to keep training new employees. Because of this problem, the employer tried to reduce the productive process to a series of steps that did not require a high level of training or skill.

Shop production. The factory system was a direct result of the economic advantages to be derived from "shop production"—housing each stage of the production process under one roof. During the early industrial period, when transportation was a major problem, it paid the manufacturer to locate his plant as close as possible to everything he needed, including labor and the products of other manufacturers. In modern terms, however, "one roof" has organizational rather than physical connotations; it refers to a single system of supervision and control.

By centralizing the system for producing goods, employers could impose much more effective controls on labor. In the putting-out system, a man set his own pace. In the factory system, he worked at the pace set by his supervisor and his machine. The shop concept also made it possible to use capital much more effectively. Concentrating production facilities in one strategically located building made it easy to move partially finished goods from step to step in the production process and to exercise effective control over quality.

With increasingly efficient machines, more dependable sources of power, expanding markets, greater amounts of investment capital, and a rapidly developing technology, the factory system of industrial production was well under way by the early decades of the nineteenth

The traditional craftsman of past societies was both designer and executor of his work, and he took pride in the fact that the end product of his efforts was serviceable as well as artistic. With the advent of the factory system, however, quality was often replaced by quantity, and the task that any individual performed became only one small part of a total operation. In today's world of mass production, traditional craftsmanship, as indicated by this Sudanese worker, has all but given way to assembly-line techniques.

century. As this organization of work continued to grow and spread, it had numerous consequences and implications for society as a whole.

THE RISE OF THE CORPORATION

Although the idea of the corporation was part of the culture base prior to the eighteenth century, this convenient means of multiple ownership and risk sharing did not come into its own until industrial capitalism developed around the factory system in the nineteenth century. Corporate ownership—that is, ownership of collective property by the fictitious "person" known as a corporation—tended to replace personal ownership as industrial enterprises increased in size and complexity.

A share in a corporation is, in a sense, a "piece of the company." The general principle of shareholding is that an investor owns and potentially controls a corporation to the extent that he owns a larger or smaller number of shares in it. Issuing such shares is not only a method of raising investment capital; it also limits the risks of ownership. If the business fails, only the assets of the corporation itself fall into the hands of creditors. The personal property of shareholders is protected, as it is if the corporation is sued.

Ownership and control. The advantages of corporate ownership over personal ownership were particularly obvious to industrialists in the United States, where the rise of manufacturing was paced by the rise of corporations. The greatest expansion took place after the Civil War, when the country was opened up to commerce by the railroads. Indeed, by the last quarter of the nineteenth century the success of such giant industrial enterprises as Armour and Company, U.S. Steel, and Standard Oil was causing so much public concern that some attempt was made to regulate them, notably through the Sherman Antitrust Act of 1890. This was the classic piece of antitrust legislation that defined "restraint of trade" as a federal offense.

But who is to be held responsible for the offenses of corporations? The stockholders who

"own" them? The truth is that the role of the stockholder is an ambiguous one. About a third of all the stock purchases in the United States—millions of shares each day—are held for less than six months.[4] Clearly, such shareholders can exercise little practical control over the corporations of which they are legally, if briefly, part-owners. Nor, for that matter, can the great majority of the longer-term shareholders, for whom active participation is limited to returning proxy forms that grant power to vote their shares. Many investors put their money into mutual funds, which are typically collections of stock holdings in perhaps a hundred different companies. In such cases the individual does not even choose the stocks that are bought and sold, and personal concern over any given corporation in the portfolio is unlikely.

Increasingly, the owners of stock in American corporations are not individuals but other organizations. Besides the mutual funds, these include universities, religious bodies, unions, foundations, and a great variety of other groups. Corporations gain control over other corporations, and these in turn are controlled by still other corporations. Thus it is becoming more and more difficult to specify precisely the structure of industrial ownership. One thing is clear, however: the corporation has swiftly become the most significant organizational form in the industrial structure.

The thesis that ownership and control of a corporation are essentially separate functions performed by separate groups of people was first argued systematically by Adolf A. Berle, Jr., and Gardiner C. Means in *The Modern Corporation and Private Property* (1932). There was much historical justification for this view. By the time of the Sherman Antitrust Act, the highly personal control of the old "robber barons" of industry was giving way to the more unobtrusive, collectivized methods of the investment bankers. When economists and historians asked themselves who was really responsible for the economic chaos that accompanied the stock market collapse of 1929, they found that they had to make a sharp distinction between the comparatively few men engaged in running commerce and industry and the millions who owned shares in commercial and industrial enterprises.

Surprisingly, Berle drew an optimistic conclusion from this. Separation of ownership from control, he thought, would mean that corpora-

---

4. Andrew Hacker, ed., *The Corporation Take-Over* (New York: Harper & Row, Inc., 1964), p. 6.

tions could be run by men for whom profit was not the primary concern. Even if these men did not now fully realize their public responsibilities, they would come to do so in time. For this view—as much an article of faith as a sociological prediction—he has been severely criticized. Nevertheless, it is a noteworthy fact that since the 1930's leading corporations have at least paid more lip-service to public responsibility than they did previously. What has not changed is the truly awesome concentration of economic power that they represent.

The new corporatism. Berle and Means also tried to find out who actually owned most of the country's wealth. According to their tabulations, in 1930 the two hundred largest corporations (excluding banks) controlled almost half the corporate wealth (again, with the exception of bank holdings) and almost a quarter of the total wealth. After examining the pattern of control industry by industry they concluded that 65 percent of American industry was owned by about six hundred corporations, whose active management could not amount to more than two thousand men. The trend has continued. Today, approximately 50 percent of American manufacturing facilities are held by about 150 corporations.[5] Given the great wealth of these corporations, the men who direct them (but who may have little or no part in their ownership) wield enormous power and influence. Some students of American society see this as a growing threat. C. Wright Mills, for example, concluded that major corporation heads, along with top government officials and military brass, formed a "power elite" that controlled national decision-making.[6] (For a critical analysis of this thesis, see Chapter 14, "The Political System," pages 465–466.)

It should be noted that most American workers still earn their livelihoods outside corporate structures and that it will apparently be some time before small businesses, education, and various other work structures—especially federal and local governments—are surpassed as employers by corporations. Nevertheless, because these other structures depend increasingly on stocks to finance pension funds and other long-term projects, very few segments of American society can remain indifferent to the economic health of the major corporations. At the same time, a growing number of Americans are becoming concerned about the far-reaching effects that corporate policies may have on the overall fabric of national life.

INDUSTRIAL ORGANIZATION: MANAGEMENT

In recent years sociologists have tended to concentrate on what goes on in economic organizations, and a large body of research has accumulated under the general head of "formal organizations." We shall use the distinction between formal and informal organizations that was developed in Chapters 1 and 2 as the main theme in this necessarily brief account of people's behavior in modern work settings.

THE FORMAL BUREAUCRATIC STRUCTURE

Although most studies of modern industrial organization have been made at lower levels, let us begin our review at the top. Nothing could be more rational, in a Weberian sense, than the managerial structure of a corporation—on paper. In practice, however, executives and managers depart from their prescribed roles in many ways.

First, what are these prescribed roles? At the top of the managerial pyramid, or hierarchy, is the chief executive, the company president. Just below this command role is a second level consisting of *top managers*—vice-presidents in charge of such divisions and functions as sales, manufacturing, research and development, and so forth. Next come various levels of *middle management*. While policy is formulated at the first two levels, it is implemented at this broad middle level. Here are the assistant vice-presidents, chiefs of sales divisions, and plant managers. Finally, at the lowest level of management, are the *first-line* supervisors: foremen, crew leaders, office managers, etc. Occupants of these roles are in regular face-to-face contact with the rank-and-file workers engaged in the actual process of production.

5. A. A. Berle, Jr., "Economic Power and the Free Society," in *ibid.*, pp. 101–102.

6. C. Wright Mills, *The Power Elite* (New York: Oxford University Press, 1956).

VIEWPOINTS GOVERNMENT AND THE ECONOMY

During most of the twentieth century, there has been a continual sporadic extension of governmental control over economic life. This trend reflects the widespread tendency to turn to government to remedy real or supposed evils, the centralizing effects of two world wars, and a shift in the intellectual climate of opinion away from individualism towards collectivism. The major economic challenge facing the United States in the coming decades is the reversal of this trend through the maintenance and strengthening of competitive private enterprise. A successful response is essential both for continued economic progress and, what is even more important, for the preservation of a free society.

The immediate position is in some ways more favorable than it has been for many decades. The magnificent post-World War II record of free-enterprise economies, the disappointing performance of central "planning" particularly in Britain but also in other western countries, and the glaring example offered by Russia of the suppression of personal freedom under this leading type of central planning, have all served to disillusion intellectuals and others about the merits of collectivistic solutions to economic problems. There is widespread recognition that government intervention is not a panacea. There is renewed understanding of both the efficiency of the market mechanism and its important role in the dispersal of power and the preservation of freedom. . . .

The major source of strength is the deep and abiding belief in personal and civil freedom that is so central a feature of Western thought in general and American thought in particular. Extension of governmental intervention in economic affairs threatens this freedom. . . .

In the American tradition, the "free" in free enterprise does not mean that established enterprises shall be "free" to do whatever they want including keeping out competitors by cartels, price-fixing arrangements and the like. It means "freedom" to compete, the "freedom" of anyone to set up an enterprise. Free enterprise means that the new entrant shall have neither special advantage nor disadvantage; it means a clear field for all, without governmental favors for any. . . .

There is little chance that competitive private enterprise will be destroyed by deliberate intent. The real problem is rather that a lack of understanding of both its importance and its meaning will lead to the adoption of policies that undermine it by inadvertence.

Milton Friedman
"Minimizing Government Control to Strengthen
Competitive Private Enterprise"

We have come to the point where the economy can be purposefully ordered for the common good. . . .

The important point is not the machinery of economic regulation but rather the widespread recognition that the basic characteristics of the economy are matters of public interest and responsibility. The sovereign importance of the market is a thing of the past. Even if it were to furnish a perfectly equilibrated price structure, the market would resolve few if any of our fateful dilemmas. No one has claimed that it would provide full employment, housing, schools, an equitable distribution of wealth, or a proper division between public needs and private wants. No one has claimed that an "unintervened" market would result in a rate of national growth commensurate with obligations to our own citizens and to those abroad whose situation is both desperate and of selfish importance to us. Such basic economic decisions will have to be brought into the realm of public responsibility. This means bringing economic activity under the legal order and making it a first responsibility of government and law. Otherwise our future as a nation will be determined by economic choices made privately, choices having to do with domestic matters such as the rate of growth and type of capital investment and internationally with the amount of foreign investment and the type of regime with which business is to be done.

How to achieve general acceptance of the necessity for purposive governmental policies in the economic order is a hard question. Americans want to feel free of constraints and obligations, especially those of government, but their world is increasingly and inescapably crisscrossed with the strands of mutuality. The biggest facts of their lives—air, water, power, security, noise, traffic, communication, income, home-building, crops, education, milk, drugs—are so complicated that government has already had to become heavily involved in them. Americans do not want to be caught up in multi-national responsibilities; they prefer not to think about the intricacies of multinational trade and finance. Yet these too are the necessary conditions of their existence and far more so those of their children. Since such momentous matters cannot be left in private hands, they end in government's hands. And since the decisions about such urgent and difficult matters are more and more to govern our common life, a new philosophy of government is necessary to meet the need.

W. H. Ferry
The Economy Under Law

Policy making. The president of a corporation is usually appointed and indirectly supervised by a board of directors. His central task is coordination in the face of change.[7] To insure the survival, prosperity, and growth of a business corporation, its president is expected to lead his top managers in the collective formulation of policy. Thus he works mainly with people, and his skill at judging their motives and capabilities may be as important to the corporation's welfare as any strictly technical knowledge he possesses. He also plays a key role in deciding which parts of the organization shall have what share of its resources, and he has to provide solutions for problems his subordinates cannot handle—for instance, emergencies. In so doing, he may have to decide if an exception can be made to policies he himself has formulated.[8]

A top manager also enjoys considerable autonomy, since he has full responsibility for planning, supervising, and coordinating activities for his division of the company. Even if the chief executive tells his top managers exactly what to do, he will probably not tell them much about how it should be done.

Middle management. The function of middle managers, who have their own bureaucratic hierarchy, is to implement the policy decisions they receive from above. They are normally not party to these decisions, nor are they in contact with workers to any significant extent. They make routine administrative decisions within the framework of established procedures, prepare reports of a mainly factual nature, and solve a lot of day-to-day problems that top managers have neither the time nor the inclination to deal with and that foremen are not supposed to deal with. The complexity of the middle management hierarchy—and it can become impenetrably complex—depends mainly on the size of the organization.

Line supervision. The largest single managerial group is made up of foremen, straw bosses, supervisors, office managers (in small offices), and inspectors. They are the last link in the hierarchy of administration—the final interpreters of executive orders. These orders, however, are spelled out to them by middle management in terms of their individual supervisory functions, not in terms of the overall policy being implemented.

INFORMAL PATTERNS OF INTERACTION

In theory, everyone in management has his place in the hierarchy, knows his place, and performs his proper function. Superiors direct subordinates, who carry out the instructions they receive. Equals cooperate for the good of all. But in fact, every managerial role involves characteristic problems, tensions, and frictions, some of which have been studied by sociologists.

The man at the top. The president of a corporation works with people, and the people he works most closely with are his own top managers. He adjudicates between competitive factions within the managerial group, hoping to maintain the loyalty and enthusiasm of each. He attempts to motivate greater commitment and encourage subordinates to greater effort. And he strives to keep in touch with what is going on at lower levels.

The leadership styles of chief executives vary considerably with the types of economic organization and the historical period. The personal, authoritative style of leadership that we associate, for instance, with the "tycoon" or "captain of industry" seems to have given way to the managerial "team" that operates through consensus.[9] But this may be mainly a difference of manner. The fact that a president establishes policy by conferring with his top lieutenants rather than shouting out orders does not necessarily alter the realities of power.

The power struggle. Relationships at the vice-presidential level are in many ways competitive. Change introduced into the operations of one division of the organization will inevitably have an impact on those of another. If such change makes a top manager's task more difficult or appears to place his division at a disadvantage, it is likely to be covertly or overtly resisted. Miller and Form maintain that vice-presidents often withhold information from the chief executive:

7. Burleigh B. Gardner and David G. Moore, *Human Relations in Industry*, rev. ed. (Homewood, Ill.: Richard D. Irwin, Inc., 1950), p. 62.

8. Delbert G. Miller and William H. Form, *Industrial Society*, 2nd ed. (New York: Harper & Row, Inc., 1964), p. 175.

9. Peter M. Blau, *Bureaucracy in Modern Society* (New York: Random House, Inc., 1956), p. 76.

Fear and distrust may grow as vice-presidents vie for power. Upward communications are likely to be highly filtered. A subordinate's future in an organization is often influenced appreciably by how well he senses and communicates to his boss information which fits the latter's orientation.[10]

Thus a vice-president's responsibility to make his division of the organization successful, plus his personal ambitions, introduces variables that lead to a conflict system within the organization and a consequent struggle for power. Although these social realities are not consistent with the cherished ideal of smooth teamwork and harmonious relationships, they may benefit the organization—but only if the competition is kept within bounds.

An important key to understanding relationships between heads of various divisions within an economic organization is the distinction between *line* and *staff* segments of the overall structure. Line divisions are those responsible for producing the things or processing the cases that constitute the organization's product. In a household appliance manufacturing corporation, for example, the refrigerators, washing machines, freezers, stoves, etc., that were assembled by workers would constitute the product and would be the responsibility of line divisions. Other divisions or departments are more or less supportive or ancilliary to actual processes of production, and their services are often called staff functions. In theory, these groups serve the line divisions so that a better product can be produced efficiently and marketed in effective ways. In practice, because of limiting perspectives on both sides, relationships between such segments of the organization are sources of considerable conflict.[11] At the center of these conflicts are the vice-presidents in charge of the various divisions.

The kinds of conflicts that can be generated between these various parts of an organization can be illustrated with an actual example from a firm that had decided to develop and market a new model of refrigerator. The engineering department was asked to work out a design for a moderately priced machine. Market research was given the task of assessing consumer acceptance of the new model. Accounting was

instructed to make a cost analysis so that the product could be produced at a competitive price. The sales division had to develop a suitable advertising campaign. The line division—manufacturing—was instructed to retool and add employees in readiness for producing the new refrigerator efficiently. But quarrels among the staff divisions over questions of cost and styling delayed actual production. Finally, when the first refrigerators began to come off the assembly line, the accounting division showed that the cost of production was still too high for the company to realize the needed margin of profit, and the staff divisions had to repeat the entire process of working out a mutually acceptable design.

Relationships between the heads of divisions, in other words, are likely to be strained and difficult because of the pressure each is under to make a good showing. The effective accomplishment of the task of one almost invariably interferes with the activities and goals of another. For this reason, the interplay among top managers is potentially one of continuing strain and friction.

Line and staff. A large part of the antagonism between line and staff divisions can be traced to the fact that most of their respective personnel belong to different generations and come from different social backgrounds. In one study based on analyses of company records in three industrial plants, it was discovered that the apparent efforts of staff officers to impress their superiors and so win promotion irked the line officers, who were, as a group, older and more experienced but less well educated and therefore less promotable. In addition, the line officers did not feel that they had anything to learn from the "college punks," "pretty boys," and "crackpots" in such staff divisions as production planning, industrial engineering, and industrial relations.

The staff officers felt that they were under constant pressure to demonstrate their usefulness but found that their college training was not of much relevance to the jobs they were called upon to do. They also learned that their suggestions would not even be considered unless they cultivated the "right" line officers. The line officers had been doing things their own way for so long that they were likely to approve very little and to sabotage any changes their superiors forced them to accept. The staff offi-

10. Miller and Form, *op. cit.*, p. 189.
11. Robert K. Merton, "The Machine, the Worker, and the Engineer," *Science*, 105, (January 24, 1947), 79–81.

The problems of the "amorphous" middle manager are in some ways linked to the differences between Max Weber's ideal bureaucracy and its counterpart in reality. Theoretically, the roles in a bureaucratic structure call for specialized skills, and these roles make up a ranking system that is rational and efficient. The middle manager, however, often finds that his specialized skill amounts to little more than his ability to shuffle papers, attend meetings, write reports, and solve day-to-day crises. He may become disillusioned because the competent performance of his role seems unrelated to or at odds with the overall rationality and efficiency of his organization.

cers reacted by classing their line colleagues as "bull-headed old codgers" and attributing their lack of cooperation to "ignorance." Actually, the line officers understood very well what the staff officers were up to and fought to preserve the carefully nurtured informal arrangements that made their jobs tolerable.[12]

The amorphous middle. Relations between top management and middle management also involve problems. In a large corporation, a top manager's contacts tend to be limited to middle management's upper levels. If he attempts to find out what is going on at lower levels, he is likely to be given either a report from which much information has been screened out or, if he makes a personal visit, a highly selective "guided tour." In either case, middle managers are not going to volunteer information that might be damaging to them. Nor do they like to accept orders as such. One study found that downward communications from senior executives that were intended as "instructions or decisions" were almost invariably classified by subordinate managers as "information or advice"—i.e., as something they could take or leave alone.[13] One possible interpretation of this form of distortion is that it represented status protection, a rejection of subordinate status, and a self-concept of autonomy.

As in staff and line relations, so in middle management generally, the difference in education between the generations is likely to cause conflict. Nowadays most corporations recruit middle managers directly from college graduating classes. These recruits are fed into the bottom level of the middle-management hierarchy in somewhat larger numbers than the company will eventually need. The hope is that, after a year or two, the less able ones will be weeded out and the others will begin to move up the organizational ladder.

One significant result of this system is that capable individuals without college degrees who,

in an earlier generation, could have hoped to rise to the top are now automatically barred from doing so and may become demoralized and apathetic. Another result is that the bright young men who someday are going to take over the corporation are often far too bright for the jobs they are assigned. In any case, there is not enough for them to do. According to one disillusioned report:

When I left Chrysler my name was on the door and I supervised the $175 million credit and collection operation for the nationwide network of about 6500 dealers. Despite the heaps of paperwork that I shuffled (mostly functioning as a rubber stamp) and stuffed into my attaché case to handle at home, I personally did nothing but make routine passive decisions. A high school graduate could have held down the job. . . .

The company organization was a nightmare. . . . Archaic mazes of obscure systems and procedures had to be puzzled out, eternal dalliance and indecisive vacillation had to be reckoned with, and, finally, there was the perpetual (and often futile) hunt for someone who would be man enough to give you a straight "yes" or "no." . . .

The result was stagnation, with a younger generation of management people more interested in playing the system than in reforming or developing it. Their pastime was called daylighting. Rising executives took to showing up, working several hours, and spending the rest of the day socializing and dawdling around with makework and trivia.[14]

The author of this bitter article, which was published with an accompanying editorial in the *Wall Street Journal*, quit business to teach law. A number of serious students of American business believe that this type of "executive dropout" may become a familiar phenomenon in years to come.

The foreman's dilemma. The first-line supervisor has been called, with some reason, the "marginal man" of industry.[15] By virtue of his role, a foreman is expected to carry out the orders of management. But since he has (in the present state of American industry) usually been promoted from the ranks of the workers and is in any case in continual contact with them, the workers expect him to adopt their point of view in conflicts with management. His freedom of action is sharply restricted by the established power of unions and the growing power of staff

12. Melville Dalton, "Conflicts Between Staff and Line Managerial Officers," *American Sociological Review*, 15, (June 1950), 342–351.

13. Tom Burns, "The Direction of Activity and Communication in a Department Executive Group," *Human Relations*, 7, No. 1 (February 1954), 73–79.

14. Hugh Crossland, "Confessions of a Business Dropout," *Wall Street Journal* (December 13, 1967), editorial page.

15. Donald E. Wray, "Marginal Men of Industry: The Foreman," *American Journal of Sociology*, 54 (January 1949), 298–301. See also Miller and Form, *op. cit.*, p. 208.

divisions. While it is his responsibility to insure that production schedules are met and that operations under his supervision are carried out according to company policy, he actually has very little authority.

Research analysts have discovered that the foreman may respond to these role conflicts and dilemmas in four principle ways:[16]

1. He may embrace the ideology of management. If he does, the workers make life uncomfortable for him on the job and reject him socially off the job.

2. He may retain the workers' ideology. Argyris reports that the overwhelming majority of foremen who have come up from the ranks adopt this role.[17] The consequence for the foreman is that relations between him and his chief become strained, and his further advancement into the lower executive ranks is rendered unlikely.

3. He may attempt to straddle the ideologies of management *and* labor. Such dual identification appears to be most common among newly appointed foremen. Upward mobility, however, has a way of changing perspectives, and over time such foremen are usually forced into one of the two attitudes already discussed.

4. Finally, isolation through exclusive identification with other foremen is a possible response. The first-line supervisor can join a foreman's union or other such organization, restrict his social contacts to others in similar roles, and attempt to become a "third party" in the organizational power struggle. This can resolve the foreman's conflicts, but its success depends on the attitude taken by other foremen in the same organization.

INDUSTRIAL ORGANIZATION: LABOR

Sociological research into work groups began, for all intents and purposes, in 1927 when the management of the Western Electric works at Hawthorne, near Chicago, invited an Australian psychologist named Elton Mayo to come and study the effects of physical work conditions on workers' output.[18] At that time, unions had little or no legal protection, and union organizers were widely persecuted. Sociological research into unions, on the other hand, began in the very different political and social climate of the late 1940's and early 1950's. By then, unions were well established and were under political attack for allegedly misusing their power.

These two traditions of research, then, cannot be approached in precisely the same way, though efforts have been made to combine them. Both throw light on the situation of the ordinary worker but from rather different angles.

LABOR UNIONS

The rise of labor unions was a direct result of the working and living conditions created by the Industrial Revolution. In the United States about 12 percent of the labor force was organized by 1920, but by 1933 that figure had been cut in half.[19] Then union membership began a rapid rise. This could not have happened without federal recognition of the right to organize, as embodied in the celebrated Section 7a of the National Industrial Recovery Act (1933) and the Wagner Act (1935). From 1936 on, largely through the crusading tactics of the newly formed Committee for Industrial Organization, which broke with the parent American Federation of Labor to pursue a philosophy of industrial rather than craft unionism, membership soared until in 1945 fully 25 percent of the American labor force was unionized. This included over 75 percent of the workers in transportation and about 50 percent of those in other major industrial areas. Important exceptions were agriculture, trade, finance, insurance, and government.[20]

These percentages have remained relatively stable ever since, though by 1960 the unionized portion of the labor force was down to 21.9

16. Gardner and Moore, *op. cit.,* pp. 48–49.

17. Chris Argyris, *Personality and Organization,* (New York: Harper & Row, Inc., 1957).

18. See especially Fritz J. Roethlisberger and William J. Dickson, *Management and the Worker* (Cambridge, Mass.: Harvard University Press, 1939), which describes the whole series of experiments initiated by Mayo. Two of the Hawthorne studies are summarized on pages 487–489 of this chapter.

19. Arthur M. Schlesinger, Jr., *The Coming of the New Deal* (Boston: Houghton Mifflin Company, 1959), p. 385.

20. H. Gregg Lewis, "Labor Unions: Influence on Wages," *International Encyclopedia of the Social Sciences,* Vol. 8 (New York: The Macmillan Company, 1968), p. 544.

In theory, local union members hold the ultimate power of decision-making in their hands. Like other bureaucratic associations, however, the men at the bottom tend to comply with the downward directives of national union leaders. This photograph shows a local union meeting in action.

percent.[21] Efforts are now being made to organize agricultural workers, but it is too early to estimate the success of this venture.

Union organization and union democracy.

In both formal and informal structure, American unions resemble other bureaucratic associations. But as economic organizations they have one differentiating characteristic: they are supposed to be run for the benefit of their members. As a result, the formal structure is always very democratic. Local unions send delegates to state and national conventions, and these delegates elect the executive officers of the national union. All major issues—whether to strike, whether to accept a particular contract, etc.—are decided by membership vote. In union meetings, any member may speak on any topic he cares to raise.

As a bureaucracy, a local union has a formal structure not unlike that of management. Policy is formulated by the president and the top

managers who make up the executive board. Another key role in the union hierarchy is the potentially powerful one of the elected secretary-treasurer, a full-time paid position in many larger unions. In smaller unions the only full-time paid functionary is likely to be the business agent, who represents the union in all disputes concerning the administration of its wage contract. In national unions another full-time employee is the international representative (unions of national scope that include Canadian locals are often called "internationals"), who seeks to ensure that the parent group retains some control over the locals and who takes a leading role in negotiations with top management.

Much of the administration of union policy is handled by committees. Grievances, the formulation of aims, and negotiations with management over contract terms are often committee matters. Members are either appointed or elected, and the roles carry considerable responsibility.

Direct day-to-day contact with lower-level representatives of management is carried on primarily by the union stewards. These are usually elected representatives of workers in a given department of a plant. The steward is the

21. U.S. Department of Labor, *Directory of National and International Unions in the United States, 1965*, No. 1943 (Washington, D.C.: Government Printing Office, 1965), p. 53.

person to whom the union member turns first if he feels he has a grievance. If the steward cannot handle it, it goes to the grievance committee or perhaps to the business agent. The steward also monitors the activities of the company to make certain that the terms of its contract with the union are not violated within his immediate environment.

At the bottom of the union are the rank-and-file members. In theory they hold ultimate power in their own hands. They can vote a leader into or out of office, comply with or refuse to abide by his policies, and otherwise control the union and determine its direction. In fact, however, the members tend to become content with the advantages the organization gains for them and thus reduce their participation in union meetings. There has been a gradual tendency in unions, as in other types of voluntary associations, for the officers to take more and more power into their own hands—a situation that may increase efficiency but does not conform to the American model of democracy.[22]

There are notable exceptions to this pattern. In a well-known study of the International Typographical Union (ITU), sociologists Lipset, Trow, and Coleman found a vigorous two-party political system within the organization.[23] But most cases are less clear-cut. A study of international organization among oil workers focused on the problem of whether, in the face of powerful, industry-wide opposition from the major employers, the oil workers' union could reconcile its strong tradition of local autonomy with its need to increase efficiency in collective bargaining.[24]

During the New Deal period, the continually poor state of this union's finances, at a time when other industrial unions were becoming stronger, led to a revolt of the union convention against the administrative officers. This revolt mainly took the form of an amendment to the union constitution, creating an executive council (the body that makes important policy decisions between conventions) consisting of rank-and-file workers to act as a watchdog over the union's elected leadership. This was a most unusual step, since the executive councils of all other large American unions are made up of the union's president and other chief officers.

The oil workers' "nonpolitical" executive council succeeded in reducing the power of the president, but it also created administrative chaos at union headquarters. Only after some

of the president's powers had been restored and an international policy committee had been established to centralize collective bargaining policies and procedures did the union begin to make solid economic progress for its members.

It might seem that this progress was achieved at some cost to union democracy, especially since union elections virtually ceased to be contested. However, the study concludes that the problem was—and is—not one of a power-hungry central administration but of a politically apathetic membership at the local level, combined with a union convention that simply does not seem interested in the problems of international organization. Members of local unions who take an active interest in union affairs have a good chance of being chosen by their locals to serve on the executive council, which continues to fulfill its watchdog function. This is a sign that democracy in some sense continues to exist, though the union has not yet solved the problem of what *form* of democracy would best serve its interests.

Methods of control. Some sociologists have taken a comparative approach to union organization. Etzioni, drawing on all the existing sociological studies, has attempted to classify unions in terms of the type of control they exercise over their members.[25] In his view, *coercive* unions use naked force (beatings administered in bars, for example) to keep their members in line. *Pure normative* unions concentrate on indoctrinating members in some revolutionary ideology. *Social* unions rely on ostracism, which they are able to do because the majority of their members derive great social satisfaction from leisure-time association with other members. Finally, *utilitarian* unions—the category into which most American unions fall—make use of their economic power over the worker, to whom expulsion may bring severe hardship. Most unions, in Etzioni's opinion, use some combination of normative and utilitarian control.

---

22. William Spinrad, "Correlates of Trade Union Participation," *American Sociological Review,* 25 (1960), 237–244.
23. Seymour Martin Lipset, Martin Trow, and James Coleman, *Union Democracy* (New York: The Free Press, 1956).
24. Melvin Rothbaum, *The Government of the Oil, Chemical, and Atomic Workers Union* (New York: John Wiley & Sons, Inc., 1962).
25. Amitai Etzioni, *A Comparative Analysis of Complex Organizations* (New York: The Free Press, 1961), pp. 59–65.

Crisis in labor. The failure of the labor movement to grow faster than the labor force in recent years has inspired a great deal of soul-searching among union leaders and some rather gloomy speculation by researchers. Among the reasons cited for the stagnation are alleged loss of idealism and energy among top leaders; a union membership that is too prosperous to be militant and that has no memories of the Great Depression; federal legislation aimed at curbing labor's recruiting power, especially the Landrum-Griffin Act of 1959; the general change in the character of the American labor force since the 1930's from predominantly blue-collar to predominantly white-collar; and the shift of the economy from manufacturing to service industries.

Labor has not failed completely to recruit white-collar workers. The retail clerks' union, for example, is one of the fastest growing in the country. And there are even some unions of professionals. The American Federation of Teachers has enough strength to bring some local school systems to a virtual halt, and there are strong unions of journalists, actors, airline pilots, and several other highly skilled occupations. But organized labor seems far indeed from recruiting a *majority* of white-collar workers, even in those areas where it has already had some success. Thus it remains a predominantly working-class movement, even while its changing membership figures accurately reflect an America that is ceasing to be working-class:

A comparison of the ranking by size of national unions in 1954 and 1960 . . . shows that the state, county and municipal workers' union jumped from the fortieth largest union to the twentieth in this six-year span. The retail clerks' union climbed from the sixteenth largest to the eleventh; the teamsters' union gained about 250,000 members and changed from third largest to first. During this same period, the four largest unions in the American Federation of Labor–Congress of Industrial Organizations (AFL–CIO)—the auto workers, steel workers, machinists, and carpenters—had a total membership loss of slightly over 100,000 while the three AFL–CIO unions reflecting substantial growth—the electrical

brotherhood, the retail clerks, and the state, county, and municipal workers—had a total gain of approximately 330,000 members.[26]

None of this, however, worries union leaders quite as much as the spectacle of automation—machines replacing workers. There is also the highly explosive issue of recruiting blacks and members of other minority groups previously excluded. Relatively little progress has been made toward integrating these groups into the American labor movement. Even if the more farsighted union leaders want them in, it seems clear that a majority of the members do not. California agriculture, where the majority of workers are already drawn from a single ethnic group, is one of the few areas in which there may be hope of using ethnic solidarity to build union solidarity.[27]

HUMAN RELATIONS AND THE WORKER

Beginning in 1927, Elton Mayo's team of researchers at Western Electric initiated a whole tradition of research that compelled management to see the worker as a human being with human needs and problems. This may not seem a very revolutionary concept today, but at that time all the emphasis was on the worker's physiology and the strictly physical aspects of the operations he had to perform in his job. Psychologically, the worker was looked on as an isolated individual working for himself. It was assumed that if he could be shown that working harder was in his own interest, he would automatically do so, provided the work was made physically easy for him. This approach, developed by the American engineer Frederick W. Taylor and his associates, was known as "scientific management" or "Taylorism."

Discovery of the group. Management at Western Electric's Hawthorne works was trying to find out, by means of systematic experiments, whether such environmental factors as variations in the intensity of illumination could explain variations in workers' productivity and morale. The Mayo team was allowed to experiment with a small group of five experienced women workers, set apart from the rest in a special room so that their conditions of work could be systematically controlled and observed.

26. James L. Stern, "Automation—End or a New Day in Unionism?" *The Annals of the American Academy of Political and Social Science* (November 1963), p. 34.

27. Ray Marshall, "Ethnic and Economic Minorities: Unions' Future or Unrecruitable?" in *ibid.*, pp. 63–73.

The operation selected was that of assembling telephone relays. This consists in "putting together a coil, armature, contact springs, and insulators in a fixture and securing the parts in position by means of four machine screws"; each assembly takes about one minute when the work is going well.[28]

After an initial period of observation to obtain base-line data, the experimenters systematically varied the conditions under which these women worked, retaining each condition for a period of several weeks or even months. The first variation was in method of payment. A group piece-rate, specific to those in the room, was initiated. Production went up. (The experimenters were pleased.) Next, two brief rest pauses were introduced, one in the morning and one in the afternoon. Again, productivity rose. (The experimenters were happy.) Then, refreshments were served during morning and afternoon breaks. Once more, production went up. (The experimenters were delighted.) Additional breaks were instituted; the group stopped working half an hour early, then a full hour early. Each of these variations seemed to produce increased hourly output. (The experimenters were ecstatic.)

However, certain grave doubts had begun to grow in the minds of members of the research staff. They decided to return to the somewhat more repressive conditions of an earlier experimental period to see if productivity would fall. When they did so, hourly output per worker rose to new heights! It seemed that there was little or no relationship between the experimental conditions they had been systematically introducing and the productivity of the group. Further checks indicated that this was indeed the case. There was an "unexpected and continual upward trend in productivity throughout the periods, even . . . when the girls were put on a full forty-eight hour week with no rest periods or lunch . . . ."[29]

In retrospect, it is easy to see what had happened. After working together for months, the women of the relay assembly room had come to know and like each other. They visited each other after working hours and regarded their little group as something special, apart from the common run of workers. Since they had come to believe in the importance of what they were doing, they were determined to do a good job even if rather unfavorable conditions were introduced.

From management's point of view, then, the whole experiment was a failure. Sociologists, however, perceived that what Mayo and his associates had produced was a demonstration of the importance of the primary group in a context where no one had thought to look for it. The individual worker was not a social atom in a lonely crowd of other social isolates. Even in an impersonal bureaucratic setting he was tied to other workers through bonds of friendship.

Additional evidence that informal group organization can be a powerful factor in the productivity of individual workers was obtained in a study made by the Mayo team several years after the research in the relay assembly room.[30] Here, the researchers' purpose was to study workers under conditions that were as "natural" as possible. In this way they hoped to avoid some of the pitfalls of the earlier investigation. A good approximation to normal shop floor conditions was obtained by duplicating a small segment of an assembly line system within an enclosure that could be kept under observation. Fourteen men worked in this "bank wiring observation room." They were supervised by their regular foremen; they produced the same objects (segments of telephone switchboards, or "banks") as other persons in their department; they used the same materials and methods; their products were subject to the same inspection procedures. After an initial period, the men accepted the observer (who had been instructed to be as unobtrusive as possible) and behaved almost as if he were not present.

The men were paid according to a complex "group piece-work" formula. Their pay was based on the number of banks they wired or soldered in a given time period. It was soon discovered, however, that they had their own idea of what constituted a "fair day's work." They would work steadily until, some time in the afternoon, they approached their informal

---

28. Elton Mayo, *Human Problems of an Industrial Civilization* (New York: The Viking Press, Inc., 1966), p. 56; first published in 1933.

29. G. A. Pennock, "Industrial Research at Hawthorne; An Experimental Investigation of Rest, Working Conditions and Other Influences," *Personnel*, 8, No. 5 (February 1930), 304.

30. Reported in Roethlisberger and Dickson, *op. cit.*, Part 4; see also Henry A. Landsberger, *Hawthorne Revisited* (Ithaca, N.Y.: Cornell University Press, 1958) and George Homans, *The Human Group* (New York: Harcourt Brace Jovanovich, 1950), pp. 48–155.

"quota." Then they would slow down noticeably. They would engage in horseplay, tell jokes, undertake preparations for the next day, make minor adjustments on their tools, talk, and otherwise drag out their work until quitting time.

If a given individual produced more than the "quota" allowed, he was subjected to verbal abuse, name-calling, and even physical punishment, thinly disguised as a kind of game known as "binging" (pages 42–43). There was a corresponding taboo against turning out too little work; men who did this were called "chiselers." But if a man was not well or for some other reason fell behind, his fellow workers would give him some of their units to turn in. This was clearly against the rules, and it did not fit with the piece-rate incentive plan.

The foreman was quite aware of these practices but could do very little about them. The men were, on the whole, good workers, and it would not have improved their productivity to antagonize them. Moreover, they could have made the foreman's life miserable in many petty ways. Thus the workers were controlling their supervisor rather than the other way around.

Further, if a member of their group complained to the foreman about the group's behavior (as happened once during the experiment), he was ostracized by the others as a "squealer" and eventually forced to transfer to another unit.

These normative codes, systems of social control, and conceptions of the internal status system were all parts of the informal structure of the work situation. Sociological research in the industrial setting has frequently documented the way in which such mechanisms can serve to protect the worker from the full impact of supervisory manipulation and can limit production despite attempts on the part of management to stimulate it.

Overall, the modern industrial worker is far from a helpless pawn in an impersonal complex of mass production. He is surrounded by a number of rules, limitations, and protective proscriptions imposed by his union. This formal organization puts constant pressure on management to increase the worker's economic rewards and protects the worker from unwarranted manipulation. In addition, he develops primary group ties within his work group that

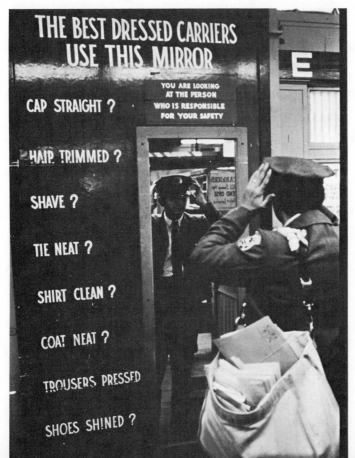

Although informal group controls can sometimes modify the power relationship between the worker and his supervisor, bringing about virtual control of the supervisor by the worker, there is usually more than adequate force behind the dictates of a formal organization. Here, a mailman makes sure that his appearance corresponds to the dress code of the United States Post Office.

make the daily task more pleasureable. The informal codes and controls that emerge in work settings do much to modify relationships between worker and supervisor, as well as between workers themselves.

The human relations era. Mayo and his colleagues had shown that the behavior of workers on the job could not be explained without reference to the values and structure of work groups, and that there were circumstances in which money was not the workers' chief concern. Unfortunately, many sociologists and industrial relations managers jumped to the conclusion that money was never a prime motivating force and that the work group was the only group affecting workers' behavior. Word spread that all management's problems with its production-level employees could be solved by administering large doses of sympathy and understanding, and research by social psychologists unconnected with Mayo's school confirmed this trend by demonstrating that a "permissive" and "democratic" style of leadership was apparently more effective with small work groups than an "authoritarian" one. Foremen were sent to training courses (sardonically referred to by union leaders as "charm schools") in order to unlearn their authoritarian ways.

Some years later, William Foote Whyte reviewed the entire field of "human relations," as this approach had come to be called, and concluded that somehow money had to be brought back into the picture.[31] He also pointed out that even though informal group organization is undoubtedly important, not all groups have the same *kind* of informal organization. Finally, he suggested that if a company wanted the kind of informal organization that would motivate its employees to work hard, it should restructure its formal organization to allow for more delegation of authority. Meanwhile, other researchers had succeeded in discrediting the notion that high morale always involved high productivity. Some groups just enjoyed being lazy, it seemed, while others apparently could be scared into working hard.[32]

These and other criticisms have resulted in a redirection of human relations research. The very term "human relations" is scarcely used anymore. Instead, researchers have attempted to look beyond the primary work group to the whole organization. For example, it has been discovered that workers simply are not fooled by a permissive style of supervision if it is clearly at variance with the company's overall policy,[33] and that a democratic first-line supervisor will not have much influence at the shop floor level unless he can make his opinion stick with management.[34] At the same time, researchers have learned to accept as a fact of industrial life the kind of restriction of output found in the Western Electric bank wiring room.

Edward Gross has pointed out that working-class people, for good reasons, do not have the same work ambitions as middle-class managers and therefore cannot be expected to react to the same kinds of incentives. On the other hand, they may cooperate with management wholeheartedly in the face of collective emergencies such as wars.[35]

THE WORKER IN INDUSTRIAL SOCIETY

Only industrial societies have what we ordinarily regard as occupations. Of course, people have always pursued various trades and callings, even in many so-called primitive societies. But occupations are far more specialized roles and cannot be conceived of as existing apart from a modern type of labor market. Modern workers, unlike those in ancient, medieval, and primitive societies, are relatively free to change their occupations and to pursue them for financial gain. They are also increasingly able to keep their work

31. William Foote Whyte, "Human Relations—A Progress Report," in *Complex Organizations: A Sociological Reader*, ed. Amitai Etzioni (New York: Holt, Rinehart and Winston, Inc., 1962), pp. 100–112.

32. See especially Leonard R. Sayles, *Managerial Behavior: Administration in Complex Organizations* (New York: McGraw-Hill Book Company, 1964); Henry A. Landsberger, *Hawthorne Revisited* (Ithaca, N. Y.: Cornell University Press, 1958); and Richard D. Mann, "A Review of the Relationships Between Personality and Performance in Small Groups," *Psychological Bulletin*, 56 (1959), 241–270.

33. Sayles, *op. cit.*

34. Donald C. Pelz, "Influence: A Key to Effective Leadership in the First-Line Supervisor," *Personnel*, 29, No. 3 (November 1952), 209–217.

35. Edward Gross, "Industrial Relations: Reward Systems," *International Encyclopedia of the Social Sciences, op. cit.*, Vol. 7, pp. 250–251.

separate from other aspects of their social existence, if they wish to do so.

Besides occupations, another familiar concept born of the Industrial Revolution is that of employment, with its opposite, unemployment. Being employed, in the sense we use the word today, is not just keeping busy. It means actually taking part in the industrial economy as a producer or distributor. In the early eighteenth century, according to a careful inquiry made at that time, the average French peasant spent at least 164 days a year without work.[36] But this should not be labeled "unemployment"; there *was* no other work, and no one expected there to be any. The life of the peasant followed the rhythm of a technologically primitive agriculture. In an industrial economy, on the other hand, "full employment" is at least theoretically possible, and most occupations involve work that is expected to be year-round.

The governments of industrial societies are interested in measuring levels of employment and unemployment, however they may define these concepts. Nearly all of them have set up statistical agencies for this purpose. In addition, most have national censuses that record, among other facts, the number of people pursuing different occupations. In the United States, detailed information on occupations is collected every ten years as part of the Census of Population. Measurement of employment and unemployment is carried out monthly, in the Current Population Survey (see Methodological Essay, page 495). By combining data from these two sources, it is possible to trace some of the important changes that have occurred in the composition of the American labor force. (See, for example, Table 7.5, page 232, showing the percentage of workers in major occupational groups from 1900 to 1969.)

Such data is very useful to the sociologist studying labor force participation, but he is also concerned with many things that statistics cannot show. He is interested in how a society defines and values work. He wants to know how technological changes create disequilibria in the social system and how this leads to other changes. He is also interested in the impact of labor force participation on the individual as he selects his occupational role, engages in work activity within the labor force, suffers unemployment, and eventually disengages from his occupation. It is to these issues that we now turn.

WORK AND ALIENATION

Some writers have maintained that during the preindustrial period man controlled his work but that after the establishment of the factory system work controlled him. Prominent among such writers is Karl Marx. Under the factory system, Marx emphasized, workers no longer owned the means of production; they could be denied a livelihood by being "locked out." In addition, the system increased the division of labor and reduced the responsibility and skill exercised by each worker. These developments, he argued, had two main results for the worker: his job became increasingly *meaningless* to him, and he himself became more *powerless*. The job was meaningless because the individual worker was simply a link—and a mechanical one, at that—in a process he was not supposed to grasp as a whole. He was powerless not only because he could not prevent the profits of his labor going to the factory owners but because, under the highly rationalized procedures of mass production, he could not even regulate the pace of his own work, much less exercise any intelligence or discretion.

Marx referred to the worker's situation in the factory system as one characterized by "alienation." To Marx, this was a highly complex philosophical concept with both objective and subjective components. It denoted not just the worker's "feelings of alienation" (in fact, he might be so "brainwashed" that he did not experience any) but his objective situation in the social structure.

One of the modern researchers' interests is the relation between job satisfaction and identification with the goals of the organization in which the job is held.[37] If *dissatisfaction* with one's job and *lack* of identification with organizational goals can be equated with alienation, then it can be demonstrated that alienation increases as rewards (in both money and prestige) decrease. Thus blue-collar workers, in nearly all the studies made so far, appear to be more alienated than white-collar workers (for exam-

---

36. The inquirer was the engineer Sebastien Le Prestre de Vauban, whose book was immediately banned.

37. See, for instance, Dwight G. Dean, "Meaning and Measurement of Alienation," *American Sociological Review,* 26 (October 1961), 753–757.

METHODOLOGY   **THE STRUCTURED INTERVIEW**

The structured interview utilizes a printed or mimeographed *schedule* that exactly specifies all the questions, explanations, and probes to be used by the interviewer, as well as the sequence in which they are to be presented to the respondent. Alternatives to this interviewing method are the questionnaire, which the respondent fills out himself, and the unstructured interview, in which each interviewer uses his own style in obtaining information.

A major advantage of the structured interview is that the use of a uniform schedule standardizes the interviewing process, controlling what each interviewer says and what each respondent hears. This greatly increases the likelihood that the measuring instrument will be *reliable*—i.e., that it will yield comparable data when used with different subjects or by different interviewers. A further advantage of the structured interview is its efficiency. Because he must adhere closely to a printed schedule, the interviewer loses little time in unnecessary discussion with respondents.

Use of the structured interview can be illustrated by a recent study exploring occupational knowledge among high-school boys. Schools of varying rural-urban characteristics in a western state were chosen to provide subjects for the study. From these schools, 400 male students were selected on a random and proportional basis through use of a strict sampling design (see page 300). A standardized schedule was then used to assess the subjects' knowledge of seven common occupations which were well represented in the labor force of the region. After certain background data were obtained, each respondent was asked a series of questions about a given occupation. The items below illustrate the nature of the schedule for the occupation of accountant. Space was provided for verbatim recording of responses:

1. What are the general kinds of work done by most accountants?
2. Do most accountants work for someone, work independently on their own, or both?
3. Name as many specialized types of accountants as you can.
4. How much formal education do accountants need?

Immediately following this series of questions about this particular role, each interviewee was asked to respond to a "Semantic Differential Scale" (shown below). For each pair of adjectives, the interviewee checked the one space that he felt best described the work of an accountant:

Work of Accountant

exciting —:—:—:—:—:—:— dull
easy —:—:—:—:—:—:— difficult
clean —:—:—:—:—:—:— dirty
ordinary —:—:—:—:—:—:— glamorous
creative —:—:—:—:—:—:— routine
low respon- —:—:—:—:—:—:— high responsibility   sibility

These procedures were repeated for each of the seven occupations under study and also for the respondent's own occupational choice. Responses to the structured questions were carefully coded into categories indicating varying degrees of understanding of each role studied. The semantic differential scales provided attitudinal profiles for each role.

The results of this study indicated that most of the boys knew little about common roles in the labor force which they were about to enter. They also entertained cultural stereotypes about such roles. Their high-school studies apparently had provided no preparation for either choosing among such roles or understanding the consequences of their choice.

The structured interview is one of the most widely used of all sociological measuring techniques. Its principal disadvantage is its inflexibility, which may somewhat lessen the validity of results. A system for measuring variables is said to be *valid* to the extent that it measures exactly what it was designed to measure. Unfortunately, the respondents to a structured interview may not always understand the standardized questions in standardized ways. Extensive pretesting of the schedule can reduce the likelihood of misunderstanding and thus increase the measuring system's level of validity, but the basic problem of inflexibility remains. A researcher must weigh this limitation of the structured interview against its advantages of precision, reliability, and efficiency.

The study of occupational knowledge cited above was conducted by Lois DeFleur and is being prepared for publication. For an appraisal of the structured interview as a research technique, see Gideon Sjoberg and Roger Nett, *A Methodology for Social Research* (New York: Harper & Row, Inc., 1968), esp. p. 193.

ple, see Table 15.1). Other studies suggest that increased rewards can reduce alienation almost regardless of the *type* of work performed.

Repetitive, mechanical jobs exist today as they did in Marx's time. But Marx, no doubt overwhelmed by the appalling conditions in nineteenth-century factories, did not foresee the modern worker's capacity for keeping his life on the job separate, if necessary, from his life off it or for deriving satisfaction from on-the-job relationships. He also appears to have neglected the strength of success as a motive. This is hardly surprising since he believed that, so long as the capitalist system remained, the workers could only get poorer.

Finally, there is some reason to doubt whether jobs that appear boring to an outsider have quite the same effect on the workers themselves. The answer seems to be that many workers, especially older ones, succeed in developing a tolerance for repetitive jobs to the point that they may even become disturbed at the thought of changing. The fact that they have adjusted to their work does not necessarily mean, however, that they find their jobs actually satisfying.

OCCUPATIONAL CHOICE AND OCCUPATIONAL MOBILITY

American values hold that a person's occupation is a matter of free and rational choice, limited only by natural ability. In fact, however, the choices people make are seldom wholly reasoned or free. Research shows that although every male child understands that he will be expected to work when he grows up, he has only a dim understanding of most occupational roles.[38] Thus his first vocational aspirations are largely fantasies. By adolescence they may be more realistic, but in general the aspirations of youth far exceed what they will eventually achieve. Most of the young people who aspire to professional and managerial roles via higher education will never be college graduates but will find employment in the skilled labor force.[39]

Ignorance of job opportunities is another limiting factor. Most workers' first jobs are the only ones they know about at the time they take them.[40] Moreover, this first step, often casually taken, can set the pattern for a lifetime of employment. Also largely fortuitous is the range of role models available to an individual; many youngsters enter an occupation in imitation of an older person whom they admire. Cultural and reference group values exert a similar influence. Underlying all these factors are variables of class and status that restrict the range within which a free choice of occupation is even conceivable.

As noted in Chapter 7, "Social Stratification," a person's position in the social hierarchy limits not only his choice of occupation but also his opportunities for advancement. Job changing appears to be more common in the United States than elsewhere. In both 1955 and 1961, two years for which census surveys are available, one in ten American workers changed jobs at least once. Other studies, using different methods, have discovered rates that are even higher. But most of this movement results in horizontal rather than vertical mobility. Movement between jobs in the same major category (using the Bureau of the Census classification of major occupational groups) is far more frequent than vertical movement into the category immediately above, while vertical mobility into the category above *that* appears to be rare indeed. In addition, some categories, such as those of "clerical and kindred workers" and "operatives

---

TABLE 15.1. **PERCENTAGE OF ALIENATION OF NONSUPERVISORY MALE WHITE-COLLAR EMPLOYEES AND BLUE-COLLAR EMPLOYEES**

ATTITUDE	WHITE COLLAR (1792 workers)	BLUE COLLAR (4788 workers)
I like my job as a whole	70	57
Satisfied with working conditions in general	75	47
Satisfied with company and job as a whole	60	51
Satisfied with present wages	39	28
Satisfied with progress in company up to now	65	64

SOURCE: D. Katz and R. L. Kahn, "Some Recent Findings in Human Relations Research in Industry," in *Readings in Social Psychology,* ed. G. E. Swanson, T. M. Newcomb, and E. L. Hartley (New York: Holt, Rinehart and Winston, Inc., 1952), p. 655.

---

38. Walter L. Slocum, *Occupational Careers: A Sociological Perspective* (Chicago: Aldine Publishing Company, 1966), pp. 186–225.

39. John C. Flanagan *et al., The American High School Student* (Pittsburgh: Project Talent Office, University of Pittsburgh, 1964).

40. Seymour M. Lipset *et al.,* "Job Plans and Entry into the Labor Market," *Social Forces* (March 1955), pp. 229–230.

and kindred workers," seem to be especially hard to get out of. The sons of "managers, officials, and proprietors," however, have a good chance of becoming professionals.[41]

Not many broad generalizations can be made with certainty in this area of intergenerational mobility, partly because of the ambiguity of the occupational categories used by the census and partly because the only way of analyzing occupational mobility through census statistics is to work in terms of age groups. One of the few studies that does include data on individuals indicated that, in a sample of the entire American labor force taken in 1957, 42.2 percent of skilled manual workers had fathers who were also skilled manual workers and that much the same father-son relationship appeared among the professionals.[42]

There is some evidence that American workers begin their working lives with unrealistically optimistic expectations about how far they can advance themselves and that, as they grow older, they become more realistic. One study of attitudes among workers in an automobile manufacturing plant found that the older workers tended to define "success" not as getting ahead but as acquiring newer and better material goods such as cars and washing machines. Less experienced workers, on the other hand, still had hopes of moving into a higher occupational category. The author of the study concluded that the older workers had come to terms with their lack of real mobility by compensating for it as consumers. The younger ones still believed in the American Dream.[43]

UNEMPLOYMENT

To the average middle-class person in this age of affluence, questions as to the consequences of unemployment may seem remote. But for several million members of the labor force they are not remote at all. These Americans are facing the consequences of being jobless. For the lower-class black, the older worker, the undereducated youth, and the worker whose skills have become obsolete, the specter of unemployment is ever present. Unemployment rates in these categories remain relatively high (see Table 15.2, page 499).

What is the impact of unemployment? Is it simply economic, or does it have other sig-

nificant dimensions? The merit of work is an integral part of the belief system of our society. Occupational activity defines one's place and worth within the social structure. The money one earns is, of course, important since it provides the essentials for survival. But the mere fact of having a job and performing it satisfactorily supplies an important element of the self-image. A man who can work and support his family in this society is a far different figure, to himself as well as to others, than the man who cannot find work or who is fired from his job for whatever reason. The ethic of work defines the unemployed man as a *moral* failure, regardless of whether his unemployment is of his own making or the product of impersonal social and economic forces.

How does one handle the feelings of personal inadequacy and self-recrimination that are generated by unemployment? One may rebel, join a militant movement, and fight the system that has limited his opportunity. This mode of response occurred in Europe in the interwar period and has been adopted recently by some blacks in urban America.[44] In the United States during the Depression years, studies of the unemployed male family head showed that he suffered not only lowered self-esteem but actual loss of authority within the family.[45] Political extremism was apparently far from his thoughts, even though up to 25 percent of the labor force was without work.

We may contrast this mode of response with another, observed in a contemporary American setting—the response characteristic of those who form a so-called subculture of un-

41. See the comprehensive (but now somewhat outdated) study by Seymour M. Lipset and Reinhard Bendix, *Social Mobility in the Industrial Society* (Berkeley, Calif.: University of California Press, 1959).

42. Elton F. Jackson and Harry J. Crockett, Jr., "Occupational Mobility in the United States: A Point Estimate and Trend Comparison," *American Sociological Review*, 29 (1964), 7.

43. Ely Chinoy, "The Tradition of Opportunity and the Aspirations of Automobile Workers," *American Journal of Sociology*, 57 (1951–1952), 453–459.

44. David Street and John C. Leggett, "Economic Deprivation and Extremism: A Study of Unemployed Negroes," *American Journal of Sociology*, 57 (July 1961), 53–57.

45. Mirra Komarovsky, *The Unemployed Man and His Family* (New York: Holt, Rinehart and Winston, Inc., 1940); see also E. Wright Bakke, *Citizens Without Work* (Hamden, Conn.: Shoe String Press, Inc., 1969).

METHODOLOGY MEASURING THE LABOR FORCE

As a result of programs evolved during the 1930's and 1940's, the government of the United States now derives most of its information on employment and unemployment from labor force statistics. These are obtained by the Bureau of Labor Statistics from the monthly Current Population Survey (a sample survey covering fifty thousand households, conducted by the Bureau of the Census).

Contrary to the impression many people have, labor force statistics do *not* divide everyone into the categories of "employed" and "unemployed." In the first place, only persons over fourteen years of age are interviewed and then only if they are living in households. This provision automatically excludes all juveniles, even those who may contribute regularly to the family income (e.g., the children of migratory farm workers); it also excludes members of the armed forces and inmates of hospitals, prisons, and other such institutions. Second, under the procedures used by the Bureau of Labor Statistics, an individual cannot be classed as employed or unemployed unless he *first* qualifies for inclusion in the labor force. The minimum qualification for this is whether he looked for work during the previous week. If he did not, and if he did no paid work at all and/or was not just temporarily absent from his job, he is classified, not as unemployed, but as *not in the labor force*. On the other hand, even the smallest amount of part-time work during the previous week qualifies him for inclusion in the labor force as "employed."

Criticism of these procedures by labor economists and others, on the grounds that they systematically understate the amount of unemployment, has recently led to certain refinements. Since 1967 additional questions have been used in the survey in order to determine *why* those who are not in the labor force have failed to seek work; the unemployed are asked how they lost their last jobs; part-time employment is more carefully distinguished from full-time employment. But the basic labor force concept remains the same.

The detailed information on occupations collected every ten years as part of the general population census (see page 263) makes use of the following overall classifications:

Professional, technical, and kindred workers

Managers, officials, and proprietors, except farm

Clerical and kindred workers

Sales workers

Craftsmen, foremen, and kindred workers

Operatives and kindred workers

Laborers, except farm and mine

Private household workers

Service workers, except private household

Farmers and farm managers

Farm laborers and foremen

This schema has changed very little since it was first introduced in 1943 by Alba M. Edwards, then director of the Census. At that time, it was rightly considered a great improvement. New occupations are continually being created, however, and the need to fit all of them into the schema can sometimes produce classifications that appear rather peculiar. Why, for instance, should "dietitians and nutritionists" be classified as "professional, technical, and kindred workers," while "officers, pilots, pursers, and engineers, ship," are classified as "managers, officials, and proprietors, except farm"? Nevertheless, the schema has proved adequate for reflecting the major changes that have been taking place in the composition of the American labor force, and it has the advantage of making the censuses from 1950 through 1970 directly comparable with respect to occupational distribution.

For the latest procedures used in gathering information on employment and unemployment, see *Concepts and Methods Used in Manpower Statistics from the Current Population Survey* (Washington, D.C.: U.S. Department of Labor, Bureau of Labor Statistics, June 1967), BLS Report No. 313. The older procedures are described in *Measuring Employment and Unemployment*, President's Commission to Appraise Employment and Unemployment Statistics (Washington, D.C.: U.S. Government Printing Office, 1962). See also *Classified Index of Occupations and Industries* (Washington, D.C.: U.S. Department of Commerce, Bureau of the Census, 1960).

employment, in which engaging in petty crime or living on welfare payments is seen as a reasonable alternative to searching for regular employment. Schwartz and Henderson, among others, have suggested that this type of subculture is appearing among urban blacks in the United States, particularly those who have migrated from the rural South.[46] This segment of the population represents a combination of the factors associated with chronic unemployment. Many of its members have less than a high-school education; their skills are low; and they are the objects of racial prejudice on the part of white employers. Many are also very young: from 1961 to 1968 unemployment among nonwhite males between sixteen and nineteen actually increased by over 5 percent while unemployment in most other categories decreased by substantial amounts (Table 15.2, page 499).

It must not be thought, however, that those in the subculture of unemployment enjoy being without jobs. The reactions of this sixteen-year-old youth just back from jail are probably fairly typical:

Q. How do you feel when you don't have a job—what's the worst thing?
A. Well, I feel like, you know, when people are not working and they don't go to school there isn't anything they can do for themselves. . . .
Q. What does getting ahead mean to you—making it big?
A. It doesn't really mean much to me. I don't want to be ahead of anybody, you know. I mean, the way I stand now, I can't jump ahead of anybody, like somebody even younger than me that might be workin' now, maybe they makin' $5.00 a week by just workin' a couple o' hours a week, he still ahead of me. Even if he doesn't go to school he's still ahead of me. I'm doing nothin'.[47]

---

46. Michael Schwartz and George Henderson, "The Culture of Unemployment: Some Notes on Negro Children," in *Blue-Collar World: Studies of the American Worker*, ed. Arthur B. Shostak and William Gomberg (Englewood Cliffs, N.J.: Prentice-Hall, Inc., 1964), pp. 458–468.

47. From an interview in Edgar May, *The Wasted Americans: Cost of our Welfare Dilemma* (New York: Signet Books, 1965), pp. 85–86.

Our culture places a high value on productivity and success, and Americans are constantly reminded that it is "good" to have money and a job. Thus the person who is unemployed feels not only a financial loss but also a loss of self-esteem; he is relegated to a low social position because of his economic situation.

The unemployed black who is head of a family has exactly the same kinds of reactions to his plight as an unemployed white. Many leave home altogether; current welfare regulations make it easier for their families to obtain help if no male head is present.[48] But many unemployed black men stay on in spite of everything and succeed in retaining authority over their families.[49]

TECHNOLOGICAL DISPLACEMENT

Of the many workers displaced by technological advancements, probably not even a majority become unemployed (generalization is difficult here because systematic research on the subject has hardly begun). Nor, in spite of popular alarm about so-called automation, are electronic computers somehow speeding up labor productivity (i.e., the rate at which workers produce goods) to such an extent that few or no workers will be necessary.

All this does not, of course, prevent the impact of technological change, of whatever kind, from being utterly disastrous for workers in particular plants and regions. We have already seen how the introduction of diesel locomotives destroyed the livelihood of an entire town (pages 195–196). Whole regions have suffered, and are still suffering, the same kind of fate. For instance, the poverty of the approximately half-million people who live in the Cumberland Plateau region of eastern Kentucky (the southwestern edge of the Appalachians) is so deep and apparently so irremediable that, according to one study, 85 percent of its young people had no alternative but to leave or endure lifetimes of near-starvation.[50] This is because the mechanization of existing coal mines and the introduction of new techniques such as strip mining, in which most of the work is done by huge earth-moving machines, have destroyed for most families the only source of employment they ever knew. In 1910 the region's mines produced

most of the nation's coal, with a work force of 700,000 men. Today they employ fewer than 200,000 men and *produce more coal.*[51]

With the development of an increasingly sophisticated technology, computerized applications of cybernetics continue to emerge. In a suburb of Chicago a bakery as large as a football field is operated by machines controlled by computers, with a handful of experts monitoring the equipment:

The mixing and blending of flour, sugar, milk, butter, and all the other solid and liquid ingredients is directed and constantly supervised by the computing machine whose electronic pulses busily carry instructions to the other machines and bring information from sensory devices about conditions, performance, and progress back to the central computing machine. The mixing and blending is done according to recipes, or "programs," stored on magnetic tape, punch cards, tiny doughnut-shaped "cores," magnetic drums, or similar devices.

Apart from the mixing, blending, and baking, the computing machine controls supplies so that raw materials are ordered and thriftily kept at the proper level—not so much as to waste storage space or risk spoiling, and not so little as to keep any of the mixing and baking centers idle. Baking time and oven temperatures are computed and continually adjusted to the slightest change in outside conditions. The baking process is constantly monitored and controlled. Conveyor belts, for the transport of raw materials to mixing centers, dough to baking containers, [and] containers to ovens, cooling racks, freezing plants, dispatch centers, and trucks, are directed.

And the entire production process—from ordering of raw materials to shipping of finished goods—is only *one* of the functions of the cybernated system. The computing machine also performs management functions for the business end of the bakery operation by controlling and monitoring the component machines to calculate, for example, the optimum number of rolls to be delivered on any day to each customer—not fewer than he might sell, but not so many that he will return them—always considering weather conditions, the day of the week, impending holidays, and many other variables that might influence consumption. This calculation is transmitted to raw-material dispatch centers, mixing centers, and so forth, right [down] to the shipping department and the delivery trucks. And everywhere adjustments are made, orders corrected, space reallocated, all in order to assure the optimum efficiency and economy of operations.

48. *Ibid.,* pp. 53–58.

49. Schwartz and Henderson, *op. cit.*

50. Cited in Michael Harrington, *The Other America* (Baltimore: Penguin Books, Inc., 1963), p. 50.

51. Harry M. Caudill, *Night Comes to the Cumberlands: A Biography of a Depressed Area* (Boston: Little, Brown and Company, 1963), p. 263.

The computing machine is programmed to process the payroll for the company's diminishing number of employees and the invoices for its increasing number of customers; to compute the market prognosis, adjusted in accordance with trends in taste, seasons, advertising, and any other influences the programmers have thought of; to provide information about past experience to modify advertising; to calculate any changes thereby required in the production, purchasing, and distribution patterns; and to monitor all phases of operation to assure that instructions (with all modifications) are carried out. In other words, the system is capable of an interchange of information that permits the most complex relationships in continuous cycles of adjustments, feedback, modifications, and learning, at speeds expressed in as unfathomable a unit as a "microsecond" or a "nano-second." Still the potential applications of the system are not exhausted; and, like every other cybernated machine system in use now, it is underused.[52]

If all technologically displaced workers could move on immediately to other jobs at the same or higher levels, there might be no "problem of automation." And most workers displaced by computers seem to do just that. In fact—though we have only scattered data at present—it is possible that most of them move to other jobs in the same company. It is also possible that much of the impact of computerization is emotional and subjective, as this research study suggests:

The employees we questioned were very much aware of the potential of the computer for replacing workers. About three-quarters of them reported that machines were replacing workers in insurance companies. But, when questioned about their own job prospects, about four-fifths felt that it was very unlikely that they, themselves, would be replaced by machines. This reflected the actual work situation, in which no employees had lost jobs because of the computer installation.

More than half of the employees felt that their jobs had changed because of the new equipment. They saw themselves as having been promoted or transferred or as having the content of their job altered. The company officials and the research team, on the other hand, estimated that less than one third of the work force was affected in any significant way by the change. Apparently employees were associating many aspects of their own jobs with this very visible new influence in their lives.[53]

Actually, the rate at which white-collar employees are being displaced from their occupations by computers probably does not even begin to compare with the rate at which manual workers are being displaced by other mechanical devices, especially in agriculture. From 1959 to 1965 the rate of increase in output per worker for agriculture was 6 percent—about three times what it was in the 1930's and the highest it has ever been. This meant that agriculture was being exposed to almost the same amount of technological change as coal mining, which is a much smaller industry.[54] And like the people of the Cumberland Plateau, farm workers moved when they could: Some 8.5 million Americans left the country for the city between 1950 and 1960.[55]

Paradoxically, displaced rural workers—the younger ones at any rate—may in the long run prove more fortunate than their urbanized industrial counterparts. The former agricultural laborer who has moved to the city has at least *moved*. The skilled worker whose plant is closed down often cannot afford to move. Moreover, the descent into unemployment is made all the more demoralizing for him because he has more to lose. The fate of such workers, and of others in similar plights, was dramatically revealed by a congressional inquiry into the closing of the Oklahoma City meat packing plant of Armour and Company in 1960.[56] The plant had gradually become obsolete and unprofitable, and finally it was closed down permanently. About a third of the 325 workers thus displaced were men in their forties who owned their own homes. They had severance pay, but most also had debts. Moving in search of work was just not an economically realistic proposition for them, even if work had been available elsewhere. It could be expected that their economic—and social—position would continue to deteriorate.

In some industries and occupations workers have been able to organize in the face of tech-

---

52. Alice Mary Hilton, "Cyberculture—Age of Abundance and Leisure," *Michigan Quarterly Review*, 3, No. 4 (October 1964).

53. William A. Faunce, Einar Hardin, and Eugene H. Jacobson, "Automation and the Employee, " in *Life in Society*, ed. Thomas E. Lasswell, John H. Burma, and Sidney H. Aronson (Glenview, Ill.: Scott, Foresman and Company, 1970).

54. A. J. Jaffe and Joseph Froomkin, *Technology and Jobs: Automation in Perspective* (New York: Frederick A. Praeger, Inc., 1968), pp. 57, 63.

55. *Ibid.*, p. 58.

56. Cited in Harrington, *op. cit.*, pp. 44–45.

TABLE 15.2. **EMPLOYMENT AND UNEMPLOYMENT DEVELOPMENTS AMONG WHITES AND NONWHITES, 1961 TO 1968**

| | EMPLOYMENT | | | | UNEMPLOYMENT | | | |
| | NUMBER (in thousands) | | CHANGE, 1961–1968 | | NUMBER (in thousands) | | CHANGE, 1961–1968 | |
AGE, SEX, AND COLOR	1961	1968 (est.)	NUMBER	PERCENT	1961	1968 (est.)	NUMBER	PERCENT
Both Sexes								
Total, 16 years and over	**65,746**	**75,757**	**10,011**	**15.2**	**4,714**	**2,842**	**−1,872**	**−39.7**
White	58,912	67,600	8,688	14.7	3,742	2,247	−1,495	−40.0
Nonwhite	6,832	8,157	1,325	19.4	970	595	−375	−38.7
16 to 19 years	4,106	5,793	1,687	41.1	827	835	+8	+1.0
White	3,692	5,206	1,514	41.0	669	640	−29	−4.3
Nonwhite	414	587	173	41.8	158	195	+37	+23.4
20 years and over	61,639	69,964	8,325	13.5	3,885	2,009	−1,877	−48.3
White	55,220	62,393	7,173	13.0	3,073	1,608	−1,466	−47.7
Nonwhite	6,419	7,571	1,152	17.9	812	401	−411	−50.6
Men								
Total, 16 years and over	**43,656**	**48,044**	**4,388**	**10.1**	**2,997**	**1,437**	**−1,560**	**−52.1**
White	39,588	43,347	3,759	9.5	2,398	1,156	−1,242	−51.8
Nonwhite	4,067	4,697	630	15.5	599	281	−318	−53.1
16 to 19 years	2,313	3,243	930	40.2	478	422	−56	−11.7
White	2,055	2,899	844	41.1	384	323	−61	−15.9
Nonwhite	258	344	86	33.3	94	99	+5	+5.3
20 years and over	41,342	44,801	3,459	8.4	2,519	1,015	−1,504	−59.7
White	37,533	40,448	2,915	7.8	2,014	833	−1,181	−58.6
Nonwhite	3,809	4,353	544	14.3	505	182	−323	−64.0
Women								
Total, 16 years and over	**22,090**	**27,714**	**5,624**	**25.5**	**1,717**	**1,407**	**−310**	**−18.1**
White	19,324	24,253	4,929	25.5	1,344	1,091	−253	−18.8
Nonwhite	2,765	3,461	696	25.2	371	316	−55	−14.8
16 to 19 years	1,793	2,551	758	42.3	349	413	+64	+18.3
White	1,637	2,308	671	41.0	285	316	+31	+10.9
Nonwhite	156	243	87	55.8	64	97	+33	+51.6
20 years and over	20,297	25,163	4,866	24.0	1,367	994	−373	−27.3
White	17,687	21,945	4,258	24.1	1,060	775	−285	−26.9
Nonwhite	2,610	3,218	608	23.3	307	219	−88	−28.7

SOURCE: U.S. Department of Labor, *Manpower Report of the President,* January 1969, p. 44.

nological displacement and force their employers to retain positions and work practices that have long ceased to be either necessary or profitable. Diesel trains regularly carry "firemen"; skilled printers regularly set "dead horse" (type that will not be used but only remelted); airliners frequently have "featherbirds" (extra pilots who do nothing).

For the most part, however, technological change is not easily resisted or delayed. And it is clear that its impact is an unequal one, falling more heavily on the older worker than on the younger, on the blue-collar worker more than on the white-collar worker, on workers in declining industries more than on workers in expanding industries.

RETIREMENT

If a worker manages to survive all the everyday problems of employment in an industrial society, the time comes when he must face the last problem of all: retirement from the labor force. In our society, the conventional (and, in many occupations, compulsory) age for retirement is sixty-five. The expectation of life for an American man who survives to that age is about seventy-eight. For an American woman, it is eighty-one. In 1961 the median annual income of American couples over sixty-five was $2530, only about three quarters of what the Bureau of Labor Statistics then considered necessary for an adequate standard of living.[57] Americans over sixty-five who lived alone were far worse off. If we add to these facts the psychological strains attendant on loss of the occupational role, it is clear that growing old is the heaviest burden a worker has to bear.

There is evidence that many Americans who are past the age of retirement do not leave the labor force all at once but withdraw from it gradually.[58] This reluctance to break with the world of work is not motivated simply by financial need. In an industrial society, as we have seen, the occupational role is a central one. It links both men and women with a variety of groups beyond the immediate family, defines the male's role as breadwinner within the family, and to a great extent determines his status in the community. After losing this role, a man may literally be unable to face his former associates. Here is an example which, while involving a Britisher, is pertinent to the United States as well:

Mr. Kite was sixty-five. He had been obliged by ill health to give up his work as a brewer's labourer two years before. "I kept losing time. It was on account of my health. The work was heavy. I went to my doctor and he said I'd never be able to do any work again. The next week I got the sack. . . . I used to go out and see the boys on Saturday evenings. I'd meet my sons-in-law and we'd go out to the pub. . . . Now I can't do it. It's like being a pauper. I had to turn away from that because I didn't have a pound like I did in my pocket. I couldn't stand anybody anything [drinks]. I couldn't do my share.[59]

What do the retired do with their time? Research shows that most of them associate with members of their own age group rather than with young persons and with relatives rather than friends who are not related.[60] So-called Golden Age clubs do not attract a large proportion of the retired unless they are set up in retirement communities. There is less church attendance among persons over sixty-five than among those between sixty-five and fifty. As people grow older, there is an increase in the amount of time spent doing nothing at all—or in activities designed to conceal the fact that there is nothing to do:

Q. What did you do after supper?
A. I filled out my diary and my mail book. . . .
Q. What mail book?
A. Oh, I notice generally the mail I get and send.
Q. You keep track of it in a book?
A. Everything.
Q. The mail you receive. . . .
A. And the mail I send. . . .
Q. And that's what you did after supper?
A. Yes. It takes only a little while. And then I rest a while again, with the window open to get some

57. Earl F. Cheit, "Aging: Economic Aspects," *International Encyclopedia of the Social Sciences, op. cit.,* Vol. 1, pp. 197–198.

58. Betty V. H. Schneider, *The Older Worker* (Berkeley, Calif.: University of California, Institute of Industrial Relations, 1962).

59. Peter Townsend, *The Family Life of Old People* (Baltimore: Penguin Books, Inc., 1963), p. 165.

60. Yonina Talmon, "Aging: Social Aspects," in *International Encyclopedia of the Social Sciences, op. cit.,* Vol. 1, pp. 191–193.

Although retirement from the labor force is difficult for many people in American society, the extent to which this change becomes a crisis depends considerably upon an individual's role flexibility. Those who do not relate themselves to the social system only on the basis of their occupational roles may find the transition from the world of work to the world of leisure much easier.

wind and look at the trees, and I'm glad that I can look at them.

Q. How long did you look at the trees?

A. Oh, I can't tell you. Then I look at the television program. . . . At 10:00 generally I retire to bed with a whole lot of books.

Q. Did anybody come to the door?

A. No.[61]

One of the reasons for the loneliness of the old is that in modern industrial society they are not expected to live with their offspring, and they are accorded only low status in the community. In fact, they may be regarded by young people with amused tolerance at best.

Retirement is another crisis in working life that seems to weigh more heavily on the blue-collar than on the white-collar worker. A study

by Loether found that more than half the members of a group of retired workers in Los Angeles had worked full time or part time at some point after their initial retirement.[62] Most of the blue-collar workers said they had gone back to work to earn money. Among white-collar workers, however, the reason was enjoyment. Here are reflected different attitudes toward retirement no less than toward work. Loether summarizes the implications of his findings in the following terms:

The average white-collar worker has positive feelings about his job. Therefore, he may look with some dread at the prospect of retirement and the loss of his occupational role. But when he does retire, the transition to the retired state is smoother for him than it is for the blue-collar worker. He is able to make the transition more smoothly because he has greater role flexibility. He is able to compensate for the loss of his occupational role because he has other roles to play and because he has not put disproportionate emphasis on his occupational role as a means of relating himself to the social system.[63]

---

61. From an interview in May, *op. cit.*, p. 104.

62. Herman J. Loether, "The Meaning of Work and Adjustment to Retirement," in Shostak and Gomberg, eds., *op. cit.*, p. 532.

63. *Ibid.*

CHANGING ATTITUDES TOWARD WORK

In ancient Greece and Rome, work was generally seen as a curse; men were condemned to work because they had angered the gods.[64] Accordingly, no rational person worked if he could avoid doing so. Work was a fit preoccupation only for slaves, artisans, craftsmen, and other low types. The Latin societies generally have retained this interpretation. The phrase *trabajo es castigo* ("work is punishment") still expresses the feelings of most Spanish-speaking people, at least toward manual labor.

In ancient Hebrew society, on the other hand, attitudes toward work seem to have varied with its supposed purpose and motivation. Thus work might be condemned for interfering with spiritual devotion or valued as a form of cooperation with God. The early Christian Church saw work as "Adam's curse" but encouraged performance of it for personal need and for charity—an ideal that reached full flowering in the great religious orders of the Middle Ages. It was only with the rise of puritanism in Europe during the sixteenth century that work for gain began to be elevated into a noble activity. As Max Weber (page 181) was one of the first to point out, the development of the "Protestant Ethic," by providing a new cultural definition of work, did much to pave the way for the emergence of modern industrialism.

Recently many people have speculated about whether we are now becoming a "civilization of leisure" (or even a "civilization of pleasure"),[65] but surprisingly little information has been collected on what ordinary people think of the prospect. True, hours of work have been progressively reduced to the point at which a forty-hour, five-day week is considered normal and a thirty-five hour week not unusual. This is certainly an advance over the twelve-hour days and six-day weeks of the early industrial period, and it is one for which labor unions, in particular, fought long and hard. But did they fight for leisure as such, or for the freedom to choose between shorter hours and higher earnings? It seems likely that, given the continuing emphasis in American society upon material success and the possession of goods symbolic of material success, most workers will choose higher earnings. Indeed, they may need those increased earnings to meet the increasing cost of services, such as high-quality medical care, improved insurance coverage, and higher education for their children, which were previously beyond their economic range.

But if leisure is not about to replace work as industrial man's principal activity, it does appear that a point is reached in advanced industrial societies at which most people have to decide how important work is to be in their lives. And there is evidence that those who can afford it are spending a great deal of money on certain types of leisure activities. It is probable that the very freedom to choose between a variety of leisure pursuits will, if cultivated systematically, result in the revision of attitudes toward work.

---

64. This section on the history of attitudes toward work is indebted to Adriano Tilgher, "Work Through the Ages," in *Man, Work, and Society,* ed. Sigmund Nosow and William H. Form (New York: Basic Books, Inc., 1962), pp. 11–24.

65. See, for example, David Riesman, *Abundance For What? And Other Essays* (Garden City, N.Y.: Doubleday & Company, Inc., 1964).

SUMMARY

The historical approach to the study of industrial society traces the growth of the factory system and the beginnings of modern industrialism—developments found to depend on the existence of free labor, investment capital, and machinery driven by a power source more versatile than water. Among the most important accompaniments of the factory system were the rise of the corporation and the concentration of economic power in a few hands.

The modern industrial corporation is a special type of formal bureaucratic organization.

On the management side, the supposed rationality of corporate organization—with its division of functions between top management, middle management, and line supervision—is impaired by power struggles, staff-line conflict, and a lack of effective direction and communication at the middle levels. And this lack is compounded by typical corporation recruitment and promotion policies. A particularly unsatisfactory position is that of the first-line supervisor, who is torn between management and labor.

The sociological study of labor dates from the classic studies of industrial work groups by Mayo. The principal lesson of these studies was that the informal organization of the work group itself and the satisfaction derived from group membership had more influence on the workers' behavior than individualistic incentives such as money. This discovery initiated a new era in industrial relations, some of the excesses of which are now being corrected.

The analysis of labor force and occupational statistics in the United States depends on the technical definitions and procedures of the Bureau of the Census and the Bureau of Labor Statistics. Underlying both is the more general notion of occupation, a form of work role that did not exist before the rise of industrial society. Choice of occupation is for most Americans a rather haphazard procedure, and most young people achieve less than they think they will. Occupational mobility in American society is more often horizontal than vertical.

Unemployment in the United States is disproportionately high for young nonwhites. Unemployment is exceptionally demoralizing for male heads of families because of the stress our society places on being economically active and successful. Displacement of workers from their jobs by increased mechanization or by automation is more likely to result in unemployment and hardship among blue-collar workers than among white-collar workers. By far the greatest amount of technological displacement has occurred in agriculture.

Retirement in the United States at the present time is an economic and psychological ordeal that has not yet been substantially relieved by social legislation. The role of the retired person seems to be peculiar to industrial society. So, too, does the type of dissatisfaction with work that sociologists have labeled "alienation." This, however, should not be mistaken for dissatisfaction with work as a means to an end, since many people, given a choice between work and leisure, choose work. Even if a civilization of leisure is technologically possible, attitudes toward work will have to change before the leisure-oriented world becomes sociologically possible.

16

The Family

THE FUNCTIONS OF THE FAMILY

Regulation of Sexual Behavior and Parental Obligations. Transmission of Material Goods and Social Status. Companionship.

BASIC ORGANIZATIONAL PATTERNS

Forms of Marriage. Independence of the Marital Unit. Patterns of Family Organization. The Hopi: A Family Type.

THE CHANGING AMERICAN FAMILY

Laws and Mores Regulating Sexual Behavior. Changing Functions of the Family. Earning a Living. Education for Life. The Begetting of Children. The Religious Function. Protecting Family Members and Governing Their Behavior. Leisure and Recreation. Choosing a Marriage Partner. Love and Sex.

PRE- AND POST-MARRIAGE PATTERNS

Dating and Courtship. Marital Dissolution.

Human infants are conceived bisexually, and they will not survive unless someone tends to their immediate needs for a considerable period of time. The institution of the family, probably the oldest form of social organization, is based on these two facts. Anthropological research has revealed a variety of structural forms and patterns for the family, but all of them regulate sexual behavior, parental obligations, and property rights to food, clothing, and shelter. All provide for the socialization of children and for the adult need for companionship. Because the human infant matures slowly, much time is required to teach him the accumulated lore of the past, and at any cultural level, the institution of the family ensures that the individual will have the chance to learn whatever wisdom his ancestors have acquired. Thus the family is a basic agent for transmitting human culture.

From infancy we are all exposed to the regulatory patterns of our culture, and therefore it is not surprising that we should develop strong feelings about the "rightness" or "wrongness" of certain patterns. In no other area of sociological analysis is it so hard to avoid ethnocentrism, the feeling that the customs of other groups are quaint, queer, immoral, or unnatural. This ethnocentrism is especially obvious with regard to sexual behavior. We are likely to look askance, for example, at the homosexual relationships condoned by the ancient Greeks. Gouldner has asserted that even the *study* of Greek homosexuality has been systematically neglected by Western scholars.[1] Within American society, Kinsey found that college students defined moral behavior much differently than did respondents with less education. College students tended to condone a form of heterosexual activity called "petting"; the less educated defined petting as unnatural and immoral but condoned premarital coitus.[2] Thus the tendency toward ethnocentrism—which can be intracultural as well as cross-cultural—is a pitfall to be aware of as we begin our discussion of marriage and the family. We shall examine first the functions of the family.

1. Alvin W. Gouldner, *Enter Plato* (New York: Basic Books, Inc., 1966), p. 45.

2. Alfred C. Kinsey *et al., Sexual Behavior in the Human Male* (Philadelphia: W. B. Saunders Co., 1948).

3. Alfred C. Kinsey *et al., Sexual Behavior in the Human Female* (New York: Pocket Books, 1965), p. 101; originally published in 1953.

THE FUNCTIONS OF THE FAMILY

In all known societies the family is the primary agent of socialization during the children's early years. Obviously, parents can teach only what they already know, and thus children are socialized to the style of life and status of their parents. Since material goods are an essential element in style of life and status, the transmission of these goods is also regulated. And social control over sexual behavior and property leads to the patterning of adult needs for companionship. Let us review these areas in turn.

REGULATION OF SEXUAL BEHAVIOR AND PARENTAL OBLIGATIONS

The psychological object of human sexual behavior is orgasm, "a sudden release of neuromuscular tension."[3] But attainment of orgasm is not just another tension release mechanism. Instead, it has been the subject of detailed and occasionally severe sanctions: "If a man is found lying with a woman married to a husband, then they shall both of them die. . . ." (Deut. 22:22) If a man wishes to reduce the tension of hunger, the range of permissible behavior is comparatively wide. But sexual behavior may have consequences far beyond the immediate function of tension release: it can make the woman pregnant, and someone will have to care for the baby. Hence all societies have at least one role whose definition includes the obligation to rear children.

Among other mammals, the care and feeding of the young devolves primarily on the female because she has the equipment to give the infant a form of food it can digest. Among human beings, the situation was similar until quite recently. If a mother was unable to nurse her baby, a wet nurse was required. Now, however, every one of the operations performed to provide a baby with sustenance can be performed by a reasonably competent male. But rearing a child requires more than feeding it at appropriate intervals. Someone must provide food, clothing, and shelter for the infant and its caretaker. The man is generally expected to perform this role.

This division of labor formerly appeared rational because a woman who engaged in regular coital activity risked regular pregnancy and therefore needed to be available to feed a series of infants for about thirty years of her adult life. Doubtless it was this situation that led Marx and Engels to assert that the sex act was the beginning of the division of labor.[4] Although methods of preventing conception have been known for several thousand years,[5] only recently have they become generally reliable and—equally important—acceptable. Even today they are widely used only in the industrialized societies among the comparatively affluent. Consequently, the obligation to provide for a mother and her children is still defined as a male role.

If an infant's physical needs are not attended to with at least a minimum of efficiency, it will soon die, and evidence suggests that a child's social needs may be equally important to survival. (See the discussion of the effects of social isolation on children in Chapter 4, pages 143–146.) At the least, it is clear that if the infant does not receive some minimum of social stimulation, it will not learn how to behave as a social adult. Most persons who tend infants automatically talk to them and communicate feelings—love, anxiety, happiness, fear, hate—without being aware that they are engaged in the delicate and important task of transmitting culture to the next generation.

TRANSMISSION OF MATERIAL GOODS AND SOCIAL STATUS

The institution of the family regulates the transmission of material goods and social position to children. The child of rich parents shares their wealth, and the child of poor parents shares their poverty. Among other mammals, the children of the most efficient predators are better fed than the children of less able parents, but this advantage does not persist when the young animal becomes an adult and must fend for itself. Among human beings, the transmission of wealth and status to offspring is defined as right and just. Parents are socialized to love and provide for their children, and it seems "natural" that this feeling should persist after the children are grown. Most of us take for granted that our parents should try to provide us as adults with the same share of worldly goods they themselves

enjoyed, and we expect to do as much for our own children.

Thus economic and social opportunities depend, to a greater or lesser extent, on the accident of birth into a family rather than on individual characteristics. In industrialized societies the state claims some portion of parental wealth in the form of inheritance taxes. The transmission of social position is also more problematic in industrialized societies because many positions must be achieved rather than ascribed. The son of a physician, for example, has an advantage over other boys if he wishes to become a physician himself: he can learn some of the role requirements at home and his father's income will finance an expensive education. Yet to step into his father's role, the boy must do the necessary course work himself and possess enough ability to pass the required examinations. In traditional societies, as we have seen, wealth and status depend much more heavily on ascribed characteristics.

COMPANIONSHIP

Although rapid technological change sometimes makes us feel that we are facing problems never before faced, some aspects of family life appear to be perennial. One of these is the difficulties experienced by men and women when they must adjust to each other in a close relationship over a long period of time. Even if it is assumed that all human beings need companionship, the incompatibility of some married couples indicates that marriage is not always or necessarily the best means of satisfying the need. Yet most people appear to marry quite willingly. The advantage to the woman is that a particular man has become obliged to support her and her children. But why should men be willing to incur such responsibilities?

We can speculate that some men fall in love, and under the influence of this emotion, they may wish to ensure exclusive sexual access to a particular woman. Or they may perceive love of a woman as a multifaceted human rela-

4. Karl Marx and Friedrich Engels, *The German Ideology* (Moscow: Progress Publishers, 1964), p. 43; originally published in German in 1932.

5. John T. Noonan, *Contraception: A History of Its Treatment by the Catholic Theologians and Canonists* (Cambridge, Mass.: Harvard University Press, 1965).

Most persons who tend infants automatically talk to them and communicate feelings—love, anxiety, happiness, fear, hate—without being aware that they are engaged in the delicate and important task of transmitting culture to the next generation.

tionship entailing mutually advantageous rights and opportunities as well as responsibilities. Furthermore, fathering a family may provide a kind of immortality, a comfort in the face of certain death, and the right to transmit one's own share of worldly goods to one's offspring may also provide psychological satisfaction. In any event, men and women marry, and the ensuing emotional relationships, from passionate love to cold hatred, have been the source of inspiration for much great literature and myth. The ancient Sanskrit account of the origin of the family highlights this theme:

In the beginning, when Twashtri came to the creation of woman, he found that he had exhausted his materials in the making of man, and that no solid elements were left. In this dilemma, after profound meditation, he did as follows. He took the rotundity of the moon, and the curves of creepers, and the clinging of tendrils, and the trembling of grass, and the slenderness of the reed, and the bloom of flowers, and the lightness of leaves, and the joyous gaiety of sunbeams, and the weeping of clouds, and the fickleness of the winds, and the timidity of the hare, and the vanity of the peacock, and the softness of the parrot's bosom, and the sweetness of honey, and the cruelty of the tiger, and the warm glow of fire, and the coldness of snow, and the chattering of bluejays, and the hypocrisy of the crane, and compounding all these together, he made woman and gave her to man. But after one week, man came to him and said: Lord, this creature that you have given me makes my life miserable. She chatters incessantly and teases me beyond endurance, never leaving me alone; and she requires incessant attention, and takes all my time up, and cries about nothing, and is always idle; and so I have come to give her back again, as I cannot live with her. So Twashtri said: Very well, and he took her back. Then after another week, man came again to him and said: Lord, I find that my life is very lonely, since I gave you back that creature. I remember how she used to dance and sing to me, and look at me out of the corner of her eye, and play with me, and cling to me; and her laughter was music, and she was beautiful to look at, and soft to touch; so give her back to me again. So Twashtri said: Very well, and gave her back again. Then after only three days, man came back to him again and said: Lord, I know not how it is; but after all I have come to the conclusion that she is more trouble than a plea-sure to me; so please take her back again. But Twash-tri said: Out on you! Be off! I will have no more of this. You must manage how you can. Then man said: But I cannot live with her. And Twashtri replied: Neither could you live without her. And he turned his back on man, and went on with his work. Then man said: What is to be done? For I cannot live either with her or without her.[6]

This account has a male bias, revealing the ancient pattern of male dominance that, to a considerable extent, still survives. One of the major concerns of this chapter will be the ex-amination of changes that are occurring in male-female relationships and the influence of urban-ization and industrialization on these changes. We shall briefly discuss major types of family patterns, look at historico-legal influences on contemporary American patterns, discuss family life in the United States today, and comment on future prospects of this type of social orga-nization.

BASIC ORGANIZATIONAL PATTERNS

We have mentioned some of the biological facts that underlie marriage and family patterns. Human beings have responded to these facts in a number of ways, some of which we shall examine here.

FORMS OF MARRIAGE

Marriage occurs when the sexual union of at least one male and at least one female is sanctioned by law or tradition in order to define the relationship between them. The rela-tionships that are normatively defined involve not only sexual behavior itself but also obliga-tions toward offspring and such other matters as the proper division of labor. In some societies the marriage does not take place until the bride is pregnant. In others, such as our own, women are encouraged to marry before demonstrating fecundity. The two basic forms of marriage are *monogamy*, or the union of one man and one woman, and *polygamy*, or plural marriage. Polyg-amy may involve the union of one man with more than one woman (*polygyny*), one woman with more than one man (*polyandry*), or more than one man with more than one woman (*group marriage*).

Monogamy. Monogamy occurs in all soci-eties and is predominant even where other forms exist. The prevalence of monogamy may be due to the fact that more or less equal numbers of males and females are born and survive to the age of marriage. Moreover, supporting more than one wife and her children can be very expensive.

Monogamy was valued long before popular feeling supported equal rights for women in bed, at board, or in the polling place. Over a hundred years ago the Mormons were hounded from Illinois and attacked by the military forces of the United States largely because of Mormon sup-port of polygyny. The account of the behavior of a number of Old Testament patriarchs pro-vides some theological basis for polygyny in the Judeo-Christian tradition, but the New Testa-ment clearly favors monogamy. Although vari-ous Christian groups have experimented with other forms, eventually these forms were de-clared to be heretical, and monogamy has pre-vailed as the only "moral" form of marital rela-tionship where Christian influence is strong.

But nowhere has monogamy ever achieved perfect stability; some married persons do not remain sexually faithful to each other, and some terminate the relationship with divorce. The legal termination of marriage was a common practice among all ancient peoples of whom we have historical records, and anthropologists have found evidence of divorce among all the peoples they have studied. No adequate data exist on the prevalence of extramarital coitus in past societies, but literary and other records lead one to suppose that it has occurred at practically all times and places.

Polygamy. Polygyny, the union of one man with two or more women, is the most common form of polygamy, or plural marriage. Polyandry is much less common, and there is very little evidence to support the hypothesis that group marriage has ever been institutionalized on an intergenerational level in any society.

6. *A Digit of the Moon*, trans. F. W. Bain, in *The Family in Various Cultures*, ed. S. A. Queen *et al.* (New York: J. B. Lippincott Company, 1961), pp. 1–2.

Polygyny is as old as history and is still in evidence throughout most of the world. It is most commonly practiced today among the Muslims, whose sacred book, the Koran, specifies that under certain conditions a man may have as many as four wives. The most obvious limitation on polygyny is that it requires either a surplus of women or some wifeless men.

Polygyny might be expected to cause jealousy, conflict, and competition among the wives for the affection of the husband, but available evidence suggests that this is not necessarily so. Among the Crow Indians, for example, the first wife commonly suggested to her husband that he select a second wife to help with the household chores. The second wife might well be a sister or other blood relative whose marital prospects were otherwise dim. Thus polygyny might provide a sense of belonging for women threatened with spinsterhood.

The practice of polygyny is related to social stratification. Supporting more than one wife is an expensive business, and though Muslims are permitted more than one, most of them cannot afford it. In many instances where polygyny is practiced, only the chief of a tribe and his sons, or other males in positions of prestige and power, have more than one wife.

Polygyny is not consonant with contemporary Western values and beliefs, either religious or secular; and we may wonder whether it can persist in a world moving toward modern industrialization. Though this view may reflect ethnocentrism, there are reasons to believe that a monogamous marriage form is better suited to urban, industrialized societies. In all industrialized societies, equality of opportunity is ideologically emphasized, and one segment of this ideology is the notion that women should share the opportunity for sexual and emotional expression. Polygyny seems to offer less opportunity for women than monogamy. Furthermore, polygyny requires that if the sex ratio is about even, a certain number of men must forego marriage. In any event, the traditional values associated with polygyny, especially its reference to male prestige, income, and power and its utility as a means of increasing population size, are challenged both by egalitarian values and by the population explosion. And, the cost of maintaining a household in industrialized nations would make polygyny unattractive if not impossible for most men.

Polyandry has some utility when the means of subsistence are scarce and more than one male may be required to support one woman and her children. Under such conditions, female infanticide is sometimes practiced. Polyandry may also develop where there is a shortage of females for whatever reasons.

The common practice of the Toda of South India is for a female to marry one male and at the same time to become the wife of his brothers. This form of marriage—fraternal polyandry—makes the maintenance and generational transfer of property quite simple and assures the privilege of coitus to all or almost all adults in a society. When disparities in the sex ratio decrease and means of subsistence improve, societies that permit polyandry tend to move toward a monogamous form of marriage.

In both polygyny and polyandry, the female has low status. The norms governing behavior reflect male dominance and there is a primary concern with the satisfaction of male sexual needs while the female is assured of a home and of material provision for her children.

INDEPENDENCE OF THE MARITAL UNIT

The degree to which a married couple and their children are separated—economically, socially, and geographically—from all other kin is a major variable affecting the functioning of the family.

The nuclear family. We call a family structure *nuclear* in reference to the relations involving the husband, the wife, and their immediate children. The nuclear family is the *family of orientation* for the children, for whom it is also *consanguine,* because they are biologically related to all the other members. For the parents, the nuclear family is the *family of procreation.* It is not consanguine for them because, owing to universal incest taboos, they are not biologically related to each other.

When the nuclear family becomes isolated from its kin, family relationships are focused on a comparatively small number of persons. This fact affects role expectations. A wife may have to look to her husband to perform activities that would have been undertaken by a male member of her own family. Or she may have to do things herself or depend on her children for activities that might have been performed by an aunt or other relative. The young mother with small children in a strange city, for example, is particularly affected by the absence of relatives. She must spend a good portion of her time interacting with the children, without the companionship of any other adult. While she has the advantage (if she has enough money) of diaper service, dishwasher, and automatic washing machine, these contraptions provide no social interaction except when they break down and the repairman must be called.

The extended family. We shall call any family *extended* when it includes more than a father, a mother, and their children. Although the extended family is common in many traditional cultures, it is less common in urbanized societies because the male's choice of occupation and place to pursue it tends to be influenced by factors over which his parents have little control. Consequently the young husband and his wife are easily separated, geographically, from their kin. They are therefore not so likely to enjoy the material and social support the extended family can provide. On the other hand, as Olmsted noted, they are not so likely to be suffocated in its warm embrace.[7]

Many older family members have mourned the loss of extended family patterns. Elderly persons in uncertain health may be geographically separated from all those relatives whose role obligations would normally include providing them with a measure of aid and support. On the other hand, social structures have emerged which absorb some of the activities that used to be a part of life in the extended family: occupational groups, social and civic clubs, church and youth organizations, and the neighborhood kaffee-klatsch. And as we saw in the chapter on urban life, the extended family still has some viability even in big cities.

PATTERNS OF FAMILY ORGANIZATION

A number of patterns have evolved to meet the problems of defining parental obligations in child rearing, generational transfer of property, and location of residence. A brief description of these patterns is essential to an analysis of the contemporary Western family and may suggest some of the problems that can arise as societies with other structural patterns attempt to adopt the technological practices of industrialized nations.

The allocation of authority. Traditionally, the allocation of authority (the question of who makes the decisions) has been resolved in favor of the male. *Patriarchy,* or rule by the oldest male of the household, is the dominant pattern in many parts of the world, especially where Muslim culture exists. The essence of patriarchal authority is the high degree of arbitrary power exercised by the father of a family over his wife and children. Western society is characterized by a constantly increasing challenge to patriarchal patterns that have dominated family and community life for so many centuries.

Matriarchy, or rule by the mother, is much less common. In fact, some anthropologists have probably used this word to describe authority patterns in societies where the female was somewhat more dominant than in the anthropologist's own society. But it is doubtful that a society ever existed where the female dominated both the family and the power structure of the entire society. When maternal domination does occur, it is usually related to the absence of a male provider in the household—that is, where the father is absent or unable to provide economic support. In many parts of Latin America, for example, extreme poverty is directly related to a family structure consisting only of the mother and children.

In the United States a history of slavery and continued economic discrimination have fostered this kind of pattern among some blacks. The pattern may be expected to emerge and persist in any society where the man cannot find steady employment or where the jobs that he can find pay very low wages. Obviously, in this situation, women rule more by default than in accordance with a system of values that upholds female dominance. Moynihan reported that in the United States the proportion of nonwhite families headed by women had increased from 18 percent in 1950 to 25 percent in 1965, and was expected to increase even further.[8] This pattern, as well as the fact that a strong tie usually exists between the mother and young

---

7. Michael S. Olmsted, *The Small Group* (New York: Random House, Inc., 1959), p. 49.

8. Daniel P. Moynihan, "The President and the Negro: The Moment Lost," in *Commentary,* February 1969, p. 9.

children in *all* families, has led some scientists to argue that the basic definition of the family should be any group involving a mother and one or more children.

American middle-class families are sometimes thought to be tending toward a matricentric pattern because male occupational demands require that the father be absent from the household all day and authority over the children comes to rest almost exclusively in the wife's hands. Actually, authority over very small children tends to rest in the mother's hands in almost all societies. But in nonindustrial societies, the young male usually begins to work with his father and other adult males. Because this pattern is not normally followed in our type of society, the father loses some direct control over the adolescent male. But it does not follow that the mother gains the authority the father has lost.

Adolescents of both sexes are required by law to spend a sizable proportion of their waking hours in school, where neither parent is in control. Most adolescents seem inclined to spend the remainder of their waking hours with their peers, over whom parental control is at best remote. Because adolescents must remain in school so long in order to prepare themselves for the labor market, and because they are financially dependent upon their parents at this time, the stage is set for a family power struggle. The adolescent "squandering" of "hard-earned" parental income is painful for the parents to behold, and it is equally painful for the adolescents, who are often biologically and emotionally mature, to have to heed the tune called by those who pay the piper.

Actually, the emerging family pattern may perhaps most justly be called *egalitarian*, where authority is shared more or less equally by husband and wife and perhaps, to some extent, with the children. The nonworking wife may have the home to herself more than ever before in history, but role expectations concerning what she can do tend to limit her authority. As long as the husband's occupational role determines the family income level, place of residence, and general social standing, a truly egalitarian authority pattern is not probable, though certainly the wife has more voice in the decision-making process in the contemporary American family than in the patriarchal family.

Descent and residence. Just as people have been concerned about who shall make decisions, so also have they faced such questions as who shall own and inherit the goods that accumulate from one generation to the next. Three major structural patterns may be discerned: *patrilineal, matrilineal,* and *bilateral.* Thus, descent, family name, inheritance, performance of religious rituals, interaction with relatives, and a host of related activities may be focused on the father's side of the family, on the mother's, or on both.

About 40 percent of the societies examined by Murdock were found to have a patrilineal structure. In these societies a person's major kin relations—in essence, his family structure—and the greater part of all his social relationships are established for him in the male line. The mother's biological kin are ignored.[9] In the bilateral descent and inheritance pattern, social relationships are shared and developed through both the mother's and father's lines. This is the pattern of American society and of about 30 percent of all societies. In the matrilineal pattern the major social relations are developed through the female line, and the father's kin tend to be ignored.

Closely linked to the problem of descent is the question of place of residence. In *patrilocal* residence patterns, the norms require that all the father's male children live in or near his house. *Matrilocal* patterns require that the female children live with the mother. These patterns are also called *virilocal* or *uxorlocal* respectively, because the point at issue is whether the young couple live with his parents or hers. A *neolocal* pattern permits the couple to live away from the parents of both.

Patrilocal residence patterns may still be found in American cities among some first, second, and third generation ethnic groups. A "patriarch" may buy a large home or multi-family dwelling to house himself, his married sons, and other relatives. Patrilocal patterns predominate in more than half the societies examined by Murdock.[10] The crux of the issue is whether the young husband and wife must adapt to already established kin relations, or whether they can strike out on their own, depending primarily upon themselves for daily familial interaction.

---

9. See George P. Murdock, *Social Structure* (New York: The Macmillan Company, 1949), p. 15.

10. *Ibid.,* p. 20.

A number of points need to be made about these patterns of family organization. We have described them *as if* each were separate and distinct. Actually, several patterns may exist in the same society. While men have been dominant throughout most of history in most places, women have not necessarily been completely submissive and certainly have not lacked influence in the decision-making process, even in societies dominated by patriarchal patterns. Societies may also reveal both patrilocal and neolocal patterns simultaneously.

Some of these patterns appear to fit logically with certain other patterns. A patriarchal authority pattern appears to be well suited to a patrilineal pattern for property transfer and social relationships and to a patrilocal pattern for determining place of residence. But logic does not necessarily prevail in human organization, and matrilocality and matrilineality are not necessarily combined with matriarchy (although some authorities define a society as matriarchal if it is both matrilocal and matrilineal).[11]

Matrilineal households may be somewhat patriarchal or egalitarian in structure, as in the Hopi Indian family. Yet a tendency toward logical congruency can be discerned, and in the contemporary Western family the emerging patterns appear to be egalitarian, bilateral, and neolocal. The reader may judge from his own experience the degree to which these concepts reflect the reality of his own life experience.

THE HOPI: A FAMILY TYPE

A description of the Hopi type of family organization, which is somewhat distinct from the types found in industrialized societies, will give insight into a different style of living and help us recognize that other patterns can also regulate sexual behavior and provide family members with satisfying religious, educational, and work activities.

Ecological conditions. In the chapter on culture we discussed some of the key features of life among the Zuñi, a Pueblo Indian tribe of the American Southwest (pages 107–108). Closely related to the Zuñi are the Hopi, who inhabit a desert region of northern Arizona, about 120 miles east of the Grand Canyon.[12]

They appear to have lived in this isolated spot for more than fifteen centuries; their population numbers about four thousand, the descendants of some twenty thousand persons who inhabited the region at the time of the Spanish conquest. The Hopi kept to themselves then, as now, and are culturally homogeneous.

The Hopi eke out a precarious living based on dry farming, under constant threat of total drought or torrential downpours. They must also contend with sandstorms and rodents, and the danger of famine is always present. Few peoples have faced greater challenges in the struggle to survive.

A Hopi village consists of one or more large, terraced, multiroom dwellings built of mud, sticks, and stones. The dwelling usually has two levels, the upper for living, the lower for storage of food. The family sleeps on the floor on blankets or skins.

Family organization. Among the Hopi, the nuclear family unit is part of a larger group of related units that form a single household. The Hopi are matrilineal and matrilocal—the blood relatives are traced through the female line, and home ownership and performance of major ceremonials are based on this line of descent. The Hopi pattern of family organization emphasizes extended kin role relations, but the nuclear family is also important, as we shall see.

The Hopi plant maize, beans, and some fruit orchards. The lands and seeds for planting are owned by the matrilineal household, and the crops are worked by members of that household. Men are expected to work the cornfields while women tend the gardens. The male role also includes ownership and care of the sheep and cattle. The men weave clothing and make moccasins and silver jewelry, and the women care for the house and make baskets and pottery. In these activities the nuclear family works closely as a unit. Role training in economic activities is conducted by the parents.

Religion and tradition. The Hopi perceive the universe as an ordered, interrelated system of reciprocal relations dependent on man's will

---

11. Julius Gould and William L. Kolb, eds., *A Dictionary of the Social Sciences* (New York: The Free Press, 1964), p. 597.
12. This summary is taken largely from Queen *et al., The Family in Various Cultures,* Ch. 3, and Wayne Dennis, *The Hopi Child* (New York: John Wiley & Sons, Inc., 1940).

expressed in ritual and psychical acts and states. Nonhuman elements are acknowledged, but it is man's will that counts. Reciprocity is not between individuals but rather between groups, so that in a ceremonial a Hopi acts as a representative of some group. The group protects the individual as he moves through the life cycle. Ideally, Hopi norms call for unselfish, modest, unaggressive behavior.

Ceremonials are conducted by the clans, each of which consists of two or more households related through the female line. Clans are grouped in units called *phratries*. Among the important functions of the phratry are social control of marriage (marriage is not allowed within a phratry) and control over important religious ceremonials. The chief priest is the brother of the formal head of the clan—the ruling "matriarch," who keeps the symbol of ownership of the ceremonial in her home.

The village political structure is composed of the chief priests of the ceremonial societies. Their purpose is not to make new laws but rather to affirm the traditional Hopi mores in their decisions. Within the family, the mother and her brother are expected to exercise authority, and they, too, are supposed to enforce traditions and not make new rules. No competing ideologies or contrasting religious doctrines disturb the Hopi way of life.

Courtship and marriage. Courtship among the Hopi is informal. After boys and girls have endured the *rites de passage*, they are ready for courting. Boys are then considered as men and sleep in the men's ceremonial houses rather than at home. Apparently they may visit girls of their choice by night, and the girl's parents will not protest if the boy is a good prospect. A girl of marriageable age may have several suitors. If she becomes pregnant, she chooses a husband from among her suitors. (There are other ceremonial occasions when a girl may choose a marriage partner, but on these other occasions the boy is permitted to decline the honor.) Despite some dispute on this point, virginity does not seem to be a prime requisite for marriage among the Hopi.

Marriage to a person within the phratry is prohibited, and marriage to a person within one's father's phratry should be avoided. Ceremonial preparation for marriage is extensive. The ceremony is completed when the girl returns to her mother's home and her husband settles there with her—until death or divorce do them part. Divorce is accepted among the Hopi with little fanfare: the husband simply packs up and goes home to mother. The wife always retains custody of her children, and they are cared for by the household group, which, with the mother's brother, fills the gap left by the departed father. In fact, these people play an important role in the child's upbringing, even in a stable marriage. And the fact that divorce is permitted does not imply that Hopi marriages are unstable and beset with conflict. Hopi life tends to be peaceful in all respects.

Kin relationships. The terminology of kin among the Hopi gives some idea of the extensiveness of clan arrangements. The mother's blood brother and all males of his generation in the clan are called "mother's brother." All men and women of one's father's generation are called "father's brother" and "father's sister," respectively. Kinship terms and obligations are extended to cover one's own phratry and that of one's father. Hence, any single individual may be related to about half the members of a small village (i.e., one consisting of only several phratries).

These kin terms are not just quaint expressions, nor do they represent a failure in vocabulary development. Rather, they are a reflection of the roles people are expected to perform and of the attitudes they are expected to have toward one another. For example, the husband is a guest in his wife's home; in many ways his closest ties are with his mother's home, since he is "mother's brother" to his sister's children. And since if necessary he is considered to be mother's brother to all females of his sister's generation in his mother's clan, the possibility of his playing this role is greatly enhanced. Through training, he has been prepared to help his sister(s) discipline her (their) children. Just as he learned his ceremonial and clan roles from an uncle of his mother's family, so will he help his sister's children in turn to prepare to take over these roles.

Another aspect of matrilineal structure with matrilocal residence is revealed when a conjugal quarrel occurs: the wife is backed by a solid wall of kin while the husband stands alone. Thus the status of women is relatively high in Hopi society, compared to other traditional societies.

Despite the matrilineal patterns, the father-son tie among the Hopi is very close, partly

The Hopi Indians of northern Arizona have a life-style that differs considerably from most industrialized societies. The Hopi village is comprised of simple, two-level, multiroom dwellings; religious ceremonials (bottom left) are an important unifying force for the society as a whole; and Hopi family organization is an interesting combination of the nuclear and extended family. Typically, men work the corn fields and weave clothing, while women make baskets and pottery and take care of cooking and household chores. Because of the matrilineal pattern, the mother's brother is the primary disciplinarian and educator of his sister's sons. This relationship is probably the most crucial one in the development of the male self, but it also makes possible the development of a warmer and friendlier relationship between a son and his father (far left).

because the division of labor allows the father to teach his son about planting and herding. In addition, since the mother's brother has the major responsibility as disciplinarian, the father is free to develop a warm, affectionate relationship with his son. Thus every adult male has some degree of role specialization with reference to the young male. The adult male can be primarily expressive and affectionate with his son and a disciplinarian with his nephew.

According to the theory of matrilineal society, the role relationship between a mother's brother and her son should be the most crucial one in the development of the male self. With some modification, this is true among the Hopi. Mother's brother is the disciplinarian, and to make the boy a reliable worker, the uncle often resorts to drastic measures, putting the boy through all sorts of trials to prepare him for life. The mother's brother is also the key man in the boy's marriage arrangements and may even act as marriage counselor. Finally, he will eventually teach the boy the ceremonial and clan roles, thus preserving them within the clan for another generation. But when a man dies, he is buried by his son, who inherits most of his property.

Similarities to the Hopi way. When we compare the Hopi way with that of other peoples, we find some striking similarities despite the many apparent differences. The classic Jewish family also seeks oneness within an extended family pattern, with strong symbolic-religious overtones. No better example of a Christian achievement of unity through an extended pattern is to be found than in Horace Miner's study of the French Canadian parish, St. Denis.[13] There, as among the Hopi, family, work, and religion were integrated into a yearly cycle.

Although the Hopi vest the authority to make decisions in the female line, the males actually make the important decisions, as in most Western societies. If the Hopi courtship, marriage, and divorce patterns differ from our own, we can still see that sexual behavior in their society is regulated, as it is to some extent in all societies. Hopi society, like ours, has norms to guide the procreation and education of children, the bestowal of status, and daily social interaction. Such organizational forms define interaction with nonfamily members and also define the mechanisms of social control.

THE CHANGING AMERICAN FAMILY

To speak of "the" American family as though it constitutes a uniform type is somewhat ethnocentric. Anthropologists have described a wide variety of patterns among the early immigrant families to the area now called the United States—the American Indians. These patterns had no influence on contemporary patterns because a sizable proportion of the early immigrant families were killed and their land was appropriated by later immigrants, who had the advantage of superior military techniques. Most of the later immigrants arrived in a period of a little more than three hundred years commencing in 1607, the majority from western Europe and the British Isles. Their patterns provide the basis for generalizations about "the" American family pattern.

The habits and customs of this majority were influenced by the Judeo-Christian traditions: the people practiced a monogamous form of marriage with patriarchal authority patterns. The Puritan faction believed the pleasures of the flesh to be inordinately sinful, and because the Puritans and their descendants enjoyed political power out of all proportion to their number, their beliefs tended to be absorbed into the laws and mores of the entire land.

LAWS AND MORES REGULATING SEXUAL BEHAVIOR

In American society sexual morality, the law, and religious beliefs have always been closely intertwined. To discover how this came to be so, we must look back to the beginnings of Christian tradition, which was, of course, strongly influenced by the Hebraic tradition.

At first, the domestic mores of the early Christian families were not distinguishable from the Jewish, Roman, or Greek cultures of which they were a part. A distinctively Christian character to marriage and family relations began to emerge partly in response to the treatment ac-

---

13. Horace Miner, *St. Denis, A French Canadian Parish* (Chicago: The University of Chicago Press, 1939).

corded the Christians by the Romans. As the Roman emperors tried to eradicate the sect, Christian conduct became more opposed to Roman practice. Some influence can also be attributed to the older Jewish codes of sexual behavior: the sanctions were severe, and the list of proscribed behaviors was long.

Christians came to condemn easy divorce, the emancipation of women, and sexual freedom. The second coming of Christ was expected imminently, and many leaders questioned the value of marriage and family with the day of judgment so close at hand. St. Paul advised others to remain single, like him; they should marry only if aflame with an uncontrollable passion "for it is better to marry than to burn." The wife was to have a subordinate role in marriage: "Let wives be subject to their husbands as to the Lord; because a husband is head of the wife, just as Christ is head of the Church, being himself savior of the body. But just as the Church is subject to Christ, so also let wives be to their husbands in all things." (Eph. 5:22–24)

The problem of the dualism of the spirit and the flesh reached a high point in the writings of St. Augustine in the fifth century A.D. After living for years with a mistress, Augustine became a celibate priest and evolved a theology of marriage and family life that dominated Church thinking for over a thousand years. Puritan attitudes toward sex can be traced back to Augustine and other early Church Fathers. Sex was considered basically sinful except for purposes of procreation. Coitus was believed to show animal lust, and norms were developed to discourage lustful behavior. These beliefs came to play a vital role in the development of ideas about love and the role of sex in marriage until the present century. Part of the change in family life taking place today centers around this problem.

Not until the fifth century did the Christian Church decree that marriage was for life and that remarriage after divorce was to be punished by excommunication. This decree was a break with Hebrew and Roman practice—in fact, with the practices of almost all other societies. Through-

out most of Europe during the Middle Ages, the influence of the Church was so great that civil divorce was prohibited.

The impact of the Puritan Revolution. During the Middle Ages, sexual behavior proscribed by the Church was prosecuted by ecclesiastical courts. In England (but not on the Continent) such behavior became a crime during the late fifteenth and early sixteenth centuries— that is, offenders were prosecuted by the state rather than the Church. Sodomy and bestiality, for example, were made felonies in the time of Henry VIII. The Puritan Revolution in England stripped the ecclesiastical courts of all power and added adultery and incest as capital crimes, punishable in common law courts. As Ploscowe has pointed out, from measures such as these it was but a short step to prosecution and punishment for fornication and incontinent living, though these were not normally in the domain of the common law.[14]

The colonies most influenced by Puritans had the most stringent laws on sexual behavior. The Puritans of the Massachusetts Bay Colony, like their English counterparts, made adultery a crime punishable by death, though the death penalty was rarely invoked.[15] Fornicators were fined, subjected to corporal punishment, or forced to marry. The capital laws established by the General Court in Connecticut in 1642 decreed the death penalty for adultery, homosexuality, and bestiality.

The laws in colonial Virginia were more lenient. To judge by the size of the fines imposed, adultery was thought to be twice as sinful as fornication. Scott reports that prosecutions of free persons for adultery were rare, but servants were regularly called to account.[16] Servant women who bore illegitimate children were punished. The law of 1661 fixed the punishment at two years extra service, but the following year the preamble of a new law acknowledged that dissolute masters often got their servant maids with child in order to obtain extra service.

In time these laws became less severe. In 1649 the death penalty for adultery was revoked in Massachusetts, and whipping up to forty stripes, exposure on the gallows for an hour, and the perpetual wearing of the letter A—Nathaniel Hawthorne's "Scarlet Letter"—were substituted. But even today the legal codes of the various states remain relatively strict, revealing consid-

---

14. Morris Ploscowe, *Sex and the Law* (Englewood Cliffs, N.J.: Prentice-Hall, Inc., 1951), p. 138.

15. *Ibid*, p. 143.

16. Arthur P. Scott, *Criminal Law in Colonial Virginia* (Chicago: The University of Chicago Press, 1930), p. 280.

erable discrepancy between our formal and our informal norms.

Formal versus informal sexual norms. Certain kinds of behavior are almost always proscribed by law because the social danger is so obvious. Murder is an example. It is also obvious that every society has a deep interest in the survival of its children; hence the regulation of marriage and the family. Under the law, a man must provide for his family, and this law is generally enforceable. But one aspect of marriage and family law presents greater difficulties for enforcement, and this aspect is illegal sexual behavior. If the behavior involves the use of force, the victim can complain, thus bringing the behavior to the attention of legal authorities. But if the behavior occurs between consenting parties, in private, it may remain unknown, and the law forbidding it will be unenforceable. Some people argue that to have laws that cannot be enforced breeds disrespect for the law and is therefore dangerous to society. Others argue that if the law did not proscribe certain behaviors, such as adultery and homosexual contact, many more people would be likely to engage in such behavior.

Although every one of the fifty states has its own laws on sexual behavior, making generalization somewhat risky, we can safely say that the discrepancy between the actual incidence of proscribed behavior and legal punishment for it is probably very great. Adultery, for example, is defined as a felony in many states. In California it is punishable by a year in prison and/or a fine of $1000. In Massachusetts the maximum prison sentence is three years, and the fine may not exceed $5000. In Ohio a single act is not a crime, but cohabitation is punishable by a fine of $200 and a jail sentence of three months. In Tennessee adultery is not a crime.

Statutory rape occurs when a male has coitus with a female who is below the age of consent—twenty-one in Tennessee, eighteen in California and Texas, sixteen in Massachusetts, Michigan, and Ohio. Maximum punishment in these states ranges from the death penalty in Texas to ten years in Tennessee. (Fifteen other states provide for the death penalty if the victim is below a specified age, which ranges from sixteen down to seven.[17]

Some states distinguish between statutory and forcible rape (which clearly involves physical assault), while others do not. In Michigan,

for example, if the female is below the age of sixteen, statutory and forcible rape are not distinct offenses, and rape is a felony with a penalty of imprisonment for life or any term of years. The confusion of statutory and forcible rape in some state codes makes the national statistics on the incidence of rape ambiguous.

Kinsey's data give us some estimate of the incidence of adultery and statutory rape. Among married women in the sample, about one in four had experienced extramarital coitus by age forty.[18] Among married men the figure was 50 percent.[19] Three percent of the women in the total sample had experienced premarital coitus by age fifteen, and 20 percent between sixteen and twenty years of age.[20] From these data one may infer that some proportion of males, depending on the state definition of the age of consent, had violated the law.

The frequency of actual punishment for adultery and statutory rape may be indicated by Michigan data showing that from 1957 to 1961 one person was committed to prison for adultery while 423 were committed for rape. Only in 1957 were the data on forcible rape distinguished from the data on statutory rape, and in that year seventy-one persons were committed for statutory rape and seventeen persons for forcible rape.[21] If we assume that the behavior of people in Michigan during this period of time was somewhat similar to the behavior of persons included in the Kinsey samples, we may infer that considerable sexual activity that is punishable by law remains in fact unpunished in Michigan. A similar situation with respect to the law and actual behavior exists in the other states.

American laws on sexual behavior are characterized by severe penalties, owing to the Puritan heritage, and wide variation in penalties, owing to state laws. Behavior that is a felony in one state may not be even a misdemeanor in another. We can speculate that unless American behavioral norms revert to Puritan standards (in

17. Robert Bensing, "A Comparative Study of American Sex Statutes," *Journal of Criminal Law, Criminology and Police Science,* 42 (May–June 1951), 51–72.

18. Kinsey *et al., Sexual Behavior in the Human Female,* p. 416.

19. Kinsey *et al., Sexual Behavior in the Human Male,* pp. 586–589.

20. Kinsey *et al., Sexual Behavior in the Human Female,* p. 288.

21. Data supplied by the Michigan Department of Correction, showing prison commitments from 1957 to 1961.

which instance the behavior would tend to conform to the law), some effort may be made to provide a uniform, enforceable code—that is, a code whose penalties will be publicly approved and hence will be more enforceable.

CHANGING FUNCTIONS OF THE FAMILY

Some immigrant families settled in the wilderness and were forced to become highly self-sufficient. Others settled in villages and small towns where technological conditions were not much different from those in the European villages and towns they came from. The presence of a butcher, a baker, and a candlestick maker meant that some necessities did not have to be provided by the family itself. Yet all these families tended to perform services for their own members that today are performed by extra-familial agencies. In both New England and the South the household was the primary unit of social life, performing as a self-sufficient economic unit and providing educational, religious, and protective functions.

In a classic essay written more than a generation ago, William Ogburn enumerated the activities traditionally performed by the American family: affection-procreation; economic; education; religious; protective (political); status giving; and recreational.[22] In colonial days family role activities were blended to form a continuous life cycle which functioned to satisfy various human needs. The dilemma of modern times, according to Ogburn, is the loss of many of these "functions" from the family. Many activities once integral to the home are now performed away from it by persons who are not family members. Ogburn perceived that industrialization and urbanization had changed the

family from a relatively self-sufficient institution to an institution whose main function was the distribution of affection and the formation of personality.

Other social scientists offered different explanations for the changes. At Harvard both Sorokin and Zimmerman developed elaborate historical theories of a cyclical nature.[23] Instead of portraying the development of the contemporary Western family as a linear movement greatly influenced by technology and urbanization, they perceived a cycle in which the family was as much the cause as the effect of change. The family was seen to be crucial to the existence of society and, in this process, losing its activities. At a certain point the family becomes "atomized," the cultural pattern becomes "sensate," and as delinquency, family disorganization, increasing divorce, and sexual promiscuity become dominant patterns, the society disintegrates. In Zimmerman's words:

This is the basic theme of family and civilization. Civilization grows out of familism; as it grows it loses its original connection with the basic spring which furnished the essence of civilization. When this process has gone too far, the civilization soon exhausts its inventory of social "material." Then occurs a reaction or decay. The amount of reaction and decay and the length of these "Dark Age" periods seem to depend upon how quickly the culture finds its way back to the fundamental mother-source—familism.[24]

Both Sorokin and Zimmerman found the family and society in a state of decay which could be countered only by a return to the moral values and norms of the traditional family type. But other scholars have questioned whether the fact that the family was changing necessarily meant that it was declining in importance or that it was in a state of moral decay.[25] They argue that the family is adapting and modifying itself to the changing society of which it is a part. Thus, according to Burgess and Locke:

The form of the family that appears to be emerging in modern society may be called the companionship family because of its emphasis upon the intimate interpersonal association as its primary function. Other characteristics of the companionship family are: the giving and receiving of affection; the assumption of equality of husband and wife; democracy in family decisions, with a voice and a vote by

22. William F. Ogburn with Clark Tibbitts, "The Family and Its Functions," in *Recent Social Trends,* by the President's Research Committee on Social Trends (New York: McGraw-Hill Book Company, 1934), pp. 661 ff.

23. See esp. Carle C. Zimmerman, *Family and Civilization* (New York: Harper and Brothers, 1947); and Pitirim Sorokin, *The Crisis of Our Age,* (New York: E. P. Dutton & Co., Inc., 1941).

24. Zimmerman, *op. cit.,* p. 783.

25. Ernest W. Burgess and Harvey J. Locke, *The Family: From Institution to Companionship* (New York: American Book Company, 1960); Talcott Parsons and Robert F. Bales, *Family, Socialization and Interaction Process* (New York: The Free Press, 1955).

VIEWPOINTS   MARRIAGE AS A CHANGING INSTITUTION

"American marriage is in real trouble today," a young American husband wrote me a few weeks ago. I think I'd put it, instead, that men and women feel the need of new and mutual understanding. They are trying to achieve a new unity in an ancient institution. In other countries and other times, marriage has been a convenience, a necessity for economic and family, as well as personal, reasons. In our country and in our age, at least the economic reasons for marriage are disappearing. Men and women separately can now earn good livings, can make houses into pleasant homes. . . . Marriage today is increasingly for individual satisfaction, companionship and love, and for the chosen joys of children and family. The old ideas of heirdom and carrying on a clan name, so motivating in Asia, have all but ceased to exist in our country. Personal fulfillment through union in the highest and most complete sense is what we hope for in marriage. It is a manifold hope, and to realize it requires real effort from man and woman.

I realize that I am influenced by my own American marriage to believe that a good marriage is the natural source of happiness for both man and woman. I admire men and women who build fine, fruitful lives without marriage, but perhaps they would have been better still, because happier, if they had had the experience of good marriage. Yet nothing is more dreadful, more stultifying, more defeating than an unhappy marriage. It degrades both man and woman and there should be a decent and legitimate escape from it. But a good marriage!

. . . The more each knows of the other, the happier both will be. And you will never know everything, either of you, for in this mutual teaching—from the smallest detail, as for example how he likes his coffee, to the deepest and most profound matter of private love—you will discover that you are both growing and developing and reaching new levels of emotion and intelligence. There is nothing so fertilizing to the growth of the individual man and woman as love between them, a growing, living love, which is to say, true love. He will never stop loving you if he finds something always new in you, and through you, in himself. Nor will you ever stop loving him. Love dies only when growth stops. . . .

You may test the truth of your love by your own growth as a woman and his as a man. If you are both growing in happiness, improving in mind and body, then your way of loving is the eternal way.

Pearl S. Buck
To My Daughters, with Love

The truth as I see it is that contemporary marriage is a wretched institution. It spells the end of voluntary affection, of love freely given and joyously received. Beautiful romances are transmuted into dull marriages, and eventually the relationship becomes constricting, corrosive, grinding, and destructive. The beautiful love affair becomes a bitter contract.

The basic reason for this sad state of affairs is that marriage was not designed to bear the burdens now being asked of it by the urban American middle class. It is an institution that evolved over centuries to meet some very specific functional needs of a nonindustrial society. Romantic love was viewed as tragic, or merely irrelevant. . . .

The purposes of marriage have changed radically, yet we cling desperately to the outmoded structures of the past. Adult Americans behave as though the more obvious the contradiction between the old and the new, the more sentimental and irrational should be their advice to young people who are going steady or are engaged. . . .

Clearly, in middle-class America, the trend is ever toward more romantic courtship and marriage, earlier premarital sexual intercourse, earlier first marriages, more extramarital affairs, earlier first divorces, more frequent divorces and remarriages. The trend is away from stable lifelong monogamous relationships toward some form of polygamous male-female relationship. Perhaps we should identify it as serial or consecutive polygamy, simply because Americans in significant numbers are going to have more than one husband or more than one wife. Attitudes and laws that make multiple marriages (in sequence, of course) difficult for the romantic and sentimental among us are archaic obstacles that one learns to circumvent with the aid of weary judges and clever attorneys.

Now the absurdity of much of this lies in the fact that we pretend that marriages of short duration must be contracted for life. Why not permit a flexible contract perhaps for one or two or more years, with periodic options to renew? If a couple grew disenchanted with their life together, they would not feel trapped for life. . . . Instead of a declaration of war, they could simply let their contract lapse, and while still friendly, be free to continue their romantic quest. Sexualized romanticism is now so fundamental to American life —and is bound to become even more so—that marriage will simply have to accommodate itself to it in one way or another.

Mervyn Cadwallader
"Marriage as a Wretched Institution"

the children; the personality development of its members as a family objective; freedom of self-expression which is consistent with family unity; and the expectation that the greatest happiness is to be found in the family.[26]

Burgess and Locke have managed to avoid a temptation to see one particular form of family life as "natural" and preferable. They were not dismayed by the fact that family activities had changed. A look at some of these past and present activities of the American family may help us better understand its changing organization.

EARNING A LIVING

Murdock reports from his study of 250 societies throughout the world that family organization always combines the rights and privileges of sexual intercourse with norms and roles for a division of labor designed to satisfy the needs for food, shelter, and clothing. For the Hopi as for the ancient Hebrew, the family is a producing as well as a consuming unit. Men and women work close to the home, and children learn their economic roles from their parents. In an important sense, the family earns its own living.

In modern Western society and increasingly in other parts of the world, the family is now mainly a consuming unit. The division of labor to satisfy basic needs may require that both husbands and wives be away from home much of the day. The mother no longer has to make all the clothes, preserve a large part of the year's supply of food, and help the father with gardening and caring for the livestock. The father's labor brings forth not agricultural produce—a good harvest and fat cattle—but an abstract medium of exchange—money—or, more often than not, an even more abstract check representing the money, most of which he will never actually see.

But the husband is not the only member of the family earning a paycheck today. In 1900 only about 4 percent of American married women worked outside the home for wages and salaries. By 1950, this figure had risen to 24 percent, by 1960 to more than 30 percent, and

by 1970 to about 40 percent. This change, which has struck such a hard blow at the aphorism that "a woman's place is in the home," is due to several factors. The rapidly expanding economy has created new roles that men and women have both been able to fill, and World Wars I and II so disrupted the industrial labor force as to give great impetus to women to work outside the home. Apparently they liked the new work roles, which, among other things, broadened their daily interaction with other people. At the same time the urban economy was producing more and more goods for the home that women used to have to make themselves. Thus, the industrial economy was simultaneously making obsolete many activities of their traditional household role and developing new roles that were attractive to women. We will consider other dimensions of the changing role of women as we examine other family activities.

In an important sense, the family has lost the productive activity: it no longer produces its own material goods. *Consumption* of goods and services is still very much family oriented, however. All family members are allowed, even encouraged, to participate. Whereas previously they worked together, now they shop together. Children learn early the ways of the marketplace. As was suggested in the chapter on socialization, the challenge to the family seems to lie not in seeking a return to the past but in devising a means by which young people can adjust to changing roles in societies with an increasingly complicated division of labor.

EDUCATION FOR LIFE

Research seems to indicate that as the family becomes less central for some aspects of education, it may become more important for others. Parsons argues that the family continues to be the prime agent for a sense of social solidarity for the individual, both in his own family and in society:

In socialization the family is above all the agency for establishing cathexes and identification, for integration into the series of social systems in which the child will function as an adult. Above all, perhaps, it is the primary agency for developing his capacity to integrate with others, to trust and be trusted, to exercise influence, and to accept legitimate influence.[27]

26. Burgess and Locke, *op. cit.*, p. 651.
27. Talcott Parsons in *Man and Civilization*, ed. Seymour M. Farber *et al.*, (New York: McGraw-Hill Book Company, 1965), p. 44.

The influence of family socialization is especially obvious in courtship and mate selection. Early family training puts limits on so-called free choice. Generally speaking, our society continues to be marked by intraracial, intraethnic, intrareligious, and intraclass marriages. Studies on mate selection show that people with similar interests and backgrounds marry each other more often than they marry those with dissimilar interests and backgrounds. What parents teach about race, ethnicity, and the like may be expected to continue to have great influence on their children, especially if the home is harmonious.[28]

Family socialization is influential in other ways. The factor found to correlate most consistently with successful adjustment in marriage is the harmony in the home life of husbands and wives in their premarital days. Parents serve as role models with whom they are able to identify. Lazarsfeld and his colleagues, in their famous study *The People's Choice,* reported that the family was one of the most important influences on the voting behavior of their respondents.[29] And Davies in summarizing the literature on political socialization states: "The family's central role in forming the individual's political personality derives from its role as the main source for the satisfaction of his needs. The child therefore tends to identify with his parents and to adopt their outlook toward politics."[30]

However, the educational function of the family has clearly been altered. The school, mass media, and other social agents will probably increase their roles in training the young. Some conflict may occur if what the family teaches the child is contradicted by these other agencies. (Science courses may contradict racial and ethnic beliefs.) Some dismay may occur when the schools teach the child things that the parent cannot understand. (The introduction of the new math, for example, caused considerable anguish to parents who had always thought themselves to be competent with figures.) In the meantime, the occupational structure changes so rapidly that both parents and schools have difficulty giving the child adequate training and advice for the world he will face.

THE BEGETTING OF CHILDREN

Prior to the nineteenth century most families all over the world were small. Women generally bore three to five children, of whom two or three on the average would survive to adulthood. Family size was in large part controlled by high death rates, especially of infants. Throughout history, the nuclear family probably averaged only four or five persons.

By the middle of the nineteenth century, however, mortality rates were beginning to drop markedly, first in Europe and then in the United States. One consequence was that women lived longer and could bear more children. In the United States seven or eight became the average, and three to five of these survived to adulthood, helping to increase family size as well as the rate of population growth. In the early years of the Industrial Revolution when the labor of children in mills and factories was essential to the family's earning power, and during America's westward movement when many hands were needed to develop homesteads, the larger family could be seen as a benefit. But as child labor diminished and urbanization increased, married couples adopted various forms of birth control, thereby countering the consequences of lower mortality rates, especially at the younger age levels. People who lived in cities found the ideal of a large family to be incongruent with urban living and its opportunities for increased personal freedom, to say nothing of the fact that changing economic patterns made children an economic liability rather than an asset. And so family size decreased to its earlier level, and a smaller family was defined as the new ideal.[31]

Urbanization and industrialization have made small family size both possible and convenient. Parents can be fairly sure that the children they have will live to grow up, and a small family is easier to support than a large one. These facts have consequences: a woman's role as mother is completed long before she is too old to be economically and socially productive. On the average, American women bear their last child before they are thirty. By the time she is in her mid-forties, the average woman must find

28. See Ruth S. Cavan, *The American Family,* 3rd ed. (New York: Thomas Y. Crowell Company, 1963), pp. 320 ff.

29. Paul F. Lazarsfeld, Bernard Berelson, and Hazel Gaudet, *The People's Choice,* in William Petersen, ed., *American Social Patterns* (Garden City, N.Y.: Doubleday & Company, Inc., 1956), esp. pp. 161–163.

30. James C. Davies, "The Family's Role in Political Socialization," *The Annals of the American Academy of Political and Social Science* (September 1965), p. 10.

31. Judith Blake, "Ideal Family Size Among White Americans: A Quarter of a Century's Evidence," *Demography,* 3, No. 1 (1966), 172.

something to fill her time that is an adequate substitute for the mother role. Some women enter the labor market. Others engage in volunteer work. Still others intensify their domestic labors and resurrect productive activities—like knitting sweaters and making jellies—that are no longer necessary but that may result in better goods than technology supplies. Some writers believe that today's woman is lucky to have so many choices, but others have observed that her attempts to find worthwhile, satisfying activities are often frustrated.

The fact that the labor energy of children is less needed around the house also gives rise to problems. Children are often set to doing little jobs not because their help will save the mother's time and energy but because the chore is alleged to be good for the child's character. Some mothers have the patience to supervise the work and make it attractive to the child. But children often see such make-work activity for what it is. As children enter adolescence, it is somewhat easier to find things for them to do that are actually helpful to adults. Boys can have newspaper routes, for example, and girls can baby-sit. But meaningful work for adolescents is hard to find, and the long summer vacation can be a trial both to them and to their parents. Fortunately, the length of the school year and the mountains of homework (alleged to be good for intellectual growth) help make the situation bearable the rest of the time.

THE RELIGIOUS FUNCTION

A popular aphorism says that "the family that prays together stays together." Evidence to support this saying is found in the fact that the divorce rates of those couples who share the same religious beliefs are lower than the rates of those who have different religions or lack a formal church affiliation. But the aphorism hardly explains the nature of the relationship between religion and family. Can the rise in divorce rates and general family disorganization be attributed to the loss of religious activity within the family? And to what extent has religious activity been lost to the home? Are other activities as important as religion in keeping a family together?

It seems clear that ritualistic religious practices such as fasting and observing special days of prayer have lost some of their significance to the family as a group. And while the *rites de passage* at birth, young adulthood, marriage, and death are still religious family functions, they lack some of the significance they once had. Relatives are more likely to be spectators to these events than central role players with long-range mutual obligations and expectations. The family religious practices that have held such a central place in Jewish tradition—such as the observation of dietary laws, the lighting of the Sabbath lights by the wife, and the reciting of the *kiddush* by the husband—seem to have suffered a particularly sharp decline in American society.[32]

Among Christian families in America, the most common form of religious family worship has been the saying of grace at meals. Apparently, this practice is still common, varying somewhat by religious denomination. For example, in a recent study of eight religious denominations in Oklahoma, the number of respondents who reported that they said grace or table prayers at least once daily ranged from a high of 100 percent among members of the Assembly of God to a low of 40 percent among the members of the Christian Church. A majority in six of the eight denominations reported daily grace at meals. But family Bible reading seems to have disappeared from most American homes.[33]

Until recently, at least, church membership has been rising in the United States. It was estimated to have reached a steady 63 percent between 1950 and 1958,[34] and by 1960 it was higher than it had been at any other time in this century. But it has been charged that religion in American society is now relegated to Sunday morning and has ceased to be meaningful in the daily lives of most families. Questions have also been raised in recent years about the impact of the parochial school system and its relation to family life. It is true, for example, that about half the Catholic children in the United States are enrolled in parochial schools, but a recent study by Greeley and Rossi revealed that the parochial school appeared to

---

32. See Mannheim S. Shapiro, "Jewish Family Values," in *Council Woman*, a publication of the National Council of Jewish Women (February 1965).

33. Unpublished study by William V. D'Antonio, James Davidson, and Joseph Schlangen, "Protestants and Catholics in Two Oklahoma Communities" (University of Notre Dame, 1966).

34. Richard Lambert, "Current Trends in American Religion—A Summary," *The Annals of the American Academy of Political and Social Science* (November 1960).

Not long ago the labels "breadwinner" and "homemaker" were indicative of the clearly defined roles that a man and a woman assumed in marriage. Today, however, the roles frequently overlap. A wife often puts in as many hours at the office as does her husband, and thus the couple may share such household chores as doing the laundry. Decision-making, too, has become a cooperative effort, with husbands and wives typically collaborating on important family matters. Recently, even the question "who should raise the children" has caused considerable controversy. In the United States the responsibility of child rearing still rests primarily with the woman, but some countries—such as Israel—have experimented with various forms of communal families (left), which relieve the mother of some of this responsibility.

be most effective religiously with students who came from homes with religious parents. And apparently only a minority of the students studied came from such homes.[35]

Despite these changes, the home continues to be the source of basic values and beliefs, many of which continue to have religious overtones. The current religious revolution has involved the attempt to make religious beliefs relevant to the secular city, to preach a gospel of concern for one's neighbor. If religious leaders succeed in their quest, it will be because families have accepted this social gospel as part of the socialization process and as part of their role obligations.

PROTECTING FAMILY MEMBERS AND GOVERNING THEIR BEHAVIOR

Father used to rule the roost, with some help from mother. He was obliged to protect his wife and family from external dangers, and he often had power of life and death over family members. It was *his* business if his children, or his wife, needed a good whipping. We now have police, city, county, and state organizations to handle many of the protective activities males used to be responsible for. In the process of change, the father's power has been drastically reduced. Local, state, and federal governments have all passed laws that to some extent free his wife from inferior status, and his children's behavior is subject to extra-familial discipline as well.

The reciprocal role obligations by which parents protected children and in turn were given help in old age have also broken down. The parents' protective function is more indirect; much of it is purchased for the children by the taxes the parents pay. At the same time, pension retirement plans and social security benefits have reduced the protective role of children in the parents' old age.

LEISURE AND RECREATION

Some people bemoan the passing of the good old days when the family spent its leisure time together. But we must remember that in earlier times the working day was a lot longer, no one had much leisure time, and there were relatively few ways to spend it. We cannot doubt that families do spend less time together, but whether this has serious consequences for the family as an institution is another matter.

For example, dating as a form of recreation has become a part of teen-age and young adult culture in American society. As recreation, it is consistent with the emphasis on freedom from adult supervision, independence training, and the idea that young people should have *fun* together. At the same time, dating serves as an important form of socialization. In a society that values freedom in mate selection, dating serves as a mechanism by which young people can come to know each other, develop interpersonal competency, and see themselves in their respective sex roles. Thus, while the manifest function of dating may be recreation, its latent function as socialization may be vital to family stability in the future.

CHOOSING A MARRIAGE PARTNER

Mixed marriages—interclass, interethnic, interfaith, and interracial—have been opposed throughout history. The main reason for opposition has been the ethnocentric belief that "we are better than they" and that therefore "*we* should not besmirch the family name by allowing any of *our* members to marry into *that* family." The findings of sociologists might lead society's members to oppose mixed marriages, but for different reasons. Sociological findings support the generalization that "the greater the sociocultural differences between the partners the less likely are chances for success in marriage."

The class factor. Most marriages in America, as well as in other Western societies, are intraclass. As Hollingshead showed in his study of Elmtown's youth, teen-age dating patterns are very much class-oriented, so the probability that young people will become seriously involved with persons not of their class-status position is greatly reduced before serious dating occurs.[36]

---

35. Andrew Greeley and Peter H. Rossi, *The Education of Catholic Americans* (Chicago: Aldine Publishing Company, 1966).

36. A. B. Hollingshead, *Elmtown's Youth* (New York: John Wiley & Sons, Inc., 1949).

It would seem that colleges and universities are so organized socially as to minimize cross-class dating. Where fraternities and sororities abound, they act as a filtering mechanism to insure a minimum of cross-class dating and marriage. In other cases, the very homogeneity of the student body mitigates against the development of breaks in the class dikes. Finally, it should be remembered that children from the lower classes still don't get to college with the frequency of middle- and upper-class children, further insuring against a widespread pattern of cross-class marriages. Still, with our movement toward a predominantly middle-class society, it is evident that young people have a greater range of possible marriage mates today than ever before.

Ethnicity. The movement toward middle-class life has been a major factor in the breakdown of ethnic ghettos. As one third-generation American put it: "When I was young 'marrying out' meant marrying someone who was not of the same ethnic group." In American cities during the early years of this century, there were as few mixed marriages between Irish and Italian and Polish Catholics as there were between any one of them and non-Catholics. To a great extent the values, beliefs, and sentiments that held these ethnic ghettos together have broken down as these groups have become assimilated into the broader context of American life.

From the sociological viewpoint, the important thing is to try to comprehend the social forces that work to foster or discourage inter-ethnic marriages. Does the breakdown of old barriers reflect an increasing cultural consensus, a homogenization of the society? Does the process reveal trends that may become predictive of new patterns in interfaith and interracial marriages?

Interfaith marriages. All major religious groups strongly oppose interfaith marriage for these basic reasons:

1. Differences in religious beliefs furnish "fundamental" differences for individual and family value systems, posing constant threats to the maintenance and development of conjugal love and family unity.

2. Among the values that may bring on conflict in the family is that centering around the religious training of children. In what religion shall the children be brought up? The Catholic Church may require non-Catholics who marry Catholics to agree that the children will be brought up in the Catholic faith. In a sense, this forces the non-Catholic to acknowledge that his religious values are not as significant or valid as those of his marriage partner.

3. Kin loyalties and church loyalties may clash. (This reason may have had more validity in times when married couples were more closely tied to their kin.)

4. The spiritual aspect of marriage may suffer from the fact that each partner has different beliefs and values.

Despite such objections to interfaith marriage, unions between Catholics, Protestants, and Jews, and even between believers and non-believers, have been steadily increasing in American society and in Western societies generally. It is estimated that at least 30 percent of all American marriages validated by the Catholic Church are mixed. The percentage of mixed marriages for Protestants as a general category is somewhat lower, and Jews report the lowest percentage of all, between 5 and 10 percent. Such factors as ethnic cohesiveness, socio-economic status differences, and plain prejudice have been found to be related to these various rates.[37]

Truxal and Merrill have suggested that the increasing rates of interfaith marriage in the United States, principally between Catholics and Protestants, may mean one or both of two things: (1) the population is becoming more homogeneous; thus religious barriers are breaking down; (2) there is a possibility that marital conflict is increasing partly as a result of the increase in interfaith marriages.[38]

In a study of interfaith marriages in New York City, Heiss found that many of those involved had nonreligious parents and came from troubled homes.[39] But some partners in interfaith marriages come from harmonious, closely knit families in which they were indoctrinated with their parents' religious beliefs. Probably most have also been indoctrinated with the gen-

---

37. John L. Thomas, "The Factor of Religion in the Selection of Marriage Mates," in *Sourcebook of Marriage and the Family,* ed. Marvin Sussman (Boston: Houghton Mifflin Company, 1968), pp. 243–246.

38. A. Truxal and F. E. Merrill, *The Family in American Culture* (Englewood Cliffs, N.J.: Prentice-Hall, Inc., 1947), pp. 607–610.

39. Jerold S. Heiss, "Premarital Characteristics of the Religiously Intermarried," *American Sociological Review,* 25, No. 1 (February 1960), 47–55.

MEASURING CONJUGAL INTERACTION PATTERNS

One of the most useful methods for measuring the quality of interaction between a husband and wife is the *Revealed Difference Method* developed by Fred L. Strodtbeck. Strodtbeck based his approach on a procedure known as *Interaction Process Analysis,* a technique worked out by Robert F. Bales for measuring interaction in small groups. In Interaction Process Analysis (IPA), the investigator observes the participants in a small-group discussion and scores each interpersonal "act" (statement) in terms of both general and specific categories: *positive socio-emotional reactions* (e.g., those showing solidarity or agreement), *negative socio-emotional reactions* (e.g., those showing hostility or disagreement), *task-oriented answers* (e.g., suggestions or opinions), and *task-oriented questions* (e.g., requests for suggestions or opinions). By determining the relative occurrence of each type of "act" during the course of a problem-solving situation, the investigator is able to measure both individual and group characteristics.

Strodtbeck adapted this basic scoring technique from the IPA to his Revealed Difference Method for evaluating husband-wife interaction patterns. With this technique, the investigator presents a husband and wife with a series of stories, each of which contains some problem that a couple might typically encounter. For every problem two alternate solutions are given, and the spouses are asked to choose independently the solution they prefer. After several stories have been presented to the couple, the investigator determines the problems on which husband and wife disagree (hence the name *Revealed Difference Method*). The spouses are then asked to discuss each of the problems for which they have picked opposing solutions in order to arrive at a solution that is mutually acceptable. These discussions are tape-recorded and then scored by the technique used in Bales' IPA. (A less commonly used system of scoring is to have a panel of judges rate the participants on a series of specific interpersonal dimensions.)

This method for measuring the quality of interaction between spouses is based on the assumption that a husband and wife will reveal their customary modes of relating to each other as they discuss a problem and try to agree on a solution to it. The method enables the investigator to assess how different interpersonal variables in the interaction process vary from one married couple to another, among different socioeconomic groups within a society, or even between different societies. It is possible, for instance, to determine if the husband has a great deal more power than his wife and also what effect this has on the general orientation of each spouse to the other (e.g., couples in which one spouse has considerably more power than the other will manifest, on the average, less affection and more hostility in their interaction than couples where the power differential is not so great). The Revealed Difference Method also permits the investigator to determine how particular types of conjugal characteristics are related to other variables in which he may be interested.

Critics of the Revealed Difference Method argue that it does not provide a true measure of interaction patterns between a husband and wife because the experimental situation introduces the element of artificiality. Thus the participants' behavior toward one another is something less than "real." Although this criticism is not without merit, it does not completely refute the validity of the technique. General interpersonal orientations are not readily altered, even in an experimental situation. The Revealed Difference Method can be especially useful in supplementing other means of gathering data (such as interviews) since it permits a much more quantifiable indicator of husband-wife interaction patterns. Because it is essentially a culture-free instrument, it is particularly valuable in cross-cultural work. It has been used successfully by Liu among the Chinese in Hong Kong and by Hutchison in the Philippines, as well as by Strodtbeck among different cultural groups in the United States.

For elaborations of the Revealed Difference Method and the IPA, see Fred L. Strodtbeck, "Husband-Wife Interaction over Revealed Differences," *American Sociological Review,* 16 (August 1951), 468–473; and Robert F. Bales, *Interaction Process Analysis: A Method of Study of Small Groups* (Cambridge, Mass.: Addison-Wesley Publishing Company, 1950). For a criticism of the Revealed Difference Method, see Arthur J. Vidich, "Methodological Problems in the Observation of Husband-Wife Interaction," *Marriage and Family Living,* 18 (August 1956), 234–239. For applications of the method in cross-cultural studies, see W. T. Liu, "Family Interactions among Local and Refugee Chinese Families in Hong Kong," *Journal of Marriage and the Family,* 28 (August 1966), 314–323; and Ira W. Hutchison, *Husband-Wife Interaction and Fertility Patterns in the Philippines* (Unpublished Ph.D. dissertation, University of Notre Dame, 1970).

eral cultural belief that the choice of a marriage partner is a purely personal decision and that "love conquers all." Other social factors may also encourage an interfaith marriage. The proposed spouse may be a "good" person, with assets to offset the religious difference. Willingness to accept a prenuptial agreement to bring up the children as Catholics might be a major offsetting factor to a Catholic. Parents may prefer an interfaith marriage that guarantees upward mobility for their child to an intrafaith marriage that does not. Given the impetus to change already present in our society and the fact that there is discussion among Protestant and Catholic theologians and church leaders of possible easing of proscriptions, it may be expected that interfaith marriages will become increasingly common.

Race. The most highly proscribed form of mixed marriage in the United States continues to be interracial marriage, particularly marriage between blacks and whites. Here, centuries of strong prejudice minimize the probability of any great amount of intermarriage in the foreseeable future. It may be hypothesized that much of the resistance by whites to integrated housing is based on the fear that it will lead to interracial marriage.

Even though state laws forbidding racially mixed marriage have recently been declared unconstitutional, the mores against it remain strong, and they are broken very infrequently. In California, there were only 455 racially mixed marriages during the first thirty months after the repeal (in 1948) of a state law prohibiting such unions. This represented just .56 percent of all marriages. A recent study by Heer showed slight increases in interracial marriage in California, Hawaii, Michigan, and Nebraska—the only states for which recent data were available—but the rate of frequency was still very low. In no case did the percentage of whites marrying

blacks reach even *one* percent. The highest reported rates for blacks marrying whites were in Hawaii (16 percent) and California (2.58 percent).[40]

Data from a number of studies show that black men marry white wives almost four times more frequently than black women marry white husbands. What factors might help explain this pattern? It has been hypothesized that most black men who marry white wives come from higher occupational strata than the average for blacks and that they marry women who come from somewhat lower economic strata.[41] In such case the black man might perceive a gain in social status by marrying a white wife, and the white woman might perceive an improved economic position as worth any possible lessening of status. The black women who might be interested in marrying a white man, by contrast, would probably have more to lose than to gain by marrying someone with a lower position in the economic scale. And like her male counterpart, she is unlikely to find a white spouse of equal class standing.

Despite some increase in interracial dating, especially on college campuses, most blacks as well as most whites continue to have a strong preference for marriage with someone of their own race and social background. There seems little basis for predicting a rapid increase in racially mixed unions in the near future.

LOVE AND SEX

In American society romantic love is widely regarded as the basis of a successful marriage. A young man and woman are "meant for each other"; for each, the other is the "one person in the world who can bring happiness." The relationship is predestined; it is "love at first sight." Popular music, novels, movies, soap operas, and innumerable advertisements for an endless variety of goods and services have all contributed to the creation of role models heightening the illusion that love can conquer all.

Unfortunately, there have been no studies that would show the percentage of couples whose marriages grew out of romantic love or whose social relationships in marriage were reflections of this ideal. But some research findings are suggestive. For example, a recent study of some six hundred married women in

40. David M. Heer, "Negro-White Marriage in the United States," *Journal of Marriage and the Family,* 28, No. 3 (August 1966), 262–273.

41. A recent study in Indiana tends to cast doubt on this hypothesis. Pavela found in his study of ninety-five interracial marriages that the occupational distribution of the spouses was the same as for Indiana as a whole. Even in Pavela's sample, however, black husbands outnumbered black wives by about three to one. See Todd H. Pavela, "An Exploratory Study of Negro-White Intermarriage in Indiana," *Marriage and Family Living,* 26 (May 1964), pp. 209–211.

and around Chicago revealed that they selected "mother" as the most important female role, with "wife" a poor second.[42] More than 60 percent of the older women perceived "bread-winner" rather than "husband" as the most important male role.

Still more indirect evidence against the theory of romantic love is provided by other studies of marital adjustment. The factor most consistently associated with successful adjustment is that of perceived happiness of parents' marriages. Other factors that have consistently correlated with such adjustment—e.g., adequate length of acquaintance, courtship, and engagement; adequate sex information in childhood; mature and similar chronological age[43]—do little to support romantic love as the keystone to successful marriage.

In fact, Bell argues that writers of marriage manuals who romanticize sexual union in marriage may make it difficult for couples to adjust to reality. Such passages as the following may set off unrealistic expectations, especially for the wife:

In concrete terms a woman might compare sexual love with a mountainside which she and her husband climb together because they want to share the adventures along the upward path and the superb view from the summit—they adjust their pace to each other, ascend the last steep slope side by side and share the sudden beauty of the valleys and skies at the moment they reach the peak.[44]

Bell analyzed data which showed that between 20 percent and 29 percent of married women in various studies had overestimated the place of sex in their married lives. At the same time, while a majority of women in all studies, and a great majority of college-educated women, reported being satisfied with sex in their lives, about one fourth of married women studied claimed that their sexual needs were not being fully met.[45]

Further criticisms of the romantic love complex are found in the writings of Joseph Folsom, who argues that "cardiac-respiratory" or excited love is only a temporary phenomenon.[46] This love is manifested in the sense of breathlessness and trembling, fear and pleasure that comes over the lover at the mere presence of the beloved. According to Folsom, many couples mistake it for true love and refuse to accept the fact that excited love will abate. They want a perpetual romance. Thus "love at first sight" becomes their prerequisite for marriage. But Folsom argues that learning the techniques of competent sexual intercourse may be a much more certain road to marital happiness. And the strong emphasis on personal happiness in the romantic complex can easily lead to sexual exploitation by either partner, whether intended or not.

Nelson Foote has attempted to provide a sociological definition of the concept of love. He states that "love is that relationship between one person and another which is most conducive to the optimal development of both."[47] This development is to be measured in terms of their interpersonal relations, and in a total social sense, not only with each other but with all others with whom they come into contact.

According to Foote, these interpersonal relations are marked by "social equality and reciprocity." Social equality refers to the way in which a couple learns to share in certain valued experiences. It is not exploitative, nor can it develop in an atmosphere of super-subordinate relations. Reciprocity involves the recognition of the value of the other's attempt to do something for you. Reciprocity is basic to much if not all of social interaction. People in love are constantly performing reciprocal acts for one another, as an expression of their love. Where one or another spouse does not or cannot reciprocate, then only a dependency relationship can develop.

In contemporary American society, and increasingly throughout the world, something akin to this kind of interpersonal relationship now called conjugal love is gaining ascendency as a basis for marriage and the family. It is built on sexual attractiveness but not exclusively.

42. Marya Mannes, "I, Mary, Take Thee, John, as . . . What?" *The New York Times Magazine,* November 14, 1965.

43. Clifford Kirkpatrick, *The Family as Process and Institution,* 2nd ed. (New York: The Ronald Press Company, 1963), pp. 384 ff.

44. Robert R. Bell, *Premarital Sex in a Changing Society* (Englewood Cliffs, N.J.: Prentice-Hall, Inc., 1966), p. 136.

45. *Ibid.,* p. 137.

46. Joseph K. Folsom, "The Romantic Complex and Cardiac-Respiratory Love," in *Selected Studies in Marriage and the Family,* ed. R. F. Winch and R. McGinnis (New York: Holt, Rinehart, and Winston, Inc., 1953), pp. 354–362.

47. Nelson Foote, "Love," *Psychiatry,* 16 (1953), 245–251; quote from p. 247.

More important, it is built on norms for mutual self-development, which include the physical, intellectual, emotional, and spiritual nature of man. More and more, love is coming to be perceived as a basic psychic need, which, if fulfilled, provides the individuals with a sense of security vitally necessary for life in modern urban society. Perhaps being loved, besides making it possible to love oneself as well as others, makes it easier for an individual to win a sense of belonging in a group.

In March 1970, this poster of a pregnant man, clutching his bulging stomach, appeared at one thousand Family Planning Association clinics throughout England. A "sign" of changing sexual norms, the poster was part of a nationwide campaign aimed at encouraging male responsibility for unwanted children.

The Health Education Council LTD

Would you be more careful if it was you that got pregnant?

Contraception is one of the facts of life.

Anyone married or single can get advice on contraception from the Family Planning Association. Margaret Pyke House, 25-35 Mortimer Street, London W1 N 8BQ. Tel. 01-636 9135.

PRE- AND POST-MARRIAGE PATTERNS

In traditional societies, marriages were commonly arranged by the parents. In industrialized societies, young people are fairly free to do their own mate-selecting. But sometimes the selection fails to work—the marriage terminates in divorce. The majority of marriages end when one partner, more often the male, dies. In this section we shall discuss the problems related to both pre-marriage and post-marriage patterns.

DATING AND COURTSHIP

When the family arranged marriages, the feelings the young people had toward one another were relatively unimportant. In contemporary America, young people generally arrange their own marriages, and the mechanism whereby they test out their ideas of each other is called *dating*. The date is usually initiated by the male, and he is expected to pay for the entertainment. (The expense of the clothes the female wears to attract the male tends to balance the expense the male incurs.)

Dating provides young people with a chance to learn to know persons of the opposite sex. A problematic aspect of a date (compared to other forms of social interaction) is sexual behavior. The sexual tensions of adolescents are high, and a date offers some opportunity for sexual expression. But what form of expression is appropriate? In older Western societies, the answer was none, or not very much. A female was supposed to be a virgin at the time of her marriage. Religious norms called for male chastity as well, but in practice no one was much concerned about it. Males would often have recourse to prostitutes, or to "loose" women who were not defined as marriageable. When the negative sanctions for premarital coitus are heavy for the female and light or nonexistent for the male, we say that a *double standard* exists.

In American society, the double standard and other traditional norms regarding premarital sex were already being challenged by the 1920's, and since that time there have been increasing pressures for change. Just what the current norms are is unclear. As Ehrmann noted at the end of the 1950's, "That there is not a clearly defined code is epitomized in the fact that so many young people raise questions as to what is right."[48] This questioning continues to-day, despite the growing acceptance of more permissive attitudes toward premarital sexual behavior.

A number of studies in the last few decades have reported that about one fourth of the fe-males and one half of the males had experienced premarital coitus. Reiss points out that "Major studies show little evidence of behavior changes in coital rates but they do show changes in petting rates."[49] Reiss also feels that the per-missiveness-with-affection standard is found increasingly and shows a greater emphasis on affection than on personal pleasure—the old male emphasis. Along the same lines, Ehrmann reported that his most important empirical finding was that more and more women related their sexual expression to love.[50]

Most research supports the hypothesis that promiscuity is no more common than it ever was and that the premarital sexual behavior of many young people focuses around "love" or a "meaningful relationship." The major shift of attitude and behavior concerns the proportion of young women who are "in love" rather than out on a casual date and who are now willing to engage in intercourse before marriage. But by 1970 this behavior still involved only a minority of females and did not appear to be precipitated by the availability of the Pill. Rather, it appeared that "it is after they decide to have sex that they go get the pill."[51] It is still an open question how far the new freedom of discussion and attitudes will go with regard to still more permissive behavior. Cross-cultural research conducted by Christensen and others suggests that the United States may be following the pattern of coitus with affection already well established in the Scandinavian societies.[52]

MARITAL DISSOLUTION

Another consequence of the changes that have taken place in the United States has been the rapid rise in the divorce rate. However, while the divorce rate has risen dramatically, the death rate has dropped, and the result has been an actual reduction in the frequency of marital dissolutions: in 1890 the annual rate of marital dissolution from death and divorce was thirty-two per thousand married couples; in 1950, thirty-one per thousand. In sixty years the rate of dissolution by death fell from thirty to less than twenty per thousand married couples, while the divorce rate rose from two to eleven. Since 1950 the divorce rate has dropped to around ten per thousand.

Divorce. The following facts stand out about divorce in the United States:[53]

1. "Divorces occur mostly to young persons after a short period of married life . . . ."

2. The increase in divorces in recent years has been "partially due to reasons other than the growth of the married population."

3. Among the major nations of the world, the United States has the highest rate of divorce.

According to the *Divorce Statistics Analysis* of 1963, about half of all divorces are granted to men and women between the ages of twenty and thirty-five. The modal age for husbands is 25–29 years and for wives it is 20–24. "These data indicate that the likelihood of divorce for younger couples is higher than for older couples. Almost one-half of the wives divorced in these six states [states providing the most complete statistics and upon which much of the analysis was based] were married in their teens." Only one of four divorced wives was married at age twenty-five or older.

Approximately three out of four couples never get divorced. At the other extreme, some 6 percent of husbands and wives report having

48. Winston Ehrmann, *Premarital Dating Behavior* (New York: Henry Holt and Co., 1959), p. 173.

49. Ira L. Reiss, *The Social Context of Premarital Sexual Permissiveness* (New York: Holt, Rinehart and Winston, Inc., 1967), p. 15.

50. Ehrmann, *op. cit.*, p. 269.

51. William A. McWhirter *et al.*, "The Arrangement at College," *Life*, May 31, 1968, p. 62.

52. For a summary of this research, see Harold T. Christensen, "Toward a Theory of Normative Sexual Morality," in *Family and Fertility*, ed. William T. Liu (South Bend, Ind.: University of Notre Dame Press, 1967), pp. 47–67.

53. The following statements including quotations are based on *Divorce Statistics Analysis, United States 1963*, Public Health Service Publication, No. 1000, Series 21, No. 13, pp. 6–39.

three or more marriages. Thus the likelihood of divorce is higher for those remarrying than for those marrying for the first time.

There has been an increasing tendency for divorces to involve families with children. While the number of divorces granted annually increased by 10 percent between 1953 and 1963, the number of children involved increased by 77 percent. While only 45 percent of divorcing couples had children in 1953, almost two thirds of such couples had children in 1963.

The most common legal grounds for divorce are cruelty, nonsupport, desertion, and combinations of these. But since state laws largely determine the nature of the legal grounds, there is probably a significant difference between real causes and legal causes.

As with other aspects of human social life, no single factor can account for the high or low divorce rates in society. Besides age, the following factors have been consistently correlated with divorce: alcoholism; economic instability; religious differences; personality maladjustments; and sexual incompatibility. A study by Idaho lawyers found that financial nonsupport accounted for 20 percent of all divorces, adultery 19 percent, and drunkenness 18 percent. A number of sociologists have found strong support for the hypothesis that "there is a rough inverse relationship between economic status and the divorce rate."[54] The fact is that in total numbers and by rate, the lower economic strata experience more divorces than the upper, despite the expense of legal services.

In lower socioeconomic strata *marital strain,* from whatever source, tends to end up in *economic strain* and then divorce. The economic strain is expressed in terms of withdrawal of economic support by the husband. When he begins to spend time and money elsewhere, the wife may withdraw sexual favors. Strongly aggressive action between spouses, which is even taught to the children, is more common to the lower rungs of the economic ladder than to any other strata. In general, the social setting of the lower class family is conducive to many forms of tension and conflict that are simply not found among the other classes.[55] Such tensions increase the probability that the family will be headed by a woman. This situation is especially noticeable today among black ghetto families, as Moynihan has pointed out.[56]

Most of us, influenced by the Western tradition, tend to view divorce as something "bad," to be avoided if possible. Even supposedly dispassionate social scientists speak of the "alarmingly high divorce rate." An important part of the problem is the effect of divorce on children. For a long time it was assumed that the effect was negative and that the children of divorced parents were more likely to become delinquent or fail to "adjust" to society. Recent research casts doubt on this assumption.[57] Unhappy unbroken homes often seem to cause more problems than broken homes.

Further research in this area is needed, but it presents extraordinary difficulties for two reasons: First, what we really need to know is what kind of adults the children of divorce turn out to be, and measuring their adjustment a year or two after the divorce gives an inadequate answer. Tracking the children down years later when they are grown is expensive and hard to do. Second, this kind of research assumes that the investigator knows what kind of adults society needs. Within certain limits, we probably all agree on some types that society doesn't need—alcoholics, homicidal maniacs, paranoid schizophrenics, and the like. And we may all agree that we want productive types with some sense of social responsibility. But at this point consensus may break down. Does society need young men with scraggly beards who want to change society, or does it need young men with brief cases who are willing to keep their suburban yards free of crabgrass? The measurement of social adjustment is undergirded with a host of value assumptions.

Death. Today about eleven million persons in the United States have lost their marriage partners through death, and about 80 percent

54. See A. B. Hollingshead, "Social Class and Family Stability," in Sussman, *Sourcebook of Marriage and the Family;* and William J. Goode, *The Family* (Englewood Cliffs, N.J.: Prentice-Hall, Inc., 1964).

55. For a powerful documentary on these forces and their disruptive consequences see Elliot Liebow, *Tally's Corner: A Study of Negro Streetcorner Men* (Boston: Little, Brown and Company, 1967); and Daniel P. Moynihan, "The Negro Family: The Case for National Action," U.S. Department of Labor (March 1965), p. 78.

56. Moynihan, *op. cit.*

57. See, for example, Lee G. Burchinal, "Characteristics of Adolescents from Unbroken, Broken, and Reconstituted Families," *Journal of Marriage and the Family,* 26 (February 1964), 44–51; and Ivon F. Nye, "Child Adjustment in Broken and Unhappy Broken Homes," *Marriage and Family Living,* 19 (November 1957), 356–361.

of them are women.[58] The proportion of widows has risen steadily in the last decades and will probably continue to rise because women live longer than men, are usually younger than their husbands, and are less likely to remarry.

Some of the problems created by the death of a marriage partner are more difficult for women than for men. Income maintenance and employment are the best examples. Although women are reported to be the beneficiaries of 80 percent of all life insurance policies, few of them are "wealthy widows." Three fourths of the policies, a recent study showed, were for less than $5,000, and an additional 20 percent were for less than $10,000. Because the widow has to pay funeral expenses and medical bills and because she is likely to be over sixty-five years of age and unable to earn an adequate income for herself, her economic situation is precarious.

Widows of working age are frequently not prepared to enter the labor market. Many have never acquired a marketable skill and can therefore find work only at low-skill jobs that pay very low wages. Yet even the woman who has no pressing financial need for employment may discover that any kind of job at any wage is preferable to lonely days at home, keeping house only for herself. Greater emphasis on the need to acquire a marketable skill would undoubtedly be fruitful in the socialization of females. Too often women are left with the idea that marriage removes the need for acquiring competence in an area that may be attractive to employers.

Some of the problems of widowhood are common to both sexes. The survivors tend to be socially isolated. Even if squabbling had been the most common form of daily interaction in the marriage, people become dependent on their partners, and the isolation appears to have physical consequences. The widowed die sooner than nonwidowed of the same age, the tendency toward suicide is increased, and mental illness is more common.

Although men and women both may suffer loneliness at home, widowhood (like divorce) hinders social interaction more for women than for men. An extra man is always in demand at social gatherings, but an extra woman is often defined as a fifth wheel. Much American social life is designed for couples, and the woman who is widowed is not only deprived of male companionship at home but may find herself excluded from heterosexual social gatherings as well. If she lives long enough, this fact will no longer constitute a problem because at advanced ages heterosexual social events are rare, not because of the structure of American social life but because women are more durable than men. Thus far, advances in medical technology have served only to increase the disparity in the ages at which men and women die. A possible solution would be for women to marry men five or more years younger than themselves, but few people appear to be attracted to the rationality of this approach.

---

58. The following discussion draws heavily on Felix M. Berardo, "Widowhood Status in the United States: Perspectives on a Neglected Aspect of the Family Life-Cycle," *The Family Coordinator*, 17 (July 1968), 191–203.

SUMMARY

In all known societies, the family serves as a primary agent for the transmission of culture through the socialization of children. Marriage defines responsibility to particular children. Sexual behavior, the inheritance of material goods, and adult companionship are everywhere regulated to some extent, apparently because such regulation makes the system of assigning responsibility for children more workable.

But the basic organizational patterns that serve to ensure biological and cultural survival show great differences. Although the most common form of marriage is monogamy, many societies have practiced polygamy—particularly polygyny. In traditional societies the extended family is fairly common, but in industrialized societies, families tend to be nuclear, owing in part to the geographical and occupational mobility required by advanced technology. Male dominance diminishes as women enter the labor market and become less dependent economically, while at the same time the development of effective contraceptive devices enables women to devote fewer years to child rearing. Parental domination of children becomes problematic as the educational system assumes the task of preparing young people for the occupational system.

In the United States the laws governing sexual behavior developed from the Puritan tradition and appear discrepant with actual behavior. In many instances, as in the private behavior of consenting adults, sex laws are inherently difficult to enforce. In other instances, laws remain unenforced because public opinion apparently does not support the severity of the sanctions. This situation raises the question of the appropriate relationship of formal to informal norms.

In response to technological changes, the American family is becoming a consuming rather than a producing unit. Families spend less time together. The occupational roles of the parents are performed away from home, and the children are prepared for their occupational roles in the schools. Occupational socialization thus tends to be removed from parental control, though it is still subject to parental influence. But the family remains the prime source of influence on the personality formation of the child. This influence can be seen in mate selection; even though American dating patterns reflect a minimum of direct family control, parental influence is seen in the restrictions on interclass, interethnic, interreligious, and interracial marriage.

As women become less dependent economically, emphasis on the companionate aspect of marriage increases. Divorce terminates about one American marriage in four. Death terminates fewer marriages among younger people than formerly, but the medical technology responsible for this fact has also increased the length of widowhood for women. Both divorce and the death of one's spouse create the need for resocialization to new life roles.

17
Religion

There have been endless debates over what types of human activity can properly be called religious. Some scholars would apply the term *religion* only to convictions about the existence of a god or gods. Others would define religion as almost any kind of belief system to which people are deeply committed. For example, communism has often been referred to as a religion. Morris Cohen, a well-known American philosopher, argued seriously that baseball could be considered a religion in the United States because it served to integrate American society.[1]

The sociologist approaches religion within an institutional framework. He sees it not only as behavior that includes personal and shared beliefs about the supernatural but also as a complex of culture traits, a kind of group behavior, a basis for both social integration and social conflict, and a reflection of differing life styles. These topics will be reviewed in the present chapter.

Émile Durkheim, in the classic work *The Elementary Forms of Religious Life*,[2] has provided a useful definition of religion:

All known religious beliefs, whether simple or complex, present one common characteristic; they presuppose a classification of all things, real and ideal, of which men think, into two classes or opposed groups, generally designated by two distinct terms which are translated well enough by the words *profane* and *sacred*.[3]

To Durkheim, the distinction between the sacred and the profane was absolute. These were two totally distinct classes with nothing in common. The sacred consisted of things "set apart, and forbidden"—that is, things and ideas thought of as in some way transcendent or ultimate. The profane was defined simply as everything else.

Within this conceptual framework, systems of religious belief can be regarded as means of defining and relating to the sacred. The doctrines and scriptures of Christian, Jew, Muslim, and Buddhist, and even the myths of primitive man

aim first and foremost at these goals. Once the sacred has been defined, rites and rituals can be developed as rules of conduct that will bring man into the presence of the sacred.

Durkheim included one additional and very important factor in his definition of religion. He insisted that the beliefs must be shared by an *organized group*: "Religious beliefs are always common to a determined group, which makes a profession of adhering to them and of practicing the rites connected with them."[4] This is the factor that most sharply distinguishes religion from magic. The magician, too, cultivates supernatural beliefs and rites; there are magical myths, dogmas, functionaries, and ceremonials. But on one point there is an essential difference: the magician's knowledge is *secret*, not shared. If it were made public, its value would be lost. Thus the magician may have a clientele, but he does not have a congregation.

The definition of religion, then, begins with religious belief, which makes clear the nature of the sacred. From this, the meaning of rites and rituals relating the individual to the sacred can be understood. Finally, beliefs and rituals do not exist in the abstract but are forms of conduct that people share in groups, within a framework of norms, roles, and other organizational components. Defining religion in this way focuses attention upon religious *behavior*. For the sociologist, the proper study of religion involves not only what various types of people *believe* but also how they act, individually and collectively, upon those beliefs.

RELIGION AS INDIVIDUAL BEHAVIOR

There is abundant evidence that religious behavior varies greatly from one individual to another. This is true even in societies that support only one institutionalized system of religion, and it is particularly apparent in a society like ours, where the variations are almost endless. Another complication is that the more personal or "inner" aspects of religious experience can never be subjected to direct scrutiny. But in spite of these and related research difficulties, a number of objective conclusions about religious behavior have been reached. Some of the major *dimensions of religiosity* have been identified;

---

1. Morris R. Cohen, *The Faith of a Liberal* (New York: Henry Holt and Company, 1946), pp. 334–336.

2. Émile Durkheim, *The Elementary Forms of Religious Life* (New York: The Macmillan Company, 1926); originally published in 1912.

3. *Ibid.,* p. 36.

4. *Ibid.,* p. 41.

The system of religious beliefs known as spiritism is still a powerful ideology in some parts of the world. This burial ceremony in New Guinea, for example, reflects the tribesmen's belief in the survival of their ancestors' "spirits." They paint their bodies with grey paint and wear cave-like frames on their heads, which are plastered with mud and often decorated with human or dog's teeth. This costume—and the accompanying ritual—commemorates a battle in which their ancestors were forced into a river by a marauding tribe and then emerged covered with mud to frighten off the attackers.

typologies of religious experience have been proposed; and individual and social consequences of religious commitment have been identified. Each will be illustrated in the sections that follow.

DIMENSIONS OF RELIGIOSITY

A number of attempts have been made to analyze the essential characteristics of religious behavior.[5] One dimension of religiosity that can be readily identified is the particular body of beliefs that an individual has internalized. The rituals that he practices constitute another aspect of his religious behavior, as do his subjective religious experiences. Among those people who feel in direct communion with the supernatural, religious behavior may also involve a sense of calling to reveal the divine word. These dimensions of religiosity, sometimes referred to as the ideological, the ritualistic, the experiential, and the revelational, provide a convenient framework for discussion.

Ideology. Both the content of an individual's religious beliefs and the intensity with which he holds them are sometimes referred to as the ideological dimension of religiosity. Such beliefs are, of course, the very core of religion.

Some scholars believe that the earliest form of religious belief was fetishism, the conviction that some inanimate object has mysterious or magical power (often called mana). The continued popularity of such objects as lucky coins, charms, religious medals, and amulets shows that this belief still survives in modern industrial society. A somewhat more complex form of religious ideology is animism, the belief that natural objects are infused with consciousness. Primitive man, living close to nature, attributed quasi-human personality to trees, mountains, rocks, and rivers. Industrial man, separated from nature by an elaborate technology but very dependent upon mechanical devices, still shows traces of animism. He refers to boats and airplanes as "she" and may praise, scold, pat, or even kick his automobile, which is as important to his way of life as primitive man's hunting complexes were to him.

5. Charles Y. Glock and Rodney Stark, Religion and Society in Tension (Chicago: Rand McNally & Company, 1965), pp. 20–21.

Still more complex is *spiritism.* Its principal feature is a dualistic conception of man in which the "spirit" survives the death of the physical body. Ancestor worship and other beliefs that attribute to the "souls of the dead" a special significance for the living are found in many religious systems. Spiritism survives in the contemporary world among those who fear ghosts, graveyards, and haunted houses or who consult a "medium" to try to communicate with someone who has died.

The world's major religions are either polytheistic or monotheistic. *Polytheism* is the belief in a plurality of gods. The polytheism of classical Greece, with its elaborate pantheon of more and less powerful gods, was hardly a religion at all by modern Western standards. It had no sacred scriptures or doctrines and said almost nothing about morality. Different versions of the same legend would be told in different localities; there was no authority to pronounce on which was the correct one. The very identity of a god was sometimes in doubt. People came to assume that the god worshiped as Zeus in one part of Greece was the same Zeus who was worshiped in other parts—but they could never be sure.

Monotheism, on the other hand, is a set of beliefs based on the idea of a single, all-powerful, pervasive god. Most monotheistic religions have highly developed theologies—that is, explanations of man and his place in the cosmos plus prescriptions and proscriptions for human behavior. Judaism, Christianity, and Islam, the principal monotheisms of the contemporary world, originated in areas that had been dominated by polytheism and various forms of magic. There is a tendency in the West to view the transition from polytheism to monotheism as progress to a "higher" form of religion, but the rigorously monotheistic religion of Judaism, with its voluminous scriptures and scriptural commentaries, is far older than either Christianity or Islam and at least as old as Greek polytheism. Thus, it is probably safe to assume only that a religion with an elaborate but unified theology is at a later stage of development than one that consists of an assortment of irreconcilable myths and legends.

For the sociologist, theology is merely the starting point for analyzing the ideological dimension of religious behavior. He is primarily concerned with what individuals actually believe, as distinct from what the leaders of their religion say they should believe. One of the most comprehensive studies in this area was carried out by Glock and Stark in four metropolitan counties of northern California.[6] Over three thousand members of Christian churches were questioned about some of Christianity's basic doctrines. One of these was the doctrine that God exists. Since each respondent in this survey identified himself as a member of a recognized Christian denomination, either Protestant or Catholic, one might presume that asking this question would be an idle academic exercise. However, the results were surprising.

For one major Protestant denomination, only 41 percent of those questioned indicated that they subscribed without reservation to a belief in the existence of God. For Protestants as a whole, less than three fourths unreservedly accepted it. For Catholics, the figure was 81 percent. It appears, then, that even among persons sufficiently interested in religious matters to maintain a church membership when under no compulsion to do so, a large proportion had doubts of one kind or another concerning the existence of the very deity to which their formal doctrines, rituals, and organizations were dedicated.

These same people were asked whether they had any doubts that "Jesus is the Divine Son of God." Again, there was a substantial range of responses. Only about two thirds of Protestants as a whole (69 percent) said that their belief was completely firm, and only 40 percent of one denomination subscribed to the idea without reservation. Among Catholics, 86 percent were completely certain. Such statements as "The miracles the Bible reports are true," "Jesus walked on water," and "There is a life beyond death" met with substantial skepticism, and there was much hesitation over accepting the biblical account of the birth of Jesus. When asked if it was completely true that "Jesus was born of a virgin," southern Baptists expressed certain belief in 99 percent of the cases studied, but theirs was the only resoundingly affirmative response. At the other extreme only one fifth (21 percent) of the Congregationalists accepted the virgin birth literally.

What are the implications of such data? The fact that those surveyed were church members showed that they considered themselves religious to some degree, even though they might be unable to make a full commitment. There is

6. *Ibid.,* pp. 86–122.

also the likely interpretation that, for the individual, belonging to a church satisfies many needs, of which gaining a setting for the expression of his personal religious beliefs is only one. The study does not show that religion is undergoing a decline in the United States. Indeed, there is evidence that Americans in general are still a very religious people. For instance, a poll taken in August 1965, found that 97 percent of the American public expressed belief in God, and 72 percent expressed belief in an afterlife. Only 27 percent, however, were prepared to call themselves "deeply religious," and about 42 percent said that they did most of their praying outside any church.[7] Moreover, another study completed in 1966 found that belief in God had declined since 1952.[8]

In any case, sociological research is beginning to provide a basis for understanding better the role of personal belief in the totality of an individual's religious behavior. Some persons, it is clear, engage in religious practices either partly or mainly because in this way they can satisfy certain psychological and social needs which are not provided for by other means.

Ritual. The ritualistic dimension of religiosity refers to the practices prescribed by various religious groups for their members. Religious rituals include an almost unlimited variety of behaviors. What most of them have in common is the purpose of symbolizing, honoring, and reminding participants of some aspect of their faith. Typical examples of ritual are observing diets and routines of prayer, manipulating sacred objects, wearing distinctive clothing, and following unique modes of living.

Descriptive studies of religious ritual are numerous.[9] Elaborate analyses have been made of religious practices in societies at all stages of development. The most conspicuous characteristic of these many systems is their almost incredible variety. Some make heavy demands on their members. Sexual celibacy, a life of poverty, extensive daily prayer, and humble service to the sick and poor are all required by a number of religious orders. Others may permit normal family life but require members to live in communities isolated from the main society. Still others require little beyond occasional attendance at formal services plus modest financial support.

On the whole, modern students of ritualism have been most impressed by its more dramatic

and symbolic forms. The demonstration of religiosity through self-mutilation, human sacrifice, and cannibalism has been analyzed to yield far-reaching theories of religious behavior.[10] Although it might be thought that such practices are too exotic to throw light on religion in modern America, even here there are groups that cultivate extreme forms of ritualism, in the hope of finding evidence that they are following the true faith. For example, within recent years a number of people have died and others have become seriously ill because of their literal interpretation of this passage from the New Testament:

And these signs shall follow them that believe; In my name they shall cast out devils; they shall speak with new tongues;

They shall take up serpents; and if they drink any deadly thing, it shall not hurt them; they shall lay hands on the sick, and they shall recover. (Mark 16: 17–18)

In 1967, for example, a twenty-five-year-old male factory worker was bitten by a rattlesnake as he handled it during the services of the Free Holiness Church of God, of Covington, Kentucky. Believing that no harm would come to him as long as he maintained his faith, he refused medical aid and died within a few hours.

In most religious groups in the United States the degree of ritual observance varies sharply among different types of members. For example, Fichter reports a study of the extent to which 8363 white urban Catholics observed such ritual prescriptions as attending Mass, performing Easter duties, taking Holy Communion, accepting only Church-validated marriage, and sending children to parochial schools.

---

7. Louis Harris, "Religion in the U.S.: A Harris Poll," *New York Post*, August 16, 1965.

8. In 1966 the Gallup organization made a comparison of the strength of religious beliefs in 1952 and 1966. For some of the findings of this study, see Daniel Callahan, "The Quest for Social Relevance," in *Religion in America*, eds. William G. McLoughlin and Robert N. Bellah (Boston: Beacon Press, 1968), p. 366, note 44.

9. For a survey, see William J. Goode, *Religion Among the Primitives* (New York: The Free Press, 1951).

10. See especially Sir James Frazer's multivolume classic, *The Golden Bough* (1890), available in a one-volume abridgement (New York: The Macmillan Company, 1955); and Arnold van Gennep, *The Rites of Passage* (Chicago: The University of Chicago Press, 1960); this was originally published in 1909.

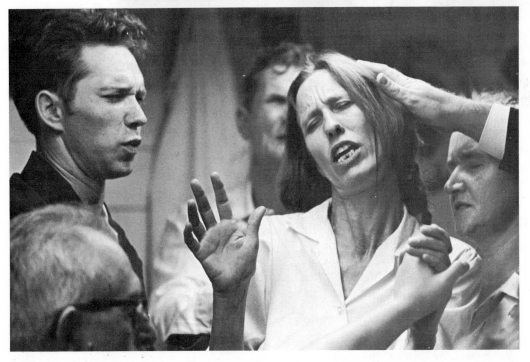

The various religious rituals of America are not as staid as one might imagine. At the pentecostal Scrabble Creek Church in West Virginia, for example, impassioned sermons are supplemented by brief, if hysterical, periods of snake-handling. With religious ecstasy at a peak, a rattlesnake, venom and all, is passed through the hands of the believers. The Scrabble Creek rituals pale in comparison, however, to the practices of the snake-handlers at the Church of Jesus in nearby Jolo. There, handfuls of rattlesnakes are placed under clothing or worn as crowns. Overcome by emotion and the Holy Spirit, the woman above speaks in tongues.

It was found that the extent of observance varied according to educational level, residential mobility, sex, age, and income.[11] Few studies, however, probe as deeply as this one. Usually, people of different faiths are compared in much simpler terms, such as weekly attendance at religious services. A number of investigators have found that Jews are the least ritualistic of our major groups. In one extensive study, only 10 to 12 percent of the Jews sampled indicated that they went to a synagogue every week. The Catholics were far more ritualistic, with about 70 percent reporting that they attended Mass on a weekly basis. Protestants were intermediate, with 30 to 40 percent reporting weekly attendance.[12]

None of these figures can be taken to mean that one group or the other is more or less religious in any absolute sense, because such ritualistic behavior is only one dimension of religiosity. For example, Lenski has found that Jews are far more involved in what he calls the "communal" aspects of religion (i.e., marrying and forming friendships within the Jewish community). Catholics rank lowest in this respect, with Protestant groups intermediate.[13]

The degree to which the members of any religious group actually carry out the detailed rituals of their faith (with the exception of church attendance) appears to follow a characteristic pattern. A majority of members conscientiously follow the rituals that have been established as normative in their church, lesser numbers of people partially conform, and some people conform not at all. This general pattern can be illustrated by data from a study in which a large number of worshippers were observed as they entered a Catholic cathedral. A careful count was made of how many people dipped their fingers in the font of holy water and how many made the sign of the cross upon entering the church. Of the more than fifteen hundred people observed, 62.7 percent performed both rituals. Another 10.7 percent followed one or the other, and the remaining 26.6 followed neither. A similar pattern of conformity (and nonconformity) has been noted with respect to many other kinds of normative behavior, such as obeying traffic regulations or coming to class on time.[14]

Experience. The "experiential" dimension of religiosity has been defined as consisting of all those "feelings, perceptions and sensations" of the individual that involve "some communication, however slight, with a divine essence, i.e., with God, with ultimate reality, with transcendental authority."[15] Such religious experiences are to a considerable degree shaped by the individual's beliefs and by the rituals he follows. Because such beliefs and rituals are shared with others and are products of the individual's socialization, his religious feelings, perceptions, and sensations are strongly influenced by his social and cultural background. Thus, people who have been brought up to believe that God is terrifying are apt to look upon feelings of terror as an authentically religious inner state. For others, with different prior socialization, some experience of sublime joy might be seen as an authentic indicator of contact with the deity. Still others might find a truly religious experience in humility, exaltation, or peacefulness. In short, people can feel that they are in contact with a supernatural agency in many ways and to a greater or lesser degree.

Some individuals who regard themselves as deeply religious may never experience such contact. This is the condition known to theologians as spiritual aridity or dryness. Others, even those who have not previously been much concerned with religion, may be suddenly overwhelmed with an intense feeling of the divine presence. Here is the description of such an experience by a young man who felt that he "had no religion . . . no sense of personal relationship to God." During a summer vacation he took an afternoon walk alone.

I was in the empty unthinking state in which one saunters along country lanes, simply yielding oneself to the casual sights around which give a town-bred lad with country yearnings such intense delight. Suddenly I became conscious of the presence of someone else. I cannot describe it, but I felt I had as direct a perception of the being of God all round about me . . . . It came unsought, absolutely unexpectedly. I remember the wonderful transfiguration of the far-off woods and hills as they seemed to blend in the infinite Being with which I was thus brought

11. Joseph H. Fichter, *Dynamics of a City Church: Southern Parish* (Chicago: The University of Chicago Press, 1951).

12. Gerhard Lenski, *The Religious Factor* (Garden City, N. Y.: Anchor Books, 1963), pp. 35–50.

13. *Ibid.*

14. Floyd H. Allport, "The J-Curve Hypothesis of Conforming Behavior," *Journal of Social Psychology,* 5 (1934), 141–183.

15. Glock and Stark, *op. cit.,* p. 20.

into relation. This experience did not last long. But it sufficed to change all my feeling. I had not found God because I had never looked for him. But he had found me. . . .[16]

Several interesting and fairly widespread variations of the experiential dimension of religiosity have been identified. For example, one type of experience is said to provide "a sudden feeling, knowing, or intuition that the beliefs one holds are true."[17] This can be called a *confirming* experience. For some persons, it amounts to little more than rather vague and diffuse feelings of reverence or awe such as often accompany participation in solemn religious rituals. In other cases, the individual becomes convinced that he is actually in the presence of his god. In another common type of religious experience the individual not only perceives himself to be in the presence of the divinity but feels that the divinity has become aware of him. This can be called the *responsive* type of religious experience. It may convince the believer that he belongs to a "chosen" group or has been "saved" by timely conversion to the true faith. He may also become convinced that he has been healed or cured or that his life has been saved through divine intervention.[18]

A third expression of the experiential dimension, the *ecstatic,* is often accompanied by violent physical and psychological manifestations, such as uncontrollable urges to jump, scream, twitch, roll on the floor, and "speak in tongues." Such "visitations" of the supernatural often occur in a group context. The classic American example is the revival meeting.

Revelation. The fourth and last major dimension of religiosity, less common than the others, is the *revelational.* Here, the individual not only believes he is in communication with divinity but feels he has been taken into the divine confidence by receiving a sacred "message" of some kind, often through the mediation of visions and voices. Historically, those receiving such messages have been regarded with wonder and reverence, and special significance has been attached to the sites where their revelations occurred. Ancient Hebrew prophets, Muhammad (the founder of Islam) and many Christian saints experienced revelation. Outstanding among religious leaders who have claimed divine inspiration in modern times was Joseph Smith, founder of the Church of Jesus Christ of the Latter Day Saints, who by his own account discovered and translated the Book of Mormon at the direction of an angel.[19]

FUNCTIONS OF RELIGIOSITY

One aspect of individual religiosity has been the object of so much sociological inquiry that it deserves separate treatment here. This is the *functional* aspect, the aspect that is implied if we ask: What consequences does religion have for the individual? How does the individual, *as a consequence of his religiosity,* orient himself to the world around him in ways different from those of the nonreligious person? This is an enormously complex question, and here we can only give a few of the more obvious answers.

Security. Most religions provide the individual with an ideology that enables him to make sense of his life. Illness, injustice, poverty, death—all may be comprehensible if they are part of a benevolent deity's divine plan. Or they may simply be unimportant in comparison with the eternal realities.

Crisis. The lives of most men are periodically touched by crises. Whether these crises stem from social or natural sources, they create fears and anxieties that must be handled. The individual's religious beliefs and practices offer him ways of managing crises without overwhelming psychological cost. Rituals such as prayer and sacrifice often take the form of appeals for divine intervention on behalf of the sufferer. This permits the believer to feel he is "doing something"—as indeed he is. If the crisis is averted, the efficacy of the rituals is affirmed. If the catastrophe occurs, it can be regarded as having been divinely ordained, perhaps as just punishment for past transgressions. Either outcome provides the individual with an interpretation of the crisis, which otherwise might crush him through its seeming senselessness.

16. Quoted in A. C. Bouquet, *Religious Experience—Its Nature, Types and Validity* (Cambridge, England: Heffer, 1932), pp. 11–12.

17. Glock and Stark, *op. cit.,* p. 43.

18. See the examples collected in William James, *The Varieties of Religious Experience* (New York: The Macmillan Company, 1961); originally published in 1902.

19. A standard sociological account of Mormonism is Thomas F. O'Dea, *The Mormons* (Chicago: The University of Chicago Press, 1957).

MEASURING RELIGIOSITY

What images are associated with the label *religious?* Does it connote a person who is pious or a conscientious objector, one who has ecstatic experiences or simply knows his Bible, an individual whose major motive is to love his neighbor or one who carefully attends to the prescribed obligations of his denomination? Prior to the classification of these dimensions of religiosity, single items—such as church membership or attendance—were used as sole indicators of religious commitment. Now, however, the researcher has at his disposal multidimensional indices that focus on different levels of analysis: individual, institutional, and societal.

1. Individual—Charles Y. Glock identified five dimensions of individual religious commitment within which all the diverse manifestations of religiosity could be ordered: *ritualistic* (attendance, prayer, etc.); *intellectual* (knowledge about basic tenets); *ideological* (belief); *experiential* (feeling); and *consequential* (effect).

2. Institutional—Joseph Fichter classified the members of a Roman Catholic parish with respect to their attachment to the church as an institution. Visualized in concentric zones, *nuclear* (most involved) members are at the core, with *modal* (average) members followed by *marginal* and *dormant* (noninvolved) members.

3. Societal—N. J. Demerath and others focused upon the association between religiosity and socioeconomic factors, suggesting that churchlike and sectlike tendencies are closely related to socioeconomic status.

Following Glock's analysis of individual religious commitment, many researchers began to study the relationships between all five of Glock's individual dimensions. The results of this body of research suggest that no two dimensions of religious commitment overlap by much more than 30 percent. In other words, if one tries to predict a man's ritual involvement on the basis of his ideological fervor (or any dimension of religiosity on the basis of another), the results will not be very accurate.

Some researchers have taken one of Glock's dimensions and subdivided it. *Orthodoxy,* for instance, is considered one subdimension of ideology. To measure orthodoxy, sociologists have used various research questions, which usually focus on the certainty of belief in: the existence of a personal god; the divinity of Jesus; the authenticity of Biblical miracles; and the existence of the Devil. Critics have charged that this measure is neither theologically nor methodologically valid, because no theologically literate person could correctly respond to questions which force a choice between very extreme and simple-minded positions. Others contend that the questions asked are not really measures of orthodoxy and that they do not focus on authentic Christianity.

Some studies have also used several religious dimensions in an attempt to show an individual's total relationship to the religious institution. Thus, if one person scores 5 on ritual and 1 on orthodoxy, while another scores 1 on ritual and 5 on orthodoxy, both have average scores of 3 and rank equally as "modal" members.

Overall, the tendency of research on religiosity has been in the direction of ever more subtle dimensions. The crucial question is whether or not new refinements and indices lead to increased understanding of religious behavior. The structure and number of such dimensions remains an open issue, but one thing is certainly clear: researchers can never again be satisfied with a single, convenient indicator of religiosity.

Charles Y. Glock and Rodney Stark, *Christian Beliefs and Anti-Semitism* (New York: Harper & Row, Inc., 1966) and *Religion and Society in Tension* (Chicago: Rand McNally & Co., 1965); Charles Y. Glock, "On the Study of Religious Commitment," *Religious Education,* Research Supplement, 42 (July–August, 1962), 98–110, Joseph Fichter, *Social Relations in the Urban Parish* (Chicago: The University of Chicago Press, 1954); N. J. Demerath, *Social Class in American Protestantism* (Chicago: Rand McNally & Co., 1965).

Death. Most religions, primitive and modern, have something to say about life after death. Some speak of a miserable hereafter in which the spirits of the dead wander about wailing and moaning, but others—including Christianity and Islam—hold forth inviting visions of paradise, at least for the deserving. Belief in personal immortality in a happy setting makes the deaths of loved ones more tolerable and the prospect of one's own death less terrifying. Hope of a happy hereafter can also help to reconcile the individual to a life of deprivation in this world, since earthly existence is looked on as no more than a temporary state leading to eternal bliss. The fact that a belief in immortality is found in nearly all societies has led some writers to suggest that it may fulfill a basic social need.[20]

Social values. Research tends to show that individuals who are strongly linked through religious commitment to traditional norms and values gain a source of moral strength and behavioral stability.[21] Under such conditions, the individual is more willing to comply with the norms of his society, especially if he interprets them as having divine sanction, and is more likely to interpret social deviance as a form of religious deviance. For centuries, kings and emperors claimed to be God's chosen representatives (or, in some cases, to be divine themselves), thereby making rebellion against the Crown synonymous with defiance of God's will. Belief in sacred kingship helped maintain political and social stability.

Other functions. There have been a number of recent attempts to trace ways in which religion influences the daily lives of people in modern urban-industrial society. In an extensive study of the major socioreligious groups in a large American city, Lenski was able to show that membership in any one of them (white Protestants, black Protestants, white Catholics, and Jews) was associated with many significant variations in behavior:

Depending upon the socioreligious group to which a person belongs, the probabilities are increased or decreased that he will enjoy his occupation, indulge in installment buying, save to achieve objectives far in the future, believe in the American Dream, vote Republican, favor the welfare state, take a liberal view on the issue of freedom of speech, oppose racial integration in the schools, migrate to another community, maintain close ties with his family, have a large family, complete a given unit of education or rise in the class system. These are only a few of the consequences we have observed to be associated with differences in socioreligious group membership, and the position of individuals in these groups.[22]

Of course, to speak of "consequences" as Lenski does is to assume the presence of a causal relationship. But, as Lenski admits, the nature of this relationship—the intervening group processes and variables, including complex subcultures, socialization practices, and the like—is not at all clear. Nor can we really tell from this kind of evidence which of the supposed "consequences" of religious affiliation are functional and which dysfunctional. (See the discussion of functional analysis in Chapter 1, pages 48–49.) Nevertheless, it is beyond dispute that when Americans are grouped according to their religious affiliations, significant differences in behavior can be observed from one religious category to another.

RELIGION AS GROUP BEHAVIOR

Experimental social psychology clearly indicates that beliefs gain credibility in proportion to the degree in which they are shared.[23] Even such extraordinary beliefs as the conviction that the world is in imminent danger of a cosmic catastrophe can become acceptable to otherwise conventional people if the predictions are supported by a trusted group.

Festinger and his associates report on the case of an American housewife who claimed to be receiving messages predicting a vast catastrophe. These messages, she said, were sent by the inhabitants of another planet. The catastro-

---

20. Ashley Montagu, *Immortality* (New York: Grove Press, Inc., 1955), pp. 31–67.

21. Carl G. Jung, *Psychology and Religion* (New Haven, Conn.: Yale University Press, 1938).

22. Lenski, *op. cit.,* p. 320.

23. Solomon E. Asch, "Effects of Group Pressure Upon the Modification and Distortion of Judgments," in *Readings in Social Psychology,* eds. Eleanor E. Maccoby, Theodore M. Newcomb, and Eugene L. Hartley (New York: Holt, Rinehart and Winston, 1958), pp. 174–183. See also Chapter 5, "The Socialization Process," esp. pp. 150–153.

phe was to take the form of a flood that would completely inundate the west coasts of both North and South America. But she and those who believed her would be rescued by a flying saucer. A number of persons did believe her. As the time predicted for the catastrophe drew near, the prophetess and most of her followers began to spend all their time together.

When the time came and there was no flood, the prophetess did not abandon her convictions. After a few hours of soul-searching, she announced that God had decided to spare the earth from destruction. Those who were with her were glad to accept this explanation. They believed even more than before in the truth of her messages and made no attempt to conceal the fact. But those who, although they had believed, were not with her when she explained the apparent failure of her prophecies, tended to abandon membership in her group and to keep quiet about their experiences in it.[24]

As we have already noted, Durkheim maintained that "truly religious beliefs are always common to a determined group."[25] Sociologists are interested in finding out what kinds of groups develop and maintain various kinds of religious beliefs and practices. This section will be concerned with some of the major forms of such groups, the ways in which they are organized, and the types of individuals who lead them. Discussion will be confined to analyses based on Christian groups. As one experienced scholar has pointed out, "virtually all attempts to develop a typology of religious groups have been concerned with Christian materials; their applicability to other religions has yet to be tested adequately."[26] This restriction, while limiting, has the advantage of permitting variations in religious organization to be discussed within the same general context of religious belief.

SOURCES OF RELIGIOUS VARIATION

One problem in discussing religion as group behavior is to account for the multiplicity of groups with basically similar religious doctrines. A theoretical formulation that is helpful in understanding this phenomenon, especially as it occurs in Western society, was advanced some years ago by the German sociologist Ernst Troeltsch.[27] Troeltsch contrasts two funda-

mental forms of religious organization—*church* and *sect*. These concepts, as he uses them, do not purport to describe any particular groups, nor are they simply a means of classifying actual religious organizations. Rather, they are ideal types (page 86) representing opposite ends of a continuum. As such, they provide the basis for a theory of religious variation.

The religious establishment. The church, in Troeltsch's theory, is a large, formal association with an elaborate status hierarchy. Its manifest goals are to perpetuate its creeds and to extend its control over the spiritual life of as large a portion of the population as it can—ideally, over all. Its system of norms, roles, sanctions, and status distinctions is highly conventionalized, widely accepted, and deeply institutionalized. The church is, in short, the entrenched religious establishment.

The church defines itself as coextensive with society. First, it draws its membership from the broadest possible social spectrum. Second, it attempts to merge its own power with the principal sources of secular power in the society. Therefore, while it makes every effort to appeal to all classes in its creeds and operations, in order to insure its own survival it makes its closest alliances with the principal holders of economic and political power.

Because of its broad membership base and varied power alignments, the church must always be ready to *compromise*. In particular, it must be willing to accommodate itself to the emergence of new power groups, such as economic or military elites. As Troeltsch put it:

The fully developed church . . . utilizes the State and the ruling classes, and weaves these elements into her own life; she then becomes an integral part of the existing social order; from this standpoint, then, the church both stabilizes and determines the social order; in so doing, however, she becomes dependent upon the upper classes and their development.[28]

---

24. Leon Festinger, Henry W. Riecken, Jr., and Stanley Schachter, *When Prophecy Fails* (Minneapolis: University of Minnesota Press, 1956).

25. Durkheim, *op. cit.,* p. 41.

26. J. Milton Yinger, *Religion, Society and the Individual* (New York: The Macmillan Company, 1957), p. 143.

27. Ernst Troeltsch, *The Social Teaching of the Christian Churches,* (New York: The Macmillan Company, 1931).

28. *Ibid.,* p. 331.

Idealists of all social levels are likely to be offended at the compromises made by the church in adapting to changes in the secular power structure. For example, many Catholics were distressed when the Vatican reached a compromise with the Fascist political leader Mussolini in the Lateran Treaty of 1929 and when the pope failed to place the full moral authority of Catholicism in opposition to Hitler's genocidal policy toward the Jews. The very mechanisms by which a church works for its own survival and seeks to preserve or extend its power in the secular society are almost guaranteed to be interpreted as corrupt by those to whom the secular society is anathema. It is for this reason that protest groups emerge within the church and demand reform.

The sectarian protest. A group that repudiates the compromises of the church in order to institute its own forms of worship and belief is known in Troeltsch's schema as a *sect.* This is generally a small group with voluntary membership. The program of the sect often includes the manifest goal of protest against church dogma. But points of dogma as such are likely to be less important than the fact that human needs are not being satisfied by existing arrangements within the church. Meeting such needs is a latent goal of the sect. Such unmet needs may result from many factors: widespread poverty, powerlessness (the proclivity of the lower classes to form sects testifies to this), intellectual confusion and a need for certainties (both more likely to arise among the middle and upper classes), guilt over personal inadequacies, and sheer boredom with life, such as may overwhelm an elite too secure in its privileges. There are also the pressures generated by social change. Yinger has described the conditions leading to the emergence of sects in the following terms:

When due to compromises with the secular powers, rigidity of ecclesiastical structure, the failure of doctrine and ritual to change as prevailing personality inclinations change (what are appealing symbols to one generation may lack meaning to another), when, that is, the religious system loses some of its ability to satisfy various individual and group needs, it promotes sectarian development.[29]

---

29. Yinger, *op. cit.,* p. 145.

At first, the organizational pattern of the sect is very informal. Simply because it is new, its norms, roles, social control, and ranking patterns are not deeply institutionalized. On the contrary, interaction within it is likely to be spontaneous and emotional. Its ranking system generally consists of a leader, with perhaps a few lieutenants, and a group of followers whose power and status remain undifferentiated. In their religious orientations, sectarians nearly always stress a return to more fundamental beliefs and practices. Thus the so-called Shaker sect established a number of utopian communities in isolated rural areas of the United States so that its members could more closely approximate the simple life of Christ. Through geographical isolation, limited economic dependence on the outside society, celibacy, extensive segregation by sex, and other practices, the Shakers minimized the temptations of the wicked world. By group living in an isolated community setting, they maximized the opportunity to engage in their own forms of worship without censure from nonmembers. However, the Shakers never completed the sect-to-church cycle largely because they failed to provide for marriage and childbearing. They were dependent upon recruiting from the outside. Most Shaker colonies had died out by the early part of this century.

One of the ironies with respect to the development of a sect is that, if it survives, sooner or later it loses its ability to meet the needs of its members as effectively as it did when it was newly formed, and its case becomes much the same as that of the church from which it seceded. Any religious group that persists over time and has more than a handful of members has to cope eventually with the same problems as the church. For example, members expect the sect to solemnize and record births, marriages, and deaths. For these and other purposes, formalized rituals are necessary—rituals usually modeled after those of the rejected church.

Furthermore, the second generation of sect members has not experienced the problems that caused the sect to be formed in the first place, and its members may not so willingly accept its discipline. New forms of social control must therefore be designed in order to retain the purity of beliefs and practices. This means increasing formalization. The original leader dies. Others struggle for control, and the winner must

During the 1840's, when the Shaker sect reached its peak, there were about six thousand members living in eighteen isolated villages throughout the United States. Today only two communities are still active, and there are less than twenty members—all of whom are women. The Shakers have abandoned the raucous singing and frenetic dancing that gave the sect its name, but the rule of celibacy remains a part of their beliefs. If there are no new converts, the youngest Shaker (at left) may become sole custodian of the faith. The photograph below shows a segregated stairway at the once-active Shaker village in Pleasant Hill, Kentucky.

consolidate his position. This means institutional politics. These and other difficulties cause the sect to lose its original spontaneity and informality. It begins to look increasingly routinized. Finally, some of its members leave to found a sect of their own. The original sect has become a church.

CLASSIFICATION OF RELIGIOUS GROUPS

Because of the great diversity of religious groups in Western society, there is need for a more descriptive typology than Troeltsch's, which simply defines the opposite ends of a continuum. While it should be recognized that the variety of religious groups within Christianity alone is nearly endless, the following schema has been found useful.

The universal church. Calling a church "universal" means that it has no serious competitors in the society where it exists; for all practical purposes, the entire population belongs to it. It is closely integrated with the social order and relatively successful in meeting the needs of its members. This type of religious structure is most often found in socially homogeneous societies that are not characterized by high rates of change or internal conflict. A classic illustration is the Catholic Church of the thirteenth century.[30] An outbreak of heresy had subsided and for a time all society in Christian Europe— artist and architect, scholar and philosopher, peasant and knight, monarch and monk— seemed functionally unified by a shared religious orientation. This was "the high point of the medieval synthesis."[31]

The ecclesia. The Greek word *ecclesia*, from which our *ecclesiastical* is derived, originally meant "assembly," especially an assembly of adult male citizens. The early Christians regularly used it to mean "church." In our usage it

denotes an established church that does not succeed in being universal but is the religion of the "respectable majority." Its ethical system therefore corresponds more or less closely to that of the secular world.[32] Nottingham has suggested that the present-day Anglican Church in England and the Lutheran Church in Sweden are good examples.[33]

The denomination. Although class, racial, or regional boundaries can figure prominently in the sociological description of a denomination, it is usually a relatively large group, well established within its society and widely accepted as respectable. The denomination has accommodated itself to the secular world. It is relatively tolerant of other denominations, though it may be quite intolerant of sects. Membership is usually acquired by birth; emotional conversions are rare. Services are conventionalized. Spontaneous expressions of religious fervor, if they occurred, would be considered out of place or even vulgar. The denomination is the most familiar religious group of all in American society. Examples range from the conservative Baptists to the relatively unconventional but still "respectable" Unitarians.

The sect. The origins and organizational characteristics of the sect have already been discussed. It is a relatively small group that has broken away from a more established group; it is usually loosely organized, voluntary, and lacking a professionally trained clergy; its members pay less attention to formalistic doctrine than to spontaneous commitment. Sects are often both unable and unwilling to accommodate themselves to the secular order and therefore tend to be rejected by it. (Table 17.1, page 550, summarizes and contrasts the essential characteristics of the sect with those of the denomination.)

The cult. At the farthest extreme from the universal church are a number of small, unconventional groups organized around unconventional leaders. Such groups generally deviate substantially from established religious doctrine. Their membership tends to be drawn from alienated and rootless urban people in search of esoteric experience. Cult members represent only a small proportion of society, and cult doctrines and practices have little or no influence on the society as a whole.

---

30. Yinger, *op. cit.,* p. 148.

31. Norman F. Cantor, *Western Civilization: Its Genesis and Destiny* (Glenview, Ill.: Scott, Foresman and Company, 1969), p. 348.

32. Leopold von Wiese, *Systematic Sociology* (New York: John Wiley & Sons, Inc., 1932), p. 625.

33. Elizabeth K. Nottingham, *Religion and Society* (New York: Random House, Inc., 1954), p. 63.

TABLE 17.1.   CHARACTERISTIC DIFFERENCES BETWEEN SECTS AND DENOMINATIONS

CHARACTERISTIC	SECT	DENOMINATION
Size	Small	Large
Relationship with other religious groups	Rejects—feels that the sect alone has the "truth"	Accepts other denominations and is able to work in harmony with them
Wealth (church property, buildings, salary of clergy, income of members)	Limited	Extensive
Religious services	Emotional emphasis—try to recapture conversion thrill; informal; extensive congregational participation	Intellectual emphasis; concern with teaching; formal; limited congregational participation
Clergy	Unspecialized; little if any professional training; frequently part-time	Specialized; professionally trained; full-time
Doctrines	Literal interpretation of scriptures; emphasis upon other-wordly rewards	Liberal interpretations of scriptures; emphasis upon this-worldly rewards
Membership requirements	Conversion experience; emotional commitment	Born into group or ritualistic requirements; intellectual commitment
Relationship with secular world	"At war" with the secular world which is defined as being "evil"	Endorses prevailing culture and social organization
Social class of members	Mainly lower class	Mainly middle class

SOURCE: Glenn M. Vernon, *Sociology of Religion* (New York: McGraw-Hill Book Company, 1962), p. 174.

RELIGIOUS LEADERSHIP

What kind of people lead religious groups? In what ways do they relate to their followers? These and numerous other questions have stimulated research and inquiry into the phenomenon of religious leadership.

In the present section, two types of religious leaders will be discussed: religious innovators—those who start new systems of belief—and clergy—leaders of established religious groups. Roughly the same questions can be asked with respect to both types. Each type, however, provides a very different style of leadership.

Religious innovator. Individuals who start religions seem to come from a variety of social backgrounds. Often, they are of humble origin. More important, it seems, are the social conditions under which they live. It is during periods of social unrest, when established systems of

values begin to crumble, that founders of new faiths are likely to emerge. In particular, mass migration, rapid urbanization, industrialization, wars, and other social upheavals provide conditions conducive to the formation, or attempted formation, of new religions.

Two major types of religious innovators can be discerned: the "prophet" and the "messiah." (The meanings of these terms are not intended to be identical with their usage within established religious groups.) To their followers, both prophets and messiahs appear to have special powers or qualities that sociologists refer to as *charisma* (see Chapter 6, pages 182–184). In other respects, however, they differ considerably. Vernon has summarized the major behavior patterns associated with the role of prophet in the following terms:

An individual typically comes to believe that he is in communion with his deity or deities and has received divine mandates to perform certain tasks or "missions." He then defines himself as being the mouthpiece or instrument of divine will, having learned his deity's wishes through visions, dreams, trances, direct verbal communication or other means.[34]

The messiah is also a religious innovator who possesses great charisma. However, unlike the prophet (who merely claims to speak for a divinity), the messiah claims that he personally is a divine being. Further, instead of calling for reform in the existing social or religious system, he predicts the total collapse of the system and the coming of a millenium when the entire world, or at least his society, will be utterly transformed.

There have been numerous individuals in the history of the United States who started successful sectarian groups by playing the role of prophet or messiah. A good example of the prophet is Georgia-born Elijah Poole, who as Elijah Muhammad, the "Messenger of Allah," founded the Black Muslim sect.[35] Another black leader, Father Divine, provides an example of the messiah. Father Divine also came from humble origins in the South, where his name was George Baker. His career began after he migrated to New York and announced that he was a divine being—in fact, God himself! He developed the Peace Mission Movement, which spread to many urban centers and became very successful financially.[36]

Clergy. We have already seen how any religious group that persists through time tends to become institutionalized. If the group grows in size, a formal division of labor and a hierarchy of leadership become necessary, and a class of religious specialists develops. While such specialists are variously referred to as priests, rabbis, ministers, or pastors, depending upon which denomination or major religion they serve, they are alike in many ways. Thus they can be grouped together under the general heading of clergy.

The activities of the clergy make up a considerable variety of roles—teacher, preacher, scholar, master of ritual, counselor, institutional representative, and administrator. All these roles are played in some measure by all members of the clergy.

The relationship between the clergyman and those he leads in the typical Protestant denomination differs from the relationship in the Catholic parish. The minister is directly responsible to the members of his congregation, and the democratic power structure leads to an emphasis on service roles for clergymen, such as counseling and organizing social functions. It may also mean adapting the ritualistic and doctrinal aspects of the faith to the interests of particular congregations. Many ministers deal little with theological issues in their sermons, speaking instead on current secular themes.

In contrast, the Catholic priest's main responsibility has traditionally been to higher church authority. His parishioners have generally had little or no voice in how the church was run, nor have their interests had any influence on the service. Today, there are numerous signs of challenge and change, but the image of the priest is still that of the shepherd in charge of his flock.[37]

In terms of formal training, both Jews and Catholics make extensive demands on prospective clergymen. The typical Catholic priest must spend several years in advanced study after the equivalent of graduation from college, and the rabbi must spend from four to six years in rabbinical school after completing college. Protestant standards, by contrast, range from no formal educational requirements at all to advanced training equivalent to that of the Catholic and Jewish clergy. In general, the educational level of the American Protestant clergy declined steadily from colonial times until about 1930, when the trend began to reverse itself.

Reasons given for entering the clergy vary somewhat among the major religions. In certain Protestant groups the individual is expected to have been "called" to the ministry by "a subjective emotional experience which semi-miraculously reveals God's will that one should become a clergyman."[38] Such experiences are not regarded as so important by Catholics and Jews (although these faiths definitely emphasize the

34. Glenn M. Vernon, *Sociology of Religion* (New York, McGraw-Hill Book Company, 1962), p. 174.

35. E. U. Essien-Udom, *Black Nationalism: The Search for an Identity* (Chicago: The University of Chicago Press, 1962).

36. Robert A. Parker, *The Incredible Messiah: The Deification of Father Divine* (Boston: Little, Brown and Company, 1937).

37. On the revolution in Catholic thinking see especially Thomas F. O'Dea, *American Catholic Dilemma* (New York: The New American Library, Inc., 1962); and the same author's *The Catholic Crisis* (Boston: Beacon Press, 1969).

38. David O. Moberg, *The Church as a Social Institution* (Englewood Cliffs, N. J.: Prentice-Hall, Inc., 1962), p. 484.

duty of the faithful to at least consider the religious life as a vocation) and are somewhat more typical of the sectarian than the denominational Protestant groups. However, in a study of 1704 students from fifty-seven Protestant seminaries, "a definite call of God" was given by more than a third as a reason for entering the ministry.[39]

While clergymen are drawn from every social stratum, there are certain preconditions that seem to increase the probability that an individual will decide to enter the ministry. Some researchers have attempted to trace this decision to psychological factors,[40] but it can also be explained as a product of purely social influences. It is known that homes in which the father is a minister provide twenty-five times as many clergymen as other homes. Close friendship with a respected member of the clergy appears to be another important influence. In short, many of the same kinds of factors appear to influence prospective members of the clergy as influence prospective doctors, dentists, lawyers, and other apprentice professionals.[41]

Historically, in Protestant England the Anglican Church offered one of the few careers open to the younger sons of gentry, whose first-born sons inherited the family estates. On the Continent, for centuries, the Catholic Church provided the sole opportunity for advancement for boys of the lower class. While conditions were very different in nineteenth-century America, here, too, the priesthood offered poor boys a chance to achieve positions of respect and authority. Home influence also played an important role. For the immigrant mother in particular, having a son become a priest was often a matter of the greatest pride and satisfaction.

RELIGION AND THE SOCIAL ORDER

The most ambitious attempt by a contemporary sociologist to relate the social and political order with religious belief is *Religion and Regime* by Guy E. Swanson. In this work, Swanson has proposed a sociological explanation of why some European countries adopted Protestant beliefs during the Reformation while others did not. The key to his explanation is the concept of *immanence*, the belief that spirits or spiritual values are "actually incorporated in particular times, places, and things."[42] He traces the differences between Catholics and Protestants to their respective attitudes toward immanence: broadly speaking, Catholics believe that God is immanent in the world through the church and the sacraments, while Protestants do not. Whole populations, he argues, were predisposed toward either the Catholic or the Protestant point of view by the behavior of their central governments. If a government seems to act only for its own distinctive purposes, as in a traditional monarchy, then it is easy for the people who live under such a government to believe in a God who acts in the same way. If, on the other hand, the government is clearly a product of compromise between various special interests—indeed, if legitimate special interests exist at all outside the government—then the notion of an immanent God may seem less convincing.

Opinions may differ about Swanson's success in proving his case, but there can be little doubt that the kind of approach his work represents will become increasingly influential. This approach is not without precedents. In fact, it may be seen as a combination of two well-established fields of inquiry: the part played by religion in social integration—i.e., the creation and maintenance of social order—and its part in the opposite phenomenon, social conflict.

RELIGION AND SOCIAL INTEGRATION

The fact that society is orderly, for the most part, and that human beings voluntarily accept rules for interaction has been a continuing source of speculation for students of human society. Many explanations for the basis of this order have been proposed. Perhaps the best-known example is the "social contract" theory (page 5), which was very popular among political philosophers during the seventeenth and eighteenth centuries.

More recently, social scientists have suggested that religion may be one of the key ele-

---

39. Ralph A. Felton, *New Ministers* (Madison, N. J.: Drew Theological Seminary, 1949), pp. 15–17.

40. Moberg, *op. cit.,* p. 485.

41. *Ibid.,* pp. 482–483.

42. Guy E. Swanson, *Religion and Regime: A Sociological Account of the Reformation* (Ann Arbor, Mich.: University of Michigan Press, 1967), p. viii.

NOTICE: PLEASE LEAVE PETTY AND DOCTRINAL DIFFERENCES ALONE BELIEVING THE CREATOR OF THE WHOLE UNIVERSE & ALL THEREIN, IS NOT AS NARROW AS OUR THINKING & REMEMBER THIS IS A FELLOWSHIP MEETING. (The Goal) TO PROMOTE A BELIEF IN A JUST ETERNAL CREATOR—OR STIMULATE WHAT YOU ALREADY HAVE, TO GAINING A LOVE TOWARDS ALL MEN, HATEING NONE, THOUGH WE DETEST OUR & THEIR EVIL WAYS SO MUCH, THAT WE PRAY TO OVERCOME EVIL WITH GOOD, TO THE GAINING OF RIGHTEOUSNESS, FAITH, REPENT-ENCE & HOPE—TO FINALLY CHARITY, AS PER 1 COR.13—YES THE CROWNING PURE LOVE VIRTUE. WE WILL TRUST YOU TO COOPERATE UNTIL PROV-ING DIFFERENTLY. SIGNED: MARL KILGORE – PRESIDENT WILLIAM HILLES – SECRETARY

Regardless of their truth or falsity, religions are important to society because they generally reinforce the basic mores, norms, and laws upon which the social order rests. As this sign from a Lutheran Fellowship meeting indicates, religions may be not only a source of ethical codes for their members but also an integrating force for society as a whole.

ments in the maintenance of the social machinery. Religions define sacred values and prescribe behavioral codes by which these values can be obtained. Thus, for the society that supports it, religion provides an effective basis for a system of mores—an essential prerequisite to social orderliness. Social order also depends upon law; but law, the more formal and codified system of societal norms, is closely related to and dependant upon the mores, as was explained in earlier chapters.

There is, in short, a direct line of dependency between the powerful sentiments of reverence, awe, and fear that religious beliefs generate and the rules that religions prescribe for leading a life that will assure divine approval. These rules in turn become important aspects of societal organization in the form of shared mores. At some point, these rules may be translated into law if social change or other processes threaten to make them ineffective. Thus reli-

gions define, reinforce, and reaffirm the elementary human responses upon which the social order ultimately rests.

For the sociologist, such functions of religion are of central importance. He is interested in the consequences that religious systems have for individuals and societies, not whether their definitions of the sacred or their accounts of the events of the world are "correct." As the English anthropologist Radcliffe-Brown has put it:

The hypothesis we are considering is that the social function of a religion is independent of its truth or falsity, that religions which we think to be erroneous or even absurd and repulsive, such as those of some savage tribes, may be important and effective parts of the social machinery, and without these "false" religions, social evolution and the development of modern civilization would have been impossible.[43]

In addition to being a source of ethical codes, in what other ways are religions socially integrating? For one thing, the sharing of some common set of beliefs *about almost anything* is in

---

43. A. R. Radcliffe-Brown, *Structure and Function in Primitive Society* (New York: The Free Press, 1952), p. 154.

itself integrating. That is, it tends to reduce the ways in which people can perceive themselves as "different" from each other. Shared religious beliefs can be especially integrating if they set the believers apart from the outside world. For example, the Mennonites, whose beliefs deviate in many respects from those of most American Christians, are highly integrated. "They are proud to be known as 'peculiar people' who live in isolated communities away from the mainstream of sinful, secular society."[44]

RELIGION AND SOCIAL CONFLICT

The presence of different religions in the same society can result in violent and tragic conflicts. The persecution of religious minorities has been a familiar fact throughout history. At the beginning of the Christian era, followers of Christ were persecuted by the Roman government. Then, after Christianity became the official religion of the Roman Empire, non-Christian groups were no less energetically persecuted. In later centuries "religious" wars wracked both East and West, though often economics and

TABLE 17.2. **ESTIMATED RELIGIOUS COMPOSITION OF THE ADULT POPULATION OF THE UNITED STATES**

RELIGIOUS GROUPS	PERCENT OF ADULT POPULATION
Protestants	72%
Baptists	21%
Methodists	17%
Lutherans	7%
Presbyterians	6%
Episcopalians	3%
Other Protestants	18%
Roman Catholics	22%
Jews	3%
Other Religions	1%
No Religion or Religion not reported	2%
Sample Size	5,827
U.S. Adult Population	108,051,172

(as reported by the 1960 Census of Population)

SOURCE: Bernard Lazerwitz, "Religion and Social Structure in the United States," in *Religion, Culture, and Society,* ed. Louis Schneider (New York: John Wiley & Sons, Inc., 1964), p. 427. Based on data obtained by the University of Michigan Research Center in 1957 and 1958, from a sample of the civilian population twenty-one years old and over.

politics had at least as much to do with the struggles as religion. Christians clashed with Muslims, Catholics with Protestants, Protestants with other Protestants.

After World War II, at the time of the partition of India and Pakistan, tens of thousands were killed and millions made refugees in the explosive conflict between Muslims and Hindus. For years, Jews and Arabs have battled in the Middle East. And in 1969, Catholics and Protestants turned adjacent neighborhoods in northern Ireland into warring camps.

In the United States, where freedom of religion is guaranteed by the Constitution, religious conflict is usually nonviolent today, but religious prejudice and discrimination are by no means dead. There are still tensions between Christians and Jews, between Protestants and Catholics, among some branches of Protestantism, and between believers and nonbelievers. There is also tension at times between the government and some religious groups. Legal confusion with respect to the precise relationship between religion and the state can be found in such areas as prayer in public schools, tax exemptions for church property, federal support for parochial schools, abortion, artificial insemination, divorce, and military conscription.

The Society of Friends (the Quakers) has always taught its members that they should not bear arms. This teaching caused trouble for American Quakers in the colonial period. When the United States drafted men for military service, Quakers and other pacifist religious groups found themselves in direct conflict with the law. In time, a system was set up whereby those whose religious training and belief would not permit them to fight could be given noncombat assignments in the armed forces, and those who would·not accept any military assignment could fulfill their obligations through civilian service. Since a Supreme Court decision in June 1970, it has become possible to fulfill military obligations through civilian service on the basis of personal conviction as well as on the basis of religious affiliation. But some groups, notably the Jehovah's Witnesses, have refused all such arrangements and, unless granted unqualified exemption, have preferred to go to jail.[45] During the Vietnam war the former heavyweight boxing

44. W. Seward Salisbury, *Religion in American Culture* (Homewood, Ill.: The Dorsey Press, 1964), p. 325.
45. *Ibid.,* pp. 329–330.

champion of the world, Cassius Clay (Muhammad Ali) claimed exemption as a minister of the Black Muslims; but the claim was rejected, and he was sentenced to jail for refusing to serve in the armed forces.

RELIGION IN AMERICA

Because the Constitution of the United States prohibits government interference in religious matters, Congress has always refused to authorize official inquiries into church membership. As a result, the best available data on the religious composition of the American population are only estimates, made at irregular intervals by a variety of agencies. Table 17.2 shows one such estimate, based on a study by the University of Michigan Survey Research Center. An estimate made by the Bureau of the Census in 1957, based on a sample of 119,333 persons over fourteen years old, showed a very similar distribution (66.2 percent Protestant, 25.7 percent Roman Catholic, and 3.2 percent Jewish).

When America's religious composition is examined in terms of place of residence, certain ecological patterns emerge. Jews tend to be concentrated in the larger urban centers, particularly in the Northeast. The same is true of Catholics, but to a lesser extent. Of the Protestants, Baptists are heavily represented in the South; it is much harder to generalize about the other denominations. The less well established sectarian groups tend to be found in cities, particularly among blacks.

RELIGION AND SOCIAL CLASS

Studies of the relationship between religion and social class fall into two main categories. In the first, statistical indices of social class position, such as years of education or occupational group, are used to give a *quantitative* overview of class variations in religious affiliation. In the second, the same kinds of variations are examined from a *qualitative* viewpoint—that is, in terms of what religious experiences *mean* to the persons in question.

The quantitative approach. Tabulation of membership by education and occupation reveals substantial class differences among major religious groups. The University of Michigan survey cited above showed that Protestant denominations such as the Episcopalian, Presbyterian, and Methodist churches had more college-educated members than the others (Table 17.3) and were also more heavily represented in managerial and professional occupations (Table 17.4, page 556). Other Protestants, as well as most Roman Catholics, tend to be of the middle or lower-middle class, as measured by either

TABLE 17.3. **EDUCATION ATTAINMENT OF ADULTS IDENTIFYING THEMSELVES WITH MAJOR RELIGIOUS GROUPS IN THE UNITED STATES**

RELIGIOUS-GROUPS	SAMPLE SIZE	0–8 GRADES	SOME HIGH SCHOOL	4 YEARS HIGH SCHOOL	1–3 YEARS COLLEGE	4 YEARS OR MORE OF COLLEGE	TOTAL (%)
Nation	5827	33	20	28	10	9	100
Protestants	4185	33	21	27	10	9	100
All Baptists	939	44	24	21	7	4	100
Baptists: Whites	713	39	26	24	7	4	100
Baptists: Negroes	226	63	20	11	3	3	100
Methodists	730	31	20	28	10	11	100
Lutherans	328	35	22	29	9	5	
Presbyterians	272	18	17	29	20	16	100
Episcopalians	119	8	14	25	25	28	100
Roman Catholics	1270	34	20	32	9	5	100
Jews	188	21	13	33	17	16	100

SOURCE: Lazerwitz, *op. cit.,* p. 428.

TABLE 17.4. OCCUPATIONAL STATUS OF ADULTS IDENTIFYING THEMSELVES WITH MAJOR RELIGIOUS GROUPS IN THE UNITED STATES

RELIGIOUS GROUPS	SAMPLE SIZE	WITHOUT AN OCCUPATION	FARMERS	UNSKILLED	SEMISKILLED	SKILLED	CLERICAL AND SALES	OWNERS, MANAGERS, AND OFFICIALS	PROFESSIONS	TOTAL (%)
Nation	5827	18	9	9	15	18	10	12	9	100
Protestants	4185	17	10	10	15	17	10	12	9	100
All Baptists	939	18	11	15	20	16	7	8	5	100
Baptists: Whites	713	16	12	8	19	19	9	11	6	100
Baptists: Negroes	226	18	8	34	21	10	4	1	4	100
Methodists	730	21	9	8	14	16	11	11	10	100
Lutherans	328	14	15	8	14	18	13	11	7	100
Presbyterians	272	17	4	8	7	17	14	20	13	100
Episcopalians	119	13	2	4	6	12	17	23	23	100
Roman Catholics	1270	15	4	10	20	22	10	11	8	100
Jews	188	14	0	1	9	9	16	32	19	100

SOURCE: Lazerwitz, *op. cit.,* p. 428.

education or occupation. Jews, on the other hand, vary considerably in education but have very strong representation in the upper occupational categories. Of all the major groups, the Baptists apparently draw most heavily from the bottom of the social structure; a large proportion of their members are poorly educated and in low-status jobs. The data from which these generalizations are drawn are reasonably consistent with other nationwide surveys of religious identification and are also paralleled by data from studies of specific American cities.[46]

It should not be concluded from these data, however, that religious affiliation is simply a class phenomenon. All groups draw *some* of their members from each social stratum. Another statistical generalization that should be interpreted with caution is the finding that upper- and middle-class people are more likely to be formal members of a church and to attend services with some regularity than are lower-class people.[47] This, again, is not a simple or invariant relationship; some lower-class people are ardent churchgoers, while some upper- and middle-class people attend rarely or not at all.

The qualitative approach. Figures on church attendance tell us nothing about the quality of the experience of those who attend. Some clues to the kinds of needs the churches fulfill for their members are provided by the

styles of worship. People attending the services of fundamentalist and evangelical sects often exhibit spontaneous forms of emotional behavior. In some other denominations, by contrast, services are highly formal, thoroughly institutionalized, and completely without spontaneity. (In a statistical survey, both types of service would be tabulated simply as "Protestant.")

In some religious groups people "speak in tongues," shake, scream, jump, faint, roll on the floor, and give unsolicited testimony of their religious salvation. Here is a first-hand account:

After Mrs. Rogers had been preaching for about fifteen minutes, an old lady got up and started screaming and shouting, "Help me, Lord Jesus!" She was still throwing her arms up and shouting for Jesus to help her when a younger woman jumped up and hollered, "Precious Lord Jesus, save me!" Mrs. Rogers' voice was getting louder all the time. For two hours, she preached—and for two hours, people were getting up, shouting, jumping up and down, calling

---

46. Herbert W. Schneider, *Religion in Twentieth Century America* (Cambridge, Mass.: Harvard University Press, 1952), p. 288; Lenski, *op. cit.,* pp. 79–81; Donald O. Cowgill, "The Ecology of Religious Preference in Wichita," *Sociological Quarterly,* 1 (1960), 87–96.

47. Bernard Lazerwitz, "Some Factors Associated With Variations in Church Attendance," *Social Forces,* 39 (1961), 301–309.

to Jesus for help and salvation, and falling out exhausted. Some of these "Holy Rollers," as Dad called them, would fall to the floor and start trembling rapidly; some of them even began to slobber on themselves. When I asked Mama what was wrong with those people and what they were doing on the floor, she told me that the "spirit" had hit them. When Carole heard this, she began to cry and wanted to get out of there before the spirit hit us.[48]

H. Richard Niebuhr has this to say about religious expression:

Where the power of abstract thought has not been highly developed and where inhibitions on emotional expression have not been set up by a system of polite conversation, religion must and will express itself in emotional terms. Under these circumstances spontaneity and energy of religious feeling rather than conformity to an abstract creed are regarded as the tests of religious genuineness.[49]

What is being suggested here is that religious behavior at the bottom of the socioeconomic hierarchy is closely connected both with the nature of social life more broadly, as lower-class people experience it, and with the needs, tensions, and frustrations it generates. This can be clearly seen in the type of sectarian religious movement known as *millenarism*.[50] Millenarian movements are those that announce the coming of a period of great happiness and prosperity—a *millennium*—in which all believers will share. Christianity itself, according to modern biblical scholars, was once such a movement, appealing chiefly to members of the lower class. But the phenomenon is not confined to Western culture. Anthropologists have classified both the American Indian "ghost dance" (page 355) and the Melanesian "cargo cult" as essentially millenarian and have noted that they appeared at a time when the native cultures from which they arose were threatened with extinction by the spread of Western culture.[51]

Scholars have also pointed out that the number of millenarian sects in Western society seems to increase sharply in times of economic depression. Such was the case along the American frontier as the nineteenth-century westward movement continued and, more recently, in the Appalachian coal fields.[52]

The struggle for economic survival, the emotional distress caused by an unstable social environment, the hopelessness of seeking a better way of life, the threat of cultural extinction—all, it seems, may underly the appeal of millenarian sects. The black American; the white rural migrant to the impersonal city; the farm family whose means of subsistence have been wiped out by technological change—these are the ready recruits for revivalist and pentecostal sects, for obscure store-front churches where it is preached that the poor are the chosen people and the meek shall inherit the earth. In these groups people with little social status can find religious status. In addition, the emotionality of the services provide them with a means for working off their pent-up feelings of frustration. The formalism of the established denominations has little appeal for such people.

To the middle class, by contrast, sectarian religious behavior often seems ludicrous. Most middle-class people are more concerned with the amenities of life than with economic survival. The pleasant and dignified atmosphere of the Sunday service held in a building that "looks like" God's house, where there is a chance to socialize with "nice" people after the service, fits their needs very comfortably. Thus the distinctive human needs generated at different levels of the social structure find expression and satisfaction within different types of religious groups.

THE FUTURE OF RELIGION

Societies and their religions undergo change together. This does not imply that one is necessarily "determined" by the other; religion may change society or vice versa. At the present time in the United States, the traditional beliefs and practices of all major religious denominations are being challenged not only by an increasingly secularized society but also by churchmen

48. Claude Brown, *Manchild in the Promised Land* (New York: Signet Books, 1966), pp. 25-26.

49. H. Richard Niebuhr, *The Social Sources of Denominationalism* (Hamden, Conn.: Shoe String Press, 1954), pp. 27-28.

50. Norman Cohn, *The Pursuit of the Millennium* (New York: Harper & Row, Inc., 1961).

51. Peter Worsley, *The Trumpet Shall Sound: A Study of Cargo Cults in Melanesia* (New York: Schocken Books, Inc., 1968); Anthony F. C. Wallace, "Revitalization Movements," *American Anthropologist*, 58 (1956), 264-281.

52. Yinger, *op. cit.*, pp. 156-194.

Airplanes are the only contact that these natives in New Guinea have with Western civilization. Since the "strange birds" bring food, medicine, tobacco, and alcohol, they have, in effect, ushered in a millennium—a period of prosperity for the tribesmen. Not surprisingly, however, this sudden appearance of cargo is also a source of some consternation to the natives. Thus they have developed a cargo cult which explains the arrival of the supplies in terms of their existing beliefs. Because ancestor worship is an important part of their ritual, most tribesmen believe that the goods are sent by their ancestors.

themselves. What does this imply for the future of religion?[53]

Secularization. With scientific and industrial progress, societies tend to become increasingly secular in their basic value orientations. American churches, especially the Protestant ones, have reacted to this situation by becoming less otherworldly. Clergymen today are increasingly involved in the nonreligious affairs of their communities. The heavy participation of the clergy in the civil rights movement is an outstanding example. Less controversial has been the involvement of virtually all urban churches (and increasingly the suburban ones too) with such social problems as juvenile delinquency, poverty, and drug addiction.

Secularization does not necessarily mean, however, that religion is declining in importance. Indeed, over the last one hundred years the proportion of the American population belonging to a recognized church has risen steadily. Of course, this may not imply an increasingly deep commitment to religious faith. It may be simply that as American society increases in affluence and middle-class values spread, church membership is seen as more desirable from a purely social point of view. On the other hand, there has been a clear increase in the amount of religious literature that is bought and consumed by the public; books of an inspirational nature continue to appear on best-seller lists.[54] The

53. For a discussion of the various challenges currently facing the major religious denominations of the United States, see Harvey Cox, *The Secular City*, rev. ed. (New York: The Macmillan Company, 1966), and Peter Berger, *The Sacred Canopy: Elements of a Sociological Theory of Religion* (Garden City, N.Y.: Doubleday & Company, Inc., 1967).

54. Louis Schneider and S. M. Dornbusch, *Popular Religion* (Chicago: The University of Chicago Press, 1958).

coverage of religious activities in the mass media also remains extensive. However much religion may be changing in our time, then, it apparently has not lost the interest of most Americans.

Adaptation. It seems possible to conclude that religion in America is not dying out but rapidly assuming new forms that will assure its survival in a changing society. Religious faiths have often adapted themselves to changing circumstances in the past. For example, there are now three major varieties of Judaism in the United States, representing three general degrees of acculturation to American society. Orthodox Jews maintain their religion much as it was in their area of origin—usually eastern Europe—resisting the impact of American culture. So-called Conservative Jews maintain strong ties with traditional Jewish beliefs and traditions but also permit numerous modifications of traditional worship, religious organization, and doctrine. Finally, the proponents of Reform Judaism, while continuing to regard themselves as Jews, have abandoned many of the traditional features of their religion.

The challenge of science. There is one final trend that pertains not only to the United States but to other nations as well. As explanations of events in the physical world, in the social order, and in man's psychological functioning become increasingly sophisticated because of the advance of the sciences, traditional religious beliefs are increasingly subject to question. But whether this means an actual decline in the felt need for religion is another matter.

Some of the more heated debates between churchmen and scientists that accompanied the development of the physical and biological sciences in the nineteenth and early twentieth centuries have now largely subsided. American churchmen, by and large, appear to be taking the view that the major differences have either been resolved or were based upon false premises in the first place. On the other hand, while it may no longer be fashionable to continue these controversies in public, a number of scientists persist in the conviction that two systems of thought, one based upon faith and revelation and the other upon scientific logic and empir-

ical evidence, can never really achieve a rapprochement.[55]

An interesting dimension of the problem of dealing with the environment in scientific rather than supernatural terms is revealed in a study done some years ago by the anthropologist Malinowski on a primitive society.[56] The Trobriand islanders of the Southwest Pacific were expert fishermen. Fish were a major food for the entire society. These people knew how to harvest fish from both the quiet lagoon and the more dangerous open sea around their island. Harvesting fish in the lagoon was simple and foolproof. They had developed a reliable technology, using a poisonous substance that killed the fish but left them completely fit for human consumption.

Malinowski noted that these island people did not practice any form of religious rituals or magic rites to aid in this task. That is, they did not attempt to manipulate or appeal to supernatural powers in connection with their lagoon fishing. But fishing in the open sea was an entirely different story. Deep-sea fishing could yield great catches of highly desirable fish, or the fisherman could come home empty-handed. Moreover, the sea could be hazardous for fishermen in open canoes. Therefore extensive rites and rituals were practiced in order to ensure safety and a good catch.

These observations suggested to Malinowski that primitive men develop reliable technical knowledge that can replace magical beliefs and practices. Their knowledge is more a product of trial and error, a result of hard experience and traditional wisdom, than a result of an accumulation of systematic theory and empirical research; but it is dependable knowledge that gives them command over various aspects of their environment.

Whether primitive or sophisticated, however, when men attempt to deal with phenomena for which their technical knowledge is inadequate or unreliable, they invent rituals, magical rites, superstitions, myths, or other forms of culture concerning the supernatural. These cultural forms permit them to feel more secure in the face of the unknown. If this thesis is correct, the accumulation of scientific knowledge may present an increasing challenge to religious beliefs.

On the other hand, an equally good case can be made that no matter how sophisticated science may become, there will always remain unknown frontiers which man will have to deal

55. Glock and Stark, *op. cit.,* p. 263.

56. Bronislaw Malinowski, *Science, Magic, and Religion* (Garden City, N.Y.: Anchor Books, 1954).

VIEWPOINTS   THE CHURCH AS A SOCIAL FORCE

What is the church's primary mission? Is it redemptive or social—or both? There are those who hold that even evangelism should be reinterpreted along the lines of social engineering and political pressure.... When most major Protestant denominations have their annual councils, assemblies, or conventions, they make pronouncements on matters having to do with disarmament, federal aid to education, birth control, the United Nations, and any number of social and political issues. Very rarely are any resolutions passed that have to do with the redemptive witness of the Gospel.

... Certainly there is a sense in which the church is to advise, warn, and challenge by proclaiming the absolute criteria by which God will judge mankind—such as the Ten Commandments and the Sermon on the Mount, by proclaiming God's divine purpose through government in a fallen society, and by preaching the whole council of God, which involves man's environment and physical being as well as his soul.... [But] we have been trying to solve every ill of society as though society were made up of regenerate men to whom we had an obligation to speak with Christian advice. We are beginning to realize that, while the law must guarantee human rights and restrain those who violate those rights, whenever men lack sympathy for the law they will not long respect it even when they cannot repeal it. Thus the government may try to legislate Christian behavior, but it soon finds that man remains unchanged.

The changing of men is the primary mission of the church. The only way to change men is to get them converted to Jesus Christ. Then they will have the capacity to live up to the Christian command to "Love thy neighbor."

... There are certain issues we know to be wrong—racial injustice, crime, gambling, dishonesty, pornography. On these matters we must thunder forth as the prophets of God.... [B]ut it becomes a different matter when the church speaks as the church on every social and political issue that comes along, especially when the issue settled either way is not a moral or spiritual problem....

I am convinced that if the church went back to its main task of preaching the Gospel and getting people converted to Christ it would have far more impact on the social structure of the nation than it can have in any other thing it could possibly do.

Billy Graham
World Aflame

Christianity is a movement of change within the world, a movement which seeks to transform the institutional relations between men in order the better to express the relationships which constitute them as human: this movement is to be hated by the world, is to come in conflict with the power structure of the world, but is eventually to "overcome the world." "This is the victory that overcomes the world, our faith." It therefore seems not unreasonable to describe the Church as a revolutionary movement within the world. The preaching of the gospel is a danger to the values of the world and to the economic and political structures which embody these values....

[The] revolutionary mission of the Church... cuts deeper than what would ordinarily be called the political revolution. The Christian is entitled to feel that the political revolution, precisely because it does not reach to the heart of the matter, to the ultimate alienation of sin, is liable to betray the revolution itself. The achievements of the political revolution, insofar as they are thought of as ultimate aims and not as pointers toward an absolute future, may themselves become forms of the dominative society. The mission of the Church is to be ... the revolution in the revolution. To proclaim the gospel is to interpret the revolution in revolutionary terms, not to see it as merely the substitution of one imaginable social order for another.

... The fact that the Church's task is, in a sense, a political task, should not make us see it as essentially a job for the laity, with the clergy acting as back-room boys or as the army supply corps. We should, rather, see it as a task for the Church as such, in its structures. If the bishop is a leader in the Church, it is only because he has been given the task of being a leader in the revolutionary struggle against the values and political forms of the world. Insofar as he neglects this primary task it becomes increasingly difficult to take him seriously as a merely ecclesiastical leader. ... The business of the priest is to be one jump ahead of the Christian life of his age; it is his job to be constantly representing to the Christian people and to the world, the evangelical, revolutionary significance of their Christian, secular lives....

[The] "credibility" of the Church is to be judged, not according to whether it is a community in which we can begin to satisfy our personal need for warmth and kindness and decent personal relations, but according to whether it is an effective force in the revolutionizing of the world.

Herbert McCabe
"Priesthood and Revolution"

with in terms of his faith. Science by its nature admits of uncertainty, and though it has forced changes in particular religious beliefs, it has hardly shown religion itself to be irrelevant to human life. Religion remains the social institution through which man seeks to understand those things that are beyond science, including the meaning of his own existence.

SUMMARY

Religion, the institution that defines the sacred and outlines man's responses to it, is a group-centered phenomenon that forms part of society's culture. Individual religious behavior can be discussed in terms of four dimensions of religiosity: ideology, ritual, experience, and revelation. Religious affiliation often seems to exist without support from religious ideology, indicating that religion fulfills needs other than ideological ones. The function of ritual is mainly symbolic, and observance varies greatly within the major religious groups. Individual religious experience, which may be confirming, responsive, or ecstatic, contains a strong social element. Revelation is the dimension of religiosity known to prophets, saints, and the founders of religions. At the individual level, religion provides security, aids in the management of crises and in adjustment to death, provides personal values, and has other, less easily specified functions.

Religious beliefs gain in credibility in proportion as they are shared. Ernst Troeltsch's church-sect continuum provides the basis for a theory of religious variation. In Troeltsch's analysis, the church is the religious establishment, which allies itself with the status quo. The sect is a protest movement that breaks away from the church. In time the sect usually becomes a church, giving rise to other sects.

Christian groups, in spite of their great variety, can be classified in five main categories: the universal church, the ecclesia, the denomination, the sect, and the cult. Religious leaders can be categorized as the innovators—the prophets and messiahs—and the clergy. Prophets see themselves as instruments of the divine will, while messiahs claim that they themselves are divine. The clergy—the religious specialists—receive different amounts of training and have different relationships with the groups they lead, depending on the church they represent. Prospective members of the clergy appear to be influenced by many of the same kinds of factors that influence those choosing other professions.

From the perspective of society as a whole, a major function of religion is the contribution it makes to social stability and social integration. Indeed, religion can be the principal means of sustaining group identity. But religion is also a source of social conflict: from ancient times to the present day, religious groups have clashed with each other incessantly. Sometimes religious beliefs are also a source of conflict with the state.

From two thirds to three quarters of all Americans can be described as Protestants, from one fifth to one quarter as Roman Catholics, and about 3 percent as Jews. In general, different types of religious groups meet the needs generated at different levels of the social structure. Millenarism is a type of religious movement that satisfies the needs of the lower class, especially when its members are suffering economic and social insecurity.

With the growth of industrialism, American society has become increasingly secularized, and so have most religious groups and their clergy. Nevertheless, church membership has increased steadily, and public interest in religion shows no sign of diminishing. The major faiths in the United States have shown a tendency to adapt to changing conditions and attitudes; and while there is a possibility that science will someday replace religion, there is at least an equal possibility that man's need for some type of religious faith will always remain.

18

Education

In every society, ancient or modern, men have provided for the education of their children. Without training in the ways and skills of his society, the individual could not long survive, and unless its members were trained in these ways, the group would be doomed to extinction. Today we tend to think of education as systematic training conducted in formally established schools by specialized teachers. It should be recognized, however, that for the majority of citizens, even in Western societies, the school has only recently become the key group in the educational institution. Although formal academies and schools of various kinds have existed for a long time, until little more than a century ago the ordinary person in Europe or the United States had few prospects of ever attending one. Most people remained illiterate. Only the elite were able to send their offspring to formal academies or to hire trained tutors.

This does not mean, however, that children in earlier societies received no training. The male child in the primitive society, for example, had to internalize complex aspects of culture and social organization including the making and use of weapons, the arts of war, and the mysteries and magic of secret groups. In short, he had to acquire all the skills and lore needed to play an adult role among his people. For girls, the management of food was a matter of supreme importance, as mismanagement could mean starvation. Even the improper preparation of skins for clothing could spell disaster under certain conditions. All these aspects of culture had to be learned.

For the most part, adult males trained the boys with patience and care, while the girls received systematic instruction from the women. Thus the educational institution was integrated closely with the institution of the family. It varied greatly from society to society, but these early cultures required no specialized role of teacher and no specific building for learning.

As societies grew more complex, it became increasingly difficult for the family to pass on to the child all of the knowledge and skill that he would need as an adult. Industrialization and urbanization made it necessary for a child to find his way into an industrial labor force rather than

learn to till the soil as his forefathers had. Not only was there an ever increasing demand for *general* skills, such as reading and writing, but an ever increasing necessity to be able to perform some *specialized* role within the division of labor. The school, with a corps of trained educators and a bureaucratic organization to coordinate its activities, was developed to provide the needed training experiences.

This chapter will focus on the structures, trends, and problems of contemporary formal education in the United States—America's elementary and secondary schools, colleges, and universities. As was pointed out in Chapters 5 and 6, the American educational system is primarily an agent of socialization. Indeed, "planned socialization" is a large part of what most Americans mean when they speak of education. It is hardly surprising, then, that education today, in America as in other countries, is torn between the divergent aims of socialization—assuring societal continuity and encouraging ordered social change.

THE FUNCTIONS OF EDUCATION

The purposes and consequences of education may be viewed from the perspectives of both the society and the individual.[1] From society's point of view, the functions of education include transmitting the cultural heritage, providing trained individuals who can assume specialized roles within the division of labor and, in some instances, developing new knowledge.

The American educational system also serves certain less obvious, but nevertheless important functions. It effectively relieves the mother of child-care for long periods of time by providing a kind of systematic "baby-sitting" service. At somewhat older age levels, it becomes a place where the two sexes learn to relate to each other during the courtship period. Schools operated by religious groups serve to perpetuate distinct subcultural traditions, and vocational schools obviously emphasize distinctive content. And so on.

Under certain conditions, schools can serve as important agents of social change. Literacy can open up the modern world to people who have been shut off from the printed page. In our

---

1. An excellent treatment of the functions of education in American society can be found in: David A. Goslin, *The School in Contemporary Society* (Glenview, Ill.: Scott, Foresman and Co., 1965).

own society, social change is sometimes deliberately sought by the schools through the use of such techniques as operating rural extension courses and busing ghetto students to schools outside their neighborhoods. Social change and social reform, therefore, must be considered when evaluating the functions of the school for the society.

From the standpoint of the individual, the school has obvious functions. Education is the principal means by which status can be gained in a society that generally stresses achievement, acquisition of skills, and upward mobility. Whereas in earlier times youths needed only a minimum of formal schooling to get a job, the social consequences of dropping out of school today are well nigh disastrous.

How well the American school system performs its functions is debatable, but some facts are clear. First of all, the United States offers a range of educational opportunity unmatched by any other country. It was calculated in the early 1960's that 2.5 percent of all Americans were then being educated at the college level or beyond. The corresponding figure for the Soviet Union was .8 percent, and this was much higher than the figures for France, West Germany, and England.[2] The figure for England—.2 percent—clearly reflected the traditional English policy, modified only recently, of restricting higher education to a small governing elite. It is a fact that, in 1960, a young American black living in the South had a better chance of attending college than a young Englishman.[3]

It is also a fact that the American school system has failed black Americans, along with American Indians, many Spanish-speaking Americans, and the very poor generally. How to provide the child of the urban or rural slum with the education he must have if he is ever to escape that slum is a problem the schools have not solved. And it is also true that, in high schools and colleges, growing numbers of students are dissatisfied with courses, rules, and procedures that seem to them irrelevant to the times and to their needs.

EVOLVING FUNCTIONS

Over the years, America's schools have been forced to discard some old functions and take on new ones. Changes in educational phi-

losophy have taken place not primarily because of any abstract considerations but in response to changing social conditions. The history of American education can be reduced, at the risk of some oversimplification, to an account of how one central function gave way to another in successive periods.[4]

Training political elites. Education under colonial rule was compulsory only in the sense that some of the colonies required their towns to provide schools and teachers. Many parents sent their children to school in the fear that otherwise the youngsters might grow up knowing nothing of civilization. Except in New England, education was not free. By and large, the property-owning class considered free public education a form of welfarism with potentially dangerous consequences.

Public education in the colonial period meant elementary education. Only in the older towns and cities of the Northeast did a demand for education beyond the primary level begin to make itself felt, and the secondary schools that resulted were private institutions, which concentrated on subjects useful to the very small minority headed for college.

After independence, private institutions of higher learning began to flourish, and many new colleges were founded. By 1799 the United States had twenty-five, including two state universities—far more institutions of higher learning than England had at that time. But the function of higher education in America (when it was not preparation for the ministry) was still similar to that in England: training political leaders, of which the new nation was in great need.

During this early period, the federal government's most notable contribution to education was the Northwest Ordinance of 1787, which required every town set up in the Northwest Territory to reserve part of its land for the use of public schools. The government did not begin to make widespread grants of land for education until over seventy years later, and the first *state* to require its towns to actually provide schooling was Massachusetts in 1834.

---

2. Ben J. Wattenberg and Richard M. Scammon, *This U.S.A.* (New York: Pocket Books, 1967), p. 276.
3. *Ibid.*, p. 279.
4. Henry J. Perkinson, *The Imperfect Panacea: American Faith in Education, 1865 to 1965* (New York: Random House, Inc., 1968) is the main source for the following discussion.

Spreading equality. American education began to break out of the British mold as the mass of white Americans sought a larger share in democracy. In the troubled atmosphere of the 1820's was born the idea of free public education for all. But it was not until the 1830's that "common schools," as free public elementary schools were called, began to appear in large numbers outside New England, and some states did not provide them until the 1850's or later. The principal reason for the delay was the resistance of the property-owning class.

There is no doubt that the educational reformers of this period were aiming at greater social equality.

The object of the common school system is to give every child a free, straight, solid pathway by which he can walk directly up from the ignorance of an infant to a knowledge of the primary duties of a man, and can acquire a power and an invincible will to discharge them.[5]

So wrote Horace Mann in his first annual report as secretary of the first state board of education, set up in Massachusetts in 1837. Over great opposition from both teachers and legislators, Mann established the first "normal," or teacher-training, school. Along with the adoption of his system of schooling by grades, this began the movement for the professionalization of teaching. Thus, through the efforts of Mann and other reformers, the groundwork was laid for the American system of education as we know it today:

By 1850, . . . there had been formulated and, to some extent, established, the basic principles of American education: (1) that free public and secondary schools should be available to all children; (2) that teachers should be given professional training; (3) that all children be required to attend school up to a certain age, but not necessarily the free public school, religious and other bodies having complete liberty to establish their own educational systems at their own cost. These privileges as yet were only

imperfectly extended to women, and even less to Negroes.[6]

Although new colleges sprang up everywhere during the 1850's and 1860's, over 80 percent of them closed for lack of pupils. Even so, when the Civil War broke out, colleges outnumbered public high schools.[7] America was not yet ready for universal education beyond the primary level.

Promoting—and preventing—integration. Crises over integration of the races in public schools have occurred repeatedly for more than a century. By the end of the Civil War, most southern schools were closed. And the majority of the newly freed blacks had never had any schooling. As northern reformers saw it, the South should become culturally closer to the North, and its black citizens should immediately be uplifted so that they could take their rightful place in society. Both goals, they thought, could be met through education.

The movement to educate the southern black included the idea of racially integrated or "mixed" schools. (The private charitable and religious organizations that financed the flow of teachers to the South were not disturbed by the fact that most northern school systems were racially segregated.) School buildings were constructed by the so-called Freedmen's Bureau, a federal agency set up to care for ex-slaves, and were financed from the sale of requisitioned Confederate real estate. By 1869, the peak period, the Bureau had employed 9503 teachers in these schools, including many southern blacks trained by northern whites.[8]

At first, southern whites simply avoided the mixed schools; later they openly harassed and persecuted the teachers. During the Reconstruction Period (1867–1877), Louisiana, Florida, Mississippi, and Arkansas had black educators in charge of their school systems for considerable periods; but already, during the federally supervised state constitutional conventions of 1867–1868, it had proved impossible to persuade southern whites to support mixed schools with their taxes. When state assemblies with black majorities voted in favor of integrated schools, white parents withdrew their children from school altogether.

All the southern states had been "reconstructed" by the late 1870's, and all had instituted, or reinstituted, systems of free elementary

5. Alice V. and Lester D. Crow, eds., *Vital Issues in American Education* (New York: Bantam Books, 1964), p. 41.

6. Samuel Eliot Morison, *The Oxford History of the American People* (New York: Oxford University Press, 1965), p. 291.

7. David M. Potter in Louis B. Wright *et al.*, *The Democratic Experience* (Glenview, Ill.: Scott, Foresman and Co., 1968), p. 225.

8. Perkinson, *op. cit.*, p. 15.

education. As white conservatives regained control of the legislatures in state after state, however, they began to pass laws establishing segregated public school systems. Methods were found to divert public funds so that the schools for blacks received the lesser share. The final blow to black educational hopes was the omission of any provision for integrated schools in the Civil Rights Act of 1875. By 1896, after twenty years of northern indifference and southern determination, the political climate was ripe for the Supreme Court's historic decision in *Plessy* vs. *Ferguson* that the "separate but equal" facilities in the South were indeed constitutional. The facilities were not equal, and the separation rested on a philosophy of racism. Nevertheless, this legal basis for segregation was not changed until 1954.

Americanizing. Curiously enough, it was just as Reconstruction was drawing to a close that compulsory education laws, which might have saved integrated schools in at least some parts of the South, began to be introduced into the North. (Massachusetts had had a form of compulsory education since 1852, but at the time the concept was too progressive even for the other New England states.) In 1874 a compulsory education law was passed in the state of New York. The two principal reasons behind this revolutionary measure—and it should be noted that it *was* a revolution in the history of relations between government and the citizen—were that the cities were growing rapidly and that their newest inhabitants were mostly immigrants. In the half-century after 1860, America's population increased by over sixty million. In six of the ten years between 1905 and 1914 the *annual* total of immigration exceeded one million.[9]

Especially after the closing of the western frontier, the tremendous growth in population was most evident in the cities. Urban problems associated with the immigrants were the most pressing domestic issue of the times:

Confronted with the deterioration of their cities, many native urban Americans placed the blame on the newcomers. . . . Their kids were everywhere, especially in the streets. . . . The schoolroom was where these young hoodlums belonged. It was scandalous that many of these "future citizens" could hardly speak English, let alone read or write it. They needed to be civilized and Americanized. . . .[10]

Another reason for keeping immigrant children off the streets was that they formed a pool of cheap labor that depressed wage levels. Urban workers were in no mood to encourage the entry of immigrant children into the labor market, even if employers held the opposite point of view. Thus it came about that, by 1900, thirty-one states had enacted compulsory schooling laws. Their purpose was clear: the children of immigrants were to be "civilized and Americanized." From this era dates the beginning of the social and cultural gap between the average urban teacher and his pupils. Yet it was the schools, above all, that were charged with the task of making Americans out of these new citizens.

Restoring community. By the turn of the century, it was obvious that large cities were to be a characteristic feature of the American scene, and that they would continue to grow. Recognizing this fact, the more thoughtful educators and reformers began to extend their concern with the immigrant—particularly the urban immigrant—to the entire quality of urban life.

The most influential educator of the period—indeed, of any period in American education up to the present—was John Dewey, whose epoch-making *School and Society* was published in 1899. To Dewey, *education* was synonymous with what we have called socialization; *schooling* was any formalized teaching or learning of particular academic skills. Thus schooling was only part of education and not necessarily the most important part. What *was* important, if children were to become true citizens of a democracy, was that they should learn to trust in their own experience. And one of the things that their experience should teach them was the value of cooperation, which Dewey saw as the basis of democracy. Here, he thought, was a chance for the school—especially now that attendance was compulsory—to take over where society had failed. It could provide a democratic community in which the individual child could develop into a worthy citizen.

Critics have argued that, by making teachers into agents of primary socialization as well as academic instructors, Dewey placed on them a burden that they should not have been asked to bear. But at least in the large northern cities,

---

9. Morison, *op. cit.,* p. 813.
10. Perkinson, *op. cit.,* p. 68.

teachers had already been bearing part of this burden. Indeed, for many immigrant children the school teacher was the earliest and most influential representative of American culture they encountered. Only in recent years has sociological research begun to question the depth of the Americanization thus achieved and to give proper weight to the socializing influence of both family and neighborhood.

During the latter part of Dewey's teaching career, drastic changes were wrought in American society by the First World War and the restriction of immigration. Further drastic change came with the Great Depression. But Dewey's influence remained strong, extending to curricula and teaching methods, on the one hand, and to the relationship between school and society, on the other. In Dewey's philosophy, the school was never just the agent of society; it was an independent source of social change. This conception clearly underlay the Social Frontier Movement, a program begun in the early 1930's by some of Dewey's former colleagues at Columbia University. The movement tried to involve both teachers and students more closely with society and simultaneously bring them to a clearer recognition of what they needed to ask of society.[11]

Allied with the idea that the school could take a direct hand in helping to reconstruct society was the idea of the community school. The heads of some school systems—usually in medium-sized cities—carried Dewey's theory of the school as an embryonic community one step further by attempting to use the community outside the school as an educator. In practice, this usually involved lectures by city officials and student "projects" on such topics as local housing problems. The most lasting effects of both the Social Frontier and the community school movements were in enlarging school curricula.

Vocational sorting. With compulsory schooling, education had to please far larger numbers of people, most of whom wanted their children to find better jobs than their own. And somehow the educational system had to satisfy the demands of these parents within the framework of traditional American values. Gradually the public schools became involved in the deli-

cate process of vocational sorting. The old goals of Americanization and equalization were still honored, particularly at the elementary level, but more and more schools devised arrangements for sorting students into categories as soon as they approached the age to be thinking about careers. Some were pointed toward management and the professions, others toward the typist's desk and the carpenter shop. For the college-bound, the question of how best to prepare for college began to be asked earlier and earlier.

The importance of career preparation became a major issue that the National Education Association tried to resolve by appointing a Commission on the Reorganization of Secondary Education. The Commission's report, published in 1918, emphasized that "vocation" should be only one of seven major aims of education, which it listed as (1) health, (2) command of fundamental processes, (3) worthy home membership, (4) vocation, (5) citizenship, (6) worthy use of leisure time, and (7) ethical character. These aims were to be realized through "common courses for all in general education, common extracurricular activities, and the comprehensive high school."[12]

In general, this has remained the official program of American secondary education, though critics have pointed out that it is a somewhat ambivalent position:

American educators tried to have it both ways. They would work in a system that selected students for different careers, but the teachers would focus their efforts on the task of equalizing or unifying the students. The compromise, of course, was largely a verbal one. It marks the beginning of the substitution of educational slogans for concrete educational policies in America. . . . The structure of the educational system—a selective system—defeated all rhetoric and strategems.

Study after study of the American schools revealed that they failed to equalize; they merely sorted and selected students for different careers, different ways of life.[13]

Educating the expert society. In the 1950's and 1960's the compromise between equalization and vocationalism almost broke down. For a while, especially after Sputnik I and the National Defense Education Act of 1958, it looked as if vocationalism had won out. America had to "catch up" with the Soviet Union by producing more scientists, engineers, and technicians.

11. *Ibid.*, pp. 205–210.
12. *Ibid.*, pp. 148–149.
13. *Ibid.*

VIEWPOINTS TEACHING AND LEARNING

[The] whole controversy about teaching the *subject* versus teaching the *child* would seem side-splittingly funny to every educator who ever lived prior to 1900. They took for granted that you taught the subject *to* the child and they went ahead and did it—they didn't argue about it.

. . . Our teachers and administrators are just as talented and just as intelligent as they ever were, probably more so, but since the takeover of my profession about 35 years ago by the burning-eyed, thin-lipped disciples of one Dr. John Dewey, . . . school people . . . have been told over and over again, with all the persistence of a Chinese water torturer, that culture was of no consequence whatsoever in education. . . . An administrator like me has to know psychology, curriculum, finance, school law, but nobody could care less whether I've ever heard of the Platonic Absolutes or the Nicomachean Ethics. And any schoolman can get a doctoral degree from virtually any institution in the land without having anyone even asking him if he can distinguish between Bizet and Puccini; between Galileo and Copernicus, or between the Wars of the Roses and the Flowering of New England. In such a Philistine environment, . . . it's a living wonder to me that such a large number of our teachers and school administrators are as literate and as cultured as they are.

What is needed to restore the public school to its proper place in our American Heritage, then, is a complete and total change in our national and state educational philosophy, an altering of our intellectual climate. We are going to need people increasingly in high professional places who will stand up and say for all to hear that certain things in this life, this world, this universe are important in themselves just because they exist; not just for what they can do for us personally, or for how much money they are worth. We need to be told once again that the real purpose of education is, always has been and always will be, to pursue the truth—just that, but in order to do this, we must supply our children with the intellectual tools which the race over the centuries make indispensable. We will need to know that adjustment to one's environment, that fetish and shibboleth of my profession for a generation and more, is not the soul, nor even a defensible goal of education, but rather an outworn and exploded relic of past thinking and antiquated practice.

Max Rafferty
"Today's Challenge in Education"

It seems stupid to decide a priori what the young ought to know and then to try to motivate them, instead of letting the initiative come from them and putting information and relevant equipment at their service. It is false to assert that this kind of freedom will not serve society's needs—at least those needs that should humanly be served; freedom is the only way toward authentic citizenship and real, rather than verbal, philosophy. Free choice is not random but responsive to real situations; both youth and adults live in a nature of things, a polity, an ongoing society, and it is these, in fact, that attract interest and channel need. If the young, as they mature, can follow their bent and choose their topics, times, and teachers, and if teachers teach what they themselves consider important—which is all they can skillfully teach anyway—the needs of society will be adequately met; there will be more lively, independent, and inventive people; and in the fairly short run there will be a more sensible and efficient society.

It is not necessary to argue for free choice as a metaphysical proposition; it is what is indicated by present conditions. Increasingly, the best young people resolutely resist authority, and we will let them have a say or lose them. And more important, since the conditions of modern social and technological organization are so pervasively and rigidly conforming, it is necessary, in order to maintain human initiative, to put our emphasis on protecting the young from top-down direction. The monkish and academic methods which were civilizing for wild shepherds create robots in a period of high technology. The public schools which did a good job of socializing immigrants in an open society now regiment individuals and rigidify class stratification.

Up to age twelve, there is no point to formal subjects or a prearranged curriculum. With guidance, whatever a child experiences is educational. Dewey's idea is a good one: It makes no difference *what* is learned at this age, so long as the child goes on wanting to learn something further. Teachers for this age are those who like children, pay attention to them, answer their questions, enjoy taking them around the city and helping them explore, imitate, try out, and who sing songs with them and teach them games. Any benevolent grownup—literate or illiterate—has plenty to teach an eight-year-old; the only profitable training for teachers is a group therapy and, perhaps, a course in child development.

Paul Goodman
"Freedom and Learning: The Need for Choice"

Then equalization began to reassert itself in the form of demands for compensatory education for the disadvantaged. Once again, America had to "keep the kids off the streets"—particularly those in the black ghettos who dropped out of school and could find no jobs. Faced with the dual problem of unemployed youth and a shortage of skilled workers, educators in the 1960's concluded that their system, far from overemphasizing vocational sorting, was not vocational enough.

The number of individuals undergoing education in the "expert society" of the computer age was as unprecedented as it was awe inspiring. In 1968, for example, some 57.6 million Americans—over a quarter of the total population—were receiving formal schooling. But the end product of all this education did not generate much confidence. Critics charged that, in or out of school, Johnny was unable to read, speak, or write decently, handle figures, or begin to grasp what modern science was all about. Course content, teaching methods, textbooks, even such fundamentals as the grade system and the grading system underwent critical appraisal; and a period of reform, innovation, and experiment began, supported to an unprecedented extent during the 1960's by federal funds. After some dramatic successes—particularly in curricula—and some disastrous failures, attempts continue to be made to determine what functions American education should, and can, perform.

THE PROBLEM OF PURPOSE

For American education, the tension created by the conflicting tendencies toward equilibrium and change is represented in conflicting sets of goals. On the one hand, schools are expected to maintain the status quo by socializing youth in traditional ways of acting and thinking; on the other, they are expected to nurture creative talent, carry on an endless quest for truth, and provide leadership in areas of change that may alter not only their own structure but the structure of the whole society. Moreover, the society that supports the educational system is itself divided as to what directions should be followed and what kinds of activities should be given

14. *Life*, May 16, 1969, pp. 22–42.

priority. There is even considerable disagreement as to what the purpose of education should be. Frequently, parents and teachers hold opposing views. Even more frequently, students and their parents are in opposition.

This disagreement is clearly shown in the results of a recent Harris Poll.[14] The purpose of the survey was to examine the American high school through the eyes of students, parents, and teachers and administrators. Concerning the function of the school, 62 percent of parents believed that maintaining discipline should take priority over student self-inquiry; only 27 percent of teachers agreed. Seventy percent of parents—but only 46 percent of teachers—believed that homework requiring memorization was good and useful. But the "generation gap" emerged when all three groups were asked whether race should be discussed more in the classroom. A majority of students—52 percent—said yes; only 36 percent of teachers and 27 percent of parents agreed.

According to this poll, most teachers and principals "would agree that schools are not the place to foster controversy or to challenge prevailing standards," and most parents think that the schools "should keep the children passive and disciplined, and provide them with the tools that lead to college and a job." But the students "are beginning to want to challenge and change the schools, as their older brothers and sisters are challenging and changing the colleges."

One of the challenges the high-school student shares with the college student is that of the school's right to dictate curriculum, rules, discipline, and all the rest. At both levels, students want to participate in establishing policy. According to the Harris Poll, 58 percent of high-school students want more participation. Only 20 percent of parents and 35 percent of teachers agree that they should have it. Fifty-four percent of the students think that such participation is very important. Again, only 25 percent of parents and 30 percent of teachers agree.

By 1970, college students had pretty much won their freedom from *alma mater* in personal affairs, as was evidenced by the virtual ending of restrictions on male-female visiting in dormitory rooms. They had begun to influence the curriculum, in some cases forcing the inclusion of new programs of Black Studies and new courses in racial and urban problems. And more and more, students were struggling for a place

The period of educational innovation that began in the 1950's was largely based on the premise that our teaching techniques were simply not motivating students to learn. Thus many of America's schools began to experiment with team teaching, non-grading, computerized instruction, and new philosophies that tried to account for the needs of the student as an individual (far right). In England, almost fifty years ago, A. S. Neill started a school known as Summerhill (all other photos), which has become famous for educational innovation and the philosophy of its founder: "I'm not trying to produce any kind of person here. I'm only trying to let people be themselves without outside interference. . . . I believe that if they can govern themselves and are free from fear, free from compulsion to develop a sincerity and a character of their own, the rest will take care of itself." . . .

in policy-making—on boards of regents, boards of trustees, and curriculum, faculty, and admissions committees. Frequently they achieved seats on boards and committees, but their power to influence what was taught, how it was taught, and who taught it remained extremely limited. In the great majority of cases, they either had no vote or were so outnumbered that their vote was meaningless. In some cases, too, they gained the right to participate, then failed to use it.

Meanwhile, the public looked on with much head-shaking. Again, principles and practice clashed. The schools taught students to believe in representative democracy, in which all citizens should take part. They taught that it was desirable for the individual in a free society to exercise initiative, to exert leadership, and to work for a better world, ever closer to the democratic ideal. But when the students took the teachings seriously and sought to apply them in the educational institution itself, they found themselves up against established concepts of bureaucratic authority and responsibility.

These are only two examples of conflicting attitudes toward the proper functions of education, but there are many others. Who should be educated, and what should be taught? What teaching methods should be used? Should education be general or specialized? Should it be predominantly humanistic or scientific? At the university level, should the instructor place research before teaching or vice versa? Is it the role of the scholar to seek and dispense truth, or does he also have the responsibility to attempt to solve the critical problems his society is facing? Should he remain professionally neutral in the political debates of his times, or should he speak out for the causes he believes in? Can he put his talents at the service of government or private industry without accepting some responsibility for the policies and activities of his employer?

Many of these issues are centuries-old. What is new is that large numbers of students—in the colleges and universities and also in the public high schools—are taking an active part in the debates. And the great majority of the most active student debaters obviously believe that education is serving the wrong purposes, is performing the wrong functions. In the conflict between equilibrium and change, these students are in favor of change. Most parents and many of the less active students oppose them. The ranks of the educators are split.

EDUCATION AND SOCIAL STRATIFICATION

The quantity and quality of education an individual receives play a significant part in determining the outcome of his struggle for upward mobility. Education, then, is linked to stratification in two ways: position in the class structure helps determine what education the individual gets, and the education he gets helps determine his future position in the class structure.

THE CHANCES OF BECOMING EDUCATED

There is no doubt of the importance of education to the individual American: it is his best opportunity to improve his position in life. In theory, that opportunity is equal for all. In practice, the individual's chances of becoming educated are determined to a considerable degree not by his native potential but by the type of instruction he receives and by the circumstances into which he is born.

Place of residence and income. An individual's place of residence has a definite effect on the kind of education he receives because the amount of money allotted to education varies considerably from state to state (Table 18.1). In 1969, for example, the highest expenditure per pupil was $1140, in New York; the lowest, $432, in Alabama. The highest per capita expenditure was $343, in Alaska; the lowest, $114, in Alabama. In a related study by the Office of Education, educational expenditure was compared to proportion of failures on the Armed Forces Qualification Test. The results of the study showed that the regions that spent the least per pupil had the highest rates of failure.

In part, at least, the differences in per capita rates of expenditure at the state level reflect differences in the incomes of the residents, and this is also true at the local level. Despite state aid, the major responsibility for financing public schools remains with the school district. Thus the quality of a district's schools reflects the ability, as well as the willingness, of the residents of that district to be taxed. Public pressure

TABLE 18.1. **ESTIMATED PUBLIC SCHOOL EXPENDITURES, 1969, BY STATES**

STATE	TOTAL EXPENDITURES (in millions)	AVERAGE EXPENDITURES PER PUPIL IN AVERAGE DAILY ATTENDANCE		SCHOOL EXPENDITURES PER CAPITA	
		AMOUNT (in dollars)	RANK	AMOUNT (in dollars)	RANK
United States	**35,511**	**696**	—	**178**	—
New England	**1,908**	**747**	—	**167**	—
Maine	143	567	36	147	38
New Hampshire	107	624	32	152	36
Vermont	82	677	18	193	15
Massachusetts	885	748	12	162	32
Rhode Island	159	840	4	174	23
Connecticut	532	826	5	180	22
Middle Atlantic	**7,577**	**952**	—	**205**	—
New York	4,216	1,140	1	233	2
New Jersey	1,352	852	3	191	17
Pennsylvania	2,009	743	14	171	25
East North Central	**7,032**	**687**	—	**178**	—
Ohio	1,704	634	30	161	33
Indiana	965	635	29	191	17
Illinois	1,893	755	11	172	24
Michigan	1,647	665	21	188	19
Wisconsin	823	787	7	195	14
West North Central	**2,855**	**673**	—	**178**	—
Minnesota	812	767	9	223	4
Iowa	532	723	16	192	16
Missouri	705	645	28	152	36
North Dakota	103	585	35	164	30
South Dakota	109	589	34	166	29
Nebraska	205	510	44	142	40
Kansas	388	647	26	169	27
South Atlantic	**4,782**	**597**	—	**159**	—
Delaware	118	745	13	221	5
Maryland	850	775	8	226	3
District of Columbia	172	920	—	213	10
Virginia	739	600	33	161	33
West Virginia	233	521	42	129	44
North Carolina	676	505	45	132	43
South Carolina	340	478	48	128	45
Georgia	618	530	39	135	41
Florida	1,037	647	26	169	27
East South Central	**1,577**	**482**	—	**120**	—
Kentucky	381	538	38	118	49
Tennessee	499	498	46	126	46
Alabama	407	432	50	114	50
Mississippi	290	462	49	124	48
West South Central	**2,780**	**541**	—	**145**	—
Arkansas	248	486	47	125	47
Louisiana	610	632	31	164	30
Oklahoma	341	516	43	135	41
Texas	1,582	526	41	144	39
Mountain	**1,485**	**642**	—	**188**	—
Montana	142	761	10	205	12
Idaho	108	559	37	154	35
Wyoming	68	715	17	216	8
Colorado	374	662	23	183	21
New Mexico	210	676	19	209	11
Arizona	285	648	24	171	25
Utah	202	527	40	195	14
Nevada	97	648	24	216	8
Pacific	**5,515**	**681**	—	**215**	—
Washington	653	673	20	199	13
Oregon	435	793	6	217	6
California	4,189	665	21	217	6
Alaska	94	987	2	343	1
Hawaii	144	724	15	185	20

SOURCE: *Statistical Abstract of the United States, 1969,* Table 167, p. 116.

for economy is considerable,[15] and the concept of efficiency in education tends to be interpreted in a narrowly financial sense.

Although the individual's chances of becoming educated depend to a degree on the wealth of his state and school district, his parents' income is considerably more important in determining the quality of his elementary and secondary education. The most detailed study of how parental income affects education is Patricia Sexton's *Education and Income*.[16] Sexton found the average family income in each school area of a large midwestern city ("Big City") and then compared the area's income level with all the detailed information she could obtain on the area's public schools. She classified the schools studied into four groups. Those in Group I were in areas where average family income ranged from $3000 to $4999 annually. The corresponding ranges for the other groups of schools were: Group II, $5000 to $6999; Group III, $7000 to $8999; and Group IV, $9000 or above.

Sexton discovered that as income went down so did the quality of education. The educational facilities provided to students in Groups I and II were definitely inferior. Over three times as many "emergency substitute" teachers—i.e., teachers who were not fully qualified—were regularly employed at these levels than at the two levels above. The science facilities were either nonexistent or substandard in 47 percent of the schools in Groups I and II but in only 2 percent of the schools in Groups III and IV. Over 50 percent of the school buildings in Group I were rated "poor" or "fair," as compared with only about 5 percent of the buildings in Group IV. One particularly shocking effect of these substandard physical facilities was that nearly 40 percent of the poorest children could not take advantage of the city's free-lunch program. Their schools had no lunch rooms.

There were other factors that handicapped the poorer children. For one thing, the lower income families were more geographically mobile; thus their children's education was more often disrupted by moves. Health was also a major problem. The diphtheria rate in Group I was fifteen times what it was in Group III, while there were no diphtheria cases at all in Group IV. Only about half of the students in Group I had health examinations when they entered the first grade, but 93 percent received examinations in Group IV. And even when the children in the lowest income category had illnesses diagnosed by the school nurse, they were only half as likely to receive treatment as those in the highest category.

In view of these conditions, it is not surprising that the poorer children had lower performance scores than the children from the higher income levels. For example, IQ scores—which are mainly measures of learned verbal skill—were notably higher for children in the upper-income groupings. Tests measuring other forms of student achievement showed similar results. It is significant, however, that the gap in performance widened noticeably with age. This shows that the performance differences resulted *not* from lower levels of "natural" ability on the part of the children in lower income areas but from the lower quality of their educational facilities and educational experience.

The remarkable increase in federal aid to education after 1963 was designed to help remedy the kind of conditions described by Sexton. Some forty important federal education bills were passed between 1965 and 1969, increasing the amount appropriated or budgeted for education from about $2 billion in 1960 to over $10 billion in 1968. It cannot be claimed, however, that equal educational opportunity was suddenly legislated into existence. For instance, by 1967 only about a third of the federal loans available under the Higher Education Act of 1965 and similar programs were going to college students from families with annual incomes of less than $6000. Over a quarter of them were going to students from families with annual incomes of over $10,000. Moreover, by 1969 the rate of increase in federal spending was being drastically cut. For instance, budget requests for school books and library services had been reduced by 66 percent over the previous year. Other educational programs were terminated altogether.[17]

One example of the efforts made by government during the last half of the 1960's was Operation Head Start, a program administered through the machinery set up by the Economic Opportunity Act of 1964. Educators and public officials—not to mention the informed pub-

15. James B. Conant, *Slums and Suburbs* (New York: Signet Books, 1961), pp. 31–38.

16. Patricia Sexton, *Education and Income* (New York: Compass Books, 1964).

17. Summarized in *Publisher's Weekly*, April 28, 1969, pp. 62–63.

lic—had been disturbed by research reports suggesting that by the time a child was ready for kindergarten, his chances of being able to benefit from the public school system had already been largely determined. Head Start sought to compensate for physical and cultural deprivation by providing preschool children in poverty areas with nutritious food and special instruction.

For a time the program was thought to be a great success; but an evaluation published in 1969 reported no improvement in academic aptitudes,[18] and the possibility of improving school performance by such means was seriously questioned. On the other hand, Head Start has shown some positive results. Several studies indicate that participants in Head Start have higher test scores in subsequent school years than nonparticipants from the same area.[19]

At the local level, unlike the federal, large additional sums cannot suddenly be appropriated for education without major changes in the tax structure. Usually such changes are either politically difficult to obtain or, because those whose taxes would be raised would move elsewhere, likely to prove self-defeating. It often happens, therefore, that the only drastic measure open to a community suddenly faced with demands to improve its schools is to find a new way to use its old facilities. One such measure—busing—involves transporting a certain proportion of the children to schools outside their own neighborhoods. It has worked well in a few relatively prosperous communities with long-established traditions of harmonious race relations. Some school systems have achieved good results by busing only the children in the elementary grades. But in many areas, there is wide-spread opposition to busing from self-segregated white parents.

Family background. Aside from the income of one's parents, the family influences the individual's chances of becoming educated in other ways. For example, the educational attainment of a person's father is related to the educational

18. Robert B. Semple, *New York Times*, April 14, 1969, p. 1.

19. James S. Coleman, *Equality of Educational Opportunity* (Washington, D.C.: Government Printing Office, 1966), pp. 491–523.

20. Robert J. Havighurst *et al., Growing Up in River City* (New York: John Wiley & Sons, Inc., 1962). See also J. S. Davie, "Social Class Factors and School Attendance," *Harvard Educational Review*, 23 (1953), 175–185.

TABLE 18.2 **FATHER'S EDUCATION AND SON'S EDUCATION**

SON'S EDUCATIONAL ATTAINMENT	EDUCATIONAL STATUS OF FATHER			
	NOT HIGH-SCHOOL GRADUATE	HIGH-SCHOOL GRADUATE BUT NO COLLEGE	SOME COLLEGE	COLLEGE GRADUATE
No high-school diploma	42.6	10.3	6.5	4.0
High-school diploma but no college	34.1	36.1	23.8	8.2
At least some college attendance	23.3	43.7	69.7	87.9

SOURCE: Murray Gendell and Hans L. Zetterberg, eds., *A Sociological Almanac for the United States*, 2nd ed. (New York: Charles Scribner's Sons, 1964), p. 80; based upon men twenty to twenty-four years of age, October 1960.

level he himself is likely to reach. Table 18.2 shows that of men aged twenty to twenty-four, less than a fourth of those with fathers who did not graduate from high school had themselves attained any college credits. Among those whose fathers had graduated from college, on the other hand, almost nine out of ten had been to college. These figures obviously do not mean that every person whose father has had limited educational attainment will himself have limited attainment, but they show that the level of education an individual attains is statistically related to his family's educational background.

Other aspects of a person's social origins have been shown to be related to his prospects for completing a given level of education. The social status of the family is inversely related to the probability of dropping out of school. That is, the lower the socioeconomic level of the family, the higher the probability that education will be terminated early.[20] This is due in part to a lack of motivation. The adolescent living in a small town, an urban slum, or a working-class neighborhood is under far less pressure to attend college than the youngster in a middle-class suburb, where college attendance is the norm for his peers.

Teachers' expectations and values. Perhaps from the point of view of many middle-class whites, slum children, regardless of color, have no "culture"—only a set of undesirable habits. In fact, however, people who live in slums generate and act out patterns of culture that display great creativity. The variety of English spoken in slums, for example, may be ungrammatical by middle-class standards, but it is not non-grammatical. It has its own grammar and syntax, as well as a rich vocabulary.

Nevertheless, teachers are likely to expect little from slum children, and they are likely to get what they expect—their prophecy is self-fulfilling. Rosenthal and Jacobson conducted an experiment with some self-fulfilling prophecies of their own.[21] They singled out an elementary school in a working-class district and obtained permission to give three kinds of IQ tests to each of the 650 pupils. They told the teachers that these tests would predict which children were about to "bloom," or "spurt," intellectually. After the testing, they used a random process to select a certain proportion of names in each class as those of "potential spurters." The names of these "special children" were then given to the teachers, in order to influence their expectations. The other children were used as the control group, though of course the teachers did not know this.

Rosenthal and Jacobson retested all of the children at regular intervals, the last being two academic years after the first testing. Through this retesting process, they were able to measure the special children's "expectancy advantage"—i.e., how much their gains in IQ exceeded those of the control group. At the end of one year an expectancy advantage too great to be the result of chance was indeed detected, especially among children in the two youngest grades. The following year the expectancy advantage of the younger children disappeared, but that of the older children increased. As these results indicate, the expectations of a teacher may have a definite effect on a child's school performance.

In addition to the effect of teachers' expectations, sociologists and educational theorists have also been concerned with the extent to which the personal *values* of teachers affect teaching-learning interaction. Essentially, the theory that there is value-influence on the teaching role boils down to a set of generalizations, some of which are assumptions and some of which have rather solid data to support them. The basic argument can be stated in the following terms:

1. *There are social class differences in personal values.* This generalization is strongly supported by empirical research, a substantial amount of

which has already been discussed. (See, for example, Chapter 5, pages 156–158.) We noted that middle-class people are more oriented than lower-class people toward long-range goals, rational planning of resources, political conservatism, individual responsibility, achievement, personal control of aggression, manners, conventionality of dress, and the importance of education.

2. *Teachers are drawn mainly from the middle class and hold middle-class value orientations.* Studies of the social origins of teachers have for many years indicated middle-class backgrounds.[22] It is less clear, however, that the teaching profession systematically attracts those who hold the most central values of the middle class.[23]

3. *Teachers use middle-class values in assessing the relative merits of middle- and lower-class students.* This is the heart of the matter. As has been stated by W. Lloyd Warner:

Since the teachers' judgments of the children and of standards of performance are inevitably based on their own personal standards, buttressed by those set up by the school as an institution, the lower-class child is at a disadvantage when competing with children from the middle class.[24]

It is, of course, an assumption that the teacher "inevitably" uses middle-class values to judge the children he teaches. On the other hand, it would be difficult to imagine persons with the social origins and educational backgrounds of most teachers using some alternative value system, completely foreign to their prior experience, as a basis for judging their charges. Overall, the assumption is probably correct.

Given these theoretical generalizations (and recognizing their potential limitations), one must turn to the actual role performance of the teacher to understand the impact that his middle-class values can have on the child. Psychologists Davis and Dollard outlined some years ago the way in which the social-class standards of the

---

21. Robert Rosenthal and Lenore Jacobson, *Pygmalion in the Classroom* (New York: Holt, Rinehart and Winston, Inc., 1968).

22. W. W. Charters, Jr., "Consequences of Educators' Social Position on the Teaching-Learning Process," in *Handbook on Teaching*, ed. N. L. Gage (Chicago: Rand McNally & Company, 1963), pp. 722–740.

23. *Ibid.*, p. 577.

24. W. Lloyd Warner, *American Life: Dream and Reality* (Chicago: The University of Chicago Press, 1953), p. 177.

METHODOLOGY   STATISTICAL ANALYSIS

Professional sociologists use statistical analysis extensively for describing and comparing groups and social categories. In brief, a set of statistics is a group of numerical measurements arranged in some meaningful way. The numerical values are produced by observation—by counting or measuring some phenomenon. The most important task of statistics, in fact the real meaning of the term *statistics,* is to summarize in a single numerical value some quality, trend, or property of an array of measures. This summarizing number is called an *index* number or a *coefficient* and is computed by applying a mathematical formula to an array of measures.

Statistical coefficients have many uses: some are used to describe a situation for which data is complete; some to make inferences from a sample. As an example of a descriptive coefficient, let us assume that we wanted to describe with precision the *central tendency* of a set of observations. At least three different coefficients can be used for this purpose: the *mode,* the *median,* and the *mean.* The *mode* is the numerical value that occurs most frequently in a given set of measures. Thus, in the set 100, 17, 2, 8, 17, 15, the mode (though not the average) is 17. The *median* is the value above and below which precisely half of the entries in a given array will fall. Thus in the above array the median (but, again, not the average) is 16. The *mean* is the coefficient that corresponds to the average. Let us use the mean (symbolized $\bar{X}$) to determine the central tendency of the sample in the figure below:

Measures	Conventional symbols:
4	X = the numerical value of any
3	measure (4, 3, etc.)
7	n = the number of measures (in
1	this case, n = 11)
4	Σ = "sum up all numerical
2	values"
6	$\bar{X}$ = the symbol for the mean
3	
5	*Computational formula:*
4	
5	$\bar{X} = \dfrac{\Sigma X}{n}$ or $\dfrac{44}{11}$ or 4
$\overline{44}$ = Sum	

What is the mode of the above array? What is the median of the above array?

We can summarize the mathematical formula used to obtain the mean ($\bar{X}$) as follows: *The mean is obtained by adding up all the values in an array of measures and then dividing the obtained sum by the number of measures in the array.* To define this very simple statistic we have had to use twenty-nine words; many commonly used statistics would require several paragraphs. As indicated by our figure, however, the definition of the mean can be given in conventional statistical notation as: $\bar{X} = \Sigma X/n$, which requires only six symbols.

Another aspect of statistics involves the degree of "scatter" or *variability* that exists in an array of measures. In the array indicated in the figure at the left, there is relatively little dispersion or scatter. Note that the lowest and highest entries are only 3 points away from the mean. However, if we included measures as high as 100 or even larger, we would increase the variability greatly (and, of course, change the central tendency).

Statisticians indicate the degree of variability in an array by using an index of scatter. One such index is the *standard deviation,* which is symbolized by the small sigma σ and has the following formula:

$$\sigma = \sqrt{\frac{\Sigma(X - \bar{X})^2}{n}}$$

Prepare a verbal description of this formula and then compute the standard deviation of the array given in the figure at the left. Remember that Σ means to sum up a whole series of individual items and that X means each individual numerical value. Notice also that you are to square *each* term and not the sum of the terms.

Another important statistical problem involves showing the *association* between variables. This requires two measures for every person or object that is to be studied. The goal is to summarize in a single coefficient the degree to which a high or low score on one measure also implies a high or low score on another. There are dozens of these statistical coefficients—which are referred to as coefficients of "correlation"—and some are available for use with multiple sets of measures, such as data from two different experiments or surveys.

STATISTICAL CONTROL OF VARIABLES

It is difficult at best to analyze the relationships between the variables commonly studied in sociological research. Human behavior is the most complex of all objects of scientific study, and a sociologist is seldom certain that he has taken into account all the factors that can lead people to behave as they do. Often, a researcher uncovers additional influencing variables, making it necessary to revise his earlier interpretations.

One way that sociologists attempt to understand complex social processes is to control certain variables *statistically* while studying the influence of others. The difficulties one may encounter in this method will be apparent if we examine the problem of explaining why certain types of educational institutions seem to produce so many graduates who go on to take the doctor of philosophy degree. There are innumerable variables from which to construct tentative explanations of this phenomenon. One hypothesis (popular among smaller schools) is that the small liberal arts college provides a rich educational environment that stimulates students to undertake graduate work. In fact, many distinguished scholars did receive their undergraduate degrees from just such schools. But more recent research has suggested that this may merely reflect initial student ability. Indeed, it can be hypothesized that able students, who would do well anywhere, are attracted to small liberal arts schools because of prevailing beliefs about their influence. According to this hypothesis, the number of Ph.D.'s who spend their undergraduate years at these colleges merely reflect a "self-fulfilling prophesy."

To study this problem, and to control for the influence of student ability, Astin carried out a large-scale research project on a sample of 265 colleges and universities. He obtained data on selected characteristics of all incoming freshmen. The schools studied included all types of bachelor's programs in the United States (except for certain very small colleges and those with extremely low levels of student ability). From official records on all Ph.D.'s granted in the United States during a specific three-year period, he determined how many doctoral recipients earned their undergraduate degrees from each of the 265 institutions. He then obtained data on all bachelor's degrees awarded by each institution during a three-year span just six years earlier. From these data he was able to calculate simple Ph.D. "output rates." Some schools produced no graduates who went on to receive Ph.D.'s. As many as 23 percent of the graduates of other schools went on to take the advanced degree.

The problem was to find out whether individual or institutional attributes had resulted in these differences. To do this, the researcher needed to know the influence of a student's individual characteristics on continuing to a Ph.D. Earlier studies gave partial answers. For example, completion of the doctorate was clearly related to sex, IQ, and undergraduate major, and males were far more likely to obtain the degree than females. High IQ students had clear advantages over those with lesser ability, and some majors were more likely to continue than others (e.g., psychology versus business).

With these relationships understood, the "student input" factor was controlled statistically to see if the differences in the Ph.D. output rates could be attributed to the type of institution. To do this, Astin devised a way of predicting what output rate a particular institution *should* have, given the characteristics of its entering students. He computed an "expected" Ph.D. output rate for each institution, based upon student intelligence, percent of males, and distribution of majors. He then compared each school's *actual* rate with its *expected* rate to see if it was "overproducing" or "underproducing" Ph.D.'s, given its student input.

Astin's results showed that some institutions produced far more Ph.D.'s than their expected rates, and his findings seriously challenged many popular assumptions. In general, the larger, state-supported, coeducational institutions overproduced, while most small colleges—especially those with religious affiliations—made a poor showing. The all-male and all-female schools of all sizes tended to underproduce. Among the lowest producers were Harvard, Princeton, and Dartmouth. Among the highest were Brooklyn College, Yeshiva, Brigham Young, Utah, and Utah State. The latter finding pointed to the need for further controls. Socioeconomic, ethnic, and religious factors appeared to be significant variables for further study.

Alexander W. Astin, "'Productivity' of Undergraduate Institutions," *Science* (April 13, 1962), pp. 129–135.

teacher could handicap the child of the lower class.[25] In the application of positive and negative sanctions in the classroom, these authors argued, the teacher tends to use the child's social-class membership rather than his actual performance as a basis for distributing rewards or punishments. The middle-class child, whose family training is supportive of the same values approved by the teacher, gets immediate reward for what he does in school. The lower-class child, whose standards of dress, manners, cleanliness, grammar, etc., do not resemble those of the favored children, gets much less approval for what he does, *even if he does it correctly.* The lower-class child, in other words, is discriminated against for what he *is* rather than for what he *does.*

This theory implies that school is a punishing experience for the lower-class child and a relatively rewarding experience for the middle- or upper-class child. The middle-class child receives "positive reinforcement" for his approved behavior and thus learns how to succeed in school. The lower-class child gets "negative reinforcement." Friedenberg describes this process as "the ceaseless corrosive drizzle of social disapproval."[26]

Somewhat similar conclusions may be drawn from Stinchcombe's study of a high school in a small California college town.[27] Stinchcombe was interested in explaining the attitude toward the high school of those who were still attending it; he did not study dropouts as such. After administering a questionnaire to virtually all the school's 1600 students, he analyzed the responses of those who seemed by three criteria (receiving flunk notices, skipping school, and being sent out of class by a teacher) to be rebelling against the school as a social system. He decided that the principal reason for this rebellious behavior lay neither in the student's home life nor in such personal attributes as a low IQ score but rather in what he called "poor articulation between present activity and future status increments." In other words, the

expectations that the rebellious students were supposed to fulfill in school had little or no connection with what the students themselves expected to be doing in adult life.

The author found that most of the rebels were either boys who expected to be manual workers or girls whose main interest was in early marriage. Students in these categories were especially likely to rebel if they had low IQ scores, lived in slums, or were members of ethnic minorities. An additional factor making for rebellion, especially among the boys, was that the labor market they were about to enter was a "universalistic" one—i.e., one in which they would be judged not as individuals with certain human qualities but as possessing or lacking certain universally accepted "qualifications." Other factors were involved, but these were the main ones.

School was hard on these youngsters because it judged them in terms of the achievement-oriented, middle-class culture that defined anything less than getting into college as some kind of failure. Finding this culture irrelevant to their needs and threatening to their self-esteem, these students withdrew into an "expressive alienation" that made itself known by, among other things, claims for the privileges of adult status. Smoking, drinking, driving fast cars, and "making out" with girls, all of which were likely to get them into trouble at school, if not with the police, were actually the means by which these young people sought a sense of self-identity and personal worth denied them by their school.

Although research continues on this issue, the teachers' role performance in the classroom is, at best, a difficult subject to study systematically. Interviews with teachers concerning their practices suggest that the theory of class influence has merit, but it must still be regarded as somewhat conjectural.[28] In any event, if one turns to the mass of empirical evidence concerning who succeeds within the American educational system, it is overwhelmingly clear that it is primarily the children of the upper and middle classes.

There is also substantial evidence that the children of the upper and middle classes, rather than the children at the bottom of the social structure, receive the services of the best educated and most experienced public school teachers. For example, Havighurst, in his study of Chicago teachers, found that 89 percent of the

25. Allison Davis and John Dollard, *Children of Bondage* (Washington, D.C.: American Council on Education, 1940); see esp. Ch. 13.

26. Edgar Z. Friedenberg, *The Vanishing Adolescent* (New York: Dell Publishing Company, 1962), p. 121.

27. Arthur L. Stinchcombe, *Rebellion in a High School* (Chicago: Quadrangle Books, 1969).

28. Howard S. Becker, "Social Class Variations in the Teacher-Pupil Relationship," *Journal of Educational Sociology,* 27 (1953), 128–141.

teachers in higher-status elementary schools had six or more years of experience, whereas only 52 percent of those in lower-status schools had similar qualifications.[29]

Thus it is not only teachers' role performance but also personal preferences that make it difficult for school systems to equalize the quality of teaching for all segments of the community. Teachers' preferences influence their choice of working environment, and there is a deep ambivalence about serving in a "problem" school in an area of low income and high transiency. It is here that the greatest challenges can be found, but it is also here that the teaching role can be most difficult to perform. In any case, it is clear that, under our present system, the more difficult schools tend to be staffed by teachers with lesser qualifications.

Education and race. In the United States race more than any other factor has been a limiting influence on the individual's chances for education. Table 18.3 shows one index of the differential impact of unequal opportunity within the educational institution of the United States. Older nonwhites, in particular, were channeled out of the schooling process. According to the 1960 census, there were about 145,000 nonwhite college graduates as compared with about 5.7 million white ones. If nonwhites had had the same proportion of college graduates as whites, the total of nonwhite college graduates would have been more than half a million.

As we have seen, many factors—place of residence and income, family background, teachers' expectations and values—serve to help or hinder a child's educational experience, regardless of his natural ability. The nonwhite child tends to be hindered by these factors, and the problem is compounded by racial segregation.

THE ADVANTAGES OF EDUCATION

Year by year, our society requires fewer unskilled and semi-skilled workers and much larger numbers of professional and technical workers. The individual who terminates his education early faces an increasingly education-oriented labor force and a lessening demand for lower-level skills. The days when the self-made man could rise in the occupational structure without formal education are rapidly coming to a close. Some insight into the importance of educational attainment as a factor in channeling workers into different levels of the labor force can be gained from examining Table 18.4. In 1960 at least 80 percent of unskilled workers had not obtained a high-school diploma. At the other extreme, a full three fourths of professional and technical workers had attended college.

The significance of education in modern society can be seen in other ways. Miller has reported trends in income as related to educational attainment over a twenty-year period. In 1958, a man in his middle years (45–54) who had not completed elementary school earned $3000 a year. By comparison, a man in the same age range who had completed college was earning more than $12,000 a year. In today's dollars, the range would remain comparable. The individual with a seriously limited education must normally accept an income about one fourth that of his better-educated fellow citizen.[30]

The same author notes that average income does not increase uniformly with each year of schooling but jumps with the completion of each *level* of education. In 1959 a man with one to three years of high school averaged about $4600 in annual earnings, but a man who had completed high school averaged nearly $5600. Sim-

TABLE 18.3 **PERCENT OF THE POPULATION WHO WERE ILLITERATE BY AGE AND COLOR IN 1959**

AGE	WHITE	NONWHITE
14–24 years	0.5	1.2
25–34 years	0.7	4.2
35–44 years	0.9	6.1
45–54 years	1.3	10.2
55–64 years	2.3	13.0
65 years and over	5.1	25.5

SOURCE: Bureau of the Census, *Current Population Reports,* Series P–20, Nos. 45 and 99.

29. Robert J. Havighurst, "Teachers in Chicago Schools," in *School Children in the Urban Slum,* ed. Joan I. Roberts (New York: The Free Press, 1967), p. 556.

30. H. P. Miller, "Annual and Lifetime Income in Relation to Education, 1939–1959," *American Economic Review,* 50 (1960), 962–986.

TABLE 18.4.   EDUCATION AND LEVEL OF OCCUPATION, 1960

TYPE OF OCCUPATION	LEVEL OF EDUCATION			
	PERCENT WITH NO HIGH-SCHOOL DIPLOMA	PERCENT WITH HIGH-SCHOOL DIPLOMA	PERCENT WITH SOME COLLEGE	MEDIAN YEARS OF EDUCATION
White collar workers				
Professional and technical workers	6	19	75	16.2
Proprietors and managers	38	33	29	12.4
Clerical or sales workers	25	53	22	12.5
Blue collar workers				
Skilled workers	59	33	8	11.0
Semi-skilled workers	70	26	4	9.9
Unskilled workers	80	17	3	8.6

SOURCE: U.S. Department of Labor, *Manpower: Challenge of the 1960's*, 1960, pp. 11–17.

ilarly, a full four years of college brought in over $2000 more than one to three years.

To graduate from either high school or college, then, is to advance to a new income level; the diploma seems to have commercial value in itself.[31] But the reason for this is not always clear. While it can be argued that individuals who have the persistence to finish what they begin are likely to become superior employees and deserve higher pay, it is still hard to see why possession of a high-school diploma should ensure at least another $1000 a year in brick laying or why lack of a college diploma should prevent admission to an executive trainee program. According to Nicholas von Hoffman,

Smarter kids from reasonably good high schools have caught on to the fact that what goes on in many—not all—colleges has an attenuating and vanishing connection with their future work. They see that the B.A. doesn't prepare you to do anything, that it only certifies you as one who no longer has to be kept off the job market and is now employable.[32]

The fact is, however, that the employer—who stands between the school and the job—is free to demand whatever qualifications he may desire, regardless of whether or not they are necessary for, or even relevant to, performance of the job. The number of years of education completed by a young inexperienced job applicant tends to determine not only his chances of obtaining a particular kind of job but his employability in general. In fact, number of years of education completed is now the single best predictor of an individual's economic performance. This makes the problem of the school dropout all the more serious.

THE SCHOOL AS A SOCIO-CULTURAL SYSTEM

In studying the educational institution, sociologists attempt to assess the meaning of that institution both for the society as a whole and for the individual within the society. In addition, they often focus on the school itself as a human group. Examination of the school from this point of view is an exercise in the study of social organization. Here, again, more than one level of analysis is possible. The school can be viewed as a bureaucratic structure, with formalistic goals, norms, social control, and other organizational features; and it can also be analyzed from the standpoint of the individual who takes up his life's work within such a system.

31. For the nonwhite, the commercial value of a diploma is by no means equal to its value for the white. But one study suggests that the benefits of a college education to nonwhites are increasing rapidly. See Melvin Borland and Donald E. Yett, "The Cash Value of College," *Trans-action*, November 1967, pp. 44–49.

32. "Is College Necessary?" *Providence Sunday Journal*, December 28, 1969, p. T-5.

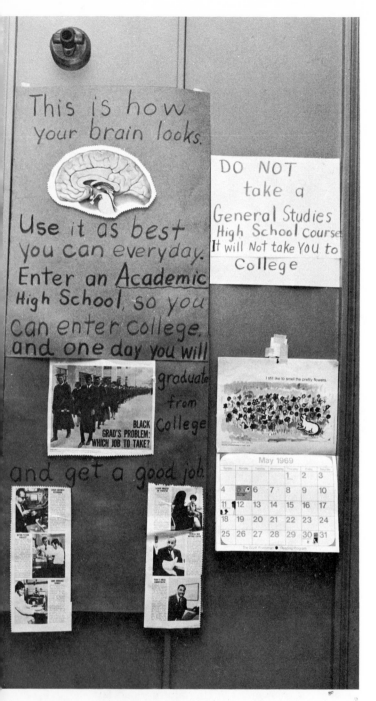

For lower-class youngsters, black or white, the necessities of food and work often overshadow the dreams of educational attainment. Thus students at the bottom of the socioeconomic scale must be highly motivated to aim for a college degree. The display shown here attempts to provide this kind of motivation by emphasizing the commercial value of the diploma.

THE SCHOOL AS BUREAUCRACY

The public schools provide an excellent illustration of the trend in our society toward rationality and large-scale bureaucratic organization. In frontier America most schools had only one room, with a schoolmaster or a schoolmarm in charge of all grades, subjects, and activities. As the number of students grew and the complexity of the educational task increased, these simple arrangements were gradually replaced by the multi-teacher school, complete with administrator and various adjunct personnel. Soon, school systems were organized, each with an administrative hierarchy responsible for implementing policies formulated by a school board and with a staff of teachers responsible for educating the students on a day-to-day basis.

This transformation of our educational institution at the primary and secondary levels has taken place within the memory of many living Americans. In 1930 there were still about 150,000 one-room schools. Today, such schools are found only in remote, sparsely populated areas, and the number of school districts has been drastically reduced through consolidation.[33] Efficiency and economy demand the consolidated superschool, the large-scale school system, and the corps of professional school administrators.

Manifest and latent goals. As a formal bureaucratic structure, the school does not differ in principle from other large-scale groups, but certain of its features merit comment. We have noted that the school's general purpose includes not only transmitting the cultural heritage to all the young but also providing specialized training so that our labor force can be continually restocked. Other formal goals of the school relate to students' health, recreation, future participation in the political institution of the society, and so on.

These manifest goals are within the experience of anyone educated in an American public school. But certain latent goals may not be so obvious. At the college level, for example, men and women are brought together manifestly for the improvement of their minds. In a latent sense, what they accomplish in the way of sort-

---

33. Patricia C. Sexton, *The American School: A Sociological Analysis* (Englewood Cliffs, N.J.: Prentice-Hall, Inc., 1967), p. 72.

ing and interacting with potential spouses may be as important to their later lives as whatever they learn in the classroom. Similarly, for the younger student, the school is an important milieu where the child learns to cope with society in microcosm.

If the child has not learned about authority, social control, role expectation, and status by the time he first arrives at the door of the school, he will do so very quickly thereafter. Through informal interaction with his fellow students, he develops a knowledge of human nature as this is defined within his particular society. He learns what provokes anger or compassion in others and how logical arguments are presented in everyday terms. He discovers the nature of humor within his peer-group subculture, and he masters a host of other interactional subtleties that he cannot pick up from parental contact. The extensive primary group involvement that the individual has with his age peers within the school setting is as significant a set of socialization experiences as are the formal lessons he gets from adults in the classroom.

The school as bureaucracy serves goals not only for the society and for its students but for the individuals who work within its system. For many it is a place to make a living. In this sense, schools are big business. In 1969, expenditures for public schools in the United States amounted to more than $35 *billion.* Teaching is also the largest of our professional fields, with nearly 2 million people finding employment in primary and secondary teaching and another 200,000 earning a living on the faculties of colleges and universities. Every year, a full third of our college graduates expect to find employment in primary and secondary education.[34] This work force deals daily with about one fourth of our population—the students enrolled in our schools.

Roles and norms. In viewing the role system of the school from the standpoint of those who earn their living in it, a key word is *specialization.* The proliferation of subject matters, services, and responsibilities that have developed within our schools has made our teachers as specialized as the employees of any large-scale industry. In the colleges, with their tight

departmental structure, specialization reaches its apex. Even within a given department, a professor who teaches courses and does research in a particular subfield of his discipline may be considered ill-equipped to teach and do research in anything else—including most other subfields in the same discipline.

The system of norms within which schools operate are a combination of legal statutes that offically govern their responsibilities, sources of funds, lines of authority, and the like; and formal and informal norms that are developed within the system itself. Like all bureaucracies, schools, colleges, and universities abound in rules, directives, policies, and regulations.

Formal norms arise out of pressures toward *standardization,* another key concept in bureaucratic systems. The bureaucratic pressure toward rationality demands that operational procedures be as uniform as possible. This is to ensure predictability, fair treatment, and orderly processing. Thus, the host of rules and regulations governing faculty activities, student conduct, degree requirements, payrolls, the administration of grants, the purchasing of needed materials, and so forth are seen by their designers as responsible procedures for getting the job done with a minimum of conflict and a maximum of efficiency.

Many schools and colleges have also standardized their operations in other ways. The classroom format, the 50-minute lecture, the 700-page textbook, the multiple-choice test, designated hours of credit, and a rigid time plan for the academic year are all examples of bureaucratic standardization in conducting educational activities. Again, they are intended to be rational and efficient.

Community control. Serious doubt concerning the efficiency with which some school systems—especially in large cities—have performed their task of "people-processing" has been one factor in the growing debate over so-called community control. The issue has many ramifications—political, sociological, and economic. In general, however, it seems fair to say that it has arisen from the failure of a highly bureaucratized educational system to modify or abandon arrangements that were valuable when first introduced but no longer meet the needs of the times.

Over a century ago, city schools *were* run by locally appointed boards. The system tended

34. James A. Davis, *Great Aspirations,* Vol. 1, "Career Decisions and Educational Plans During College" (Chicago: National Opinion Research Center, 1963), No. 90.

to be corrupt because the board members, who raised money for schools and appointed teachers, were usually themselves appointed by the political leaders of each ward or district. As education at all levels became more professionalized, a movement developed to take it out of politics. It was also clear that, at least in the big cities, the separate districts could not cope with the pressures created by mass immigration and compulsory school attendance.

Most cities attempted to deal with all these problems at once by taking power away from the district boards and consolidating it in the hands of a city board, which in turn delegated much of its authority to a professional, the city superintendent of schools. Organizationally, the result was greater centralization and bureaucratization (including greater financial efficiency). But the concept of the neighborhood school remained in full force. This structural contradiction between localized attendance and centralized administration remained a potential source of conflict even during periods when centralization was working well. Nor was education taken out of politics; it was merely transferred from the ward clubhouse to city hall. The impact of these problems can be readily seen in a recent example.

One leading feature of a centralized, bureaucratized school system is that rules for the hiring, firing, and promotion of teachers are uniform in every school district under the jurisdiction of the system's board. In April 1968 the governing board of the Ocean Hill-Brownsville Demonstration Project, an experiment in community control set up in New York City, recommended the dismissal of one school principal, five assistant principals, and thirteen teachers from schools in the Ocean Hill area of Brooklyn. The area's population was about 75 percent black and about 25 percent Puerto Rican, most of whom lived under slum conditions. This governing board had had a number of special powers delegated to it by the city Board of Education as part of the experiment; but firing teachers was not one of those powers.

There is some confusion over the actual circumstances surrounding the governing board's attempts to obtain these dismissals.[35] What is certain, however, is that relations between the governing board and the United Federation of Teachers—relations that were already bad, since the board was upsetting all the normal rules for teacher appointment and tenure—soon

degenerated into the bureaucratic equivalent of war. Before the year ended there had been three strikes by the teachers' union (UFT) against the city school system, all of them aimed at the Ocean-Hill project, where the schools stayed open under nonunion teachers. After the second of these strikes, union teachers returned to work at Ocean Hill under the protection of over a thousand police. The third strike kept at least seven eighths of the city's schoolchildren out of school for five weeks; the issues went far beyond the Ocean-Hill experiment to include the decentralization plan the city Board of Education was going to put before the state legislature.

It was generally agreed that the New York City school system had grown far too large for its centralized bureaucracy to respond effectively to local needs, especially the needs of minority groups.[36] But the question of how to decentralize not only divided the system against itself but involved it in a head-on clash with its social environment.

TEACHING AS A CAREER

At the elementary level, teaching is mainly woman's work. Men who teach in elementary grades are outnumbered by women by about six to one and are more likely than women to drop out and enter other occupations. There are two principal reasons for the systematic elimination of men from the elementary school teaching role, one is social-psychological and the other is economic. School teaching has been so much a woman's occupation since the early days of public education that the female school teacher is a deeply ingrained cultural stereotype. (See inset, "The Teacher Image," opposite.) As a result, men who enter such work must cope with problems of status and self-concept. In addition, the pay scale is less acceptable to men than to women. Most women teachers are either supplementing their husband's income or are single and therefore not dependent on their salary to provide for a family. For men, particularly family breadwinners, the pay traditionally associated

35. Martin Mayer, *The Teachers Strike: New York, 1968* (New York: Harper & Row, Inc., 1969). Contrast Nat Hentoff in *Civil Liberties*, February 1969.

36. David Rogers, *110 Livingston Street: Politics and Bureaucracy in the New York City School System* (New York: Vintage Books, 1969).

THE TEACHER IMAGE

Today's female school teachers are radically different from those of the 1920's, but the cultural stereotype of the old-fashioned schoolmarm still lingers on. The following requirements from a 1923 teachers' contract in Cook County, Illinois, shed some light on the question of how the teacher "image" became deeply ingrained in American society.

1. Do not get married. (This contract becomes null and void immediately if the teacher marries.)
2. Do not keep company with men.
3. Be home between the hours of 8 p.m. and 6 a.m. unless in attendance at a school function.
4. Do not loiter downtown in ice cream stores.
5. Do not leave town at any time without permission of the chairman of the board.
6. Do not smoke cigarettes. (This contract becomes null and void immediately if the teacher is found smoking.)
7. Do not drink beer, wine, or whiskey. (This contract becomes null and void if the teacher is found drinking beer, wine, or whiskey.)
8. Do not get in a carriage or automobile with any man except your brother or father.
9. Do not dress in bright colors.
10. Do not dye your hair.
11. Do not wear dresses more than two inches above the ankles.
12. Wear at least two petticoats.
13. Keep the schoolroom neat and clean: (a) Sweep the floor at least once daily. (b) Scrub the floor at least once weekly with hot water and soap. (c) Clean the blackboards at least once daily. (d) Start the fire at 7 a.m., so the room will be warm by 8 a.m.

with elementary level teaching was not attractive; and even with the considerable improvements of recent years, it fails to attract and hold many men.

Above the elementary level, teaching becomes increasingly a male occupation. At the secondary level, roughly half the teachers are men. The percentage of women increases among experienced teachers because men who stay in public education as a career tend to move up into the administrative ranks.

Teaching is one of the least stable of the occupations requiring substantial formal preparation. Many women perceive teaching as a dignified occupational role to fill their time before marriage and as a pleasant job to return to at a later life-stage. Thus, they use teaching as a kind of in-and-out career. Many men, on the other hand, see teaching in an up-or-out perspective. If they move up in the system and become administrators, they tend to remain in education; if not, they turn to other occupations.

Other factors contribute to the instability of the teaching career. By comparison with medicine, law, or even college teaching, the public-school teacher has only a limited claim to professional status. The physician, lawyer, and professor must complete years of study and earn specific degrees beyond the bachelor's level before becoming fully qualified to practice their professions. For elementary and secondary teachers, standards vary considerably. Most states require a college education, and some school systems virtually demand a master's degree; but there are also areas where one can teach with only a few college credits. In any case, there is limited prestige in having clients who are compelled by law to receive one's services and who make no direct payment for them.

Teachers also experience a considerable amount of internal role conflict. They are expected to display the same sense of responsibility as physicians but are often paid less than skilled blue-collar workers. They are hired for their qualifications, but parents and politicians think they can tell them what to do. They are trained to be educators but often find their real job is keeping order.[37] Associations of teachers are considered "professional" only as long as they do not make a serious effort to safeguard and improve their members' interests. In short, the nature of the teaching role itself is a source of social instability.

37. James Herndon, *The Way it Spozed To Be* (New York: Bantam Books, 1969).

SUBCULTURES IN THE SCHOOLS

Subcultures develop when people of similar interest and with similar problems come into repeated contact with each other. In modern society the school brings together children and adolescents who share similar problems and interests; and they come to look to each other, rather than to the adult community of parents and teachers, to fulfill their individual and social needs. They develop their own goals, norms, role expectations, techniques of social control, and criteria of status. Thus, the young constitute a society within a society.

One might argue that young people have always developed ways of behaving and believing that set them apart from younger children on the one hand and from adults on the other. To a certain extent this is true. In today's society, however, there are indications that the forces that generate subcultures among adolescents and young adults are operating with particular intensity. The high-school subcultures that have recently appeared in our midst have characteristics not found in those of earlier times, and the same appears to be true of college subcultures.

High-school subcultures. The young now remain in school and out of the labor force longer than ever before. Even though they gain sophistication at an earlier age, they remain socially dependent for a longer period than any previous generation. At the same time, the adolescent role itself has been changing. Because of increasing affluence and new norms concerning adult supervision, adolescents in America now have a degree of autonomy much greater than that of other generations.

It can be argued, however, that teen-agers today are really no more free to do as they wish than are most adults. Pushed together in the schools, student hangouts, and other gathering places, the young have worked out complex social and cultural expectations that are as structured and demanding as those of the adult world. The subculture of the adolescent defines goals, specifies norms, and provides controls and systems of ranking that pose rigid restrictions on behavior. The adolescent competes for rewards and status within this system, and failure to achieve goals in the subsociety can be as damaging as in any other walk of life.

The high school serves as the focal point around which teen-age society is organized.

In many ways the world of the adolescent parallels its adult counterpart, for young people typically work out complex systems of roles, norms, and social ranking. But the adolescent subculture is also a distortion of the adult world. It selects from the larger culture those behaviors that seem glamorous or sophisticated, while generally rejecting those that require adult responsibility.

Within each school, an elaborate, informal structure develops that supports a subculture somewhat specific to the local group. This subculture borrows many of its traits selectively from the larger society, but it also depends upon inventions produced from within. Occasionally, it seems almost to amount to a *contra-culture,* a subculture deliberately designed to flout adult norms and definitions. For the most part, however, the teen culture parallels, draws upon, and distorts the adult world. It selects from the larger culture those behavior complexes and traits that seem glamorous or sophisticated, while generally rejecting those that require adult responsibility.

Like the cultures of all modern societies, that of the teen-ager is constantly changing. Fads and fashions in clothing, speech, hairstyles, music, and dancing come and go, sometimes with amazing rapidity. These aspects of teen culture often amuse adults, who sometimes engage in reverse borrowing, selectively adopting dress, slang, music, and dance styles and incorporating them back into the general culture.

But the adolescent subculture is much richer than it might appear on the surface. It goes beyond the clothing crazes, the rapidly changing hairstyles, the soon-forgotten argot, and the never ending parade of popular singers. It is a subculture that supports a definite set of values. It defines who and what is important; it provides frameworks within which parents, teachers, school, and many other aspects of the larger society can be judged.

Perhaps the most extensive sociological study of the adolescent subculture in recent years is that of James Coleman.[38] In a study of ten high schools in communities of various sizes and socioeconomic levels, Coleman assembled a vast amount of quantitative information on values, attitudes, heroes, orientations toward school, sports, sociometric patterns, and many other aspects of the adolescent society. He found that in the adolescent society, as in its adult counterpart, the patterns of role expectations, interests, and values for males and females differed greatly. Highest in the interests of boys were organized sports, hobbies, and outdoor activities. Among girls, being with friends was a favored activity. Both boys and girls used the mass media extensively and were deeply interested in popular music, television, and movies. School-related activities such as clubs did not rank high among boys but appealed somewhat to girls.

The proportion of these adolescents involved in delinquent and antisocial behavior was negligible, but there was evidence that some of the vices of the adult world—such as smoking and drinking—were well represented in their society. Sex behavior ranged from exploratory necking on the part of the younger students to full heterosexual participation. A double standard was very much in evidence. A boy suffered no loss of status if it became known that he had engaged in intercourse. For a girl, even gossip to this effect was devastating.

Cars are of great significance to adolescent boys, just as they are to adult males. For the youth, the car is a combination hobby, extension of self, and status symbol—an important indicator of the transition from dependence to independence. The objects of greatest importance to girls are boys, and many facets of the female adolescent subculture are woven around this central theme. Having the "right clothes," an "attractive personality," "good looks," the proper cosmetics and hairstyles, and maintaining just the right balance between being sexually interesting and having a tarnished reputation are significant components associated with the main boy-girl complex. Being in with the "right crowd" is also a significant consideration, more pressing for girls than it is for boys. The "in crowd" is composed of persons who are socially, rather than academically, successful. The criteria for membership are related to clothes, reputation, personality, and appearance.

But what is the significance of the adolescent society for the American educational institution as a whole? For one thing, the adolescent subculture places generally low valuation on activities and goals that are held in highest esteem by the larger community. Scholastic achievement and systematic preparation for later adult responsibilities consistently rank low as criteria of success or status among teen-agers themselves. In this sense, the adolescent society is one which orients the youth *away from,* rather than *toward,* those interests and achievements which will be most significant for him in later life.

But perhaps equally important, the adolescent society can be a frustrating and unpleasant world for those who do not meet its criteria for

---

38. James S. Coleman, *The Adolescent Society* (New York: The Free Press, 1961).

status and do not have access to its inner circles. As Coleman notes, the struggle for popularity is often detrimental to the goals of the school, even the goal of "social adjustment."

It is commonly assumed, both by educators and by laymen, that it is "better" for boys and girls to be in school together during adolescence—if not better for their academic performance, then at least better for their social development and adjustment. But this may not be so. . . . Coeducation in some high schools may be inimical to *both* academic achievement *and* social adjustment. The dichotomy often forced between "life adjustment" and "academic emphasis" is a false one, for it forgets that most of the teen-ager's energy is not directed toward either of these goals. Instead, the relevant dichotomy is cars and the cruel jungle of rating and dating versus school activities, whether of the academic or life adjustment variety.[39]

College subcultures. Colleges, like high schools, support institution-wide subcultures. These are derived in part from the history of the institution itself and in part by what new generations of students bring with them to the campus. Since the college draws its students from many racial, religious, socioeconomic, and regional backgrounds, its student body is generally much more diverse than that of a local high school. The general college subculture contains many of the traits, values, and behavior patterns that are found broadly in the adolescent world, but it is by no means the same. The selective processes that work to bring some high-school graduates to the campus and leave others behind also seem to operate with respect to cultural themes and traits. In many schools the undergraduate subculture continues to stress rating and dating, athletics, popularity, and other features of the teen-age world. In other schools these become patterned after more adult models and modified by the special characteristics of the institution itself. Furthermore, many elements are present in the life of the undergraduate that are neither a part of the teen-ager's life nor a part of life in the broader community.

An interesting attempt to classify different types of college peer groups and to identify some of their major subcultural patterns is that of Clark and Trow.[40] After examining a wide variety of data and previous sociological research, these sociologists developed the typology that in modified form, provides the basis of the following discussion. Clark and Trow caution that they have tried to identify types of subcultures, *not* types of students: a given individual may participate in several subcultures. Furthermore, the peer groups on a given campus may be formed around some mixture of the patterns they describe. Like all typologies, this one tends to oversimplify reality, but the following subcultures are readily recognizable on many college campuses.

Long established on the American campus, the *collegiate* subculture fits most closely with the stereotype of college life. It is one in which football, fraternities, dating, drinking, and campus fun play a central part. There is evidence that as higher education extends downward in the social structure, many of today's students lack interest (or the finances to participate) in these activities. But the collegiate subculture is still a part of campus life, particularly at larger state institutions among middle- and upper-middle-class students.

This type of subculture does not orient the individual away from scholastic and academic matters entirely (the fraternity and sorority member must maintain minimal standards in order to remain in good standing), but academic concerns are definitely low in the hierarchy of preferences. Such groups are relatively indifferent to the more serious values of the college and its faculty. The collegiate subculture does not encourage active participation in the world of intellectual affairs, nor is it much concerned with career lines over the long range.

The *vocational* subculture often flourishes on campuses that recruit ambitious and mobility-oriented students from the working- and lower-middle classes. The main goals of such students are to complete the courses, accumulate the credits, and get the diploma that will mean a better job than they could otherwise command. Many of these students are married, and some have full-time jobs. This is particularly true at urban universities, where students tend to have little attachment to the college as such, regarding it mainly as a convenient place to pick up what they need in the way of academic credentials.

These busy, hard-pressed students have little time either for sports and social activities

39. *Ibid.*, p. 51.
40. Burton R. Clark and Martin Trow, "The Organizational Context," in *College Peer Groups: Problems and Prospects for Research*, ed. Burton R. Clark and Martin Trow (Chicago: Aldine Publishing Company, 1966), pp. 17–70.

Students in a nonconformist subculture tend to be highly critical of existing social arrangements and often advocate changing them to suit their ideological convictions. Many adopt deviant forms of dress and appearance.

or for the more scholarly concerns of the faculty. The pursuit of knowledge for its own sake is a luxury they cannot afford. In this sense, the practical, vocational culture may be as divorced from active participation in intellectual affairs as is the collegiate subculture.

There is on every campus a subculture that stresses serious academic concerns. Taking its values from those of the faculty, the *academic* subculture orients students toward completing course work, getting top grades, earning scholarships, planning for graduate school, and exploring the world of ideas. For these individuals the significant features of the college are its library, the kinds of teaching and research represented on the campus, and the depth of the available course work.

The academic subculture stresses the importance of scholarly and scientific habits of mind, which are seen as significant attributes for a person aiming at a future professional role. Although students in this group share with the vocationally oriented an interest in their careers after college, they are not so narrowly focused on specific vocational training. The significant qualities that distinguish the academic subculture from the other types are the strong concerns with course work beyond the minimum required for passing and the identification with the faculty.

Most campuses have some kind of *nonconformist* subculture, labeled at various times as "bohemian," "beatnik," "protest," "radical," "alienated," or "New Left." Nonconformists are often deeply involved with ideas, but they are not the same ideas as those that preoccupy the academic subculture. For the nonconformist, ideologies are more significant than empirically derived knowledge. Students in this group tend to be highly critical of existing social arrangements and often advocate changing them to suit their ideological convictions. Many adopt deviant forms of dress and appearance. There is apparently little concern for postcollege vocational plans.

The nonconformists often assume a posture of critical detachment toward the faculty and one of generalized hostility toward the administration. Because such groups are highly visible and very outspoken, they are often able to exert influence far beyond what one would expect on the basis of their small numbers. For some students, such groups offer an interesting and challenging alternative to the more conforming orientations.

Peer group subcultures such as those described here provide guidelines and orientations for the student concerning the academic system around him. They intervene in various ways to dilute or strengthen the official goals and values of the institution, and they give different types of meaning to the individual's college experience.

THE STUDENT PROTESTS

Every generation has its special educational problems. The late 1940's saw our colleges flooded with GI's returning from World War

II. In the early 1950's, conservative elements in American society saw a Communist lurking behind every academic bush. Then came the civil-rights decision and its impact on the schools. Later in the decade, Sputnik I sent shock waves through the American educational institution. For a time, student apathy and complacency were identified as significant symptoms of educational malaise. More recently, student protests have shaken higher education.

The number of Americans aged eighteen to twenty-four remained fairly constant from the late 1920's to the 1960's and then increased rapidly, thanks to the "baby boom" of the late 1940's and the 1950's. But the proportion of those of college age to the total population changed very little. What did change was the proportion of college-age youth attending college. College students now comprise about one fourth of their age group and will increase to one third in a few more years. And what makes this student group important is that, by and large, it will provide the leaders of tomorrow—yet the values, attitudes, and beliefs of the students are increasingly at variance with those of their own age group who are not in college and with those of the adult public generally.

Prior to the nationwide student strikes of May 1970, campus disruptions had occurred at only a small minority of America's more than three thousand colleges and had involved only a small minority of their millions of students. Thus, a survey conducted by the Gallup organization in the fall of 1969 turned up what seemed to be some surprising results.[41] Interviewing over a thousand students on fifty-seven campuses, ranging from major universities to small junior colleges, the polltakers found that 36 percent claimed to have participated in a campus demonstration of some sort, and 12.5 percent said they had broken a law or a campus regulation as part of a protest. At the same time, when the students were asked to rate nine American institutions, they gave the highest favorable vote—68 percent—to universities. (A majority also considered the family, business, and Congress good or excellent; but less than 50 percent approved the courts, the police, high schools, and organized religion, and a scant 18 percent had a good word for political parties.)

A survey of the eighteen-to-twenty-four age group published in January 1969 revealed that 58 percent of college students were "practical-minded" with regard to their college educa-

tion, looking upon it as a means to economic and social ends, but 40 percent identified themselves with the statement, ". . . College for me means something more intangible, perhaps the opportunity to change things rather than make out well within the system."[42] Such students might be looked upon as "forerunners" of leaders and citizens to come.

Among the forerunners, two thirds approved of civil disobedience and draft resistance. Only 14 percent supported going to war to keep national commitments. Fully half had less faith than their parents in democratic processes. Indeed, half of them believed that the United States is a sick society.

Social factors. Empirical research has shown that student activists are highly intelligent, good-to-outstanding scholars, who come from politically liberal families whose humanistic value orientations have helped shape a higher level of social and political conscience than has been found in any preceding generation.[43] While their activism may be seen as part of a worldwide phenomenon, our concern here is to try to delineate the factors within American society that have fostered the development of this movement and to relate the phenomenon to trends on campus.

America's college campuses have experienced a two-phase movement, which has been summarized as follows:

In phase one, the student movement embodied concern, dissent, and protest about various social issues, but it generally accepted the legitimacy of the American political community in general and especially of the university. In those years, many students believed that the legitimacy of the existing political structure was compromised by the undue influence of corporate interests and the military. They made far-reaching criticisms of the university and of other social institutions, but their criticisms were usually directed at the failure of the American political system and of American institutions to live up to officially proclaimed values. . . .

41. *Newsweek*, December 29, 1969, pp. 42–45.
42. *Fortune*, January 1969, pp. 70 ff.
43. These comments are derived from "Students Protest," *AAUP Bulletin* (Autumn 1969), pp. 309–326, which is Ch. 3 in *The Politics of Protest: Violent Aspects of Protest and Confrontation*, a staff report to the National Commission on the Causes and Prevention of Violence.

In phase two of the student movement, a considerable number of young people, particularly the activist core, experienced a progressive deterioration in their acceptance of national and university authority.[44]

According to a staff report to the National Commission on the Causes and Prevention of Violence, the 1960's witnessed a gradual change in the way student activists perceived authority. There was a decline in the legitimacy that some students were willing to attribute to either the university or the larger society. The report cited the following events and the way they were perceived as reasons for the gradual increase in student activism and dissent:[45]

1. *The nonviolent southern civil rights movement.* On the one hand, the students were shocked to witness at first hand the repressive treatment of blacks by southern whites. But they also gradually came to question the sincerity of the federal government's announced desire to achieve full implementation of civil rights for the blacks.

2. *The "War on Poverty."* Again, student hopes and expectations for massive reform and change were dashed by what they perceived to be bureaucratic ineptness and political ploys to preserve power and the status quo.

3. *The events at Berkeley.* As the student movement developed, Berkeley came to symbolize all that was bad in the multiversity: too large, too conservative, serving the interests of the establishment, uninterested in undergraduate education, and fundamentally hostile to humane values. Thus, the students came to see the university as being as much in need of reform as any of the other social organizations or institutions of the society.

4. *Escalation of the war in Vietnam.* President Johnson had been elected in 1964 in part because he promised not to get the United States unnecessarily involved in Vietnam. Increasing involvement throughout his administration, and the political and military rhetoric used to justify it, helped create a "credibility gap" that came to be as disturbing to many activists as the fact of the war itself.

5. *Cooperation by academic institutions with the war effort and with military agencies generally.* The 1960's were a decade in which the varied activi-ties of the university with intelligence agencies and the Defense Department were brought out into the open. More and more students came to question the moral position of administrations and faculties.

6. *The draft.* Again, the draft brought town-and-gown problems together. Activist college students questioned the morality of their special privileged status vis-à-vis contemporaries who were not in college. The moral quandary became ever more complicated: conscientious objection; avoiding the draft by seeking out occupations defined by the Selective Service as draft-exempt; conscription into service by a political system in which they had no voice.

7. *Race, poverty, and urban decline.* The failure of American society to have brought freedom and equality to all citizens by the middle of the 1960's made American claims to be fighting for human freedom in Vietnam seem hypocritical to many students. White activists were increasingly challenged by blacks to face up to this hypocrisy. And both came to argue with increasing vigor that the billions of dollars being used to fight a war in Vietnam should be used instead to confront the problems of urban America.

8. *Police on campus.* Increasingly throughout the 1960's, the most radical activists were able to obtain support from student moderates and the noncommitted because of the harsh treatment meted out to them by the police. Police actions on campus led some to believe that university administrators were more concerned with reasserting their authority than with confronting basic issues.

College policies. Campus riots are not new in America. Harvard experienced them in the 1700's, and there were scattered outbursts of violence through the nineteenth century. But disruptive *political* activity by students, while common enough in Latin America, Europe, and Asia, is a relatively new phenomenon in the United States. Until recently, American campus riots have traditionally been expressions of youthful exuberance or frustration, triggered by football triumphs, winter doldrums, or intimations of spring. In 1964, however, came mass demonstrations at the University of California at Berkeley, protesting an administration ban on further political "advocacy" at the main entrance to the campus. In the succeeding years, external

44. *Ibid.,* p. 317.
45. *Ibid.,* pp. 318–319.

The classroom format, the fifty-minute lecture, the multiple-choice test—these and other bureaucratic procedures have caused some students to challenge the decisions of university administrators and to demand a voice in determining school policy.

causes—civil rights, Vietnam, etc.—and internal college policies have continued to be interwoven in campus unrest. Indeed, the student strikes of May 1970 were, to a large extent, the combined result of an external policy—the intervention into Cambodia—and a college policy—the use of police and guardsmen on campus.

Since World War II, American colleges and universities have grown much larger, and the number of different activities in which they engage has greatly increased. A major increase has been in commissioned research for outside clients, primarily the federal government. World War II had hardly ended when various universities were given such jobs as running laboratories for the Atomic Energy Commission. Since then, as a result of the Cold War, military spending has grown ever greater, and a considerable share of the enormous expenditures has gone to the universities. "Limited" wars have continued to break out; the threat of total nuclear destruction has continued; and in laboratories and "think-tanks" the game of weapon, counterweapon, and counter-counterweapon goes on.

Such, in outline, are the conditions that have led some students to argue that the contemporary university, by cooperating with a society so involved instead of attempting to change it, is betraying its traditional functions. Clark Kerr, former president of the University of California, felt they were using the school as a whipping boy: "I think really, basically, they, the students, are asking more of society than they are of the university. They just happen to be around the university, and their grievances are basically against society, not the university."[46]

Some students have also become concerned with the relations between their schools and the communities in which they are situated. One of the three principal issues in the confrontations at Columbia University in April and May 1968 was the university's decision to construct a gymnasium in a Harlem park.[47] Since the park was a public facility, the city had stipulated that the ground floor of the gym was to be reserved for the public. Columbia was then empowered to construct a university gymnasium above the public gymnasium by the legal device of leasing the "air rights" from the city at a nominal rent.

All this offended several community organizations, already angered by Columbia's decision to replace low-rent slum property with more university buildings. The gymnasium issue became similar to the issue of community control of public schools, and the issue of racial discrimination was also prominent. These issues were taken up by student organizations at Columbia and fused with the issue of whether the university should sever its connection with the Institute of Defense Analysis, an agency of the Defense Department.

The third major issue was nonpolitical: amnesty for student demonstrators. What this and similar demands elsewhere often amount to is a claim that students have a right to participate in determining school policy. Some student demonstrators view the school as a kind of community in which students form the majority of the citizens, not as an institution that can "process" them as it sees fit. This ideal of a university community seems to have arisen in reaction to the impersonal bureaucratization of American campuses. Administrations have consistently been criticized more than faculties; for some students, their procedures dehumanize the learning process and reduce the individual to a set of holes in an IBM card.

But there is also dissatisfaction with an educational experience that some find overly rigid in organization and irrelevant in content. The Gallup survey found that dissatisfaction among students increased from freshman to senior year and that more than half thought their schools had "serious shortcomings." These included oversized classes, too few courses, and dull lectures. Other observers have suggested that many undergraduates feel cheated because, for the most part, they are actually being taught and graded not by the scholars on the faculty but by graduate teaching assistants:

Here they—and their families—are paying out thousands of dollars for a college education, much as they might have paid high prices for good seats at a national championship football game, only to discover that they are not to watch the stars play the game, but that the teams today are using their second- or third-string substitutes.[48]

In response to student criticism, a number of schools have offered student-designed courses

46. Quoted in Jerrold K. Footlick, "The College Scene Now," *The National Observer* (May 1967), 19.

47. *Crisis at Columbia,* the Cox Commission Report (New York: Vintage Books, 1968).

48. John Keats, *The Sheepskin Psychosis* (New York: Dell Publishing Company, 1966), p. 51.

and taken other steps to resolve the student-administration problems. Where the schools have failed to respond, students have sometimes organized "free universities" of their own.

Dissent, sociology, and public opinion. Student dissent, then, covers a very wide range. As we said in the chapter on politics, the group committed to political revolution is small. The Gallup survey found considerable student disillusionment with the revolutionaries, particularly because of their internal wrangling and their increasing violence; and black militants on campus have tended to reject alliance with them. Much larger is the unorganized body of students who distrust and dislike the American middle-class system of values, the institutional structures that have been built on these values, and the groups and individuals who run things in American society. Finally, in addition to the many who do no dissenting at all, there are those whose protests are particular and parochial, concerned with such things as curfews, parking regulations, and administration refusals to permit beer to be sold in the student union.

The clash in values between a bright, articulate college minority and the American public generally is a matter of some concern. So, too, is the response of a great many Americans—mostly middle and working class but including some scholars and intellectuals—who react to the challenge to the status quo by condemning *all* dissenters—even, in some cases, all college students.

The sociologist can look on college unrest as collective behavior. As we noted in Chapter 11 (page 356), if existing social arrangements do not meet the needs of the individuals who act within them, general dissatisfactions are produced. Against this background of chronic disaffection, acute strains bring discontent into more immediate focus. Incidents provide the immediate precipitating situation around which collective behavior develops. Emotional contagion, rumor, agitation by leaders, selective perception, and many other aspects of the dynamics of collective behavior have played their part in shaping the behavior of students in specific instances of protest or demonstration.

The campus protests also exhibit many of the characteristics of an incipient social movement. Protests at one or two major universities in the United States were quickly followed by parallel outbreaks in some smaller schools. Shortly after these forms of behavior spread in fadlike manner across the country, similar outbreaks occurred in European universities—and some went far beyond the American model.

Major campus disruptions decreased during the first part of the 1969–1970 academic year and then increased sharply, but there is scant indication of what the future holds in this regard. Nor can one say what the final outcome of the campus protests will be. They have had considerable effect at many schools, bringing about not only internal changes in regulations and curriculum but also changes in policy concerning relations with the surrounding community and with government and industry. As a force for change, then, the protests have, to a degree, performed their function.

In the controversy over student protest, the generation gap has been involved, particularly between student and parent and between student and administrator, but also, in many cases, between younger and older faculty members. In the larger society the same gap is apparent to some extent, but young people who are not in college are often as strongly critical of the protesters as the middle-aged. Thus the gap is social and economic as well as chronological. The citizen of any age who works for a living and, regardless of his income, finds it a struggle to remain solvent, frequently sees the student protesters as ungrateful, unproductive, possibly Communist-inspired, and probably even un-American. He may also make heroes of those school administrators and politicians who "crack down" on campus dissent with tear gas and nightsticks. Finally, he may turn on higher education itself, for failing to perform the function of assuring societal continuity.

SUMMARY

Every society provides for the training of its young. But it is only rather recently—since the impact of urbanization and industrialization—that school systems have become necessary to provide individuals with the knowledge and skills of their society. Today education is torn between the divergent aims of socialization—assuring societal continuity and encouraging social change.

Since colonial times American education has emphasized a succession of different functions, depending on the needs of society. Although socializing the young remains a fundamental function, there are differences of opinion as to just what the schools should be doing. Many adults, chiefly concerned with social stability, want their children taught discipline and prepared for lucrative careers. Growing numbers of the young, in high school and college, question and challenge the status quo both within the schools and in the adult world generally.

Education in America is linked to social stratification. The individual's position in the class structure helps determine what education he gets, and the education he gets helps determine whether he rises, sinks, or remains at the same level in the class structure. Place of residence, family income, family background, and teachers' expectations and values all have their effects. Race is particularly influential: the child of black parents is less likely than the white child to receive a decent education.

Education pays in the United States. Not only does the college graduate earn considerably more than the high-school graduate, but graduation at either level means an appreciably better income than the dropout at that level can expect. Number of years of education completed is now the single best predictor of an individual's economic performance.

As a formal, bureaucratic structure, the school has such manifest goals as transmitting the cultural heritage and restocking the labor force. In addition, it has latent goals—e.g., teaching the child to cope with society and providing young men and women with an opportunity for mate selection. Specialization marks the role system of the school, and standardization is the typical bureaucratic trend. Recently, in some urban centers, there has been a counter move toward community control.

Among the professions, teaching ranks low. In the public school system, it is an in-and-out career for women, an up-or-out career for men. For a variety of reasons, role conflict is considerable. Both the high schools and the colleges have their subcultures. Both are, in some respects, opposed to the values of adult society.

Campus unrest has been a matter of serious concern to the American public. Many of those who take part are potential future leaders, yet they not only reject the values of the society but question the legitimacy of its authority. They seek basic changes, in the policies of their schools and in the policies of their country. Reacting against them is adult society generally and also those in their own age group who are not in college. Here, again, the force for the status quo and the force for change create tension and instability.

The Sociologist In Contemporary Society

THE SCOPE AND QUALITY OF SOCIOLOGICAL KNOWLEDGE

THE RESPONSIBILITIES OF THE SOCIOLOGIST

The Ethics of Research. The Sociological Dilemma. Activism and Scholarship: A Latent Reciprocity.

ACTIVISM IN THE MATURING SOCIOLOGY

The Academic Setting. Engineering for the Underdog. Evaluating Social Programs. National Policy Planning.

In this text we have viewed sociology from a number of perspectives. In addition to summarizing available data and discussing major concepts and theories, we have tried to portray sociology as a new venture in human thought—an attempt to bring the objectivity of science to the study of man in society.

The founders of sociology hoped to develop a science of society that would provide a complete guide to the solution of social problems and the achievement of a just and harmonious social order. It is obvious that sociology has fallen far short of these goals. In fact, society as a whole still remains rather uncertain as to the legitimate place of sociology's contributions. Even within sociology itself, there are numerous areas of disagreement. The boundaries of the field are by no means clear. There is no complete consensus as to which research methods can be regarded as most useful for assembling reliable data. Even the mode of reporting sociological observations and expressing sociological theories (in humanistic style, statistical summaries, mathematical models, etc.) remains a topic of debate.

As sociologists have continued to struggle with these problems, new questions have emerged concerning the ethical responsibilities of the sociologist. These center around such issues as the ethics of the research process; the legitimate uses of sociological data; and the proper relationship that should prevail between the sociologist and those whom he studies and those to whom he turns for the financial support of his research. Similar controversies concerning goals and moral perspectives have been common to all scientific disciplines. Following the development of the nuclear bomb in World War II, physicists suddenly found themselves in the midst of a heated debate concerning the ethical implications of their work. In earlier years, controversy flared over the evolutionary theories of the biologist. Very recently, ethical issues have arisen over the implications of organ transplants, chemical and germ warfare, the use of insecticides, the meaning of abortion, and the prolongation of human life.

These controversies suggest that there is a relationship between the level of maturity of a given science and its importance to the society within which it flourishes. When enough knowledge is assembled within a field to provide keys to the achievement of some type of *change*—either technological, biological, or social—it begins to have potentially significant consequences for a great many people. The scholarly ideal that knowledge should be pursued mainly for the sake of knowing may have much merit. However, when the knowledge of a given field can be *used*, this knowledge becomes relevant both to those who press for change and to those who seek to preserve the status quo. And when such a transition does take place, it brings forth a host of new responsibilities for practitioners of the developing field.

It now appears that contemporary sociology is reaching this stage of development. In spite of its limitations, sociological knowledge can already provide objective assessments of many of society's problems. To some degree it can also provide useful explanations as to their origin and even practical information on ways to bring about needed amelioration. Moreover, sociology deals directly with the sociocultural phenomena that lie at the very center of social life. Self, sex, status, conformity, deviance, work, politics, religion, family—these are the anchors of human existence. As reliable knowledge accumulates about such matters, implying an ability to alter existing arrangements, a certain amount of societal concern over the ethical perspectives of sociologists is inevitable. What the sociologist finds out and what he does about it will undoubtedly be a continuing subject of controversy.

In the sections that follow we will attempt to assess the present scope and quality of sociological knowledge and then review ways in which sociologists have oriented themselves to the ethical implications of their work. Finally, we will examine some possible directions for the future.

THE SCOPE AND QUALITY OF SOCIOLOGICAL KNOWLEDGE

What is the *scope* of sociological knowledge today? The present text is partly an answer to that question. It has brought together a broad sweep of fact and theory on such matters as social organization, social conflict, and social change. It has discussed man's relation to his society, problems of deviance and conformity, intergroup relations, communications, demography, and urbanization. It has examined in detail the social institutions of society. Throughout, a variety of illustrative studies have been cited to make clear the kinds of data sociologists obtain through the use of different research procedures.

Contemporary sociology, of course, extends beyond the broad topics we have discussed and into literally dozens of subfields and specialties. As was suggested above, sociology straddles almost all of the significant social concerns that men share. As Smelser and Davis note, the very breadth of the field may help to explain why the general public has such confused notions as to what sociology is all about:

To some people the word "sociology" means investigators going around and asking people personal questions; to others it means urban renewal; to others it means doing social work with underprivileged people; to others it smacks of radical politics; and to still others it is numbers and statistics about social life.

In part, this diversity arises because sociology is a very heterogeneous enterprise. Sociologists study an extraordinary variety of topics, and it is difficult to gather all their interests into a single, convenient definition that would immediately convey the essence of the field. Another part of the diversity of meaning stems from the fact that sociologists often study things that excite strong positive or negative feelings—race relations, crime, family relations, and the like. Because of this, there is a tendency for some persons to pick out one aspect of sociology about which they feel strongly and to identify this aspect with the whole of the discipline.[1]

In spite of misconceptions on the part of the general public and the existence of disagreement among sociologists themselves, sociology has an underlying unity. Whatever their particular orientations, sociologists work within the same general conceptual frameworks and draw upon the same methodological tools. The areas of theory and research that have been summarized in the present text represent a definition of the scope and substance of sociology with which most sociologists would generally agree.

Another important question is how *trustworthy* is sociological knowledge. Obviously, many of the explanatory formulations of sociology are in a state of only partial verification. The research findings of sociology range in validity from those about which very little doubt remains to those that are extremely tentative. It is for this reason that we have provided an introduction to research procedures and techniques as well as to traditional areas of conceptualization. Sociological knowledge is difficult to evaluate without knowing how it was obtained. Data assembled through controlled observation and assessed by quantitative techniques appear generally to be more trustworthy than information gained through less systematic procedures. Quantitative techniques can never eliminate the need for creative theory-building. Nevertheless, sociological knowledge will become increasingly trustworthy as sociologists continue to develop statistical procedures, computer applications, and other sophisticated methods for gathering and analyzing their data.

THE RESPONSIBILITIES OF THE SOCIOLOGIST

If it is accepted that contemporary sociology is beginning to assemble important knowledge about societal concerns, what special responsibilities does this imply for the sociologist? First, as the pace of social research quickens, the ethics of the research process itself need further clarification. If human lives can be influenced by sociological research, then it is very important that such research be conducted according to principles that provide maximum protection both for the groups and individuals under study and for the discipline of sociology. The problem here closely parallels that of other professions, such as law and medicine, which have a significant impact on the human condition. The second major question of responsibility concerns the sociologist's part in directing social change and social policy. In the following sections we will examine each of these issues in turn.

---

1. Neil J. Smelser and James A. Davis, *Sociology* (Englewood Cliffs, N.J.: Prentice-Hall, Inc., 1969), p. 5.

METHODOLOGY   **COMPUTER SIMULATIONS OF SOCIAL SYSTEMS**

In many kinds of sociological studies, researchers use computers because of their ability to digest information, process it rapidly, and provide answers to complex problems. The application of computers to problems of social-systems analysis is relatively new, however, and it is a use that promises to aid greatly in the development of certain types of sociological theory. If a given theory can be formalized and fed into a computer, the computer can *simulate* the social systems or processes to which the theory refers, and the logical implications of the theory can then be explored.

Essentially, computer simulation requires a model of a social system that can be manipulated by the computer. To design such a model, a researcher begins by carefully defining the concepts and relationships in a set of generalizations. Then a set of symbols is formulated for representing the theoretical system in such a way that it has "built-in" rules for logical manipulation. The computer can be programmed to accept such symbolic representations and to follow any internally consistent set of rules. Thus programmed, the computer can be used to trace out the consequences of any set of conditions introduced into the model.

While such simulations are usually complicated, we can illustrate the basic idea by considering a set of sociological concepts and generalizations that could actually be programmed. For example, we will assume that prior sociological studies had yielded the following generalizations concerning the members of *two unlike groups:*

1. Increasing "social contact" (SC) increases mutually "favorable attitudes" (FA).

2. Increasing "favorable attitudes" (FA) decreases "social distance" (SD).

3. Decreasing "social distance" (SD) increases "social contact" (SC).

These propositions can be stated in the indicated symbols (with *inc* and *dec* signifying increasing and decreasing causal relationships respectively). Thus far, we have:

$$inc \ SC \ inc \ FA$$
$$inc \ FA \ dec \ SD$$
$$dec \ SD \ inc \ SC$$

This is an extremely simple model, but it has certain logical consequences. We need no computer to determine these relationships: *inc* SC *dec* SD, and *inc* FA *inc* SC. Common sense tells us that this miniature system is internally consistent. Gathering relevant data, however, would enable the researcher to prove that the derived propositions were valid. And it is clear that if the model *were* correct, two groups in such a system of relationships would eventually merge, becoming one group with a high degree of social cohesion and with little or no social distance between members. (The reader should trace this out.)

Given this model, a researcher could introduce various hypothetical conditions and make logical predictions as to what the outcome of each condition would be. For instance, if he were to introduce a condition X, such as a college policy that deliberately assigned roommates so as to mix the groups fully, this would increase contact rates between members of the groups. What would be the result? If, on the other hand, he were to introduce condition Y, a policy of segregating the groups, this would decrease contact rates and tend to maintain the existing boundaries between the two groups.

Suppose that the model were then made more complex with the introduction of numerous factors and conditions that had known influences on each of the major variables in the model. At this point, a computer would be needed to trace out all the possible derived propositions. If the model were both internally consistent and a good representation of reality, the computer could simulate *all possible conditions* (even those that could not be found in real groups). It would then be possible to forecast how any given condition (such as roommate selection) would have an impact on the social system.

In a truly complex simulation—such as one of nations at war or of a city undergoing specified patterns of social change—one could predict (with adequate models) what would happen under a great variety of circumstances and conditions. Thus the advantage of this type of computer simulation is that policy decisions can be designed ahead of time to meet eventualities that might turn up later in reality. Since the outcome of a decision can be predicted, such simulations are useful not only for theory development but also for practical decision-making.

For further information, see Harold Guetzkow, ed., *Simulation in Social Sciences: Readings* (Englewood Cliffs, N.J.: Prentice-Hall, Inc., 1962).

THE ETHICS OF RESEARCH

In the past, little systematic effort has been directed toward establishing a formal code of ethics for sociologists. Recently, however, the American Sociological Association formulated a set of ethical principles covering both the research process and the applications of sociological findings. This code, which has now been officially adopted by the membership of the ASA, establishes the following guidelines:

1. *Objectivity in Research.* In his research the sociologist must maintain scientific objectivity.

2. *Integrity in Research.* The sociologist should recognize his own limitations and, when appropriate, seek more expert assistance or decline to undertake research beyond his competence. . . .

3. *Respect of the Research Subject's Rights to Privacy and Dignity.* Every person is entitled to the right of privacy and dignity of treatment. The sociologist must respect these rights.

4. *Protection of Subjects from Personal Harm.* All research should avoid causing personal harm to subjects used in research.

5. *Preservation of Confidentiality of Research Data.* Confidential information provided by a research subject must be treated as such by the sociologist. . . . Even though research information is not a privileged communication under the law, the sociologist must, as far as possible, protect subjects and informants. . . . The obligation of the sociologist includes the use and storage of original data to which a subject's name is attached. When requested, the identity of an organization or subject must be adequately disguised in publication.

6. *Presentation of Research Findings.* The sociologist must present his findings honestly and without distortion. There should be no omission of data from a research report which might significantly modify the interpretation of findings.

7. *Misuse of Research Role.* The sociologist must not use his role as a cover to obtain information for other than professional purposes.

8. *Acknowledgement of Research Collaboration and Assistance.* The sociologist must acknowledge the professional contributions or assistance of all persons who collaborated in the research.

9. *Disclosure of the Sources of Financial Support.* The sociologist must report fully all sources of financial support in his research publications and any special relations to the sponsor that might affect the interpretation of the findings.

10. *Distortion of Findings by Sponsor.* The sociologist is obliged to clarify publicly any distortion by a sponsor or client of the findings of a research project in which he has participated.

11. *Disassociation from Unethical Research Arrangements.* The sociologist must not accept such grants, contracts, or research assignments as appear likely to require violation of the principles above, and must publicly terminate the work or formally disassociate himself from the research if he discovers such a violation and is unable to achieve its correction.

12. *Interpretation of Ethical Principles.* When the meaning and application of these principles are unclear, the sociologist should seek the judgment of the relevant agency or committee designated by the American Sociological Association. Such consultation, however, does not free the sociologist from his individual responsibility for decisions or from his accountability to the profession.

13. *Applicability of Principles.* In the conduct of research the principles enunciated above should apply to research in any area either within or outside the United States of America.[2]

This code is a preliminary attempt at clarifying the ethical responsibilities of the sociologist. As new issues arise in the course of research, the code will undoubtedly become increasingly specific and elaborate.

THE SOCIOLOGICAL DILEMMA

There is a growing recognition on the part of the federal government and other groups that sociological knowledge may have considerable utility for those whose task it is to formulate new social policies. Such groups are quite aware of sociology's limitations, but they see the discipline as a better guide to understanding human social behavior than such alternatives as folk wisdom or undisciplined observation. A recent report of the National Academy of Sciences stated the matter as follows:

Behavioral science knowledge is a source of understanding about social and individual behavior that has been confirmed by as careful observation, testing, or statistical analysis as possible. Much of the knowledge of the behavioral sciences is fragmented, much is based on limited verification, and many

---

2. From a pamphlet distributed by the American Sociological Association to its voting members in 1970.

propositions are only approximate explanations of complex social and behavioral phenomena. The behavioral sciences are, nonetheless, an important source of information, analysis and explanation about group and individual behavior, and thus an essential and increasingly relevant instrument of modern government. At the same time there is a need to be concerned as much with the development of the behavioral sciences as with their use; indeed, to see both the development and the use of the behavioral sciences as parts of a total and continuing problem.[3]

These two characteristics of contemporary sociology—its growing utility and its need for increased rigor—pose a dilemma for sociologists: they must reconcile the call for social action with the call for scientific detachment. The growing utility of sociology would seem to demand that sociologists devote their main efforts to reforming society. If the field is to move forward as a science, however, a major effort must be directed toward increasing the level of objectivity and the rigor of sociological research. Must a sociologist choose between these alternatives? What are the consequences of such a choice?

If a sociologist chooses to be a disengaged analyst who assembles knowledge but never takes part in decisions as to how it will be used, he artificially isolates himself from the society of which he is a part. In fact, it is doubtful that thorough disengagement or detachment is possible. Like other individuals, sociologists have personal values, loyalties, commitments, likes and dislikes, and even some outright prejudices. While physical scientists probably have no emotional commitments to the chemical elements, geological strata, or microscopic organisms that they study, the sociologist is deeply involved with his subject matter—his fellow human beings. Thus, it is difficult for him to remain completely objective.

On the other hand, if a sociologist actively enters the struggle to change society, he may lose his scientific identity and become a *partisan*—committed to some kinds of changes and not to others. While partisanship may have an altruistic intent, it is dictated by personal values and not by the logic of the scientific method. An individual who attempts to persuade others to adopt social innovations dictated by ideological premises—whatever their merits—is difficult

to perceive as a disinterested investigator. His value as an "expert witness" and supplier of trustworthy knowledge becomes subject to question.

The sociologist thus finds himself on the horns of a dilemma. If he opts for the scientific role, he may be shirking his social responsibility. If he chooses to take an active part in rearranging the social order, he may lose credibility as a scientist. Although this dilemma has no perfect solution, the efforts of the social scientist and the social ameliorist are, as we shall see, in many ways complementary.

ACTIVISM AND SCHOLARSHIP: A LATENT RECIPROCITY

In many respects, the contemporary debate over activism versus scholarship is a modern version of the old split between social amelioration and social science that has characterized sociology from its beginnings. As we noted in the Prologue, one of the reasons for sociology's ready acceptance among intellectuals in Europe and for its rapid growth in the pragmatic setting of American society was that it held forth the promise of solutions to pressing social problems. As the discipline matured during the first half of the twentieth century, emphasis shifted to the task of developing sociology as a basic science. Today, the thrust toward social action has been renewed. These differences, however, have been differences only in emphasis. The goal of social amelioration has always been clearly present in the research problems that scientifically oriented sociologists have selected. And a dedication to the scientific method has been widely advocated by activist sociologists from the late nineteenth century to the present.

The current debate over activism and scholarship, however, includes a number of new political and ideological dimensions. For example, serious questions have been raised about what types of research should properly be undertaken by sociologists. That is, what problems among what groups should be studied for whom?

---

3. *The Behavioral Sciences and the Federal Government*, No. 1680 (Washington, D.C.: National Academy of Sciences, 1968), p. 2.

Sociologists, like scientists in other fields, have existed mainly on the largesse of the federal government and industry. Funds for social research come mainly from such groups as the National Institute of Mental Health, the National Science Foundation, the military, a few private foundations, and a limited number of businesses. Critics charge that because of these lines of support, sociological research has been directed primarily at maintaining the status quo in the power structure of American society. Whatever the validity or invalidity of this charge, it does illustrate the way in which the selection of research topics, the seeking of financial support for research, and even the use to which research findings may be put can have ethical, political, and ideological overtones. It also illustrates that whether he may wish it or not, the scholar who develops knowledge about society is drawn into an almost inescapable affinity with those who wish to apply it.

Social engineering as activism. Some forms of activism have been with us a long time without becoming subject to serious debate. For example, social scientists have long been working with rural populations to help them take advantage of changes in agricultural technology.[4] Demographers have taken an active part in encouraging control of population growth, and medical sociologists have improved the organizational aspects of medical service.[5] All of these endeavors are part of an activism that might best be called *social engineering.*[6] This form of activism is highly *instrumental,* centered mainly on *technological* change, and usually carried on through established *bureaucracies* (e.g., University Extension Services and various departments or agencies of government). Agricultural economists, penologists, family-life specialists, and numerous others who try to alter

specific behavior patterns among particular categories of people fall into this classification.

Effective social engineering is dependent upon effective scholarship. Basic research into the nature of groups, into the socialization process, and into numerous other sociocultural issues yields data which can be essential for those who want to alter the behavior of populations in specified ways. Although the (inverse) dependency of scholarship on social engineering is not so obvious, it too exists. Investigations that probe into sociological issues for practical goals almost always yield information related to basic sociological theories. Indeed, a substantial part of existing sociological knowledge has been developed from research that was originally supported for applied purposes. Thus, a more-or-less reciprocal relationship exists between the social engineer and the social scientist. Scholarship and this form of activism are not mutually exclusive; though somewhat distinct activities, each supports the other.

Protest as activism. In recent years a different form of activism has been represented by those who have protested, on moral or ideological grounds, some aspect of the existing social order. Among sociologists and others, this new activism has centered around such broad issues as the war in Vietnam, the draft, the continuing inequalities of social life, the pollution of the environment, and the exclusion of the average citizen from the important decision-making processes that affect his life. Some of this activism has been merely rhetorical, but much of it has been aimed at effecting specific social changes—giving students a voice in the administration of a college, increasing the participation of neighborhood residents in an urban renewal program, altering laws pertaining to marijuana, organizing the poor of a community into effective pressure groups, forcing manufacturers to provide consumer protection. It has involved not only demonstrations and petition-signing but also fact-finding and hard work.[7]

Despite its diversity of goals and methods, protest activism has some common denominators that distinguish it from social engineering. Like social engineering, the new activism is *instrumental* in that it seeks to modify existing social structures or situations so that social behavior will conform more closely to some specified ideal. But the goals of the protest activists tend to be *ideological* rather than technological,

4. C. Arnold Anderson, "Trends in Rural Sociology," in *Sociology Today,* ed. Robert K. Merton *et al.* (New York: Basic Books, Inc., 1959), pp. 360–375.

5. See Irene B. Taeuber, "Population and Society," in *Handbook of Modern Sociology,* ed. Robert E. L. Faris (Chicago: Rand McNally & Company, 1964), pp. 83–126; and Saxon Graham, "Sociological Aspects of Health and Illness," in *ibid.,* pp. 310–347.

6. Philip M. Hauser, "Social Science and Social Engineering," *Philosophy of Science,* 16 (July 1949), 209–218.

7. For an extensive discussion of the whole question of activism, see William V. D'Antonio, "Academic Man: Scholar or Activist," *Sociological Focus,* 2, No. 4 (Summer 1969), 1–25.

and they typically are pursued through informally organized groups or some kind of *voluntary* association rather than through an officially approved bureaucratic agency. Perhaps the most distinguishing characteristic of the new activism, however, is that those involved seek change because they perceive such change to be *morally necessary*. The social engineer, on the other hand, seeks change because it is technologically efficient and consistent with official policy. This is not to imply that those who formulate and implement such policies have no underlying moral commitments. Indeed, their commitments may closely parallel those of activists.

The relationship between protest activism and social science is not as clear as that between social engineering and social science, but it exists nonetheless. For example, insofar as social science has been able to assemble reliable information on social issues such as the impact of prejudice and discrimination, differential treatment of the poor under the law, and numerous other inequities, it has already made a contribution to responsible protest activism. Presumably it can continue to make such contributions in the future. Activists who decry and seek to correct existing social problems need trustworthy data to make their arguments more convincing. They also need to evaluate their proposed solutions against whatever objective evidence the social sciences have to offer, ensuring as best they can that the changes they recommend will in fact help alleviate a particular problem rather than introduce new difficulties.

Protest activism, for its part, can make an indirect contribution to scholarship by calling attention to social conditions that have been largely bypassed in terms of research. Long before the recent upsurge of activism, a great many sociological studies were directed toward problems of social concern—prison conditions, discriminatory treatment of the poor by the police and the courts, racial prejudice, problems of the homosexual, problems of migratory workers, problems of the aged. The activists can take a certain amount of credit, nevertheless, for raising the priority of problem-oriented research and for directing it toward areas where the need for understanding is most urgent. In the 1970's, it no longer seems so crucial to analyze the conditions that lead American farmers to adopt more efficient agricultural techniques or that make for more productive groups on the assembly line. Although these problems are legitimate areas of sociological concern, they have received a disproportionate emphasis in the past, largely because funds were readily available to support this type of research. Thus the protest movement has challenged sociologists not only to reorder their priorities but also to examine more carefully the problem of research support.

Though most contemporary sociologists would probably agree that there is a reciprocal relationship between social science and social activism, not many would accept the proposition that sociologists should turn *en masse* to the task of pushing for social reform and cease trying to conduct objective research. There is no need to belabor the point that a sociologist's special effectiveness in pointing the way toward social reform depends on his command of trustworthy knowledge about social processes and institutions. However much the emphasis of sociology may shift to meet the needs of the times, the scientific method remains relevant. Furthermore, there is a need in sociology as in other activities to maintain some division of labor. Not every sociologist is interested in working for social reconstruction. Some enjoy doing research within the framework of science; they see a deeply satisfactory challenge in attempting to reach conclusions about the workings of groups within the canons of evidence and the logic of inquiry to which social scientists subscribe. Viewed within the perspective suggested above, however, it appears that activism and scholarship can be mutually supportive in many ways.

ACTIVISM IN THE MATURING SOCIOLOGY

Over the past fifty years, American sociologists have tended to emphasize basic research rather than social engineering or other types of social activism. Uncertain of sociology's claim to acceptance as a science and uncertain even of the validity of its findings, most sociologists avoided confrontations in which they might have been called upon to demonstrate the accomplishments of their field. As the discipline continues to develop, however, sociologists are becoming less hesitant to add their voice to those of other expert witnesses who can aid in the shaping of social policy. Activism based on sociological knowledge, in other words, becomes increasingly acceptable to sociologists as the scientific stature of their discipline becomes more secure. Today, most sociologists are willing to make their views known on public issues whether or not they wish to become actively involved in seeking social reform.

It is possible, therefore, that the maturing sociology will bring about a new kind of activism—one that is very firmly tied to sociological research findings. It will not be primarily a means of implementing official bureaucratic policies regarding technological change; neither will it be motivated mainly by moral or ideological considerations. Rather, it will flow from the fact that the sociologist as an individual has become increasingly confident of his own specialized knowledge.

We can expect the "typical" sociologist of the future to perform two kinds of functions in addition to his role as researcher. First, he will make himself available as a competent consultant for those who collectively wish to alter their existing social arrangements in ways that will make their group life more satisfying and harmonious. Relevant codes of ethics, already formulated in part, will insure that such activities are carried on in a responsible manner. Second, sociologists will increasingly take the initiative in making known their position on public issues. For the lack of a better name, such a new orientation to the use of research knowledge might be called *sociological activism.*

But in what specific ways might sociological activism be brought to bear in the immediate future? In fact, are there areas of social life in which sociologists are already beginning to play such a role? It can be argued that sociological activism has long been a part of the academic setting. It is beginning to be a part of the sociologist's role in working with lower socioeconomic strata. And it probably will be increasingly a part of the formation of national policy.

THE ACADEMIC SETTING

Social science courses can and probably do have a dual purpose: to teach students to see their social worlds more objectively, and to transform the "unformed and uninformed [students] into decision-making persons. In short, to transform a passive 'mass' into an active 'public.'"[8] The scholar who subscribes to this view of his teaching activities is very much an activist, even if he limits his efforts to the classroom and maintains the highest standards of scholarship in the process.

Beyond the classroom, there lies the question of the governance of the college or university. How shall decisions be made, and who shall do the governing? An increasing number of faculty, students, and administrators believe it can be governed more democratically and are struggling for changes that will allow students as well as faculty to participate in the governing process. The college or university thus becomes a kind of sociological laboratory itself, providing its members with an opportunity to learn something of the limits of living together and of the organizational forms most conducive to the enrichment of human life. During the 1970's the campus may be the locus for discovering new forms of decision-making across age and status lines. Sociologists may play an important role in studying these forms, and sociological activism may play a significant part in determining the direction of change.

ENGINEERING FOR THE UNDERDOG

Achieving social changes that will enhance the way of life for those now at the bottom of the social structure offers unlimited opportunities for sociological activism. Sociologists are already well advanced in the art of consulting for business and industry, but seldom have they served as consultants for the poor. Today a growing number of sociologists are beginning to turn in this direction.

Social engineering for the underdog is not simply a vague goal for the future. Roy Francis has proposed, for example, that it is the responsibility of sociologists to bring their knowledge to bear to help educate the police so that they will not discriminate against the poor and the downtrodden.[9] Ideally, sociological activists committed to such a goal would not be either pro- or anti-police but scholars sharing the best of their knowledge for the purpose of achieving social changes consistent with democratic principles. The task of bringing genuine equality to the process of law enforcement implies a vast

---

8. Irving Horowitz, *Professing Sociology* (Chicago: Aldine Publishing Company, 1968), p. 134.

9. See Roy Francis, "Sociological Relevance and the Police," *The American Sociologist,* 4, No. 1 (February 1969), 52; and Alvin Gouldner, "The Sociologist as Partisan: Sociology and the Welfare State," 3, No. 2 (May 1968), 103–116.

effort at restructuring the police as a form of social organization. It probably also requires an extensive analysis of the sociocultural environments from which police personnel are drawn.

If social engineering on this scale seems totally unrealistic, we might recall that some of the projects that have resulted in modification of our physical environment have been no less ambitious in scope. The TVA system and the reclamation of the Columbia River Basin through technical know-how and expenditures of billions of dollars are cases in point. In the future, the restructuring of sociocultural systems may seem no more utopian than transforming vast regions of unproductive land into useful crop areas or lowering high mortality rates.

EVALUATING SOCIAL PROGRAMS

One of the most significant contributions that can be made by a sociological activist is the evaluation of new solutions to old problems. More and more scholars are becoming involved in the evaluation of such programs as "Headstart" and "Upward Bound." As increasing attention is given to domestic issues by government, opportunities to perform such services will expand.

Evaluation research is not greatly different from the kinds of activities that most research sociologists are now doing. Thus a sociologist who may not be personally interested in leading a cause for some social reform can still help policy-makers in their evaluation of new programs. At present, government programs tend to be seen within a simple "success-failure" framework. But a sociologist is equipped to use more meaningful criteria, enabling him to unravel the actual contributions that a program may have made toward understanding or ameliorating a given problem even though a complete "solution" was not obtained. There seems little doubt that as political leaders become increasingly aware of sociology's ability to provide responsible assessments of new programs, evaluation studies will be increasingly common.

NATIONAL POLICY PLANNING

In recent years there have been many proposals for increasing the involvement of social scientists in the planning of national policy and for making systematic use of relevant sociological data. For decades the federal government has made use of economic indicators such as the Gross National Product, employment and unemployment trends, new housing starts, imports, exports, department-store sales, and automobile production in assessing the economic health of the nation and in formulating economic policy. The development of comparable indicators to measure the nation's *social* health is now a realistic possibility. Indeed, steps have already been undertaken by the federal government to develop such a set of indicators.[10] The Department of Health, Education, and Welfare, for example, has assembled a report that examines trends concerning health and illness, mobility, the quality of the physical environment, income and poverty, public order and safety, learning, science and art, and alienation.[11] Another agency, the Office of Statistical Policy in the Bureau of the Budget, has been assigned the responsibility of assembling and disseminating an even more elaborate and coherent system of social indicators.[12] The utility of such indicators has been summarized in a recent report of the National Academy of Sciences:

Such indicators could serve several purposes. They would be warning signals of dangerous and undesirable trends in the nation, such as increases in crime or poverty, that could call attention to the need for remedial action before the problems reached a critical stage. They could help assess the performance of our social institutions and of special programs or policies established to remedy social ills and to move toward a more ideal society. They could serve as the basis for more informed and enlightened forecasting and action by both public and private agencies.[13]

Needless to say, data derived from sociological research will play a significant part in these new developments.

10. For an introduction to the problem of developing social indicators, see Raymond A. Bauer, ed., *Social Indicators* (Cambridge, Mass.: The M. I. T. Press, 1967), and Eleanor B. Sheldon and Wilbert E. Moore, eds., *Indicators of Social Change: Concepts and Measurements* (New York: Russell Sage Foundation, 1968).

11. U.S. Department of Health, Education and Welfare, *Toward a Social Report* (Washington, D.C.: Government Printing Office, 1969).

12. *The Behavioral and Social Sciences: Outlook and Needs* (Washington, D.C.: National Academy of Sciences, September 1969), p. 104.

13. *Ibid.,* pp. 101–102.

In recent years many sociologists have become actively involved in the planning of national policy. The sociologist pictured here, for instance, was particularly involved on May 13, 1970, when a member of the Underground Press Syndicate hurled a cottage cheese pie into his face during a hearing conducted by the President's Commission on Obscenity and Pornography.

The sociological activists of the future will probably also play a more direct role in shaping national social policies than they do today. Horowitz has suggested that every congressman have a social scientist consultant on his staff to aid in the formulation of policy. He also advocates the active involvement of sociologists in similar roles at local and state levels.[14] More important, there have been numerous proposals from many sources for the establishment of a national council of social advisers, which would be composed of sociologists, anthropologists, psychologists, and political scientists. These would occupy a position in national policy-making which would parallel that of the current Council of Economic Advisers. The social advisers would provide the President with a perspective on national and international affairs that is now badly lacking.[15] Finally, many scholars argue that policy-formulating study groups and groups representing divergent viewpoints are urgently needed within the formal structure of the American Sociological Association and perhaps even within its regional affiliates.

Only the future will show what impact the expert knowledge of the sociologist and the efforts of the sociological activist will have on national and local policy-making. Meanwhile, as sociology continues to mature as a science, it will probably follow the same general paths that have been taken by older sciences. That is, the sociologist will remain essentially a scholar whose central task will be to gather more and more knowledge of increasing validity about a growing variety of sociocultural phenomena. At the same time, he will enter more directly into the affairs of his society and bring his knowledge to bear on decisions and policies that will help shape the society of the future. The authors of the present text hope that many of their readers will join with them in these exciting ventures.

---

14. Horowitz, *op. cit.*; Amitai Etzioni makes a similar proposal in "On Public Affairs Statements of Professional Associations," *The American Sociologist*, 3, No. 4 (November 1968).

15. For example, of the eleven commissioners who were members of the National Advisory Commission on Civil Disorders, seven were lawyers, two were businessmen, one was a labor leader, and one, Roy Wilkins, was presumably chosen to represent blacks. For a more extensive discussion of this issue, see Scott Greer, *The Logic of Social Inquiry* (Chicago: Aldine Publishing Company, 1969), esp. Ch. 16, "Social Science and Social Policy," pp. 186–195.

Picture Credits

COVER   Ann Douglass from Photo Research, Inc.

PROLOGUE

Opening photograph: p. xiv Tom Medcalf.

p. 2 James L. Ballard. *p. 10* Museum of the City of New York. *p. 11 top left and right:* Lewis W. Hine, George Eastman House Collection; *bottom left:* Library of Congress. *p. 16 top:* Charles Gatewood, New York; *bottom right:* James L. Ballard; *bottom left:* George Dunbar Photo, Scarborough, Ontario. *p. 17 right:* photograph by Charles Biasiny; *left:* Susan Opton, Portland, Oregon. *p. 23* Ernest Harburg, Ann Arbor, Michigan.

PART ONE

Opening photograph: p. 28 Jonas Dovydenas, Chicago.

Chapter One. *p. 30 top:* Ken Molino, Courtesy Pacific Telephone Magazine, San Francisco. *p. 39* Don Bronstein from Max Siegel and Associates, Chicago. *p. 44 right:* Arnold Zann, Chicago; *left:* Harshe-Rotman & Druck, Inc., for the Academy of Motion Picture Arts. *p. 45 top:* John Yang, New York; *bottom:* photograph by Roger Malloch © 1969 MAGNUM PHOTOS. *p. 49* Gerry Adler, New York. *p. 52* Photo *Chicago Daily News,* Paul E. Sequeria. *p. 56* photograph by Roger Malloch © 1969 MAGNUM PHOTOS.

Chapter Two. *p. 64* Odeda from Bethel, New York. *p. 65* Warren D. Jorgensen, Bronx, New York. *p. 68* UPI. *p. 74* photograph by Elliott Erwitt, MAGNUM PHOTOS. *p. 80* Associated Press. *p. 84 The New World,* Chicago. *p. 91* Peter Gould from PIX, Inc. *p. 94 top:* Michael Budrys from *The Chicago Tribune; bottom:* UPI.

Chapter Three. *p. 102* French Tourist Office. *p. 103* Staffan Wennberg for *Pace* Magazine. *p. 105 top right:* University of Notre Dame; *top left:* PIX, Inc.; *bottom right:* Tom Medcalf; *bottom left:* Barnaby Picture Library, London. *p. 112* Benedict J. Fernandez; North Bergen, New Jersey. *p. 116 top right and top left:* Reprinted from *Parade* Magazine, New York; *bottom:* Bonnie Freer from Photo Researchers, Inc. *p. 121* Wide World.

PART TWO

Opening photograph: p. 124 Benedict J. Fernandez, North Bergen, New Jersey.

Chapter Four. *p. 130* Ken Heyman. *p. 138 top right:* photograph by Roger Malloch, MAGNUM PHOTOS; *top left:* Lawrence Fink from Nancy Palmer Photo Agency; *bottom:* Art Shay, Deerfield, Illinois. *p. 140* photograph by Eve Arnold © 1969 MAGNUM PHOTOS. *p. 142* Radio Times Hulton Picture Library, London. *p. 143* Graeme Hardie from *Pace* Magazine.

Chapter Five. *p. 151* Ben Ross from Photo Researchers, Inc. *p. 154 right:* Rita Freed from Nancy Palmer Photo Agency; *left:* Mark Vlach. *p. 159* photograph by Charles Harbutt © 1963 MAGNUM PHOTOS. *p. 162* UPI. *p. 170 top:* photograph by Leonard Freed © 1969 MAGNUM PHOTOS; *bottom:* Rita Freed from Nancy Palmer Photo Agency. *p. 171 top:* photograph by Cornell Capa © 1970 MAGNUM PHOTOS; *bottom:* Rita Freed from Nancy Palmer Photo Agency.

PART THREE

Opening photograph: p. 174 Charles Moore from Black Star.

Chapter Six. *p. 182 top:* Pictorial Parade; *bottom:* John Bryson from Ralpho Guillumette. *p. 187* Wide World. *p. 194* Scott, Foresman. *p. 197 top right:* James L. Ballard; *top left:* Courtesy Chicago Historical Society; *bottom right:* Tom Medcalf; *bottom left:* Alfred W. Mueller, Galena, Illinois. *p. 203* Mark Riboud, MAGNUM PHOTOS.

Chapter Seven. *p. 213* Radio Times Hulton Picture Library. *p. 214* photograph by Leonard Freed © 1969 MAGNUM PHOTOS. *p. 217 top:* Charles Gatewood, New York; *middle:* George W. Gardner; *bottom:* Wayne Schiska. *p. 222 Washington Post. p. 238 top right and top left:* photographs by Rene Berry © 1970 MAGNUM PHOTOS; *bottom:* Blau from PIX, Inc. *p. 239 top:* Ernest Cole from PIX, Inc.; *bottom:* Ian Berry from PIX, Inc.

Chapter Eight. *p. 246* Edward Rice from Photo Trends. *p. 251* World Health Organization photo by T. S. Satyan. *p. 252* U.S. News & World Report. *p. 260* Courtesy of Horizon *History of China. p. 261* from *China: Empire of the 700 Million* by Harry Hamm, translated by Victor Anderson, Copyright ©️ 1966 by Harry Hamm. Reproduced by permission of Doubleday & Co., Inc. *p. 265* Department of Commerce. *p. 272* photo by Arthur Rickerby ©️ Time, Inc., 1965. *p. 274 top:* Agency for International Development, Washington, D.C.; *bottom:* The Ford Foundation, New York.

Chapter Nine. *p. 282* Spence Air Photos, Los Angeles. *p. 296* Robert W. Cottrol, New York. *p. 297 top:* George W. Gardner; *bottom:* James L. Ballard. *p. 303 top:* from *Central Park Country* by N. and R. Johnston, Sierra Club; *bottom right:* Marvin E. Newman from Multi-Media Photography, New York; *bottom left:* Charlotte Livingstone, New York. *p. 306* Paul Almasy, Neuilly-sur-Seine, France.

PART FOUR

Opening photograph: p. 310 Bernie Boston photo *Washington Evening Star.*

Chapter Ten. *p. 316* Anti-Defamation League, New York. *p. 319* Charles Gatewood, New York. *p. 322* UPI. *p. 323* Jim Taylor, Chicago. *pp. 328–329* June Finfer, Chicago. *p. 334 top left:* Robert M. Lightfoot III, Van Cleve Photography, Evanston, Illinois; *bottom,* Wide World. *p. 335 top and bottom:* Martin J. Dain, Scope Associates, Inc., New York. *p. 337* Wide World. *p. 340* UPI.

Chapter Eleven. *p. 351* Arturo Mellet from PIX, Inc. *p. 352* Wide World. *p. 355* Howard D. Simmons, Chicago. *pp. 358–359* photographs by *The Seattle Times. p. 360* Courtesy *Daily Journal-Gazette,* Mattoon, Illinois. *p. 364 Long Beach Independent-Press-Telegram. p. 368 top:* Wide World; *bottom:* Los Angeles Times. *p. 369 top and bottom:* Los Angeles Times.

Chapter Twelve. *p. 376* Library of Congress. *p. 377* Howard Harrison from Nancy Palmer Photo Agency. *p. 380* Wide World. *p. 384 top:* Steve Schapiro from Black Star; *bottom:* Charlotte Livingstone, New York. *p. 403* Hal A. Franklin, Chicago. *p. 405* photograph by Leonard Freed ©️ 1969 MAGNUM PHOTOS.

Chapter Thirteen. *p. 413* NET. *p. 416* a European news service. *p. 419 right:* World Health Organization; *left:* American Heart Association. *p. 424* UPI. *p. 425* Wide World. *p. 434 top:* NASA; *bottom:* NBC. *p. 435* copyright ©️ 1963 by Bob Jackson, *Dallas Times Herald.*

PART FIVE

Opening photograph: p. 438 photograph by Elliott Erwitt, MAGNUM PHOTOS.

Chapter Fourteen. *p. 445* photographs by Charles Harbutt ©️ 1969 MAGNUM PHOTOS. *p. 446* MAGNUM from the book *America in Crisis* published by Ridge Press & Holt, Rinehart & Winston. *p. 453* Charles Gatewood, New York. *p. 454* UPI. *p. 459* George W. Gardner. *p. 464 Ebony* Magazine. *p. 466* Dorothea Lange, The Oakland Museum Collection. *p. 469* June Finfer, Chicago.

Chapter Fifteen. *p. 476 top:* photograph by Rene Burri, MAGNUM PHOTOS; *bottom:* Photo Sudanese National Commission for UNESCO. *p. 482 top:* Bob Adelman, *Look; center:* Burk Uzzle, ©️ 1968 MAGNUM PHOTOS; *bottom:* photograph by Burk Uzzle, MAGNUM PHOTOS. *p. 485* photograph by Charles Harbutt ©️ 1966 MAGNUM PHOTOS. *p. 489* Tom McCarthy, New York. *p. 496 Insight* from University of Notre Dame. *p. 501* Kosti Ruohomaa from Black Star.

Chapter Sixteen. *p. 507* Charles Gatewood, New York, *p. 514 top:* Museum of Northern Arizona; *bottom:* Dick Kent photography. *p. 515 top:* Courtesy of the Arizona State Museum; *bottom right:* Museum of Northern Arizona; *bottom left:* Dick Kent photography. *p. 524* Enrico Sarsini, *Life* Magazine ©️ Time, Inc. *p. 525 top:* Lynn McLaren for Photo Researchers; *bottom:* Michael Gorkin, New York. *p. 531* The Health Education Council, London.

Chapter Seventeen. *p. 538* S. Toth, New Guinea. *p. 541* James R. Holland, Boston. *p. 548* John Loengard, *Life* Magazine ©️ Time, Inc. *p. 553* George W. Gardner. *p. 558* S. Toth, New Guinea.

Chapter Eighteen. *p. 570* photos from *Neill & Summerhill: A Man and His Work* by John Walmsley, Penguin Books, Ltd., London. *p. 571 center:* photo from *Neill & Summerhill: A Man and His Work* by John Walmsley, Penguin Books, Ltd., London; *right:* Carol Ann Bales, Chicago. *p. 582* Joe Molnar, New York. *p. 585* from Des Moines, Iowa paper, 1970. *p. 586* Charles Gatewood, New York. *p. 589* photograph by Burk Uzzle ©️ 1970 MAGNUM PHOTOS. *p. 592 top:* Documentation Française, Paris; *bottom:* Charles Gatewood, New York.

Opening photograph: p. 596 Charles Gatewood, New York. *p. 607* Wide World.

Name Index

Subject Index